Third Edition

MW00718076

Marketing Principles and Best Practices

K. Douglas Hoffman
Colorado State University

Michael R. Czinkota
Georgetown University

Peter R. Dickson
Florida International University

Patrick Dunne
Texas Tech University

Abbie Griffin
*University of Illinois-
Urbana-Champaign*

Michael D. Hutt
Arizona State University

Balaji C. Krishnan
University of Memphis

Robert F. Lusch
Texas Christian University

Ilkka A. Ronkainen
Georgetown University

Bert Rosenbloom
Drexel University

Jagdish N. Sheth
Emory University

Terence A. Shimp
University of South Carolina

Judy A. Siguaw
Cornell University

Penny M. Simpson
University of Texas-Pan American

Thomas W. Speh
Miami University-Ohio

Joel E. Urbany
University of Notre Dame

THOMSON
———✦———™
SOUTH-WESTERN

Australia · Canada · Mexico · Singapore · Spain · United Kingdom · United States

THOMSON

SOUTH-WESTERN

Marketing Principles and Best Practices, 3e

K. Douglas Hoffman, Michael R. Czinkota, Peter R. Dickson, Patrick Dunne, Abbie Griffin, Michael D. Hutt, Balaji C. Krishnan, Robert F. Lusch, Ilkka A. Ronkainen, Bert Rosenbloom, Jagdish N. Sheth, Terence A. Shimp, Judy A. Siguaw, Penny M. Simpson, Thomas W. Speh, and Joel E. Urbany

VP/Editorial Director:
Jack W. Calhoun

VP/Editor-in-Chief:
Michael P. Roche

Senior Publisher:
Melissa S. Acuña

Senior Acquisitions Editor:
Steven W. Hazelwood

Developmental Editor:
Mary H. Draper, Draper Development

Marketing Manager:
Nicole Moore

Production Editor:
Emily S. Gross

Manufacturing Coordinator:
Diane Lohman

Media Developmental Editor:
Peggy Buskey

Media Production Editor:
Pam Wallace

Design Project Manager:
Chris Miller

Photography Manager:
John Hill

Production House:
Stratford Publishing Services

Cover Designer:
Chris Miller

Cover Image:
© Getty Images

Internal Designer:
Chris Miller and Ramsdell Design

Photo Researcher:
Susan Van Etten

Printer:
Quebecor World Versailles
Versailles, KY

For permission to use material from this text or product, contact us at
Tel (800) 730-2214
Fax (800) 730-2215
http://www.thomsonrights.com

For more information, contact South-Western,
5191 Natorp Boulevard
Mason, Ohio, 45040.
Or you can visit our Internet site at:
http://www.swlearning.com

To the students of Marketing-
past, present, and future:

It is our collective wish that this text play some role toward improving marketing practice throughout the 21st century.

The *Marketing Principles and Best Practices* author team

Brief Contents

Contents

Chapter 3: Marketing Ethics and Social Responsibility   66
Peter R. Dickson, Florida International University

Chapter 4: International Marketing   96
Michael R. Czinkota and Ilkka A. Ronkainen, Georgetown University

Part 2: Understanding the Market   131

Chapter 5: Marketing Research and Information Systems   132
Peter R. Dickson, Florida International University

Chapter 6: Consumer Behavior   174
Jagdish N. Sheth, Emory University, and Balaji C. Krishnan, University of Memphis

Part 3: Product Strategy 269

XIV   CONTENTS

POWER.
The Power of 16 Experts

Marketing Principles and Best Practices, 3e has raised the bar in marketing education by delivering content by an inspired collaboration of marketing experts, speaking in one, clear and unified voice. At the same time, each expert brings a passion for his or her area of expertise to the text, along with unique personal experiences and insights into the latest marketing trends. This intensified presentation will capture, engage, and sustain your students' interest and enthusiasm from cover to cover.

Marketing is like Playing Chess in a Thunderstorm...

POSITION.
The Power of the Environment

Marketing Principles and Best Practices, 3e works within a new framework integrated into each chapter focusing on the macro-environmental forces that can affect marketing strategy. The **Environmental Forces Framework** stresses the critical importance of monitoring the total marketing environment while developing and implementing marketing strategy. The new edition examines not only the typically covered competitive pressures but the economic, political/legal, technological, natural, and sociocultural factors as well. This new framework allows the reader to see and understand how outside forces can instantly and drastically change your marketing plan. Much like playing chess in a thunderstorm, where environmental forces can change the outcome of the game, the same holds true in marketing—environmental forces can alter your strategy instantly.

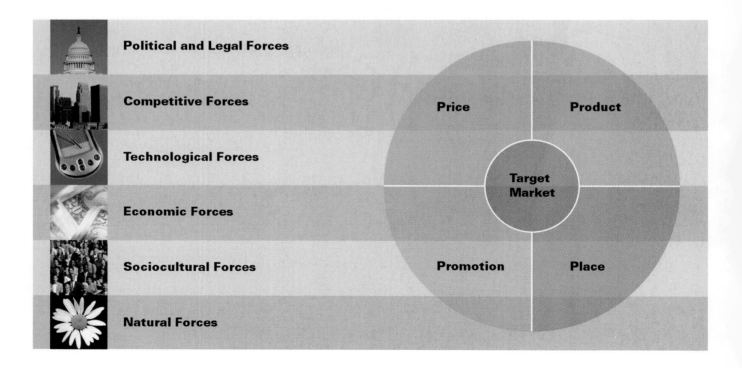

Political and Legal Forces

Competitive Forces

Technological Forces

Economic Forces

Sociocultural Forces

Natural Forces

Price · Product · Promotion · Place

Target Market

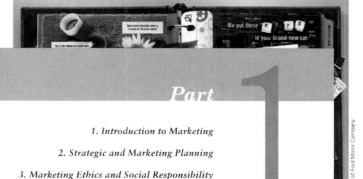

Ford Motor Company recycles trash into brand new parts like battery housings, splash shields, and lamp bodies in an effort to conserve resources and protect the planet.

© Courtesy of Ford Motor Company

Part 1

1. Introduction to Marketing

2. Strategic and Marketing Planning

3. Marketing Ethics and Social Responsibility

4. International Marketing

The Marketing Environment

Sociocultural Forces

A nationwide poll of adults ages 18–65, undertaken by Duffey Communications and RoperASW in 2002, revealed that "unrealistic standards of beauty" was the biggest criticism that customers had of advertising.

Political and Legal Forces When the market fails to be "sufficiently" inventive, the federal government has to step in, for example, by requiring washing machine manufacturers to invent, manufacture, and market new models that use 35% less energy, all of this by 2007.

Competitive Forces In economies where industries are protected or where distribution monopolies are granted, it is unlikely that the marketing distribution system will be as efficient as it can and should be.

Technological Forces New technology succeeds by creatively destroying an old, inferior technology. This is good for society, but new technology also can create new ethical dilemmas, such as those related to privacy on the Internet and the cloning of stem cells to be used in lifesaving medical research.

Economic Forces Economic forces may be considered when SBUs, classified as dogs, are being considered for divestiture. Decision makers may "maintain" a "dog" to sustain the economic vitality of the local community.

Sociocultural Forces A nationwide poll of adults ages 18–65, undertaken by Duffey Communications and RoperASW in 2002, revealed that "unrealistic standards of beauty" was the biggest criticism that customers had of advertising.

Natural Forces The European Union has developed an ecolabel, the EU flower, to "stimulate both the supply and demand of products with a reduced environmental impact." Ecolabels are driven both by pragmatism (reduced ability to deal with waste) and demand (by environmentally conscious consumer groups).

3 **LEARNING OBJECTIVE**

1

Every chapter includes examples of the environmental forces, identified by icons to increase awareness of the marketing environment.

PERFORMANCE.
Powerful Topics of Today

Marketing Principles and Best Practices 3e, covers the contemporary topics in marketing today. The new edition includes the latest coverage on the issues and trends in the field of marketing that can affect decision and strategy in today's environment. Here are just some of the hot topics and examples discussed in the new edition:

- **Customer Relationship Management—** The authors take an in-depth look at customer relationship management as it relates to business-to-business marketing, services marketing, personal selling, and sales management.

- **Marketing Strategy—**The third edition examines marketing strategy and planning— including the nature and scope of strategic planning, the steps involved in the strategic planning process, as well as the fundamentals of marketing planning.

- **Customer Satisfaction and Quality—** The text examines customer satisfaction, the cornerstone of marketing, as the desired result in the consumer decision-making process. It then discusses how customer satisfaction relates to service quality.

- **International Marketing—**The authors place special emphasis on the importance of international marketing in the business world and the need to adapt marketing strategy to meet the needs of new, global markets.

BEST PRACTICES IN E-MARKETING

The Wi-Fi Revolution

College students a half century ago listened to music on stereos which, at the time, were referred to as Hi-Fi players, which stood for high-fidelity performance. College students today, along with millions of other people around the world, can gain access to the Internet via Wi-Fi, which is short for wireless fidelity. Wi-Fi enables computers to connect to the Internet via low-power radio signals instead of cables. Thus, users can have Internet access at base stations, or so-called "hot zones," that are Wi-Fi equipped. As long as he has a Wi-Fi-enabled laptop computer (and most new laptops, and even desktops, now come Wi-Fi ready), the user can surf the Net at public access points throughout the United States and elsewhere around the world. In addition to Internet access, Wi-Fi technology allows computers within the same hot zone to communicate with each other. It is estimated that by 2006 there will be well over 100,000 public hot spots in the U.S.

What are the MarCom implications of Wi-Fi? Early developments in Wi-Fi usage portend future applications that are even more exciting than present uses. Perhaps the most outstanding application of Wi-Fi technology at this time is the availability of hot zones at Starbucks coffee shops. Wireless connections are available in more than 2,000 S_ in the U.S. and Europe. Early experien__ ers who purchase Wi-Fi ac__

← Every chapter addresses the impact of technology in marketing today. **Best Practices in E-Marketing** examines how new technologies affect the field of marketing and the latest trends.

ETHICS AND SOCIAL RESPONSIBILITY

The Campaign Against Music Piracy

Is downloading music from the Internet for personal use stealing, or is it just taking advantage of the capabilities of today's available technology? Hip-hop queen Mary J. Blige believes it's stealing: "If you create something and someone takes it away, that is stealing." Blige has been joined recently by the likes of Shakira, Britney Spears, Elton John, Eminem, the Dixie Chicks, Madonna, and Sheryl Crow to form a group of 90 artists organized as the Music United for Strong Internet Copyright Coalition (MUSIC). MUSIC's purpose is to use artist clout to convince consumers that file-sharing and downloading music for free is il[legal]. [According] to MUSIC, illegal downloading is taking its t[oll on the] industry. CD shipments were down 5% in 2[001 and an] additional 9% in 2002. In 2003, global recor[d sales] were expected to fall another 6%, mar[king the] straight year of sales declines. To make its p[oint, MUSIC] placed full-page ads in *The New York Times*[, *Los Ange-*] *les Times,* and policy-maker publications s[uch as Roll Call] asking the question "Who Really Cares abo[ut illegal down-] loading?"

According to music-industry estimates, [some 2.6] billion music files are downloaded illegally fr[om the Internet] each month through "peer-to-peer" services [such as KaZaA,] Morpheus, and Gnutella. Consumer surve[ys reveal that] those who download the most are buyi[ng significantly] fewer CDs than those who do not engage [in the activity] by a two to one margin. In addition, one su[rvey of online] consumers indicated that 35% of responde[nts were more] likely to download a song they really liked th[an buy the] CD. Hilary Rosen, Chief Executive Officer [of the Recording] Industry Association of America (RIA[A), laments that] many people don't realize that wh[en they] download [music] you like from a peer-to-peer [network or other unautho-] rized Internet so[urce ...]

In a **NEW** feature, *Marketing Principles and Best Practices* showcases currently underserved markets that may become markets of the future. **Focus on Emerging Markets** reinforces the dynamic nature of what lies ahead in marketing.

Students have the opportunity to make real-world ethical choices concerning the kinds of controversial dilemmas they may encounter as marketers in the **Ethics and Social Responsibility** in Marketing feature.

FOCUS ON EMERGING MARKETS

Do Retailers Really Understand the Latino Consumer?

It is important that all marketers understand the purchase behavior of their targeted Latino consumer, their attitudes and beliefs, and the size of the opportunity, before they can think of successfully marketing to Latinos. Given the size of the opportunity and its importance to the future growth of many companies, it is crucial that food marketers begin to understand the Latino consumer now or potentially miss out on the largest opportunity of this century.

Consider, for example, the grocers catering to Latino consumers. One of the very successful operators is San Jose's Mi Pueblo Foods. While many outside observers would attribute Mi Pueblo's success to the layout and design of its stores—an intricate floor-tile pattern, stucco textured walls, faux windows, adobe roof tiles, faux balconies, large bins of beans, walls of spices, and hanging sides of meat—that is not the case. What really sets Mi Pueblo apart from other grocers is its understanding of the Latina female and her shopping habits.

Most grocery stores in the United States, recognizi[ng the] time poverty of the average household, fea[ture prepared] foods. Yet, as a study by ACNielsen and [....] found out, this is not alway[s the case.] Latina women feel it i[s....]

TECHNOLOGY.
Now You're Teaching with Power

14

Marketing Principles and Best Practices has the most powerful technology package available. The new edition has a plethora of online support for the reader to have additional resources for further assessment and learning at their fingertips.

Xtra!

This web-based learning tool enhances students' educational experience with interactive learning activities designed to help them improve their course grades and develop

✗tra!

the complex decision-making skills required in the professional marketing role. Included on Xtra! are the Interactive Learning Activities, Xtra! quizzing, digitized videos, and much more.

Interactive Marketing Activities

Innovative and interactive activities open every chapter and place students in the role of the marketing manager for several well-known companies. Students read the scenerios, go online to Xtra! and respond to a series of questions, choosing from a variety of marketing strategies aimed at achieving market growth. They then see the consequences of their choices and learn from experience about the vital role of strategy in marketing. Clues are identified throughout the chapter by chess icons to help students understand the best decision.

WebTutor Advantage

We've harnessed the power of the Internet to deliver this interactive, web-based course management student supplement on WebCT and BlackBoard. Its innovative learning approach actively engages students. As instructor, you can incorporate WebTutor Advantage as an integral part of your course, or simply let students use it on their own as a study guide.

InfoTrac College Edition

We give your students 24-hour access to a library brimming with more than ten million full-text articles from more than 4,000 journals, popular periodicals, and newspapers such as Newsweek, Time, USA Today—20 years of content updated daily.

http://bestpractices.swlearning.com

The *Marketing Principles and Best Practices, 3e* web site offers a robust variety of activities and resources that build on and reinforce your students' knowledge of marketing principles. This online

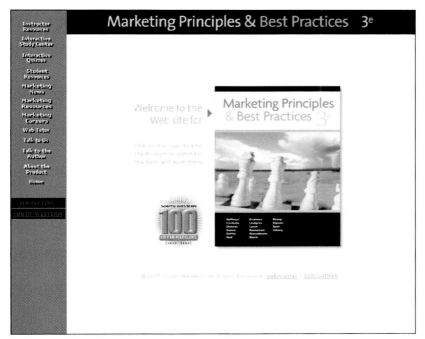

resource includes Marketing in the News—a continuously refreshed supply of relevant news stories that demonstrate the application of key marketing topics, quizzing, flash presentations, as well as the ability to download the instructor supplements.

SUPPLEMENTS.
Powerful Support Package

Instructor's Manual

Marketing Principles and Best Practices Instructor's Manual contains an in-depth lecture guide, insights into the opening vignettes, key teaching points of the chapter, and much more to enhance your lecture.

Video Package

Captivating video segments feature companies like Kodak, Krispy Kreme, ESPN, and Timberland with engaging dramatizations. The marketing strategies featured in these video cases allow readers to make marketing strategy decisions and to evaluate those made by well-known companies.

Test Bank with ExamView Computerized Testing Software

100%-accurate test bank has been carefully rewritten and verified for total accuracy. ExamView computerized testing software contains all the questions in the printed test bank. Its easy-to-use test-creation software, compatible with Microsoft Windows, allows you to add or edit questions, instructions, and answers.

PowerPoint Lecture Slides

The third edition comes with three versions of PowerPoint Lecture Slides, giving you much more ease and flexibility. Choose from light to detailed content with various levels of graphic, animation, and video.
- Quick Pick PowerPoint Slides
- Total Pack PowerPoint Slides
- Total Pack with Videos

Other instructor ancillary material include:
- Instructor's Resource CD-ROM
- Transparency Acetates
- Best Practices Web Site
  http://bestpractices.swlearning.com
- WebTutor Advantage on WebCT and Blackboard

Student Supplements include:
- Study Guide
- Xtra! Online Access
- Best Practices Web Site
  http://bestpractices.swlearning.com
- WebTutor Advantage for Blackboard and WebCT

Marketing Principles and Best Practices
...It's Your Move!

Preface

Welcome to the third edition of *Marketing Principles and Best Practices*! This innovative text combines the expertise of 16 leading marketers into one high-powered principles of marketing textbook. Our author team consists of current South-Western textbook authors and marketing professors who are specialists in their respective fields. The end result is a principles text that successfully communicates a strong sense of passion in each and every chapter, raising the bar and setting a new standard for principles of marketing textbooks. *Marketing Principles and Best Practices* is full of "added-value" insights into the latest marketing trends and issues, such as customer-relationship management, emerging markets, ethical issues, and technological advances, while equipping students with a solid foundation in principles of marketing that is beyond compare.

Voice of the Expert

The team of expert marketers who have collaborated on this innovative textbook present the best practices in marketing in a cohesive, well-illustrated format. Each chapter begins with the author's personal message to the student that emphasizes the importance and value of studying each area of marketing. While each chapter reflects the distinct flavor of each author, the format, writing style, and pedagogy are consistent and unified. Reviewers have praised the clear writing style, and we thank Doug Hoffman for his role in ensuring a consistent and streamlined presentation. Ultimately, *Marketing Principles and Best Practices* provides the means to showcase our team of authors' areas of expertise. Writing is our forté—throughout our collective careers we have published more than 125 books and 1,100 articles. As a group, we are genuinely excited about collaborating with each other and having the opportunity to influence, educate, and challenge students of marketing at all levels—students and instructors alike.

Environmental Forces

It may seem like a cliché to say so, but many would agree that today's business climate is more turbulent than ever. Compelling events continue to change the face of business, including economic turmoil, competitive pressures, political and legal developments, technological innovation, sociocultural shifts, and the depletion of natural resources. Consequently, this third edition of *Marketing Principles and Best Practices* has purposely focused on the impact of macroenvironmental forces on marketing strategy. As the cover of the text illustrates, we are asking students to consider marketing as a game of chess played in a thunderstorm. Within their control are chess pieces that can be strategically moved to carry out their plan of attack (marketing strategy). Beyond their control are the chess pieces of their opponent (the competition) and the thunderstorm that rages around the game itself (other environmental forces) that may alter the outcome of the game. This analogy is simple yet powerful—the player most adept at coordinating strategy and adapting to changing environmental forces dominates the board (the marketplace). In essence, marketing becomes a game of "survival of the fittest." This analogy is threaded throughout the text.

Chapter 1 fully explains the marketing environment, with a new emphasis on the environmental forces that affect marketing strategy. Each subsequent chapter reveals how these environmental factors shape decision making and create awareness of the forces that influence marketing decision making. To link this organizational framework throughout the text and demonstrate the importance of these forces to the student, icons are placed next to these forces as they are discussed. This new organizational framework stresses the critical importance of monitoring the marketing environment while developing and implementing marketing strategy. Below are the environmental icons and the environmental forces that they represent.

 Political/legal forces consider traditional issues such as antitrust regulation and consumer protection, as well as the impact of political upheaval occurring throughout the world.

 Competitive forces include existing competitors and new forms of emerging competition.

 Sociocultural forces reflect demographic and other developments that bring about changes in customer attitudes, beliefs, norms, customs, and lifestyles.

 Economic forces include business cycles, inflation, and fluctuations in personal income.

 Natural forces reflect the impact of diminishing resource availability and the often unintended consequences that products and production have on the environment.

 Technological forces represent the application of science to solve problems and to perform tasks in consumer and business markets.

Coverage of Contemporary Market Topics

The reviewers have spoken and the third edition of *Marketing Principles and Best Practices* has responded! Extensive reviews were commissioned to prepare for the third edition from instructors teaching principles of marketing and specialists in each area of marketing. When asked to identify the marketing topics they considered "extremely important" for introductory students to study, the response was unanimous—customer-relationship management, customer satisfaction, marketing ethics and social responsibility, international marketing, marketing and technology, identifying and reaching new emerging markets, and marketing strategy and planning. The authors have fully and comprehensively addressed these marketing topics in the third edition.

Customer-Relationship Management

Customer-relationship management is introduced and defined in Chapter 1 and discussed in further detail as it relates to business-to-business marketing (Chapter 7), services marketing (Chapter 10), and personal selling and sales management (Chapter 14).

Customer Satisfaction

Customer satisfaction is a cornerstone of marketing. Without customers, a business has little reason to exist. Customer satisfaction's relationship with the marketing concept is introduced in Chapter 1, further explained as a desired result in the consumer decision making process in Chapter 6, and discussed in detail as it relates to service quality in Chapter 10.

Marketing Ethics and Social Responsibility

With renewed emphasis on ethical business practice and social responsibility, the third edition of *Marketing Principles and Best Practices* dedicates an entire chapter to marketing ethics and social responsibility (Chapter 3). In addition, new box features, titled "Ethics and Social Responsibility in Marketing," have been developed in every chapter that describe real-world, controversial ethical dilemmas and prompt students to make an ethical choice. Each feature includes two questions for students to consider that point out the controversial nature of topic.

International Marketing

This new edition of *Marketing Principles and Best Practices* places international marketing coverage where it should be—front and center. Covered as a separate topic in Chapter 4, international marketing is presented early in this text to recognize the importance of international marketing in today's business world. The international marketing chapter illustrates the importance of modifying marketing strategy to meet the needs of new, global markets. In addition, international marketing examples are integrated throughout the text.

Marketing and Technology

The impact of technology on marketing strategy is woven throughout the text. For example, technological forces are represented as a macroenvironmental variable in Chapter 1, integrated as an environmental forces icon in almost every chapter, and discussed as a factor that influences marketing research (Chapter 5), consumer and business-to-business decision making (Chapters 6 and 7), market segmentation and new product development (Chapters 8 and 9), and so on. In fact, the influence of technology on marketing is discussed within the text of virtually every chapter. In addition, "Best Practices in E-Marketing" box features have been developed in every chapter that specifically address how new technologies are currently affecting the field of marketing.

Emerging Markets

To develop an awareness of the potential of emerging markets, the third edition includes a new feature called "Focus on Emerging Markets." This innovative box feature showcases markets that are currently underserved today that may very well be the major markets of the future. These features present strategies for serving the Latino, African American, and Asian markets, and explore the potential in hybrid technology markets, international markets, and marketing to the world's poor. This eye-opening feature reinforces the dynamic nature of the world's markets and provides insight into the question: What lies ahead?

Marketing Strategy and Planning

All too often, introductory marketing students equate marketing with sales and advertising. Consequently, it is important to explain early on that sales and advertising are simply visible tools that are used to carry out the marketing plan. Strategic and marketing planning seeks answers to the questions, "Where does the organization want to go?" and "How do we get there?" Given the importance of marketing strategy and planning, a new Chapter 2, "Strategic and Marketing Planning," has been developed that discusses the nature and scope of strategic planning, the fundamental steps and content of the strategic planning process, and the fundamentals of marketing planning.

Interactive Learning (http://bestpracticesxtra.swlearning.com)

This third edition of *Marketing Principles and Best Practices* features Xtra!, a Web-based learning environment that enhances the student's educational experience. With access to Xtra!, students have an abundant supply of interactive learning experiences that have the potential to help them grasp the complex decision making required by marketers and improve course grades. Xtra! includes these features:

> *Interactive Marketing Activities.* Innovative and unique, these interactive marketing activities, designed and written by marketing professors, provide an interactive, educational learning experience for marketing students. These activities, found on the first page of each chapter, place students in the role of a marketing manager of well-known companies. By responding to a series of prompts, students choose various marketing strategies they believe provide the greatest potential for market growth. Once they choose a strategy, students immediately learn the consequence of their choices and are given additional opportunities to learn from their experience.

> *Xtra! Quizzing.* These practice exams give students an opportunity to test their knowledge in preparation for midterms and final exams. Each question includes feedback for right and wrong answers and textbook page references to ease further study.

> *Chapter Case Video Segments.* These video segments bring the chapter video cases to life.

Fresh Content and New Examples Selected by the Experts

One of the great advantages of a team of expert authors is that each is keenly tuned into the latest developments in his or her area of specialty. In addition, each expert has a treasure trove of rich examples of actual marketing strategies collected while doing consulting work and researching the successes and failures of marketing strategies used by leading businesses. Pulling the very best examples from their collective experiences, the authors enrich each chapter with new, interesting, real-world applications. No other principles-of-marketing author team can provide this collective knowledge about marketing or the application of marketing in business today. Highlights of new content in the third edition are summarized below:

- **New opening vignettes** in each chapter highlight the latest applications of marketing strategy and feature companies and brands such as Crest, Honda, Microsoft, Viacom, Newton, Altoids, and IBM.
- **New chapter cases** in each chapter provide a fresh opportunity for students to apply their knowledge and analyze marketing strategies in businesses well known for their goods and services.
- **New boxed features** that provide vivid, interesting examples of "Best Practices in E-Marketing," "Ethics and Social Responsibility in Marketing," and "Focus on Emerging Markets" create a comprehensive, well-rounded learning experience for students.

- **Integration of the new environmental forces framework** in every chapter is accomplished with the use of margin notes that illustrate the impact of environmental forces on each aspect of the marketing program.

- **The new Chapter 1, "Introduction to Marketing,"** introduces marketing and the macro-environmental forces that shape marketing strategy and serves as the foundation for the rest of the chapters. The chapter gives students a fundamental understanding of marketing and acquaints them with marketing concepts and terminology. The chapter also illustrates and describes the environmental forces and their impact on all aspects of the marketing program.

- **The new Chapter 2, "Strategic and Marketing Planning,"** which has been consistently praised by reviewers, discusses the nature and scope of strategic planning, the fundamental steps and content of the strategic planning process, and the fundamentals of marketing planning.

- **Chapter 5, "Marketing Research and Information Systems,"** includes new coverage of the technological enhancements in customer research, including electronic observational research, decisions-support systems, and Web-based marketing research.

- **Chapter 6, "Consumer Behavior,"** has been reorganized around the consumer decision process and highlights the psychological, situational, social, and technological factors that affect the process. This chapter includes more examples of the application of consumer behavior concepts and new coverage of culture's and subculture's impact on the consumer buying-decision process.

- **Chapter 7, "Business-to-Business Marketing,"** includes expanded coverage of governmental customers with new coverage of the U.S. Departments of Defense and Homeland Security's purchasing operations and e-government initiatives. This chapter also includes new coverage of customer-relationship-management (CRM) systems and the central components of a profitable CRM strategy.

- **Chapter 9, "Marketing's Role in New Product Development and Product Decisions,"** includes more coverage of branding strategies for business-to-business firms and new coverage of the applicability of the product life cycle.

- **Chapter 13, "Integrated Marketing Communications: Advertising, Promotions, and Other MarCom Tools,"** includes new coverage of the Internet as an advertising medium and more detail on major sales-promotion methods.

- **Chapter 14, "Personal Selling and Sales Management,"** presents personal selling as a critical component of promotion and introduces new coverage of the pros and cons of team selling.

- **A new "Marketing Arithmetic" Appendix** introduces the marketing arithmetic concepts that are important for all principles students to understand. The topics in this appendix include the components of an income statement return-on-investment percentage, a strategic profit model, the break-even point cost per thousand (CPM) for advertising media, the lifetime value of a customer, and the amount that should be profitably spent to acquire new customers.

Chapter Pedagogy

Drawing upon their vast teaching experience and their very best classroom examples, the author team has created a powerful pedagogy that creates a compelling and sustained learning experience. The pedagogy in the third edition of *Marketing Principles and Best Practices* exemplifies the best practices used to teach marketing by our team of expert teachers in universities around the country.

Opening Vignette

The best classroom examples are those that fully engage students and demonstrate marketing strategies in companies that students consider "hip, cutting edge, or intriguing." We believe that it's important to begin each chapter with an opening vignette that generates ideas, questions, and appreciation for smart marketing decision making. In the third edition, opening vignettes feature a variety of companies that students recognize, including services, technology, and manufacturing, and describe the very best practices in marketing in companies such as Honda, Palm, Starbucks, ExxonMobil Speedpass, Philip Morris, IBM, and Procter & Gamble.

An Interactive Opening Vignette with Xtra! (http://bestpracticesxtra.swlearning.com)

These new interactive marketing activities, available with Xtra!, guide students in evaluating and assessing various marketing strategies for actual companies. The benefit to the student is that these activities allow them to build decision-making skills and to observe the outcome of various marketing strategies. As students select options, they will learn more about the impact of their decisions.

Voice of the Expert

On the first page of each chapter, each author shares a personal message in "Voice of the Expert." Based on their research, teaching, and consulting experiences, each author describes why the chapter topics are important from a personal viewpoint. In essence, "Voice of the Expert" personalizes each chapter and conveys the author's passion for and unique insights into chapter materials.

Environmental Framework

Given the importance of environmental forces on marketing strategy, icons have been developed to symbolize each of the environmental forces. Throughout the text, these icons will appear in the chapter margins and highlight chapter content that illustrates the impact of environmental forces on marketing strategy. Environmental icons are used to remind students that marketing is a dynamic planning process and that modifications to marketing strategy are often needed to take advantage of opportunities and/or offset threats that develop within the marketing environment.

Best Practices in E-Marketing

E-marketing uses a flood of new technologies to create interesting and innovative ways to provide customer value. Fundamentally, e-marketing has influenced traditional marketing strategy in two ways. First, the electronic tools being used by marketers have increased the efficiency of traditional marketing practices. Secondly, the technology of e-marketing has transformed many marketing strategies—new business models have emerged; innovative services have been developed; pricing strategies have been literally turned upside down; new distribution practices now create tremendous efficiencies in supply-chain management; and the Net facilitates communication internally to employees and externally to customers in B-to-B and B-to-C markets. The "Best Practices in E-Marketing" feature provides specific examples of how technology is being used in today's business world.

Ethics and Social Responsibility in Marketing

This new feature will reinforce the message that ethics, values, corporate responsibility, and integrity are the new watchwords in today's business. Each chapter presents an ethical dilemma faced by marketing managers today. The purpose of this feature is to generate discussion about behaviors that cross the line of right and wrong and aid students in making ethical decisions.

Focus on Emerging Markets

What are the new markets of the future? What companies are leading the way by tapping into emerging market segments? New "Focus on Emerging Markets" boxed features create an awareness of the diverse and rich cultural issues in marketing. These new features will highlight how companies are adjusting their marketing strategies to respond to the sociocultural (e.g., ethnic, gender, age, income) and technological changes in the domestic and international marketplace.

New Photos/Ads

Photo captions reinforce chapter topics and a new emphasis has been placed on including additional timely advertisements to illustrate marketing in practice.

Key Terms

Each chapter contains approximately 20–25 key terms. For ease of use and understanding, key terms are bold-faced and defined within the chapter, as well as in the margin and the end-of-chapter glossaries. Other important terms (not designated as key terms) are italicized in the text for emphasis.

Questions for Review and Discussion

End-of-chapter review questions query students on chapter content, while discussion questions provide the means for students to apply their knowledge base to thought-provoking marketing issues.

New In-Class Team Activities

For those instructors wishing to increase and enhance student interactivity, in-class team activities have been added to the third edition as end-of-chapter material to facilitate in-class group discussions.

Internet Questions

End-of-chapter Internet activities tie the Net to chapter materials, providing hands-on exercises for students who wish to explore the latest developments in Web applications as they relate to marketing strategy.

Chapter Cases

All new end-of-chapter cases bring the fundamentals of marketing to life. Chapter cases enhance the currency of this edition, since cases feature such intriguing subject matter as TiVo, Yao Ming, the plight of tobacco retailers, International Truck and Engine Corporation (formerly Navistar), Apple Computer Corporation, Ferrari, and Javelin Executive Jet, among others.

New Videos and Updated Video Cases

Four new video cases are featured that significantly enhance the package's current selection of fifteen great choices. Caribou Coffee illustrates the real-life importance of marketing strategy and planning. Ping Golf takes students through its operations as the company develops and manages new products. Krispy Kreme takes an inside look at market segmentation and answers the question: "Who is eating all those Krispy Kreme doughnuts?" And Wahoo's Fish Taco explains its unique recipe for success.

Comprehensive Instructor Resources

Great news! The "best practices" concept of having experts write chapter content has been expanded to the authors of our ancillary materials. Each ancillary is now written by specialists as well. The third edition of *Marketing Principles and Best Practices* includes comprehensive instructor's resources that provide a wide range of lecture-enhancement material for both new and veteran instructors.

Instructor's Manual

The Instructor's Manual, written by Debra Laverie at Texas Tech University, has been greatly expanded to include the following lecture-enhancement materials:

- In-depth lecture guide, organized by section with reference to textbook pages and PowerPoint slides.
- Insights into the chapter's opening vignette and key teaching points.
- Teaching goals of the Xtra! interactive marketing activity, found on the first page of each chapter and included with Xtra!

- Answers to "Questions for Review and Discussion," "Internet Activities," and "Team Activities."
- Solutions to chapter case and video case.
- Additional lecture material and cases.
- Transparency masters.

Instructor's Resource CD-ROM

This CD includes the Instructor's Manual, Test Bank, ExamView, PowerPoint, and other teaching resources in one convenient source.

Test Bank

Recognizing the critical importance of a comprehensive, 100% accurate test bank, the third-edition test bank has been carefully rewritten and verified for accuracy. The test bank includes true-false, multiple-choice, and fill-in-the blank questions that test knowledge of chapter concepts. Each question is identified by a learning objective and textbook page reference where the question is answered. In addition, test questions about the interactive marketing activities are included in the test bank. The test bank was written by Tom Quirk, Webster University.

ExamView

This computerized testing software contains all of the questions in the printed test bank. This program is an easy-to-use test-creation software compatible with MicroSoft Windows. Instructors can add or edit questions, instructions, and answers and select questions by previewing them on the screen, selecting them randomly, or selecting them by number. Instructors can also create and administer quizzes online, whether over the Internet, a local area network (LAN), or a wide area network (WAN).

PowerPoint Lecture Slides

In response to requests from instructors teaching this course, this new edition of *Marketing Principles and Best Practices* offers three different versions of the Power-Point slides to provide flexibility and simplify lecture presentation. With these three options, instructors may choose light or detailed chapter content with varying degrees of graphics, animations, and video. The PowerPoint slides, developed by Jack Lindgren, University of Virginia, are available in these three versions:

- *Quick Pick PowerPoint Slides.* When you want to present just the core concepts and key terms from each definition, these Quick Pick slides are the best option for explaining the major concepts and key terms in each chapter. These slides are available at the Instructor's Web site and on the PowerPoint CD-ROM.
- *Total Pack PowerPoint Slides.* The Total Pack includes comprehensive coverage of content delivered in a dynamic, graphics-rich presentation. These slides are available at the Instructor's Web site and on the PowerPoint CD-ROM.
- *Total Pack with Videos.* The Total Pack with Videos includes all of the slides in the Total Pack plus video segments that illustrate key chapter points. The videos feature well-known commercials shown during the Superbowl and other commercials from 2003 that students will recognize. The Total Pack with Videos is only available on the PowerPoint CD-ROM.

Video Package

Video segments, featuring companies like Polaroid, Krispy Kreme, ESPN, and Timberland, illustrate the marketing strategies featured in the end-of-chapter video cases. Located at the end of each chapter, each video case is supported by discussion questions that prompt students to make marketing-strategy decisions and evaluate those made by well-known companies. The Instructor's Manual contains suggested solutions to the video case solutions. With Xtra!, students have access to the video segment, case questions, and e-mail functionality to e-mail video case solutions to instructors.

Best Practices Web Site (http://bestpractices.swlearning.com)

The Best Practices textbook-support Web site offers a variety of activities and resources that build on and reinforce knowledge of marketing principles. Supplement downloads, online activities, PowerPoint slides, Marketing in the News, and many other resources are available for instructors at http://bestpractices.swlearning.com.

Marketing in the News

This new feature provides instructors with a continuously refreshed supply of relevant news stories that demonstrate the application of key marketing topics. This valuable resource organizes marketing news stories by chapter to save research time. Available at the Instructor's portion of the textbook-support Web site at http://bestpractices.swlearning.com, Marketing in the News will have a library of marketing news stories and will be refreshed monthly with new marketing events and applications.

Transparency Acetates

Color acetates that summarize chapter topics and key marketing terminology are available in the transparency acetate package.

WebTutor Advantage

WebTutor is an interactive, Web-based, student supplement on WebCT and/or BlackBoard that harnesses the power of the Internet to deliver innovative learning aids that actively engage students. The instructor can incorporate WebTutor as an integral part of the course, or the students can use it on their own as a study guide. Benefits to students include automatic and immediate feedback from quizzes and exams; interactive, multimedia-rich explanation of concepts; on-line exercises that reinforce what they've learned; flashcards that include audio support; and greater interaction and involvement through online discussion forums. In addition, **WebTutor Toolbox** provides students with links to the rich content from our companion Web sites.

Student Resources

Best Practices Xtra! (http://bestpracticesxtra.swlearning.com)

With access to Xtra!, students have an abundant supply of interactive learning experiences that have the potential to help them grasp the complex decision making required by marketers and improve course grades. Xtra! includes these features:

- *Interactive Marketing Activities.* The interactive marketing activities, designed and written by marketing professors, place students in the role of a marketing manager of well-known companies. By responding to a series of prompts, students choose various marketing strategies that they believe provide the greatest potential for market growth. Once they choose a strategy, students immediately learn the consequence of their choices and are given additional opportunities to learn from their experience.
- *Practice Exams.* These practice exams give students an opportunity to test their knowledge in preparation for midterms and final exams. Each question includes feedback for right and wrong answers and textbook page references to ease further study.
- *Chapter Case Video Segments.* These video segments bring the chapter video cases to life.
- *PowerPoint Slides.* These in-depth slides present important chapter topics and include rich illustrations and advertisements.
- *Marketing Planning Template.* This Word file provides an easy-to-use template for a professionally organized and designed marketing plan.

Study Guide

The Study Guide is designed to enhance student understanding and provide additional practice applying chapter concepts. Each chapter includes a summary of chapter learning objectives, experiential exercises, and in-depth quizzes on chapter content and vocabulary. The study guide also includes answers to study guide questions and page references where study guide answers may be found in the textbook.

Best Practices Web Site (http://bestpractices.swlearning.com)

The Best Practices Student Web site offers a variety of activities and resources that build on and reinforce knowledge of marketing principles. Interactive quizzes, online activities, career information, PowerPoint slides, key term review, and many other resources are available for students at http://bestpractices.swlearning.com.

Free InfoTrac® College Edition

Students receive an entire library for the price of one book. With InfoTrac® College Editions, they are given complete, 24-hour-a-day access to more than 10 million full-text articles from more than 4,000 journals and popular magazines and newspapers such as *Newsweek, Time,* and *USA Today.* The database is updated daily with full-length, substantive articles representing more than 20 years of content. Because Info-Trac® is accessible from any computer with Internet access, it is perfect for all students, from dorm dwellers to commuters and distance learners.

PowerPoint Slides

These slides are available for use by students as an aid to note taking and as a tool for reviewing key chapter topics. These are available as a download from the Web support site and with Xtra!

Acknowledgments

Marketing Principles and Best Practices, Third Edition, greatly benefited from the quality of reviews provided by numerous colleagues representing a variety of academic institutions. In particular, the author team is very grateful to the following colleagues for giving their time and insightful direction:

Aaron Ahuvia
University of Michigan Dearborn

John Benavidez
University of New Mexico

Paul Canfield
University of Wisconsin Eau Claire

Alka V. Citrin
Georgia Tech University

Anthony Di Benedetto
Temple University

Gary L. Frankwick
Oklahoma State University

Douglas C. Friedman
Penn State Harrisburg

Gabriel R. Gonzalez
Colorado State University

Barbara Gross
California State University Northridge

Susan Forquer Gupta
University of Wisconsin Milwaukee

John C. Hafer
University of Nebraska at Omaha

Dorothy Harpool
Wichita State University

Cathy L. Hartman
Utah State University

Eric J. Karson
Villanova University

James J. Kellaris
University of Cincinnati

Maria Kniazeva
University of San Diego

Debra A. Laverie
Texas Tech University

Larry Lowe
Bryant College

Michael L. Mallin
Kent State University

Gordon G. Mosley
Troy State University

Thomas A. Myers
University of Richmond

Terry Paul
Ohio State University

Dennis Pitta
University of Baltimore

Jan Napoleon Saykiewicz
Duquesne University

Jeffrey B. Schmidt
The University of Illinois at Urbana-
Champaign

Newell D. Wright
James Madison University

We have also benefited from the quality reviews provided on previous editions by numerous colleagues and thank them for their time and constructive suggestions:

Tim Aurand
Northern Illinois University

Arni Authorsson
College of St. Francis

Mike Barone
Iowa State University

Francine Beaty
Miami University

Mark Bennion
Bowling Green University

Edward Bond
Bradley University

Anne Brumbaugh
Wake Forest University

Bill Carner
University of Texas—Austin

Jerome Christia
Coastal Carolina University

Janice Cox
Miami University-Ohio

Erwin Daneels
Worcester Polytechnic Institute

George Dollar
Clearwater Christian College

Carl Dresden
Coastal Carolina University

Sean Dwyer
Louisiana Tech University

Dave Fallin
Kansas State University

Dwayne Gremler
University of Idaho

Steve Grove
Clemson University

Diane Hambley
University of South Dakota

Charles Harrington
Pasadena City College

Braxton Hinchey
University of Massachusetts—
Lowell

Earl Honeycutt
Old Dominion University

Susan Meyer
Colorado State University

Ina Midkiff
Austin Community College

Russ Moorehead
Des Moines Area Community
College

Terry Paul
Ohio State University

Tom Pritchett
Kennesaw State University

Glen Reicken
East Tennessee State University

Alan Sawyer
University of Florida

Regina P. Schlee
Seattle Pacific University

Don Schreiber
Baylor University

Jane Sojka
Ohio University

Ruth Taylor
Southwest Texas State University

John Weiss
Colorado State University

Rama Yelkur
University of Wiscon—Eau Claire

Joyce Young
Indiana State University

We would also like to extend our heartfelt thanks to the many good folks at South-Western, many of whom we have had the pleasure of knowing for many years through our other text projects. Special thanks to Jack Calhoun, VP/Editorial Director; Mike Roche, VP/Editor-in-Chief; Melissa S. Acuña, Senior Publisher; Steve Hazelwood, Senior Acquisitions Editor; and Nicole Moore, Marketing Manager, for generating and maintaining the level of support and enthusiasm associated with this project throughout the entire process.

We would especially like to thank Mary Draper—Developmental Editor beyond compare. South-Western presented the author team with a great gift when they asked you to develop this project. You are the best of the best and epitomize the spirit of best practices!

Additional thanks are extended to Emily Gross, Production Editor; Chris Miller, Design Project Manager; John Hill, Photography Manager; Susan Van Etten, Photo Researcher; Vicky True, Media Technology Editor; Peggy Buskey, Media Developmental Editor; Pam Wallace, Media Production Editor; Diane Lohman, Manufacturing Coordinator; and Susan Petrie and Kathy Glidden (Stratford Publishing Services), for putting the project together—no small task!

A number of other good people focused on putting together the Instructor's Manual, PowerPoint Lecture Slides, Test Bank, and Study Guide. We would like to extend our special thanks to Debra Laverie, Texas Tech University; Jack Lindgren, University of Virginia; and Tom Quirk, Webster University, for their support and dedication to the project. We acknowledge the contributions of Notre Dame MBA student Celina Celada who conducted research for features in Chapter 15.

We would also like to thank the South-Western sales force for supporting this unique project and stirring up the worldwide principles-of-marketing market. We truly appreciate your efforts in bringing this package to the marketplace and offer our assistance in support of your efforts.

This project continues to generate a great deal of interest in the academic and publishing communities. We thank the parent company of Thomson Learning for wholeheartedly and enthusiastically accepting and supporting the project.

To Lise Johnson, Director of Marketing, and Bill Schoof, Regional Account Manager—there is a little bit of you two in every book that the majority of us write. Many thanks to you both!

Finally, each of us would like to thank our families, friends, and colleagues for their support. Writing a text is a time-consuming experience that often takes us away from those who mean the most in our lives. Thank you for your understanding, patience, and encouragement.

K. Douglas Hoffman, Colorado State University

Chapter 1 Introduction to Marketing
Chapter 2 Strategic and Marketing Planning
Chapter 10 Services Marketing

K. Douglas Hoffman earned his master's and doctorate degrees from the University of Kentucky and his bachelor's degree from The Ohio State University. He has been formally recognized for teaching excellence and has served as past education coordinator for the services marketing special interest group of the American Marketing Association.

Dr. Hoffman currently is a professor of marketing and has taught such courses as Principles of Marketing, Services Marketing, E-Marketing, Retail Management, and Marketing Management. His primary teaching and research passion is services marketing. He launched the first services-marketing classes at Mississippi State University, the University of North Carolina at Wilmington, and Colorado State University.

Prior to his academic career, Dr. Hoffman served as a distribution analyst for Volkswagen of America and worked as a research analyst for Parker Hannifin Corp. His current research and consulting activities are primarily in the areas of customer service/satisfaction, service recovery, and services-marketing education. Dr. Hoffman has coauthored two other South-Western/Thomson Learning texts: *Essentials of Services Marketing* (2nd edition) and *Managing Services Marketing* (4th edition), both with John E. G. Bateson.

Michael R. Czinkota, Georgetown University

Chapter 4 International Marketing

Michael R. Czinkota earned his doctorate degree in logistics and international business from The Ohio State University. He has received honorary degrees from Universidad Pontificia Madre y Maestra in the Dominican Republic and Universidad del Pacifico in Lima, Peru. Dr. Czinkota is a former U.S. deputy assistant secretary of commerce, former head of the U.S. delegation to the Organization for Economic Cooperation and Development (OECD) Industry Committee in Paris, and a member of the Board of Governors of the Academy of Marketing Science. He is also a former board member and vice president of the American Marketing Association. He has authored *International Marketing* (6th edition), *International Business* (6th edition), and *Global Business* (3rd edition), all from South-Western.

Peter R. Dickson, Florida International University

Chapter 3 Marketing Ethics and Social Responsibility
Chapter 5 Marketing Research and Information Systems

Peter R. Dickson is the Knight-Ridder Eminent Scholar in Global Marketing at Florida International University. He was previously the Arthur C. Nielsen, Jr. Chair of Marketing Research at the University of Wisconsin-Madison Nielsen Center for Marketing Research and the Crane Professor of Strategic Marketing at The Ohio State University. Dr. Dickson is heading up the National Hispanic Corporate Council/Florida International University (NHCC/FIU) Hispanic Market Research project, is the Academic Director of the Master in International Business, and is leading the launch of the Masters in Sales Management at the Chapman Business School, Florida International University. He is the past chairman of the marketing strategy special interest group of the American Marketing Association. Dr. Dickson has won numerous awards for his undergraduate and graduate teaching and four of his most recent academic papers won national awards. Recent, relevant papers to the two chapters that he wrote are a coauthored paper that reviewed the impact of the Internet on market research and a paper on the dubious origins of the Sherman Antitrust Act, a cornerstone of marketing law in the United States. In his spare time, Dr. Dickson is an entrepreneur, sailor, landscape gardener, and collector of Georgian silver.

Patrick Dunne, Texas Tech University

Chapter 12 Retailing and Wholesaling

Patrick Dunne, an associate professor of marketing at the Jerry Rawls College of Business at Texas Tech University, received his MBA and PhD from Michigan State University and his BS in Business Administration from Xavier University.

In more than 30 years of years of university teaching at Michigan State, Drake, Oklahoma, and Texas Tech, Dr. Dunne has taught a wide variety of marketing and retailing courses at both the undergraduate and graduate levels. In addition to authoring more than a dozen retailing textbooks, he has published articles in many of the leading academic journals.

Professor Dunne has been honored with several university teaching awards and is actively involved in professional training programs. He is also an active consultant to a variety of retailers and wholesalers.

Abbie Griffin, University of Illinois, Urbana-Champaign

Chapter 9 Marketing's Role in New Product Development and Product Decisions

Abbie Griffin earned her PhD in management from the Massachusetts Institute of Technology, her MBA from Harvard University and her BS in Chemical Engineering from Purdue University. She is editor of the *Journal of Product Innovation Management,* and serves as director of the Product Development and Management Association. She received the 1997 Marketing Science Institute Best Paper Award, the 1993 John D. C. Little Best Paper Award, and the 1994 Frank M. Bass Dissertation Paper Award for "Voice of the Customer." Dr. Griffin teaches product development and business-to-business marketing.

Her research interests include measuring and improving new-product-development processes, obtaining customer inputs for new-product development, decreasing the time needed to commercialize products, and managing technology.

Dr. Griffin's professional experience includes consulting in marketing, strategic planning, and technology management to technology-dependent firms. She is on the Board of Directors of International Truck and Engine (formerly Navistar).

Michael D. Hutt, Arizona State University

Chapter 7 Business-to-Business Marketing

Michael D. Hutt (PhD, Michigan State University) is the Ford Motor Company Professor of Marketing at the W. P. Carey School of Business, Arizona State University. He has also held faculty positions at Miami University (Ohio) and the University of Vermont.

Dr. Hutt's teaching and research interests are concentrated in the areas of business-to-business marketing and strategic marketing. His current research focuses on the cross-functional role that marketing managers assume in formulating strategy. Dr. Hutt's research has been published in the *Journal of Marketing, Journal of Marketing Research, MIT Sloan Management Review, Journal of Retailing, Journal of the Academy of Marketing Science,* and other scholarly journals. For his 2000 contribution to *MIT Sloan Management Review,* he received the Richard Beckhard Prize. He is the coauthor of *Business Marketing Management* (South-Western), now in its eighth edition, and of *Macro Marketing* (John Wiley & Sons).

Balaji C. Krishnan, University of Memphis

Chapter 6 Consumer Behavior

Balaji C. Krishnan is an assistant professor of marketing in the Fogelman College of Business and Economics at the University of Memphis, where he teaches in the undergraduate, graduate, international MBA, and executive MBA programs. His research interests are in the areas of pricing and price promotions, branding and brand equity, services marketing, and cross-cultural issues in marketing. He has published in the *Journal of Public Policy and Marketing,* the *Journal of Business Research,* and the *Journal of Services Marketing.*

Robert F. Lusch, Texas Christian University

Chapter 12 Retailing and Wholesaling

Robert F. Lusch is Distinguished University Professor and Dean of the M. J. Neeley School of Business at Texas Christian University. Previously, he served on the faculty of the University of Oklahoma for 24 years, where he held the Helen Robson Walton Chair in Marketing Strategy and was George Lynn Cross Research Professor. A prolific author, he has published 16 books and more than 150 articles and is best recognized for his work in marketing and retailing strategy. In 1996, he received the Harold Maynard Award for Theoretical Contributions to the Marketing Literature, and in 1997 was named the Distinguished Marketing Educator of the Year by the Academy of Marketing Science. He is also the past editor of the *Journal of Marketing,* which is the oldest academic marketing journal (founded in 1936), and past chairperson of the American Marketing Association, the largest professional association of marketing educators and practitioners in North America.

Ilkka A. Ronkainen, Georgetown University

Chapter 4 International Marketing

Ilkka A. Ronkainen earned his doctorate and master's degrees from the University of South Carolina and an additional master's degree from the Helsinki School of Economics. He has served on the review board of the *Journal of Business Research, International Marketing Review,* and the *Journal of International Business Studies.*

He is a former North American coordinator for the European Marketing Academy and is also a former board member of the Washington International Trade Association. Dr. Ronkainen serves as a docent of international marketing at the Helsinki School of Economics. He has served as a consultant to IBM, the Rank Organization, and the Organization of American States. In addition, he maintains close ties with a number of Finnish companies and their internationalization and educational efforts.

Bert Rosenbloom, Drexel University

Chapter 11 Marketing Channels and Distribution

Dr. Bert Rosenbloom is Professor of Marketing and holds the Rauth Chair in Electronic Commerce at Drexel University. Before coming to Drexel, he served on the faculty of the City University of New York.

Dr. Rosenbloom is a leading expert on the management of marketing channels and distribution systems. *Marketing Channels: A Management View,* seventh edition is one of his eleven books. His book *Retail Marketing* (Random House), a pioneering text on the application of modern marketing methods to retail channels, has had a major impact on distribution throughout the U.S. and other countries around the world. Another of his books, *Marketing Functions and the Wholesaler Distributor* (Distribution Research and Education Foundation) has been acclaimed in the wholesaling sector for providing the industry with new concepts and analytical methods for increasing productivity in wholesale marketing channels.

Dr. Rosenbloom's research has been widely published in the major professional journals of marketing such as *Journal of Marketing, Journal of Retailing, Journal of the Academy of Marketing Science, Business Horizons, Industrial Marketing Management, Journal of Consumer Marketing, Journal of Personal Selling and Sales Management, Management Review, Long Range Planning, European Journal of Marketing* and numerous others.

Dr. Rosenbloom served as the editor of the *Journal of Marketing Channels* and served on the editorial boards of the *Journal of Consumer Marketing, Journal of the Academy of Marketing Science,* and *Journal of International Consumer Marketing,* and on the ad hoc review boards of the *Journal of Marketing Research, Journal of Marketing,* and *Journal of Retailing.* He also served for nine years as Academic Consulting Editor for the Random House series of books on marketing. In addition, he has served as the Vice President of the Philadelphia Chapter of the American Marketing Association, on the Board of Governors of the Academy of Marketing Science, and was awarded an Erskine Fellowship. He also served as President of the International Management Development Association.

Jagdish N. Sheth, Emory University

Chapter 6 Consumer Behavior

Jagdish (Jag) N. Sheth is the Charles H. Kellstadt Professor of Marketing at the Goizueta Business School and the founder of the Center for Relationship Marketing (CRM) at Emory University. He has also taught at the University of Southern California, the University of Illinois, Columbia University, and the Massachusetts Institute of Technology. Dr. Sheth is nationally and internationally known for his scholarly contributions in marketing, customer satisfaction, global competition, and strategic thinking.

Dr. Sheth has received numerous awards, including the Outstanding Marketing Educator award of the Academy of Marketing Science, the Outstanding Educator Award of Sales and Marketing Executives International, and the P. D. Converse

Award for outstanding contributions in marketing theory from the American Marketing Association. He has been recognized as a Distinguished Fellow of the Academy of Marketing Science and a Distinguished Fellow of the International Engineering Consortium. Dr. Sheth is also a Fellow of the American Psychological Association (APA).

Terence A. Shimp, University of South Carolina

Chapter 13 Integrated Marketing Communications and Other MarCom Tools

Terence A. Shimp is a professor of marketing, W.W. Johnson Distinguished Foundation Fellow, and chair of the Marketing Department at the University of South Carolina. Dr. Shimp holds a doctorate in business administration from the University of Maryland. He is an award-winning teacher, having won the AMOCO teaching award in 1990 that is presented annually to a single faculty member at the University of South Carolina. In 2001, the American Academy of Advertising honored Dr. Shimp with a Lifetime Contributions to Advertising Award. He also has been recognized for outstanding articles in the *Journal of Consumer Research* and the *Journal of Advertising*. He is past president of the Association for Consumer Research and president of the *Journal of Consumer Research* policy board. Dr. Shimp serves on the editorial review boards for the *Journal of Consumer Research*, the *Journal of Consumer Psychology*, and *Journal of Marketing*, the *Journal of Public Policy and Marketing*, *Marketing Letters*, and the *Journal of Marketing Communications*.

After serving on the faculty of Kent State University for four years, Dr. Shimp has been a faculty member at the University of South Carolina for 25 years. He teaches marketing communications at both the undergraduate and graduate levels and research methods to PhD students. His primary areas of research are consumer learning, persuasion, and response to marketing and advertising communications. He is the author of *Advertising, Promotion, and Supplemental Aspects of Integrated Marketing Communications*, sixth edition, from South-Western.

Judy A. Siguaw, Cornell University

Chapter 14 Personal Selling and Sales Management

Judy A. Siguaw earned her master's and doctorate degrees from Louisiana Tech University and her bachelor's degree from Lamar University. She has been awarded the Chancellor's Excellence in Teaching Award from the University of North Carolina at Wilmington; research grants from the Marketing Science Institute, American Express, and the American Hotel Foundation; and research awards from the Chartered Institute of Marketing, Cornell University, and the Academy of Marketing Science. She serves as the faculty advisor for the Cornell student chapter of the Hotel Sales and Marketing Association International and also as a trustee of the Hotel Sales and Marketing Association International Foundation Board.

Dr. Siguaw's research interests include sales/sales management, distribution channels, market orientation, and innovation. She has published in the *Journal of Marketing*, the *Journal of Marketing Research*, the *Journal of the Academy of Marketing Science*, the *Journal of Business Research*, the *Journal of Marketing Education*, *Industrial Marketing Management*, and others. She is a coauthor of *American Lodging Excellence: The Key to Best Practices in the Lodging Industry* and *Introducing LISREL*.

Prior to entering academia, Dr. Siguaw spent 10 years in the corporate environment, including a sales position with General Foods Corporation, now a division of Philip Morris known as Kraft Foods. Today, Dr. Siguaw provides executive education and consulting in the area of sales.

Penny M. Simpson, University of Texas-Pan American

Chapter 8 Market Segmentation and Target Markets

Penny Simpson earned her DBA in marketing from Louisiana Tech University and currently teaches at University of Texas-Pan American. Dr. Simpson has received several teaching awards and was previously selected as the David D. Morgan United Teacher Associates Insurance Company Endowed Professor. She serves on the editorial board of *Teaching Business Ethics* and has reviewed articles and books for other journals including the *Journal of Business Research* and the *Journal of the Academy of Marketing Science*. She has also published research in a number of journals, including the *Journal of Marketing*, the *Journal of the Academy of Marketing Science*, the *Journal of Marketing Channels*, the *Journal of Business Research*, and the *Journal of Marketing Education*. Dr. Simpson's wide area of research interests and publications range from health care and tourism to promotion and distribution channels, including the Internet. All of these research interests have focused on understanding targeted markets and the effects of various factors on their responses. Dr. Simpson also worked several years in management in the savings and loan industry and has consulted with a number of regional banks. Her primary consulting activities involve the development and success of small businesses in a competitive environment.

Thomas W. Speh, Miami University-Ohio

Chapter 7 Business-to-Business Marketing

Thomas W. Speh is the James E. Rees Distinguished Professor of Marketing and Associate Dean of Academic Affairs at the Richard T. Farmer School of Business, Miami University, Ohio. Dr. Speh earned his PhD from Michigan State University.

Dr. Speh has published articles in a number of scholarly journals, including the *Journal of Marketing, Harvard Business Review,* the *Journal of the Academy of Marketing Science,* the *Journal of Business Logistics,* and others. He is also the recipient of several teaching awards, including the Effective Educator award from the Miami University Alumni Association. Dr. Speh has served as president of the Warehousing Education and Research Council and is currently the president of the Council of Logistics Management.

Prior to his tenure at Miami University, Dr. Speh taught at the University of Alabama and Michigan State University. He is the coauthor of *Business Marketing Management* (South-Western), now in its eighth edition.

Joel E. Urbany, University of Notre Dame

Chapter 15 Pricing Strategies and Determination

Joel E. Urbany earned his PhD from The Ohio State University. In 1998, he was awarded *Business Week*'s Most Popular Professor Rating for the MBA program at the University of Notre Dame. In 1993, he received the Outstanding Second-Year Professor award for the MBA program from the University of South Carolina, and in 1988 he won the Alfred G. Smith Award for Teaching Excellence from the University of South Carolina. Dr. Urbany is a member of the editorial review boards of the *Journal of Consumer Research* and *Marketing Letters,* and serves as an invited reviewer for several publications, including *Marketing Science,* the *Journal of Marketing,* the *Journal of Marketing Research,* and the *Journal of Retailing.*

Dr. Urbany's research focuses on information economics, managerial decision making, and buyer behavior. He has consulted with and conducted executive education programs for a wide variety of companies, including Bayer; Flagstar, Inc.; Donnelly Corp.; Milliken; Marsh Supermarkets; and Ambac International.

Third Edition

Marketing Principles and Best Practices

In Chapter 1, **Douglas Hoffman**, Colorado State University, introduces marketing as a business philosophy and discusses marketing's active role in facilitating exchange relationships. Students will learn how marketing strategy becomes a game of "survival of the fittest," meaning that those businesses that are best able to adapt to changing environmental forces are the ones that will survive and thrive in the future. In Chapter 2, Professor Hoffman explains how strategic and marketing planning offers decision makers frameworks to organize information that ultimately lead to more informed decision making.

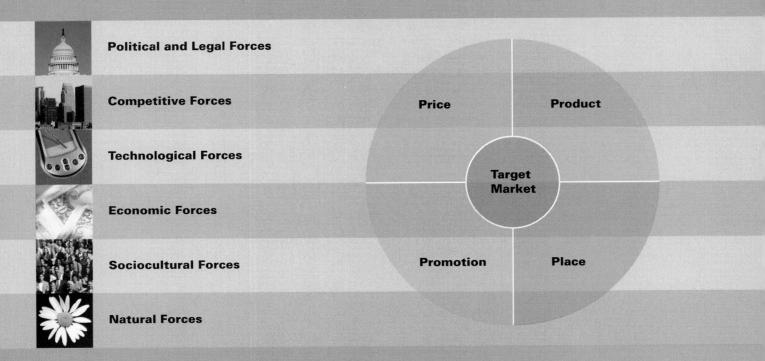

Political and Legal Forces

Competitive Forces

Technological Forces

Economic Forces

Sociocultural Forces

Natural Forces

Price

Product

Target Market

Promotion

Place

Given the renewed emphasis on socially responsible and ethical business behavior, **Peter Dickson**, Florida International University, introduces in Chapter 3 the four aspects of marketing social responsibility and the rules and regulations that govern the elements of the marketing mix. In Chapter 4, **Michael Czinkota** and **Ilkka Ronkainen**, both of Georgetown University, deal with the opportunities and challenges of international marketing and illustrate the importance of modifying strategy to meet the needs of new global markets.

The Marketing Environment

 Political and Legal Forces When the market fails to be "sufficiently" inventive, the federal government has to step in, for example, by requiring washing machine manufacturers to invent, manufacture, and market new models that use 35% less energy, all of this by 2007.

 Competitive Forces In economies where industries are protected or where distribution monopolies are granted, it is unlikely that the marketing distribution system will be as efficient as it can and should be.

 Technological Forces New technology succeeds by creatively destroying an old, inferior technology. This is good for society, but new technology also can create new ethical dilemmas, such as those related to privacy on the Internet and the cloning of stem cells to be used in lifesaving medical research.

 Economic Forces Economic forces may be considered when SBUs, classified as dogs, are being considered for divestiture. Decision makers may "maintain" a "dog" to sustain the economic vitality of the local community.

 Sociocultural Forces A nationwide poll of adults ages 18–65, undertaken by Duffey Communications and RoperASW in 2002, revealed that "unrealistic standards of beauty" was the biggest criticism that customers had of advertising.

 Natural Forces The European Union has developed an ecolabel, the EU flower, to "stimulate both the supply and demand of products with a reduced environmental impact." Ecolabels are driven both by pragmatism (reduced ability to deal with waste) and demand (by environmentally conscious consumer groups).

Introduction to Marketing

The age of typical buyers of Honda vehicles has steadily increased over the years, and the company is concerned about future sales growth if the trend continues. To combat the "age creep," Honda embarked on a plan to create a younger, more hip image for Honda by implementing an ambitious marketing plan designed to capture the hearts and minds of 18–35-year-old males. The plan includes the development of a new product—an innovative sport utility vehicle, the Element—specially designed for the needs of young outdoor enthusiasts.

You Decide. After reading the opening vignette and paying special attention to the sections of this chapter marked with the chess piece, answer these questions:

1. Honda has developed the Element, a new product to appeal to younger male consumers. Which business philosophy did they appear to use?

2. The strategy used to market the Element included identifying a specific target market and designing a marketing mix that meets targeted consumer needs and reinforces the product-positioning strategy. This strategy is best seen in Honda's implementation of which marketing-mix elements?

3. The introduction and marketing of the Honda Element was a marketing strategic response to which external environmental force?

Courtesy, © 2003 American Honda Motor Company

**Honda and the
Art of Tailoring
the Marketing Mix**
According to *USA Today*'s Test Drive editor, James R. Healy, the Honda Element "is funky looking, fun to drive, useful beyond belief and a delightful poke in the eye of all those over-complicated, overpriced machines that have become the norm."[1] In other words, the Honda Element is one of the coolest new vehicles on the market today.

The Element is Honda's most recent attempt to attract young males ages 18–35 who are outdoor enthusiasts. The product was introduced primarily in response to two trends. First, Honda wanted to combat the "age creep" among its customer base. Across all Honda automotive products, the brand's median owner age is 43. Additional indications are that the brand's median age will continue to rise. Case in point: The median age of Honda's Civic sedan buyers has risen from 37 to 41 in the past four years. As a result, the Element was purposely designed to appeal to a younger demographic. The Element's second primary objective is to attract male consumers. Unlike most cars, Hondas are increasingly sold to women. Consequently, despite Honda's record sales, its marketing personnel are betting on the Element to broaden its customer base and insure future sales growth. Ultimately, the Element has been designed to attract younger buyers who may make the brand hipper. Honda needs a youth-oriented product to compete with import competitors.

Honda is implementing a marketing strategy purposely tailored for its target market—young outdoor enthusiasts. The Element is Honda's first completely American-designed and -developed sport utility vehicle. The Element's product strategy is specifically designed with the young and active consumer in mind. First, as shown, the Element features cubic styling, which Honda believes is masculine. Part Hummer H2 and part Mercedes G-wagon, the Element features cargo-friendly side-door openings, 39 inches of rear-seat legroom, a rear seat that splits in two or folds up completely against the sides of the vehicle—leaving ample sleeping space for those nights locked out of the house, and a split tailgate that provides shelter from the rain and a place to sit while the driver is putting on his ski boots or scuba gear (the bottom portion of the tailgate will support 440 pounds). The upholstery is best described as FXC—fabric for extreme conditions—and the rest of the vehicle is appointed with a wipe-clean interior.

The Element's pricing strategy is in line with what its target market can afford. Models range in price from $16,500 for the basic model to $21,310 for the deluxe EX model that includes everything from MP3 jacks to rear power outlets, and AM/FM/CD stereo with subwoofer to a removable skylight above the rear seat and cargo space designed to accommodate tall cargo.

The Element's distribution strategy is consistent with the rest of Honda's product line. The Element is distributed to the marketplace through Honda's authorized dealers. Honda expects to deliver 50,000 Elements a year and can produce as many as 70,000 a year.

The Element's promotional strategy is specifically targeted to young males who are outdoor enthusiasts. The Element's first ads appeared on *Monday Night Football,* featuring targeted males on surfboards and mountain bikes. Other ads will run on shows such as Fox TV's *The Simpsons* featuring the Element with props such as kayaks, bongos, and sleeping bags. Additional ads are scheduled to appear on cable networks such as *Comedy Central* and network TV's Super Bowl pre-game programming. A print campaign is also scheduled to appear in sports magazines dedicated to snowboarding, surfing, and skateboarding; music magazines such as *The Source* and *Blender,* and male-oriented magazines such as *Maxim.*

Honda's positioning of the Element as a young male-oriented sport utility vehicle may face some interesting challenges. Vehicle

VOICE OF THE EXPERT
K. Douglas Hoffman, Colorado State University

Welcome to Chapter One of Marketing Principles and Best Practices! Within this chapter, the origins of marketing as a business philosophy, marketing's impact on society, and the fundamentals of marketing strategy are presented. Successful businesses view marketing strategy as a dynamic process that is able to flex with changing environmental forces such as the economy, competition, and even customers themselves. As an analogy, consider marketing as a game of chess played in a thunderstorm. Within your control are chess pieces that can be strategically moved to carry out your plan of attack (marketing strategy). Beyond your control are the chess pieces of your opponent (the competition) and the thunderstorm that rages around the game itself (other environmental forces). The player most adept at coordinating strategy and adapting to changing competitive and other environmental forces dominates the board (the marketplace). It's a game of "survival of the fittest." Those best able to adapt to changing conditions not only survive, but thrive.

enthusiasts are predicting that the Element will also attract hordes of "old guys" who have fond memories of their most beloved vehicles, such as the 1940s Willys Overland wagon, the 1950s Volkswagen Bus, and the 1960s International-Harvester Scout. The Element evokes feelings associated with all of these classics. Additionally, plenty of female snowboarders, surfers, and outdoor enthusiasts would also love to own an Element. The Element's position in the marketplace will ultimately be defined by the brand's customers.

What is Marketing? Ask 20 experts and you're likely to get 20 different answers. A Google™ search of the term "marketing" generates an astounding 35.4 million matches and the phrase "marketing defined" yields a smaller but still spectacular 1.63 million matches.[2] From this search, it becomes readily apparent that the scope of marketing is vast and wide, as "marketing," the term, is connected with a variety of descriptors, such as green marketing, social marketing, sports marketing, Internet marketing, health care marketing, database marketing, niche marketing, strategic marketing, viral marketing, hospitality and tourism marketing, business-to-business marketing, consumer marketing, government marketing, relationship marketing, integrated marketing, direct marketing, customer relationship marketing, e-mail marketing, industrial marketing, and agri-marketing, among others.

Clearly, the practice of marketing is applicable to businesses big and small that range from the world's most admired companies, such as Wal-Mart, Southwest Airlines, BMW, Sony, and Nokia, to mom-and-pop type operations, such as family-owned restaurants, florists, and hardware stores, to neighborhood kids who mow lawns, provide child care, tend gardens, and sell lemonade from homemade lemonade stands.[3] It is also apparent that marketing applies to a variety of economic sectors, whether they are agricultural, manufacturing, or service-related. In addition, marketing applies to the public sector as well as to the private sector and is equally applicable for nonprofit firms (promoting social causes such as energy conservation, responsible drinking, funding for medical research), as it is for for-profit companies.

So, what is Marketing? The common theme that surrounds the vast majority of marketing definitions is that marketing is the planning and implementation of almost everything an organization does to facilitate an exchange between itself and its customers. As it facilitates exchange, marketing looks beyond its own organizational boundaries and takes into account external forces that exist in the business environment. Marketing efforts are then adjusted accordingly to facilitate exchange under the new set of conditions. As conditions continue to change, so does the marketing effort. Consequently, marketing is a continuous and dynamic strategic decision-making process.

The primary objective of this chapter is to acquaint students with a fundamental understanding of marketing and marketing concepts. As such, the chapter introduces marketing as a business philosophy and discusses marketing's active role in facilitating exchange relationships. As a business philosophy, marketing affects customers' lives and the communities where they live, work, and play; consequently, the societal impact of marketing is also presented. Finally, as Honda illustrated in the opening vignette, marketing is a dynamic strategic process that matches the firm's strengths and resources to potential opportunities that exist within the marketing environment. Hence, the fundamentals of marketing strategy conclude the chapter and provide the basis for *best practices* in marketing decision-making.

Marketing as a Business Philosophy

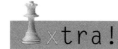

1 LEARNING OBJECTIVE

The sophisticated modern marketing practices implemented by Coca-Cola, Procter & Gamble, Mitsubishi, and other dominant market players did not develop overnight. They evolved over time by trial and error, through turbulent economic and other market forces, and continue to be refined today.[4] Traditionally, introductory marketing textbooks present the historical and philosophical development of marketing in terms of eras defined by specific periods in time. However, scholars have recently discounted this "periodization view." In fact, ample evidence exists to indicate that business practices thought to have been developed in recent decades were in fact practiced centuries ago. Similarly, approaches to markets that were thought to end decades ago still continue today and for good reasons.

In an effort to enhance our understanding of marketing as a business philosophy, it is helpful to compare four orientations, or business philosophies, that businesses have embraced as they sought success in the marketplace. It is important to note that these four orientations could easily fall along a continuum with endpoints ranging from an inner-directed approach to an outer-directed approach reflecting each orientation's inclusion of customer and other key player input into organizational decision making (see Figure 1.1). Based on the continuum, many of today's companies could be described as more or less *product-oriented, sales-oriented, market-oriented,* or *relationship marketing-oriented.*

Product Orientation: If We Build It, They Will Come

Firms that adopt a product orientation channel their efforts and resources into the efficient production of their products, with little or no input or direction from customers. Typically, these firms embrace the **production concept**, which means that they choose to pursue a business philosophy that focuses on making products that are widely available, affordable, and require little selling effort. These firms are usually manufacturing-oriented and emphasize improved production requirements over customer research. For example, the early days of the cell phone and personal computing industry during the 1990s appear to have followed a production philosophy. Products were mass produced to make them more available and affordable and product improvements were primarily driven by internal forces such as engineering and manufacturing. Businesses that adopt a product orientation are most successful when demand exceeds supply and competitive pressures are few. In other words, a

Production concept
Is based on the belief that products that are widely available and affordable will sell themselves.

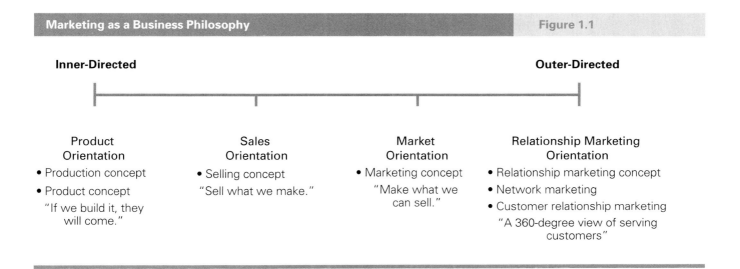

Marketing as a Business Philosophy   Figure 1.1

Inner-Directed   **Outer-Directed**

Product Orientation	Sales Orientation	Market Orientation	Relationship Marketing Orientation
• Production concept	• Selling concept	• Marketing concept	• Relationship marketing concept
• Product concept	"Sell what we make."	"Make what we can sell."	• Network marketing
"If we build it, they will come."			• Customer relationship marketing
			"A 360-degree view of serving customers"

product orientation supports the viewpoint that "if we build it, they [customers] will come!" Those following a product orientation commonly believe that distribution is a secondary concern best left to wholesalers and retailers so that the business can focus on its primary goal of production.

A secondary belief of the product orientation is that "good products will sell themselves." This point of view is known as the **product concept** and is based on the idea that customers will always prefer and therefore purchase the best products on the market. Although the product concept initially makes sense, (i.e., why wouldn't customers desire the best products on the market?), it is readily apparent that customers either cannot afford or are not willing to pay for continuous quality improvements that they really do not need or want. For example, if the computing speed of a Dell personal computer can be improved by 50%, those who support the product concept believe that customers should be readily willing to replace their current computing systems. However, if that 50% improvement translates into a savings of an eighth of a second of processing time, many customers are not likely to reinvest in new systems, since this product improvement is of little benefit to most customers. Ultimately, customers primarily look to purchase value—the best product for the best price that best suits their needs and wants.

Sales Orientation: Selling What We Make

Traditionally, businesses that are unsuccessful pursuing a product orientation make the transition into a sales orientation because they are faced with unsold inventories. Consequently, the business is presented with the challenge of convincing customers to purchase products it has already produced. With a sales orientation, distribution activities begin to take on a higher priority. Hence, in comparison to the production concept's notion of "if we build it, they will come," and the product concept's idea that "good products will sell themselves," the **selling concept** promotes the business philosophy of "selling what we make." Examples of the selling concept in action can be found in many of today's automobile dealerships, where sales representatives are more motivated to sell existing inventory than to place new manufacturing orders that meet specific customer needs and wants. The selling concept is also widely practiced on the Internet through the use of pop-up ads that appear in a separate window and overlay the Web site that the user had intended to view. The mass distribution of unsolicited e-mail advertising would also qualify as a sales-oriented approach.

Although sales-oriented businesses communicate with the market, the communication tends to be unidirectional (one-way), with the seller being the primary source of the communication. Little if any information communicated from the buyer to the seller is incorporated into the selling strategy. Compared to a product orientation, the cost of communicating to customers and the price reductions offered to sell off unsold inventories add to the cost of pursuing a sales orientation and take their toll on profit margins.

A harsh perspective of a sales-oriented business is a firm that pursues a "hard- or high-pressure sales strategy"—pressuring customers to purchase products even though the customer originally neither wanted nor needed the product. However, over the years, many firms have come to realize the shortsighted wisdom of high-pressure sales tactics and are pursuing more long-term-oriented and consumer-friendly approaches to sales. Today's professional personal selling approaches are much more in tune with meeting customer needs and wants and providing value to customers.

Market Orientation: Make What We Can Sell

In contrast to product and sales orientations, market-oriented firms gather, share, and use information about "the market" (customers, competitors, market trends, etc.) to make decisions before engaging in the sales process.[5] In other words, a

Product concept
Also known as the better-mouse-trap fallacy, is the belief that customers will favor the best-quality products on the market.

Selling concept
Promotes the business philosophy of "selling what we make."

market-oriented firm's relationship with its customers is a reciprocal (two-way) relationship. As such, market-oriented firms actively seek out customer needs and wants and then develop and provide products that satisfy previously identified or anticipated shortages and desires. For example, Honda's marketing efforts that were described in the opening vignette demonstrate how knowledge obtained from the marketplace was integrated into the Element's development. Formally defined, market-oriented organizations can be described as those businesses that practice the three pillars of the **marketing concept** (see Figure 1.2):

1. Customer focus
2. Coordinated marketing effort
3. Long-term success.

Customer focus pertains to obtaining information about customer needs and wants and then providing products that fulfill these shortages and desires. As further discussed in Chapter 6, *needs* are unsatisfactory conditions that prompt the customer to take action to make the condition better. Needs are basic and reflect shortages of necessities such as food, water, shelter, and transportation. In comparison, *wants* are desires to obtain more satisfaction than is absolutely necessary to improve the unsatisfactory condition. For example, a customer may need transportation to attend classes and a Huffy bicycle may suffice; however, what the customer may really want is a Honda Element to fulfill his or her transportation requirement. In addition, once customers' basic needs are met, their wants seemingly appear to expand exponentially. The next time you shop at a grocery or department store take notice of the vast array of products available today. Do most of these products satisfy needs or wants? Clearly, many more "wants" than "needs" are being targeted by today's product offerings.

In sharp contrast to the sales concept of "selling what we make," the marketing concept promotes the business philosophy of "making what we can sell." Practitioners of the marketing concept understand that obtaining a customer focus goes far beyond basic customer research that collects information about customers' current sets of needs and wants. Obtaining a customer focus should also include gathering marketing intelligence on environmental forces such as competitive, economic, sociocultural, technological, political/legal, and natural forces that affect customer needs and wants. In addition, businesses that practice a customer focus obtain information

Marketing concept
Promotes the business philosophy of "making what we can sell" and is built upon the three pillars of customer focus, coordinated marketing, and long-term success.

Customer focus
Pertains to obtaining information about customer needs and wants and then providing products that address these needs and wants.

The Three Pillars of the Marketing Concept	Figure 1.2

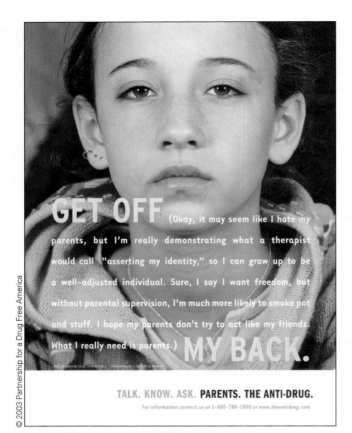

Non-profit organizations such as the Partnership for a Drug-Free America utilize marketing to fight drug abuse.

Coordinated marketing effort

Represents the business mindset that adopting and implementing a market orientation should not be the sole responsibility of the marketing department.

Long-term success

Focuses on building and maintaining customer relationships that can last a lifetime.

Relationship marketing concept

Seeks to create and sustain mutually satisfying long-term relationships not only with customers but also with other key players, such as employees, suppliers, distributors, retailers, the surrounding community, and society as a whole.

pertaining to customers' future needs and wants, as well as their current set of needs and preferences. Hence, over the years, the concept of customer focus has broadened and taken on more of a strategic nature.

Market-oriented organizations also practice the second pillar of the marketing concept—a **coordinated marketing effort**. In its simplest form, a coordinated marketing effort represents the business mindset that adopting and implementing a market orientation should not be the sole responsibility of the marketing department. In essence, coordinated marketing means that achieving a market orientation is a group effort and that a variety of departments throughout the organization should be involved in the process. Marketing intelligence should be gathered and disseminated throughout the organization, and a variety of departments should work together to respond to the set of customer needs and wants identified. For example, the research and development department needs market intelligence to design and develop new products, production personnel need to be kept informed so they can gear up their manufacturing facilities and produce the new product, purchasing needs information about the parts needed to build the product so it can establish relationships with suppliers, and finance needs information for developing budgets to fund production and marketing activities. Clearly, a business will never be market-oriented without a coordinated marketing effort that transcends the various functional departments.

The third pillar of the marketing concept practiced by market-oriented businesses is a focus on **long-term success**. Although scholars disagree whether long-term success is a component or a consequence of the market orientation philosophy, it is important to note that the vast majority of businesses achieve long-term success buy conducting *customer-oriented* business practices. Long-term success distinguishes itself from short-term success in that the former tends to focus on building and maintaining customer relationships that can last a lifetime. For example, as a child you most likely opened a checking and/or savings account with a local bank. As your needs and wants grew with you, your relationship with your bank most likely began to expand in the form of an ATM card, a debit or credit card, or even a car loan. As you continue to mature, your relationship with your bank may be further solidified as you obtain a home loan and then a home equity loan to remodel the kitchen or apply to other purchases. In addition to your banking needs, most banks are now expanding into insurance and other financial products (such as retirement planning) to capitalize on their existing customer relationships and provide one-stop shopping for all of your banking, insurance, and other financial product needs. Finally, it is important to note that long-term success is not necessarily defined solely in terms of profitability and may alternatively be defined in terms such as market share, sales growth, and/or new product success. In addition, there are literally thousands of nonprofit firms that are very effective marketers for which long-term success is defined in nonmonetary terms, such as Planned Parenthood, Mothers Against Drunk Driving (MADD), and the Red Cross, to name a few.

Relationship Marketing Orientation: A 360-Degree View of Serving Customers

Compared to the marketing orientation, which integrates customer needs and wants into its business philosophy, the **relationship marketing concept** seeks to create and sustain mutually satisfying long-term relationships, not only with its customers but also with other key players, such as employees, suppliers, distributors, retailers, the surrounding community, and society as a whole. Currently referred to as a "360-degree view of serving customers," relationship marketing considers the impact of operations on a much broader set of stakeholders and focuses increasingly on sustaining long-term relationships with the firm's most profitable customers.

Companies such as Hewlett-Packard (HP) that practice relationship marketing develop marketing networks to compete in the marketplace. A **marketing network** includes the company and its stakeholders, who form mutually profitable business relationships. In HP's case, its marketing network includes such companies as Intel, the highly respected Pentium chip manufacturer; Nokia, the Finnish wireless technology innovator; Celestica, the manufacturer of printed circuit boards; and Agilent Technologies, which specializes in testing and measurement products and standards. HP has also forged relationships with universities that supply its talented workforce. In addition, HP actively encourages its workforce to become involved in community outreach programs which demonstrates the company's commitment to social corporate citizenship. Ultimately, marketing networks create environments that facilitate technological and marketing synergies among companies and institutions, which can lead to the development of innovative new products and a vast variety of other operational improvements aimed at increasing profits.

Marketing network
Includes the company and its stakeholders, who form mutually profitable business relationships.

Firms engaged in relationship marketing activities are also often actively involved in the practice of **customer relationship management (CRM)**—the process of identifying, attracting, differentiating, and retaining customers. CRM applications cover a wide array of business activities, such as sales force automation, partner relationship management, data warehousing, and customer profiling and segmentation.[6] As such, CRM is discussed in greater detail in later chapters that deal with topics such as business-to-business marketing, services marketing, personal selling, and sales management. Essentially, the goal of CRM is to provide seamless coordination among all customer-facing functions by integrating people, process, and technology to maximize relationships with all customers. In other words, regardless of whether a Southwest Airlines passenger is conducting a face-to-face conversation with an inside ticket agent, a curbside baggage handler, or one of Southwest's call center cus-

Customer relationship management (CRM)
is the process of identifying, attracting, differentiating, and retaining customers.

tomer service representatives, each of these employees should have access to the same information regarding the customer's travel plans, frequent flyer status, personal preferences (seating, meals, beverages), and billing information. Similar interfaces with the airline's business-to-business partners are also established. Effective CRM systems help firms customize the customer experience, which leads to increased customer satisfaction, customer retention, sales growth, and profitability. In addition, business-to-business transactions become more cost-efficient and effective. Customer relationship management is viewed as the wave of the future.

LEARNING OBJECTIVE 2

Marketing as an Exchange Process

Exchange process
Takes place when two or more parties give something of value to each other to satisfy needs or wants.

As our *Google*™ search of the phrase "marketing defined" uncovered, facilitating exchange between buyers and sellers is at the crux of every definition of modern marketing. Simply stated, the **exchange process** takes place when two or more parties give something of value to each other to satisfy needs or wants. Ultimately, marketing exchanges exist because they are beneficial to both parties, whether it be cash in exchange for products or products exchanged or bartered for other products. Marketing's role in facilitating the exchange process is clearly stated in today's most accepted definition of marketing provided by the American Marketing Association.[7]

Marketing
Is the process of planning and executing the conception, pricing, promotion, and distribution of ideas, goods, and services to create exchanges that satisfy individual and organizational goals.

Marketing is the process of planning and executing the conception, pricing, promotion, and distribution of ideas, goods, and services to create exchanges that satisfy individual and organizational goals.

Facilitating Exchange through Marketing Activities

Marketing facilitates the exchange process by providing a variety of *marketing activities* that benefit customers, producers, and marketing channel intermediaries—namely wholesalers and retailers (see Figure 1.3). Traditionally, marketing activities include the following:

- Buying: Marketers buy an assortment of products from many different manufacturers that are made available to customers under one roof. For example, the typical U.S. supermarket carries more than 15,000 items purchased from more than 500 manufacturers. Buying activities help simplify consumer decision making and make purchasing products a much more efficient process.

Figure 1.3	Marketing Facilitates Exchange

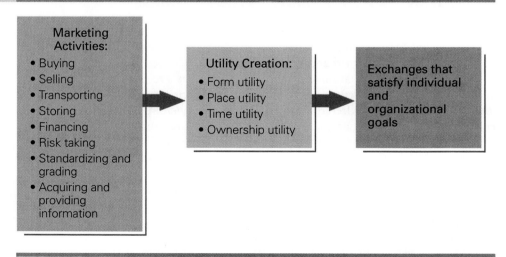

- Selling: Channel intermediaries, such as wholesalers and retailers, play a key selling role, effectively reducing the number of transactions that need to take place between producers and customers. By eliminating the need for customers to have direct contact with the manufacturer, producers are free to focus on their core competency—production. Without channel intermediaries, the number of transactions between customers and producers would be enormous. Wal-Mart is the world's largest retailer and offers a broad selection of products at discount prices. Surprising to many, Wal-Mart is also the number one jewelry retailer, toy retailer, and grocery retailer.[8]

- Transporting: Transportation activities, also often referred to as *logistics* or *physical distribution,* facilitate the exchange process by moving the right amount of product to the right place at the right time to enhance customer satisfaction. Showmotion, a proven leader in the entertainment transportation industry, uses its crack staff of "road warriors" to provide specialized transportation for touring acts such as Destiny's Child and John Mayer, mobile marketing campaigns for products such as Jolly Rancher, and special event productions.[9]

- Storing: The quantities in which products are manufactured are usually too large for any individual consumer to use immediately. Hence, channel intermediaries, such as wholesalers and retailers, physically hold products between the time they are produced and the time they are needed by final consumers. Grocers such as King Soopers, Safeway, and Albertsons store products on their shelves and in their freezers until consumers are ready to buy.

- Financing: Financing arrangements facilitate the exchange process by enticing customers to buy today and/or enabling customers who do not have adequate funds to purchase products. For example, General Motors' offer of 0% financing for 60 months for all new vehicle purchases and Ethan Allen's offer of "six months same-as-cash" for new furniture purchases make their products more affordable. Financing activities facilitate the speed with which the product is consumed in the marketplace and provides producers with the capital needed to produce additional products.

- Risk taking: Marketing intermediaries, such as wholesalers and retailers, take title to and physically hold products until they are sought by customers. By purchasing products from producers before they are actually sold, wholesalers and retailers assume the risk that the product will actually sell in the marketplace. Intermediaries are willing to assume the risk in order to make a possible profit.

- Standardization and grading: Marketing intermediaries also facilitate the exchange process by sorting products by their size and quality. Examples of the wide array of products that have undergone standardization and grading include beef, eggs, and diamonds. Standardization and grading activities allow consumers to make more informed choices when comparing alternatives. The U.S. Department of Agriculture (USDA) conducts mandatory inspections paid for by tax dollars to assess the wholesomeness of America's beef and poultry products. In contrast, grading for quality is voluntary and is requested and paid for by meat and poultry producers and processors.[10]

- Information acquisition and provision: Marketers collect, organize, and act on information pertaining to customers, competitors, distribution channel members, and regulators. For example, Nielsen Media Research, the world-famous TV ratings company, collects and distributes information pertaining to television and radio audience measurement, print readership, and customized media research services.[11] By obtaining and providing pertinent information, marketers are able to not only create a strategic competitive advantage over their competitors but also facilitate the efficiency and effectiveness of the exchange process. Marketers also facilitate exchange by providing consumers with information through promotional campaigns that create product awareness and communicate product benefits.

Facilitating Exchange by Narrowing Separations

Ultimately, the marketing activities described above facilitate the exchange process by bridging together the natural *separations* that exist between buyers and sellers. By carrying out the marketing activities described above, marketers create and provide utility (value) to their customer base. A seller creates utility for a buyer in only two ways: by increasing the benefits to the buyer in terms of the buyer's cost and by decreasing the buyer's cost compared to the buyer's benefits.[12] Each of the marketing activities presented above contribute to the creation of one or more of the utilities that further facilitate the exchange process. Four of the most fundamentally important utilities that marketers provide include form utility, time utility, place utility, and ownership utility.

Form utility

Pertains to the transformation of raw materials and/or labor into a finished product that the consumer desires.

Form utility pertains to the transformation of raw materials and/or labor into a finished product that the consumer desires. Although the actual creation of form utility is accomplished through the production process and is not directly attributable to marketing, marketing does play a key role in influencing the size, shape, design, and quality of products, as well as the quantity and assortment of products produced. Marketers can influence form utility through marketing activities such as *information acquisition and provision* that take place during the new product development process. For example, in Chapter 9, which is dedicated to product decisions and new product development, we will learn that the actual size of the original Palm Pilot™ was determined by the size of a man's Hathaway dress shirt pocket—the smallest shirt pocket on the market as determined by customer research.

Place utility

Makes the product available where the consumer wants or needs it.

Place utility makes the product available where the consumer wants or needs it. A natural separation exists between where products are produced and where they are ultimately consumed. For example, if you purchase a McDonald's Big Mac in the Ukraine, the beef patties were likely obtained from Hungary, the bun from Russia, the sesame seeds from Mexico, the special sauce and pickles from Germany, the onions from the United States, and the lettuce from the Ukraine.[13] Production facilities are typically not built where customers reside but are generally located to take advantage of available raw materials, reduced labor costs, and/or access to a variety of modes of transportation. Marketing activities such as *selling* and *transporting* facilitate the exchange process by closing the natural separation that exists between where sellers produce the product and where buyers wish to purchase it, thereby allowing consumers to purchase products produced by distant manufacturers.

Time utility

Makes the product available when the customer wants or needs it.

Time utility makes the product available when the customer wants or needs it. A natural separation exists between when products are produced and when they are consumed. Most products are not manufactured for immediate consumption or use. Marketing activities such as *storing* provide time utility by physically holding products between the time they are produced and the time they are needed by final consumers. The marketing activity of *risk taking* also creates time utility when marketing intermediaries purchase products from producers before they are actually sold to final consumers. The risk-taking activity provides the capital necessary for producers to manufacture product efficiently throughout the year even though consumer sales of the product may be seasonal in nature, such as sales of snowboards and skis.

Ownership utility

Involves transferring the title for a product from producer to consumer.

Ownership utility involves transferring the title for a product from producer to customers. Channel intermediaries, such as wholesalers and retailers, perform marketing activities such as *selling* that provide ownership utility by selling to numerous customers in a single location and eliminating the need for individual customers to transact business with individual manufacturers. For example, without Chevrolet car dealerships, consumers who wish to purchase a Chevrolet Corvette would be forced to travel to the Corvette's production facility in Bowling Green, Kentucky, to purchase and take ownership of the vehicle. In addition, the marketing activity of *financing* provides ownership utility by enabling customers who do not have adequate funds to purchase the product.

Marketing's Impact on Society

As a business philosophy, for better or worse, marketing affects society in numerous ways. Chapter 3, which addresses the relationship between marketing and social responsibility, discusses marketing's impact on society in detail. Noting marketing's powerful impact on society, many of today's most influential marketing organizations have further refined the marketing concept and are now openly conducting business based on the societal marketing concept. Simply stated, the **societal marketing concept** is defined as satisfying customer needs and wants in a manner that is in the best interest of customers and society-at-large. Practiced in its purest form, the marketing concept could be interpreted to promote the notion that business should provide customers everything they need and want regardless of whether it was good or bad for the individual or society. However, the societal marketing concept looks beyond the customer's short-term self-interests and considers the customer's, as well as society's, long-term welfare.

Marketing affects society on a number of levels. Consider the following examples as a brief overview of marketing's influence.

- Marketing provides jobs. Half of every retail dollar spent by customers goes to cover the marketing costs associated with the product.[14] This is due to the many marketing activities performed before the product arrives on store shelves. Although estimates vary, approximately 25–33% of the U.S. civilian workforce performs marketing activities. Selecting marketing as a career offers a wide array of occupational choices, including product development, brand management, promotion management, market research, personal selling, sales management, packaging, transportation, warehousing, wholesaling, and retailing. Jobs pay salaries and salaries provide workers with a higher standard of living.
- Marketing provides customers with alternatives. Marketers collect assortments of products from many different manufacturers and make them available to customers through worldwide distribution systems. As a result, customers have multiple alternatives available to them in most product categories to enhance their way of life.

Societal marketing concept
Is defined as satisfying customer needs and wants in a manner that is in the best interest of consumers and society-at-large.

The makers of Crest toothpaste support causes that are directly related to the needs of its emerging market consumers by providing mobile dentist's offices that offer free dental care to inner-city children.

© Jim Cummins/CORBIS

The Campaign Against Music Piracy

Is downloading music from the Internet for personal use stealing, or is it just taking advantage of the capabilities of today's available technology? Hip-hop queen Mary J. Blige believes it's stealing: "If you create something and someone takes it away, that is stealing." Blige has been joined recently by the likes of Shakira, Britney Spears, Elton John, Eminem, the Dixie Chicks, Madonna, and Sheryl Crow to form a group of 90 artists organized as the Music United for Strong Internet Copyright Coalition (MUSIC). MUSIC's purpose is to use artist clout to convince consumers that file-sharing and downloading music for free is illegal. According to MUSIC, illegal downloading is taking its toll on the music industry. CD shipments were down 5% in 2001, and fell an additional 9% in 2002. In 2003, global recorded-music sales were expected to fall another 6%, marking the fourth straight year of sales declines. To make its point, MUSIC has placed full-page ads in *The New York Times*, the *Los Angeles Times*, and policy-maker publications such as *Roll Call*, asking the question "Who Really Cares about Illegal Downloading?"

According to music-industry estimates, more than 2.6 billion music files are downloaded illegally from the Internet each month through "peer-to-peer" services such as KaZaA, Morpheus, and Gnutella. Consumer surveys indicate that those who download the most are buying significantly fewer CDs than those who do not engage in downloading, by a two to one margin. In addition, one survey of teenage consumers indicated that 35% of respondents were more likely to download a song they really liked than purchase the CD. Hilary Rosen, Chief Executive Officer of the Recording Industry Association of America (RIAA), believes, "Too many people don't realize that when you download a song you like from a peer-to-peer network or some other unauthorized Internet source, what you are doing is stealing music. And not only is that against the law, it also hurts the very artists and songwriters most downloaders prefer and love."

Given the lavish lifestyles of many popular artists, it may be hard for consumers to get too concerned about whether Britney Spears and Madonna are going to make enough money to see themselves through retirement. However, the industry may be able to capture more consumer support and make a stronger case for the downsides of downloading songs if it changes its focus from the livelihoods of the artists to the livelihoods of the songwriters, studio musicians, sound engineers, coproducers, and retail music store clerks who may lose their jobs if CD sales continue to decline. Best Buy closed 107 stores in early 2003, due in large part to the music industry's troubles. Five hundred more music stores of all types are expected to close shop throughout the remainder of 2003. In addition, given current trends, the music industry's big five—Universal, Sony, Warner, EMI, and BMG, which account for 70% of sales—may be less willing to take risks on supporting new artists or may abandon their current support of niche music markets. In the end, consumers may be listening to fewer artists and a more limited variety of music genres.

DISCUSSION QUESTIONS

1. Is downloading music from the Internet for personal use stealing, or is it just taking advantage of the capabilities of today's available technology?
2. If it were your job to discourage consumers from downloading music for free, how would you approach the issue? Do you think the music industry's current approach will be successful? Why or why not?

Sources: Jason Gelman, "Shakira and Mary J. Blige Among Artists Campaigning Against Music Piracy" (26 September 2002), http://lauch.yahoo.com/read/news.asp?contentID+210616, accessed 25 January 2003.

Joe D'Angelo, "Britney, Nelly, Missy Elliott Want You to Quit Stealing Music," (26 September 2002), http://www.vh1.com/news/articles/1457802/09262002/spears_britney.jhtml, accessed 25 January 2003.

Bernhard Warner and Merissa Marr, "Battered Record Execs Set to Face the Music," Reuters (17 January 2003), http://www.publicbroadcasting.net/kunc/news.newsmain?action=article&ARTICLE_ID=4 . . ., accessed 25 January 2003.

Q. Todd Dickinson, "The Costs of Internet Piracy for the Music and Software Industries" (19 July 2000), http://usinfo.state.gov/topical/econ/ipr/ipr-ectodd.htm, accessed 25 January 2003.

Reuters, "Big Music Chains Launch Bid to Sell Music Online" (27 January 2003), http://www.publicbroadcasting.net/kunc/news.newsmain?action=article&ARTICLE_ID=446753, accessed 25 January 2003.

- Marketing helps make products affordable. Effective marketing practices lead to the mass consumption of many products. The greater the customer demand, the less expensive it is for manufacturers to produce the product, because manufacturers are able to obtain discounts on supplies due to higher volume purchases. The less it costs to make the product, the lower the price at which it can be sold to customers. The lower the price of the product, the more customers purchase, and so on. Ultimately, marketing helps generate demand and make products affordable through *economies of scale*, which means that the individual costs of each product decrease as production quantities increase.
- Marketers must be mindful of limited natural resources. Marketers have a social responsibility to conserve the world's scarce resources, such as water, energy, packaging materials, or a particular species of fish. Innovative product develop-

ment has led to new technologies in product construction that have helped to conserve scarce resources. Examples include the use of recycled packaging, production that uses recycled materials that can be recycled again upon disposal, the development and use of solar and wind power to produce electricity, and additional proactive strategies such as Starkist's promise that its tuna is caught using dolphin-protective fishing methods.

- Marketers must be mindful of unintended social consequences. They must consider the impact their products and promotional campaigns have on customers and ask themselves if their products are in the best interest of society as whole. The unintended social consequences of tobacco and alcohol products are classic examples. However, more subtle examples exist. For example, the use of attractive female models to promote products has led society to place a higher value on appearance, which may be directly related to an increase in eating disorders among females. Should marketers use more typical-looking models to promote their products?

- Marketing promotes societal causes. In addition to generating demand for household consumer and business products, marketers also promote the causes supported by a host of nonprofit institutions, such as hospitals, churches, and social services and other philanthropic organizations. In addition, for-profit corporations also support causes that are particularly relevant to their customers, such as Crest toothpaste's support of traveling dentist's offices to meet the needs of inner-city children.

- Marketing fuels the global economy. Effective marketing practice that takes place across national borders stimulates global economic growth. To prosper in a world of abrupt changes, newly emerging environmental forces, and unforeseen dangers from abroad, marketers must develop strategic responses. As discussed in Chapter 4 which is dedicated to international marketing, successful international marketing holds the promise of higher profits, an improved quality of life, a better society, and perhaps, due to the increase linkages among nations, even a more peaceful world. Marketing facilitates trade, and historically, trade facilitates peace!

Marketing as a Dynamic Organizational Process

4   LEARNING OBJECTIVE

Thus far, we have learned about marketing's origins, how marketing facilitates exchanges by narrowing the natural separations that exist between buyers and sellers, and marketing's impact on society. The remainder of this chapter is devoted to increasing your understanding of marketing as an organizational process. As an organizational process, marketing offers guidelines on how to develop and implement marketing strategy within a business climate marked by frequently changing environmental forces.

As depicted in Figure 1.4, marketing strategy is the birthplace of a product's **value proposition**—the bundle of benefits the product provides to fulfill customer needs and wants. For example, the value proposition of a bottle of Coca-Cola may include, among other benefits: the refreshing taste of the beverage itself, the product's temperature, the convenience of purchase locations, product price, and the carefully constructed brand identity associated with the Coca-Cola name. Coca-Cola's value proposition is bought and sold (exchanged) in the marketplace. Satisfied customers often become loyal customers and demonstrate their loyalty by returning to the market to purchase additional product. In addition, loyal customers often tell others of their satisfying experiences and these potential customers may begin to purchase the product as well. In turn, customer loyalty leads to achieving organizational objectives such as sales growth and profitability and/or nonprofit objectives. Marketing intelligence is gathered at each step along the way and marketing strategy is modified accordingly to ensure future success. Finally, it is important to note that

Value proposition
Is the bundle of benefits the product provides to fulfill customer needs and wants.

Figure 1.4	Marketing Strategy in Action

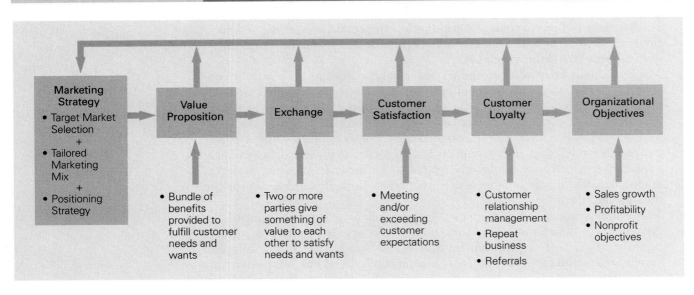

Market
Is any individual, group of individuals, or organization willing and able to purchase a firm's product.

Market segmentation
Is the process of dividing markets into distinctive groups based on homogeneous (similar) sets of needs.

Target market
Is the specific group of customers toward which a firm directs its marketing efforts.

marketing strategy as an organizational process does not take place in a vacuum, but is a dynamic process that is affected by environmental forces.

The Fundamentals of Marketing Strategy

Before a product is introduced into the marketplace, a viable market should be identified prior to the product ever being produced. A **market** is any individual, group of individuals, or organizations willing and able to purchase a firm's product. Generally, within each market, different groups of customers have differing needs (heterogeneous demand) for specific products. For example, in the early days of toothpaste, the product market consisted of three distinct groups of end-users—those who wanted fresher breath, those who wanted whiter teeth, and those who wanted fewer cavities. This process of dividing markets into distinctive groups based on homogeneous (similar) sets of needs is called **market segmentation**. Most companies cannot be all things to all people because they simply do not have the resources to produce enough products for every group of customers. Market segmentation enables the firm to focus its marketing efforts on a more narrowly defined market. More formally, the specific group of customers toward which a firm directs its marketing efforts is referred to as the firm's **target market**.

As is the case with the toothpaste market, many of today's product markets are becoming increasingly *fragmented*. In other words, marketers are continuing to identify and pursue smaller and smaller market segments and target markets. For example, in the toothpaste market, we now have toothpaste specifically targeted to smokers, toothpaste for those who are concerned about gingivitis, toothpaste for those who have sensitive teeth, and toothpaste such as AquaFresh that provides a breath freshener, a whitener, and a cavity fighter all in one product. Moreover, AquaFresh communicates to its customers that it provides all three benefits by making each of three streams of toothpaste a different color and packaging the toothpaste in a clear plastic package. It should be noted that as markets become increasingly fragmented in hopes of differentiating products from the competition, the potential payoff becomes smaller and smaller because the market segments become smaller and smaller as well. Extensive coverage of market segmentation and target marketing is provided in Chapter 8.

In the effort to reach particular target markets, marketers develop specific marketing mixes tailored to meet the needs and wants of the desired target markets. The **marketing mix** comprises four key areas of decision making—product, place (distribution), promotion, and price, also known as *the four Ps*. Key to developing the appropriate marketing mix is the positioning strategy selected for the product. **Positioning** is the image customers have about a product in relation to the product's competitors. Consequently, **marketing strategy** involves: (1) identifying target markets, (2) tailoring marketing mixes that meet the needs and wants of each specific target market, and (3) developing marketing mixes that reinforce the product's desired positioning strategy in the marketplace (see Figure 1.4). For example, as presented in the opening vignette of this chapter, the Honda Element is being introduced to the marketplace. The target market for the Element has been clearly defined as young males who enjoy a variety of outdoor activities. Similarly, Honda has chosen to position the Element as the vehicle of choice for young adults who pursue an active outdoor adventure-filled life. Consequently, in the minds of consumers, the Element may be seen as an alternative to more broadly defined sport utility vehicles. Accordingly, Honda's marketing mix for the Element includes the product itself, which is uniquely designed to attract young males; a distribution strategy (place) provided through Honda's nationwide dealerships that gives the target market physical access to the Element; a promotional campaign that reinforces the positioning strategy by featuring the target market using the vehicle for its intended purposes; and appropriate pricing so that the target market can afford to purchase the product. *Ultimately, a synergy should exist among the marketing mix elements that appeals to the target market and reinforces the product's positioning strategy.*

Marketing Strategy and the Marketing Mix

A firm's marketing mix represents the *controllable* aspects of the firm's marketing strategy. Successful businesses constantly monitor ever changing environmental conditions and modify their marketing mixes accordingly. As a primer to the extensive coverage of each of the marketing mix variables provided throughout the remainder of the text, a brief introduction to each of the marketing mix variables is provided below.

Product Decisions

For our purposes, the term **product** refers to goods, services, people, places, and ideas. More specifically, a product could be a tangible good like a Sony PlayStation, an intangible service such as a visit to a physician, a person such as a political candidate, a place such as a European travel destination, and/or an idea such as water conservation or HIV protection. Products are marketed to customers, which for our purposes are further delineated into two categories—**household consumers**, defined as the consuming public, and **business-to-business customers**, including commercial, institutional, and government markets and defined as customers who resell the product (e.g., wholesalers, retailers, government exchanges), customers who use products as component parts for the production of finished products (e.g., manufacturers), and customers who are final users of products such as paper, staples, and fax machines in their daily business operations (e.g., most businesses). When marketing products to household consumers and business customers, marketing strategy must be adjusted to reflect each group's different decision-making processes. For example, household consumer decision making follows a much different path than government buying processes. Given the importance of each of these customer markets and their unique differences from each other, Chapter 6 is dedicated to household consumer behavior, while Chapter 7 explores business-to-business marketing.

Ultimately, products consist of a bundle of benefits developed through often extensive *product decisions* and a *new product development process*. Product decisions involve a wide array of issues such as product quality, product design, product

Marketing mix
Comprises four key areas of decision making—product, place (distribution), promotion, and price—also known as the four Ps.

Positioning
Is the image customers have about a product in relation to the product's competitors.

Marketing strategy
Involves: (1) identifying target markets, (2) tailoring marketing mixes that meet the needs and wants of each specific target market, and (3) developing marketing mixes that reinforce the product's positioning strategy in the marketplace.

Product
Refers to goods, services, people, places, and ideas.

Household consumers
Are defined as the consuming public.

Business-to-business customers
Are defined as customers who resell the product, customers who use products as component parts for the production of finished products, and customers who are final users of products in their daily business operations.

variety, product features, branding, packaging, labeling, product support, warranties, return policies, and managing the product throughout its life cycle. The bulk of these issues are discussed in detail in Chapters 9 and 10, which focus on product decisions, new product development, service as a competitive advantage, and the marketing of services.

Place (Channel Strategy) Decisions

Marketing channel
Is the network of organizations that create time, place, and ownership utilities for household consumers and business customers.

Marketing channel strategy (place), along with the other three Ps of the marketing mix—product, price, and promotion, must be developed and coordinated to meet the needs and wants of target markets. A **marketing channel** is the network of organizations that create time, place, and ownership utilities for household consumers and business customers. A traditional marketing channel consists of the *manufacturer* who produces the product and sells it to a wholesaler, the *wholesaler* who resells the product to a retailer, and the *retailer* who sells the product to the household consumer. Marketing channels make available the vast array of products, whether they are automobiles, food products, clothing, electronics, or cleaning supplies, to billions of people and millions of business customers all over the world.

The importance of place decisions in formulating marketing strategy cannot be overstated. In today's marketplace, the remaining three Ps of product, promotion, and price can be easily duplicated. For example, consider the product, price, and promotional strategies of the electronic retail giants Best Buy and Circuit City. Each of their strategies are virtually identical—each retailer pursues a "me-too" strategy by selling the same products for the same price and by promoting their products primarily through advertising circulars distributed in Sunday newspapers. In contrast, if one of these retailers is able to control its distribution costs and/or create enhanced time, place, or ownership utility through its channel strategy, then it has created a differential advantage that is difficult to duplicate. For example, Wal-Mart and Kmart sell virtually identical products for very similar prices. So, why is Wal-Mart so much more profitable? Wal-Mart's profitability is due in large part to its very efficient and highly effective channel strategy.

Supply chain management
Also known as logistics and physical distribution, refers to the planning, implementation, and control of the physical flows of materials and finished products from points of production to points of use.

Most customers do not give much thought to how products end up on store shelves, but it's truly an amazing feat when one considers that the average U.S. supercenter carries more than 80,000 items under one roof. It's even more astonishing to consider that there are approximately 3.1 million retail establishments in the U.S., which generate nearly $3.3 trillion in sales annually.[15] How is all that product moved around the country and the rest of the world? The planning, implementation, and control of the physical flows of materials and finished products from points of production to points of use is known as logistics, physical distribution, or **supply chain management**. Supply chain management consists of activities such as transportation, materials handling, order processing, inventory control, warehousing, and packaging. Given the importance of marketing channel strategy, supply chain management, and retailing and wholesaling functions as they pertain to marketing strategy, Chapters 11 and 12 are dedicated to these important subjects.

Promotion Decisions

Perhaps the most visible element of the marketing mix is promotional strategy, also known as *marketing communications*. In fact, the public often mistakenly equates marketing with promotional activities such as advertising. Although advertising is certainly a part of marketing, it does not come remotely close to describing marketing in its entirety. As an analogy, advertising is to marketing what a fighter plane is to an aircraft carrier. Advertising and the fighter plane are simply used as tools to implement a much broader strategy.

In general, the primary roles of marketing communications are to *inform, persuade,* or *remind* customers about the product being offered and to position the product in the marketplace. Customers cannot be expected to use a product they do not know about; therefore, a primary objective of promotion strategy is to create consumer awareness (*informational promotions*) and provide information about where to obtain and how to use the product. Even when awareness of the product exists, customers may need additional encouragement through *persuasive* promotional efforts to try it. Finally, people forget. Just because customers have been told something once, it does not mean that they will necessarily remember it over the course of time. *Reminder* promotional campaigns such as Kellogg's Corn Flakes' "try us again for the first time" promotional campaign refresh customers' memories.

Communicating the firm's product offering to the target market is most effectively accomplished through a program of **integrated marketing communication (IMC)**. IMC is a system of management and integration of marketing communication elements—*advertising, publicity, sales promotion, personal selling, sponsorship marketing,* and *point-of-purchase communications*—with the result that all elements adhere to the same message. Regardless of the product category or type of business, promotional strategy is critical to a company's overall marketing strategy and represents a major determinant of its success. As such, Chapters 13 and 14 discuss in detail the individual components of promotion strategy and IMC as a strategic process.

FUEL YOUR OWN ECONOMIC RECOVERY.

Wendy's 99¢ Super Value Menu. The Best 99¢ You Can Spend.

Wendy's promotes its value menu to lure value-conscious customers into its restaurants.

Pricing Decisions

Of the four marketing mix variables coordinated to influence targeted customers' purchase decisions, effective pricing strategies perhaps remain the most elusive. Today, price remains one of the least researched and mastered areas of marketing.[16] Pricing decisions are complex and are driven by a variety of considerations, including customer demand, costs, information availability, competition, profit motives, product considerations, and legal considerations. Each consideration should be carefully weighed as pricing strategy is formulated.

Effective pricing strategy understands the bundle of benefits provided by the product's value proposition and the value placed by customers on these benefits. For example, Federal Express offers guaranteed overnight delivery of letters and packages for a premium price. Although customers have less expensive shipping alternatives available, Federal Express has been very successful in terms of sales growth and profitability. The Federal Express pricing strategy has effectively captured the value that customers place on guaranteed overnight delivery.

Customer perceptions of **value** represent the trade-off between the perceived benefits of the product to be purchased and the perceived sacrifice in terms of the costs to be paid (see Figure 1.5). Customer costs include more than the *monetary cost* paid for the product. Other costs include *time costs, energy costs,* and *psychic costs,* which reflect the time, physical energy, and mental energy the customer expends to acquire the product. Similarly, the perceived product benefit extends beyond *product benefits* (the benefit derived from the product itself), and includes *service benefits* (warranties and guarantees), *personnel benefits* (employee competency), and *image benefits* (the perceived value of the brand). Chapter 15 provides an overview of pricing strategy, with a focus on factors that influence base prices, and discusses the key reasons why base prices are adjusted over time.

Integrated marketing communication (IMC)
Is a system of management and integration of marketing communication elements—advertising, personal selling, publicity, sales promotion, sponsorship marketing, and point-of-purchase communications—with the result that all elements adhere to the same message.

Value
Represent the trade-off between the perceived benefits of the product to be purchased and the perceived sacrifice in terms of the costs to be paid.

| Figure 1.5 | The Fundamental Components of Value |

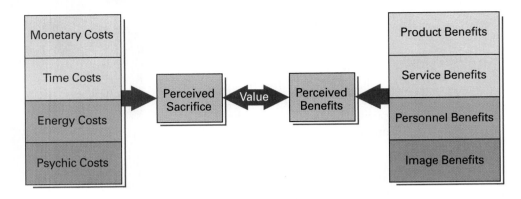

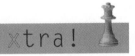

Environmental forces
*Exist outside the walls of the firm,
are less controllable, and include
sociocultural, economic, natural,
technological, political/legal, and
competitive forces.*

Environmental scanning
*Identifies important trends in the
environment and considers the
potential impact of these changes
on the firm's existing marketing
strategy.*

Marketing Strategy and Environmental Forces

Throughout this chapter, it has been noted that environmental forces have a major impact on marketing strategy. For our specific purposes, **environmental forces** exist outside the walls of the firm, are *less controllable*, and include *sociocultural, economic, natural, technological, political/legal,* and *competitive* forces. Successful businesses track environmental forces by a process known as environmental scanning. **Environmental scanning** identifies important trends in the environment and considers the potential impact of these changes on the firm's existing marketing strategy. As indicated in the beginning of the chapter, marketing strategy becomes a game of "survival of the fittest," meaning that those businesses best able to adapt to changing environmental forces are the businesses most likely to survive and thrive in the future (see Figure 1.6).

Given the importance of environmental forces on marketing strategy, icons have been developed to symbolize each of the environmental forces discussed below. Each icon is illustrated and located next to its respective section. Throughout the remainder of the text, these icons will appear in the chapter margins to illustrate the impact of environmental forces on marketing strategy. The world is a dynamic marketplace, and marketers play a large role in adapting business practice to volatile environmental forces that offer both challenges and opportunities.

| Figure 1.6 | The Impact of Environmental Forces on Marketing Strategy |

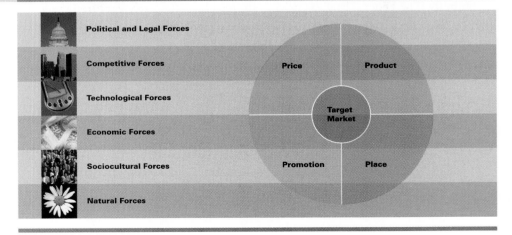

Competitive Forces

Competitive forces have a dramatic impact on marketing strategy.[17] One competitor may lower prices in an attempt to capture more market share, such as Taco Bell's strategy in the quick-serve industry. Another competitor may invest more in research and development in hopes of generating new products and establishing their position in the marketplace as an innovator such as Philips Electronics' investment in flat-panel televisions. A third competitor may begin to bypass traditional channels of distribution and sell directly to consumers through manufacturer-owned retail outlets or conduct direct selling via the Internet, such as Dell Computer Corporation and Amazon.com. Finally, a fourth competitor may engage in an aggressive promotion campaign aimed at increasing brand awareness and preference, thereby strengthening the value of its brand and hopefully leading to increases in sales, such as MCI's intense and enduring promotional campaign in the telecommunications industry. Competitive forces can affect all aspects of marketing mix and marketing strategy.

Competitive Forces

When monitoring competitive forces, marketers should research the market, identify current and potential competitors, and attempt to anticipate competitive actions.

- *Researching the market* can be accomplished by examining some basic questions. What is the core benefit provided to customers? How old is the market? What business philosophy does the market seem to follow—product orientation, sales orientation, or market orientation? Has the orientation changed over time? What marketing-mix adaptations have occurred over time? How have environmental forces affected the market in the past? Why did early market leaders fail? Why are current market leaders succeeding?
- *Identifying current and potential competitors* involves identifying the key contenders in the marketplace and analyzing their marketing mixes. In today's market, competition is as intense as it has ever been, as competitors can be solely online (http://www.CDNow.com), offline (local music store), or both, as is the case with "brick and click" firms such as Tower Records that operate out of both physical and virtual locations (http://www.towerrecords.com). In addition, traditional retail formats such as grocery stores and drug stores are seemingly engaged in an ever expanding selection of nontraditional products. For example, customers can now rent DVDs from their local drug and grocery stores, as well as from traditional video rental stores such as Blockbuster. Consequently, when identifying current and potential customers, online and offline, as well as traditional and nontraditional, competitors must be considered.
- *Anticipating competitive actions* to changes in marketing strategy is another important competitive consideration. For example, if one competitor lowers prices in hope of gaining more market share and other competitors simply lower theirs as well, current market share distributions will likely not change and the industry as a whole will generate less revenue. The airlines are a classic example of an industry that almost always matches competitive actions, particularly when it comes to competitive pricing.

The impact of competitive forces on marketing strategy is evident in the battle between Home Depot and Lowe's—the two giant do-it-yourself (DIY) home improvement chains. Lowe's was first to make the conscious decision to alter its marketing strategy of attracting professional contractors to a new focus on catering to the needs and wants of women. The switch in strategy made good sense, since 80% of home improvement projects are initiated by females. As a result, the primary difference between Lowe's and Home Depot became that at Lowe's, presentation counts. Lowe's aisles are wider and product selection shifted to higher-margin goods, such as Laura Ashley paints and high-end bathroom fixtures. As further evidence, Lowe's, which used to sell $99 gas grills and compete with the likes of Wal-Mart and Kmart, now sells $899 stainless steel Jenn-Air models. Lowe's customer service was

Hispanic vs. Latino: What Is the Difference?

Hispanics are now the largest "ethnic" group in the United States, but the pan-ethnic label 'Hispanic' obscures or erases the enormous diversity in this fast-growing group. Hispanics are the only large minority group in the United States categorized by their language—Spanish. While this common language may be what binds them, many speak limited Spanish or speak only English. Hispanics constitute people (or their ancestors) who came from about two dozen different countries and whose ethnicity ranges from pure Spanish to mixtures of Spanish blood with indigenous Latin American, African, German, and Italian, among other combinations. When individuals are asked directly, there is no single preferred label, but it is clear that the term 'Hispanic' is uniformly disliked. What's more, nearly 85% preferred a national-origin label term (such as Puerto Rican or Cuban) over an umbrella term. Of the umbrella terms, "Latino" ranked higher in preference than any other. Examples of the labels chosen by individuals to identify themselves are presented in the table "California Latino Descriptors."

Several key characteristics help distinguish "Latino" subcultures in the United States today. Three defining "Latino" characteristics are: *national origin, regional clustering,* and *class and generational citizenship status.* First, the different Latino nationalities reflect vast differences in the types of food they eat, clothes they wear, music they listen to, etc. For example, the traditional Mexican music genre "ranchera" is very different from the "salsa" listened to by Puerto Ricans or Cubans. Second, national groups have historically clustered in different parts of the U.S., resulting in regional clustering— with Mexicans and Central Americans in the Southwest, Puerto Ricans and Dominicans in the Northeast, and Cubans in Florida. Within these regions, each group has developed distinct cultural patterns. As a result, some may identify themselves more specifically as Nuyorican (New York-Puerto Ricans) or Tejano (Texas-Mexicans). Third, subgroups are marked by class and generational citizenship status. For example, within California, first-generation Mexican immigrants are different from middle-class second- and third-generation Mexican-

Americans. The first generation may identify themselves as Mexican and live by the cultural norms they brought with them from Mexico, whereas second- and third-generation Mexican-Americans might refer to themselves as "Chicano," reflecting their coexistence between American and Mexican cultures.

Marketers, particularly those that produce and promote food, music, and apparel products, must be cognizant of Latino subculture preferences. Clearly, within the Latino population, who and what are valued varies among subcultures. Marketers who are best prepared to identify and incorporate subculture preferences into their marketing strategies will be the most successful in attracting and retaining this lucrative market.

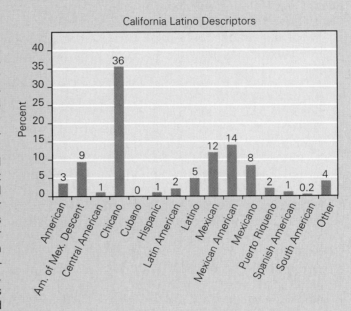

California Latino Descriptors

Sources: Daniel L. Roy *Strangers in a Native Land: A Labyrinthine Map of Latino Identity* Rept. No. 66045 (Lawrence, KS: Univ. of Kansas, 1998). Graph used with permission.

Marie Arana "The Elusive Hispanic/Latino Identity," *Nieman Reports* 55 (Summer 2001), 8–10.

Linda Robinson "Hispanics Don't Exist," *U.S. News and World Report,* 124 (18) 1998, 26–31.

also improved. According to one female Lowe's customer, "At Home Depot, you can't find anyone to help—and if you do, they just point." Lowe's strategy has paid off. In the late 1980s, 13% of Lowe's customers were female. Today, females represent more than 50% of Lowe's customers. In addition, Lowe's store sales, profitability, and stock performance are outperforming Home Depot's numbers. What is Home Depot's next move? You guessed it—Home Depot is upgrading its stores and merchandise to cater to females! The duel between these two DIY giants has been called one of the best shows in retailing today.[18]

Sociocultural Forces

Sociocultural Forces

Sociocultural forces are best defined as demographic and other developments that bring about changes in customer attitudes, beliefs, norms, customs, and lifestyles. Environmental scanning of sociocultural forces includes analyzing demographic

The tremendous growth of emerging markets within the U.S. has had a profound impact on the U.S. food industry.

market profiles and keeping track of emerging trends and activities. More specifically, we have chosen to focus on global population growth, emerging markets within the U.S., family structure, and the effects of aging on the marketplace. Tracking sociocultural forces is important because customer markets can be more effectively segmented, markets with greater profit potential can be identified, and marketing efforts can be more efficiently and effectively targeted.

Population Growth

Globally, the world is experiencing rapid population growth. In 2000, the world's population was estimated to be approximately 6.1 billion. Within the next 25 years, that number is expected to exceed 7.9 billion.[19] Although it is readily accepted that the world consists of different kinds of people with different needs and wants, many are surprised when they discover just how many differences really exist. Consider the following description of the world's population if it consisted of 1,000 people:

If the world consisted of 1000 people, 480 would be men and 520 would be women, 330 would be children, but only 60 would be over the age of 65. In addition, 335 would know how to read and write as adults, but only 10 would be college graduates. Within this world of 1000 people, it would contain 583 Asians, 133 Africans, 94 Europeans, 83 Latin Americans, 55 Russians, and 52 North Americans. Communication would be challenging as 165 people speak Mandarin, 86 English, 83 Hindi, 64 Spanish, 58 Russian, 37 Arabic, and the rest of the world would speak in over 200 different languages. There would be 3 Jews, 45 atheists, 62 Buddhists, 132 Hindus, 167 nonreligious, 178 Moslems, 329 Christians, and 84 others.[20]

Truly, the world comprises many different kinds of people who hold different attitudes, beliefs, norms, customs, and lifestyles that help determine the products they most need and desire.

Emerging Markets

Within the U.S., changes in our demographic and ethnicity composition continue to affect societal values.[21] According to the 2000 U.S. Census, minority markets, now more accurately termed *"emerging markets,"* account for approximately 80 million of 281 million Americans. Emerging markets now represent more than half the population of America's largest cities. By 2005, emerging-market populations are expected to exceed majority populations in California, Hawaii, New Mexico, Texas, and the District of Columbia. In 2010, one-third of the U.S. population is forecasted to be composed of African-American, Latino, Asian-American, and Native American

Sears' bilingual market approach has made the giant retailer a favorite among Latino customers.

populations. By 2050, America's emerging markets will likely surpass the majority population throughout the U.S.

Due to the rapid growth of emerging markets in the U.S., there has been a growing interest in ethnic marketing in recent years. Latinos, African-Americans, and Asian-Americans account for nearly 13%, 12%, and 4% of the U.S. population, respectively. The purchasing power of these three groups combined is forecasted to be a trillion-dollar growth market. As a result, half of the Fortune 100 companies have established marketing programs geared toward emerging markets; however, progress has been slow. For example, emerging markets account for 30% of the U.S. population, but they only receive 6–10% of direct-mail promotions. Successful marketers need to develop and implement multicultural marketing programs that produce and promote original products. Case in point: NBC has recently purchased Telemundo, the second-largest Spanish-language television network. The simple truth is that there is a large Latino population within the U.S. that watches Spanish-language television and purchases products featured in Spanish-language commercials. Companies such as Sears and Colgate-Palmolive, which have dedicated a significant portion of their marketing budget to the Spanish-speaking population, have seen tremendous returns on their investments.

Family Structure

The classic nuclear family consisting of a married couple living with their children now represents 23.5% of all American households, compared with 45% in 1960. However, marriage and family remain valued ideals. According to a recent survey sponsored by the Institute for American Values, 83% of college-age women say that "being married is an important goal." Other statistics of interest pertaining to marriage and family include the following:[22]

- At some point in our lives, nine out of 10 of us say "I do."
- Today's average bride is 25 years of age. The average groom is 26.
- The average cost of a wedding is $22,360, a 47% increase since 1990. Weddings now generate $50 billion annually.
- The average married couple has an average of 1.9 children, down from 2.4 in 1965.

Nestlé stresses the connection between baking cookies and family relationships when marketing its semi-sweet morsels.

© Susan Van Etten

- Half of all U.S. marriages end in divorce and the likelihood of failure increases with time. Twenty percent of marriages end in the first five years, 33% within 10 years, and 43% within 15 years. Among the 75% who remarry, 60% will divorce again.
- Happily married people live longer and are less likely to experience surgery or deaths due to illness, from depression to heart attacks.

The marketing implications of delayed marriage and an increased divorce rate include an increase in single-adult households, which has repercussions for builders and providers of products found in every household, such as appliances, carpet, tile, roofing supplies, and plumbing, among many other product categories. Delayed marriage may also translate into good news for the wedding industry, as older couples are more financially secure and spend more on wedding-related goods and services. Delayed marriage also translates into delayed parenthood, which means that these new parents may be in a better financial position to purchase a wider array of upscale baby products.

Women's changing attitudes toward their roles has also affected the sociocultural environment. For example, 70% of women between the ages of 25 and 54 are in the labor force. Today, women head nearly one in three households, compared to one in seven in 1950. Additionally, an increasing share of women are remaining single into their 30s because of their disenchantment with marriage and more educational and employment opportunities. All of these factors have led to lives characterized by a shortage of time. Successful marketers consider changes in the family structure, both in marketing their products and in reaching target markets. For example, a traditional approach to reach women would be to advertise products on daytime television; however, this would not be an effective approach to reach working women in today's marketplace. Direct mail, content-specific magazines, and radio may prove more effective in reaching this market. In addition, time-saving product markets such as dry-cleaning services, kitchen appliances, ready-to-serve meals, restaurants, children's day care, online banking, mail-order catalogues, lawn care, and house-cleaning services are just a few of the products now valued by this time-pressed market.

Stouffer's marketing to Generation Y has taken on a whole new twist.

Aging Population

In addition to population growth, emerging markets, and changes in the U.S. family structure, the aging of America is another example of a sociocultural force.[23] The median age of Americans is increasing. In 1970, the median age was 28; in 2000, the median age had risen to 36. Consider that by 2008, 40% of the workforce will comprise baby boomers who will, in growing numbers, experience physical impairments due to the natural aging process. In addition, the number of people age 65 and older is expected to more than double by the year 2050. Consequently, marketers can expect more demand for products such as health care, assistive technologies, recreation, travel and tourism, retirement housing, and food products designed for the special dietary needs of aging baby boomers and the elderly.

On the other end of the spectrum is the U.S. youth market, otherwise known as Generation Y. Born between 1979 and 1994, Generation Y at 60 million is more than three times the size of Generation X (17 million) and rivals the size of the Baby Boom generation at 72 million. More important to marketers is that Generation Y will soon rival the Baby Boom generation in buying clout. However, Generation Y is unlike any generation marketers have ever experienced. For instance, one in three Ys is not Caucasian, one in four lives in a single-parent household; and three of four have working mothers. Generation Ys have considerable financial freedom, are Internet savvy, and are commonly heavily involved in family purchase decisions. Many of the brands favored by Generation Y, such as *Mudd, Paris Blues, In Vitro, Cement,* and *Delia's,* are unrecognizable to older generations. The question remains whether the brands of the future will be created by new firms, or will existing brands be able to make the transformation and reinvent themselves as they adapt to changing sociocultural forces.

Economic Forces

Economic Forces

Economic forces greatly affect both a firm's marketing strategy and customer purchasing decisions.[24] For our purposes, *economic forces* are best described in terms of business cycles, inflation, and income. *Business cycles* reflect dynamic economic conditions that run from prosperity (low unemployment, high income and consumer spending) to recession (high unemployment, reduced consumer spending), to eventual recovery (declining unemployment, increased consumer spending). From 1994 to 2000, the U.S. experienced solid increases in real output, low inflation rates, and an unemployment rate of less than 5%. Times were good, if not great, and customers spent accordingly. However, in 2001, the bottom fell out of the economy, with the assistance of the terrorist attacks of September 11, both in terms of performance and psychologically. In 2002, approximately 1.4 million U.S. workers lost their jobs. A moderate recovery is expected in the years that lie ahead.

Successful marketers alter their marketing strategy to adapt to various business cycles. In times of recession, when discretionary income decreases, consumers are more value conscious and often are more thoughtful about purchase decisions as they seek out the best products for the best prices. In response, grocery stores increase shelf space for their own private-label (store) brands, which offer a better price for consumers and increased profit margins for the grocer. In times of prosperity, consumers can be more frivolous and seek out products that fulfill wants as much as needs. Consequently, marketers are more successful promoting designer clothing, expensive watches, and luxury automobiles during times of prosperity.

Inflation is another important economic force that deserves marketers' careful attention. Inflation is a rise in price levels and decreases consumer purchasing power. Luckily, inflation within the U.S. has been relatively stable, increasing at a rate of 2–3% a year. Global markets have not been as fortunate, as some have seen triple-digit increases in inflation. As in the case of recessions, customers respond to increases in inflation by making purchases based on value and are more likely to forgo a familiar manufacturer's brand name for the savings of a value-oriented brand.

Economic forces are also characterized by consumer *income*. According to the 2000 U.S. Census, the median household income is $41,994, with 62% of households earning between $15,000 and $75,000. Those earning a median income of $75,000 or more represent an additional 23% of households. However, since 1975, practically all the real gains (taking inflation into account) in household income have gone to the top 20% of households. In other words, 80% of U.S. households have seen little or no gain in household income since 1975. It is little wonder that value-oriented marketers like Wal-Mart and Target continue to not only survive but also thrive even through tough economic periods. Household income figures also indicate that the incomes of the fairly large upper-middle and upper class continue to rise. Marketers of upscale products continue to target these markets.

Natural Forces

Natural Forces

The impact of *natural forces* on marketing strategy is the result of diminishing resource availability and the often unintended consequences that products and production have on the environment.[25] Resource and environmental product issues span every phase of a product's life cycle and can include issues such as industrial water pollution, destruction of the ozone layer and rain forests, hazardous waste, oil spills, air pollution, global warming, and threats to endangered species. A *life-cycle inventory* (LCI) can be conducted that helps marketers track the use of energy, resources, and emissions to the environment associated with a product throughout its life cycle. As such, an LCI commonly accounts for the environmental impact of raw-material procurement, manufacturing, packaging, and distribution, as well as the effects of consumption and disposal.

For example, an LCI of cotton versus disposable diapers would consider the resource and environmental costs of each alternative. In the case of the cloth diaper, the amount of pesticides and water used to grow cotton, the water and energy needed to manufacture and transport the diapers to stores and homes, and the amount of water and energy required to launder cloth diapers would be assessed. In comparison, an LCI of disposable diapers would take into account the environmental implications of cutting down and processing trees for wood pulp, along with the environmental costs associated with the extraction and refining of the petroleum required to produce the plastic back sheets. Finally, it would quantify the energy used in manufacturing and transportation, as well as the amount of solid waste eventually sent to landfills. Figure 1.7 presents the results of an LCI commissioned by Procter & Gamble comparing the relative environmental impacts of cloth versus

The Environmental Impact of Cloth versus Disposable Diapers			Figure 1.7
	Cloth	**Disposable**	
Raw material consumption (lb.)	3.6	25.3	
Water consumption (gal.)	144	23.6	
Energy consumption (BTUs)	78,890	23,290	
Air emissions (lb.)	0.860	0.093	
Water pollution (lb.)	0.177	0.012	
Solid waste (lb.)	.24	22.18	

Source: Arthur D. Little, Inc. Disposable versus Reusable Diapers: Health, Environmental, and Economic Comparisons. Report to Procter & Gamble, March 16, 1990.

Marketers must be mindful of limited natural resources and the unintended social consequences of their products.

paper disposable diapers. Experts in industry, government, and academia are now working to legitimize the use of life cycle inventory and other cradle-to-grave approaches as marketing tools.

Businesses that have been successful in countering the effects of natural forces have done so through the implementation of a variety of strategies. In many cases, the end result has been lower production costs, new and improved products and/or packaging, enhanced brand image, and the promise of future sales growth. Examples of environmentally friendly strategies are described in brief below.

- Minimize direct environmental impact. Earth's Best Organic Baby Food produces a flavorful product that is free of synthetic pesticides, fertilizers, antibiotics, growth hormones, salt, refined sugar, and modified starches. In addition, the product is packaged in a glass jar that is made from recycled content and is recyclable itself.
- Use sustainable sources or raw materials. Collins Pine Company, with forests in California, Pennsylvania, and Oregon, divides each forest into sections that are harvested on a 10-year cycle. No more timber is cut than was produced the previous decade.
- Source-reduce products and packaging. This is accomplished through light-weighting products and packaging, super-concentrating products, such as laundry detergent, so it can be sold in smaller packages, and selling products in containers that are refillable.
- Conserve natural resources, habitats, and endangered species. Frigidaire washers and Waterpik showerheads have created sustainable competitive advantages by purposely engineering their products with water conservation in mind.
- Use recycled content. It is estimated that each American throws away 4.3 pounds of garbage a day, most of which could be recycled. Recycling cuts pollution, conserves natural resources and energy, can be cost-competitive with traditional methods of disposal, and creates jobs.
- Make products energy efficient. Forty percent of the energy produced in the U.S. is consumed by individuals for use in automobiles, heating and cooling equipment, and appliances. This produces approximately 40 thousand pounds of carbon dioxide emissions a year. The California Energy Commission estimates that cost-effective investments in energy-efficient products could reduce total U.S. electricity demand by 40–75%.
- Make products and packaging that can be composted. According to the U.S. Environmental Protection Agency, 40% of solid wastes disposed of in the U.S. could be effectively turned into humus, which can enrich gardens and agricultural soils.

Clearly, the impact of natural forces on marketing strategy should be continuously evaluated to ensure future resource availability and a healthy environment for future generations.

Technological Forces

Technological Forces

Technological forces represent the application of science to solve problems and to perform tasks.[26] Phenomenal developments in technology—particularly the Internet—have led to fundamental changes in marketing strategy. The most significant change has been that power in the marketplace has shifted from sellers to buyers. Customers have more choices, more information, and are becoming increasingly demanding. Accordingly, markets have had to become more accessible and more responsive. Less than 10 years ago (in about 1996), the obsession with the Internet began. Thousands of businesses, customers, employees, and partners got wired to one another and began conducting business processes online—also known as *e-business*. Eventually, more and more customers (business and household) became wired and formed a critical mass. Through repeated usage, customer trust has dramatically increased, and the Net has become a viable means for revenue production and economic growth. In 2002, 531 million people, representing 8.5% of the world's population, had access to the Internet. Within the U.S., 182 million people (64% of the population) are Internet users, and 103.7 million (57% of all U.S. users) visit online retailers. Of those who visit online retailers, 92.8 million (51% of all U.S. users) conduct an average of 10 transactions a year and spend $460 per capita online.

Technological advances (both online and offline) have led to increased business efficiencies and effectiveness, provided value-added features for existing products, and generated new business models and products. The primary sources of business efficiencies include automated online purchasing with suppliers; automated order processing with customers; e-mailing communications to customers and stockholders, which saves printing and mailing costs; posting products online, which saves the cost of printing and mailing brochures; and conducting business intelligence. Technology has also facilitated business effectiveness by enabling innovative business processes such as customer relationship management, supply chain management, and enterprise resource planning.

Marketers have also used technology to provide added-value features to their existing product lines, as illustrated in these examples:

- Lands' End customers can build models of themselves at http://www.landsend. com and virtually try on the retailer's merchandise.
- Diet-conscious consumers can access http://www.weightwatchers.com to learn about healthy recipes and share their diet secrets with other Weight Watcher's members.
- Cadillac customers can go to http://www.cadillac.com and take a 360-degree tour of the inside of a CTS model and check specific dealership inventory and pricing information before seeking out an actual Cadillac dealership.
- BMW customers can go to http://www.bmwfilms.com to stream a series of short action films that feature BMW automobiles, which enables the company to target specific groups for specific BMW models.

Technology has provided access to information that has never been made available to customers before. In turn, marketers are able to provide their products with greater exposure and conduct business with a more informed customer.

In addition to efficiency, effectiveness, and value-added enhancements, advances in technology have also led to new business models and products. In simple terms, there are four types of e-business models—*content sponsorship, direct selling, infomediary,* and *intermediary* models.

- The *content sponsorship* model creates Web sites that contain content aimed at special interest groups. For example, http://www.gurl.com is aimed at females in their early teens. The content sponsorship model generates revenue by selling advertising space to marketers that wish to reach the early-teen female market.
- The *direct selling* model bypasses traditional middlemen such as retailers and wholesalers and generates revenue by selling directly to customers. Dell, a direct seller of personal computers and related accessories http://www.dell.com, has been very successful at implementing the direct selling model.
- *Infomediaries,* such as http://www.doubleclick.com, collect and distribute online market information for a fee.
- *Intermediaries* create a virtual marketplace where buyers and sellers come together, negotiate, and complete transactions. For example, Priceline.com (http://www.priceline.com) and eBay (http://www.ebay.com) are classic examples of

online intermediaries that generate revenue through commissions and/or listing fees and who have turned traditional pricing strategy on its head. Finally, there are just too many new, technologically innovative products to go into much detail about all of them. However, those that seem to be making the biggest impact on marketing strategy and society as a whole include cell phones, e-mail, CD burners, and video playback machines such as TiVo and ReplayTV that can delete marketing messages (see End-of-Chapter Case).

Political and Legal Forces

Political and Legal Forces

Marketers must also be cognizant of the *political and legal forces* that surround their operations.[27] Marketers must be fully aware of and conform to all laws affecting marketing strategy. Two vital areas within the political and legal environment that relate to marketing strategy are antitrust regulation and consumer protection.

Antitrust regulation encourages competitive conduct and protects competition among rivals in the marketplace. In the years following the Civil War, business enterprise enjoyed tremendous growth and operated without government control or regulation. It was thought that business would take care of itself, as competition would weed out the unscrupulous and prevent any single business from dominating the marketplace. However, unscrupulous practices did prevail and industry monopolies quickly formed, making it next to impossible for small business and new business to compete. In response, the U.S. Congress enacted major laws to promote competition. These laws are summarized in Figure 1.8.

Consumer protection involves regulation that protects consumers from deception, fraud, and harmful products and is primarily directed toward producers of food, pharmaceuticals, automobiles, and children's products, as well as public utilities and advertisers. The primary regulatory agencies charged with protecting consumers include the Food and Drug Administration (FDA), the Environmental Protection Agency (EPA), the National Highway Traffic Safety Administration (NHTSA), the Consumer Product Safety Commission (CPSC), and the Federal Trade Commission (FTC). Examples of major laws aimed at protecting consumers are included in Figure 1.9.

Figure 1.8	**Laws Enacted to Promote Competition**

Sherman Antitrust Act

Outlaws monopolies and prohibits any contract, combination, or conspiracy that restrains trade.

Clayton Act

Originally passed to strengthen the Sherman Antitrust Act, the Clayton Act prohibits price discrimination, exclusive dealer arrangements, tying contacts, and other behaviors that substantially lessen competition or tend to create a monopoly.

Federal Trade Commission Act

Established the Federal Trade Commission (FTC) and charged the commission with regulating unfair business practices.

Robinson-Patman Act

Focused exclusively on outlawing the practice of price discrimination, where sellers were offering different prices or price-related deals to different customers. It should be noted that price discrimination regulation applies to business-to-business and not to business-to-household consumer transactions.

Wheeler-Lea Act

Expanded the powers of the FTC and prohibited business practices that not only were injurious to competition but also injured the public.

Laws Enacted to Protect Consumers	Figure 1.9

Child Protection Act
Protects children from the sale of hazardous toys.

Fair Packaging and Labeling Act
Provides that specific information be provided on all labels and packaging, such as product content, manufacturer or distributor mailing address, and quantity of contents.

Consumer Credit Protection Act
Requires credit-granting institutions to fullly disclose annual interest rates to consumers.

National Environmental Protection Act
Created the Environmental Protection Agency (EPA) and charged the agency with protecting consumers from air, water, and noise pollution and regulating hazardous waste.

Consumer Product Safety Act
Established the Consumer Product Safety Commission and charged the agency with establishing safety standards for consumer products.

Although these laws were enacted decades ago, political and legal forces are constantly changing and are affecting marketing strategy in today's marketplace. The development of a national do-not-call list; Internet privacy; tobacco advertising, promotion, and regulation; children's advertising and promotion; deceptive advertising and remedies; environmental marketing claims; and warnings and disclosures are just some of the political and legal forces that marketers need to keep a close watch on over the next few years.

Chapter Summary

Learning Objective 1: *Understand the concepts associated with and the fundamental differences among business philosophies based on product orientation, selling orientation, market orientation, and relationship marketing orientation.* To enhance our understanding of marketing as a business philosophy, it is helpful to compare four orientations or business philosophies that businesses have embraced as they have sought success in the marketplace—product orientation, sales orientation, market orientation, and relationship marketing orientation. Product-oriented firms are manufacturing-oriented, focusing largely on the product itself. Businesses that are unsuccessful pursuing a product orientation are often faced with unsold inventories. Consequently, the business is faced with becoming sales-oriented and communicating to the market why its product would be of interest to consumers. In contrast to product orientation and/or sales orientation, market-oriented firms gather, share, and use information about "the market" to make decisions. Hence, marketing as a business philosophy is best described by those businesses that practice the three pillars of the marketing concept—customer focus, coordinated marketing, and long-term success. Finally, relationship marketing seeks to create and sustain mutually satisfying long-term relationships not only with its customers but also with other key players such as employees, suppliers, distributors, retailers, the surrounding community, and society as a whole.

Learning Objective 2: *Appreciate how marketing facilitates exchange by executing marketing activities that help bridge the natural separations that exist between buyers and sellers.* Facilitating the exchange process between buyers and sellers is at the crux of every definition of modern marketing. Marketing facilitates the exchange process through a variety of marketing activities that include buying, selling, transporting, storing, financing, risk taking, standardizing and grading, and acquiring and providing information. Ultimately, marketing activities facilitate the exchange process by bridging the natural *separations* that exist between buyers and sellers through the creation of form, time, place, and ownership utilities.

Learning Objective 3: *Develop an appreciation of marketing's impact on society.* As a business philosophy, marketing affects society in numerous ways. For example, marketing provides jobs, marketing provides customers with alternatives, marketing helps make products affordable, marketers must be mindful of limited natural resources, marketers must be mindful of unintended social consequences, marketing promotes societal causes, and marketing fuels the global economy. Noting marketing's powerful impact on society, many of today's most influential marketing organizations have further refined the marketing concept and are now openly conducting business based on the societal marketing concept—satisfying customer needs and wants in a manner that is in the best interest of customers and society-at-large.

Learning Objective 4: *Recognize marketing's role as a dynamic strategic process that is able to adapt to changing environmental forces.* As a strategic process, marketing offers guidelines on how to develop and implement marketing strategy within a business climate marked by frequently changing environmental forces. Marketing strategy involves: (1) identifying target markets (2) tailoring marketing mixes that meet the needs and wants of each specific target market and (3) developing marketing mixes that reinforce the product's positioning strategy in the marketplace. Environmental forces have a major impact on marketing strategy. Environmental forces exist outside the walls of the firm, are less controllable, and include sociocultural, economic, natural, technological, political/legal, and competitive forces. Environmental scanning identifies important trends in the environment and considers the potential impact of these changes on the firm's existing marketing strategy.

Key Terms

For interactive study: visit http://bestpractices.swlearning.com.

Business-to-business customers, 17
Coordinated marketing effort, 8
Customer focus, 7
Customer relationship management (CRM), 9
Environmental forces, 20
Environmental scanning, 20
Exchange process, 10
Form utility, 12
Household consumers, 17
Integrated marketing communication (IMC), 19

Long-term success, 8
Market, 16
Market segmentation, 16
Marketing, 10
Marketing channel, 18
Marketing concept, 7
Marketing mix, 17
Marketing network, 9
Marketing strategy, 17
Ownership utility, 12
Place utility, 12
Positioning, 17

Product, 17
Product concept, 6
Production concept, 5
Relationship marketing concept, 8
Selling concept, 6
Societal marketing concept, 13
Supply chain management, 18
Target market, 16
Time utility, 12
Value, 19
Value proposition, 15

Questions for Review and Discussion

1. How does a firm's relationship with its customers change as the firm makes the transition from a product-oriented to a sales-oriented to a market-oriented to a relationship-marketing-oriented business philosophy?

2. You wish to start a business that practices the marketing concept as a business philosophy. What steps would you need to take to implement the marketing concept?

3. Marketing facilitates the exchange process through a variety of *marketing activities*. Describe four of the marketing activities (there are eight in total) as they would relate to Barnes & Noble or Borders bookstores.

4. Describe the natural separations that exist between most manufacturers and their customers. How does an intermediary such as Best Buy narrow these separations and facilitate the exchange process?

5. In your opinion, what have been the unintended social consequences of marketing's use of attractive female models to promote products? Do you believe that marketers should seriously consider ending the practice of using "super models" to promote their products? Why or why not?

6. Explain the principle and importance of market segmentation. Based on your observation of the break-fast foods aisle in a supermarket, how is the breakfast foods market segmented?

7. Select a favorite restaurant and discuss how its marketing mix reinforces the restaurant's positioning strategy.

8. Discuss how the terms positioning, target market, marketing strategy, and marketing mix relate to one another.

9. What is the difference between a household consumer and a business customer? How might these differences affect marketing-mix decisions?

10. Marketing strategy is affected by environmental forces that surround business operations. If couples are waiting longer to get married and subsequently have children later in life, what product markets are likely to be affected by this trend in the sociocultural environment?

In-Class Team Activities

1. As young entrepreneurs, you have come up with a great business idea and want to get started on developing a marketing strategy. As a group, select a product category of interest and then discuss and record the decisions you need to make for each of the three development steps of marketing strategy.

2. As a group, discuss the relevance of each of the six environmental forces specific to your area of the country. How might these affect your marketing strategy in opening a landscaping service or other new business?

Internet Questions

1. Go to http://www.hummer.com. Use the Web site to determine the different positioning strategies for the H1 and the H2. How is the marketing mix for each model different based on: product, place, promotion, and price?

2. Visit the Campbell's Soup Web site, http://www. soupathand.com. Compared to Campbell Soup's tra-ditional target market, what is the new product's target market? How has the marketing mix been altered to attract this new market? Do you think there is enough need for this product to make it a permanent feature?

CHAPTER CASE

ReplayTV and TiVo: Are Digital Video Recorders Marketable?

On the surface, digital video recorders (DVRs), such as those developed and marketed by ReplayTV and TiVo, are similar to VCRs, with the exception that they are tapeless. More specifically, ReplayTV and TiVo are digital video recorders that can record as much as 13 videotapes' worth of programming on a hard drive and eliminate the clutter and hassle of dealing with traditional videotapes. (A TiVo demonstration is available by accessing http://www.tivo.com/1.0.asp and selecting one of the demonstration formats provided in the upper-right-hand corner).

Look below the surface and users will find that ReplayTV and TiVo offer a number of additional benefits over traditional VCR technology. For example, users no longer have to fast-forward through a videotape to locate a particular show. DVRs provide an electronic program guide that is available on the user's TV screen. Users simply highlight the desired programming, click, and watch. Program recording is conducted in a similar fashion. Another intriguing benefit is the "live broadcast pause," which enables users to pause, rewind, slow-mo, or instant-replay live TV. Need to answer the phone, grab a snack, put the kids to bed? No problem! Users can just pause live TV, tend to what needs to be tended to, and return to watch their favorite shows at the exact point they terminated their viewing. Even better for most users, commercials recorded during the "live broadcast pause" can be bypassed if desired, either manually by selecting fast-forward, or by selecting "commercial advance," which skips commercials automatically. DVRs also offer a number of other features, such as TiVo's Season Pass™, which automatically finds and records every episode of a series for a complete season; WishList™, which locates and records users' favorite actors, directors, teams, or even topics; and Smart Recording, which automatically detects programming changes and suggests programming to viewers that matches their interests.

Pricing of TiVo and ReplayTV includes a fixed price for the DVR unit itself plus a monthly fee for the accompanying service. Each DVR maker offers a variety of models that increase in unit price with recording-space capability. The monthly fee remains the same regardless of the model purchased. Specific details pertaining to pricing and product information can be accessed at TiVo's (**http://www.tivo.com**) and ReplayTV's (**http://www.sonicblue.com**) Web sites.

In a recent article entitled, "More U.S. Homes have Outhouses than TiVos," the writer of the story asks the question, "Who will win the battle of TiVo vs. ReplayTV?" The answer may be neither one. Industry observers, such as Tom Edwards, senior analyst and researcher at NPDTechworld, question the viability of stand-alone DVRs. Mr. Edwards believes that the technology will become an unbranded feature incorporated directly into televisions, DVDs, and satellite receivers. TiVo and ReplayTV are currently licensing their technology for such uses.

Other challenges, in the form of legal actions and consumer privacy concerns, lie ahead. Jamie Kellner, Chairman and CEO of the Turner Broadcasting division of AOL Time Warner, had this to say about consumers who are using DVRs to skip commercials:

"[Skipping commercials is] theft. Your contract with the network when you get the show is you're going to watch the spots. Otherwise you couldn't get the show on an ad-supported basis. Any time you skip a commercial . . . you are actually stealing the programming."

Of particular concern to the network television industry is ReplayTV's "commercial advance" feature that senses the beginning and end of commercials in digitally recorded TV programs. Users can simply push a button and skip an entire series of commercials. In fact, once the ReplayTV software catches on that this is how you want

to watch your show, it will advance automatically for you.

Media giants such as Disney, Paramount Pictures, ABC, NBC, and CBS have recently filed suit against SONICblue, the makers of ReplayTV claiming that commercial skipping and file sharing "deprive plaintiffs of the means of payment for their works and erode the value of plaintiff's copyrighted programming." Legal experts believe that the plaintiffs do not have much of a case since VCR technology has basically the same capabilities and rulings on its acceptable use (based on the fair use doctrine) have been pronounced upon by the Supreme Court. However, in a recent court ruling, a magistrate judge has ordered SONICblue to collect all available information regarding every program its users record, every commercial that is skipped, and every file that is shared. Consequently, ReplayTV users may feel their privacy is being compromised, much like TiVo customers felt when it was revealed that TiVo was collecting information about its customers' viewing habits. The Federal Trade Commission has noted that "most consumers are not comfortable with having someone or something watch them while they watch television."

The magistrate judge's ruling is subject to review by a U.S. District Court judge presiding in the case. Given citizens' rights to privacy, which are protected by the First Amendment, the case could also eventually find its way to the U.S. Court of Appeals. The question that remains is whether TiVo's and ReplayTV's future looks very promising or will be plagued by difficult challenges that lie ahead.

Case Questions

1. What are the major benefits provided by DVRs such as ReplayTV and TiVo?
2. Develop a marketing strategy for digital video recorders. Select a target market who would desire a specific benefit listed in the answer to question 1. Develop a marketing mix tailored to your selected target market. Discuss your positioning strategy.
3. Go to ReplayTV's (**http://www.sonicblue.com**) and TiVo's (**http://www.tivo.com**) Web sites and discuss the pricing strategy for each of the DVRs. Does the pricing approach seem to be appropriate for your target market? Please explain.
4. Based on the information provided in the case, discuss how your marketing strategy may be affected by sociocultural, political/legal, economic, technological, and competitive environmental forces.

Sources: Joe Bauke, *Replay TV—A Second Look,* http://www.reviewboard.com/Section/Technology/replaytv2, accessed 26 January 2003.

Chris Springman, "Are Personal Video Recorders, Such As Replay TV and TiVo, Copyright-Infringement Devices?" FindLaws Legal Commentary (9 May 2002), http://writ.news.findlaw.com/commentary/20020509_springman.html, accessed 26 January 2003.

Eric W. Lund, "*Replay TV vs. TiVo,*" http://www.egotron.com/ptv, accessed 26 January 2003.

Bradley Johnson, "More U.S. Homes Have Outhouses than TiVos," http://www.adage.com/news.cms?newsId=36471, accessed 26 January 2003.

"TiVo . . . So Easy, Everyone Can Use It," http://www.tivo.com/1.0asp, accessed, 26 January 2003.

VIDEO CASE

Goya Helps Latinos Maintain Mealtime Traditions

Eighty years ago, Latino immigrant Prudencio Unanue and his wife longed for the comfort foods of their home, so they started an import business to satisfy the need. However, a few years later, the Spanish Civil War broke out, and they could no longer obtain the foods they wanted for their business. So they began importing sardines from a cannery in Morocco. "He had to do something. He had four kids, and we had to eat," recalls his son, Joseph A. Unanue, now in his 70s. The elder Unanue bought the brand name, Goya, along with the sardines. The name cost an extra dollar. Throughout the years, Unanue added olive oil, olives, and other products the Latino community in America requested. During the 1960s, Goya began canning everything from beans to coconut juice. Today, Goya serves up entire menus of beans, rice, pasta, seasonings, beverages, and a variety of specialties.

On the surface, it might seem to be a simple matter to import and manufacture food products to serve what appears to be a niche community. But it isn't. First, the Latino population, including immigrants and descendants, now accounts for 13% of the U.S. population. By 2050, Latinos will make up about 25% of the population. Thus, Latino consumer tastes are becoming more and more a part of the mainstream, not to mention a huge segment of purchasing power. Second, there is no such thing as a single Latino population. Although Goya was founded originally to serve consumers of Spanish descent, American Latinos come from a variety of countries, from Puerto Rico and Mexico to Nicaragua and Cuba. Their cultures, family structures, attitudes, and tastes in food are different. "Latinos from different countries eat different foods," notes Andy Unanue, Joseph's son and likely successor as CEO. But Goya is ahead of other marketers in pinpointing the location of different populations. "Luckily, we have a big arm out in the field who acts as the census. We know which Latinos are moving into what regions before anybody else," says Andy.

Of course, Goya often ends up serving different groups of Latino consumers within the same geographical region. But its marketers know that Cubans prefer black beans, while Nicaraguans want small chili beans and Mexicans will buy pintos. So they provide all three—and more.

Changing roles in Latino families have also reflected a change in purchasing habits, and Goya has adeptly kept up with the times, serving both the young and the old. Latino seniors still want to create their own meals from scratch; they don't want packaged or prepared foods. So

Goya offers a full complement of ingredients for this market. But "the younger people are busy, they are used to the microwave, and they want to eat those things they grew up on that they don't have time to make or can't make as well as their mothers," explains Mary Ann. So Goya provides a wide range of rice-and-bean mixes and other foods that can be prepared quickly by working mothers or fathers. The company Web site offers even more help for this new generation: a section with favorite recipes that includes menus for holiday celebrations and other occasions.

By being first to the grocery shelves decades ago, Goya established itself as the premiere Latino food brand, and it has been discovered by more and more non-Latino consumers whose food tastes are changing. Moreover, Goya has managed to ward off attempts by larger companies to tread on its turf by simply producing higher-quality, more authentic products. "We firmly believe that Latinos like buying things they consider their own, that are authentic," remarks Andy Unanue. "And we are. We're Latino and we give them authenticity." Not only do Latino consumers prefer Goya's authenticity, but so do non-Latinos. Thus, after failed attempts to introduce their own Latino food lines, giants like Campbell's Soup are trying to compete by purchasing genuine Latino food businesses. Goya is watching carefully.

Goya remains a privately owned business steeped in strong family tradition, with no plans to change the way it operates. Although Goya products generally represent low-involvement purchase decisions, consumers relate strongly to the traditions these products represent. When they fill their shopping carts with Goya rice, olives, and salsa, they feel like members of a community.

Case Questions

1. Of the six environmental forces presented in the chapter, discuss the forces that most greatly affect Goya's marketing strategy.

2. Why is it so important for Goya marketers to understand the different sub-groups within the Latino community?

3. What might be some pros and cons of Goya's attracting more and more non-Latino consumers to its products?

Sources: Goya Foods Web site, *http://www.goya.com,* accessed 4 March 2000.
  "Venezuela's Flood Victims Desperately Waiting for Aid," *PR Newswire,* 3 January 2000; Bill Saporito, "Food Fight," *Corporate Board Member,* Autumn 1999, http://www.boardmember.com.
  "Goya Foods," *Hispanic Online,* January/February 1999, *http://www.hispaniconline.com.*

2

Strategic and Marketing Planning

Viacom is the parent company of many successful media, retail, and recreation companies, including CBS television, Paramount Pictures, Nickelodeon, MTV, VH-1, BET, Blockbuster, and Simon & Schuster, among many others. Viacom is considered the clear leader in entertainment, news, sports, and music. For example, the very popular cable television channel Nickelodeon is viewed by more than 471 million households worldwide and claims 41 of the top 50 programs targeted at children 2–11. Two of Nickelodeon's top-rated shows are *SpongeBob SquarePants* and *The Fairly OddParents*. The success of these shows has spawned huge volumes of related merchandising, and SpongeBob has developed a large following among children and adults, especially gay men. Further, a full-length SpongeBob movie is set for release in 2004.

You Decide. After reading the opening vignette and paying special attention to the sections of this chapter marked with the chess piece, answer these questions:

1. What would be the best way to define Viacom's strategic business units?

2. Which opportunity for growth has been the focus of the developers of *SpongeBob SquarePants*?

3. If you were asked to develop a marketing plan for *SpongeBob SquarePants,* which primary issue would you take into consideration?

AP Topic Gallery

Viacom Inc. & SpongeBob SquarePants

Viacom, a leading global media company, produces programming and related products that appeal to every demographic across all media. It's very likely that you have encountered one of the products of this media empire. Viacom's business portfolio includes the following:

Broadcast Television:	CBS Television, Viacom Television Stations Group, Paramount Television, and UPN (United Paramount Network)
Cable Television:	MTV, MTV2, Nickelodeon, BET (Black Entertainment TV), Nick at Nite, TV Land, Noggin, VH-1, TNN, CMT, Comedy Central, Showtime, The Movie Channel, Flix, and the Sundance Channel
Motion Pictures:	Paramount Pictures, Paramount Home Entertainment
Retail & Recreation:	Blockbuster, Paramount Parks, Famous Players, and United Cinemas International
Radio & Outdoor:	Infinity
Publishing, Online, & More:	Simon & Schuster, Viacom Interactive Ventures, MTV.com, VH1.com, Nickelodeon.com, CBS.com, CBSNews.com, Viacom Consumer Products, and Famous Music

Clearly, Viacom is a leader in the creation, promotion, and distribution of entertainment, news, sports, and music. For example, MTV reaches more than 377.3 million households in 166 countries and territories, Nickelodeon is viewed in more than 471 million households worldwide, and VH-1 reaches an additional 100 million households. Other Viacom business units are equally or more successful.

LEARNING OBJECTIVES

After you have completed this chapter, you should be able to:

1. *Recognize the nature and scope of planning, including the five key elements that are crucial to planning activities.*

2. *Understand each of the fundamental steps involved in developing a strategic plan.*

3. *Appreciate the fundamentals of marketing planning.*

Who Lives in a Pineapple Under the Sea?

One of Viacom's latest and greatest success stories involves an unlikely buck-toothed sea sponge who lives in the underwater town of Bikini Bottom. Nickelodeon's *SpongeBob SquarePants* is a huge hit! In fact, SpongeBob has become so pervasive in American pop culture that SpongeBob costumes were the number one Halloween costume for 2002. Kevin Kaye, Executive Vice President of Production at Nickelodeon, reports that SpongeBob is the top-rated cable show for kids ages two to 11 and has been since the third quarter of 2001. However, SpongeBob's appeal does not stop with kids. In July 2002, SpongeBob attracted 61.5 million viewers, including 26.8 million kids ages two to 11, 14.7 million "tweens ages 9 to 14," and 21.8 million adults, ages 18 to 49. *SpongeBob SquarePants* attracts more adults than any other Nickelodeon programming and both Nickelodeon and Viacom's MTV have aired SpongeBob episodes as late as 11:30 p.m. to specifically reach older viewers.

Much of SpongeBob's success has been credited to the simple uncomplicated story lines involving an innocent yellow sea sponge who has boundless, yet nerdy, optimism. SpongeBob's optimism is credited with attracting yet another market—gay men. In a recent story printed in *The Wall Street Journal (WSJ)*, SpongeBob is reported to be "the biggest phenomenon to capture the imagination of gay men since the purple Teletubby named Tinky Winky started carrying a purse." Novelty shops frequented by gay customers are now stocking SpongeBob plush toys, lunch boxes, and key chains alongside their regular merchandise and are having trouble keeping enough stock on the shelves. The *WSJ* article has stirred a lot of questions about whether Nickelodeon is directly targeting gay audiences. Nickelodeon's response to queries is that the show is strictly aimed at kids two to 11. However, Tom Kenny, the voice of SpongeBob, who recently appeared on *Late Night with Conan O'Brien*, reported, "It's never been addressed by us on the show . . . [jokingly adding], all the main characters are hiding horrible secrets of their own."

Capitalizing on the show's success, SpongeBob has become a merchandising bonanza, with current sales estimates at $500 million, including items such as paper towels, beach towels,

VOICE OF THE EXPERT
K. Douglas Hoffman, Colorado State University

The three fundamental components of marketing strategy introduced in Chapter One—target market selection, marketing mix development, and positioning strategy—do not exist in a vacuum. Marketing strategy should logically flow from the strategic planning process and is more fully developed and implemented through marketing planning. Strategic and marketing planning offers decision makers frameworks to organize a vast array of information that should ultimately lead to more informed decision making. It is important to recognize that even well-developed strategic and marketing plans do not guarantee success—they are not mystical crystal balls that see clearly into the future. As such, there will always be a certain amount of risk inherent in decision making. However, strategic and marketing planning increases the decision maker's odds of success. Finally, it should be noted that the actual exercise of developing a strategic and marketing plan may be as useful, if not more so, than the completed plans themselves. Both planning processes force decision makers to organize their thoughts on a number of different levels across the organization, as well as to consider the impact of environmental forces on the firm's overall strategy. Ultimately, strategic and marketing planning identifies strategic windows where the organization's core competencies are matched with opportunities that exist within the marketplace.

macaroni-and-cheese dinners, ties, pajamas, and even SpongeBob thongs with the town of Bikini Bottom emblazoned on the front. So much for targeting the two-to-11 kids market! In addition, script development is currently under way and *SpongeBob—The Movie* (not likely the real title) is scheduled to appear in theatres in late 2004. However, there is some concern that the show's creator and head writer, Stephen Hillenburg, will not be able to write new episodes while working on the movie. Consequently, SpongeBob fans may be faced with reruns, which they will most likely optimistically endure.

Viacom's Nickelodeon is betting its future success on new shows such as *The Fairly OddParents,* which follows the adventures of a 10-year-old boy and his peculiar fairy godparents. The company has already signed deals with manufacturers to produce approximately 100 products that will be tied to the show. However, Nickelodeon stands firm on its stance that merchandising comes second to quality programming. Who can argue with success? Last year, Nickelodeon claimed 41 of the top 50 TV programs on both network and cable television appealing to children ages two to 11. According to Nielsen Media Research, *SpongeBob SquarePants* was rated as the No.1 show, while *The Fairly OddParents* was rated as No. 2.[1]

Strategy is ultimately about finding a fit between an organization and its environment. After reading Chapter 1, you should have a clear understanding of how environmental forces can have an impact on an organization's success or failure within the marketplace. Strategic decision making pertains directly to the organization's ability to adapt to changing environmental forces and match organizational capabilities to the opportunities that exist within the current marketing environment. As a result, strategic and marketing planning seeks answers to the questions, "Where does the organization want to go?" and "How do we get there?"

Strategic and marketing planning occurs within and across all levels of the organization and is critical in achieving organizational objectives such as securing customers' preference for the organization's products over competitive products; developing a sustainable competitive advantage; and, perhaps most importantly, corporate survival and growth. Given the importance of strategic and marketing planning, this chapter discusses the nature and scope of planning in general, the fundamental steps and content of the strategic planning process, and the fundamentals of marketing planning. Consequently, after reading Chapters 1 and 2, you should understand the fundamentals of marketing, as well as the fundamentals of strategic and marketing planning.

LEARNING OBJECTIVE 1

The Nature and Scope of Planning

Planning is the basis for sound decision making in any situation in life. Whether you are planning a wedding, a vacation, or a multimillion-dollar sponsorship program, numerous efforts pertaining to the particular activity must be coordinated and planned well in advance. Without planning, the activity may have disastrous results.[2]

Consider, for example, a wedding. John and Susan get engaged, and then announce in March that they wish to marry in June because they simply can't wait any longer. The bride, groom, and their parents meet to discuss the wedding. In making a list of things to do, the top priorities are to secure the church and reception site for the desired date. Once those details are set, invitations, flowers, the bride's and

The key elements to any planning activity, including wedding planning, include timing, tasks, responsibility, follow-up, and budgeting.

© Susan Van Etten

bridesmaids' dresses, and tuxedos must be ordered. Next, the music, menus, cake, and invitation list must be decided on. And finally, table seating, the rehearsal dinner, and the honeymoon must also be planned.

If any of these elements are overlooked or not followed up on, John and Susan's wedding day will be ruined in their eyes. For example, if the responsibility of ordering the flowers is not assigned to a particular person, there is a risk that no flowers will be displayed at the church or on tables at the reception. If the responsibility of ordering and mailing invitations is not assigned to someone, there is a risk that no guests will attend the wedding. John and Susan want everything perfect for that day, so tasks are assigned to the bride, groom, and parents, and the group decides to meet in two days to discuss their progress.

When they next meet, John and Susan are very upset. The preferred church and the reception site are both booked on their desired date. John and Susan learn that most engaged couples have secured these details many months in advance. Susan also discovers that the dress she wants will take six months to order. And Susan's parents find that the cost of the reception with the desired number of guests far exceeds their budget. The group is forced to rethink their original plan and make the necessary modifications, allowing for these environmental factors.

This example demonstrates several elements that are key to any planning activity:

- *Timing.* Planning must occur well in advance of the activity. Planning postponed until the last minute will produce only negative results.
- *Tasks.* Every activity consists of a number of specific tasks. All details about each task must be planned in order for the entire activity to be successful.
- *Responsibility.* Every task needs a specific coordinator. If one person is not held accountable, the task may not get done.
- *Follow-up.* Even if responsibility for each task has been delegated, one individual must follow up on and coordinate the progress of the overall activity. Even the most responsible person can slip up and forget something.
- *Budgeting.* Budgeting is essential in planning. Plans that are too expensive for an individual or organization can have serious financial consequences. Through planning, costs are estimated and deemed acceptable or unacceptable.

These elements are critical in business planning. However, business planning has more far-reaching consequences than a wedding. Thousands of jobs and millions of dollars rely on solid planning efforts by management.

The Scope of Planning

Although the phrase and title of this chapter "Strategic and Marketing Planning" is frequently used in business discussions, there is often confusion concerning the difference between *strategic planning* and *marketing planning*.[3] For our purposes, **strategic planning**, or the organization's overall game plan, has a longer planning horizon (typically three to five years) than marketing planning and is primarily performed at the *corporate* and *business* levels of the organization. *Corporate strategy* takes place at the highest levels of the organization and seeks answers to the question, "What businesses should we be in?" As presented in the opening vignette, Viacom's business portfolio includes motion pictures, broadcast television, cable television, radio, outdoor, retail, recreation, publishing, online, and more. In comparison to corporate strategy, *business strategy* attempts to achieve and maintain competitive advantages in specific product-market domains. For example, one of Viacom's corporate holdings within its broadcast television business is CBS Television. Business strategy within CBS Television includes the product-market domains of CBS Entertainment, CBS News, CBS Sports, and CBS Enterprises. In sum, strategic planning typically takes place at the corporate and business levels of the organization, encompasses the firm's long-range goals, and dictates direction for all departments in the firm pertaining to issues such as mission direction, development of objectives, assessment of organizational growth opportunities, product markets to be served, and competitive advantage (see Figure 2.1).

In contrast to strategic planning, **marketing planning** has a shorter planning horizon (typically one year) and is performed at the marketing level, or what otherwise could be termed the product or product-line level of the organization. In keeping with our CBS example, within the business level of CBS News, the network

Strategic planning
Or the organization's overall game plan, has a longer planning horizon (typically three to five years) than marketing planning and is performed at the corporate *and* business *levels of the organization.*

Marketing planning
Has a shorter planning horizon (typically one year) and is performed at the marketing level or product or product-line level of the organization.

Figure 2.1	The Scope of Strategic and Marketing Planning

PepsiCo's overall strategic plan could easily encompass over a hundred companies and hundreds of brands.

engages in *marketing strategy* for such shows as *CBS Evening News with Dan Rather, 60 Minutes, 60 Minutes II, 48 Hours,* and *The Early Show.* In essence, marketing planning is the game plan for a particular product or product line. The marketing plan is the detailed scheme of the marketing strategies and includes target market selection, tailoring of the marketing mix, and product positioning.

Tactical planning is another level of organizational planning that takes place at the marketing level. **Tactical planning** involves *specifying details* that pertain to the organization's activities *for a certain period of time.* For example, the scheduled dates for a radio or television campaign for the third quarter would be included in a tactical plan. So, too, would the details regarding the fourth-quarter price deal offered to dealers. The production department's tactical plan may include the testing of a new quality-control program on a packaging line. The tactical plan is a detailed account of the firm's short-term activities as outlined in the strategic and marketing plans.

In summary, the strategic plan represents the company's overall plan, while the marketing plan details the marketing efforts and strategies as outlined in the strategic plan. As illustrated in Figure 2.1, corporate, business, and marketing strategy have distinctive and overlapping domains. Business strategy logically flows and overlaps corporate strategy and marketing strategy flows from and overlaps both corporate and business strategy. For example, complementary mission statements can be developed at the corporate (CBS Television) and business (CBS News) levels, and competitive advantage can be formulated at both the business (CBS News) and marketing (*60 Minutes*) levels. The end result is that strategic and marketing planning does not necessarily follow a strict hierarchy where corporate strategy dictates business strategy and business strategy dictates marketing strategy. Instead, the three levels of planning are interrelated and reinforce one another.

Tactical planning
Involves specifying details that pertain to the organization's activities for a certain period of time.

Fundamentals of Strategic Planning

2 LEARNING OBJECTIVE

Strategic planning at the corporate and business levels is an effective way for an organization to coordinate efforts among various departments, analyze its competitive position within its environment, and allocate its resources. The strategic planning

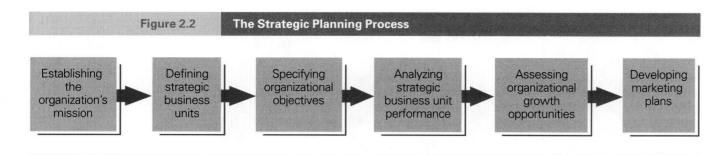

Figure 2.2 | **The Strategic Planning Process**

process causes all employees involved in the process to thoroughly think through the strategies that will prove most effective in achieving company goals. The fundamental steps involved in strategic planning include the following (see Figure 2.2):

- Establishing the organization's mission
- Defining strategic business units
- Specifying organizational objectives
- Analyzing strategic business unit performance
- Assessing organizational growth opportunities
- Developing marketing plans

Establishing the Organization's Mission

An organization's mission is the most important element in strategic planning. As part of the mission statement, the organization must define its business, or what makes it different from its competition. The entire strategic plan is built around this element. By focusing on its mission, management can concentrate their energies on making sound decisions, allocating resources, and generating profits in the long run. A **mission statement** is a guideline for the organization's decision making for both the short and long run. The mission provides direction to the strategic planning and marketing planning processes, as is illustrated in Starbucks Corporation's mission statement (see Figure 2.3).[4]

Starbucks states its purpose through its mission statement and its direction through six guiding principles. Starbucks' mission statement and accompanying guidelines encompass a broad range of issues that are typical of corporate mission statements. For example, the first two guidelines address Starbucks' commitment to providing a positive work environment while embracing diversity. The third guideline is directed at Starbucks' channel strategy and applies to procurement, production, and delivery activities. Guidelines four and five address Starbucks' relationship

Mission statement
Is a guideline for the organization's decision making for both the short and long run and provides direction to the strategic planning and marketing planning processes.

Natural Forces
Starbucks' appreciation for the impact of natural forces on its operations is evident in the firm's environmental mission statement.

Figure 2.3 | **Starbucks' Mission Statement**

Establish Starbucks as the premier purveyor of the finest coffee in the world while maintaining our uncompromising principles while we grow.
The following six guidelines will help us measure the appropriateness of our decisions:

- Provide a great work environment and treat each other with respect and dignity.
- Embrace diversity as an essential component in the way we do business.
- Apply the highest standards of excellence to the purchasing, roasting, and fresh delivery of our coffee.
- Develop enthusiastically satisfied customers all of the time.
- Contribute positively to our communities and our environment.
- Recognize that profitability is essential to our future success.

Source: http://www.starbucks.com/aboutus/environment.asp, accessed 13 February 2003. Used with permission.

with its stakeholders, including customers, the communities in which it operates, and the environment. Finally, the sixth statement specifies the company's primary objective—profitability. By effectively implementing the first five guidelines, the company believes that profitability will follow. Once the mission is accomplished and profitability is obtained, much of these funds are invested back into the company to achieve even greater levels of accomplishment across all six guidelines.

In addition to its corporate mission statement, Starbucks' commitment to environmentally friendly business practices is demonstrated in a separate environmental mission statement (see Figure 2.4). Starbucks actively attempts to minimize its environmental impact and creates opportunities for environmentally friendly business in a variety of ways. First, the company has adopted purchasing guidelines to buy environmentally friendly products from companies that share their concern for the environment. In addition, the company purchases lead-free ink, engages in paperless administration systems when possible, practices minimal packaging, recycles post-consumer materials, recycles coffee grounds obtained from roasting and extract operations into compost, incorporates energy conservation practices into its retail and manufacturing locations, voluntarily tracks and reduces its greenhouse gas emissions, and actively educates employees about Starbucks' commitment to the preservation of the environment.

Starbucks has developed a corporate mission statement as well as an environmental mission statement.

Starbucks' corporate and environmental mission statements and guidelines provide excellent examples of how these documents provide organizational focus and direction. By focusing in on its mission, management can concentrate their energies on making sound decisions, allocating resources, and generating long-term profits. Mission statements drive strategic planning.

Defining Strategic Business Units

Large companies like PepsiCo that offer diverse product lines and/or operate in several countries often create **strategic business units (SBUs)**, or smaller divisions, to facilitate planning and general operations. Smaller companies also use SBUs as a way to organize operations. Ultimately, an SBU can be one specific product, one product line, or a particular business. For example, an SBU at PepsiCo could be all of the Frito-Lay brands at the corporate level, or the business levels subsidiary Frito-Lay Dorito®, or a specific brand of Doritos® Brand Tortilla Chips such as Doritos® Brand

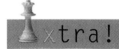

Strategic business units (SBUs)
Facilitate planning and have a clear market focus, an identifiable set of competitors, independent management teams, and SBU-specific operational goals.

Starbucks' Environmental Mission Statement	**Figure 2.4**

Starbucks is committed to a role of environmental leadership in all facets of our business. We fulfill this mission by a commitment to:

- Understanding of environmental issues and sharing information with our partners.
- Developing innovative and flexible solutions to bring about change.
- Striving to buy, sell, and use environmentally friendly products.
- Recognizing that fiscal responsibility is essential to our environmental future.
- Instilling environmental responsibility as a corporate value.
- Measuring and monitoring our progress for each project.
- Encouraging all partners to share in our mission.

Source: http://www.starbucks.com/aboutus/environment.asp, accessed 13 February 2003. Used with permission.

AP Topic Gallery

A strategic business within the Frito-Lay division of PepsiCo could be the entire product-line of Doritos Brand of Tortilla Chips or a specific brand within the product-line such as Salsa Verde!

SMART
Refers to well-developed organizational objectives that are specific, measurable, achievable, relevant, and time-bound.

Competitive Forces
Competitive position objectives such as market share are commonly stated objectives in most strategic plans.

Salsa Verde![5] Each SBU establishes its own mission statement, objectives, and strategic and marketing plans independent of other SBUs in the organization. As such, the SBU operates as a separate entity. Typically, the individual SBUs have a *clear market focus,* an *identifiable set of competitors, independent management teams,* and SBU-specific *operational goals,* while maintaining common management and production facilities with the remainder of the company.

Specifying Organizational Objectives

Ultimately, an organization's mission statement directs the objectives of the organization's strategic business units. All strategic and marketing plans flow from these objectives. Each department and SBU can have its own objectives, but these objectives must be guided by the organization's overall corporate and business-level objectives.

Overall, well-developed organizational objectives should be **SMART**—*specific, measurable, achievable, relevant,* and *time-bound.*[6]

- *Specific* organizational objectives are stated in terms of specific outcomes that are clearly defined. These objectives may include units to be sold, awareness levels to be reached, or a specific dollar amount of sales to be generated.
- *Measurable* organizational objectives are stated in quantitative terms that are capable of being assessed. Qualitative objectives such as "let's go do a good job this year" or "let's be nicer to customers this year," although worthy, are not specific or measurable when stated in this form. According to an old cliché, if you can't measure it, you can't manage it. In fact, if you can't measure it, managers and front-line employees alike seem unable to pay attention to it.
- *Achievable* objectives are motivating, realistic, and consistent. For example, asking employees to maximize sales volume while simultaneously meeting per-unit profitability objectives is most likely not an achievable objective.
- *Relevant* organizational objectives are appropriate and pertinent. In other words, the objectives stated in a strategic plan that involve corporate and business goals may not be relevant when stated as objectives in a marketing plan being developed for a specific brand.
- *Time-bound* organizational objectives are to be reached within a specific time frame. Much like qualitative objectives, organizational objectives with open-ended time frames will most likely never be achieved.

Organizational objectives vary depending on the type of organization. For example, a retailer such as Barnes & Noble bookstores may state market and financial objectives that are further divided into customer patronage objectives (sales, customer retention, store traffic); competitive position objectives (market share, image, channel relations); productivity objectives (labor, space, merchandise); and profitability objectives (return on investment, earnings, dividends). In addition, objectives will also vary based on the functional department within the organization developing its part of the strategic plan. For example, an objective for the marketing department may be "to obtain a 15% market share and maintain a profit margin of 20% by the end of the fiscal year" for a specific product or product line. In comparison, an objective for the production department may be to "reduce the level of rework from packaging from 5% to 3% by the end of the fiscal year."

Analyzing SBU Performance: Allocating Resources in the Product Portfolio

Strategic planning tools are available to help managers in their strategic and marketing planning efforts. Careful planning efforts are acutely important to most large organizations that are structured into multiple SBUs with many product offerings. The fundamental issue is one of resource allocation and prioritization. Which products (SBUs) are most, and least, deserving of additional investments? The situation faced by business planners can be compared to that which confronts medical personnel in times of war and medical crises, when these personnel are faced with the wrenching task of determining which of many injured people should receive immediate aid. *Triage* is the medical practice used in times of medical crisis. Patients are prioritized in terms of how badly they require immediate medical care, and how likely it is that their lives can be saved. Those patients who badly need care and are likely to survive are the top priority for assistance, whereas those who either are unlikely to survive or are not in desperate condition are lower in the priority scheme.

Similarly, an organization's product mix can be viewed as a portfolio, with each product having a different growth rate and market share, thus requiring different amounts of attention and characterized by differing performance potentials. Product-portfolio analysis offers suggestions for appropriate marketing strategies to best use an organization's scarce cash and other limited resources.[7] The fundamental issue is one of resource allocation and prioritization. In other words, which products (SBUs) are most, and least, deserving of additional investments? Additional investments are provided or withheld through the implementation of five resource allocation strategies:

Organizational objectives for a retailer such as Barnes & Noble may pertain to a variety of goals including customer patronage, competitive position, productivity, and profitability.

- **Build Strategy**—The goal of a *build* strategy is to improve the SBU's position in the marketplace by investing additional resources. The SBU is identified as worthy of the additional investment based on current and/or future performance potential compared to other SBUs in the product portfolio.
- **Maintain Strategy**—The goal of a *maintain* strategy is to hold the SBU's current position steady in the market place. Hence, some investment may continue to fund the SBU, but the aim is to neither lose nor gain ground in the marketplace. A maintain strategy may be implemented when other SBUs with more potential exist and the company wants to provide additional resources elsewhere.
- **Niche Strategy**—The goal of a *niche* strategy is to narrow the focus of the SBU's intended market. Some SBUs struggle in the marketplace as they attempt to meet the needs and wants of too many different types of customers. Niching often increases an SBU's performance by scaling back the scope of its objectives and focusing in on smaller, more well-defined target markets whose needs can be met more effectively and efficiently. For example, a software company that develops broad-based accounts-receivable software may begin focusing on accounts-receivable software for pharmacies.
- **Harvest Strategy**—The goal of a *harvest* strategy is to use the SBU primarily to generate resources for other SBUs. The organization does not completely pull its support from SBUs that are being harvested. However, some harvested SBUs are generating more resources than they could ever effectively use, or are so dominant in the marketplace that sustaining their current position requires minimal investment.

Build strategy
Refers to the resource allocation strategy for which the goal is to improve the SBU's current position in the marketplace.

Maintain strategy
Refers to the resource allocation strategy for which the goal is to hold the SBU's current position steady in the marketplace

Niche strategy
Refers to the resource allocation strategy where the scope of the SBU is more narrowly focused on smaller, more well-defined target markets.

Harvest strategy
Refers to the resource allocation strategy in which an SBU is primarily used to generate resources to fund other SBUs.

Developing an Effective Web Strategy: The 7Cs of Customer Interface

The customer's online experience will likely be a key consideration for many organizations' marketing plans. A customer's online experience progresses over time through four unique stages: (1) Functionality—"The site works well," (2) Intimacy—"The site understands my particular set of needs," (3) Internalization—"Visiting the site is part of my daily life," and (4) Evangelism—"I love to tell others about the site." As the customer makes the transition through each stage, the experience moves from a general reaction (functionality) to a personal reaction (intimacy and internalization) to an outer-directed action (evangelism). In other words, as customers move through each of the stages, loyalty to the organization increases, purchasing intensifies, customers willingly provide more feedback, and they are more likely to share their positive experiences with others. The challenge for marketers is how to help customers make the transition through each of the stages within an online environment.

Effective Web designs incorporate the 7Cs of customer interface:

- *Context*—What is the look and feel of the screen-to-customer interface? Is the context purely functional-dominant such as **http://www.altavista.com** or is it more aesthetic-dominant such as **http://www.axis-media.com**?
- *Content*—What is the digital matter posted on the Web site? Content includes the organization's offering mix (products and information) and multimedia mix (text, audio, images, and graphics).
- *Community*—The site should provide the means to build a closer relationship between the customer and the firm, and between the customer and other customers (e.g., chat rooms).

- *Customization*—The site should have the ability to modify itself based on the customer's past usage behavior (personalization), or provide the ability for customers to modify the site based on their own preferences (tailoring).
- *Communication*—The customer should be provided with multiple ways to communicate with the Web site. Examples include the posting of toll-free numbers, e-mail, self-help capabilities, online help desks, and the organization's mailing address.
- *Connection*—What other sites are connected to the main Web site? Connections can vary from destination sites such as **http://www.nytimes.com** (which has few connections to other sites) to a hub site such as **http://www.drkoop.com** (which provides a balance between internal and external [linked] content) to a portal site such as **http://www.ceoexpress.com** which provides almost exclusively links to other sites.
- *Commerce*—The site should be constructed so that customers can easily conduct transactions. Commerce involves all aspects of the interface supporting transactions such as order confirmation, shipping confirmation, easy payment options, order fulfillment, handling questions, and handling returns.

Each of the 7Cs should reinforce one another and be specifically designed with the organization's target market in mind as they transition through the four stages of the online experience.

Sources: Rafi A. Mohammed, Robert J. Fisher, Bernard J. Jaworski, and Aileen Cahill, *Internet Marketing: Building Advantage in a Networked Economy* (Boston: McGraw-Hill Irwin, 2002), 622–624.
Ron Zemke and Tom Connellan, *E-service* (New York: AMACOM, 2001).

Divest strategy
Refers to the resource allocation strategy where investment in an SBU is discontinued.

- **Divest Strategy**—The goal of a *divest* strategy is to discontinue all investment in an SBU so that resources can be redirected to other SBUs in the product portfolio that show more performance potential.

The following section discusses one of the most well-known strategic planning tools that managers can use in the practice of triage as they attempt to make resource allocation decisions among their own product portfolios. The Boston Consulting Group's (BCG) Product-Portfolio Analysis—more commonly known as the BCG Matrix—aids decision makers in determining each SBU's current market situation and resource requirements.

BCG's Product-Portfolio Analysis

The BCG matrix (see Figure 2.5) classifies products from the perspective of a single company and its particular products or SBUs. Classification is based on two dimensions. The horizontal axis represents the relative market share that a particular product realizes vis-à-vis the dominant brand in the category. This axis delineates relative share into "high" and "low" categories.

Consider, for example, a product category with four brands and the following market shares: Brand A, the industry leader, enjoys a relative market share that is

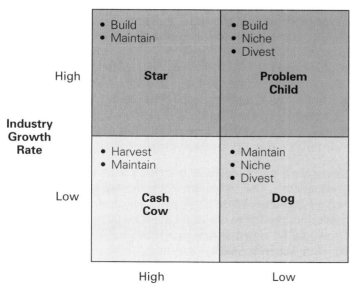

Boston Consulting Group (BCG) Matrix

Figure 2.5

twice as large as its nearest rival, Brand B. Comparatively, Brands B, C, and D realize relative shares of 0.5 (i.e., 25/50), 0.4 (20/50), and 0.1 (5/50), respectively. If the point of division between the right and left quadrants of the matrix is at a relative share of 1.0, Brand A has a relatively high market share, whereas Brands B, C, and D are all relatively low.

The vertical axis in the BCG matrix is based on the product, market, or industry growth rate. Here, the dividing point between upper and lower quadrants is traditionally set, albeit arbitrarily, at 10%. Realizing that the population growth rate in the United States is around 2% per annum, many staple products (e.g., milk, bread, industrial commodities) generally grow at a rate commensurate with the population, and, as such, are considered relatively low on the scale. It is in the area of new technologies and fads that growth rates are high. Innovative new products experience growth rates of 50% or higher in early years, and then eventually decrease over time.

With these distinctions in mind, Figure 2.5 categorizes four general types of products, and gives each a metaphoric name, suggesting the implications that each holds for a firm's marketing strategy: cash cows (to be milked), stars (to sustain their ascendancy), problem children (to treat with caution), and dogs (to avoid).

Problem Children. Problem children are strategic business units that enjoy rapid growth but are characterized by low market shares and poor profit margins. When it comes to resource allocation decisions, SBUs classified as problem children present a real quandary for decision makers—thus the name. On the one hand, problem children have enormous demand for cash, and risk becoming dogs, since growth inevitably will slow if cash is not forthcoming. On the other hand, if effectively supported, problem children have the potential of transforming themselves into stars. Strategically, marketers of a problem child may employ a *build* strategy and invest heavily in an attempt to increase market share. Other strategic options include employing a *niche* strategy, whereby the SBU can focus in on more well-defined markets whose needs can be met both more effectively and efficiently, or decision makers may employ a *divest* strategy if other SBUs are available that look more desirable and are more deserving of funding.

Problem children
Are SBUs that enjoy rapid growth but are characterized by low market shares and poor profit margins.

Stars
Are SBUs characterized by high market-growth rates and high market shares.

Stars. Problem children that improve their position in the marketplace through increased market share become **stars**. Stars are SBUs characterized by high market-growth rates and high market shares. Stars are market leaders that generate substantial profits. However, stars require a large resource investment to generate any significant growth. Strategically, resource allocation decisions for SBUs classified as stars are generally to *build* or *maintain* the SBU's position. Employing a build strategy makes sense in cases where the SBU has recently entered the star category and has room to grow and/or new markets for the product category have been identified and are expanding rapidly. A maintain resource allocation strategy is appropriate for stars that are, for lack of a better term, superstars. These stars are dominating the high-growth market and continue to do so over time. In this instance, the maintain strategy is used to sustain the SBU's current position in the market.

Cash cows
Are SBUs that enjoy high market share but undergo low levels of market growth.

Cash Cows. Stars that experience a steady decrease in market growth may eventually become **cash cows**. Consequently, cash cows are SBUs that enjoy high market share but undergo low levels of market growth. Cash cows are generally very profitable and generate more cash than needed to maintain their market share. Strategically, corporatewide efforts should be aimed at managing cash cows by investing in improvements to *maintain* their superior market position, and/or *harvesting* the excess cash that cash cows produce to support development of other SBUs within the organization's product portfolio. In essence, cash cows are "milked" to fund other projects—thus the name.

Dogs
Are SBUs characterized by low market shares and low market-growth rates.

Dogs. **Dogs** are SBUs characterized by low market shares and low market-growth rates. Dogs operate at a cost disadvantage and have few opportunities for growth because the markets are not growing and there is little new business. Marketers of dog products can pursue several strategies: (1) focus on a particular segment of the market by pursuing a *niche* strategy and attempt to outperform competitors in that segment; (2) *divest* the product by selling the business to a competitor or by eliminating the product from the product portfolio; or (3) *maintain* the product for social responsibility reasons, in instances where break-even or better conditions exist, to sustain economic vitality in the community in which the business is located.

Ideally, an organization should have a balance of products in its portfolio to be successful. Products that generate cash offset those products that require additional investment for growth. If a firm has too many cash cows or dogs, overall company growth is unlikely and future prospects are lacking. Likewise, if the organization has a disproportionate number of stars or problem children, the resource demands may be too excessive to provide sufficient support for these products. The logic underlying product portfolios is similar to financial investment logic: Don't place all your eggs in one basket! Having only a single type of security in one's investment portfolio can lead to disaster if the market for that one offering experiences a sudden decline. Similarly, possessing only cash cows or stars and problem children is severely shortsighted.

Economic Forces
Economic forces may be considered when SBUs, classified as dogs, are being considered for divestiture. Decision makers may "maintain" a "dog" to sustain the economic vitality of the local community.

Limitations of Portfolio Models
Although strategic planning tools, such as the BCG product-portfolio analysis model and others like it, are a useful starting point for analyzing product portfolios, they should be viewed and used with some caution.[8] Clearly, pros and cons are associated with their use. On the positive side, portfolio models provide a rational systematic method for resource allocation decisions that should overcome the obstacles of irrational and emotional decision making based on sunk costs and personal attachments to particular business units. On the downside, portfolio models such as the BCG matrix assume a causal relationship between market share and profitability that does not necessarily exist. In addition, the distinction between cell descriptors of "high" and "low" are highly subjective. As a result, two different managers can recommend two different resource allocation strategies given the same scenario. A third limitation of portfolio models is that they do not take into account synergies that may possibly exist among the various SBUs within the product portfolio. Consequently,

divesting one SBU may lead to the unforeseen demise of other more promising SBUs. Finally, the cell labels themselves (problem children, stars, cash cows, and dogs) may introduce irrational emotions into the decision-making process. For example, managers may not want to be on the management team of an SBU known as a dog or a problem child!

Industry use of portfolio models has met with mixed results. For example, several studies have reported that firms using portfolio models have reported a lower return on capital than those firms not using them. Of course, it could be argued that struggling firms finally turn to portfolio models for salvation, but, alas, it's too late. On the other hand, in another study of Fortune 1000 companies, virtually all of the respondents believed that their use of formal portfolio models had a positive impact on their decision making. In the end, portfolio models help decision makers organize their thoughts and make more informed decisions. Managers should supplement portfolio-based decision making with their own specialized knowledge pertaining to the SBU being evaluated and consider their own gut instincts as well.

Assessing Organizational Growth Opportunities

Established products are the lifeblood of most companies. But a company that depends solely on its current products may be headed for trouble. Aggressive competitive activity or a major change in technology can cause a rapid decline in sales for even the most successful product. Growth is fundamental to the long-term success of any organization and an integral part of the planning process. Opportunities for growth (see Figure 2.6) can be explored through three avenues: developing growth within current operations (*intensive growth strategies*), achieving growth by acquiring other businesses directly related to existing operations (*integrative growth strategies*), and developing growth by acquiring other businesses not directly related to existing operations (*diversification growth strategies*).

Intensive Growth Strategies

Growth opens up new sales and profit opportunities for a firm while reducing dependence on existing products for its success. Companies can pursue a number of growth options within their current operations. Figure 2.7 presents four such options: market penetration, market development, product development, and product diversification.

Market Penetration. A firm may first attempt to grow its business through **market penetration** by selling more of its *existing products* to *existing markets*. The main objective of this strategy is to convince existing customers to purchase and use more of the firm's product. This strategy is used most often for mature products in mature markets. Firms attempt to penetrate markets either by improving quality, dropping prices, increasing distribution, or engaging in aggressive advertising and other promotional activities. For example, although Starbucks' growth has taken place on a number of fronts, one example of the company engaging in a market-penetration strategy involves its Loyalty Card program.[9] Scott Waltmann, a Merrill Lynch analyst for Starbucks, notes, "The Starbucks card has a lot of usability—the average

Market penetration
Represents the firm's attempt to sell more of its existing products to existing markets.

Technological Forces
Starbucks' technologically enabled loyalty cards allow customers to prepay for their purchases electronically and have proven to be an effective market penetration strategy.

Organizational Growth Strategies		Figure 2.6
Intensive Growth Strategies	**Integrative Growth Strategies**	**Diversification Growth Strategies**
• Market Penetration	• Backward Integration	• Concentric Diversification
• Market Development	• Forward Integration	• Horizontal Diversification
• Product Development	• Horizontal Integration	• Conglomerate Diversification
• Product Diversification		

Figure 2.7	Intensive Growth Strategies

	Existing Markets	New Markets
Existing Products	Market Penetration	Market Development
New Products	Product Development	Product Diversification

Sociocultural Forces

As a result of women's increasing concerns over their own hair loss, Rogaine™, which had been exclusively targeting men, is now actively marketing its hair-loss remedy to women.

Market development

Represents the firm's attempt to sell more of its existing products to new markets.

Product development

Represents the firm's attempt to sell new products to existing markets.

Product diversification

Represents the firm's attempt to sell new products to new markets.

office worker may go downstairs for coffee two to three times a day. The card locks in the customer, because if they have a balance on the card, they're more likely to walk past another coffee purveyor to go to Starbucks."[10] Over five million customers have signed up for the Starbucks card since it was introduced.

Market Development. Firms that find *new markets* for *existing products* are pursuing **market development**. This strategy is undertaken when (1) new uses are discovered for mature products, such as baking soda's repositioning as a deodorizer, carpet cleaner, and toothpaste, among other uses; (2) new users are found due to a change in consumer behavior or demographics, such as Rogaine™, the hair-loss remedy for men, now being marketed to women with thinning hair; or (3) new markets are entered with an existing product such as Starbucks' international division, which is rapidly opening new locations throughout the world.

Product Development. Firms that develop *new products* that they feel will appeal to *existing markets* are pursuing a **product development** strategy. In this scenario, a firm seeks to provide its existing market with a variety of new choices. Once again, a significant portion of Starbucks' growth strategy can be tied to product development. The company has expanded by developing numerous new products that appeal to its existing markets, such as the introduction and sales of Frappuccino® blended beverages; music CDs based on the extremely popular in-house music programs; deli-style sandwiches; and Starbucks Barista Quattro™ thermal coffeemaker, a fully automated home espresso machine.

Product Diversification. The riskiest option for growth is **product diversification**, which develops *new products* for *new markets*. Product diversification enables a company to depend less on any one product or product line; however, the strategy is risky for two reasons. First, the firm is delving into an area that is outside its recognized expertise and customers may reject its presence in the new marketplace. For example, customers might find that an automobile manufactured by Harley-Davidson is a laughable idea. However, this is exactly the transition Honda made nearly 25 years ago when the motorcycle maker began producing Honda Civics. Today, Honda and its luxury spin-off product line, Acura, are among the most recognized and admired automobile manufacturers in the world. The second reason that product diversification is risky is that customers might be correct—the company may just not have the expertise to successfully market a new product in a new marketplace. For example, PepsiCo, the marketer of Pepsi-Cola branded products, among others, originally purchased KFC, Pizza Hut and Taco Bell to increase its market share of U.S. cola fountain sales. PepsiCo eventually sold its fast-food restaurant business to Yum! Brands, Inc.—a Fortune 300 company and the world's largest quick-serve restaurant company in terms of number of restaurant units.[11] Yum! Brands, Inc., with more than 30,000 restaurants around the world in more than 100 countries and territories, commands the quick-serve restaurant expertise that PepsiCo lacked.

Integrative Growth Strategies

Integrative growth opportunities, defined as growth through the acquisition of other businesses directly related to existing operations, present themselves in the form of *backward integration, horizontal integration,* and *forward integration.* All three methods of acquisition have one aspect in common—they all represent acquisitions of other businesses that are directly related to the firm's current operations. As such, all three forms of integrated growth represent acquisitions of other businesses that enhance the current operation's **value chain** (see Figure 2.8). The value chain includes all businesses that are upstream and downstream from the manufacturer. For example, located downstream from the manufacturer is the traditional *marketing channel* consisting of wholesalers and retailers. Looking upstream from the manufacturer is the traditional *supply chain* consisting of suppliers and producers of raw materials. Hence, the value chain is formed by combining the supply chain with the marketing channel and represents what most practitioners are talking about when discussing *supply chain management.*

Backward integration occurs when a business acquires a firm upstream in the value chain. For example, if a manufacturer purchases a supplier, then backward integration has transpired. Firms typically engage in backward integration to control their costs of supply, or to generate additional profits, as well as for quality-control reasons. In contrast, if the manufacturer begins to purchase retailers located downstream in the value chain, forward integration has occurred. Firms may engage in forward integration as a growth strategy to enhance their profit opportunities, as well as to gain additional control over marketing activities. Acquiring competitors at the same stage along the value chain characterizes horizontal integration. In other

Courtesy of Ferrero U.S.A., Inc.

Nutella pursues a market penetration strategy by engaging in advertising and price promotions for its hazelnut spread.

Value chain

Is formed by combining the supply chain with the marketing channel and represents what most practitioners are talking about when they discuss supply chain management.

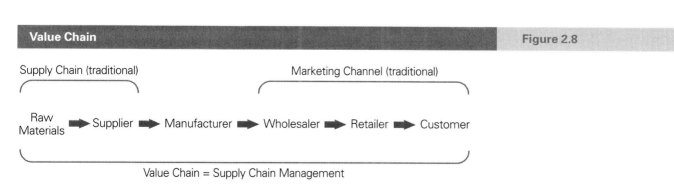

Figure 2.8

Value Chain = Supply Chain Management

Source: Judy Strauss and Raymond Frost, *E-Marketing* (Upper Saddle River, NJ: Prentice-Hall, 2001), 189.
© 2001. Reprinted by permission of Pearson Education, Inc., Upper Saddle River, NJ.

Starbucks' Commitment to Corporate Social Responsibility

As specifically addressed in Starbucks' corporate and environmental mission statements, Starbucks believes that giving back to the community is vitally important. The company proves its commitment through its *community building* and *Commitment to Origins*™ programs, as well as through The Starbucks Foundation. Partners (employees) at all levels are involved in these initiatives, with the goal of improving the resources and well-being of those areas that surround Starbucks' operations.

The goal of community-building programs is to integrate Starbucks' corporate culture with its surroundings. "It is the goal of Starbucks' corporate and regional community building initiatives to involve partners as decision-makers, volunteers, and leaders in the initiatives they support." The company openly encourages and rewards participation in neighborhood cleanups, walkathons, and other community leadership activities. Specific examples of past partner involvement include grants to local parks, violence protection programs, cash and product donations, and participation in local literacy organizations. Recently, Starbucks teamed up with Earvin "Magic" Johnson to form a joint venture known as Urban Coffee Opportunities to encourage retail vitality and economic opportunity in underserved urban neighborhoods.

Starbucks also demonstrates its involvement with the communities of its coffee growers through its Commitment to Origins™ program. According to Starbucks' corporate Web site (http://www.starbucks.com), the Commitment to Origins™ initiative involves assisting "producers, their families, and communities, and the natural environment to help promote a sustainable social, ecological, and economic model for the production and trade of coffee." Programs that have been developed under the Commitment to Origins™ initiative include the creation of a Fair Trade Certified™ brand of coffee that rewards farmers who form and participate in democratically run cooperatives in exchange for guaranteed premium prices. Starbucks committed to purchase one million pounds of Fair Trade Coffee™ in 2002–2003 and to expand its distribution of the brand throughout North America and internationally. Other Commitment to Origins™ programs include Conservation Coffee™, which supports the production of shade-grown coffee using ecologically sound growing practices, and Starbucks' involvement with CARE—a relief organization that distributes Starbucks funds in response to emergencies and natural disasters in coffee- and tea-origin countries.

The Starbucks Foundation, established by Starbucks Chairman Howard Schultz in 1997, is yet another example of Starbucks' community involvement. The foundation is dedicated to "creating hope, discovery, and opportunity in communities where Starbucks lives and works." The primary focus of the foundation is to improve young lives through literacy programs for children and families. The Starbucks Foundation has provided numerous grants to local community organizations serving low-income, at-risk families. In addition, the foundation recently made a four-year commitment to help support "Jumpstart." Jumpstart, a nonprofit organization, provides one-on-one tutoring to at-risk preschoolers enrolled in Head Start programs. Through the work of the foundation, Starbucks believes it can nurture youth and "create a more just, compassionate and sustainable world today and in the future." Clearly, Starbucks demonstrates on a daily basis that it has become much more than a coffee house. Starbucks is actively attempting to improve people's lives and the environment in which they live, work, and play. Simultaneously, Starbucks' strong commitment to corporate social responsibility has provided it with a sustainable competitive advantage in the marketplace.

DISCUSSION QUESTIONS

1. As a member of the consuming public, were you aware of Starbucks' commitment to the community and environment of its customers and coffee growers? Should Starbucks' actively promote its commitment to the community and the environment? Why or why not?
2. Organizations often support societal causes directly related to the interests of the business' customers and employees. Do you believe that Starbucks is strictly following this school of thought? Why or why not?

Sources: http://www.starbucks.com/aboutus/csr.asp.
http://www.starbucks.com/aboutus/community.asp.
http://www.starbucks.com/aboutus/origins.asp.
http://www.starbucks.com/aboutus/fairtrade.asp; accessed 14 February 2003.

words, a retailer acquiring a competitive retailer or a manufacturer acquiring another manufacturer would be considered horizontal integration. The benefits of horizontal integration as a growth strategy include increased market share, additional profit opportunities, and the cost savings associated with economies of scale that may arise due to a larger volume of business transactions.

Diversification Growth Strategies

Diversification growth opportunities, defined as growth through the acquisition of other businesses not directly related to existing operations, can be accomplished through *concentric diversification, horizontal diversification,* and *conglomerate diversification.* In other words, diversification growth strategies represent acquisitions of other businesses that are not directly related to the existing business' value chain. As such, concentric diversification represents the acquisition of other businesses that have technological and/or marketing synergies with existing operations. For example, when PepsiCo acquired Pizza Hut, KFC, and Taco Bell, it did so to increase its market share of cola fountain sales in the marketplace, even though it lacked expertise in operating quick-serve restaurants. Hence, marketing synergies existed between the two types of businesses and the acquisition was completed. As mentioned previously, PepsiCo eventually sold the three restaurant chains to Yum! Brands, Inc., which specialized in the quick-service restaurant industry. Growth through horizontal diversification can be achieved by acquiring companies who market different products to the same market targeted by the acquiring firm. For example, if PepsiCo acquired Tower Records it would be due in large part to the common target market that both products serve, even though technological synergies would not exist. Finally, a business may wish to grow and diversify its product portfolio by engaging in conglomerate diversification. Conglomerate diversification is characterized by acquiring other businesses that have nothing in common with current customers, technology, or products. For example, if PepsiCo decided to acquire companies that specialized in the production of enabling technologies (e.g., wheelchairs, heart-monitoring equipment, etc.) for the elderly, they would indeed be pursuing a growth opportunity through conglomerate diversification.

Developing Marketing Plans

The final step in strategic planning is developing the marketing plan at the marketing level. Marketing plans emanate from and are inspired by the overall strategic plan. Marketing plays an instrumental role in determining the strategic plan, and, in turn, marketing plans are influenced and directed by the strategic plan. The fundamental steps in developing a marketing plan are discussed in detail below.

Fundamentals of Marketing Planning

3 LEARNING OBJECTIVE

Once the strategic plan is developed and approved, marketing planning at the marketing level takes place.[12] As stated in the beginning of this chapter, the marketing plan is the detailed scheme of marketing strategies and activities associated with each product's marketing mix. Hence, the strategic plan is the company's overall plan, while the marketing plan details the marketing efforts and strategies outlined in the strategic plan.

Variations in Marketing Planning

The most successful marketing efforts are driven by a formal marketing plan, which includes specific objectives, necessary resources, planned activities, and expected results. However, marketing plans take different forms and follow many formats. For example, practitioner development and use of marketing plans can vary in scope, length, and formality.

Marketing Plans Vary in Scope

Marketing plans can be created for an entire product category or for specific brands, depending on the size of each and its intended target market. For example, Procter & Gamble's marketing plan for Pringles Potato Chips probably includes the entire line of Original, Sour Cream & Onion, Sweet Mesquite BBQ, Cheezums, Pizzalicious, and so on.[13] There is no need to develop a complete marketing plan for each of these products since they are varieties of a single product line that are likely to be targeted to the same market. On the other hand, even though it is a brand within the same product line, Diet Coke probably has a marketing plan of its own separate from

Coca-Cola, since the two beverages are targeted toward different markets and require different marketing mixes to effectively appeal to their respective markets.

Marketing Plans Vary in Length

Some companies require only an outline of the overall plan, with details provided on a quarterly basis in a tactical plan. Other companies require a complete product history with a detailed plan covering the upcoming year. In addition, most marketing plans are short-term, covering a one-year period. Other marketing plans are much longer, encompassing a period of two to 10 years. A combination of the two, which pairs a one-year operational plan with a section on long-range goals and plans, represents the best of both worlds.

Marketing Plans Vary in Formality

Some companies do not require a formal marketing plan. In instances such as these, a marketing budget is assigned to a product, and the product manager simply submits proposals as potential promotions arise. In this case, management is taking a *reactive* or "Band-Aid" approach to marketing—competitive "fires" are put out with a quick-and-dirty promotional effort. These companies fail to realize, though, that many of these fires could be avoided if proper *proactive* planning had taken place well in advance.

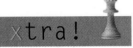

The Traditional Marketing Plan

A detailed marketing plan is critical in creating and coordinating effective marketing activities. The seven major components of a traditional marketing plan are depicted in Figure 2.9 and include:

- Executive Summary
- Market Situation Analysis
- SWOT Analysis
- Specification of Marketing Objectives
- Formulation of Marketing Strategies
- Preparation of Action Programs and Budgets
- Development of Control Procedures

In the discussion that follows, a marketing plan will be simulated for a fictitious consumer product—Twisty Pretzel.[14] This oversimplified marketing plan is provided to illustrate the important components of a typical marketing plan. Keep in mind that an actual marketing plan will likely be much longer and more detailed.

Executive Summary

The Executive Summary is a synopsis of the entire marketing plan. Usually included in the Executive Summary are a recap of the product's performance during the previous 12 months, the objectives of the plan, a list of planned activities, and the resources required to support the plan. The Executive Summary is useful for those in upper management who need to be aware of these facts and figures, but who are not

Figure 2.9   Components of the Marketing Plan

Executive Summary → Market Situation Analysis → SWOT Analysis → Specification of Marketing Objectives → Formulation of Marketing Strategies → Preparation of Action Programs and Budgets → Development of Control Procedures

Twisty Pretzel is the dominant brand in the fastest growing category within the salty snack industry.

directly involved with the implementation of the details. In its barest essentials, an Executive Summary statement for Twisty Pretzel might look something like this:

The Twisty Pretzel product line increased sales from $122 million in 2002 to $181 million in 2003, a jump of 48% over the prior year. The increase was achieved by the introduction of the brand's first national ad campaign, increased trade support, and new product introductions. Sales for the next 12-month period are expected to be $208 million, an increase of 15% over the prior year. Sales increases are projected on the basis of increased sales to existing markets through in-ad coupons and trade allowances, expanded distribution to new markets via slotting allowances, and the introduction of a new low-fat pretzel nugget to the marketplace. In addition, the national ad campaigns scheduled to run in two of the four quarters will facilitate sales across the board. The estimated budget to support these activities is $22.5 million, an increase of 12% over the prior year.

Since the Executive Summary is a synopsis of the marketing plan, it should be written last, even though it is the first document in the marketing plan. Furthermore, when extracting the Executive Summary from the marketing plan, several issues should be considered. First, the marketing plan itself is a summary document of product-related issues; consequently, the Executive Summary may sometimes gloss over important details that senior executives need to know and comment on. As such, precautions should be taken to ensure that the Executive Summary is not too general in nature. In addition, the Executive Summary may be written mistakenly as a political document attempting to convince upper management of the merits of the plan, as opposed to a decision-making instrument that presents the straight facts. Developers of the marketing plan must keep in mind that the plan is a decision-making tool so that the document's and the developer's credibility remain intact.

Market Situation Assessment

The Market Situation Assessment is a breakdown of the brand's current status in the marketplace. It reviews brand-related trends in the industry, the brand's situation within the company itself, including current marketing strategy, as well as pertinent information about customers and existing distribution channels. The assessment of the

Political and Legal Forces

Political and legal forces, as well as other environmental forces, are considered in the Market Situation Assessment of the marketing plan.

market situation also addresses the impact of environmental forces relevant to the brand's marketing efforts, including competitors (existing and potential), technological developments, economic conditions, natural forces, political and legal developments, and sociocultural trends. In essence, the Marketing Situation Analysis component of the marketing plan acts as the "state of the union" for the brand. Within the analysis, the prior year's activities are reviewed and analyzed. Additionally, actual sales results as compared to the stated objectives in the prior year's plan are included. An analysis of Twisty Pretzel's situation might be along the following lines:

Pretzels currently represent a $1-billion dollar industry. They are considered the salty snack industry's fastest-growing category. However, environmental forces, particularly economic and sociocultural, continue to affect the industry. The Twisty Pretzel brand is the market leader, with a market share of 18%. Twisty Pretzel's closest competitor, Falcon brand pretzels, maintains its 7% share of the market. Twisty Pretzel's sales increased 48% over the prior year. In 2001, the brand had no ad support. In 2002, a national ad campaign supported the brand with Matthew Perry, also known as Chandler Bing of NBC TV's Friends, *as the spokesperson. Four trade promotions were run, one per quarter. Coupons were distributed twice during the year. Falcon brand pretzels matched the Twisty Pretzel deal levels to the trade, but ran no supporting media or promotional efforts. All of these factors contributed to the huge increase in sales in 2003 and the Twisty Pretzel brand's market dominance. Currently, Twisty Pretzel is looking to improve on its noteworthy distribution efforts and to effectively control quality issues at one of its production facilities.*

SWOT Analysis

Information obtained from the Market Situation Assessment can be effectively organized through a SWOT Analysis. The SWOT Analysis organizes the information from the situation assessment into four categories—*strengths, weaknesses, opportunities,* and *threats*. Strengths and weaknesses represent *internal assessments* of the firm's current capabilities and address questions such as:

Strengths:
- What are our core competencies—what do we do best (e.g., production capabilities, distribution, finance, human resources, research and development, marketing, etc.)?
- What do employees think that we do well (e.g., training, benefits package, rewarding performance, etc.)?
- What do customers think the organization does best (e.g., customer service, handling complaints, handling returns and exchanges)?
- What is the organization's reputation in the marketplace (e.g., involved in the community, reputable business practices, vital to the local economy)?

Weaknesses:
- What areas of the business need the most improvement (e.g., production capabilities, distribution, finance, human resources, research and development, marketing, etc.)?
- What are employee suggestions for improvements (e.g., training, benefits package, rewarding performance, etc.)?
- How do customers think we could improve our business (e.g., customer service, handling complaints, handling returns and exchanges)?
- Compared to competitors, what is the organization's reputation in the marketplace (e.g., involved in the community, reputable business practices, vital to the local economy)?

In contrast, opportunities and threats represent *external assessments* of the firm's marketing environment. Typically, opportunities and threats emerge from the Market Situation Assessment of environmental forces and their potential impact on the brand's future survival or demise. Opportunities and threats address questions such as:

Building Customer Relationships in the African-American Market

The American consumer market is changing rapidly. Where the market was dominated by Caucasians just a generation ago, ethnic populations are growing quickly and now represent approximately 30% of U.S. consumers. Of particular interest is the African-American market. Outpacing overall U.S. population growth, the African-American population grew by almost 20% during the 1990s and now represents approximately 12% of the population. Today, the African-American population is estimated at 35.5 million and controls 8% of the buying power in the U.S.—an estimated $572 billion. In addition, African-American-owned businesses have also increased, growing at a rate of 46% from 1987 to 1997. Despite the buying power of African-American consumers and businesses, they have been virtually overlooked by many marketers. According to some estimates, marketers have spent little more than 1% of their advertising budgets targeting this group.

Marketing to African-American consumers and businesses involves understanding the group's priorities and culture, offering the right mix of products at the right prices, and building relationships based on trust. For example, the insurance industry is now beginning to understand the specific insurance-related priorities of the African-American culture. These priorities include access to screening tests and treatments for breast cancer and prostate cancer. Medical research has shown that African-American women have a higher-than-average incidence of mortality from breast cancer, and African-American men have the highest prostate cancer rates in the world. In addition, the latest U.S. Census figures indicate that the number of households headed by single African-American women increased by 2.3 million during the 1990s. As a result, the right mix of insurance products for this market includes cancer and critical illness plans that include benefits for yearly mammograms and prostate examinations, and income-replacement products such as disability insurance to protect the children of single-parent households.

The single biggest obstacle to marketing to ethnic groups is building trust. This is particularly true if you are not a member of the ethnic group. Building trust is primarily a function of taking the time to listen to consumers and getting involved in the community. Listening not only identifies the specific needs of the market but also signals to the market that the marketer cares. Hence, the relationship transforms itself from a pure sales relationship (short-term) to more of a counselor relationship, where the marketer is looking after the long-term needs of its customer. Similarly, community involvement indicates that the marketer is a supporter of the community and a friend, and also provides the opportunity to meet potential future customers. Past research indicates that ethnic markets are immensely loyal to marketers that have earned their trust and cater to their needs.

Sources: "Retailers Look to Sharpen Ethnic Marketing Focus," *Drug Store News* 23 (8) (25 June 2001), 78–81.

Bill Hill, "Tapping the African-American Market, *National Underwriter/ Life & Health Financial Services* 106 (23) (10 June 2002), 8–9.

Opportunities:
- As environmental forces affect the marketplace, what opportunities are emerging (new markets, new suppliers, decreased operating costs)?
- Are changes in the competitive, sociocultural, and natural environment creating new opportunities (e.g., fewer competitors, changing consumer taste, drought conditions that lead to new business opportunities, etc.)?
- Are changes in political and legal, economic, and technological forces creating new market opportunities (e.g., procompetitive legislation, economic recovery, e-commerce, etc.)?

Threats:
- As environmental forces affect the marketplace, what new threats are emerging (declining markets, fewer suppliers, increasing operating costs)?
- Are changes in the competitive, sociocultural, and natural environment creating new threats (e.g., new emerging competitors, changing consumer taste that adversely affects our current product mix, drought conditions that lead to declining opportunities, etc.)?
- Are changes in political and legal, economic, and technological forces creating new threats (e.g., national do-not-call lists, inflation, growth of online competitors, etc.)?

A SWOT Analysis does not have to be an exhaustive examination of every fact uncovered in the market situation assessment. Practitioners suggest that only those strengths, weaknesses, opportunities, and threats that are most relevant to the brand should be considered. Consequently, the typical marketing plan may only consider five to 10 issues in each category of the SWOT Analysis. Twisty Pretzel's SWOT Analysis, in simplified terms, may look something like the following:

Strengths:
- Twisty Pretzel enjoys a dominant market share in the salty snack industry's fastest-growing category
- Twisty Pretzel enjoys an 85 ACV (all-commodity volume) level of distribution, according to the latest Nielsen figures, and reaches 472,000 retail outlets weekly in more than 120 countries.[15]
- With the backing of its parent company, Twisty Pretzel is in a strong financial position and is able to offer incentives to enhance the product's acceptance in distribution channels.

Weaknesses:
- Inconsistent quality has been found in the pretzels produced at the XYZ site.
- Twisty Pretzel is struggling with its distribution efforts in the Southwest.

Opportunities:
- Consumers are becoming increasingly health-conscious and prefer low-fat and fat-free snacks.
- Due to recent changes in the economic environment, consumers are becoming increasingly value-conscious.

Threats:
- A major supermarket chain in the Midwest has threatened to discontinue the Twisty Pretzel line.
- Falcon brand is being highly promoted in the Northwest and is taking some Twisty Pretzel market share away.
- Older consumers are beginning to decrease their consumption of snack foods targeted to younger generations.

Specifications of Marketing Objectives

This section of the marketing plan details the objectives on which the marketing plan is based. Similar to establishing objectives for the strategic plan, well-developed objectives for the marketing plan should be SMART—specific, measurable, achievable, relevant, and time-bound. Twisty Pretzel's marketing objectives, meeting the SMART requirements, might be stated as follows:

The objective of the Twisty Pretzel marketing plan in the upcoming 12 months is to:
- *Increase sales of the Twisty Pretzel product line by 15% to $208 million.*
- *Increase market share from 18% to 21%.*
- *Achieve a 90 ACV for the product line.*
- *Maintain a 19% profit margin for the product line.*
- *Introduce a new low-fat pretzel nugget.*

Formulation of Marketing Strategies

The Formulation of Marketing Strategies details how the marketing objectives will be accomplished. On a general level, marketing strategy formulation should flow logically from the Market Situation Assessment as organized in the SWOT Analysis. Possible strategies to be considered are formulated by matching strengths to opportunities (*SO strategies*) and strengths to threats (*ST strategies*). Additional strategies to be considered are generated by considering approaches that overcome the brand's weaknesses and take advantage of opportunities (*WO strategies*) or minimize threats (*WT strategies*) created by environmental forces (see Figure 2.10).

On a more specific level, strategy formulation engages in a narrowing-down process where specific target markets are outlined, as are the marketing mixes that will be used to satisfy the needs of these target markets. All activities included in the plan are detailed in full. This section acts as the brand's building process blueprint, which will take place over the next 12 months. Twisty Pretzel's strategy might appear in abbreviated form as follows:

Formulating Marketing Strategy Figure 2.10

	Opportunities: O_1 O_2 O_3 . . . O_n	Threats: T_1 T_2 T_3 . . . T_n
Strengths: S_1 S_2 S_3 . . . S_n	**SO Strategies:** Strategies that use the firm's strengths to take advantage of opportunities that exist in the marketplace.	**ST Strategies:** Strategies that use the firm's strengths to offset threats that exist in the marketplace.[a]
Weaknesses: W_1 W_2 W_3 . . . W_n	**WO Strategies:** Strategies that offset the firm's weaknesses and enable the firm to take advantage of opportunities that exist in the marketplace.	**WT Strategies:** Strategies that offset the firm's weaknesses and counter threats that exist in the marketplace.[a]

[a] *When effectively managed, threats can be offset and also turned into potential opportunities.*

- *The national ad campaign introduced in 2002 will carry forward. Matthew Perry will be maintained as the brand's spokesperson, since he continues to have great appeal. Throughout the national ad campaign, we will continue to stress that: (1) Twisty Pretzel products are low in fat because they are baked; (2) they are a good value; and (3) they appeal to all age groups.*
- *A new low-fat pretzel nugget is being pursued by R&D. Samples of several types are available and being tested in focus groups. The new product will be introduced into the market by the end of the year. The introduction will be supported by trade allowances.*
- *Promotional incentives will be introduced to offset the concerns of the Midwest supermarket chain and the threats posed by Falcon brand's increased marketing efforts in the Northwest. Additional incentives will also be offered to those accounts in the Southwest that do not currently carry the line, in an effort to increase distribution.*
- *New procedures need to be established to prevent further inconsistencies at XYZ production site.*

Preparation of Action Programs and Budgets

This section of the marketing plan details any programs designed to result in some specific action, as well as the budget required to support the marketing activities created to achieve the company's objectives. Action programs are *tactical planning* documents that specifically outline who does what, by when, and how much it will cost.

Marketing plans that include comprehensive budget information tend to get more attention from senior management and other decision makers. At the corporate level, marketing plans are investment opportunities that make their case for resource allocations. Marketing plans that clearly state their case financially, as well as strategically, are more likely to be funded, as management tends to believe that such plans will yield a positive return on investment. An example of Twisty Pretzel's Action Program and Budget would look as follows:

The national ad campaign introduced in 2002 will continue. Ad flights will be scheduled twice a year, in June and December, the peak selling periods for salty snack foods.

Sales and marketing efforts will focus on a major supermarket chain in the Midwest that has threatened to discontinue the Twisty Pretzel line. Additional support will be provided to the supermarket chain in the form of in-ad coupons. Since Falcon brand is being effectively promoted in the Northwest, the Falcon trade allowances will be met by Twisty Pretzel and the situation will be reviewed on a monthly basis. Otherwise, trade allowances at the current level of $1.20 per case will be continued once per quarter, except in the Northwest where the Falcon's level of $1.80 per case will be met. Additional sales force efforts will focus on the Southwest, where distribution is the lowest. Slotting allowances in the amount of $5,000 per store will be offered to those accounts in the Southwest that do not currently carry the line, in an effort to increase distribution. Finally, efforts in the Northeast will focus on cracking a major wholesaler that controls $50 million in sales of salty snack foods.

One new line extension, in the form of a low-fact pretzel nugget, will be added in the second quarter. The introduction will be supported by trade allowances of $1.50 per case.

New quality-control procedures have been developed and are being implemented to prevent further inconsistencies at XYZ production site.

In total, Twisty Pretzel's required budget for the upcoming 12 months is as follows:

	(in millions)
Ad campaign	*$ 5.5*
Trade allowances	*13.0*
Special slotting allowances	*1.0*
Introduction of pretzel nugget	*1.5*
Production site upgrades	*.5*
Regional in-ad coupon support	*1.0*
Total	*$22.5*

Special distribution programs as outlined above are scheduled for the first quarter. Heavier allowances in the Northwest are scheduled for the second quarter.

Development of Control Procedures

This final section of the marketing plan details how results of the plan will be measured on an ongoing basis. For example, management may require a monthly or quarterly update of sales measured against projections. If sales are far from projections, the marketing plan can be modified midstream in hopes of increasing sales productivity. The development of control procedures is smart business practice. Developers of the marketing plan should monitor progress through the stated period of the plan. Is the implementation of the plan being rolled out as scheduled? Are environmental forces acting as predicted? Have new opportunities or threats presented themselves? Ultimately, control procedures keep the marketing plan on course and facilitate making adjustments to the plan if necessary. Twisty Pretzel's control procedures are stated as follows:

Sales of Twisty Pretzel will be monitored on a monthly basis. Actual case sales for the month and cumulative year will be compared to the prior year same period and to objectives. Achievement of the market share and distribution figures will be reviewed semiannually, when Nielsen figures are updated and available. Since Nielsen figures are a few months behind in reporting, final judgment as to the achievement of these goals will be delayed until the Nielsen figures for the entire year are released. Profit-margin figures will be judged on the basis of total revenues less total costs for the brand.

Final Thoughts on Marketing Planning

In addition to the marketing strategies and tactics specified by the marketing plan, the exercise of actually putting a marketing plan together is a very useful process. The marketing plan helps decision makers organize their thoughts on a number of different levels across the organization, as well as consider the impact of environmental forces. Ultimately, the marketing plan is a plan of action that facilitates the exchange process discussed in Chapter 1 by providing customers what they want, where they want it, and when they want it, at a price they can afford. However, the marketing planning process goes beyond just meeting customers' needs. Effective marketing planning identifies *strategic windows* in the marketplace by matching the company's *core competencies* (what the company does best) with the opportunities that present themselves in the marketplace. Consequently, effective marketing planning ensures that what is good for the customer makes sense for the organization as well.

Chapter Summary

Learning Objective 1: *Recognize the nature and scope of planning, including the five key elements crucial to planning activities.* Planning is the basis for sound business decision making. Key elements that are critical to any planning activity include: timing, specifying tasks, assigning responsibility, following up, and budgeting. Thousands of jobs and millions of dollars rely on solid planning efforts by management.

Confusion often exists over the difference between *strategic planning* and *marketing planning*. Strategic planning, or the organization's overall game plan, has a longer planning horizon (typically three to five years) than marketing planning and is performed at the *corporate* and *business* levels of the organization. Marketing planning has a shorter planning horizon (typically one year) and is performed at the *marketing* or *product* or product-line level of the organization. *Tactical planning* is another level of organizational planning that takes place at the marketing level. Tactical planning involves *specifying details* that pertain to the organization's activities *for a certain period of time.*

Learning Objective 2: *Understand each of the fundamental steps involved in developing a strategic plan.* Strategic planning is an effective way for an organization to coordinate efforts among various departments, analyze its competitive position within its environment, and allocate its resources. Strategic planning comprises six fundamental steps: (1) establishing the organization mission (how an organization defines its business or what makes it different from the competition); (2) defining strategic business units (smaller divisions created to facilitate planning and general operations); (3) specifying organizational objectives (specific, measurable, achievable, relevant, and time-bound); (4) analyzing strategic business unit performance (using strategic planning tools such as the BCG model to guide resource allocation strategies); (5) assessing organizational growth opportunities (explored through intensive, integrative, and diversification growth strategies); and (6) marketing planning (which includes specific objectives, necessary resources, planned activities, and expected results for a specific product).

Learning Objective 3: *Appreciate the fundamentals of marketing planning.* Marketing planning occurs at the marketing or product level and emanates from and is inspired by the overall strategic plan. Marketing plans vary in scope, length, and formality. A marketing plan can cover a specific product or an entire product line or category. A typical marketing plan includes an executive summary, an analysis of the marketing situation, an assessment of opportunities and threats, specification of marketing objectives, a formulation of marketing strategies, the preparation of action programs and budgets, and the development of control procedures.

Key Terms

For interactive study: visit http://bestpractices.swlearning.com.

Build strategy, 45	Market penetration, 49	SMART, 44
Cash cows, 48	Marketing planning, 40	Stars, 48
Divest strategy, 46	Mission statement, 42	Strategic business units (SBUs), 43
Dogs, 48	Niche strategy, 45	Strategic planning, 40
Harvest strategy, 45	Problem children, 47	Tactical planning, 41
Maintain strategy, 45	Product development, 50	Value chain, 51
Market development, 50	Product diversification, 50	

Questions for Review and Discussion

1. Define and discuss the five key elements necessary for a successful planning activity as they relate to the marketing of SpongeBob SquarePants merchandise.

2. Organizational planning consists of three levels: strategic planning, marketing planning, and tactical planning. How are they different from one another and how are they interrelated?

3. What are the six fundamental steps involved in strategic planning? Explain how each affects the overall goals of the company.

4. Possible resource allocation strategies for an SBU classified as a "dog" within the Boston Consulting Group matrix include niching, divesting, and maintaining. Explain the rationale for each strategy as it pertains to SBUs classified as "dogs." Why would harvesting and building be inappropriate resource allocation strategies in this instance?

5. CBS News is currently airing a news broadcast that appeals to Generation Y (a high-growth market), but at the moment commands a small market share of the Generation Y market. How would this broadcast be categorized within the Boston Consulting Group matrix and what would be the appropriate resource allocation strategies available to CBS, given the broadcast's current categorization?

6. Based on Starbucks' corporate and environmental mission statements provided in Figures 2.3 and 2.4,

how is the company abiding by its missions based on the information provided in the Ethics and Social Responsibility text box?

7. Northwood Golf Course is a family-owned nine-hole golf course located in Champion, Ohio. The family is considering a number of growth opportunities. Based on the intensive growth options discussed in the text, provide specific examples of how the golf course could enhance its growth opportunities in the future.

8. The value chain is formed by combining the supply chain with the marketing channel and represents what most practitioners are talking about when they discuss *supply chain management*. If an organization chooses to grow by acquiring another firm within its value chain, what type of growth opportunity is occurring? Discuss each of the three types of organizational growth opportunities under this strategy.

9. As explained in the chapter, marketing plans can vary in scope, length, and formality, but a traditional plan will contain what seven components? Briefly discuss each component.

10. Develop a SWOT analysis for your college of business or other disciplines. Develop and state two strategies for each of the following categories: SO, ST, WO, and WT.

1. Each group is going on a camping trip. In order for the trip to go well, you must address the key planning elements. What details will you have to decide on as you prepare. Answers should be based on the five key elements: timing, tasks, responsibility, follow-up, and budgeting.

2. Your team is responsible for marketing the college of business. Develop a SWOT matrix pertaining to the issues that face the college. Based on your SWOT analysis, develop a list of strategies that will guide the college's future. Compare answers with other groups.

1. Visit the E*Trade (http://www.etrade.com) and the Ameritrade (http://www.ameritrade.com) Web sites and compare and contrast the mission statement for each company. Hint: If you have trouble locating the mission statement, try using the search/tell me more functions.

2. Go to http://www.mplans.com and look at some of the sample marketing plans. Select one that is interesting to you (and available online) and explain how they have segmented the market. This information can be found in the Situation Analysis section of the plan.

CHAPTER CASE

Yao Ming: The Next Sports Marketing Icon?

Some National Basketball Association (NBA) fans call him "Yao, baby!"; others call him "The Great Wall of Houston." Regardless of his new nickname, Chinese native Yao Ming, a 7'5" rookie center for the Houston Rockets, has given the NBA a much needed boost on two continents. Over the last several years, fan interest in the NBA has been waning. In a poll of 1,000 randomly selected Americans, only 7.7% indicated that they were very interested in the NBA, while 62.1% indicated that they were not at all interested. Of the 37.7% of respondents who expressed some interest in the NBA, 40% indicated that their interest has declined over the past five years. Fan support has decreased over the years for a variety of reasons, including the beliefs that some players don't play hard every night, today's players are less charismatic than past players, many players are more interested in the money than winning, and the on- and off-court behavior of NBA players has gotten worse instead of better. In essence, much of the fans' disenchantment with the NBA is beyond the control of the NBA itself.

On the positive side, fans are increasingly interested in the influx of international players who have recently joined the NBA and believe the game of basketball is better because of it. In addition to Yao Ming's recent arrival to the Houston Rockets, a number of other international players have joined the ranks of the NBA, including the Dallas Mavericks' forward Dirk Nowitzki (Germany), Peja Stojakovic (Yugoslavia) of the Sacramento Kings, and Memphis Grizzlies' forward Pau Gasol (Spain).

In terms of global marketing appeal, Yao Ming could break all the rules and become a sports-marketing icon on two continents. Since Yao's arrival to the league, NBA's Asia operations are suddenly exploding. Twelve regional channels in China (a.k.a. the Land of 1.3 Billion) now televise NBA games—last year two regional channels broadcasted NBA games. Thirty of the 120 broadcasts of NBA games in China featured Yao Ming's Houston Rockets during the 2002–2003 season. Within the U.S., Yao's arrival has spurred an increase in ticket sales wherever he plays. At home in Houston, game attendance at the Compaq Center has increased by 2,000 ticket sales per game this year. It appears that Yao appeals not only to Chinese-Americans but also to other Asian-Americans. Last year, 0.05% of the Houston Rockets group ticket sales were to Asians. This year, that number has profoundly jumped to approximately 12% of ticket sales. When Houston plays on the road, the opposing teams' venues benefit as well. For example, in locations that have large Asian populations, such as Seattle and Oakland, opposing teams have developed and successfully sold ticket packages that feature Yao's appearances.

What does Yao Ming think about all of this media attention? So far, he's kept a low profile. Although he does speak understandable English, he generally uses an interpreter to speak to large groups. In addition, five strategists guide his career and believe that too many endorsements, photo shoots, and interviews too soon will stretch him too thin. As a result, access to Yao Ming is currently restricted. What little the public does know about his personal life off the court is that he doesn't drink alcohol and he is very interested in new technologies. On the court, Yao Ming gives it his all every game and has a great smile.

Other obstacles may detract from Yao's full marketability. First, players who receive the top sports endorsements are usually championship caliber. According to the CEO of a Dallas-based sports and marketing consulting firm, "For an athlete to move product in America, he either needs to perform extremely well or be recognized as the reason his team does." Although Yao has had his moments, such as blocking the first three shots taken by the L.A. Lakers' Shaquille O'Neal in their first outing together, Yao is not currently recognized as a dominant center and his team is not predicted to make the playoffs. However, time and experience may change

all that. Another obstacle is that, to date, the NBA's "big men" are not traditionally appealing to the shoe market. Endorsement contracts from shoe companies such as Nike, Reebok, and Adidas are where the big money lies. For example, the projected value for LeBron James' first shoe contract is $5 million per year and Kobe Bryant's newly negotiated contract is estimated to be in the $15-million range.

What is to become of the NBA and Yao Ming? Only time will tell what fortunes lie ahead.

Case Questions

1. Develop a possible mission statement for Yao Ming.
2. Based on the information provided, develop a SWOT analysis for Yao Ming.
3. Guided by Yao Ming's mission statement developed in the first question and using the SWOT analysis, formulate five possible marketing strategies for Yao Ming to pursue and discuss the advantages and disadvantages of each strategy.

Source: Jack McCallum, "Sky Rocket," *Sports Illustrated* 98 (5) (10 February 2003): 34–38.

VIDEO CASE

A Whole Lotta Latté

If strategy is about finding the best fit for a company and its business environment, Caribou Coffee knows where to look. Started in 1992 by John and Kim Puckett in Minneapolis, Minnesota, the company now boasts 218 stores in nine states. Now the nation's second largest specialty coffee retailer, it consistently beats coffee giant Starbucks as the java of choice in many markets, including Ohio, Minnesota, Michigan, and Wisconsin, as well as Atlanta, Chicago, and Washington, DC.

So how did Caribou dare to go toe-to-toe with Starbucks? "The secret is strategy," says Caribou CEO Don Dempsey. All planning is done in the fall and the entire organization is involved. "Our strategic planning is based on one year out with hard numbers and three years out on overall strategy."

Every aspect of the business is analyzed during these planning sessions. Company expansion is high on the list. Decisions are made on the number and location of new stores, as well as budget allocations for additional staffing and equipment. Provisions are made in the budget for moving into new markets. Asset management, including the remodeling of existing stores; the marketing budget; and general administrative needs are other critical elements of the company's overall strategic plan.

With the rest of the year devoted to the execution of these planning decisions, Dempsey acknowledges there is

a gulf between predictions and reality. "Flexibility is key to a successful plan, because in the real world we are not dealing with facts, we are dealing with assumptions. Details of our strategic plan are always changing—it is a constant process of review and correction."

So what happens when things don't go according to plan and problems arise? "Start-up entities are fragile, and when a company is small and young little mistakes can kill it," Dempsey says. "That's why profits drive everything. The more profitable a business is, the less vulnerable it is. It can absorb mistakes more easily. And contingency planning is also very important. You have to anticipate disastrous events and be prepared for them. If your building burns down, you better have some other place to roast your coffee."

Profitability is a favorite topic of Dempsey's. "There are only two ways to generate profits," he says. "You must either increase sales or cut costs, and there is only so much cost-cutting a business can do before it affects its ability to deliver a quality product. In a retail business, there are only two ways to generate sales—build more stores or increase sales in the ones you already have."

One way to increase sales is to serve the best coffee, and the best coffee starts with the best beans. Caribou works on a "just-in-time" philosophy. Its master roasters focus on craft and work small, ensuring that Caribou serves the freshest and best-tasting coffee on the market.

With competition in the coffee industry at the boiling point, businesses have to go the extra mile to impress customers. Although Caribou keeps a watchful eye on what the competition is doing, Dempsey believes the real challenge is staying focused on its own business.

Staff is well trained and well paid for better retention. Caribou's layers of supervisory personnel take care of the stores. District managers make the rounds of stores in their region to check on overall operations. Shift supervisors are responsible for store cleanliness, staff friendliness and attitude, and for making sure that customers are happy. In all areas where it shares a market, Caribou beats Starbucks on quality, service, and ambiance.

Caribou is so confident of its product, the company's marketing campaign is focused on getting coffee lovers into its stores to try its coffee. Based on a strategy to use a limited marketing budget to the greatest effect, the advertising team came up with a hugely effective campaign entitled the Great Coupon Roundup. With the purpose of generating both buzz and business, close to life-size cardboard caribous are randomly placed around town and in office-building elevators. With coupons attached offering "coffee for the entire herd"—up to 10 free cups—the customer must bring the caribou into a Caribou store to redeem the coupons.

When discussing expansion into new markets, Dempsey emphasizes the high costs and initial operational inefficiencies. "When you expand into a new area, you have to fly people there to recruit and train staff and stay around to "district-manage" a single store. You're shipping in less product, so unit shipping costs are higher."

Because of the enormous costs involved, new markets are strategically analyzed and carefully chosen. Demographic factors such as size and type of market and opportunities for further expansion are important considerations.

For example, Washington, DC was strategically chosen because it is a coffee-drinking market that would provide a "beachhead" for further East Coast expansion. Caribou now has stores in Maryland, Virginia, and North Carolina, all within driving distance of Washington.

"Brand precedes Starbucks wherever they go domestically," says Dempsey, "and although we are the brand leader with 100% brand awareness in Minnesota, everywhere else in the country the reverse is true." Dempsey knows that brand awareness increases in direct correlation to greater market penetration, but says it is a slow build. "In new markets, we have to build the brand and our company's reputation store by store." With its offerings of quality coffee, good service, and a pleasant environment, Caribou is winning customers over, one coffee lover at a time.

Case Questions

1. How does Caribou Coffee approach its planning? Explain.
2. How has Caribou Coffee used strategy to differentiate itself from other coffee makers?
3. Where is the company's strategic marketing campaign focused? Why has it been so successful?
4. How does Caribou Coffee strategically select new markets in order to further the company's expansion goals?

Sources: Adapted from material in the video "Caribou Coffee" and on the Caribou Coffee corporate Web site, http://www.cariboucoffee.com.

3

Marketing Ethics and Social Responsibility

xtra!
Interactive Marketing Activity

Go to Xtra! to access this Interactive Marketing Activity at http://bestpracticesxtra.swlearning.com.

The irresponsible actions of many financial analysts and their companies helped to proliferate and prolong the financial disaster of 2002. Generally, these financial advisors would recommend that their clients continuously buy stocks, even if they knew the stocks were likely to be "losers." Many of these stock "experts" did not research the stocks they were recommending, and, in some cases, they were misrepresenting the recommended stocks. Since financial advisors are usually paid based on commissions for each transaction, it is likely these analysts were encouraging so much buying to pad their own pockets.

You Decide. After reading the opening vignette and paying special attention to the sections of this chapter marked with the chess piece, answer these questions:

1. Which marketing responsibilities did financial advisors violate in the financial disaster of 2002 and why?

2. The financial disaster of 2002 might have been averted had financial advisors asked which ethical questions when making stock-trade recommendations to clients?

3. What is the best way to improve the social responsibility of financial analysts?

© electraVision/Index Stock Imagery

The Fraud of the Century: A Massive Failure of Social Responsibility

A fraud is a person or thing that is not what it seems or pretends to be. Many of us have committed some degree of fraud. If you have ever sold a used car, you may have hesitated in revealing the car's defects, which were hidden by a new paint job. Or some have unethically chosen to exaggerate their education or experience when applying for college or a new job. Similarly, advertising is known for *puffery,* the tendency to exaggerate the performance of a product. Laws and regulations have curbed advertising puffery, especially in the pharmaceutical industry, where puffery can cause injury or death to trusting customers.

One of the worst types of fraud perverts important economic markets, creating macroeconomic effects that reverberate down the decades. When this happens, it can result in a loss of trillions of dollars in capital from the stock market and retirement funds. For working folks, the result of this type of catastrophic fraud is an economic downturn, which leads to higher unemployment and the loss of comprehensive health care.

The U.S. economy is still recovering from such a fraud that Wall Street perpetrated on stockholders, which left many Americans believing that American capitalism had rotted at its very core. The major players in this financial scheme were fined $1.4 billion for their behavior in December 2002, but this was a knuckle rap compared to what they could have been fined for the damage their market manipulation did to the largest and most sophisticated economy in the world. Here is what they did.

In 1998, two full years before the stock market crash, *Business Week* featured a story on the unscrupulous behavior of financial analysts in its cover story called "Wall Street's Spin Game."[1] Financial analysts recommend to customers what stocks to buy, what stocks to hold, and what stocks to sell. Analysts are expected to understand the fundamental trends in particular industries and identify the winners and losers and the value of their stocks based on their long-term prospects. But, as

Business Week reported, analysts were not conducting market research, such as studying customers, suppliers, and competitors. Instead, they played up good news and sugarcoated bad news about the financial performance of companies.

The facts speak for themselves. In the early 1980s, "buy" recommendations to customers equalled "sell" recommendations (the rest were "hold" recommendations). But by 1998, buy recommendations outnumbered sell recommendations by more than 10 to 1. Buy, buy, buy recommendations fed a financial bubble based on the New Economy's greater-fool theory of economics rather than on fundamental economic theory. The greater-fool theory is that you buy the stock that is greatly overvalued because next week there will be a greater fool who will buy it from you at an even higher price. In this case, the customer was treated like a fool rather than someone who is valued, respected, and served. Ridiculously inflated price-earning ratios were fraudulently explained away as indicating the New Economy, where the old standards of performance and rules no longer applied. No one explained why.

Even more outrageously, an e-mail trail caught financial analysts selling stocks to their customers that they knew were real dogs. Financial analysts had become stock sales people, participating in a fraud on unsuspecting customers, instead of consultants who helped customers make wise investment decisions.

The financial disaster of 2000 was compounded by the irresponsible behavior of industry regulators. In February 2001, *Fortune* magazine reported on the continuing fraud. The tech bubble started to burst in April 2000, but even as late as February 2001, just before another general fall of the market, the top 10

LEARNING OBJECTIVES

After you have completed this chapter, you should be able to:

1. *Understand that marketing's contribution to society includes improving the efficiency and effectiveness of the economic process through the creation of exchanges, markets, products, and trading innovations. Explore why marketing is frequently criticized for socially irresponsible behavior.*

2. *Recognize why the self-centered behavior of millions of businesses and consumers around the world has a detrimental impact on supply and demand.*

3. *Appreciate the role of personal ethical behavior and learn the major theories of marketing ethics.*

4. *Understand that rules and regulations govern each element of the marketing mix.*

5. *Understand that marketing has a role in promoting worthy public causes and how cause-related marketing is used to achieve this goal.*

VOICE OF THE EXPERT
Peter Dickson, Florida International University

The purpose of this chapter is to introduce you to four aspects of marketing social responsibility. The first recognizes that spaceship earth has limited and dwindling resources. What we waste today deprives future generations. Marketing's responsibility is to continue to improve the efficiency of exchange, improve our economy's use of scarce resources, and consider the unintended, collective, economic, social, and political consequences of its practices. Marketing's second responsibility is to obey the law; sadly, law is often created by scandals where industry self-regulation has failed.

The third responsibility of marketing is to behave ethically. But what is ethical behavior? The best minds over the last 3,000 years have struggled with this question. My conclusion is that our minimum ethical responsibility is to always ask whether what is proposed is ethical and to come to a personal answer about this question. If we don't bother to ask and then answer the question before we act, then we are not even being honest with ourselves. The fourth responsibility of marketers is to use their skills to promote social causes: to give back to society by doing good deeds. But this is more of a personal responsibility than a firm responsibility. Our moral compasses vary greatly in the directions they point us. I promise you that this chapter will get you thinking. But whether it changes your future behavior is very much up to you.

brokerage houses were recommending 7,033 buys and only 57 sells. The fraud was still being perpetrated. Where were the regulators in the late 1990s when it was obvious that many analysts were no longer independent and could not justify the stock prices? Why didn't they step in earlier and require written substantiation for analysts' recommendations, based on economic performance? Were under-the-table fees being used to promote new start-ups? Exporters are not allowed to use bribery in their global marketing—it is against the law. Why, at the heart of Wall Street, were analysts allowed to be bribed to promote stocks to their customers? Where were the regulators? Were their political masters bought off by the lobbyists? Closing the barn door after the horse has bolted is hardly good enough.

What about the mutual fund managers, the managers who are professional experts at managing the funds? They manage hundreds of billions of Americans' retirement savings. Where were their heads? Didn't they notice the stock market bubble? Why didn't they ask for more substantiation based on market research from analysts before buying company stocks? Mutual fund managers get paid several percentage points of the fund's value for managing the fund. Did they act responsibly during the bubble or did they also get carried away?

In the first two chapters we learned how successful firms adapt to changes in the marketing environment by adjusting one or more of their marketing-mix elements (product, place, promotion, and price). But firms that are successful in the long term respond to these changes and opportunities in a socially responsible manner. Failure to do so puts an individual company, even a whole industry, at risk. Many individual investors no longer trust stockbrokers and their analysts. Some of this distrust will probably last a lifetime. Thousands of stockbrokers have also lost their jobs or their high incomes. These represent some of the long-term consequences that reverberate through an industry that is socially irresponsible. Similarly, the accounting audit industry is also coming under much tighter regulation as a result of the failure of the accounting profession to regulate its own audit practices. When ethics decline in an industry, more regulation almost always follows. Freedom is not free in markets and marketing—its price is social responsibility and, when it is not paid, a market becomes more controlled and less free.

Social responsibility

Is the collection of marketing philosophies, policies, procedures, and actions intended primarily to enhance society's welfare.

Social responsibility is the collection of marketing philosophies, policies, procedures, and actions intended to enhance society's welfare. Although the general notion of social responsibility has been around for quite some time, it has taken on new resurgence throughout much of the business world. Here in the U.S., Business Strengthening America (BSA) was recently formed with the goal of encouraging civic engagement and volunteer service in corporate America—"do well by doing good." BSA, which started within the confines of the White House, was organized as a direct result of the Enron and other corporate scandals.[2]

The social responsibility of marketing has several sides. Marketing activities must be efficient and effective and not squander scarce resources. Marketing executives must be mindful of the unintended social consequences of their efforts on cultures, and subcultures. Marketing executives, along with all other executives in a firm, have to obey the law and participate responsibly in the making of laws. But simply abiding by the law is only a first step, and marketing executives are expected to have a strong moral compass that guides their behavior. In short, they are expected to behave according to the canons of ordinary or common decency. Finally, professional marketers are expected, as public citizens, to give back to society. The *social contract* says that we should use our skills in promoting societal causes and in other ways that benefit the whole society of humankind, such as bringing AIDS education to Africa, or helping the International Red Cross develop a more efficient global distribution system for the aid it sends to disaster areas. In this chapter, we discuss each of these dimensions of social responsibility.

Marketing's First Social Responsibility: Strive to be More Efficient and Effective

Marketing's first responsibility to society is to advance life, liberty, and general happiness by creating exchanges, markets, and product and trading innovations that increase the efficiency and effectiveness of the economic process. In short, the first responsibility of marketers is to keep learning to do their jobs more efficiently and effectively. This is undertaken in the selfish pursuit of profit. But as 18th century economist Adam Smith pointed out more than 200 years ago, such self-improvement also makes markets more competitive, makes our lives as workers and customers more productive, and wastes less of the earth's scarce resources that need to be preserved for future generations.

Many people believe that marketing is not fulfilling this first social responsibility very well. They believe a lot of products that are marketed are not needed and that a lot of marketing effort, particularly advertising, is wasteful and becoming less, rather than more, effective. In this section, we address these criticisms.

Too Many Unneeded Products Are Marketed That Fail

Although it is almost impossible to assess what percentage of new products succeed, it has been estimated that about half of the resources earmarked for developing and marketing new products is spent on failures.[3] It is very probable that better marketing research and marketing planning could increase the success rate, but it must always be appreciated that success often comes as a result of lessons learned through failures. Babe Ruth, during his baseball career, hit more home runs than any baseball player in history. He also struck out more times than any baseball player in history. In other words, new product development and marketing are always risky, and the price of occasional great success is frequent failure.

Each year, tens of thousands of new products fail. But do you think the marketers of these products believed they would be unwanted and unneeded? Did they purposefully and deliberately intend to waste all of their money and effort in such ways? Presumably not. This waste of money, blood, sweat, and tears is an argument for *better marketing, not less marketing*. But even the best marketing efforts often fall short. Companies can misunderstand customer preferences, fail to anticipate competitors' lowering prices, or miss the clues that foreshadow the unveiling of a product even better than their own. The responsibility of marketers is to keep learning how to improve their market research, new product development, and marketing processes. Whether the art of marketing is getting better as fast as it could is perhaps an open question. In this sense, marketing may not score very high on its first responsibility, which is to strive as hard as it can to become ever more efficient and effective in its many and varied activities.

Too Many Unneeded Products Are Marketed That Succeed

The role of research and development in marketing is to invent, design, manufacture, and market new products that customers prefer over currently used products. That is part of the natural evolution of markets, where ever better products replace inferior alternatives. Who would argue against the marketing of better painkillers, cancer

Technological Forces

New technology succeeds by creatively destroying an old, inferior technology. This is good for society, but new technology also can create new ethical dilemmas, such as those related to privacy on the Internet and the cloning of stem cells to be used in lifesaving medical research.

Shell Oil Company funds natural resource conservation projects in the Gulf of Mexico in a partnership with the National Fish and Wildlife Foundation. This ad, part of a series of print and broadcast ads that feature Shell people around the world, demonstrates Shell's values in action.

Planned obsolescence
Is the design of a product with features that the company knows will soon be superseded, thus making the model obsolete.

treatments, and safer, more fuel-efficient cars? There are also several reasonable and rational answers to the criticism that other successful products are just not needed and are a waste of the earth's dwindling resources and poor people's meager earnings.

The individual freedom to pursue life, liberty, and happiness is one of the most noble principles and "rights" of the age of enlightenment, which started in the 18th century and continues through today. Millions of men and women have given their lives to defend this "right" and extend it to people who have not possessed such freedom. *Freedom and free choice* do not simply mean the right to choose the political leadership of a society. They involve freedom to pursue a desired education, freedom to pursue a vocation and career in a free labor market, and freedom to spend one's earnings and savings as one chooses. If we believe in such freedoms, then we must allow the expression of this freedom in other people's choices of products. For example, it is a slippery slope to criticize disposable diapers as a waste of trees that could be better used to produce books on enlightened thinking. The slope ends in a managed economy where the powerful elite prescribes what is good and bad for everyone else. Again and again, such a system of top-down dictatorship, no matter how well-meaning, has been tested and has failed, most recently in communist economies.

History offers a long and tragic litany of fanatics closing the minds of their followers, removing freedoms and rights, and viciously exterminating any threats to their tyranny. In the United States, consumers live with the fact that every supermarket has a full aisle of pet foods containing hundreds of choices. Is it wrong that many families spend more on their pets than on donations to feed starving children in other parts of the world? Perhaps. Do these same families have the right to choose to spend their money this way and to respond more positively to pet food marketing campaigns than charities' marketing campaigns? We may not agree with their choices and priorities, but, yes, they have this right, and it is a right that many have died for.

An extension of the "do we need this product?" criticism is that marketing encourages planned obsolescence by coming out with new, "improved" models too often (e.g., Microsoft 2000 or XP). **Planned obsolescence** is the design of a product with features the manufacturer knows will soon be superseded, thus making the model obsolete. But customers do not need to buy the new model, and they often do not. Women do not always buy into the latest spring or fall fashions. If customers are concerned about the rapid obsolescence of their purchase, they often postpone their purchase. Such a concern also creates a marketing opportunity for an enterprising seller to introduce an innovative leasing scheme that enables customers to easily trade in and upgrade to the latest technology. This is precisely what Gateway did with its "Your:) ware" marketing campaign. But this leasing solution was not that popular, proving that obsolescence was not a major concern to personal computer buyers.

Sometimes products are criticized for being too shoddy, with built-in components that fail too quickly. The answer to this is that quality always wins out when it is desired. The big three domestic automobile manufacturers (General Motors, Ford, and Chrysler) learned this lesson the hard way in the 1980s, when they cared little about product quality. Should they have learned this lesson at the expense of their customers and shareholders? No, but such behavior always catches up with companies in free markets. For example, nearly a year after Microsoft's latest version of its

Windows XP had been found to contain at least 12 separate problems the company itself referred to as "critical," customers were still unknowingly purchasing new computers that contained the same defect-plagued software. Taking notice of Microsoft's business practices, *Forbes* magazine reported to its readers what Microsoft was up to and labeled Microsoft's business practice in this instance as "absurd."[4] Consequently, businesses engaged in shoddy business practices run the risk of damaging their reputations for years and, in some cases, decades. On the other hand, many critics of the modern market economy complain that product parts last too long and that manufacturers should be required to dispose of their products at the customer's request and recycle the materials. The free-market answer to this criticism is the creation of a new service market where firms compete to dispose of and recycle such products.

Market Distribution Systems Are Inefficient

There has been a long tradition of criticizing the inefficiency of distribution systems, which has its roots in the complaints of farmers who, for example, calculate that they are paid only 20 cents for the corn that is finally sold by the supermarkets as cornflakes for $3 or more. Does this seem fair? Who is making all the profits in the added-value process from the farm to the breakfast table, and how much "added value" are they really adding?

It is hard not to have sympathy for the average farmer, particularly if you come from a farming heritage. But to ask whether each player in the chain deserves its margins, and to try to calculate some efficiency measure, is to ask the wrong question. The right question is: Have the distribution systems evolved as a result of the forces of free-market competition? If they have, then by the laws of competition, the existing distribution systems are efficient. A further very important truth is that a great deal of innovation and learning have occurred in physical distribution in the United States over the last 30 years, so much so that the percentage of the gross domestic product spent on the cost of physical distribution (order processing, transportation, and inventory storage) has dropped from around 15% to under 10%. At the same time, the reliability and quality of these services have greatly increased. This came about because deregulation of the transportation and communication industries in the late 1970s led to an incredible burst of competition and innovation that reduced the cost of transportation and communication services and increased their quality. The cost of distribution has also benefited from stable and low interest rates and fuel costs. No other major sector has increased its efficiency, as measured by its reduced share of the gross domestic product, by anything like physical distribution's improvement.

Has enough innovation occurred in physical distribution to make it "efficient"? Again, this is a silly question because it cannot be answered. What is clear is that competitive forces are forcing supermarkets, mass merchandisers, and department stores to adopt the new technologies of distribution. If they do not, then fierce competitors who are trendsetters in innovating new, more efficient distribution processes, such as Wal-Mart, will take away their business.

The current distribution system will last until a better system is invented or developed. The current system replaced an earlier system, which replaced an even earlier system, and so on, back to primitive distribution systems. As long as this evolution continues, we know that distribution is becoming more efficient. We see this occurring everywhere: Cars are being marketed by super-dealerships; vacations are being booked using travel agents identified by Web searches; books are being purchased through online stores on the Web. We see an increase in mail-order catalog sales. We saw Kmart replace Sears as *the* mass merchandiser, and now Wal-Mart has replaced Kmart. But stores such as Meijer and Target are now challenging Wal-Mart. We see major new airports being built, major container ports being expanded, and trains stacking containers two high.

Competitive Forces

In economies where industries are protected or where distribution monopolies are granted, it is unlikely that the marketing distribution system will be as efficient as it can and should be.

Of course, firms that stubbornly cling to outdated distribution systems will be viewed as betraying the first social responsibility of marketing, which is to strive to improve and become more efficient. These firms are blights on marketing, just as doctors who refuse to improve their practices and teachers who refuse to improve their teaching are blights on their profession. But how long will the inefficient distributor survive before a new, more efficient, competitor enters the marketplace? Not as long as the inefficient doctor or teacher who is protected from competition. If marketing is socially irresponsible because it does not try hard enough to improve the efficiency of its distribution systems, then the medical and teaching professions presumably face much greater condemnation because their comparative improvement in performance over the last 30 years has seemed pitiful to some. The reason is also clear: Doctors and teachers have too little competition to force better customer service at lower cost. So let's give at least two cheers for marketing's role in distribution, rather than complaining about the cost of distribution.

A Lot of Advertising Is Wasteful Expenditure

One frequent criticism of marketing is its use of mass advertising to reach a large number of customers. But mass advertising is inherently inefficient in reaching interested customers, so this inefficiency exposes products to customers who are not at all interested in the product. Hence, advertising is viewed as intrusive and wasteful, even alien to some customer values.[5]

For example, let us consider a typical commercial break that consists of a pod of six 30-second television commercials. Even if the advertiser has targeted a program that has a high percentage of its target market as viewers, it is unlikely that more than 20% of the viewing audience are *potential buyers* (that is, they are current satisfied users of the brand or are open to switching to the brand). What percentage of such a viewing audience will be interested in three or more of the advertisements in the pod of six commercials? The answer is less than 10%. No wonder so many people say that television advertising, junk mail, and telephone marketing waste money and intrude on their privacy. It is because advertising and marketing use **inefficient targeting** to identify interested audiences, not because they are too efficient, skilled, and manipulative.

Inefficient targeting
Results when advertising and distribution reach too broad an audience, most of whom are not interested in the product.

In fact, the phrase "being turned off" by advertising may not simply describe a negative attitude. It may actually describe the psychological mechanism that customers in a "high-consumption" materialistic society develop, from an early age, to cope with the irrelevance and inefficiency of advertising and sales pitches. It is very evident that we learn to develop attention mechanisms that allow us to tune out advertising, just as we tune out so many other stimuli that are competing for our attention day in and day out.

How do advertisers cope with the increased tuning out of customers? They increase their efforts to try to get us to tune in, through more powerful attention-grabbing mechanisms. This explains why television advertisements have become ever more expensive and elaborate productions, crafted to gain and keep our attention, often by using popular celebrities or zany humor. It also explains why direct marketing has developed more devious ways of getting us to open the mail: A common ruse is to disguise the mail as coming from a friend or from the Internal Revenue Service. It is also likely that we are not fooled for long. In response, customers have developed ever more powerful and selective tuning-out mechanisms to cope with these increasingly attention-grabbing mechanisms. Thus, the cost of creating advertising that gains our attention is spiraling upward with little or no long-term increase in its effectiveness. It is not just that mass advertising is becoming more expensive. A greater percentage of the money is being spent on gaining our attention than on explaining why the product is better than other alternative products.

A development that may save the image and cost efficiency of advertising is the evolution of very specialized digital TV channels and specialized electronic and print magazines aimed at particular demographic (age, income, gender, ethnic, education, lifestyle) groups. If this results in a much better overlap of the product target market and the audience, the average ratings of advertising would become more positive. If the overlap were strong enough that an average of 50% of the viewing audience would be interested in any particular advertisement, this would result in two-thirds of the audience reporting interest in three or more of the ads in a pod of six 30-second commercials. The audience would also learn to pay more attention to such advertising because it is of interest. In short, a major answer to the criticism of advertising's social value is better targeting of interested audiences, which requires the invention of communication channels that are better targeted to the "interested" audience.

Marketers' Self-Interested, Unintended Consequences on Supply

2   LEARNING OBJECTIVE

In a free market, the individual activities of producers can have a cumulative effect that is often not intended and can lead to harmful effects on others or society at large. This is called the **tragedy of the commons** because the issue was first described in the context of the common grazing area (sort of equivalent to the modern public park) that villages in England used to make available for local residents to graze their sheep. To each village household, it did not seem unreasonable to increase its small flock of sheep, but across a hundred households, this pursuit of individual self-interest led to such severe overgrazing that all of the grass on the commons died. Now no one was able to graze sheep on the commons, and everyone's sheep starved and died. Modern examples of "the tragedy of the commons" are everywhere. The world's fish resources are running out because fishermen have used modern technology to increase their fishing capabilities, and each individual fisherman does not believe that his individual behavior will ruin fishing for everyone. But cumulatively, such behavior has led to such a destruction of supply that many varieties of fish have fallen below a sustainable breeding population. This is a prime example of supply-side market failure. **Supply-side market failure** results when the individual activities of a supplier inadvertently lead to destructive effects on the overall supply. The incremental self-interested behavior of millions of businesses and consumers around the world is threatening the supply of trees, fresh water, and fresh air. Normally, as Adam Smith famously pointed out, the individual pursuit of self-interest benefits the collective interest of society, but not in today's worldwide fisheries.

Yet how do you tell a family in China not to burn coal to heat their house, or a utility not to burn coal to generate electricity when families and utilities in Europe and North America have done so for hundreds of years, creating much of the ozone problem? It is not easy. Figure 3.1 presents earth's three *socioecological* classes. As the economies of China, India, and other countries experience very rapid growth over the next 20 years, a billion "sustainers" will become "overconsumers," and the stresses on the earth's environmental resources will be tremendous. Markets will have to be regulated, and marketers will have to obey these regulations. If the abilities and resources of marketing are spent on fighting (or finding ways around) regulation, we will face a "tragedy of the commons" of global proportions. Government programs and policies can help encourage sellers to market more earth-friendly products. Such efforts make everyone more environmentally conscious. But note that it is not just marketers' but everyone's responsibility to save our supply of scarce resources for the hundreds of generations of our descendants.

Not all is doom and gloom. Between 1980 and 1995, water use in the United States dropped by 9% even with population growth of 16%.[6] Using innovative recycling programs, industry water use dropped by 35% during the same period. Water use for farm irrigation dropped by 11%, primarily because farmers switched from

Tragedy of the commons
Is the name given to the process in which individuals, pursuing their own self-interest, overuse a common good to such an extent that the common good is destroyed.

Supply-side market failure
Results when the individual activities of a supplier inadvertently lead to destructive effects on the overall supply.

Natural Forces
The responsibility of marketers is to promote conservation, recycling, and product innovations that save energy, air, water, trees, fish, and other scarce resources.

Figure 3.1	Earth's Three Socioecological Classes		
	Overconsumers **1.1 Billion** **> US $7,500 per capita** **(cars, meat, disposables)**	**Sustainers** **3.3 Billion** **US $7,500 per capita** **(living lightly)**	**Marginals** **1.1 Billion** **< US $700 per capita** **(absolute deprivation)**
	Travel by car and air	Travel by bicycle and public surface transport	Travel by foot, maybe donkey
	Eat high-fat, high-calorie, meat-based diets	Eat healthy diets of grains, vegetables, and some meat	Eat nutritionally inadequate diets
	Drink bottled water and soft drinks	Drink clean water, plus some tea and coffee	Drink contaminated water
	Use throwaway products and discard substantial waste	Use unpackaged goods and durables and recycle wastes	Use local biomass and produce negligible wastes
	Live in spacious, climate-controlled, single-family residences	Live in modest, naturally ventilated residences with extended/multiple families	Live in rudimentary shelters or in the open; usually lack secure tenure
	Maintain image-conscious wardrobe	Wear functional clothing	Wear secondhand clothing or scraps

Source: Based on Alan Durning, *How Much Is Enough?* (Washington, D.C.: Worldwatch Institute, 1993.) Reprinted by permission. Copyright 1993, www.worldwatch.org.

Political and Legal Forces

When the market fails to be "sufficiently" inventive, the federal government has to step in, for example, by requiring washing machine manufacturers to invent, manufacture, and market new models that use 35% less energy, all of this by 2007.

Demand-side market failure

Is the cumulative effect of the marketing practices of many thousands of advertising campaigns, which has a residual negative impact on the values of buyers and the demand for various products (e.g., voting).

rotary sprayers (which waste a lot of water) to underground systems that water the roots. Household use stayed steady, but innovations such as the short-flush toilet began to make a difference. The answer to gloom and doom is, again, the invention and marketing of clever new innovations.

Marketers' Self-Interested, Unintended Consequences on Demand

Other self-destructive forces exist in free markets. Over the last two decades in the United States, market research tools such as focus groups and continuous political polling have been used to target voter concerns and issues and market political candidates. But instead of being used to guide the creation of innovative new programs and policies, the resulting customer insights have often been used to create negative advertising that attacks the values and character of political opponents. Today, voters get most of their information about candidates running for election from TV ads, yet more than 90% of adults believe that the claims made in these ads are mostly (or at least partially) false.[7] The result has been to greatly reduce voters' respect for politicians and the electoral process: "I'm so sick of these ads . . . because nine out of 10 are negative" is a typical response. Such turn-off has resulted in **demand-side market failure**, the cumulative effect of the marketing practices of many thousands of advertising campaigns that has a residual negative impact on the values of buyers and demand for various products. The participative democracy market is in danger of failing because of the marketing practices of candidates and political parties. Short-term self-interest is literally destroying long-term public interest.

More generally, the cumulative effect of the marketing practices of many thousands of advertising campaigns has been claimed to have a residual negative impact on the values of certain demographic groups. This surfaces in T-shirts worn by women that read "There are 9 supermodels and 3 billion other women on this earth." The point, which is immediately understandable to tens of millions of women (if not men), is that the extensive use of these supermodels in advertising sets impossible standards for girls and women to aspire to in their appearance. The result

Ford Motor Company recycles trash into brand new parts like battery housings, splash shields, and lamp bodies in an effort to conserve resources and protect the planet.

is lower self-esteem and self-confidence and a higher rate of eating disorders. A quite reasonable reaction is for women to be turned off by fashion and "look-ism," and to turn to other self-esteem-boosting activities. Demand is again being killed by the accumulated negative impact of advertising. For example, Miller Lite's "Catfight Ad" that featured two attractive women tearing each other's clothes off and fighting in a pit filled with wet concrete created a controversy. Laura Ries, an image guru, noted: "Every time I see it I cringe. It's explicit. It's degrading. It has no real message, except all men are idiots and all they think about are girls and mud wrestling."

The problem is that marketers have found that using attractive models sells. Miller Brewing executives report that the "Catfight Ad" was a big hit with its target market—21- to 31-year-old beer drinkers. Tom Bick, Miller Lite's brand manager, feels that the target market sees the ad for what it really is—"a light-hearted spoof of guys' fantasies." The bottom line is that consumers, both men and women, respond to marketing that features beautiful models.[8] If this were not true, marketers would not spend billions of dollars on marketing campaigns using such models. Should we then limit the opportunities for people to make a living from their beauty? Should we limit the ability of advertisers to use beauty to sell because it makes ordinary folks feel more ordinary? Again, this is a slippery-slope question. What if great writers, painters, composers, athletes, and heroes inspire us, enrich our dreams, and lift the human spirit, but they also make our own achievements seem very ordinary? Should their works be banned? This at least raises an issue of whether critics of marketing apply the same ethical standards and codes to marketing as they do to other fields of human achievement and activity. This brings us to the second major social responsibility of marketing.

Sociocultural Forces

A nationwide poll of adults ages 18–65, undertaken by Duffey Communications and RoperASW in 2002, revealed that "unrealistic standards of beauty" was the biggest criticism that customers had of advertising.

Marketing's Second Social Responsibility: Behave Ethically

3   LEARNING OBJECTIVE

The second major social responsibility of marketing is to conduct business in an ethical manner. Most companies do live up to this responsibility; however, some do not. Consider the following examples that have tragically affected the lives of children:

- Cosco and Safety 1st, two of the country's largest makers of baby products, were fined $1.75 million in civil penalties for failing to report product defects to the

In 1999, about 15 million computers were sent to the landfill in the United States. Since then, this number has increased by at least 10% each year. While this represents a small portion of the total solid waste stream (less than one-half of 1%), computers contain a variety of hazardous materials that can adversely affect the environment. For instance, monitors and televisions with cathode ray tubes (CRTs) possess significant amounts of lead, an element that can damage the nervous system, especially in children. The U.S. Environmental Protection Agency reported that 24% of all lead in the municipal waste stream is attributable to CRTs. Other computer components that contain hazardous materials include mercury switches, cadmium batteries, and lead solder.

As a result of the rapid obsolescence of computers and worries about their environmental impact, governments around the world are crafting regulations to keep electronic equipment out of landfills. As of July 1, 1999, the Commonwealth of Massachusetts, for example, banned businesses and households from putting CRTs into local landfills. European countries are also pursuing far-reaching "take back" legislation that requires manufacturers to bear the full cost and responsibility of unwanted electronic equipment disposal.

Driven by this environmental concern and by government regulation, a whole new industry of electronic recycling has emerged. The largest such firm is Aurora Electronics of California. In 1995, it posted revenues of $95 million: $52 million from the resale of spare computer parts and $43 million from recycling and refurbishing. Envirocycle of Pennsylvania recycled more than 500,000 monitors in 1996, and its full-service demanufacturing operation is growing at more than 40% each year. Additionally, hundreds of small firms have been formed in recent years around the world to refurbish, demanufacture, and recycle electronic waste. These companies succeed by regularly forming strategic alliances with the original equipment manufacturers (OEMs) to process their surplus inventory, warranty returns and off-spec products, and offer full-service asset management disposition to businesses and municipalities that generate electronic waste.

Electronic asset recovery programs excel in the marketplace for two reasons. First, they satisfy the growing demand by consumers for more environmentally friendly products. Second, they provide services that result in cost savings and avoid liability claims to OEMs and other waste generators. These issues propelled Xerox to institute its own asset recovery and remanufacturing program. "The switch to asset recovery was not done primarily because of environmental considerations, although we realized that would be a benefit," notes Jack Azar, Manager of Environmental Design and Resource Conservation for Xerox. "We saw competitive advantage coming from this program." From 1991 to 1995, Xerox reaped $200 million in raw material and parts savings, and reduced its landfill and potential liability costs by more than $450,000 annually. These cost savings are shared with customers.

Electronics recycling firms are finding treasure in other people's electronic trash. By responding to a market demand created by the growth of a "waste" product, new government regulations, consumers' environmental concerns, and operational cost-reduction projects at OEMs, these businesses are able to earn a profit while providing a beneficial service to the environment.

government. According to the Consumer Product Safety Commission, the companies attempted to quietly fix problems associated with their car seats, cribs, electric baby-wipe warmers, high chairs, strollers, and walkers that reportedly contributed to the deaths of two infants and injured more than 300 children.[9]

- Lane Company, a manufacturer of cedar chests, was fined $900,000 for earlier models of its products that latched automatically when shut. The fine settled allegations that the company failed to report in a timely manner that children could become trapped inside the chests. According to reports, Lane had received information that five children suffocated inside older models of its product line.[10]

- Peg Pergo USA Inc., a manufacturer of children's ride-on toys, was fined $150,000 for failing to report in a timely manner that certain models of its products presented a fire hazard and/or failed to stop. The company was aware of approximately 20 incidents, two of which involved burn injuries and $55,000 in property damages to three houses and a garage. Other injuries included a concussion, scratches, bumps, and bruises as products failed to stop and continued on to hit trees, trucks, poles, and other stationary objects.[11]

Despite these and other more well-publicized exceptions (e.g., the cigarette industry, Firestone, Enron, and Arthur Andersen) that the media have used to help create an image that business is unethical, many companies in the United States today are moral enterprises, led by men and women of impeccable character. The moral rudder of most enterprises is under the very solid control of senior executives, particularly the chief executive officer and senior vice presidents of sales and marketing, who lead by example and encourage a corporate culture of honesty and decency.

These enterprises often have written codes of ethics. It has been estimated that about 60% of U.S. companies have written codes of ethics that all employees agree to abide by. They are commonly accepted as a "given" by all employees.[12] Some larger companies have appointed an ethics officer to further promote ethical behavior. These individuals help executives in tough decisions, and provide a safe haven (and source of support) for whistle-blowers. Figure 3.2 presents a summary of the business conduct guidelines of IBM and Procter & Gamble (P&G). The guidelines reflect concern about treating customers (and everyone in the marketplace) in a fair and decent way, but they also express more general concerns, such as respecting the intellectual property rights of others, caring about the environment, and encouraging community service. Notice that the IBM code focuses more on trading ethics, whereas the P&G code is a more general social contract.

Figure 3.3 summarizes the content of some two hundred company ethics statements. United States companies are more concerned about intellectual property rights (such as not stealing patents, copyrighted material, and confidential information) and about ethical purchasing practices. Does this mean that some companies are more concerned about making sure that their buyers do not take bribes and indulge in other unethical behavior, and less concerned about the ethical behavior of their own marketing practices (such as offering bribes)? Whatever your opinion, this figure reminds us that ethical trading requires both the seller and the buyer to behave ethically. European companies seem to address purchasing and marketing ethical issues in about the same proportion.

Natural Forces

Canadian companies are somewhat more concerned about environmental issues than U. S. companies, suggesting that concern over the environment is a more important part of the "social contract" and culture in Canada.

Business Conduct Guidelines for IBM and for Procter & Gamble	Figure 3.2

IBM	Procter & Gamble
Do not make misrepresentations to anyone you deal with.	To provide customers with superior benefits.
Do not use IBM's size unfairly to intimidate or threaten.	To listen and respond to customer opinions.
Treat all buyers and sellers equitably.	To ensure products are safe for intended use and anticipate accidental misuse.
Do not engage in reciprocal dealing.	To strive for fair and open business relationships with suppliers and retailers.
Do not disparage competitors.	
Do not prematurely disclose an unannounced offering.	To help business partners improve performance.
Do no further selling after competitor has the firm offer.	To reject illegal or deceptive activities anywhere in the world.
Keep contact with the competition minimal.	To safeguard the environment.
Do not illegally use confidential information.	To encourage employees to participate in community activities.
Do not steal or obtain information by willful deceit.	To be a good neighbor in communities in which business is done.
Do not violate patents or copyrights.	To provide employees a safe workplace.
Do not give or accept bribes, gifts, or entertainment that might be seen as creating an obligation.	To show concern for the well-being of all employees.
	To create opportunities for employee achievement, creativity, and personal reward.
	To provide a fair annual return to the owners.
	To build for the future to maintain growth.

Sources: Gene R. Laczniak and Patrick E. Murphy, *Marketing Ethics* (Lexington, MA: Lexington Books, 1985), 117–123; and Jan Willem Bol, Charles T. Crespy, James M. Stearns, and John R. Walton, *The Integration of Ethics into the Marketing Curriculum* (Needham Heights, MA: Ginn Press, 1991), 27.

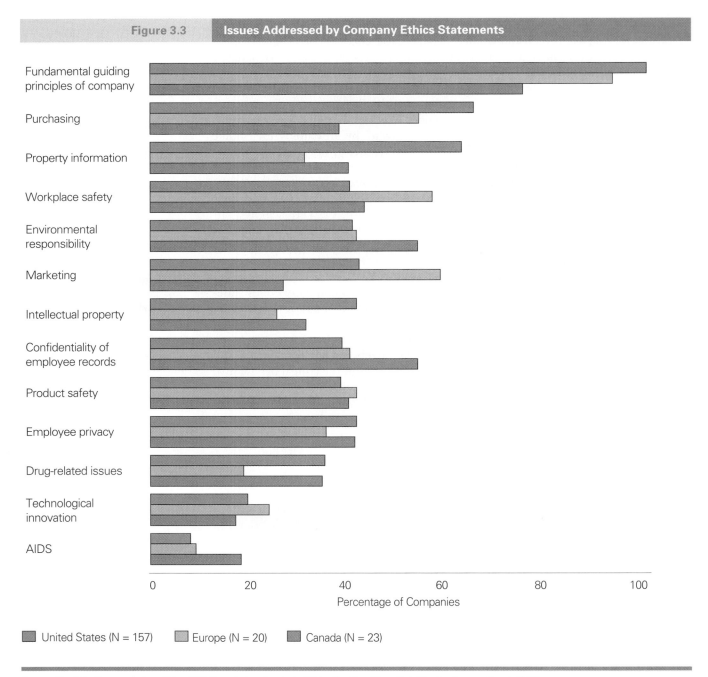

Figure 3.3   **Issues Addressed by Company Ethics Statements**

Percentage of Companies

☐ United States (N = 157)   ☐ Europe (N = 20)   ☐ Canada (N = 23)

Source: Reprinted by permission of Ronald E. Berenheim, *Corporate Ethics Practices* (New York: The Conference Board, 1992).

Personal Codes of Ethics

Company codes of ethics are often stated in general terms, leaving specific interpretation up to the individual salesperson or marketing executive. However, ethical dilemmas often arise during the implementation of marketing strategy. When this happens, decisions must be made without an opportunity to consult superiors. Such situations throw heavy responsibility on the marketing manager, product manager, and sales force. This ethical stress on the marketing executive can be greatly heightened by the presence of a company double standard. A company must make clear what action it will take against unethical behavior and establish credibility by fol-

Motivated by her personal code of ethics, Sherron C. Watkins alerted her boss at Enron of shady accounting practices that led to the discovery of Enron's corporate crime.

lowing through. It must walk the walk. If actions are taken only when a company's unethical behavior is discovered and publicly challenged, then the company sends the worst signals to its marketing executives. What it says is that the company does not really mind what an executive does to achieve financial goals, as long as someone from outside does not find out. If the misconduct becomes public, the executive in question will take the fall. As evidence, whistle-blowers often lose their jobs or are branded troublemakers or fortune seekers by the company. Unfortunately, many marketing decision makers face this conflict to varying degrees. It places great demand on their personal code of ethics. It also often greatly undermines their respect for senior executives and their motivation, which cannot be good for the organization's competitiveness.

The famous Nuremberg trials of Nazi subordinates at the end of World War II established a new principle of ethical accountability. All of the evil could not be blamed on Adolf Hitler, nor was the excuse "If I did not obey orders, then I would have been punished" found acceptable. We are all accountable for the lawfulness and decency of our trading decisions and behavior. Subordinates are responsible for their own behavior, even if following orders or under the threat of dismissal. Advertising agencies are accountable for the honesty of the messages they create for their clients. Ignorance is no excuse. No one gets an easy way out. To take a stand may put a promotion, a business contract, a trading relationship, or even a job at risk. To not take a stand is to sell out one's values, self-respect, and soul. To pass the responsibility on to senior executives may be construed as weakness, or worse, setting up the boss. When orders and ethics collide, a trusted mentor in the organization can be invaluable. That is why the position of **ethics ombudsman** has been created. An ethics ombudsman is someone senior in the organization whom managers can go to and know they will receive a sympathetic hearing: someone who can help them with their quandary, take up the concern, and protect the manager (whistle-blower) from any negative repercussions.

The American Marketing Association also has developed a code of ethics that marketing professionals can turn to for guidance and direction (see Figure 3.4). The emphasis is on ethical trading behavior, and approximately half of the points mentioned

Ethics ombudsman

Is someone senior in an organization whom managers can go to and know they will receive a sympathetic hearing: someone who can help them with an ethical quandary, take up the concern, and protect the manager (whistle-blower) from any negative repercussions.

Figure 3.4	American Marketing Association (AMA) Code of Ethics

AMA CODE OF ETHICS

Members of the American Marketing Association are committed to ethical professional conduct. They have joined together in subscribing to this Code of Ethics embracing the following topics:

RESPONSIBILITIES OF THE MARKETER

Marketers must accept responsibility for the consequences of their activities and make every effort to ensure that their decisions, recommendations and actions function to identify, serve and satisfy all relevant publics: customers, organizations, and society.

Marketers' Professional Conduct must be guided by:

1. The basic rule of professional ethics: not knowingly to do harm;
2. The adherence to all applicable laws and regulations;
3. The accurate representation of their education, training and experience; and
4. The active support, practice and promotion of this Code of Ethics.

HONESTY AND FAIRNESS

Marketers shall uphold and advance the integrity, honor, and dignity of the marketing profession by:

1. Being honest in serving consumers, clients, employees, suppliers, distributors, and the public;
2. Not knowingly participating in conflict of interest without prior notice to all parties involved; and
3. Establishing equitable fee schedules including the payment or receipt of usual, customary and/or legal compensation for marketing exchanges.

RIGHTS AND DUTIES OF PARTIES IN THE MARKETING EXCHANGE PROCESS

Participants in the marketing exchange process should be able to expect that:

1. Products and services offered are safe and fit for their intended uses;
2. Communications about offered products and services are not deceptive;
3. All parties intend to discharge their obligations, financial and otherwise, in good faith; and
4. Appropriate internal methods exist for equitable adjustment and/or redress of grievances concerning purchases.

It is understood that the above would include, but is not limited to, the following responsibilities of the marketer:

In the area of product development and management:

- disclosure of all substantial risks associated with product or service usage;

- identification of any product component substitution that might materially change the product or impact on the buyer's purchase decision;
- identification of extra cost-added features.

In the area of promotions:

- avoidance of false and misleading advertising;
- rejection of high-pressure manipulations, or misleading sales tactics;
- avoidance of sales promotions that use deception or manipulation.

In the area of distribution:

- not manipulating the availability of a product for the purpose of exploitation;
- not using coercion in the marketing channel;
- not exerting undue influence over the reseller's choice to handle a product.

In the area of pricing:

- not engaging in price fixing;
- not practicing predatory pricing;
- disclosing the full price associated with any purchase.

In the area of marketing research:

- prohibiting selling or fundraising under the guise of conducting research;
- maintaining research integrity by avoiding misrepresentation and omission of pertinent research data;
- treating outside clients and suppliers fairly.

ORGANIZATIONAL RELATIONSHIPS

Marketers should be aware of how their behavior may influence or impact the behavior of others in organizational relationships. They should not demand, encourage or apply coercion to obtain unethical behavior in their relationships with others, such as employees, suppliers, or customers.

1. Apply confidentiality and anonymity in professional relationships with regard to privileged information;
2. Meet their obligations and responsibilities in contracts and mutual agreements in a timely manner;
3. Avoid taking the work of others, in whole, or in part, and representing this work as their own or directly benefiting from it without compensation or consent of the originator or owner; and
4. Avoid manipulation to take advantage of situations to maximize personal welfare in a way that unfairly deprives or damages the organization of others.

Any AMA member found to be in violation of any provision of this Code of Ethics may have his or her Association membership suspended or revoked.

Source: http://www.marketingpower.com, American Marketing Association, AMA Code of Ethics, 2003. Reprinted by permission.

are associated with honesty and disclosure. The code can help bolster an executive's belief that the stand that he or she is taking is ethical and socially responsible. However, the American Marketing Association, unlike some other "professional" organizations, is not in a position to provide legal support to its members who face a conflict between their personal ethics and what they are being asked to do. This places a great deal of responsibility on the individual marketing executive. Exercising this responsibility requires an understanding of what is prescribed as right and wrong. It requires an understanding of where such values and rules originate, as well as the issues and moral philosophy that underlie personal and organizational ethics.

Theories of Marketing Ethics

It is no accident that both primitive and advanced civilizations have ethical and moral codes that constrain group and individual behavior and attempt to maintain the social fabric of the culture. The enlightenment of a civilization is often measured by its underlying ethics. When ethical codes break down, societies cease to function and ultimately collapse from within (for example, the decline and fall of the Roman Empire, the collapse of communist systems) or under external pressures (for example, the defeat of the Third Reich in World War II).

The great philosophers of the Enlightenment, Jean-Jacques Rousseau and Thomas Hobbes, argued that society needs a set of ethical rules, a morality accepted by all, called a **social contract**, for it to function effectively. If you want to be part of society, you obey the rules. If entrepreneurs and firms wish to trade in a society and profit from such trade, then they have a social and moral obligation to accept the general ethical rules of the society, and not undermine them with unacceptable trading practices. This section describes underlying principles and beliefs that form the foundation of marketing ethics in society.

The Principle of Utility—Choosing the Most Good for the Most People

Three other famous philosophers, David Hume, Jeremy Bentham, and John Stuart Mill, developed the principle of utility. The **principle of utility** is that "ethical behavior" is the behavior that produces the most good for the most people in a specific situation. At first glance, this sounds like a very good rule. But in practice, this ethical principle is hard to apply. First, how do you calculate the most good for the most people? How do you add up all of the good and bad? Can you measure *good* by adding up all the positive outcomes, then subtracting all the negative outcomes? For example, is it allowable to have two out of every 1,000,000 consumers die from the side effects of the smallpox vaccine if the chances of being exposed to smallpox are very slight (less than one in a million)?

The utility principle can be twisted into some interesting interpretations. It can lead an otherwise ethical company to decide that it must sink to the lowest ethical standards among a group of competitors. "If we were to be more ethical," a company might argue, "we, as a good guy, might go out of business, and what good would be gained from that? It is in the interest of our employees, our customers, and society (that is, the total good) that we, who are basically an ethical firm, stay in business even if it means that we have to stoop to the unethical practices of our rivals." This kind of thinking can become moral quicksand. It can mean being dragged down to the ethics of the most desperate competitor. How common is this dilemma? It is as common as the occurrence of paying off government officials in many markets around the world. It is as common as competing against companies that have lower costs because they are not using scrubbers or other technology to reduce pollution, again another common event.

Another harsh reality is that the more desperate the company or personal situation is, the lower the applied ethical standards will be, and the more the decision maker will be fixated by how his or her company will benefit. Again, the rationalization is

Social contract
Is a philosophical belief that part of the price you pay or what you owe for being able to conduct business in a society and profit from such business is to care about the society and contribute to its betterment.

Principle of utility
That "ethical behavior" is the behavior that produces the most good for the most people in a specific situation.

Economic Forces

In economic terms, marketing ethics is a *normal good* because demand for ethical behavior in a firm increases as the net income of a company increases. Thus, in wealthy economies, business behavior is likely to be more ethical than in poorer economies where firms are struggling to survive. It also means that in hard times, ethical standards are often lowered.

The Battle to Ban Online Gambling

One in $10 of all the money spent in the United States on recreation is spent on gambling: about $47 billion a year in total. Gambling is very big business. Las Vegas is booming, and Native American tribes are building casinos around the country. As a form of "compensation" for the theft of their tribal lands in the 1800s, small regional tribes have become rich off their "right" to run casinos. According to surveys by respected market research firms, more than 90% of adult Americans find casino gambling acceptable, particularly those local residents who benefit from the employment and entertainment that casinos create. The typical casino gambler has a slightly higher income than the national norm, but otherwise is very average.

Why, then, is there so much objection to gambling on the Internet? Such gambling might ultimately require prepayment using a credit card that would make it difficult for children to participate. It is not even clear that children would find gambling more attractive than video games. Providing the gambling Web sites were audited by government agencies for the fairness and integrity of their games, as casinos are now, the risk of widespread corruption and fraud would be very low. Currently, 36 states run their own lotteries, so it is hard for state legislators to object to Web-based gambling on moral grounds. Given that, why has the National Association of Attorneys General created a special committee to draw up federal regulation to make Internet gambling illegal? Why has the state of Nevada already passed legislation banning Internet gambling? The reason seems simple: Internet gambling would pose a long-term serious competitive threat to existing gambling products marketed by casino companies and state governments. It is banned to restrict competition. How long will such a ban last?

Legitimate and respectable Internet gambling companies operating from the Caribbean, as well as from other countries that allow such businesses and regulate them appropriately, cannot be prevented from offering the excitement of their gaming sites to Americans, and for that matter to the rest of the world. Furthermore, there is no way that governments anywhere can stop their citizens from using credit cards to purchase such entertainment. When this happens, the major casino companies and their software suppliers will be more than ready to enter the market, and the federal and state regulations will fade into the sunset. In a recent survey, only 15% of online gamblers indicated that online casinos are more fun than traditional Vegas casinos, and almost a third were dissatisfied with the online gambling experiences they have had. When they play for money, 60 percent think that the online gambling sites are fixed. The most frequently visited gambling sites are **http://www.freelotto.com**, **http://www.gamesvillelycos.com**, **http://www.prizecentral.com**, **http://www.goldenpalace.com**, and **http://www.virtualvegas.com**.

DISCUSSION QUESTIONS

1. Surveys show that people believe casinos should be responsible for offering programs to help compulsive gamblers. What unique problems exist in requiring Internet gambling services to be responsible for offering programs to rehabilitate compulsive Internet gamblers?

2. Do you think those who are attempting to restrict gambling on the Internet are behaving ethically? When do you think the traditional casino gambling companies such as Harrah's will change sides and lobby for legalizing online casino gambling? What advantages do well-known names such as Harrah's have in setting up online gambling sites?

Sources: Philip P. McGuigan, "Stakes Are High in Battle to Ban Internet Gambling," *The National Law Journal,* 3 November 1997, B8.
Greenfield Online, Wilton, CT. Results were presented in *Marketing News,* 12 February 2001, 12.

---

that behaving unethically is for the total good, and that the means justifies the ends, such as saving the jobs of employees. Sometimes it seems that only successful companies and executives can afford a conscience.

Categorical Imperative—What If Everyone Did It?

The philosopher Immanuel Kant's famous categorical imperative offers an alternative to the utility principle. The **categorical imperative** asks whether the proposed action would be right if everyone did it. What would happen to the social fabric? This view of ethics asks us to think about the social destructiveness of trading practices that, if only we engage in them, seem hardly to be serious violations. For example, consider the use of advertising puffery (exaggerated claims). If only done occasionally by a few, it does not seem so serious, but if everyone did it all the time, then advertising would lose its integrity and credibility, and end up destroying the usefulness of a major marketing tool. It would also greatly reduce the efficiency of markets, because markets rely on advertising to transmit information to everyone about prices, availability, new innovations, and quality. Some would say that this is

Categorical imperative
Asks whether the proposed action would be ethical and right if everyone did it.

precisely what has happened to advertising. What would happen if the one-million-plus companies in the United States each made several hundred unsolicited phone calls each evening? Would that be socially responsible and fair? What would happen if you were constantly on the receiving end of such ethics? At a global marketing level, many companies lobby their government to erect trade barriers to protect them from foreign competitors. But what happens if all countries erect such barriers? Global trade would be killed, and the world would be plunged into a depression such as occurred in the 1930s.

This approach takes most of the situation or context out of the ethical evaluation and, in that sense, is more explicit than the utilitarian principle. **Situational ethics** is that societal condition where right and wrong are determined by the specific situation, rather than by universal moral principles. It also has elements of "do unto others what you would have them do unto you." But the categorical imperative still requires the decision maker to *see* the universal wrong or evil in the act if everyone did it, including doing it to them. Depraved individuals, caring nothing for society or even their family, may answer that, yes, it would be fine for society, and that others are welcome to act in the same way toward them, their children, and their grandmothers. The basic point is that both utilitarian situational ethics and the categorical imperative still require a basic set of values. Whose responsibility is it to instill such values in marketing decision makers?

Situational ethics
Is that societal condition where "right" and "wrong" are determined by the specific situation, rather than by universal moral principles.

Religious Beliefs as the Foundation for Basic Values

Basic decency and morality are taught on or across a father's or mother's knee, with grandmothers, grandfathers, uncles, aunts, and other surrogate parents helping out. If not taught by extended family members, such basic values are taught to us as children by respected teachers and coaches and through organizations such as the YMCA, Boy Scouts, and Girl Scouts. Finally, ethical teachings are provided to us at our church, synagogue, mosque, or other source of our spiritual and religious beliefs. But what if, somehow as adults, some of us seem to have missed these lessons? Some say it is too late to teach adults about the basic ethics of honesty, decency, and consideration for others. Others seem to expect companies to take on this impossible task for their employees. But is that really a company's responsibility? Are parents, schools, and the world's great religions becoming lax in living up to their side of the social contract to teach children basic values?

One of the distinguishing characteristics of different civilizations, countries, societies, and tribes is their dominant religion. It often has great impact. For example, the predominant religion of the United States is Christianity. The Judeo-Christian creed, along with "enlightenment thinking" (some of which can be traced to the Islamic enlightenment of 900–1300), has greatly influenced the Constitution, common law, and system of justice in the United States. Thus, it can be argued that marketers in the United States fulfill the social contract by adopting a code of marketing ethics based on Judeo-Christian religious beliefs that have defined our society's law and morality.

But what happens to those who believe in the ethical code of a different religion, such as the seven million Americans who are believers in Islam? Certainly, individuals living in a free society will apply their own set of religious beliefs to all situations, including marketing decision making. This exercise of different religious beliefs and values increases the variability in ethics we are likely to observe in the marketplace. One economic reason we should use the "predominant religion" values as the common core for our society's ethics, even if we are not followers of that religion, is that the universal acceptance of its code enables us to predict the likely behavior of other parties in the market. Predictability leads to an increase in certainty and a sense of confidence and control that the market is orderly and fair, and thus reduces the costs of doing business.

Sociocultural Forces

The dominant religion in a country will shape its citizens' opinions of marketing practices. Citizens in Muslim countries may consider advertisements from western Christian cultures quite immoral.

Notice that this creates a fundamental ethical dilemma: a trade-off between freedom of religion, beliefs in different ethical codes, and the efficiency of the market. An example of this problem has occurred in diamond trading around the world. For years, a fundamental sect of Jews dominated the global trading of these precious gems. The ethical behavior of these diamond traders in their trading among themselves was very high for centuries. A trader's word was his bond. But now the sect's religious ethics do not have the same hold on some younger generations of traders, and new traders from Russia and Asia have entered the market. The result is that there is much less trust in the diamond-trading business than there used to be, and this has increased the risk and cost of diamond trading.

If the clearly dominant and underlying religious creed in a society or among a group of specialized traders is not to be used as the foundation for a generally accepted code of business ethics, then what should be used? It would be extraordinarily difficult to argue that some other religious or moral philosophy should be substituted.

More generally, a serious and unresolved situational-ethics problem often occurs in global marketing. No international code of business ethics exists because each society's ethics vary, some slightly and others greatly. Fortunately, most of the world's major religions and cultures share common norms and ethics and would answer the questions on an ethical checklist similarly. In some countries, though, bribery, kickbacks, and dishonesty in advertising, selling, and dealing are much more acceptable than in others. How should American firms behave in such markets? If they do not tolerate such standard practices, they risk not doing business, and, furthermore, may be hated for arrogantly imposing their values where they are not wanted. For example, should American garment manufacturers be concerned about the working conditions in the offshore factories that produce many of their clothing lines? Liz Claiborne makes unscheduled visits to its suppliers to ensure they meet the company's standards and attempts to work with those suppliers that provide the best working conditions. Presumably, other companies are less particular, only caring about price and output quality. But just how much American companies should be held responsible for the human rights abuses of their suppliers is unclear, particularly if caring puts the American company at a competitive cost disadvantage.

The quick and easy answer to the situational-ethics problem, "When in Rome, do as the Romans do," is no real answer for at least two reasons. First, international business is carried out in two places at once, for example, between a seller in New York and a buyer in Rome. What is the social contract in this situation? Is it determined by the accepted norms of the American or the Italian trading partner's political economy? Regulating the Internet is tied up in this very knot. An international body called the Hague Convention is trying to decide who has jurisdiction and how a common law is ultimately developed across 200 countries. It has been working for 10 years and has gotten nowhere.

Second, this philosophy suggests abandoning one's own "moral compass," and replacing it with the ethical standards of a trading partner—not a comfortable or natural position to be in. With the increase in global marketing comes a pressing need to adopt an international code of ethics. Unethical behavior will always exist, but it can be defined the same way and condemned by every society. Even if this occurs some time in the future, international marketing decision makers still will have to reconcile their personal moral compass with situational issues and trade-offs among interest groups and stakeholders they are paid to serve. All of the above issues make it very difficult to prescribe answers to the ethical questions and dilemmas that surround marketing and trading practices.

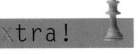

Personal Ethical Choices

A personal ethics checklist for marketers is illustrated in Figure 3.5. By answering these questions, a decision maker or decision-making team seeks to develop its own ethical standards. Although most questions are self-explanatory, others need some brief explanation or raise issues worth exploring.[13] It seems that the least society should require of marketing executives is that they ask these questions. Sometimes not asking a question can be as wrong as asking and giving a poor answer. For example, not considering the safety of a toy being marketed seems to be as irresponsible as considering the safety and deciding to sell the toy anyway. The effects are often the same.

One of the most common situations in which marketing executives suffer a lapse of ethics is when they have to make a quick decision because they are preoccupied with other concerns. The ethical sufficiency of the decision is simply not examined. **Ethical vigilance** means, in practice, asking hard questions. It means paying constant attention to whether one's actions are right or wrong. And if wrong, asking why one is behaving in that manner. It is important to confront excuses and reasons for violating personal ethics. Avoiding or shelving the answers to such questions is no solution. Decision makers who ask why they do or do not behave in certain ways are more honest with themselves about their true intentions. This is the essence of executive responsibility, and it also can be the first step down the path of change. Such questions lead people to recognize that most of us have at least two codes of ethics: (1) the set we espouse and want others to apply in their behavior toward us and (2) the code of ethics that, for whatever rationalizations, we actually live up to. The more we recognize the differences between them, the closer we come to understanding how easy it is to talk about ethics in black and white, while practicing in shades of gray.

The list of questions shown in Figure 3.5 is organized in approximate order of importance and by the nature of the ethical or moral principles involved. The first question in the table is the first and last question the ethical minimalist will ask. The

Ethical vigilance
Means paying constant attention to whether one's actions are "right" or "wrong," and if ethically "wrong," asking why one is behaving in that manner.

A Personal Ethics Checklist for Marketers	Figure 3.5

☐ Am I violating the law? If yes, why?

☐ Are the values and ethics that I am applying in business lower than those I use to guide my personal life? If yes, why?

☐ Am I doing to others as I would have them do to me? If not, why not?

☐ Would it be wrong if everyone did what I propose to do? Why?

☐ Am I willfully risking the life and limb of consumers and others by my actions? If yes, why?

☐ Am I willfully exploiting or putting at risk children, the elderly, the illiterate, the mentally incompetent, the naive, the poor, or the environment? If yes, why?

☐ Am I keeping my promises? If not, why not?

☐ Am I telling the truth, all the truth? If not, why not?

☐ Am I exploiting a confidence or a trust? If yes, why?

☐ Am I misrepresenting my true intentions to others? If yes, why?

☐ Am I loyal to those who have been loyal to me? If not, why not?

☐ Have I set up others to take responsibility for any negative consequences of my actions? If yes, why?

☐ Am I prepared to redress wrongs and fairly compensate for damages? If not, why not?

☐ Are my values and ethics as expressed in my strategy offensive to certain groups? If yes, why?

☐ Am I being as efficient in my use of scarce resources as I can be? If not, why not?

This set of questions can be used as the basis for a team's or an individual's mental model to perceive and recognize an ethical issue associated with a proposed goal, strategy, program, or tactic.

Government Corruption and the Offering of Bribes Across Countries

One of the sad realities in poor countries is that the level of corruption is very high. Corruption is a huge friction in an economic system. It makes the system much less efficient because resources are being diverted to unproductive individuals who are not part of the added-value chain. The following table lists the levels of corruption and bribery in various countries. The scores relate to perceptions of the degree of corruption and propensity to pay bribes in the country and ranges between 10 (highly clean) and 0 (highly corrupt).

When there is a lot of corruption, there can be a lot of inefficiency, including the collapse of markets. But corruption is not always such a great friction. According to the 2002 Corruption Perceptions Index, South Korea and Taiwan, two of the great economic success stories of the last 50 years, have quite a high level of government corruption and their companies also are more likely to offer and pay bribes in their marketing in emerging economies.

There are at least two ways of thinking about bribery in marketing in emerging markets. One is to recognize that if the government (the politicians, bureaucrats, and courts) is corrupt in a country, then it will very likely keep business corrupt and it is very hard to change the system. Another consideration is that countries whose exporters offer bribes or pay bribes in emerging markets are the cause of the problem continuing, if not the initial cause of the problem (see table).

Source: Data compiled from *Transparency International Bribe Payers Index 2002*, http://www.transparency.org, Corruption Surveys and Indexes. Reprinted by permission of Transparency International.

Corruption and Bribe Payers Indexes

Country	Corruption Index[1]	Bribe Payers Index[2]
Australia	8.6	8.5
Sweden	9.3	8.4
Switzerland	8.5	8.4
Austria	7.8	8.2
Canada	9.0	8.1
Netherlands	9.0	7.8
Belgium	7.1	7.8
UK	8.7	6.9
Singapore	9.3	6.3
Germany	7.3	6.3
Spain	7.1	5.8
France	6.3	5.5
USA	7.7	5.3
Japan	7.1	5.3
Malaysia	4.9	4.3
Hong Kong	8.2	4.3
Italy	5.2	4.1
S. Korea	4.5	3.9
Taiwan	5.6	3.8
China	3.5	3.5
Russia	2.7	3.2
Correlation	0.802212	

[1]The above index is based on a poll of surveys undertaken by seven independent research institutions from around the world. The higher the score the lower the corruption of public officials.

[2]More than 800 business experts in 15 leading emerging countries were asked, "In the business sectors with which you are most familiar, please indicate how likely companies from the following countries are to pay or offer bribes to win or retain business in this country." The higher the score, the lower the propensity to pay bribes.

---

second question addresses the application of a double standard and the basis for such a double standard. The third question addresses the extent to which marketers apply the Golden Rule: "Do unto others as you would have them do unto you." A prominent British chief executive officer has suggested that a better way of posing the question is to look at oneself and ask, "What would I think of someone who has my business ethics or took the action that I propose to take?"[14]

Marketing's Third Social Responsibility: Obey the Law

As discussed in Chapter 1, political and legal forces affect the marketing environment to which the marketer must adapt. It is the job of government to establish the rules and regulations to which businesses must conform. These rules and regulations affect each element in the marketing mix. Marketers must therefore be aware of and conform to all laws affecting their business. This often involves getting lawyers to review marketing-mix plans.

As individual citizens, our behavior is constrained by the law and by our individual views of right and wrong. It is no different for firms and marketing decision makers that compete in domestic and international markets. Marketplaces are full of

The Consumer Product Safety Commission, an agency created under the Consumer Product Safety Act, protects the public against risks of injuries with consumer products. Kidd Safety, a feature at its Web site, offers guidelines for using scooters safely. (http://www.cpsc.tov)

rules. Many are written into law, some are stated in professional codes of ethics, and others are stated in company rules of good conduct. This section asks you to think about some of the legal issues that affect marketers in order to lay a foundation or framework for your understanding of marketing law. Such considerations may seldom be specifically stated in actual written marketing plans or decisions, but they are important.

Despite the fact that the U.S. marketplace is one of the most open and free in the world, federal, state, and local laws and agencies impose numerous constraints. The great surge of consumerism that occurred in the 1960s resulted in several new agencies, including the Consumer Product Safety Commission, and numerous new laws. More regulation means more restrictions, and more crusading regulators mean higher legal expenses and the risk of a company losing its reputation if a case is tried in the press.

While the political/legal environment can frustrate initiative, in general it is positive for business. For example, in the United States, many of the laws that affect marketing practice are in place to encourage competition and protect consumers. For example, long before Firestone recalled millions of tires because of separating treads, dozens of individuals had sued the company for identical reasons. The public was unaware of the potential danger because all parties involved agreed that once claims were settled, the papers would be sealed. As a result, the Transportation Recall Efficiency, Accountability and Documentation Act (TREAD Act) was passed to force tire manufacturers to report possible product defects and to provide tire-pressure-monitoring devices and warning lights, which are mandated to become standard equipment on all new U.S. vehicles manufactured after November 2003.[15] Figure 3.6 summarizes the major laws affecting marketing. Moreover, the current plague of lobbyists, who buy the influence and the votes of local, state, and national politicians in many and various ways, exists because thousands of companies and industries are trying to have laws passed and laws interpreted to favor the competitiveness of their particular firm or industry. In other words, if it is your law that is passed, then regulation is good; if it is someone else's law, then it is bad.

Political and Legal Forces

While we may complain about too many laws in the U.S., the opposite is much worse. In many African countries, there is little trade with the outside world because there are no laws or courts to uphold the law and trading contracts. A successful business culture needs to be protected by a strong and fair legal system.

Political and Legal Forces

The Library of Congress has calculated that the annual cost of completing, filing, and handling an estimated 15,000 different government forms is $40 billion, well over the national expenditure for all research and development. Clearly, some of this paperwork is worth the cost, but much is not.

Figure 3.6	Major Laws That Affect Marketing
Acts	**Prohibitions**

Major Laws That Protect Consumers

Child Protection Act of 1966	Prohibits the sales of hazardous toys.
Fair Packaging and Labeling Act of 1967	Requires certain information to be listed on all labels and packages, including product identification, manufacturer or distributor mailing address, and the quantity of contents.
Consumer Credit Protection Act of 1968	Requires the full disclosure of annual interest rates on loans and credit purchases.
National Environmental Policy Act of 1970	Established the Environmental Protection Agency to deal with organizations that create pollution.
Consumer Product Safety Act of 1972	Created the Consumer Product Safety Commission and empowered it to specify safety standards for consumer products.
Nutritional Labeling and Education Act of 1990	Prohibits exaggerated health claims and requires all processed foods to provide nutritional information.
Americans with Disabilities Act (ADA) of 1991	Protects the rights of people with disabilities; prohibits discrimination against the disabled (illegal in public accommodations, transportation, and telecommunications).
Brady Law of 1993	Imposes a five-day waiting period and a background check before a customer can take possession of a purchased gun.

Laws That Encourage Competition

Sherman Antitrust Act of 1890	Prohibits restraint of trade and monopolization; delineates a competitive marketing system as a national policy.
Clayton Act of 1914	Strengthens the Sherman Act by restricting such practices as race discrimination, exclusive dealing, tying contracts, and interlocking boards of directors where the effect may be to substantially lessen competition or tend to create a monopoly.
Federal Trade Commission Act of 1914	Prohibits unfair methods of competition; established the Federal Trade Commission, an administrative agency that investigates business practices and enforces the FTC Act.
Robinson-Patman Act of 1936	Prohibits price discrimination in sales to wholesalers, retailers, or other producers. Also prohibits selling at unreasonably low prices to eliminate competition.
Miller-Tydings Resale Price Maintenance Act of 1937	Exempts interstate fair trade contracts from compliance with antitrust requirements.
Wheeler-Lea Act of 1938	Amended the FTC Act to further outlaw unfair practices and give the FTC jurisdiction over false and misleading advertising.
Celler-Kefauver Antimerger Act of 1950	Amended the Clayton Act to include major asset purchases that decrease competition in an industry.
American Automobile Labeling Act of 1992	Requires a vehicle's manufacturer to provide a label informing consumers of where the vehicle was assembled and where its components originated.
North American Free Trade Agreement (NAFTA) of 1993	International trade agreement existing between Canada, Mexico, and the United States. Encourages trade by removing tariffs and other trade barriers among these three countries.

The point is that marketers can be just as shortsighted about changes in the political/legal environment as they can be about changing customer needs and technological innovations. A hostile attitude toward the political/legal environment that is generalized into a hostile attitude toward public policy is unreasonable, and if it encourages a marketing strategy that willfully frustrates the letter or intent of the law, it can be disastrous. For example, Toys "R" Us lost market share after the Federal Trade Commission pressed charges that the toy giant was violating antitrust regulations.[16] Bill Gates and Microsoft faced similar backlash effects when the government pursued its antitrust campaign against the computer software monolith.

Companies also have to be farsighted in their promotion of self-interest and in their lobbying for special regulation to protect their interests. Indeed, even the original Sherman Antitrust Act, the granddaddy of all market competition law, was initially supported by the "robber barons" of the day because it was deliberately vaguely worded so as to be uninterpretable and, hence, unconstitutional.[17] They did not expect a future Supreme Court to come along and interpret the vagueness as an invitation to make law from the bench designed to serve the needs of the time. They created a monster that ultimately broke up their giant monopolistic trusts. The lesson is that self-interested lawmaking often comes back to haunt the original sponsor through unintended and unanticipated consequences.

Marketing's Fourth Social Responsibility: Help Market Good Causes

5   LEARNING OBJECTIVE

The fourth important dimension of marketing's social responsibility is to encourage its use in the promotion of worthy public causes.[18] Today's marketers have come to recognize, as has been confirmed in a recent Roper poll, that in many markets a company's media expression of social responsibility influences consumer behavior more than advertising.[19] You do well by doing good. It also helps if your product can be associated with your socially responsible contributions. Clothing designer Ralph Lauren donated $13 million to restore the 184-year-old "Old Glory" American flag that flew in the rockets' red glare and inspired the national anthem. Kimberly-Clark sells disposable diapers and builds children's parks and playgrounds. McDonald's works with environmental groups to increase its recycling. Shell Oil's TV advertising features conservationists that it employs to protect the environment surrounding its drilling operations.

Some companies have started up their own nonprofit organizations, and these are not always cynical efforts to buy public relations. They are mostly initiatives suggested by their workforce and welcomed by management who recognize that they will build company morale and are a positive expression of a company's ethics. They are a way of expressing what should be done by a socially responsible organization. An issue that the marketing professional has to face is whether marketing good causes is the responsibility of firms or individuals with the resources and capabilities to do so. The drug firm Merck is widely admired for its corporate social responsibility. It has donated hundreds of millions of dollars' worth of vaccines to poor countries and sells its AIDS drug in poor countries at an 85% discount off the price charged in the United States. The needs of people have been put in front of profits, but is it the responsibility of firms to help the poor of the world or is this responsibility better faced by the rich owners of companies and their charitable giving? Whatever you may think about the social responsibility of Microsoft, its founder Bill Gates and his wife Melinda (an ex-marketing executive) have been extraordinarily generous in their philanthropy. Their foundation has given or pledged a colossal $23 billion in the last five years, mostly to eradicate certain diseases around the world.

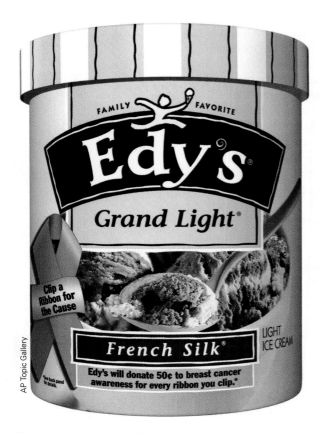

Demonstrating its commitment to social responsibility, Edy's Ice Cream is partnering with ice cream lovers across the nation to raise up to $250,000 for the detection and cure of breast cancer.

Cause-related marketing
Is an activity that governments, public service organizations, companies, and individuals undertake to encourage target customer participation in socially redeeming programs.

On the other hand, the highly respected super-investor Warren Buffett, who plans to leave some $30 billion to his foundation on his death, believes that, for now, the best way he can help good causes is to make as much money as a businessman as he can so he can leave more for his foundation.[20] The point is that socially responsible marketers should try to help market good causes, either through their firm *or* as individuals giving their time and expertise.

Cause-Related Marketing

Cause-related marketing includes those activities that governments, public service organizations, companies, and individuals undertake in an effort to encourage target customer participation in socially redeeming programs. These efforts are usually delivered through educational campaigns and provide free or low-priced services at convenient times and places. The following are examples of cause-related marketing:

- How should future societies deal with the issue of using inexpensive genetic testing to reduce genetic disabilities? Genetic disabilities create very high medical care costs that are carried by everyone participating in health insurance pools and great anguish to families, not to speak of the misery of those afflicted with such disabilities. Education campaigns might inform and persuade individuals to take the tests, and might then target those with the flagged genetic markers with further education about the value of choosing not to have children. Marketing campaigns would be more proactive, setting up testing sites at convenient times and locations, providing professional counseling on test results, and, as an alternative, offering special adoption priority programs coupled with voluntary sterilization.[21]

- Advertising campaigns sponsored by public service organizations and liquor companies are undertaken around holiday seasons to discourage drinking and driving. Over the years, these campaigns have become much more aggressive, targeted at the friends of problem drinkers, suggesting appropriate behaviors such as taking the keys away from those at risk, and creating a designated driver in a group. Market research found that targeting the problem drinker had no effect. What sort of products might be invented to support such communication campaigns? Some communities have sponsored free taxi services and encouraged bars to offer more recreational activities, such as providing pool tables and dancing to reduce the amount of liquor consumption in an evening. Other "social marketers" have encouraged the invention of devices that can be installed in problem drinkers' vehicles that require a "breath test" to start the engine.

The challenge for social marketing is coming up with alternative products that can be marketed to those at risk. Some suggestions, based on experts' extended study of the problem, are designed to lessen the evil, but are still considered too controversial. Examples of such products are providing free, less addictive drugs or clean needles for drug addicts and free birth control pills or abortions to teenagers. The marketing of new technologies, such as new medications to treat drug addicts or new forms of contraception such as the morning-after pill, is often argued to be unethical because these products promote or encourage, rather than reduce, the socially undesirable behavior. The problem is that the critics do not have good alternative solutions, or their solutions are draconian new laws and punishment. On the other hand, there have been many successful social marketing programs that can be used as benchmarks of best practice for marketing professionals interested in using their talents for good causes.

Chapter Summary

Learning Objective 1: *Understand that marketing's contribution to society includes improving the efficiency and effectiveness of the economic process through the creation of exchanges, markets, products, and trading innovations. Explore why marketing is frequently criticized for socially irresponsible behavior.* Marketing's first responsibility is to be efficient, because, if it is not, it is wasting scarce resources that will no longer be available for future generations. Marketing is sometimes inefficient, but in competitive markets it is generally about as efficient as it has learned to be, and hence can be. Marketing also has to be honest because markets are not efficient when they are dishonest. As marketers respond to the marketing environment, they must do so in a manner that reflects their concern for the welfare of others. This was termed the *social contract* by the great philosophers of the Enlightenment, Jean-Jacques Rousseau and Thomas Hobbes. The social contract has stood the test of time in moral philosophy. It is a responsibility marketing (and for that matter every other business discipline) cannot escape.

Budweiser uses marketing to reduce drinking-related car accidents through its Alert Cab program.

Learning Objective 2: *Recognize why the self-centered behavior of millions of businesses and consumers around the world has a detrimental impact on supply and demand.* The world faces several potential "tragedy of the commons" effects on clean air, fresh water, trees, fish, participatory democracy, and young women's self-esteem and happiness with themselves. This is because the pursuit of entirely selfish interests by businesses and consumers does not always work for the best. All functions of a firm, including marketing, have to be sensitive to such unintended effects. The enlightened leadership that marketing planners are expected to display is most put to the test when they are faced with ethical dilemmas created by conflicts of interests among customers, employees, owners, and future generations of humanity. How they choose to resolve such dilemmas tells them a lot about themselves.

Learning Objective 3: *Appreciate the role of personal ethical behavior and learn the major theories of marketing ethics.* Several theories or perspectives on marketing ethics are presented in this chapter. Some are more absolute than others in their prescriptions and they are often based on religious convictions. While these theories may differ on some issues and judge behavior differently, they tend to agree on the sort of questions that need to be asked and answered. At some time in the future, you will need to come to terms with where you stand ethically, because the ethical behavior of firms comes down to the ethical behavior of individuals. Like any marketing skill, the skill of behaving ethically and with social responsibility develops with practice: the practice of asking the right questions, answering them honestly, and resolving dilemmas by balancing short- and long-term interests at 4 A.M. (in other words, losing a little sleep over them!).

Learning Objective 4: *Understand that rules and regulations govern each element of the marketing mix.* Numerous national, state, and local laws regulate marketing practices. Marketers are expected to have a general understanding of these laws and consult their company lawyers for advice on specifics. Many of these laws are created because industry self-regulation failed. Regulations are an important environment variable that have to be considered in marketing planning.

Learning Objective 5: *Understand that marketing has a role in promoting worthy public causes and how cause-related marketing is used to achieve this goal.* We learn from this chapter that the principles of marketing (e.g., understand your target customer) also apply to the marketing of worthy causes and that the promotion of worthy causes can benefit a company's image. But firms have to limit their support of marketing social causes and good deeds because they are spending their owners' money and are accountable to them. There are no such limits on the extent to which marketing professionals, as individuals, can give of their time, talents, and resources to market worthy social causes.

Key Terms

For interactive study: visit http://bestpractices.swlearning.com.

Categorical imperative, 82	Inefficient targeting, 72	Social responsibility, 68
Cause-related marketing, 90	Planned obsolescence, 70	Supply-side market failure, 73
Demand-side market failure, 74	Principle of utility, 81	Tragedy of the commons, 73
Ethics ombudsman, 79	Situational ethics, 83	
Ethical vigilance, 85	Social contract, 81	

Questions for Review and Discussion

1. In 1999, recycled disposable medical equipment had sales of $40 million out of a total $60-billion market for medical disposables. Recyclers buy, chemically wash, rinse, dry, sterilize, pack, and resell instruments, such as used catheters for $250 (half the cost of new ones). The Food and Drug Administration (FDA) regulates the new drug and equipment markets by setting standards and putting its stamp of approval on production and marketing practices. Normally, entrepreneurs hate government regulators that add millions of dollars of expense to business processes, but entrepreneurs in the recycled disposable medical equipment market begged the FDA to hold hearings about regulating their industry. The hearings began in December 1999 and resulted in an August 2000 announcement that the FDA would regulate the industry. The larger disposable medical equipment recyclers celebrated the FDA decision to regulate, and they had good reason to celebrate. Why would these sellers welcome such government regulation?

2. A competitor's disgruntled employee mails you plans for what looks like a promising new product. Should you throw the plans away? Send them to your R&D people for analysis? Notify your competitor about what is going on? Call the Federal Bureau of Investigation?

3. All-terrain vehicles were involved in 1,500 deaths and 400,000 serious injuries during the 1980s—20% of these affecting children 12 and under. The automobile industry stopped selling the three-wheel version and notified dealers to instruct buyers that the vehicles should not be driven by children under 16. However, many dealers have ignored the direction. The industry view is that because state laws allow children to use the vehicle, it is the parents' responsibility to supervise their children's use. Should the product be banned?

4. In the late 1970s, credit card interest rates rose to 18–20% because of inflation. Through the 1980s and 1990s, many credit card interest rates remained at around 18–20%, long after inflation had cooled and the cost of money had dropped to under 7%. Many banks have argued that the cost of servicing credit card debt is high, but some banks charge only 10% on their cards. The merchant is charged a fee (2–5%) for each purchase made on a card. This covers the cost of the transaction and some of the risk of card theft and bad debt. Is it ethical for companies to continue charging 18–20% interest?

5. Increasingly, prescription drugs are being marketed directly to consumers, as if they were soap powder.

How might such marketing be socially responsible? How might it be socially irresponsible?

6. A supermarket serving a low-income African-American market charges higher prices for its staples (such as bread and milk) than do supermarkets in the suburbs. Consumer groups have complained that this practice exploits the poor. The store argues that suburban shoppers buy more profitable luxuries, allowing suburban stores to lower their prices on staples. The store's management also can prove that there is a greater incidence of shoplifting and vandalism in its store, resulting in hardly any profit, even at the higher prices. Should the store lower its prices? Should it simply close down if it would lose money by lowering its prices? What other creative options does the store have?

7. A Save the Children Fund (SCF) ad featured little Pedro with the sad eyes and Joanne Woodward saying, "Imagine, the cost of a cup of coffee, 52 cents a day, can help save a child." But SCF has not been in the business of directly sponsoring children for many years. It is involved in community development work, such as building playgrounds and providing start-up loans for small businesses. The problem is that community development does not pull cash donations the way that little Pedro does. Only about 35% of the funds raised are actually spent on charitable projects;

the rest is spent on marketing and overhead.[22] Was SCF's behavior ethical? Should SCF be held to a higher or lower standard than would be applied to a for-profit organization?

8. You are in a foreign country where bribing government officials and businesspeople is essential to doing business, and bribery is not outlawed as it is in the United States. Officials from the country approach you, saying that there are many buyers for your products and you could make good profits in their country. Would you do business and pay the bribes? Would you hide the practice, hoping that no one in the United States would find out? Would you pay a distributor in the country a set fee to take care of everything for you, pretending not to know what "taking care of everything" means?

9. Every February, audiences for the major networks' programs are measured. These ratings are used to compute audience size and what advertisers will be charged for advertisements placed during these programs. During "Sweeps Week," all of the networks advertise new episodes to boost their audiences. Before and after Sweeps Week, however, the networks present reruns of shows or episodes, sometimes out of sequence. How ethical is the Sweeps Week practice of the networks? How should audience measurement be undertaken?

In-Class Team Activities

1. A major U.S. bank in Chicago has been approached by an Arab sheik who wishes to make a major investment in its New Ventures Mutual Fund that has been brilliantly managed by a 35-year-old female executive. The bank is very keen to make the sale, but the sheik will only do business with men. Normally, the female mutual funds manager would travel to meet such a client. Should the bank send her anyway? What if a major commission is involved in making the sale? Would it make any difference if the sheik was visiting the United States and refused to meet the female executive? Within your team, choose one person to play the role of the sheik and present his perspective, another to play the role of the female star manager and present her perspective, and another the role of the male who would replace her and his perspective. Be prepared to present each perspective, and then discuss what the group thinks should be done.

2. The cigarette industry has been under attack for more than 30 years for marketing cigarettes that are addic-

tive and cause lung cancer. Even though its own scientists confirmed these accusations, the CEOs of the industry testified under oath that tobacco was not addictive. These CEOs later admitted they lied under oath at the advice of their corporate lawyers. Company officials also assured the public that their advertisements were not directed toward children. Yet, independent market research revealed that 90% of children 8–13 years old could recognize Joe Camel.[23] Later, court documents revealed that the cigarette manufacturers did target children with their advertising. The World Heath Organization estimates that 200–300 million children and young people under the age of 20 today will eventually be killed by tobacco. Clearly, the cigarette industry needs to change decades of socially irresponsible marketing. As a group, discuss and decide whether you would take a high-paying job in the marketing department of a cigarette company? What if it were your only job opportunity?

Internet Questions

1. Pornography, one of the biggest businesses on the Web, naturally attracts the interest of children. Banning such sites is very difficult because it would require enforceable international laws and would not be popular. The most sensible solution is for parents and teachers to monitor the sites that children visit. A survey undertaken by *Family PC* found that 71% of parents say they monitor their children's use of the Internet, but only 26% say they use either built-in or commercial filtering or monitoring software. Imagine you have an easy-to-use monitoring software and operating system that operates on any PC and that tracks the sites that your PC visits. It could be sold on a disk for $3 per unit in bulk to a distributor. How might you use several nonprofit organizations to distribute this product to families with young children for under $10? The alliance has to be consistent with the goals of the organization and would earn badly needed income. It also has to avoid unnecessary controversy.

2. A problem with the Internet is that it is very good at spreading rumors very fast. For example, a rumor started by a "Nancy Markle" accused the artificial sweetener aspartame of causing Alzheimer's disease, birth defects, brain cancer, diabetes, Gulf War syndrome, lupus, multiple sclerosis, and seizures.[24] The site http://urbanlegends.miningco.com presents many other socially irresponsible slanders on the products we use. Reliable health sites such as http://mayoclinic.com, http://www.medhelp.org, http://www.oncolink.org, http://cancer.gov, and http://navigator.tufts.edu give excellent information on nutrition and illnesses. They are required to back up their advice and information with credible scientific research. How can the spread of false or unsubstantiated health claims that create great fear and distress be controlled on the Web? What long-term effect might such rumor-mongering have on Internet use?

CHAPTER CASE

The Great Subliminal Persuasion Lie

Is it fair if companies insert messages such as "Drink Coke" and "Eat Popcorn" into single frames of a motion picture and through such subliminal messages (messages we cannot detect) lead moviegoers like sheep to the theater's overpriced concession counter? Of course not. Such behavior would be outrageous manipulation and very unethical. Vance Packard, the popular 1950s sociologist, used this marketing practice as the central premise of his book *The Hidden Persuaders* (1957), which took modern marketing practices to task for their unethical behavior and lack of social responsibility. The book was a huge hit and was widely talked about in magazines and the broadcast media. It sold millions of copies and seriously damaged the reputation of the advertising and marketing profession. Its sweeping condemnation was picked up uncritically by the popular press and mass media and led several states to pass laws against subliminal persuasion. This manifesto of the manipulative sneakiness used by marketers and the capitalist system is still being taught in high school classrooms.

There is just one "tiny" little problem with this story. It is based on an outrageous lie and libel. The practice of such subliminal persuasion has absolutely no basis in fact. When challenged, Packard and his publisher were never able to document where and when such practices occurred, and cognitive psychologists, in search of notoriety, fame and fortune, have never observed such effects. Even trying their hardest, cognitive psychologists have

only been able to create an occasional barely significant effect in controlled experiments. Vance Packard and his publisher made millions. The image of all-powerful marketing tactics manipulating a vulnerable and gullible customer was indelibly burned into the folklore of American culture. Vance Packard became a rich folk hero, and modern marketing, despite all the wonderful products it has helped bring to the modern world, was vilified. The irony is that one of advertising's biggest social irresponsibilities is not deliberate misuse of its power, but that much deliberate use of its power is ineffective. A lot of money and resources are wasted on ineffective advertising campaigns.

Case Questions

1. Was the publisher of *The Hidden Persuaders* acting ethically when it published this book?
2. Why was the general public so fearful of such marketing tactics in the late 1950s?
3. Some marketers say that claims of subliminal persuasion are ridiculous because of the observed, generally very weak influence of advertising on consumer behavior. Do you agree?

For a review of the lack of evidence, see Timothy E. Moore, "Subliminal Advertising: What You See Is What You Get," *Journal of Marketing* 46 (Spring 1982): 38–47. For an interesting discussion of how the media persists in believing in subliminal messages in advertising and music, see John R. Vokey and J. Don Read, "Subliminal Messages: Between the Devil and the Media," *American Psychologist* (November 1985): 1231–1239.

VIDEO CASE

Timberland's Slogan: Pull on Your Boots and Make a Difference

Timberland makes boots—all kinds of boots, from work boots to hiking boots to mountain biking shoes. They come in all shapes, sizes, and colors. Timberland also churns out backpacks for school children, outerwear, and leather fashion boots for women. Most of these products come at a premium—a pair of hiking boots can cost more than $100. Consumers like the image that Timberland products evoke—love of the outdoors, rugged individuality, health consciousness, and fashion.

But Timberland has taken its product image a step farther, integrating the company with socially responsible activities. Touting the virtues of volunteerism, Timberland encourages both its customers and its employees to give their time and effort to create a better world. "With your boots and your beliefs, you will be able to interact responsibly and comfortably within the natural and social environments that all human beings share," says the company's Web site. In other words, Timberland boots aren't just boots, they are vehicles for good works.

Timberland doesn't just talk the talk; the company walks the walk, in its own boots. Through its Path of Service Program, all full-time Timberland employees receive 40 hours of paid time a year to volunteer within their community. By the year 2000, employees had performed more than 80,000 hours of service. Timberland employees have renovated day-care facilities, cleared hiking trails, cleaned streets, worked at animal shelters, installed playgrounds, and even assisted in hurricane relief efforts. Timberland gives employees a wide range of volunteer options to suit their skills and interests, or they can participate in City Year, a nationwide program designed to get young people more involved in restoring inner-city communities. In addition, Timberland keeps in close contact with various United Way organizations, matching employee volunteers to organizations that need help.

Some Timberland employees take the volunteer mandate even further and head up individual activities. Glenn Myers of New Hampshire spearheaded a fund-raising effort that collected $18,000 in relief for the people of war-torn Kosovo. Timberland matched his efforts, so that a check for $36,000 was presented to the Red Cross. Then Myers offered to temporarily house a Kosovo refugee in his home. When two entire families arrived instead, he and several Timberland coworkers arranged for the families to occupy an apartment. When winter arrived, Myers conducted a clothing drive throughout the Timberland headquarters in Stratham, New Hampshire, and delivered boxes of warm clothing to the Kosovo families. "Timberland believes in the power of the individual," notes the company Web site. "That one voice can and must make a difference." Employees like Glenn Myers take this message to heart.

Timberland is well known for its corporate donations to socially responsible causes, ranging from local events such as a road race to benefit an elementary school parent-teachers organization, to the expansion of a homeless shelter, to its support of the City Year program, which has received more than $10 million from Timberland.

What about Timberland's economic responsibilities? The company now earns more than $800 million per year in revenues and continues to announce growth in revenues. Company president and CEO Jeffrey Swartz notes that the formula for social responsibility works just as well on the bottom line. "I am pleased to report Timberland's fourth consecutive year of record revenue and improved earnings," he stated in 2000. "Results in 1999 reflect Timberland's continued focus on developing a portfolio of businesses that are diversified by product, geography, and channel."

Timberland's careful balance between social responsibility and economic responsibility has earned the company a spot on *Fortune*'s list of 100 best companies to work for. With roughly 4,000 employees worldwide, nearly 49% of whom are women and 31% of whom are minorities, the New Hampshire bootmaker needs to combine a cosmopolitan and local outlook in the way it presents itself to the public. In doing so, the company has managed to sell both its footwear and its social mission in one slogan: "Pull on your boots and make a difference."

Case Questions

1. How well do Timberland's social responsibility activities complement the interests of Timberland's intended target market?
2. How does Timberland use social responsibility to promote its products? Is this ethical? Why or why not?
3. How does Timberland balance its philanthropic actions with its economic responsibilities?
4. As stated in the chapter text, "Socially responsible marketing is the collection of marketing philosophies, policies, procedures, and actions intended to enhance society's welfare." Explore Timberland's Web site (http://www.timberland.com). Does Timberland's site effectively work towards this goal? Explain your answer.

Sources: Timberland Web site, http://www.timberland.com, accessed 16 February 2000.

Kate Barbera, "Reaching Out to the Homeless," *Portsmouth Herald*, 13 February 2000, http://www.seacoastonline.com.

"Timberland Announces Record Fourth Quarter and Full Year Revenue and Earnings," *Business Wire*, 3 February 2000.

"100 Best Companies to Work For," *Fortune*, 10 January 2000, http://www.fortune.com.

"Here and Abroad, People Are Doing Wonders for Relief Effort," *Portsmouth Herald*, 18 November 1999, http://www.seacoastonline.com.

Christine Gillette, "Agency Plans Center," *Portsmouth Herald*, 28 June 1999, http://www.seacoastonline.com.

4

International Marketing

xtra!

**Interactive
Marketing Activity**

*Go to Xtra! to access this
Interactive Marketing Activity at
http://bestpracticesxtra.swlearning.com.*

In the early days of the entertainment industry, movies and television shows from the U.S., backed by large-budget production companies, dominated the world market. In recent years, movies and television shows from different countries are increasingly professional, finding audience support in both their home markets and abroad. Some of these productions are now being customized in one country to meet local preferences in other countries to better meet all audience needs. For example, the Disney Channel show, *Art Attack,* is filmed in a single format,with parts of each show destined for different countries. The show, appearing in 26 different languages, contains some film clips that appear in all show versions and some clips that are only shown in the destination country or region, so that the show appears to be "local."

You Decide. After reading the opening vignette and paying special attention to the sections of this chapter marked with the chess piece, answer these questions:

1. What is the greatest potential proactive reason for marketing movies and television shows internationally?

2. Which international marketing environmental factors probably present the greatest challenge to marketing movies and television shows internationally?

3. Movie and television producers could most effectively implement a globalization approach to international marketing by customizing which marketing-mix element?

© PhotoDisk/GETTY IMAGES

Cultural Imperialism Does Not Sell In International Markets

The dominance of U.S. cultural exports is felt everywhere. In *USA Today*'s 2001 list of top movies, U.S. films took 49 of the top 50 places in a list that included only one non-English-language film, *Crouching Tiger, Hidden Dragon.* Given the marketing power of Hollywood, many are worried that diversity will not survive and that the end result of globalization will be "Americanization." Quite the opposite is actually taking place in the entertainment world and international market for popular culture.

During the initial stages of television in any country, the domestic industry has only fledgling production capabilities, and cheap imports, especially from the United States, tend to fill the time slots. With time, however, homegrown production develops and its market share increases. The top TV show in South Africa is *Generations* (a soap opera); in France, it is *Julie Lescaut* (a police series); and in Brazil, it is *O Clone* (a soap opera). The more the world globalizes, the more people embrace the distinctiveness of their own cultures. U.S. shows do have some appeal in foreign markets, however. Blockbuster Hollywood action movies, cartoons (easy to dub), and certain hit series travel well across cultural barriers. The #1 hit among German teenagers is *Buffy im Bann der Dämonen,* while Chinese children enjoy newly introduced Mickey Mouse cartoons.

Art Attack, an art show for the Disney Channel (which is seen around the world), included 216 episodes shot in 26 different languages. A single format (a set that features oversized paint pots and paint brushes, in fuchsia pink and lime green) is reshaped for each country to give it a local feel. About three-fifths of each show is made up of shared footage: close-ups of the hands of one artist (British). The rest of the show is filmed separately for each country, the heads and shoulders of local presenters seamlessly edited in. Even though the local presenters are all flown into one central studio in the United Kingdom, the show costs only one-third of what it would take to produce separately for each country. Local viewers in each place consider the show to be theirs.

In Europe, U.S. films are the hands-down favorite of moviegoers for several reasons. Hollywood blockbusters, such as *Spiderman* or *Star Wars: Attack of the Clones*, are made with budgets beyond the Europeans' wildest dreams. In addition, spending for marketing has soared, doubling since the mid-1990s to an average of $3.2 million per movie. Finally, U.S. studios depend increasingly on overseas revenues and are investing more to push their movies in foreign markets. Lately, French moviemakers, who have long resented the overwhelming popularity of Hollywood movies on their home turf, have begun to fight back. *Le Fabuleux Destin d'Amélie Poulain*, a French-made romantic comedy, recently recaptured the French box office to the tune of $37.7 million in receipts. It was one of four French films released in 2001 that sold more than five million tickets, beating a record set in 1947. For the first time in decades, French films stood their ground against American imports. With higher budgets and better production values, the new films were created by a wave of young directors with Hollywood experience.

What is even more interesting is that films that are successful in their home markets are also more acceptable to the big-money U.S. market. In 2001, French-language films enjoyed their best year in the United States, grossing $28 million—small by overall standards but a huge improvement over $6.8 million in 2000. The boost in U.S. audience for foreign films in general comes squarely from the youth market, a dramatic change from the art-house crowd of the past. To reach this audience, studios use

VOICE OF THE EXPERT

Michael R. Czinkota and Ilkka A. Ronkainen, Georgetown University

International marketing takes place all around us every day, has a major effect on our lives, and offers new opportunities and challenges. International marketing is necessary because economic isolationism has become impossible. Failure to participate in the global marketplace assures firms and nations of declining economic capability and consumers of a decrease in their standard of living. Successful international marketing, however, holds the promise of higher profits, an improved quality of life, a better society, and, perhaps, due to increased linkages among people, even a more peaceful world.

Within the last three decades, world trade has expanded from $200 billion to almost $7 trillion annually. Trade growth on a global level has outperformed the growth of domestic economies, which has made many countries and firms become participants in international marketing. Every billion dollars of exports supports the creation of 11,500 jobs, and these jobs are usually better paying than those catering purely to domestic customers. Similarly, firms that export have been shown to be more profitable and grow faster than their domestic counterparts.

the Internet as a marketing tool, offering prizes, as well as trailers and synopses.

Top local TV programming created around the world is making its way into the U.S., too. Most shows on Univision, America's Spanish-language TV network, including the hugely popular telenovelas, are made by Mexico's Televisa. The BBC, while expanding its own programming in the U.S., co-produces much of the natural-history content on Discovery. Even Arte, a Franco-German culture channel, is no stranger to American airwaves.

The trade in entertainment is no longer a one-way street that makes all who watch and listen clones of each other. Much of the U.S. content going abroad is adjusted, as is the material coming into the United States. Britain's "Bob the Builder" has hammered his way into U.S. homes having lost his Staffordshire accent. Since its introduction in May 2001, 2.9 million videos of this animated series have been sold.[1]

The objective of this chapter is twofold. First, we discuss the opportunities and challenges that face marketers as they expand into international markets. This chapter is presented early in the text in recognition of the importance of international marketing in today's business world. Secondly, this chapter provides a glimpse of "marketing strategy in action." So far in this textbook, Chapters 1, 2, and 3 have provided the fundamental building blocks of marketing strategy and social responsibility. This chapter reinforces the concepts presented in the first three chapters by demonstrating the importance of modifying marketing strategy to responsibly meet the needs of new, global markets.

LEARNING OBJECTIVE 1

The Nature of International Marketing

International marketing
Is the process of planning and conducting transactions across national borders to create exchanges that satisfy the objectives of individuals and organizations.

International marketing is the process of planning and conducting transactions across national borders to create exchanges that satisfy the objectives of individuals and organizations. International marketing has forms ranging from export-import trade to licensing, franchising, joint ventures, wholly owned subsidiaries, and management contracts.

As this definition indicates, international marketing retains the basic marketing tenets of "satisfaction" and "exchange." The fact that a transaction takes place "across national borders" causes the international marketer to be subject to new sets of environmental forces, to different constraints, and quite frequently to conflicts resulting from different laws, cultures, and societies. The basic principles of marketing strategy still apply, but their implementation, complexity, and intensity may vary substantially. It is in the international marketing field that one can observe most closely the role of marketing as a societal process and as an instrument for the development of socially responsible business strategy. One look at the emerging market economies of central Europe shows some of the many new challenges that confront international marketers. How does the marketing concept fit into these societies? How should distribution systems be organized? How can one get the price mechanism to work? Similarly, in the international areas of social responsibility and ethics, the international marketer is faced with a multicultural environment with differing expectations and often with inconsistent legal systems when it comes to monitoring environmental pollution, maintaining safe working conditions, copying technology, or paying bribes.[2] The ability to master these challenges successfully affords a company the potential for new opportunities and high rewards.

The definition of international marketing also focuses on international transactions. Marketing internationally is an activity that needs to be aggressively pursued. Those who do not actively participate in the transactions are still subject to the changing influences of international marketing. The international marketer is part of the exchange, recognizes the changing nature of transactions, adjusts to a constantly moving target, and reacts to shifts in the business environment. This need for adjustment, for comprehending change, and, in spite of it all, for successfully carrying out transactions highlights the fact that international marketing is as much art as science.

To achieve success in the art of international marketing, it is necessary to be firmly grounded in its scientific aspects. Only then will consumers, policy makers, and business executives be able to incorporate international marketing considerations into their thinking and planning and make decisions based on the answers to such questions as:

1. How will my product fit into the international market?
2. What marketing-mix adjustments are or will be necessary?
3. What threats from global competition should I expect?
4. How can these threats be turned into opportunities?

The integration of international dimensions into each decision made by individuals and by firms can make international markets a source of growth, profit, and needs/wants satisfaction, and can also lead to a higher quality of life.

Opportunities in International Marketing

To prosper in a world of abrupt changes, newly emerging forces and dangers, and unforeseen influences from abroad, firms need to prepare themselves and develop active responses. New strategies need to be envisioned, new plans need to be made, and the way of doing business needs to be changed. To remain players in the world economy, governments, firms, and individuals need to respond aggressively with innovation, process improvements, and creativity.

The growth of international marketing activities offers increased opportunities. By integrating knowledge from around the globe, an international firm can build and strengthen its competitive position. Firms that depend heavily on long production runs can expand their activities far beyond their domestic markets and benefit from reaching many more customers. Market saturation can be avoided by lengthening or rejuvenating product life cycles in other countries. Plants can be shifted from one country to another, and suppliers can be found on every continent. Cooperative agreements can be formed that enable all parties to bring their major strengths to the table and emerge with better products than they could produce on their own. In addition, research has found that firms that export grow faster, are more productive, and have employees who tend to earn more.[3] At the same time, international marketing enables customers all over the world to find greater varieties of products at lower prices and to improve their lifestyles and comfort.

Competitive Forces

Many newly founded firms are global from the very beginning, giving rise to the term *"born global."* With the advent of electronic process technology, these smaller players are able to compete on price and quality—often with greater flexibility.

A Ukrainian Big Mac® sandwich is made from ingredients from all over the world. McDonald's relies on overseas operations, like the one in the Ukraine, to generate half of its sales.

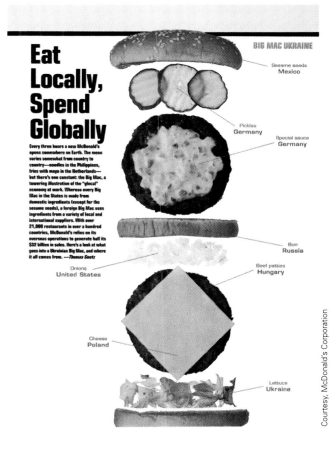

Courtesy, McDonald's Corporation

Challenges in International Marketing

International opportunities require careful exploration and an awareness of global developments, an understanding of their meaning, and a development of the ability to adjust to change. Firms must adapt to their international markets if they are to be successful.

Many firms do not participate in the global market. Often, managers believe that international marketing should only be carried out by large multinational corporations. It is true that there are some very large players from many countries active in the world market, as shown in Figure 4.1. But smaller firms are major players, too. For example, nearly 97% of U.S. exporters are small and medium-sized enterprises.[4]

Those firms and industries that do not participate in the world market have to recognize that in today's trade environment, isolation has become impossible. Today, most firms and individuals are affected directly or indirectly by economic and political developments that occur in the international marketplace. Those firms that refuse to participate are relegated to react to the global marketplace, and therefore are unprepared for harsh competition from abroad.

Figure 4.1	The World's Largest Publicly Held Manufacturing Companies		
Rank	**Company**	**Headquarters**	**Revenues ($ millions)**
1	Exxon Mobil	US	204,506.0
2	General Motors	US	186,763.0
3	Royal Dutch/Shell Group	UK/Netherlands	179,431.0
4	BP	UK	178,721.0
5	Ford Motor	US	162,586.0
6	DaimlerChrysler	Germany	156,135.0
7	General Electric	US	131,698.0
8	Toyota Motor	Japan	126,002.0
9	Total Fina Elf	France	107,031.0
10	Chevron Texaco	US	99,049.0
11	Volkswagen	Germany	95,075.0
12	Siemens	Germany	89,075.0
13	IBM	US	81,186.0
14	Philip Morris	US	80,408.0
15	Verizon Communications	US	67,625.0
16	Hitachi	Japan	66,676.0
17	Nestlé	Switzerland	65,346.0
18	Fiat	Italy	64,013.0
19	Sony	Japan	63,210.0
20	Honda Motor	Japan	61,410.0
21	Vivendi Universal	France	59,872.0
22	Matsushita Electric Industrial	Japan	57,358.0
23	ConocoPhillips	US	57,224.0
24	Hewlett-Packard	US	56,588.0
25	Peugeot	France	55,223.0
26	Boeing	US	54,069.0
27	Merck & Co.	US	51,790.0
28	Nissan Motor	Japan	51,689.0
29	Eni	Italy	51,148.0
30	Unilever Group	UK	50,384.0

Source: Data compiled from http://www.industryweek.com/iwinprint/iw1000/2003/database/iw03Enter.asp accessed 16 October 2003.

The International Marketing Environment

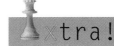

International environmental forces will have similar, but most likely more powerful, impacts on the development of international marketing strategies when compared to purely domestic ones. Not only are these international environments different from the domestic ones, but they usually differ considerably between individual country markets (or even within them). Key international environments are the sociocultural and political/legal environments.

Sociocultural Environment

The cultural environment of a country includes its languages, values, and attitudes. Marketing managers need to account for these cultural factors when developing marketing strategies. In addition, the marketer needs to consider how these factors shape customer behavior and affect the implementation of marketing programs in individual markets and across markets. When *Sesame Street* expanded into international markets, the program was adapted by local producers to reflect local language, customs, and educational systems.[5] The Russian version of *Sesame Street* is 70% locally produced and features Aunt Dash, a quintessential Russian character who lives in a traditional cottage and spouts folklore and homespun wisdom. The creators of the joint Israeli-Palestinian production hope that the exploits of Dafi, a purple Israeli Muppet, and Haneen, an orange Palestinian one, will help teach mutual respect and understanding by exposing children to each other's culture and breaking down stereotypes. The name of the show has also been changed to *Sesame Stories,* since a street is considered an unsafe place to play. A new Muppet recently introduced in the South African edition reflects the reality in that country, where one in every nine people is afflicted with AIDS. These adaptations were made to *Sesame Street* so it would appeal to local markets.

The international marketer is a **change agent** trying to impress on a local consumer the need to adopt a new product. The propensity to change will be a function of (1) customers' cultural lifestyles in terms of how deeply held their traditional beliefs and attitudes are, and also which elements of culture are dominant; (2) the power of opinion leaders and change agents themselves; and (3) communication about new concepts from sources ranging from reference groups and government to commercial media.[6]

Change agent
Is a person or institution that facilitates change in a firm or in a host country.

It has been argued that differences in cultural lifestyle can be accounted for by four dimensions of culture. These dimensions consist of the following:

- **Degree of individualism**—the extent to which individual interests prevail over group interests.
- **Level of equality**—the extent to which less powerful members accept that power is distributed equally.
- **Uncertainty avoidance**—the degree to which people feel threatened by ambiguous situations and have created beliefs and institutions to try to avoid these feelings.
- **Material achievement**—the extent to which the dominant values in society are success, money, and personal possessions.[7]

For example, northern Europe features very high individualism, high equality, low uncertainty avoidance, and low focus on material achievement. For a marketing manager, this means there will be relatively low resistance to new products, strong consumer desire for novelty and variety, and high consumer regard for environmentally friendly and socially conscious solutions.[8] Similar analyses can and should be performed for markets and regions targeted for marketing action.

To foster cultural sensitivity and acceptance of new ways of doing things within the organization, management must institute internal training programs. These programs may include (1) culture-specific information (e.g., data in the form of video packs or

© Mitchell Gerber/CORBIS

Sesame Street's Big Bird is popular around the world and is known by children in over 140 countries. In China, new characters were added to Sesame Street to reflect local color, including Little Berry, "Xiao Mei."

culturegrams covering other countries); (2) general cultural information (e.g., values, practices, and assumptions in countries other than one's own); and (3) self-specific information that involves finding out one's own cultural paradigm, including values, assumptions, and perceptions about others.[9] The Internet can also play a role in preparing marketing people for the international marketplace. While it cannot replace real-life interaction as an experiential tool, Web-based training can provide materials such as detailed scenarios and relevant exercises tied to the learner's background.[10]

These cultural dimensions can be looked at not only as a challenge but also as an opportunity to make the marketer's efforts more effective, not only in one market but throughout the world. The Dockers® line of casual wear originated at Levi Strauss's Argentine unit and was applied to loosely cut pants by Levi's Japanese subsidiary. The company's U.S. operation later adopted both, making Dockers® the leading brand in the category. Similar success has followed in more than 40 countries' markets entered since the mid-1980s.[11] Suggestions on how culture can be used as a marketing tool are provided in Figure 4.2.

In addition to understanding cultural forces, an international marketer needs to understand a country's socioeconomic environment, particularly the age distribution of the population, income, and economic infrastructure. Part of this analysis includes studying population projections in specific geographic locations and analyzing their possible implications. For example, the total population of industrialized countries (Japan, the United States, western Europe) is leveling off and is aging. This is good news for marketers. Consumers in the 45- to 55-year-old age group are among the most affluent consumers of all, having reached the peak of their personal earnings potential. Emerging markets (such as Brazil, China, and India) will soon have the majority of their huge populations in prime working age, driving both economic and consumption growth. For example, the Coca-Cola Company now derives 37% of its revenue from Africa, Asia, and Latin America, and these markets contribute 49% of its operating profits. Low per-capita incomes should not deter marketing efforts. Unilever learned that low-income Indians, usually forced to settle for low-quality products, wanted to buy high-end detergents and personal-care products but could not afford them in the available formats. In response, the company developed extremely low-cost packaging material and other innovations that allowed the distribution of single-use sachets costing the equivalent of pennies rather than the $5 regular-sized containers. Having the same brand on both product formats built long-term loyalty for the company.[12]

Another socioeconomic factor that should be studied by international marketers is the number of women in the paid workforce. Women who work outside the home create a demand for labor-saving devices, packaged and prepared foods, and household services. Working women typically have smaller households and greater disposable income. Infrastructure will also determine market opportunity. The diffusion of Internet technology into consumer lifestyles has been rapid, with the number of users evening out around the globe. Computers priced at less than $500 will boost ownership and subsequent online potential. Developments in television, cable, phone, and wireless technologies not only will make the market broader but also will enable more services to be delivered more efficiently. For example, with the advent of third-generation mobile communications technology, systems will have a 100-fold increase in data transfer, allowing the viewing of videos on mobile phones.

Making Culture Work for Marketing Success   **Figure 4.2**

Culture should not be viewed as a challenge but as an opportunity that can be exploited. This requires, as has been shown in this chapter, an understanding of the differences and their fundamental determinants. Differences can quite easily be dismissed as indicators of inferiority or approaches to be changed; however, the opposite may actually be the case. The following rules serve as a summary of how culture and its appreciation may serve as a tool to ensure marketing success.

- **Embrace local culture.** Many corporate credos include a promise to be the best possible corporate citizens in every community in which the company operates. For example, in 3M's plant near Bangkok, Thailand, a Buddhist shrine, wreathed in flowers, pays homage to the spirits that Thais believe took care of the land prior to the plant's arrival. Showing sensitivity to local customs helps local acceptance and builds employee morale. More importantly, it contributes to a deeper understanding of the market and keeps the marketer from inadvertently doing something to alienate constituents.

- **Build relationships.** Each market has its own unique set of constituents who need to be identified and nurtured. Establishing and nurturing local ties at the various stages of the market-development cycle develops relationships, which can be invaluable in expansion and countering political risk. 3M started its preparations for entering the China market soon after President Nixon's historic visit in 1972. For 10 years, company officials visited Beijing and entertained visits of Chinese officials to company headquarters in Minneapolis-St. Paul. Such efforts paid off in 1984, when the Chinese government made 3M the first wholly owned venture in the market. Many such emerging markets require long-term commitment on the part of the marketer.

- **Employ locals to gain cultural knowledge.** The single best way to understand a market is to grow with it by developing the human resources and business partnerships along the way. Of the 7,500 3M employees in Asia, fewer than 10 are from the United States. As a matter of fact, of the 34,000 3M employees outside of the United States, fewer than 1% are expatriates. The rest are locals who know the local customs and purchasing habits of their compatriots. In every way possible, locals are made equals with their U.S. counterparts. For example, grants are made available for 3M employees to engage in the product-development process with concepts and idea development.

- **Help employees understand you.** Employing locals will give a marketer a valuable asset in market development; i.e., in acculturation. However, these employees also need their own process of adjustment (i.e., "corporatization") to be effective. At any given time, more than 30 of 3M's Asian technicians are in the United States, where they learn the latest product and process advances while gaining insight into how the company works. Also, they are able to develop personal ties with people they work with. Furthermore, they often contribute by infusing their insights into company plans. Similar schemes are in place for distributors. Distributor advisory councils allow intermediaries to share their views with the company.

- **Adapt products and processes to local markets.** Nowhere is commitment to local markets as evident as in product offerings. Global, regional, and purely local products are called for and constant and consistent product-development efforts on a market-by-market basis are warranted to find the next global success. When the sales of 3M's famous Scotch-Brite® cleaning pads were languishing, company researchers interviewed housewives and domestic help to determine why. Traditionally, floors are scrubbed with rough coconut shells. 3M responded by making its cleaning pads brown and shaping them like a foot. In China, a big seller for 3M is a composite to fill tooth cavities. In the United States, dentists pack a soft material into the cavity and blast it with a special beam of light, making it as hard as enamel in a matter of seconds. In China, dentists cannot afford this technology. The solution was an air-drying composite with similar effects in a matter of minutes. However, its relative expense is minimal.

- **Coordinate by region.** The transfer of best practice is critical, especially in areas that have cultural similarities. When 3M designers in Singapore discovered that customers used its Nomad™ household mats in their cars, they spread the word to their counterparts throughout Asia. The company encourages its product managers from different parts of Asia to hold regular periodic meetings and share insights and strategies. The goal of this cross-pollination is to come up with regional programs and "Asianize" or even globalize a product more quickly. Joint endeavors build cross-border *esprit de corps*, especially when managers may have their own markets' interests primarily at heart.

Sources: For corporate codes of conduct, see, for example, Johnson & Johnson's credo at http://www.jnj.com/our_company/our_credo/index.htm; 3M examples are adopted from John R. Engen, "Far Eastern Front," *World Trade*, December 1994, 20–24. See also "3M Operational Facts, Year-End 2002," available at http://www.mmm.com.

A significant factor influencing international marketing is economic integration. Some countries enter into trade relationships with other nations to facilitate exchange among member countries and provide larger markets for member-country companies. These relationships include bilateral trade agreements (such as between

How does a small business enter into worldwide markets that demand its products? How does a sales staff of only three people serve clients across the globe with efficiency and a personal touch? The answer comes in the form of e-commerce, the digital-age solution to international marketing.

Evertek Computer Corporation is a San Diego-based company that sells new and refurbished computers and parts in more than 80 countries worldwide. The 12-year-old company has undertaken some export sales since its earliest days and these sales now comprise 20% of its total revenues.

The key to Evertek's success has been its well-established sales network, whose centerpiece is an e-commerce web site that loads rapidly, provides real-time inventory, and allows potential new distributors to fill out an online application. The success of this site relies on the hands-on sales approach of John Ortley, Evertek's International Sales Manager, who writes countless personal e-mails a day to current and potential clients and spends hours on the phone fostering relationships with every one of his clients.

Ortley enhanced his already thriving sales network by becoming a member of BuyUSA.com (**http://www.buyusa. com**), an e-commerce Web site backed by the powerful guarantee of the U.S. government. The Web site, which represents many U.S. businesses interested in promoting their goods and services abroad, serves 90 countries and over 20,000 customers. BuyUSA.com also promotes Evertek at overseas information technology trade shows.

Evertek requires that buyers pay in advance before their products are shipped. However, many of Evertek's customers operate in emerging markets, and cannot afford to pay in advance and risk losing that money. BuyUSA.com, backed by the U.S. government, promises customers that their investment will not be lost. If they do not receive the promised products, they can contact their local U.S. Embassy's commercial section for help.

Evertek has established a successful sales network and has grown its revenues considerably, thanks to export sales. This has all been due, in large part, to the growing global demand for Evertek's competitively priced computers and parts. However, Evertek's products would not be available were it not for the appropriate sales strategy it has adopted: Clients worldwide, from developing to industrialized nations, are quickly connecting to the Internet, taking advantage of the convenience and reliability of e-commerce Web sites like BuyUSA.com. Says Ortley, "We are an e-commerce business and we're thriving. The world is shrinking, and it's getting easier and less expensive to do business on a global basis."

Source: "A San Diego Company Uses the Internet to Go Global." U.S. Commercial Service, About What's New 081802, *http://www.usatrade.gov/website.nsf/ WebBySubj/Main_WhatsNew081802*, accessed 25 October 2002.

Chile and Canada), free-trade areas (such as the North American Free Trade Agreement [NAFTA]), common markets (such as the Southern Cone Common Market [MERCOSUR]), and economic unions (such as the European Union [EU]). Membership in these agreements lowers barriers and increases access to new markets. In more advanced stages of economic integration, the regulation of marketing environments is standardized and participating countries share a common currency. In 2002, 12 members of the EU launched the euro as the EU's official currency. This makes marketers' operations easier due to a standardized currency, but at the same time competitively more challenging as more member-country companies compete for the same clients. Figure 4.3 shows the members of the European Union, MERCOSUR, and NAFTA.

Figure 4.3	Members of the European Union, MERCOSUR, and NAFTA				
	European Union Members*			**MERCOSUR** **Members**	**NAFTA** **Members**
	France	Germany	Italy	Argentina	United States
	Belgium	Netherlands	Luxembourg	Brazil	Canada
	Great Britain	Portugal	Greece	Uruguay	Mexico
	Ireland	Denmark	Spain	Paraguay	
	Austria	Finland	Sweden		

*Additional 10 countries to join in 2004: Cyprus, Czech Republic, Estonia, Hungary, Latvia, Lithuania, Malta, Poland, Slovakia, and Slovenia

Political/Legal Environment

Political and legal forces often play a critical role in international marketing activities. Even the best business plans can go awry as a result of unexpected political or legal influences, and the failure to anticipate these factors can be the undoing of an otherwise successful business venture.

Of course, a single international political and legal environment does not exist. The business executive must be aware of political and legal factors on a variety of levels. For example, although it is useful to understand the complexities of the host-country legal system, such knowledge does not protect against a home country's imposed export embargo.

Many laws and regulations not designed specifically to address international marketing issues can have a major impact on a firm's opportunities abroad. Minimum wage legislation, for example, affects the international competitive position of a firm using production processes that are highly labor-intensive. Other legal and regulatory measures, however, are clearly aimed at international marketing activities. Some may be designed to assist firms in their international efforts, while others may protect the international marketer from adverse activity in another country. For example, the U.S. government is quite concerned about the lack of safeguards on intellectual property rights in China, where counterfeiting of CDs, books, and films is widespread. *Intellectual property rights* provide protection to patents, copyrights, and trademarks, and ban illegal copying or counterfeiting. Counterfeiting includes selling inferior products sold under fake logos. Ultimately, this activity may damage the reputation of the company and reduce the chances that an innovative firm can recoup its investment in research and development through the sale of newly spawned products. In 2002, when China joined the **World Trade Organization** (**WTO**), the institution that administers international trade and investment accords, it agreed to honor the legal ground rules for international trade, which include safeguards on intellectual property rights. It is expected that the problems of imitation and theft will decrease as a result.

Countries differ in their laws, as well as in their use of these laws. For example, in the United States, institutions and individuals are quick to take a case to court. As a result, court battles are often protracted and costly, and simply the threat of a court case can reduce marketing opportunities. In contrast, Japan's legal tradition tends to minimize the role of the law and lawyers.

From an international business perspective, the two major legal systems worldwide can be categorized into common law and code law. **Common law** is based on tradition and depends less on written statutes and codes than on precedent and custom. Common law originated in England and is the system of law found today in the United States. On the other hand, **code law** is based on a comprehensive set of written statutes. Countries with code law try to explicitly spell out all possible legal rules. Code law is based on Roman law and is found in the majority of the nations of the world. In general, countries with the code law system have much more rigid laws than those with the common law system. In the latter, courts adopt precedents and customs to fit the cases, allowing the marketer a better idea of the basic judgment likely to be rendered in new situations.

Although broad in theory, the differences between code law and common law, and their impact on the international marketer, are not always as broad in practice. For example, many common-law countries, including the United States, have adopted commercial codes to govern the conduct of business.

Host countries may adopt a number of laws that affect a company's ability to market, including laws affecting the entry of goods, such as tariffs and quotas. Also in this category are **antidumping laws**, which prohibit below-cost sales of products, and laws that require export and import licensing. In addition, many countries have health and safety standards that may, by design or by accident, restrict the entry of foreign goods.

World Trade Organization (WTO)
Is the institution that administers international trade and investment accords. It supplanted the General Agreement on Tariffs and Trade (GATT) in 1995.

Common law
Is based on tradition and depends less on written statutes and codes than on precedent and custom.

Code law
Is based on a comprehensive set of written statutes.

Antidumping laws
Are designed to help domestic industries injured by unfair competition from abroad due to imports being sold at less than fair value.

Political and Legal Forces

In Egypt, foreign motion pictures are subject to a screen quota, and a distributor may import only five prints of a foreign film.[13]

Other laws may be designed to protect domestic industries. For example, some governments restrict foreign investment for projects that are not in line with national economic development goals. For example, the Egyptian government places limits on foreign equity in construction, insurance, and transport services. In addition, the employment of nonnationals is restricted to 10% of the personnel employed by a company.

Very specific legislation may also exist to regulate where a firm can advertise or what constitutes deceptive advertising. Many countries prohibit specific claims by marketers comparing their product to that of the competition and restrict the use of promotional devices. Some countries regulate the names of companies or the foreign-language content of a product's label.

International law plays an important role in the conduct of international business. Although no enforceable body of international law exists, certain treaties and agreements, respected by a number of countries, profoundly influence international business operations. The World Trade Organization defines internationally acceptable economic practices for its member nations. Although it does not directly affect individual firms, it does influence them indirectly by providing a more stable and predictable international market environment.

Sociocultural Forces

Opportunities and costs of market entry are often tied to distance beyond geography. Common language increases trade between two countries by 200%, common currency by 340%, and common membership in a trading bloc by 330%.

Selecting an International Market

When a firm decides to expand into the international marketplace, it needs to determine which countries offer the best opportunity for success. The process of evaluating countries and selecting those with the highest market and sales potential is called *target market selection*. In addition to identifying the international market, the firm needs to determine if its market-expansion strategy involves expanding into a small number of markets or into a large, diverse number of markets.

Screening and Identifying International Markets

A four-stage process is used to screen and analyze international markets, as illustrated in Figure 4.4. The process begins by using general criteria to evaluate a country's market and sales potential. This information may include demographics, income distribution, population size, etc. This type of information is called *secondary data* because it is available from many published sources and Web sites. Later in the process, when the marketer needs answers to specific questions about a target market, primary data will be required. As will be described in Chapter 5, *primary data* answer questions that secondary data do not and include information collected for the first time.

The four-stage process used to screen and analyze international markets includes these steps:

Stage One: Conduct preliminary screening. The preliminary screening process relies on existing data about the country, industry, and current products on the market. Country-specific factors typically include those that indicate the market's overall buying power, such as population, gross national product in total and per capita, and total exports and imports. Product-specific factors narrow the analysis to the marketer's operations. A company such as Motorola, manufacturing for the automobile aftermarket, is interested in the number of passenger cars, trucks, and buses in use. The statistical analyses must be accompanied by qualitative assessments of the impact of cultural elements and the overall climate for foreign firms and products. Internally, the marketer must decide on the strategic fit of a market as well. In some cases, an individual market may not be attractive in its own right but may have some other significance, such as being the home market of the most demanding customers (thereby aiding in product development) or being the home market of a significant competitor (presenting a preemptive rationale for entry). Furthermore, the

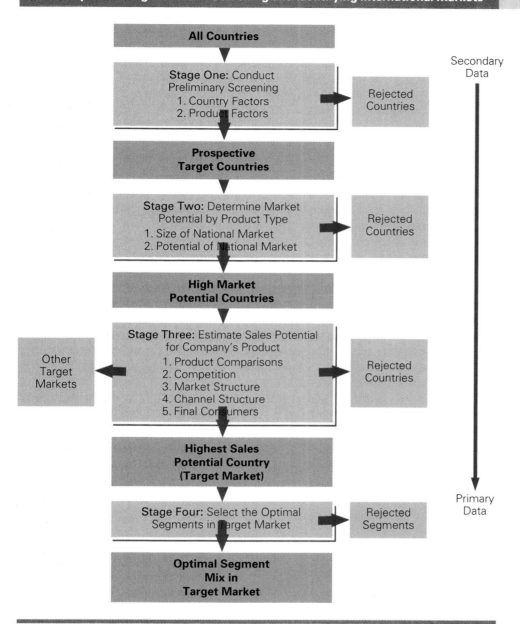

Four-Step Screening Process in Screening and Identifying International Markets   Figure 4.4

time dimension will have to be incorporated into the analysis. An insignificant market may turn into an emerging market, and those with a foothold may reap the benefits.

Stage Two: Determine total market potential. Total *market potential* is the sales, in physical units or in monetary terms, that might be available to all marketers in an industry. The marketing manager needs to assess the size of existing markets and forecast their future growth. Two general approaches are used. *Analytical techniques* based on the use of existing data include using indexes to measure potential through proxy variables that have been shown (by research or by intuition) to correlate closely with the demand for a product. For example, an index for consumer goods might involve population, disposable personal income, and retail sales in the market concerned. In addition to quantitative techniques, marketers use various survey techniques. These are especially useful when marketing new technologies. A survey of end-user interest and responses may provide a relatively clear picture of the possibilities in a new market. A second commonly used approach to assess the size of existing markets is *estimating by analogy*—where demand patterns in one market are expected to repeat themselves in other markets as a function of indicators such as disposable income.

Stage Three: Estimate sales potential. *Sales potential* is the share of the market potential that the marketer can reasonably expect to gain in the long run. To arrive at an estimate, the marketer needs to collect data on perceptions of the product (as far as its relative advantage, compatibility, ease of use, trialability, and the extent to which it lends itself to word-of-mouth communication); competition (its strength and likely responses); market factors (such as barriers to entry); channel structure (including access and support of intermediaries such as wholesalers and retailers); and final consumers (their ability and willingness to buy something new and non-local). The marketer's questions can never be fully answered until the commitment has been made to enter the market and operations have commenced. The mode of entry has special significance in determining the final level of sales potential.

Stage Four: Select the optimal segment within the target market. Once a market has been selected, the marketer must further define the portion of the market it will reach with its product. Therefore, further refinement of the market is required. Some of the information that may be useful in narrowing the market includes data about the wants, resources, geographical location, attitudes, and buying practices of consumers. Initially, the decision may be made to enter one or only a few segments (e.g., major coastal cities in China, the government market, or the premium-priced segment) and later expand to others.

Choosing a Concentration or Diversification Strategy

Diversification strategy
Is the market-development strategy that involves expansion to a relatively large number of markets.

Concentration strategy
Is the market-development strategy that involves focusing expansion on a smaller number of markets.

When Amazon.com (http://www.amazon.com) decided to expand into the global marketplace, it chose to launch its online bookstore in five countries—Germany, Japan, the United Kingdom, France, and Canada. By selecting this large number of markets, Amazon.com chose a diversification strategy. A **diversification strategy** is the market development strategy that involves expansion to a relatively large number of markets. On the other hand, a **concentration strategy** focuses on a small number of markets.[14] The decision to concentrate or diversify is driven by market factors such as market growth, sales stability, competitive lead time, and extent of restraints. The decision may be driven by marketing-mix-related factors, such as the extent to which the same mix can be used across borders. Finally, the diversification strategy may be based on company factors that include resources available and the level of direct control the marketer wants to exert on local operations.

Both concentration and diversification strategies are applicable to market segments or to mass markets, depending on the marketer's resource commitment. One option is a *dual-concentration strategy,* in which efforts are focused on a specific segment in a limited number of countries. This option is ideal for small firms or firms that sell market-specialized products to clearly defined markets, such as ocean-capable sailboats. *Dual-diversification* strategy is an option where a firm markets to most segments in most available markets. This strategy is frequently used by large consumer-products companies, like General Electric, that have abundant resources to support large market coverage.

LEARNING OBJECTIVE 4

The Internationalization Process

Initiating international marketing activities takes the firm in an entirely new direction, quite different from adding a product line or hiring a few more people. Going international means that a fundamental strategic change is taking place. The first step in developing international commitment is to become aware of international marketing opportunities. Management may then decide to enter the international marketplace on a limited basis and evaluate the results of the initial activities. An international business orientation develops over time. This section looks at the major motivations and strategies for expanding a business across national borders.

Management's Role in International Expansion

The type and quality of a firm's management are key to whether and how it will enter the international marketplace. Management dynamism and commitment are crucial in the first steps toward international operations.[15] Conversely, the managers of firms that are unsuccessful or inactive internationally usually exhibit a lack of determination or devotion to international marketing. The issue of *managerial commitment* is a critical one because foreign market penetration requires a vast amount of market development activity, sensitivity toward foreign environments, research, and innovation. It can take as long as two years for a novice firm to successfully complete its first export order. Therefore, a high level of export commitment is of key importance to endure occasional setbacks and failures.[16]

Motivations to Go Abroad

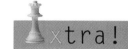

A variety of motivations can push and pull individuals and firms along the international path. An overview of the major motivations that have been found to make firms go international is provided in Figure 4.5. Proactive motivations represent firm-initiated strategic change. Reactive motivations describe actions that result in a firm's response and adaptation to changes imposed by the outside environment. In other words, firms with proactive motivations go international because they want to; those with reactive motivations do so because they have to.

Proactive Motivations

Profits are the major proactive motivation for international marketing. Management may perceive international sales as a potential source of higher profit margins or of more added-on profits. Of course, the profitability perceived when planning to go international is often quite different from the profitability actually obtained. In international start-up operations, initial profitability may be quite low, particularly since unexpected influences, such as shifts in exchange rates, can change the profit picture substantially.

Unique products or a technological advantage can be another major stimulus. A firm may produce products that are not widely available from competitors. The global expansion of H&M clothiers serves as an example of a firm with unique products and an approach that has met with success around the world. Special knowledge about foreign customers or market situations may be another proactive stimulus. Such knowledge may result from particular insights by a firm, special contacts an

Political and Legal Forces

Governments provide a wide array of support to exporters through promotional activities such as information and assistance in assessing readiness to go abroad and financing to help keep exports competitive, as well as environmental facilitation by intervening on behalf of firms to ensure market entry and a level playing field.

Major Motivations to Internationalize Small and Medium-Sized Firms		Figure 4.5

Proactive	Reactive
Profit advantage	Competitive pressures
Unique products	Overproduction
Technological advantage	Declining domestic sales
Exclusive information	Excess capacity
Economies of scale	Saturated domestic markets
	Proximity to customers and ports

Source: Michael R. Czinkota, Ilkka A. Ronkainen, and Michael H. Moffett, *International Business, Update 2003* (Mason, OH: South-Western, 2003), 279. Reprinted with permission of South-Western, a division of Thomson Learning: www.thomsonrights.com. Fax 800-730-2215.

individual may have, in-depth research, or simply from being in the right place at the right time (for example, recognizing a good business situation during a vacation trip).

One major proactive motivation involves economies of scale. International activities may enable the firm to increase its output and therefore ride more rapidly on the learning curve. The Boston Consulting Group has shown that the doubling of output can reduce production costs by up to 30%. Increased production for international markets can therefore help to reduce the cost of production for domestic sales and make the firm more competitive domestically as well.

Reactive Motivations

Reactive motivations occur when a firm enters the international market because it is responding to environmental forces rather than attempting to blaze new trails. Competitive pressures are one example of a reactive motivation. For example, General Mills agreed on a marketing alliance with Nestlé to retain its position in the world marketplace versus Kellogg's. A company may fear losing domestic market share to competing firms that benefit from the economies of scale gained through international marketing activities.

Overproduction can result in international activities. During downturns in the domestic business cycle, foreign markets have historically provided an ideal outlet for excess inventories. International expansion motivated by overproduction usually does not represent full commitment by management, but rather a safety-valve activity. As soon as domestic demand returns to previous levels, international activities are curtailed or even terminated.

Declining domestic sales or a saturated domestic market have a similar motivating effect. Firms may attempt to prolong the product life cycle by expanding the market. Excess capacity can also be a powerful motivator. If equipment for production is not fully used, firms may see expansion abroad as an ideal way to achieve broader distribution of fixed costs.

Physical and psychological closeness to the international market can often play a major role in the international marketing activities of the firm. For example, a firm established near a border may not even perceive itself as going abroad if it does business in the neighboring country. Except for some firms close to the Canadian or Mexican border, however, this factor is much less prevalent in the United States than in many other nations. Most European firms automatically go abroad simply because their neighbors are so close.

In general, firms that are most successful in international markets tend to be motivated by proactive—that is, firm internal—factors. Proactive firms are also frequently more service-oriented than reactive firms. Furthermore, proactive firms are more marketing-strategy-oriented than reactive firms, which have operational issues as their major concern.

Alternative Entry Strategies

The key entry strategies used by the majority of firms to initiate international business activities are indirect exporting and importing, direct exporting and importing, licensing, and franchising. Once firms are established in the international market, other modes of expansion are used, such as direct foreign investment, joint ventures, and contract manufacturing.

Indirect Exporting and Importing

International intermediaries
Are marketing institutions that facilitate the movement of goods and services between the originator and the customer.

Indirect exporting and importing means that the firm participates in international marketing through an **international intermediary** and does not deal directly with foreign customers or firms. While such indirect activities represent a form of international market entry, they are unlikely to result in growing management commitment to international markets or increased capabilities in serving them.

Many firms are indirect exporters and importers without their knowledge. As an example, merchandise can be sold to a domestic firm that in turn sells it abroad. This is most frequently the case when smaller suppliers deliver products to large multi-national corporations, which use them as input to their international sales. Foreign buyers may purchase products locally and send them to their home country. At the same time, many firms that perceive themselves as buying domestically may in reality be buying imported products. They may have long-standing relations with a domestic supplier who, because of cost and competitive pressures, has begun to find sources for products abroad rather than produce them domestically. In this case, the buying firm has become an indirect importer.

Direct Exporting and Importing

Firms that opt to export or import directly have more opportunities ahead of them. They learn the competitive advantages of their products more quickly and can therefore expand more rapidly. They also have the ability to control their international activities better and can forge relationships with their trading partners, which can lead to further international growth and success.

However, these firms faced obstacles avoided by those that indirectly access international markets. These hurdles include identifying and targeting foreign suppliers and/or customers and finding retail space, processes that can be very costly and time-consuming. Some firms overcome such barriers through the use of intermediaries or "storeless" distribution networks (such as mail-order catalogs and Web sites).

International Intermediaries

Both direct and indirect importers and exporters frequently make use of intermediaries that can assist with troublesome yet important details, such as documentation, financing, and transportation. Intermediaries also can identify foreign suppliers and customers and help the firm with long- or short-term market-penetration efforts. Two major types of international intermediaries are export management companies and trading companies.

Export management companies (EMCs) specialize in performing international business services as commission representatives or as distributors. EMCs have two primary forms of operation: They take title to goods and operate internationally on their own account, or they perform services as agents. They often serve a variety of clients; thus, their mode of operation may vary from client to client and from transaction to transaction. An EMC may act as an agent for one client and as a distributor for another. It may even act as both for the same client on different occasions. An **agent** is a marketing intermediary that does not take title to the products, but develops marketing strategy and establishes contacts abroad.

When working as an agent, the EMC is primarily responsible for developing foreign business and sales strategies and establishing contacts abroad. Because the EMC does not share in the profits from a sale, it depends heavily on high sales volume, on which it charges commission. EMCs that have specific expertise in selecting markets because of language capabilities, previous exposure, or specialized contacts appear to be the ones most successful and useful in aiding client firms in their international marketing efforts.

An EMC may also serve as a **distributor**, a marketing intermediary that purchases products from the domestic firm, takes title, and assumes the trading risk. Selling in its own name, it has the opportunity to reap greater profits than when acting as an agent. The potential for greater profit is appropriate, because the EMC has drastically reduced the risk for the domestic firm while increasing its own risk. The domestic firm selling to the EMC is in the comfortable position of having sold its merchandise without having to deal with the complexities of the international market, but it is less likely to gather much international expertise.

A second major intermediary is the **trading company**, a marketing intermediary that exports, imports, countertrades, invests, and manufactures. Today, the most

Export management companies (EMCs)
Specialize in performing international services as commissioned representatives or as distributors.

Agent
Is a marketing intermediary that does not take title to products, but instead develops marketing strategy and establishes contacts abroad.

Distributor
Is a marketing intermediary that purchases products from the domestic firm and assumes the trading risk.

Trading company
Is a marketing intermediary that undertakes exporting, importing, countertrading, investing, and manufacturing.

Nike Investments: Global Working Conditions

Nike, the footwear company, is based in Beaverton, Oregon. One hundred percent of its footwear is produced by subcontractors, most of them outside the United States. Nike's own people focus on the services part of the production process, including design, product development, marketing, and distribution. For example, through its "Futures" inventory control system, Nike knows exactly what it needs to order early enough to plan production accordingly. This avoids excess inventory and assures better prices from its subcontractors.

To achieve both stability and flexibility in its supplier relationships, Nike has three distinct groups of subcontractors in its network:

- Developed partners, the most important group, participate in joint product development and concentrate on the production of the newest designs. Traditionally, they have been located in the People's Republic of China and the Republic of China but, given rising labor costs, some of the more labor-intensive activities have been moved out to countries with lower labor costs.
- The second group of Nike's suppliers are called developing sources and offer low labor costs and the opportunity for Nike to diversify assembly sites. Currently, they are located in the People's Republic of China, Indonesia, and Thailand. Nearly all are exclusive suppliers to Nike and receive considerable assistance from the company, with a view to upgrading their production. They will be the next generation of developed partners for Nike.
- The third group, volume producers, are large-scale factories serving a number of other independent buyers. They generally manufacture a specific product for Nike, but they are not involved in any new product because of fears they could leak proprietary information to competitors. Orders from Nike for suppliers in this group fluctuate, with variations of 50% between monthly orders.

Over time, Nike's outsourcing activity has followed a geographic pattern, as has its overall market participation. A "Nike index" has been developed by Jardine Fleming to track a country's economic development. Development starts when Nike products manufacturing starts there (e.g.,

Indonesia in 1989, Vietnam in 1996). The second stage is reached when labor starts flowing from basic industries, such as footwear, to more advanced ones, such as automobiles and electronics (Hong Kong in 1985, South Korea in 1990). An economy is fully developed when a country is developed as a major market (Japan in 1984, Singapore in 1991, and South Korea in 1994).

Nike's outsourcing has been a source of concern. In Indonesia, for example, where Nike's contract manufacturers produce 70 million shoes annually in 12 factories, there have been complaints about low wages and inhumane working conditions. These complaints have led to major debates about Nike's contribution to and exploitation of developing countries.

In response, Nike developed a code of conduct and is enforcing it in countries where it has outsourcing activities. For example, apparel workers now need to be at least 16 years old. Factory indoor air quality is now being measured and improved. Meal and transportation allowances, education subsidies, and health-care services are provided. Yet criticism of its outsourcing practices has not died down, much to Nike's frustration. When his alma mater, the University of Oregon, aligned itself with an anti-sweatshop group, Worker's Rights Consortium, Nike Chairman Phil Knight withdrew a planned $30-million contribution to the University's athletic fund.

DISCUSSION QUESTIONS

1. When opening operations in a developing country, should a multinational company orient its wages to prevailing indigenous wage levels or offer substantially higher wages?
2. Should working conditions for multinational firms be the same all over the world? Why or why not?

Sources: "Pangs of Conscience," *Business Week,* 29 July 1996, 46–47.
United Nations, *World Investment Report 1994: An Executive Summary* (New York: United Nations, 1994), 15; and "Nike Contract Factory Owners Increase Minimum Wage in Indonesia," *http://www.nikebiz.com,* 14 April 2000.
Stephen Greenhouse, *The New York Times,* 25 April 2000, *http://www. corpwatch.org,* 17 April 2001.

Licensing agreement
Is an arrangement in which one firm permits another to use its intellectual property in exchange for compensation, typically a royalty.

Royalty
Is the compensation paid by one firm to another under licensing and franchising agreements.

famous trading companies are the *sogoshosha* of Japan. Names such as Mitsubishi, Mitsui, and C. Itoh have become household words around the world. A trading company engages in a wider variety of activities than an EMC. It can purchase products, act as a distributor abroad, or offer services. It can provide information on distribution costs, handle domestic and international distribution and transportation, book space on ocean or air carriers, and handle shipping contracts.

Licensing

Under a **licensing agreement**, one firm permits another to use its intellectual property for compensation, usually a royalty. A **royalty** is the compensation paid by one firm to another under this type of agreement. The recipient firm is the licensee. The property licensed might include patents, trademarks, copyrights, technology, technical know-how, or specific business skills. For example, a firm that has developed a bag-in-the-box packaging process for milk can permit other firms abroad to use the same process. Licensing therefore amounts to exporting intangibles.

Licensing has intuitive appeal to many would-be international managers. As an entry strategy, it requires neither capital investment nor detailed involvement with foreign customers. By generating royalty income, licensing provides an opportunity to earn income from research and development investments already made. After initial costs, the licensor can reap benefits until the end of the license contract period. Licensing also reduces the risk of **expropriation**, a government takeover of a company's operations, because the licensee is a local company that can provide leverage against government action. Licensing also may provide a means by which foreign markets can be tested without major involvement of capital or management time.

Licensing is not without disadvantages. It is a very limited form of foreign market participation and does not guarantee a basis for future expansion. In fact, quite the opposite may take place. In exchange for the royalty, the licensor may create its own competitor, not only in the market for which the agreement was made but also in third-country markets.

Franchising

Franchising is the granting of the right by a parent company (the franchiser) to another independent entity (the franchisee) to do business in a prescribed manner. The right can take the form of selling the franchiser's product; or using its name, production, preparation, and marketing techniques, or general business approach. The major forms of franchising are manufacturer/retailer systems (such as car dealerships), manufacturer/wholesaler systems (such as soft drink companies), and service-firm/retailer systems (such as lodging services and fast-food outlets).

To be successful in international franchising, the firm must be able to offer unique products or unique selling propositions. With its uniqueness, a franchisee must offer a high degree of standardization. In most cases, standardization does not require 100% uniformity, but rather, international recognizability. Concurrent with this recognizability, the franchiser can and should adapt to local circumstances. Food franchisers, for example, will vary the products and product lines offered depending on local market conditions and tastes. The need to do so, however, has to be researched. TGI Friday's® (TGIF) assumed that Korean customers would expect to see kimchi (a kind of pickled cabbage that is a staple in Korean restaurants) on TGIF menus as well. They quickly found out that customers in American restaurants wanted only American food.[17]

Foreign Direct Investment

All types of firms, large or small, can carry out global market expansion through foreign direct investment or management contracts, and they are doing so at an increasing pace. **Foreign direct investment** involves buying property and businesses in foreign nations. It is an international entry strategy that is achieved through the acquisition of foreign firms. For example, British-Dutch Unilever acquired Bestfoods and Ben & Jerry's in the United States in 2000. Key to the decision to invest abroad is the existence of specific advantages that outweigh the disadvantages and risks of operating so far from home. Because foreign direct investment often requires substantial capital and a firm's ability to absorb risk, the most visible players in the area

© Ilona Czinkota

International franchising offers owners immediate product recognition, established customer loyalty, proven business processes, and established distribution channels. Wendy's has successfully expanded into the Hungarian market through franchising.

Expropriation
Is a government takeover of a company's operations, frequently at a level lower than the value of the assets.

Franchising
Is a form of licensing that grants a wholesaler or a retailer exclusive rights to sell a product in a specified area.

Foreign direct investment
Is an international entry strategy achieved through the acquisition of foreign firms.

Multinational corporations
Are companies that have production operations in at least one country in addition to their domestic base.

Displacement
Is the act of moving employment opportunities from the country of origin to host countries.

are large **multinational corporations**, which are defined by the United Nations as "enterprises which own or control production or service facilities outside the country in which they are based."[18] They come from a wide variety of countries, depend heavily on their international sales, and in terms of sales generate revenues that exceed the gross domestic products of many nations.

Many of the large multinationals operate in well over 100 countries. For some, their original home market accounts for only a fraction of their sales. For example, Nestlé's sales in Switzerland are only 2% of total sales. Through foreign direct investment, multinational corporations create economic vitality and jobs in their host countries, but also cause displacement in some economies. **Displacement** occurs when employment opportunities move from the country of origin to the host country.

Reasons for Foreign Direct Investment. Marketing considerations and corporate desire for growth are major causes of foreign direct investment. Today's competitive demands require companies to operate simultaneously in the "triad" of the United States, western Europe, and Japan. Corporations therefore need to seek wider market access in order to maintain and increase their sales. This objective can be achieved most quickly through the acquisition of foreign firms. Through such expansion, the corporation also gains ownership advantages consisting of political know-how and expertise.

Foreign direct investment permits corporations to circumvent current barriers to trade and operate abroad as a domestic firm, unaffected by duties, tariffs, or other import restrictions. Furthermore, local buyers may wish to buy from sources that they perceive as reliable in their supply, which means buying from local producers. Another incentive is the cost factor, with corporations attempting to obtain low-cost resources and ensure their sources of supply. Finally, once the decision is made to invest internationally, the investment climate plays a major role. Corporations will seek to invest in those geographic areas where their investment is most protected and has the best chance to flourish. Often, government incentives also play a role in guiding the investment location of firms.

As large multinational corporations move abroad, they are quite interested in maintaining their established business relationships with other firms. Therefore, they frequently encourage their suppliers to follow them and continue to supply them from a foreign location. Many Japanese automakers have urged their suppliers in Japan to begin production in the United States in order for new U.S. plants to have access to their products. As a result, a few direct investments can gradually form an important investment preference for subsequent investment flows.

A Perspective on Foreign Direct Investors. All foreign direct investors, and particularly multinational corporations, are viewed with a mixture of awe and dismay. Governments and individuals praise them for bringing capital, economic activity, and employment, as investors are seen as key transferers of technology and managerial skills. Through these transfers, competition, market choice, and competitiveness are enhanced.

At the same time, many consider a dependence on multinational corporations detrimental to the local economy. International direct investors are accused of actually draining resources from their host countries. By employing the best and the brightest, they are said to deprive domestic firms of talent, thus causing a brain drain. Once they have hired locals, multinational firms are accused of not promoting them high enough and of imposing many new rules on their employees abroad. By bringing in foreign technology, they are viewed either as discouraging local technology development or as perhaps transferring only outmoded knowledge. By increasing competition, they are declared the enemy of domestic firms. There are concerns about foreign investors' economic and political loyalty toward their host government. And, of course, their sheer size, which sometimes exceeds the financial assets that the government controls, makes foreign investors suspect. Clearly, a love–hate relationship exists between governments and the foreign direct investor. As the firm's size and investment volume grow, the benefits it brings to the economy increase. At the same time, the dependence of the economy on the firm increases as well.

Types of Ownership

A corporation has a wide variety of ownership choices, ranging from 100% ownership to a minority interest. The different levels of ownership will result in varying degrees of flexibility for the corporation, a changing ability to control business plans and strategy, and differences in the level of risk assumed. Often, the ownership decision is either a strategic response to corporate capabilities and needs or a necessary result of government regulations.

Full Ownership

Full ownership of a foreign firm may be desirable, but not a necessary prerequisite for international success. At other times, it may be a necessity, particularly when strong linkages exist within the corporation. Interdependencies between and among local operations and headquarters may be so strong that anything short of total coordination will result in a less-than-acceptable benefit to the firm as a whole. This may be the case if centralized product design, pricing, or advertising is needed. Yet, increasingly, the international environment is growing hostile to full ownership by multinational firms. Many governments exert political pressure to obtain national control of foreign operations. Ownership options are limited either through outright legal restrictions or through measures designed to make foreign ownership less attractive—such as profit repatriation limitations. **Profit repatriation limitations** are restrictions set up by host governments based on a company's ability to pay dividends from its operations back to its home base. The international marketer is therefore frequently faced with the choice of either abiding by existing restraints and accepting a reduction in control or losing the opportunity to operate in the country.

Profit repatriation limitations
Are restrictions set up by host governments in terms of a company's ability to pay dividends from its operations back to its home base.

Joint Ventures

Joint ventures are a collaboration of two or more organizations for more than a transitory period.[19] The participating partners share assets, risks, and profits. Equality of partners is not necessary. The partners' contributions to the joint venture can also vary widely and may consist of capital, technology, know-how, sales organizations, or plant and equipment. Joint ventures can help overcome existing market access restrictions and open up or maintain market opportunities that otherwise would not be available. If a corporation can identify a partner with a common goal, joint ventures may represent the most viable vehicle for international expansion.

Joint ventures
Result from the participation of two or more companies in an enterprise in which each party contributes assets, owns the new entity to some degree, and shares risk.

Joint ventures are valuable when the pooling of resources results in a better outcome for each partner than if each attempted to carry out its activities individually. This is particularly the case when each partner has a specialized advantage in areas that benefit the joint venture. For example, a firm may have new technology, yet lack sufficient capital to carry out foreign direct investment on its own. By joining forces with a partner, the technology can be used more quickly and market penetration is easier. Similarly, one of the partners may have a distribution system already established or have better access to local suppliers, either of which permits a greater volume of sales in a shorter period of time. Greater experience with the culture and environment of the local partner may enable the joint venture to be more aware of cultural sensitivities and to benefit from greater insights into changing market conditions and needs. For example, New United Motor Manufacturing (NUMMI), based in Fremont, California, is a joint venture between General Motors and Toyota that helped introduce the Toyota production system and teamwork-based working environment while taking advantage of GM's marketing expertise. In addition to producing the Toyota Corolla, Toyota Tacoma, and Pontiac Vibe, NUMMI also makes the right-hand-drive Toyota Voltz, which is exported to Japan.

Joint ventures, such as New United Motor Manufacturing (NIMMI), allow two or more organizations to pool their resources. NUMMI utilized Toyota's superior production and teamwork system and GM's marketing expertise.

© Michael Yamashita/CORBIS

Joint ventures also permit better relationships with local organizations—government, local authorities, or labor unions. If the local partner can bring political influence to the undertaking, the new venture may be eligible for tax incentives, grants, and government support, and may be less vulnerable to political risk. Negotiations for certifications or licenses may be easier because authorities may not perceive themselves as dealing with a foreign firm.

Problem areas in joint ventures, as in all partnerships, involve implementing the concept and maintaining the relationship. Eventually, most joint ventures fall short of expectations and are disbanded. The reasons for the failures include conflicts of interest, problems with disclosure of sensitive information, and disagreement over how profits are to be shared. In some cases, managers dispatched to the joint venture by the partners may feel differing degrees of loyalty to the venture and its partners. Reconciling such conflicts of loyalty is one of the greatest human-resource challenges for joint ventures.[20]

Strategic alliances

Strategic alliances
Are informal or formal arrangements between two or more companies with a common business objective.

Strategic alliances are informal or formal arrangements between two or more companies with a common business objective. They are more than the traditional customer–vendor relationship but less than an outright acquisition. The great advantage of such alliances is their ongoing flexibility, since their form, although stable at any given point in time, is subject to adjustment and change in response to environmental shifts.[21] In essence, strategic alliances are networks of companies that collaborate to achieve a given project or objective. However, partners for one project may well be fierce competitors in another situation.

Companies must carefully evaluate the effects of entering such a coalition. The most successful alliances are those that match the complementary strengths of partners to satisfy a joint objective. Often the partners have different product, geographic, or functional strengths that the alliance can build on to achieve success with a new strategy or in a new market. Figure 4.6 shows how some firms have combined their individual strengths to achieve their joint objective. In light of growing international competition and the rising cost of technology, strategic alliances are likely to continue their growth in the future.

Strategic Alliances That Blend Strengths of Partners					Figure 4.6

Partner	Strength	+	Partner	Strength	=	Joint Objective
Pepsico	Marketing clout for canned beverages		Lipton	Recognized tea brand and customer franchise		Sell canned iced tea beverages
Philips	Consumer electronics innovation and leadership		Levi Strauss	Fashion design and distribution		Outdoor wear with integrated equipment for fashion-conscious consumers
KFC	Established brand and store format and operations skills		Mitsubishi	Real estate and site-selection skills in Japan		Establish a KFC chain in Japan
Siemens	Presence in a range of telecommunications markets worldwide and cable-manufacturing technology		Corning	Technological strength in optical fibers and glass		Create a fiber-optic-cable business
Ericsson	Technological strength in public telecommunications networks		Hewlett-Packard	Computers, software, and access to electronic channels		Create and market network management systems

Sources: "Portable Technology Takes the Next Step: Electronics You Can Wear," *The Wall Street Journal,* 31 July 2000, A3, A14; Joel Bleeke and David Ernst, "Is Strategic Alliance Really a Sale?" *Harvard Business Review* 73 (January-February 1995): 97–105; and Melanie Wells, "Coca-Cola Proclaims Nestea Time for CAA," *Advertising Age,* 30 January 1995, 2. See also http://www.pepsico.com; http://www.lipton.com; http://www.kfc.com; http://corningcablesystems.com; http://www.ericsson.com; and http://www.hp.com.

Contractual Arrangements

Firms have found contractual arrangements to be a useful alternative or complement to other international options, since they permit the international use of corporate resources and can also be an acceptable response to government ownership restrictions. Such an arrangement may take the form of **complementary marketing**, where the contracting parties carry out different activities. For example, Nestlé and General Mills have an agreement whereby Honey Nut Cheerios and Golden Grahams are made in General Mills' U.S. plants, shipped in bulk to Europe for packaging at a Nestlé plant, and then marketed in France, Spain, and Portugal by Nestlé.[22] Other contractual arrangements exist for **outsourcing**, in which a firm enters into long-term arrangements with its suppliers. For example, General Motors buys cars and components from South Korea's Daewoo, and Siemens buys computers from Fujitsu. As corporations look for ways to grow and focus simultaneously on their competitive advantage, outsourcing has become a powerful new tool for achieving these goals. Firms increasingly also develop arrangements for **contract manufacturing** that allow the corporation to separate the physical production of goods from the research, development, and marketing stages, especially if the latter are the core competencies of the firm. Such contracting has become particularly popular in the footwear and garment industries. For example, Nike, the footwear company based in Beaverton, Oregon, has 100% of its footwear produced by subcontractors, most of them outside the United States. Nike's own people focus on the services part of the production process, including design, product development, marketing, and distribution.[23]

Complementary marketing
Is a contractual arrangement where participating parties carry out different but complementary activities.

Outsourcing
Is using another firm for the manufacture of needed components or finished goods or delivery of a service.

Contract manufacturing
Is using another firm to manufacture goods so that the marketer may concentrate on research and development, as well as the marketing, aspects of the operation.

Markets at the Bottom of the Income Pyramid

Marketers are facing a challenging time as they start the 21st century: Domestic markets are not experiencing growth and many of the promising international markets have been struck by recession or by financial crises. The time may have come to look at the four billion people in the world who live in poverty, subsisting on less than $1,500 a year (see figure below). Despite initial skepticism, marketers are finding that they can make profits, while at the same time having a positive effect on the sustainable livelihoods of people not normally considered potential customers.

Annual Per Capita Income*	Tiers	Population in Millions
More Than $20,000	1	75–100
$1,500–$20,000	2 & 3	1,500–1,750
Less Than $1,500	4	4,000

*Based on purchasing power parity in U.S.$.
Source: U.N. World Development Reports

The first order of business is to learn about the needs, aspirations, and habits of targeted populations for which traditional intelligence-gathering may not be the most effective. Hewlett-Packard has an initiative called World e-Inclusion which, working with a range of global and local partners, aims to sell, lease, or donate $1 billion worth of satellite-powered computer goods and services to markets in Africa, Asia, eastern Europe, Latin America, and the Middle East.

In the product area, marketers must combine advanced technology with local insights. Hindustan Lever (part of Unilever) learned that low-income Indians, usually forced to settle for low-quality products, wanted to buy high-end detergents and personal-care products, but could not afford them in the quantities available. In response, the company developed extremely low-cost packaging material and other innovations that allowed for a product priced in pennies instead of the $4–$15 of the regular containers. The same brand is on all of the product forms, regardless of packaging.

Coca-Cola has introduced "Project Mission" in Botswana to launch a drink to combat anemia, blindness, and other afflictions common in poorer parts of the world. The drink, called Vitango, is like the company's Hi-C orange-flavored drink, but contains 12 vitamins and minerals chronically lacking in the diets of people in developing countries. The project satisfies multiple objectives for the Coca-Cola Company. First, it could help boost sales at a time when global sales of carbonated drinks are slowing, and, secondly, it will help establish relationships with governments and other local constituents that can serve as a positive platform for brand Coca-Cola.

Due to the economic and physical isolation of poor communities, providing access can lead to a thriving business. In Bangladesh (with annual income levels of $200), GrameenPhone Ltd. leases access to wireless phones to villagers. Each phone is used by an average of 100 people and generates $90 in revenue a month—two or three times the revenues generated from wealthier users who own their phones in urban areas.

The emergence of these markets presents a great opportunity for international marketers. It also creates a chance for business, government, and civil society to join together in the common cause of helping the aspiring poor join the world market economy.

Sources: "Making the Web Worldwide," *The Economist,* 28 September 2002, 76.
C. K. Prahalad and Stuart L. Hart, "The Fortune at the Bottom of the Pyramid," *Strategy and Business,* First Quarter 2002, 35–47.
"Drinks for Developing Countries," *The Washington Post,* 27 November 2001, B1, B6.
Dana James, "B2–4B Spells Profits," *Marketing News,* 5 November 2001, 1, 11–12.

Level of Managerial Commitment

Regardless of the entry strategy selected, the central driver of internationalization is the level of managerial commitment. This commitment will grow gradually from an awareness of international potential to the adaptation of an international strategic direction. It will be influenced by the information, experience, and perception of management, which in turn are shaped by motivations and corporate concerns.

Management's commitment and its view of the capabilities of the firm will then trigger various international marketing activities that can range from indirect exporting and importing to more direct involvement in the global market. Eventually, the firm may expand further through foreign direct investment measures such as joint ventures or strategic alliances. All of the developments, processes, and factors involved in the overall process of going international are linked to each other. A comprehensive view of these linkages is presented schematically in Figure 4.7.

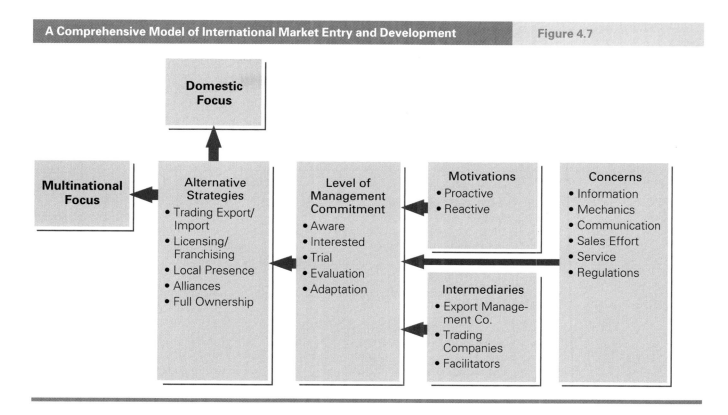

A Comprehensive Model of International Market Entry and Development Figure 4.7

Tailoring the International Marketing Mix

5 LEARNING OBJECTIVE

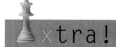

As described in Chapter 1, marketers develop specific marketing mixes tailored to meet the needs and wants of the desired target markets. In international markets, the marketing mix—the product, distribution, promotion, and price—may need to be adjusted to accommodate local markets. Marketers may use one of the three following strategies when determining adjustments to the marketing mix:

- **Standardized approach.** No special provisions are made for the international marketplace. Instead, the target market is identified and a product is chosen that can easily be marketed with little or no modification.
- **Multidomestic approach.** Marketers who choose the multidomestic approach completely alter the marketing mix to fully adapt to local conditions in each and every target market.
- **Globalization approach.** In this approach, regional and global strategies are developed that allow for local differences in implementation.

Ideally, the marketing manager should "think globally and act locally," not by focusing on the extremes of full standardization or full localization, but rather by exploiting good ideas, strategies, and products on a wider regional basis. The adaptation decision will also have to be assessed as a function of time and market involvement. The more exporters learn about local market characteristics in individual markets, the more they are able to establish similarities and, as a result, standardize their marketing approach. This market insight gives exporters legitimacy with local representatives in developing a common understanding of the extent of standardization vs. adaptation.[24]

Product Decisions

While there are arguments for an increasing amount of product standardization from an economies-of-scale perspective, international marketing managers have to

Standardized approach
Is the approach to international marketing in which products are marketed with little or no modification.

Multidomestic approach
Is the approach to international marketing whereby local conditions are adapted to in each and every target market.

Globalization approach
Is the approach to international marketing in which differences are incorporated into a regional or global strategy that will allow for differences in implementation.

balance these considerations against factors that may call for adaptation. In many cases, the marketing manager has no choice but to make the adaptations. For example, Murray Ohio Manufacturing had to make its lawn mowers quieter for the European market because of the noise standards imposed by the European Union.[25] In some cases, the choice is based on customer preferences (e.g., Tefal, the world leader in cookware, makes pans available with detachable handles in Japan to enable storage in the traditionally tighter spaces of Japanese kitchens). The general expectation is that products should be economical in terms of purchase, use, and maintenance.[26]

Increasingly, quality standards may be imposed on marketers, especially in business marketing. The EU has chosen the **International Organization for Standardization (ISO)** 9000 as a basis to harmonize varying technical norms of its member states, thereby making it necessary for all marketers interested in the EU to comply.[27] The ISO is a nongovernmental organization that promotes the development of standardization to facilitate the international exchange of goods and services. Increasing environmental concern is leading some governments to require marketers to take responsibility for their packaging waste, thereby resulting in attempts to redesign products and their packaging, reducing the waste generated, recycling it, and reusing it. This has resulted in car marketers introducing models that are, to a large extent, recyclable.[28]

International Organization for Standardization (ISO)
Is a nongovernmental organization that promotes the development of standardization to facilitate the international exchange of goods and services.

Design Considerations

The climate and geography of international markets can have an impact on product design. For example, the marketing of chocolate products is challenging in hot climates and has led three companies to take different approaches to their marketing-mix adaptation. Nestlé's solution was to produce a slightly different Kit Kat bar for Asia, reducing the fat content to raise the chocolate's melting point. Cadbury Schweppes has its own display cases in retail outlets to reject heat and humidity, while Toblerone has confined its distribution to air-conditioned outlets.

The international marketer must also make sure products do not contain ingredients or features that might be in violation of legal requirements or religious or social customs. In Islamic countries, for example, animal fats have to be replaced by ingredients such as vegetable shortening.

Branding Considerations

The use of standardization in branding is strongest in culturally similar markets; for U.S. marketers, this means Canada and the United Kingdom. Standardization of product and brand do not necessarily move hand in hand; a global or regional brand may well have local features (such as Ford's Escort), or a highly standardized product may have local brand names (e.g., Snuggle, Cajoline, Kuschelweich, Mimosin, and Yumos). While the same brand name may be used, additional dimensions may have to be considered. Chinese consumers expect more in terms of how the names are spelled, written, and styled, and whether they are considered lucky. Chee-tos® are marketed in China under the Chinese name *qi duo* (roughly pronounced "chee-do") that translates as "Many Surprises."[29] Segmentation decisions will affect branding as well. At Whirlpool, the Whirlpool brand name is used as the global brand name to serve the broad middle-market segment, while regional and local brands cover the others. Throughout Europe, the Bauknecht brand is targeted at the upper end of the market seeking a reputable German brand. Ignis and Laden are positioned as price-value brands—Ignis Europewide, Laden in France.[30]

Packaging Considerations

With packaging, marketers have to worry about the protective, promotional, and user-convenience dimensions of the function. Packaging needs to vary as a function of transportation mode, transit conditions, and transit time. Promotional features take into consideration regulations and customer preferences, while package sizes take into account purchase patterns and market conditions.

Labeling Considerations

The country of origin has considerable influence on the perceptions of a product's quality. For example, when Canon changed its supply of copiers sold in the Russian market from their Japanese production facilities to their newly opened Chinese plant, sales slumped, and Canon's dealers started importing Canon copiers from around the world that displayed the "Made in Japan" label. This **gray marketing** of its copiers forced Canon to switch its procurement for Russia back to the Japanese source.

Promotion Decisions

To customize the promotional plan for a market, the international marketer should consider issues related to positioning and advertising copy.

Positioning Considerations

The most important category of adaptations is based on local behavior, tastes, attitudes, and traditions—all reflecting the marketer's need to gain customers' approval. The product itself may not change at all; only its positioning may need to be adjusted. For example, Coca-Cola launched Diet Coke in Japan by changing its name to Coke Light and shifted the promotion theme from "weight loss" to "figure maintenance." Japanese women do not like to admit that they are dieting by drinking something clearly labeled *diet*. On occasion, market realities may cause a shift in the product's positioning. Panda, a northern European chocolate and sweets maker, had to place its licorice products in the United Kingdom in health care stores upon finding traditional channels at British daily-goods retailers blocked by competition.

Copy Considerations

Frequently, the copy in advertisements needs to be adjusted to appeal to the international customer. For example, France requires the use of French in any offer, presentation, or advertisement, whether written or spoken, including Web sites. While some advertisements may share common graphic elements, the copy in the ad may need to be customized for the local culture. Marriott used similar ads to reach business travelers in the U.S., Saudi Arabia, Latin America, and German-speaking Europe. However, the copy was modified based on the local consumer's needs. While the common theme, "When You Are Comfortable, You Can Do Anything," was

Gray marketing
Is the marketing of authentic, legally trademarked goods through unauthorized channels.

Natural Forces

The European Union has developed an ecolabel, the EU flower, to "stimulate both the supply and demand of products with a reduced environmental impact." Ecolabels are driven both by pragmatism (reduced ability to deal with waste) and demand by environmentally conscious consumer groups.

International marketers customize advertising copy to appeal to the local market. While retaining similar graphic elements, these Marriott ads were uniquely designed and written to appeal to the different cultures of Japan, Latin America, and Portugal.

used worldwide, local creative emphases varied; for example, the Latin American version stressed comfort, while the German version focused on results.

Similarly, ads for cosmetic products marketed in countries such as Saudi Arabia need to be sensitive to local moral standards. While a global creative approach can be used, the copy and images used in promotions may require some adjusting. For example, Guy Laroche's ad for Drakkar Noir shows a man's hand clutching the perfume bottle and a woman's hand seizing his bare forearm. This version, used around the world, was adjusted for Saudi Arabia to show the man's arm clothed in a dark suit sleeve, and the woman's hand merely brushing his hand.

Distribution Decisions

While distribution decisions continue to be mostly tactical and made on a market-by-market basis, marketing managers may need to adjust the distribution strategy. Distribution formats are crossing borders, especially to newly emerging markets. While supermarkets accounted for only 8% of consumer nondurable sales in Thailand in 1990, the figure today is over 50%. The other trend is that intermediaries themselves have embarked on globalization efforts either independently or through strategic alliances. Entities such as Toys "R" Us from the United States, Galeries Lafayette from France, Marks & Spencer from the United Kingdom, and Takashimaya and Isetan from Japan have expanded worldwide.[31]

Some markets may require unique approaches to developing global products. At Gillette, timing is the only concession to local taste. Developing markets, such as China, eastern Europe, and Latin America, are first introduced to the older, cheaper products before the latest, state-of-the-art versions are sold. In a world economy where most of the growth is in developing markets, the global products' inevitable premium pricing may keep them out of the hands of the average consumer. As a result, Procter & Gamble figures out what consumers in various countries can afford and then develops products accordingly. In Brazil, the company launched a diaper called Pampers Uni, a less-expensive version of its mainstream product. The strategy is to create price tiers, hooking customers early, then encouraging them to trade up as their incomes and desire for better products grow.[32]

The monitoring of competitors' approaches—determining what has to be done to meet and beat them—is critical. In many markets, the international marketer is competing with local manufacturers and must overcome traditional purchasing relationships or face large multinational marketers that have considerable resources to commit. BBN Technologies, a marketer of interactive data-processing equipment and support services, is facing competitors such as Siemens and Philips and will have to prove not only that its products are competitive in price and quality but also that the company will honor its commitments and provide the necessary after-sales service.[33] This may mean that the marketer has to establish a sales office and employ its own personnel in selected target markets, rather than relying on independent distributors as is done at home.

Pricing Decisions

International competitiveness in price is a challenge for the marketing manager in two broad ways. First, exported products are threatened by price escalation—the combined effect of costs incurred in modifying products to the international marketplace, operational costs in exports (such as shipping), and market-entry costs (such as tariffs and taxes). Second, marketers may also face unfavorable foreign-exchange rates. The marketing manager has two options to ensure that prices remain competitive: either absorb the price increases, especially when customers are felt to be price-elastic, or pass through, which means that the customer bears the added costs but is still willing to buy the product due to its other attractive features. With the introduction of the euro, the common European Union currency, foreign-currency fluctuations will no longer present a challenge to marketers from the 12 member countries that are using the common currency.

Natural Forces

In India, 30% of personal care products are sold in single-serve packages. Without innovation in packaging, waste problems could escalate quickly. Dow Chemical and Cargill are experimenting with an organic plastic that is totally biodegradable. If successful, this process could revolutionize packaging everywhere in the world, not just in India.

Implementing Marketing Programs Worldwide

With world markets rapidly converging and merging, marketers have to make sure that their organizations are capable of taking advantage of the resulting opportunities. The necessary actions relate to management processes, organizational structure, and corporate culture, all of which should ensure the successful implementation of marketing programs both across borders and within individual markets.

The new realities of the global marketplace require, by design, a balance between sensitivity to local needs and deployment of technologies and concepts across borders. This means that neither headquarters nor country managers can call the shots alone. If decisions are not made in a coordinated fashion, or if standard procedures are forced on country operations, local resistance in the form of the *not-invented-here syndrome* may lead to the demise of potentially attractive innovation. Resistance may stem from opposition to any idea originating from the outside, from lack of involvement in strategy development, or from valid concerns about the applicability of a concept to that particular market. Without local commitment, no global marketing effort can survive.

Management Processes

In the multidomestic approach, marketing managers at the country level had very little incentive to exchange ideas or coordinate activities with their counterparts. Globalization, however, requires transfer of information both between the headquarters and country organizations and within the country organizations themselves. By facilitating the flow of information and sharing best practices from around the world, whether through regular meetings or use of corporate intranets, ideas are exchanged and organizational values are strengthened.[34] IBM, for example, has a Worldwide Opportunity Council that sponsors fellowships for employees to listen to business cases from around the world and develop global platforms and solutions. At Levi Strauss, as with most successful global marketers, marketing personnel are supported through electronic networking capabilities and are encouraged to adopt ideas from other markets. Headquarters exercises its control only when necessary, for example, in protecting brand identity, image, and quality.

Part of this global marketing readiness is personnel exchange. Many companies encourage (or even require) marketing managers to gain experience abroad during the early or middle levels of their careers. The more experience people have in working with others from different regions and ethnic backgrounds, the more able a company is to locally integrate its global philosophy, strategy, and actions.

The role of headquarters staff should be that of coordinating and leveraging the resources of the corporation worldwide. This may mean activities focused on combining good ideas that come from different parts of the organization to be fed into global planning. Many companies employ world-class advertising and market-research staffs whose role should be to assist country organizations with upgrading their technical skills and focusing their attention not only on local issues but also on those with global impact.

Globalization calls for a substantial degree of centralization in marketing decision making, far beyond that in the multidomestic approach. Once a strategy has been jointly developed, headquarters may want to permit local managers to develop their own programs within specified decision-making boundaries. These programs could then be subject to headquarters' approval, rather than forcing local managers to adhere strictly to the formulated strategy. For tactical elements of the marketing mix, such as choice of distribution channels or sales-promotional tools, decisions should be left to the country managers. Colgate-Palmolive allows local units to use their own ads, but only if they can beat the global "benchmark" version. With a properly managed approval process, effective control can be exerted without unduly dampening country managers' creativity and initiative.

Technological Forces

Companies that support global networking capabilities, such as intranets and centers of excellence, have been shown to be more successful than their counterparts that do not make similar investments. For example, employees at Levi Strauss can join an electronic discussion group with colleagues around the world, watch the latest commercials, or comment on the latest marketing program or plan.

Organization Structure

Various organizational structures have emerged to support global marketing efforts. Some companies have established global or regional product managers and their support groups at headquarters. Their task is to develop long-term strategies for product categories on a worldwide basis and to act as the support system for the country organizations. This matrix structure focused on customers is considered more effective in today's global marketplace by companies that have adopted it than the traditional country-by-country approach it replaced.

Whenever a product group has global potential, firms such as Procter & Gamble, 3M, and Henkel create strategic-planning units to work on the programs. These units, such as 3M's EMATs (European Marketing Action Teams), consist of members from the country organizations that will market the products, managers from both global and regional headquarters, and technical specialists.

Local marketing organizations are absorbing new roles as markets scan the world for ideas that can cross borders. The consensus among marketers is that many more countries, in addition to the strategic leaders, are now capable of developing products and solutions that can be applied on a worldwide basis. This realization has given birth to centers of excellence. Ford's centers of excellence have been established with two key goals in mind: to avoid duplicating efforts and to capitalize on the expertise of specialists on a worldwide basis. Located in several countries, the centers work on key components for cars. For example, one works on certain kinds of engines, while another engineers and develops common platforms. Designers in each market then style the exteriors and passenger compartments to appeal to local tastes.

Chapter Summary

Learning Objective 1: *Understand the importance of international marketing and its opportunities and challenges.* International marketing is the process of planning and conducting transactions across national borders to create exchanges that satisfy the objectives of individuals and organizations. International marketing offers many new opportunities for growth for both large and small firms. Some of these opportunities include a strengthened competitive advantage, greater exposure to new markets, and opportunities to partner with new global suppliers. Both large and small businesses should consider participating in the world market.

Learning Objective 2: *Recognize the effect of the global environment on international marketing activities.* Managers need to understand and cope with a new set of environmental forces that consist of varying sociocultural dimensions and divergent and sometimes even conflicting political and legal approaches. The cultural environment of a country includes its languages, values, and attitudes. The socioeconomic environment of a country includes the age distribution of the population, income, and economic infrastructure. While globalization may have brought about significant convergence to markets, the marketer is still subject to a variety of sociocultural and political/legal forces that may affect a firm's opportunities abroad.

Learning Objective 3: *Understand the process of international market selection.* In investigating global market opportunities, the firm must first identify and screen markets internationally based on general country factors and firm-specific criteria. After identifying specific desirable markets, management must then choose between concentrated or diversified expansion approaches to these markets. A diversification strategy is the market-development strategy that involves expansion to a relatively large number of markets. A concentration strategy focuses expansion on a small number of markets.

Learning Objective 4: *Recognize the process of internationalization and the different forms of market entry.* The initiation of internationalization depends heavily on managerial commitment to the international strategy and on the firm's motivation for going international. Initial modes of entry are typically exporting or importing and licensing and franchising, and are often assisted by intermediaries. Over time and with growing experience, firms then expand through direct foreign investment, joint ventures, or contract manufacturing.

Learning Objective 5: *Comprehend the international adjustment of the marketing mix.* In international markets, the marketing mix (product, distribution, promotion, and price) may need to be adjusted to accommodate the local markets. Three strategies are available to marketers as they tailor the international marketing mix: the standardized approach, the multidomestic approach, and the globalization approach. Products may need to be redesigned to meet different needs of the international market. Both positioning strategies and advertising copy may need to be tailored to appeal to the international customer. Pricing decisions are particularly challenging for the international marketer. Exported products are threatened by price escalation, the combined effect of costs incurred in modifying products, operational costs in exports (shipping), and market-entry costs (tariffs and taxes). Also, marketers may face unfavorable foreign-exchange rates.

Learning Objective 6: *Understand the steps necessary to implement an international marketing strategy.* Managerial processes, as well as the organizational structure, need to be reviewed and adjusted to enable worldwide implementation of marketing programs. The ability to leverage resources across regions and markets has become a significant marketing tool for many global marketers.

Key Terms

For interactive study: visit http://bestpractices.swlearning.com.

Agent, 111
Antidumping laws, 105
Change agent, 101
Code law, 105
Common law, 105
Complementary marketing, 117
Concentration strategy, 108
Contract manufacturing, 117
Degree of individualism, 101
Displacement, 114
Distributor, 111
Diversification strategy, 108

Export management companies (EMCs), 111
Expropriation, 113
Foreign direct investment, 113
Franchising, 113
Globalization approach, 119
Gray marketing, 121
International intermediaries, 110
International marketing, 98
International Organization for Standardization (ISO), 120
Joint ventures, 115
Level of equality, 101

Licensing agreement, 112
Material achievement, 101
Multidomestic approach, 119
Multinational corporations, 114
Outsourcing, 117
Profit repatriation limitations, 115
Royalty, 112
Standardized approach, 119
Strategic alliances, 116
Trading company, 111
Uncertainty avoidance, 101
World Trade Organization (WTO), 105

Questions for Review and Discussion

1. What are the principal differences between domestic and international marketing?

2. Is it beneficial for nations to depend more on each other?

3. Discuss the different effects that code law and common law can have on the international marketer.

4. Why is management commitment so important to export success?

5. What determines the mode of market entry of a firm?

6. What is the purpose of export intermediaries?

7. Suggest criteria on which international marketing managers can base their market choice.

8. Why are more marketers forming alliances with other companies to achieve their goals?

9. If there is a love–hate relationship between governments and foreign investors, what marketing approaches can be taken to present the investor as a contributor to its host country?

10. With more companies adopting global or regional marketing strategies, how can the participation of country-level marketers be ensured in the implementation of those strategies?

In-Class Team Activities

1. A Gallup poll conducted in nine Muslim countries in 2001–2002 revealed that respondents considered the United States as "ruthless, arrogant, aggressive, and biased against Islamic values," and most thought that U.S. culture was a corrupting influence on their societies. Outline the basic marketing tasks necessary to improve the U.S. image abroad in general and in Muslim countries in particular. Tasks can include: (a) what the U.S. brand promise should be, (b) how the audience should be segmented, (c) what types of messages/ programs should be developed, and (d) what range of marketing communication tools should be used.

2. From 1997 to early 2002, the high value of the U.S. dollar compared to the euro made exporters' marketing tasks challenging (for example, the $/€ exchange rate varied between .82 and .98). Since then, the rate has climbed to 1.08 (in early 2003). Develop strategies for exporters to take advantage of this new situation in the Euro-zone. At the same time, speculate as to how European exporters are adjusting their strategies for the U.S. market. Strategy proposals should naturally include both price-based and non-price-based alternatives.

Internet Questions

1. The software industry is the hardest hit by piracy. Using the Web site of the Business Software Alliance (http://www.bsa.org), assess how marketers are tackling the problem.

2. Compare and contrast international marketers' home pages for presentation and content; for example, Coca Cola (at http://www.coca-cola.com) and its Japanese version (http://www.cocacola.co.jp), as well as Ford Motor Company throughout the world (http://www.ford.com).

3. Imagine you are a marketer trying to enter the Asian market and have decided to use a sogoshosha as a facilitator. Using the Web site of the Sumitomo Corporation (http://www.sumitomocorp.co.jp), establish what information is available about the countries of your choice.

CHAPTER CASE

The Gray Ferrari

"We can put a man on the moon, but we can't retrofit a Ferrari. It's crazy!"

Robert L. Johnson, founder and CEO of
Black Entertainment Television

The Situation

It all started when Robert L. Johnson had dinner at Mr. K's Chinese restaurant with Michael Jordan of the Washington Wizards and David Falk, the leading sports agent. When the discussion turned to cars, Johnson mentioned his interest in buying a Ferrari. Both Falk and Jordan recommended their respective dealers, but said they had found the going tough. Only a select number of Ferraris are made annually and the automaker limits the number sold by U.S. dealers to about 1,000. In practice, anyone placing an order would have to wait more than two years for delivery of a car that costs $200,000 to $300,000, depending on the model. A New Jersey dealer had a Ferrari available, but Johnson felt the price was too high at $300,000. Michael Jordan's dealer had a 360 Modena

available for $160,000. He bought it, although it was not exactly what he had wanted, given that the Modena is not a convertible. Franco Nuschese, the owner of Georgetown's Café Milano, referred Johnson to a dealer in Munich who had Ferrari 360 Spiders available at $190,000. Johnson wired the money to Munich and expected to receive the car within days.

The Standards

Only after the purchase of the 360 Spider did Johnson discover that it needed to conform to certain government standards, mainly those relating to emissions and safety— a fact that made Johnson's Ferrari sit in a dealer warehouse for months. The hardest part is satisfying the rules of the Office of Vehicle Safety Compliance (OVSC), a branch of the National Highway Traffic Safety Administration (NHTSA) in the U.S. Department of Transportation (DOT).

Nonconforming import cars (from outside the United States and Canada) are reported to the OVSC by registered importers (RI) on behalf of the buyer. In 2002, the NHTSA reported that 23 RIs "specialize in European or gray-market cars." The RIs then submitted petitions explaining how they would replace foreign parts with U.S. parts and adjust the engineering. The bumpers, for example, are thicker on North American versions, and seat-belt warning systems have to be added, as well as speedometers adjusted from kilometers to miles. Petitions are available for public comment, although they are extremely rare. From 1991 to 2001, fewer than 10 objections were filed.

There has been a substantial increase in the number of nonconforming vehicles entering the United States. An ever-growing gray market for automobiles, especially luxury models, has emerged. Gray-market goods are defined as items manufactured abroad and imported into the United States without the consent of trademark holders. Gray-market goods are not counterfeits; however, differences may exist between these goods and those goods produced for U.S. or North American sale. In 2001, a total of 199,431 nonconforming vehicles were imported (up 15% from 173,841 in 2000). The number of RIs has also increased as a result. Automakers could not look away as they had in the past. In Ferrari's case, the drivers of interest in gray-market cars were the low number of cars authorized for import and the high value of the dollar (from 1997 to early 2002). The strong dollar meant savings of 30–40% in some cases.

Ferrari's Response

In late June 2001, Ferrari took the unprecedented step of asking DOT to halt importation of 2001 Ferrari Mode-

nas and 550 Maranellos until the company could prepare its objections to gray-market imports. On August 6, Ferrari's formal brief stated that gray-market imports differ from their North American counterparts in "hundreds" of ways and cannot be readily modified to meet U.S. requirements. This meant a request for federal intervention in denying imports of Ferraris not originally intended for the United States.

In the technical documentation provided by Ferrari, a total of 234 parts, with a suggested retail price of $56,584, were needed to bring a 2001 non-U.S. model 550 into compliance. A total of 306 parts ($68,021) were needed for a 360. As a result, Ferrari had serious reservations about whether RI-proposed modifications to non-U.S. cars would be sufficient to meet emission and safety requirements. For example, the RI's petition may state that doors on all 550s are identical, but doors on non-U.S. cars are not fitted with side-impact protection bars. Enzo Francesconi, Ferrari NA's Director of Technical Services, said the company was not taking the action for business reasons, but because it was concerned about safety.

In a related move, Ferrari informed potential buyers of its limited-production $258,000 550 Brachetta that they would be required to sign an agreement prohibiting them from reselling the car to anyone but their Ferrari dealer within the first year of ownership. The reported rationale is to prevent speculation in these exotic cars.

Ferrari alleges that gray imports have no impact on authorized dealers' profits and that the actions taken are really to protect the company's reputation. It categorically rejects owners' and dealers' allegations of profiteering.

Vehicle Importation Guidelines

The following provides information about the importation of a passenger car, truck, trailer, motorcycle, moped, bus, or MPV built to comply with the standards of a country other than the U.S. or Canada. Importers of motor vehicles must file form HS–7 (available at ports of entry) at the time a vehicle is imported to declare whether the vehicle complies with DOT requirements. As a general rule, a motor vehicle less than 25 years old must comply with all applicable federal motor vehicle safety standards (FMVSS) to be imported permanently. Vehicles manufactured to meet the FMVSS will have a certification label affixed by the original manufacturer in the area of the driver-side door. To make importation easier, when purchasing a vehicle certified to the U.S. standards abroad, a buyer should make sure that the sales contract verifies the label is attached and present this document at the time of importation.

A vehicle without this certification label must be imported as a nonconforming vehicle. In this case, the importer must contract with a DOT-Registered Importer (RI) and post a DOT bond for one-and-a-half times the

vehicle's dutiable value. This bond is in addition to the normal U.S. Customs entry bond. Copies of the DOT bond and the contract with an RI must be attached to the HS-7 form.

Under the contract, the RI will modify and certify that the vehicle conforms with all applicable FMVSS. Before an RI can modify a vehicle, NHTSA must have determined that the vehicle is capable of being modified to comply with the FMVSS. If no determination has been made, the RI must petition NHTSA to determine whether the vehicle is capable of being modified to comply with the FMVSS. If the petitioned vehicle is not similar to one sold in the U.S., this process becomes very complex and costly. A list of vehicles previously determined eligible for importation may be obtained from an RI or from the NHTSA Web site.

Since the cost of modifying a nonconforming vehicle, or the time required to bring it into conformance, may affect the decision to purchase a vehicle abroad, we strongly recommend discussing these aspects with an RI before buying and shipping a vehicle to the U.S.

Source: National Highway Transportation Safety Administration at *www.nhtsa.dotgov/cars/rules/import/gray0202.html*

The Reaction

Reaction from RIs, as well as (would-be) owners, was swift and vehement. Rich Goings, a Ferrari owner and Chairman of Tupperware Corporation, filed a letter with OVSC stating: "The case currently being presented by Ferrari NA is nothing more than an attempt to continue to artificially influence market demand to support inflated profit margins. Should this continue, I feel compelled to leverage the influence of companies such as mine with the legislative branch to launch an investigation." In a letter to his Congressman, Doug Pirrone, President of Berlinetta Motorcars Ltd. in Huntington, New York, alleged that Ferrari's goal "is to control market, ensure a monopoly, fix the prices, and eliminate all competition."

In the meantime, many RIs have felt the strangling effect of Ferrari's action on their businesses. "It's on life-support now," said Lois Joyeusaz, CEO of J.K. Technologies, one of the RIs registered with DOT. The dealer had to start storing cars, such as Mercedes-Benzes, Porsches, and Ferraris, on a remote farm 90 miles away during its wait for government approval.

Government in the Middle

The OVSC found itself caught in a predicament between Ferrari owners and Ferrari itself. Kenneth Weinstein, Associate Administrator for Safety Assurance at the NHTSA, who oversees the OVSC, stated that the office "wanted to give everyone the right opportunity to make their points" even if that caused delays in approvals and owners getting possession of their cars. As far as RIs' complaints about their ever-growing inventories of imports that could not be delivered to rightful owners, Weinstein stated: "We are doing our job, and if they made a financial commitment that we would be done reviewing their petitions by a particular time, that is not the government's responsibility."

A Side Note

In a rare comment from the public during the petition processes, the head of the Original Automobile Manufacturers' Association, John Linder, took exception to many of the RIs' comments. However, a number of people investigating the matter were unable to find any evidence of such an association or of a person called John Linder. A person who identified himself as John Linder contacted *The Washington Post* and stated that his motive was that he was not too keen on the idea of rich people trying to bring in luxury cars that he believes violate safety standards. He avowed no affiliation with Ferrari or with authorized dealers.

The Decision

April 10, 2002, the following decision was announced by NHTSA, effective immediately: "This notice announces the decision by NHTSA that 2001 Ferrari 360 passenger cars not originally manufactured to comply with all applicable Federal motor vehicle safety standards are eligible for importation into the United States because they are substantially similar to vehicles originally manufactured for importation into and sale in the United States and certified by their manufacturer as complying with the safety standards, and are capable of being readily altered to conform to the standards." The same decision was made with respect to the 550 model.

The landmark petition on which the decision was based was made by J. K. Technologies and generated 21 responses, of which 19 were in favor and two against. Mr. Linder's comment was not responded to, given that he proved to be a "fictitious entity." Ferrari suffered a setback with this decision.

Case Questions

1. Gary Roberts, a Costa Mesa, California, importer stated: "Ferrari's control freaks ought to cooperate with importers and let the free market take care of itself." Describe your reaction to this statement.
2. Is Ferrari's case a good argument for requiring that products be delivered only through approved distribution channels to ensure the highest quality for the customer?
3. Given its loss, what alternative actions are open to Ferrari?

Sources: This case was written by Ilkka A. Ronkainen using publicly available materials. These include: U.S. Department of Transportation, "Decision That Nonconforming 2001 Ferrari 360/550 Passenger Cars are Eligible for Importation," *Federal Register* 67 (10 April 2002): 17479–17486.

Alec Klein, "Life in the Stalled Lane," *The Washington Post,* 6 January 2002, A1, A5.

Bob Gritzinger, "Ferrari NA Wants to Block Gray Imports," *AutoWeek,* 19 August 2001, 45–46.

For general information on gray-market imports, see The Better Business Bureau/New York at *http://www.newyorkbbb.org/library/publications/subrep45. htm,* and Anti-Gray Market Alliance at *http://www.antigraymarket.org.*

VIDEO CASE

ESPN's Worldwide Reach

It began by mistake. Back in the late 1970s, Bill Rasmussen decided to launch a cable station to broadcast Connecticut-area sports. With the assistance of his partners, Rasmussen leased a building in Bristol from which to broadcast and then bought some satellite time. Only after signing the agreement did he learn that his satellite coverage was national—and his small-scale plan of New England sports coverage began to grow. The early name for the channel—Entertainment and Sports Programming Network—proved too much of a tongue twister and, in 1985, they settled on the ESPN acronym as the corporate name. The letters now stand for nothing—except a sports phenomenon.

Since those early days during which the network scrambled to televise whatever it could—from a men's pro, slow-pitch softball game to its first NHL game in 1979—the organization has grown dramatically, filling what Will Burkhardt of ESPN says is now a saturated market for televised sports in the United States and rapidly moving overseas. "We reach 150 to 155 million households around the world [excluding the United States]; that encompasses about 180 markets and territories," says Burkhardt. ESPN reaches all seven continents, including one of the scientific stations located in Antarctica. The expansion has taken place over the last 15 years, beginning when ESPN provided groundbreaking coverage of the America's cup international sailing race from Australia in 1987. That race seemed to be a turning point not only for ESPN, but for cable broadcasting itself. From there, ESPN purchased a majority interest in the European Sports Network (called Eurosport) and began service to 25 Middle Eastern and North African nations. In addition to its Eurosport market, ESPN's largest international markets have become China, India, and Argentina.

Burkhardt notes that ESPN entered the international marketplace because of a "desire to grow outside of the U.S. borders and to take what we had learned in the United States in terms of people's passion for sport . . . and bring that to the international marketplace." This was around the same time that cable and satellite television were expanding around the world, so ESPN's timing seemed perfect.

However, marketing around the world isn't easy. For instance, although India has a huge middle-class population, middle class in that country means that a family might earn about $1,800 per year, as opposed to an American middle-class family's earnings of $35,000 per year. Thus, attracting viewers to pay for television is more difficult in India. In addition, the infrastructure for cable television is very different from that of the United States, which requires more effort for ESPN marketers. India has tens of thousands of cable entrepreneurs serving approximately 100 customers each, instead of a giant like AOL Time Warner, which serves 13 million. Still, ESPN thinks that serving India is worth the effort and tailors its programming to the single most-watched sport in the nation: cricket.

In the burgeoning South American markets, where sports fanatics thrive, viewers can watch all kinds of programming—Argentine rugby, Argentine polo, Brazilian basketball, and Brazilian tennis, to name a few. But Burkhardt emphasizes that ESPN starts with a regional marketing strategy, "building a bed or programming

from which you then start to localize." Currently, most broadcasts are in English or the local language, but dealing with some countries' multiple local dialects is extremely difficult. In addition, consumers in smaller markets want to see broadcasters of their own nationality instead of ESPN's standard crew of broadcasters. "There is no question that people in Mexico would prefer all of our commentators to be Mexican, instead of some who are Argentine," remarks Burkhardt. ESPN simply can't afford to provide this degree of customization yet.

Ultimately, ESPN's goal is to reach as many households worldwide as possible, despite any difficulties in penetrating new markets. For example, the company landed a huge deal that gave it distribution rights in Latin America for all four rounds of the Masters Golf Tournament. ESPN Latin America alone is now distributed in more than 11 million households in 41 countries and territories, broadcasting in English, Spanish, and Portuguese.

In spite of victories like the Masters broadcast, perhaps one of the greatest challenges to ESPN is that the company must, in large part, make its pitch to cable and satellite television operators before its programming ever reaches the consumers themselves. Those operators conduct business in different ways, they lack rating systems, and some even replace ESPN programming with home-grown shows. Then there are political challenges, such as when ESPN was thrown off Chinese cable after the United States mistakenly bombed a Chinese embassy in Eastern Europe. And there are legal tangles in each country that need to be dealt with, as well. But sports are an international language that tries to provide entertainment without political ramifications, and people everywhere love to watch. "We're obviously not trying to promote any kind of political message through showing an American baseball game," says Burkhardt. And perhaps that is the key to ESPN's success—its ability to bring sport to everyone, everywhere, anytime.

Case Questions

1. How have environmental forces affected ESPN's worldwide marketing efforts?
2. Why is it important for ESPN to be global? What might be some barriers to trade for ESPN?
3. How would you describe ESPN's global marketing strategy?
4. Search ESPN's Web site at *http://www.espn.go.com* and summarize what it is doing in international markets.

Sources: Telephone interview with Will Burkhardt of ESPN, January 2000: "TV Listings," 8 February 2000, *http://www.espn.go.com*.
"ESPN International Lands Masters for Latin America," company press release, 11 November 1999, *http://www.espn.go.com*.
Michael Hiestand, "Did You Know? ESPN is 20 Today," *USA Today*, 7 September 1999, *http://www.usatoday.com*.
"Looking Back, Back, Back . . . ," company press release, 6 September 1999, *http://www.espn.go.com*; Rudy Martzke, "ESPN at 20," *USA Today*, 18 August 1999, 2c.

Peter Dickson, Florida International University, presents the market research process in Chapter 5 and explains that companies with superior market research and information systems will gain a better understanding of the market and build a comprehensive base of knowledge to improve decision making. In Chapter 6, Jagdish Sheth, Emory University, and Balaji Krishnan, University of Memphis, describe how marketers can achieve better results by studying consumer behavior and the psychological and social factors that influence the consumer buying decision process. Because of the unique characteristics of

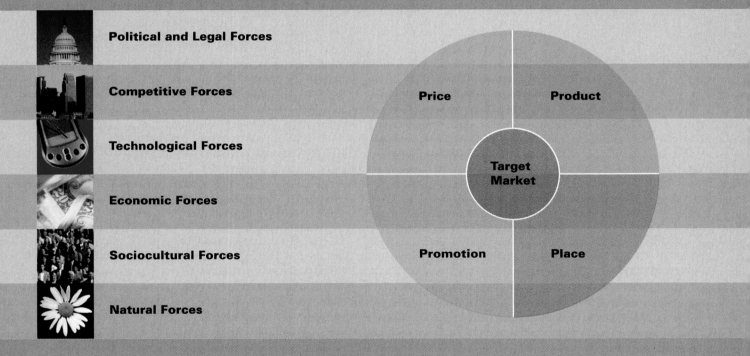

Political and Legal Forces

Competitive Forces

Technological Forces

Economic Forces

Sociocultural Forces

Natural Forces

Price

Product

Target Market

Promotion

Place

the business market and the vast opportunities it presents to marketers, Michael Hutt, Arizona State University, and Thomas Speh, Miami University—Ohio, introduce students to the distinctive characteristics of the business market and how organizations make buying decisions in Chapter 7. Penny Simpson, University of Texas—Pan American, presents the concept of target marketing in Chapter 8 and explains how it is implemented in consumer, business, and international markets.

Understanding the Market

 Political and Legal Forces Some of the practices of target marketers, such as using Joe Camel to reach vulnerable markets with potentially harmful products, have been banned. As the result of lawsuits brought against cigarette manufacturers, cigarette makers may no longer use cartoon characters to promote their products.

 Competitive Forces Firms should understand all the competitors vying for a market segment's limited dollars. Certainly, Coca-Cola is aware of the different types of drinks, including Pepsi, Red Bull, and even water that Generation Y drinks.

 Technological Forces The Internet is also expanding the volume of information available to purchasing managers and transforming the way buyers and sellers come together.

 Economic Forces During periods of recession, customers want additional information before making purchase decisions. The Internet provides sellers with a low-cost means of providing information to consumers.

 Sociocultural Forces The population in Europe is expected to age, while the population in Asia is getting younger. This has led to a number of companies focussing their attention on the growing Asian market as they prepare for the future.

 Natural Forces Ever wonder why European cars are so much smaller than those sold in the United States? The roads in many European countries are narrow, constrained by the environment. So most cars sold in France, for example, are about the size of the Geo Metro.

5

Marketing Research and Information Systems

© Kim Kulish/CORBIS

If You Fly Blind, You Are Likely to Crash and Burn

Just five years ago, there was a contagious belief that the new communication technologies, particularly the Internet and wireless phones, would transform the way we lived. Many senior executives who embraced this belief tried to convince investors that the online experience would replace the entertainment dominance of television and music.[1] Curiously, these senior executives had very little market research to back up their convictions. Where was the market research, for example, to support the claim that Internet use would double every 100 days? How about the claim that consumers would use the Internet extensively for shopping? What about the substantiation of claims that Amazon.com would dominate the book retail trade and that broadband would have profound effects on the advertising industry? There were plenty of consultants and experts who predicted extraordinary growth in the sales and use of the new technologies. Few supported their claims with solid market research to reveal trends in consumer usage and demand. Five years later, a thousand Internet company start-ups have gone broke, thousands more are struggling, and 100,000 jobs have been lost in Silicon Valley alone.

At first glance, it appears that the market research industry failed to provide factual information about trends in demand and new product potential. This may lead some to believe that the market research industry failed to do its job. Although the quality of data provided by market research greatly increased during the 1990s due to new Internet-based methodologies, senior executives and boards of directors decided to invest in huge advertising budgets and not on quality consumer research. Why? They did not believe it would provide valuable insights into trends. Worse, as sometimes happens with market research, they may have considered such research a threat to their agendas. The private and public use of such research would have greatly moderated the irrational exuberance of investment in the high-tech sector. Senior management and boards flew blind and many of their companies crashed and burned.

Some argued that they did not conduct market research because it was not reliable and valid, since consumers lacked the necessary knowledge and experience to appreciate the true potential of the new product concept, prototype, or service. There is some truth to this concern. But in the absence of high-quality market research, the personal opinions of industry gurus and development engineers about the potential of the new technology markets held sway. The problem with this is that the engineers who most understood the product and its potential uses inevitably became too close to their invention and overly optimistic in forecasting its future. This fed the tech bubble that burst when investors realized that even the most successful dot.coms, like Amazon.com, were not profitable. They observed that large numbers of Internet firms were going belly up as they ran out of cash. They had spent a huge amount of investors' money in start-up marketing campaigns (including a lot of TV advertising) and when they had spent all their owners' and lenders' money, they went broke. How could quality consumer research have prevented some of the "irrational exuberance?"

LEARNING OBJECTIVES

After you have completed this chapter, you should be able to:

1. *Appreciate the importance and scope of market research and information systems.*

2. *View traditional customer research as a step-by-step decision-making method prescribed by the market-research process.*

3. *Understand the issues surrounding data collection, such as the differences between qualitative and quantitative data and the importance of sampling and question design.*

4. *Appreciate how new technologies are transforming the market-research process from a discrete to a continuous activity.*

5. *Recognize that market-research extends beyond traditional customer research to the study of competitors.*

6. *Explore the growing importance of conducting channel research and the methods used to study these channels and individual trade partners.*

VOICE OF THE EXPERT
Peter R. Dickson, Florida International University

This chapter gives you a brief introduction to the world of market research, the eyes and ears of marketing. A company that undertakes quality marketing research, listens to the results, and takes action to respond to the results is like an animal with superior vision and hearing. It is genetically superior and, all other things being equal, will flourish. My experience at the Nielsen Center for Marketing Research, where I interacted with leading users of market research and leading research firms, has led me to the conclusion that market research needs to be more appreciated and used by senior managers in their decision making.

More companies need to involve market researchers in their strategic discussions. Similarly, market researchers need to be proactive and market their services. They need to seek out involvement in important strategic decisions. They need to minimize the number of marketing managers and consultants between them and the decision maker(s). They also need to demonstrate how market research has a useful impact on a firm's strategic plans. As future marketers I hope you take this message to heart. Learn about market research and learn to use it effectively. It will serve you well. Good, sensible market research will greatly benefit your firm and the clever use of market research is an excellent path to promotion.

In this chapter, you will gain an appreciation for the importance and scope of market-research and information systems. Over the years, traditional customer research has been guided by a step-by-step decision-making method prescribed by the market-research process. However, strict adherence to the market-research process is now changing as technological enhancements such as electronic observational research, decision-support systems, and Web-based marketing research have transformed the research process from a discrete activity to a continuous process. The chapter concludes by highlighting the simple fact that the scope of market research and information systems should extend beyond customer research and include competitor and channel research.

LEARNING OBJECTIVE 1

Importance and Scope of Marketing Research and Information

Firms that adjust their marketing strategies faster than competitors to reflect environmental changes in domestic and international markets are able to sustain a competitive advantage. The key to this advantage often lies in the firm's ability to collect, organize, and act on information gathered through *market research* and *marketing information systems*. The competitive importance of market research and analysis cannot be overstated. For example, Shell Oil commissioned a study of 30 companies that had survived in business for more than 75 years.[2] What impressed the Shell Oil researchers the most was the ability of these long-standing companies to learn about their changing marketplaces and to adapt their marketing strategies accordingly. These successful companies had developed a shared way of thinking about customers, competitors, distributors, and themselves. The managers in these companies were able to change their thinking about the marketplace faster than their competition. Such fast insight and learning also gave them more time to innovate, imitate, and avoid crisis management. Ultimately, companies that embraced market research and the development of marketing information systems combined with superior decision-making skills created a strategic competitive advantage over their rivals.

The scope of market research and marketing information systems extends beyond basic customer research. From a sociological and political economy perspective, a market is made up of many diverse players, each with its own distinct interests and behavior. Successful marketing decision-making teams obviously think a lot about how customers will react to a new product or business tactic. But they also think about how other "players" in the marketing environment will react to the firm's change in marketing strategy. It is like a card game where you have to anticipate how the different players will react to your move. Some will welcome your moves, others will be indifferent to them, and still others will contest your moves. Simultaneously, you then have to think about how customers will react to your rivals' reactions.

A change in the firm's marketing strategy is likely to set off a chain reaction of events. Successful marketers think through these likely events before marketing strategy is modified. Who is most likely to react to a firm's change in marketing strategy? A market typically contains four players—customers, competitors, distribution-channel members, and regulators that monitor the marketplace. Therefore, it is generally recommended that the study of the market be divided into four topics: customer research, competitor research, channel research, and public policy research. Formally defined, **market research** is the process of gathering information pertaining to customers, competitors, channels, and public policy for the purpose of specific decision making. Market research technically differs from marketing information systems in that market research collects information for a specific purpose. In contrast, **marketing information systems (MIS)** provide organized and continuous data collection and analysis for the purpose of providing ongoing marketing intelligence.

Market research
Is the process of gathering information pertaining to customers, competitors, channels, and public policy for the purpose of specific decision making.

Marketing information systems (MIS)
Provide organized and continuous data collection and analysis to facilitate ongoing marketing intelligence.

To fully maximize the impact of market research on a firm's marketing decision-making, it is important that the market research process not end at the presentation of results. Researchers should continue to be involved in the decision-making process and the implementation of the decisions.

As such, marketing information systems may highlight potential threats and opportunities that exist in the marketplace, whereas follow-up market research might be used to explore a specific threat or opportunity in depth. Firms that broaden the scope of their market research and marketing information systems beyond traditional customer research have a better understanding of the market and a more comprehensive base of knowledge to improve decision making. Market research and marketing information systems are not a panacea for guaranteed success. However, they do significantly decrease the level of risk and increase the odds of success associated with decision making.

Customer Research and the Marketing Research Process

2 LEARNING OBJECTIVE

Customer research encompasses the study of business-to-business customers and household consumers. Customer research can take many and varied forms, with arguments for and against the effectiveness and cost efficiencies of different practices. However, regardless of the specific research methods used, traditional customer research tends to follow a path prescribed by the market-research process.

The **market-research process** presented in Figure 5.1 offers a systematic approach to designing, collecting, interpreting, and reporting information that helps marketers explore opportunities and make specific marketing decisions. It is important to note that the market-research process is not set in stone and that the process itself may indeed be adapted based on the requirements of each project. Typically, the market research process includes the following steps:

1. Problem Definition
2. Research Design
3. Data Collection
4. Data Analysis and Interpretation
5. Presentation of Results

In the following sections, we expand on the major steps in the market-research process.

Market-research process
As presented in Figure 5.1, offers a systematic approach to designing, collecting, interpreting, and reporting information that helps marketers explore opportunities and make specific marketing decisions.

Figure 5.1	The Marketing Research Process

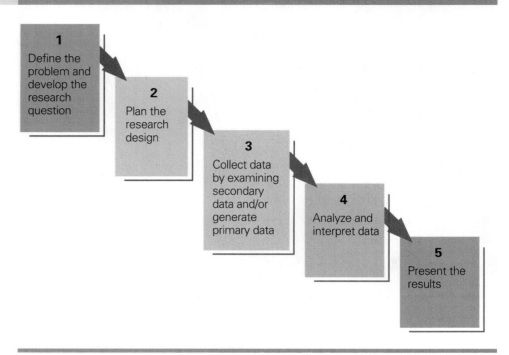

Problem Definition

The primary objective of the problem-definition stage of the market-research process is to develop the *research question*. Problem definition is often mentioned as the most important and difficult step in the process, as it involves recognizing that a problem exists and then attempting to define the specific problem—not an easy task. In fact, the problem may be redefined based on information collected in latter stages of the market-research process. One of the challenges in defining the problem is differentiating between *symptoms* and *problems*. Sometimes decision makers believe that a symptom is the problem, whereas in actuality the symptom is an indicator of a much more important issue that needs to be addressed. For example, the symptoms of declining sales and employee turnover may be indicators of larger concerns such as a poor location decision or weak middle-management skills, much like a runny nose and a cough are symptoms of a cold. Consequently, marketers need to carefully examine the facts surrounding the issue of concern to determine the correct problem definition. Poor problem definition results in wasted expense, time, and effort and, perhaps even more tragically, the original problem not getting solved.

Research Design

After the problem has been defined and the research question has been formed, researchers proceed to the research-design step of the market-research process. Simply stated, research design is the master plan for the research study. Research design addresses the type of research needed to investigate the research question, determines the need for primary or secondary data, and ensures that the end results of the research study are reliable and valid.

Types of Research

The nature of the research question determines whether exploratory, descriptive, or causal research is the appropriate research method to generate the data needed to address the research question. **Exploratory research** is appropriate when the research

Exploratory research
Is appropriate when the research question needs to be further defined and/or if researchers want additional information before they venture into more formal and extensive data-collection procedures.

question needs to be further defined and/or if researchers want additional information before they venture into more formal and extensive data-collection procedures. Exploratory researchers explore internal records and data and discuss the issues surrounding the research question with informed sources, such as customers and suppliers. Exploratory research tends to be less formal, less time-intensive, and less expensive than its descriptive and causal counterparts.

Descriptive research is characterized by a more formal research process of exploration and is typically used for product-usage and customer-satisfaction research. Descriptive research typically queries respondents about their demographic characteristics (e.g., age, income, marital status, occupation, etc.); media habits; place-of-purchase habits; usage behavior; competitive considerations; and purchasing criteria; as well as their current level of satisfaction with existing products and future needs. Descriptive research can be further defined as cross-sectional or longitudinal. *Cross-sectional research* addresses customers' responses at a specific point in time. For example, if respondents were asked "How satisfied are you with the college of business?" the respondents' responses would reflect their current feelings. In contrast, *longitudinal research* addresses customer responses over a period of time. For example, if the same college of business satisfaction question were asked of respondents while they were freshmen, and then asked again while they were sophomores, juniors, and seniors, changes in respondent satisfaction could be assessed over time. The longitudinal study would likely provide a richer understanding of respondents' satisfaction levels, as their satisfaction with the college likely changes as their wants and needs change over time.

In contrast to exploratory and descriptive research, **causal research** is used when the research question specifically hypothesizes that X "causes" Y. Also known as, "cause-and-effect" studies, examples of causal research have included the study of music tempo as it relates to time spent in restaurants. Past research has indicated that when the music is more upbeat, tables turn over more quickly and overall sales volume increases, since more diners can be seated and served. Slow down the music and patrons stay longer and purchase more desserts and after-dinner beverages, thereby increasing the profit margins on a per-table basis.[3] Other causal studies might include the effects of price decreases on sales, pay raises as they relate to employee satisfaction, and the practice of thanking customers by name as it relates to customer satisfaction.

Types of Data

During the research-design stage of the market-research process, researchers must also determine if the information they need is currently available from existing sources or if new research must be conducted. **Secondary data** refers to data that already exists. As such, secondary research is generally associated with the advantages of being inexpensive, quickly collected, and provided from multiple perspectives (thereby limiting the potential bias of a single source). Secondary data can be further defined as internal secondary data and external secondary data. *Internal secondary data* refers to published records that already exist within the organization, such as sales records, financial performance reports, and cost analyses. In contrast, *external secondary data* pertains to data that resides outside the firm such as *Consumer Reports*, trade publications, and government reports.

If secondary data sources have been scrutinized and the information needed by market researchers has not been uncovered and/or additional information is desired, the need for primary data may be determined. **Primary data** pertains to the generation of new data that is collected to address specific market-research problems. Although more time-intensive and expensive than secondary data, primary data are generally associated with the advantages of fitting the specific needs of the researcher, being controllable, having known data-collection procedures, and ensuring privacy (the firm that collects the information has no obligation to share the information). Specifics relating to the collection of secondary and primary data are discussed later in the chapter.

Descriptive research
Also known as survey research, is characterized by a more formal research process of exploration and is typically used for product-usage and customer-satisfaction research.

Causal research
Also known as cause-and-effect studies, is used when the research question specifically hypothesizes that X "causes" Y.

Secondary data
Refers to data that already exist.

Primary data
Pertain to the generation of new data collected to address specific market-research problems.

Reliability

Is a measure of the stability or consistency of customer responses. In other words, a research technique is reliable if it produces almost identical results when the same question is asked again of the same respondents, or when several similar customer questions produce similar customer responses.

Validity

Refers to the relevance of the measure

Research Reliability and Validity

Research design also includes the steps necessary to ensure that research findings are reliable and valid. **Reliability** is a measure of the stability or consistency of customer responses. In other words, a research technique is reliable if it produces almost identical results when the same question is asked again of the same respondents, or when several similar customer questions produce similar customer responses. Research techniques that are reliable are not necessarily valid. For example, a study may reliably predict that New York City's crime rate increases with the city's ice cream sales. Interpreted literally, the city should ban sales of ice cream to reduce the crime rate. However, what the study should have really measured was how the crime rate varied by season or temperature. New York City's crime rate, like its ice cream sales, increases during the warmer months. Hence, **validity** refers to the relevance of the measure. In other words, valid research techniques measure what they are supposed to measure. Considered jointly, reliability and validity address the fundamental question: Does the research technique consistently measure the true opinions and behavior of the respondent?

LEARNING OBJECTIVE 3

Data Collection

The third step in the market-research process involves the collection of data. Data collection can be accomplished by examining secondary research that already exists and/or by generating new data through primary research using qualitative and/or quantitative research techniques. This section addresses each of these topics, as well as sampling and questionnaire design.

Secondary Data

One of the largest providers of secondary data is the U.S. Census Bureau. In fact, the U.S. Census Bureau is the largest market-research organization in the world and compiles masses of information about household trends. Almost every public library has the bureau's reports, and the bureau has offices in large cities, with specialists whose job is to help businesspeople find out what they need to know. *American Demographics* magazine also presents analyses of census data, in addition to other analyses on population trends and changes in values, habits, hobbies, and entertainment. The U.S. Government Printing Office (Washington, DC 20402) has a subject bibliography index that lists free government publications on some 300 subjects. The Library of Congress (202–707–5000) also specializes in helping people find information. The U.S. government produces three- to 30-page annual industry reports on more than 300 industries covering both national and global trends in supply and competition. These *U.S. Industrial Outlook* reports provide references for further information, as well as the names and phone numbers of the government researchers who prepared the report. Other important government publications are *Statistical Abstract of the United States* and the transcripts of industry studies undertaken by the Federal Trade Commission, the Justice Department, and the U.S. International Trade Commission. The best free source of advice on obtaining secondary information is your local library.

Requesting Secondary Data from the Government or Trade Associations

Calling and asking for secondary information from a government expert or a staffer at an industry trade association is an important market-intelligence skill that is seldom taught. Some general contact process rules are listed here:

- Politely and cheerfully introduce yourself, give your name and the name of the person who recommended that you call, and state the purpose of your call. Credible compliments go a long way in obtaining the help of an information expert.

- Initially, ask specific questions. Be open, enthusiastic, optimistic, humble, courteous, and grateful (don't interrupt too much!).
- Use a list of questions if you have a number of questions, but try not to make it too obvious that you are following a list. An apparent lack of structure encourages spontaneous insights and allows for bond-forming casual discussion.
- Send a thank-you note (you may wish to call again), and offer to return the favor.
- Be persistent. Keep generating leads. *Calling a cooperative expert is by far the best $10 value for the money in market research and analysis.*[4]

To find trade associations, journals, and newsletters associated with a particular industry, consult the *Directory of Directories,* the *Encyclopedia of Associations,* the *Encyclopedia of Business Information Sources,* and the *Nelson Directory.* Trade associations often publish information on industry sales by geographical region, year, and product category, as well as general studies of consumer behavior that are published in trade magazines.

Technological Forces

Cooperative technological experts are a great source of information for marketing planners. It may take 10 such calls before you find the "true" expert who is willing to share his or her expertise and secondary data.

The Web as a Source of Secondary Data

The World Wide Web has revolutionized the use of secondary data in market research because of its ability to search for relevant information for a low cost. Examples of important data sources on the Web are the U.S. Census Bureau site (http://www.census.gov) and STAT-USA (http://www.stat-usa.gov), another comprehensive source of government statistics that focuses on trade and economic information. Figure 5.2 lists other valuable sites that provide information about customer trends. Some databases are free and others charge a fee for access to information.

Web Sources of Secondary Data	Figure 5.2

Web Site	Information Available
ACNielsen http://www.acnielsen.com	Television audience, supermarket scanner data, and more
Gartner, Inc. http://www.gartner.com	Specializes in e-business and usually presents highlights of its latest findings on its Web site
Arbitron http://www.arbitron.com	Local market and Internet radio audience data
Information Resources, Inc. http://www.infores.com	Supermarket scanner and new product purchasing data
Dun & Bradstreet http://www.dnb.com	Database on more than 50 million companies worldwide
Stat-USA http://www.stat-usa.gov	U.S. Department of Commerce source of international trade data
U.S. Patent Office http://www.uspto.gov	Provides trademark and patent data for businesses
World Trade Organization (WTO) http://www.wto.org	World trade data
International Monetary Fund (IMF) http://www.imf.org	Provides information on many social issues and projects
U.S. Securities and Exchange Commission (SEC) http://www.sec.gov	Edgar database provides financial data on U.S. public corporations
U.S. Small Business Administration (SBF) http://www.sba.gov	Features information and links for small business owners

continues

Figure 5.2	*continued*

Federal Trade Commission (FTC) http://www.ftc.gov	Shows regulations and decisions related to consumer protection and antitrust laws
U.S. Census Bureau http://www.census.gov	Provides U.S. population statistics and trends
Lexis-Nexis http://www.lexis-nexis.com	Articles from business, consumer, and marketing publications
Hoovers Online http://www.hoovers.com	Business descriptions, financial overviews, and news about major companies worldwide
Forrester Research http://www.forrester.com	Identifies and analyzes emerging trends in technology and their impact on business
Gallup Organization http://www.gallup.com	Pioneering political public opinion polling company that offers general and industry-specific consumer studies
NFO WorldGroup http://www.nfow.com	World's largest provider of Internet-based research and the world leader in customer satisfaction and stakeholder-management research
Harris Interactive http://www.harrisblackintl.com	Worldwide market research and consulting firm, best known for *The Harris Poll*® and for its pioneering use of the Internet to conduct scientifically accurate market research

Source: Judy Strauss, Adel El-Enasry, and Raymond Frost, *E-Marketing*, 3rd Ed. (Upper Saddle River, NJ: Prentice Hall, 2003), 165–166. © 2003. Reprinted by permission of Pearson Education, Inc., Upper Saddle River, NJ.

Primary Data: Qualitative Research

Primary research is generally conducted on a basic level before it proceeds to a full-blown primary market-research study. Typically, basic primary research includes methods such as extensive in-depth interviews with customers, customer visits, and focus groups. These types of research methods are often referred to as *qualitative research* because they are more descriptive in nature and do not generate data that can be quantitatively analyzed with much confidence.

In-Depth Interviews and Customer Visits

One of the most basic and important qualitative research activities a firm can use is to meet face-to-face with customers. Talking directly to customers seems so obvious, yet some firms have lost themselves in sophisticated, arm's-length customer research. The problem with traditional survey research, for example, is that too many steps and interpretative judgments separate customers and decision makers. The vivid impact of listening to customers' own words and of seeing how they use a product in their homes, in their offices, or on their production lines is lost if customers are not observed using the product. As a consequence, customer concerns then have less impact on decision making: Visits allow the **voice of the customer** to be heard, and make this voice audible throughout the organization.[5] As fully described in Chapter 9, the voice of the customer is a structured, in-depth, probing, one-on-one situational interview technique that uncovers both general and detailed customer needs.

Companies are often very creative in the ways they observe customers. Fisher-Price, the toy manufacturer, has a special play laboratory and a waiting list of several years for children to participate in their new product testing, which is observed through one-way mirrors. Other toy manufacturers spend a lot of time visiting day-care facilities and watching how children play with toys. Day-care employees, who

Voice of the customer (VOC)
Is the expression of the preferences, opinions, and motivations of the customer that need to be listened to by managers.

J.D. Power and Associates surveys millions of consumers and business customers, listening to the voice of the customer. Awards, such as the one given to Enterprise Rent-A-Car in 2002, serve as positive reinforcements to top performers in an industry.

are "professional" observers, are great sources of ideas for product improvements. In general, the millions of salespeople whose business it is to observe consumers and shoppers are great sources of information.

For several decades, Japanese firms such as Panasonic and Sony have used **hands-on consumer research** that focuses on the way current customers use specific products and brands.[6] For example, one appliance manufacturer took hundreds of photos of actual Japanese kitchens and concluded from the photos that the major problem manufacturers have to address when designing new appliances is the extreme shortage of space in many kitchens. This observation might not have been made had researchers not visited the homes in person and taken the photographs. Such photos should be displayed on the walls of the room where the research team meets. They are a constant reminder of the customers' usage situation that can be "revisited" by simply looking up from the meeting table.

A major camera company used *observational research* as a clever way to improve the design of its camera line. Research and development engineers searched through thousands of prints being processed at one-hour processing labs and counted the most common problems with the photos, such as poor focus adjustment, poor lighting, incorrect film speed, and double exposures because the film was not wound forward. From the situations captured in the photo, they could observe when and where these problems occurred. This led to design improvements in the cameras and better advice in the camera instruction manuals.

Other market researchers encourage consumers to take photos that describe how they use the product and then tell the story the photo illustrates. This encourages consumers to reveal the deeper meaning and significance of the product in their lives. This in-depth technique, called **motivational research**, can sometimes be taken too far. It can lead management to attribute too much meaning to customer involvement with a product or brand because the rich and fanciful stories of a minority of customers are highlighted in the research reports to management. An example of motivational research going too far was when, in the 1950s, researchers concluded that baking a cake was a surrogate for having a baby.

Hands-on consumer research
Is conducted by managers directly observing the way current customers use specific products and brands. The opposite is arm's-length research, which is undertaken by external suppliers.

Motivational research
Is directed at discovering the conscious or subconscious reasons for a person's behavior.

Advanced Technology Makes Survey Research Fast and Easy

When a company needs to conduct a quick assessment of a market segment or test a new product idea, the best research option may be a Web survey. Web surveys provide fast, low-cost access to feedback from large groups of respondents. Survey Professionals (http://www.SurveyPro.com) offers breakthrough technology that gives companies easy, step-by-step tools to create customized, self-administered Web surveys. According to SurveyPro.com, "experienced and inexperienced researchers prefer our simple, risk-free environment for testing and evaluating their topic of interest. More experienced users appreciate our powerful tools and our easy upgrade path to more advanced research solutions."

SurveyPro.com has developed a vast library of survey templates that can be copied or customized, depending on the research objectives. The Survey Template Library includes hundreds of free surveys created to test customer or employee satisfaction and solicit product and service evaluations. The surveys are designed for unique industries and a variety of occupations and lifestyles. Using this library, market researchers have the choice of copying a survey, modifying it as needed, or writing their own survey from scratch.

SurveyPro.com has also made it easy to track results from respondents. As e-mail responses come in, researchers can view results and analyze data in real time—even as data are being collected. Continuously updated reports indicate who has viewed and taken your survey. One click produces various presentations, including tables, charts, and graphs. Data may also be saved to Excel for additional analysis. According to J. Ogden, a Public Relations specialist, "We built our survey, and at 10:30 a.m. the mailing went out to 5,000 people. By 5:30 that afternoon, we had 1,048 completed responses. This is a great product for great results. It was exciting to watch the responses come in and do the analysis immediately online."

Web surveys are an efficient, cost-effective research option, and SurveyPro.com has the advanced technology required to meet the research needs of large clients, including Microsoft, Yahoo, Intel, IBM, and Carnival Cruise Lines. Using advanced technology, personalized messages with a customized survey can accurately reach a large, global audience with the assurance of anonymity. According to L. Baum, a Ph.D. student at the University of Utah, "As an academic researcher of vulnerable populations, I have been especially concerned about participant burden and confidentiality. Surveypro.com is convenient, efficient, and user-friendly and has several features for assuring respondent privacy. They even offered my participants technical support, which can be important when working with an international sample. I think it is well worth adding to the budget section of a funding proposal or scholarship application."

Source: http://www.surveypro.com, accessed 15 May 2003.

Customer Visits in Business-to-Business Marketing

The customer visit is particularly crucial for business-to-business marketing because a few key customers often account for 80% of a firm's business. DuPont's customer-oriented culture goes beyond having its cross-functional teams visit with its customers. Its "Adopt a Customer" program encourages manufacturing process workers to visit a customer once a month and represent the customer's needs on the factory floor.[7]

If they can, marketing executives should also get firsthand experience in being a customer of competitors' products. For example, a team of Marriott executives spent six months on the road, staying in economy hotels and learning about competitors' strengths and weaknesses. The result was the $500-million launch of the Fairfield Inn chain, which immediately achieved an occupancy rate 10 points higher than the industry average.[8] Japanese companies have been known to send up-and-coming executives to the United States for several years to do nothing but travel and study the market for their products firsthand. The importance of creating a company culture that encourages direct contact with the customer explains why the chief executive officer of United Airlines spends time at the ticket counter, and why senior executives at 3M spend several days a month visiting customers, and not just big accounts. Below are several guidelines for planning direct visits with customers:

- **Have customer visits arranged by the sales force.** Cooperation between factory engineers and the sales force is crucial. No one likes someone else in a company doing anything behind his or her back, particularly a sales representative whose commissions depend on customer trust and goodwill.

Rubbermaid conducted qualitative research to learn more about consumers' opinions about plastic food storage containers. In response, Rubbermaid created StainShield™ containers, the first affordable food storage containers that won't stain or absorb food odors.

- **Visit 10 to 20 randomly chosen customers, as well as important customers who are leaders in adopting new technology.** This reduces the impact of an extreme, atypical opinion in later decisions.
- **Use jargon only if the customer uses the same jargon.** Listen carefully, and note the way customers talk about the product. This gives you clues about the benefits they seek, how they think about the benefits, what problems they confront, and how to design the product to gain a competitive advantage. Rather than asking a customer to adopt your jargon, you should be adopting the customer's words and metaphors. This is how a team changes its thinking about the customer and related decisions. Do not talk in front of customers using jargon that makes them feel like outsiders.
- **Learn to listen and observe; do not treat the visit as a sales call.** This is something the sales representative will find hard to accept. Do not engage in disparaging the competition when the customer praises them. Instead, be open to ideas that can be quickly imitated.
- **Define your research objectives in advance, and use a discussion guide based on these objectives.** Write a report on the visit that addresses the research objectives. Report separately on the serendipitous information. "Report" means informing key people within your organization about what you saw or heard.
- **Observe the product in use in every situation.** Note and photograph how an innovative customer has adapted your product, package, or service to improve its performance in a particular usage situation. This may suggest a promising new design feature to better serve a market niche.
- **If possible, have two or three members of the team make the visit together.** The time spent talking while traveling before and after the visit is invaluable. Shared expectations, perceptions, and insights are best when made close to the customer visit. Members of the team also discover what they did not see or hear and thus learn from each other how to become better observers and listeners.

Focus Group Research

Next to observation and in-depth discussions with customers, the most common way of undertaking customer research is the use of *focus groups*. A **focus group** is a

Focus group

Is a carefully recruited group of six to 12 people who participate in a freewheeling, one- to two-hour discussion that focuses on a particular subject, such as product usage, shopping habits, or warranty experiences.

In a focus group, customers reveal their opinions about product usage, shopping habits, or other consumer experiences. Focus groups reveal valuable information but seldom represent the opinions of the total market.

© Spencer Grant/PhotoEdit, Inc.

carefully recruited group of six to 12 people who participate in a freewheeling, one- to two-hour discussion that focuses on a particular subject, such as product usage, shopping habits, or warranty experiences. Managers observe the discussion through a one-way mirror or on videotape. In recent years, it has been found that smaller focus groups are often more effective because the individuals in them are more talkative and they can be conducted in more casual locations, such as hotel suites. Young marketing executives often spend one or two weeks a year crisscrossing the country doing three or four focus groups a day. In more formal focus groups, a skilled, trained conversationalist called a *moderator* often conducts the session to encourage conversation and debate and members of the cross-functional decision team watch the discussion through a one-way mirror or on closed-circuit television.

Focus groups can be used successfully by following these best-practice process suggestions:

- The random calling and screening of participants based on their product usage experience and target *demographics,* such as age and education, can be expensive, sometimes nearly $1,000 to find 30 to 50 willing participants. Consider spending more to create a longer list of willing, qualified participants that can be drawn from at fairly short notice. This will greatly speed up the process of running future focus groups. Take care to check how frequently they have participated in focus groups; avoid professional participants.

- Expect to pay at least $50 per participant to cover travel expenses and two to three hours of his or her time. Professionals such as doctors and architects may expect to be paid several hundred dollars for participating.

- Find a good moderator who can relate to your target group, and develop a long-term relationship with the moderator. Do not conduct focus groups yourself unless you have had professional training and can remain emotionally detached from the subject. Talk to the moderator afterwards about his or her interpretation of the reactions of the focus-group participants.

- Listen to what is said, but also note the interest or emotion behind what is said. Are the participants excited and interested or really only politely lukewarm?

- Encourage the cross-functional team and senior management to watch the focus group. The focused attention and the discussion that ensues have an immediacy that will have a long-term impact on decision making. This also enables questions to be passed to the moderator during a break when focus groups are watched live.

- Continue to run focus groups until no new, important insights are learned from the last focus group that is run. This often means only three or four focus groups need to be run.
- The concept of focus groups has been taken a step further in new product development, with experts recruited to participate.

Although focus groups are great at bringing to the surface issues, problems, and the range of services and features desired, they are seldom completely representative of the thoughts and opinions of a firm's total target market. Typically, focus groups are followed up by more formal survey research of a representative sample of the target market. Focus groups can help identify market segments, but survey research is needed to estimate the size of the segments.

Primary Data: Quantitative Research

If the answer to the research question developed in the problem-definition stage of the market-research process is not provided from qualitative research, or if reassuring confirmation is sought, then more thorough descriptive or causal research is likely to be undertaken that can provide *quantitative* answers. Since descriptive research is more common in business than causal research, we focus our discussion on descriptive-research methods. Descriptive research, also commonly referred to as *survey research,* involves the sampling and surveying of a population of customers using a carefully prepared set of questions. Surveys of individuals or households are normally taken to study and categorize the variation in buyer values, lifestyles, product usage, benefits sought, and beliefs about product performance (see Chapter 6). This categorization process helps marketers segment consumers into subgroups that share similar preferences and behavior (see Chapter 8). Figure 5.3 compares the major survey-research approaches.

These days, survey research is often used to track customer satisfaction. In a competitive market, customer loyalty and satisfaction are leading indicators of future sales. If they begin to decrease, then it is likely that future sales will also decrease. Therefore, in an effort to avoid losing customer sales, marketers are increasingly conducting surveys of customer satisfaction.[9] Figure 5.4 presents an example of such an analysis. It categorizes customers by their past loyalty. A slip in satisfaction from a company's most loyal customers is much more serious than a decline in satisfaction among customers who have never been very loyal. The most rigorous customer satisfaction index (CSI) counts the percentage of "happy" customers in a satisfaction survey. Happy customers say (1) they are completely satisfied, (2) they would definitely recommend the product to friends, and (3) they definitely plan to continue to be loyal customers. The two major issues in survey research are sampling and questionnaire design.

Sampling

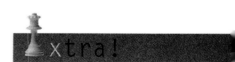

To determine if the opinions expressed in focus groups and in-depth interviews represent the true opinions, attitudes, interests, beliefs, and behaviors of the larger population of customers, market researchers may survey a sample of the population. But how is a sample drawn, and what are the advantages of the different methods of selecting a sample of the overall population? These questions are best addressed by discussing the advantages and disadvantages of probability sampling and nonprobability sampling.

Probability Sampling. A probability sample is an umbrella term used to describe sampling techniques where respondents have a known (nonzero) chance of being chosen. Three common types of probability samples include simple random samples,

Figure 5.3	Major Survey Research Methods				
Criteria	**Direct/Cold Mailing**	**Mail Panels**	**Telephone**	**Personal In-Home**	**Mall Intercept**
Complexity and versatility	Not much	Not much	Substantial, but complex or lengthy scales difficult to use	Highly flexible	Most flexible
Quantity of data	Substantial	Substantial	Short, typically lasting 15–30 minutes	Greatest quantity	Limited to 25 minutes or less
Sample control	Little	Substantial, but representativeness may be a question	Good, but non-listed households can be a problem	In theory, provides greatest controls	Can be problematic; sample representativeness may be questionable
Quality of data	Better for sensitive or embarrassing questions; however, no interviewer is present to clarify what is being asked		Positive—interviewer can clear up any ambiguities; negative—may lead to socially acceptable answers 60–80%	The chance of cheating arises	Unnatural testing environment can lead to bias
Response rates	In general, low; as low as 10%	70–80%	60–80%	Greater than 80%	As high as 80%
Speed	Several weeks; completion time will increase with follow-up mailings	Several weeks with no follow-up mailings, longer with follow-up mailings	Large studies can be completed in three to four weeks	Faster than mail but typically slower than telephone surveys	Large studies can be completed in a few days
Cost	Inexpensive; as low as $2.50 per completed interview	Lowest	Not as low as mail; depends on incidence rate and length of questionnaire	Can be relatively expensive, but costs vary considerably	Less expensive than in-home, but higher than telephone; again, length and incidence rates will determine cost
Uses	Executive, industrial, medical, and readership studies	All areas of marketing research, particularly useful in low-incidence categories	Particularly effective in studies that require national samples	Still prevalent in product-testing and other studies that require visual cues or product prototypes	Pervasive-concept tests, name tests, package tests, copy tests

stratified samples, and cluster samples. Companies are often interested in finding out whether their best customers are very satisfied, how the customer service they experienced could be improved, and what other goods or services might be sold to them. In this case, the company might generate a simple random sample of customers from the company's customer database by selecting those customers who have purchased

Customer Satisfaction by Past Loyalty					Figure 5.4
	Current Satisfaction				
Past Loyalty	**Completely Satisfied**	**Somewhat Satisfied**	**Neutral**	**Dissatisfied**	**% of Sales**
Firm friends	7%	3%	0%	0%	10%
Core loyal	10	5	5	5	25
Loyal switchers	10	10	10	10	40
Buy-on-price customers	0	5	10	10	25
Overall	27%	23%	25%	25%	100%

$1,000 or more worth of goods and services in the last year. Hence, a **simple random sample** is a probability sample where respondents are chosen from a complete list of the population. Simple random samples are often generated through the assistance of computer programs that use random number generators. Typical samples range in size from 400 to 1,000 participants, but can be generated into the tens of thousands from customer lists that can consist of hundreds of thousands.

Continuing with this example, if the company was particularly interested in its female clientele, then a stratified sampling technique would be appropriate. A **stratified sample** is a probability sample where researchers divide the complete population into groups and then use simple random-sampling techniques on the subgroups. In other words, the customer database would be stratified into males and females. A simple random sample would then be selected from the list of female respondents. Somewhat similar to stratified samples, **cluster samples** are probability samples where researchers randomly choose geographic clusters and then randomly select samples within the clusters. For example, a large upscale retailer such as Nordstrom may want to randomly select five stores within each of the company's sales regions and then randomly sample customers from each of these stores.

The primary advantage of probability samples is that they greatly reduce the potential for biasing error in the results. In addition, sampling can be much more cost-effective than surveying the whole population and has the additional advantage of not constantly bothering the entire population of customers for feedback. Probability samples also enable confident estimation of the behavior and attitudes of the entire population of interest given the random-sample result. For example, if the random-sample survey of 400 customers indicates that 50% of those surveyed are satisfied, then the true incidence of satisfaction in the entire population of this group of customers is almost certain (at least 99% certain) to be 42.5–57.5%[10]. With a larger random sample of 1,600 indicating 50% satisfaction, the true incidence of satisfaction in the entire population of customers is almost certain (99% certain again) to be 46–54%. A sample of 10,000 that reports that 50% are satisfied brings the precision of the estimate to 48.5–51.5%.[11]

The primary disadvantage of random sampling is that it is rare to obtain a list of the entire target population of interest. If researchers are very lucky, they may find friendly distributors who will allow them to study competitors' customers by sampling from databases of customers who have recently purchased rival products. In this case, though, the results generalize only to customers of a particular distributor. If researchers wish to study why some customers are product-category nonusers, they need to find a specific list of this population of interest, which may be impossible.

To offset the difficulties associated with generating probability samples, many market research firms offer access to *panels of households*. Put together by the research firm itself or through third-party research suppliers, each panel is pre-identified or prequalified as possessing specific sociodemographic and buying behavior characteristics (e.g., representing the population of all households across the United States).

Simple random sample
Is a probability sample where respondents are chosen from a complete list of the population.

Stratified sample
Is a probability sample where researchers divide the complete population into groups and then use simple random-sampling techniques on the subgroups.

Cluster samples
Are probability samples where researchers randomly choose geographic clusters and then randomly select samples within the clusters.

The firm will then randomly sample from these panels, or be provided with an entire panel of 5,000 households that have already been randomly selected to provide a demographic representation of the U.S. population. This is by far the most convenient and probably the best way of undertaking sampling and survey research—a marketer can purchase answers to individual questions in **omnibus surveys**, in which several firms studying different product markets participate in the same survey.

Nonprobability Sampling. In contrast to probability samples, nonprobability samples are arbitrary sampling techniques where respondents have an unknown or zero chance of being chosen for the sample. Three common types of nonprobability samples include convenience samples, quota samples, and judgment samples. To get a sense of demand in different geographical regions of the United States for a premium brand of Columbian coffee called Grower Reserve, how might a marketer undertake taste tests against a premium supermarket brand such as Starbucks? One approach might be to survey a sample of 100 adults intercepted in a shopping mall by a local market-research firm that has a testing facility at the mall. Because these customers are conveniently available to survey as they walk through the mall, this type of sampling is called a **convenience sample**. A convenience sample is a nonprobability sample because respondents are not chosen from a complete list of the population, but on the basis of their availability. For example, people who are systematically too busy because they work long hours at white-collar jobs in offices (where they also drink a lot of premium coffee) would be underrepresented in such a survey, creating a *nonresponse* or *participation bias*—a common disadvantage of nonprobability samples.

The above sample design might be further limited to three upscale malls in each of the seven regions of the United States (New England and Northeast, South, Midwest, Mountain and High Prairies, Southwest, California, and Northwest). Hence, the total sample consists of 2,100 respondents (7 regions × 3 malls × 100 respondents). This sample continues to constitute a nonprobability sample because the malls chosen are not selected randomly from the population of all malls available, all mall visitors are not randomly sampled, and nonmall visitors are not included.

Nonprobability-sampling techniques also include quota and judgment samples. *Mall interceptors,* individuals who select and survey respondents, may be asked to fill quota samples—say, 100 men and 100 women—to ensure that men are not underrepresented in the sample. **Quota samples** are nonprobability samples where researchers conveniently match characteristics in the population with quotas to ensure that respondents are not under- or overrepresented. In addition, mall interceptors may be called upon to survey only individuals who appear to be premium-coffee drinkers. In this instance, **judgment sampling**, where the respondent's selection is based on the arbitrary judgment of the researcher, would be used. Clearly, while nonprobability samples are more convenient, they create the opportunity for far greater research bias.

Sampling Challenges. The major problem with sampling is the risk of **nonresponse error** or *participation bias,* which occurs when a particular customer group is under- or overrepresented in a sample. For example, in an effort to study what Americans eat, the U.S. Environmental Protection Agency (EPA) hired the market-research firm National Analysts. The firm scientifically selected 6,000 households of all incomes and 3,600 low-income households.[12] Accurate results were important because EPA planned to use the results to measure ingestion of pesticides through consumption of different agricultural products (e.g., corn and potatoes) and, based on results, set agricultural pesticide regulations. Future government support of school lunch and food stamp programs also depended on the results. The questionnaire took up to three hours to complete, and respondents were paid $2 to participate. In the end, only 34% of those who initially agreed to be surveyed actually participated. The problem with this particular study was that households should

Omnibus surveys
Refers to the sampling method whereby several firms studying different product markets participate in the same survey.

Convenience sample
Is a sample of consumers who are not randomly sampled from a population (e.g., users of the product) but who are readily available.

Quota samples
Are nonprobability samples where researchers conveniently match characteristics in the population with quotas to ensure that respondents are not under- or overrepresented.

Judgment sampling
Refers to a nonprobability sampling technique where the respondent's selection is based on the arbitrary judgment of the researcher

Nonresponse error
or participation bias occurs when a particular customer group is under- or overrepresented in a sample.

Keeping the Promise of Confidentiality

A large automobile dealership decided to undertake a customer-satisfaction survey of 5,000 of its recent customers. Customers were told that the questionnaire was confidential and anonymous. However, each return envelope had an identification label so that customer satisfaction could be linked to the salesperson who sold the car and the car's service history. The data from this service was collected and stored in the dealership's customer-relationship database.

The manager of the dealership was very surprised at the high level of customer dissatisfaction. Several hundred of the respondents indicated they were very unhappy with the quality of the service they received. Fearing that the dealership would lose their business unless something was done to respond to their concerns, and genuinely wanting to make

things right, the manager instructed the sales and service managers to call these several hundred customers, listen to their complaints, and try to make amends. The dealership had promised that the surveys were anonymous and confidential. Yet, by contacting the customers, the dealership staff let them know that the anonymity and confidentiality promise was violated, despite the fact that the dealership's intentions were honorable.

DISCUSSION QUESTIONS

1. What should the sales or service manager say if a customer asks if the dealership is calling because of the survey's open-ended questions?
2. Do you believe that the customers' responses remained confidential?

have been paid more—$20 to $30—to encourage participation. For an additional cost of $250,000, the response rate would have been about 90%, particularly in the low-income sample. And while $250,000 might sound like a lot of money, when billions of dollars spent on pesticides and school lunches were at stake, not spending $250,000 on incentives was a huge mistake.

A more general problem with sampling is that many populations have been over-surveyed or taken in by bogus market-research studies that are merely sophisticated sales pitches. The Council of American Survey Research Organizations estimates that about one-third of households now refuse to participate in phone surveys because of inconvenience or a suspicion that the call is really selling under the guise of research (called **sugging**), which has been made illegal by the Federal Trade Commission. In addition, Americans have less time to participate in such studies because they generally work longer hours today than in the past. As a result, it takes a lot of incentives to avoid the risk of nonresponse bias and the consequent accusations (of course, almost always made by those who disagree with the findings) that the research was biased.

Sugging
Refers to the illegal practice of selling under the guise of research.

Question Design

When designing a survey, market researchers should carefully compose the questions so that they are precise and understandable and help reveal the information required by the researcher. Figure 5.5 presents examples of various question types used to measure customer beliefs and attitudes. Sometimes questions can be combined to create a new measure. In the example of a *Likert agreement scale* shown in Figure 5.5, each respondent's ratings of Bank One on the seven-point semantic differential scale in the table can be weighted by the relative importance the respondent assigns to each feature, then summed to create an overall evaluation of Bank One. This overall evaluation measure has been found to be a good predictor of choice.

The *ratio scale* presented was developed to track the changes in shoppers' perceptions of prices in their neighborhood supermarkets and to study whether loyal customers of each store had different price perceptions. The difference between a *ratio scale* and an *interval scale* is that a ratio scale has a meaningful, natural zero point and is a continuous measure, rather than measured in discrete intervals. A study of the reliability of survey measures did not find that any one of the types of measures presented in Figure 5.5 was any better than any other, but that the reliability of the measure increased as the number of points in the scale increased.[13] Thus, a 10-point scale is more reliable than a seven-point scale, which is more reliable than a five-point scale. This same study also found that it was better to use several

Figure 5.5	Types of Survey Questions

Likert agreement scale, which measures a bank's performance beliefs:

	Strongly Disagree	Disagree	Somewhat Disagree	Neither Agree nor Disagree	Somewhat Agree	Agree	Strongly Agree
Bank One offers courteous service	—	—	—	—	—	—	—
Bank One has conveniently located ATMs	—	—	—	—	—	—	—
Bank One offers low interest rates	—	—	—	—	—	—	—
Bank One has an easy-to-use Internet site	—	—	—	—	—	—	—

Semantic differential scale, which measures a bank's performance beliefs:

Bank One is discourteous	:__:__:__:__:__:__:	Bank One is courteous
Bank One ATMs are inconveniently located	:__:__:__:__:__:__:	Bank One ATMs are conveniently located
Bank One has low interest rates	:__:__:__:__:__:__:	Bank One has high interest rates
Bank One's Internet site is not easy to use	:__:__:__:__:__:__:	Bank One's Internet site is easy to use

Importance scale:

Using a 10-point importance scale, where 1 = not important, 5 = moderately important, and 10 = very important, how important are the following to you in evaluating a bank?

Courteous service	—
ATM location convenience	—
Interest rates	—
Convenient Internet site	—

To indicate their relative importance in evaluating a bank, please allocate 100 points across the following four performance features: (e.g., 25, 25, 25, 25 would indicate equal importance):

Courteous service	—
ATM location convenience	—
Interest rates	—
Convenient Internet site	—
Total	100

Specialized ratio scales (a ratio scale has a natural zero point):

If a shopping basket full of groceries costs $100 at Publix, how much would that same basket of groceries cost at:

Kroger	$___
Winn-Dixie	$___
Kmart	$___
Wal-Mart	$___

measures, such as the three-item CSI scale mentioned earlier that tracks satisfaction, rather than just a single measure of a belief, behavior, or attitude. Using a market-research process that involves multiple measures of customer satisfaction increases the reliability of the responses and the validity of the result.

A useful follow-up question in satisfaction-survey research is to ask an *open-ended question* such as, "How can we improve?" The answers to this question can then be used to increase the quality of the product and reduce dissatisfaction. For example, for several years United Parcel Service (UPS) questioned customers about their satisfaction with the speed and reliability of the shipping service. When the company asked how the service could be improved, it discovered that customers wanted more face-to-face contact with UPS drivers; they wanted a person to front the service whom they could get to know, ask for advice on shipping, and personally approach with problems and emergencies. As a result, the company is now giving its 62,000 drivers an additional 30 minutes a day to spend time with customers, as well as a small commission on any leads they generate.[14] The program initially cost about $6 million in extra drivers' hours and commissions, but generated tens of millions in additional revenue.

Like samples, questions can be biased or subject to nonresponse (because a particular question cannot be answered or the respondent chooses not to answer). Consequently, survey questions have to be carefully designed to avoid "leading" respondents. For example, if a question starts with an explanation of how a company has recently spent $50 million on training its employees to be more friendly and responsive, then the answers are likely to overstate customer satisfaction with employee responsiveness, because the respondents will have been led. Even top business schools are not above trying to destroy the objectivity of consumer survey research. The annual rankings of business schools, such as those by *Business Week,* have become big business. When a school's ranking rises dramatically, so do its applications. This has led some otherwise very respectable business schools to ask their graduates who are surveyed by such rating services to rate the school very highly on customer satisfaction questions: High ratings increase the reputation of the school and hence the value of the alumni's degrees. Imagine the fuss that would be created if it were discovered that the validity of J. D. Power surveys of new-car customer satisfaction were similarly corrupted by a car manufacturer asking all of its new car buyers to rate a particular model highly because doing so would increase the resale value of the car?

The only sure way of detecting whether questions are confusing, hard to follow, unanswerable because respondents cannot remember their behavior, or not answered because they are too personal is to pretest the survey using a small sample from the population. The *pretest* is administered in the same way that the full survey will be administered. After the respondent has completed the survey, the market researcher interviews the respondent, talking through the survey and the responses item by item. This method can reveal problems with understanding and interpretation and potentially identify reasons for customer nonresponse.

A commonsense approach should always be adopted in undertaking survey research. For example, before a firm undertakes regular surveys of customer satisfaction, it should develop a program to monitor customer-dissatisfaction complaints registered with the company through letters and phone calls. Unsolicited consumer complaints send red-alert signals about problems with product design or after-sales service. Tracking service requests is another way of identifying customer dissatisfaction. The downtown Chicago Marriott hotel, for example, discovered that two-thirds of its guest calls to housekeeping were for an iron and ironing board. Instead of replacing the black-and-white televisions in the bathrooms of concierge-level guest rooms (housekeeping had received no calls requesting color televisions in the bathrooms), the hotel spent $20,000 putting irons and ironing boards in all guest rooms.[15]

Data Analysis, Interpretation, and Presentation of Results

After data have been collected, the fourth and fifth steps in the market-research process involve data analysis and interpretation and the presentation of results. During these last two steps, the collected data must be analyzed, interpreted, and presented to the decision makers who charged the researchers with the original task of investigating the research question generated during the problem-definition stage. Data analysis typically involves the use of statistical techniques to determine average responses and responses that deviate from the average. For example, a market-research study may determine that the average amount of time customers spend on a shopping trip to the grocery store is approximately 20 minutes. However, upon further examination, researchers conclude that the average time spent by male shoppers is 15 minutes, while female shoppers spent an average of 25 minutes. These findings may be further interpreted as an indication that females consider more information when making grocery purchasing decisions. As such, females may be more receptive to grocer advertisements and place a greater importance on the manufacturer's labeling information.

Presentation of results is the fifth and final step of the market-research process. The presentation of results is generally presented in a formal written report and/or an oral presentation. Much like the executive summary of a marketing plan, the written research report begins with an overview of the study's findings and recommendations. Time-pressured decision makers prefer reports and presentations that are clear, concise, and nontechnical in nature. Consequently, prior to the presentation, researchers must make a conscious decision about how much detail and supporting documentation to present. The presenter's job is easier if he or she has a keen understanding of the needs and expectations of the decision makers and presents the research findings accordingly. The remainder of the report documents the study's progress through the research process and provides the more technically minded decision maker with the supporting documentation for the study's findings and recommendations.

Modern best practice suggests that the market-research process should not stop at the presentation and delivery of the report. Both those who are doing the research and those who will use the research need to work together to design and implement any action taken as a result of the findings and to track the results of the action. By working together in this way, they can ensure that the results of the study are more likely to be acted on. In addition, both the researchers and the users will learn together how to undertake more actionable research in the future.

Technological Enhancements in Customer Research

Technological innovations such as electronic-observation research, decision-support systems, and the World Wide Web have revolutionized market research. These particular innovations are transforming market research from a discrete activity to a continuous process. Consequently, many marketers are starting to question the conventional problem-oriented market-research process described in Figure 5.3. In today's world of rapidly changing supply and demand, the conventional customer-research process, with its problem-solving emphasis, is being challenged by a process that emphasizes the continuous observation and tracking of consumer behavior. The reason is simple. Once a significant problem is detected that requires extensive study to be fully understood, it is too late to respond effectively. Continuously gathering marketing intelligence detects a problem almost immediately, allowing more time for an effective response.

Electronic Observational Research[16]

In the mid-1970s, consumer packaged-goods companies and grocery retailers settled on a system of bar codes called the **Universal Product Code (UPC)** that is now on almost all items. These bar codes are read by scanners at the checkout counter and have greatly increased the efficiency and speed of checkout processes. Today, the UPC and the **European Article Numbering (EAN)** systems are used in stores and libraries in North America and Europe and are expected to be used worldwide in almost all product categories in the next 20 years.

A very important side benefit of this technology is that it allows companies to electronically track what is purchased in retail stores. The data about sales are now purchased by two major market-research companies, ACNielsen and IRI, which combine all of the individual retailers' data into massive syndicated databases that can report on sales of tens of thousands of items in more than 70 metro markets. The top 100 packaged-goods companies each spend an average of $5 million a year on

Universal Product Code (UPC)

Is a bar code on a product's package that provides information read by optical scanners.

European Article Numbering (EAN)

Is the European version of the Universal Product Code on a product package that provides information read by optical scanners.

such market-research information. As part of their service, Nielsen and IRI researchers work with clients to analyze buying trends on a week-to-week basis in product categories of interest to each client. For example, the Gatorade brand spends about $4 million a year studying the supplement-drink category, which generates more than $1 billion in annual sales. Ultimately, almost all consumer retail sales will be tracked by such syndicated services, which already account for about 20% of all spending on market research.

Both IRI and ACNielsen also collect other information that they combine with their scanner data. For example, the IRI BehaviorScan service, which operates in more than a dozen markets, uses a device that attaches to a household's TV sets and controls which TV advertisements are shown in the household. This allows IRI to undertake field experiments that track the impact of advertising campaigns. The purchasing behavior of a randomly chosen sample of households from the IRI household panel is compared against a random sample of households that is not exposed to the advertising campaign (the *control sample*). Hundreds of such field experiments have revealed that TV advertising campaigns are usually effective only for new products and do very little for established brands.[17]

ACNielsen has household panels that track the total purchases of a household and its exposure to various marketing campaigns carried by TV, radio, magazines, newspapers, the Internet, and direct mailings. Such panel behavior can then be combined with *geodemographic information* to make predictions about the behavior of households in different parts of a city or a county, known as *census blocks. Geodemographic analysis* is based on two premises. The first is that any two people who live in the same neighborhood are more likely to share similar lifestyles and demographic characteristics than any two people who live far apart. The second is that a number of market-research firms have used *cluster analysis* on household census data, enabling them to "label" neighborhoods by their demographics and lifestyles. These names can be quite colorful, such as Blue Blood Estates, Pools and Patios, Shotguns and Pickups, and Family Ties. Figure 5.6 lists ways that geodemographic market

Applications of Geodemography	Figure 5.6
Application	**Description**
Repositioning	A geodemographic system was used to determine if changing the title of a national magazine from *Apartment Life* to *Metropolitan Home,* along with upscaling its format, would induce a shift in readership. Subscriptions before and after the change were classified by geodemographic segment to track subscriber trends.
Recruiting	Branches of the U.S. armed forces classify their recruits by geodemographic segment to determine where to locate recruiting centers and to decide what media and appeals work well to attract young men and women into the military.
Locating	A national chain of boutiques analyzed its clientele by geodemographic segment to determine the type of shopping center in which to locate to maximize store traffic. Supplemental analyses were used to select in-center locations and a store format.
Linking Research and Strategy	A household appliance manufacturer interested in coordinating distribution and media coverage for a new product linked each positive response from a national telephone survey to the respondent's geodemographic segment. Program results focused the manufacturer's new product roll-out, media selection, and distribution decisions.
Qualifying Lists	Direct marketers classify current clientele by geodemographic segment. A marketer then identifies segments that contain particularly high concentrations of those clients exhibiting superior purchase volumes. The marketer then identifies new lists that target these geodemographic segments.
Fund-Raising	Organizations seeking funds to support medical research, literacy programs, or other causes classify previous givers by geodemographic segment. Mailing and telephone contact lists with high concentrations of sympathetic segments are used to expand the program's donor base.

research has been used in marketing. Information from ACNielsen panels, combined with geodemographic analysis, enables companies to better pinpoint what types of households are heavy buyers of certain product categories and specific brands.

Decision-Support Systems

Decision-support system (DSS)

Is a set of computer software programs built into a user-friendly interface package, such as Windows, that helps a manager make marketing-mix decisions.

A **decision support system (DSS)** is a set of computer software programs built into a user-friendly interface package, such as Windows, that helps a manager make marketing-mix decisions. Essentially, a DSS taps into the firm's existing market-information system (MIS) along with other third-party databases to make the information more accessible to and usable by decision makers. For example, the DSS enables a user to answer state-of-the-market questions, undertake market forecasts, and create simulations showing what might happen if tactics were changed. Behind the interactive user-friendly icons, frameworks, prompts, and pull-down guide screens are major online market and accounting databases full of millions of observations of individual consumer behavior provided by companies such as ACNielsen and IRI, but also generated from a company's own records of customer trading exchanges. These databases are "mined" for insights by powerful spreadsheets, statistical programs, and mathematical models. Some companies use these systems to target individual customers with special promotions through direct marketing, as illustrated in Figure 5.7.

Figure 5.7	Database Mining and Direct Marketing

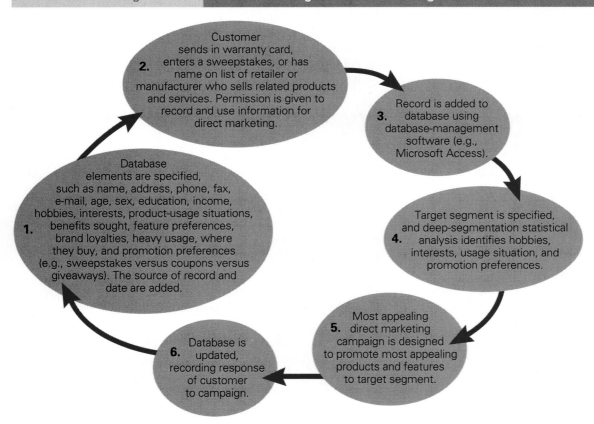

Direct database marketing is a tool for direct communication with target customers of a special product and promotion offer that has a high chance of appealing to customers. It combines the fundamentals of deep market segmentation with modern database technology and the implementation of microcommunication promotions offered to thousands of hot prospects, rather than millions of mostly indifferent customers. As the database records the history of interactions with each customer, customer segmentation can go beyond a deep understanding of heavy users and identify the sort of marketing interactions and trading relationships that groups of customers wish to have with the company.

The Growing Latino Market

While marketers are focusing on emerging markets in China and Eastern Europe, they may be overlooking a major emerging market at home, the Latino market. Latinos are already a larger minority than African-Americans and it is estimated that one out of three Americans will have close Latino relatives in 10 years' time. The Latino influence on food, music, entertainment, and sports is already evident. What impact Latinos will have on expenditures for child rearing and investment markets down the road is a very open question.

The tables present results from a U.S. Census Bureau Current Population Report published in March 2000.[a] From these tables, what do you conclude is somewhat different about the Latino population and what impact will these demographic differences have on particular markets in the U.S.? Please think about as many markets as you can.

If you wished to study what is unique about the Latino culture that is not explained by differences in age, education, income, and family size, how would you go about doing so by controlling for age, education, income, and family size? Construct a cross-tab table to illustrate how you might present the results.

Among Latinos, extended families of grandparents, parents, and children live together more often than in other U.S. households. What effect do you think this has on their children learning English and the adults assimilating into their workplaces and the broader U.S. culture?

Young Latinos are more fashion conscious[b] than the general U.S. population. The language preference of Latinos from 14 to 24 is 57% English, 28% Spanish, and 14% either.[c] Latino adolescents and young adults watch 17 hours of English TV (nine hours of Spanish) and listen to 16 hrs of English radio (nine hours of Spanish radio). If you were in the fashion clothing market for young adults, would you target the Latino segment and, if so, how? Why are young Latinos likely to become fashion trend setters? How might you use market research to study whether they are becoming fashion trendsetters?

[a]Melissa Therrien and Roberto R. Ramirez, The Hispanic Population in the United States Current Population Reports p. 20–535, U.S. Census Bureau, Washington, D.C.: March 2000.
[b]Michael Marx "Hispanics and Financial Services: Challenges and Opportunities," Strategic Research Institute Report Marketing to U.S. Hispanics and Latin America, January 2003.
[c]"Language and Markets in the U.S.," Hispanic Business, December 2002, 16–26.

Full-Time, Year-Round Workers With Annual Earnings $35,000 or More by Detailed Latino Origin: 1999
(in percentages)[1]

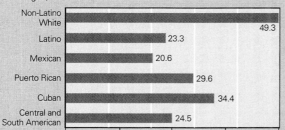

[1]Each bar represents the percentage of individuals, of the specified origin, who earned more than $35,000 for full-time year-round work. Data for other Latinos not shown.
Source: U.S. Census Bureau, Current Population Survey, March 2000.

Population by Latino Origin and Educational Attainment: 2000
(as a percentage of each population 25 years and older)

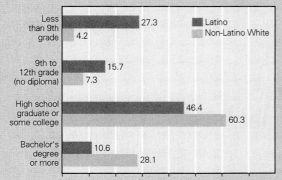

Source: U.S. Census Bureau, Current Population Survey, March 2000.

Family Households With Five or More People by Detailed Latino Origin: 2000
(in percentages)[1]

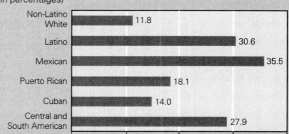

[1]Each bar represents the percentage of family households of five or more people whose householder was of the specified origin. Data for other Latinos not shown.
Source: U.S. Census Bureau, Current Population Survey, March 2000.

Population by Latino Origin and Age Group: 2000
(as a percentage of each population)

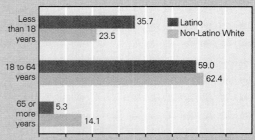

Source: U.S. Census Bureau, Current Population Survey, March 2000.

Similarly, *Transaction-Based Information Systems (TBIS)* link, communicate, and process all of the transactions with a company's distributors/customers. The TBIS has evolved out of the *electronic data interchange (EDI)* among businesses. Examples are McKesson's ECONOMIST system for its drugstore customers and American Airlines' Sabre reservation system for its travel agents. Transaction-based information systems are having a dramatic effect on channel and business-to-business customer relationships. By speeding up transaction communication and increasing the monitoring and control of sales and orders, TBISs have greatly reduced the working capital tied up in inventory and the risks of obsolete inventory. Beyond saving billions of dollars a year by reducing warehousing and inventory costs, they have enabled retailers and manufacturers to become much more responsive to market demand, because a TBIS provides the manufacturer with online information about what is "hot" and what is not. This type of data-mining market research can immediately be used to change manufacturing schedules and the procurement of supplies.

Web-Based Market Research

Market researchers have been quick to embrace the Internet as a tool for conducting market research and planning and reporting on Web-based market research. Web-based market research has had a total quality management (TQM) effect for the following reasons:

1. Web-based market research has increased the quality of market research by reducing errors in the market-research process. For example, direct data entry from the Web site reduces random and systematic errors in the data and statistical analysis.
2. Web-based market research has significantly reduced the cost of research by 20–50%.
3. Web-based research has significantly sped up the whole market-research process, from weeks to days.

Online market surveys are designed to study consumers' preferences for new products, services, and technology.

© Lucidio Studio, Inc./CORBIS

An issue associated with the quality of Web-based market research has been how representative the sample is. In other words, are online respondents representative of the firm's target market? But studies have shown that properly conducted Web-based studies, as described in the end-of-chapter case study, are as good, if not better, at sampling specialized markets and enable a much richer multimedia information environment for testing product concepts and product extensions.[18] There is more of a concern over controlling who is participating. For example, Web-based research often needs checks to make sure that children are not participating in studies targeted to the family head of household.

To ensure that Web-based survey respondents represent target markets, market researchers often identify them from customer databases and invite them by e-mail to participate in a Web-browser survey. Typically, these individuals are paid $3–20 or offered frequent-flier miles for 15–20 minutes of their time. Dell has taken Web-based product-promotion testing right to their customer Web site, where they have tested a new promotional campaign for advanced Intel chips. Their study (which won an Explor Award for innovation in Web-based market research) demonstrated that a mild promotional message was just as effective at encouraging customers to trade up to a more powerful chip in their computer than a harder sell.

Every 24 hours, a sample of 50,000 AOL subscribers receive invitations to participate in ongoing customer-satisfaction surveys.[19] Using data from approximately two million responses over a period of 18 months in the late 1990s, AOL gauged customer reaction to new AOL services. Although AOL has had its share of problems, they have not stemmed from a lack of information about its customers!

But perhaps the most important advantage of Web-based market research is that it allows firms to quickly study a segment of the target market and test new ideas. This rapid response from customers provides a dynamic link between customers and management in a timely, cost-effective manner. Figure 5.8 summarizes the advantages and disadvantages of online survey research. Figure 5.9 presents the results of a survey of 200 firms using online primary research. More than 80% of the respondents have used online surveys to learn more about market behavior.

Advantages and Disadvantages of Online Survey Research	Figure 5.8

Advantages	Disadvantages
Fast and inexpensive	Sample selection/generalizability
Diverse, large group of Internet users worldwide to small specialized niche	Measurement validity (e.g. different browsers, computer screen sizes, resolution settings)
Computer entry reduces researcher data-entry errors	
Honest responses to sensitive questions	Self-selection bias
Anyone-can-answer, invitation-only, or password-protected	Respondent authenticity uncertain
	Frivolous or dishonest responses
Electronic data are easy to tabulate	Duplicate submissions
Less interview bias	Steep learning curve for Web developers

Source: Judy Strauss, Adel El-Enasry, and Raymond Frost, *E-Marketing,* 3rd Ed. (Upper Saddle River, NJ: Prentice Hall, 2003), 179. © 2003. Reprinted by permission of Pearson Education, Inc., Upper Saddle River, NJ.

Figure 5.9	Proportion of 200 Firms Using Online Primary Research

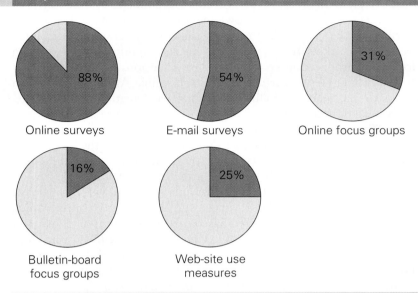

Source: Adapted from Judy Strauss, Adel El-Enasry, and Raymond Frost, *E-Marketing*, 3rd Ed. (Upper Saddle River, NJ: Prentice Hall, 2003), 173.

LEARNING OBJECTIVE 5

Competitive Forces

Often, the market is defined by the way market researchers are able to collect sales and market-share information. This information is often supplied by government agencies, trade associations, or market-research firms that survey all of the firms in a market.

Competitor Research

The first question almost every company asks in its decision-making process is, "Who are the major players in the market?" That is, who has what share of market sales? *Market share* is measured as a percentage of total industry sales over a specified time period. Before determining the major players, we must define the *market*. Clearly, problems exist in defining the market. A company's market share can change dramatically depending on whether the market is defined as global, a particular export market, the U.S. market, a region of the United States, a city, or a segment of users or usage. The scope of the market is normally specified by a realistic assessment of company resources and by company growth objectives.

Some of the different types of markets a product competes in are illustrated in Figure 5.10. The closest and most immediate competition comes from rivals' products targeted at the same segment that share similar, specific design features (e.g., a 12-ounce can of diet cola). The next level of product-category competition comes from products that share some similar features (e.g., soft drinks). More general competition comes from products that satisfy a core benefit (e.g., thirst-quenching or pick-me-up drinks). The most distant competition is for consumers' discretionary spending. At this level, a new car may compete against a new deck for the house or an overseas trip, particularly during economic downturns, when consumers tighten their belts.

The historical problem with research into competition has been too much focus on measuring the number of current competitors, the concentration of market share (the combined market share of the largest three competitors), and the current balance-sheet assets of major competitors. The emphasis needs to be placed on market dynamics, such as who is introducing new manufacturing, distribution, and product-development processes into the market. Competitive insight comes from explaining successful changes in the market, not from knowing who has the largest market share. The acid test for such insight is whether an executive wants to know what company has the largest market share (*static thought*) or what company has experienced the largest change in market share (*dynamic thought*).[20]

Competitor-research efforts seldom require defining market share out to the last share point (1% of market share) because defining the exact bounds of the market is

Examples of Levels of Competition Figure 5.10

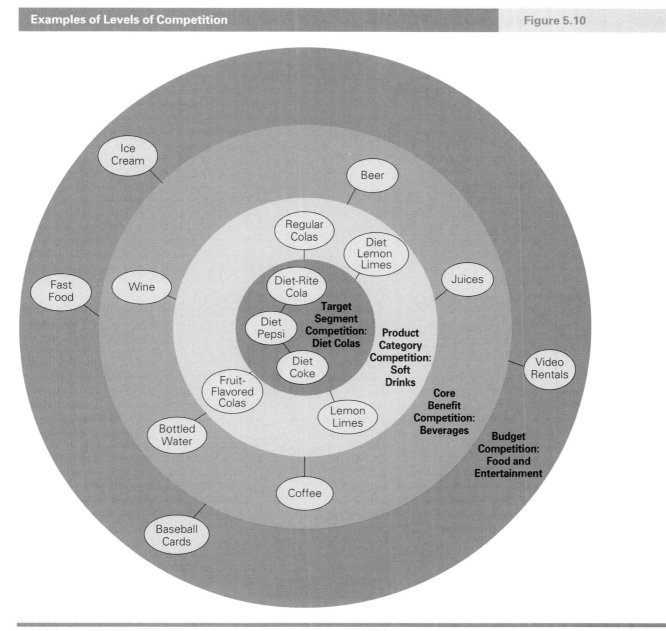

Most managers just consider their segment or product category competition and are sometimes blindsided by the success of less direct competition (e.g., bottled water and iced tea's effect on diet cola sales).
Source: Adapted from Donald R. Lehmann and Russell S. Winer, *Analysis for Marketing Planning* (Homewood, IL: Irwin, 1991), 22.

seldom that precise. Competitor-research efforts are better spent finding out which established competitor or new start-up is using radical new product or process technology to increase customer satisfaction and reduce costs. The history of technology suggests that small start-up companies often revolutionize a market.[21] For example, the typewriter was invented by Christopher Sholes, working in Milwaukee as a civil servant, and not for a printing or publishing company. The electric typewriter was developed and enhanced by IBM, and not by Remington or Underwood, the market leaders in manual typewriters. In turn, it was Wang and Apple, rather than IBM, that developed the computer word-processing and desktop-publishing market. Amazon.com was started in 1994 by a Wall Street analyst working out of his home, and not by a leading book retailer or publisher.

The change in market share over time is a vital indicator of the competitive environment. However, market share is not the only measure of competitiveness. The following measures are often used as leading indicators of a likely change in future sales and profits.

1. *Mind share:* The percentage of customers who name the brand when asked to name the first brand that comes to mind when they think about buying a particular type of product. This indicates the consumer's top-of-mind brand awareness and preferences. How is it changing among different segments?
2. *Voice share:* The percentage of media space or time a brand has of the total media share for that industry, often measured simply as dollars spent on advertising. This is likely to lead to a change in mind share (but not always, if the messages are weak). How and why is it changing?
3. *Research and development (R&D) share:* A company's R&D expenditure as a percentage of the total industry's R&D expenditure. This is a long-term predictor of new product developments, improvements in quality, cost reductions, and thus market share. It is an important measure of future competitiveness in many high-technology markets. How is it changing, and what is it being spent on?

Researching the History of the Market

A study of the recent history of the product market identifies the marketing mix and product dimensions on which sellers have competed most strongly to serve the interests of resellers and consumers. In some markets, this competition may have resulted in a price war. In others, sellers have competed with each other to improve product quality. Often, a technological improvement made by an innovator forces every competitor to respond. This occurred when Duracell introduced the alkaline battery. All of its competitors were forced to match the new technology. The history of the product market is seldom recorded. It is often carried around in the heads of experienced executives, and the invaluable insights they can provide are lost when they retire.

An industry often has standard marketing tactics and rules that are universally adopted. Examples are certain formulas for cost-plus pricing and spending a certain percentage of the previous year's sales on advertising in the next year. Sales-force commissions and incentives are also often standardized in an industry. These rules of doing business make the market more predictable and stable. If the market "learns" and has moved toward more efficient ways of making and marketing its products, then these rules and processes should reflect such learning, and thus make sense. Knowing how and why standard industry practices and decision rules came about enables a firm to better understand whether the rules are based on continuous market learning or whether they have simply become established practice.[22] If they are based on market learning, then a competitor can better understand what works and what does not in the marketplace and why. However, if the rules are based on old-fashioned agreements to restrain competition, then violating them represents an opportunity for the aggressive firm.

Michael Porter's pioneering text *Competitive Strategy* changed the way many companies think about their competition.[23] Porter identified five forces that shape competition: *current competitors, the threat of new entrants, the threat of new substitutes, the bargaining power of distributors (or business-to-business customers),* and *the bargaining power of suppliers.* This structure can be reduced further to include simply current competitors and potential competitors and substitutes. The way distributors and suppliers behave determines the threat posed by immediate and potential competition. Distributors and suppliers are therefore not separate competitive elements but moderators or amplifiers of competition (see Figure 5.11). Generally, suppliers and distributors are business partners that form alliances used to gain

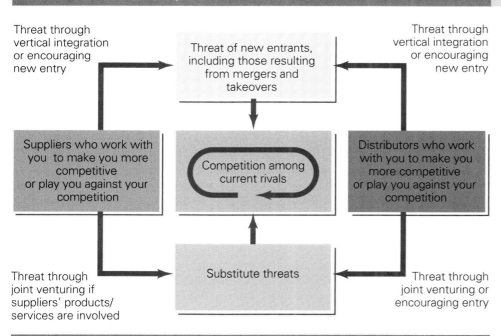

Current and Potential Competition

Figure 5.11

competitive advantage and should be seen in this light. That is why distributor and channel research should be undertaken separately from competitor research. It is true that at times distributors and suppliers have to be directly considered in a competitive analysis, but only when they threaten to become a new direct competitor. A company must be on guard against new entrants and others up and down the supply chain. This concern is best addressed in competitive research by asking and answering the questions presented in Figure 5.12.

Auditing Current Competitors

For most companies, it is not possible to put all current competitors under the microscope and undertake an in-depth analysis of their competitive strengths and weaknesses. However, particular competitors are always worthy of such attention, either because they are attacking with a new product or because a firm has decided, in a previous plan, to attack them. The isolation of "aggressors" or "targets" usually requires a preliminary analysis that identifies which rivals you are gaining business from and which competitors you are losing business to. This is the way you identify your immediate current competition, which may or may not be using similar technology.[24] For example, many major U.S. cities now have only one daily newspaper, yet such monopolies have not inflated profits for the publisher. The reason is simple. Although other major newspapers may have died, competition for advertising has increased from the suburban weeklies, direct marketing, and other media. Television, radio, and local magazines also have become more competitive with their news and features. The mistake that newspaper publishers made was not identifying these competitors early on when they could have taken countermeasures.[25]

Figure 5.13 presents a competitor-analysis template a company can use as a basis for its own unique competitor-analysis form. The competitive strategy guru Michael

Competitive Forces

The initial investment in time, effort, and expense necessary to audit competitors may be very high (amounting to several weeks or even months of an executive's or consultant's time), but it should be treated as an investment. The results will produce a report that can be built on from year to year with constantly expanding details and insights. This file then becomes part of the collective memory of your organization, to be passed on to successive managers.

Figure 5.12   **New Competitive-Threats Audit**

The key to identifying potential new competition is to
ask a series of questions that narrows in on the most
likely competitor and its situation.

New Technology—Converging Markets Threat

- What price changes in other technology markets appear to influence our sales? Is this effort changing?
- Which new technology or service is starting to be considered as a substitute for our product by consumers? Is this occurring in any particular usage situation or by any particular group of buyers? Are our existing channels encouraging such substitution?
- What is our closest new technological or service competition?
- Who is the major mover and shaker in this new industry?
- What appears to be its current objective and strategy?
- What is its growth rate?
- What has been its effect on our sales?
- What further threat does it pose?
- What constraints does it face?

Channel Integration Threat

- Which supplier is most likely to become a downstream direct competitor in the near future? Why? How would it do it? Is there any evidence of this occurring?
- Which customers are most likely to become upstream, do-it-themselves competitors in the near future? Why? How would they do it? Does any evidence of such plans exist?

Competitor Takeover—Merger Threat

Which mergers, takeovers, or trading coalitions among competitors or from inside pose
the greatest threat to our position? What evidence exists that this is likely to occur?

Porter has argued that competitive advantage in product quality and costs can come
from one or more of the following stages in the added-value chain:[26]

1. Inbound logistics processes
2. Operations processes
3. Outbound logistics processes
4. Marketing and sales processes
5. Service processes

The implication is that a rival's competitive standing at all stages of the added-value chain, from inbound logistics to after-sales service, must be studied. The analysis form presented in Figure 5.12 addresses characteristics of these processes. This analysis should involve at least three types of information. The first type of information is a rating of the rival's performance compared or *benchmarked* against the very best in the industry. The second type of information is the direction this performance is moving (improving indicated by an up arrow and declining indicated by a down arrow beside the rating). The third type of information should be a detailed explanation as to what is unique and interesting about the rival's behavior or product, or at least the name and e-mail address of someone who can provide such detail.

This brings us to the question of how competitor research is undertaken. It is seldom gathered through James Bond methods of industrial espionage, using sources of doubtful reputation. Interestingly, the market-research company ACNielsen started business in 1923 by doing competitive market research for machinery manufactur-

A Competitor Analysis Template	Figure 5.13

Competitor _____ Analyst _____ Date _____

Summary of Competitor's Position

- Goals and major competitive strategy _____
- Current success story _____
- Current mistakes _____
- Competitive advantages/disadvantages _____

Benchmarking Analysis*

Financial Position
Cash flow, cost structure, access to capital, profits _____

Market Position
Major geographical markets, target segments _____

Product Position
Raw material, manufacturing, design quality, features _____
Brand strength and image with target markets _____

Price Position
How much above/below average, types of promotions _____

Inbound Logistics Process
Sources of supply, purchasing skills, inventory flow _____

Production Processes
Production capacity, adaptability, efficiency, quality, costs _____
Labor adaptability, skill, loyalty _____

Outbound Logistics Processes
Order-delivery time, inventory flow, special services _____

Trade Relations Processes
Major channels used, channel relationships _____

Advertising and Promotion Processes
Message themes, media usage, campaign schedules _____

Sales-Force Processes
Sales-force management, morale, training, incentives _____
Use of technology, service quality, efficiency _____

*Comparative benchmarking rating; direction of change; what processes, technology, people are driving its performance improvement

ers. It was not until 1928 that it started to undertake consumer research. Figure 5.14 reports on the most useful sources and types of competitor information. The following is a description of how many firms make sense of the information they gather about competitors:

We gather about 10 people in a room, twice a month, in long (think-tank) sessions, anything from three hours to a couple of days. The sessions have no formal structure. We examine and massage the latest competitor and industry information to determine where things are going and what we should be doing. There are a lot of people in the business unit who know something about a competitor. But it's almost like the three blind men and the elephant: Each one examines a small part of the whole. When you put them all together in a room, they are amazed about how much they know. That coalesces into one or two sheets of paper presenting all we know about a competitor's strengths and weaknesses, and our judgments with respect to a competitor's strategies and measures of success. That is the beginning of a competitor file.[27]

Figure 5.14	**Competitor Intelligence**

Most Useful Source of Information (by type of market)

Percent Distribution

	Total	Industrial Products	Consumer Products	Both Consumer and Industrial
Sales force	27%	35%	18%	23%
Publications, databases	16	13	15	22
Customers	14	13	11	17
Marketing research, tracking services	9	3	24	9
Financial reports	5	7	3	1
Distributors	3	4	1	1
Employees (unspecified)	2	2	6	—
Analysis of products	2	1	3	3
Other	8	6	8	13
No answer	14	16	11	11
	100%	100%	100%	100%
Number of responding companies	308	158	72	78

Most Useful Type of Information (by type of market)

Percent Distribution

	Total	Industrial Products	Consumer Products	Both Consumer and Industrial
Pricing	23%	26%	20%	19%
Strategy	19	20	15	22
Sales data	13	11	18	12
New products, product mix	11	13	8	10
Advertising/marketing activities	7	3	19	4
Costs	6	8	3	5
Key customers/markets	3	3	6	1
Research and development	2	2	1	3
Management style	2	1	3	1
Other	4	4	—	8
No answer	10	9	7	15
	100%	100%	100%	100%
Number of responding companies	308	158	72	78

Source: Howard Sutton, *Competitive Intelligence* (New York: The Conference Board, 1988).

LEARNING OBJECTIVE 6

Conducting Channel Research

The pioneering professional market researcher Charles Parlin started business in 1911 conducting distribution-channel research and not consumer research. He studied the distribution channels for agricultural instruments and then for textiles. Interest in researching channels of distribution increased greatly in the 1990s for at least two reasons. The first is that retailing had become much more competitive because the market was becoming saturated with stores. Management Horizons, a retailing consulting company, estimates that in the 1990s the amount of retailing square footage increased from about 15 square feet for every person in the United States to 20 square feet. By comparison, for every person in the United Kingdom, there are only an estimated two square feet of retail space per person. So much available retail space is competing for consumer dollars that rivalry between retailers has become ferocious. This explains why otherwise well-managed retailers such as The Gap or Home Depot have run into hard times—they built too many stores. The second reason for undertaking distribution market research is that, in the next few years, many experts predict that Web direct marketing will gain 10–30% of sales in certain product categories, such as computer software and hardware, recorded music, books, videos, and air travel. How are traditional distribution channels going to respond to this threat?

The suggested procedure for learning about distribution channels is to first address a number of questions about the drivers of change in the channel (see Figure 5.15) and then to zero in on a detailed audit of some key resellers (sometimes called trade customers). Figure 5.15 lists several questions that address the impact on the distribution channel of (1) changes in technology, (2) new entrants, (3) changes in established channel relations, and (4) changes in the way existing channel members do business. The recorded-music market provides an excellent example of how such changes affect product marketing.

In the 1950s and early 1960s, record retailers allowed consumers to play new records in the store. This was an important way of exposing a new artist or title to the public, because enthusiasts and opinion leaders did most of this in-store sampling. But as popular music took off with rock and roll and the spending power of baby boomers increased, chain stores opened record bars that did not provide sound booths for sampling, but undercut the record stores in prices. Consumers would often listen to the music in the record store and buy at the chain store. To compete, the record stores dropped the sound booths, but offered a generous return policy. Eventually, even the return policy was dropped.

As a result of the termination of in-store sampling, popular radio stations became critical in marketing records. But radio was also going through a transition. Increased competition was forcing stations into top 20 or top 40 formats, where hit-parade music was played continuously at the expense of new artists and songs. This program format kept audiences and advertisers happy, but forced recording

---

Channel Change Audit · **Figure 5.15**

- **Who are the latest new entrants in the reseller market?**
  What is their competitive advantage?
  Which existing resellers are being most affected?
  How has it affected us?

- **What new trading coalitions among resellers are occurring?**
  What will be their competitive advantage?
  How will it affect us?

- **What changes in order-processing technology are now occurring?**
  What impact will they have on the way business is done?
  What competitive advantage do they provide?

- **What changes in transportation technology are now occurring?**
  What impact will they have on the way business is done?
  What competitive advantage do they provide?

- **What changes in warehousing technology are now occurring?**
  What impact will they have on the way business is done?
  What competitive advantage do they provide?

- **What changes in payment technology are now occurring?**
  What impact will they have on the way business is done?
  What competitive advantage do they provide?

companies to buy airtime to advertise their new releases (where previously such exposure was free). This increased the cost of launching a new release, thus giving a major competitive advantage to larger recording studios and distributors. MTV pulled the recording industry out of the doldrums in the early 1980s, but this new promotion channel also forced studios into a whole new marketing activity: video production. The music video component has become an important new competitive element in selling compact discs and a further entrance barrier for new competition. But free music sites on the Internet have again revolutionized the distribution of music. It is also now possible for individual musicians to make their own digital recordings and distribute them directly from their own Web site to consumers who download the music for a small fee. What effect is this having/will this have on the traditional music-distribution system? The role of distribution research is to find out what new forms music retailing is taking, conduct consumer research to assess their potential, and then undertake further distribution research to assess the profitability and competitiveness of various types of Web-based music retailing. The whole future of the popular music industry depends on finding both a popular way to sell music on the Internet and a way to reduce but not completely eliminate music sharing between friends. The best minds in the music industry have not yet found the way.

Researching Individual Trade Customers

Once the general channel-change audit has started, important trade customers and business partners will have been identified for further study. Clearly, not all of these resellers can be studied, and some good managerial judgment is needed to make sure greater attention is paid to the major players and innovators. When a manufacturer's sales force uses an account-management approach for its major retail trade accounts, it should be relatively easy to complete audits of such trade customers. However, care must be taken that day-to-day operating relations do not drive the evaluations of those who are in constant contact with representatives of suppliers and resellers. The reseller audits require the auditor to stand back, assess the changes that have occurred over the past trading year, and explain some of the basic reasons for predicting longer-term changes.

The individual distributor audit in Figure 5.16 starts with a summary "partner" evaluation that can also be used as a short-form audit when the product team does not have the time or interest to fully evaluate particular resellers. A paragraph can be written to provide responses to the concerns listed. The evaluation can be updated on a regular basis (normally annually), so the major investment is in preparing the initial evaluation. The detailed evaluation questions have been categorized into those dealing with the reseller's trading performance, marketing position, competitive effort, and purchasing behavior. Understanding what is going right or wrong in a channel *partnership* relationship almost always involves taking information and putting it together like a jigsaw puzzle. That is why it is important to add depth to the audit by answering as many questions as possible, using facts, good judgment, and best guesses. Trying to understand the reasons for a channel member's change in performance or behavior often means tracing back from its buying behavior, through trading and operating indicators, to its competitive effort and market position. Distribution market research also must forecast distributors' future competitive strengths and weaknesses.

Individual Distributor Audit	Figure 5.16

Company Name: _____

Date: _____

Summary Evaluation

- Image and reputation
- Geographical markets/customer segments served
- Major strength, unique value, importance of this reseller
- Major weakness and failure of reseller
- Special personal relations with distributor

Detailed Evaluation

Trading Performance

- Annual Sales
- Annual sales of our products
- Contribution earned from sales to this reseller
- Average stock-turn of our products
- Past average stock-turn of our products
- Profit performance

Competitive Selling Effort

- Quality of locations
- Quality of advertising
- Quality of premises
- Quality of sales staff
- Sales staff knowledge of our products
- Inventory management
- Extent we are treated as preferred supplier
- Special marketing efforts and cooperation

Purchasing Behavior

- Recent ordering history
- Volume deals/discounts sought and given
- Other allowances and considerations sought and given:
    - Freight
    - Cooperative advertising
    - Promotions
    - Returns
    - Push money and sales contests
    - Special credit terms

Chapter Summary

Learning Objective 1: *Appreciate the importance and scope of market research and information systems.* Firms that adjust their marketing strategies to reflect environmental changes in domestic and international markets faster than competitors are able to sustain a competitive advantage. Often the key to this advantage lies in the firm's ability to collect, organize, and act on information gathered through *market research* and *marketing information systems*. The scope of market research and marketing information systems extends beyond basic customer research. A market typically contains four players—customers, competitors, distribution-channel members, and regulators that monitor the marketplace. Therefore, it is generally recommended that the study of the market be divided into four topics: customer research, competitor research, channel research, and public policy research.

Learning Objective 2: *View traditional customer research as a step-by-step decision-making method as prescribed by the market-research process.* The market research process offers a systematic approach to designing, collecting, interpreting, and reporting information that assists marketers in exploring opportunities and making specific marketing decisions. Typically, the market-research process includes the following steps: problem definition, research design, data collection, data analysis and interpretation, and presentation of results. It is important to note that the market-research process is not set in stone and that the process itself may indeed be adapted based on the requirements of each project.

Learning Objective 3: *Understand the issues surrounding data collection, such as the differences between qualitative and quantitative data and the importance of sampling and question design.* Data collection can be accomplished by examining secondary research that already exists, and/or by generating new data through primary research using qualitative, and quantitative research techniques. Basic primary research includes extensive in-depth interviews with customers, customer visits, and focus groups. These types of research methods are often referred to as qualitative research because they are more descriptive in nature and do not generate data that can be quantitatively analyzed with much confidence. If the answer to the research question developed in the problem-definition stage of the market-research process is not provided from qualitative research, or if reassuring confirmation is sought, then more thorough descriptive or causal research is likely to be undertaken that can provide quantitative answers.

Qualitative and quantitative research data are collected by sampling the population of interest. A probability sample is an umbrella term used to describe sampling techniques where respondents have a known (nonzero) chance of being chosen. Three common types of probability samples include simple random samples, stratified samples, and cluster samples. Nonprobability samples are arbitrary sampling techniques where respondents have an unknown or zero chance of being chosen for the sample. Three common types of nonprobability samples include convenience samples, quota samples, and judgment samples.

Learning Objective 4: *Appreciate how new technologies are transforming the market-research process from a discrete to a continuous activity.* Market research is being transformed from a discrete activity to a continuous process because of new technologies, including electronic observation research, decision-support systems, and Web-based market research. The Universal Product Code (UPC) and European Article Numbering (EAN) are examples of electronic-observation research systems that track retail purchases. Two major market-research companies, ACNielsen and IRI, combine the data tracked by these systems into massive databases that can report on sales of thousands of items in 70 metro markets. Information from ACNielsen panels, combined with geodemographic analysis, enables companies to better pinpoint what types of households are heavy buyers of certain product categories and specific brands. Decision-support systems (DSS) tap into the firm's existing market-information system (MIS), along with other third-party databases, to make the information more accessible to and usable by decision makers. Web-based market research has increased the quality of market research by reducing errors in the market-research process, significantly reducing the cost of research by 20–50%, and speeding up the whole market-research process from weeks to days.

Learning Objective 5: *Recognize that market research extends beyond traditional customer research and also involves the study of competitors.* Competitor research is the study of the major competitors in a market, the market share each holds, and the change in market share over time. Another critical aspect of competitor research is tracking innovative products and new process technology that competitors have developed that increase customer satisfaction and reduce costs. When researchers target current competitors, they identify those they are attacking with an innovative new product or those competitors that are attacking them.

Learning Objective 6: *Explore the growing importance of conducting distribution-channel research and the methods used to study these channels and individual trade partners.* Distribution-channel research has increased since the 1990s because retailing has become more competitive and because Web direct marketing is expected to gain 10–30% of sales in select product categories. To develop a full understanding of the channel, researchers need to study both the distribution channel and the important trade customers/partners within that channel.

Key Terms

For interactive study: visit http://bestpractices.swlearning.com.

Causal research, 137	Judgment sampling, 148	Reliability, 138
Cluster samples, 147	Marketing information systems	Secondary data, 137
Convenience sample, 148	(MIS), 134	Simple random sample, 147
Decision-support system (DSS), 154	Market research, 134	Stratified sample, 147
Descriptive research, 137	Market-research process, 135	Sugging, 149
European Article Numbering (EAN), 152	Motivational research, 141	Universal Product Code (UPC), 152
	Nonresponse error, 148	Validity, 138
Exploratory research, 136	Omnibus surveys, 148	Voice of the customer, 140
Focus group, 143	Primary data, 137	
Hands-on consumer research, 141	Quota samples, 148	

Questions for Review and Discussion

1. In the mid-1980s, Pepsi overtook Coke in supermarket sales with its highly successful "Take the Pepsi Challenge" marketing campaign. In blind taste tests, consumers tasted the two colas and identified Pepsi as the one they preferred. In response, Coke developed a new cola that beat Pepsi in blind taste tests. After 200,000 taste tests, it settled on New Coke, a sweeter, smoother flavor that beat Pepsi and old Coke in the blind taste tests. The result was a marketing disaster. In 1985, New Coke replaced Classic Coke on the shelves, and tens of thousands of angry Coke customers called Coke to complain. Coca-Cola brought back Classic Coke alongside New Coke and insisted that it had not made a mistake. Five years later, New Coke was dead. What mistake did Coca-Cola make in the market research it undertook? (Hint: Did it not do enough research, or did it do the wrong sort of research?)

2. Imagine that you were part of the cross-functional team developing the Depend® adult disposable diaper. Several members of the team seem to have a problem understanding consumer complaints about the existing product in the market. What market intelligence–gathering activity might you suggest to raise their understanding?

3. When researching customer needs, would it be better for a product designer to visit customers personally or to read a survey-research report on customer needs, beliefs, and behaviors? What biases are inherent in each approach that might lead to misunderstanding consumer behavior?

4. How would a company that combines a bar with a laundry service use geodemographic analysis?

5. In a case brought against Microsoft charging that it monopolizes the PC software market, Microsoft claimed that 80% of software developers are happy with the situation as it is. This result was based on a yes/no question that followed a 350-word statement describing all of the advantages of the current situation and none of the disadvantages. The dean of the business school of the Massachusetts Institute of Technology defended the question, saying that he saw nothing wrong with it. What is wrong with such a question?

6. Figure 5.12 presents information about the usefulness of competitive intelligence and the most useful sources of such intelligence. Why do you think price information is rated as being more important than strategy

information? List several reasons. What do the results of the most useful sources tell us about how we should set up an intelligence-gathering operation?

7. The State Department is in charge of more than 100 U.S. embassies and consulates scattered around the globe. How are the U.S. diplomatic service and the State Department likely to change if the predominant conflict between countries in the 21st century becomes economic rather than ideological?

8. "To outguess them, [General George] Washington sought the best strategic advice and had no pride of ownership. The excellence and not the origin of the plan was decisive with him. He learned by listening well, or by observing and reflecting. During the greater part of the struggle, he had to be his own chief intelligence officer, and he did so with considerable success. Always he tried to learn what was not happening as well as what was, and he frequently undertook the careful analysis, in person, of conflicting intelligence reports."[28] If General George Washington could, with his "now you see it, now you don't" army, win a war and a nation's freedom against the world's superpower of the time by doing this, why would a CEO of a modern corporation not lead in a similar way?

9. In new markets that are emerging because of breakthrough technological innovations, it is critical that growth and expansion grow at the same pace as consumer demand. If you underproduce, customers turn to competitors to satisfy demand. If you overproduce, your operating costs skyrocket and your prices may go up, again driving customers to competitors. The only way to track the pace of consumer demand is through market research. What this means is that strategic market research in industries such as fiber-optic communications should accurately forecast the increase in demand and the increase in supply and advise senior management when they should make huge investments in production capacity. Apparently the fiber-optic industry was not so informed by its market researchers. Why do we know this to be so? Because currently less than 20% of fiber-optic capacity is being used in part because of clever new compression and parallel-signaling innovations in the use of optical fiber. The industry was overbuilt and too much fiber-optic cable was laid. In this case, the industry, investors, and companies such as Lucent Technologies did not pay nearly enough attention to supply-side (competitor) market research that would have revealed the emerging imbalance between demand and supply. To estimate changes in supply, how would you find out about the amount of cable being laid? Who would you talk to? Identify the sources who could provide estimates. What role might a trade association play in undertaking such research?

10. In the fiber-optic market situation described above, why do supply decisions need to be made before you know what the demand will be? What new technology threatens demand for fiber-optical communication?

In-Class Team Activities

1. In the chapter opener, it is suggested that a panel of households should have been studied to track the evolving use of the Internet. Why do you think it was important to study how everyone in the household, and not just the head of the household, used the Internet? What do you believe the results of this study would have shown?

2. Why do you think that many firms fail to involve their market researchers in the design and implementation of new plans and programs based on the results of market research?

Internet Questions

1. The PC revolution has led to executives doing a lot of their own typing, letter writing, and report writing, rather than relying on an executive assistant or secretary to do the work. The Internet provides a huge source of information about markets, countries, consumers, products, and technologies that can be searched easily using key words. Schoolchildren learn from a very early age today how to search the Internet for research projects. How will this change the demand for market researchers and market analysts in the future? How will their jobs change?

2. An infamous bank robber was asked why he robbed banks. He said, "Because that is where the money is." Some have argued that a similar but much more legal principle applies to Internet marketing. The prime targets for marketers are wealthy online customers. The rich of the world are online, while the poor are not and

may never be. Search Web sites so that you can participate in a class discussion of the following two questions:

a. Are the world's rich, those with the top 10% of incomes, already connected to the Internet wherever they live in the world? Are the wealthy in India, Africa, China, Russia, and South America already connected to the Web? If they are, what impact will this have on the marketing of premium brands to the world's wealthy? (Hint: Start searching U.S. government or Internet company sites.)

b. Which group of very wealthy Americans has the Internet and Internet shopping barely penetrated yet? How will this change in the future?

3. The following survey presents examples of different types of questions that can be used to learn about Internet usage. Identify any problems with the measures. If you were taking the survey, would you find the questions ambiguous, hard to answer, or biased toward a particular response?

Dichotomous Questions

Have you ever browsed the Internet?

Yes   No

Open-Ended Questions

Microsoft has been prosecuted for unfair business practices, such as trying to drive competitors out of business. What is your opinion of Microsoft's browser?

_____
_____
_____
_____

"The most important consideration for me in choosing a browser is . . ."

_____
_____
_____
_____

Multiple-Choice Questions

Which one of the following products have you purchased from a Web site:

Books	Software
Music CDs	Airline tickets
Clothing	X-rated material
Stocks	Computers and peripherals

Intention-to-Buy Scale

How likely is it that next Christmas Holiday Season you will buy a gift for a family member or a friend from a Web site:

Definitely will buy	Probably will buy
Maybe will buy	Not certain
Probably will not buy	Definitely will not buy

Rating Scales

Amazon.com's Web site is:

Excellent   Very good   Good   Fair   Poor

On a scale of 1 to 10, where 10 is excellent and 1 is a dog, how would you rate the Amazon.com Web site? _____

Semantic Differential Scale

Amazon.com's Web site is:

Easy to use	:___:___:___:___:___:___:	Hard to use
Fun	:___:___:___:___:___:___:	Boring
Modern	:___:___:___:___:___:___:	Old-fashioned
Friendly	:___:___:___:___:___:___:	Unfriendly
Laid back	:___:___:___:___:___:___:	Pushy
Soft sell	:___:___:___:___:___:___:	Hard sell
Helpful	:___:___:___:___:___:___:	Unhelpful
Cluttered	:___:___:___:___:___:___:	Uncluttered

Importance Scale

How important is it for you to pay a price in Web shopping that is less than regular retail?

Extremely important	Very important
Somewhat important	Not very important
Not important at all	

Likert Scales

"Amazon.com is very easy to learn to use compared with other shopping sites."

Strongly disagree	Disagree
Somewhat disagree	Neither agree nor disagree
Somewhat agree	Agree
Strongly agree	

"You learn more about products when you Web shop than when you shop in a regular store."

Strongly disagree	Disagree
Somewhat disagree	Neither agree nor disagree
Somewhat agree	Agree
Strongly agree	

CHAPTER CASE

AOL's Opinion Place

In September 1995, America Online (AOL) and a prominent research firm called The M/A/R/C Group launched a joint venture called Digital Marketing Services (DMS). This partnership gave market researchers access to millions of AOL subscribers who represented "mainstream America." Client companies have found that a major advantage of this research is the ability to reach very specialized target populations, given AOL's wide reach across millions of consumers.

In an area called Opinion Place, only two clicks away from the AOL Welcome Screen, AOL customers volunteered to participate in a 15-minute survey in exchange for AOL Rewards, such as frequent-flier miles. Within the first two years of existence, DMS had completed hundreds of surveys and more than one million interviews.

Opinion Place attracts hundreds of thousands of respondents per week. DMS qualifies each respondent, ensuring that he or she is part of the target population to be sampled. Upon entering Opinion Place, a respondent is qualified and sent into the survey. In this way, DMS ensures that the target market is studied and that the sample is randomly chosen from the appropriate sampling frame. If respondents do not qualify, they are sent to a randomly chosen survey for which they qualify. Respondents do not select the surveys, because this would cause a serious self-selection bias.

Major companies are finding that online market research increases the quality of survey data, reduces data-collection time, and reduces the cost of the study. Low costs lead to more studies, and iterative research (new research that is built upon the findings of past studies) to refined ideas. JCPenney tested 60 styles of women's swimsuits in a survey, allowing complex branching and asking different follow-up questions depending on earlier answers. A study can take only days from start to finish, with all study materials sent to and from a client by e-mail. In fact, a major packaged-goods manufacturer works with DMS to get feedback on concepts from thousands of consumers in less than 24 hours. They take the iterative approach to idea refinement, learning from each study. The velocity of this volume of information is unattainable through other research methods.

Finally, DMS claims that it charges 30–50% less for an equivalent survey undertaken in a mall or by mail. Proponents of online survey research point out that this capability is only about five years old and that it will ultimately have its greatest impact in the area of global market research. For example, companies are increasingly interested in the preferences and behavior of the emerging economic elite in countries such as China, where they can contact those who are highly educated, tech-savvy, and, most importantly, "wired" to the Internet. Companies as diverse as Coca-Cola, Avon, the Discovery Channel, Hewlett-Packard, Hickory Farms, Kodak, Sprint, Starbucks, and Warner Bros. use DMS's services and the services of other firms that offer online marketing research.

The main argument against online marketing research is that participants do not represent the entire population of U.S. households. For example, AOL's Opinion Place respondents are younger, more highly educated, and somewhat more affluent than the average U.S. adult. They appear more likely to buy name brands, try new products, and influence others' purchase decisions. But the questions companies must ask themselves remain: Does the sample validly represent the desired marketing target? Can any method attract a sample representative of the U.S. population? Maybe the critics of online research (who are mostly research companies using telephone, mail, or mall-intercept methods) are encountering their own problems as new technologies and changing attitudes impede interviews.

Case Questions

1. What types of target customers are most easily reached by online market research? What target customers are not reachable by online market research?
2. What are the greatest advantages of online market research?
3. Almost all transactions between retailers and manufacturers and between other types of businesses will be done on the Internet within 10 years. What invaluable market-research information will this generate to complement online market research?

VIDEO CASE

The Market Research Behind Fisher-Price's Rescue Heroes

The toy business isn't child's play. It's a marketing environment in which competition is tough, consumers are fickle, and truly new ideas are hard to come by. Shelly

Glick Gryfe, director of marketing research at Fisher-Price, knows all that, yet she still enjoys searching for that perfect product, the one that children and their parents will buy—and buy again—with fierce loyalty. Gryfe and her colleagues at Fisher-Price believe in the value of marketing research to bring a new toy to store shelves. But they don't conduct research indiscriminately; they carefully choose which types will be most useful and stick to the budget.

Through exploratory research, Fisher-Price marketers discovered that there was a gap in toys available for preschool and early elementary schoolboys. Little boys liked the idea of action figures that their older brothers and friends played with, but those toys were difficult for them to understand and handle. And their moms clearly did not want their young children playing with toys that had violent overtones. The research caused Fisher-Price to coin the term KAGOY—Kids Are Getting Older Younger—meaning that younger children want more grown-up toys. Yet those toys must be designed for little hands and young imaginations. "So we were then looking for something that might move away from the [traditional Fisher-Price playset] and be more specifically action figure, but in a way that was more appropriate for preschool boys on many dimensions," explains Gryfe.

Fisher-Price marketers combined the idea of action figures with an age-appropriate context, and the idea for a new group of figures—Rescue Heroes—was born. Fisher-Price used a combination of in-house and outside researchers to obtain primary data on the concept, and later the toy itself. First, marketers conducted in-house focus groups they called "mom talks." Gryfe explains, "A mom talk is basically a focus group that we do in-house. It's done very early in the process to see if we're on the right track. . . . We do this before we spend lots of money on out-of-house focus groups and prototypes." During the mom talks, marketers interviewed mothers to find out what they wanted—and didn't want—in a new toy. They learned quickly that mothers liked the idea of imaginative play, but didn't want their children playing with aggressive or violent toys. Gryfe admits that these in-house focus groups tend to be subject to sampling bias, because the people who participate are those who want to have an impact on products; they aren't necessarily representative of the general buying public. She also believes that participants may edit their responses when they are on site, whereas they may be more candid when they participate in focus groups elsewhere. Once they got some answers, Fisher-Price marketers refined their research and took it on the road. They hired outside moderators to conduct focus groups, often in shopping malls.

Once they had prototype Rescue Heroes, Fisher-Price marketers invited children to the on-site "play lab" to test the figures, each of whom represents an occupation in which a hero rescues people in need—such as firefighters Billy Blazes and Wendy Waters, emergency medical assistant Perry Medic, alpine guide Cliff Hanger, and scuba diver Gil Gripper. In the play labs, boys played with Rescue Heroes and other toys while researchers observed them through a one-way mirror. During these sessions, marketers learned that the figures needed to have oversized feet to stand on their own and not topple over. Similar studies were conducted off the premises to refine the products, including one at Simon Fraser University in British Columbia, Canada, which involved 28 families with boys aged three to six. Later, Fisher-Price actually sent the toys home with children to play with for a week and then interviewed the mothers about their boys' activities. Finally, marketers interviewed parents about whether they would buy the toys and whether they were comfortable with the price.

One nagging theme that emerged from all this research was, "Who are the rescuers? Whom do they rescue? Are there stories behind them?" Marketers realized that they needed to create a scenario for the figures, so little synopses about the characters were developed and printed on the backs of the packages. Then CBS decided that the Rescue Heroes would make a terrific basis for a new children's animated series, and the Saturday morning show of the same name was launched. With careful marketing research behind them, it looks like the Rescue Heroes are going to stand on their own two feet after all.

Case Questions

1. Why was it important for Fisher-Price marketers to define their problem through exploratory research?
2. Do you think that Fisher-Price's methods for collecting primary data are effective? Why or why not? Describe other techniques that might be effective.
3. In what ways might Fisher-Price use secondary data in its research?
4. Go to the Fisher-Price Web site (**http://www.fisherprice. com**) and see what Rescue Heroes information and/or activities are available. Describe what you found at the Web site. Does the site contain any elements that would allow it to collect further research on this product?

Sources: Fisher-Price Web site, http://www.fisherprice.com/us/rescueheroes/products, accessed 28 February 2000.

Karl Taro Greenfeld, "Mattel: Some (Re)Assembly Required," *Time,* 25 October 1999, http://www.time.com.

"Rescue Hero Toys Offer Positive Influence," Simon Fraser University Web site, 31 May 1999, http://www.sfu.ca.

Consumer Behavior

Recognizing that there was a significant need for a good wine that was affordably priced, Jess Jackson founded Kendall-Jackson Wine Estates in 1982. Before introducing his wines into the marketplace, Jackson first identified the unique character and taste that he thought the wines should have and then set out to produce the wines at a cost that would allow affordable pricing for the mass market. Kendall-Jackson has since become one of the most successful wine brands in the United States simply because the founder identified consumer needs and wants in the wine market and then met those needs.

You Decide. After reading the opening vignette and paying special attention to the sections of this chapter marked with the chess piece, answer these questions:

1. Which step in the individual consumer decision-making process did the initial introduction of Kendall-Jackson wines best address?

2. Which of the factors that affect individual consumer decision making would probably have the strongest influence on a consumer's purchase of wine for a dinner party with friends?

3. Which source of information should Kendall-Jackson try to affect, since it would be the most effective in influencing consumers' wine selection?

© Susan Van Etten

Kendall-Jackson Wine Estates

Companies that *anticipate* changes in consumer behavior and respond with new goods and services are likely to achieve long-term health and profitability. But companies that *change* consumer behavior have the opportunity to make major breakthroughs in new markets and industries.

Kendall-Jackson Wine Estates broke into the wine market by carving out a new niche for a moderately priced bottle of wine, becoming the number-one brand of table wine in the United States, with more than $600 million in retail sales. By studying consumer buying habits and actually altering consumer buying behavior, Kendall-Jackson established itself as an industry leader.

Kendall-Jackson was founded by Jess Jackson, a successful attorney in San Francisco. Jackson recognized a huge gap in the wine market and was responsible for closing this gap between the super-premium wines and the jug wines. According to Jackson, "I realized there was a hole in the market I could drive a truck through. The market needed really good wines that the average person could afford." Knowing that his new wine needed to be priced at $5 per bottle, he explored different options for producing a high-quality, moderately priced wine. Jackson started by defining the complex, subtle, and unique taste profile and character of the wine he wanted to produce. He was betting that a breakthrough in the technical aspects of wine making would lead consumers to care more about the taste of the wine itself than the specific vineyard from which it came.

Instead of producing the grapes for the wine, Jackson purchased grapes from the open market with guidance from highly skilled wine makers. These wine makers also guided Jackson in carefully blending the wines to predetermined tastes. This process allowed him to price his wine at $5, between the $10-plus price of the boutique wines and the $2 price of economy wines in 1982.

In the 20 years since he founded his company, Jackson has adapted and extended his winning model to new offerings selling at a premium with the Kendall-Jackson label and to wines from far-flung countries, such as Chile and Australia. Kendall-Jackson continues to innovate knowing that competitors are never far behind. "It used to be that a major advance in wine making came every 50 years or so," Jackson says. "That fell to every 20. Now it's every three to four years. Styles in taste and methods of production seem to become obsolete every 10 years. We have to keep reinventing ourselves."

By identifying a need in the market, Kendall-Jackson managed to open up a whole new market for wines in the U.S. Today, Kendall-Jackson constantly seeks ways to improve its product and production process. Companies such as Kendall-Jackson succeed largely due to their ability to anticipate consumers' latent needs and create consumer demand by offering products with a mass appeal, as well as prestige.[1]

LEARNING OBJECTIVES

After you have completed this chapter, you should be able to:

1. *Understand the three roles consumers play when buying goods and services, and appreciate the consumer buying-decision process.*

2. *Understand how psychological factors—perception, learning, motivation, and psychographics—may affect the consumer buying-decision process.*

3. *Recognize how social factors—reference groups, family, and culture—may affect the consumer buying-decision process.*

4. *Appreciate how physical surroundings, time, and mood shape consumer's buying decisions throughout each stage of the buying-decision process.*

5. *Comprehend how technology may affect the consumer buying-decision process.*

VOICE OF THE EXPERT

Jagdish N. Sheth, Emory University
Balaji C. Krishnan, University of Memphis

As we begin the new millennium, understanding the consumer will be the key to business success. Companies are in business to serve the customer. Those that do so efficiently and effectively are the ones that make a profit. The study of consumer behavior provides the basic knowledge necessary for successful business decisions.

Studying and understanding consumer behavior open several avenues for a student embarking on a career in the field of marketing. A person with a good understanding of consumer behavior understands the underlying reasons why consumers are loyal to a brand or a store. Knowing about the psychology and sociology of consumers helps a manager prepare business strategies. Studying consumer behavior can lead to a career in sales, market research, brand management, or the retail sector.

Similarly, understanding the psychology of consumers can help you secure a position as an account executive in an advertising agency. Knowing how consumers will react to certain types of cues should help determine the advertising strategy for different brands in different industries.

If a student has strong quantitative and analytical skills, a course in consumer behavior in conjunction with marketing-research courses will be useful in securing a market-research analyst position. As a market-research analyst who understands consumer behavior, you can provide deeper insight into what the numbers mean, which can result in better recommendations for top management.

Recently the concept of customer-relationship management (CRM) has come to the forefront. A number of companies are interested in deploying some sort of CRM strategy in their firms. An understanding of consumer behavior is a prerequisite to implementing a successful CRM strategy.

By studying consumer behavior, marketers can better understand their target markets and be better equipped to achieve results through their marketing strategies.

When the marketers at Kendall-Jackson Wine Estates recognized the need for a moderately priced bottle of wine, they began to study how and why consumers purchase wine. How did they select a bottle of wine? Was the wine purchased as a gift? When were consumers willing to pay a premium price? By studying consumer behavior, marketers gain insight into consumer buying decisions and improve their marketing strategies. This chapter presents the general principles behind consumer behavior. First, the chapter defines three roles that consumers play and presents the consumer buying-decision process. Next, the effect of psychological and social factors on consumer buying decisions is addressed. Finally, the chapter explores how physical surroundings, time, and mood influence consumers during the various stages of the consumer buying-decision process.

Consumer behavior deals with how consumers behave when buying both goods and services. Since Chapter 10 deals with services marketing, this chapter will focus mainly on consumer behavior as it relates to marketing goods. Similarly, although our definition of consumer behavior includes business customers, the focus in this chapter is on household consumers. The buying behavior of business-to-business customers is covered in Chapter 7.

The Roles of Consumers and the Consumer Buying-Decision Process

Consumer behavior is the process by which individuals or groups select, use, or dispose of goods, services, ideas, or experiences to satisfy needs and wants. This definition of consumer behavior includes a variety of activities and a number of roles that people hold as consumers.

Three Roles of Consumers

To fully understand consumer behavior, it is helpful to begin with a review of the different roles consumers play. As **users** of a product, consumers are concerned about product features and how successfully the product can be used. **Payers** are consumers who pay for a product and are concerned with its price and the inherent financial considerations. Ads claiming "0 down and 0% interest till 2005" are targeted toward payers, because these messages appeal to their sensitivity to price. **Buyers** focus on the logistics of purchasing the product. Buyers, for example, determine whether to purchase a product at a traditional retail center, by phone, or online. It is estimated that more than 65% of L'eggs panty hose are ordered by mail or phone, even though they are available in most supermarkets, which are open 24 hours a day! It is the buyer who decides where the panty hose will be purchased.

Consumer behavior
Is the process by which individuals or groups select, use, or dispose of goods, services, ideas, or experiences to satisfy needs and wants.

Users
Are the consumers who actually use the product.

Payers
Are the consumers who actually pay for the product.

Buyers
Are the consumers who actually purchase the product.

The Consumer Buying-Decision Process

In each of these roles, consumers constantly face choices—how much to spend, what product to acquire, and where to purchase the product. Marketers need to have some understanding of how these decisions are made in order to develop appropriate marketing strategies. The **consumer buying-decision process**, illustrated in Figure 6.1, is a five-stage process by which consumers make buying decisions. As you can see, the buying-decision process is influenced by psychological factors, situational factors, social factors, and technological factors, which are explained later in this chapter.

This consumer buying-decision process addresses decisions about *whether* to purchase, *what* to purchase, *when* to purchase, from *whom* to purchase, and *how* to pay for it. For example, a consumer decides whether to buy a car, what make or model to buy, when to buy it, where to buy it (Internet or dealer), which dealer, and how to pay for it. Consumers have finite resources in terms of money and time, so they have to constantly weigh the possibility of either postponing or forsaking the

Consumer buying-decision process
Typically involves whether to purchase, what to purchase, when to purchase, from whom to purchase, and how to pay for a purchase.

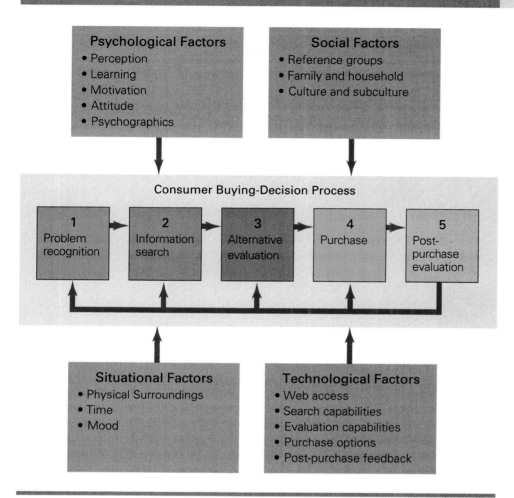

Psychological Factors
• Perception
• Learning
• Motivation
• Attitude
• Psychographics

Social Factors
• Reference groups
• Family and household
• Culture and subculture

Consumer Buying-Decision Process

| 1 Problem recognition | 2 Information search | 3 Alternative evaluation | 4 Purchase | 5 Post-purchase evaluation |

Situational Factors
• Physical Surroundings
• Time
• Mood

Technological Factors
• Web access
• Search capabilities
• Evaluation capabilities
• Purchase options
• Post-purchase feedback

purchase of a product. Also, most purchase and usage decisions are repetitious. Therefore, consumers tend to conserve their transaction costs by not deliberating at each step. Thus, they end up short-circuiting the process. For example, a student may have to scrap his plan to attend tonight's game to study for a test. Similarly, he may have to postpone buying a BMW until he has made enough money to afford it. Thus, we constantly make decisions about whether to purchase and what to purchase at the product level.

An important consumer behavior at this decision level is *mental budgeting*—how the budget consumers set for a product category guides their subsequent behavior as a consumer. The payer plays the most important role in mental budgeting, as the user is constrained by what the payer has budgeted and whether the product is within the budget. This occurs subconsciously, even when one consumer is playing both the payer and user roles. Travelocity.com appeals to this predisposition by allowing you to specify the amount you are willing to spend on a vacation and then coming up with alternative vacation packages from which you can choose. Similarly, Priceline.com understands that consumers make mental budgets and lets you select the price you are willing to pay for airline tickets and hotel rooms.

After making the choice at the product level, the consumer makes another what-to-purchase decision—a choice among brands. For example, if the product-category–level decision is to take a vacation, the next decision is which brand to purchase—that is, which travel destination to select, how to get there, and so on. It is important

Economic Forces

An economic downturn may affect the behavior of payers, buyers, and users. The payer may not have the money to make purchases. Buyers, who may be working longer hours or at two jobs, may have limited time to shop. Users, therefore, will have less access and exposure to new goods and services.

This Colgate advertisement is an example of an external stimulus that kindles the desire in customers for strong, white teeth.

Problem recognition
Is a consumer's realization that he or she needs to buy something to get back to a normal state of comfort.

Needs
Are unsatisfactory conditions that prompt consumers to an action that will make the conditions better.

Wants
Are desires to obtain more satisfaction than is absolutely necessary to improve an unsatisfactory condition.

for marketers to understand how a consumer selects a brand. This insight may help the marketer determine appropriate strategies to motivate consumers to buy one brand instead of another.

Step 1: Problem Recognition

Consumers typically make purchase decisions to satisfy a particular need or want. A consumer, for example, could realize that she is hungry and thus has to buy some food, or that the leaking faucet needs to be fixed. A consumer problem can be any state of deprivation or discomfort felt by a consumer. **Problem recognition**, the first step in the consumer buying-decision process, occurs when consumers realize that they need to do something to get back to a normal state of comfort.

Consumer Needs and Wants

To understand consumer behavior, we need to understand how consumers perceive, learn, and make decisions to satisfy their needs and wants. It is important to understand what the needs and wants of users, payers, and buyers are. **Needs** are unsatisfactory conditions that prompt the consumer to an action that will make the condition better. **Wants** are desires to obtain more satisfaction than is absolutely necessary to improve an unsatisfactory condition. The difference between a need and a want is that need arousal is driven by a person's discomfort with physical and psychological conditions. For example, if someone is hungry, he physically needs food; if he is stressed and cannot sleep, he is psychologically discomforted. Wants occur when people want to take their physical and psychological conditions beyond the state of minimal comfort. Thus, food satisfies a need, while gourmet food satisfies a want. Similarly, any car will satisfy the need for transportation from your apartment to school. But a Miata or a Porsche satisfies the desire (or want) for superior performance, prestige, and/or a positive self-image. Only when needs are satisfied do wants surface.

Types of Problems: Routine and Latent

There are two types of problems that consumers may face. One is a routine problem that can be recognized. For example, if you know you are going to run out of milk, you make a note to yourself to replenish this product. The second type of problem is latent. You may not be aware that you have a problem because you may not have given it enough thought. For example, marketers send reminders about regular or preventive maintenance for automobiles, or they may offer new and attractive price or promotion offerings that make you reconsider your habitual behavior. This is a common practice for marketers of long-distance phone services and preapproved credit cards.

Problem recognition can occur due to either an internal stimulus or an external stimulus. *Internal stimuli* are perceived states of discomfort—physical (e.g., hunger) or psychological (e.g., boredom). *External stimuli* are informational cues from the marketplace that lead the consumer to realize the problem. They could be an advertisement or a friend's comment that triggers the process by which the consumer realizes the problem.

The payer, the buyer, or the user can recognize the problem. VCRs were not considered needs until they were made widely available. There was no obvious problem

Most of us visit the local video store or order a movie from a satellite service when we want to watch a movie. Netflix, one of the few bright spots on the dot-com horizon, wants to change all that. Netflix is an online DVD rental firm that is using innovative marketing strategies to change consumer behavior. Thanks to the marketing efforts of Leslie Kilgore, vice president of marketing, Netflix is creating a buzz among movie fans by selling movie subscriptions to DVD owners. The most popular plan is a $19.95 monthly subscription for three DVDs. Customers can keep a DVD as long as they want, or, once they view a DVD, they can exchange it for a new rental. The faster customers view and exchange movies, the more videos they can watch each month.

Kilgore's primary marketing efforts are geared toward getting nonsubscribers to experience the benefits of an online rental subscription. "Our marketing goal is to profitably get owners of DVD players to try Netflix for free," she explains. "Remarkably, of the people who try Netflix, 90% go on to become paying customers," she says. To make sure that the free trials turn into subscriptions, Netflix emphasizes service, not the movies, to ensure that customers have a great experi-ence. In addition to free trials, Netflix is using happy customers to spread the word about online subscriptions. Customers can spread the word about Netflix in several ways: They can tell friends via e-mail from a "Tell a Friend" auto-mated form on netflix.com, inform fellow movie buffs on special-interest Web sites, link from commercial sites, or even refer music enthusiasts from an audio file-sharing site like 3WK.com.

"In the last couple of years, customers have been our largest source of growth," Kilgore says. "We also have very strong affiliation programs with extremely large online sites, but more of our customers come from a whole host of small sites run by Netflix customers." Netflix recently signed up its biggest affiliate to date, Best Buy, in a deal that involves online and offline efforts. In addition to promotional partnerships, Netflix has been doing some online advertising on major sites such as Yahoo! and MSN. With a subscriber base of more than 670,000, Netflix appears to be successfully changing the way we rent movies.

Source: Steve Ditlea, http://www.technologymarketing.com, November 2002.

that VCRs solved. However, once they were available, consumers could use them to view programs they had missed and the "need" to be able to watch a program at your convenience was recognized. Thus, although the "need" existed, it was not rec-ognized until the advent of VCRs. The same is true for products such as TiVo, Post-it® Notes, and personal digital assistants (PDAs). These products serve the *latent needs* of the consumer in the user role.

Consumers typically had to go to a store or restaurant to buy pizza before home delivery was made available. The convenience of being able to order a pizza from home is one solution to buying a pizza. This serves the needs of consumers in the buyer role. For the payer, the availability of leased automobiles has improved afford-ability. Also, the availability of credit makes many consumers recognize the "need" to buy a new car or furniture. Similarly, to "help" consumers identify these prob-lems, marketers promote credit-card use by sending consumers preapproved cards.

Marketers can use their knowledge of how consumers recognize problems to their own advantage. They can send consumers reminders for routine problem recognition. Moreover, to expedite actions by consumers, marketers may provide coupons along with the reminders. If consumers have not yet recognized the prob-lem, marketers can educate them about the benefits of using a product such as a PDA or TiVo. Some marketers also let consumers sample or "test drive" products in an effort to educate them about the benefits of their products.

Step 2: Information Search

The **information-search** stage of the consumer buying-decision process can be as simple as scanning your memory to remember what product/brand you bought the last time you made a similar purchase decision. This can be a subconscious search for information. However, more often than not, we specifically seek information to solve the problem that has been identified. This search rarely includes every brand in

Technological Forces
The "need" for technology-related products is often not recognized by consumers until after the product is introduced into the marketplace.

Information-search
Is the stage in the consumer buying-decision process when consumers collect information on a select subset of brands.

Consumers may seek out independent sources of product information during the information search stage of the consumer buying-decision process. Consumer Report is a comprehensive source for unbiased advice about products and services, and other consumer concerns.

Competitive Forces

Firms compete with each other to get their brands into consumers' consideration sets. Sometimes they achieve this by changing the criteria consumers use to make their decision.

existence. Consumers usually consider only a select subset of brands, organized as follows:

- The *awareness set* consists of brands a consumer is aware of.
- An *evoked set* consists of brands in a product category that the consumer remembers when she is making a decision.
- Of the brands in the evoked set, not all are deemed to fit the need. Those considered unfit are eliminated right away. The remaining brands are termed the *consideration set*—the brands a consumer will consider buying.

Initially, consumers seek information about the consideration set of brands. New information can bring additional brands into the awareness, evoked, and consideration sets.

Different sources of information are used in the information-search process. These sources of information may be categorized as marketer or nonmarketer. When the source of the information is the marketer/manufacturer, it is termed a *marketer source*. This information may be from advertising, packaging, in-store displays, or other product literature made available to consumers. Lately, most companies have set up Web sites to facilitate consumers' search for information.

Nonmarketer sources are independent of the marketer's control. They include personal sources and independent sources, such as information provided by *Consumer Reports* and friends and acquaintances. Since these sources have no personal interest in biasing the information (unlike marketer sources), they are deemed to be more credible. The information provided by friends and acquaintances is also called word-of-mouth and plays a critical role in consumers selecting products.

Lately, the Internet has become an important source of information for many consumers. Other than marketer sources, such as company Web sites, many news groups discuss products, including music[2]. There are also tools available on the Internet for obtaining comparative information on a number of different brands. One such Web site is **http://www.dealtime.com**.

Sometimes consumers may not go through such a long and conscious search strategy. They may use a contrasting search strategy called heuristics. *Heuristics* are quick rules of thumb and shortcuts used to make decisions. Heuristics can be implemented in a variety of ways:

- Broad inferences are quickly drawn from partial information (e.g., the product price or store image may be used to judge quality).
- Past experiences are considered adequate.
- Opinions from friends and family are adopted as the final choice.
- Brand names are heavily relied on.

Although these strategies are not systematic, they are also not irrational. They are rational to their users in terms of the cost-versus-benefit trade-offs they perceive. If they are short on time, many consumers are likely to use the heuristics route to guide them in their information search.

Consumers' choice of information sources depends partly on their search strategy. A search strategy is the way consumers search for information to help them make decisions. Since acquiring information takes time, as well as physical and mental effort, consumers weigh these "costs" against what they are likely to gain from acquiring information. That comparison helps them decide how much information they will acquire and from what sources.

Marketers can influence this stage of the consumer buying-decision process by educating consumers about their own product or sharing information with them. For example, Procter & Gamble mails free samples of detergent to consumers, encouraging them to try the product. Progressive provides customers with insurance quotes from its competitors. In this case, Progressive is trying to help its customers by simplifying the information search. The company hopes that consumers will value this service and return the favor by purchasing insurance with Progressive.

Step 3: Alternative Evaluation

Once consumers conduct an information search, how do they use that information as they proceed through the **alternative-evaluation** stage of the consumer buying-decision process and ultimately make a product choice? Consumers select one of several alternatives (brands, dealers, and so on) available to them. The process and steps involved in evaluating products are called *choice models*. For example, let us consider a consumer who is planning to buy an automobile. Let's say she has four brands in her consideration set. She rates them in four different categories—price, mileage, power/speed, and aesthetics. The rating for each automobile is shown in Figure 6.2.

There are two broad categories of choice models: compensatory and noncompensatory.

Compensatory Model

In the *compensatory model,* the consumer arrives at a choice by considering all of the attributes of a product (or benefits of a service) and mentally trading off the alternative's perceived weakness in one or more attributes for its perceived strength in other attributes. If the consumer decides to assign weights for the criteria she is using as 40% to price, 30% to mileage, 20% to power/speed, and 10% to aesthetics, she will arrive at the following perceived values:

$$\text{Brand A} = 0.4\,(6) + 0.3\,(8) + 0.2(6) + 0.1(7) = 6.7$$
$$\text{Brand B} = 0.4\,(7) + 0.3\,(9) + 0.2(4) + 0.1(6) = 6.9$$
$$\text{Brand C} = 0.4\,(8) + 0.3\,(7) + 0.2(5) + 0.1(8) = 7.1$$
$$\text{Brand D} = 0.4\,(5) + 0.3\,(8) + 0.2(8) + 0.1(8) = 6.8$$

Using the compensatory model of evaluating alternatives, the consumer would decide to buy Brand C, although it is the worst brand as far as mileage is concerned.

Noncompensatory Models

While there are several *noncompensatory models* that have been identified, four are the most common and useful. These are the conjunctive, disjunctive, lexicographic, and elimination-by-aspects models.[3] In the *conjunctive model,* the consumer begins

Alternative-evaluation
Is the stage in the consumer buying-decision process when consumers select one of several alternatives (brands, dealers, and so on) available to them.

A Consumer's New-Car Alternative Evaluation				Figure 6.2

	Attribute			
Brands	**Price**	**Mileage**	**Power/Speed**	**Aesthetics**
A	6	8	6	7
B	7	9	4	6
C	8	7	5	8
D	5	8	8	8

Note: Each attribute is rated on a scale of 1 to 10; 10 represents the best rating an attribute can get.

During the alternative evaluation stage, marketers may introduce strategies that ease the decision process. Recognizing that choosing a new car is a difficult decision, GM introduced the 24 Hour Test Drive that allows new car shoppers to spend a whole day or night with one of its new vehicles.

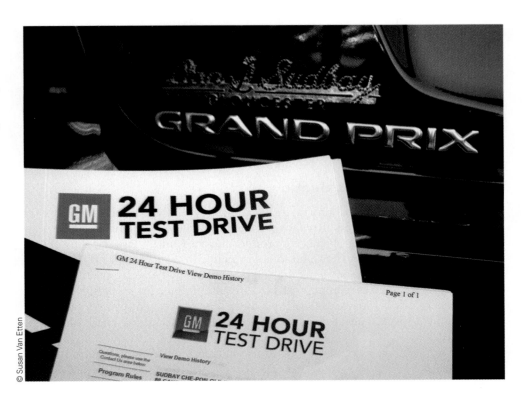

© Susan Van Etten

by setting the minimum cutoffs for all salient attributes. Each alternative is then examined on each attribute, and any alternative that meets the minimum cutoffs for all attributes can potentially be chosen.

If the consumer uses a cutoff of 6, by examining Figure 6.2 it is clear that the only brand that meets the cutoff for every criterion is Brand A. Thus, she will choose Brand A, if she uses the conjunctive model to make the decision.

The *disjunctive model* entails trade-offs between aspects of choice alternatives. Sometimes the consumer is willing to trade off one feature for another. For example, a car buyer might say that the automobile she is willing to consider buying should have good pickup or, if it has less pickup, it should be fuel efficient. Although similar trade-offs are made with the compensatory model, there are differences. First, the disjunctive model considers the sheer presence or absence of attributes, rather than the degree or amount to which these attributes are present. Second, in the compensatory model, the attributes traded off need not serve the same purpose, while they tend to in the disjunctive model.

Another model consumers use to make a choice is the *lexicographic model*. In this model, attributes of alternatives are rank-ordered in terms of importance. Consumers examine all alternatives on the most important criterion and identify the ones that surpass a threshold level. If more than one alternative remains in the choice set, they then consider the second most important criterion and examine the remaining alternatives with respect to that criterion's threshold level. The process continues until only one alternative remains. Using this approach, the consumer would have decided on Brand C, as it scores the highest (8) on the most important attribute—price.

The *elimination-by-aspects (EBA) model* is similar to the lexicographic model, but with one important difference: Consumers rate the attributes in order of importance and, in addition, define cutoff values. They then examine all alternatives first on the most important attribute, further considering only those that satisfy the minimum cutoff level on this most important attribute. If more than one alternative meets the requirement, they go on to the next aspect, appraising the remaining alternatives on the second attribute. In our example, if the consumer has a cutoff of 6 for the first attribute (price), Brand D would be eliminated because it does not meet the criterion. All the remaining brands meet the second criterion of mileage. Thus, the consumer would proceed to the third attribute, where Brands B and C have scores less than the cutoff; thus, Brand A would be selected.

Consumers may use any of these choice models independently or use a combination of the choice models. For more important decisions, a consumer might first use a noncompensatory model and then, to further identify the choice, use a compensatory model. The noncompensatory model could be used to eliminate choices and narrow down the set of alternatives for closer comparisons.

Marketers can play a very important role in the alternative-evaluation phase of the decision-making process. They could highlight new criteria that the consumer has not originally considered. For example, Volvo emphasizes the safety of its cars. In this case, the consumer is likely to reevaluate the different models, using safety as a criteria. Similarly, some late entrants into the automobile market, such as Kia and Hyundai, have improved the warranty on their automobiles to affect their consumers' alternative-evaluation process.

Step 4: Purchase

Once the consumer has evaluated the alternatives, she makes a **purchase**. This appears to be a straightforward step, but even here consumer behavior at times becomes intriguing. The consumer, for example, may use one of the alternative-evaluation techniques to determine the brand she is going to purchase. At this stage, she arranges for the terms of the transaction, seeking and obtaining the transfer of title or ownership from the seller, paying for the automobile, and receiving possession of the product commitment from the seller. While the steps described here are automatic in the case of groceries, they become more significant in the case of purchases such as automobiles or homes. In the case of rare artifacts, implementing the purchase, including finding a seller, may be a long drawn-out process. The Internet auction retailer eBay attempts to make this simpler for consumers by matching buyers and sellers.

Sometimes the consumer purchase process may be derailed when a consumer changes her mind. The preferred brand may be out of stock, thus forcing the consumer to buy a different brand than the one identified or to postpone the purchase. Second, new in-store information may reopen the evaluation process. Third, financing terms may render a purchase infeasible, forcing the consumer as payer either to abandon the purchase altogether or to substitute a lower-priced model for the intended brand or another brand that is available with better financing terms. Fourth, unexpected situations may lead to a postponement of the purchase. For example, the consumer may learn that the company he is expecting to hire has a recruitment freeze, and thus he is not sure of where or when he is going to be employed.

Marketers try to influence the purchase stage of the decision process by providing price-matching schemes. After considering all the alternatives, a consumer may still be apprehensive about buying a costly product. This is because the price of products varies from store to store and also over time. In order to get a consumer to make the purchase rather than postpone it, companies such as Best Buy and Circuit City have come up with schemes to expedite the purchase stage for the consumer. They agree to match competitors' prices, as well as provide a guarantee that they will match prices for 30 days after the purchase date.

© Susan Van Etten

Circuit City attempts to expedite the purchase stage of the decision process by offering to match competitors' prices for thirty days after the date of purchase.

Purchase

Is the stage in the consumer buying-decision process when transaction terms are arranged, ownership title is transferred, the product is paid for, and the consumer takes possession of the product from the seller.

Step 5: Postpurchase Evaluations

The purchase of the product is followed by a post-purchase evaluation stage. When consumers' expectations are not met by the product performance, they get dissatisfied. When performance meets their expectations, consumers are satisfied, and when consumers' expectations are surpassed by performance, they are delighted. Thus, marketers should be concerned not only with the performance of their product but also with consumers' expectations, knowing that consumer satisfaction will affect future purchase decisions.

Postpurchase behavior
Is the last stage in the consumer buying-decision process, when the consumer experiences an intense need to confirm the wisdom of that decision.

Postpurchase behavior is the last stage in the consumer buyer-decision process, when the consumers experience an intense need to confirm the wisdom of their decision. Postpurchase behavior may include *cognitive dissonance*, the doubt and regret the buyer may feel about the purchase choice. One of the methods of reducing cognitive dissonance and confirming the soundness of one's decision is to seek further positive information about the chosen alternative and avoid negative information about the chosen alternative.

Following a satisfactory or dissatisfactory experience, consumers have three possible responses: *exit*, *voice*, or *loyalty*. If consumers are dissatisfied with their experience with a brand, they may decide never again to buy that brand. This places them back at the start of the decision process the next time the problem arises. Some dissatisfied consumers complain and then decide either to give the brand or marketer another chance or simply to exit. If consumer complaints are addressed, then the consumer is more likely to buy that brand again. If the complaint is not successfully addressed, the negative feelings may intensify beyond what they would have been had the consumer not made the complaint in the first place.

The third response is, of course, loyalty. Consumer loyalty means the consumer buys the same brand repeatedly. It is fair to assume that satisfied consumers are more likely to be loyal. However, some consumers exhibit switching behavior, despite being satisfied with the current brand.

Depending on any new information they may be exposed to, consumers may decide to collect more information before they purchase the same product. Recently, there has been a recall of products that contain phenylpropanolamine. This new information may cause consumers to either check the ingredients of cold medications before buying one or research the side effects of this ingredient. Similarly, based on your level of satisfaction or dissatisfaction with a product such as an automobile, you may include new criteria in the alternative-evaluation phase or weight the existing criteria differently. In either case, the alternative you select may be different. In some cases, you may be satisfied with the product. However, you may not be satisfied with the retailer because of the poor service you got at the store. In this case, postpurchase evaluation may lead you to buy the same brand from a different store.

As discussed earlier, a number of factors affect the consumer buying-decision process. They can broadly be classified as psychological factors, social factors, and situational factors. Each of these will be discussed in the following sections.

LEARNING OBJECTIVE   2

×tra!

Psychological Bases of Consumer Behavior

A number of psychological factors affect the consumer buying-decision process. Marketers study these factors with the objective of influencing the decision process in their favor.

Perception

Perception
Is the process by which an individual senses, organizes, and interprets information received from the environment.

The objective reality of a product matters, but what matters even more is the consumer's perception of a product or experience or a brand. **Perception** is the process by which an individual *senses*, *organizes*, and *interprets* the information he or she receives from the environment. Marketers seek to understand the sources of consumer perceptions and to influence them. For example, cereals are made darker in color to make them appear more masculine, while mouthwash is colored green or blue to connote a clean, fresh feeling. Similarly, consumer perception is the reason that clear colas failed to succeed in the marketplace.

When a consumer decides to eat at a restaurant, the ambience and the smell and taste of the food affect his senses and overall perception of the restaurant. He organizes this information as being similar or dissimilar to prior experiences. Having organized the information according to criteria such as food quality, service, and ambience, he interprets this information as being either good or bad depending on whether he likes the experience.

Taco Bell restaurants, for example, feature a bright purple-and-green color motif in their interiors, replacing the somewhat lackluster past look of the chain. When Taco Bell made this change some years ago, the new colors were so significantly different from before that most consumers inevitably sensed the change. Moreover, given the prior associations most people have with bright neon colors, consumers readily interpreted the new motif as signifying youthfulness and an upbeat ambience.

Learning

Learning is a change in the content of long-term memory. Most consumer behavior is learned behavior. We learn consciously and subconsciously from a number of sources. We learn from our prior experiences, our peers, mass media, or family and friends. Learning helps us respond better to our environment. A child who accidentally puts his hand on a hot electric bulb learns to never again touch anything resembling that object. Thus, human learning is directed at acquiring a potential for future adaptive behavior. A consumer, for example, who takes advantage of a going-out-of-business sale and buys a substandard product that can not be returned learns about the futility of buying a nonreturnable product.

When a consumer runs out of cereal, she knows she has to restock the next time she shops for groceries. She knows exactly where the cereal is located and picks up a box of the same brand on the next shopping trip. This type of decision making does not involve much explicit thought. However, if she decides to purchase a cellular phone, she will try to acquaint herself with the various offers and options available. Thus, the learning process for a purchase that involves merely replenishing existing goods is vastly different from the learning process where the purchase involves a specific problem that has to be solved.

Motivation

Motivation is what moves people—it is the driving force for all human behavior. **Motivation** is the state of drive or arousal that drives behavior toward a goal-object. Thus, motivation has two components: (1) *drive or arousal,* and (2) a *goal-object.* The arousal or drive is akin to stepping on the gas pedal in an automobile, while the goal-object is analogous to steering of the vehicle. A gas pedal without a steering wheel is dangerous, while a steering wheel without a gas pedal is useless.

Emotions and the level of involvement consumers have with products are important motivating factors, as described next.

The large, juicy strawberry in this Knudsen advertisement creates the perception that this novel, new combination of cottage cheese and fruit will satisfy any sweet tooth.

Learning
Is a change in the content of long-term memory.

Motivation
Is the state of drive or arousal that moves us toward a goal-object.

This advertisement for Earthbound Farm Organic vegetables stirs customer's emotions and appeals to their need to provide safe, healthy food for their children.

Emotions
Are strong, relatively uncontrolled feelings that affect our behavior.

Involvement
Is a product's degree of personal relevance to a consumer.

Attitudes
Are learned predispositions to respond to an object or class of objects in a consistently favorable or unfavorable way.

Consumer Emotions

Needs and emotions are closely related. **Emotions** are strong, relatively uncontrolled feelings that affect our behavior.[4] Emotions are often triggered by environmental factors or events. Many of us felt sad and insecure after the events of September 11, 2001. These emotions changed the travel and flying habits of many consumers. Some emotions may be internally generated. Emotions are typically accompanied by physiological changes, such as dilation of the pupils of the eyes, rapid breathing, or an increase in blood pressure. We all seek positive emotional experiences and avoid negative emotional experiences. Much product consumption and use is driven by and immersed in emotions.

We cuddle a baby because we feel love for her or him. We swear at a rude driver who cuts in front of us because we feel anger and frustration. Although we have all experienced emotion, it is not easy to define. The reason is that emotion is a complex set of processes that happen concurrently in multiple systems. Emotions have three response components: cognitive, emotional, and physiological. *Cognitive responses* are the thought processes of individuals, and include beliefs, categorization, and symbolic meaning. *Emotional responses* do not involve thinking; they simply happen, often inexplicably and suddenly. Specific songs, for example, may make individuals feel happy or sad or recreate other past feelings associated with the particular piece of music. In contrast to cognitive and emotional responses, *physiological responses* are often described in terms of physical pleasure or discomfort.

Involvement

Involvement can be defined as the degree of personal relevance of an object or product to a consumer. Involvement is a matter of degree—how relevant or how central a product is. Accordingly, we can expand the notion of involvement to refer, beyond relevance, to the degree to which a consumer finds a product interesting. While both salt and cosmetics are relevant to some people, it is quite likely that consumers would be more involved in a decision about cosmetics than in one about salt.

Involvement, defined as the degree of interest, has two forms: enduring involvement and situational involvement. *Enduring involvement* is the degree of interest a consumer feels about a product on an ongoing basis. In contrast, *situational involvement* is the degree of interest the consumer has in a specific situation or on a specific occasion, such as when buying a product or consuming something in the presence of an important client or friend. A consumer may have no particular interest in vacuum cleaners. However, when her vacuum cleaner breaks down and has to be replaced, she gets very involved in the decision to buy a vacuum cleaner. This involvement is temporary, though, and ceases to exist once the problem is solved. Thus, her involvement with the vacuum cleaner is situational. However, the same consumer may be a "techie" and interested in knowing more about computers, regardless of whether she needs to purchase one. This kind of involvement does not depend on the situation, but is enduring in nature.

Attitude: Definition and Characteristics

Gordon Allport, a psychologist, defines **attitudes** as "learned predispositions to respond to an object or class of objects in a consistently favorable or unfavorable way."[5]

The definition has several implications:

1. Attitudes are learned. That is, they get formed on the basis of some experience, with or without information about the object.
2. Attitudes are predispositions. As such they reside in the mind.
3. Attitudes cause consistent response. They precede and produce behavior.

Because attitudes precede and produce behavior, they can be used to predict behavior. For example, if we know that a person's attitude toward George W. Bush running for president is positive, then we can predict that he/she is more likely to vote for him. Marketers use attitude measures before launching new products. Behavior also can be used to infer the underlying attitudes. In everyday life, we observe somebody's behavior toward us and use that observation to infer whether that person likes us; we then use that inferred attitude to predict how the person will behave toward us in the future. Marketers, too, often use this logic. When consumers buy a product, their purchase behavior is used to infer a favorable attitude toward the related product class, which in turn is deemed to be an indicator of the potential purchase of an item in a related product class.

In this advertisement, Egg Beaters are promoted as "real eggs." Marketers strive to reinforce positive attitudes and change negative attitudes toward their brands.

Attitudes, then, are our evaluations of objects—people, places, brands, products, organizations, and so on. People evaluate objects in terms of their goodness, likeability, or desirability. Consumers may hold attitudes about salespeople in general (e.g., "Salespeople are basically all hucksters"), and about specific companies (e.g., "Company X makes good appliances, but not computers"). Attitudes do change with time and marketers strive to influence consumers' attitudes. Marketers try to change negative consumer attitudes toward their brand and reinforce positive consumer attitudes toward their brand.

Psychographics

Another facet of motivation is **psychographics**, characteristics of individuals that identify them in terms of their psychological and behavioral makeup—how people occupy themselves (behavior) and what psychological factors underlie their activity pattern. For example, a consumer's need to seek affiliation or peer approval may make him become a member of a golf club or go to theaters. Theatergoing or playing golf thus becomes part of his psychographics. This psychographic in turn drives him to buy golf equipment or do whatever is needed to implement that particular psychographic. The psychographic thus becomes motivational. Psychographics have three components: values, self-concept, and lifestyles.

Psychographics
Are characteristics of individuals that describe them in terms of their psychological and behavioral makeup.

Values

When you think about what is important to you in life, you are thinking about your values. Values are end-states of life, the goals you live for. Psychologist Milton Rokeach has identified two groups of values: terminal and instrumental. *Terminal values* are the goals we seek in life (e.g., peace and happiness), whereas *instrumental values* are the means or behavioral standards by which we pursue our goals (e.g., honesty).

Consumer researcher Lynn Kahle and his associates developed a list of values (LOV) directly relevant to everyday consumer behavior:

© John Henley/CORBIS

A person's lifestyle influences the pattern of our activities and how we spend time and money. Marketers who sell cellular phones to college students need to consider how lifestyle decisions influence consumer buying decisions.

Self-concept
Refers to a person's self-image.

VALS™
Is a psychographic profiling scheme developed by SRI Consulting Business Intelligence.

1. Self-respect
2. Self-fulfillment
3. Security
4. Sense of belonging
5. Excitement
6. Sense of accomplishment
7. Fun and enjoyment
8. Being well respected
9. Warm relationships with others[6]

Consumers are clustered in three groups, depending on which of these terminal values are more important to them. They are *internals* if they value self-fulfillment, excitement, a sense of accomplishment, and self-respect. These people like to be in control of their lives. In marketing terms, internals take proactive steps, such as looking at nutritional labels while buying products. The second group is *externals,* who value a sense of belonging and security and being well respected. These people like to conform and thus are more likely to buy products they think most people buy. Externals are brand-conscious people who buy a popular brand because everybody else is buying it. Finally, *interpersonals* value warm relationships with others, as well as fun and enjoyment.

Self-Concept

Everyone has a self-image—a perception of who they are. This is called **self-concept**. Furthermore, self-concept includes the individual's idea of who she currently is and what she would like to become. These two components of self-concept are called *actual self* and *ideal self,* respectively.

Self-concept deeply influences people's consumption, for people express their self-concept in large measure by what they consume. For example, in his senior year, a student may begin to think of himself as a professional and thus begins to dress like one, retiring his baseball caps and sneakers. Many Generation Xers, now well past their teen years, have begun to nurture a self-concept of being grown-up, responsible people, and, consequently, they are flocking to dermatologists to take off their tattoos—the same tattoos they have proudly sported for many years.

Individuals' self-concepts vary according to which of the three consumer roles described earlier—users, payers, and buyers—they are playing. A user may have a self-concept of being a very discerning connoisseur or a very involved user. The payer may have a self-concept of being thrifty or financially prudent, or of being nonchalant, with a money-is-no-object-to-me attitude. Finally, the buyer may have a self-concept of being a convenience or service seeker or very time conscious.

Lifestyle

Up to this point, we have looked at how we think of ourselves and what we value. Now we will focus on the way we live—our *lifestyle*. A good way to determine a person's lifestyle is to look at the products and brands he consumes. Lifestyle is a function of (1) a consumer's personal characteristics, namely, genetics, race, gender, age, and personality; (2) personal context, namely, culture, institutions, reference groups, and personal worth; and (3) needs and emotions. These three sets of factors together influence the pattern of our activities—how we spend time and money.

Values and Lifestyles (VALS)

One of the most widely used psychographic profiling schemes is called **VALS™**. Developed by SRI International, and currently run by SRI Consulting Business Intel-

Do Consumers Really Care About Regulating Internet Privacy?

Dozens of bills are pending in Congress to regulate Internet privacy, often based on the assumption that privacy fears are stifling the growth of the Internet. Proponents like to trot out surveys in which consumers overwhelmingly express concern about Internet privacy. In a June 2002 report by Jupiter Research, 70% of online consumers said they were worried about online privacy. In another survey, 93% of e-commerce users said it was very important that sites disclose their privacy practices.

But what do these surveys really prove? Consumers may tell survey takers they fear for their privacy, but their behavior belies it. People don't read privacy policies, for example. In a survey taken last year by the Privacy Leadership Initiative, a group of corporate and trade association executives, only 3% of consumers said that they read privacy policies carefully, and 64% said they only glanced at—or never read—privacy policies.

Another indication that privacy is a false concern: Relatively few consumers have bought privacy-management tools, such as software that allows them to browse anonymously and manage Internet cookies and e-mail. Many vendors are now migrating away from consumer-centric business models. So, although consumers can take technological control over their own situation, few of them do.

Plus, as most online marketers know, people will "sell" their personal data incredibly cheaply. As Internet pundit Esther Dyson has said, "You do a survey, and consumers say they are very concerned about their privacy. Then you offer them a discount on a book, and they'll tell you everything." Indeed, a recent Jupiter report said that 82% of respondents would give personal information to new shopping sites to enter a $100 sweepstakes.

Clearly, consumers' stated privacy concerns diverge from what consumers do. Two theories might explain the divergence.

First, asking consumers what they care about reveals only whether they value privacy. That's half the equation. Of more interest is how much consumers will pay—in time or money—for the corresponding benefits. For now, the cost-benefit ratio is tilted too high for consumers to spend much time or money on privacy.

Second, consumers don't have uniform interests. When it comes to online privacy, consumers can be segmented into two groups: activists, who actively protect their online privacy, and apathetics, who do little or nothing to protect themselves. The activists are very vocal, but appear to be a tiny market segment.

Using consumer segmentation, the analytical defect of broad-based online privacy regulations becomes apparent. The activists, by definition, take care of themselves. They demand privacy protections from businesses and, if they don't get them, use technology to protect themselves, or take their business elsewhere.

In contrast, mainstream consumers don't change their behavior based on online privacy concerns. If these people won't take even minimal steps to protect themselves, why should government regulation do it for them?

DISCUSSION QUESTIONS

1. Do you believe that the majority of consumers have privacy concerns when Internet shopping?
2. What specific concerns do you believe are most important?

Source: Eric Goldman *assistant professor, Marquette University Law School; former general counsel, Epinions.com*, 14 October 2002.

---

ligence (SRIC-BI), the first version introduced in 1978 (VALS I) segmented the entire U.S. adult population into nine groups based on the identities they seek and implement via marketplace behaviors. According to SRIC-BI, "People pursue and acquire [goods], services, and experiences that provide satisfaction and give shape, substance, and character to their identities."[7] In 1989, VALS 2 was introduced, with eight groups to reflect the changes that had taken place, as well as to improve the segmentation principles for advertising and marketing applications, as illustrated in Figure 6.3.

Strugglers, who are at the bottom of Figure 6.3, are passive consumers who are generally not well educated and have limited resources. Typically, they are more concerned with safety and security and represent a modest market for products. *Makers* are the do-it-yourself (DIY) category of consumers. They are value conscious and buy products they can use to build things they would like to use. They are conservative and suspicious of government intrusion. *Strivers* constantly seek the approval of their peers and people around them. They are typically people of limited means and bemoan this fact.

Believers, on the other hand, have limited but sufficient resources to meet their limited needs, and are conservative in their decision making. They value church, family, and community very much and are more likely to buy American products.

Figure 6.3	VALS™ Network

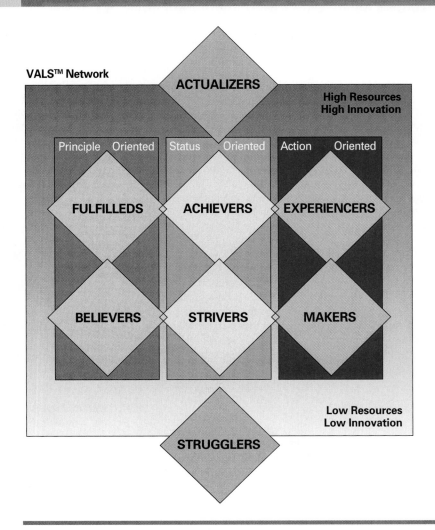

Experiencers are young, enthusiastic, and rebellious. They seek variety and excitement in the products they consume. They are more likely to spend a substantial amount of their money on clothing, fast food, movies, and videos. *Achievers* are successful career people who value stability and status quo. They are likely to be politically and economically conservative. Their lives revolve around their family and church. They are more likely to buy products that enhance their sense of prestige and exhibit their success to their peers. *Fulfilleds* are mature, successful consumers who are well educated and are in (or have recently retired from) professional jobs. They are fairly knowledgeable about world events and are socially conscious. They are practical consumers who look for durability and value in the products they purchase. *Actualizers* are "take charge" people with high self-esteem and plentiful resources. While image is important to these consumers, they do not use it to impress others, but to reflect their taste and character. They are established or emerging business or government leaders and are open to new ideas and change. They are socially conscious and have a diverse and rich life.

You can take the VALS survey at the SRI Consulting Business Intelligence Web site **http://www.sric-bi.com** to find out in which VALS category you belong. Consumers tend to be dynamic—as their available resources, as well as the pressures on these resources, change, their VALS category may also change. However, the psychological motivations measured by VALS are enduring traits, lasting on the order of 15 years or more.

Social Bases of Consumer Behavior

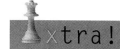

Some consumers are influenced by the group of people they look up to and some people are influenced by other members of their family, while culture and subculture play an important role in some consumers' decision-making process.

Reference Groups

All the formal and informal groups that affect a consumer's purchase decision are called **reference groups**. There are three main types of reference groups that affect purchase decisions. They are *membership groups, aspirational groups,* and *dissociative groups.* The amount of influence these groups have on consumers varies by product category, as well as by individual consumer. Some consumers are likely to be influenced more by such groups than others. Likewise, some product categories may be associated with these groups and thus consumers are likely to be influenced more in their purchase decision in this situation. For example, a biker may get a tattoo to feel like part of the group.

Membership groups are groups to which the consumer belongs. They can be formal groups such as church groups or informal ones such as family or colleagues. While these groups may play an important role in each of the five consumer decision-making processes, they play a critically important role in the information search and alternative evaluation. For example, if a consumer were to be in the market for a product about which he has little knowledge, he may depend on the views of such groups to gather information. This is done by soliciting information about these products.

Aspirational groups are groups that a consumer wants to belong to. As illustrated earlier in the chapter, many Gen Xers who are entering the job market start dressing more conservatively in an effort to look "the part." People hoping to be promoted start dressing like their bosses. Many middle-aged people try to recapture their youth by buying sports cars. They do this in an effort to identify with the group they want to belong to—youth. Marketers use this concept of aspirational groups in many of their communications. For example, famous athletes endorse athletic shoes. The message here is, "If you want to be like this athlete, use these shoes."

Dissociative groups are those groups that consumers do not want to be associated with. Consumers may decide to not buy certain products because they are associated with a particular group of people. Some years ago, motorcycles were associated with the Hell's Angels image. Bikers were not portrayed positively, which led to a number of people not buying motorcycles. Honda tried to change this with its "The Nicest People Ride Hondas" campaign. In this case, Honda was trying to break the dissociative-group effect by emphasizing that "regular" people drive Hondas, and so should you. Now many professionals ride motorcycles as a hobby.

Family and Household

Households are the basic unit of buying and consumption in our society, despite the fact that what constitutes a household has changed drastically with the passage of time. A household is a consumption unit of one or more people identified by a common location and address. While a number of consumer decisions are made by individuals concerning personal consumption (e.g., buying food during your lunch hour), more significant purchase decisions are made jointly by members of a household, with the product intended to be used by some or all of the members of that household.

Reference groups
Are the formal and informal groups that affect a consumer's purchase decision.

Household decision making
Occurs when significant decisions are made by individuals jointly with other members of their household and purchases are made for joint use by the members of the household.

Sociocultural Forces

Family size varies from culture to culture and from subculture to subculture. In some cultures, the family extends beyond the immediate nucleus to include grandparents, aunts, and uncles.

Sociocultural Forces

The population in Europe is expected to age, while the population in Asia is getting younger. This has led to a number of companies focusing their attention on the growing Asian market as they prepare for the future.

Household decision making is likely to be different from individual decision making. **Household decision making** occurs when significant purchasing decisions are made by individuals jointly with other members of their household, and products are bought for joint use by some or all of the members of the household. In the individual decision-making process, all three roles—buyer, user, and payer—are more likely to reside in one person, while in the household, the three roles are more likely to be assumed by separate individuals. The separation of the three roles makes household buying behavior somewhat complex to track and influence. Moreover, these role allocations are dynamic, varying from time to time from one product to another and from one family type to another.

Family composition is also dynamic and changes with time and place. Years ago, a typical U.S. household would have been described as the traditional nuclear family, with a husband, a wife, and 2.5 children. In 1970, married couples with children comprised 41% of all households in the U.S. By 2000, such households had declined to 23.5%. On the other hand, the number of single-parent households rose from 6% in 1970 to 9.3% in 2000.[8] Consequently, the "typical" family has changed dramatically, and households display much more diversity.

Steps in Family Buying Decisions

If you think back to a recent marketplace decision made in your family, you might recall that various members undertook different activities en route to the final decision. Based on research and observations, scholars have identified and described the family buying process as consisting of the following steps.[9]

1. Initiating the purchase decision
2. Gathering and sharing information
3. Evaluating and deciding
4. Shopping and buying
5. Managing conflicting opinions

The first four steps are self-explanatory and are similar to the steps described for individual consumers. The fifth step is particularly salient in the context of family decision making. Also, within the family the actual dynamics involved in the first four steps are more involved than in individual decision making. Different members of the family play different roles in the decision process. One member might initiate the purchase decision by making a product request. Another member of the family might collect information. A third member might evaluate and decide. Yet another member might make the actual product purchase. Finally, someone might take the responsibility of resolving any differences in preference and conflicts that may arise. Such conflicts not only arise before the decision is made but also may continue or arise anew after the purchase. Interspousal and intrafamily influence can vary from step to step.

Conflict in Family Decisions

Family decision making may give rise to conflict, whether the consumer roles are distributed among or shared by family members. Conflict among distributed roles arises when the user, payer, and buyer roles are played by different family members and different alternatives satisfy each person. Conflict also arises when a single role is shared by multiple family members and their goals diverge. For example, in the case of a family car, one parent may be interested in the high performance of a turbo engine, while the other parent may want a minivan that is safe and roomy enough for small children.

Conflicts will inevitably arise if there is disagreement among family members on either goals or perceptions. The nature of the conflict will differ according to whether there is disagreement in one or both of these areas. Four strategies of conflict resolution have been suggested by scholars: problem solving, persuasion, bargaining, and politicking. *Problem solving* entails family members trying to gather

Children between the ages of 8 and 14 influence about $300 billion in annual spending by their parents, including their parents' choice of vacation destinations.

more information or add new alternatives. When motives/goals are congruent and only perceptions differ, obtaining and sharing information often suffice to resolve conflicts. *Persuasion* requires educating about the goal hierarchy; one parent might argue how a large, safe car is in the best interest of the whole family, since the car is needed to transport children. *Bargaining* entails trading favors (wife gets to buy the house of her choice as long as the car bought is one the husband prefers). When goals and perceptions are so divergent that even bargaining is infeasible, families resort to *politicking*. Here, members form coalitions and subgroups within the family and by doing so simply impose their will on the minority coalition. Incidentally, it is not unusual for parents to find themselves part of the minority coalition.

Children's Influence in Family Decision Making

In 2000, U.S. children between the ages of 8 and 14 spent about $155 billion a year and influenced another $300 billion in spending by their parents. Children's influence increases with age. Children influence household buying in three ways. First, children influence household purchases by having individual preferences for products paid for and bought by parents. Second, children in their teens begin to have their own money and become payers and buyers of items for self-use. Third, children influence their parents' choice of products meant for shared consumption (e.g., family vacation), or even products meant solely for parental consumption, by exerting expertise influence (e.g., high-tech products or the latest clothing fashions).

Culture and Subculture

Culture is pervasive. It is everywhere around us, sometimes without our knowledge. Different scholars have defined it differently, including one which is "the man made part of the environment." It is a dynamic, learned behavior. Some of the essential components of culture are values, language, customs, rituals, arts, and literature. A common misconception is that cultural differences exist only across geographic borders; there are cultural differences within the borders of a single country, such as the United States. A New Yorker is likely to experience culture shock when visiting Louisiana, as the values and customs of both places are quite different. In fact, it has been found that there are nine different "nations" in North America.[10]

FOCUS ON EMERGING MARKETS

Billions of Third World Buyers Are Rich Opportunity

Allen Hammond, chief information officer for Washington-based think tank World Resources Institute (WRI), likes to play a game with the company execs he meets. He asks whether their domestic markets are experiencing rapid growth (typical response: "No"). He then asks if they're interested in a hot new market overseas that doesn't have their products (typical response: "Of course"). Once he has them hooked, he throws the curve ball: This "hot new market" is the four billion people worldwide who live in abject poverty, subsisting on less than $150 a year. Typical response: "Are you joking?"

But Hammond and others are quite serious. Hewlett-Packard Co. is so serious, in fact, that last year it launched an initiative called World e-Inclusion which, working with a range of global and local partners, aims to sell, lease, or donate a billion dollars' worth of satellite-powered computer products and services to underserved markets in Africa, Asia, Eastern Europe, Latin America, and the Middle East.

Whether or not the emergent trend is dubbed B2–4B (business-to-four billion), selling to the "bottom of the pyramid," or selling to premarkets (not yet developed enough to be considered a consumer market), companies such as HP, Unilever, and Citibank are latching on to the idea that they can turn a profit while having a positive effect on the sustainable livelihoods of people not normally considered potential consumers. Doing so, however, requires companies to form unconventional partnerships—with entities ranging from local governments and nonprofit organizations to pop stars—to gain the community's trust and understand the environmental, infrastructure, and political issues that may affect business. Providing affordable, high-quality products and services means new packaging and pricing structures; for example, they may allow customers to rent or lease rather than buy.

Ultimately, however, Third World initiatives don't require huge amounts of cash. Labor and materials are generally inexpensive, and so is marketing: Residents of underdeveloped areas often have limited access to media, so word-of-mouth is the supreme marketing tool, followed by education and product demonstrations. While experts caution that success ultimately depends on a long, sustained effort by companies, low costs mean potentially big profits, albeit on volume sales with razor-thin margins.

"To market to these populations requires a lot of energy and imagination. You have to forget a lot that you already know," says C. K. Prahalad, a professor at Ann Arbor's University of Michigan Business School and an international expert on the subject. "Four billion people are joining the premarkets of the world, and they are yearning for a way of life they see on TV and the Internet," he says. "They can see how the rest of the world lives, and they are eager to become consumers."

"It's where there will be growth in the next 10 to 20 years," says Diane Osgood, a London-based environmental economist and independent consultant who works with companies looking to develop sustainable businesses in poor nations. A few positive trends don't diminish the challenge. Many of the world's poor earn less than $4 a day and rarely have extra cash lining their pockets. They often live in remote areas, where they shop at small kiosks. Many are illiterate or nearly so. Their access to and ability to use products often is determined by available infrastructure—water, roads, and electricity—or lack thereof. Says Hammond, "You're going to have to price your product, package it, and market it in totally different ways than for your Fortune 500 product."

Culture is dynamic because it is constantly changing. We see these changes all around us. The main driving force of many changes today is information technology. The growth of the mass media and associated technologies has made communication far easier. It has also opened the eyes of a number of people to events around the world. Thus, we have a global market of teenagers today who are influenced by the same movies and television programming, such as MTV. The explosive growth of the Internet in remote parts of the world, which has led to communication and idea sharing in open forums, has also become a driving force in cultural change.

Culture is a learned behavior, as we observe people around us and learn what is acceptable and unacceptable behavior. To a large extent, our eating habits and our behavioral norms are defined by people around us, such as parents, siblings, friends, and teachers. In America, we learn that Super Bowl parties are a tradition, even if we do not follow football with any great interest. We learn to drive on the right side of the road and that a handshake must be firm. However, in other cultures people drive on the left side of the road and a firm handshake is considered aggressive.

Marketers have noted the cultural changes in this country and are already incorporating a number of marketing methods to acknowledge these changes. In the last couple of years, firms increasingly offer bilingual communication options to consumers, an acknowledgement of the large numbers of Spanish-speaking consumers. Similarly, TV ads are being produced in Spanish for use on the fast-growing Spanish-language cable channels.

Situational Bases of Consumer Behavior

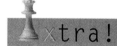

A number of situational factors affect the consumer buying-decision process. Some of the important ones are physical surroundings, time, and consumer moods. Each one of these influences different parts of the consumer buying-decision process. For example, a consumer may not gather as much information as she had planned to do because of lack of time. Similarly, a consumer in a happy mood is more likely to buy more products.

Physical Surroundings

Since it is very important for consumers to feel comfortable when they are shopping, retailers attempt to make shopping an enjoyable experience. They pay particular attention to details such as lighting, the store temperature, music, and smell. A consumer who is comfortable is likely to take more time to shop and spend more money at the store.

Physical surroundings can also be used to remind consumers about products they need to purchase. Music stores play the latest songs in an effort to encourage more CD purchases, while grocery stores try to attract consumers to their bakery by allowing the smell of their products to permeate the rest of the store. Thus, marketers can alter the physical surroundings of a store to help promote sales of their products.

Beside the physical surroundings in the store, a number of factors such as store layout and store decor, including colors, are likely to affect consumer purchase decisions. In a grocery store, consumers look for related products to be together. Thus, you are likely to find baking soda in both the toothpaste aisle and the aisle with deodorizing agents. Similarly, aisles need to be reasonably wide so the consumer does not feel claustrophobic. In order to make shopping more enjoyable, some marketers provide a separate children's play area so parents can take their time to shop. This allows the parents to enjoy the experience of shopping, knowing that their children are enjoying themselves and have an adult supervising them.

The external appearance of the store matters, too. Many consumers judge the store by its colors, as well as other aspects of its appearance. Marketers can vary the store's external appearance based on the clientele they are seeking. One of the main problems with visiting a restaurant is the time it takes to wait for a table. Since consumers judge the waiting time by looking at the number of cars in the parking lot, some restaurants put their parking lot where it is not visible from the street. The restaurant owners believe that if consumers drive into their parking lot, the chances of them staying to dine in their restaurant is higher.

Time

As an important resource to consumers, time plays an important role in different phases of the consumer decision-making process. The information search and alternative evaluation may be curtailed due to the paucity of time to make the decision. Similarly, the purchase decision itself may be made in a hurry if the consumer is pressed for time. As was pointed out earlier, sometimes people tend to buy a product again even though they are not completely satisfied with it because they do not have the time to evaluate alternatives and make a different decision. Thus, time affects most of the stages of consumer decision making.

Sometimes the lack of time leads to consumers making a suboptimal decision. Thus, lack of time may be an advantageous situation for the marketer. Some marketers try to take advantage of this by creating an artificial time pressure for their

Natural Forces

Ever wonder why European cars are so much smaller than those sold in the United States? The roads in many European countries are narrow, constrained by the environment. So most cars sold in France, for example, are about the size of the Geo Metro.

consumers. Many telemarketers offer an apparently good deal, but then mention that the deal will not be available once the phone call is completed, not giving the consumer the time to think through his options or consider alternatives. Similarly, some dot-com companies provide a fixed period of time (e.g., 30 minutes) to buy the airline ticket you are considering. After the 30-minute time period passes, the price for the ticket is not valid any more. This has the effect of reducing the consumer's option to look for other sources of information and evaluate alternatives.

Mood

Do you recall the last time you really enjoyed shopping? Maybe you were in a bookstore such as Borders, and some especially mellow music was playing. You relaxed and lingered on, browsing through the books on the "new release" shelves. Maybe you ended up buying four books that day. That is the power of positive mood! This is the same reason many online storefronts have audio files attached, so that when you visit their Web site you hear music playing in the background.

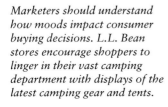

Moods
Are emotions that are less intense and transitory.

When an emotion is less intense and transitory, it is termed a **mood**. We are in a particular mood or another all the time. We may be in a happy, sad, positive, negative, or introspective mood at any given point of time. Since consumer moods are so prevalent, it is important for marketers to understand consumer moods.

Just like emotions, moods are induced both by external stimuli and by internal autistic thinking—that is, recalling some past incident or fantasizing about some event. The store ambience, salespeople demeanor, advertising tone and manner are all marketing stimuli that can affect a person's moods. For example, a consumer may get into a good mood when a helpful saleswoman pays personal attention to him. This cheerful mood may induce the consumer to buy products that he was ambivalent about when he entered the store.

Mood states have consequences in terms of favorable or unfavorable consumer response to marketing efforts. We generally do not buy anything from salespeople who put us in an unpleasant mood—for example, by not showing that they care about our business. Research indicates that consumers linger longer in positive-mood environments, recall advertisements better that created good moods, and feel more positive toward brands based on advertising that created feelings of warmth.[11]

Marketers should understand how moods impact consumer buying decisions. L.L. Bean stores encourage shoppers to linger in their vast camping department with displays of the latest camping gear and tents.

Technological Bases of Consumer Behavior

Technology has always played an important role in defining consumer behavior. Improvements in air transportation, for example, allowed products to be shipped across great distances. Wider product availability changes consumer behavior, since it gives them more options to choose from. Similarly, advances in packaging materials allowed perishable goods such as fruits to be purchased in areas where they are not grown. Similarly, the level of Internet technology available to a consumer is increasingly becoming an important criterion that determines some purchase-decision processes.

Technological Forces

The explosive growth of the Internet has had a profound effect on each stage of consumer decision making.

Web Access and Problem Recognition

In the United States alone, nearly 150 million people have access to the Internet. In other parts of the world, the growth in the number of people accessing the Web is staggering. Some people use the Internet to buy products, but a greater number do so to collect information for making a purchasing decision. While young males were more likely to access the Internet in its initial years, that is not the case now. Young women, as well as middle-aged men and women, are beginning to use the Internet in larger numbers.

The Internet has made the concept of the "global village" a reality. Current information about any part of the world is available at the click of a mouse. This allows consumers from one part of the world to be aware of what is happening in other parts of the world and the goods and services that are available. This easy dissemination of information becomes an additional source of problem recognition for consumers in many parts of the world.

Enhanced Search Capabilities

The Internet plays a very important role in the information-search stage. In fact, many consumers use the Internet primarily to search for information. These are the *browsers*. Recent research indicates that men are more likely to be *browsers* who surf the Internet, while women are more likely to be *seekers* who purchase specific products on the Internet. Search engines such as Google and Yahoo! are used extensively to search for product information. Moreover, a number of companies also provide information from their customers in the form of reviews. These become an important source of information for a consumer who is about to make a purchase decision. Some companies use techniques such as collaborative filtering to help consumers gather information. For example, based on the products a customer has browsed, Lands' End's Web site (http://www.landsend.com) recommends products that would be of interest to that customer. The objective is to make it easier for consumers to collect information that will help them make a purchase decision. Similarly, Amazon.com recommends books that might interest a consumer based on her purchase history.

Economic Forces

During periods of recession, customers want additional information before making purchase decisions. The Internet provides sellers with a low-cost means of providing information to consumers.

Expanded Evaluation Capabilities

The huge amount of information available on the Internet may make the information-gathering stage a rather lengthy one, leading to information overload. To avoid this situation and postponement of the purchase, a number of Web sites called *shopbots* have emerged. These Web sites enable consumers to evaluate their alternatives rather easily. Shopbots such as DealTime.com, shopper.com and mySimon.com allow consumers to compare features and prices of electronics, personal care items, jewelry, clothing, and books. Thus, the Internet not only increases the amount of information available to the consumer but also organizes this information to allow comparisons of goods and services.

Alternative Purchase Options

Most dot-com companies focus on converting the people browsing for information into their customers. As noted earlier in the chapter, many consumers make purchases on the Internet and this number is increasing rapidly. In a number of product categories, such as books, music, and travel, purchasing on the Internet has become an attractive option for consumers due to the extremely competitive prices offered. Moreover, the Internet also makes the role of buyer an easy one, since it allows buyers to search for information, evaluate alternatives, and make the purchase in a relatively short time span without expending much effort. Consumers who make purchases on the Internet typically have privacy and security concerns. Similarly, they like to make purchases without having to go through a number of Web pages, which delays their purchase. Recent studies also indicate that consumers would like to know the amount of the shipping and handling fees up front, rather than just prior to the purchase. Marketers that can provide assurances that consumer information is safe with them and will not be shared are likely to be the ones that will succeed. To make the purchase process easier, a number of firms allow consumers to select products, stack them in a virtual shopping cart, and then purchase the products with one click on the shopping cart.

Enriched Postpurchase Feedback Opportunities

Web sites are also becoming an increasingly important tool that firms use to solicit feedback in an efficient and effective manner. Consumers use the Internet to e-mail or post their comments, grievances, or opinions about a company's goods/services. Some consumers post their complaints or grievances on Web sites established for this purpose. This is similar to the word of mouth we encounter in daily life, except that this is in cyberspace. For example, consumers accessing babycenter.com post product reviews of products they have bought for their children. This gains added salience since it is a nonmarketer source of information found close to the link to buy the product. Marketers would do well to pay close attention not only to direct feedback but also to feedback on their products from such neutral Web sites.

Technological Forces

Most companies now recognize the importance of having an Internet presence. As part of an integrated marketing-communications effort, Web sites are frequently promoted on product labels and packaging and as a means of offering sales promotions and obtaining customer feedback.

Chapter Summary

Learning Objective 1: *Understand the three roles consumers play when buying goods and services, and appreciate the consumer buying-decision process.* Consumer behavior is the process by which individuals or groups select, use, or dispose of goods, services, ideas, or experiences to satisfy needs and wants. Consumers fill different roles in the consumer buying process (users, payers, and buyers). While these three roles are unique, the same person may play all three roles in some purchase decisions.

The consumer buying-decision process includes five distinct activities, including problem recognition, information search, evaluation of alternatives, purchase, and postpurchase activities. When purchasing some products, each of these activities is identifiable, while with others, it may seem like consumers are skipping steps. Marketers can influence the decisions consumers make in each of these five activities.

Learning Objective 2: *Understand how psychological factors—perception, learning, motivation, and psychographics—may affect the consumer buying-decision process.* The psychological factors that affect the consumer buying-decision process include perception, learning, motivation, attitude, and psychographics. By understanding perceptions, marketers can begin to influence them. Learning is a change in the content of long-term memory, and most consumer behavior is learned behavior. Motivation is the driving force behind all human behavior and includes two components: drive and goal-object. By studying attitudes and how they are formed, marketers are better equipped to predict consumer behavior. Psychographics are another facet of motivation and they include characteristics of individuals that identify them in terms of their psychological and behavioral makeup.

Learning Objective 3: *Recognize how social factors—reference groups, family, and culture—may affect the consumer buying-decision process.* The social factors consist of reference groups, family and household, and culture and subculture. Many purchase decisions are made with input from reference groups and family members. The groceries someone buys may be a function of the eating habits of her spouse and children. Culture and subculture affect consumer behavior significantly. Culture is a learned behavior, as we observe people around us and learn what is acceptable and unacceptable behavior.

Learning Objective 4: *Appreciate how physical surroundings, time, and mood shape consumers' buying decisions throughout each stage of the buying-decision process.* Marketers may be able to influence consumer buying behavior by making adjustments to consumers' physical surroundings, being aware of time constraints and pressures that consumers face, and altering consumer moods through store ambience and salespeople demeanor. Each of these factors affect the decisions consumers make during the five-step process.

Learning Objective 5: *Comprehend how technology may affect the consumer buying-decision process.* The level of technology available to consumers is becoming an increasingly important criterion that determines consumer decision processes. In the recent past, the explosive growth of the Internet has had a profound effect on each stage of consumer decision making. Information, and current information at that, about any part of the world is available at the click of a button. This easy dissemination of information becomes a source of problem recognition for consumers in many parts of the world. The Internet has a very important role in the information search stage as well as search engines and collaborative filtering techniques help consumers with information gathering. With respect to alternative evaluation, Shopbots such as DealTime.com, shopper.com and mySimon.com allow consumers to compare features and prices of products rather easily. The Web has also provided consumers with additional purchase options. In a number of product categories, like books, music, and travel, Internet purchasing has become an attractive option due to the extremely competitive prices being offered. Finally, Web sites are increasingly becoming an important tool for firms to solicit feedback in an efficient and effective manner. Marketers would do well to pay close attention to not only what is being provided as direct feedback to them, but also to monitor consumer feedback on neutral Web sites.

Key Terms

For interactive study: visit http://bestpractices.swlearning.com.

Alternative evaluation, 181
Attitudes, 186
Buyers, 176
Consumer behavior, 176
Consumer buying-decision process, 176
Emotions, 186
Household decision making, 192
Information search, 179

Involvement, 186
Learning, 185
Moods, 196
Motivation, 185
Needs, 178
Payers, 176
Perception, 184
Postpurchase behavior, 184
Problem recognition, 178

Psychographics, 187
Purchase, 183
Reference groups, 191
Self-concept, 188
Users, 176
VALS™, 188
Wants, 178

Questions for Review and Discussion

1. What are the different sources of information that a consumer uses to make a purchase decision? Which of these is more important as a source of information? How do they differ from each other?

2. Describe compensatory and noncompensatory choice models. Give examples of each type.

3. Contrast individual consumer decision making and family buying decisions.

4. How do needs differ from wants? Are needs internally realized or can others (marketers) make us realize our needs?

5. What is VALS? What are the eight categories of people represented in VALS 2? Which of these profiles do you fit? Why?

6. How can conflicts that arise from family buying decisions be resolved?

7. Marketers are often criticized for targeting children with their advertisements. Why do you think marketers like to target this segment?

8. If Bill buys groceries for the apartment he shares with Bob and another student, is that household buying or individual buying behavior? Why?

In-Class Team Activities

1. Form groups of five to discuss the following: "The Internet has fundamentally changed the ways consumers behave. This is an irreversible process that is likely to affect the way we feel, think, and act in the purchasing process."

2. Discuss in groups if the five-stage process discussed in the text applies to impulse purchases. If so, discuss the salient stages in this process. If not, what alternative model may apply?

Internet Questions

1. Select a product you are likely to buy in the near future. Go to Google (http://www.google.com) and search for the product. Visit three Web sites that carry information about this product. For each of the three sites, answer the following questions:

   a. How useful is the site for the information search stage of decision making?
   b. Is the site useful for the alternative-evaluation stage of decision making?
   c. Does the site allow you to purchase the product?
   d. Is this site promoting the product category or promoting a specific brand?

2. In 1978, the research and consulting firm SRI Consulting Business Intelligence developed a psychographic segmentation system called VALS, which stands for values and lifestyles.

   a. Go to SRI's home page (http://www.sric-bi.com) and link to the VALS 2 survey.
   b. Complete the survey to place yourself in a VALS segment.
   c. Do you agree with the results? Why or why not? What values and lifestyle issues are dominant for you as a consumer?
   d. How do companies use the VALS information to infer consumer behavior?

CHAPTER CASE

The Butterflies Are Coming

During the 1990s, prospects were excellent for luxury-goods companies like Dior, Ralph Lauren Polo, Gucci, Tiffany & Co., and Armani. The economy was strong, the stock market was climbing ever higher, and, for these firms, average annual revenue growth of 10% to more than 20% was the norm. Baby boomers, among the biggest luxury consumers, were in their peak earnings years. Secure in their lifestyles and content to "cocoon," or turn inward, they spent heavily on luxury items for themselves and their homes.

Their free-spending ways came to an abrupt end when the September 11 terrorist attacks forced many consumers to reevaluate their concepts of luxury. The same luxuries they bought a month earlier now seemed frivolous, and the conspicuous consumption and self-indulgence of years past gave way to a less materialistic attitude. With the subsequent downturn in the economy, sales growth for luxury goods fell to 4.4% in 2001. Among households with base incomes of more than $50,000—a group that accounts for 53% of total household spending, or $1.7 trillion annually overall—44% sharply curtailed spending, and a mere 9% believed that they needed to purchase luxury goods to appear successful.

Breaking free from their self-imposed cocoons, consumers wanted to reconnect with and relate to the outside world. "Empty-nesting boomers are now connecting with the outside world and emerging . . . from the cocooning lifestyle that has been their focus these past 20 years," Pam Danziger, president of Unity Marketing, a consulting firm that specializes in consumer insights for luxury marketers, explains. Dubbing this new psychographic group "Butterflies," Danziger believes that it will drive trends in luxury-goods marketing.

These findings are the result of Unity Marketing's *Luxury Market Report 2003,* which identified three distinct market segments for luxury goods:

- *Cocooners:* Inwardly focused, want to make their nests more luxurious.
- *Luxury Aspirers:* Conspicuous consumers who have not yet reached the level of luxury to which they aspire.
- *Butterflies:* Least materialistic, most highly evolved; looking for new ways to get meaning into their lives.

Cocooners currently account for about 40% of luxury consumers, followed by Luxury Aspirers at 33% and Butterflies at 25%. Danziger expects Butterflies to become the dominant group as Cocooners and Luxury Aspirers evolve into Butterflies. By understanding what motivates this new group and developing appropriate marketing strategies to reach them, luxury-goods companies can position themselves to benefit from the changing consumer behavior in their target markets.

Who are these Butterflies? They are an interesting group, full of contradictions. Butterflies are the least materialistic of all luxury consumers, understanding that possessions don't bring happiness. Yet they spend the most on luxuries, have the highest average income, and buy the most expensive houses. They have a more personal definition of luxury; it is in the eye of the beholder and not defined by brand. They strongly believe that luxury isn't about how much something costs but how much it means to you personally. Their view of luxury is democratic: It is for everyone and different for everyone. Their definitions of luxury will change over time as their lifestyles, life stage, and circumstances change. They also believe that having wealth brings social responsibility.

Most Butterflies are part of the baby-boom generation and are approaching or in the empty-nester stage of their lives. In these peak earnings years, they have more to spend on personal luxuries. Perhaps more important, says Danziger, "As you get older, you move from 'things' to 'experience.' The thing they are buying becomes a means to an end." Danziger believes that luxury marketing is all about selling a feeling. She cites the example of Starbucks, which took a very ordinary product—a cup of coffee—gave it a luxury image, and created an upscale coffee-drinking experience.

Butterflies exhibit different spending priorities than Cocooners or Luxury Aspirers. Personal luxuries, such as fashion and fashion accessories, jewelry and watches, fragrance and beauty products, and automobiles, are their largest purchases. They spend less on home-related luxuries (furniture, art and antiques, appliances, housewares), which for Cocooners account for more than half of their luxury purchases. Butterflies also spend more on luxury services than the other groups. For example, their desire to connect makes them big purchasers of travel and entertainment services. Personal luxury services such as housecleaning and lawn care are another priority, freeing them from these mundane tasks so they can get out more.

The outlook is good for sellers of products like luxury automobiles, jewelry, apparel, beauty products, sporting goods, and similar products, and for luxury-service providers—spas, cosmetic and beauty treatments, travel, and landscaping. Along with these main categories, opportunities will open up for products to support Butterflies' interests. Consumers who develop passions for gourmet cooking and wine will want better cookware, equipment, wine glasses, reference books and videos, wine racks, and storage vaults. To more fully experience these passions, they may take wine tours or attend cooking classes in Italy.

What do these findings mean for luxury-goods marketers? "Experience" and "connection" are the key words. Marketers must find ways to develop meaningful two-way communication with their target customers, positioning their products as ways to achieve the desired emotional connection as consumers pursue their passions. They must also incorporate the experience into the buying process. Linking luxury goods to luxury services—offering interior-design services at an upscale furniture store, for example—will attract Butterfly consumers. Luxury retailers that sell directly to consumers have an edge as well, because they have two profit opportunities: direct sales plus sales through third party retail outlets. Coach Inc., which sells its luxury accessories at major department stores and its own retail stores, is a good example of a savvy marketer.

Product-focused companies also need to adjust their marketing strategies to reach Butterflies by adding an experiential dimension and taking a customer-centric view of their products. Rolf Jensen, a futurist, says consumers are not just buying products, but rather lifestyles. The luxury product becomes the means to an end—the lifestyle—not the end. Instead of emphasizing product features, he recommends selling luxury goods like luxury services. The focus should be on how purchasing the product will make the consumer feel.

Case Questions

1. Summarize the characteristics of the Butterfly. Do you agree with Danziger that this group will be the dominant consumer of luxury goods? Explain your answer.

2. "Luxury marketing is about passion, and everything from marketing materials to the selling environment, packaging, the delivery of the product to the actual experience of it must enhance the luxury experience," says Danziger. How could you, as a marketer of luxury cars, implement these ideas in your marketing strategies?

3. Would adventure or themed travel appeal to Butterflies, and why or why not? What needs would it meet?

Sources: "The Cocoon Cracks Open," *Brandweek,* 28 April 2003, 32–36.
Frank Green, "Malls Are the Place to Go," *San Diego Union Tribune,* 5 June 2003, C1, C5.
"Luxury Business Newsletter Debuts from Unity Marketing," *Business Wire,* 19 November 2002, http://www.findarticles.com (accessed May 2003).
"Meet the Butterflies: The Emerging Luxury Market," *Unity Marketing,* http://www.unitymarketingonline.com/news2 (accessed May 2003).
"The Next Big Marketing Opportunity: Luxury, According to Unity Marketing Study," *Business Wire,* 25 February 2003, http://www.findarticles.com (accessed May 2003).

VIDEO CASE

Wahoo's Fish Taco: Success of the Surfer Dudes

Mix together three brothers who love to surf, a craving for the fish tacos they gobbled up when they surfed in Mexico, and a lot of marketing and business savvy and you get Wahoo's Fish Taco, a fast-casual restaurant featuring healthy food and a lively ambience. Today, the chain has 28 locations in Southern California and Colorado and is growing selectively in other areas as well.

Don't let the brothers' "surfer bum" attitude and appearance—Wing Lam sports long hair, a Fu Manchu mustache, shorts, and sandals—fool you. Each has a business degree and speaks several languages. Marketing director Lam has been the driving force in Wahoo's success. He is joined by his younger brothers: Mingo Lee is finance director and Eduardo Lee is planning director. Recently, they tapped experienced restaurateur Steve Karfaridis to be director of operations. He has developed an infrastructure to support the chain's growth, such as an inventory-control system and other more standardized systems.

The chain has developed a personality true to the brothers' Southern Californian roots. It's noisy, friendly, even chaotic. The walls are plastered with real surf gear and posters from surf, skateboard, and snowboard com-panies—a custom that began when employees at local surfing-apparel manufacturers put up banners to mark their favorite booths. Wahoo's became the cool place to eat. "Instead of importing what's fashionable in New York, we're exporting our own culture," Lam says.

Each location feels unique and is bursting with energy. The close-packed tables provide a nonverbal signal: Come to Wahoo's and you belong to the boarding tribe. Yet thanks to Karfaridis, underneath the apparent chaos is a well-orchestrated program of service supported by the right systems and employee training. It allows Wahoo's employees to have fun while they serve up excellent food, quickly, with smiles on their faces. For example, the company's "10-seconds rule" trains employees to recognize the value of that short time period. Ten seconds is the maximum time that a plate of food can wait on the pass-through or a customer should stand in front of the register before someone approaches them.

Wahoo's menu features large portions of healthy food that goes beyond its signature fish tacos to include Mexican appetizers like quesadillas and combination plates, soups, salads, sandwiches, and teriyaki or Cajun-seasoned rice bowls. Prices are reasonable—the average check is $7. The target customer is males from 18 to 25, a group that eats out almost six times a week, making it the largest consumer of commercially prepared food in the U.S., according to the National Restaurant Association. As one Wahoo patron commented, "It's embarrassing how much I come here!"

What makes Wahoo stand out in the crowded restaurant field? It appeals to the "Boarding Tribe"—surfers, snowboarders, skateboarders, and other extreme-sports enthusiasts—and is a natural fit with Southern California's surf-and-skateboard industry. "They have created a mystique and a cultlike following," says Janet Lowder, a restaurant consultant. The timing was right, too; Wahoo's was one of the earliest "fast-casual" restaurants, an increasingly popular category that offers diners a step up from fast food.

Financially, Wahoo's has surpassed most of its industry peers, with annual unit sales of about $1.1 million and a per-square-foot return on investment that is off the charts. About 300,000 diners eat at the average Wahoo's each month, and most of the company's restaurants break even within three months of operation.

How did they do it? Savvy marketing and understanding their customers were key. But in the beginning, it was all about trusting their instincts.

The initial idea arose because the brothers wanted to start a simple business so they could make a living while surfing between shifts. "As we got older, most of the surfers we hung out with made fewer and fewer surf trips to Mexico," says Lam. "But we missed the food. So instead of going there, I brought the fish taco here."

In 1988, the brothers opened the first small Wahoo's Taco store in Costa Mesa, California. Growing up in the restaurant business—their family had owned Chinese restaurants in Brazil and nearby Newport Beach, California—they thought it would be easy to attract customers. But with startup funds of just $30,000, they couldn't afford to advertise. Just 40 customers a day came in at first.

To get the word out, Wing Lam handed out menus at local businesses, many of which were surf-related, and invited everyone to come and try his food. "I soon had guys from Billabong, Quiksilver, and O'Neill dropping by," Lam said. Aligning Wahoo's with these popular brands turned out to be a smart move. Wahoo's, too, became associated with cool sports and surfing and skateboarding stars.

Next, Lam gave away a lot of food. Because surfers and skateboarders were a core-market group for the restaurant, Wahoo's sponsored local sporting events like the U.S. Surfing Open in Huntington Beach and served up its fish tacos to competitors. When the area's first rock-climbing gym opened, Wahoo's did an event that helped launch that business and at the same time promoted its own. "Rock climbers accepted us," said Lam.

While giving away free food is expensive for a small business, marketing the company in more traditional ways is even more costly. Lam believes that getting into the community and giving out product samples is not only cheaper but more effective. "Once they taste it, see it, smell it, and touch it, they connect it to you," he explains. "Everyone wants to support local business, as opposed to a large corporate entity that they are not attached to. They see you being a part of the community and want to interact with you, support you because you are supporting the community. The giving comes back tenfold."

The freshness of the food attracted customers, but it was more than the menu that brought customers into Wahoo's time and time again. "It's the package, an experience," says Lam. "We were confident in our menu. We wanted people to experience something, a getaway to our favorite spots in Baja." So the brothers created a place where customers could hang out and get great food.

What brings customers back to Wahoo's? A salesman and surfer who's been eating there for more than 10 years credits two things: "the real Baja flavor" and the restaurants' "good vibe."

Case Questions

1. Explain how Wahoo's marketing mix demonstrates its understanding of its target consumers.
2. Which psychological factors does Wahoo tap in its marketing strategy? Which VALS 2 consumer segments would most typify Wahoo's target customers? Please explain.
3. How does Wahoo's Tacos use reference groups and physical surroundings to shape consumer behavior?

Sources: Adapted from material in Small Business School 2001 video "Wahoo's Tacos" and Marc Ballon, "Wahoo's to Become a Bigger Fish Food," *Los Angeles Times*, 6 September 2001, http://www.bigchalk.com, accessed May 2003.

Lori Doss, "Wahoo's Fish Taco: Surf's Up for Brothers Who Turn Love of Mexican Vacation Snack into Flourishing Fast-Casual Concept," *Nation's Restaurant News*, 28 January 2002, http://www.findarticles.com, accessed May 2003.

Bruce Horovitz, "Color Orange County the New Capital of Cool, *USA Today*, 6 September 2002, 1B.

Carlotta Mast, "Avid Surfer Shares with Colorado Students How He's Made Fish Taco Chain Work," *Daily Camera* (Boulder, Colorado), 23 January 2003, http://www.bigchalk.com, accessed May 2003.

Business-to-Business Marketing

More than half of IBM's total revenue now comes from its information technology services component, IBM Global Services. This component works with each of the different types of businesses—commercial, government and institutions—to provide customized information technology (IT) solutions for their customers. One goal of the company's B2B efforts is to be the dominant (if not the only) IT provider for each of its customers. This is best accomplished by satisfying customer needs and developing trusting, mutual commitments that lead to long-term business relationships.

You Decide. After reading the opening vignette and paying special attention to the sections of this chapter marked with the chess piece, answer these questions:

1. An initial critical task in customer-relationship-management strategy is to identify the most valuable customers. As a whole, which business classification offers the greatest long-term value to IBM Global Services?

2. A number of factors affect the business purchasing process. Which influencing factors should IBM Global Services use or leverage to best acquire and keep customers?

3. Many corporate buyers routinely evaluate potential suppliers. Which factor should be considered most important in selecting a business service provider, such as IBM Global Services?

IBM Global Services
International Business Machines Corporation (IBM) manufactures and sells computer services, hardware, and software. IBM Global Services, which accounts for more than half of IBM's corporate revenue, is the world's largest information technology (IT) service provider, with more than 125,000 employees operating in 160 countries. The unit integrates all of the firm's capabilities—services, hardware, software, and research—to help business customers in areas such as IT system design, e-commerce, management consulting, and traditional maintenance and support. In turn, many customers rely on IBM Global Services to directly manage critical processes for them. To illustrate, at IBM's Web-hosting facility in Boulder, Colorado, 6,500 employees run applications and store information for thousands of customers pursuing e-commerce strategies.[1]

Rather than serving individuals or household consumers, IBM Global Services is a leading-edge business-to-business firm that markets its goods and services to organizations: commercial enterprises (e.g., manufacturers, banks, and retailers); governmental units (federal, state, local); and institutions (e.g., universities and health-care organizations). Marketing managers at IBM give special attention to transforming complex technology goods and services into concrete solutions that enhance the efficiency and effectiveness of the customer's business. Here are a few customer solutions IBM has delivered.

How many times have you received a catalog in the mail that you immediately threw away because it did not address your needs and preferences? Lands' End, a global direct marketer and leading Internet retailer (http://www.landsend.com), wanted to gain a deeper understanding of customer behavior in order to better target prospects and respond to their unique needs.[2] IBM helped Lands' End develop a customer relationship management system that has significantly boosted its bottom line by reducing unprofitable catalog mailings, lowering the cost of acquiring customers, and increasing the average revenue per customer transaction. In turn, government at all levels is launching Internet initiatives (i.e., e-gov) that allow constituents to locate services quickly, easily, and at any time. For example, when the state of Michigan decided to make all government agencies and services easily accessible online at one Internet site, government officials considered proposals from 16 vendors and chose IBM to develop the technology solution. Says Stephanie Comai, e-Michigan's director, "Within 90 days IBM had the Michigan.gov portal launched and live. I don't know of any state government that's been able to get its site up and running that quickly."[3] Finally, Washington Mutual, a profitable and rapidly expanding bank, is included among IBM's lengthy list of customers in the financial services industry. In recent years, Washington Mutual has pursued an aggressive acquisition strategy and turned to IBM Global Services for assistance in integrating the acquired banks into an existing information technology infrastructure and in launching Internet-based strategies.[4] Consistent with a 12-year service agreement, IBM provides continuing service and support to Washington Mutual's data centers and branch banks.

In serving customers like Lands' End or Washington Mutual, business marketers such as IBM attempt to define the customer's needs and goals, identify *key buying influentials* within the organization, and deliver a solution that responds to those requirements. Rather than an immediate sale, business marketers attempt to build *long-term relationships* with customers by delivering on their promises and responding to the customer's changing requirements over time. Likewise, because business marketers like IBM serve *fewer but far larger customers* than consumer product marketers (for example, Coca-Cola), special attention must be given to monitoring customer satisfaction and, above all, customer loyalty. To that end, one goal for IBM is to gain an increasing share of a customer's total information technology expenditures (that is, share of wallet). Larry Schiff, an IBM strategist, notes: "If you delight your customers and are perceived to provide the best value in your market, you'll gain loyalty and market/wallet share."[5] While loyal customers are likely to be satisfied, all

LEARNING OBJECTIVES

After you have completed this chapter, you should be able to:

1. *Identify the major types of customers that comprise the business market and the massive buying power these customers represent.*

2. *Appreciate the importance of developing close buyer-seller relationships in business-to-business marketing.*

3. *Understand the decision process that organizational buyers apply as they confront different buying situations and the approach organizational buyers use to evaluate the performance of business marketers.*

4. *Appreciate the environmental, organizational, group, and individual forces that influence the buying decisions of organizations.*

VOICE OF THE EXPERT

Michael D. Hutt, Arizona State University
Thomas Speh, Miami University—Ohio

In the business market, the customers are organizations (businesses, governments, and institutions) and these customers represent a huge market opportunity. While we think of companies like Procter & Gamble (P&G), Sony, or Ford as sellers, they are also buyers that annually spend billions of dollars each on goods and services sold to them by other businesses. They buy enormous quantities of raw materials and manufactured component parts; they make large investments in buildings, equipment, and information technology; and they continually purchase supplies and business services to support operations. Building and maintaining a close relationship with a customer like P&G means paying careful attention to details, meeting promises, and swiftly responding to new requirements.

The purpose of this chapter is to introduce you to business-to-business marketing by identifying the distinctive characteristics of the business market, exploring the way in which organizations make buying decisions, and isolating the requirements for marketing strategy success. The chapter also provides a perfect vehicle for profiling leading business marketing firms such as IBM, Cardinal Health, Cisco Systems, Dell Computer, and others that demonstrate best practices in marketing strategy. Because more than half of all business school graduates are employed by firms that compete in the business market, many business-to-business firms make regular recruiting visits to your campus. To that end, the chapter might suggest a new career path or help you make a more informed career choice. That's our wish.

satisfied customers will not remain loyal. Business marketers earn customer loyalty by providing superior value to ensure high satisfaction and by nurturing trust and mutual commitments.

This chapter explores the unique characteristics of the business market and the special opportunities and challenges that it presents for marketers. What are the different types of customers that comprise the business market? What are the distinguishing features of business markets? What types of buying decisions do business (organizational) buyers make? Who participates in the buying process? What factors influence the buying behavior of organizations?

LEARNING OBJECTIVE 1

X tra!

Business market
Consists of all organizations that buy goods and services for incorporation into other goods for consumption, use, or resale.

The Business Market: Size and Scope

Business marketers serve the largest market of all: The dollar volume of goods and services purchased in the business market significantly exceeds that of the household consumer market. In the business market, a single customer can account for an enormous level of purchasing activity. For example, the General Motors purchasing department spends more than $125 billion annually on goods and services—more than the gross domestic product for countries such as Ireland and Greece.[6] Indeed, the business market consists of millions of organizations—large and small, public and private, profit and not-for-profit—that collectively buy trillions of dollars' worth of goods and services.

The **business market** consists of all organizations that buy goods and services for incorporation into other goods (e.g., component parts); for consumption (e.g., office supplies, consulting services); for use (e.g., production equipment); or for resale. The factors that distinguish business marketing from household consumer marketing are the nature of the customer and how that customer uses the product. Figure 7.1 summarizes the characteristics of business market customers.

Figure 7.1	Characteristics of Business Market Customers
Characteristic	**Example**
Business market customers comprise commercial enterprises, institutions, and governments	Among Dell's customers are Boeing, Arizona State University, and numerous state and local government units
A single purchase by a business customer is far larger than that of an individual consumer	An individual may buy one unit of a software package upgrade from Microsoft, while Citigroup purchases 10,000
Business market customers in some industries tend to be geographically concentrated	Auto manufacturing in the United States is largely concentrated in Michigan, Ohio, and California
Relationships between business marketers tend to be close and enduring	IBM's relationships with some key customers span decades
Business market customers are using the Internet to advance purchasing efficiency and effectiveness	Purchasing managers are using the Internet to search for suppliers, conduct auctions, and communicate with suppliers
While serving different types of customers, business marketers and consumer-goods marketers share the same job titles	Job titles: marketing manager, product manager, sales manager, account manager

In business marketing, the customers are organizations: commercial enterprises, governments, and institutions, as shown in Figure 7.2. Commercial enterprises (businesses) buy products to form or facilitate the production process or as components for other goods and services. Government agencies and institutions (for example, hospitals) buy goods to maintain and deliver services to their own market: the public.

Commercial Enterprises as Customers

Commercial enterprises include manufacturers, construction companies, service firms (e.g., hotels); transportation companies (e.g., airlines); selected professional groups (e.g., dentists); and resellers. *Resellers* include wholesalers and retailers. *Wholesalers* are businesses that purchase products to sell to organizational users and retailers. In turn, *retailers* are businesses that sell to household consumers. A detailed discussion of wholesalers and retailers is provided in Chapter 12.

Commercial enterprises
Are the sector of the business market represented by manufacturers, construction companies, service firms, transportation companies, professional groups, and resellers that purchase goods and services.

A Concentration of Customers

Manufacturers are the most important commercial customers, spending more than $1.5 trillion on materials each year. A startling fact about manufacturers is that there are so few of them. There are approximately 360,000 manufacturing firms in the United States. And although only 10% of these manufacturers employ more than 100 workers each, this handful of firms ships more than 75% of all products manufactured in the United States.[7] Because of this concentration, the business marketer normally serves *far fewer but far larger* customers than a consumer-product marketer. For example, Intel sells microprocessors to a few manufacturers, such as Dell and Hewlett-Packard, who, in turn, target millions of potential computer buyers. Because each large firm has such vast buying power, the business marketer will often tailor a marketing strategy for each customer. In addition to concentration by size, *business markets are geographically concentrated.* More than half of the manufacturers are concentrated in eight states: California, New York, Ohio, Illinois, Michigan, Texas, Pennsylvania, and New Jersey.

Small Business Customers

Smaller manufacturing firms also constitute an important sector for the business marketer. In fact, nearly two-thirds of all manufacturers in the United States employ fewer than 20 people.[8] In addition to small manufacturers, there are more than five million small businesses in the U. S. with fewer than 10 employees.[9] Based on sheer numbers, small businesses represent a dominant category of business market customers, but a market that is often difficult to serve. Because small business buyers have differing needs and often a different orientation, the astute marketer will develop a customized strategy for this target segment. To illustrate, FedEx wanted to

Types of Organizational Buyers		Figure 7.2
Commercial Customers	**Institutional Customers**	**Governmental Customers**
Manufacturers	Schools, colleges, universities	Federal government
Construction companies		• General Services Administration
Service firms	Health-care organizations	• Defense Supply Agency
Transportation companies	Libraries	State government
Selected professional groups	Foundations	Local government
	Art galleries	• Counties
Wholesalers	Clinics	• Townships
Retailers		

To reach small business shippers, FedEx has developed many new services to reach this dominant category of business market customer. The FedEx Small Business Center (www.fedex.com) provides information on tracking shipments, packaging, and guidelines for international shipping. In addition, FedEx makes it easy for small shippers to drop off packages, placing them in convenient locations as shown here.

Economic Forces

On average, more than half of every dollar earned from sales of manufactured products is spent on materials, supplies, and equipment needed to produce the goods. The 250 largest industrial firms (from a purchasing standpoint) annually spend more than $1.4 trillion on a wide array of goods and services.[12]

increase its share of the small-shipper segment but recognized that picking up packages at a small business is expensive. To cost-effectively reach these customers, FedEx encouraged small shippers to bring their packages to conveniently located FedEx drop-off points.[10] The strategy was successful.

Significant Buying Power

Every firm, regardless of its organizational characteristics, must procure the materials, supplies, equipment, and services necessary to operate the business successfully. The magnitude of expenditures by large corporations is staggering—in one year, Chrysler spent $2.1 billion on car seats alone, Intel doled out $960 million on production equipment, and Black & Decker spent $100 million on batteries.[11] When a customer buys a $24,000 sport-utility vehicle from Ford, the automaker has already spent more than $12,000 to buy steel, paint, glass, fabric, aluminum, and electrical components to build that product.

Professional and Group Purchasing

Rarely do individual departments in a corporation do their own buying. Procurement is usually administered by an individual whose title is manager of purchasing or director of purchasing. The purchasing manager is responsible for administering the purchasing process and managing relationships with suppliers. The day-to-day purchasing function is carried out by buyers, each of whom is responsible for a specific group of products (e.g., personal computers or office supplies). Organizing the purchasing function in this way permits buyers to acquire a high level of expertise on a limited number of items. The salesperson works closely with buyers and develops relationships with personnel from other departments who may influence purchase decisions.

E-procurement systems
Enable individual employees to buy online while the company retains control of the entire purchasing process.

E-Procurement. Like consumers who shop at Amazon.com, purchasing managers use the Internet to find new suppliers, communicate with current suppliers, or place an order. **E-procurement systems** enable individual employees to buy online, with the company retaining control of the entire purchasing process. While providing a rich base of information, purchasing over the Internet is also very efficient. It is estimated that purchase orders processed over the Internet cost only $5, compared to the current average purchase order cost of $100. For example, IBM has moved all of its purchasing to the Web and has created a "private exchange" that links its suppliers together. A private exchange allows a company such as IBM to automate its purchases and collaborate in real time with a specially invited group of suppliers.[13] By handling nearly all of its invoices electronically (some 400,000 e-invoices a month), IBM saves nearly $400 million per year using its more efficient Web purchasing strategy.

Purchasing managers are also using the Internet to conduct online reverse auctions. Rather than one seller and many buyers, a **reverse auction** involves one buyer who invites bids from several prequalified suppliers. For example, FreeMarkets Inc. offers an independently run auction site that enables buyers of industrial parts, raw materials, and services to find and screen suppliers and to negotiate with those suppliers through a dynamic, real-time competitive bidding process. To illustrate, Cooper Industries, a worldwide producer of electrical tools and hardware, recently used the site to solicit bids for its air-freight service requirements.[15] During the event, 11 suppliers placed more than 50 bids, and the winning bid provided Cooper with cost savings of 26%. Reverse auctions are best suited for commodity-type items such as packaging materials, diesel fuel, metal parts, and motor freight.

Demand Issues

The demand for business products differs from the demand for consumer products in that business demand is derived and fluctuates. In addition, B2B marketers often stimulate household consumer demand, even though they do not sell directly to consumers.

Derived Demand. **Derived demand** refers to the direct link between the demand for an industrial product and the demand for consumer products: *The demand for industrial products is derived from the ultimate demand for consumer products.* Consider the materials and components that are used in a Harley-Davidson motorcycle. Some of the components are manufactured by Harley-Davidson, but the finished product reflects the efforts of more than 200 suppliers or business marketers

Technological Forces
The Gartner Group projects business-to-business online purchasing will reach $8.5 trillion by 2005.[14]

Reverse auction
Involves one buyer who invites bids from several prequalified suppliers.

Derived demand
Is the direct link between the demand for an industrial product and the demand for consumer products.

Consumers of Harley-Davidson motorcycles stimulate the derived demand for component parts and services that are provided by more than 200 suppliers.

© McPherson Colin/CORBIS SYGMA

that deal directly with the firm. In purchasing a Harley-Davidson motorcycle, the consumer is stimulating the demand for a diverse array of products manufactured by business marketing firms, such as tires, electrical components, coil springs, aluminum castings, and other items.

Economic Forces
A decline in mortgage rates can spark an increase in new home construction and a corresponding increase in appliance sales.

Fluctuating Demand. Because demand is derived, the business marketer must carefully monitor demand patterns and changing buying preferences in the household consumer market, often on a worldwide basis. Retailers generally respond by increasing their stock of inventory. As appliance producers such as Maytag increase the rate of production to meet the demand, business marketers that supply these manufacturers with items such as motors, timers, and paint experience a surge in sales. A downturn in the economy creates the opposite result. This explains why the demand for many industrial products tends to fluctuate more than the demand for consumer products.

Stimulating Demand. Some business marketers must not only monitor household consumer markets but also develop a marketing program that reaches the ultimate consumer directly. Aluminum producers use television and magazine ads to point out the convenience and recycling opportunities that aluminum containers offer to the consumer—the ultimate consumer influences aluminum demand by purchasing soft drinks in aluminum, rather than plastic, containers. More than four billion pounds of aluminum are used annually in the production of beverage containers. Since September 11, 2001, Boeing has promoted improved airport security and the convenience of air travel in a media campaign targeted to the consumer market to create a more favorable environment for longer-term demand for its planes. Similarly, DuPont advertises to ultimate consumers to stimulate the sales of carpeting that incorporates its product.

Governmental Units as Customers

Governmental units
Comprise the sector of the business market represented by federal, state, and local governmental units that purchase goods and services.

Federal (one), state (50), and local (87,000) governmental units generate the greatest volume of purchases of any customer category in the United States. **Governmental units** comprise the sector of the business market represented by federal, state, and local governmental units that purchase goods and services. Collectively, these units spend more than $1.7 trillion on goods and services each year—the federal government accounts for $590 billion, and states and local governments contribute the rest.[16] Governmental units purchase from virtually every category of goods and services—office supplies, personal computers, furniture, food, health care, and military equipment. Business marketing firms, large and small, serve the government market. In fact, 25% of the purchase contracts at the federal level are with small firms.[17]

Government Buying

The government uses two general purchasing strategies: formal advertising (also known as open bid) or negotiated contract. With *formal advertising*, the government solicits bids from appropriate suppliers. This strategy is followed when the product is standardized and the specifications are straightforward (e.g., 20-pound bond paper or a personal computer with certain defined characteristics). Contracts are generally awarded to the lowest bidder; however, the government agency may select the next-to-lowest bidder if it can document that the lowest bidder would not responsibly fulfill the contract. Following the lead of the private sector, government buyers are using online reverse auctions to purchase a range of products. For example, the Internal Revenue Service (IRS) held a reverse auction for 11,000 desktop PCs and 16,000 notebook PCs. The prebid pricing started at $130 million; when the auction closed, the price was down to $63.4 million.[18]

In contrast, a *negotiated contract* is used by the government to purchase goods and services that cannot be differentiated on the basis of price alone (such as complex scientific equipment or R&D projects) or when there are few potential suppli-

Lockheed Martin and Boeing often compete against one another for U. S. military contracts. Lockheed Martin was recently awarded the contract to manufacture the Joint Strike Fighter—a contract worth more than $200 billion and involving the production of 3,000 planes.

ers. There may be some competition, because the contracting office can conduct negotiations with competing suppliers simultaneously. The purchasing decision for the government is much like that for a large corporation. Which is the best possible product at the lowest price, and will the product meet performance expectations?

For example, Lockheed Martin emerged as the winner in a five-year battle with Boeing to manufacture the Joint Strike Fighter, an agile radar-evading aircraft intended as the standard fighter for the U.S. Air Force.[19] The competition included a fly-off where each of the firms demonstrated the performance of its plane. After the contest, the Pentagon conducted a thorough analysis of cost and performance data before picking Lockheed as the prime contractor for this lucrative contract—a project expected to total more than $200 billion and involve the production of 3,000 fighters over the next four decades.

Defense and Homeland Security. The U.S. Department of Defense (DOD) spends a large portion of the federal government's total procurement budget. DOD's purchasing operation is said to be the largest business enterprise in the world. The era of declining defense budgets was quickly reversed with the September 11 terrorist attacks on the U. S. Defense and homeland security have since become priorities in the federal budget.

E-Government. Across all levels of government, officials are embracing the Internet as the best means of delivering services to constituents. E-government, then, involves transferring traditional government operations to an integrated Internet environment for improved public sector accessibility, efficiency, and customer service. For example, http://www.govbenefits.gov now provides users with access to information about 200 special government benefit programs and http://www.recreation.gov provides a description of all publicly managed recreation sites in the U.S.

Institutions as Customers

Institutional customers comprise the third sector of the business market. **Institutional customers** comprise the sector of the business market represented by health-care

Political and Legal Forces
Many states are launching creative e-government initiatives to deliver services to citizens.

Institutional customers
Comprise the sector of the business market represented by health-care organizations, colleges and universities, libraries, foundations, art galleries, and clinics that purchase goods and services.

organizations, colleges and universities, libraries, foundations, art galleries, and clinics that purchase goods and services. Institutional buyers make up a sizable market—total expenditures for public elementary and secondary schools alone exceed $640 billion annually and national health expenditures exceed $1.3 trillion.[20] Schools and health-care organizations make up a sizable component of the institutional market.

On the one hand, institutional purchasers are similar to governments in that the purchasing process is often constrained by political considerations and dictated by law. In fact, many institutions are administered by governmental units—schools, for example. On the other hand, other institutions are privately operated and managed like corporations; they may even have a broader range of purchase requirements than their large corporate counterparts. Like commercial enterprises, institutions are ever cognizant of the value of efficient buying and are adopting sophisticated approaches to purchasing, such as e-procurement.

Institutional Buying

Many institutions are staffed with professionals—doctors, professors, researchers, and others. Depending on its size, the institution may employ a purchasing agent and, in large institutions, a sizable purchasing department. Business marketing and sales personnel, in formulating their marketing and personal selling approaches, must understand the needs of the full range of participants in the buying process. Often, the salesperson must carefully cultivate the professional staff in terms of product benefits, while developing a delivery timetable, maintenance contract, and price schedule to satisfy the purchasing department. Leading business marketers also use the Internet to provide added value to their customers. For example, Cardinal Health, Inc. has embraced the Internet as the centerpiece of its marketing strategy and provides an online catalog, daily Internet specials, and a host of services for its customers—purchasing managers at hospitals and health-care facilities worldwide.

An important factor in institutional buying is group purchasing. Hospitals, schools, and universities may join cooperative purchasing associations to secure purchasing efficiencies. Group buying allows institutions to enjoy lower prices, improved quality (through improved testing and supplier selection), reduced administrative costs, and greater competition. Moreover, for-profit hospital chains, which are a growing force in health care, can achieve many of these economies by consolidating purchases through a centralized purchasing function. In addition to responding to the needs of individual institutions, the business marketer must be prepared to meet the special requirements of cooperative purchasing groups and large hospital chains.

International Business-to-Business Markets

A complete picture of the business market must include a horizon that stretches beyond the boundaries of the United States. As introduced in Chapter 4, the demand for many industrial goods and services is growing more rapidly in many foreign countries than in the United States. Countries like Germany, Japan, Korea, and Brazil offer large and growing markets for many business marketers. Countless small firms and many large ones—such as GE, 3M, Intel, Boeing, Dow Chemical, and Motorola—derive a significant portion of their sales and profits from international markets. For example, Motorola is helping China leapfrog one stage of industrial evolution for which Western nations have invested billions of dollars—the need to tie every home and business together with copper wire. The firm's sales in China now exceed $3 billion annually. The Chinese buy more cell phones than consumers anywhere else in the world—there are more than 200 million mobile-phone users in China![21] Going forward, the market opportunity for Motorola is huge, but the competition will be fierce from strong rivals such as Finland's Nokia and Sweden's Ericsson.

The Chinese buy more cell phones than consumers anywhere else in the world. Motorola, Nokia, and Ericsson are engaged in a fierce, competitive battle in an attempt to win over China's 200 million plus mobile-phone users.

The Purchasing Process of International Customers

The process of purchasing, including the formal procedures, negotiations, and personnel, may differ markedly from one country to another. To illustrate, decision making is often a slow and deliberate group process in many Asian countries. Frequently, Asian buyers will go to extraordinary lengths to avoid individual action on any decision and will work to achieve a group consensus. In this type of decision-making climate, patience and a low-pressure selling approach are the keys to success. Although similarities exist in the business marketing process across countries, the marketing strategy must be targeted to the culture, product usage, and buying procedures of international buyers. However, when customers in different countries around the world want essentially the same type of good or service, the opportunity exists to market a global good or brand.

Sociocultural Forces

Some research suggests that, compared to consumer goods, industrial and high-technology products (e.g., computers) may be more appropriate for global brand strategies.[22]

Business-to-Business Classification Systems

Marketers can gain valuable strategy insights by identifying the needs and requirements of different types of commercial enterprises or business customers. The *North American Industrial Classification System (NAICS)* organizes business activity into meaningful economic sectors and identifies groups of business firms that use similar production processes.[23] The NAICS is a result of the North American Free Trade Agreement (NAFTA); it provides for standardization among Canada, Mexico, and the United States in the way that economic data are reported. Every plant or business establishment is assigned a code that reflects the primary product produced at that location. The new system, which includes traditional industries while incorporating new and emerging technology industries, replaces the Standard Industrial Classification (SIC) system that was used for decades.

Figure 7.3 illustrates the building blocks of the system. Observe that the first two digits identify the economic sector and, as more digits are added, the classification becomes finer. For example, all business establishments that create, disseminate, or provide the means to distribute information are included in the Information sector: NAICS Code 51. Nineteen other economic sectors are included in the system. More specifically, U.S. establishments that produce paging equipment are assigned an

Cisco: An E-Commerce Innovator

Cisco, Systems, Inc. provides the networking solutions that are the foundation of the Internet and of most corporate, education, and government networks on a global scale. Virtually all messages or transactions passing over the Internet are carried efficiently and securely through Cisco equipment. Cisco provides the hardware and software solutions for transporting data, voice, and video within buildings, across campuses, or around the world.

A recognized leader in e-commerce, Cisco generates more than 50,000 page views per week on its Web site (http://www.cisco.com) and captures 90% of its revenue from the Internet. Cisco's Web site provides existing or potential customers with self-service access to a rich base of information, including technology solutions for different types of businesses, technical service and support, and online customer training. As the Web site was enriched, the company learned something important about Cisco customers—they are anx-ious to help each other. To illustrate, potential customers who visit the site are encouraged to post a question if they are unable to find the information they require. Often, before Cisco's technical staff finds the answer, another Cisco customer posts the desired response. Many of these customers have completed Cisco's online training course and are anxious to demonstrate their knowledge. By further promoting this sense of community, thousands of technical questions to Cisco each week are now answered by customers.

By helping themselves—whether configuring products or securing training or service support—Cisco's customers help the company save an estimated $250 million per year and achieve the highest profit margin in the industry.

Source: Don Tapscott, "An Open Letter to CEOs," *Digital 4Sight,* September 2002, http://www.cisco.com, accessed 1 February 2003.

NAICS Code of 513321. The six-digit codes are customized for industry subdivisions in individual countries, but at the five-digit level they are standardized across the three countries.

If a manager understands the needs and requirements of a few firms within a classification category, requirements can be projected for others that share the same category. Each group should be relatively homogeneous in terms of raw materials required, component parts needed, and manufacturing processes used. The NAICS provides a valuable tool for identifying new customers and for targeting profitable segments of business buyers.

Figure 7.3	North American Industrial Classification System

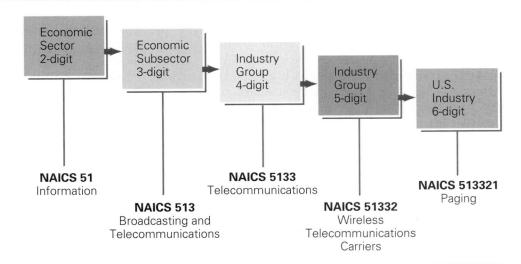

NAICS 51
Information

NAICS 513
Broadcasting and Telecommunications

NAICS 5133
Telecommunications

NAICS 51332
Wireless Telecommunications Carriers

NAICS 513321
Paging

Developing Close Buyer-Seller Relationships

Relationships in the business market are often close and enduring. Rather than providing the end result, a sale in the business market signals the beginning of a relationship. By convincing a chain of sporting-goods stores to use its computers, IBM initiates a potential long-term business relationship. More than ringing up a sale, IBM creates a customer. To maintain that relationship, the business marketer must both develop an intimate knowledge of the customer's operations and contribute unique value to the customer's business.

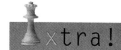

Customer Relationship Management (CRM)

For many business marketing firms, all customers are not equal; some account for a disproportionate share of sales or profit. Managers often refer to this as the *80/20 rule,* meaning 20% of the customers account for 80% of the sales. This means that the firm's most valuable customers deserve special attention.

To meet the specific needs of their most profitable customers, business marketing firms, large and small, are making substantial investments in *CRM systems*—enterprise software applications that synthesize customer information from all of a company's contact or touch points, including e-mail, call centers, and sales and service representatives—to support subsequent customer interactions and to inform market forecasts and marketing strategy.[24] Strategy experts contend that many CRM initiatives fail because executives mistake CRM software for a marketing strategy. It isn't. CRM software can help, but only after a customer strategy has been designed and executed. (Chapter 10 provides an expanded discussion of the pros and cons of CRM.) Figure 7.4 highlights the central components of a CRM strategy.

To develop a profitable customer strategy, special attention must be given to the following activities:[25]

Technological Forces
CRM systems identify the firm's most profitable customers and help the firm to treat them accordingly.

1. *Acquiring the right customers.* A customer strategy requires a clear understanding of customer needs, a tight grasp on the costs that will be incurred in serving different types of customers, and an accurate forecast of profit potential. The goal for the business marketer is to identify the most valuable customers and prospects.

Creating a Customer Relationship Management Strategy			Figure 7.4	
CRM Priorities				
Acquiring the Right Customers	**Crafting the Right Value Proposition**	**Instituting the Best Processes**	**Motivating Employees**	**Learning to Retain Customers**
Critical Tasks				
• Identify your most valuable customers • Calculate your share of their purchases (wallet) for your goods and services	• Determine the goods or services your customers need today and will need tomorrow • Assess the goods or services that your competitors offer today and will offer tomorrow • Identify new goods or services that you should be offering	• Research the best way to deliver your goods or services to customers • Determine the service capabilities that must be developed and the technology investments that are required to implement customer strategy	• Identify the tools your employees need to foster customer relationships • Earn employee loyalty by investing in training and development and constructing appropriate career paths for employees	• Understand why customers defect and how to win them back • Identify the strategies your competitors are using to win your high-value customers

Companies such as SAS actively market CRM systems which enable businesses to identify and retain their most profitable customers.
Reproduced with permission of SAS Institute, Inc., Cary, NC, USA.

Value proposition
Is a program of goods, services, ideas, and solutions that a business marketer offers to advance the performance goals of the customer organization.

Supply-chain management
Is a technique for linking a manufacturer's operations with those of all its strategic suppliers, key intermediaries, and customers to enhance efficiency and effectiveness.

2. *Crafting the right value proposition.* The **value proposition** includes the goods, services, ideas, and solutions that a business marketer offers to advance the performance of the customer organization. To succeed, business marketers require a deep knowledge of what customers need today and will need tomorrow and what competitors are offering today and are likely to offer tomorrow.

3. *Instituting the best processes.* Frontline employees, such as salespeople, are responsible for creating satisfied, loyal customers because of their role in executing the strategy.

4. *Motivating employees.* Dedicated employees are the cornerstone of a successful customer strategy. Employee loyalty is earned by organizations that invest heavily in training and development and that align employee incentives to company performance measures.

5. *Learning to retain customers.* Customer loyalty and retention are important to business marketers because the cost of serving a long-standing customer is often far less than the cost of acquiring a new customer.[26] Why? Established customers buy more goods and services from a trusted supplier and, as they do, the cost of serving them declines. The business marketer also learns how to serve them in a more efficient manner and spots opportunities for expanding the relationship. So, customer profitability tends to increase over the life of a relationship.

Supply-Chain Management

Figure 7.5 further illuminates the importance of building close buyer-seller relationships by illustrating the chain of suppliers involved in the creation of an automobile. Consider Honda and Ford. At its Marysville, Ohio, auto assembly plant, Honda spends more than $5 billion annually for materials and components from some 300 North American suppliers.[27] These expenditures by the 300-member purchasing staff at Honda of America represent 80% of the firm's annual sales. Similarly, Ford relies on a vast supplier network, including firms such as TRW and Johnson Controls, to contribute half of the more than 10,000 parts in a typical Ford car. The relationships between these auto producers and their suppliers fall squarely into the business marketing domain. Similarly, business marketers such as TRW rely on a whole host of others farther back on the supply chain for raw materials, components, and other support. Each organization in this chain is involved in the creation of a product, marketing processes (including delivery), and support and service after the sale. In performing these value-creating activities, each also affects the quality level of the Honda Accord or Ford Explorer.

Supply-chain management is a technique for linking a manufacturer's operations with those of all of its strategic suppliers, key intermediaries, and customers to enhance efficiency and effectiveness. The Internet allows members of the supply chain all over the world to exchange timely information and engineering drawings during new product development, and synchronize production and delivery schedules. A buyer like Honda, following a supply-chain management strategy, will reach several tiers back in the supply chain to assist second-, third-, and fourth-tier suppliers in meeting cost, quality, and delivery requirements. The goal of a supply-chain strategy is to improve the speed, precision, and efficiency of manufacturing and delivery through strong supplier relationships.[28] This goal is achieved through information sharing, joint planning, shared technology, and shared benefits. If the business marketer can become a valued partner in a customer's supply chain, the rewards are substantial: a long-term profitable relationship in which the supplier is viewed as

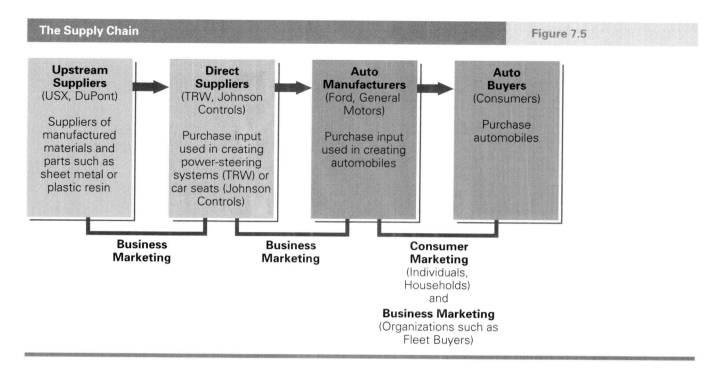

The Supply Chain   Figure 7.5

Upstream Suppliers (USX, DuPont)	Direct Suppliers (TRW, Johnson Controls)	Auto Manufacturers (Ford, General Motors)	Auto Buyers (Consumers)
Suppliers of manufactured materials and parts such as sheet metal or plastic resin	Purchase input used in creating power-steering systems (TRW) or car seats (Johnson Controls)	Purchase input used in creating automobiles	Purchase automobiles

Business Marketing   **Business Marketing**   **Consumer Marketing** (Individuals, Households) and **Business Marketing** (Organizations such as Fleet Buyers)

an extension of the customer's company. To achieve these results, the business marketer must demonstrate the ability to meet the customer's precise quality, delivery, service, and information requirements.

Just-in-Time Systems

A strategy of purchasing, production, and inventory practiced in many manufacturing firms is referred to as *just-in-time* or *JIT*. The essence of the concept is to deliver defect-free parts and materials to the production process just at the moment they are needed. Consider Dell's JIT system.[29] Most of Dell's suppliers have warehouses near

Dell's success in the computing industry can be directly linked to its effective use of just-in-time systems. Most of Dell's suppliers have warehouses near the firm's manufacturing plants that provide Dell the supplies it needs, when it needs them.

the firm's manufacturing plants. When Dell receives an order for a personal computer, it transmits the requirements to suppliers, who pick the proper parts and pack them in reusable bins. Following a continuous loop between suppliers and Dell, trucks deliver the carefully sorted parts to the computer maker's plant for final assembly. The goals of JIT are to minimize inventory costs, improve product quality, maximize production efficiency, and provide optimal levels of customer service. To illustrate, JIT practices have allowed Dell to provide prompt service to its rapidly growing base of customers—a PC is shipped three days after the order is received.

JIT systems are built on trust, demonstrated performance, and a close supplier–customer relationship. To illustrate, Owens-Illinois is the primary supplier of glass containers to the J. M. Smucker Company, the jam and jelly manufacturer. To reduce container inventory costs, Smucker's maintains only enough glass containers to run the production line for a few hours. Production managers at Smucker's have learned that they can count on Owens-Illinois for deliveries that permit a seamless production process. Such consistent delivery performance to Smucker's standards has created a long-standing customer for Owens-Illinois.

LEARNING OBJECTIVE 3

The Organizational Buying Process

Organizational buying behavior is a process rather than an isolated act. Tracing the history of a procurement decision in an organization uncovers critical decision points and evolving information requirements. In fact, organizational buying involves several stages, each of which yields a decision.[30] Figure 7.6 lists the eight major stages in the organizational buying process.

Similar to the consumer decision-making process discussed in Chapter 6, the business-to-business purchasing process begins when someone in the organization recognizes a problem that can be solved or an opportunity that can be captured by acquiring a specific product. Problem recognition (Stage 1) can be triggered by internal or external forces. Internally, a firm like Pillsbury may need new high-speed production equipment to support a new product launch. Or a purchasing manager may be unhappy with an equipment supplier's price or service. Externally, a salesperson can precipitate the need for a product by demonstrating opportunities for improving the organization's performance. Likewise, business marketers also use advertising to alert customers to problems and demonstrate how a particular product may provide a solution.

The Organizational Buying Process	Figure 7.6

Stage 1: Problem Recognition

Example: Managers at Pillsbury need new high-speed packaging equipment to support a new product launch.

Stage 2: General Description of Need

Example: Production managers work with a purchasing manager to determine the characteristics needed in the new packaging system.

Stage 3: Product Specifications

Example: An experienced production manager helps a purchasing manager develop a detailed and precise description of the needed equipment.

Stage 4: Supplier Search

Example: After conferring with production managers, a purchasing manager identifies a set of alternative suppliers that could satisfy Pillsbury's requirements.

Stage 5: Acquisition and Analysis of Proposals

Example: Alternative proposals are evaluated by a purchasing manager and a number of members of the production department.

Stage 6: Supplier Selection

Example: Negotiations with the two finalists are conducted, and a supplier is chosen.

Stage 7: Selection of Order Routine

Example: A delivery date is established for the production equipment.

Stage 8: Performance Review

Example: After equipment is installed, purchasing and production managers evaluate the performance of the equipment and the service support provided by the supplier.

During the organizational buying process, many small or incremental decisions are made that ultimately translate into the final choice of a supplier. To illustrate, a production manager might unknowingly establish specifications for a new production system that only one supplier can meet (Stages 2 and 3). This type of decision early in the buying process dramatically influences the favorable evaluation and ultimate selection of that supplier. The remaining stages of the organizational buying process are described here.

Identifying Suppliers and Analyzing Proposals

Once the organization has defined the product that will meet its requirements, attention turns to this question: Which of the many possible suppliers can be considered promising candidates? The organization will invest more time and energy in the supplier search when the proposed product has a strong bearing on organizational performance. When the information needs of the buying organization are low, Stages 4 and 5 occur simultaneously, especially when standardized items are under consideration. In this case, a purchasing manager may merely check a catalog or secure an updated price from the Internet. Stage 5 emerges as a distinct category only when the information needs of the organization are high. Here the process of acquiring and analyzing proposals may involve purchasing managers, engineers, users, and other organizational members.

Selecting a Supplier and Evaluating Performance

After being selected as a chosen supplier (Stage 6) and agreeing to purchasing guidelines (Stage 7) such as required quantities and expected time of delivery, a marketer faces further tests. A performance review (Stage 8) is the final stage in the purchasing process. The performance review may lead the purchasing manager to continue, modify, or cancel the agreement. A review critical of the chosen supplier and supportive of rejected alternatives can lead members of the decision-making unit to reexamine their position. If the product fails to meet the needs of the using department, vendors screened earlier in the procurement process may be given further consideration. To retain a new customer, the marketer must ensure that the needs of the buying organization have been completely satisfied. Failure to follow through at this critical stage leaves the marketer vulnerable.

The flow of stages in this model of the procurement process may not progress sequentially and may vary with the complexity of the purchasing situation. For example, some of the stages are compressed or bypassed when organizations are making routine buying decisions. However, the model provides important insights into the organizational buying process. Certain stages may be completed concurrently; the process may be discontinued by a change in the external environment or in upper-management thinking. The organizational buying process is shaped by a host of internal and external forces such as changes in economic or competitive conditions or a basic shift in organizational priorities.

Types of Buying Situations

The same product may elicit markedly different purchasing patterns in various organizations with various levels of experience and information. Therefore, attention should center on buying situations rather than on products. Three types of buying situations have been identified: (1) new task, (2) straight buy, and (3) modified rebuy.[31]

New-Task Buying Situation

New-task buying situation
Is a purchase situation that results in an extensive search for information and a lengthy decision process.

In the **new-task buying situation**, the problem or need is perceived by organizational decision makers as totally different from previous experiences. Therefore, decision makers must explore many alternative ways of solving the problem, and then search for appropriate suppliers. To illustrate, a large health insurance company placed a $600,000 order for workstation furniture. The long-term impact on the work environment shaped the six-month decision process and involved the active participation of personnel from several departments.[32] New-task buying decisions can be extremely important to the firm—strategically and financially.

When confronting a new-task buying situation, organizational buyers operate in a stage of *extended problem-solving*.[33] The buying influentials and decision makers lack well-defined criteria for comparing alternative products and suppliers, but they also lack strong predispositions toward a particular solution. In the consumer market, this is the same type of problem-solving an individual or household might follow in buying a first home.

Strategy Guidelines. The business marketer confronting a new-task buying situation can gain a differential advantage by participating actively in the initial stages of the procurement process. The marketer should gather information on the problems facing the buying organization, isolate specific requirements, and offer proposals to meet the requirements. Ideas that lead to new products often originate not with the marketer but with the customer.

Marketers that are presently supplying other items to the organization ("in" suppliers) have an edge over other firms; they can see problems unfolding and are familiar with the "personality" and behavior patterns of the organization. The successful business marketer carefully monitors the changing needs of organizations and is prepared to respond to the needs of new-task buyers.

Straight Rebuy

When there is a continuing or recurring requirement, buyers have substantial experience in dealing with the need, and they require little or no new information. Evaluation of new alternative solutions is unnecessary and unlikely to yield appreciable improvements. Therefore, the organization is likely to undertake a **straight rebuy**, routine ordering from the same supplier of a product that has been purchased in the past.

Routine problem-solving is the decision process organizational buyers use in the straight rebuy. Organizational buyers have well-developed choice criteria to apply to the purchase decision. The criteria have been refined over time, and the buyers have developed predispositions toward the offerings of one or a few carefully screened suppliers. This process is termed *routine problem-solving*. In the consumer market, this is the same type of problem-solving that a shopper might use in selecting 30 items in 20 minutes during a weekly trip to the supermarket.

Strategy Guidelines. The purchasing department handles straight-rebuy situations by routinely selecting a supplier from a list (formal or informal) of acceptable vendors and then placing an order. The marketing task appropriate in this situation depends on whether the marketer is an "in" supplier (on the list) or an "out" supplier (not among the chosen few). An "in" supplier must reinforce the buyer–seller relationship, meet the buying organization's expectations, and be alert and responsive to the changing needs of the organization.

The "out" supplier faces a number of obstacles and must convince the organization that significant benefits can be derived from breaking the routine. This can be difficult, because organizational buyers perceive risk in shifting from the known to the unknown. The organizational spotlight shines directly on them if an untested supplier falters. Testing, evaluations, and approvals may be viewed by buyers as costly, time-consuming, and unnecessary.

The marketing effort of the "out" supplier rests on an understanding of the basic buying needs of the organization: Information gathering is essential. The marketer must convince organizational buyers that their purchasing requirements have changed or that the requirements should be interpreted differently. The objective is to persuade decision makers to reexamine alternative solutions and to revise the preferred list to include the new supplier.

Modified Rebuy

In the **modified-rebuy** situation, organizational decision makers feel that significant benefits may be derived from a reevaluation of alternatives. Several factors may trigger such a reassessment. Internal forces include the search for quality improvements or cost reductions. A marketer offering cost, quality, or service improvements can trigger the reassessment. The modified-rebuy situation is most likely to occur when the firm is displeased with the performance of present suppliers (e.g., poor delivery service).

Limited problem solving best describes the decision-making process for the modified rebuy. Decision makers have well-defined criteria, but they are uncertain about which suppliers can best fit their needs. In the consumer market, college students buying their second computer might follow a limited problem-solving approach.

Straight rebuy
Is routine reordering from the same supplier of a product that has been purchased in the past.

Modified rebuy
Is a purchase where the buyers have experience in satisfying the need but feel the situation warrants reevaluation of a limited set of alternatives before making a decision.

Strategy Guidelines. In a modified rebuy, the direction of the marketing effort depends on whether the marketer is an "in" or an "out" supplier. An "in" supplier should make every effort to understand and satisfy the procurement need and move decision makers into a straight rebuy. The buying organization perceives potential payoffs from a reexamination of alternatives. The "in" supplier should ask why and act immediately to remedy any customer problems. The marketer may be out of touch with the buying organization's requirements.

The goal of the "out" supplier should be to hold the organization in modified-rebuy status long enough for the buyer to evaluate an alternative offering. Knowing the factors that led decision makers to reexamine alternatives could be pivotal. A particularly effective strategy for an "out" supplier is to offer performance guarantees as part of the proposal.[34] To illustrate, the following guarantee prompted International Circuit Technology, a manufacturer of printed circuit boards, to change to a new supplier for plating chemicals: "Your plating costs will be no more than x cents per square foot, or we will make up the difference."[35] Pleased with the performance results, International Circuit Technology now routinely reorders from this new supplier.

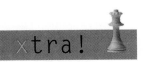

Evaluating Potential Suppliers

The business marketer must understand how organizational buyers measure value and evaluate supplier performance. To develop profitable relationships with organizational customers, the value offerings developed by the business marketer must be based on skills and resources that provide value *as perceived by customers.*

The Total Cost of Ownership

To address the needs of business customers of all types, the marketer requires an understanding of the goals and priorities that occupy the attention of purchasing managers. Given rising competitive pressures, purchasing managers use rigorous cost-modeling approaches to identify factors that drive the total cost of ownership of purchased goods and services. The **total cost of ownership** considers not only the purchase price but also an array of other factors, such as transportation and acquisition costs, as well as the quality, reliability, and other attributes of a product over its complete life cycle.[36] Based on this perspective, paying a premium price for a higher-quality product could be justified because the initial purchase cost will be offset by fewer manufacturing defects, lower inventory requirements, and lower administrative costs. To illustrate:

> *Honda of America reduced the cost of the purchased content that goes into the Accord by setting cost targets for each component—engine, seats, chassis, and so on. Then purchasing managers worked with suppliers to understand the cost structure of each component, observed how it was manufactured, and then identified ways to reduce cost, add value, or do both. The result? Honda achieved a 20% cost reduction in the external purchases that are embodied in the current Accord.[37]*

Measuring Value

Accurately measuring value is crucial to the purchasing function. The principles and tools of **value analysis** aid the professional buyer in approaching this task. For example, Ferro Corporation developed a new coating process that allows Maytag to paint a refrigerator cabinet in 10 minutes, compared to the old process, which took three hours.[38] Dramatic cost savings were achieved by Maytag. Value is achieved when the proper function is secured for the proper cost. Because functions can be accomplished in a number of different ways, the most cost-efficient way of fully accomplishing a function establishes its value.

Total cost of ownership
Considers not only the purchase price but also an array of other factors, such as the quality and other attributes of a product over its complete life cycle.

Value analysis
Is a method of weighing the comparative value of materials, components, and manufacturing processes from the standpoint of their purpose, relative merit, and cost in order to uncover ways of improving products, lowering costs, or both.

Evaluating Supplier Performance

Once a contract is awarded to a supplier, buyers formally rate supplier performance to assess the quality of past decisions and to guide future vendor selections. The *weighted point plan* is a supplier rating system widely used by organizations.

For example, DaimlerChrysler Corporation uses this system to "grade" suppliers of electronic components.[39] Suppliers can be awarded a total of 100 points, including up to 40 points for quality, 25 points for competitive pricing, 25 points for responsive delivery, and 10 points for technical assistance. Working with other departments such as production, purchasing calculates a performance score and regularly sends each supplier a report card. Those scoring 91 or higher become preferred suppliers. As this illustration demonstrates, customers in the business market are interested in the total capabilities of a supplier and how these capabilities might assist them in improving their competitive position—now and in the future.

Major Forces Affecting Organizational Buying Decisions

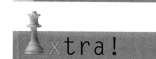

4 **LEARNING OBJECTIVE**

As illustrated in Figure 7.7, the buying decisions of organizations are influenced by environmental forces (e.g., the growth rate of the economy); organizational forces (e.g., the size of the buying organization); group forces (e.g., patterns of influence in the buying center); and individual forces (e.g., personal preferences).

Environmental Forces

A projected change in business conditions, a technological development, or a new piece of legislation can drastically alter organizational buying plans. Collectively,

| Forces Influencing Organizational Buying Behavior | Figure 7.7 |

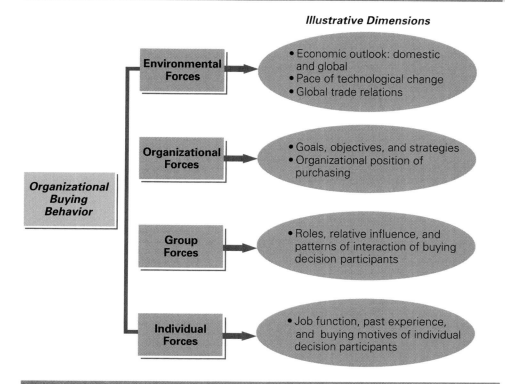

SafePlace Corporation

In February 2002, a guest staying at the Hilton in Cherry Hill, New Jersey, died while attending a convention. Several other guests were sent to the hospital amid fears of an outbreak of Legionnaires' disease or an anthrax attack. Later, it was determined that the guest had died from pneumonia and a blood infection unrelated to the hotel. The alarm surrounding this incident illustrates how important safety and security have become to a hotel's business, particularly since September 11, 2001.

In response to this need, John C. Fannin III, a fire protection and industrial security expert, formed the SafePlace Corporation to serve a range of customers in the business market. The firm is an independent provider of safety accreditation for lodging, health-care, education, and commercial facilities. Like the "Good Housekeeping Seal of Approval," SafePlace® accreditation requirements are based on the security, fire protection, and health and life safety provisions of selected nationally recognized codes, standards, and best practices. Among the areas the firm reviews in awarding accreditation are each site's fire protection measures, use of video surveillance, food handling and storage, employee screening, and emergency management training.

The Hotel du Pont in Wilmington, Delaware was the first lodging facility in the United States to receive the SafePlace® seal of approval. Such an accreditation process involves a rigorous inspection of the facility and identifies the best practices that should be employed by the hotel, such as: the use of key cards (as opposed to keys); self-closing doors; smoke detectors and sprinklers in the guest rooms; throw-bolt locks on the doors; excellent water quality; and safe work and food-handling practices among the hotel staff. The Hotel du Pont, which paid a $45,000 fee for the inspection and consulting services, displays the SafePlace® seal in the lobby and plans to feature the credential on all of the hotel's marketing materials.

Since launching its program in March 2002, SafePlace is receiving inquiries from more than 25 hotels a week. In turn, John Fannin, the firm's President and CEO, feels there is a huge opportunity in the education market, particularly with colleges and universities (for example, the safety accreditation of dormitories). Says Fannin, "Through third-party accreditation, SafePlace strives not only to provide the public with a means to measure the relative safety of one facility over another, but gives organizations the opportunity to promote their superior safety to the general public."

Source: "Hotel du Pont Receives Accreditation for Putting Safety First," *Du Pont Daily News* (9 May 2002), http://www.safeplace.com, accessed 22 January 2003.

---

such environmental forces define the boundaries within which buyer-seller relationships develop in the business market. Among the most influential types of environmental forces that shape organizational buying behavior are economic and technological influences.

Economic Forces

Marketers that serve broad sectors of the business market must be particularly sensitive to the differential impact of selective economic shifts on buying behavior.

Economic Forces

Because of the derived nature of industrial demand, the marketer must also be sensitive to the strength of demand in the ultimate consumer market. The demand for many industrial products fluctuates more widely than the general economy. Firms that operate on a global scale must be sensitive to the economic conditions that prevail across regions. For example, as the U.S. economy moves out of a recession, the European economy may continue to sputter. A wealth of forces dictate the vitality and growth of an economy.

The economic environment influences an organization's ability and, to a degree, its willingness to buy. However, shifts in general economic conditions do not affect all sectors of the market evenly. For example, a rise in interest rates may damage the housing industry (including lumber, cement, and insulation), but have minimal effects on industries such as paper, hospital supplies, office products, and soft drinks.

Technological Forces

The Internet is also expanding the volume of information available to purchasing managers and transforming the way buyers and sellers come together.

Technological Forces

The rate of technological change in an industry influences the composition of the decision-making unit in the buying organization. As the pace of technological change increases, the importance of the purchasing manager in the buying process declines. Technical and engineering personnel tend to be more important to organizational buying processes in which the rate of technological change is great. Recent research also suggests that buyers who perceive the pace of technological change to be more rapid will (1) conduct more intense search efforts and (2) spend less time on their overall search processes.[40] Why? "In cost-benefit terms, a fast pace of change implies that distinct benefits are associated with search effort, yet costs are associated with prolonging the process" because the acquired information is "time sensitive."[41]

Organizational Forces

An understanding of the buying organization is based on the strategic priorities of the firm, the role that purchasing occupies in the executive hierarchy, and the competitive challenges that the firm confronts.

Advancing the Customer's Goals

Organizational buying decisions are made to facilitate organizational activities and to support the firm's mission and strategies. A business marketer who understands the strategic priorities and concerns that occupy key decision makers is better equipped to respond to customer needs. For example, IBM centers attention on how its information technology and assorted services can improve the efficiency of a bank's operations or advance the customer-service levels of a hotel chain. Alternatively, a supplier to Hewlett-Packard will strike a responsive chord with executives by offering a new component part that will increase the performance or lower the cost of its ink-jet printers. To provide such customer solutions, the business marketer needs to have an intimate understanding of the opportunities and threats the customer confronts.

Strategic Role of Purchasing

In many firms, purchasing strategy is becoming more closely tied to corporate strategy. To illustrate, purchasing executives at Motorola have a clear understanding of the firm's objectives, markets, and competitive strategies. As purchasing assumes a more strategic role in the firm, the business marketer must understand the competitive realities of the customer's business and develop a value proposition unique to the customer. A value proposition is a program of goods, services, ideas, and solutions that a business marketer offers to advance the performance goals of the customer organization. For example, Motorola is keenly interested in working with suppliers that can contribute technology or component parts to enhance the value of the firm's cellular handsets for customers and that strengthen its competitive position.

Organizational Positioning of Purchasing

An organization that centralizes procurement decisions approaches purchasing differently from a company where purchasing decisions are made at individual user locations. When purchasing is centralized, a separate organizational unit is given authority for purchases at a regional, divisional, or headquarters level. For example, Wendy's International, Inc. operates a centralized purchasing system from its Columbus, Ohio, headquarters that supports the entire Wendy's network—all corporate and franchise restaurants on a global basis. The centralized staff manages the purchasing of all direct materials for all of the restaurants—food, packaging, and supplies. Says Judith Hollis, Vice President of Supply Chain Management: "We view our job as developing supplier partnerships that are going to assist Wendy's with sustaining our competitive advantage. We look to companies that are involved in technological innovation in quality, food, safety, and preparation efficiency."[42] A marketer that is sensitive to organizational influences is better equipped to identify buying influences and target marketing strategy for both centralized and decentralized organizations.

Group Forces: The Buying Center

Buying decisions typically involve not one, but several members of the organization, whether the decisions are made by commercial enterprises, institutions, or governmental organizations. The decision-making unit of a buying organization is called

Buying center
Consists of those individuals who participate in the purchasing decision and who share the goals and risks arising from the decision.

the **buying center**. The buying center consists of those individuals who participate in the purchasing decision and who share the goals and risks arising from the decision.[43] The size of the buying center varies, but an average buying center will include more than four persons per purchase; the number of people involved in all stages of a purchase may be as many as 20.[44]

The composition of the buying center may change from one purchasing situation to another and is not prescribed by the organizational chart. A buying group evolves during the purchasing process in response to the information requirements of the specific purchase situation. Because organizational buying is a process rather than an isolated act, different individuals are important to the process at different times.[45] A design engineer may exert significant influence early in the purchasing process when product specifications are being established; others may assume a more dominant role in later phases. Again, the composition of the buying center evolves during the purchasing process, varies from firm to firm, and varies from one purchasing situation to another. To be successful, the business marketer must identify the organizational members who comprise the buying center and understand each participant's *relative influence* and the *evaluative criteria* important to each member in reaching a decision.

Isolating the Buying Situation

Defining the buying situation and determining whether the firm is in the early or later stages of the procurement decision-making process are important first steps in defining the buying center. The buying center for a new-task buying situation in the not-for-profit market is presented in Figure 7.8. The product, intensive-care monitoring systems, is a complex and costly purchase. Buying center members are drawn from five functional areas, each participating to varying degrees in the decision process. Moreover, each buying center member emphasizes different evaluation criteria. Administration and purchasing are concerned with price and cost issues, while physicians are concerned with product quality and service. A marketer that concentrated exclusively on the purchasing function would be overlooking key buying influences.

Salespeople who frequently encounter new-task buying situations generally observe the following:

The buying center is large, slow to decide, uncertain about its needs and the appropriateness of the possible solutions, more concerned about finding a good solution than getting a low price or assured supply, more willing to entertain proposals from "out" suppliers and less willing to favor "in" suppliers, more influenced by technical personnel, [and] less influenced by purchasing agents.[46]

Figure 7.8	The Involvement of Buying Center Participants at Different Stages of the Procurement Process

| Buying Center Participants | Stages of Procurement Process for a Medical Equipment Purchase | | | |
	Identification of Need	Establishment of Objectives	Identification and Evaluation of Buying Alternatives	Selection of Suppliers
Physicians	High	High	High	High
Nursing	Low	High	High	Low
Administration	Moderate	Moderate	Moderate	High
Engineering	Low	Moderate	Moderate	Low
Purchasing	Low	Low	Low	Moderate

Source: Reprinted from *Industrial Marketing Management* 8, Gene R. Laczniak, "An Empirical Study of Hospital Buying," p. 61, ©1979, with permission from Elsevier.

By contrast, salespeople facing more routine purchase situations (that is, straight and modified rebuys) frequently observe buying centers that are "small, quick to decide, confident in their appraisals of the problem and possible solutions, concerned about price and supply, satisfied with 'in' suppliers, and more influenced by purchasing agents."[47]

Buying Center Roles

Members of the buying center assume different roles throughout the purchasing process: users, influencers, buyers, deciders, and gatekeepers.[48] As the name implies, *users* are the personnel who will be using the product in question. Users' influence on the purchase decision may range from inconsequential to extremely strong. In some cases, users initiate the purchase action by requesting the product. They may even develop the product specifications.

Consider Clark Equipment Company, which manufactures forklift trucks for the business market.[49] They found that equipment operators (users) assume an important role in the buying decision. Users spend a considerable part of their workday operating the equipment and often receive financial incentives tied to their performance. This means that driver comfort and equipment reliability (minimal equipment downtime) are central to the buying decision. In designing a new line of forklifts, Clark Equipment is giving an unprecedented level of attention to driver comfort, reduced engine-noise level, and product reliability.

Gatekeepers control information to be reviewed by other members of the buying center. The control of information may be accomplished by disseminating printed information, such as advertisements, or by controlling which salesperson will speak to which individuals in the buying center. To illustrate, the purchasing agent or an administrative assistant might perform this screening role by opening the gate to the buying center for some sales personnel and closing it to others.

Influencers affect the purchasing decision by supplying information to help with evaluating alternatives or by setting buying specifications. Typically, those in technical departments, such as engineering, quality control, and R&D, significantly influence the purchase decision. Sometimes, individuals outside the buying organization can assume this role. For high-tech purchases, technical consultants often assume an influential role in the decision process and broaden the set of alternatives being considered.[50]

Deciders are the individuals who actually make the buying decision, whether or not they have the formal authority to do so. The identity of the decider is the most difficult role to determine: Buyers may have formal authority to buy, but the president of the firm may actually make the decision. A decider could be a design engineer who develops a set of specifications that only one vendor can meet.

The *buyer* has formal authority to select a supplier and implement all procedures connected with securing the product. The power of the buyer is often usurped by more powerful members of the organization. The buyer's role is often assumed by the purchasing agent, who executes the administrative functions associated with a purchase order.

One person could assume all roles in a purchase situation or separate individuals could assume different buying roles. To illustrate, as users, personnel from marketing, accounting, purchasing, and production may all have a stake in which information technology system is selected.

Identifying Buying Influentials

Multiple buying influences and **key buying influentials** are critical in organizational buying decisions. Key buying influentials are those individuals in the buying organization who have the power to influence the buying decision. A central challenge for the business marketer is to identify the patterns of influence in the buying center. Except for repetitive buying situations, key influencers are frequently located outside the purchasing department. However, research provides some valuable clues for

Key buying influentials
Are those individuals in the buying organization who have the power to influence the buying decision.

identifying powerful buying center members.[51] To illustrate, organizational members tend to assume an active and influential role in the buying center when they have an important personal stake in the decision, possess expert knowledge concerning the choice at hand, have direct access to top management, and are central to the flow of decision-related information.

Individual Forces

Individuals, not organizations, make buying decisions. Each member of the buying center has a unique personality, a particular set of learned experiences, a specified organizational function, and a perception of how best to achieve both personal and organizational goals.[52] Organizational members are influenced by both rational and emotional motives when choosing among competing offerings.

Rational and Emotional Motives

Rational motives are usually economic, such as price, quality, and service. *Emotional motives* include such human factors as the desire for status within the organization, salary increases, and increased job security. For example, a purchasing manager may be intrigued by the quality or price offered by a newly created supplier firm, but fear the personal consequences if the new supplier stumbles. A marketer concentrating exclusively on rational motives has an incomplete picture of the organizational buyer.

Differing Evaluative Criteria

Evaluative criteria
Are specifications that organizational buyers use to compare alternative goods and services.

Evaluative criteria are specifications that organizational buyers use to compare alternative goods and services; however, these may conflict. Organizational product users generally value prompt delivery and efficient servicing; engineering values product quality, standardization, and testing; and purchasing assigns importance to cost savings and delivery reliability.[53] Product perceptions and evaluation criteria differ among organizational decision makers as a result of differences in educational backgrounds, source and type of information exposure, interpretation and retention of relevant information, and level of satisfaction with past purchases.[54] Engineers have an educational background different from that of plant managers or purchasing agents; they are exposed to different journals, attend different conferences, and possess different professional goals and values. For example, engineers may be most interested in choosing a new piece of equipment that represents state-of-the-art technology, while purchasing managers are concerned with price and operating costs. A sales presentation that is effective with purchasing may be entirely off the mark with engineering. Knowledge of the buying criteria that key buying influentials emphasize allows the business marketer to tailor marketing strategies to the needs of individual customers.

Chapter Summary

Learning Objective 1: *Identify the major types of customers that comprise the business market and the massive buying power these customers represent.* In business-to-business marketing, the customers are organizations. More specifically, the business market can be divided into three major sectors: commercial enterprises; governments (federal, state, and local); and institutions. Commercial enterprises include manufacturers, construction companies, service firms, transportation companies, selected professional groups, and resellers. Of these, manufacturers account for the largest dollar volume of purchases. Governmental units also make substantial purchases of products. Two general purchasing strategies are used by government buyers: the formal advertising approach for standardized products and negotiated contracts for unique requirements. Institutional customers, such as health-care organizations and universities, comprise the third sector of the business market. Across business market sectors, purchasing managers are using the Internet to identify potential suppliers, conduct online reverse auctions, and communicate with suppliers.

Learning Objective 2: *Appreciate the importance of developing close buyer-seller relationships in business-to-business marketing.* Business market customers are developing closer relationships with fewer suppliers than they have used in the past, and they expect these suppliers to provide defect-free products at the moment they are needed. These trends place a premium on the customer relationship management and supply chain capabilities of the business marketer. Firms that excel at customer relationship management identify their most valuable customers and then develop the right value proposition and processes to retain them in a longstanding relationship. Supply chain management links a manufacturer's operations with those of all its strategic suppliers and its key intermediaries and customers to enhance efficiency and effectiveness.

Learning Objective 3: *Understand the decision process that organizational buyers apply as they confront different buying situations and the approach organizational buyers use to evaluate the performance of business marketers.* Knowledge of the process that organizational buyers follow in making purchasing decisions is fundamental to responsive marketing strategy. As a buying organization moves from the problem-recognition phase, in which a need is defined, to later phases, in which suppliers are screened and ultimately chosen, the marketer can play an active role. The nature of the buying process followed in a particular situation depends on the organization's level of experience with similar procurement problems. There are three types of buying situations: (1) new task, (2) modified rebuy, and (3) straight rebuy. Each requires a unique problem-solving approach, involves unique buying influentials, and demands a unique marketing response. Purchasing managers center on the total cost of ownership in evaluating products, rely on tools such as value analysis to make informed decisions, and use a weighted point plan to evaluate supplier performance.

Learning Objective 4: *Appreciate the environmental, organizational, group, and individual forces that influence the buying decisions of organizations.* A wealth of forces—which can be classified as environmental, organizational, group, and individual—influence the buying decisions of an organization. A central challenge for the business marketer is to identify the organizational members who comprise the buying center.

Key Terms

For interactive study: visit http://bestpractices.swlearning.com.

Questions for Review and Discussion

1. Describe the major categories of customers that comprise the business market.

2. Compare and contrast the two general procurement strategies used by the federal government: (1) formal advertising and (2) negotiated contract.

3. DuPont, one of the largest industrial producers of chemicals and synthetic fibers, spends millions of dollars annually on advertising its products to final consumers. For example, DuPont invested more than $1 million in a TV advertising blitz that emphasized the comfort of jeans made of DuPont's stretch polyester-cotton blend. Because DuPont does not produce jeans or market them to household consumers, why are large expenditures made on consumer advertising?

4. The goal of a supply-chain strategy is to improve the speed, precision, and efficiency of manufacturing through strong supplier partnerships. Explain.

5. General Electric (GE) has embraced e-purchasing and has saved more than $500 million per year by conducting online reverse auctions in buying a range of goods, including office, computer, and maintenance supplies. What new challenges and opportunities does this auctioning process present for business marketers who serve GE?

6. Mike Weber, the purchasing agent for Smith Manufacturing, views the purchase of widgets as a routine buying decision. What factors might lead him to alter this position? More important, what factors will determine whether a particular supplier, such as Albany Widget, will be considered by Mike?

7. Harley-Davidson, the U.S. motorcycle producer, recently purchased some sophisticated manufacturing equipment to enhance its position in a very competitive market. First, what environmental forces might have been important in spawning this capital investment? Second, which functional units were likely to have been represented in the buying center?

8. Millions of notebook computers are purchased each year by organizations. Identify several evaluative criteria that purchasing managers might use in choosing a particular brand. In your view, which criteria would be most decisive in the buying decision?

9. Describe the weighted-point plan and discuss how a purchasing manager at Xerox might use it to evaluate the performance of a component-parts supplier for the firm's high-speed photocopier.

10. Evaluate this statement: Both rational and emotional factors enter into the decisions that organizational buyers make.

In-Class Team Activities

1. Dell Computer has excelled with a fast-paced build-to-order approach that involves taking customer orders online, orchestrating production tailored to each customer, and forging a one-to-one relationship with the customer after the sale. Some auto industry executives have turned to Michael Dell, the company founder, for advice on how to make their businesses look like his.

   Senior executives at Ford, for example, envision a future where customers will order online and factories will build to order, eliminating billions of dollars of inventory costs (for example, large stocks of vehicles on hand). All of those mass-produced cars sitting for weeks on dealer lots represent a massive investment that yields no return until a buyer comes along.

   a. Evaluate the feasibility of a build-to-order system for an automaker like Ford and outline the key

requirements Ford must meet to make the strategy work for a potential customer like you.

   b. How would a build-to-order system alter the way in which suppliers (business marketers) serve Ford as a customer?

2. Consider some leading-edge producers of consumer products, like Procter & Gamble, Gillette, or Coca-Cola. What major differences would you expect to find in comparing the marketing-strategy patterns used by these consumer-products companies to those of leading business marketing firms such as Intel, 3M, or Dow Chemical? Next, describe the similarities and differences that emerge when comparing the distinctive attributes of a leading-edge marketer of consumer products to a firm that demonstrates superb skills serving customers in the business market.

Internet Questions

1. The Internet is transforming the way in which firms are managing the supply chain. Covisint, an online auto parts exchange, represents one of the auto industry's most ambitious attempts at e-commerce. This exchange is a joint venture of Ford, General Motors, DaimlerChrysler, Nissan, and others. Go to http://www.covisint.com to (a) identify the mission of this organization and (b) describe how this online exchange could reduce supply-chain costs for the automaker and for suppliers.

2. Dell Computer has been wildly successful in selling its products over the Internet to customers of all types, including every category of customer in the business market: commercial enterprises, institutions, and government. Assume that the library at your university is planning the purchase of 25 new desktop computers.

Go to http://www.dell.com to the Dell Online Store for Higher Education and:

a. Identify the price and product dimensions of two desktop systems that might meet your university's needs.
b. Provide a critique of the Web site and consider the degree to which it provided access to the information that a potential buyer might want.

3. Siebel Systems provides customer relationship management software solutions to all sectors of the business market. Go to http://www.siebel.com and review success stories in order to:

a. Identify a particular Siebel corporate customer.
b. Describe the benefits that this customer received from the software solution.

CHAPTER CASE

The Javelin Executive Jet and a Potential Homeland Security Solution

Aviation Technology Group, Inc. (ATG), based in Englewood Colorado, unveiled the full-scale mock-up of its executive jet in July 2001—the Javelin (http://www.avtechgroup.com). George Bye, President of ATG, describes the concept: "I saw the opportunity to build a jet that would be professionally different, one that would give civilian pilots access to the same kind of style and performance previously only found in military fighter jets." The Javelin, a visually striking all-metal jet, is equipped for two occupants (pilot and passenger) and is targeted to the pilot-owner market. According to the firm, the jet is designed to fly faster, farther, and safer, and do so at a lower operating cost per mile, than any other light business jet on the market. The 600-mile-per-hour jet climbs at more than 10,000 feet per minute to a certified ceiling of 51,000 feet with a range of 1,250 nautical miles. The operating cost of the Javelin is $0.72 per mile.

Jet Prestige

Market research studies indicate that a large number of pilot-owners fly their own business jets on a trip or are accompanied by only one other passenger. The Javelin allows a pilot-owner business executive to fly point-to-point in less time and with lower operating costs than any other current commercial or business jet. The Javelin's ability to fly higher and faster than competing jets in its class also makes it very attractive to those who need to get to a destination quickly. The company also believes that the Javelin's sleek design adds to the prestige of ownership.

The jet will be tested for FAA certification and the first customer delivery is due in 2005. There will be 26 aircraft produced the first year, for $1.88 million each. The price increases to $2.2 million for the following year's product. By contrast, the purchase price of a Lear Jet is $6.8 million and the 10-year cost of ownership is twice as high as that of the Javelin. However, the Lear jet can accommodate several passengers.

Homeland Security: A New Market Opportunity

In the wake of the September 11, 2001, terrorist attack on the United States, ATG is pursuing the development of a single-seat version of the Javelin business jet as a low-cost air-defense aircraft. Tentatively named the Homeland Defense Interceptor (HDI), the aircraft will provide a high-performance, economic-interceptor, and surveillance platform for homeland security against airborne threats of various types, including airliners, business jets, helicopters, and crop-dusting planes. The HDI is an all-metal, high-speed, light military aircraft capable of all weather, day/night, intercept and surveillance missions.

The Mach 1.6 (maximum-speed) HDI will be equipped with air-to-air radar, advanced instrumentation, and a secure military radio, and armed with a 7.62mm minigun with tracer rounds and two short-range heat-seeking missiles.

A Possible Solution

While the U.S. is well equipped to defend against conventional military air threats, the new challenges posed by terrorists place a strain on the existing fleet of air-defense aircraft. By deploying a dedicated, low-cost homeland defense interceptor, ATG asserts that the U.S. Air Force could reduce the demands on its F-15 and F-16 fighter units, thereby delaying the replacement costs for these expensive aircraft and freeing them to pursue their primary military mission. The base unit cost of an F-16 is $26.9 million, versus $4.5 million for the HDI. Fuel and operating costs for the HDI are approximately $700 per flight hour, compared to $3,600 per flight hour for the F-16.

Case Questions

1. Some potential executive jet buyers will find the Javelin more appealing than other business owners. Describe the characteristics of the best customer prospects for the Javelin.
2. Given a limited marketing budget, what marketing strategies could ATG use to reach the best prospects in the executive jet market?
3. While the Javelin will target executives who are experienced pilots, the HDI concept will have to be sold to the U.S. Department of Defense. Evaluate the HDI concept and consider the challenges that ATG must overcome to win a government contract.

Sources: "Javelin Business Jet Seeks New Air Defence Role," http://www.flightdailynews.com/farnborough2002/07_24/defence/javelin.shtm, accessed 22 January 2003.

"Sleek New Jet Unveiled," http://www.avtechgroup.com, accessed 15 January 2003.

Press release by Aviation Technology Group, Inc.

VIDEO CASE

Beyond Shipping: UPS's Role in the Supply Chain

Nearly a century ago, United Parcel Service (UPS) drivers began delivering packages for Seattle department stores from Model T Fords and the backs of a few motorcycles. Today, UPS employees are easy to spot, in their crisp brown uniforms and lumbering brown trucks that have earned the company just one of its nicknames: the brown bear. Although everyone reading this has probably received a package delivered by UPS at one time or another, perhaps UPS's biggest impact is behind the scenes as it helps businesses and nonprofit organizations of all sizes get rolling.

UPS delivers about 12 million packages a day around the world for 2.5 million customers, using 225 jets and nearly 160,000 trucks. But UPS wants to do more for its business customers than just drop a box at the front desk. "We want to increase our global footprint across the entire supply chain," says CEO James Kelly. UPS has spent a whopping $11 billion on upgrading its technology in the last decade—on everything from mainframes, PCs, wireless communication devices, cellular networks, and 4,000 programmers and technicians. The reason? With this huge investment in technology, UPS is setting itself up to help its customers cope with different types of demand by assisting them in managing inventory, by offering warehouse services, and even by helping repair products. For instance, UPS has set up an "end of runway" facility near its air hub in Louisville, Kentucky. Computers and

other electronic devices in need of repair are trucked from the airport to the facility close by, where technicians repair them on site for customers like Hewlett-Packard and then reship them quickly either to HP itself or to one of its customers. In addition, UPS has revived the old-fashioned COD service for large customers such as Gateway, but it is doing so in high-tech fashion. UPS drivers collect payments from customers and deposit the funds directly into Gateway's bank through electronic funds transfer. No other shipping company currently offers that type of service.

UPS intends to be a major player in e-commerce, where it already dominates shipping by Internet retailers. UPS stocks shoes and other clothing for Nike.com in its Louisville warehouse and fulfills orders every hour. A UPS call center in San Antonio actually handles customer orders from Nike.com. In this way, UPS grows its own business by handling more of Nike.com's operations, while Nike.com reduces its overhead and reaps the benefits of reliability and quick turnaround from UPS. Still, this isn't enough for UPS, which launched UPS e-Ventures to act as the research and development division of the company's e-commerce initiatives. The first project, among many to come, is e-Logistics, which will be designed to provide end-to-end business logistics solutions for small- and medium-sized Web businesses. "UPS recognizes the power the Internet has to impact business-to-business and business-to-consumer commerce," notes Mark Rhoney, president of UPS e-Ventures.

To assist its business customers, UPS must communicate with them to get them to think about logistics on a larger scale. One challenge faced by UPS as it develops these B2B efforts has been to increase customers' awareness of ways that UPS can make them more successful. But UPS must reach more people within an organization than just those who are directly involved in the company's transportation or shipping. "We need to work deeper in our customers' organizations," notes Ed Buckley, vice president of marketing, Europe. "There are people [within an organization] who don't see any connection to shipping; we try to get them to think differently." For instance, the UPS product called Document Exchange provides a secure venue for executives to transmit information.

One way the company raises its profile is to team up with very visible sports organizations such as the Olympic Games and NASCAR, both of whom are customers of UPS. UPS has been a worldwide partner of the Olympic Games since 1994 and the official express delivery sponsor of the NFL since 1993. Most recently, the company sealed an agreement with NASCAR that includes customer promotions, hospitality events, a souvenir program, and a specially designed UPS package delivery car. If nothing else, affiliations like these might get other potential customers to think about UPS as more than a big brown truck.

Case Questions

1. How might derived demand affect UPS's business?
2. Choose a company or nonprofit organization that interests you—say, Holiday Inn, Kentucky Fried Chicken, Old Navy, Hard Candy cosmetics, Harley-Davidson motorcycles, or the Red Cross. In what ways could UPS serve the organization you've chosen?
3. The UPS Web site (http://www.ups.com) includes links to click for tracking, shipping, transit time, pick up, drop off, and supplies. If you were an entrepreneur starting a small business, in what ways would these be helpful to you? Are there any categories you would add to make the site more useful?

Sources: UPS Web site, http://www.ups.com, accessed 7 March 2000.

"UPS Takes to the Track as Official Express Delivery Company of NASCAR," *Business Wire,* 17 February 2000.

Jennifer Couzin, "UPS Tests Its Peddle's Mettle," *Industry Standard,* 7 February 2000.

Sandeep Junnarkar, "UPS Delivers e-Commerce Unit," *CNet News,* 7 February 2000, http://www.cnet.com.

Kelly Barron, "Logistics in Brown," "At Ground Level," and "Addicting the Customer," *Forbes,* 10 January 2000, http://www.forbes.com.

"Out of the Box at UPS," *Business Week Online,* 10 January 2000, http://www.businessweek.com.

Scott Kirsner, "Venture Vérité: United Parcel Service," *Wired,* 9 September 1999, http://www.wired.com.

8

Market Segmentation and Target Markets

Teeth-whitening systems can only whiten teeth by removing stains and bringing back the original tooth color. The largest single market segment for teeth whiteners is baby boomers, who have consumed teeth-staining food, coffee, and tea for years. Other potential consumers include teens, young brides, and young professionals who are concerned about their appearance and have the money to spend on such "vanity" products. Procter & Gamble (P&G) targeted some of these groups in the Whitestrips initial product launch through QVC, and by giving samples to teens, brides, and gay men.

You Decide. After reading the opening vignette and paying special attention to the sections of this chapter marked with the chess piece, answer these questions:

1. P&G used a differentiated strategy in a brilliant launch of the new Crest Whitestrips by selecting a few market segments and customizing marketing mixes for each. What is the key advantage of this strategy and why?

2. Which targeted segments pose the greatest risk to company marketing efforts and why?

3. Which segmentation variable is most appropriate for this teeth-whitening product?

© Susan Van Etten

Taking a Bite Out of White Teeth

The big winners in today's marketplace are the companies that best identify market segments with unmet needs and wants and address those needs and wants with compelling products. For instance, consider the huge toothpaste-products market, a $1.3-billion market in 2001 in the U. S. alone. Firms in this highly competitive industry are continually looking for new product characteristics that will strike a chord with special market segments to either grow the total market or increase the firm's market share. Consider how the toothpaste industry has developed products for each of its different markets: toothpastes for pets, for rejuvenating gums, for kids, for "night mouth" and even for medical conditions such as fibromyalgia and chronic fatigue. One of the most successful of these toothpaste segments is teeth-whitening products.

The first major whitening toothpaste by Rembrandt came onto the market in 1990. Since that time, almost all major toothpaste manufacturers, and some minor ones, have developed multiple products that contain whiteners. The reason is clear: By March 2002, sales of whitening toothpastes exceeded $570 million and sales of dental accessories (including whitening kits/strips) exceeded $253 million, while sales of other toothpastes declined 10.5% for the year. More importantly, experts predict that sales of whitening-system products will reach $400 million in 2003. The growth in this market is not surprising, considering that nearly 74% of adults believe that a "bad smile" and yellow teeth harm career success, and 92% believe that their teeth and smile are important in social situations, according to research by the American Academy of Cosmetic Dentistry.

Bolstered by the belief that at least half of all Americans wanted whiter teeth—a market potential of 150 million consumers—and that their needs were not being met, Procter & Gamble began efforts in

1997 to develop a new teeth-whitening system. The system was to be an inexpensive, at-home product that really worked and that would replace much more expensive in-dentist-office whitening treatments. The result was Crest Whitestrips. More than $200 million worth of the innovative new product was sold in the first year, one of the most successful new product launches for P&G in the past 20 years.

To maximize its potential for success, P&G developed a product that met the needs of a large market segment. It also designed a narrowly targeted marketing launch. P&G initially spent little to advertise Crest Whitestrips, preferring to sell the product over the Internet and in dentists' offices. Initial sales in these two channel outlets alone amounted to $23 million. The company also turned to QVC to reach a slightly older demographic and sold 44,000 kits in just 24 hours. Another key component of the product launch was targeting the product innovator segments with free samples. These targeted groups were identified as teens, brides, gay men, and consumers who were gossipy trend-setters known as "aspirational individuals." The results of this and other public relations strategies were impressive: The product received more than 1.1 billion mentions in the media, such as a statement on CNN Headline News that "Crest Whitestrips are, like, the hottest new product on the market," which resulted directly in 33% of sales, according to company estimates.

Other companies, such as Colgate, are rapidly responding to the huge "teeth whitening" market. Research by Colgate suggests that only 3.4% of households in the U. S. use whitening products, largely because consumers see them as too difficult and too expensive to use. This research was the basis for their competitive response to Crest Whitestrips—Colgate Simply White, a gel that is brushed onto teeth and left on for 30 minutes. The company hopes its easy, inexpensive whitening product will generate $187 million a year, reaching $400 million by 2003. BriteSmile

LEARNING OBJECTIVES

After you have completed this chapter, you should be able to:

1. *Understand the basic concepts and importance of segmenting and targeting markets.*

2. *Explain advantages and disadvantages of segmentation and target marketing.*

3. *Identify and explain the process of target-market selection, including criteria for segmentation, bases for segmentation, profiling market segments, and positioning.*

4. *Appreciate how segmenting business markets differs from segmenting consumer markets.*

5. *Identify special considerations in segmenting global markets.*

VOICE OF THE EXPERT
Penny Simpson,
University of Texas–Pan American

The focus of a successful marketing program is the customer. The process of understanding the customer and designing a specialized marketing mix for that customer is target marketing. Only through this targeting process can marketers develop a total needs-based product package that is desired by the customer, delivers the messages they want to hear, is available at the precise time the customer wants it, and is priced right.

The importance of target marketing is even more apparent in light of the post September 11 economy, in which companies have increasingly faced the need to cut costs and provide customers with better value. Target marketing allows companies to do a better job of using resources efficiently and effectively by concentrating efforts on likely customers and disregarding unlikely ones. As an added benefit, this targeting process improves the value that customers receive because marketing efforts are designed to meet their specific needs.

has also entered the market through a chain of teeth-whitening "spas" and affiliations with selected dentists. Considering that future users of these whitening products are mostly baby-boomer women looking to reverse years of coffee- and tea-stained teeth, the high sales projections for teeth-whitening products looks warranted.[1]

This chapter will help you understand the importance of target marketing and explain how it is implemented in consumer markets, business markets, and international markets. Those of you who truly understand the concepts of segmenting and targeting markets and appreciate the balancing act of customization versus mass marketing will be better positioned to succeed in the constantly changing marketing environment.

LEARNING OBJECTIVE 1

Markets and Target Marketing

Market
Is any individual, group of individuals, or organizations willing, able, and capable of purchasing a firm's product.

A **market** is any individual, group of individuals, or organizations willing, able, and capable of purchasing a firm's product. For example, if you want to buy a new car, you are in the new car market. Before a firm can effectively market its products to you, or to any other member of the market for that matter, it must fully understand your needs and wants from that product. However, the needs and wants from a product are not the same for everyone in a market. For example, you and your mother may both want a new car, so you are both in the new-car market; but you probably each want a different type of car. You may want a small, fast, red sports car, while your mother would like a large, safe, dependable, white car that gets good mileage.

Heterogeneous demand
Occurs when a group of consumers have differing needs from a specific product.

Generally, different groups of customers have differing needs and wants from specific products, or **heterogeneous demand**. For example, teens may want blue jeans that are stylish, construction workers want jeans that are durable, and older "gray" consumers want jeans that are comfortable. Real differences in product preferences exist. This means that a company wanting to reach these different groups of consumers must divide the market into distinct groups based on these differences, then analyze in detail each group it wants to reach so it understands what customers need and want from the products they buy. Only then can a company tailor products and messages about the products efficiently and effectively for the most likely buyers. For example, Ford has developed two different advertising messages for the Focus to appeal to two different markets: active adults ages 18–49, with a household income less than $75,000, and Latino youth, male and female.

Market segmentation
Is the separation of markets into distinctive groups based on some similar trait or traits.

As introduced in Chapter 1, the separation of markets into distinctive groups based on homogeneous (similar) characteristics is called **market segmentation**,[2] and is critical to reaching customers who need different things from a product. Each of the divided markets, or **market segments**, that a company selects to reach with its marketing efforts is a target market. More formally, the specific group of customers toward which a firm directs its marketing efforts is the firm's **target market**. This process of matching a specialized marketing mix with the needs of a specific market segment is critical to the marketing success of a product and is called **target marketing**. To illustrate, just imagine the likely success (or failure) when market needs do not match the marketing mix, such as Rogaine advertised to adolescent girls in *Teen* magazine, heavy metal music playing in upscale hotel lobbies, or mascara advertised in *GQ* magazine.

Market segment
Is a group of consumers that are alike based on some characteristic(s).

Target market
Is the specific group of customers toward which a firm directs its marketing efforts.

Target marketing
Is the process of matching a specialized marketing mix to the needs of a specific market segment.

A firm will not generally want to try to appeal to *all* members of a total market in the same way, but may rather concentrate on selected groups of customers. Depend-

- Targeting multiple markets generally increases marketing costs.
- Efforts toward personalization and individualization of markets can lead to proliferation of products, which can become overly burdensome and costly to manage.
- Efforts to overly segment markets into too-small niches may be viewed cynically by the targeted individual and negatively affect consumer response to marketing efforts. After seeing letters to all your friends from Publishers Clearing House, your letter arrives stating that: "Yes, you, Lucky W. Inner, from Muleshoe, Texas, have won $10 million, if . . ." You may be a little skeptical, or even immune to such personalized tactics, and come to resent companies that engage in the practice. One writer terms this practice "Faux Segmentation" and asks "Who do these guys think they're fooling?"[8]
- Efforts to personalize marketing efforts require that vast amounts of data about each consumer be collected and analyzed. This amassing of personal information may be viewed as a violation of privacy that may have negative effects on firms or on the discipline of marketing in general.
- Narrowly segmenting a market to target customers may actually prevent a product from developing brand loyalty. One researcher argues that the only way to build a large, sustainable brand-loyal customer base is to build broad brand popularity. More to the point, he says:

  It is very clear, however, that building loyal frequent buyers means broadening brand appeal to more and more different kinds of households rather than narrowing it through segmentation to a small, homogeneous group. One can go further to say that to successfully build a base of loyal frequent buyers a brand must also become broadly popular among category users. This is the opposite of segmentation. It is integration, building brand popularity.[9]

Figure 8.4	**Advantages and Disadvantages of Target Marketing**	
	Advantages	**Disadvantages**
	Defines the market for further analysis	Increased costs
	Allows creation of a customized marketing mix	Increased number of products
		Faux segmentation
	Aids in assessing potential demand	Amassing of personal data may violate privacy
	Aids identification of competitors	
	Increases sales effectiveness and efficiency	May decrease brand loyalty
	Aids in positioning products	Some practices considered unethical
	Aids in identifying opportunities	Proliferates stereotyping

Political and Legal Forces

Some of the practices of target marketers, such as using Joe Camel to reach vulnerable markets with potentially harmful products, have been banned. As the result of lawsuits brought against cigarette manufacturers, cigarette makers may no longer use cartoon characters to promote their products.

- Target marketers have been widely criticized for unethical or stereotypical activities.

The most public criticism of segmenting and target marketing comes from minority and consumer groups who claim that the practice of aiming potentially harmful products at disadvantaged or vulnerable markets is highly unethical. Popular examples of such practices include Camel cigarettes' Joe Camel character, which was accused of targeting children; the widespread practice of using extremely thin, waiflike models in advertisements targeting the identity-seeking, vulnerable teenage-girl market; and beer companies targeting underage college students. The consumer perception of targeting potentially harmful products, such as cigarettes, alcohol, and lottery tickets, toward vulnerable consumers, such as children, poor, or uneducated consumers, may have negative effects, including negative word-of-mouth and boycotts against the marketing firms.

Finally, the process of segmenting and targeting markets is akin to stereotyping and has been criticized for that reason. Recently, for example, the Miller Lite TV advertisement, called "Catfight," showed two women fighting over whether the beer is less filling or tastes great. The ad, as discussed in a previous chapter, was a portrayal of women in a male "fantasy" and sparked criticism that the ad degrades women. Critics note that images such as these further proliferate stereotyping and may actually alienate potential customers.

These criticisms and potentially negative and positive effects of segmenting and targeting markets are important for firms to consider when developing marketing strategies. A summary of these advantages and disadvantages appears in Figure 8.4.

LEARNING OBJECTIVE 3

The Target-Market Selection Process

The process of selecting a potential market and then segmenting, analyzing, and profiling the market to better target it with a customized marketing mix is the *target-market selection process*. This process consists of the eight interrelated tasks shown in Figure 8.5. Although depicted as a series of sequential steps, the process's ordering of tasks varies in practice, with some tasks actually occurring simultaneously or in a completely different order. Moreover, the target-market selection process is a continuous, ongoing process because markets are dynamic and constantly changing.[10] Consequently, firms may need to revise their marketing mix based on the segments' changing needs or identify new markets to replace shrinking ones.

Not only is the segmentation process continuous, it may be either a priori or post hoc. *A priori* segmentation occurs when variables for segmenting markets, such as age or income, are selected first and then customers are classified accordingly. For example, a car manufacturer could identify a large number of golf-playing consumers with incomes greater than $75,000 as a potential market and then develop a car aimed at that group of consumers. *Post hoc* segmentation involves

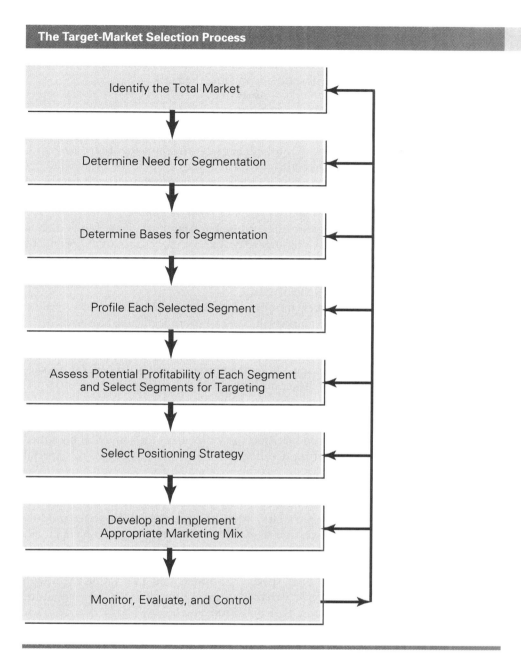

The Target-Market Selection Process

Figure 8.5

Identify the Total Market

Determine Need for Segmentation

Determine Bases for Segmentation

Profile Each Selected Segment

Assess Potential Profitability of Each Segment and Select Segments for Targeting

Select Positioning Strategy

Develop and Implement Appropriate Marketing Mix

Monitor, Evaluate, and Control

examining existing customer data and then segmenting it to classify the customers into segments, or clusters, based on similarities of variables.[11] A bank may use post hoc segmentation to analyze its existing customer database, determine which customers have the largest savings, and then develop special programs to reach these segments. Some evidence suggests that post hoc segmentation is more common than a priori among businesses, especially small businesses, that actually create and offer a product and then examine their customers in efforts to revise and refine their marketing mix.[12]

Identify the Total Market

The first step in the target-market selection process is to specifically define the total market of all potential customers for a product category. Market purchase patterns and whether the product user is the same person as the buyer are two of the factors that should be considered when defining the total market. For example, recent research shows that men are increasingly responsible for buying household products. For example, men buy 25% of all frozen breakfasts, 24% of canned stews, and 23% of wart and corn removers.[13] This means that companies that strictly identify women as their market may be substantially missing the mark.

Determine Need for Segmentation

Another important task in the market-segmentation process is determining whether the total market needs to be divided into segments for the purpose of targeting with special marketing programs; after all, not all markets need to be segmented. In general, for segmentation to be warranted, *there must be differences with respect to customer needs or demands, potential product variations must be cost-effective (profitable), and implemented product differences must be apparent to customers.*[14] For example, the market for sugar is huge. Most kitchens stock sugar but is there a need to segment markets when selling sugar? Probably not, because of the product's homogeneity of demand and little perceived difference among brands.

Criteria for Successful Segmentation

Differences in demand preferences are only one criterion that firms must consider when deciding whether to divide markets into one or more segments. Segments being considered for targeting with a customized marketing mix should be analyzed according to five criteria for successful segmentation, along with various strategic and external factors, before making the segmentation decision. In general, to successfully segment a market, the market must have these characteristics:[15]

- Heterogeneous—Clear differences in consumer preferences for a product must exist. If all consumers in the market use the product in the same way and want the same benefits from the product, such as with sugar, there may be no added value from dividing the market into segments for special targeting.

American Express and the Cayman Islands Department of Tourism are targeting families with children in this ad, a consumer segment that is heterogeneous, measurable, substantial, actionable, and accessible.

Courtesy, Cayman Islands Department of Tourism.

- Measurable—Different preferences for a product must be identifiable and capable of being related to measurable variables, such as age, gender, lifestyle, product usage, and so on. A number of consumers have larger-than-average feet and require large shoe sizes, such as a man's size 20 or a woman's size 12. However, identifying these special consumers and associating them with specific variables, such as age, income, or geographic region, is virtually impossible.
- Substantial—The proposed market segment must have enough size and purchasing power to be profitable. The benefits of altering the marketing mix must exceed the costs incurred from the changes.
- Actionable—Companies must be able to respond to different preferences with an appropriate and profitable marketing mix. Although a marketing mix directed toward consumers with larger-than-average feet or toward all anaconda owners could be developed, the cost of finding those consumers and then marketing products only to them may outweigh the benefits derived from the revenue generated.
- Accessible—The proposed market segment must be readily accessible and reachable with targeted programs. Consider the problems of reaching homeless consumers with information about discounted food and clothing or of inexpensively reaching only those male consumers who wear a size 20 shoe.

Segmentation Strategy

A firm must consider the appropriate, viable segmentation strategy for reaching market segments. Companies might develop one marketing-mix strategy that is appropriate for all members of the total market, known as an **undifferentiated targeting strategy**. Generally, this strategy is effective when all members of the market have homogeneous demand with respect to the product, as is the case with sugar. This means that differentiation of the product by brand is difficult because, in general, all consumers derive the same benefits from different brands and there is little perceived difference between brands. Salt, flour, and fresh vegetables are examples of products where there is virtually no difference in brands or the benefits that consumers derive from those brands.

Where heterogeneity of demand exists, and thus multiple market segments, marketers may adopt either a concentrated strategy or a differentiated strategy. A **concentrated strategy** is where only one marketing mix is developed and directed toward a few, or perhaps one, profitable market segments. In contrast, a **differentiated strategy** exists when a firm develops different marketing-mix plans specially tailored for each of two or more market segments. Each of the three types of segmentation strategies a firm might adopt are shown in Figure 8.6. Obviously, marketing costs increase as the number of market segments targeted increases, so that firms must examine the resource requirements for segmenting in light of available resources.

External Factors

Firms must also consider external factors that may affect the success of segmentation. Examples include the age of the product, profitability, market share, the competition, the product itself, and the market, which can each affect segmentation strategy. The fierce competition between Coke and Pepsi, for example, has prompted Pepsi to partner with Sony Music Entertainment in a "Drink Pepsi, Taste Stardom" campaign. The partnership concept involves exclusive appearances by some popular Sony artists, such as Jennifer Lopez, in an effort to capture the youth market through an affiliation with music. U.S. and world cola market leader, Coke, is connecting to younger consumers through sports.[16]

Determine Bases for Segmentation

To divide a market into segments, firms may use *segmentation variables* that describe the characteristics of each part of the market. Segmenting means dividing markets into homogeneous, or like, groups based on similar characteristics or traits. Any one or combination of a number of variables or descriptors of the market, such as astrological sign[17] or attitudes toward the past,[18] can serve as a basis for segmenting

Undifferentiated targeting strategy
Is the targeting strategy where one marketing-mix strategy is used for all members of the total market.

Concentrated strategy
Is the target-marketing strategy where only one marketing mix is developed and directed toward one market segment.

Differentiated strategy
Is the target-marketing strategy where a firm develops different marketing-mix plans specially tailored for each market segment.

Competitive Forces
Competition between Coke and Pepsi is fierce. Almost any change in marketing efforts by one results in a significant change in marketing efforts by the other.

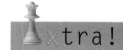

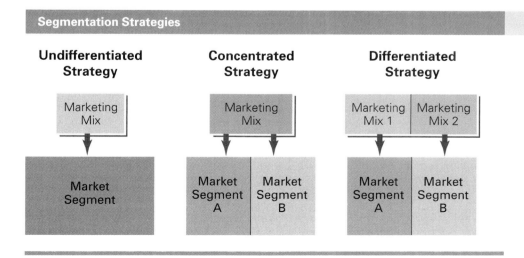
Segmentation Strategies Figure 8.6

Figure 8.7	Segmentation Variables

Demographic Segmentation
- Age
- Income
- Family life cycle
- Family size
- Religion
- Race
- Nationality

Geographic Segmentation
- Country
- Region
- State
- City
- Neighborhood
- Rural
- Urban

Psychographic or Lifestyle Segmentation
- Values
- Motives
- Lifestyle
- Self-concept

Benefits-Sought Segmentation
- Preferences for specific characteristics of products

Situational Segmentation
- Physical surroundings
- Social surroundings
- Time allotted for purchase
- Reason for purchase
- Purchaser's mood

Behavior or Usage Segmentation
- Degree of loyalty
- Consumption pattern
- Heavy, medium, or light user

Demographic segmentation
Is the division of groups of consumers into segments based on demographic characteristics such as age, income, gender, ethnic background, and occupation.

Family life cycle (FLC)
Is a segmentation variable that incorporates income and lifestyle to explain differences in spending patterns based on family role and transitions among roles.

markets. The most generally accepted bases for segmenting markets, however, are demographics, geographics, psychographics, benefits sought, situation, and behavior or usage patterns. Figure 8.7 summarizes these segmentation variables.

Demographic Segmentation

The division of groups of consumers into segments based on age, income, occupation, level of education, race, gender, family life cycle, family size, religion, race, and nationality is known as **demographic segmentation**. The Gap, GapKids, and babyGap segment according to age; Lord & Taylor segments by income; and 1st African Clothing segments by race.

Another less well-known but important demographic variable is the family life cycle. The **family life cycle** (FLC) model presented in Figure 8.8 describes the stages

Figure 8.8	Family Life Cycle

Bachelor I
Bachelor II
Newlywed
Single Parent (young and middle-aged)
Full Nest I (child < 6)
Delayed Full Nest (child < 6)
Full Nest II and III (youngest child ≥ 6)
Childless couple (no children at home)
Older Couple
Bachelor III

Source: As shown in Charles M. Schaninger and William D. Danko, "A Conceptual and Empirical Comparison of Alternative Household Life Cycle Models," *Journal of Consumer Research* (March 1993): 580–594. Used by permission of University of Chicago Press.

Who is the Real Big Brother?

This chapter speaks to the issue of identifying prospective customers and truly understanding and targeting them through the process of profiling. Unfortunately, this means obtaining and maintaining vast amounts of personal data about customers. Examples of information contained in these databases include items bought, frequency of purchases, where purchases are made, payment method, home address, magazine subscriptions, and even whether or not an item was purchased as a gift. This information is used, in part, by numerous companies such as Citibank, Wells Fargo, Verizon, and Sears to identify specific spending patterns that may help them efficiently target potential customers, suggest other products customers may want, determine credit risk, predict bankruptcy and other behaviors, and even determine how much time and effort to devote to a customer. Despite its widespread use, the acquisition, use, and sale of this personal data about individual consumers are considered unethical and a violation of privacy by some consumers and consumer advocate groups.

Advocate groups are also charging the federal government with violating individual privacy and playing "Big Brother" by using the same profiling tactics that big business uses, as outlined above. Although criminal justice agencies have used "criminal profiling" for decades, the September 11 tragedy has spurred the U.S. government to adopt the business practice of "profiling" in a widespread coordinated way to identify potential terrorists before they attack. Efforts are currently under way by the Defense Advanced Research Projects Agency to develop a system that will track customer-spending patterns through credit-card purchases, phone calls, travel, e-mail, medical records, and other information. Based on the idea that terrorists will follow a specific spending pattern, computer technology may be used to quickly spot these patterns, identify the source, and initiate a timely investigation.

DISCUSSION QUESTIONS

1. Do you believe it is ethical for companies to accumulate and use vast amounts of consumer data for targeting consumers? For governments to use this information? Explain.
2. Do you believe there is a difference between a company's accumulation and use of personal consumer information and the government's accumulation and use of it? Explain.

Sources: Elaine Monaghan and Tim Reid, "US to Set Up Big Brother Citizen Database," *The Times*, 22 November 2002, 19.
Elisa Williams, "The Man Who Knows Too Much," *Forbes*, 11 November 2002, 68–69.

or evolution of the typical consumer over his or her lifetime. The FLC variable incorporates income and lifestyle to explain differences in spending patterns based on family role and transitions among roles.[19] Typically, consumers evolve from single, to married, to married with children, to no children, to retired, and finally to single again. Quite obviously, consumers' needs for different products vary with each of these stages in the FLC. For example, singles buy canned vegetables in individual-serving sizes, families with babies buy strained vegetables, and retired older persons may "buy" their vegetables by eating out in family-style restaurants.

Geographic Segmentation

Geographic regions may be used to segment markets for specialized marketing efforts. Types and brands of products purchased vary greatly by regions of the world, country, state, city, or neighborhood, and by urban and rural locations. Obviously, snow sleds are common purchases in northern sections of the United States, while outdoor furniture is popular in the South. Not so obvious is that consumers in different regions of the U.S. often have different preferences in products. For example, wine consumers in San Francisco prefer different types of wines than those preferred by consumers in Atlanta. Preferences for wines even differ by neighborhoods within cities. Interestingly, one researcher has identified nine distinctively different regions of the United States based on individual values called "nations of North America."[20]

Generally, **geographic segmentation**, the division of groups of consumers into segments based on where those consumers live, is used in conjunction with other segmentation descriptors. For example, companies may target teenagers in Dallas. Combining demographics with geographics like this is called **geodemographics**. Or marketers may target tennis-playing teenagers in New York City, which combines geodemographics and psychographics (lifestyle) information. Not surprisingly, the

Geographic segmentation
Is the division of groups of consumers into segments based on where those consumers live.

Geodemographics
Is the combination of demographic and geographic segmentation.

Technological Forces

With the technological development of location-based marketing, imagine walking or driving past a Starbucks or Dunkin' Donuts and immediately receiving a text message offering 50 cents off the price of a cup of coffee. Already, AT&T Wireless allows its network users to geographically locate other AT&T users who have agreed to participate.

Psychographic segmentation

Is the segmentation of markets by social class, lifestyles, and psychological characteristics, such as attitudes, interests, opinions, and values.

best source of demographic and geographic data is the U. S. Census. Best of all, the information is free. Go online to http://www.census.gov and access demographic profiles for different areas of the U.S. A map of various age groups by county in the U.S. is shown in Figure 8.9. Using the map as a guide, where would you recommend that companies selling baby products focus their marketing efforts?

Advances in technology, such as cell phones and the Internet, may alter the way that marketers look at geographic segmentation. The Federal Communications Commission is now requiring that U.S. cell phone carriers be able by 2005 to determine the approximate geographic location of its customers to within 100 meters of the nearest tower for emergency services purposes. Since your cell phone carriers will know where you are whenever your cell phone is activated, they may reach out to you through "location-based" or "location-sensitive" marketing.

Psychographic or Lifestyle Segmentation

Segmenting markets by social class, lifestyles, and psychological characteristics, such as attitudes, interests, and opinions (frequently called *AIO*), and values is called **psychographic segmentation** (or psychographics) as explained in Chapter 6. Increasingly popular, psychographics often creates a better picture of market segments than does demographic or geographic segmentation. These segmentation bases allow the marketer to truly understand the inner workings of potential consumers before developing a marketing mix aimed at those consumers.

The importance of lifestyle segmentation is illustrated by the increasing number of carmakers using the variable to develop and market new car products. The 2003

Figure 8.9	U.S. Counties by Age

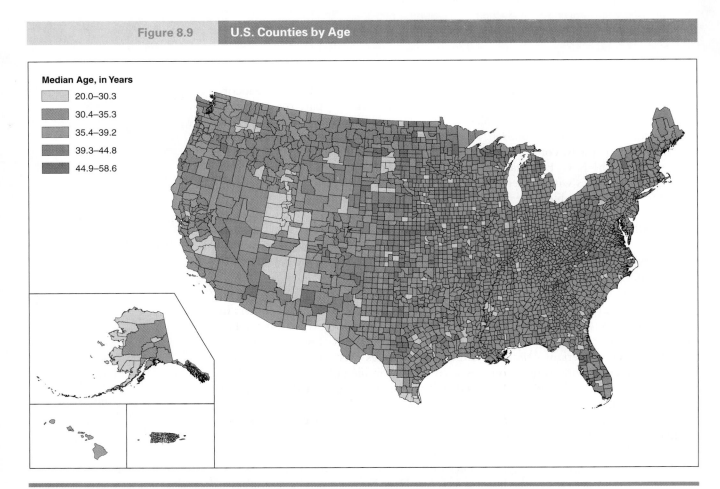

Median Age, in Years
- 20.0–30.3
- 30.4–35.3
- 35.4–39.2
- 39.3–44.8
- 44.9–58.6

Source: http://factfinder.census.gov/servlet/BasicFactsServlet, accessed 17 January 2003.

Toyota 4Runner now targets consumers "who aspire to reach the ultimate peak."[21] Saab targets educated, independent thinkers. The 2003 Honda Element, called a "dorm on wheels," targets young, active members of Generation Y. The 2003 Ford Escape aims for young-at-heart, adventurous urban professionals. And the Jeep Wrangler targets the true outdoor adventurer who strives for a challenge, demands personal freedom, and "speaks their own language."

Psychographics is routinely used in concert with demographic and geographic data. Notable private sources of such data are SRI Consulting, with its VALS™ product, discussed previously in Chapter 6, and ESRI Business Information Solutions' (formerly CACI Marketing Systems) ACORN.™ ESRI Business Information Solutions uses its own ACORN™ lifestyle segmentation tool to describe residential neighborhoods by zip code. Visit http://www.esribis.com to get a "sample" profile of your zip code area similar to the one shown in Figure 8.10 for the neighborhood around the University of Texas in Austin, Texas.

Profile of Austin, Texas 78701	Figure 8.10

The ESRI Business Information Solutions profiling application, ACORN™, describes the 78701 zip area in this way: "This is the youngest and smallest consumer market, comprising the dormitories and student housing located around universities. Their budget goes to college expenses or an active social life. Top-ranked for take-out fast food, having ATM cards, and making long-distance calls using calling cards, their purchase decisions are based on price. They rank highest for watching sports on TV."

Demographically, the 78701 zip code area, as compared to national averages, is:

	Zip 78701	National Average
Total Population	3,597	285,412,400
Male	67.7%	49.1%
Female	34.3%	50.9%
Median Household Income	$31,996	$41,369
Average Home Value	$290,592	$165,558

© Stewart Cohen/Index Stock Imagery

Benefits-sought segmentation

Is the segmentation of markets based on consumer preference for a specific product attribute or characteristic.

Benefits-Sought Segmentation

Markets can also be segmented based on consumer preference for a specific product attribute or characteristic. This type of segmentation is called **benefits-sought segmentation**. Nowhere is this more apparent than in the toothpaste-product category mentioned in the opening vignette. Other examples of product benefits that can serve as a basis for segmentation are airplanes divided into first, business, and coach classes; restaurants divided into smoking and nonsmoking sections; and mail delivered by regular or express mail. Based on preferences for each of these items, customized marketing mixes can be developed.

Most segmentation strategies should include the benefits-sought variable. After all, marketers must understand the benefits their consumers want from a product before an appropriate marketing mix can be tailored to a specific segment. Then, consumers must understand how that product will meet their needs before they buy it. Many experts maintain that the benefits sought from a product are more predictive of consumer purchase behavior than any other segmentation variable.[22]

Situation segmentation

Is segmentation of markets based on purchase situation or occasion.

Situation Segmentation

The purchase situation or occasion can also serve as a basis for segmenting markets. Think, for example, about purchasing a meal and what might influence the purchase decision. A meal purchased by a busy student to eat in the 10 minutes between classes would likely be much different from a meal purchased for a long-anticipated first date, or even a meal purchased for a night at home alone watching TV. Each of these situations or purchase occasions represents a different market segment that is potentially suitable for targeting.

Situation segmentation is segmentation of markets based on purchase situation or occasion. Five different situational characteristics may affect purchase behavior and serve as a descriptor for a market segment. These situational characteristics and examples are:

1. Physical Surroundings—Is the store or salesperson pleasant or offensive?
2. Social Surroundings—Are friends or parents watching the purchase?
3. Temporal Perspective—How much time is there to make the purchase?
4. Task Definition—Why is this product being purchased? Is it a gift? If so, is it a gift for a girlfriend? boyfriend? parent? boss?
5. Prepurchase Attitude—What is the purchaser's mood at the time of purchase: happy or sad?[23]

These situational variables may serve as the basis for a unique marketing mix. For example, in today's time-poor society, marketers can define segments based on the temporal perspective—consumers who are time-conscious or pressed for time—and develop a marketing mix tailored toward them that emphasizes convenience and time savings.

Behavior or usage segmentation

Is the segmentation of markets based on usage patterns, such as heavy users, medium users, and light users, or loyalty toward a product, or the way in which a customer uses a product.

80/20 principle

States that about 20% of a firm's customers are responsible for generating 80% of the firm's revenue.

Behavior or Usage Segmentation

Loyalty toward a product, the way a product is used, and usage patterns (heavy, medium, or light users) may also serve as a basis for segmenting markets. A major factor to consider here is the **80/20 principle**, which holds that only a small percentage (20% or less) of a firm's customers are responsible for generating most (80%) of the firm's revenue. In one real-life example, 80% of Diet Coke sales derive from 13% of its customers.[24] The principle, in general, means that firms must pay special attention to developing and maintaining close relations with this "best" 20% of their loyal customers, keeping in mind the following warning.

For more than a decade now, many marketers have preached that loyalty leads to higher profits, citing claims that profits may increase by as much as 100% simply by keeping 5% of customers who would otherwise defect.[25] The idea is that loyal customers cost less to keep, are willing to pay higher prices, and will spread favorable word-of-mouth. More recent research, however, suggests that loyal customers may not be the most profitable ones, at least the ones who demand, and receive, extra perquisites, where the costs of delivering these extras exceed the benefits derived from these "old friend" customers.[26] These study findings simply suggest that firms carefully examine their loyal customers in terms of revenue generated versus resources required for retention.

Sources of Segmentation Data

Information for segmenting markets may be obtained from internal or external sources. Internally, most companies create and retain information about their existing and potential customers in a database. However, to expand their customer base, firms need to get new prospective customers into their database for targeting from external sources.

Internal Database Sources

Customer and marketing databases may contain vast amounts of both personal and purchasing-pattern information about customers. Examples of customer information collected in an internal database are date of birth (age), educational attainment, profession, credit rating, purchases, purchase patterns, and so forth. Companies may use the information to classify customers into segments based on selected attributes or characteristics in an increasingly popular process called data mining.

Data mining is exploring data for patterns and relationships. These patterns can be used to target specific groups with special programs to create greater marketing efficiency. For example, American Express could examine the data from all of its customers who purchased an airline ticket using their credit card in the last year. Their ticket-purchase patterns—time of day, day of week, destination, frequency of travel, or even class of travel—and purchases made while traveling could be explored to determine patterns or segments. The company could then separate consumers with similar purchase patterns into segments for targeting with special catalogs and direct mail about travel clubs and special products, such as luggage and vacation travel packages.

Data mining has also been used by companies such as Wal-Mart to customize product offerings in individual stores to local community needs and by one financial company to find out that consumers completing credit applications in ink were less likely to default than those completing applications in pencil.[27] Internal data are readily available to firms and can be extremely valuable in developing customized marketing mixes.

External Data Sources

Databases have been shown to be extremely useful for firms profiling their *existing* customers. In order to grow, however, firms need to expand their customer base. A useful way to acquire these prospects is to buy mailing lists. There are a wide variety of such lists, including magazine or catalog subscribers, association members, voters, and postal residents, and they are available for a myriad of consumer types and interests. For example, *The Lifestyle Market Analyst* published by Standard Rate & Data Service contains a section on consumer magazines and direct mail lists sorted by lifestyle. These consumer-interest lists include everything imaginable—from consumers interested in art, casino gambling, or yachting to contributors to specific political campaigns.

Lists of consumer e-mail addresses by demographic or geographic characteristics can also be obtained from listing companies or by using software that searches the Web with a technique called *spidering*.

A large number of private organizations, trade associations, and magazines offer market-research data and segmentation profiling. For example, ESRI Business Information Solutions publishes *The Sourcebook of Zip Code Demographics* and *The Sourcebook of County Demographics*; Standard Rate & Data Service publishes *The*

Data mining
Is a technique of exploring data for patterns.

Technological Forces
The use of data mining over the past decade has saved companies $75 billion and will likely yield an additional $500 billion from increased sales and decreased costs over the next decade, according to one expert.[28]

Technological Forces
Spidering software allows automated Web site searches for key variables. Possible search variables can include profession, state, city, or even countries. Personalized e-mail can then be sent to the individual names collected.

Lifestyle Market Analyst; and Simmons Market Research Bureau, Inc. publishes an annual study of media and markets. Magazines such as *American Demographics* and *Sales & Marketing Management* often contain useful data about various types of markets.

Much useful information is in the public domain and available at no charge. One of the best sources of geodemographic information about market segments is the U.S. Census Bureau. The TIGER/Line Files with LandView Mapping capabilities can be used to access census data and are used by most profiling organizations. The TIGER/Line Files and other U.S. Census Bureau data are available online and at any Federal Repository Library.

Profile Each Selected Segment

Profile
Is a detailed picture of a market segment based on multiple segmentation descriptors.

Before a marketing program aimed at a specific market segment can be developed, the marketer must truly understand the typical customers in that market—their wants and needs, interests, attitudes, etc. A detailed picture of a market segment is called a **profile**. The profile should paint a clear picture of the typical customer for the company's product, using all applicable segmentation variables discussed previously—demographic, geographic, psychographic, benefits sought, situation, and usage. Although this profile is a *generalized average* of the typical customer in the segment, it helps marketers discover and understand who the potential users of the product are, so that the best marketing mix for that customer may be developed. One way of profiling markets is to use a table such as that shown in Figure 8.11.

A now classic example of profiling comes from the "Don't Mess with Texas" antilitter campaign. Research had indicated that the typical deliberate litterer in Texas was a male between the ages of 18 to 34 who drove a truck, liked sports, and

| Figure 8.11 | Profile of Market Segments Form |

Profile of Market Segments Form

	Segment		
	A	**B**	**C**
Size			
Number of consumers			
Growth rate			
Profile			
Demographic characteristics			
Geographic characteristics			
Psychographic characteristics			
Benefits sought			
Product Usage			
Favorite brands			
Quantities consumed			
Occasions of use			
Etc.			
Communications Behavior			
Media used			
Frequency of media usage			
Etc.			
Purchasing Behavior			
Distribution channel preferred			
Outlet preference			
Purchase infrequency			
Price range			
Etc.			

did not typically respond to appeals to civic duty. The "Don't Mess with Texas" antilitter campaign developed from the profile of this Texas "Bubba" involved using sports celebrities and country music and rock stars in a macho appeal to these Texans' sense of pride in their state. Littering was reduced by an amazing 29% within nine months after the campaign began.[29] The success of the campaign came directly from a true understanding of the "typical litterer" and how to reach him. A profile of typical college students is seen in Figure 8.12. Do you fit this profile?

Assess Potential Profitability of Each Segment and Select Segments for Targeting

Once segments have been identified and clearly distinguished, a firm must determine the profitability of customized marketing efforts aimed at these segments and determine the cost of implementing specialized marketing efforts.

Determine Forecast Demand

The first step is to determine the potential demand for a product within each segmented target market. For example, a company targeting undergraduate business students in Louisiana would need to determine that Louisiana has 23 public colleges and community colleges and that the total enrollment in these schools in Fall 2002 was 186,009 students, with 25,742 declaring undergraduate business management and administration majors.[30] If the company expects a 50% share of the market, the sales forecast would be 12,871 units.

Firms must consider expected growth and competition in forecasting future sales. A large market share in a small, fast-growth market may mean more long-term profits than a small market share in a crowded, stagnant, large market. Imagine trying to

A consumer profile helps marketers establish a clear picture of their target market. With this ad, Carnival is trying to convey the wide variety of choices available to its target market as part of its "Today's Carnival" product enhancement strategy.

How Average Are You?	Figure 8.12

A recent study surveyed 2,930 American college students aged 18 to 30. The study found that there were 8.7 million female and 6.6 million male students in the U.S., with 8 million of them full-time students, 3.3 million part-time, 6.9 million pursuing four-year degrees and 3.8 million working toward two-year degrees. On average, college students are in class 1.7 hours each day, spend 1.6 hours a day studying, work 2.6 hours, and then sleep 6.8 hours each day. When they are not working or studying, students are engaged in various activities. For example, 90% of the college students surveyed surf the Internet every day, while 99% surf at least several times a week. At least several times a week, these surveyed students were involved in listening to self-selected music (87%), watching TV (86%), talking on the phone (85%), listening to the radio (80%), reading newspapers (44%) or magazines (36%), and hanging out with friends (60%). Not all college student activities are sedentary, however, as 52% exercise several times each week

College students also have money to spend on anything they like—on average, $287 per month. Altogether, college students make a significant impact on firms' revenues, as they spend $3 billion a year for CDs and tapes, $4 billion for personal-care goods, and more than $11 billion each year on snacks and beverages. Part-time college students tend to have even more discretionary money than full-time students. Considering the activities of the typical college student listed here, how and where do you think marketers should reach them?

Source: Rebecca Gardyn, "Educated Consumers," *American Demographics,* November 2002, 18–19.

Products are positioned based on the ways in which they are used. Soft Scrub may be used in a number of different ways as this advertisement demonstrates.

This Chick-Fil-A campaign positions chicken products against the entire beef product class.

compete in the fast-food hamburger market against McDonald's, with its 13,000 stores in the U.S. and 6,000 in Europe.[31]

Estimate Costs

The projected cost of developing and implementing specialized marketing efforts must also be determined. In the Louisiana college-student example described earlier, the added costs of reaching this market might include revising the product to meet Louisiana college-student needs, changing the price to fit the budgets of these college students, changing distribution channels by offering the product for sale in Louisiana college bookstores, and advertising in Louisiana college newspapers. Additional costs of the specialized targeted-marketing program must be weighed against the estimated revenue to be gained from the market segments, company objectives, and the resources required to generate those revenues.

Select Positioning Strategy

Positioning

Is the image that consumers have about a product, especially in relation to the products' competitors.

After the target markets have been selected and are fully understood, the marketing mix that best suits the target can be developed. Key to developing the appropriate marketing mix is the **positioning** strategy of the product. Creating and sustaining a strong, clear, and consistent customer image of the product in comparison with its competitors is key to *differentiating* the product, which is essential to developing a brand image that leads to customer loyalty. Numerous products have been successful in creating these strong brand images in consumers' minds. What do you think of when you think of the following brands?: Coca-Cola (the real thing), Olay cosmetics (for women of all ages), IAMS dog food (for every stage of your pet's life), Cheer laundry detergent (protects against fading), and Ivory (pure).

Effective positioning means determining (1) what consumers currently think about the product, especially in relation to competing products; (2) what the marketer wants consumers to think about the product; and (3) which positioning strategy will elevate consumers' current product image to the desired product image. In other words, where are we now, where do we want to go, and how do we best get there, bearing in mind the product position relative to competitors.

Determining what consumers think of a product often involves market research. A firm may want to survey its potential customers to determine what they think

Keebler claims that FudgeShoppe Clusters "don't fudge on the fudge" in a direct comparison with other fudge cookies.

Clorox Wipes are positioned directly against Windex Wipes in this advertisement.

about the product based on several selected criteria, such as color, taste, freshness, etc. Criteria selected should be both important to consumers and helpful to the firm in creating a unique advantage or position for a product in the marketplace. A commonly used method for this is **perceptual mapping**.

Perceptual mapping involves creating a visual depiction about consumer perceptions of a product on two or more dimensions in relation to competitors. An example of a perceptual map, shown in Figure 8.13, was created from hypothetical data for clothing brands. In this example, consumers rated six different clothing brands according to their perceptions of how "old and dated" or "young and cool" each brand is

Perceptual map
Is a commonly used multi-dimensional scaling method of graphically depicting a product's performance on selected attributes, or the "position" of a product against its competitors on selected product traits.

Hypothetical Perceptual Map of Clothing Brand Names　　　**Figure 8.13**

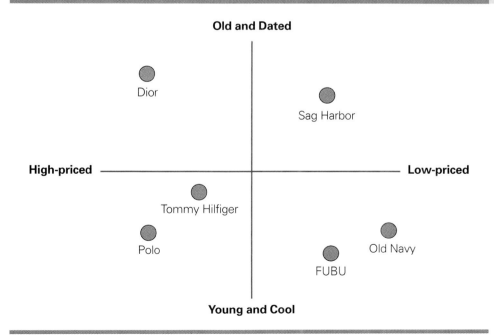

and how low- or high-priced it is. The map of consumer perceptions of product characteristics helps answer the where-are-we-now question, and the gaps help provide possible answers to the where-do-we-want-to-go question. The Figure 8.13 map shows that the hypothetical consumers surveyed view FUBU and Old Navy as fairly inexpensive brands suitable for young, aware consumers, while Dior is considered a very high-priced clothing brand for older folks. Can you spot some gaps in the perceptual map that competitors could enter for a competitive advantage? Interested students may want to create their own perceptual map using the demonstration of the Market Visioner tool at http://www.dssresearch.com/perceptualMap.

Not only must the positioning strategy determine where a company wants to go, it must also specify how to get there by positioning the product in any one, or combination, of the following ways:

- Price/Quality—Positioning by price/quality emphasizes the value derived from the product, in terms of its quality, price, or both. Wal-Mart stores are positioned based on everyday low pricing (EDLP) and good value, while Neiman Marcus stores offer unique, high-quality products for sale.
- Product Attributes—The characteristics or attributes of a product may serve as the basis for positioning the product. Some Colgate-Palmolive toothpastes are positioned by their attributes: Colgate Tartar Control Plus Whitening has both an antitartar and a whitening formula for "clean, white teeth," and Colgate Total toothpaste helps prevent cavities, gingivitis, plaque, and tartar, and provides "long-lasting fresh breath protection." These toothpastes are clearly positioned in consumers' minds based on product attributes.
- Product User—The typical user of a product can also be used to position a product. Marlboro cigarettes, with their Marlboro man, appealed to the rugged individual and the advertisement for Skechers shows images of different types of Skechers wearers.
- Product Usage—Products can be positioned based on the ways in which they are typically used. For example, the advertisement for Soft Scrub on page 254 shows different places where the product can be used.
- Product Class—Some products are positioned against another type of product or product class. Budweiser is the "King of Beer" and the popular Chick-Fil-A campaign in which cows invite viewers to "Eat More Chikin" positions chicken products against beef.
- Competition—Comparing a product to its competition, either directly or indirectly, is another form of product positioning. Burger King and McDonald's often compare their products to each other, as do Ragu and Prego spaghetti sauces, while Imodium AD is positioned against the "white stuff" and the "pink stuff." Product advertisements do not have to name a competitor, however, to be positioned based on competition. Tide claims to "clean better" and Avis says, "We Try Harder" suggesting the "place" of the products in comparison with all other brands in the product category. The ad shown for Clorox Wipes is clearly positioned against its major competitor.
- Symbol—Occasionally, companies use a symbol or icon to position their product in the minds of consumers. Over time, the symbol can become synonymous with the company or product, as with the Maytag Man, the golden arches of McDonald's (or Ronald McDonald), the Pillsbury Doughboy, the Jolly Green Giant, and, of course, the Nike swoosh. In each of these cases, most adult consumers have a clear image about the product or company by merely seeing the symbol.

Repositioning
Is the process of creating a new image about an existing product in consumers' minds.

As the needs of companies, competitors, and consumers evolve over time, brand positions may also need to change. This process of creating a new image about an existing product in consumers' minds is called **repositioning**. Repositioning, which involves changing existing attitudes and beliefs about a product, is much more difficult and costly than establishing a position for a new product, and companies have tried it with different degrees of success. One successful repositioning story comes from PepsiCo's Mountain Dew, first considered a "hillbilly" drink when it was introduced in the 1960s. After changing the targeted market and the way it appealed to the market in 1992, sales rose dramatically. By 1997, Mountain Dew was in the number-four position in the carbonated-drink market, ahead of Coca-Cola Company's Sprite, now ranked fifth. The success of Mountain Dew in the highly competitive soft-drink market is attributed to a consistent, strong image that links teenagers, the major market segment, with the outdoors, outrageousness, high energy, and the drink's ability to quench thirst.[32]

More recently, Procter & Gamble has been repositioning its Pert shampoo against successful competitor Suave by changing the image to "lighter and livelier" and by cutting the price. Makers of the 30-year-old Mr. Coffee coffeemaker are repositioning that brand to appeal to a younger market by retaining MTV star Carson Daly and snowboarder Christ Klug as spokespersons. Are these two efforts likely to work?

Develop and Implement Appropriate Marketing Mix and Monitor, Evaluate, and Control

The final steps in the target-market selection process are to develop and implement a marketing mix matched to the needs of the target market and evaluate and control the plan. This means developing a specific plan of action and timeline—who will do what, when, where, how, and why. Concrete and measurable indicators of marketing effectiveness, such as sales and consumer perceptions, must be specified for each marketing-mix component and continually monitored and evaluated at predetermined times to assess effectiveness of the marketing mix in meeting desired plan objectives. New segments, new needs, and new opportunities may be identified through continual monitoring of target markets and changes in the mix may be made accordingly.

Segmenting Business Markets

4 LEARNING OBJECTIVE

The previous section discussed segmenting and targeting individual consumer markets. As with consumer markets, business marketers often need to segment their markets. As explained in Chapter 7, key factors that distinguish business markets from household consumer markets are the nature of the customer and how that customer uses the product. For example, Weyerhaeuser makes wood products, such as particleboard. It can sell this product to furniture manufacturers for building furniture, or it can sell the product directly to lumber yards for sale to household consumers. Each of these business customers has a different set of needs for the particleboard. An understanding of each of the two markets will help Weyerhaeuser tailor an effective marketing mix that will satisfy each customer's needs.

Segmenting the business market can help a firm analyze the market, select the best markets for targeting, and manage marketing programs.[33] While the steps in the target-market selection process are essentially the same for business markets as those shown in Figure 8.5, there are three major differences in segmenting business markets. Those differences include the following:

- The purchasing process, which differs greatly from the household consumer market.
- The use of different segmentation variables.
- The differences in how the segmentation is implemented.

The business-to-business purchase process was discussed in detail in Chapter 7. This section explains the way business markets are segmented.[34] The segmentation variables used to segment business markets include demographics, operating characteristics, purchasing approaches, product usage, situational factors, and buyers' personal characteristics.

Demographics

The demographic components of the business market include the *industry*, the *size* and *growth* potential, and the *location* of the targeted firm's operations. Although some firms sell products to companies in the same industries, such as Nike selling shoes to Foot Locker or Footaction USA, some companies sell products to many different industries. Xerox, for example, sells its copiers to businesses in all industries, ranging from small independent restaurants to multinational heavy-equipment manufacturers. By grouping segments into industry types, the selling firm can learn more about an industry in order to better develop a marketing mix that will help solve the market's needs.

Selling firms may need to segment their business markets by company size and tailor their marketing efforts accordingly. For example, Xerox would certainly not devote the same resources to selling a copier to one restaurant in a small town as it would to selling thousands of machines to an international corporation. Finally, location is often an important descriptor for segmenting business markets. The proximity of the segment to sales offices or manufacturing facilities, or the geographic concentration of the market segment, may substantially affect marketing efforts.

Operating Characteristics

The operating characteristics of a business include *company technology*, *product* and *brand-user status*, and *customer capabilities*. Obviously, the product type and brand a business uses affects the way in which a selling firm will market the product to that business. Also, a supplying firm may want to approach loyal or heavy product users differently than it approaches infrequent product users. The business customer's technology and capabilities will also affect the types of products that firm buys and what it needs from supplying firms and thus may serve as a segmentation basis. For example, the computer needs of a large multinational firm with its own extensive, in-house computing specialists would differ greatly from those of a small-town restaurant. A firm selling computers to these two distinctively different markets would need to tailor the marketing mix to the specific needs of each.

Purchasing Approaches

Firms purchase goods and services in a variety of ways. The approach a firm takes with purchasing decisions may be distinguished by the *level in the organization* at which products are purchased; *purchasing policies; purchasing criteria,* such as the speed of delivery; the size of the order; and the *nature of the buyer-seller relationship*. A firm's purchase process, the policies and criteria for purchasing, and how formalized or centralized the process is can each affect a customer's special needs. For example, a large fast-food restaurant may purchase products at its main headquarters and disperse those products to each individual member of the chain, or each store may buy certain products individually. Each of the two purchasing approaches requires different marketing tactics from suppliers. Different type of firms and specific policies for purchasing also require special marketing efforts. Some private firms and governmental agencies often require bids on all purchases over a set dollar figure or require that prices be based on supplier cost.

The stage in the purchase process can also serve as a basis for segmenting business markets. There are three distinct stages that may each represent a different market segment, regardless of the industry. These stages are first-time prospects, novices or new users, and sophisticates or long-time users.[35] Buyers in each of these buying categories have a different set of needs that the supplying firm can fulfill, so marketing mixes customized to the needs of each segment should be developed.

New Face of America

The face of America has changed dramatically over the past few decades. As the table below reveals, a sizable proportion of the population is non-Caucasian: Latino, African-American, Asian, multicultural, and even Native American. The ratio of ethnics to Caucasians will continue to shrink, as age-distribution statistics indicate that the proportion of the non-Caucasian population in age groups under 34 is much greater. The statistics also show other differences between the non-Caucasian ethnic groups. Asians, for example, have the highest average income and education level, Native Americans are poorest, and Latinos are least likely to have a high school diploma. The map of the U.S. below reveals another difference—geographic location of non-Caucasian ethnic groups in the U.S. Note the concentrations of African-Americans in the southern and eastern regions of the U.S., of Latinos west of the Mississippi River, and of Native Americans in Oklahoma, Arizona, Alaska, and the north-central U.S. To confuse the issue even more, clear differences within ethnic groups exist as well. For example, the Asian population comprises Koreans, Japanese, Vietnamese, and Chinese, among others, with each group having a different language. The Latino subculture is just as diverse, with members who originate from Mexico, Puerto Rico, and Central America, among other countries.

For marketers, the increasing diversity of the U.S. represents both a challenge and a competitive advantage. Considering that the spending power among Latinos, African-Americans, and Asians alone is expected to reach more than $1.2 trillion by 2007, those firms able to segment and respond to the needs of the different groups best will be the major winners. To better market to these different ethnic groups, some companies, such as Frito-Lay, Kraft, and DaimlerChrysler, have created organizational divisions or teams specifically charged with targeting various ethnic and urban groups and are substantially increasing spending on ethnic marketing. Just a few specific ethnic marketing efforts under way by selected companies are:

Latinos
- Frito-Lay is targeting Latinos in urban areas with a line of snacks, Sabritas, that feature the flavors found most appealing to Latinos: chili, citrus, and cheese.
- General Mills' Haagen-Dazs brand has developed a caramel-and-cream ice cream called Dulce de Leche.
- Gatorade has launched a line of Xtremo sports drinks with flavors such as mango and tropical punch.
- Kraft has introduced mayonnaise with lemon and gelatin with milk products called Mayonesa con Limon and Gelatina par Leche, respectively.

Asians:
- Under the Stockpot brand, Campbell's Soup has added three Asian-flavor broths and soups, including a Vietnamese broth known as pho.
- Unilever has launched a line of Asian-flavor dishes under the Lipton brand.
- EthnicGrocer.com (**http://www.ethnicgrocer. com**) sells Japanese, Thai, and Indian meal kits.

continues

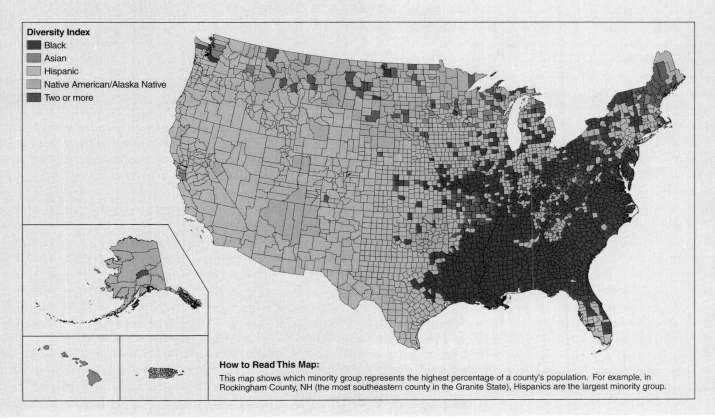

Diversity Index
- Black
- Asian
- Hispanic
- Native American/Alaska Native
- Two or more

How to Read This Map:
This map shows which minority group represents the highest percentage of a county's population. For example, in Rockingham County, NH (the most southeastern county in the Granite State), Hispanics are the largest minority group.

- Charles Schwab & Co. has employees in its call centers who speak different Asian languages.
- Honda is targeting Chinese and Koreans with in-language ads using Chinese calligraphy.

African-Americans
- Pepsi has replaced pop star Britney Spears with Destiny's Child R&B singer Beyoncé Knowles, who appeals to a broader market.
- Kmart uses targeted brands, location, and a new campaign featuring Chakka Khan and BeBe Winans.

Sources: "Vendor News," *DSN Retailing Today*, 10 June 2002, 59.
Hassan Fattah, "Asia Rising," *American Demographics*, July/August 2002, 38–42.
Rebecca Johnson, "Frito's More Inclusive Party," *Advertising Age*, 3 June 2002, S-2.
Alison Stein Wellner and John Fetto, "Our True Colors," *American Demographics*, November 2002, S2-S20.
Debra Aho Williamson, "Foreign Flavors, Mainstream Taste," *Advertising Age*, 8 July 2002, 2–3.

	Total	Latinos	African-Americans	Asians	Native Americans	Caucasians	Multi-cultural
Percentage of the Total Population*		12.5	12.3	3.6	0.9	75.1	2.4
Income Level:							
< $25,000	28.7	36.4	42.9	22.3	41.7	27.6	35.4
$25,000–$49,999	29.4	32.7	29.2	24.2	30.5	27.7	30.3
$50,000–$74,999	19.5	16.5	15.4	19.0	15.8	18.8	17.4
$75,000–$99,999	10.2	7.5	6.8	12.5	6.6	11.4	8.3
$100,000 +	12.3	7.0	5.6	21.9	5.4	14.8	8.7
Average Income:	$42,228	$33,565	$29,470	$53,635	$30,599	$44,517	$35,587
Education Level:							
Less than HS diploma	19.6	47.6	27.7	19.6	29.1	16.4	26.7
HS graduate	28.6	22.1	29.8	15.8	29.2	29.5	25.2
Some college	21.0	15.6	22.5	14.0	23.6	21.5	22.0
Associate's degree	6.3	4.3	5.8	6.6	6.6	6.5	6.6
Bachelor's degree	15.5	6.7	9.5	26.7	7.6	16.6	12.6
Graduate degree	8.9	3.8	4.8	17.4	3.9	9.5	7.0
Age Distribution:							
Gen Z (< 5)	7.0	10.5	8.1	6.5	8.6	6.1	13.9
Gen Y (5–24)	29.01	37.9	34.8	28.6	37.0	26.2	39.7
Gen X (25–34)	14.4	18.4	14.9	18.9	15.1	13.4	14.6
Baby Boomers (35–54)	29.1	23.4	27.7	30.6	27.4	30.4	21.9
Empty Nesters (55–64)	8.4	4.8	6.8	7.6	6.4	9.5	4.9
Seniors (65 +)	12.0	4.9	8.1	7.8	5.6	14.4	5.0

*The percentage of the total population of all groups totals more than 100% because some respondents were evaluated under multiple ethnic groups.

Product Use or Usage Situation

The way in which a product is used by a business and the level of service a customer needs can also determine the marketing efforts required to effectively reach that business market. Weyerhaeuser's sale of particleboard to different markets, mentioned at the beginning of this section, is an example of product-use segmentation. The Ryan's Family Steakhouse chain has a service technician who visits each site and maintains equipment, such as ice makers, while a single, independent restaurant in a small town may need the equipment seller to maintain that equipment. Accordingly, selling firms can devise different marketing plans based on different needs for services from the supplying firm.[36]

Situational Factors

As with household-consumer market segmentation, a myriad of temporary, situational factors can affect purchasing needs of the business-to-business market. Most obviously, special product uses and special physical distribution requirements, such as order size and urgency of delivery, can affect the purchase process, and thus serve as bases for segmenting the market.

Buyers' Personal Characteristics

Finally, the individual personal characteristics of the participants in the purchase process can influence a buyer's needs. For example, some buyers are afraid to take risks and require a lot of time and information to make a decision, or a buyer could have a brother-in-law who also sells the needed product. In the first case, the supplier may need to develop a marketing mix that provides this type of buyer with testimonials and substantial evidence of product benefits to reassure the buyer, while in the second case, the supplier may not want to waste valuable resources targeting this buyer.

As with segmenting consumer markets, a combination of these segmentation variables are generally needed to draw a profile of business-market segments. Once the potentially profitable segments are profiled, specialized marketing-mix programs can be implemented to meet their special needs and the plan can be monitored, evaluated, and controlled.

Segmenting Global Markets

5 LEARNING OBJECTIVE

Increasingly, companies must reach out to foreign countries to prosper as opportunities for domestic growth in many industries decline. Just as in domestic markets, firms must understand who their customers are through market segmentation and match the marketing mix they deliver with the needs of their customers before entering these new global markets.

In general, the target-market selection process and the segmentation descriptors are the same for global markets as for household-consumer markets. Like domestic consumer markets, global markets may be segmented based on demographics, geographics, psychographics, benefits-sought, situation, and usage. A common approach is to segment international markets geographically by country, combined with the demographics or general lifestyle of the country, although some research indicates that combining geographics with consumer-purchase behavior patterns is preferable.[37] Other variables that are generally considered in defining homogeneous demand segments in international markets include economic, political/legal, and cultural factors.

Economic Factors

The country's stage of industrial development may affect the ability, willingness, capability, and purchase patterns of individuals in the market. For example, consumers in poorer developing countries spend proportionally more of their incomes on basic consumer goods and services, while consumers in more prosperous developing countries spend more on durable goods.

Political and Legal Factors

A country's political/legal environment may affect a firm's ability to market to its customers, so that specialized marketing programs must be revised to meet those requirements. For example, the French government requires that marketers get special permission from the Commission Nationale Informatique et Liberté before creating a customer database[38] and proposed legislation in Mexico would prohibit companies from sharing or selling customer information without specific customer permission.[39] The stability and type of government must also be considered in defining segments and determining the way in which products are marketed in different countries.

Cultural Factors

Culture and language can pose real challenges to firms targeting customers in different countries. Cultural and religious factors can also affect consumer needs for goods and services in ways that marketers must consider. The Islamic religion's proscriptions

Figure 8.14	Summary of Segment Variables by Marketing Type		
	Consumer Market	**Business Market**	**Global Market**
	Demographic	Demographic	Demographic
	Geographic	Operating Characteristics	Geographic
	Psychographic	Buyer's Personal Characteristics	Psychographic
	Benefits-Sought	Purchasing Approaches	Benefits-Sought
	Situation	Product Use/Usage Situation	Situation
	Behavior/Usage		Behavior/Usage
			Economic
			Political/Legal
			Cultural

for female dress would certainly affect a clothing firm's offerings in Muslim countries. Similarly, certain colors have different meanings in different countries. For example, white, a symbol of purity in America, is a symbol of death in Asian countries.

As with household-consumer markets and business markets, the best market-segment profiles are derived from a combination of segment variables. A summary of these variables for the consumer, business, and global markets is shown in Figure 8.14. However, firms deciding to target international markets may have difficulty finding the data needed to define segments. Many countries do not have a standardized routine census of citizens to provide reliable demographic and geodemographic data about potential consumers. Also, data needed for some segmentation variables are very difficult to obtain or nonexistent. Finally, an effective target-marketing program evaluates potential segments for profitability, then continuously monitors the effectiveness of both the marketing mix for meeting customer needs and the environment for opportunities and changes in the market.

Chapter Summary

Learning Objective 1: *Understand the basic concepts and importance of segmenting and targeting markets.* Successful firms must truly understand the markets they serve and match their marketing mix to the needs and wants of the market in a process called target marketing. A market is an individual, group of individuals, or organizations willing, able, and capable to purchase a firm's product. A market may be subdivided into any number of smaller markets, called segments. The number and the size of markets a firm may select for targeting can vary greatly from a mass market to one individual.

Learning Objective 2: *Explain advantages and disadvantages of segmentation and target marketing.* The target-marketing process is extremely important to businesses because it allows firms to identify and analyze their customers, develop tailored marketing mixes to meet customer needs, identify market demand, identify competition, increase operating efficiencies, improve product positioning, and identify opportunities. Despite these advantages, there are some disadvantages to target marketing. Most notably, some firms have targeted disadvantaged, poor, or uneducated consumers with illegal or unethical products; others have portrayed some market segments stereotypically and offensively; and in doing so both groups have created cynicism toward target-marketing practices. These firms may have actually inhibited brand popularity and loyalty, and wasted money and effort.

Learning Objective 3: *Identify and explain the process of target-market selection, including criteria for segmentation, bases for segmentation, profiling market* *segments, and positioning.* Nevertheless, the target-marketing process is important and begins with: (1) identifying the total market; (2) determining the need for segmentation based on criteria for segmentation, strategic factors, and external factors; and (3) determining the bases for segmentation using demographic, geographic, psychographic, benefits-sought, situation, and behavior (usage) descriptors. The firm must then collect segmentation data. These sources may be internal (from the company's database) or external (from research, other firms, or the government). The target-marketing process continues with the following steps: (4) profiling each selected segment; (5) assessing potential profitability of each segment and selecting segments for targeting; (6) selecting the positioning strategy on the basis of price/quality, product attributes, product user, product usage, product class, competition, or symbols; (7) developing and implementing an appropriate marketing mix; and (8) monitoring, evaluating, and controlling the selection process.

Learning Objective 4: *Appreciate how segmenting business markets differs from segmenting consumer markets.* Firms that target other businesses can segment their markets using the same process used in consumer market segmentation. However, the bases for segmentation for business markets include demographics, operating characteristics, purchasing approaches, product use or usage situations, situational factors, and buyers' personal characteristics.

Learning Objective 5: *Identify special considerations in segmenting global markets.* Targeting global markets also requires the same target-market selection process but has slightly different segmentation variables. Along with the consumer-market segmentation descriptors, global segments should be profiled using economic, political/legal, and cultural factors.

Key Terms

For interactive study: visit http://bestpractices.swlearning.com.

Behavior or usage segmentation, 250
Benefits-sought segmentation, 250
Concentrated strategy, 245
Data mining, 251
Demographic segmentation, 246
Differentiated strategy, 245
Family life cycle (FLC), 246
Geodemographics, 247
Geographic segmentation, 247
Heterogeneous demand, 236

Market, 236
Market segment, 236
Market segmentation, 236
Micromarketing, 237
Micromarkets, 237
Niche, 237
Niche marketing, 237
Perceptual map, 255
Positioning, 254
Profile, 252

Psychographic segmentation, 248
Repositioning, 256
Situation segmentation, 250
Target market, 236
Target marketing, 236
Undifferentiated targeting strategy, 245
80/20 principle, 250

Questions for Review and Discussion

1. Explain the four different size classifications of market segments on the segmentation continuum.

2. Explain advantages and disadvantages of target marketing. Would you recommend segmenting markets for potentially harmful products such as cigarettes? Why?

3. Explain the steps in the Target-Marketing Selection Process.

4. Select a market or product class, such as bottled water, and determine total sales for the market, competitors

in the market, and market share of each competitor in the market.

5. Using Figure 8.3 as a guideline, select and profile a target market for LitTalk, an audiotape copy of great literature, such as *Great Expectations* and *War and Peace,* covered in popular college literature textbooks. Use as many bases of segmentation variables as possible.

6. Since everyone drinks water, explain why you would or would not segment the "water" market if you were

selling Naya bottled water. What if you were selling prune juice? Justify your answers using the criteria for successful market segmentation.

7. Which segmentation variable(s) is most important? Why?

8. Find articles in the library or online that discuss the target market for a particular brand, such as Nike or Ralph Lauren, and profile the market for that brand. Include as many of the segmentation bases as possible.

9. Understanding what consumers are looking for in a product, or benefits sought, is an important way of segmenting markets. Ask five friends what they most want from their shampoo and then identify possible benefits-sought market segments for shampoo.

10. Find an advertisement that represents positioning based on each of the seven ways discussed in the chapter. Explain each selection.

11. Compare and contrast segmentation for consumer markets, business markets, and international markets.

In-Class Team Activities

1. Identify needs you may have as a college student that you think are not being met. Discuss the types of goods or services that could be developed to meet those needs.

2. Determine several likely segments for cosmetic surgery and profile each.

3. The toilet paper market is huge, but growth is stagnant and competition is fierce. This competitive environment has led some top manufacturers to develop new products to meet previously unfulfilled needs. For example, some companies have developed toilet paper with baking soda to absorb smells or added aloe for softness. The most recent trend in toilet paper is premoistened wipes. Develop a positioning strategy for a new premoistened toilet paper product.

Internet Questions

1. Profile your hometown by visiting the U.S. Census Bureau Web site at http://www.census.gov/main/www/access.html.

2. Visit http://www.visa.com and http://www.mastercard.com. How do these companies target college students? Explain your suggestions for improving their targeting efforts.

3. Visit http://www.gap.com and http://www.dior.com. Tell how each site successfully (or unsuccessfully) targets its unique market segment.

CHAPTER CASE

Fishing for New Markets

Traditionally, fishing and hunting enthusiasts gained their appreciation for these sports by growing up with the activities as a part of family life. Not the case with members of today's Generations X and Y, who may be more likely to think of "bass" as a type of guitar than a fish. In 2001, only 13% of 18- to 24-year-olds participated in these outdoor sports, as compared with a 20% participation rate in 1991. What's more, Latinos and African-Americans are even less likely to be involved in the sports than Caucasians. The number of days spent hunting and fishing each year has also declined from 25 in 1987 to 16.5 days in 2001.

A number of reasons may account for the decline in fishing and hunting among this age group. Most notably:

- A lack of time—modern families are often headed by either single mothers who work and raise their family alone or two parents, both of whom work. This often means that families rarely have time for outdoor activities after taking care of the normal day-to-day requirements.
- Sedentary lives—more and more, computers and television are mainstays of daily life. This devotion to electronics means that fewer hours are available for other activities, such as hunting and fishing.
- Competition for limited time—more and varied activities, ranging from video games to extreme sports, exist today than in the past, and each competes for the limited amount of time available to the 18- to 24-year-old segment.
- Crowding out of exurban areas—many previously available hunting and fishing grounds are being incorporated into cities and developed. This means a decreasing supply of public lands available for such outdoor activities.

Even with the decline in numbers of people participating in fishing and hunting, 53.8 million people participated in these sports in 2001, mostly Caucasian men over the age of 34, generating $70 billion in revenue. With such large revenues at stake and future participants uninvolved, many fishing- and hunting-related businesses and enthusiasts worry about getting young people interested in these activities again. A few programs across the nation have begun in response to this concern. For example, organizations as diverse as Disney and the U. S. Forest Service have sponsored "camping" trips for urban youth to encourage outdoor activities, The National Wild Turkey Federation transports more than 7,000 urban youth to its conventions annually, the Recreational Boating and Fishing Foundation and the Ohio Division of Wildlife have run ads of a young boy begging, "Take me fishing—because I'm growing up too fast," and the Big City Mountaineers take inner-city teens in Miami on fishing and camping trips. These efforts to attract young consumers to fishing and hunting have met with some success, but industry experts are still concerned that unless more boys and girls of all backgrounds become involved in these outdoor activities, the industry will surely die.

Case Questions

1. Would you advise fishing and hunting industry marketing officials to segment the market based on age? Why? What segmentation descriptors would you suggest using other than age?
2. Thinking about each element of the marketing mix, how would you advise fishing and hunting industry officials to market fishing and hunting activities to 18- to 24-year-old males and females of all socioeconomic and ethnic backgrounds?
3. How would you position the fishing and hunting industry to better appeal to 18- to 24-year-olds?

Source: Pamela Paul and Katarzyna Dawidowska, "Hook & Bait," *American Demographics* (November 2002), 36–39.

VIDEO CASE

Who Wants a Krispy Kreme? Everyone!

It's a scene repeated numerous times around the United States—and now in Canada and Australia as well. Eager customers line up hours in advance, waiting for the newest Krispy Kreme Doughnut store to open. When the doors open at 5:30 in the morning, they rush in to be the first to enjoy the Hot Original Glazed doughnuts as they come out of the oven. Local television news teams and radio personalities will be on hand to cover the event. In the store's first week, it will sell as many doughnuts as most of its rivals sell in a year.

"I think we have tremendous customer loyalty, and it's the result of 65 years of brand equity, starting with a one-of-a-kind taste treat," explains Stan Parker, senior vice president of marketing for Krispy Kreme. "We had a man in Springfield, Missouri, camp out for 12 days to be the first in line to get a hot doughnut."

Started in 1937 in the Southeast, the Krispy Kreme chain remained a southern secret for almost 50 years. Travelers spread the word about the melt-in-your mouth confections, and in 1995 the North Carolina-based company began a national expansion program. By mid-2003, the company was selling more than 7.5 million doughnuts every day in more than 290 company-owned and franchise stores in 38 states, Canada, and Australia. Fans can also find Krispy Kreme donuts at select "off premises" locations like grocery and convenience stores.

So who's buying all these doughnuts? Extensive research revealed that "Our customer is everyone, everywhere," says Parker. "Kids of all ages enjoy them." In the morning, a dad buys breakfast for himself, a mom takes a dozen to share with coworkers, or a salesperson delivers several dozen of the sweet treats to clients. Later in the day, that same mom rewards her son for doing well on a spelling test. In the early evening, the soccer team celebrates its latest win. These family traditions arose naturally. "It's not something we went out and created," Parker points out.

Jimmy Strickland, franchise owner and the area developer for western Missouri and the state of Kansas, agrees. "Demographically, we certainly appeal to families," he says. "The whole 'doughnut theater,' being able to see the whole process happening—we're not marketing to one particular segment, one particular group or income. Our product crosses all boundaries." The Kansas City area, for example has 28 municipalities and is very segmented geographically. The broad product appeal—very few people don't like the taste of Krispy Kreme—creates a regional draw; the average customer drives seven miles to get a Krispy Kreme doughnut.

To select new store sites, Strickland first looks at car counts. "We try to have at least 35,000 cars a day [pass] in front of our stores," he says. Next is household income; the ideal is not too high or low, in the $45,000 to 50,000 range. Because families incorporate the Krispy Kreme experience into other activities, store developers want a certain number of homes and retail businesses in the neighboring area. For example, after seeing a movie or going shopping, the family can then stop by Krispy Kreme for doughnuts. It becomes part of a planned event. Locations near family-oriented stores such as Toys "R" Us and Babies "R" Us draw well.

The company uses its broad appeal in its low-key marketing strategy. It has no national advertising budget, but instead emphasizes local grassroots marketing, public relations, and community relations. Prior to opening a store in a new market, Krispy Kreme boxes off hot doughnuts to radio and television stations and newspaper offices. Programs like its good grades program, which gives a free doughnut for every A on a child's report card, create goodwill and bring families back. Krispy Kreme stores sponsor youth sports teams in local markets, handing out doughnuts to players who stop by in uniform after the game. Non-profit groups can buy doughnuts at a discounted price to sell at fundraisers. Tours for school groups are very popular. Children love watching the in-store doughnut factory, where they can see how doughnuts are shaped, baked, and glazed. Kids get their own Krispy Kreme paper hats and "make" a donut, dipping it in glaze and sprinkles.

The universality of Krispy Kreme doughnuts was proven yet again in 1999, when the company opened its first California stores. How would health-conscious southern Californians react to the sugary treats? Surprisingly, they loved them, and southern California has become one of Krispy Kreme's most successful markets. Likewise, Canadians and Australians have embraced the Krispy Kreme experience.

"As we enter a market, we look at what plays and what doesn't," explains Steve Bumgarner, director of marketing. "Krispy Kreme is about the hot doughnut experience; that is core to the brand and won't change. Things that are "extended" personality—heritage, history, Americana—we may play up in certain markets." For example, in Japan, Americana would be a draw, whereas it wouldn't be in Canada. "We stay true country to country, city to city," he says. When the company opened its first stores in New York City, it reached out to southern transplants, interviewing them about where they had their first Krispy Kreme doughnuts. This publicity generated interest, so that New Yorkers flocked to the stores to try Krispy Kreme for themselves.

Krispy Kreme's popularity is tied to the brand's emotional appeal. "Walk into a Krispy Kreme store and people are always smiling," Parker says. They want to share the Krispy Kreme experience, like the Canadian who had tasted a Krispy Kreme in Texas. When the company opened its first Canadian store outside Toronto, he was so excited that he brought his friends to the store to share in the Krispy Kreme experience.

"People from all walks of life and different nationalities come into our stores and wax rhapsodic about the doughnuts," comments company CEO Scott Livengood. "Our product doesn't really skew toward any particular demographic group. We're a reflection of America, a universal product. It's a pretty simple experience."

Case Questions

1. Describe Krispy Kreme's approach to market segmentation. Where on the continuum of market segmentation (Figure 8.1) does it lie? Do you think this is an appropriate strategy for this company? Explain your answer using the five criteria for successful segmentation.

2. How does Jimmy Strickland apply segmentation variables when choosing new store locations in Kansas City? Which factors are most important to Krispy Kreme?

3. How should Krispy Kreme approach its global markets in terms of market segmentation and target marketing?

Sources: Adapted from material in the video: *Market Segmentation and Consumer Behavior: Who Is Eating All Those Krispy Kreme Doughnuts?*

Carlye Adler, "Would You Pay $2 Million For This Franchise?" *Fortune Small Business*, 1 May 2002, http://www.fortune.com, accessed June 2003.

Krispy Kreme corporate Web site, http://www.krispykreme.com; accessed 9 June 2003.

Andy Serwer, "The Hole Story," *Fortune*, 7 July 2003, pp. 53–62.

From David Shook and Scott Livengood, "His Doughnut Stores Are His 'Children'," *Business Week Online*, 9 December 2002, http://www.businessweek.com, accessed June 2003.

In Chapter 9, **Abbie Griffin**, University of Illinois at Urbana-Champaign, presents strategies for new product development that include uncovering unmet consumer needs and problems, developing a competitively advantaged product, and shepherding products through the firm. Professor Griffin then explores how marketers reinforce a product's competitive position in the minds of consumers through branding, packaging, and labeling and then manage a product through its life cycle.

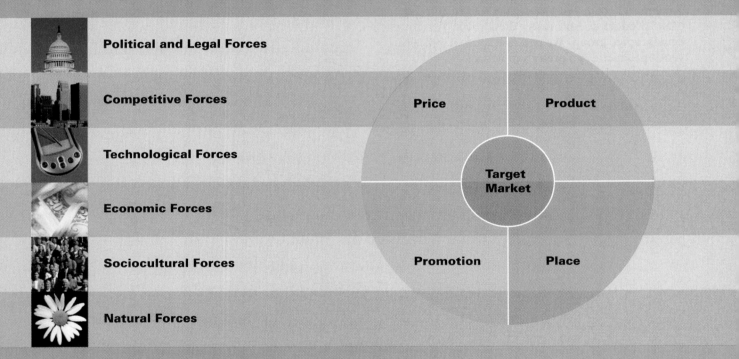

Political and Legal Forces

Competitive Forces

Technological Forces

Economic Forces

Sociocultural Forces

Natural Forces

Price

Product

Target Market

Promotion

Place

With much of the world economy dominated by the service sector, Chapter 10 focuses on the unique challenges involved in marketing and managing service operations. In this chapter, **Douglas Hoffman**, Colorado State University, emphasizes that businesses with unmatched, unparalleled customer service can experience a strategic competitive advantage in the marketplace.

Part 3

Product Strategy

 Political and Legal Forces The events of September 11 have led JetBlue Airlines to develop an innovative strategy to manage passenger stress, which has been heightened since the terrorists' attacks. JetBlue passengers are now provided with instructional cards on how to perform "Airplane Yoga" to ease their anxieties.

 Competitive Forces British Airways uses its servicescape to differentiate itself from the competition by featuring the first fully flat bed for passengers traveling business class.

 Technological Forces Wave Pick Technology has enabled L.L. Bean to fulfill 100% of its orders within 24 hours from order to delivery. The company is held in high esteem as a best-practices example of excellence in order fulfillment processes.

 Economic Forces Due to rising labor costs and lower customer discretionary spending, gross margins have been reduced to 5–10% in many industries. This has led many companies to take a serious look at which of their customers are the most profitable, with plans to treat them accordingly.

 Sociocultural Forces Americans love their pets and marketers have responded accordingly. DogFriendly.com (**http://www.dogfriendly.com**) has published the California and Nevada Dog Travel Guide. The guide includes dog-friendly accommodations, emergency veterinarians, and attractions such as parks, beaches, and stores that allow dogs to accompany their owners.

 Natural Forces Traditional electric water heaters consume 20% of the average annual household's energy expenditure, resulting in an expenditure of approximately $450 for the average household. Envirotech Systems Worldwide, Inc. has developed an award-winning tankless water heater that heats water on demand and significantly decreases the costs of and energy used by traditional water heaters.

Marketing's Role in New Product Development and Product Decisions

While designing the new Palm Pilot, 3Com obtained input from potential customers and then used reliable, existing technology to produce a means for handwritten input. Next, the Palm team integrated the product with other computer and software products, so that the Palm functioned as part of a system to solve customer problems of capturing, organizing, and communicating information. Then, the developers of the Palm supported the positioning of the product through its choice of branding and packaging strategies. Finally, the makers of the Palm expanded the Palm line to reach other market segments with slightly different needs. Consequently, 3Com perceives its Palm line as very successful.

You Decide. After reading the opening vignette and paying special attention to the sections of this chapter marked with the chess piece, answer these questions:

1. The success of new products can be evaluated using four items that span three dimensions. Which item has 3Com most likely used to measure the success of the Palm line?

2. Which of the three product-development activities most likely presented the greatest challenge to 3Com prior to introducing the Palm Pilot?

3. What has been the most important product decision the Palm creators have made?

© Novastock/Index Stock Imagery

New Product Development: The Evolution of the Palm

The Newton personal digital assistant (PDA) was conceived by the advanced research group at Apple, evolving out of their development effort to eliminate keyboard entry into computers. The Newton's core benefit proposition (CBP) was to capture, organize, and communicate ideas and data, without requiring keyboard entry.[1] The advanced research group and Apple management defined Newton's form and features without first asking how people in the target market were capturing information and what unsolved problems remained. In the end, Apple found that the $800 asking price bought a lot of pens, Post-it® Notes, paper, calendars, and even electronic address books. Newton did not solve peoples' remaining information-use problems in a cost-effective way. Newton sales were dismal, and the product ultimately was withdrawn from the market.

Contrast Newton's failure to the runaway success of the Palm Pilot (now known as the "Palm"), another PDA. The Palm's CBP also captures, organizes, and communicates ideas. However, the Palm provides value to customers not only by replacing paper or electronic address books and calendars, but also by replacing computer-based time-management systems. Individuals are therefore willing to pay the $200 to $400 purchase price. The product is so successful that it has spawned a whole host of look-alike competitors.

Why was the Palm successful while the Newton was a dismal failure? There are three major differences between the Newton and the Palm, each of which contributed to the Palm's success. First, the Palm team obtained input from potential customers while developing the design. For example, they obtained size and carrying reactions from one of the employees in the business development group: He wore Brooks Brothers shirts, which have the smallest pockets of any major shirtmaker. Additionally, the Palm's buttons, which allow users to switch instantly from one application to another, say from the calendar to the to-do list, are arranged according to information gathered from customers about the frequency of use for each application.

Second, the handwriting-recognition technology in the Palm, although less sophisticated than Newton's, works much more effectively. Palm users must learn a simple, but rather intuitive, alphabet (called "Graffiti") to make written inputs. For example, writing "⌐" with the stylus produces a "t." Palm created a product from proven technologies that requires users to modify writing behavior to conform to a standard form, but that works reliably when they do so.

The third success contributor is that the Palm seamlessly integrates with other standard products, including both computers and software. The development team thought through solutions to peripheral details of information-management problems, rather than just thinking of the PDA as the total answer. The PDA was one piece in a full system that solved the full set of problems around capturing, organizing, and communicating information. The data-exchange cradle and desktop software create a system that functions effectively, both in and away from the office. Overall, by soliciting customer input to guide the design, using proven technology to deliver the design, and ensuring seamless integration with other already available products, the Palm was quickly accepted (with sales of more than one million units by year three) in a way the Newton never was.

Palm not only designed an effective and useful new product, it also supported the positioning of the product in the market through its branding and packaging strategies—some of the product-management decisions marketing makes. Palm created a brand, the original "Palm Pilot," which was evocative of the

LEARNING OBJECTIVES

After you have completed this chapter, you should be able to:

1. *Classify products by who the buyer is and the purpose for which the product is being bought.*

2. *Understand the benefits associated with creating a portfolio of products that provides appropriate product depth and width for your target customers.*

3. *Define new and successful products and understand why products fail so that the stage for successful product development is set.*

4. *Develop successful new products through uncovering unmet needs, using proven development methods, and managing the project through the organization's infrastructure.*

5. *Make decisions about brand names, packaging, and labeling.*

6. *Manage products for profitability from their introduction through growth and into maturity and decline.*

VOICE OF THE EXPERT
Abbie Griffin, University of Illinois at Urbana-Champaign

Without a product, there is no firm. Without new products, there is no growth. Without growth, there is no shareholder value. Thus, the long-term basis for the success of a firm relies on its ability not only to market one product well, but also to continue to grow and prosper by developing new products for the marketplace. This chapter provides information about how to develop and then manage successful new products through their life cycle to profitably contribute to the growth of the firm and drive shareholder value.

For many marketers, product development is a transitional assignment. It is one of the major ways that marketers obtain functional breadth as they grow into general management positions. All marketers, however, will benefit from a strong understanding of the new-product-development process and product-management issues that you'll study in this chapter.

product's purpose and size (packaging)—it piloted you through your day, while fitting in the palm of your hand.

But the Palm team didn't stop there. The original Palm used a simple yet effective design philosophy with intuitive interfaces to deliver a clearly defined and somewhat narrowly focused set of benefits to the target market—business professionals with complex schedules, networks, and lives. While the original Palm Pilot has been retired, the product line has expanded over time to reach other segments with slightly different needs, which has allowed the Palm portfolio of products to continue to grow sales over the product life cycle. For example, the Palm IIIx targeted those with higher performance needs (more storage, more interactivity). The Palm V is more aesthetically streamlined, with increased screen contrasts. Its more sophisticated packaging appeals to more mature and upscale business professionals. Business professionals requiring continual wireless contact are targeted by the Palm VII, which is positioned between two-way pagers and wireless Internet–accessing laptops. The M100 and M105 are "cooler" Palm models with functions, features, and prices more appropriate for teenagers and college students—whose lives seem to be more complicated than ever. Finally, the new Tungsten, with a color screen, collapsible chassis, and further enhanced performance is the next platform to appeal to those wanting the highest levels of performance.

The Palm story is an excellent example of a business unit that set the stage for product success by first uncovering customer needs, and then developing a competitively advantaged product that delivered effective, obvious answers to those needs. The company followed up by creating a brand name and package that appealed to the target market and captured the essence of the product's purpose. Finally, Palm has developed a portfolio of products over time that spreads the brand's appeal from the initial target market to many others, which has allowed the division to grow, profit, and prosper over the life cycle of the product, even in the face of numerous entering competitors.

Products

Are the set of features, functions, and benefits that customers purchase. Products can be goods, services, people, places, and ideas.

Features

Are the way that benefits are delivered to customers. Features provide the solution to customer problems.

Brands

Are the name, representative symbol or design, or any other feature that identifies one firm's product as distinct from another firm's. Trademark is the legal term for a brand. Brands may be associated with one product, a family of products, or with all of the products sold by a firm.

This chapter provides information about new product development and product management decisions. It begins with information about different kinds of products, definitions of product newness and new product success, and managing product portfolios. The chapter then discusses how to set the stage for achieving new product success and the steps necessary for developing competitively advantaged products. Marketing decisions about product branding, packaging, and labeling are also presented. The chapter ends with a discussion of managing products through their life cycle.

LEARNING OBJECTIVE 1

Classifying Products

Products[2] are the core of every organization. Whether it be a good, service, person, place, or idea, organizations need a product to offer. In general, products offer customers a bundle of benefits that address a set of needs. The benefits may include the product's **features**, its package and **brand** name, the service that supports product performance, on-time delivery, courteous and effective customer relations, an adequate warranty, and so on. Over time, customers choose products with the set of features that deliver the maximum benefit for them. Based on differences in markets, buyer attitudes and motivations, purchase patterns, and product characteristics, products can be categorized into several groups, with important implications for marketing-mix decisions.

In general, products can be classified as either consumer or business-to-business products, depending on *who the buyer is* and *for what purpose the product is being bought*. If a consumer purchases a product for his or her own household use, the product is called a *consumer product*. Consumer products are classified further into categories based on how the consumer views and shops for the product. Products purchased by organizations to be used in producing other products or in operating their businesses are classified as *business-to-business products*. Business-to-business products are further divided into categories based on how the products will be used.

Consumer Products

Examples and the marketing-mix implications of the four kinds of consumer products are summarized in Figure 9.1.

- *Convenience products* are typically inexpensive items consumers purchase with little effort that are used on a frequent basis. Consumers spend little time shopping for convenience products.
- *Shopping products* are more expensive than convenience products, so the decision to purchase them is more important. The consumer will spend more time searching for information before selecting a particular brand, and compare prices and benefits among brands offering similar features.

Classifications and Marketing-Mix Considerations for Consumer Products   Figure 9.1

Marketing-Mix Considerations	Consumer Product Type			
	Convenience	**Shopping**	**Specialty**	**Unsought**
Product Examples	Soda and other soft drinks, milk, toothpaste, soap	Clothing, computers, appliances, furniture	Luxury items: Rolex watch, Jaguar cars	Insurance, medical trauma services
Consumer Attitudes	Low involvement, minimize time and decision effort, feature and price focus	Moderate to high involvement, balance between image and features/functionality	Very high involvement, image (brand) far more important than features	Unaware, possibly avoiding learning about category
Consumer Purchase Behavior	Frequent purchases, no planning, routine decisions	Less frequent purchases, planned shopping, compare along multiple dimensions	Infrequent purchases, special purchase effort, little brand comparison	Infrequent purchases, comparison shopping (features and brand) when made aware of need to purchase
Place (Distribution)	Widespread, with convenient locations	A large number of more selective outlets	Limited and exclusive, few outlets per market	More selective outlets, from few to many
Price	Inexpensive, low price	More expensive, moderate price	Very expensive, high price	Varies
Promotion	Mass communication, focus on price, availability, awareness	Mass communication and personal selling, focus on features, differentiation	Targeted communication, stress brand and status	Aggressive ads to create awareness, personal selling to close sale

Installations such as chemical facilities are customized, expensive, and purchased infrequently. The selling process is typically longer, more complex, and more challenging than for other business-to-business products.

© Benelux Pres/Index Stock Imagery

- *Specialty products* are high-involvement consumer purchases, where the product reflects the consumer's personality or self-image. Thus, consumers are willing to spend a great deal of time to acquire one particular brand. Substitutes are not an option.
- *Unsought products* are either unknown or known to the buyer but are not being actively sought at this point in time. Consumers do not search for unsought products until they need or are made aware of the products.

Business-to-Business Products

The five categories of business-to-business products vary in how they are used, as well as the closeness, or strength, of the relationship between the buyer and seller, as explained in Chapter 7.

- *Raw materials* are unprocessed products that become part of a company's finished goods. Almost all raw materials are commodities. Farm products such as milk, eggs, corn, wheat, and processed sugar are considered raw materials for the food industry, as are oil and gas for the chemical and petroleum industries. Because there is little or no differentiation between sellers, buyer-seller transactions are conducted at arm's length.
- *Supplies* are used to support business operations, but are not part of the finished product. Supplies are standardized, purchased often, and are inexpensive compared to other product categories. Examples include pens, paper, Post-it® Notes, cleaning solutions, and lubricating oil. Buyer-seller interactions for supplies are arm's length, with little or no ongoing relationship between the firms.
- *Accessories* are usually standardized pieces of equipment that support the overall running of factories and businesses. They are purchased more frequently than installations (described below), but far less frequently than supplies. Examples include printers, copiers, retail display cases, and delivery trucks. While accessories frequently are bought through arm's-length transactions, some firms have developed stronger relationships with one or two suppliers to try to reduce overall costs. For example, USX (formerly US Steel) has a long-term supply relationship with Compaq for all the firm's PCs.

- *Component parts and materials* are products that are partly assembled or already processed to be ready for assembly into the finished product. Hamburger patties, buns, ketchup, onions, and pickles are all component parts/materials for both McDonald's and Burger King. Tires, seats, and engines are components used in manufacturing new automobiles. Firms are trending toward closer buyer-seller relationships with their suppliers of components and materials, using relationship marketing to try to capture competitive advantages through differentiation and product-design efficiencies.

- *Installations* are major capital goods. Usually, installations are customized, expensive, and purchased infrequently. Products such as buildings, laboratories, and major computer systems are all considered installations. The selling process is typically longer, more complex, and more challenging than for any other type of business-to-business product. The practices of relationship marketing are the norm for installations.

Managing the Product Portfolio

2 LEARNING OBJECTIVE

Few companies are successful by relying on a single product. Most companies manufacture and market a variety of products. This portfolio of products may be targeted to just one set of customers, or may target multiple segments. It can consist of products within just one product category, or products from multiple categories.

Product Mix Decisions[3]

All of the products a company markets can be thought of as its **product mix**. The mixture of products typically includes various items that are related in terms of the raw materials used to create them, the products' end uses, or the customers targeted. A group of related items in a company's product portfolio constitutes a **product line**. The following example illustrates the number of product-mix decisions marketers must make.

The Purex Corporation had a relatively small product mix when it opened its doors. The company primarily manufactured bleach and a few powdered laundry detergents. Over the years, through new-product development and acquisitions, Purex extended its product mix by offering fabric softeners (StaPuf®), fabric softener sheets (Toss'n Soft), Brillo® soap pads, Sweetheart soaps, Sweetheart Dish Liquid, Mildew Stain Remover, and sponge products (Dobie® pads). These products all relate to household cleaning.

The *product-mix width* is the number of different product lines a company offers. The width of Purex's product mix included detergents, fabric softeners, cleansers, scouring pads, bleach, dish liquids, soaps, ammonia, and toilet-bowl cleaners. The *product-mix depth* refers to the number of brands within each product line. The depth of Purex's detergent product line included Purex Powdered, Purex Liquid with Fabric Softener, Trend Powdered, Trend Liquid, Dutch Powdered, and Dutch Liquid.

Any company limits its growth potential if it chooses to concentrate on a single product line. Companies that offer multiple product lines enjoy numerous benefits:

- *Protection against competition:* If a company relies on one product for success, a competitor can enter the market, undercut its price, and steal market share. A company with more than one product line will not be devastated by the effects of a competitor's actions in any one particular area.

- *Increase growth and profits:* Companies offer more than one product line to boost market growth and company profits. If a product category is mature, with little to no growth, a company may find it difficult to increase its share and profits unless it is willing to spend more to take market share away from a competitor.

Product mix
Is the full set of a firm's products across all markets served.

Product line
Is the set of products a firm targets to one general market. These products are likely to share some common features and technology characteristics or be complementary products. They also are likely to share several elements of the marketing mix, such as distribution channels.

- *Offset sales fluctuations:* Companies that offer products with seasonal variations find that multiple product lines help to offset these fluctuations in sales.
- *Achieve greater impact:* Multiple product lines allow a company to achieve greater market impact. A company with multiple lines of products is often more important to both consumers and channel members.
- *Enable economical resource usage:* Multiple product lines enable the economical use of resources. Spreading operational costs over a series of products enables a manufacturer to reduce the average production and marketing costs for all of its products; this results in lower prices to customers.
- *Avoid obsolescence:* Companies offering more than one product line avoid becoming obsolete when one product line reaches the end of its life cycle.

LEARNING OBJECTIVE 3

Setting the Stage for Successful New Product Development

As we saw in the previous section, firms have many types of products they can choose to develop. To set the stage for new product development, three issues must be thoroughly examined: defining the type of new product to launch, establishing how its success will be measured, and anticipating potential reasons for possible failure.

Defining New Products

Line extensions
Are new products that are developed as variations of existing products.

The next time you are at a grocery store, go to the cereal section and count the number of cereals you do not recognize. Some of these products will be totally new types of cereals. Others are variants, or line extensions, of current products. **Line extensions** are new products developed as variations of existing products. Honey Nut Cheerios is a line extension of Cheerios. Walk around the store and look at the packages that declare a product is "New and Improved." One dimension of newness is how new a product is in the eyes of the market. This can range from small, incremental changes to improve one aspect of performance or to provide choice variety, to totally new types of products that solve problems never before solved for consumers.

A second dimension of newness is how new the product is to the firm. Theme parks are familiar products for consumers, but a theme park based on cars would be a very new product for Ford Motor Company to produce. It would require much more effort for Ford to develop a new theme park than for Disney, which has built them before, just as it would require much more effort for Disney to develop a new car than it would for Ford. While it may not make strategic sense for Ford to develop a new theme park, it might make sense for Ford to diversify beyond cars and trucks into the motorcycle market. Again, motorcycles are not new to consumers, but they would be new to Ford, and likely would require more time, effort, and risk to develop than a new car.

Overall, "newness" is a combination of newness to the market and newness to the firm. Products that are newer on either dimension are riskier to develop and commercialize. "*New-to-the-world*" products—products that create an entirely new market—are the riskiest of all, but present enormous profit potential because they represent monopoly opportunities, at least in the short term. On average, only 10% of products commercialized by firms are new-to-the-world. As shown in Figure 9.2, most of the projects in firm portfolios are *improvements to products* already on the market, additions to existing lines (*line extensions*), and products new to the firm but already manufactured by competitors (*new product lines*).[4] Fully 70% of the average firm's products focus on changing or adding to current products.[5] Ultimately, however, a new product is any product a firm spends money on to change, improve, or reduce cost.

The Average Project Portfolio   Figure 9.2

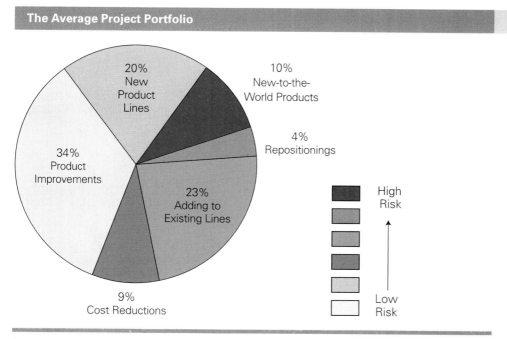

Source: Adapted from Abbie Griffin, "PDMA Research on New Product Development Practices: Updating Trends and Benchmarking Best Practices," *Journal of Product Innovation Management* 14 (1997): 429.

Firms do not commercialize a product and then just reap ongoing profits. Once a product is developed and introduced to the market, competitors introduce products that improve on the initial product's performance. New technologies also become available over time that solve additional customer problems not addressed by the first-generation product. In actuality, changes in any of the environmental forces can induce a need to redevelop products to address those changes. These change events require that firms manage products and product development as an ongoing spiral, as shown in Figure 9.3.[6] Product development does not take place just once, but must be repeated over and over for a firm to stay in business in the long run. Some development cycles may consist only of small, incremental changes in the product. For example, in each of the two years after Ford introduced the 1986 Taurus, they made small changes in a number of components. Some changes were made to reduce costs, while others were to improve quality and performance. In other cycles, more radical changes were made, as when Ford totally redesigned the Taurus for its 1996 reintroduction. The target market for the Taurus remained unchanged, as did its *core benefit proposition (CBP)*. A **core benefit proposition (CBP)** is the primary benefit or purpose for which a customer buys a product. However, with the Taurus redesign, both the styling and many components and subsystems were updated, some with newly available technology (air bags) or materials (engineered plastics). These design changes in turn caused manufacturing changes. Just keeping pace with competitors requires repeatedly reinvigorating products to make them new in the eyes of customers.

Defining Successful Products

Developing new products is time- and resource-consuming, as great care must be taken to ensure the best decisions are made *before* the product reaches channel members and final consumers. Much of this chapter looks closely at the process and management of product development. However, before discussing methods for new product development (NPD), it is first important to consider what firms are actually attempting to achieve by introducing new products to the market. Quite frankly,

Core benefit proposition (CBP)
Is the primary benefit or purpose for which a customer buys a product. The CBP may reside in the physical good or service performance, or it may come from augmented dimensions of the product.

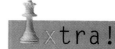

Figure 9.3	The New Product Development Spiral

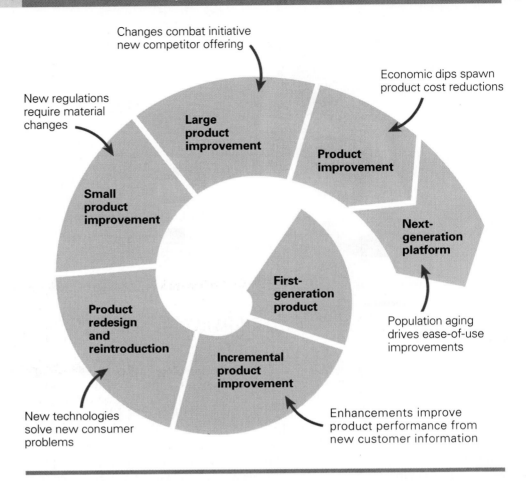

NPD success is difficult to define. Whereas most firms' ultimate objective is financial success, some product-development projects have goals that are more than just financial. The Ford Taurus, for example, achieved a high market share, although it had the lowest long-run quality of any Ford car or truck in 20 years, and did not break even on recovering development expenses for many years. However, in Ford's eyes, and in the eyes of many customers, the Taurus was very successful. How, then, should product success be measured?

NPD managers evaluate *NPD project success* using four items that span these three dimensions:[7]

1. **Financial Success.** Most firms measure financial success by profitability. Other measures of financial success include margin improvement (for cost-reduction projects) and return on investment (ROI), which is most frequently used for new-to-the-world products.
2. **Technical Performance Success.** New products frequently are evaluated on their competitive advantage from a technological or performance point of view. For example, a new Intel processor may be 20% faster than the competitor's current processor. The specific performance measure used depends on which features and specifications are important to consumers.
3. **Success from the Customer's Perspective.** Both *market share* and *customer satisfaction* are used to evaluate a product's success from the customer's perspective. A new product in the ready-to-eat cereal category is considered a success if it

Political and Legal Forces

Reacting to couples desire to be "closer" in times of world crisis, the Cupplerobe has been introduced to allow couples to engage in "crisis-cocooning." The hood of the Cupplerobe accommodates two heads, side-by-side, and two front center openings on the robe allow both occupants to have full use of both hands. The Cupplerobe has recently experienced a great deal of interest from an unexpected market segment: marriage counselors. For more information, go to www.Cupplerobe.com.[8]

Product development processes are moving to the Internet, slowly but surely. However, e-development is very much in its infancy. It is thus very unclear how to use the technologies to best advantage. At this point in time, firms are using the Internet and other information technologies in very different ways.

In its simplest implementation, the Internet is being used to improve project management. A number of companies have developed software that allow project progress to be tracked over time, with the data stored on the Internet, or on a firm's intranet. As each team member completes a step of the process, the data indicating completion are entered into the software, which is updated immediately. All team members have access to the project, so each can see where bottlenecks are occurring and who is doing what, at any point in time. If a team member is late in finishing an item or entering data, the system sends out a reminder to that person and notifies the team leader as well. Team members can log on to the project site from wherever they are located, whether at a different location within the company or traveling on business.

One more advanced firm, a division of a large chemical company, maintains a proprietary database of customer information. Anyone who deals with customers is allowed access. All information from any kind of customer contact is recorded in this database, including performance requirements and new business-development opportunities. When new products are developed, information from this system is used to build the business case. If 300 out of 400 customers want a certain product or feature, that information is in the system. In addition, customer contact is tracked in this system through the entire market-development process. Everything in the database is searchable, including text documents and information about customers, competitors, and products. This database is consulted during the entire product-development process. While the company has not linked its database into an Internet-based project-management system, it intends to in the future.

Other firms are collecting market-research data, including both qualitative and quantitative data, on the Internet. In this manner, data from worldwide sources can be gathered at lower costs. Systems for conducting conjoint studies, which quantitatively determine the preference trade-offs among different features, have demonstrated that a key to online research is making sure that the pictures and videos of products (or potential products) are as realistic as possible. Broadband communications are allowing firms to demonstrate the dynamics of product use before the product is even developed, using simulation and visualization software. The one codicil to marketing data gathered from the Internet is that these consumers may not be representative of the target market, as only 60% of the U.S. population currently connects to the Internet.

achieves only a 1% share of this highly fragmented market. On the other hand, in more concentrated industries such as pickup trucks, firms look for a new truck to obtain a 20–25% market share.

Achieving product success along one dimension does not necessarily mean the product will achieve success along another. For example, superior technical-performance levels may not lead to a significant market share or customer satisfaction. As the Taurus example shows, a product can even achieve high levels of customer satisfaction without achieving profitability, if either development spending or product cost is not controlled. Unfortunately, the perfect product-development project that achieves high levels of success on all three dimensions, known as the *silver bullet*, rarely exists. Firms frequently sacrifice some level of success on one dimension to achieve success on another. For instance, the objective of one project may be to increase customer satisfaction; for another, it may be to raise the technical-performance bar for the product category. Although profits need not be the primary goal of any particular project, the firm does need to generate a profit across the portfolio of products that comprise its product mix.

Anticipating New Product Failure

Achieving product success is difficult. Even though firms over the last 20 years have improved the probability that a project that starts the new-product-development process will succeed, it still takes almost five projects to create one market success,[9] as Figure 9.4 illustrates. Projects are abandoned during development for a number of

| Figure 9.4 | **Project Mortality** |

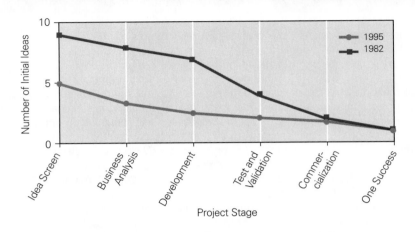

reasons. Sometimes available technology is unable to meet desired performance specifications or a desired price point. At other times, a firm's strategy changes, rendering the product no longer interesting, or a competitor beats the firm to the market. A firm may uncover information that suggests the product as conceived would not solve customer problems, and thus customers would not purchase it. Sometimes, the development team is unable to interest marketing or management in commercializing the product.

Even if a product makes it to market, it can be a failure. On average, only about 55% of products launched are categorized as successes by the commercializing firms.[10] Products can fail due to either strategic or development process factors, or some combination of the two. Strategic reasons that products fail in the marketplace include:

- Failure to provide an advantage or performance improvement over products already available to customers.
- Lack of synergy with the technologies and manufacturing processes of the firm, requiring that the firm learn about how to design and make new technologies.
- Marketing synergies lack necessary distribution channels, promotion and selling practices, or pricing policies, often because the product targets a group to whom the firm has never before marketed a product.

Additionally, products may not be successful in the marketplace because different aspects of the NPD process were not executed effectively. The most important aspects to manage effectively in the process are the predevelopment stages (idea generation and screening, preliminary investigation, and detailed investigation) and the proficiencies of both the technological and marketing-related activities within them. Failure also results when a firm fails to develop a well-thought-out *project strategy* at the outset of the process. The **project strategy** addresses the attributes the product is expected to have, the target market, and the purpose behind commercializing the product. Lack of strategy can lead to a mistargeted product, or one that lacks benefit. Finally, projects that have not garnered upper-management support throughout the development process are more likely to be failures in the marketplace. Lack of management support can lead to performance that is not quite high enough to win sales, or inadequate marketing expenditures to create adequate awareness and trial when the product is launched.

The next sections of the chapter provide insights into how to prevent most of these failures.

Project strategy
Sometimes called a protocol, is a statement of the attributes the project is expected to have, the market to which it is targeted, and the purpose behind commercializing the product.

Developing Successful New Products

4   **LEARNING OBJECTIVE**

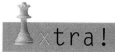

The objective for marketing professionals and NPD teams is to create a series of product successes for their firm. Effective product development requires that a firm successfully complete three activities:

1. Uncover unmet needs and problems.
2. Develop a **competitively advantaged product**, a product that solves a set of customer problems better than any competitor's products.
3. Shepherd products through the firm.

These three activities are simple in concept. Unfortunately, none of them is easy to complete. Further, if any one activity is not fully completed, the product is unlikely to succeed in the marketplace. Each activity requires that the firm master a different set of complex issues. Each issue also must be addressed across functional lines. Marketing cannot address the issues alone; neither can engineering or any other functional area. For example, developing a competitively advantaged product requires: (1) input from customers on unmet needs; (2) input from marketing as to what the competition is doing to address the need; (3) input from manufacturing about what the firm can currently build; (4) input from engineering as to what additional technologies are available; (5) input from R&D about new ways of potentially addressing the need; and (6) input from finance about costs. Excelling at NPD activities requires cooperation across multiple departments, which is still difficult to achieve in many corporations.

Another difficulty in implementing these activities arises because firms do not undertake product development solely for one purpose. Growing a business over time requires a process of repeatedly recommercializing old products to maintain (or grow) the firm's presence in current markets while also commercializing new products to expand the firm's market presence. The activities required for sustaining current business through NPD, however, may differ from those needed for expanding market presence.

A project sustaining a business is constrained by past designs, but may be narrower and more focused in nature. For example, a product-development team working on the next-generation Palm product starts from an already available base of features, software, and manufacturing assets. All of these must be taken into account in developing a new version, so that already obtained economies are not lost. The task for the next cycle may be to gather more in-depth customer information, but in a narrower area of function or use, as the team already has a great deal of knowledge concerning the needs of potential customers. Alternatively, the team may need to incorporate new competitively available features or technological possibilities into the project.

When developing products to grow new markets, fulfilling all three requirements for successful NPD results in profits, market share, and customer satisfaction. Take the case of Procter & Gamble's Pert+™. The product's core benefit proposition—to simultaneously clean and condition hair—originally targeted women who were either traveling or showering at a health club after a workout, because it allowed them to stop carrying two hair-care products. While other companies had previously tried to fulfill this CBP, none had. One firm's failed attempt consisted of supplying both conditioner and shampoo in one bottle, like an oil-and-vinegar salad dressing. Using it required shaking vigorously to mix the two parts into one consistent fluid. Unfortunately, like oil-and-vinegar dressings, the first few uses of a new bottle usually contained a lot more shampoo than conditioner, and the last few uses had more conditioner than shampoo. Although the need was well known, achieving cleaning *and* conditioning had been an unsolvable technical problem. Indeed, it took researchers at Procter & Gamble nearly 10 years to discover a technical solution—a radically different surfactant system (wetting agent) than had ever been considered.

Competitively advantaged product
Is a product that solves a set of customer problems better than any competitor's product. This product is made possible due to this firm's unique technical, manufacturing, managerial, or marketing capabilities, which are not easily copied by others.

Natural Forces
Traditional electric water heaters consume 20% of the average annual household's energy expenditure, resulting in an expenditure of approximately $450 for the average household. Envirotech Systems Worldwide, Inc. has developed an award-winning tankless water heater that heats water on demand and significantly decreases the costs of and energy used by traditional water heaters. It is estimated that $25 billion is spent in the U.S. annually on heating water that is never used.[11]

Once the technical problem was solved, the project-management system at Procter & Gamble moved the product to market. This very different technology has provided Procter & Gamble with a sustainable competitive advantage and has resulted in a successful entry in the shampoo category, both in terms of share and profits.

Uncovering Unmet Needs and Problems

Products fail that don't solve customer problems, or don't solve them at a competitive cost. This section details the customer-needs information firms must uncover to produce better products, and outlines three techniques for obtaining an in-depth knowledge of consumer and potential consumer needs.

Defining Customer Needs

Customer needs are the problems that a person or firm would like to solve. They describe what products let you do, not how they let you do it. Products deliver solutions to customers' problems, but there usually are many different kinds of solutions for each customer need. General needs are relatively easy for firms to uncover and design a solution for. As an illustration, one general need people have is to "be able to communicate with others when we are not together." Phone service solves the problem of communicating with others when you are far away, as long as the other person also has a phone and you know the phone number. The traditional phone systems' wires deliver the general function of "transporting my voice from here to there." New services may use satellites. Both solve the general problem.

Customers also have very specific needs, or details of the general need, that a product must address to be truly successful. These detailed needs can be difficult to uncover, because most detailed needs are specific to particular contexts in which the product is used. For example, phones are used in many different situations. Some of the detailed needs include, "Let me talk to someone when I'm in the kitchen," ". . . in the bedroom," ". . . in the living room," and ". . . outside sitting on my porch." Features provide the ways in which products function. Wiring multiple rooms in the house for phone service and installing multiple phones solves these problems. Or one can talk in all of these places (and many more) by purchasing a cordless phone rather than multiple wall phones. Consider the detailed need of "let other people here participate in the conversation." This can be delivered through multiple extensions, or, alternatively, by using a speakerphone. Different sets of features may better address each of these detailed needs.

Customer problems are complex and frequently different needs conflict. For example, while I want to be able to talk on the phone from any room in the house, my teenager may want to ensure that his conversations are private. Yet, with extensions everywhere in the house, anyone can pick up a phone and listen. Alternative solutions to this problem include installing another phone line or getting the teen his own mobile phone. Yet, because both of these solutions are rather expensive, they directly conflict with the need to talk cheaply with others.

Clearly, no product is perfect. Each product is a compromise, in that it only partially solves a complex set of customer problems. Ultimately, products are sets of features that deliver extremely well for some needs, adequately for others, and do not deliver at all for others. Over time, customers choose products with the set of features that delivers the maximum benefit for them. Although technologies and competitors evolve, customer needs tend to be more stable than product features.

The lessons gleaned from this example are threefold. First, customer needs are complex. Second, developing successful products requires understanding the details of needs. Finally, while needs are rather stable, the "best" (most successful) solutions change over time. Solutions may change as a result of changes in any of the six environmental forces. New technologies enable new features. As a case in point, cell technology has enabled wireless communication. Deregulation of phone companies increased the number of competitors, which in turn decreased prices and increased

Sociocultural Forces
Americans love their pets and marketers have responded accordingly. DogFriendly.com (http://www.dogfriendly.com) has created and published the California and Nevada Dog Travel Guide. The guide includes dog-friendly accommodations, emergency veterinarians, and attractions such as parks, beaches, stores, and outdoor restaurants that allow dogs to accompany their owners.[12]

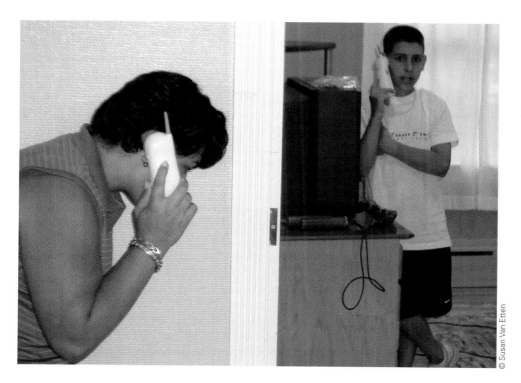

Details of needs are complex and often conflicting. While the family may want to be able to talk on the phone from any room in the house, we may also want to ensure that any conversation is kept private.

the number of people who could afford to make long-distance calls and the breadth of services offered. Through it all, the sociocultural need to communicate with others has remained stable. To deal successfully with these changes as they take place, firms must repeatedly return to the drawing board to understand which new set of compromises customers prefer, given the current environmental context. Providing product-development teams with a rich understanding of complex and detailed customer needs and problems prepares them to select the best technology and feature compromises to continue delivering successful products in the future.

Methods for Understanding Customer Needs

Realistically, customers cannot tell firms exactly what products to develop. Customers are unlikely to have the technical understanding necessary to describe new features or technologies a product should have or forecast what features will best solve their problems in the future. They also cannot provide reliable information about anything with which they are not personally familiar or with which they have no experience. By definition, then, customers are not familiar with a new product a firm may be thinking of developing, and cannot provide fully reliable information when asked to react to a **concept** or **prototype**, a product concept in physical form.

Does that mean that firms should not try to understand customer needs and problems? Not at all. Customers can indeed provide reliable information about products they have used and situations they have experienced. They will readily talk about problems they have had and product uses relevant to them. They can discuss which products and features they currently use to meet their needs—where these products fall short, where they excel, and why.

Customer needs are often ascertained initially through qualitative market research. As discussed in Chapter 5, qualitative market research is often conducted with a small number of customers. Three methods are especially useful for gathering customer needs qualitatively: *becoming the people with the problems* the firm wants to solve, *critically observing those with the problems* of interest, and *talking to (interviewing) people in depth about their problems*. Each method produces slightly different kinds of information. No one technique is sufficient to produce a full

Concept
Is a written description or visual depiction of a new product idea. A concept includes the product's primary features and benefits.

Prototype
Is a product concept in physical form. A prototype may be a full working model that has been produced by hand or a nonworking physical representation of the final product. It is used to gather customer reaction to the physical form (aesthetics and ergonomics) or to initial operating capability. It is also used in internal performance tests to ensure that performance goals have been met.

understanding of needs. The best results are obtained when a product-development team uses multiple methods to understand people's problems in great detail. Once a full set of needs has been gathered, then a number of different quantitative market-research techniques can be used to predict which needs are more important.

Becoming the Customer: Discovering Problems. An enormous amount of customer knowledge and understanding can be gained by putting development team members into situations where they "become" customers and experience the problems the firm is trying to solve firsthand. This method encourages team members to use the firm's products, and all competitors' products, in everyday as well as extraordinary situations.

For example, the product-development team for a feminine hygiene pad at one company is known for the extent to which they try to fully understand and identify with customer problems. The entire team—both men and women—personally tests relevant products from both their own firm and the competition. Both male and female team members wear pads underneath armpits and in shoes to test chafing and odor elimination. They also wear pads in the anatomically appropriate area to simulate normal use. New team members are sent on expeditions to purchase the product.

This technique applies not just to consumer products, but with a bit of creativity is useful for many firms selling business-to-business products. For instance, team members at firms that supply McDonald's with cooking equipment are encouraged to work in the kitchens, both on current equipment and with development prototypes. McDonald's readily assigns the development people to shifts because they hope to get improved products. Of course, all kitchen-equipment firms have test kitchens in which they operate their equipment during development. However, operating a system in a laboratory setting simply does not provide the same breadth of operating experience as working in a real McDonald's—crammed in a kitchen full of teenagers flipping burgers on a Friday night after the local high school football game has ended, with hordes of other teenagers demanding to be fed quickly. By working full shifts during different time periods, development personnel learn about shift startup and cleanup, and the effects of different volume levels on operation, breakage, and fatigue. They are exposed to a random day's worth of the strange things that can happen in a fast-food kitchen that affect both the operator and the equipment.

Having employees become actively involved customers is the best way, sometimes the only way, to transfer *tacit knowledge* to the product development team. **Tacit knowledge** is knowledge that is implied by or inferred from actions or statements. Becoming a routine customer for all the different products in a category may also be the most efficient way to expose development teams to the trade-offs others have made in their products and the effects these decisions have had on product function. While this technique brings rich data to the product-development team, it has several inherent problems:

Tacit knowledge
Is knowledge implied by or inferred from actions or statements.

- The firm must learn how to transfer one person's experience and tacit knowledge to another.
- If experiences are not recorded, retaining personal knowledge becomes a critical issue if team members frequently shift jobs or leave the firm.
- Project management must take steps to ensure that team members understand that their own needs differ from the "average" customer's needs in unexpected ways.
- Being a customer takes time, money, and personal team-member effort.

While personally gathering customer information is not possible in all product areas, with a little imagination it is more feasible than many firms currently realize.

Anthropological Excursions: Living With and Critically Observing Customers. Product developers who cannot become customers may be able to "live with" their

Counterfeiting = Stealing

Brands, logos, and product designs are the property of the companies that develop them. Companies invest millions in developing just the right image, obtaining optimal performance in a product, or creating a distinctive "look and feel" for their product. For example, Rolex watches have a very distinctive look and feel compared to other watch brands. To protect their rights of ownership, brands are trademarked and logos are copyrighted, meaning that the owning firm retains the sole right to use those brands and logos as identifying marks. Other material associated with products also is frequently copyrighted, such as the words and notes of songs and movies. Nothing that is copyrighted or trademarked may be used without the express permission of the firm that developed it. Usually, obtaining this permission requires paying usage fees to the firm that owns the material.

Some firms and individuals seem not to recognize the creating firms' right of ownership. They make and sell "knock-offs" or counterfeit goods that resemble or copy the original products, violating trademark and copyright laws. Examples include counterfeit "Gucci" handbags and "Rolex" watches, which can be purchased on the streets of almost any major city in the world. Additionally, the Internet makes it easier for those who want to acquire access to digital products without paying for them. For example, DVDs of the recently released movie *Chicago* were sold on the streets of Hong Kong the day it was released into theaters in the U.S.

Counterfeit goods cause two problems for the firms owning the purloined brands and logos. First, they cause direct damage to the companies, as counterfeit products take potential customers away from them, causing losses to revenue and profit streams. Second, because many brands that are counterfeited are expensive brands, like Rolex and Gucci, a cheap imitation can adversely impact the brand's image.

DISCUSSION QUESTIONS

1. If you discovered that your employer produced "knock-off" or counterfeit products, such as "Rolex" watches, how would you react? Would you take steps to end it?
2. Do you believe it is ethical to download music from the Internet and create a CD or tape without paying the royalty? Why or why not?

customers, observing and questioning them as they use products to solve problems. Developers of new medical devices for doctors cannot act as doctors and personally test devices in patient situations. However, they can observe operations, even videotape them, and then debrief doctors about what happened and why.

Sometimes observing customers in their natural settings leads directly to new products or features. Developers at Chrysler observed that many pickup truck owners had built holders for 32-ounce drinks into their cabs, so starting in 1995 Ram trucks featured cup holders appropriate for 32-ounce drinks. In other instances, observation points out a problem. The team must determine whether the problem is specific to a particular individual or applies generally across the target market, and, if so, develop an appropriate solution. Another Chrysler engineer watched the difficulty his petite wife had wrestling children's car seats around in the family minivan. It took him several years to convince management that his innovative solution—integrating children's car seats into the car's seating system—would solve a major problem for a large number of customers.

Critical observation, rather than just casual viewing, is a major key to obtaining information by watching customers. Critical observation involves questioning *why* people are performing each action rather than just accepting what they are doing. The best results are achieved when team members spend significant time with enough different customers to be exposed to the full breadth of problems people encounter. They must spend enough time observing customers to uncover both normal and abnormal operating conditions. Using team members responsible for different functions is important because people with different training and expertise "see" and pay attention to different things.

Anthropological excursions identify tacit information and expose team members to customer language. It is the most effective means for gathering work-flow or process-related information. These customer needs are particularly important for firms marketing products to other firms. The products they develop must fit into the work flow of those firms, which means the processes must be fully understood. Even when questioned in detail, people frequently forget steps in a process or skip over them. Although forgotten in the course of interviews, these steps may be crucial to product design trade-offs.

Observing and living with customers is not especially efficient. Its problems include:

- Significant team-member time and expense. Events and actions unfold slowly in real time, and there are no shortcuts.
- "Natural" actions may not be captured. Videotaping or observation, no matter how well designed and intentioned, is intrusive by nature and may change behavior.
- Observations must be interpreted through the filter of team members' own experiences. It is a challenge for the team to turn observed actions into words that reliably capture customer needs.

Being customers and critically observing customers are powerful techniques for gathering rich, detailed data on customer problems. However, both activities require significant amounts of time that may not be available in every product-development project. These techniques are best used in an ongoing way to continually expand a group's knowledge of customer problems. When time is short, the only means to rapidly gather customer needs is to talk to customers and have them tell you their problems.

Voice of the customer (VOC)

Is a one-on-one interviewing process used to elicit an in-depth set of customer needs.

Talking to Customers to Learn Needs and Problems. By talking to customers, NPD teams can gather needs faster and more efficiently than by being or observing customers. A structured, in-depth, probing, one-on-one, situational-interview technique called **voice of the customer (VOC)** can uncover both general and very detailed customer needs.[13] This method differs from standard qualitative techniques in the way questions are asked. Rather than asking customers "What do you want?" directly, VOC uses indirect questions to discover wants and needs by leading customers through the ways they currently solve particular problems. VOC asks questions about functions rather than about products.

For example, one study asked customers *what* they used to transport food they had prepared at home to be consumed at another location, especially if the food was to be stored for some period of time before it was eaten. Picnic baskets, coolers, and ice chests were the items most frequently suggested to fill this general function. However, asking *how* they fulfilled the function, rather than about a particular product, yielded information about many different and unexpected products customers used—including knapsacks, luggage, and grocery store bags with handles—and the reasons *why* they used them. Detailed probing reveals specific features, drawbacks, and benefits of each product. Most important are questions delving into why various features of products are good and bad. What problem does each feature solve, and does a particular feature cause any other problems? Probing *why* uncovers needs.

One advantage of interviewing is that many different use situations can be investigated in a short period of time, including a range of both normal and abnormal situations. Each different use situation provides information about additional dimensions of functional performance. A good way to start an interview is to ask customers to tell you about the last time they found themselves in a particular situation. The food transportation study began, "Please tell me about the most recent time you prepared food in your home, to be shared by you and others, and then took the food outside your home and ate it somewhere else later." By asking customers to relate specifics—what they did, why they did what they did, what worked well, and what did not work—both detailed and general customer needs are obtained indirectly.

After customers relate their most recent experiences, they are asked about the specifics of how they fulfilled the function in a series of other potential use situations. These use situations attempt to cover all the performance dimensions across which customers may expect a product to function. In the food-transportation example, customers were asked about the last time they took food with them:

Individuals who use products to transport food for a romantic picnic will talk about very different performance needs than those who are taking food and drink to a college football tailgate party. New product development teams will uncover different needs by asking about specific product uses.

- On a car trip
- To the beach
- To a football or baseball game
- On a romantic picnic
- On a bike trip
- Hiking or backpacking
- Canoeing or fishing

They also related the most disastrous and marvelous times they ever took food with them. The set of situations constructed varies the different dimensions of expected performance as widely as possible. In the food study, the amount, types, and temperatures of the food taken varies; the outside temperature varies; and different aesthetics are covered, as is a large range of ease of mobility and transportability. Buried in the stories customers tell about specific uses are the nuggets of needs. While no customer experiences all situations, the food-transporting and -storage needs resulting from each situation were uncovered fully by interviewing 20 to 30 people.

VOC provides a much larger list of very detailed and context- or situation-specific customer needs than other qualitative market-research techniques. This is because the objective of VOC is to obtain a level of detail that enables teams to make engineering trade-offs during product development.

There are several keys to successfully obtaining the voice of the customer. First, it is critical to ask about functions (what customers want to do), not features (how it is done). Continually probing about why a feature is wanted or works well reveals underlying needs. Only by understanding functional needs can teams make appropriate technology and feature trade-offs in the future. A second key is that VOC only covers reality. People who have never been on a romantic picnic cannot accurately tell you what they would like on one because they really do not know. Anything they say is conjecture. The final key to success is to ask detailed questions about specific uses. General questions (tell me about going on picnics) elicit general needs. General needs are not as useful to the development team for designing products as are details of needs, which are obtained through using specific questions (tell me about the last time you went on a romantic picnic). Customers can provide tremendous levels of detail when asked to relate the story of a specific situation that occurred in the last year.

While VOC provides numerous verbal details about problems directly useful to the team, it has several drawbacks:

- The development team obtains a better understanding of a fuller set of detailed needs if the team interviews customers, but this adds to the team's development tasks.
- Interviewing customers is a nontraditional task for many team members (e.g., engineers, accountants).
- Extreme care must be taken to maintain the words of the customer and not translate individual problems into solutions before understanding the full set of customer needs.
- Tacit (hard-to-articulate) needs and needs associated with process operations may not be complete.

No one technique easily provides the entire customer-needs knowledge that product-development teams seek. Tacit needs are best discovered by being a customer. Process-related needs are identified most easily by critically observing customers. In-depth interviewing is the most efficient means to obtain masses of detailed needs, but may not provide needs that are hard to articulate. Unfortunately, few projects afford the time and expense of fully using all of these processes. Development teams need to use the most appropriate one(s) given the project's informational requirements, budget, and time frame. Once needs have been gathered, the team can turn to developing a competitively advantaged product that fully solves customers' problems.

Developing a Competitively Advantaged Product

Developing competitively advantaged products consistently over time is aided by having a strategy for what will be done and a process for how it will be accomplished. Firms with both an NPD strategy and a formal process for doing so demonstrate superior performance in terms of percentage of sales for new products, success rates, and meeting sales and profit objectives.[15]

Product-Development Strategy

"If you don't know where you are going, any road will get you there." New product strategy provides the long-term destination for where the firm is going. Effective strategies for product development flow from the overall business strategy of the firm (Figure 9.5). For example, if the firm's stated strategy is to be a low-cost manufacturer, then an effective new-product strategy for the business unit probably is not to develop a continuous stream of technologically leading-edge products. A more effective new-product strategy might be to continually improve the cost-effectiveness of the manufacturing processes.

Effective strategies consist of clear new-product goals that derive directly from the overall business strategy. Areas of strategic focus can be defined in a number of ways, including:

- Markets or market segments
- Product types or categories (such as newness categories)
- Product lines
- Technologies or technology platforms

Areas of strategic focus are then selected and prioritized, and a plan for how to attack each area is developed. A plan of attack defines the way in which the firm will compete in each strategic arena. For example, in the 1980s, Ford Motor Company's plan of attack for the family-sedan market was to be the industry design and styling innovator. Thus, successive generations of Taurus styling have been radically different from other family sedans on the market. However, different plans of attack may be adopted across different strategic arenas of a firm. In the minivan product category, Ford has chosen more of a fast-follower strategy behind Chrysler. Here they

Sociocultural Forces

Originally developed for the Hawaiian market, where year-round tropical heat and active outdoor lifestyles provide a challenging environment for deodorant manufacturers, Body Mint® has developed an all-natural, all-body deodorizer tablet. The Body Mint works from the inside out to reduce bad breath and underarm and foot odor and provides customers with greater confidence and improved self-image. For more information, go to **http://www.bodymint.com**.[14]

Aligning Product-Development Strategy with Firm Strategy Leads to Success	Figure 9.5

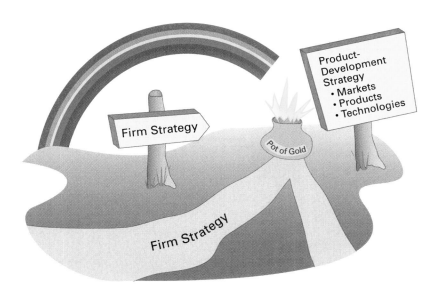

have allowed Chrysler to innovate and have chosen to compete using a "second but better" design.

Project Strategy

Even after the NPD strategy for the business unit is set, a strategy for each individual product-development project must be developed. A project strategy is the specific plan for how this project will proceed and why. An effective project strategy states the reasons the firm is undertaking a project and identifies specific business goals for the product. For example, it outlines whether the firm is undertaking this project to meet a previously unmet customer need, to update performance for a current product, or to counteract share losses from a newly commercialized competitive product. Each project's goals will depend, in part, on why the project is being undertaken. For example, the goal for a performance-improvement project may be increased share or customer satisfaction while maintaining profitability.

The project strategy also describes the target market and core benefit proposition for the product. It details the firms or individuals who are expected to purchase the new product. Some project teams draw pictures or create collages of people in the target market, **customer prototypes**, and hang them on the walls to remind themselves who the target market is as the project moves forward.

Finally, successful strategies require a schedule to establish key milestones, including the planned market-introduction date. The schedule helps keep the team task-focused, and helps managers across the company identify key resources and activities required to achieve success. Once the team and management agree on the project purposes, goals, timing, and required resources, the team is ready to proceed to development.

A Framework for Managing Product Development

A formal **product-development process**, such as that illustrated in Figure 9.6, outlines the normal way NPD proceeds at the firm. It defines what functions (i.e., marketing or engineering) are responsible for performing what tasks, in what order, and in conjunction with what other tasks and functions. A formalized process institutionalizes learning about what works and does not work, and how interdependent

Customer prototypes
Are the detailed pictures and descriptions of individuals or firms in the target market for a product. Creating these descriptions helps firms envision how products and the marketing mix might best be combined to maximize profits.

Product-development process
Consists of a clearly defined set of tasks and steps that describes the normal means by which product development proceeds. The process outlines the order and sequence of the tasks and indicates who is responsible for each.

Figure 9.6	NPD Process Tasks and Road Map

Is a common new product-development process that divides the repeatable portion of product development into a time-sequenced series of stages, each of which is separated by a management-decision gate.

steps must be completed. Projects that follow a formalized product-development process are more successful, and firms that are the best at NPD are more likely to use a formalized process for new product development.[16] Firms without formalized NPD processes depend on one or a few product-development "craftsmen" who "just know how to do it." If they leave the firm, NPD knowledge leaves with them.

Most firms use a formal *stage-gate™ process* to organize the tasks for developing new products (see Figure 9.7). The **stage-gate™ process** is a common NPD process that divides the repeatable portion of product development into a time-sequenced series of stages separated by a management-decision gate. Stage-gate™ processes are organized and consistent, and can be understood and deployed by all those involved in NPD projects at a firm. Personnel responsible for each function complete tasks related to that function at each stage. The process acknowledges that different functions require a different expertise in each stage, all of which are necessary to successfully complete the stage. Thus, it encourages cross-functional teamwork and problem solving. As the goals for each stage are completed, management reviews progress at a gate meeting, determines whether the criteria necessary to move forward have been met, approves the tasks and resources for the next stage (go), asks for more information (recycle), or stops the project (kill). A well-designed process ensures that senior management participates in the NPD process where there is a significant jump in risk or cost.

Activities in Stage-Gate™ Processes

Individual firms implement the stage-gate™ process differently, personalizing it to meet the needs of their corporation. Figure 9.8 shows four actual NPD processes. For example, CalComp uses a five-stage process that does not include idea generation or post-introduction review. In contrast, the other three firms all use different six- and seven-stage processes. Traditionally, the most common tasks and stages that may be included in the firm's NPD process include the following activities.[17]

A Stage-Gate™ Approach to NPD   Figure 9.7

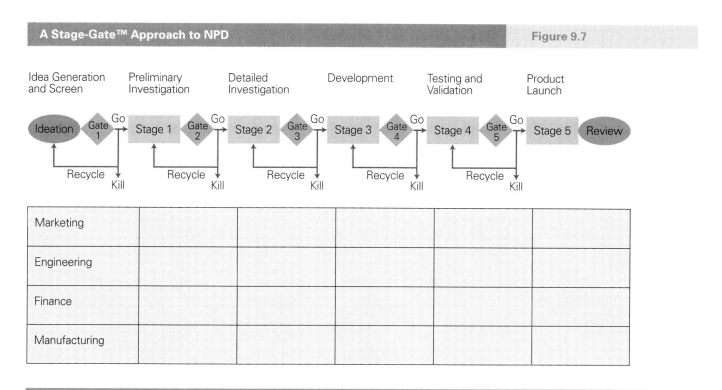

Generate and Screen Ideas. The objective of this stage is to create one or more "interesting" new product ideas. An interesting idea solves customer problems, fits the business unit's strategy and capabilities, and presents a profit-making opportunity at reasonable risk, given the size of the profit potential. In this step, ideas are first generated and then screened against a set of criteria to determine which provide the greatest opportunity for the firm. At the end of this stage, a small number of ideas that have been screened for fit and potential reward will be ready to move forward into the next stage of development.

Stages Used by Firms   Figure 9.8

Stage	CalComp	Xerox	Exxon Chemical	Keithley Instrument
Generate ideas		Preconcept	Idea	Concept
Preliminary investigation	Market requirement Specification Design	Concept	Preliminary assessment	Study
Detailed investigation			Detailed assessment	Definition
Development	Engineering model Prototype	Design	Development	Design
Test and validate	System verification Manufacturing verification	Demonstration Production	Validation	Prototype Pilot
Launch	Production	Launch	Commercial launch	Introduction
Maintenance	End of life	Maintenance		
Review			Postreview	

Sources: Public presentations and brochures.

Ideas come from many sources. Customers may ask directly for a new product or feature. Competitors may introduce a new product that sparks an idea to counteract their effort. Employees frequently have new-product ideas they are eager to suggest. Alternatively, creativity sessions can be held specifically to generate new ideas. Frequently the problem is not generating ideas but gathering ideas from a wide variety of sources so they can be evaluated. Some firms use a database or construct a new product idea bulletin board on their intranet to collect and retain ideas over time.

The objective of idea screening is to evaluate new product ideas rationally and consistently over time, and to maintain the integrity of the process as product-development team membership evolves. Initial idea screening is done based on what management already knows, rather than on information specifically developed for the project. Many firms develop a standard set of criteria that managers can use to consistently evaluate ideas. Figure 9.9 lists AT&T's idea-screening criteria.

Idea generation and screening can be completed relatively quickly, sometimes in days or hours. The resources required usually are minimal, consisting predominantly of management time, the cost of developing and maintaining an idea database, and the cost of running creativity sessions.

Conduct Preliminary Investigation. This stage develops preliminary market assessments, technical feasibility assessments, and financial assessments. This is the up-front homework necessary before detailed design work can start. Typically a small, focused, multifunctional core team of marketing and technical specialists performs this step using available resources and knowledge. At the end of the preliminary investigation, the team will know whether unknowns exist, and thus whether the project must be routed back through a research step to demonstrate feasibility, or whether the project can proceed to a detailed investigation that builds a business case based on new and more detailed information.

The preliminary market assessment is a quick-and-dirty market study using data that can be assembled quickly to answer several questions: market attractiveness and potential, probable customer acceptance of the concept, and competitive intensity. The preliminary technical assessment identifies the key technical risks and how each might be overcome. The firm's technical staff—R&D, engineering, and manufacturing—develop rough initial technical and performance specifications and pinpoint specific technical risks in both product and manufacturing process design. Regulatory issues and competitors' patent situations also are reviewed. The preliminary financial assessment is an initial check that the project has enough revenue and profit potential to warrant continuation. At this point, potential volume, revenue, cost per item, and total development cost are extremely speculative, so these estimates are no more than ballpark figures.

Figure 9.9	Potential Idea Evaluation Criteria

- **Will the market care?**
  How will consumers benefit?
  What is the total market potential?

- **Will it be important to this firm?**
  Does it fit with our strategy and goals?
  Will it create shareholder value?
  Can we obtain sufficient market share?
  Will it provide us with a comparative advantage?

- **Does it fit with our firm's capabilities?**
  Does it match our technology infrastructure?
  Does it match our marketing capabilities?
  Can we produce it at a cost that will provide profits?

"Appropriate" Products and Technologies

Products suitable for a developed country may not be suitable for an emerging market. Products may be inappropriate for a number of reasons:

- The problem that the product solves isn't as pressing in emerging nations as it is in developed ones.
- The technology in the product requires an infrastructure not available in the emerging country.
- Culture or religion makes the product as originally designed inappropriate to the emerging country.

For example, as indicated in this chapter, manual typewriters are still used extensively in countries where electrical power is limited, such as in a number of the emerging countries in the Caribbean. The original Beetle was produced and driven in South America long after it was withdrawn from the U.S. The simplicity of the air-cooled engine fit well with the level of technological sophistication in those countries.

Significant changes may need to be made for products to be appropriate for an emerging market. For example, McDonald's entered India in 1996. Currently, there are 34 McDonald's restaurants in the country. However, as the company says: "We entered the market without the brand's flagship product, the Big Mac. Keeping in mind the religious sentiments of the local population, we made a commitment not to introduce beef or pork products into our menu. We instead created a product similar to the Big Mac with mutton and chicken patties and christened them the Maharaja Mac™ and Chicken Maharaja Mac™. With the vegetarian population in mind, we created an entire vegetarian range in the menu. We also developed a mayonnaise that was eggless, which made our vegetable burgers vegetarian in the true sense of the term" (http://www.mcdonalds.com/countries/india/india.html).

Alternatively, some products just may not find that an emerging market is an appropriate venue for them for years, or even decades, until the technological and environmental infrastructure provides the necessary underpinnings for success.

Research has repeatedly shown that the quality of the up-front effort in preliminary investigation is strongly associated with increased new-product success. Because the information used in the analyses is readily available within the firm, preliminary investigation can be completed relatively quickly, generally within a few weeks. However, this step requires input from manufacturing, technologists, marketers, and financial analysts. Thus, a lack of support by management, or from any of these functional units, can delay completion and reduce the quality of the execution.

Conduct Detailed Investigation. Detailed investigation builds a business case for the project that provides enough solid information to upper management so they can approve the resources necessary for product development. The business case defines and justifies the project, and details the plan for completing the project. The cross-functional team that develops the business case becomes the core of the team that will take the project through development and into the marketplace. At the end of this stage, management has all the information it needs to make a go or kill decision on the project, and the team will be poised to move rapidly into the more expensive phases of development.

Justification requires completing a *market analysis, technical assessment, concept test, competitive analysis,* and *detailed financial analysis.* Each of these analyses requires gathering and generating new information, rather than relying on what a firm already knows. The market analysis determines customer needs in detail, quantifies market size and growth, and analyzes market segments and buyer behavior. A competitive analysis identifies competitors and competing products, including details of product strengths and deficiencies. The team analyzes competitor strategies, position in the market, and performance. These serve as inputs for developing the marketing strategy for product commercialization. The financial analysis includes a cash-flow analysis that takes into account the required timing and level of investment. This is possible because the team now has a much more detailed definition of the product specifications.

The final component of the business case is the plan of action. This includes a go/kill recommendation and a detailed plan for how physical development, testing, and manufacturing development will proceed. The plan also specifies the intended launch date for the product.

The detailed investigation stage has high levels of interdependency across tasks and is the first stage that requires a reasonable investment of time, money, and people to provide quality results. The resources required will depend on the size, complexity, and degree of uniqueness of the project. A firm can expect that even the smallest projects may require a team of three to five individuals (because each function must be represented), working at least half-time over a period of one to four months. Larger, more complex projects, however, may require four to six people working full-time for up to six months to a year. Spending enough time, money, and personnel resources during this stage, in order to produce high-quality definitions, justifications, and plans, saves a much larger amount of spending later to fix problems that arise because they were not dealt with in the initial phases of the project.

Develop Product. The actual design and physical development of the product takes place during the development stage. The outputs of this stage are:

- A prototype that has been tested in-house for performance and in a limited way with customers for preliminary reaction.
- A mapped-out manufacturing process, with critical aspects pilot tested.
- A marketing launch plan.
- A test and validation plan.

In development, team size and resource consumption peak. Different parts of the project move forward in parallel, completed by different subgroups of the team. While some tasks can be completed by one function relatively independently, many others still require extensive interaction across functions. At the heart of a successful development stage is a plan that drives the process by organizing the efforts of all those involved. It includes a chronological listing of tasks and the individuals responsible for completing them, with expected stop and start dates. Successful project leaders expect team members to adhere to the time lines and milestones, and proactively manage the project based on them. Project-management plans can only be followed when the unknowns have been eliminated from the project prior to development.

Development time increases with the size and complexity of a project. Additionally, the relative newness of a project affects development time. New-to-the-world projects average about 3.5 years to complete, new-to-the-firm projects take just over two years, major revisions of current projects require 1.5 years, line extensions need one year, and incremental improvements take about nine months.[18] Team size ranges from two to three people for incremental improvements to relatively simple products, such as shampoos or other customer packaged goods, to hundreds, or even thousands, of people when a large and complex new-to-the-firm or new-to-the-world project is undertaken. Boeing assembled an entire hierarchy of teams in developing the 777 airplane, with the total staff involved numbering in the thousands.

Test and Validate. This stage provides final project validation. The product, production process, and marketing strategy plan are all put through verification tests. The objectives are to provide management with final proof that expectations for the project in terms of performance, volume, and profit will be met, and to eliminate any final bugs in the product, process, and marketing plan. The product typically undergoes customer field trials for performance verification, and test marketing or limited rollout for testing the marketing plan. Pilot or trial production of the manufacturing process is used to produce the products tested with customers to ensure the process operates as designed. Finally, based on the results from the field and plant trials, the expected financial outcomes are updated. Results from the field, plant, and financial analyses are presented to management for a final go/kill decision, and to obtain the investment for a full market launch.

The time and effort required for testing and validation varies greatly with the size, complexity, and newness of the project. Field-testing with customers can require as little as a week for a limited test with a few customers to as much as a year for a full test market. The expense can be as little as the cost of producing one or two products, or run as much as 5% of the estimated expense of going to market.

Commercialize and Launch. The final activity in new product development is commercialization, the beginning of full production and commercial selling. Some of the team members on the project may change as the marketing and sales functions ramp up activities to implement the communications plan, marketing launch plan, and sales plan. Manufacturing also may add people to the team as production is deployed to one or more plants. However, to counterbalance these additions, some of the technical development team may move to a more limited role. While large amounts of money may be spent on advertising and communications at this stage, the project finally starts generating income.

Shepherding Products Through the Firm

Even if a firm has uncovered a customer problem and developed a competitively advantaged product that solves the problem, it still may not be able to profit from that effort if it cannot bring the product to market through its own corporate infrastructure. Shepherding products through the firm is done by putting in place appropriate organizational processes, which includes developing project leaders to lead the NPD process and navigate the politics of the organization, providing appropriate organizational structures within which to manage projects, and ensuring upper management support.

Leading NPD Projects

NPD project leaders fulfill a number of roles. The leader ensures that the NPD process is followed, that tasks are assigned to those who can complete them, and that those tasks are completed in a timely manner. The leader may help protect the team from external interference and may ensure that necessary resources are available to the team. Generally, the leader represents the team in formal meetings and reviews with management. Leaders can also play other roles, including coaching and developing team personnel. Project leadership can take several forms, including: project leaders, champions, and, more recently, NPD process owners. These leadership types differ in the ways in which they fill leadership roles.

Project leaders, the most frequently used leadership type in NPD, are appointed by upper management and given formal power and authority to complete the project. They guard the project's objectives, continuously communicate with team members, serve as a translator across different functions, and are the primary management contact point. The project leader manages the efforts of team members from the different functions. In a "lightweight" team, the leader coordinates work through liaison functional representatives, but has little influence over the work. In a "heavyweight" team, the leader exerts a strong, direct, integrating influence across all functions. Shifting to heavyweight teams has been credited with reducing NPD cycle time and increasing development productivity in the automotive industry.[19]

Champions generally work outside official roles and processes to informally influence others' actions, taking an acute interest in seeing that a particular project is pursued. The role may vary from little more than stimulating awareness of the opportunity to extreme cases where the champion tries to force a project past strongly entrenched internal resistance. The champion's role in NPD has been a topic of discussion for more than 30 years, with champion use reported by more than 40% of firms. While some specific NPD successes may be due to the efforts of a particular champion, using a champion does not raise the probability that any particular project will be a success.[20]

Process owners administer the formal NPD process across business groups within the firm.[21] Process owners build and maintain expertise in the NPD process, facilitating NPD process use for all projects in the firm, and in some projects additionally serve in leadership roles. Process owners may not be responsible for the successful outcome of a project, just for the implementation quality of the NPD process used. Even though this leadership type is a relatively recent development, about 12% of reporting firms claim that process owners lead NPD projects.

Mustering Management Support for NPD

A consistent key to producing successful new products is tangible and visible top management commitment to NPD. While top managers formally control the budgets and plans of NPD groups only loosely, they exert considerably tighter control over them informally in the way they allocate top management attention and contact. The NPD team's goal, then, is to obtain and retain top management commitment to the project by keeping their attention.

Getting a project favored and approved over others requires managing more than just a rational decision-making process. It requires managing the personalities and politics of the upper managers supporting NPD to convince them that the value of a particular project warrants the necessary resources they must provide. The NPD team thus needs to continually communicate with top management about the project. Firms usually have mechanisms for formally communicating with management through gate meetings and design reviews, and during the annual budgeting process. However, communication also needs to occur informally between the team and management. Some strategies include:

- Interviewing specific managers for their view of project expectations or customer needs.
- Sending out brief (one to two paragraphs) weekly e-mail updates.
- Inviting managers with particular areas of expertise to participate as consultants to the project.
- Requesting management presence in the laboratory as new prototypes are unveiled.
- Using one or more managers as subjects in various phases of testing.
- Creating a weekly or monthly project lunch and inviting managers to attend.
- Inviting managers to after-hours team functions, such as project picnics and parties.

The objectives of some interactions are to exchange information, such as informing management about the status of the project, obstacles that are creating roadblocks, or small successes, such as beating completion time to a milestone. At other times, the objectives of an interaction will be more persuasive in nature. Examples include the team interacting to sell the project to a potential project sponsor, bargaining for different or additional resources, or defending the project from criticism by another group within the firm.

Successful product development is a multifunctional effort. Marketing has an important role to play in this effort, but by themselves marketing staff cannot ensure success. Indeed, marketing will not even lead many product-development efforts. However, there are other product-related decisions over which marketing does exert control. The remainder of the chapter covers the types of product-related decisions that are solely marketing's responsibilities.

LEARNING OBJECTIVE 5

Making Product Decisions: Branding, Packaging, and Labeling[22]

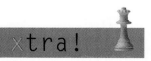

Prior to the commercialization and launch stage of new product development, marketing is responsible for making a number of decisions that will help reinforce a product's competitive position in the minds of consumers.[23] These include decisions about branding, packaging, and labeling.

Branding Decisions

Customers handle an enormous amount of information in the course of their daily activities. Consequently, they develop efficient ways of processing information to make purchasing decisions. Brands are one of the most fundamental pieces of information customers use to simplify choices and reduce purchase risk. Brand names assure customers that they will receive the same quality with their next purchase as they did with their last. Buyers are willing to pay a premium for that branded quality and assurance. For this reason, branding has become an essential element of product strategy.

Brands serve important communication functions and, in doing so, establish beliefs among customers about the attributes and general image of a product. After a brand has been established, the *brand name* (letters or numbers used to vocalize the brand), *logo* (symbols such as Prudential's rock and the Nike swoosh), and *trademark* (legally protected brand name and/or logo) serve to remind and reinforce the beliefs that have been formed. To arrive at this point, the firm must have made good on its promises. A good brand name, logo, or trademark has four important characteristics. It should:

1. Attract attention.
2. Be memorable.
3. Help communicate the positioning of the product.
4. Distinguish the product from competing brands.

Companies competent in branding use their brands and logos consistently across products, packages, and marketing messages, including advertising and collateral materials like brochures, service manuals, and price lists. For example, McDonald's places its golden arches logo consistently across its product packages, worker shirts and hats, and signage. Intel positions its "Intel Inside" logo on all products, front and center on its Web page, and even requires computer customers to put it on each computer with an Intel processor. This company has made its brand and logo more memorable by creating a tune that engages auditory attention, in addition to the visual attention of the logo.

Brand Equity

Successful brands develop **brand equity**. The financial value of brand equity can be enormous. For example, Kohlberg Kravis Roberts purchased RJR Nabisco for $25 billion (double its book value) and Philip Morris paid $12.9 billion for Kraft (four times its book value) and $5.7 billion for General Foods (more than four times its book value). Even under the generous notion that the tangible assets of these companies were undervalued by 50%, this still means that the reputation and goodwill of their brand names—their brand equity—were worth billions.

Brand equity
Is the marketplace value of a brand based on reputation and goodwill.

In addition to its financial value, brand equity also has very important strategic value. For example, from market research with their customers in the early 2000s, Navistar, a $7-billion manufacturer of diesel engines and medium and heavy trucks, found that its "International" brand meant high quality, durability, and total value. The company had changed its name from International Harvester to Navistar after selling the agricultural products division off in the mid-1980s, but had kept the International brand name for its products. However, because market research found that the brand equity of the firm was in the "International" name, and not Navistar, they changed the firm's name to International Truck and Engine in 2001 to capitalize on that equity and create a consistent message to the market.

Manufacturers have become increasingly interested in marketing new products under the umbrella of well-established brand names already familiar to consumers. New products marketed under well-established brand names are more likely to be accepted by channel members (e.g., wholesalers and retailers) due to the proven

Technological Forces
Kawasaki Motors Corporation is further expanding its brand equity through video games. Chasma, Inc., a leading producer of mobile games for wireless devices, has signed an exclusive agreement with Kawasaki to feature several of Kawasaki's trademark vehicles, such as the company's all-terrain vehicles and popular Jet Ski® watercraft, in its games. Kawasaki believes this association with Chasma provides tremendous potential for reaching active, youthful consumers with Kawasaki's brand message.[24]

track record of the brand and disenchantment with the risks involved in launching new brands. Strong brand equity is not only used to roll out new products, but also helps companies break into new markets. For example, Kodak used its film brand equity to break into the camera market, and Lipton tea used its brand equity to launch soup mixes. Finally, brand equity can be strategically used as an effective barrier to entry, making it difficult for competitors to enter or expand in the market.

Branding Strategies: Individual Versus Family Branding
When selecting branding strategies, marketers essentially have two options. The first option is to pursue an *individual brand name strategy,* where each product in a company's product mix is given a specific brand name. Procter & Gamble and General Mills are often cited as prime examples of companies that use an individual brand name strategy. The advantage of an individual brand name strategy is that it allows a firm to develop the best brand name possible for every product. In addition, an individual brand name strategy diversifies the firm's risk by not allowing individual product failures to tarnish the reputation and image of the company's other products. The downside of an individual brand name strategy is that the firm is not taking advantage of the brand equity of existing brands that may facilitate channel and consumer acceptance of new products.

The other branding option is to use a *family brand name strategy* where all, or a significant portion, of a company's products are associated with a family brand name. The primary advantage of a family brand name strategy is that it can be used to launch new products. Firms typically extend their family brand names in two ways:

1. The family brand is extended into product categories used in the same situation as the original branded product or used by consumers of the original branded product (e.g., Coke, Diet-Coke, and Vanilla Coke).
2. The family brand is extended to help the company introduce products into new product categories (e.g., Fisher-Price toys introduces Fisher-Price playwear).

Over the years, variations of the family branding strategy have evolved. The three most common include:

1. Blanket family name for all products; this strategy is followed by General Electric and Heinz.
2. Separate family names for types of products; this strategy is followed by Sears Roebuck, which markets Kenmore appliances, Craftsman tools, and DieHard batteries.
3. Family names combined with individual brand names; this strategy is pursued by Kellogg's (e.g., Kellogg's Raisin Bran and Kellogg's Corn Flakes).

Consumer firms sometimes start out with a family branding strategy, as Coca-Cola and Pepsi did. However, when new products or product categories are added, they are likely to create new brands for those product lines. For example, newer Coke brands include Sprite, Dasani water, and Fanta.

Business-to-business firms seldom use individual brand names. They are more likely to use family brand names, and the family brand is usually the firm's name. For example, Intel uses its firm name as the family brand name, and then creates product-model names such as the 386, 486, and Pentium processors. Other examples of firm names as brands include Cisco, Boeing, SAP, and International Truck and Engine. General Electric's firm name is used across both consumer (GE Appliances) and business-to-business divisions (GE Medical Systems), using brand consistency across the entire firm to produce economies of scale in marketing. Another firm that employs this strategy is Black & Decker, which markets tools to both the consumer and professional markets, all under the Black & Decker brand.

A strong family brand name will grab customer attention and may lead to product trial. It provides a foot in the door. Family branding is most effective when it is

Successful and Unsuccessful Brand Extensions	Figure 9.10

Successful Brand Extensions to New Product Categories

Base Brand	Brand Extension
Kodak film	Kodak cameras and batteries
Coleman camping lamps	Coleman stoves, tents, sleeping bags
Ivory soap	Ivory shampoo, dishwashing liquid
Woolite detergent	Woolite carpet cleaner
Jell-O gelatin	Jell-O pudding pops
Barbie dolls	Barbie games, furniture, clothes, magazines
Odor-Eater foot pads	Odor-Eater socks
Minolta cameras	Minolta copiers
Honda bikes	Honda cars, lawnmowers, rototillers, generators
Fisher-Price toys	Fisher-Price playwear
Lipton tea	Lipton soup mixes

Unsuccessful Brand Extensions to New Product Categories

Base Brand	Brand Extension
Dunkin' Donuts	Dunkin' Donuts cereal
Jacuzzi baths	Jacuzzi bath toiletries
Stetson hats	Stetson shirts, umbrellas
Levis jeans	Levis business wear
Certs candy	Certs gum
Mr. Coffee coffeemakers	Mr. Coffee coffee

applied to a product that is complementary in usage to the original branded product, an approach evidenced by the successful brand extensions presented in Figure 9.10.

Packaging Decisions

Each year, companies spend more on packaging than on advertising. As markets have matured and competitive differentiation has narrowed, packaging has become a very important component of marketing strategy. Sometimes a firm forgets that it is the packaged product, not just the product that is sold and purchased. A product's package is often its most distinctive marketing effort. Packaging performs a number of essential functions.

- *Protection:* A package must protect the product in several different situations: in the manufacturer's warehouse, during shipment to the wholesaler and retailer, in the seller's warehouse, and in transporting the product from the seller's store to the consumer's final point of consumption.
- *Identification:* Distinctive packaging helps customers identify the product in a crowded marketplace. The classic case of an eye-catching display was the L'Eggs point-of-purchase stand with hundreds of plastic eggs in different colors.
- *Information:* The package provides another means of communicating with the customer. An informed customer gets the very best performance out of a product.
- *Packaging to enhance usage:* Several very innovative packages have added real convenience to product use. For example, when Beech-Nut apple juice switched from cans to bottles (onto which plastic nipples for babies could be attached), sales quadrupled. Another example involved Chesebrough-Ponds, which put nail polish in a special type of felt-tip pen. The new packaging helped increase sales by more than 20%.
- *Packaging to enhance disposal:* A package that is biodegradable, or made from recycled materials, will appeal to environmentally conscious market segments.

Courtesy of Nestlé USA-Beverage Division and Dailey & Associates Advertising

Packaging that makes a product easier to use may increase product usage. Nestea's innovative packaging for its new iced tea concentrate makes great-tasting iced tea without the mess of tea bags.

Downy's change to milk carton refills for fabric softener was to minimize plastic waste.

- *Packaging to enhance channel acceptance:* New shipping and warehouse technology may require standard package dimensions. *Cubic efficiency* is how efficiently a package occupies storage, transportation, and display space. Boxes are more efficient than cans, and cans are more efficient than most bottles. Packaging that suits the needs of channel members is more apt to be adopted than competitive packaging that does not.

Ultimately, effective packaging adds to the value of a product. For instance, opening and resealing, pouring, mixing, processing, and cooking may all be enhanced or made easier by creative packaging. A package also continues to communicate on the kitchen shelf, workshop bench, and, most importantly, during product use. Firms that underestimate the power of a product's packaging are making a major tactical mistake.

Labeling Decisions

A customer can tell a lot about a company by the labels it places on its products. If the label appears to be an afterthought, and contains only what is legally required, then the customer will likely conclude that the company doesn't care. On the other hand, a customer-oriented label is likely to serve the following six functions:

1. Identify the manufacturer, country of origin, and ingredients or materials in the product.
2. Report the expiration date and the contents' grading based on a prescribed government standard (as on cartons of eggs).
3. Explain how to use the product.
4. Warn about potential misuse.
5. Provide easy-to-understand care instructions.
6. Serve as an important communication link among users, eventual buyers, and the company.

A quality label signals a quality product. Often the label must also be designed for a particular market segment. For example, seniors need labels with large lettering. Furthermore, because many customers toss instructions and packaging away, often the only way a customer can reach a manufacturer is through the information (e.g., toll-free number, Internet URL) provided on the label.

Product life cycle

Is the cycle of stages that a product goes through from birth to death: introduction, growth, maturity, and decline.

Managing Products Through Their Life Cycles

A product now has been designed, developed, and tested; brand, label, and package decisions have been made. As product development nears completion, product management is just beginning. The product must now be introduced to the market, and strategies for generating profit over the life of the *product category* (all brands that satisfy a particular need) must be developed and implemented. Figure 9.11 shows the general pattern of expected sales and profit over the **product life cycle**, the cycle of stages that a product goes through from birth to death. The stages include introduction, growth, maturity, and decline. *Innovators* and *early adopters,* customers generally willing to take more risk, buy the product shortly after introduction. During growth, product purchase begins to spread to the *early majority* of the mass market,

The Product Life Cycle	Figure 9.11

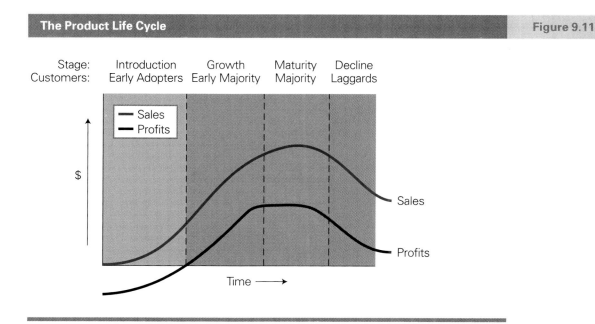

with full penetration and adoption by the *late majority* occurring primarily in the maturity stage. Near the product's decline, only *laggards* are left purchasing the product. Marketing strategy and tactics must be adapted not only to deal with changes in the environmental forces over the life cycle but also to meet the special opportunities and challenges presented by each stage of the life cycle, as illustrated in Figure 9.12.

Introduction Strategies

The introduction stage starts when a new product is presented to the market. Initial sales are slow, as potential customers must go through a learning process about the new product and its benefits before they purchase. Creating customer learning requires heavy expenditures on advertising, sampling, promotion, distribution, and personal selling, all of which contribute to profit losses at this stage. The set of marketing tactics used must work together to make customers aware of the product and encourage them to try it.

Marketing Tactics and Outcomes throughout the Product Life Cycle				Figure 9.12
Outcomes	**Introduction**	**Growth**	**Maturity**	**Decline**
Sales	Low	Fast growth	Slow growth	Decline
Profits	Negligible	Positive to flat	Flat to declining	Low or zero
Cash flow	Negative	Moderate	High	Low
Customers	Innovators	Early majority	Late majority	Laggards
Competitors	Few	Growing	Many rivals	Declining number
Tactics	**Introduction**	**Growth**	**Maturity**	**Decline**
Strategic focus	Expanded market	Market penetration	Defend share	Productivity
Expenditures	High	High (declining %)	Falling	Low
Emphasis	Product awareness	Brand preference	Brand loyalty	Selective
Distribution	Patchy	Intensive	Intensive	Selective
Price	High	Decreasing	Lowest	Rising
Product	Basic	Differentiated	Differentiated	Rationalized

The Individual Adoption Process

Customers go through several distinct stages of learning before purchasing a new product. Ideally, a firm's marketing program helps customers move through these stages, thereby decreasing their risk in purchasing a new product. The stages customers generally go through in the *adoption process* include:

- *Awareness:* Realizing that a new product exists
- *Knowledge:* Building an understanding of what the product does, what benefits it provides, and how it works
- *Liking:* Developing positive feelings toward the product
- *Preference:* Coming to prefer this product over any other, if one were to buy
- *Purchase:* Making the decision to buy and acting on it

To encourage adoption of a new product, firms use their marketing programs to lead potential customers through each successive stage. Before customers can develop knowledge about what a new product does, they must first be aware that it exists. Frequently, product introductions are accompanied by large initial advertising campaigns designed specifically to create awareness. Only after people develop knowledge about a product can they come to a conclusion as to whether they like it. Preference can only develop for products a person likes, which may lead to eventual purchase. The time frame required for new product acceptance varies widely from product to product. Some of the factors that influence this rate of adoption are listed in Figure 9.13.

The elements of the marketing program in the introduction stage of a new product's life cycle are designed to move more innovative customers (early adopters) swiftly through the learning process to purchase. Customers will be slower to adopt products that are more radically innovative, such as microwave ovens when they were first introduced in the 1970s, and products that are expensive, such as HDTVs. More innovative and expensive products require higher marketing effort, especially in the introduction stage.

The Diffusion Process

Broad *product diffusion* into the mass market results from three processes. First, a firm's marketing program induces innovators and early adopters to purchase and try the product, as outlined above. Then, if the design team has developed a product that meets the needs of these customers, they will be satisfied with their purchase and tell other potential customers, generating free word-of-mouth product advertising. Finally, positive word-of-mouth endorsements work in concert with the firm's marketing program to help provide less innovative (more imitative) customers, who make up the bulk of most markets, with enough understanding of and confidence in the product to purchase it. For a more complete understanding of the various types of customers that together create the market, see Figure 9.14.

Figure 9.13	Factors Influencing the Rate of New Product Adoption

- **Relative Advantage:** The greater the relative advantage—the lower price, ease of use, savings in time—the faster the adoption process.
- **Compatibility:** The greater the compatibility—consistent with values, needs, and experiences of potential users—the faster the adoption process.
- **Complexity:** The more difficult a new product is to understand and use, the longer it will take to be adopted.
- **Trialability:** The greater the degree to which the new product can be used on a trial basis, the faster the adoption process.
- **Observability:** The greater the degree to which the results of using a product are visible to others, the faster the adoption process.

Source: Adapted from Everett M. Rogers, *Diffusion of Innovations,* 5th Edition (New York: Free Press, 2003).

Customer Profiles	Figure 9.14

- **Innovators:** Innovators, 2.5% of all potential adopters, tend to be younger, higher in social status, more cosmopolitan, and better educated than later adopter groups.
- **Early adopters:** Early adopters, 13.5% of potential adopters, enjoy the prestige and respect that comes with owning new products, but are less venturesome and more concerned with group norms and values than innovators.
- **Early majority:** The early majority, 34% of potential adopters, spends more time deciding whether to try new products and seeks the opinions of the innovators and early adopters.
- **Late majority:** The late majority, 34% of potential adopters, is less cosmopolitan and responsive to change than any of the previous groups.
- **Laggards:** Laggards, 16% of all potential adopters, tend to be conservative, older, low in socioeconomic status, and suspicious of change.

Word-of-mouth approvals from customers reinforce the messages sent by the firm, giving them credibility. Hearing one's colleagues at work rave about their new Palm Pilot and how it changed the way they organize their life is much more powerful for many people than reading about what the product does in a print ad. Of course, if the product does not live up to expectations, negative word-of-mouth will be generated. This will almost certainly guarantee market failure, regardless of the quality of the marketing program used to launch the product. When Apple's Newton routinely failed to recognize the handwriting of early customers, negative word-of-mouth spread rapidly. Small articles and cartoons poking fun at the problem were even published in the business press, which further contributed to market failure.

Diffusion is only partly under a firm's control. Diffusion is aided early in the development process by ensuring that the product solves the problems customers want solved, and by getting the details of the product right. Once launched, the firm can speed diffusion by developing a marketing program that maximizes the number of people who become early adopters. More early adopters mean that there are more users who can spread positive word-of-mouth endorsements to more potential customers early in the marketing cycle. Finally, a firm can encourage mechanisms to spread word-of-mouth endorsements throughout the target market. For example, Amazon.com allows readers to write and post book reviews that other Amazon.com customers can access. Whatever mechanisms the firm develops must work in concert with the rest of the marketing program surrounding the product launch.

Growth Strategies

The growth stage of the product life cycle is initially characterized by rapidly increasing product demand, new competitors entering the market in response, and rapidly increasing profits for the product varieties that customers decide best meet their needs. The firm's emphasis shifts to building and holding a set of loyal customers and distribution-channel members, and sustaining sales growth as long as possible. To do this, the firm may invest in product improvements and in expanding and strengthening distribution channels. As overall spending increases to offset competitive pressures, profits begin to level off as the product category leaves the growth stage and enters the maturity stage.

Maturity Strategies

Most product categories can be assigned to the maturity stage; therefore, marketing managers most often deal with mature products. During the maturity stage, sales initially increase, but at a slower rate as the market becomes saturated and as competitive pressures reach their peak. Sales and profits typically decline in the latter half of the maturity stage.

Using the marketing program to maintain customer loyalty and satisfaction is important for maintaining profitability throughout the maturity stage. Airline frequent-flier programs, hotel honored-guest programs, and grocery store frequent-shopper programs were developed to maintain customer loyalty and improve profits. The objective is to take the pressure off price reductions as a way to keep customers by using other tactics in the marketing mix. Several strategies can be used, even in maturity, to attempt to grow the market. For example, a firm can find new users (*market development*) or increase the usage rate per user (*market penetration*). Another mechanism for growth in the mature stage is to offer significant improvements on a routine basis (*product development*). Each of these intensive growth strategies was introduced in Chapter 2.

Decline Strategies

Even if new users are found and usage rates are increased, product sales may eventually start a long-term decline, as when a substitute product that offers a superior set of benefits displaces the "old" product. Products based on new technologies frequently lead to a current product's demise. For example, 35 years ago nearly every student going to college brought along a typewriter. First, the electric typewriter caused the decline of manual typewriter sales. Then word-processing machines started making inroads into the electric typewriter market. But the real deathblow to typewriter sales was dealt by the advent of the PC and easy-to-use word-processing programs like Write, WordPerfect, and Word. Some offices still use a few forms that require a typewriter. However, the majority of offices and students now depend on PCs and word-processing programs for producing easily readable written communication.

One strategy firms can use to reduce decline is to take the product, or even a simplified version of the product, into an emerging or developing country where technology or the environmental infrastructure may not be as sophisticated as in a developed country. For example, typewriters are still much more prevalent in India, China, and parts of the Caribbean, where electrical power may be much less certain. Note that these machines may be manual, rather than electric. When the original

A brand's decline may not be permanent. The new VW Beetle has been significantly improved with new technologies, but retains the brand equity associated with the name.

© Susan Van Etten

Volkswagen beetle was withdrawn from the U.S. market because it no longer met pollution or safety requirements, it was still a strong seller in South America. The simplicity of its air-cooled engine—the cause of its not meeting U.S. pollution requirements—is a benefit in less technologically sophisticated countries. South American sales provided income to see the firm through until it could develop a series of new cars (Golf, Jetta, and Passat) that did meet the needs of the more stringent U.S. regulations. The successful reintroduction of the "new Beetle" to the U.S. market in 1999 demonstrates how firms can come full circle through the life cycle and restart it.

Reduced sales do not necessarily mean that a firm should exit the business immediately. The higher a firm's competitive strength in an industry, the longer it will want to stay in the market to reap returns from previous investments. However, the marketing tactics used at this stage will again have to be modified to maintain acceptable profitability levels. Marketing expenses, and promotion expenses in particular, will need to be reduced. IBM divested its typewriter division in the 1990s so that it could continue operations without being burdened by the large overhead costs associated with IBM's traditional business structures. The new firm's lower overhead allows it to profitably produce low-cost typewriters for developing economies. Products in decline continue to sell, but customer satisfaction (and thus loyalty) and word-of-mouth become more important generators of sales than marketing campaigns.

Applicability of the Product Life Cycle

Some marketing academics question the applicability of the product life cycle. They point to very long-lived product categories such as bar soap, grand pianos, and cars as counterexamples, suggesting that after more than 100 years, they are still in maturity. Certainly, the car market fluctuates with economic cycles, but is still steadily trending up. Currently, there is no real competing technology for cars. Personal helicopters or transporting devices to supplant car use have not yet been invented. When they are, perhaps the car market will start into an overall decline. However, as partial support for the applicability of the product life cycle in this market, there are shifts and movements across different segments of the overall car market. Station wagons, the car of preference for families in the 1950s to 1980s, are nearly defunct, having given way to minivans. Enormous luxury sedans, like the Crown Victoria, have declined in favor of enormous luxury SUVs. Thus, the product life cycle is more appropriate at some levels of analysis than others. If one considered the "product" to be cars in general, perhaps the life cycle is less important, as critics claim. However, even though the overall market is stable, demand shifts across segments, suggesting that this may be a more appropriate level at which to apply the concept of life cycles.

Chapter Summary

Learning Objective 1: *Classify products by who the buyer is and the purpose for which the product is being bought.* Products are the lifeblood of every organization, whether they are goods, services, people, places, or ideas. In general, products can be classified either as consumer or business-to-business products. Consumer products include convenience, shopping, specialty, and unsought products, all of which are characterized based on how the consumer views and shops for the product. Business-to-business products include installations, accessories, raw materials, component parts/materials, and supplies and are classified based on how the products will be used.

Learning Objective 2: *Create a portfolio of products that provides appropriate product depth and breadth for your target customers.* Few companies are successful that rely on a single product. Most companies manufacture and market a variety of products, called a product mix. This portfolio of products may be targeted to just one set of customers, or may target multiple segments. It can consist of products within just one product category, or products from multiple categories.

Learning Objective 3: *Define new and successful products and understand why products fail so that the stage for successful product development is set.* Marketing's role in successfully accomplishing new product development requires firms to continually: understand customer needs and problems, match technological capabilities to solving those problems, and move projects through the corporation and into the market. Unless all three tasks are performed well, product development is unlikely to be successful.

Changes in any of the six environmental forces (technological, competitive, political/legal, economic, natural resource, or sociocultural) can lead to the need to reevaluate the usefulness of the firm's products. Should the company's products no longer provide competitively advantaged solutions to customers at a profit, the firm will have to undertake a redevelopment program or face share, volume, and/or profit erosion.

Learning Objective 4: *Develop successful new products through uncovering unmet needs, using proven development methods, and managing the project through the organization's infrastructure.* Understanding customer needs means performing qualitative market research and making the details available to the development team. No one technique will easily provide *all* customer needs. Actually being a customer best conveys tacit needs. Process-related needs are identified most easily by critically observing customers. In-depth interviewing is the most efficient means of obtaining masses of detailed needs, but may not provide tacit and process-related information. Development teams must use the most appropriate customer need–identification technique(s), given the informational requirements, budget, and time frame for their project.

Effectively using technological capabilities to solve problems requires implementing a strategy for the NPD program overall, strategies for each project, and a product-development process. Commercializing new products consists of repeatable tasks and less repeatable tasks. Firms that use a formalized new-product process to help complete the more repeatable tasks in a consistent manner tend to have greater NPD success.

Shepherding products through the firm requires implementing effective leadership, providing an organizational structure that allows projects to move forward efficiently, and developing mechanisms to maintain management support over the life of projects. Project leaders, champions, and process owners all have been used to lead projects effectively. NPD in firms is organized through two different structures, each providing better ways to organize depending on the "newness to the organization" of the project being developed. No one structure seems to be associated with consistently higher performance.

Learning Objective 5: *Make decisions about brand names, packaging, and labeling.* Product decisions must be made in the areas of branding, packaging, and labeling. Strong brands that provide both financial and strategic equity to the firm are memorable, attract attention, communicate the product's position, and distinguish the product from competing products. While most business-to-business firms use their firm name as a family brand, consumer-product firms are more likely to develop individual brand names. Good brands develop packages and labels that are consistent with the brand image, and provide all the protection and information needed by both customers and other channel members.

Learning Objective 6: *Manage products for profitability, from their introduction through growth and into maturity and decline.* Once launched, marketing must manage profitability throughout the product life cycle by modifying marketing-mix elements to achieve the objectives of different life-cycle stages. The objective in the introduction stage is to make potential early adopters aware of the product and persuade them to try it. During growth, the objective is achieving maximum market share. Profitability is the primary objective during both maturity and decline.

Key Terms

For interactive study: visit http://bestpractices.swlearning.com.

Brand equity, 297
Brands, 272
Competitively advantaged product, 281
Core benefit proposition (CBP), 277
Concept, 283
Customer prototypes, 289

Features, 272
Line extensions, 276
Product-development process, 289
Product life cycle, 300
Product line, 275
Product mix, 275
Products, 272

Project strategy, 280
Prototype, 283
Stage-gate™ process, 290
Tacit knowledge, 284
Voice of the customer (VOC), 286

Questions for Review and Discussion

1. How do the differences between consumer products and business-to-business products affect the way new-product development is managed and organized?

2. Several examples were given in the chapter of products that were successful along one dimension of success, but not along another. What are some other examples, and along what dimensions were they less successful? Why did the companies undertake these projects?

3. NPD teams always seem to want to include every feature possible in a new product. The restraint shown by the Palm Pilot team in not adding infrared technology to the first-generation product is unusual. What steps can be taken to keep NPD teams from "over-featuring" the product?

4. Why do NPD processes need to be "personalized" for each firm? What are the factors that will contribute to the way in which a firm personalizes the process for its use?

5. What is the weakest aspect of our understanding about how to manage NPD?

6. In which types of NPD projects might a heavyweight project manager not be successful? A champion?

7. Hewlett-Packard started as a firm that developed and sold scientific measurement equipment like oscilloscopes. Over the years, the company has increased the width of its product mix to include computer equipment and medical equipment. Name three other companies that have increased their product-mix width, and name the sets of product lines they sell.

8. Since Procter & Gamble is such a highly revered company and strong marketer, why does it follow an individual branding strategy rather than take advantage of a family brand name?

9. In what stage of the product life cycle are family sedans? Station wagons? Minivans? Sports cars? If these are all segments of the car market, how is it possible for them to be at different stages of the product life cycle?

10. Is the product life cycle a useful concept in product management?

In-Class Team Activities

1. Laptop computers fulfill the general need of "allowing me to do all of my work, wherever I am." Break into small groups of three to four people. Develop a set of five to six use situations for laptops that stretch the capabilities one would need to develop across different performance dimensions. These are the situations the team could use for interviewing laptop users to obtain the voice of the customer.

2. In small groups of three to four people, fill in the tasks that each function needs to undertake in each step of the stage-gate process for product development outlined in Figure 9.7.

Internet Questions

1. Go to the Web site http://www.pdma.org. This is the Web site for the Product Development & Management Association (PDMA), a nonprofit association whose mission is to seek out, develop, organize, and disseminate leading-edge information on the theory and practice of product development and product-development processes. How does PDMA's Web site, and the associated hotlinks, help fulfill that mission?

2. The Internet is changing the way some firms gather customer information. See if you can find a company that is using the Internet to gather information on customer needs. What evidence on their site suggests that they are using the information gathered to aid in developing new products? What are the benefits of gathering information on customer needs from the Web? What are the drawbacks? For what kinds of industries might this information be most useful or appropriate to use? Least useful or appropriate?

3. What information about innovation can be obtained from the following Web sites: http://www.inside.com, http://www.creativemag.com, http://www.fastcompany.com, http://www.idsa.org, http://www.pachamber.org? How would you use this information in developing a new product?

CHAPTER CASE

Developing a "Next-Generation" Truck at International Truck and Engine

International Truck and Engine Corporation is a leading North American producer of heavy-duty trucks (Class 8, or semis, where the tractor is separate from the trailer); medium-duty trucks (Class 5–7, where the cab is integrated into the body of the truck, as in beverage and parcel-delivery trucks); severe-service trucks (dump trucks and interstate snow plows), and school buses. In the 1980s, International (originally named International Harvester and then renamed Navistar) focused management efforts on attaining operational excellence in truck manufacturing. These actions reduced product costs, radically improved manufactured-truck quality, and put the company on a solid performance track. By the early 1990s, the company was mean and lean, but hadn't commercialized a new product since 1978.

In 1991, the company instituted a new product program to refresh the interiors of International's reliable, but aging, medium-duty trucks. While the refresh program helped sustain the business, International considered this just a scrimmage for the real goal—developing an entirely new product line. The company knew it needed to design and develop an entirely new truck platform—a "next-generation vehicle"—that would deliver significant additional customer benefits to better meet needs, while taking advantage of platform economies of scale to truly grow the business.

In early 1997, the company assigned Mark Stasell to lead a cross-functional team to collect customer input and create the line's core benefit proposition (CBP). As in many business-to-business markets, the customer research project was complicated because the team had to uncover needs from different kinds of people affected by the product: those who drive the trucks, sometimes for many hours a day; those who maintain and repair the trucks; and the trucks' owners, who are interested in profiting from ownership. Based on input about what all these different types of customers value, the CBP became "vehicles that distinguish themselves by establishing new benchmarks for life cycle value and performance." The overall goal was to develop a product that "excites drivers, delights maintainers, and enriches owners."

After developing an initial understanding of customer needs, the team turned to all the other tasks associated with a major product-development planning effort in the preliminary investigation phase of development. Over the next few months, they constructed modularity strategies, estimated development expenses and product manufacturing costs, and completed and made preliminary design decisions for structural aspects of the product. Producing a vehicle that delivered life-cycle value required defining and then developing a total benefit package that provided higher overall customer value and profitability over the life cycle of product ownership, even though the initial cost would be higher than competing products. Improvements in driving up-time and reductions in maintenance cost were designed to allow initially higher prices for owners to be recouped over the life of the vehicle. Increased fuel efficiencies through streamlining the hood and cab to minimize drag were also planned to contribute to increasing profits, while simultaneously giving the truck a distinctive and aerodynamic look. Strategies to use modular parts in a number of components were developed to delight the maintainer by simplifying part replacements. Significant numbers of interior changes were designed to drastically increase driver comfort and safety.

The team got formal board approval in October 1997 for this "bet the company" endeavor to produce a new truck. International formed a new center, called the Next-Generation Product Center, to develop this platform that would apply across its four product lines. The Center's mandate was to produce an underlying truck platform that would have significant structural and component commonality across the four business units, while still successfully meeting the very different needs of each product line. Thus, the Product Center consisted of two different sets of teams. Four program teams, one for each business unit (heavy, medium, severe-service, and school bus), focused on creating vehicles that would suit the needs of their specific customers. Simultaneously, 17 systems teams (cab chassis, electrical, etc.) concentrated on developing systems modules that would be common across the platform for all business units. Significant use of modules was planned to increase economies of manufacturing scale for the components, decreasing both development and production cost, while increasing quality.

Over the next two-and-a-half years, teams of engineers designed, tested, and redesigned all the elements of the first product in the platform to launch—the medium-duty truck. International followed a structured stage-gate™ process personalized to the complexities of truck development. Stasell's team benchmarked several companies, including Honda, Chrysler, and Case, to uncover a number of best practices, which they also adopted.

Model-based product development was used to create virtual trucks well in advance of physical prototypes becoming available. Computer-aided engineering and simulation software programs, the backbone of model-based product development, allowed components and subsystems to be tested for structural integrity and physical behavior earlier in the product-development process than ever before.

In addition to testing the components and subsystems in a simulated environment, the product-development process included three other kinds of tests. First, laboratory-based tests were run on the simulation-optimized components and subassemblies to ensure that actual performance equaled predicted performance. Complete vehicle testing was then done on International's proving grounds outside of Fort Wayne, Indiana. Very early, several prototypes were built and put into field tests with actual truck drivers driving them in real situations. For example, one truck was made into a beverage-delivery truck used in city delivery of soft drinks. Customer insights from those driving these early prototype trucks were used to refine features and driving performance. Ultimately, more than 50 vehicles were seeded into various use applications for in-field durability and driving performance testing prior to launch.

Two of the team's strategies acted jointly to increase quality and decrease costs. First, the strategic decision to "not be all things to all people," as Internationals' legacy trucks had tried to be, allowed the company to integrate and optimize components to focus on life-cycle value and specific use applications for the medium-duty truck. For example, customers of the legacy truck could specify 850 engine/transmission combinations. This made it difficult to optimize performance across the two components, created production-quality problems on the manufacturing line, and increased component costs, as no one component had high enough volumes for large discounts from suppliers. The new product limited choice to 34 engine-and-transmission combinations, each of which was optimized to deliver superior drivability. Drivers of the customer prototype units indicated that the medium truck "drove as well as my SUV." Higher volumes of fewer different choices, combined with the strategy to develop modules that ultimately could be used across all four platforms, again increasing total volumes needed, allowed the team to attract larger and more capable suppliers and negotiate volume discounts. The team believed that lower variability on the manufacturing line, combined with higher quality from suppliers, would vastly increase the straight ship rate—the percentage of trucks shipped straight from the end of the assembly line to customers without needing defects fixed.

The cab team's goal was to design a best-in-class driver environment. First, information allowing them to do so was gathered from multiple drivers. This was translated into requirements for instrument-panel structure and was used to make decisions regarding location and operation of driver controls. These decisions were tested with drivers in prototypes and adjustments were made based on their feedback. From Nissan, they sourced an intelligent body-assembly system for the cab. This automated assembly system would allow the standard cab, the longer extended cab, and the travel crew cab to be built through one framing station. This flexible assembly system also would allow the company to change designs more often. Because design changes could be implemented merely by reprogramming the equipment on the line, the plan for the future was to "refresh" each product line every five years and develop brand new platforms every 10 years.

By the summer of 2000, the team was ready to go to the board of directors to request the nearly $200 million necessary for final manufacturing ramp-up and product launch in February 2001. This money was needed to finish installing and debugging equipment on the line, start training employees on the operation of new equipment, develop and reproduce the final marketing and sales materials, and finance the customer launch event. The team wanted to invite the majority of dealers and customers to a blow-out launch party that included test-track drive comparisons of the next-generation vehicle to both legacy and competitive products.

In addition, the team needed to propose to the board the timing for moving the new platform over to each of the other three business units. On the one hand, the full impact of scale economies could not be realized until all four product lines used the modular components developed in this program. On the other hand, each of these development projects would require additional tens and hundreds of millions of dollars of investment. The team would need to propose to the board the level of investment for each of the next several years, and both how many and which business units to migrate the platform to in what order.

Taken in a vacuum, it might seem obvious that the board would have no choice but to approve the appropriation request, and even recommend plunging full speed ahead on modifying the base platform to meet the needs of the other three business units. But product development doesn't happen in a vacuum. Environmental forces, such as the state of the economy, interact with decisions made for all elements of the marketing mix, including product-development decisions. Total truck industry retail sales in 1999 were 465,500 units for Class 5–8 trucks, a new record high. However, by mid-2000, the economy already had started to decline, and the volume forecast for the year was down more than 5%, to 440,000 units. The prognosis for 2001, the launch year and a year that the team wanted the company to spend hundreds of millions more in platform migration to the other business units, was forecast to be dismal—somewhere on the order of 325,000 units. While net profits for the company in 1999 were at a record high of $544 million, International already was preparing for far lower profitability in 2000 and the possibility of losses should the economy remain in a recession.

Case Questions

1. Should International launch the next-generation vehicle during this downtime in the economy? What are the pros and cons?
2. When is the "best" time to launch a new product— during downtimes or during growth periods?
3. How should Mark Stasell make the argument to the board? What facts are important to marshal when seeking board approval?
4. How does a product-development team convince a board of directors to continue to invest large amounts of money in product development when the future holds potential losses due to economic factors that have nothing to do with the company's abilities?
5. Think about how to migrate the new platform across business divisions, given financial investment constraints. Remember that full financial (and brand image) benefits do not accrue to the company until all units use the new platform. What factors are important in determining the order in which you migrate it? How should the team go about making the decision?

Source: As reported on *World Business Review, 2003*. The video of this program can be viewed at: http://www.internationaldelivers.com/site_layout/news/special-report.asp (accessed December 2002).

VIDEO CASE

PING—The Sound of Innovation

Karsten Solheim's desire to improve his golf game convinced the former General Electric engineer to try to build a better golf club. Named for the recognizable "ping" sound, which is heard when the ball makes contact with the putter's club face, PING golf clubs are praised by golfers of all skill levels for their innovative design and performance.

Conceived by Solheim using the laws of physics and engineering, the first PING putter was introduced in 1959 and revolutionized golf club design. Seven years later, his Anser putter racked up more than 500 wins and changed putting forever. Since then, golfers using PING putters have won more than 1,900 professional tour events, including 47 major tournaments.

From humble beginnings working in his garage, Solheim became the most widely copied golf club designer in the world. Today the company he built, Karsten Manufacturing (now called PING Inc.), is run by his son, president and CEO John Solheim, and employs 900 people at its 30-acre corporate headquarters in Phoenix, Arizona.

History has shown that innovators are often punished for challenging the establishment, and PING was no exception. The U.S. Golf Association (USGA) outlawed all of its putters except one until PING made some minor adjustments to its clubs. As televised coverage of tournaments increased, so did public awareness of PING's putters. Golf fans started asking about the "funny-looking" putters used by such golf greats as Jack Nicklaus and Gary Player.

PING realized that an educated consumer would be its best customer, so it started bringing customers into its plant to teach them about the unique features of its clubs and other golf equipment. A key component of PING's product-development strategy was Solheim's belief that custom-fitted clubs would enhance a golfer's performance and enjoyment of the game.

His revolutionary concept was responsible for the company's specialization and leadership role in developing and manufacturing custom-fitted golf clubs. Today, more than 2,200 trained club fitters, who must complete an intensive three-day club-fitting seminar at the company's headquarters, help customers choose the right PING clubs designed to fit their own personal specifications. The golfer's swing is measured for length, lie, loft, and grip, and wrist-to-floor measurements are taken.

Once the fitting process is complete, the customer's specifications are sent to PING's production department. The "PING man," a mechanical golfer, tests clubs for the small modifications that can make all the difference to a player's game, and all aspects of production are handled on site. The company even has its own metal foundry to make sure its clubs meet its stringent tolerances.

A custom set of clubs can be manufactured and shipped out in just two days, imprinted with the customer's unique serial number. The company's sophisticated tracking system keeps tabs on the whereabouts of all clubs and their specifications. If a customer loses a club, it can quickly and easily be replaced.

In late 2002, PING became the first golf-equipment company to allow golfers to design their clubs online. By visiting **http://www.pinggolf.com/specify**, customers can select the look, style, feel, and weight of their own custom-designed PING SPECIFY putter. "With the interactivity that the World Wide Web provides, this is a natural opportunity to move golfers from the putting green to the computer screen to create their own SPECIFY putter," says John Solheim. Once the putter is created, the golfer can either print a picture of it or have a large image of the putter e-mailed to him from PING.

There is no cost involved until the customer actually places an order for the SPECIFY putter of his or her choice. Using the site's Retailer Locator, buyers can order their putter directly from their nearest retail location. "This new online program not only helps the consumer understand the options available with the SPECIFY putter, it is another example of how our company supports its retailers with innovation and service," says Solheim.

In addition to insisting on the very best equipment, today's golfers are extremely conscious of fashion trends and new apparel technologies. The PING Apparel Collection translates PING's technological excellence in equipment into apparel. Imagine six rounds in five days in Ireland with only rain and fog for company. The Tour Rainsuit was designed with these weather conditions in mind, providing players with freedom of movement and protection from the elements. The Rainsuit includes such special features as an adjustable collar designed to reduce dripping down the player's back and specially shaped cuffs to shed water away from the club's grip. Each suit is a technological marvel—and is numbered to prove it. On the inside pocket, a label states which suit out of 600 an individual has. Only 50 PING Collection Tour Rainsuits, costing $1,000 each, will be available to consumers in the United States this year.

As a privately held company, PING does not have to answer to shareholders, and John Solheim likes it that way. The company has recently chosen to move in another new direction—forming strategic marketing alliances with complementary specialty license brands like NASCAR. Racing has a higher brand loyalty than golf—72% against golf's 42%—and PING believes there are major benefits to be gained from this alliance.

PING continues to explore new marketing opportunities to complement its powerful product-plus-service bundle that enhances the golf-playing experience for its customers. The PING vault at company headquarters is filled with replicas of winning putters plated in gold, attesting to the company's successful product-development and marketing strategies and efficient delivery systems. PING's marketing and product-development philosophy is simple—give people what they want and they will buy it. Its deep respect for the game and its players can only mean more winning products for the country's 25 million golfers using the next generation of PING products.

Case Questions

1. What role has PING's marketing played in developing new products? Explain.
2. Describe the unique benefits of the company's custom golf club tracking and delivery system.
3. How has PING's commitment to innovative marketing concepts benefitted its customers?

Sources: Adapted from material in the video: "PING-Karsten."

PING-Karsten corporate Web site, http://www. ping.com, accessed 7 May 2003.

"PING Introduces Web Site for Golfers to Create Their Own SPECIFY Putter," *PRNewswire*, 9 December 2002.

http://www.findarticles.com; accessed June 2003.

"PING Named Top Custom-Fitting Golf Equipment Company By National Survey of Golfers," *PRNewswire*, 24 October 2001, downloaded from http:// www.findarticles.com; accessed June 2003.

Technology-enabled loyalty programs are now being implemented via scanner cards. These cards benefit consumers by saving them time in the purchase process. The cards benefit businesses because they encourage customer retention, higher purchase amounts, and greater purchase frequency. For example, consumers using the Starbucks card can place credit on their card at the Starbucks Web site. Each time the customer swipes the card to make a Starbucks purchase, the appropriate amount is deducted from the card. Consumers who use the cards can get in and out of the store faster and are more likely to bypass a competitor to purchase from Starbucks since their money has already been invested in the card. Although implementing a loyalty program is expensive, the rewards of enhancing the customer's experience can far outweigh the costs.

You Decide. After reading the opening vignette and paying special attention to the sections of this chapter marked with the chess piece, answer these questions:

1. Of the four unique characteristics that differentiate services from goods, which one is especially related to the benefits provided by technology-enabled loyalty cards?

2. Implementing a loyalty program provides the company with a database of customers. What would be a firm's greatest advantage in using this database for customer-relationship management (CRM)?

3. Technologically enabled loyalty cards may best help to narrow which service-quality gap?

© Susan Van Etten

Loyalty Gadgets: The Marriage Between Technology and Loyalty Marketing

One of the most recent innovations in loyalty marketing has been the development of techno-logically based loyalty devices. Examples of such gadgets include the Starbucks stored-value card, ExxonMobil Speedpass (a miniature plastic transponder that can be attached to the customer's key chain), and Vail Resort's Colorado Card. Loyalty devices offer convenience by enabling customers to conduct transactions both faster and easier than ever before. However, the real secret of their popularity for customers and marketers alike lies in their ability to create a sense of belongingness. Ruth P. Stevens, president of New York-based E-Marketing Strategy agrees: "They are a beautiful way to create a sense of belongingness. Other than the physical (and) practical benefits of saving time (and) convenience, you also get a feel that, 'This is my store and I am a member of the club.'"

Many loyalty devices are much like the gift cards sold at many of today's major retailers. However, customers are able to reload their loyalty cards by accessing the sponsoring company's Web site, such as http://www.starbucks.com, and charge their card-replenishment amounts to their personal credit cards. Better yet, many of these cards, such as the Colorado Card (http://www.snow.com), can be tied directly to the customer's credit-card account. In general, loyalty cards streamline the customer's payment activities. For example, Colorado Card holders pay a base fee for unlimited skiing at a number of Vail resort properties, such as Arapahoe Basin, Breckenridge, Keystone, and Vail itself. In addition, since the Colorado Card can be tied to the customer's credit card, it can also be used at numerous ski rental, merchandise, and food and beverage locations on the slopes.

Cardholders obtain several benefits by purchasing and using the Colorado Card. First, the customer no longer has to stand in line to purchase a lift ticket. Colorado Card holders simply ski directly to the lift itself, where a resort employee scans a bar code on the Colorado Card. Once the card has been scanned, the customer is free to begin skiing immediately. Essentially, the Colorado Card removes cash from the skiing experience, which is a huge benefit to customers wearing cumbersome ski clothes. The Colorado Card is also combined with six "Ski-with-a-Friend" tickets, which encourages Colorado Card holders to bring along their friends (who are able to purchase lift tickets at a discounted rate). Finally, cardholders are also rewarded Peak Points for using their Colorado card that can be redeemed for free lift tickets and/or a variety of ski rental, merchandise, and dining discounts.

From a marketing perspective, loyalty-based programs offer a number of worthwhile benefits. First, they speed up a necessary action—payment. Second, they provide novelty to the service experience and in some instances may be perceived as "cool." For example, more than five million customers have signed up for the Starbucks card since it was introduced in November 2001. Flashing the card has become part of the Starbucks experience. As the name implies, loyalty cards facilitate customer retention and increase purchase amounts and purchase frequency. Scott Waltmann, a Merrill Lynch analyst for Starbucks, notes, "The Starbucks card has a lot of usability—the average office worker may go downstairs for coffee two to three times a day. The card locks in the customer, because if they have a balance on the card, they're more likely to walk past another coffee purveyor to go to Starbucks." ExxonMobil has noted similar results with Speed-pass. Speedpass customers, now numbering in excess of five million, spend 15% more on gasoline purchases and visit the station one more time a month than non-Speedpass customers. In essence, it appears that customers spend more when they don't see the money! Interestingly, Speedpass is now usable at more

LEARNING OBJECTIVES

After you have completed this chapter, you should be able to:

1. *Understand the fundamental differences between the marketing of goods and the marketing of services.*

2. *Master the major factors that influence the creation of the service experience.*

3. *Understand the components of customer satisfaction and distinguish the pros and cons of customer-relationship management.*

4. *Appreciate the managerial significance of the gap model of service quality.*

5. *Recognize the importance of customer retention and identify tactics that help firms retain customers.*

VOICE OF THE EXPERT
K. Douglas Hoffman, Colorado State University

Today, much of the world economy is dominated by the service sector. In the U.S., approximately 80% of the labor force, 75% of the GDP, 45% of an average family's budget, and 33% of exports are now accounted for by services. The primary purpose of this chapter is to introduce you to the field of services marketing and acquaint you with specific customer-service issues. The business world now demands, in addition to traditional business knowledge, increasing employee competence in customer satisfaction, service quality, and customer service, skills that are essential in sustaining the existing customer base.

It is my personal belief that this chapter will heighten your sensitivity to services, and because of that belief, I leave you with this promise. After completing this chapter, you will most likely never look at a service experience in the same way again. This new view will become increasingly frustrating for most of you, as you will encounter many service experiences in your own lives that are less than satisfactory. Learn from these negative experiences, relish the positive encounters, and use this information to make a difference when it is your turn to set the standards for others to follow. As an apostle of services marketing, I could ask for no greater reward.

than 500 McDonald's restaurants and customers can now purchase Speedpass-enabled Timex watches.

Implementing a loyalty-based program does not come cheaply. Expenses include press releases and advertising, card reload costs, synchronizing the provider's inventory-management system, and, of course, the cost of the scanning technology. However, nontechnologically based loyalty cards are much less costly to implement. For example, a simple paper card such as a Buy-10, Get-One-Free Card is a great example of a low-cost alternative that also builds customer loyalty. The beauty of any loyalty program is that it enhances the customer's overall experience through added convenience and a sense of belongingness.[1]

In this chapter, you will gain an understanding of the unique challenges involved in marketing and managing service operations. You will learn the four fundamental differences between the marketing of goods and the marketing of services, how customers derive service benefits through the experience created for them, and how the economic value of a product increases as products transform themselves from commodities to goods to services to compelling experiences. Within this chapter, you will also gain valuable insights into managing and measuring customer satisfaction and service quality, the pros and cons associated with customer-relationship management, the value of customer retention, and the importance of developing a service-recovery program. Finally, and perhaps most importantly, you should gain an appreciation for the notion that regardless of whether one is marketing a good or a service, service aspects associated with any product can lead to a strategic competitive advantage in the marketplace.

LEARNING OBJECTIVE 1

The Fundamentals of Services Marketing

Competitive Forces

Due to product parity among competitors, business is now using service as a competitive advantage. For example, Hewlett-Packard has embraced this strategy through their tagline: "A Box Without Service is Just a Box."

Services are everywhere we turn, whether we are visiting the doctor, responding to e-mail messages, eating at a favorite restaurant, or attending college classes. Simply put, the global service economy is booming. More and more, the so-called industrialized countries are discovering that their service sector is generating the majority of their gross national product. However, the growth of the service sector does not just arise within traditional service industries such as business services, the hospitality industry, health care, and other professional services. Traditional goods producers such as automotive, computer, and numerous other manufacturers are now turning to the service aspects of their operations to establish a competitive advantage in the marketplace. These previously unexplored service aspects also generate additional sources of revenue for their firms. In essence, these companies, which used to compete by marketing "boxes" (tangible goods), have now switched their competitive focus to providing unmatched, unparalleled customer services.

Ample evidence documents this transition from selling boxes to service competition.[2] For example, the traditional goods-producing automotive industry now emphasizes the service aspects of its businesses: low-APR financing, attractive lease arrangements, bumper-to-bumper factory warranties, low-maintenance guarantees, and free shuttle services for customers. Simultaneously, automotive firms are saying less about the tangible aspects of vehicles, such as gas mileage, acceleration, and leather seats, in their marketing communications. Similarly, the personal computer industry promotes in-home repairs, 24-hour customer service, and leasing arrange-

The automobile industry is now turning to the service aspects, such as special low financing arrangements, to establish a competitive advantage.

© Susan Van Etten

ments, and the satellite television industry now touts the benefits of digital service, pay-per-view alternatives, and security options to prevent children from viewing certain programming.

What Is a Service?

Services include a vast array of businesses ranging from profit to nonprofit services, private to government services, and unskilled to professional services (see Figure 10.1). However, the distinction between goods and services is not always perfectly clear. In fact, providing an example of a pure good or a pure service is very difficult in today's market economies. A pure good implies that any benefits received by the consumer contain no elements supplied by service. Similarly, a pure service would contain no benefits provided by tangible elements.

In reality, many services contain at least some "goods," or tangible elements, such as the menu selections at an Outback Steakhouse, a MasterCard statement from MBNA, or the written life insurance policy that State Farm Insurance issues. Also, most goods at least offer "services," or intangible elements. For example, table salt is delivered to the grocery store, but a company such as Morton Salt that sells it

Types of Services			Figure 10.1
Government Services	**Nonprofit Services**	**For-Profit Services**	**Professional Services**
Police and fire protection	Community hospitals	Car rental	Legal
IRS	United Way	Movie theater	Medical
Social Security	American Red Cross	Car wash	Insurance
Social services	Credit unions	Dry cleaning	Financial
Public transportation	Civic organizations	Landscaping	Architectural
U.S. Postal Service	Humane societies	Taxi service	Accounting
Department of Motor Vehicles		Airlines	Consulting
		Salon	

to thousands of retailers may offer innovative invoicing services that further differentiate it from competitors. The distinction between goods and services is blurred even further because a number of firms conduct business on both sides of the goods/services fence. For example, General Motors, the goods-manufacturing giant, generates 20% of its revenue from its financial and insurance businesses, and the carmaker's biggest supplier is Blue Cross and Blue Shield, not a parts supplier of steel, tires, or glass, as most people would think.[3]

Despite the confusion, the following definitions should provide a sound starting point for developing an understanding of the differences between goods and services. In general, **goods** are objects, devices, or things, whereas **services** are deeds, efforts, or performances.[4] Ultimately, the primary difference between goods and services is the property of **intangibility**—lacking physical substance. Because of intangibility, a host of marketing problems for services arise that are not always adequately solved by traditional goods-related marketing solutions. For example, how would you (1) advertise a service that no one can see; (2) price a service that has no cost of goods sold; (3) inventory a service that cannot be stored; or (4) mass-produce a service that needs to be performed by an individual (e.g., dentist, lawyer, physician)? Clearly, managing a service operation seems much more complicated than managing a firm that primarily produces and markets goods.

The Product Continuum

One helpful approach to looking at the differences between goods and services is provided by the *product continuum*.[5] This scale, presented in Figure 10.2 displays a range of products based on their tangibility and illustrates that there is really no such thing as a pure good or a pure service. All products have some tangible and intangible aspects. Goods are *tangible-dominant*. As such, goods possess physical properties called *search attributes* that customers can feel, taste, and see prior to their purchase decisions. For example, when purchasing a car, the consumer can kick the tires, look at the engine, listen to the stereo, smell that "new-car smell," and take the car for a test drive before making the actual purchase. In contrast, services are *intangible-dominant*. As such, services are primarily characterized by *experience attributes* and *credence attributes*. Experience attributes can be evaluated only during and after consumption, such as a meal at a restaurant or the quality of a haircut.

Goods
Are objects, devices, or things.

Services
Are deeds, efforts, or performances.

Intangibility
Is a distinguishing characteristic of services that makes them unable to be touched or sensed in the same manner as physical goods.

Figure 10.2	The Product Continuum

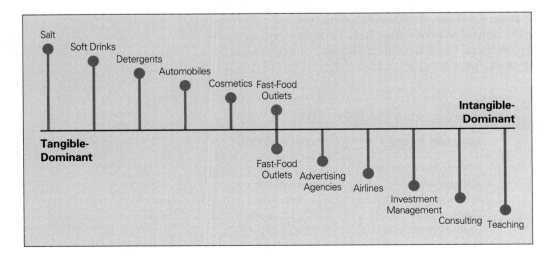

Source: Adapted from G. Lynn Shostack, "Breaking Free from Product Marketing," *Journal of Marketing* (April 1997): 77. Used by permission of the American Marketing Association.

Build-A-Bear has turned teddy bear construction into a compelling experience. Here, a child kisses her teddy bear's heart before it is placed in her new bear.

Credence attributes cannot be evaluated with certainty even after consumption of the product, such as a minister's counseling or a financial advisor's retirement investment advice. Finally, businesses such as fast-food restaurants, whose products contain both goods and services components, fall in the middle of the continuum and are characterized by a combination of search, experience, and credence attributes.

The product continuum affirms that manufacturers of tangible goods that ignore, or at least forget about, the intangible service elements of their business may be overlooking a vital differential advantage in the marketplace. By defining their businesses too narrowly, these firms have developed classic cases of *marketing myopia*. For example, the typical family pizza parlor may myopically view itself as being solely in the pizza business. However, a broader view recognizes that the business provides consumers with a convenient, reasonably priced food product in a unique atmosphere that the firm has created for its customers. Interestingly, adding service aspects to a product often transforms the product from a commodity into a *compelling experience*, and by doing so dramatically increases the revenue-producing opportunities of the product. For example, Build-a-Bear Workshops offer an experience-based business model where customers and their children or grandchildren can build and accessorize their own teddy bears. Given the option of going to a store to purchase a bear for a child or taking the child to a Build-a-Bear Workshop where they can be personally involved in producing the bear, many customers are enthusiastically opting for the latter choice.

Unique Differences Between Goods and Services

Initially, the field of services marketing was slow to develop within the business community. Many felt the marketing of services did not differ significantly from the marketing of goods. For example, it was still necessary to segment markets, identify target markets, and develop marketing mixes that catered to the needs of a firm's intended target market. However, since those early days, a great deal has been written regarding the specific differences between goods and services and their corresponding marketing implications. The majority of these differences are attributed to four unique characteristics—intangibility, inseparability, heterogeneity, and perishability.[6]

Intangibility

Of the four unique characteristics that distinguish goods from services, *intangibility* is the primary source from which the other three characteristics emerge. As a result of their intangibility, services cannot be seen, felt, tasted, or touched in the same manner that goods can be sensed. For example, compare the differences between purchasing a movie ticket and a pair of shoes. The shoes are tangible goods, so the shoes can be objectively evaluated prior to purchase. The customer can pick up the shoes, feel the quality of materials from which they are constructed, view their specific style and color, and actually sample the shoe for comfort and fit. After purchasing the shoes, the customer takes them, claiming physical possession and ownership of a tangible product.

In comparison, the purchase of a movie ticket buys the customer an experience. Since the movie experience is intangible, the movie is subjectively evaluated. For example, the customer must rely on the judgments of others (e.g., friends, movie critics, etc.) who have previously experienced the service for *prepurchase information*. Because the information provided by others is based on their own sets of expectations and perceptions, opinions will differ regarding the value of the experience. After the movie is over, the customer returns home with a memory of the experience, retaining physical ownership of only a ticket stub. In addition, the customer's evaluation of the movie will extend beyond what was seen on the screen to include their treatment by theater employees, the behavior of other customers, and the condition of the theater's physical environment.

Inseparability

One of the most intriguing characteristics of the service experience involves the concept of inseparability. **Inseparability** refers to (1) the service provider's physical connection to the service being provided, (2) the customer's involvement in the service-production process, and (3) the involvement of other customers in the service-production process. Unlike the manufacturer, which may seldom see an actual customer while producing goods in a factory, service providers are often in constant contact with their customers and must construct their service operations with the customer's physical presence in mind.

Service Provider Involvement. For many services to occur, the provider must be physically present to deliver the service. For example, dental services require the physical presence of a dentist or hygienist, medical surgery requires a surgeon, and in-home services such as carpet cleaning require an actual individual to complete the work. Because of the intangibility of services, the service provider becomes part of the physical evidence upon which the customer's evaluation of the service experience is at least partly based.

Face-to-face interactions with customers make employee satisfaction crucial. Without a doubt, *employee satisfaction and customer satisfaction are directly related*. The interaction of dissatisfied employees with customers will lower consumers' perceptions of the firm's performance. The importance of employee satisfaction within service firms cannot be overemphasized. Customers will never be the number-one priority in a company where employees are treated poorly. In fact, employees should be viewed and treated as *"internal customers"* of the firm.

Customer Involvement. Unlike goods, which are produced, sold, and then consumed, services are first sold and then produced and consumed simultaneously. For example, a box of breakfast cereal is produced in a factory, shipped to a store where it is sold, and then consumed by customers at a place and time of the customer's choosing. In contrast, services are produced and consumed simultaneously (e.g., surgery, a haircut, an amusement park ride, etc.), so consumption takes place inside the service factory. As a result, service firms must design their operations to accommodate the customer's physical presence. For example, parking lots will need to be larger and customer restrooms will need to be made available.

Inseparability
Is a distinguishing characteristic of services that reflects the interconnection among the service provider, the customer receiving the service, and other customers sharing the service experience.

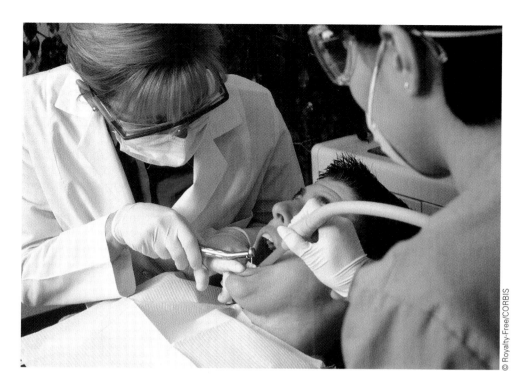

Dental services typify the insepa-rability that exists between den-tists and their patients. Both must be physically present for the ser-vice to occur.

By increasing customer participation in the service-delivery process, customers are able to *coproduce* at least part of their own service and take on the role of **partial employees**. As partial employees, customers can customize their own service and often produce it faster and less expensively than if the firm had produced it. Customers who pump their own gas, make their own salads, and prepare their own soft drinks at fast-food restaurants are classic examples of partial employees. As customers coproduce at least part of their own service, employees are freed to perform other duties, such as serving other customers who require assistance, and/or engaging in non-customer-related activities (such as completing paperwork).

Interestingly, as customer contact increases, the efficiency of an operation may decrease. This happens because the customers' involvement in the production process creates uncertainties in the scheduling of production and directly affects the *type of service* desired, the *length of the service*-delivery process, and the *cycle of service demand*. The attempt to balance consumer needs with efficient operating procedures is a delicate art. For example, imagine attempting to staff the emergency department of a hospital with exactly the right number of personnel with exactly the right qualifications on any given night.

Other Customer Involvement. The presence of other customers during the service encounter is the third defining aspect of inseparability. Because production and consumption occur simultaneously, several customers often share a common service experience. For example, other students share your learning experience in the classroom, and other customers share your entertainment experience at a Six Flags Theme Park. The marketing challenges presented by having other customers involved in the production process generally reflect the negative aspects of their involvement. For example, the popular press has been full of stories about incidents of "air rage" or "passenger-induced turbulence." Factors known to contribute to this disruptive behavior include alcohol abuse, sexual misconduct, smoking in nonsmoking areas, failure to follow boarding instructions, violating carry-on baggage restrictions, and a variety of other conditions that arise from lapses in creature comforts, crew training, and food quality. In fact, the number of incidents involving passengers interfering with flight crews has more than tripled over the last 10 years. The policing of

Partial employees
Are customers who coproduce their service via a cooperative effort with service providers.

Political and Legal Forces

The events of September 11 have led JetBlue Airlines to develop an innovative strategy to manage passenger stress, which has been heightened since the terrorists' attacks. JetBlue passengers are now provided with instructional cards on how to perform "Airplane Yoga" to ease their anxieties.

customer misconduct aboard planes is a tricky issue. According to one flight attendant, "At 37,000 feet, you don't have the option of throwing people out like you can in a cocktail lounge."[7] One would imagine that events of September 11 have inadvertently assisted the airlines in handling behavior problems. Given today's political climate, disruptive behavior aboard airplanes of any type is simply not tolerated. In fact, the events of September 11 have led some airlines, such as JetBlue, to develop innovative strategies to manage passenger stress, which has been heightened since the terrorists' attacks.[8]

The impact of other customers is not always negative. On the positive side, audience reaction in the form of laughter or screams of terror often enhances the moviegoer's experience. Similarly, a crowded pub may facilitate social interaction, and a happy crowd may make a concert an even more pleasurable event. As social creatures, humans tend to frequent and feel more comfortable in places of business that have other customers in them. In fact, the lack of other customers can act as a tangible clue that the impending service experience may be less than satisfactory. For example, when selecting from unfamiliar restaurants, would you eat at a restaurant that had no cars in the parking lot, or would you choose to eat at the restaurant down the street with a full parking lot? In the absence of other information, at which restaurant would potential customers expect to receive the better dining experience?

Heterogeneity

One of the most frequently stressed differences between goods and services is the lack of ability to control service quality before it reaches the consumer. Service encounters occur in real time, and consumers are often physically present, so if something goes wrong during the service process, it is too late to institute quality-control measures before the service reaches the customer. Indeed, the customer (and other customers who share the service experience) may be part of the quality problem. If something goes wrong during a meal in a restaurant, the service experience for a customer is bound to be affected; the manager cannot logically ask the customer to leave the restaurant, reenter, and start the meal again.

Heterogeneity is the variation in consistency from one service transaction to the next. Heterogeneity, almost by definition, makes it impossible for a service operation to achieve 100% perfect quality on an ongoing basis. Manufacturing operations may also have problems achieving this sort of target, but they can isolate mistakes and correct them over time because mistakes tend to recur at the same points in the process. In contrast, many errors in service operations are one-time events; the waiter who drops a plate of food in a customer's lap creates a service failure that can be neither foreseen nor corrected ahead of time.

Another challenge heterogeneity presents is that not only does the consistency of service vary from firm to firm and among personnel within a single firm, it also varies when interacting with the same service provider on a daily basis. For example, one Enterprise rental car franchise can have helpful and pleasant employees, while another franchise might employ individuals who process their customers like robots. Not only can this be true among different franchises, the same can be true within a single franchise on a day-to-day basis because of the mood swings of employees.

Perishability

Perishability means that a service cannot be saved, its unused capacity cannot be reserved, and it cannot be inventoried. Unlike goods, which can be stored and sold at a later date, services that are not sold when they become available cease to exist. For example, hotel rooms that go unoccupied for the evening cannot be stored; airline seats that are not sold cannot be inventoried and added to another aircraft during the holiday season when airline seats are scarce; and service providers such as den-

Heterogeneity
Is a distinguishing characteristic of services that reflects the variation in consistency from one service transaction to the next.

Perishability
Is a distinguishing characteristic of services in that they cannot be saved, their unused capacity cannot be reserved, and they cannot be inventoried.

What is e-service? Strictly speaking, *e-service* pertains to customer-service support provided on the Net. E-service plays a critical role in transforming the customer's online experience over time from a functional experience to a more personalized experience. Ultimately, e-service humanizes the Net by providing various customer-service activities while simultaneously reducing the online firm's operating costs. Examples include:

- *Electronic Order Confirmation.* Noted as one of the easiest and most cost-effective methods of increasing customer satisfaction, electronic order confirmation notifies customers within seconds or minutes that their order has been received by detailing the item purchased, quantity selected, cost, shipping charges, and order availability.
- *Package Tracking Services.* Once an order has been placed, effective e-tailers also notify customers when their purchases have been shipped and provide an expected delivery date. In addition, the best companies also provide package-tracking identification numbers so that customers can track the physical movement of their purchases through a shipper's (such as FedEx or UPS) Web site.
- *Electronic Wallets.* According to one study, two-thirds of all shopping carts are left at the virtual checkout counter. Checking out online can be a lengthy process, as customers enter their credit-card information, phone numbers, billing address, shipping address, etc. Electronic wallets have been designed for repeat customers, where the customer's credit-card and desired shipping preferences are stored on the company's server and automatically appear when the customer places an order.
- *Co-browsing.* In order to facilitate the social aspects on online shopping, e-tailers that offer co-browsing opportunities enable users to access the same Web site simultaneously from two different locations. Live text boxes are also provided so that users can chat online while making their purchase decisions.
- *Live Text Chats.* In addition to enabling customer-to-customer communications, live text chats also facilitate customer-to-e-tailer communications. Innovative outsourcing firms, such as liveperson.com, staff a number of major e-tailers' live text chats and respond to customer inquiries online, often in less than 60 seconds.
- *Merchandise Return Services.* Twenty-five percent of all merchandise purchased online is returned, and the rate is higher in industries such as apparel. Today, many e-tailers include supply return authorizations with their shipments to facilitate the return process. Other e-tailers outsource their return activities to the U.S. Postal Service's E-Merchandise Return Service, which enables customers to print return labels from the e-tailer's Web site and drop returns off at the Post Office.
- *Collaborative Filtering.* This software program facilitates suggestive selling by monitoring the purchasing behavior of like-minded customers online and then suggesting to individual users in real time what other customers have purchased. For example, based on Customer A's past purchase behavior, Amazon.com will suggests to Customer A book titles of interest based on what others have purchased who also purchased the same title as Customer A's past purchase.

Sources: Rafi A. Mohammed, Robert J. Fisher, Bernard J. Jaworski, and Aileen Cahill, *Internet Marketing: Building Advantage in a Networked Economy* (Boston, MA: McGraw-Hill Irwin, 2002).
Ron Zemke and Tom Connellen, *eservice,* (New York: AMACOM, 2001).

tists, lawyers, and hairstylists cannot regain the time lost from an empty appointment book or from customers who fail to appear at their appointed times.

The inability to inventory creates profound difficulties for marketing services. In a manufacturing setting, the ability to create an inventory of goods means that their production and consumption can be separated by time and space. In other words, a good can be produced in one location and transported for sale in another, or a good can be produced in January and not released into distribution channels until June. Most services, however, are consumed at the point of production.

Because of the effects of intangibility, inseparability, heterogeneity, and perishability, marketing plays a very different role in service-oriented organizations than it does in tangible-dominant goods organizations. Consequently, the marketing department must maintain a much closer relationship with the rest of the departments in an organization than is customary in many goods-producing businesses. The concept of operations being responsible for producing the product and marketing being responsible for selling the product cannot work in a service firm.

Understanding the Service Experience

All products, be they goods or services, deliver a bundle of benefits to the consumer.[9] The *benefit concept* is the encapsulation of these benefits in the consumer's mind. For a tangible-dominant product such as Tide laundry detergent, the benefit concept for some consumers might simply be clean clothes. In contrast to goods, services deliver a bundle of benefits through the experience created for the consumer. For example, most Tide customers will never see the inside of the manufacturing plant where Tide is produced; they will most likely never interact with the factory workers who produce the detergent or with the management staff who direct the workers; and they will also generally not use Tide in the presence of other customers. In comparison, Taco Bell's dine-in customers are physically present in the "factory" where the food is produced, and these customers *do* interact with the workers who prepare and serve the food, as well as with the management staff who run the restaurant. Moreover, Taco Bell customers consume the service in the presence of other customers who may influence their service experience.

Figure 10.3 illustrates the key factors that create the service experience for the consumer. The service experience itself creates the benefit concept for the consumer. The most profound implication of the service experience is this: It demonstrates that consumers are an integral part of the service process. Their participation may be active or passive, but consumers are always involved in the service-delivery process. Factors that influence the customer's service experience include dimensions that are visible and invisible to the customer:

* Servicescape (visible)
* Service providers (visible)
* Other customers (visible)
* Organizations and systems (invisible)

The Servicescape

Servicescape
Refers to the use of physical evidence to design service environments.

The term **servicescape** refers to the use of physical evidence to design service environments (Figure 10.4).[10] Due to the intangibility of services, customers often have trouble evaluating service quality objectively. As a result, consumers rely on the

| Figure 10.3 | Factors Influencing the Service Experience |

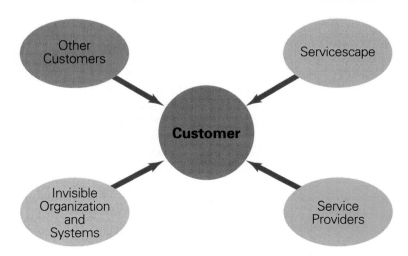

Source: Adapted from E. Langcard, J. Bateson, C. Lovelock, and P. Eiglen, *Marketing of Services: New Insights from Consumers and Managers.* Report No. 81–104 (Cambridge, MA: Marketing Science Institute, 1981).

Servicescape Dimensions			Figure 10.4
Ambient Conditions	**Space/Function**	**Signs, Symbols, and Artifacts**	
Temperature	Layout	Signage	
Air Quality	Equipment	Personal Artifacts	
Noise Level	Furnishings	Decor	
Music		Uniforms	
Odors		Award Plaques	

Source: Adapted from Mary Jo Bitner, "Servicescapes: The Impact of Physical Surroundings on Customers and Employees," *Journal of Marketing* 56, no. 2 (April 1992): 60. Reprinted by permission of the American Marketing Association.

physical evidence that surrounds the service to help them form their evaluations. Hence, the servicescape consists of *ambient conditions* such as room temperature and music; *inanimate objects* that assist the firm in completing its tasks, such as furnishings and business equipment; and *other physical evidence* such as signs, symbols, and personal artifacts like family pictures and personal collections.

The extensive use of physical evidence varies by the type of service firm. Service firms such as hospitals, resorts, and child-care centers often use physical evidence extensively as they design facilities and other tangibles associated with the service. In contrast, service firms such as insurance agencies and express-mail drop-off locations use limited physical evidence. Regardless of the variation in usage, all service firms need to recognize the importance of managing their physical evidence, because of its role in:

- Packaging the service
- Facilitating the service delivery process
- Socializing customers and employees
- Differentiating the firm from its competitors[11]

Packaging the Service

A firm's physical evidence plays a major role in packaging its service. The service itself is intangible and therefore does not require a package for purely functional reasons. However, the firm's physical evidence does send quality cues to consumers and adds value to the service when it helps customers develop positive images of the service. The firm's exterior and interior elements and other tangibles create the package that surrounds the service. The firm's physical environment forms the customer's initial impression of the type and quality of the service provided. For example, Mexican and Chinese restaurants often use specific architectural designs that communicate to customers about their firms' offerings. Physical evidence also conveys expectations to consumers. Consumers will have one set of expectations for a restaurant with dimly lit dining rooms, soft music, and linen tablecloths and napkins; they will form quite a different set of expectations for a restaurant that has picnic tables and peanut shells covering the floor.

Facilitating the Service Process

Another use of a firm's physical evidence is to facilitate the flow of activities that produce the service. Physical evidence can provide information to customers on how the service-production process works. Examples include signage that specifically instructs customers; menus and brochures that explain the firm's offerings and facilitate the ordering process for consumers and providers; physical structures that direct the flow of consumers while waiting; and barriers, such as a customer-service counter at a dry cleaners, that separate the technical core of the business (backroom operations) from the customer contact areas, where customers are actively involved in the production process.

Socializing Employees and Customers

Organizational socialization is the process by which an individual adapts to and comes to appreciate the values, norms, and required behavior patterns of an organization.[12] The firm's physical evidence plays an important part in this socialization process by conveying expected roles, behaviors, and relationships among employees and between employees and customers. Physical evidence, such as the use of uniforms, helps to socialize employees toward accepting organizational goals and affects consumer perceptions of the caliber of service provided. Studies have shown that the use of uniforms:

- Aids in identifying the firm's personnel
- Presents a physical symbol that embodies the group's ideals and attributes
- Implies a coherent group structure
- Facilitates the perceived consistency of performance
- Provides a tangible symbol of an employee's change in status (e.g., military uniforms change as personnel move through the ranks)
- Assists in controlling the behavior of errant employees

One classic example of how tangible evidence affects the socialization process of employees involves women in the military. Pregnant military personnel were originally permitted to wear civilian clothing in lieu of their traditional military uniforms. However, the military soon noticed discipline and morale problems among these servicewomen as they began to lose their identification with their roles as soldiers. "Maternity uniforms are now standard issue in the Air Force, Army, and Navy, as well as at US Air, Hertz, Safeway, McDonald's, and the National Park Service."[13]

Competitive Forces

British Airways uses its servicescape to differentiate itself from the competition by featuring the first fully flat bed for passengers traveling business class.[14]

Westin is just one example of how a hotel chain uses its servicescape as a means of competitive differentiation.

© Richard Cummins/CORBIS

Differentiating the Firm from Its Competitors

The effective management of the servicescape can also be a source of differentiation. For example, several airlines, such as American Airlines, United Airlines, and British Airways, are now expanding the amount of leg room available for passengers.[15] Similarly, JetBlue Airways offers its customers leather seats, satellite television, and blue potato chips.[16] In addition, the appearance of personnel and facilities often directly affect consumers' perceptions of how the firm will handle the service aspects of its business. Numerous studies have shown that well-dressed individuals are perceived as more intelligent, better workers, and more pleasant to engage in interactions.[17] Similarly, well-designed facilities are going to be perceived as better places to conduct business than poorly designed counterparts.

Differentiation can also be achieved by using physical evidence to reposition a service firm in the eyes of its customers. Upgrading the firm's facilities often upgrades the image of the firm in the minds of consumers and may lead to attracting more desirable market segments, which further aids in differentiating the firm from its competitors. On the other hand, note that elaborate facility upgrades may alienate some customers who believe that the firm will pass on the costs of the upgrade to consumers through higher prices. This is precisely why many offices are decorated professionally, but not lavishly.

Service Providers

The second component of the service experience involves the personnel who provide the service. Simply stated, the public face of a service firm is its service providers.[18] Unlike the consumption of goods, the consumption of services often takes place where the service is produced (e.g., hair salon, dentist office, restaurant). Even when the service is provided at the consumer's residence or workplace (e.g., lawn care, housekeeping, professional massage), interactions between consumers and service providers are commonplace. As a result, service providers have a dramatic impact on the service experience. For example, when asked what irritated them most about service providers, customers have noted seven categories of complaints:

- *Apathy:* What comedian George Carlin refers to as DILLIGAD—Do I look like I give a damn?
- *Brush-off:* Attempts to get rid of the customer by dismissing the customer completely—the "I want you to go away" syndrome
- *Coldness:* Indifferent service providers who could not care less about what the customer really wants
- *Condescension:* The "you are the client/patient, so you must be stupid" approach
- *Robotism:* When the customers are treated simply as inputs into a system that must be processed
- *Rulebook:* Providers who live by the rules of the organization even when those rules do not make good sense
- *Runaround:* Passing the customer off to another provider, who will simply pass them off to yet another provider.[19]

Service personnel perform the dual functions of interacting with customers and reporting back to the internal organization. Strategically, service personnel are an important source of product differentiation. It is often challenging for a service organization to differentiate itself from other similar organizations in terms of the benefit bundle it offers or its delivery system. For example, many airlines offer similar bundles of benefits and fly the same types of aircraft from the same airports to the same destinations. Therefore, their only hope of a competitive advantage is from the service level—the way things are done. Hence, the factor that often distinguishes one airline from another is the poise and attitude of its service providers. Singapore Airlines, for example, enjoys an excellent reputation due in large part to the beauty and grace of its flight attendants. Other firms that hold a differential advantage over competitors based on personnel include the Ritz Carlton, IBM, and Disney Enterprises.[20]

Other Customers

Ultimately, the success of many service encounters depends on how effectively the service firm manages its clientele. A wide range of service establishments such as restaurants, hotels, airlines, and physicians' offices serve multiple customers simultaneously. Hence, other customers can have a profound impact on an individual's service experience. Research has shown that the presence of other customers can enhance or detract from an individual's service experience.[21] The influence of other customers can be *active* or *passive.* For instance, examples of other customers actively detracting from one's service experience include unruly customers in a restaurant or night club, children crying during a church service, or theatergoers carrying on a conversation during a play. Some passive examples include customers who show up late for appointments, thereby delaying each subsequent appointment; an exceptionally tall individual who sits directly in front of another customer at

Hertz is addressing travelers' needs and minimizing the impact of "other customers" with programs such as Hertz #1 Club Gold® and Instant Return. Hertz #1 Club Gold® and Hertz Instant Return programs improve customers travel experiences by reducing the time it takes to pick up and return a car.

a movie theater; or the impact of being part of a crowd, which increases the waiting time for everyone in the group.

Although many customer actions that enhance or detract from the service experience are difficult to predict, service organizations can attempt to manage the behavior of customers so that they coexist peacefully. For example, firms can manage waiting times so that customers who arrive earlier than others get first priority, clearly target specific age segments to minimize potential conflicts between younger and older customers, and provide separate dining facilities for smokers and customers with children.

Organization and Systems

Technological Forces

Wave Pick Technology has enabled L.L. Bean to fulfill 100% of its orders within 24 hours from order to delivery. The company is held in high esteem as a best-practices example of excellence in order fulfillment processes.

The invisible component of the service experience, the organization and its systems, can also profoundly affect the consumer's service experience. For example, throughout the last two decades, the distribution center of L.L. Bean has been a required stop for companies engaging in benchmarking exercises.[22] Many companies, including Nike, Disney, Gillette, and DaimlerChrysler, have come to see how L.L. Bean fills orders so effectively. In fact, the center they visited is no more; it has been replaced by a completely new approach—one driven by an ever-expanding volume of orders, an increasingly global market, and a growing variety of customized products. L.L. Bean's old system built orders from the phone operations, issuing them every 12 hours to pickers. The pickers assembled the orders from around the center and then delivered them to packers, who prepared the orders for shipment.

The new system, referred to as Wave Pick Technology, operates differently. Orders come directly from the phone operators and are immediately allocated to pickers based on available capacity. Moreover, the orders are broken down by item and assigned to different pickers, who are themselves assigned to different parts of the warehouse. Order items are placed on a conveyor belt and bar-coded. Scanners then automatically assemble the orders for packing. As a result, 100% of orders can be serviced within 24 hours; from order to delivery to the on-site Federal Express depot takes only two hours.

A firm's organization and systems also involve a human component. The behind-the-scenes activities of hiring, training, and rewarding employees are directly related to how well customers are served. The United Parcel Service (UPS) believes in building trust and teamwork and making employees loyal to the company's mission.[23] UPS spends more than $300 million a year on training, pays full-time drivers more than $50,000 a year on average, and surveys its employees for suggestions. The company is virtually 100% employee-owned.

Creating Compelling Experiences

Competitive Forces

In virtually every industry, the top three to five competitors produce seemingly identical products. The development of compelling experiences such as the unique customer experience developed by Starbucks acts as a differential advantage in the marketplace and offsets the competitive effects of service commodification.

Service firms that are able to effectively mold the customer's experience via the effective management of the servicescape, service providers, other customers, and the invisible organization and system have the means to develop *compelling experiences*.[24] The development of compelling experiences is the latest competitive weapon in the war against service commodification. For example, when priced as a *commodity,* coffee is worth little more than $1 per pound. When processed, packaged, and sold in the grocery store as a *good,* the price of coffee jumps to between 5¢ and 25¢ a cup. When that same cup is sold in a local restaurant, the coffee takes on more *service* aspects and sells for 50¢ to $1 per cup. However, in the ultimate act of added value, when that same cup of coffee is sold within the compelling experience of a five-star restaurant or the unique environment of a Starbucks, the customer gladly pays $2 to $5 per cup. In this instance, the whole process of ordering, creating, and consuming becomes a pleasurable, even theatrical, experience. Economic value, like the coffee bean, progresses from commodities to goods to services to experiences. In this example, coffee was transformed from a raw commodity valued at approximately $1 per pound to a $2- to $5-per-cup experience—a markup of as much as 5,000%.

Here We Go Again!

Like Bill Murray's character in the movie *Groundhog Day*, what corporate America learned about business ethics in the 1980s, they are now forced to learn all over again. Consider the following chain of events. Andrew Fastow is ousted as chief financial officer (CFO) of Enron Corporation eight days after reporting a $618-million third-quarter loss. Less than three months later, Enron's auditing firm, Arthur Andersen, admitted that it shredded Enron-related documents. Shortly thereafter, the chief executive officer (CEO) and the CFO, Kenneth Lay and Andrew Fastow, invoked their Fifth Amendment rights as they appeared before members of Congress. Before the year was out, Arthur Andersen closed its doors and ceased to exist.

Individuals such as domestic diva Martha Stewart have also been accused of crossing the ethics line. Ms. Stewart, who was the focus of insider-trading accusations involving the sale of 4,000 shares of ImClone Systems' stock, paid a hefty price for her dealings. Her own company's stock lost 54% of its value and Ms. Stewart took a personal hit of $300 million in wealth. In addition, she vacated her highly coveted seat on the New York Stock Exchange, and the U.S. Securities and Exchange Commission (SEC) could force her to step down as chairman and CEO of her own company. The SEC also notified Ms. Stewart that civil insider-trading charges may be forthcoming.

Ethical misconduct within the service sector has been particularly rampant due to consumer vulnerability. In more specific terms, consumer vulnerability to ethical misconduct within the service sector can be attributed to several sources:

- **Services are characterized by few search attributes.** Due to the intangibility of services, consumers lack the opportunity to physically examine a service before purchasing it. Hence, consumers of services must often base their purchase decisions on information provided by the service provider.

- **Services are often specialized and/or technical.** Many services are not easily understood and/or evaluated; consequently, the opportunity exists to easily mislead consumers. As a consumer, how do you know whether your doctor, lawyer, broker, priest, or minister is competent at his or her job?

- **Some services have a significant time lapse between performance and evaluation.** The final evaluation of some services such as insurance and financial planning is often conducted only at a time in the distant future. As a result, service providers may not be held accountable for their actions in the short run.

- **Services are often provided by boundary-spanning personnel.** Many service providers deliver their services outside their firm's physical facilities and are often not under direct supervision. Hence, the opportunity to engage in ethical misconduct without repercussions from upper management increases.

- **Variability in service performance is somewhat accepted.** Variability in service performance is somewhat accepted and unethical service providers may attempt to broaden the window of acceptable performance through slightly increasing gaps in performance quality.

DISCUSSION QUESTIONS

1. Why do you think that all the news about corporate scandals and insider trading surfaced after the stock market crash, but not during the boom?
2. Based on the factors contributing to consumer vulnerability stated above, why are consumers of financial services particularly vulnerable to ethical misconduct?

Sources: Julie Creswell, "Will Martha Walk?" *Fortune* 146, 25 November 2002, 121–124.
Julia Homer, "How Did We Get Here?" *CFO* 18 (10), October 2002, 40.
K. Douglas Hoffman and John E. G. Bateson, *Essentials of Services Marketing: Concepts, Strategies, and Cases*, 2nd ed. (Mason: OH: South-Western, 2002): 105–130.

Creating compelling experiences for customers is not a new idea. The entertainment industry and venues such as those operated by Disney have been doing it for years. Other types of businesses have picked up on the idea and introduced "experience" concepts, including the Hard Rock Cafe, Build-a-Bear Workshops, and a variety of theme hotels located in Las Vegas, such as New York–New York, the Venetian, and Caesars Palace. The question facing many other service providers is how to transform their own operations into memorable experiences for the customer. One unique example involves a computer-repair firm based in Minneapolis, Minnesota. This company's team of crack technicians, formally called the "Geek Squad," intentionally dress in white shirts and sport thin black ties, pocket protectors, and badges. This firm has successfully transformed a mundane service into a memorable event that's fun for the customer. In yet another example, the Braehead Shopping Centre in Glasgow, Scotland, offers a surrogate-boyfriend service for women with uncooperative partners. "After dropping their significant other at a special lounge stocked with video games and men's magazines, women borrow a specially trained Shopping Boyfriend, who remains enthusiastic, attentive, and helpful for a few hours of mall browsing."[25]

The Quest for Customer Satisfaction

Tracking customer satisfaction in the United States is a highly complex task that is currently undertaken through the joint efforts of the American Society for Quality and the University of Michigan's business school.[26] The two groups have developed the American Customer Satisfaction Index (ACSI), which is based on 3,900 products representing more than two dozen manufacturing and service industries. Companies included in the study are selected based on size and U.S. market share, and together represent about 40% of the U.S. gross domestic product (GDP).

An overview of the best and worst companies included in the ACSI and their satisfaction ratings is presented in Figure 10.5. The H. J. Heinz Company earned top honors, while Charter Communications brought up the bottom. Qwest Communications and AT&T Corporation are Charter Communications' closest competitors, with Pacific Gas and Electric not far behind. Perhaps the most disturbing finding of the ACSI results is that the 10 companies at the top of the list produce goods, while the firms at the bottom, such as McDonald's, AltaVista, AOL Time Warner, and America Online, are service organizations. Clearly, service organizations are struggling with customer service. Findings generated from a recent McDonald's mystery-shopping exercise indicate the problems service organizations are encountering. According to a three-page document obtained by *Fortune* magazine, McDonald's mystery shoppers reported that a Raleigh, NC area franchisee only met speed-of-service standards 46% of the time and that employees were often rude, slow, unprofessional, and inaccurate.[27]

From a historical perspective, a great deal of work in the customer-satisfaction area began in the 1970s, when consumerism was on the rise. The rise of the consumer movement was directly related to the decline in service felt by many consumers. The decline in customer service and resulting customer dissatisfaction can be attributed to a number of sources. First, skyrocketing inflation during this period forced many firms to slash service in an effort to keep prices down. In some industries, deregulation led to fierce competition among firms that had never had to compete before. Price competition quickly became the main means of differentiation,

Figure 10.5	Customer-Satisfaction Ratings

The American Customer Satisfaction Index (ACSI), which measures customer satisfaction across a variety of sectors, demonstrates the added complexity of managing a service firm. All of the top companies are traditional goods manufacturers. In contrast, those scoring lowest on the ACSI are service firms.

Top Companies		**Bottom Companies**	
Company	Score (out of possible 100)	Company	Score (out of possible 100)
H.J. Heinz Company	88	McDonald's Corporation	62
Hershey Foods Corporation	87	Ask Jeeves, Inc.	62
The Quaker Oats Company	87	AltaVista Company	61
Bayerische Motoren Werke AG (BMW)	86	AOL Time Warner Inc.(Cable)	61
GM-Buick	86	AOL Time Warner Inc.(Portal)	59
GM-Cadillac	86	America Online, Inc.	58
Cadbury Schweppes plc	86	Pacific Gas and Electric Company	58
PepsiCo, Inc.	86	Comcast Corporation	56
The Coca Cola Company	85	AT&T Corporation	56
Ford Motor Company-Lincoln Mercury	84	Qwest Communications	56
Sara Lee Corporation	84	Charter Communications	53

Source: http://www.theacsi.org/overview.htm, accessed 5 December 2002. Used with permission.

and price wars quickly broke out. Here again, firms slashed costs associated with customer service to cut operating expenses.

As time went on, labor shortages also contributed to the decline in customer service. Motivated service workers were difficult to find, and who could blame them? The typical service job meant low pay, no career path, no sense of pride, and no training in customer relations. Automation also contributed to the problem. Replacing human labor with machines indeed increased the efficiency of many operating systems, but often distanced consumers from the firm, leaving them to fend for themselves.

What Is Customer Satisfaction?

Ultimately firms achieve **customer satisfaction** through the effective management of customer *perceptions* and *expectations*. If the *perceived service* is better than or equal to the *expected service,* then customers are satisfied. Because of this, firms can increase customer satisfaction by either lowering expectations or by enhancing perceptions. Note that this entire process of comparing expectations to perceptions takes place in the minds of customers. Hence, it is the *perceived* service that matters, not the *actual* service. One of the best examples to illustrate this concept involves a high-rise hotel. The hotel was receiving numerous complaints about the amount of time guests had to wait for elevator service in the lobby. Realizing that, from an operational viewpoint, the speed of the elevators could not be increased, and that attempting to schedule the guest's elevator usage was futile, the hotel's management installed mirrors in the lobby next to the elevator bays. Guest complaints were reduced immediately—the mirrors provided a way for guests to occupy their waiting time. Guests were observed using the mirrors to observe their own appearance and that of others around them. In reality, the speed of the elevators had not changed; however, the customer's perception of time had changed.

Companies can also manage expectations in order to produce customer satisfaction, without in any way altering the quality of the actual service delivered. For example, Motel 6 downplayed its service in a clever advertising campaign designed to increase consumer satisfaction by lowering customer expectations prior to purchase. The firm's advertising informs consumers of both what to expect and what not to expect: "A good clean room for $39.99 . . . a little more in some places . . . a little less in some others . . . and remember . . . we'll leave the light on for you." Many customers simply do not use the services such as swimming pools, health clubs, and full-service restaurants that are associated with higher-priced hotels. Economy-minded hotels, such as Motel 6, are carving out a niche in the market by providing the basics. The result is that customers know exactly what they will get ahead of time and are happy not only with the quality of the service received but also with the cost savings.

The Importance of Customer Satisfaction

The importance of customer satisfaction cannot be overstated. Without customers, the service firm has no reason to exist. Every service business needs to proactively define and measure customer satisfaction. Waiting for customers to complain in order to identify problems in the service-delivery system, or gauging the firm's progress in achieving customer satisfaction based on the number of complaints received, is naive. Consider the following findings gathered by the Technical Assistance Research Program (TARP):[28]

- The average business does not hear from 96% of its unhappy customers.
- For every complaint received, 26 other customers actually have the same problem.
- The average person with a problem tells nine or 10 people. Thirteen percent of dissatisfied customers tell more than 20 people.
- Customers who have their complaints satisfactorily resolved tell an average of five people about the treatment they received.

Sociocultural Forces

Over the years, customers have become tougher to please. They are more informed than ever, their expectations have increased, and they are more particular about where they spend their discretionary dollars.

Customer satisfaction

Is a short-term, transaction-specific measure of whether customer perceptions meet or exceed customer expectations.

- Complainers are more likely to do business with you again than noncomplainers: 54–70% if their problem was resolved at all, and 95% if it was handled quickly.

The TARP figures demonstrate that customers do not actively complain to the source of the failure. Instead, consumers voice their dissatisfaction with their feet, by defecting to competitors, and with their mouths, by telling existing and potential customers exactly how they were mistreated by the offending firm. The impact of dissatisfied customers on future business operations is astounding. Based on the figures above, a firm that serves 100 customers per week, and boasts a 90% customer-satisfaction rating, will be the object of thousands of negative stories by the end of the year. For example, if 10 dissatisfied customers per week tell 10 friends about the poor service they received, by the end of the year (52 weeks), 5,200 negative word-of-mouth communications have been generated.

The TARP figures are not all bad news, however. Firms that effectively respond to customer complaints are the objects of positive word-of-mouth communications. Although positive news travels at half the rate of negative news, the positive stories can ultimately translate into customer loyalty and new customers. Businesses should also learn from the TARP figures that complainers are a firm's friends. Complainers are a free source of market information, and the complaints themselves should be viewed as opportunities for the firm to improve its delivery systems, not as a source of irritation.[29] As evidence, the International Customer Service Association found that 54% of customers who had experienced a problem and complained continued to do business with the firm on a long-term basis. In comparison, only 9% of customers who experienced problems and did not complain continued to do business with the offending firm.[30]

The Benefits of Customer Satisfaction

Although some may argue that customers are unreasonable at times (see Figure 10.6), little evidence can be found of extravagant consumer expectations.[31] Consequently, satisfying consumers is not an impossible task. In fact, meeting and exceeding customer expectations create several valuable benefits for service firms. Positive word-of-mouth from existing customers often translates into new customers. In addition, satisfied customers purchase products more frequently and are less likely to be lost to competitors than are dissatisfied customers.

Companies who command high customer-satisfaction ratings also seem to be able to insulate themselves from competitive pressures—particularly price competition. Customers are often willing to pay more and stay with a firm that meets their needs than to risk moving to a lower-priced service. Finally, firms that pride themselves on their customer-satisfaction efforts generally provide better environments in

| Figure 10.6 | Is It Always Worthwhile to Keep a Customer? |

Although saving every customer at any cost is a controversial topic, and opinions are divided, some experts believe that the customer is no longer worth saving under the following conditions:

- The account is no longer profitable.
- Conditions specified in the sales contract are no longer being met.
- Customers are abusive to the point that they lower employee morale.
- Customer demands are not reasonable, and fulfilling those demands would result in poor service for the remaining customer base.
- The customer's reputation is so poor that associating with the customer tarnishes the image and reputation of the selling firm.

Source: "Is Customer Retention Worth the Time, Effort, and Expense." Sales and Marketing Management, Vol. 143, no. 15 (December 1991), 21–22.

which to work, and therefore have increased their chances to attract and retain the best and brightest employees. These positive work environments produce organizational cultures that challenge employees to perform and reward them for their efforts. Some companies even use their positive work environments to encourage employee applications. Microsoft, for example, is known for providing a remarkably challenging atmosphere for the "brainy." "Everybody gets stock options, and most professionals hired before 1992 have thus become millionaires; six became billionaires."[32]

Customer Satisfaction as It Relates to Customer-Relationship Management

One of the most recent business practices affecting customer-satisfaction levels (both positively and negatively) is customer-relationship management.[33] As introduced in previous chapters, **customer-relationship management (CRM)** is the process of identifying, attracting, differentiating, and retaining customers. CRM allows a firm to focus its efforts disproportionately on its most lucrative clients. CRM is based on the adage that 80% of a company's profits come from 20% of its customers; therefore, the 20% should receive better service than the 80%. For example, when a plastics manufacturer focused on its most profitable customers, it cut the company's customer base from 800 to 90 and increased revenue by 400%.

The increased use of CRM practices, where high-value customers are treated better than low-value customers, can be attributed to several trends. First, some believe that customers have created the situation themselves by opting for price, choice, and convenience over high-quality service. However, trade-offs arise with this focus on price and other factors at the expense of service concerns. For example, although priceline.com offers discounted tickets at significant savings, customer trade-offs include forfeiting the right to any refund, flying on whatever brand airline is available, and being forced to take connecting flights in many instances. In addition, according to one state investigation, an additional trade-off is that priceline.com is inappropriately prepared to handle customer complaints.

Another reason CRM is currently fashionable is that labor costs have risen, while competitive pressures have kept prices low. The end result is that gross margins have been reduced to 5–10% in many industries. With these kinds of margins, companies simply cannot afford to treat all of their customers equally. Consider the plight of Fidelity Investments. Ten years ago, the company received 97,000 calls a day. Half of those calls were handled by an automated phone system. Today, Fidelity receives 700,000 calls, as well as 550,000 Web site visits a day. Three-quarters of the phone calls are now handled by automated systems, which cost the company less than $1 per call. Live customer-service personnel handle the remaining calls at $13 per call. This is just one of the reasons the company contacted 25,000 of its customers to request that they use its Web site or automated phone system.

Finally, firms are expanding CRM efforts because markets are increasingly fragmented and promotional costs are on the rise. Six Continents, the owner of Holiday Inn and Inter-Continental Hotels, recently learned a valuable lesson about not treating customers equally. The company now sends its promotional mailings only to those who "bit" on earlier mailings. The end result is that the company has reduced mailing costs by 50%, while response rates have increased by 20%.

CRM Outcomes

Typical outcomes of CRM practices include **coding**, **routing**, **targeting**, and **sharing**. Each practice is typically associated with both positive and negative consequences for customers.

Coding. Firms grade customers based on how profitable the customer's business is. Service staff are instructed to handle customers differently based on their category code. Compare the following examples.

Customer-relationship management (CRM)
Is the process of identifying, attracting, differentiating, and retaining customers.

Economic Forces
Due to rising labor costs and lower customer discretionary spending, gross margins have been reduced to 5–10% in many industries. This has led many companies to take a serious look at which of their customers are the most profitable, with plans to treat them accordingly.

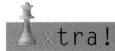

Coding
Is categorizing customers based on how profitable their past business has been.

- A New York customer travels to New Jersey to buy a table from an IKEA store. After returning home, he discovers that the table is missing necessary brackets and screws. The store refuses to mail him the missing parts and insists that he return to the store. The customer does not own a car.
- A Platinum customer of Starwood Hotels & Resorts Worldwide wants to propose to his girlfriend in India. Starwood arranges entry into the Taj Mahal after hours so that he can propose in private. Starwood also provides a horse-driven carriage, flowers, a special meal, an upgraded suite, and a reception hosted by the hotel's general manager.
- Sears Roebuck and Company's most profitable credit-card customers get to choose a preferred two-hour time window for repair appointments. Regular customers are given a four-hour time window.

Routing

Is the process of directing incoming calls to customer-service representatives in a way that ensures that more profitable customers are more likely to receive faster and better customer service.

Routing. Call centers route incoming calls based on the customer's code. Customers in profitable code categories get to speak to live customer-service representatives. Less profitable customers are inventoried in automated telephone queues. For example:

- Call this particular electric utility company and, depending on your status, you may have to stay on the line for quite awhile. The top 350 business clients are served by six people. The next tier, consisting of the next 700 most profitable customers, are handled by six more people. The next 30,000 customers are served by two customer-service representatives. The final group, consisting of 300,000 customers, are routed to an automated telephone system.
- Charles Schwab & Company's top-rated Signature clients, consisting of customers who maintain $100,000 in assets or trade at least 12 times a year, never wait more than 15 seconds to have their calls personally answered by a customer-service representative. Regular customers can wait up to 10 minutes or more.

Targeting

Involves offering the firm's most profitable customers special deals and incentives.

Targeting. Profitable customers have fees waived and are targeted for special promotions. Less profitable customers may never hear of the special deals. Consider these examples:

- Centura Bank, Inc. of Raleigh, North Carolina, ranks its two million customers on a profitability scale of 1 to 5. The most profitable customers are called several times a year for what the bank terms "friendly chats," and the CEO calls these same customers once a year with holiday greetings. Since the "friendly chats" program was implemented, the retention rate of the most profitable group has increased by 50%. In comparison, the most unprofitable group has decreased from 27% to 21% of the total customer base.
- First Bank of Baltimore, Maryland, provides its most profitable customers with a Web option that its regular customers never see. The option allows preferred customers to click a special icon that connects them with live service agents for phone conversations.
- First Union codes its credit-card customers with colored squares that flash on customer-service representatives' computer screens. A green square indicates that the customer is profitable and should be granted fee waivers and given the "white-glove" treatment.

Sharing

Involves making key customer information accessible to all parts of the organization, and in some cases selling that information to other firms.

Sharing. Customer information is shared with other parts of the organization, and information is sold to other companies. Although the customer may be new to the organization, his or her purchase history and buying potential are well-known to insiders. For example:

- A United Airlines passenger was shocked when a ticketing agent told him: "Wow, somebody doesn't like you." Apparently the passenger was involved in an argument with another United employee several months earlier. The argument became part of the passenger's permanent record that follows him wherever he flies with United. The passenger, who is a Premier Executive account holder, feels that the airline has been less than accommodating following the incident.

• Continental Airlines has introduced a Customer Information System where each of Continental's 43,000 gate, reservation, and service employees has access to the history and value of each customer. The system also suggests specific service-recovery remedies and perks, such as coupons for delays and automatic upgrades. The system is designed to provide more consistent staff behavior and service delivery.

Limitations of CRM Practices

Technology greatly enhances CRM processes by identifying current and potential customers, differentiating among high-value and low-value customers, and customizing offers to meet the needs of individual high-value customers. However, there are limitations. First, customers do not like hearing that some customers are valued more than others, especially when they are not the ones receiving the white-glove treatment. Many companies are well aware of potential customer ill will and are fairly tight-lipped about the outcomes of their respective CRM practices. In a *Business Week* lead story pertaining to CRM issues, companies such as GE Capital, Sprint Corporation, and WorldCom,

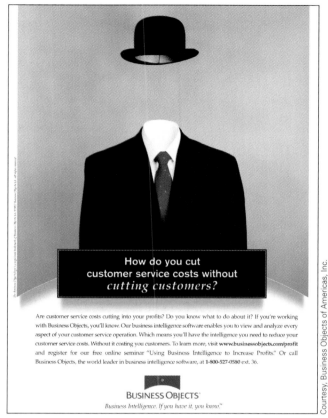

How do you cut customer service costs without *cutting customers?*

Are customer service costs cutting into your profits? Do you know what to do about it? If you're working with Business Objects, you'll know. Our business intelligence software enables you to view and analyze every aspect of your customer service operation. Which means you'll have the intelligence you need to reduce your customer service costs. Without it costing you customers. To learn more, visit www.businessobjects.com/profit and register for our free online seminar "Using Business Intelligence to Increase Profits." Or call Business Objects, the world leader in business intelligence software, at 1-800-527-0580 ext. 36.

BUSINESS OBJECTS
Business Intelligence. If you have it, you know.

Inc., declined repeated requests to speak about their service-discrimination practices.[34] Meanwhile, in service operations where service discrimination is common, such as airlines, banks, retail stores, hotels, and telecommunication companies, customer satisfaction is taking a nosedive and customer complaints are on the rise (see Figure 10.7).

Another concern relating to CRM practices involves privacy issues. How much should a company really know about its customers? When discussing its new Customer Information System, the vice president of Continental Airlines boasted, "We even know if they [the customers] put their eyeshades on and go to sleep."[35] Ironically, in this day and age of high-tech CRM systems, experts are now suggesting that if customers want better service, they should protect their privacy. In doing so, it is recommended that customers avoid filling out surveys and be protective about credit-card and Social Security information. The less companies know about customers, the less they will be able to categorize them, and the less likely customers will be treated as being low in value.

CRM is also limited by its focus on past purchase patterns. In reality, what customers spend today is not necessarily a good predictor of what their behavior will be tomorrow. How many potentially profitable customers are being eliminated today because their current purchasing behavior has them slotted and treated as "commoners"? Spurned by such treatment, how many of these customers defect to another provider that appreciates their potential and treats them appropriately? Life situations and spending habits do change over time.

Service discrimination also leads to some interesting ethical and legal questions. Should only the wealthy be recipients of quality service? Is this a form of *red-lining*— the practice of identifying and avoiding unprofitable types of neighborhoods or people? What happens when CRM-enabled companies learn that their less profitable customers who are now the recipients of substandard service are protected classes of individuals? Will CRM practices lead to an increase in lawsuits filed against companies based on claims of systematic discrimination?

CRM differentiates between high-value and low-value customers so high-value customers receive the white glove treatment. But customers don't like to hear that they are being treated differently.

Technological Forces

The use of business technologies has led to privacy concerns. According to some experts, if you do not want to be coded in a company's CRM system, be careful about what information you provide. The less the company knows about you, the less likely you will be able to be categorized.

Political and Legal Forces

Are CRM practices a form of red-lining, where only the wealthy are recipients of quality service? Will CRM lead to lawsuits based on claims of systematic discrimination?

| Figure 10.7 | Customer Satisfaction Index, 1994–2000 |

Based on annual poll of more than 50,000 customers measuring overall satisfaction with goods and services. Scale 1–100

Data: University of Michigan Business School's American Customer Satisfaction Index

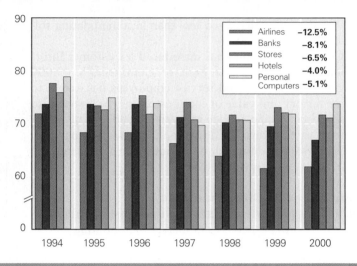

Source: Adapted from Diane Brady, "Why Service Stinks," *Business Week*, 23 October 2000, 120–121.

Service Quality

Service quality researchers agree on one issue: Service quality is an elusive and abstract concept that is difficult to define and measure.[36] The productivity of education and government services is notoriously difficult to measure. Increases in quality, such as improving the quality of education and training governmental employees to be more pleasant throughout their daily interactions with the public, do not show up in productivity measures. In contrast, providing poor quality can ironically increase the country's gross national product (GNP).[37] If a mail-order company sends a customer the wrong product, the dollars spent on phone calls and return mailings to correct the mistake will actually add to the country's GNP. However, it is readily apparent that increases in quality can have a dramatic impact on a firm's or industry's survival. As evidence, Japan did not simply bulldoze its way into U.S. markets by offering lower prices alone—superior quality compared to the competition at that time ultimately won customers over.

What is Service Quality?

Service quality
Is an attitude formed by a long-term, overall evaluation of performance.

Perhaps the best way to begin a discussion of service quality is to first attempt to distinguish service quality from customer satisfaction. Most experts agree that customer satisfaction is a short-term, transaction-specific measure, whereas **service quality** is an attitude formed by a long-term, comprehensive evaluation of performance. Service quality offers a way for competing services to achieve success. In particular, where a small number of firms, such as banks, offer nearly identical services competing within a small area, establishing service quality may be the only way for a firm to differentiate itself. Service-quality differentiation can generate increased market share and ultimately mean the difference between financial success and failure.

Goods manufacturers have already learned this lesson and over the past decade have made producing quality goods a priority issue. Improving the quality of manufactured goods has become a major strategy for both establishing efficient, smooth-running operations and increasing consumer market share in an atmosphere of increasing customer demand for higher quality. Goods quality-improvement measures have focused largely on the quality of the products themselves, and specifically on eliminating product failure. Initially, these measures were based on rigorous checking of all finished products before they came into contact with the customer. More recently, quality control has focused on the principle of ensuring quality during the manufacturing process, on "getting it right the first time," and on reducing end-of-production-line failures to zero. The final evolution in goods manufacturing has been to define quality as delivering the right product to the right customer at the right time, thus extending quality beyond the good itself and using external, as well as internal, measures to assess overall quality.

Service quality cannot be understood in quite the same way. The service experience depends on the customer as a participant in the production process, so normal quality-control measures that depend on eliminating defects before the consumer sees the product are not applicable. Service quality is not a specific goal or program that can be achieved or completed before the final product reaches the customer. Consequently, while manufacturers of goods aim for *zero defects*, the primary goal of service firms is *zero defections*. This often entails handling problems in real time as they unfold throughout the service-delivery process.

The Gap Model

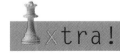

Service quality can be examined in terms of gaps that exist between expectations and perceptions on the part of management, employees, and customers (see Figure 10.8).[38]

| Figure 10.8 | Service Quality Gap Model |

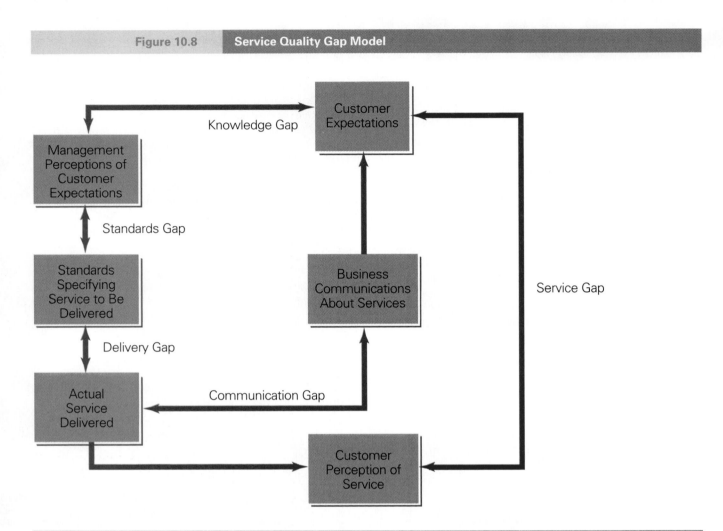

Source: Adapted from A. Parasuraman, Valerie Zeithaml, and Leonard Berry, "A Conceptual Model of Service Quality and Its Implications for Future Research." *Journal of Marketing* 49 (Fall 1985): 41–50.

Service gap

Is the gap between customers' expectations of service and their perception of the service actually delivered, which is a function of the knowledge gap, the standards gap, the delivery gap, and the communications gap.

The most important gap—the **service gap**—is between customers' expectations of service and their perception of the service actually delivered. Ultimately, the goal of a service firm is to close the service gap, or at least narrow it as much as possible. Before the firm can close the service gap, it must close or attempt to narrow four other gaps:

- The *knowledge gap*—the difference between what consumers expect of a service and management's perception of what consumers expect.
- The *standards gap*—the difference between management's perception of what consumers expect and the standards set for service delivery.
- The *delivery gap*—the difference between the standards set for service delivery and the actual quality of service delivery. For example, do employees perform the service as they were trained?
- The *communications gap*—the difference between the actual quality of service delivered and the quality of service described in the firm's external communications, such as brochures and mass-media advertising.

Hence, the service gap is a function of the knowledge gap, the standards gap, the delivery gap, and the communications gap. As each of these gaps increases or decreases, the service gap responds in a similar manner.

1. Visit ExxonMobil's homepage at http://www.exxonmobil.com.
    a. Search for Speedpass and describe the benefits of this customer loyalty program.
    b. Go to http://www.speedpass.com. How does Speedpass work at the pump? How does Speedpass work at the register? Explain the technology behind the Speedpass device.

2. Investigate http://www.liveperson.com.
    a. What products does liveperson.com offer its corporate customers?

    b. As a corporate customer, what benefits would your firm obtain from outsourcing your customer-contact duties to liveperson.com?

3. Investigate http://www.landsend.com.
    a. Access the "My Virtual Model" section of the site and build a model similar to yourself.
    b. From a marketing standpoint, what is the purpose of "My Virtual Model?"
    c. Does this unique customer-service feature transform your online experience from functional to compelling? Please explain.

CHAPTER CASE

Managing the Shared-Service Experience: Police Gas Mile High Fans

Like most service encounters, a football game is a shared experience where other fans can greatly affect, both positively and negatively, the level of enjoyment an individual derives from the event. This particular game between Colorado State University (CSU) and the University of Colorado (CU) at Mile High Stadium (the home of the NFL's Denver Broncos) was no different—except for the fact that the game ended in a police action where fans were doused with pepper spray and tear gas. Hence, the tagline: "*Police Gas Mile High Fans.*"

ESPN's Sports Center reported the story approximately as follows: At the apparent request of the Denver Broncos' ownership, police dressed in riot gear marched down the sidelines with four minutes left in the CSU vs. CU game to serve as a protective barrier between the field's goalposts and a potential onslaught of jubilant CSU students aiming to claim them as their own. CSU was in the process of trouncing its long-time intrastate rival CU to the tune of 41–14 and virtually every CSU fan who attended the game stayed until the end to enjoy every last second. In response to the armed policemen who purposely positioned themselves in front of the CSU student section, CSU students began pelting the police with everything from ice-filled soft-drink cups to the occasional can of corn and/or chili, apparently left over from earlier tailgating festivities. In response to the pelting and the attempt by a handful of students to take the field, the Denver police began discharging pepper spray in the direction of the offending students and then eventually launched teargas canisters into the stands to dissuade others from charging the field. In response to the gassing, most fans hurriedly headed for the exits, while others threw the teargas canisters that had landed in the stands back on the

field, aiming for the police. By the time the melee was over, fans young and old, the CSU pep band, players and coaches, the police, and the media were all suffering from the effects of teargas. The reputations of CSU fans and the Denver police were both tarnished by the event.

What to Do Next Year?
Now it's your turn! As one might expect, much discussion after the game centered on whether the CSU/CU game should even be played at Mile High Stadium. In fact, the mayor of Denver, the Denver police, and members of both schools' administrations met to discuss the future venue for this game. For years, the game had been played at each school's home campus and this was only the second time the teams had met in Denver (the inaugural meeting there was the year before). The factors below may help you answer the discussion questions following the case.

- Playing the game at Mile High turned it into a Colorado event instead of a campus event. The last two games had been sell-outs. Seating at Mile High accommodates approximately 76,000 fans, while the CSU stadium only holds approximately 36,000 fans.
- Beer was sold at the game and tailgating was permitted in the parking lot starting at noon. The game began at 5 p.m.
- Ever since the game has been played at Mile High, the two colleges have been less involved in managing the logistics. When the games were played on campus, each school managed traffic flow, parking, crowd control, etc.
- The University of Colorado's locker room was located beneath the CSU student section.

- The Denver police have repeatedly used pepper spray and teargas on sports fans in other situations, including post-game celebrations of the Avalanche and Broncos championship games.
- A chain-link fence stood between the field and the stands.
- College students on a number of campuses are becoming less intimidated by police.
- The Denver Broncos organization and the police denied earlier reports that the Broncos had requested police to protect the field and the goalposts.
- Prior to kick-off, CU was ranked 14th nationally. In contrast, CSU was picked to finish sixth in the newly formed Mountain West Conference. This particular game truly was an upset.
- National television coverage dictates when the game is played, and the additional revenues generated by coverage contribute greatly to the schools' athletic funds.
- Fans sitting in the alumni section at the game stated: "There was no way to escape, no warning (about the teargas or mace); there was no way to help friends."
- The CSU band director was inundated with pepper spray while attempting to help injured students. The spray permeated his uniform, blinded him, and began to burn his skin. "I asked the event staff for help, but

no one was responding. I told the band to start running up the seats and get out as fast as they could."
- The Denver police department continues to avidly defend its actions in response to drunken and overzealous fans. While many have criticized the action taken by police, many others credit the police for preventing a potential riot.

Case Questions

1. Football games are a shared service experience. List five ways "other fans" can enhance your experience and five ways they can detract from your experience.
2. If the game continues at Mile High, how would you manage this sporting event differently from how it was handled on this day?
3. Should fans have the right to tear down the goalposts at the end of a game? Should the police have the right to stop fans from doing so?
4. What unique steps does your school take to manage sporting events?

Sources: K. Douglas Hoffman and John E. G. Bateson, *Essentials of Services Marketing: Concepts, Strategies, and Cases*, 2nd ed. (Mason: OH: South-Western, 2002), 451–453.
L'Shawn Lyle, "Students Express Anger," *The Rocky Mountain Collegian* 108, (12) 8 September 1999, 1.
Eric Olson, "CSU Band Members Speak Out Against Denver PD," *The Rocky Mountain Collegian* 108, (12) 8 September 1999, 1.

VIDEO CASE

FedEx's Commitment to 100% Customer Satisfaction

If you've ever ordered anything by phone or over the Internet, chances are you've received a package delivered by a purple, orange, and white FedEx truck. Millions of other customers, both consumers and businesses, received their packages on the same day. In fact, FedEx makes three to four million deliveries each day, in more than 200 countries, 24 to 48 hours after the shipping order was placed.

Shipping a package via FedEx costs more than shipping via UPS or Airborne. But FedEx maintains its competitive position by offering security and reliability—in other words, FedEx relies on the trusting relationship it builds with customers. FedEx claims that more than 99% of its deliveries arrive on time. And when there's a mistake, the company offers a two-way, money-back guarantee: First, the customer is given a refund if the delivery is late; second, the customer receives a refund if there is any difficulty in obtaining tracking information.

Technology is the foundation of FedEx's ability to build complex, integrated relationships with its customers. FedEx maintains a database that details every aspect of each shipping transaction. With FedEx's data-

base, both the company and customer know where the package is during every moment of the transaction; if there is ever a gap in this information, the customer gets a refund. But FedEx's service goes much farther than tracking packages. Major customers, such as L.L. Bean, Dell Computer, or any of the major American automakers, can download FedEx software solutions right into their own desktop computers to customize the way they want to use the information that FedEx can provide. For instance, FedEx Ship API software allows business customers to customize the application to their own shipping needs, from generating shipping labels to tracking packages in real time.

Jeff Wyne, marketing manager for FedEx, notes that one of his organization's goals is to help other businesses be successful. One way to do this is to help a customer manage its supply chain. For instance, FedEx not only handles shipping but also owns warehouses throughout the world, where it holds inventories for companies that don't want to manage their own. FedEx has also become involved in handling international logistics for its customers, through its recently formed subsidiary, FedEx

Trade Networks Inc. "We listened to our customers, and that's what they wanted," says G. Edmond Clark, head of the new subsidiary.

If you order an anorak or a pair of hiking boots from L.L. Bean in Maine, the FedEx truck will be at your house in two days. FedEx is an integral part of L.L. Bean's entire business, from the order system on down to the customer-service system, where a representative locates a product number, fulfills the request, and generates a FedEx shipping label. Shipping personnel attach a label to the box and scan it, then place the box on the truck. Being part of the entire logistics process helps FedEx build a long-term relationship with customers like L.L. Bean—a relationship in which each company helps the other grow.

FedEx has the reputation of pulling out all the stops to get a package delivered on time, no matter what. The company has even been known to rent commercial jets when its own planes have suffered mechanical failures. If a delivery doesn't make it, not only is the customer's money refunded, a FedEx man will make a personal phone call or visit to apologize and try to find a solution to the problem. Then FedEx will study the situation to make sure it doesn't happen again. "We strive for 100% satisfaction guaranteed," says Jeff Wyne. And they'll do whatever it takes.

Case Questions

1. How does FedEx's use of technology help build relationships with its customers?
2. Go to FedEx's Web site at **http://www.fedex.com**, select "U.S.A." and then "eBusiness Tools." On that page, you'll see a link for "FedEx eCommerce Solutions" (currently found at **http://www.fedex.com/us/ebusiness/ecommerce**). Choose one of the e-commerce options described, click on its link, and read more about it. Do you think the solution is easy for customers to use? Why or why not?
3. How do FedEx and L.L. Bean benefit from the reciprocity of their relationship?
4. How does FedEx strengthen a relationship after making a mistake?

Sources: Alan Gersten, "FedEx Creates New Unit for Logistics Focus," *Reuter's Limited,* 17 February 2000.

"FedEx Trade Networks to Offer Full Range of Global Trade Services," *Business Wire,* 17 February 2000.

Brian O'Reilly, "They've Got Mail!" *Fortune,* 7 February 2000, http://www.fortune.com.

"FedEx eShipping Tools," FedEx Web site, http://www.fedex.com, accessed 4 February 2000.

Scott Kirsner, "Digital Competition—Laurie A. Tucker," *Fast Company,* December 1999, 166.

In Chapter 11, **Bert Rosenbloom**, Drexel University, takes students backstage to discover how the structure, strategy, design, and management of marketing channels give hundreds of millions of customers convenient access to a vast selection of goods and services. Professor Rosenbloom also explores how channel strategy should enhance rather than detract from the firm's product, price, and promotion strategies.

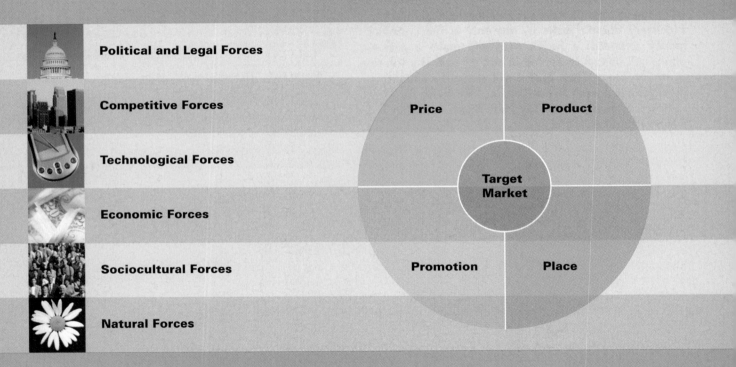

Political and Legal Forces

Competitive Forces

Technological Forces

Economic Forces

Sociocultural Forces

Natural Forces

Price

Product

Target
Market

Promotion

Place

Patrick Dunne, Texas Tech University, and **Robert Lusch**, Texas Christian University, provide an enlightening presentation of the roles of retailers and wholesalers in developing a distribution strategy in Chapter 12. In addition to presenting the differentiation strategies used by retailers to attract and retain customers, Professors Dunne and Lusch highlight the role of wholesaling in the U.S. economy.

Distribution Strategy

 Political and Legal Forces Conventional retailers often complain that online retailers get unfair tax advantages. Since by law they do not have to charge a sales tax, their net selling price to the consumer is less. In addition, since others do not have to carry inventory, they are able to avoid state property taxes.

 Competitive Forces Due to the practice of scrambled merchandising, competition often arises from nontraditional sources. For example, doughnut retailers such as Dunkin' Donuts and Krispie Kreme are now competing with nontraditional competitors such as Wal-Mart Supercenters.

 Technological Forces The emergence of the Internet as a viable channel for online shopping makes direct sales from producer to consumer more feasible for some goods and services. Thus, the length of the channel for such goods and services as CDs and airline tickets may become shorter.

 Economic Forces The total-cost approach to the systems concept of logistics attempts to achieve the desired level of customer service at the lowest cost.

 Sociocultural Forces As consumer desires for a more enjoyable car-buying experience became increasingly evident, the Saturn Division of General Motors altered its channel strategy to provide a revolutionary way of selling cars that provides consumers with detailed product information, charges one price, and offers a 30-day return policy.

 Natural Forces Many apparel retailers have seen their profits vanish when they failed to take early markdowns and, in mid-to-late July, they were still using their valuable endcaps to sell excess summerwear. This was occurring when high-markup and high-impulse "back to school" clothing was arriving at their docks.

11

Marketing Channels and Distribution

Originally, Altoids were sold through gourmet shops to a small market of British and U.S. consumers. Kraft Foods, however, wanted to expand the sales of this product to a broader market. After examining various strategies involving product, price, promotion, and place, Kraft determined that the best solution would involve a marketing channel strategy. Specifically, Kraft chose to mass-distribute Altoids by placing the product in supermarkets, chain drugstores, and mass merchandisers. Kraft surmised that consumers would appreciate the convenience of having the product available at retailers and that retail chains would welcome the additional revenue and profit margins. As Kraft had hoped, the marketing channel strategy was extremely successful in increasing sales and was highly profitable for both retailers and Kraft.

You Decide. After reading the opening vignette and paying special attention to the sections of this chapter marked with the chess piece, answer these questions:

1. In moving Altoids' channel intensity from selective to intensive, what was a primary concern for Kraft?

2. In choosing an optimal channel structure for Altoids, what criteria did Kraft likely consider the most important in the decision-making process?

3. How would Kraft best benefit by using supply-chain management rather than a traditional channel approach?

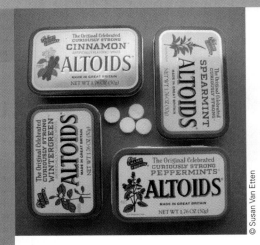

© Susan Van Etten

Altoids Marketing Channel Strategy Turned a Mint into a $100-Million Mint!
How do you go from an obscure product with annual sales of less than $10 million to an internationally recognized brand with mass appeal and annual sales of more than $100 million in less than a decade? Altoids did it with some smart marketing channel strategy.[1]

It seems that everybody now recognizes the name Altoids as the maker of those extra-strong hard-candy mints packaged in little tin boxes that seem to be sold everywhere at $2 or more a pop. But it wasn't too long ago that the "curiously strong" taste of Altoids mints was known mainly to a small cult following in England and a few aficionados in the U.S. who prowled gourmet shops. All this changed when the Kraft Foods division of Philip Morris Company (recently renamed Altria Group Inc.), the producer of Altoids, believed that its mints could enjoy a much wider appeal. For this to happen, Altoids would have to be repositioned from an obscure novelty item into a mainstream mass-market product, while still maintaining its cachet and premium price. So, the challenge became one of finding the right marketing-mix strategy to greatly expand the market for Altoids without undermining Altoid's brand equity.

Not much could be done with the first "P" of the marketing mix, product strategy, because the product was just about perfect in its present form. Consumers loved the taste of the mints and the upscale tin packaging they came in. In short, Altoids had already achieved excellent product differentiation.

Relying on the second "P"—price strategy—in the marketing mix by reducing the price of Altoids in the hope of gaining more market penetration would not be a good idea. The lower price might very likely cause consumers to view Altoids as "just another mint candy."

Moreover, lower prices would adversely affect profits.

How about emphasizing the third "P" in the marketing mix, promotion, in the form of heavy advertising of Altoids in the major media—a common strategy for penetrating mass markets? Kraft also rejected this strategy as a bad idea because it would be very expensive and could undermine the special appeal of Altoids through overexposure.

Kraft found the right marketing strategy in the fourth "P," place, by focusing on marketing channel strategy. Specifically, Kraft decided to use a mass-distribution strategy by selling Altoids in supermarkets, chain drugstores, and mass merchandisers all over the U.S. and abroad. Kraft reasoned that having Altoids readily available wherever consumers shopped would have great appeal because of the convenience factor, while the giant retail chains would welcome the additional revenue and high margins provided by a product that could be sold as an impulse item at checkout counters while taking up very little shelf space.

This mass-distribution marketing channel strategy was hugely successful. It created a win-win-win situation: Altoids maintained its mystique and premium price, retailers got a space-efficient high-profit product, and millions of additional consumers gained easy access to Altoids.

The tenfold growth in sales of Altoids is testimony to how effectively Kraft's marketing channel strategy has worked out. Indeed, while making this mint conveniently available to millions of consumers by placing it in the marketing channels where they shopped everyday, you could say that Kraft turned a tiny mint into a $100-million mint of sales and profits!

LEARNING OBJECTIVES

After you have completed this chapter you should be able to:

1. *Understand how marketing channels add time, place, and possession utilities for final customers and how channel structure evolves to provide these utilities effectively and efficiently.*

2. *Identify the five major flows in marketing channels and how each contributes to making products conveniently available to many millions of customers.*

3. *Realize that marketing channels are not only economic systems, but also social systems, in which power and conflict play an important role.*

4. *Recognize and explain all six decision areas of channel management and be familiar with the main issues associated with each of those decisions.*

5. *Appreciate the crucial role played by logistics in the creation and operation of high-performance marketing channels.*

VOICE OF THE EXPERT
Bert Rosenbloom, Drexel University

What do a tin of Altoids, a Rio Sonic Blue MP3 player, a MINI Cooper car, an Apple iPod, a bottle of Mike's Hard Ice Tea, and millions of other products have in common? The answer is surprisingly simple: They all need to be made available to final customers if they are to satisfy customer demand.[2] Everyday, literally billions of people, as well as millions of industrial companies, businesses, institutions, and other organizations all over the world, need and want millions of different products. Somehow, this vast array of products and billions of customers around the globe must be matched up so that customers can get the products they demand when and where they are needed. This may involve a consumer going to a retail store such as Gap to buy a sweater, ordering a pizza over the telephone, or using the Internet to purchase a Harry Potter book from Amazon.com.[3] In the business-to-business sector, industrial distributors, manufacturers' representatives, and sales agents may be needed to make everything from sophisticated electronic components to paper towels available to organizational customers in a broad spectrum of different industries.[4]

Most customers are unaware of the enormous effort involved in making such a vast range of products so conveniently available. Indeed, most take it for granted. A virtually limitless array of products can be purchased by simply taking a drive to the mall, picking up the telephone and ordering from a catalog, or clicking the mouse on a PC to buy online. In fact, the availability of so many products from so many sources has become a given—a routine fact of everyday life for millions of consumers and organizations. But behind this seemingly ordinary process is an extraordinary combination of businesses, people, and technologies that comprise the marketing channels that have made such efficient distribution possible.[5]

In this chapter, we go "backstage" to examine marketing channels more closely. We take a look at the concept of marketing channels—their structure, strategy, design, and management. As we peer behind the scenes to look at marketing channels, a vital and exciting part of marketing will be uncovered.

Marketing Channel Defined

Marketing channel
Is the network of organizations that creates time, place, and possession utilities.

A **marketing channel**, also referred to as a *distribution channel* or *channel of distribution,* is the network of organizations that creates time, place, and possession utilities for consumers and business users.

An example will help to clarify this definition. The updated MINI Cooper, inspired by nostalgia for the Austin MINI Cooper of the 1960s is a product that captured the public's imagination. Though designed and developed by BMW, a German automobile maker, the MINI Cooper is actually manufactured in England. As these cars roll off the assembly line and out the factory door they appear to be totally complete. But are they? Actually, they are complete only to the extent of having *form utility,* which has been provided through the manufacturing process. But as exciting and cute as these cars may be, to be of use to consumers, they must be available when and where customers want them, and arrangements must be made so consumers can actually take possession of the cars through purchasing or leasing. In other words, **time, place, and possession utilities** still need to be added to make these cars complete from the standpoint of meeting customer needs. Time, place, and possession utilities are conditions that enable consumers and business users to have products available for use when and where they want them and to actually take possession of them. Clearly, a MINI sitting on the factory lot in England is of little use to a consumer in San Francisco who wants one to traverse the hilly streets of that city. Marketing channels are what create these other utilities not just for MINI Coopers but for millions of other products as well.

Time, place, and possession utilities
Are conditions that enable consumers and business users to have products available for use when and where they want them and to actually take possession of them.

The creation of time, place, and possession utilities may result from marketing channels that are simple or complex. In the case of the MINI Cooper, the channel is fairly simple. The cars are sold by the manufacturer to retail dealers, who in turn sell the cars to consumers. The cars are transported from the factory to dealer showrooms by independent ship, railroad, or truck carriers who charge a fee for their services. Thus, the participants in this marketing channel are the manufacturers, retailers, consumers, and transportation companies. Only the first three, however, are what is referred to as the *sales channel,* which is that part of the channel involved in buying, selling, and transferring title. The transportation firms, which do not buy, sell, or transfer the title to the cars, are part of the *facilitating channel.* Public storage firms, insurance companies, finance companies, market-research firms, and several other types of firms also frequently participate as facilitating organizations in various marketing channels.

Some marketing channels are more complex than that used for the MINI Cooper. Beer, for example, which goes from manufacturers to wholesalers to retailers and then to consumers, has an extra organization (the wholesaler) in its sales channel.[6]

The simplest sales channels go directly from producers to customers, as in the case of Dell Computer Corporation, which sells all of its products directly from its manufacturing plants to customers. Dell's facilitating channel, however, which uses telephone, mail, and the Internet for order placement, as well as United Parcel Service (UPS), Federal Express, and other transportation firms to deliver its computers to customers, is more complex than its sales channel.

Both the sales and facilitating channels are usually needed to create time, place, and possession utilities. But it has become a customary practice in marketing to describe and illustrate marketing channels only in terms of the sales channel, because it is the relationship involving the functions of buying, selling, and transferring title

The participants in the marketing channels for the MINI Cooper are fairly simple and include the manufacturer, retail dealers, consumers and transportation firms.

© J. Beam Photography

where most of the strategic marketing issues emerge. For example, when setting up its sales channel, BMW faced such marketing-strategy issues as identifying and selecting the appropriate kinds of dealers to sell the new MINI Coopers, convincing them to carry sufficient numbers of the cars, motivating the dealers to do an effective job of promoting and selling the cars, and making sure that they provided good servicing and warranty support. Moreover, BMW also needed to make provisions for numerous other issues as part of its continuing relationship with independent dealers, such as future inventory levels expected of dealers, training of sales and service people, credit terms, evaluation of dealer performance, and numerous others. In contrast, BMW's efforts to arrange for transportation, storage, insurance, and similar matters, while important, are not considered strategic-marketing issues.

Marketing Channel Structure

The form or shape that a marketing channel takes to perform the tasks necessary to make products available to consumers is usually referred to as **channel structure**. Firms such as transportation companies, warehousing firms, insurance companies, and the like are usually referred to as *facilitating agencies*, because they are not involved in buying, selling, or transferring title and thus, as we mentioned earlier, are not considered to be part of the channel structure.

Marketing channel structure has three basic dimensions:

1. Length of the channel
2. Intensity at various levels
3. Types of intermediaries involved

Length of Channel Structure

Channel length is the number of levels in a marketing channel. Channel length can range from two levels, where the producer or manufacturer sells directly to consumers (direct distribution), to as many as 10 levels, where eight intermediary institutions exist between the producer and consumers. With the exception of Japan, such long channels of distribution are quite rare in industrialized countries. Much

Channel structure
Consists of all of the businesses and institutions (including producers or manufacturers and final customers) who are involved in performing the functions of buying, selling, or transferring title.

Channel length
Is the number of levels in a marketing channel.

| Figure 11.1 | Examples of the Length of Dimensions of Marketing Channel Structure for Consumer Products |

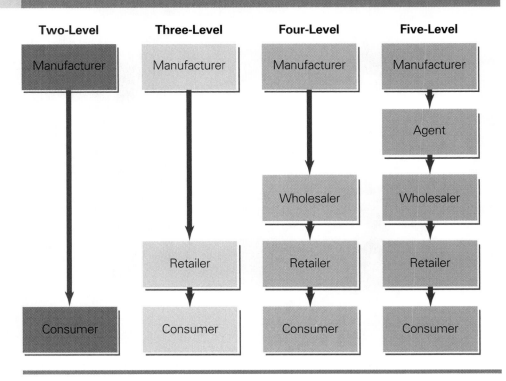

Technological Forces

The emergence of the Internet as a viable channel for online shopping makes direct sales from producer to consumer more feasible for some goods and services.[7] Thus, the length of the channel for such goods and services as CDs and airline tickets may become shorter.

Channel intensity
Refers to the number of intermediaries at each level of the marketing channel.

Intensive distribution
Occurs when all possible intermediaries at a particular level of the channel are used.

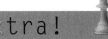

Selective distribution
Means that a carefully chosen group of intermediaries is used at a particular level in the marketing channel.

Exclusive distribution
Occurs when only one intermediary is used at a particular level in the marketing channel.

more common are channel-structure lengths ranging from two levels up to five levels. Figure 11.1 provides an illustration of typical channel-structure lengths for consumer products in developed countries.

Many customer-based factors influence the length of the channel structure, such as the size of the customer base, their geographical dispersion, and their particular behavior patterns. The nature of the product, such as its bulk and weight, perishability, value, and technical complexity, can also be very important. For example, technically complex products such as X-ray machines often require short channels because of the high degree of technical support and liaison needed by customers, which may only be available directly from the manufacturer. Moreover, length can also be affected by the size of the manufacturer, its financial capacity, and its desire for control. In general, larger and more well-financed manufacturers have a greater capability to bypass intermediaries and use shorter channel structures.[8] Manufacturers that want to exercise a high degree of control over the distribution of their products are also more likely to use shorter channel structures because the shorter the channel, the higher the degree of control. Polo, by Ralph Lauren apparel, for example, sells only through upscale department and specialty retailers, as well as its own Web site, to protect the fashion image of its products.

Intensity of Channel Structure

Channel intensity is usually described in terms of intensive distribution, selective distribution, or exclusive distribution. **Intensive distribution** means that all possible intermediaries at the particular level of the channel are used. **Selective distribution** means that a smaller number of intermediaries are used, while **exclusive distribution** refers to only one intermediary used at the particular level of the channel to cover a defined territory. The intensity dimension of channel structure can be portrayed as a continuum as shown in Figure 11.2. Although there are many exceptions, in general, intensive distribution is associated with the distribution of convenience goods, selective distribution with shopping goods, and exclusive distribution with specialty goods. Thus, inexpensive Bic pens, Gillette razor blades, and Hallmark greeting cards (convenience goods) tend to be carried by large numbers of intermediaries, particularly at the retail level, while home appliances such as Whirlpool refrigerators and apparel such as Levis jeans (shopping goods) are handled by relatively fewer retailers, and specialty goods such as Rolex watches or Rolls-Royce automobiles are featured by only one dealer in a specified geographical area (territory).

Types of Intermediaries in the Channel Structure

This third dimension of channel structure refers to the different kinds of intermediary institutions that can be used at the various levels of the channel. At the retail level, there may be many possibilities for some products. For example, a Snickers candy bar can be sold through many different types of retailers, such as candy stores, grocery stores, drugstores, supermarkets, mass merchandisers, discount department stores, and many others. For other products, such as automobiles, the choice is more limited. We should point out, however, that in recent years, with the growth of *scrambled merchandising*, where all kinds of products are sold in stores not traditionally associated with those products, the types of stores that sell various products have broadened considerably. Motor oil, for example, is now regularly available in supermarkets, while hardware items are frequently found in drugstores. Consequently, manufacturers today need to be broad-minded when considering the types of intermediaries to use in their channel structures. The conventional wisdom of particular products being distributed only through certain types of wholesalers or retailers may no longer hold.

Consumers can buy Swiss Army watches in select retail stores, including the Swiss Army store in New York's Soho district. By using the selective distribution strategy, Swiss Army limits the number of intermediaries participating in the marketing channel.

Competitive Forces

Due to the practice of scrambled merchandising, competition often arises from nontraditional sources. For example, doughnut retailers such as Dunkin' Donuts and Krispy Kreme are now competing with nontraditional competitors such as Wal-Mart Supercenters.

Determinants of Channel Structure

The structure of marketing channels, in terms of their length, intensity, and types of participating intermediaries, is determined basically by three factors:

1. The distribution tasks that need to be performed
2. The economics of performing distribution tasks
3. Management's desire for control of distribution

Distribution Tasks

Distribution tasks, also often referred to as *marketing functions* or sometimes *channel functions*, have been described by various lists for many years. Such functions as

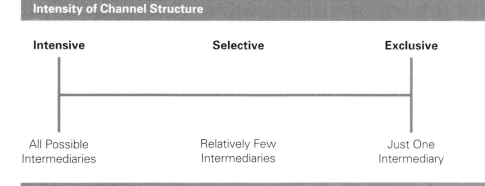

Intensity of Channel Structure   **Figure 11.2**

Intensive	Selective	Exclusive
All Possible Intermediaries	Relatively Few Intermediaries	Just One Intermediary

buying, selling, risk taking, transportation, storage, order processing, and financing are commonly mentioned. More generalized terms can also be used to describe these tasks, such as *concentration, equalization,* and *dispersion*—whereby the main tasks of marketing channels are grouped together in familial relationships—bringing products together from many manufacturers (concentration), adjusting the quantities to balance supply and demand (equalization), and delivering them to final customers (dispersion). Others describe distribution tasks in terms of a sorting process: *accumulating* products from many producers, *sorting* them to correspond to designated target markets, and *assorting* them into conveniently associated groups to ease the shopping burden for customers. Distribution tasks have also been described in much more detailed terms where specific activities sometimes unique to the particular industry are cited.[9]

Regardless of the particular list of distribution tasks presented, the rationale is the same for all of them: Distribution functions must be performed to consummate transactions between buyers and sellers. The reason is that discrepancies exist between buyers and sellers that must be overcome through the performance of distribution tasks. The channel structure the firm chooses to perform these tasks reflects how the tasks are to be allocated to various marketing institutions such as wholesalers, retailers, agents, brokers, or others. The **discrepancies between production and consumption** can be separated into four basic groups:[10]

1. Discrepancies in quantity
2. Discrepancies in assortment
3. Discrepancies in time
4. Discrepancies in place

Discrepancies between production and consumption
Are differences in quantity, assortment, time, and place that must be overcome to make goods available to final customers.

Discrepancies in Quantity. The quantities in which products are manufactured to achieve low average costs are usually too large for any individual customer to use immediately. Wrigley's chewing gum, for example, produces literally millions of packages of gum each day. Even the most ardent gum chewer could not possibly use that much gum every day! Thus, institutions in the channel structure, such as wholesalers and retailers, provide a buffer to absorb the vast output of manufacturers and provide the smaller quantities desired by individual customers.

Discrepancies in Assortment. Products are grouped for manufacturing purposes based on efficiencies of production, while customers group products based on convenience of shopping and consuming. In most cases, the production and consumption groupings are not inherently matched. For example, the thousands of items a consumer finds grouped so conveniently together in a supermarket are not, of course, produced by one manufacturer. Hundreds of relatively specialized manufacturers have made those products. The supermarket and many other intermediaries in marketing channels have performed the distribution tasks necessary to regroup this conglomeration of products, thereby overcoming the discrepancy in assortment. This enables particular manufacturers to concentrate on producing a relatively limited range of products, which when combined through marketing channels with the products of many other manufacturers, allows consumers to have wide and convenient assortments of products that greatly simplify shopping and consumption. Consumers need only stroll down the aisles and place the chosen items in their shopping cart.

Discrepancies in Time. Most products are not manufactured for immediate consumption or use. Thus, some mechanism must be available to hold products between the times they are produced and needed by final customers. A bottle of Snapple iced tea, a Tommy Hilfiger shirt, or a pair of Rollerblade in-line skates are not desired by consumers at the instant they roll off the production line. So intermediaries in marketing channels, particularly merchant wholesalers and retailers, who take title to and physically hold goods until they are needed by consumers, are crucial in overcoming this discrepancy in time.

At Lands' End Your PC Provides a Perfect Fit

The main rap against buying clothes online has been the consumer's inability to actually try on the clothing to see whether it looks good and fits right. Well, Lands' End has come up with a high-tech answer to this problem that may actually be one-up on the typical try-on booths in stores. Lands' End uses software developed by My Virtual Model Inc. that enables consumers to "try on" and check the fit of apparel online instead of in-store. With this technology, online shoppers can see how Lands' End clothing looks and fits on a computer-generated model that is practically a mirror image of themselves. Lands' End says that My Virtual Model™ will work for everything from its business suits to bathrobes, without the shopper even setting foot in a dressing room.

How does it work? You simply visit Lands' End's Web site and click on "My Model." Then select the model for women or men. Another click on "Create a Model" and you are presented with all of the features and dimensions, such as body type, height, weight, waist size, etc., needed to create a cyberspace model of yourself. You even get to give your model a name. Just a half dozen or so clicks later and your virtual model appears on the screen. You then can try a whole variety of clothing styles and colors to see how your virtual model looks in the outfits. Lands' End's version of My Virtual Model even provides style tips and advice. If you like what you see, a few more clicks of the mouse complete the purchase and the apparel you selected will arrive at your door in a couple of days.

All customers creating Virtual Models have complete privacy because, according to Lands' End, your virtual model "lives" at **http://www.myvirtualmodel.com** and only you can make contact with it. But anytime you want, you can take your model from its "home" to visit other apparel Web sites on the My Virtual Model network, which, in addition to Lands' End, includes Lane Bryant, the Home Shopping Network, Wedding Channel.com, and Kenneth Cole.

By the way, if you like, you can e-mail your virtual model to family and friends to get their opinions on how different outfits look. Try that from an in-store dressing room!

Discrepancies in Place. The location of manufacturing facilities for products is determined by such factors as raw material availability, labor costs, expertise, historical considerations, and numerous other factors that may have little to do with where the ultimate consumers of those products are located.[11] Thus, the production and consumption of products can literally take place half a world apart from each other. In fact, today it is more likely than ever that the products we buy are made in China, Singapore, Japan, Brazil, India, or some other faraway country than in some nearby factory. Channel structures evolve or are consciously designed to connect distant manufacturers and consumers by eliminating place discrepancies.

The Economics of Performing Distribution Tasks

Given that distribution tasks must be performed to overcome the four discrepancies discussed earlier, the channel structure needs to be organized to perform tasks as efficiently as possible. The development of efficient marketing channel structures is based on two principles: specialization or division of labor and transaction efficiency.[12]

Specialization or Division of Labor. The principle of **specialization or division of labor** underlies most modern production processes. Each worker in a factory focuses on performing particular manufacturing tasks and thereby develops specialized expertise and skills in performing those tasks. Such specialization results in much greater efficiency and higher output than if each worker were to perform all or most of the tasks necessary to manufacture the product him- or herself.

This 200-year-old principle, which is illustrated in Figure 11.3, applies as much to distribution as it does to production. The various intermediaries in marketing channels are analogous to production workers or stations in a factory, but instead of performing production tasks, they are performing distribution tasks. These intermediaries—whether they are wholesalers, retailers, agents, or brokers—develop expertise in distribution that manufacturers would find uneconomical to match. Moreover, many large intermediaries, such as mass merchandisers, enjoy **economies of scale and economies of scope** that would be impossible for most manufacturers to match. Home Depot, for instance, with more than 1,500 giant warehouse stores, enjoys

Specialization or division of labor
Occurs when each participant in the marketing channel focuses on performing those activities at which it is most efficient.

Economies of scale and economies of scope
Are obtained by spreading the costs of distribution over a large quantity of products (scale) or over a wide variety of products (scope).

Figure 11.3	Specialization and Division of Labor Principle: Production versus Distribution for an Electric Guitar Manufacturer

Production

Production Tasks

1. Thickening the wood
2. Shaping the body and the neck
3. Gluing and clamping the parts
4. Sanding and assembly
5. Applying the finish
6. Installing the electric components
7. Attaching the machine heads and strings
8. Adjusting the action and pickups

Distribution

Distribution Tasks

1. Buying
2. Selling
3. Transferring the title
4. Transportation
5. Storage
6. Processing orders
7. Providing information

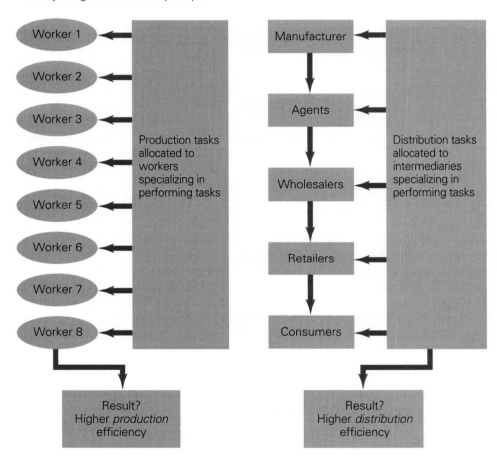

Source: Bert Rosenbloom, *Marketing Channels: A Management View,* 6th ed. (Forth Worth, TX: Dryden Press, 1999), 20. Reprinted with permission of South-Western, a division of Thomson Learning: www.thomsonrights.com. Fax 1-800-730-2215.

great economies of scale and scope because it is able to spread its operating costs over a vast quantity and variety of products.

Transaction efficiency

Refers to designing marketing channels to minimize the number of contacts between producers and consumers.

Transaction Efficiency. **Transaction efficiency** refers to the effort to reduce the number of transactions between producers and consumers. If many producers attempt to deal directly with large numbers of consumers, the number of transactions can be enormous. Paradoxically, by lengthening the channel structure through the addition of intermediaries, the number of transactions can actually be reduced. Consequently, transaction efficiency is increased. This is illustrated in Figure 11.4. As

How the Introduction of an Intermediary Reduces the Number of Transactions   **Figure 11.4**

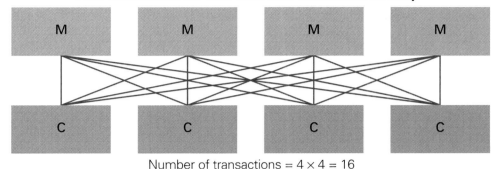

Four manufacturers deal with four consumers directly

Number of transactions = 4 × 4 = 16

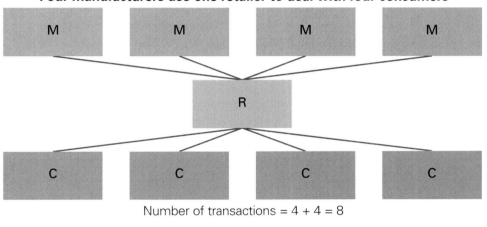

Four manufacturers use one retailer to deal with four consumers

Number of transactions = 4 + 4 = 8

shown in the figure, the number of transactions has been cut in half as a result of the introduction of the retailer into the channel structure. Given that the costs of transactions can be very high, especially if personal face-to-face meetings are necessary to consummate transactions, the reduction in contacts through the use of intermediaries in the channel structure is in many cases absolutely vital for economical distribution.

Management's Desire for Control of Distribution

Even though the economics of distribution task performance may seem to call for a particular type of marketing channel structure, a firm's desire for control of the marketing channel may outweigh the economic considerations.[13] In general, the shorter the channel structure, the higher the degree of control, and vice versa. Further, the lower the intensity of distribution, the higher the degree of control, and vice versa. For example, suppose an economic analysis, based on specialization/division of labor and transaction efficiencies, calls for a long marketing channel structure with a fairly high degree of intensity at the various levels. However, management in the manufacturing firm feels a need to protect the image of the product and also believes it is necessary to provide high levels of customer service. To do so, the manufacturer is convinced that it needs a high degree of control, and so it may opt for only one level of intermediary, with a very high degree of selectivity in appointing them as channel members, based on their willingness to take direction from the manufacturer. This is exactly the situation Gucci, the Italian maker of world-famous luxury goods, found itself in. Focusing mainly on gaining distribution efficiency, Gucci ended up selling its products through several thousand retailers. This proliferation of retailers—many of whom were not of the highest stature—although providing economies of scale in the distribution of Gucci products, adversely affected the exclusive image of Gucci. Realizing the problem, Gucci restructured its marketing channels by drastically reducing the number of retailers selling its products to less than 500 worldwide. Moreover, all of these retailers were of the highest quality, and were willing to take close direction from Gucci to project a world-class quality image vital to Gucci's long-term success. In contrast, a brand such as Fruit of the Loom underwear, which uses intensive distribution, would have far less concern about control of the channel than Gucci.

LEARNING OBJECTIVE 2 — Flows in Marketing Channels

When a marketing channel is developed, a series of *channel flows* emerge. These flows provide the links that tie channel members and other agencies together in the distribution of goods and services. The most important of these flows are the (1) product flow, (2) negotiation flow, (3) ownership flow, (4) information flow, and (5) promotion flow. These flows are illustrated for Coors beer in Figure 11.5.

The *product flow* refers to the actual physical movement of the product from the manufacturer (Coors) through all of the parties who take physical possession of the product, from its point of production to consumers. In the case of Coors beer, the product comes from breweries and packaging plants in Colorado, Tennessee, and Virginia by way of company trucks or common carriers (transportation companies) to beer distributors (wholesalers), who in turn ship the product (usually in their own trucks) to liquor stores, supermarkets, convenience stores, restaurants, and bars (retailers), where it is finally purchased by consumers.

The *negotiation flow* represents the interplay of the buying and selling tasks associated with the transfer of title to Coors products. Notice in Figure 11.5 that the transportation firm is not included in this flow because it does not participate in the negotiation tasks of buying, selling, and transferring title. Notice also that the arrows

Figure 11.5	Flows in the Marketing Channels for Coors Beer

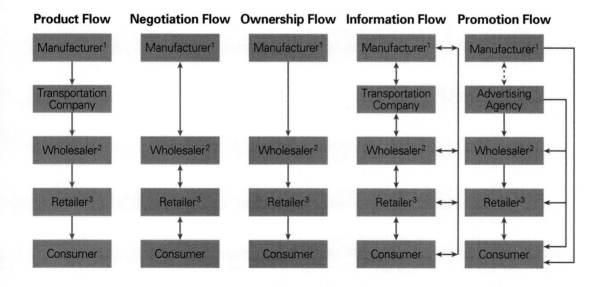

[1]Brewers and packaging plants.
[2]Beer distributors
[3]Liquor stores, supermarkets, convenience stores, restaurants, and bars.

flow in *both* directions, indicating that negotiations involve a mutual exchange between buyers and sellers at all levels of the channel.

The *ownership flow* shows the movement of the title to the product as it is passed along from the manufacturer to final consumers. Here again, the transportation firm is not involved because it does not take title to the product, nor is it actively involved in facilitating its transfer. It is only engaged in the transportation of the physical product itself.

Turning now to the *information flow,* we see that the transportation firm has reappeared, since all parties participate in the exchange of information. We also see that all of the arrows showing the flow from the manufacturer to consumers are two-directional, as the flow of information can be either up or down. For example, Coors may obtain information from the transportation company about its shipping schedule and rates, and the transportation company may in turn seek information from Coors about when and in what quantities it plans to ship the product. The flow of information sometimes bypasses the transportation firm, as shown by the arrow leading from the manufacturer (at the right-hand side of the box) directly to the wholesalers, retailers, and consumers. This route of information flow occurs when the information sought does not concern the transportation company, such as details associated with buying, selling, or promoting Coors products.[14] For example, if the manufacturer makes available to beer distributors a special reduced price on particular beer varieties, such as Coors Zima Clear Brew or Coors Extra Gold beer, this information would be passed directly to the beer distributors, and would not be of concern to the transportation firm.

Finally, the *promotion flow* refers to the flow of persuasive communication in the form of advertising, personal selling, sales promotion, and public relations. Here, a new party, the advertising agency, is included in the flow because the agency is actively involved in providing and maintaining the promotion flow, especially the advertising component of promotion. The two-directional arrow connected by a broken line between the manufacturer and advertising agency is meant to show that the manufacturer and advertising agency work together closely to develop promotional strategies. All other arrows are one-directional from the advertising agency, or directly from the manufacturer to the other parties in the marketing channel.

The concept of channel flows helps us to understand the scope and complexity of marketing channels. By thinking in terms of the five flows, it becomes obvious that marketing channels involve much more than just the physical flow of the product through the channel. The other flows (negotiation, ownership, information, and promotion) must also be coordinated to make products conveniently available to customers. Moreover, the concept of **flows in marketing channels** captures the dynamic nature of marketing channels. The word *flow* suggests movement or a fluid state, and in fact this is the nature of marketing channels. New forms of distribution emerge, different types of intermediaries appear in the channel while others drop out, and unusual competitive structures close off some avenues of distribution and open up others. Changing patterns of buyer behavior and new forms of technology such as the Internet add yet another dimension of change. Channel flows need to be adapted and managed to meet such changes.[15]

Flows in marketing channels
Are the movement of products, negotiation, ownership, information, and promotion through each participant in the marketing channel.

Marketing Channels as Social Systems

3   LEARNING OBJECTIVE

Once viewed only as economic systems, marketing channels are now seen as social systems as well because they involve people interacting with each other in different organizations and institutions. Consequently, the rules that govern channel relationships are not just a matter of economics. In the broader social-systems perspective, marketing channels are subject to the same behavioral processes associated with all social systems.[16] The behavioral processes of most significance in marketing channels are power and conflict.

Power in Marketing Channels

Marketing channel power refers to the capacity of one channel member to influence the behavior of another channel member. McDonald's, for example, as the franchiser of the world's largest chain of fast-food restaurants, has been able to exercise tremendous power over its franchisees. Indeed, it is probably not an exaggeration to say that no king or queen ever had any more power over their subjects than McDonald's enjoys over its franchisees. McDonald's operates what is known as a business-format franchise. Under this arrangement, not only the products the franchisees sell but also virtually all aspects of their operations, from the design of the restaurants to the smallest details of operating procedures, such as how long french fries should be cooked, are controlled by McDonald's. All of these provisions are included in minute detail in a franchise contract that, once signed by franchisees, means they are legally bound to abide by all of the provisions spelled out in the contract. Thus, the social system in which McDonald's and its thousands of affiliated franchisees operate is probably closer to being a dictatorship than a democracy, because McDonald's has most of the power.

For decades, most McDonald's franchisees were delighted with this unequal power relationship because a major source of McDonald's power came from its ability to reward the franchisees in the form of fat profits that turned thousands of them into millionaires. So, as long as most of the franchisees were making plenty of money, they were not very vocal about McDonald's dictatorial tactics. Recently though, some franchisees have not been content to let McDonald's rule the roost. These franchisees are especially concerned about McDonald's opening too many restaurants that takes sales away from existing franchisees as well as ill-conceived new programs such as "cook-to-order," which increased customer waiting time.

Conflict in Marketing Channels

Conflict in marketing channels is usually defined as goal-impeding behavior by one or more channel members. In other words, when one channel member takes actions that another channel member perceives as reducing its ability to achieve its goals, conflict can result. In the McDonald's case just mentioned, for example, McDonald's behavior in the form of opening so many new restaurants near existing ones was seen as goal-impeding behavior by franchisees who owned established restaurants in the same territories. They believed that McDonald's attempt to enhance its own bottom line by setting up so many new restaurants was hurting the franchisees' ability to reach their profit goals. Some of these conflicts have become so intense that lawsuits have been initiated by the franchisees.

Conflicts can also arise between producers of products and other channel members when the producer attempts to force channel members to buy a particular product as a condition for access to another product. Such *tying arrangements* were allegedly practiced by Microsoft when it forced computer makers such as Compaq and Dell to install its Internet Explorer browser software instead of rival Netscape's Navigator browser as a condition of the computer makers receiving the Windows operating system.[18] Since virtually all personal computers rely on Microsoft Windows, the computer makers had little choice but to use Microsoft's Internet Explorer. The U.S. Department of Justice found Microsoft's behavior to be illegal because it violated the Sherman Antitrust Act by creating a monopoly position for Microsoft.[19]

Other marketing channel strategies that can create conflicts among channel members include *exclusive dealing,* whereby a manufacturer requires channel members to carry only its brand; *price discrimination,* where a producer or manufacturer charges different prices to the same class of channel member for the same products; *territorial restrictions,* where a producer or manufacturer dictates where a channel member such as a wholesaler can sell its products, and *full-line forcing,* where a manufacturer requires a channel member such as a retailer to buy undesirable products from the manufacturer in order to obtain the manufacturers' most desirable products.[20]

Marketing channel power
Is the capacity of one channel member to influence the behavior of another channel member.

Political and Legal Forces
Franchises are legally required to abide by the conditions set up by the franchiser. However, some McDonald's franchisees have initiated lawsuits in the hope of using the legal system to gain countervailing power to offset McDonald's power over them.[17]

Conflict in marketing channels
Occurs when one channel member believes that another channel member is impeding the attainment of its goals.

Political and Legal Forces
Federal antitrust laws such as the Sherman and Clayton Acts were developed to limit the monopoly power of firms and promote free competition for consumers. If channel conflict fosters monopoly or reduces competition, federal antitrust officials may take notice. This is what happened to Levi Strauss Co. some years ago when it engaged in full-line forcing. The Federal Trade Commission issued an injunction against Levi Strauss to stop this anticompetitive practice.

Buying Wine Online—Are Some Channel Members Playing Dirty?

The structure of the wine industry in the United States has been changing. Thirty years ago, there were only about 100 wineries in the country, but now there are more than 2,000. At the same time, the number of wholesale wine distributors has decreased, from more than 5,000 to less than 250. The traditional marketing channel since the repeal of Prohibition in 1934 was producer to wholesaler, to retailer, to consumer. But with the dramatic growth in the number of wine producers, and the even more drastic decline in the number of wholesalers, the ability of small wine producers to make their products available to consumers through this traditional channel has been limited. It is simply not economically feasible for wholesalers and retailers to carry the wines of so many small wineries. Consequently, consumers all over the country do not have access to many fine wines from small producers.

One solution to this problem that appeared to be very promising is direct sales to consumers via the Internet. In fact, by the first year of the new millennium, this online channel seemed to be catching on very well as a means for distributing the more obscure wines from small producers.

But this was not to last for very long. In early 2000, wine wholesalers, with the support of their national trade association, successfully lobbied Congress to let states go to federal court to sue out-of-state suppliers. By gaining access to the federal courts, the wholesalers acquired even more clout in keeping out-of-state wineries from selling in their states, because it was largely the influence of the traditional

wholesalers that had resulted in states prohibiting out-of-state online sales in the first place.

So, who loses and who wins here?

Independent wineries claim that they're the big losers because they cannot sell their wine directly to consumers in most states.

But the traditional wine wholesalers claim they are doing a public service by lobbying for laws against online sellers because this helps to keep alcohol out of the hands of minors.

Consumer groups claim that the wholesalers are acting purely in their own self-interest to shield their businesses from competition. This type of protectionism limits consumer access to wine products and increases prices, they claim. In short, it's a "dirty deal," where politicians and a powerful business lobby have ganged up to hurt the interests of small wine producers and consumers.

DISCUSSION QUESTIONS

1. Do you think it is ethical for businesses to lobby government for protection from competition using a pretext such as "keeping alcohol out of the hands of minors"?

2. Is it fair for government to reduce market access to new types of businesses and limit consumer choice to protect an entrenched industry that enjoys political clout? Discuss.

Source: Based on Amy Borrus, "The Broad Backlash Against E-Tailers," *Business Week*, 5 February 2001, 102.

Marketing Channel Management

4 LEARNING OBJECTIVE

Marketing channel management, frequently shortened to the term *channel management*, refers to the analysis, planning, organization, and control of a firm's marketing channels.[21] Channel management can be a challenging and complex process, not only because many aspects are involved, but also because of the difficulties arising from the **interorganizational context** of the channel structure. That is, marketing channels are made up of independent business organizations such as manufacturers, wholesalers, and retailers, as well as agents and brokers, who, although linked together in a relationship to form a marketing channel, are still independent businesses. As such, these firms have their own objectives, policies, strategies, and operating procedures, which may or may not be congruent with those of the other members of the channel. Indeed, as mentioned earlier in this chapter, sometimes they come into outright conflict. Moreover, in marketing channels, there are usually none of the clear superior/subordinate relationships, or lines of authority, so typical of management in single-firm intraorganizational settings. Thus, managing marketing channels is frequently more challenging than managing within the intraorganizational setting of a single firm.

Marketing channel management can be viewed from the vantage points of the:

1. Producer or manufacturer looking "down the channel" toward the market
2. Retailer (or other final reseller) looking "up the channel" back to the producer or manufacturer

Marketing channel management
Refers to analyzing, planning, organizing, and controlling a firm's marketing channels.

Interorganizational context
Refers to channel management that extends beyond a firm's own organization into independent businesses.

Although either of these perspectives is valid for examining the subject of channel management, the first one (the producer or manufacturer looking down the channel toward the market) is by far the most commonly used perspective. Indeed, virtually all modern analysis and research on the subject is from this vantage point. This is probably because channel management is regarded as a part of the larger field of marketing management, which has almost universally been treated from the perspective of the producer or manufacturer. Consequently, our discussion of channel management will be from the producer/manufacturer perspective.

Decision Areas of Channel Management

Channel management viewed from the perspective of the producer or manufacturer looking down the channel toward the market can be divided into six basic decision areas:

1. Formulating channel strategy
2. Designing the channel structure
3. Selecting the channel members
4. Motivating the channel members
5. Coordinating channel strategy with the marketing mix
6. Evaluating channel member performance

Figure 11.6 provides an overview of these decision areas. The rest of this section of the chapter is organized around a discussion of each of these areas of channel management.

Figure 11.6	Major Decision Areas of Channel Management

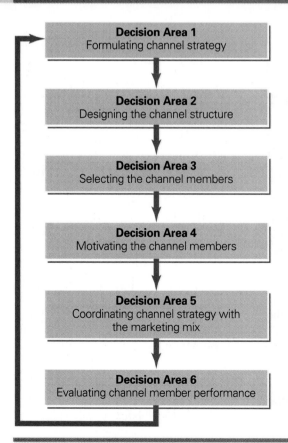

Formulating Channel Strategy

Channel strategy refers to the broad set of principles by which a firm seeks to achieve its distribution objectives to satisfy its customers. The Saturn Division of General Motors, for example, developed an innovative channel strategy to meet the needs of a large segment of customers who were dissatisfied with the car-buying experience available through existing automobile-marketing channels. These customers did not want the high pressure, sales gimmicks, and price haggling so common in traditional auto dealerships.

This channel strategy involved a huge investment and commitment by Saturn, because the new General Motors division had to plan and organize the selection and training of dealers to create an entirely new marketing channel structure and culture for selling cars that previously had not existed in automobile marketing channels. Saturn felt that such an effort was worthwhile because the firm hoped to achieve a **sustainable competitive advantage** through its innovative marketing channel strategy—believing that Ford and Chrysler would find it much more difficult and time-consuming to develop their own new marketing channels similar to Saturn's than it would be to imitate a new product feature, price incentive, or advertising campaign that Saturn might offer.

In recent years, more firms have been discovering the value of innovative channel strategy for creating a sustainable competitive advantage.[22] These firms realize that of the four Ps of the marketing mix—product, pricing, promotion, place—only place (marketing channels) provides shelter from quick imitation by competitors. Why? Simply because rapid technology transfer has made it difficult, if not impossible, to hold on to a competitive advantage based on the P of superior products; competitors, domestic or foreign, can quickly match virtually any product innovation. Holding on to the P of a pricing advantage is even more difficult, because global competition ensures that a competitor somewhere in the world will match or beat the price. The other P, promotion, also does not provide for much sustainability, because there is simply too much advertising from literally thousands of promotional messages knocking each other out of the box in short order.

So channel strategy has moved to the center stage of marketing strategy as firms seek to gain a leg up on the competition that they can hold onto for awhile. The range of firms using this approach cuts across many products and industries: WD-40, for example, the lubricating product that is present in 75% of U.S. homes, has used channel strategy to beat back such giants as 3M, DuPont, and General Electric, who for years have tried to replace WD-40 with competing products. By paying extraordinary attention to keeping retailers happy with high-profit deals and special merchandise campaigns, WD-40 created a kind of big happy family between itself and tens of thousands of retailers. The Coca-Cola company has run circles around PepsiCo all over the world through superior channel strategy, not only by focusing on giant distributors and retailers but also by paying attention to the little channel members as well.[23] In Japan, for example, Coca-Cola publishes trade magazines and holds special seminars for owners of *sakayas* (mom-and-pop stores) on how to operate more efficiently and compete with more modern outlets. In Paris, Coke uses five-foot inflatable Coca-Cola cans to help hundreds of tiny street-corner shops. Heavy earth-moving equipment manufacturer Caterpillar has emphasized channel strategy to gain a sustainable competitive advantage by building a superior dealer organization that guarantees critical-parts delivery anywhere in the world within 48 hours. This

Channel strategy
Is the broad set of principles by which a firm seeks to achieve its distribution objectives to satisfy its customers.

Sustainable competitive advantage
Is a competitive edge that cannot be easily or quickly copied by competitors in the short run.

Sociocultural Forces

As consumer desires for a more enjoyable car-buying experience became increasingly evident, the Saturn Division of General Motors altered its channel strategy to provide a revolutionary way of selling cars that provides consumers with detailed product information, charges one price, and offers a 30-day return policy.

In formulating a channel strategy, Lands' End chose to give consumers several options for purchasing its products. Lands' End products may be purchased from the catalog, from landsend.com, or at selected Sears stores.

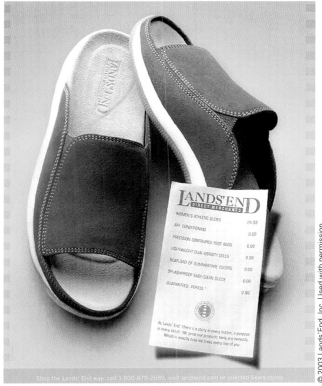

emphasis came in handy not very long ago when fierce product competition from Japanese companies threatened Caterpillar's very existence.

Designing the Channel Structure

Most businesses cannot expect to maintain the same channels they have used in the past in the face of environmental forces. Different economic conditions, sociocultural developments, new competitive structure, advancing technology, and government regulation all may influence firms to face the challenge of channel design.[24] For example, virtually all major companies have been forced by the two environmental forces of technology and competition to design online channels to augment their conventional channels.

Channel design is the process of developing new channels where none existed before, or making significant modifications to existing channels. The process of channel design can be broken down into four basic phases:

1. Setting distribution objectives
2. Specifying the distribution tasks that need to be performed by the channel
3. Considering alternative channel structures
4. Choosing an optimal channel structure

These phases are depicted in Figure 11.7.

Setting Distribution Objectives

Distribution objectives refer to what the firm would like its channel strategy to accomplish in terms of meeting the needs of its customers. At this stage of channel design, then, distribution objectives need to be stated from the point of view of the customer. This is sometimes referred to as the *bottom-up or backward approach* to channel design because the starting point for designing the channel is also the end point of the channel—the customer. This is precisely the approach taken by Saturn as discussed earlier. Saturn asked the question: "What do our customers want when they go out to buy automobiles?" The company then formulated its distribution

Figure 11.7	**Phases of the Channel-Design Process**

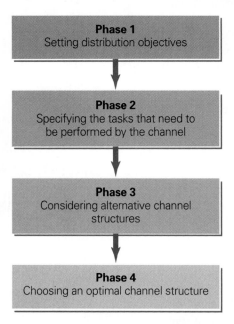

Phase 1
Setting distribution objectives

Phase 2
Specifying the tasks that need to be performed by the channel

Phase 3
Considering alternative channel structures

Phase 4
Choosing an optimal channel structure

objectives in terms of developing auto dealerships that could provide the friendly, helpful, no-haggle environment sought by customers.

Dell Computer provides another example of setting distribution objectives from the bottom up, so as to design marketing channels that meet the needs of customers better than the competition. Michael Dell founded the company after experiencing frustration when trying to buy computers from dealers who knew less about computers than he did. This frustration is what led Dell to develop a direct channel using the telephone and then the Internet. When customers called or logged in, they were able to get information and advice of much better quality than they had received from computer stores, because the people staffing the phones or responding to e-mail were knowledgeable computer salespeople rather than minimum-wage store clerks. The person-to-person interaction available in this channel enabled Dell to provide customized high-performance computers, technical support, and other value-added services to a segment of sophisticated personal computer users who wanted more than what was available from existing retail computer channels. Dell's innovative channel design of direct sales to customers via telephone and then the Internet has proved to be spectacularly successful, making Michael Dell a multibillionaire in the process.[26]

Specifying the Distribution Tasks

Making products available to final consumers—how, when, and where they want them—calls for performing numerous distribution tasks such as storage, inventory control, order processing, transportation, order tracking, and many others.[27]

Firms often make the mistake of underestimating the level of detail and subtlety involved in particular industries. Consider, for example, what happened to the Snapple Beverage Corporation soon after it was purchased by Quaker Oats Company. By tying Snapple in with its highly successful Gatorade, Quaker hoped to gain tremendous synergy for the two drinks. So, Quaker designed a channel for Snapple that paralleled the channel for Gatorade, which was from factory to retailers' warehouses, from which individual stores then ordered what they needed to keep their shelves stocked. Quaker knew this pattern well and was comfortable with it. But Quaker failed to realize that, unlike Gatorade, which was treated in the channel as a consumer packaged product such as cereal, Snapple had to compete in the soft-drink market. The channel for soft drinks places a much heavier burden on the producer and/or distributors, because individual stores do not usually place orders for soft drinks on an as-needed basis and then stock their own shelves. Instead, they rely on bottlers and distributors to perform these distribution tasks for them. Quaker had not arranged with these intermediaries to perform these tasks for retailers, so Quaker was totally out of step with industry practice. Quaker's failure to understand this distribution-task performance requirement deprived Snapple of the retail shelf space it needed to compete in the intensely competitive soft-drink market. Within a couple of years, Quaker gave up and sold Snapple at a huge loss.

Considering Alternative Channel Structures

As discussed earlier in this chapter, the form or shape the channel takes to perform the distribution tasks is referred to as the channel structure. Also recall that the channel structure has three dimensions: (1) length, (2) intensity, and (3) the types of intermediaries used.

In terms of *length*, the number of alternatives available to a firm is usually limited to three or four at a maximum. These may range from using a direct structure from manufacturer to final customer, as in the case of Dell Computer; one level of intermediary, as used by Saturn (auto retailers); two levels, as used by Coors beer (wholesalers and retailers); or three levels of intermediaries, where an agent or broker may appear in the channel structure, which is common for many imported products.

The number of alternatives in the *intensity* dimension is even more limited, because intensity is so closely related to the nature of the product in question. Thus, the only realistic alternative for products intended for mass markets, such as Gillette razor blades, is intensive distribution in order to provide adequate market coverage. At the other end of the spectrum, expensive or prestigious products, such as BMW automobiles, require highly selective or even exclusive distribution to help maintain the aura and quality image of the product.

Management's range of alternatives for the third dimension of channel structure, the *types of intermediaries* to use, is usually broader than for the first two. Within reason, management is limited only by its imagination in deciding what kinds of distributors it wants to include in its channel structure. For example, Costco, the world's largest Warehouse Club chain, sells fashion apparel such as Polo by Ralph Lauren; Waterford crystal; fine wines (it is the largest seller of Dom Perignon champagne); and diamonds valued up to $1 million![28]

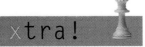

Choosing an Optimal Structure

Many different approaches have been suggested over the years for choosing an optimal channel structure. Formal management-science approaches, capital budgeting methods, and distribution-cost analysis techniques have all been offered as a means for choosing channel structure. For the most part, these methods have not found much use in the real world. Much more common are approaches that rely on managerial judgment accompanied by some data on distribution costs and profit potentials. Judgment approaches can be made more formal through explicit identification of criteria to be used in choosing the channel structure. The most basic of these are:

- *Market variables:* The location of final customers, the numbers of customers, and their density, together with their patterns of buying behavior, are the key market variables to consider.
- *Product variables:* Such factors as bulk and weight, unit value, newness, technical versus nontechnical, and perishability are product variables that are frequently important.
- *Company variables:* The financial capacity of the firm, its size, expertise, and desire for managerial control are some of the most important company variables.
- *Intermediary variables:* Cost, availability, and services provided are indicative of intermediary variables that management needs to consider.
- *Behavioral variables:* Factors such as the potential of particular channel structures to reduce conflict, while maximizing power, are key behavioral variables for management to consider.
- *External environmental variables:* Finally, variables such as economic conditions, sociocultural changes, competitive structure, technology, and government regulations are all important environmental variables to consider when choosing channel structure.

Apple Computer considered all of these variables in deciding to establish a new channel consisting of a chain of its own retail stores.[29] Market variables were considered via Apple's belief that existing independent retailers and Apple's own Web site were not covering the market sufficiently to reach Apple's target market. Product variables were of major concern because Apple felt that its highly innovative products needed a special "showcase" in the form of upscale company-owned stores staffed by knowledgeable Apple salespeople. The crucial company variable that Apple weighed was its desire for control of how its products were marketed. The company-owned-stores channel would provide such control.

Intermediary variables were examined in terms of lack of existing computer retailers that could meet Apple's desired standards for representing its products. The power to control its own destiny was the behavioral variable Apple focused on in establishing its own stores. Rather then face power struggles with giant retailers, Apple hoped to outflank them with its own stores.

Finally, at least two environmental variables played a role in Apple's decision to establish its new channel: competitive structure and sociocultural changes. Apple wanted to avoid going head-to-head in the mass market for home computers so it chose to deemphasize distribution through mass retail merchandisers where competition would be most intense. From a sociocultural perspective, Apple's vision of the computer as having unlimited possibilities for enhancing peoples' lives as they work and play called for a channel that could spark the public's imagination every time a customer set foot in one of its exciting retail stores.[30]

Selecting Channel Members

The selection of channel members, the last phase of channel design, consists of four steps:

1. Developing selection criteria
2. Finding prospective channel members
3. Evaluating prospective channel members against certain criteria
4. Converting prospective members into actual members

Developing Selection Criteria

Although general lists of **selection criteria**, such as those shown in Figure 11.8, can provide a framework, each firm needs to develop criteria for selecting channel members that are consistent with its own distribution objectives and strategies. Thus, the list of criteria for a firm practicing highly selective distribution, such as Polo by Ralph Lauren, might include such factors as the prospective channel member's reputation and the competing product lines it carries. A firm using very intensive distribution, such as Bic pens, might use little more than one criterion that consists of the prospective channel members' ability to pay the manufacturer for the products it ships to them.

Selection criteria
Are the factors that a firm uses to choose which intermediaries will become members of its marketing channel.

General Criteria for Selecting Channel Members	**Figure 11.8**

Finding Prospective Channel Members

The search for prospective channel members can use a number of sources. If the manufacturer has its own outside field-sales force, this is generally regarded as the best prospect source because of the sales personnel's knowledge of prospective channel members in their territories. Other useful sources include customers, advertising, trade shows, and the Internet. Usually, a combination of several of these sources is used to find prospective channel members at both the wholesale and retail levels.

Evaluating Prospective Channel Members

Once prospective channel members have been identified, they need to be assessed against certain criteria to determine those who will actually be selected. This can be done by an individual manager (such as the sales manager) or by a committee. Depending on the importance of the selection decision, such a committee might well include top management, up to and including the chairman of the board, if the selection decision is of great strategic importance. For example, when Goodyear Tire and Rubber Company selected Sears Roebuck and Company to sell its tires, Goodyear's CEO was involved in the decision because it had long-term strategic implications for Goodyear.

Converting Prospective Members into Actual Members

It is important to remember that the selection process is a two-way street.[31] Not only do producers and manufacturers select retailers, wholesalers, or various agents and brokers, and franchisers select franchisees, but these intermediaries also select manufacturers and franchisers. Indeed, quite often it is the intermediaries, especially large and powerful retailers and wholesalers, that are in the driver's seat when it comes to selection. Wal-Mart, for example, can pick and choose virtually any manufacturers it wants. Consequently, the manufacturers or franchisers seeking to secure the services of quality channel members have to make a convincing case that selling their products will be profitable for the channel members.

Motivating Channel Members

Motivating channel members refers to the actions taken by manufacturers (or franchisers) to get channel members to implement their channel strategy. Because efforts to motivate channel members take place in the interorganizational setting of the marketing channel, the process is usually more difficult than motivation in the intraorganizational setting of a single firm. Motivation in the marketing channel can be viewed as a sequence of phases:

1. Learning about the needs and problems of channel members
2. Offering support to channel members to help meet their needs and solve their problems
3. Providing ongoing leadership

Although the stages in the motivation process are sequential, the process repeats itself because of the continuous feedback from steps 2 and 3. This is illustrated in Figure 11.9.

Learning about Channel Members' Needs and Problems

If manufacturers or franchisers expect strong cooperation from channel members, their channel strategies should meet channel members' needs and help solve their problems. But this is easier said than done, because it is all too easy for manufacturers or franchisers to project their own views onto channel members rather than investigate the channel members' views. McDonald's fell into this trap when it tried to gain franchisee support for its ill-fated Campaign 55 strategy. Campaign 55 was introduced by McDonald's in the late 1990s and then hastily withdrawn after dismal customer response and even worse reactions by most McDonald's franchisees. The Campaign 55 promotion consisted of a special price deal on the famous Big Mac,

Motivating channel members

Is the action taken by a manufacturer or franchiser to get channel members to implement its channel strategies.

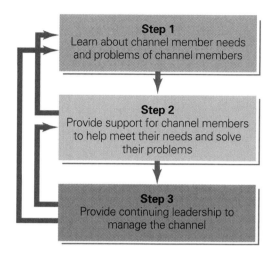

The Motivation Process in Marketing Channels — Figure 11.9

which sold for 55 cents during the promotion in honor of the founding of Mc-Donald's in 1955. But to get the 55-cent price, consumers had to buy a drink and fries along with the Big Mac. Consumers balked at the strings-attached promotion, while competitors like Burger King and Wendy's jumped on McDonald's in their advertisements by offering special deals with no strings. The franchisees were furious with McDonald's because they were not consulted and thus felt that the program was rammed down their throats. Had the franchisees been asked, most would have rejected the Campaign 55 promotion because they believed that it would be a big money loser for them. But what was most troubling was that many franchisees viewed this strategy as akin to using a "Bandaid to cure cancer." Campaign 55 was seen as a superficial, quick-fix gimmick that ignored more fundamental underlying needs and problems that franchisees were experiencing, including lack of exciting new products to sell, pricing pressures, and franchisee proliferation.

McDonald's could have foreseen the problem if it had done a better job of learning about the real needs and problems of channel members. It should have avoided the tendency to project its own views and biases onto its channel members by taking a proactive approach to learning about channel-member needs and problems.[32] This could have been accomplished through such approaches as: (1) researching channel members using in-house research teams, (2) investigating channel members using outside researchers, and (3) using channel-member advisory committees.

In-house research consists of taking the same research methods used to gather information about final customers and applying them to channel members to learn about their needs and problems. Outside research can be used by firms who do not have an in-house research capability, or by those firms that want to avoid the possible bias that can creep into in-house research. A channel-member advisory committee consists of channel-member representatives and key executives from the manufacturer or franchiser who meet on a regular basis in some neutral location. This type of close interaction can foster the kind of candid dialogue needed to uncover channel-member needs and problems, which may not emerge in the normal course of business.

Offering Support for Channel Members

Providing support for channel members can be done in a variety of ways, from an informal hit-or-miss approach to carefully planned strategic alliances.[33]

China Will Be One of the World's Largest Car Markets: Can Foreign Auto Makers Profit from This?

With more than 1.3 billion people, China has the largest population of any country in the world. Yet, as a market for cars, this emerging country is still pretty small. At present, less than 1% of China's population owns cars, compared to well over 50% in highly developed economies such as the U.S. and Germany. But China's auto market is one of the fastest growing in the world, with annual volume increases in the double digits and the number of cars sold going from 720,000 units in 2001 to well over 900,000 in 2002. Analysts expect annual sales to reach two million units by 2010.

Ten foreign carmakers have invested more than $5 billion in the Chinese car market. Most of this money has gone into joint ventures with local automobile-manufacturing companies in the form of 50% joint ventures (Chinese law allows foreign firms a maximum of 50% ownership). Among the biggest foreign investors are Volkswagen AG, DaimlerChrysler, PSA Peugeot, Citroen, and General Motors Corporation.

Although the auto market in China is already substantial and growing rapidly, it presents a very tough challenge to foreign firms when it comes to selling autos profitably in China. One problem is that most of the market is at the very low end, consisting of small, low-priced cars—the least profitable in the auto business. An even bigger problem is competing with the Chinese carmakers, who not only enjoy low labor costs but spend virtually nothing on research and design. Instead, they simply build knock-offs of foreign manufacturers' models. In fact, one of the most popular cars in China, produced by a local Chinese manufacturer, is called the Chery, which looks almost identical to the Volkswagen Jetta.

So, even though auto analysts predict that China may become the world's third largest auto market by 2025, foreign automakers are not going to reap much benefit from this growth unless they find a way to participate in the Chinese auto market profitably. Better agreements to protect intellectual property rights, as well as a growing number of middle- and upper-middle-class customers who seek the prestige associated with foreign cars, may hold the key to making money in the Chinese auto market.

Source: Based on David Murphy and David Lague, "As China's Car Market Takes Off, The Party Grows a Bit Crowded," *The Wall Street Journal*, 3 July 2002, A9.

Informal support approaches are the most common in traditional channels. Advertising dollars, promotional support, incentives, contests, and, increasingly in recent years, slotting fees (cash payments to channel members to gain shelf space) are frequently offered by manufacturers to jump-start the channel members' efforts to push the manufacturers' products. But these are often no more than cases of throwing money at a particular need or problem without thinking too deeply about it.

Strategic alliances or *channel partnerships*, however, represent a more substantial and continuous commitment between the manufacturer and channel members. Support provided by the manufacturer is based on extensive knowledge of the needs and problems of the channel members and is carried out on a long-term basis. There are often specific performance expectations that have been worked out by the manufacturer in conjunction with the channel members. Procter & Gamble and Wal-Mart, for example, have built one of the strongest strategic alliances in the consumer packaged-goods industry. This partnership emphasizes close working relationships, including stationing P&G executives permanently on site at Wal-Mart's headquarters to stay in close touch with Wal-Mart's top management. A sophisticated EDI system also provides a super-efficient means for assuring availability of P&G products in all 4,382 Wal-Mart stores.

Vertical marketing systems (VMS) provide another means through which support can be provided for channel members. VMSs have been defined as "professionally managed or centrally programmed networks, preengineered to achieve operating economies and maximum impact."[34] There are three basic types of VMSs: (1) administered, (2) contractual, and (3) corporate.[35]

An *administered VMS* is characterized by a careful and comprehensive program developed by one of the channel members to support the efforts of other channel members. Ethan Allen Interiors Inc., a furniture maker, is a good example of an administered VMS. Ethan Allen sells its furniture through more than 300 independent retailers. These retailers, called Ethan Allen Galleries, carry no competing products from other manufacturers. The appearance of the store, from architecture to lighting and display, is controlled by Ethan Allen, as is the method of selling. Rather than retail salespeople, the stores have "designers" who help customers select furniture according to the designer's decorating plan. Advertising, special events, promotions, and sales are also developed and run by Ethan Allen rather than by the independent retailers. How successful is this administered VMS? At least for Ethan Allen and its retail channel members, the payoff has been better-than-average profits by competing on quality, service, and customer assistance, rather than price, as is so common in conventional marketing channels for furniture.

Contractual VMSs consist mainly of retail cooperatives, wholesaler-sponsored voluntary chains, and franchise systems. *Retail cooperatives* are created when a group of retailers unites and agrees to pool its buying power and contribute to the operation of the cooperative by collectively supporting its own professionally managed advertising, store design, information systems, and other major management tasks. The cooperative thus operates similarly to a large corporate chain-store organization, even though each retailer in the cooperative retains its independent status. With more than 5,000 independent hardware stores, Servistar is one of the best-known retail cooperatives. The support provided by the cooperative to each of the independent retailers has enabled them to stay in business even in the face of competition from giant hardware chains such as Home Depot and Lowe's.

Wholesaler-sponsored voluntary chains are similar to retail cooperatives except that a wholesaler gets large numbers of retailers to work together. By agreeing to buy a major portion of their inventories from the sponsoring wholesaler, buying power increases and the combined association has the resources to hire professional managers to increase the operating efficiency of the voluntary association. Wholesaler-sponsored voluntary chains are most prominent in the grocery trade. Independent Grocers Alliance (IGA), Spartan, and Supervalu are some of the best-known names.

Franchising, or what in more recent years has been referred to as business-format franchising, is characterized by a close business relationship between franchiser and franchisee that includes not only the product, service, and trademark but also the entire business format itself, including marketing strategy, training, merchandise management, operating procedures and quality control. Consequently, it is a comprehensive method for distributing goods and services based on a continuous contractual relationship between franchiser and franchisee that covers virtually all phases of the business. The best-known business-format franchisers are in the fast-food market, with McDonald's being the most recognized of all, but this type of franchising is also very popular among hotels (Holiday Inn), convenience stores (7-Elevens), business services (Kinko's), and real estate agencies (Century 21). Such franchise systems combine the advantages of the large-scale and professional management of the franchiser with the entrepreneurial drive of the independent business people who are the franchisees.

A *corporate VMS* exists when a firm owns and operates the organizations at other levels in the marketing channel. The firm owning and operating the other units may be a manufacturer, wholesaler, or retailer. When it is a manufacturer that owns and operates wholesale and/or retail units, the system is usually described as forwardly integrated. When retailers or wholesalers own and operate their own manufacturing units, backwardly integrated marketing channels exists. Examples of firms operating forwardly integrated marketing channels include Goodyear Tire and the Sherwin-Williams Company, while well-known firms operating backwardly integrated channels include Sears, The Limited, and Safeway. The most important advantage of corporate VMSs, whether forwardly or backwardly integrated, is the high degree of control they provide to the corporate-channel leader because the other units in the marketing channel are owned, rather than operated as independent businesses.

Providing Continuing Leadership

Even well-conceived motivation programs, based on a thorough attempt to understand the channel members' needs and problems, coupled with a carefully targeted support program, still require leadership on a continuing basis to achieve effective motivation of channel members.[36] In other words, someone has to be in charge. Ethan Allen Interiors, cited earlier as an administered VMS, provides a good example of a firm that takes a leadership role in motivating its 300 domestic and foreign independent retailers. Not only does this furniture maker provide continuing direction and advice on all aspects of the business from inventory control to store design, it also sends all of the retailers' salespeople to the company's training school, called Ethan Allen College. At the school, salespeople learn about home-decorating techniques and, even more importantly, about the Ethan Allen way of doing things. The curriculum is designed to build teamwork and inspire confidence in the retailers to look to Ethan Allen for leadership in helping them compete successfully in the fiercely competitive home-furnishing business.[37]

Coordinating Channel Strategy in the Marketing Mix

Channel strategy is not formulated in a vacuum. The other three Ps of the marketing mix—product, price, and promotion—must all be considered as well. What is especially important is to recognize the interrelationships among these marketing-mix components, and to try to achieve synergy rather than conflict among the four Ps. Thus, channel strategy should enhance rather than detract from the firm's product, price, and promotion strategies.

Product Strategy and Channel Strategy

Product strategy often depends on channel strategy because some key product strategies interface with channel strategy in ways that can mean the difference between success or failure.[38] *Product positioning strategy,* which seeks to present products to customers in a way that gives the products a certain image compared to competitive products, illustrates the relationship between product strategy and channel strategy. Consider, for example, Gargoyles Performance Eye Wear, which makes numerous high-end sunglasses ranging in price from $85 to $200. The sunglasses are aimed at skiers, bikers, water-sports enthusiasts, basketball players, and other sports aficionados. The large range of target customers and the relatively high prices reflect a product-positioning strategy aimed at transforming sunglasses from a utilitarian product to an important fashion item associated with upscale, sports-oriented, glamorous lifestyles. Retailers play a crucial role in establishing the positioning strategy of these products. To position sunglasses as such an exciting and glamorous product with the high prices to match, retailers must create the kind of atmosphere that supports the image. If retailers simply piled these pricey sunglasses up in a bin or stuck them on Peg-Board, the special aura associated with these products would be drastically undermined. So store atmosphere, display fixturing, and attentive personal selling at the retail level are crucial to the success of this product-positioning strategy.

Pricing Strategy and Channel Strategy

Pricing strategy is closely related to channel management because pricing decisions need to take into account channel issues if the manufacturer expects strong cooperation from the channel members. Clearly, such factors as the profit margins available to channel members, the different prices charged to various classes of channel members, prices of competitive products carried, special pricing deals, changing pricing policies, and the use of price incentives are all factors of major concern to many channel members. Thus, the manufacturer needs to make sure that it knows something about the expectations of channel members for these and other relevant pricing issues before embarking on any pricing strategy.

Consider, for example, the channel-pricing strategy used by Island Def Jam Music Group, a record producer whose 70 artists under contract include new R&B

sensation Ashanti, as well as such established rock groups as Bon Jovi. In a very slow music market, Island Def Jam encouraged retailers to sell Ashanti's debut CD for only $12 by offering them a $2 rebate to help defray the relatively low retailer margins on the cut-price CD.[39] While many retailers were skeptical about the logic of introducing a hot new artist using low price as an incentive, they soon changed their minds. During the first week, Ashanti's CD sold 523,000 units, a first-week record for CD sales by a new female artist. But, after two weeks, Island Def Jam increased the wholesale price to retailers so they would have to charge consumers about $17 to maintain their margins. Did this price hike upset retailers and slow retail sales? On the contrary, sales increased and in less than a year the album went triple platinum, with three million CDs sold. Was this just a "lucky" channel-pricing strategy? Industry observers do not think so. Island Def Jam's channel-pricing strategy of getting retailers to slash prices on CDs of new artists to jump-start demand to a threshold level to create momentum and then having them raise the price to ride the wave may well become the new channel-pricing strategy for introducing CDs from new artists. Not only do artists and record companies like this strategy, retailers do as well because they get to enjoy *both* high volume and high margins on new CDs that get a boost from an initial low price.

By offering Ashanti's debut CD for only $12, Island Def Jam Music Group jump-started record sales for new artist's CD with a unique pricing strategy. After two weeks on the market, the price rose to $17 which didn't stop consumers from snatching up 3 million CDs in less than a year.

Promotion Strategy and Channel Strategy

Promotion interfaces extensively with channel strategy, because many promotions undertaken by a manufacturer require strong channel-member support and follow-through to work successfully. For example, major advertising campaigns frequently require point-of-purchase displays in stores, special deals and merchandising campaigns require channel members to stock up on extra inventory, and contests and incentives call for participation from retailers and wholesalers. When Apple launched the iMac, it spent more than $100 million on the advertising campaign for the new computer—the largest advertising expenditure for a product launch in Apple's history. But in order for this massive advertising expenditure to be successful, retailers had to be willing to inventory tens of thousands of iMacs well in advance of the release date, provide space for extensive point-of-purchase displays, and participate in special promotional events such as contests and T-shirt giveaways. Retailers also had to prep their salespeople so they could show off the new iMac to its best advantage and respond to sales objections, such as the lack of disk drives on the iMac.

Evaluating Channel Member Performance

The evaluation of channel member performance is necessary to assess how successful the channel members have been in implementing the manufacturer's channel strategies and achieving distribution objectives. Evaluations require the manufacturer to gather information on the channel members. But the manufacturer's ability to do this will be affected by its degree of control of channel members. Usually, the higher the degree of control, the more information the manufacturer (or franchiser) can gather, and vice versa.[40]

Southland Corporation, the franchiser of 7-Eleven stores in the United States, is an organization that enjoys substantial control of its franchisees. It has therefore been able to develop and implement a sophisticated channel-member evaluation system that enables Southland to monitor the performance of each of its 5,500 stores down to the smallest detail. By using a point-of-sale (POS) computer linked to headquarters, the home office can track the sales of thousands of individual products in each store. But what especially sets this channel-member performance evaluation system apart from other similar POS performance monitoring systems is the monitoring it enables Southland to maintain on the actions of individual store managers. Headquarters can keep track of how much time each store manager spends using the analytical tools contained in the system that store managers are expected to use to analyze sales data, demographic trends, and even local weather conditions to maximize sales opportunities and minimize inventory costs.

Logistics in Marketing Channels

Logistics (or physical distribution)
Is planning, implementing, and controlling the physical flows of materials and final products from points of origin to points of use to meet customers' needs at a profit.

Supply-chain management
Is managing logistical systems to achieve close cooperation and comprehensive interorganizational management, so as to integrate the logistical operations of different firms in the marketing channel.

Logistics, also often referred to as **physical distribution** (PD), is commonly defined as "planning, implementing, and controlling the physical flows of materials and final products from points of origin to points of use to meet customers' needs at a profit."[41] In more recent years, the term **supply-chain management** has been used to describe logistical systems that emphasize close cooperation and comprehensive interorganizational management to integrate the logistical operations of the different firms in the channel.[42] Although a detailed discussion of the differences between what might be referred to as the "traditional" approach to logistics and the supply-chain-management approach is beyond the scope of this chapter, Figure 11.10 provides an overview of the key distinctions. In any case, whether one chooses to use the term physical distribution, logistics, or supply-chain management, the underlying principle is building strong cooperation among channel members through effective interorganizational management.

Figure 11.10	**Comparison of Traditional and Supply Chain Approaches to the Management of Logistics**	
Element	**Approach**	
	Traditional	**Supply-Chain**
Inventory-management approach	Independent efforts	Joint reduction in channel inventories
Total-cost approach	Minimize firm costs	Channel-wide cost efficiencies
Time horizon	Short-term	Long-term
Amount of information sharing and monitoring	Limited to needs of current transaction	As required for planning and monitoring processes
Amount of coordination of multiple levels in the channel	Single contact for the transaction between channel pairs	Multiple contacts among levels in firms and levels in channels
Joint planning	Transaction-based	Ongoing
Compatibility of corporate philosophies	Not relevant	Compatible at least for key relationships
Breadth of supplier base	Large, to increase competition and spread risk	Small, to increase coordination
Channel leadership	Not needed	Needed for coordination focus
Amount of sharing risks and rewards	Each on its own	Risks and rewards shared over the long term
Speed of operations, information, and inventory flows	"Warehouse" orientation (storage, safety stock) interrupted by barriers to flows; localized to channel pairs	"Distribution center" orientation (inventory velocity) interconnecting flows, JIT quick response

Source: Martha C. Cooper and Lisa M. Ellram, "Characteristics of Supply Chain Management and Implications for Purchasing and Logistics Strategy," *The International Journal of Logistics Management* 4, no. 2 (1993): 16.

The Role of Logistics

Even the most carefully designed and managed marketing channel must rely on logistics to actually make products available to customers. The creation of time and place utilities, essential for customer satisfaction, therefore depends on logistics. The movement of the right amount of the right products to the right place at the right time is a commonly heard description of what logistics is supposed to do. But achieving this goal is no simple job. On the contrary, mass markets, with their great diversity of customer segments spread over vast geographic areas, can make the task of logistics complex and expensive. Thus, logistics has become a gigantic industry that pervades virtually all firms, from the largest to the smallest.

Logistics Systems, Costs, and Components

For many years, logistics was equated mainly with transportation. Thus, the field was narrowly defined in terms of the activities involved in shipping and receiving products and was given relatively little management attention. But in recent decades, a broader perspective, referred to as the **systems concept of logistics**, has emerged. Rather than being thought of as separate and distinct from one another, logistical factors as diverse as transportation, materials handling, inventory control, warehousing, and packaging of goods are now recognized as interrelated components of a system. Decisions or actions affecting one component have implications for other components of the logistical system. For example, a faster mode of transportation for moving a quantity of iMacs from California to New York could result in a lower level of inventory needed in New York, which in turn could result in a smaller warehouse being required. Conversely, slower transportation for shipping iMacs from California to New York might well mean that a larger inventory and a larger warehouse would be needed in New York because of the slower rate of resupply.

Systems concept of logistics
Entails viewing all components of a logistical system together and understanding the relationships among them.

The concept of logistics as a system has served as the foundation of modern logistics management. In essence, those in charge of managing logistics seek to find the optimum combination of logistics components (transportation, materials handling, order processing, inventory control, warehousing, and packaging) to meet customer-service demands.

The logistics manager also attempts to achieve the desired level of customer service at the lowest cost by applying the **total-cost approach**. This concept is a logical extension of the systems concept, because it addresses all of the costs of logistics taken together, rather than the cost of individual components taken separately, and seeks to minimize the total cost. Consequently, when designing a logistics system, a company must examine the cost of each component and how it affects other components. For instance, a faster mode of transport used to ship the iMacs mentioned earlier might increase transportation costs. But, because the inventory levels and warehouse space needed in New York would be smaller (faster transportation allows for quicker resupply), the inventory carrying costs and warehouse costs will be lower. These savings in costs may be more than enough to offset the higher transportation costs. So, from the standpoint of the total cost of the logistics system, the increase in transportation costs for the faster mode of transport may well result in a *lower* total cost for logistics.

Total-cost approach
Is calculating the cost of a logistical system by addressing all of the costs of logistics together rather than individual costs taken separately, so as to minimize the total cost of logistics.

The use of the systems concept and the total-cost approach to manage logistics is shown in Figure 11.11. This figure suggests not only that all the basic components of a system are related, but also that the systems concept and the total-cost approach provide the guiding principles for blending the components. This blending helps ensure that the types and levels of services desired by customers will be provided at the lowest total cost for the logistics system as a whole.

The basic components of a logistics system are transportation, materials handling, order processing, inventory control, warehousing, and packaging.

Economic Forces
The total-cost approach to the systems concept of logistics attempts to achieve the desired level of customer service at the lowest cost.

| Figure 11.11 | View of Logistics Management Based on the Systems Concept and the Total Cost Approach |

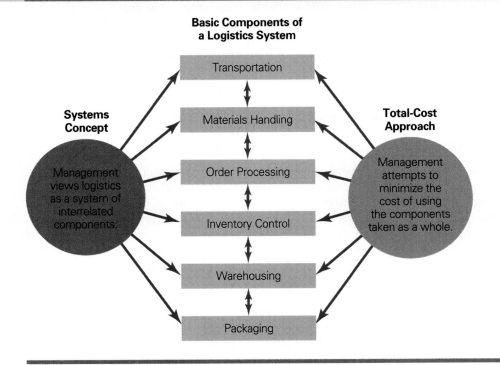

Transportation

Transportation is the most obviously necessary component of any logistics system, because in virtually all cases products must be physically moved from one location to another if a transaction is to be completed. Transportation is also often the component accounting for the highest percentage of the total cost of logistics. The five major modes of transportation are truck, rail, water, pipeline, and air. Figure 11.12 shows the expenditures on each mode of transportation from 1980 to 1999. Truck transportation has been the most dominant mode, with its share growing to 76.3% from 63.3% between 1980 and 1999. But by far the most spectacular growth has occurred for air-freight, with expenditures increasing by 553% from 1980 to 1999.

From a logistics-management standpoint, the overriding issue facing a firm is choosing the optimum mode of transportation to meet customer-service demands.

| Figure 11.12 | Total Expenditures for Various Modes of U.S. Freight Transportation in Billions of Dollars, 1980 and 1999 |

Transportation Mode	1980 Dollar	1980 Percentage of Total	1999 Dollar	1999 Percentage of Total	Growth 1980–1999
Truck[1]	94.6	66.3	304.6	76.3	222%
Rail	27.9	18.6	35.9	9.0	28.7%
Water	15.5	10.4	24.5	6.1	58.1%
Pipeline	7.5	5.0	9.1	2.3	21.3%
Air	4.0	2.7	25.3	6.3	533%
Total	149.5	100%	399.4	100%	

[1]Intercity.
Source: U.S. Census Bureau, *Statistical Abstract of the United States: 2000,* 120th ed. (Washington, DC: U.S. Government Printing Office, 2001) p. 664.

This can be a complex task because there are so many considerations. A few of these are: Should the firm use its own carriers or common carriers? What are the different rates available? What specific transportation services are offered? How reliable are various common carriers? What modes of transport are competitors using? Moreover, if the systems concept and total-cost approach are applied, the logistics manager must think in terms of how the transportation component interacts with and affects the total cost of logistics. Such decisions require specialized knowledge and expertise—not only of logistics systems, but also of the specialized needs of the industry involved and of the latest technologies available.[43]

Materials Handling

Materials handling encompasses the range of activities and equipment involved in placing and moving products in storage areas. Questions that must be addressed when designing materials-handling systems include:

- How can the distances products are moved within the warehouse during the course of receiving, storage, and shipping be minimized?
- What kinds of mechanical equipment (such as conveyor belts, cranes, and forklifts) should be used?
- How can the firm make the best use of the labor involved in receiving, handling, and shipping products?

For example, the growing use of *cross-docking* (sometimes referred to as *flow-through distribution*) has significantly enhanced materials-handling efficiency.[44] In cross-docking, products from an arriving truck are not stored in a warehouse and then resorted later to fill orders. Rather, the merchandise is simply moved across the receiving dock to other trucks for immediate delivery to stores. This eliminates the need to pick stored products at a later time. In short, products are moved directly from shipping to receiving.

In selecting a mode of transportation for hazardous chemicals, logistics managers consider safety above all other factors. In transporting other products, issues such as cost, speed, and reliability influence the transportation decision.

Order Processing

The importance of order processing in logistics lies in its relationships with *order-cycle time,* which is the time between when an order is placed and when it is received by the customer. If order processing is cumbersome and inefficient, it can slow down the order-cycle time considerably. It may even increase transportation costs if a faster mode of transportation must be used to make up for the slow order-processing time.

Order processing often appears to be routine, but is actually the result of a great deal of planning, capital investment, and training of people. When many thousands of orders are received on a daily basis, filling orders quickly and accurately is a challenging task. Indeed, in the hospital-supply industry, where medical and surgical supplies account for some 750,000 different products, developing a modern order-processing system is a nightmarish challenge, because there is no standard nomenclature for all these different products. Hence, confusion and costly mix-ups have caused large numbers of errors and hundreds of thousands of returns for credit. The industry is just now beginning to grapple with order-processing problems, but it will take years to attain the level of efficiency found in consumer-product industries.[45]

Inventory Control

Inventory control refers to a firm's attempt to hold the lowest level of inventory that will still enable it to meet customer demand. This is a never-ending battle that all firms face. It is a critically important one as well. Inventory carrying costs—including the costs of financing; insurance; storage; and lost, damaged, and stolen goods—on average can amount to approximately 25% of the value of the inventory per year. For some types of merchandise, such as perishable goods or fashion merchandise, carrying costs can be considerably higher. Yet without inventory to meet customer demand on a regular and timely basis, a firm could not stay in business for very long.

Ideally, a firm always wants to be in the position of keeping inventory at the lowest possible level while at the same time placing orders for goods in large quantities, because holding the number of its own orders to the fewest possible enables the firm to minimize ordering costs.[46] Unfortunately, there is a conflict between these two objectives. Average inventory carrying costs rise in direct proportion to the level of the inventory, while average ordering costs decrease in rough proportion to the size of the order. Thus, a trade-off must be made between these two costs to find the optimum levels for both. This point, usually referred to as the *economic order quantity (EOQ)*, occurs at the point at which total costs (inventory carrying cost plus ordering costs) are lowest. As Figure 11.13 shows, the logistics manager strives to achieve the lowest total cost by balancing inventory carrying and ordering costs.

One firm that has done a good job of controlling its inventory is Corning Consumer Products Company, a unit of Corning, Inc. Having the right quantities of each Corelle dinnerware design pattern had become a huge problem, because it is so difficult to predict consumer buying patterns, especially around Christmas. To solve the problem, Corning developed a sophisticated inventory-control system. A key feature of the system is the requirement that Corning keep a major portion of its Corelle dinnerware undecorated until it gets up-to-the-minute sales data from retailers. Soon after the system had been installed, it saved the company from a disastrous mistake. A week after a giant retail chain launched a special on 12-piece dinnerware sets, the computer-based forecasting model (a critical part of the inventory-control system) predicted that the promotion would be a flop. Corning quickly warned another retailer to cancel its own order for 160,000 of these sets and replace it with an order for a more popular design. The unfinished dishes were completed with the newly selected design and shipped out in less than two weeks.

Warehousing

The warehousing or storage component of a logistics system is concerned with holding products until they are ready to be sold. Warehousing can actually be one of the more complex components of a logistics system.[47] Quite often, when considering

| Figure 11.13 | Economic Order Quantity (EOQ) Model |

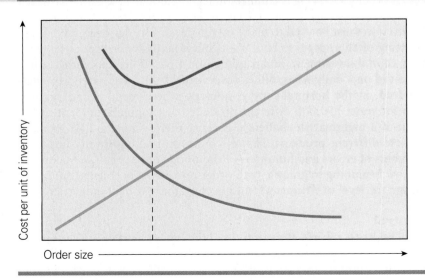

options for warehousing, the firm faces several key decisions, each of which can be difficult and complex. These decisions might include (1) the location of warehouse facilities; (2) the number of warehousing units; (3) the size of the units; (4) the design of the units, including layout and internal systems; and (5) the question of ownership. Successful decisions in each of the areas require careful planning and may require input from experts in such fields as location analysis, real estate, operations research, and industrial engineering, in addition to logistics management.

Warehousing is closely linked to the ability of firms to provide high levels of customer service. For example, with the growth of the Internet as a mode of consumer shopping, far more shipments of *eaches*—single items as opposed to product lots—will create massive numbers of *onesie transactions* in which only a single item is purchased.[48] Moreover, consumers will expect these single items to be delivered very quickly. Experts in the warehousing industry believe such demands by Internet shoppers will increase rather than decrease the need for warehousing, because most Internet retailers will be storefronts with no inventory on hand. They will instead rely on numerous well-located and efficient warehouses—either their own or third parties'—to provide the level of product availability demanded by Internet shoppers.

Packaging

Packaging and the costs associated with packaging products are relevant as a component of the logistics system because packaging can affect the other components of the system, and vice versa. For example, the type of transport used can affect packaging and packaging costs; in the case of air-freight, for instance, packaging costs are generally reduced because risks of damage are generally lower than if rail or truck transportation is used. Materials-handling and order-processing procedures and costs can also be affected by packaging because well-designed packaging can help to increase efficiencies in these components of the logistics system. Effective packaging can also help control inventory carrying costs by reducing product damage. Further, warehouse space, and thus costs, can be saved if packaging is designed to be space efficient. Therefore, packaging is far more than just a promotional device for fostering product differentiation and attracting consumer attention. Packaging has an important logistical dimension that can make a significant difference in the effectiveness and efficiency of the logistics system. Indeed, a product in distinctive and attractive packaging will have even more appeal if it is also easy to handle, conveniently stackable, and shelf-space efficient.

The Output of the Logistics System: Customer Service

Good customer service is the desired end result of virtually all business activities, and logistics is an extremely important part of these efforts.[49] This is particularly true for those aspects of customer service that are a direct function of the logistics system, including:

- Time from order receipt to order shipment
- Order size and assortment constraints
- Percentage of items out of stock
- Percentage of orders filled accurately
- Percentage of orders filled within a given number of days from receipt of the order
- Percentage of orders filled
- Percentage of customer orders that arrive in good condition
- Order cycle time (time from order placement to order delivery)
- Ease and flexibility of order placement

These logistics services are often quantified and used as **logistical service standards**, against which the manufacturer's actual performance is then measured.[50] For example, the first standard shown in the list—time from order receipt to order

Logistical service standards
Are the kinds of quantifiable distribution services performed by a logistical system to meet customer needs.

Amazon.com's customer service performance was rated 88, the highest score ever recorded for any service industry by the American Customer Satisfaction Index, (ACSI). Amazon is branching out far beyond books and is now on its way to becoming the first online department store.

shipment—might be set at 24 hours for 90% of all orders received. So, for every 100 orders received, the manufacturer must have 90 of the orders processed and shipped within 24 hours to meet the standard. The second service standard in the list—order size and assortment constraints—might be set in terms of some minimum quantity of products, and certain restrictions might be placed on mixing the various products unless specified minimum quantities of each item are ordered. A steel producer, for example, might set the minimum order for various gauges of sheet metal at two tons, and the inclusion of several gauges in a single order might require a certain combined minimum tonnage. The third standard—percentage of items out of stock, or stockouts—is almost always set in terms of a percentage of the items ordered during a given period that cannot be filled from inventory. Thus, if a manufacturer wants to fill 95% of the items ordered, its stockout percentage can be no higher than 5% to meet the standard. The other six service standards in the list can be quantified and used in a similar fashion. For more logistics services, see Figure 11.14.

In general, the higher the service standards offered, the higher the costs will be. While well-designed logistics systems and modern technology can keep these costs under control, it is usually not possible to completely escape the trade-off of higher costs for higher service standards.

A manufacturer must cover these costs either indirectly in the price it charges for products, or by passing them along to channel members in the form of service charges. In either case, there is little point in offering logistics services that channel members do not want or higher levels of service than they desire. Types and levels of logistics service that go beyond real channel-member demands simply increase costs for channel members without providing them with any desired benefits. Thus, the key issue in defining logistics service standards is to determine precisely the types and levels of logistics service desired by the channel members.

Figure 11.14	Inventory of Logistical Aspects of Customer Service

1. Delivery time
2. Consolidation allowed
3. Consistency
4. Frequency of sales visits
5. Order progress information
6. Inventory backup during promotions
7. Invoice format
8. Claims response
9. Billing procedures
10. Rush service
11. Availability
12. Competent technical representatives
13. Equipment demonstrations
14. Availability of published material
15. Terms of sale
16. Cooperation

Source: Adapted from John T. Mentzer, Roger Gomes, and Robert E. Knapfel, Jr., "Physical Distribution Service: A Fundamental Marketing Concept?" *Journal of the Academy of Marketing Science* (Winter 1988): 55.

Chapter Summary

Learning Objective 1: *Understand how marketing channels add time, place, and possession utilities for final customers and how channel structure evolves to provide these utilities effectively and efficiently.* As one of the four Ps of the marketing mix—product, price, promotion, and place—marketing channels, or place, is a key part of any firm's marketing strategy. Channel structure is the form or shape taken by the marketing channel, which consists of three dimensions: (1) length, (2) intensity, and (3) types of intermediaries. Channel structure is determined by three major factors: (1) the distribution tasks that need to be performed, (2) the economics of performing the distribution tasks, and (3) management's desire for control of the channel.

Learning Objective 2: *Identify the five major flows in marketing channels and how each contributes to making products conveniently available to many millions of customers.* Marketing channels create five flows: (1) product flow, (2) negotiation flow, (3) ownership flow, (4) information flow, and (5) promotion flow. All of these flows need to be managed to achieve effective and efficient marketing channels.

Learning Objective 3: *Realize that marketing channels are not only economic systems, but also social systems, in which power and conflict play an important role.* Marketing channel power refers to the capacity of one channel member to influence the behavior of another channel member. Conflict in marketing channels is usually defined as goal-impeding behavior by one or more channel members.

Learning Objective 4: *Recognize and explain all six decision areas of channel management and be familiar with the main issues associated with each of those decisions.* Marketing channel management consists of analyzing, planning, organizing, and controlling a firm's marketing channels. Six areas are involved: (1) formulating channel strategy, (2) designing channel structure, (3) selecting channel members, (4) motivating channel members, (5) coordinating channel strategy, and (6) evaluating channel-member performance.

Learning Objective 5: *Appreciate the crucial role played by logistics in the creation and operation of high-performance marketing channels.* The planning, implementation, and control of the physical flows of materials and final goods from points of production to points of use is referred to as logistics, physical distribution (PD), or supply-chain management. A logistics system consists of six major components: (1) transportation, (2) materials handling, (3) order processing, (4) inventory control, (5) warehousing, and (6) packaging. Logistics managers need to use the systems concept to understand the relationships among the components and the total-cost approach to determine and account for all costs of the logistical systems.

Key Terms

For interactive study: visit http://bestpractices.swlearning.com.

Questions for Review and Discussion

1. The opening of this chapter talks about the need for billions of customers around the globe to somehow be matched up with millions of products. How do marketing channels fit into this matching-up process? Explain.

2. Is the marketing channel always the most important component of the marketing mix or does it depend on the particular set of circumstances involved? Discuss.

3. What are the determinants of channel structure? Explain.

4. Why do distribution tasks need to be performed? Explain in terms of the various discrepancies.

5. Why is it important to view marketing channels as social systems, as well as economic systems?

6. Define *marketing channel management* and what is meant by the *interorganizational context* of channel management.

7. Successful motivation of channel members depends on a process that involves several steps. What are these steps and why is it important to follow them when attempting to motivate channel members?

8. The text states that "channel strategy should enhance rather than detract from the firm's product, price, and promotion strategies." What does this have to do with coordinating channel strategy in the marketing mix? Discuss.

9. Define *logistics* or *physical distribution*. In the age of electronic commerce via the Internet, is this concept still valid? Discuss.

10. What is meant by the *systems concept* and *the total-cost approach*?

In-Class Team Activities

1. Select any one of the many companies mentioned in this chapter. Go on the Internet to get some background information on the company, especially what types of marketing channels it uses to make its products available to customers. Analyze the company's marketing channels in terms of whether you think they are already optimally suited for serving their customers or whether you think changes need to be made. If you think changes are needed, how would you change the existing channel structure and why would you make those changes?

   This project can be approached using a team of six students. The team should be split into two groups of three students each. The first group should play the role of outside consultants and the second group should play the role of executives in the selected company. The consulting group should make an oral presentation of its findings to the company executives' group, followed by questions and answers. Members of both groups should do online research about the company to be well informed.

2. Online vs. "brick and mortar" is still a debate that is being played out for many different goods and services. Some consumers swear by online shopping, while others think traditional brick-and-mortar channels are the way to go.

   Pick any good or service mentioned in the chapter. Break up the class into two teams: (1) the online team and (2) the "brick-and-mortar" team. Each team will meet and discuss the good or service in question and then build a case for why online channels or bricks-and-mortar channels are best.

   Each team will then make a presentation to the other team, after which a spirited debate between the two teams should take place. In the course of the presentation and debate, many of the advantages and disadvantages of these two channel structures should be brought out.

Internet Questions

1. In the late 1990s, dot-com start-up companies claimed that the "Internet changes everything." So, there was widespread discussion about Internet-based e-commerce replacing stores and shopping malls and even paper mail-order catalogs. As we now know, of course, this did not happen. Most stores and shopping malls are still here, and more catalogs are mailed out than ever. The e-commerce online revolution never really happened. Online shopping basically became just another marketing channel alongside physical stores and mail-order channels. Moreover, even by the third year of the new millennium, online

shopping accounted for less than 2% of total retail sales.

Why do you think Internet-based online shopping did not and very likely will not replace "old-fashioned" stores and mail-order catalogs? Discuss.

2. Multichannel shopping, where consumers use different channels to shop for products in different situations, has become the norm for many people. An individual spending long hours at the office may use a few spare minutes in the workday to do shopping online. But that same individual may love to shop in stores when more time is available and to get into the spirit of the season around the holidays. This individual may also like to use catalogs while at home on the weekend in front of a fireplace, having had enough of sitting in front of a computer screen all week at the office.

What do marketers need to do to provide the right multichannel mix to satisfy channel-surfing consumers?

CHAPTER CASE

Apple Computer Corp.

Throughout Apple Computer Corp.'s two-and-a-half-decade history, from a start-up founded by Steve Jobs and Steve Wozniak in a garage, the company has been recognized as an innovator. From the early versions of the Apple II in the late 1970s, to the revolutionary Macs of the 1980s and today's PowerMacs, PowerBooks, eMacs, iMacs, and iBooks, its products have been distinctively different from the Windows/Intel (Wintel) PCs, that have dominated the worldwide market for most of the past two decades.

In spite of the company's innovative and distinctive products, Apple's market share has declined significantly since the glory days of the early 1990s, when Apple had a 10% share of the personal computer market. By 2003, Apple had less than a 3% share of the market.

Over the years, many explanations have been offered by both fans and critics of Apple about why the company's excellent products have not gained a larger market share. Some argue that Apple should have pushed its Mac operating-system software instead of concentrating on hardware. Apple's failure to concentrate on pushing its operating-system software allowed Microsoft's Windows to dominate the industry, even though Apple's system was superior. Others claim that Apple's lack of focus on the business market undermined its credibility as a serious contender to Wintel PCs. Another criticism of Apple over the years has been the lack of sufficient software applications available, compared to PCs, while others claim Apple's premium prices stunted its growth potential. Still, others have complained that Apple's advertising and promotion, while often clever, appealed only to a small segment of already loyal Apple users and did little to convert PC users to Apple users. Finally, observers have pointed out that Apple's channels have been weak, especially at the retail level, where Apple products are sold through a relatively small number of licensed Apple dealers, depart-ment stores such as Sears, and "big-box" stores such as CompUSA, where Apple products receive little attention from sales staff and even less shelf space.

Recognizing the Need for a Channel-Design Decision

While all of the factors cited above, as well as others, contributed to Apple's decline in market share, by the late 1990s, Apple's senior management, including CEO Steve Jobs, recognized that in order to grow significantly, Apple would need to convert existing Wintel users into Apple users. New-product development, aggressive pricing, and more extensive and clever advertising were all in place by the year 2000. But Apple knew that its PC-conversion strategy was not likely to succeed without stronger channels of distribution. The Apple story of superior products that are easier and more fun to use was not being communicated effectively to customers through existing retail channels. The "big-box stores," department stores, and independent stores did not devote enough display space or have sufficiently knowledgeable salespeople to create the kind of sales impact needed to convert PC users to Apple products. Moreover, Apple's licensed independent dealers lacked sufficient market coverage and incentives to push the Apple line. In fact, many of Apple's independent dealers were faced with survival problems, because Apple required the dealer to base more than 90% of their business on Apple products, yet the margins available on some of the most popular products were razor thin. An iMac that retails for $869, for example, typically yields a profit to the retailer of just $30.

As the twentieth century came to a close, Apple realized that its existing channel strategy was a weak link in its overall marketing strategy. The company knew it would need a channel strategy just as innovative as Apple products to support its bold PC-conversion strategy.

Apple's Company-Store Channel Strategy

As early as 1999, rumors began circulating in the personal computer industry that Apple was planning to open its own chain of stores throughout the United States. Apple had already been operating one retail store for a number of years at its headquarters in Cupertino, California. But its company-owned retail-store strategy was to be implemented on a much larger scale, with many stores blanketing the major metropolitan areas across the U.S.

By the fall of 2000, Apple's rumored retail strategy became a reality, as its second store opening was about to take place in Palo Alto, California, in early 2001. By mid-2001, Apple had opened 25 stores across the country and, by early 2003, the count had reached 53 stores in 24 states. More store openings are expected, but not at the torrid pace of the first 53 stores.

All of these Apple stores are located in high-traffic locations such as major regional malls. This is in contrast to Gateway Inc.'s (the only other computer maker with its own retail stores) strategy of locating many of its stores well away from major shopping destinations to minimize rental costs. Apple estimates that 85 million consumers (about a third of the total U.S. population) are within 15 miles of one of its stores.

Apple's Store Channels Customer Interface

The size of most Apple computer stores is in the 6,000–7,000-square-foot range, although some stores, such as the newly opened store in Manhattan's SoHo neighborhood, are as large as 15,000 square feet. The stores are designed to create an exciting and upscale atmosphere, with a very sparse understated look that provides a sophisticated and sleek showcase for Apple products. Apple hired famous retail designer Paco Underhill to oversee the design of the stores and Steve Jobs himself devoted considerable time to conversing with Underhill to help capture the spirit of Apple's distinctive image and style in the design of the stores. The store design organizes hardware into five sections: (1) consumer, (2) pro, (3) movies, (4) music, and (5) photo. The signs used to direct customers in the stores are simple, yet big and bold. Each store also has a service and repair section. Finally, the sales staff are a mixture of male and female "tech geniuses" who are capable of demonstrating products to their greatest advantage and who can answer virtually any question posed by customers.

To get back into the education market, which at one time Apple owned, all of the Apple stores set aside every Tuesday and Wednesday during the school year for "School Night at an Apple Store." Students and teachers at all different grade levels are invited to Apple stores to show off the kinds of projects they have done on Apple computers. If the parents of students who participate in the school night program go on to buy an Apple Computer within a month of the school night, they get $50 off the purchase price and the school gets a $50 credit toward future Apple purchases. Regular customers are still welcome in the stores during school night. Apple believes the events create added buzz that will stimulate customers' curiosity and help spark sales.

So far, Apple believes the stores have been a major success. While still not profitable (profit is expected by the end of 2003), the stores now account for almost 10% of Apple's total sales. But perhaps most important, according to Steve Jobs, half the sales at the Apple stores are to customers switching from PCs.

Case Questions

1. Do you think a network of company-owned stores was really necessary to implement Apple's PC-conversion strategy?

2. Will Apple's company-owned stores further erode the already limited effectiveness of the "big-box" department store and independent licensed-dealer channels by creating conflict?

3. Will Apple's "School Night at an Apple Store" help Apple gain further penetration into the education market for computers?

4. What other channel strategy might Apple have pursued to implement its PC-conversion strategy?

VIDEO CASE

Virtual Vineyard at wine.com

"wine.com is a direct marketing company," states wine.com's Web site, under the section that describes the company's business model. "It sources directly from producers, markets directly to customers, and manages product delivery. This gives the company control over the execution of all aspects of the ordering process, thus ensuring quality." The description makes wine.com sound like a traditional organization engaged in traditional direct marketing—but it isn't. Nor are many other companies that operate exclusively online. In fact, these companies are practically changing the definition of direct marketing because of their ability to, as wine.com cofounder Peter Granoff puts it, "collapse geography." In other words, although wine.com's target market may be fairly narrow in that it encompasses adults who are interested in wine, the market encompasses wine lovers everywhere, not just in California or New York.

If you're over 21 and want to order a bottle of wine—expensive or inexpensive—you can click on wine.com from anywhere and make your choice. If you're interested in good food or even the restaurant business, wine.com's Web site can offer you helpful information to educate you about wine. That's wine.com's major point—information. Yes, the company wants to sell eligible customers its wine products, but in doing so it wants to educate them about what they're buying. "Wine is the ideal product for the Internet," notes Granoff, because the Internet can overcome geographic obstacles and because of the amount of information that many consumers want about the products they are purchasing.

What does wine.com offer consumers that their local wine shop doesn't? First, a larger selection of wines that have been selected by experts. "We do the selecting for you," says Granoff. But it doesn't stop there. wine.com's site includes wine-tasting charts and notes from tasters. If, after making a purchase based on all this information, a consumer isn't happy with a choice, wine.com offers a money-back guarantee. Of course, says Granoff, if a consumer is looking for a bottle of wine to have for dinner that evening, the place to shop is the local bricks-and-mortar store. But for those who think ahead, want to stock up, or are planning for a special occasion, wine.com offers the widest range of choices backed by the most information, and it emphasizes customer service every step of the way.

When you visit the site, you can browse through red, white, bubbly, and rare wines; find out what's new; get suggestions for gifts; even e-mail questions to experts. Within the site, you can visit specialty shops such as the Rare Wine Shop. "We are dedicated to offering a quality selection of wines to meet the needs of a wide range of wine lovers, from novices to the more seasoned collectors," notes Bill Newlands, president and CEO of wine.com. "The Rare Wine Shop at wine.com offers us the opportunity to capitalize on the demand for world-class, hard-to-find vintages." Your neighborhood wine store is unlikely to have much—if any—inventory of rare wines because they are so expensive to stock.

Selling wine over the Internet isn't necessarily complicated, but distributing it is, due to state laws regarding alcohol sales and distribution. So, although the company calls itself a direct marketer, and began as a direct shipper, wine.com now functions within a network of in-state wholesalers and retailers to deliver wine shipments within the United States. The delivery systems must be customized to meet the regulations of each state. International shipments can be made directly to the consumer.

Recently, wine.com has entered into a number of co-marketing and cobranding agreements with such diverse companies as United Airlines, the Bloomberg Business Report, America Online, Amazon.com, and Microsoft. Granoff comments that the marketing budget is huge—upwards of $10 million per year. This hefty budget is targeted to one goal: making consumers aware of the site. Cobranding and comarketing alliances assist in boosting consumer awareness.

It's not surprising that Granoff sees wine.com's ultimate market in global terms—beyond simply shipping bottles of wine from the United States to another country. "I see a global business in the future, with global sourcing and distribution," he predicts. Undoubtedly, many of his customers would be willing to drink to that.

Case Questions

1. Based on the description provided, develop a sketch of wine.com's distribution channel.
2. Why is customer service so important to a company like wine.com?
3. With respect to time, place, and possession utilities, what do you see as the advantages of shopping for wine this way? Any disadvantages?
4. Browse through the wine.com Web site at http://www.wine.com. Do you find it to be as information-rich as Peter Granoff claims it to be? Why or why not?

Sources: wine.com Web site, http://www.wine.com, accessed March 2000.
"wine.com Pulls the Cork on Remarkable Rare Wines," company press release, 24 February 2000, http://www.wine.com.
Paul M. Sherer, "Thomas H. Lee Leads an Investment of $50 Million in Retailer wine.com," *The Wall Street Journal*, 10 November 1999, http://www.djreprints.com.
Sandeep Junnarker, "Growing Wine Rivals Pour It On," *CNet News.com*, 27 September 1999, http://www.cnet.com.
"wine.com Announces Next Phase of Wine Portal," 24 September 1999, company press release, http://www.wine.com.
Julie Landry, "Virtual Vineyard.com Goes wine.com Tasting," *Redherring.com*, 16 September 1999, http://www.redherring.com.
Sandeep Junnarker, "Virtual Vineyards Harvest Venture Cash," *Cnet News.com*, 18 June 1999, http://www.cnet.com.

12

Retailing and Wholesaling

© Bill Aron/PhotoEdit, Inc.

Supermarket managers use the art of psychology when planning the layout of their stores. Just a few examples of using psychology in retailing include the intentionally disheveled display of goods to facilitate perceptions of bargain prices and the placement of private label goods to the right of name brands. This is done because most consumers are both right-handed and right-headed and generally turn right when they enter a store. For this same reason, store managers typically locate goods that consumers can see, feel, or smell in the right-hand section of the store to stimulate hunger.

You Decide. After reading the opening vignette and paying special attention to the sections of this chapter marked with the chess piece, answer these questions:

1. Supermarket sales are not expected to match the rate of inflation in the near future. What other tactics might a supermarket manager use to improve sales and gain a competitive advantage, and why?

2. Considering the current environment surrounding supermarkets, where more supercenters and wholesale clubs are opening and Americans dine out more often, determine the stage of the retail life cycle that supermarkets are currently in.

3. Much of the opening vignette focuses on layouts and displays in supermarkets. What is the overall goal of these efforts?

Psychology: Retail Style

While it is unknown how many supermarket managers took a psychology class in college, they sure know how to practice the art of psychology as they seek to turn browsers into purchasers. On your next trip to the grocery store, see how many of the following strategies you observe being used.

Most consumers are both right-handed and *right-headed*. Since supermarkets make more money on their store's private-label brands, due to their higher margins, they stock the store brands to the right of the name brands so the consumer has to reach across the store brand to get to the name brand. Likewise, supermarkets display the higher-gross-margin merchandise on the right side of an aisle, as gauged from the predominant direction of cart traffic.

Did you know that 90% of customers who enter a store turn right? Therefore, store managers consider this section of the store prime real estate. Thus it is no accident that produce, the deli, or the bakery is the first section that a customer will reach. That is because they can see, feel, and smell the merchandise. This, in turn, will get their mouth watering and make them hungry. Any supermarket manager will tell you that their best customer is a hungry customer.

Most consumers think "neatness" counts. Thus, when you pass the snack food area, notice how all the Frito-Lay products are displayed at a right angle faced towards the flow of traffic. At times, merchants use this "neatness" trend to their advantage by trying to make their point-of-purchase displays look like a mess. These so-called "dump displays," which are affectionately known by some grocers as "organized chaos," are deliberately arranged in a haphazard fashion so the items inside look cheap and bargain-priced. The same thought process works for merchants leaving open cartons piled on top of another. Usually, the items are not on sale, they merely look like a "hot" product, or one that the retailer cannot keep in stock.

For the same reason, handwritten, legible signs create the impression of recently lowered prices, indicating that the manager did not have enough time to get printed signs. Thus, even though they do not always look great, handwritten signs move the merchandise faster than standard printed signs.

As they progress through a store, most consumers are likely to focus on a large central display. The point-of-purchase displays at the end of each supermarket aisle, known in the trade as endcaps, are usually the focus of customers' attention as they wheel their carts down the aisle. A smart retailer knows to follow the 25–25–50 rule. This rule states that 25% of all endcaps should be advertised "sale" merchandise and 25% should be unadvertised "sale" items that will cause the customer to be alert when looking at an endcap. The remaining 50% should be regularly priced seasonal or impulse merchandise. Even then, some retailers tend to violate this rule when manufacturers offer money for the right to set up their own displays.

Consumers are creatures of habit and when something is out of place they become more sensitive to their environment. Recognizing this, every supermarket will make regularly scheduled display changes for staple items such as cake mixes, salad dressings, and cereals. They do not want to move the items to new locations because that may upset time-pressed customers. However, by changing shelf displays of these staples, the grocer attracts the customer's attention and increases the chance of an impulse purchase.

There is a little bit of greed in every one of us. Supermarket managers may put a limit on the purchase of a sale item, say "Limit 4 to a Customer." Not only will consumers think that the limit restrictions mean it's a great deal, but they will often buy the limit, even if they do not need that many. Similarly, many customers will get so excited about finding a great price on a staple like peanut butter that they will fail to notice that the item's complementary products, jelly and bread, may have had their prices increased.

LEARNING OBJECTIVES

After you have completed this chapter, you should be able to:

1. *Understand the role of retailing in the U.S. economy, differentiation strategies used by retailers, and the retail life cycle.*

2. *Describe the major types of retail formats, including traditional stores and e-tailers.*

3. *Recognize the components of the retailing mix and how it is designed to attract and retain customers.*

4. *Understand the role of wholesaling in the U.S. economy.*

VOICE OF THE EXPERT

Patrick Dunne, Texas Tech University
Robert Lusch, Texas Christian University

With retail providing one out of every five jobs in today's economy, we have a strong belief that retailing offers one of the best career opportunities for today's college students. Thus, this chapter was written to convey that message, not by using boring descriptions of retailers and the various routine tasks they perform, but by making the subject matter come alive by focusing on the excitement that retailing offers its participants. Hopefully, this chapter demonstrates that retailing, as a career choice, can be fun, exciting, and challenging. This excitement arises from selecting a merchandise assortment at market, determining how to present the merchandise in the store, developing a promotional program for the new assortment, or planning next season's sales in an ever-changing economic environment. Or excitement may also arise from being an entrepreneur and launching your own retail store, perhaps a restaurant, gift shop, hobby shop, sports bar, or health and fitness club.

In keeping with our goal of maintaining student interest, we tried to limit our focus on the material that someone entering the retailing or wholesaling fields would need to know. We were more interested in telling what should happen, and what is happening, than in explaining the academic "whys" of these actions. Thus, when knowledge of a particular theory such as the retail life cycle was needed, we minimized the reasoning behind the theory and emphasized its application in the real world. In presenting these examples, we drew from a rich array of literature sources, as well as more than half a century of combined work in retailing and wholesaling.

Retailing
Consists of the final activity and steps needed to place merchandise made elsewhere into the hands of the consumer or to provide services to the consumer.

Retailing consists of the final activities needed to place merchandise made elsewhere into the hands of the consumer or to provide services to the consumer. Quite simply, any firm that sells merchandise or provides services to the ultimate consumer for personal or household consumption is performing the retailing function. Regardless of whether the firm sells to the ultimate consumer in a store, through the mail, over the phone, through a television infomercial, over the Internet, door to door, or through a vending machine, it is involved in retailing. Thus, while everybody realizes that fast-food establishments, discount stores, and florists are retailers, they often fail to recognize that a bank is also a retailer. Some experts point out the importance of retailing by noting that retailers are the marketing channel's "gatekeepers," since they are the final foot, or 12 inches, in a marketing channel that may stretch thousands of miles or even across the globe. After all, if the consumers do not buy the retailer's offering, there is no need for a manufacturer to have a marketing channel.

Wholesalers
Are persons or establishments that sell to retailers and/or other organizational buyers for industrial, institutional, and commercial use, but do not sell in significant amounts to ultimate consumers.

Wholesalers are those persons or establishments that sell to retailers and/or other organizational buyers for industrial, institutional, and commercial use, but do not sell in significant amounts to ultimate consumers. For example, a Costco outlet, even though it sells to consumers, would be considered a wholesaler, since a majority of its sales are to small business operators. As a result, the government classifies all such sales as wholesale transactions.

These channel partners—retailers and wholesalers—in conjunction with the manufacturers, have made a significant contribution to this country's economic prosperity by having the goods/services readily available in an efficient, low-cost manner. In fact, the nations that have enjoyed the greatest economic and social progress have been those with strong retail and wholesale sectors. These channel partners have become valued and necessary members of society.

In this chapter, we show the size and importance of retail marketing—the type of marketing you observe most frequently in your daily activities. We discuss the most popular types of retailing in the United States, and how retailers make their business decisions. In addition, this chapter looks at wholesale marketing. We describe the structure of wholesaling in our economy and discuss how manufacturers can market their products more effectively through wholesalers.

LEARNING OBJECTIVE   1

The Role of Retailing in the United States

Currently, there are approximately 3.1 million retail establishments in the United States, with total annual sales of nearly $3.3 trillion, or nearly $11,000 per capita.[1] The retail sector of the U.S. economy accounts for one out of every five jobs. In addition, there are 30 retail establishments for every 1,000 households, with each establishment averaging annual sales of nearly $1 million.[2] Most retailers, however, are smaller, and many have annual sales of less than $500,000 annually.

These figures, however, do not adequately reflect the changes that have occurred as a result of the number of new retail formats that developed over the last couple of decades. Most of these businesses have actually been new institutional forms, such as retailing on the Internet, warehouse club retailing, and supercenters. Change is truly the major cause of growth in retailing today. Remember, retailers are not obliged to conform to traditional ways of selling to consumers. Retailers and would-be retailers are free to forge new retailing approaches that capitalize on emerging market opportunities. This is all the more evident when we consider the fact that fashion trends, which in the past would have lasted for years, now may last only a few months.

Reaching the Consumer

When most people think of retailing, they usually think of the various types of fixed-based physical stores. After all, the overwhelming majority of retail sales occur in these stores. Today, however, retailing is much broader than simply a physical store.

Retailers are finding alternatives to having the customer travel to a fixed-based store to purchase goods and services. For example, Dell Computer, in addition to selling via the traditional retail outlets, sells its computers and peripherals to households via the Internet, through the mail, or over the phone, and still delivers within two days of the receipt of the order. Saks Fifth Avenue sells merchandise not only in its high-fashion stores, but also through its Web site. And Avon, Mary Kay, Tupperware, and other direct sellers, while selling most of their goods via in-home parties, are also now using the Internet to reach their target customers. Therefore, it is important to remember that when discussing the various types of retailers, you must first consider if they are selling from a fixed physical location or not.

Current Retail Trends

Today retailers come in many different forms and classifications. After reviewing these retailer classifications, which are usually expressed in terms of number of outlets, profit margin versus inventory turnover, and location, you will have a better appreciation of the diversity in retailing and the reasons why retailers behave as they do.

Number of Outlets and the Growth of Chain Stores

As a rule, retailers with several units are a stronger competitive threat because they can spread their fixed costs, such as distribution centers, purchasing offices, advertising, and top management salaries, over a larger number of stores, and can achieve economies of scale in purchasing. However, single-unit retailers such as your neighborhood florist, deli, and grocery store do have several advantages when competing with larger chains. These single-unit retailers, such as a locally-owned Ace Hardware, are generally owner- and family-operated and tend to have harder-working, more motivated employees. Also, they can focus all their efforts on one trade area and tailor their merchandise to that area. One strength of these stores is that in the past they were usually able to spot emerging customer desires sooner and respond to them faster than the larger multi-unit retailers operating in many diverse markets.

Any retail organization that operates more than one unit is technically a chain, but this is really not a very practical definition. The U.S. Census Bureau classifies

While large chain operations are a stronger competitive threat, single-unit retailers tend to have harder-working employees and are able to identify and respond to changing customer needs faster than larger multi-unit retailers.

| Figure 12.1 | Importance of Large Chain Operations |

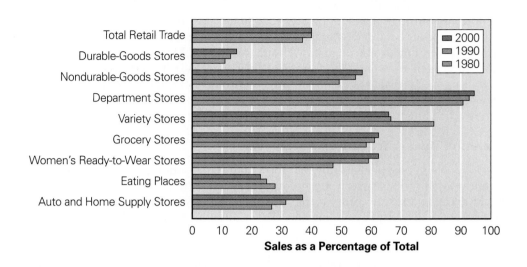

Source: U.S. Bureau of the Census, *Statistical Abstract of the United States: 2001,* 121st ed. (Washington, DC, 2001).

chain stores into two size categories: 2 to 10 stores and 11 or more. We will use the 11 or more units when we use the term *chain stores.*

Figure 12.1 shows the importance of sales by chain stores, those retail operations with 11 or more units, as a percentage of total U.S. sales for some of the different merchandise lines. The statistics in Figure 12.1 reveal that chain stores account for 41% of all retail sales (including 95% of all department-store sales and 63% of all grocery-store sales). Although large chain operations account for 57% of nondurable-goods sales, they only account for 16% of durable-goods sales, such as autos and furniture.

Not all chain operations enjoy the same advantages. Small chains are local in nature and may enjoy some economies in buying and in having merchandise tailored to their market needs. Large chains are generally regional or national and can take full advantage of the economies of scale that centralized buying, accounting, training, and information systems, as well as a standard stock list, can achieve. (A *standard stock list* requires that all stores in a retail chain stock the same merchandise.) Some national chains, such as Sears and Wal-Mart, recognizing the variations of regional tastes, use an *optional stock list* approach that allows each store the flexibility of tailoring its merchandise mix to local tastes and demands. Sears, for example, has found that stores in the Rio Grande Valley in Texas sell a preponderance of small and medium sizes in men's shirts, while in Minnesota the chain sells a preponderance of larger sizes. Wal-Mart calls this *micro-target marketing* the "store of the community," since its merchandise selection is tailored to the local market. The chain has even gone so far as to sell cans of Spamouflage—Spam in camouflage-design cans—next to hunting rifles and fishing rods in its 760 rural Wal-Marts.[3]

Chain stores have long been aware of the benefits of taking a leadership role in managing the marketing channel. When a chain-store retailer is able to achieve critical mass in purchasing, it can get other channel members—wholesalers and manufacturers—to take on additional responsibilities by acting as the retailer's *category captain.* A category captain is a vendor who helps the retailer manage its limited shelf space by determining "what kind" and "how many" units of a specific product to carry on the shelves in each store. Such action allows the entire channel to operate in the most efficient manner.

Competitive Forces

Large national retailers can still achieve scale advantages, even when using an optional stock list. For example, promotional savings will occur when more than one store can use the same advertisements, even while tailoring specific merchandise to specific stores.

In recent years, chains have relied on their high level of consumer recognition to engage in *private-label branding*. Private-label branding, sometimes called store branding, occurs when a retailer, or its wholesaler, develops its own brand name and contracts with a manufacturer to make the product with the retailer's brand on it. Overall, private branding now accounts for almost 40% of department-store sales and more than 20% of total grocery units sold, and is expected to surpass 30% of grocery sales by the year 2005. Some of the best-known private labels today include JCPenney's "Arizona Jeans," Dillard's "Roundtree & Yorke," Wal-Mart's "Great Value," and Target's "Archer Farms." Other retailers have borrowed from the success of the supermarkets and department stores with their private labels. Barnes & Noble now sells deluxe hardcover editions of many of the classics with its own publishing-house imprint. Private labels usually have lower acquisition costs, thus producing savings that can be passed on to the consumer in the form of lower prices, thereby increasing demand. But while private brands have no national advertising costs, the retailer must spend more to develop local demand for the brand. As a result, retailers and their wholesalers are now competing with the national brand manufacturers, as well as the store across the street.

The major shortcoming of using the number of outlets to classify retailers is that it only addresses those retailers operating in a traditional brick-and-mortar space. As such, this scheme ignores many nontraditional retailers such as catalog-only operators and online retailers. How many outlets does Amazon.com have? One could argue that each new online computer is a potential retail outlet for the e-tailing giant.

Margins versus Inventory Turnover

Retailers can be classified in terms of their gross margin percentage and rate of inventory turnover, as shown in Figure 12.2. The **gross margin percentage** shows how much **gross margin** (net sales minus the cost of goods sold) the retailer makes as a percentage of sales; this is also referred to as the gross margin return on sales. A 40% gross margin indicates that on each dollar of sales, the retailer generates 40 cents in gross-margin dollars. This gross margin will be used to pay the retailer's **operating expenses** (the expenses the retailer incurs in running the business, other than the cost of the merchandise, e.g., rent, wages, advertising, utilities, depreciation, insurance, etc.). **Inventory turnover** refers to the number of times per year, on average, that a retailer sells its inventory. Thus an inventory turnover of 12 times indicates that, on average, the retailer turns over or sells its average inventory once a month. Likewise, an average inventory of $40,000 (retail) and annual sales of $240,000 means the retailer has turned over its inventory six times in one year ($240,000 divided by $40,000) or every two months.

Highly successful retailers have long recognized the relationship between gross-margin percentage, inventory turnover, and profit. Briefly, retailers can make profit

Competitive Forces
While the dollar amount spent on private-label merchandise has increased by 24% over the last several years, the number of items has increased just minimally. This is the result of retailers realizing the importance of both premium price and positioning in managing their private labels.

Gross margin percentage
Shows how much gross margin a retailer makes as a percentage of sales.

Gross margin
Equals net sales minus the cost of goods sold.

Operating expenses
Are the costs a retailer incurs in running a business, other than the cost of merchandise.

Inventory turnover
Refers to the number of times per year, on average, that a firm sells its inventory.

Retailers Listed by Margin and Turnover   Figure 12.2

High Margin

High-Margin/Low-Turnover Retailers	High-Margin/High-Turnover Retailers
Low-Margin/Low-Turnover Retailers	Low-Margin/High-Turnover Retailers

Low Turnover (left)   **High Turnover** (right)

Low Margin

by earning (high gross margin percentage) and/or by turning (high inventory turnover). Retailers that can both "earn" and "turn" are high-profit performers. One can classify retailers into four basic types by using the concepts of margin and turnover.

Typically, the *low-margin/low-turnover retailer* will not be able to generate sufficient profits to remain competitive and survive. Thus, there are no good examples of successful retailers using this approach. On the other hand, the *low-margin/high-turnover retailer* is common in the United States. Brick-and-mortar (their outlets are made of bricks and mortar) examples are the discount department stores such as Kohl's and Target, the warehouse clubs such as Sam's Club and Costco, and the category killers, which will be discussed in detail later in the chapter, such as Toys "R" Us, Amazon.com, and many of the airlines' Web sites, are probably the best-known examples of low-margin/high-turnover e-tailers.

High-margin/low-turnover brick-and-mortar retailers are also quite common in the United States. Furniture stores, jewelry stores, gift shops, funeral homes, and most of the mom-and-pop stores located in small towns across the country are generally good examples of high-margin/low-turnover operations. Some clicks-and-brick (their outlets are both online computers and physical stores) retailers using this approach include Coach and Sharper Image. Finally, some retailers are able to operate as a *high-margin/high-turnover* operation. As you might expect, this strategy can be very profitable. Probably the most popular examples are convenience food stores such as 7-Eleven, Circle K, Stop & Shop, Quick Mart, or beverage and food vendors at professional sporting events. However, because most retailers are trying to achieve a high turnover rate in these early stages of Internet retailing, there are no examples of e-tailers using this strategy.

A low-margin/low-turnover retailer is the least able of the four to withstand a competitive attack because this retailer is usually unprofitable or barely profitable, and when competitive intensity increases, profits are driven even lower. On the other hand, the high-margin/high-turnover retailer is in an excellent position to withstand and counter competitive threats because its profit margins enable it to finance competitive price wars.

While the margin/turnover scheme provides an encompassing classification, it fails to capture the complete array of retailers operating in today's marketplace. For example, service retailers, such as those discussed in Chapter 10, and even some e-tailers, such as eBay and Priceline.com, have no inventory to turn over. As such, while this scheme provides a good way to analyze retail competition, it neglects these two important types of retailing—service retailers and e-tailers.

Location

Location can be a key element in a retailer's success. In fact, one retailing axiom is that "the three major decisions in retailing are location, location, and location." After all, all retail stores attract customers from a limited geographic area. For example, a convenience store attracts most customers from within a 1.5-mile radius, a drug store from within a 3-mile radius, and a discount department store from within an 8-mile radius. Even retailers selling services must pay particular attention to location. A movie theater, dry cleaner, child-care center, and barbershop will attract most of their customers from within a 3-mile area. As shown in Figure 12.3, there are four basic types of locations from which a store-based retailer can select: business districts, shopping centers/malls, freestanding units, and nontraditional locations.

As a rule, retailers selling convenience goods or services will have a smaller trade area than retailers of shopping or specialty goods and services. A physician specializing in cardiovascular diseases can attract patients from beyond his/her local community, but a general practitioner will only attract patients from his/her local community.

Business Districts. Historically, most retailers were located in their community's *central business district (CBD),* which was usually an unplanned shopping area that sprang up around the geographic point where public transportation systems con-

Political and Legal Forces
Conventional retailers often complain that online retailers get unfair tax advantages. Since by law they do not have to charge a sales tax, their net selling price to the consumer is less. In addition, since others do not have to carry inventory, they are able to avoid state property taxes.

Location is a key element in a retailer's success. Rodeo Drive in Los Angeles is popular with tourists and locals because of its proximity to cultural activities, shopping, and public transportation.

© Grantpix/Index Stock Imagery

verged. Many of the traditional department stores were located in the central business district, along with a selection of specialty stores. Stores located here drew their clientele from the entire metropolitan area and even from nonresidents visiting the city. For example, large central business districts around the world, such as New York, Paris, London, and Hong Kong, have become major shopping areas for visiting tourists. In fact, that is why dominant name-brand manufacturers, such as Christian Dior, Tiffany's, Coach, Polo, Benetton, Steuben, and Nike, open retail outlets in these CBDs.

The CBD has several strengths and weaknesses. Among its strengths are easy access to public transportation; wide product assortment; variety in images, prices, and services; and proximity to commercial and cultural activities. Some weaknesses are inadequate (and usually expensive) parking, older stores, high rents and taxes,

Types of Store-Based Retail Locations   **Figure 12.3**

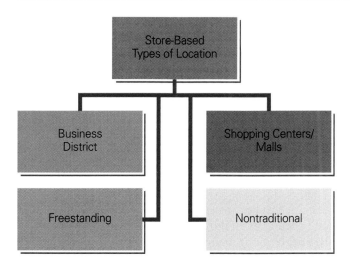

In the appliance market, Lowe's is rapidly gaining on rival Sears, in part because of location. Lowe's boxy stores are cheaper to operate than Sears department-store format. Because they may be tucked away next to apparels, appliances at Sears stores are harder to locate than the appliances at Lowe's.

traffic and delivery congestion, potentially high crime rate, and the decaying conditions of many inner cities. The *Los Angeles Times* recently reported that the world's largest retailer, Wal-Mart, which began life in the Ozarks of rural America, is building a new multilevel store in the Crenshaw Plaza in central Los Angeles. The format is expected to be symbolic of Wal-Mart's desire to find ways to push into urban areas with formats that adapt to their surroundings, but are successful because they satisfy the customers' "immediate" needs.[4]

In larger cities, secondary business districts and neighborhood business districts have developed. A *secondary business district (SBD)* is a shopping area that is smaller than the CBD and that revolves around at least one department or variety store at the intersection of two major streets. A *neighborhood business district (NBD)* is a shopping area that evolves to satisfy the convenience-oriented shopping needs of a neighborhood and generally contains several small stores, with the major retailer being either a supermarket or a variety store. An increasing number of national retail chains are finding these smaller districts an attractive location for new stores. This includes retailers such as Ann Taylor, The Body Shop, Starbucks, Crate & Barrel, Pier 1, Radio Shack, Williams-Sonoma, and Pottery Barn.

Shopping Centers/Malls. Ever since 1956, when Dayton's, now a part of Target, opened the country's first fully enclosed shopping center, Southdale Center, in Edina, Minnesota, America has had a love affair with the shopping center.[5] Today, more than 80% of Americans visit a shopping center three or more times a month. The key difference between a shopping center and a business district is that the shopping center, or mall, is a centrally owned and/or managed shopping district that is planned to have a **balanced tenancy** (the stores complement each other in merchandise offerings), and is surrounded by parking facilities. In addition, a shopping center has one or more **anchor stores** (a dominant large-scale store that is expected to draw customers to the center) and a variety of smaller stores.

Figure 12.4 lists some of the advantages and disadvantages of locating in a shopping center/mall.

Freestanding Retailer. As the name implies, a freestanding retailer is not physically connected to other retailers, but instead has an individual building and parking area. Freestanding retailers generally locate along major traffic arteries. The difficulties involved in drawing, and then holding, customers to an isolated, freestanding store

---

xtra!

Balanced tenancy
Occurs where the stores in a shopping center complement each other in merchandise offerings.

Anchor stores
Are dominant, large-scale stores that are expected to draw customers to a shopping center.

The Mall of America is not immune to the effects of change and competition. Malls, just like individual retailers, must always be reevaluating their marketing mix and the needs of their customers.

© Owaki-Kulla/CORBIS

are the reason that only large, well-known retailers should attempt it. Small retailers may be unable to develop a loyal customer base because customers may not be willing to travel to a freestanding store that does not have a wide assortment of products and a local or national reputation. Kohl's, Lowe's, Target, and Wal-Mart, as well as many convenience stores and gasoline stations, have used a freestanding-location strategy successfully in the past. Consumer electronics chains such as Best Buy and wholesale clubs such as Costco are successfully using freestanding locations today. However, when these large national chains acquire land for a freestanding store, they often acquire more land than they need and then "out-parcel," or sell, the remaining

Advantages and Disadvantages of Locating in a Shopping Center/Mall	Figure 12.4

Advantages	Disadvantages
• Heavy traffic resulting from the wide range of product offerings	• Inflexible store hours (the retailer must stay open during the center's hours, and can't be open at other times)
• Nearness to the population	• High rents
• Cooperative planning and sharing of common costs	• Restrictions as to the merchandise the retailer may sell
• Access to highway and availability of parking	• Inflexible operations and required membership in the center's merchant organization
• Lower crime rate	
• Clean, neat environment	• Possibility of too much competition and the fact that much of the traffic is not interested in a particular product offering
• More-than-adequate parking space	
	• Anchor tenant dominates smaller stores

land to smaller retailers selling complementary and/or noncompeting products. The next time you notice a new freestanding store such as a Wal-Mart or Lowe's, note the Jiffy Lube, McDonalds, or Midas Muffler outlets that spring up around the perimeter. This is because some astute local retailers, as well as small regional chains, have found it quite attractive to buy this land, even at a premium price, because of the traffic a large discounter generates.

Nontraditional Locations. Increasingly, retailers are identifying nontraditional locations that offer more place utility or locational convenience. Recognizing, for example, that a significant number of travelers spend several hours in airports, especially since September 11, and can use this time to purchase merchandise they might otherwise purchase in their local community, retailers have stepped up their airport-mall plans. One of the most unique airport malls is located within the confines of the Philadelphia International Airport—The Philadelphia Marketplace at the Airport. The mall's 33 shops include many well-known retailers (The Gap/Gap Kids, Godiva Chocolatier, and Sunglass Hut), as well as local favorites (Philly's Finest, the Philadelphia Museum Store, and DiNardo's). Similar to other malls, it is organized around a food court.[6]

On college campuses, there are an increasing number of food courts in student unions, and truck and travel stops along interstate highways are also incorporating food courts. Some franchises such as Taco Bell and Dunkin' Donuts are putting small food-service units in convenience stores and in university libraries and classroom buildings. Georgia Tech even has a supermarket on its campus.[7] Hospitals are building emergency-care clinics near where people live in the suburbs and away from the hospital, lawyers are opening storefront offices wherever there is high pedestrian traffic, and dry cleaners and copying services are locating in major office buildings.

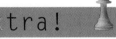

Differentiating the Retail Experience

Perhaps one of the greatest failings in retailing today is that too many retailers have concentrated on just one means of differentiating themselves from the competition—price. Price promotions usually attract, but rarely hold, customers. The customers that the retailers gain with these promotions are just as apt to switch to another retailer when that retailer cuts its prices. As a result, retailers have taught consumers that if they wait, and in many cases this wait is only a matter of days, the merchandise or services they desire will go on sale. Unless a retailer has substantially lower operating costs, lowering prices is a very dangerous strategy to use because it can easily be copied by the competition and will usually result in reduced profits, or even a loss. Some better forms of differentiation for retailers to use in attracting customers include the following:

- *Physical differentiation of the product,* such as Target's brilliant and innovative "upscale" merchandise that really catches trends before other mass merchandisers. Little wonder that Target is the discount store for many shoppers, "who do not want to be seen in a discount store." Another retailer using this strategy is Charming Shoppes. With more than 2,200 retail stores, Charming Shoppes operates the Lane Bryant, Fashion Bug, and Catherine's Plus retail chains. It has dropped its dowdy, baggy styles and refocused on body-hugging fashions that were previously marketed only to smaller-sized women. Note that service retailers such as beauty shops, health and fitness clubs, and child-care centers can also use their physical environment to differentiate their services.
- *Selling process,* such as the way Saturn auto dealers use their excellent customer service to connect with their target customers.
- *After-purchase satisfaction,* which some major retailers, such as L.L. Bean, achieve with "satisfaction-guaranteed" programs that enable customers to return clothing even after years of wear for a new item.

Has Target Hit the Bull's-Eye?

The general belief among retail experts at the beginning of the millennium was that *electronic shopping* would soon take off. Every major player in the retail industry was committed to this growth engine of the so-called "new economy." However, just as the "Y2K" problem was overrated, so were these early predictions about Internet sales. Even the great retailers such as Wal-Mart failed with ventures selling over the Internet. The cruel facts were that consumers were using the Net, but not to shop. The Internet was a revolution in communications, not distribution. *E-tailers,* as electronic retailers came to be called, found out that it was more difficult than they had planned to turn viewership of a Web site into a sales transaction.

2002 may have been the year e-marketing reached the masses. What was once an activity of the high-tech-minded elite—the average online shopper in 2000 probably was a middle-aged consumer with a household income of $100,000 or more, plus a college degree—has lost its novelty factor. Today's online shopper is older and poorer.

How did e-tailers finally find the magic bullet? Consider the success of Target's Target.com unit. This savvy e-tailer determined that while stores are for buying something for yourself, because you want to feel it and try it on, Web sites are for buying gifts for others, especially items too big or too expensive to be carried in many stores. After all, high-ticket, nonfashion items tend to work best online because of shipping and processing costs.

With the help of Amazon.com, which handles the Web site's software development and service (Target does the actual shipping of the merchandise), the site reaches beyond the typical in-store shopper of the nation's second largest retailer. And it is all because the retailer realized the difference between its in-store shopper and its electronic shopper. No wonder that more than one-quarter of its sales today come from bridal and baby registries.

During the 2002 Christmas season, Target's online sales ran about double the 1.5% for all retail sales. One of the top-selling items was a pair of faux-fur slippers. Other top-selling online gift packages sold by the e-tailer were:

- "Student Survival Kits": a movie-night package containing popcorn in a bucket, candy, soda, and a blank VCR tape.
- "Get-Well Cold Comfort Boxes": a get-well package complete with card, over-the-counter medicines, and, of course, a teddy bear.

Source: Based on information supplied by Target, Inc.

- *Location,* such as the way Dollar General and Family Dollar have used their locational advantage by placing stores that are usually located in strip centers en route to a nearby supercenter. These chains hope to intercept shoppers who would rather pick up that toothpaste and motor oil in a convenient manner instead of having to walk through a cavernous building offering tires and tomatoes, shirts and soup, and bananas and car batteries. In addition, the small size of their stores also gives these retailers advantages in negotiating leases, thus reducing their operating costs in comparison to other chains.
- *Never being out of stock,* which means being in stock with regard to the sizes, colors, and styles that the target market expects the retailer to carry. Nordstrom, for example, offers a free shirt if it is out of stock on basic sizes. For a service retailer such as a barber shop, this may equate to always having a barber available for walk-in customers.

In today's highly competitive marketplace, retailers must develop marketing strategies that separate them from their competition. Retailers must be keenly aware that not only must their marketing channel be superior to their competition but also they must make the "sale." Sam Walton, the founder of Wal-Mart, often stated that retailing was really a very simple business and had only three basic tasks:

1. Attract consumers from their trading area into their store.
2. Convert these consumers into paying customers.
3. Operate in the most efficient manner, so as to reduce costs.

While these three tasks may seem too simple to be operational, they actually summarize the strategies that every retailer must perform. It is only when a firm complicates these tasks that they get in trouble. In the chapter's third learning objective, we will discuss these tasks in greater detail.

Evolution of Retail Competition

Since it is easier to open a retail store than a manufacturing plant, in terms of entry barriers (skill, expertise, and money), new retail institutions appear continuously. Marketing scholars have developed several theories to explain and describe the evolution of competition in retailing. We will review two of them briefly.

Wheel of Retailing

Wheel of retailing theory
Is a pattern of competitive development in retailing that states that new types of retailers enter the market as low-status, low-margin, low-price operators. However, as they meet with success, these new retailers gradually acquire more sophisticated and elaborate facilities, thereby becoming less efficient and vulnerable to new types of low-margin retail competitors that progress through the same pattern.

The **wheel of retailing theory**, illustrated in Figure 12.5, is one of the oldest descriptions of the patterns of competitive development in retailing.[8] This theory states that new types of retailers enter the market as low-status, low-margin, and low-price operators. This is the entry phase and allows these retailers to compete effectively and take market share away from the more traditional retailers. However, as they meet with success, these new retailers gradually acquire more sophisticated and elaborate facilities, thereby becoming less efficient, in the trading-up phase. This creates both a higher investment and a subsequent rise in operating costs. Predictably, these retailers will enter the vulnerability phase and must raise prices and margins, becoming vulnerable to new types of low-margin retail competitors that progress through the same pattern. This appears to be the case today with outlet malls. Once bare-bones warehouses for manufacturers' imperfect or excess merchandise, outlet malls have quickly evolved into fancy, almost upscale, malls where retailers try to outdo each other's accent lighting, private dressing rooms, and generous return policies. As a result, with the operating costs at such locations increasing and with regular department stores becoming more competitive, there is now little difference in the outlets' prices and department stores' sale prices.

Holiday Hospitality Corporation, owned by Six Continents, recognizing that it could become vulnerable by constantly upgrading its lodging units, developed four distinct hotel/motel formats, Holiday Inn Express, Holiday Inn Select, Holiday Inn, and Holiday Inn Crowne Plaza. Holiday Inn Express is targeted at the in-and-out businessperson or traveler who is willing to forgo some amenities for a lower price. Holiday Inn Select is similar to the Express but is aimed at the business traveler staying for a longer period of time who desires a few more amenities, such as dataport connections and conference rooms. The traditional Holiday Inn is targeted at the middle-class market and provides higher-cost features such as a restaurant, lounge, conference rooms, and a swimming pool. The Holiday Inn Crowne Plaza is targeted

| Figure 12.5 | The Wheel of Retailing |

at the more upscale or executive business traveler and features luxurious furnishings and restaurants, health spas, and a variety of business services, conference rooms, and other amenities. Realizing that consumers may have different lodging needs depending on the circumstances, Holiday Hospitality has tied these four different formats together with the same loyalty program—the Priority Club.

Retail Life Cycle

Much like the product life cycle discussed in Chapter 9, the **retail life cycle** assumes that retail institutions pass through an identifiable cycle. This cycle includes four distinct stages:

1. Introduction
2. Growth
3. Maturity
4. Decline

Figure 12.6 lists the various stages of the retail life cycle for many of our current retail institutions.

Introduction. The retail process begins with an entrepreneur who is willing and able to develop a new approach that offers increased value to the customer. In other words, a new type of retail institution is developed at this stage. During the introduction stage profits are low, despite the increasing sales level, due to amortizing development costs.

Growth. During the growth stage, sales, and usually profits, explode. Many others begin to copy the idea. Toward the end of this period, cost pressures that arise from the need for a larger staff, more complex internal systems, increased management controls, and other requirements of operating large, multiunit organizations overtake

Retail life cycle
Is a description of competitive development in retailing that assumes that retail institutions pass through an identifiable cycle that includes four distinct stages: (1) introduction, (2) growth, (3) maturity, and (4) decline.

The Retail Life Cycle	Figure 12.6

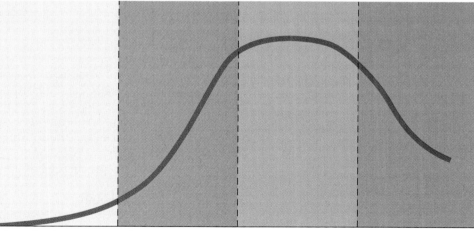

Introduction	Growth	Maturity	Decline
Internet shopping (1990s)	Food courts (1980s)	Factory outlet malls (1970s)	Cafeterias (1940s)
Recyclers (1990s)	Category killers (1970s)	Warehouse clubs (1970s)	Full-Service gasoline stations (1910s)
	Airport-based retailers (1980s)	Convenience stores (1960s)	Variety stores (1890s)
	Supercenters (1990s)	Supermarkets (1930s)	Department stores (1860s)
		Fast food (1950s)	

some of the favorable results. Consequently, late in this stage, both market share and profitability tend to approach their maximum level.

Maturity. In the maturity stage, market share stabilizes and severe profit declines are experienced for several reasons. First, managers have become accustomed to managing a high-growth firm that was simple and small, but now they must manage a large, complex firm in a nongrowing market. Second, the industry has typically over-expanded. Third, competitive assaults will be made on mature firms by new retailing formats (a bold entrepreneur offering a new value proposition, thus beginning a retail life cycle for yet another type of retail institution).

Decline. Although all types of retail institutions will inevitably reach the decline stage, retail managers try to postpone it by changing their offerings. These attempts can stave off the decline stage, but a return to earlier, attractive levels of operating performance is not likely. Sooner or later, a major loss of market share will occur, profits fall, and the once-promising idea is no longer needed in the marketplace.

Three primary inferences can be derived from the discussion of the retail life cycle:

1. Retailers should remain flexible so they are able to adapt their strategies to the various stages of the life cycle.
2. Since profits vary by stage in the retail life cycle, retailers need to carefully analyze the risks and profits of entering the various life-cycle stages or expanding their outlets at various stages in the life cycle.
3. Retailers need to extend the maturity stage. Since they will have substantial investments in a particular form of retailing by the time the maturity stage arrives, they will have a strong interest in trying to use that investment as long as possible.

The importance of these three points is reinforced by the fact that the retail life cycle is accelerating today. New retail concepts now move quickly from introduction to maturity because the leading operators have aggressive growth goals and their investors demand a quick return on investment. Larger retailers with capital and expertise in concept rollout will acquire many smaller entrepreneurs with new ideas.

LEARNING OBJECTIVE 2 | ## Major Types of Retail Formats

As pointed out in Chapter 8, once marketing managers identify a target market they must identify the most effective way to reach this market. The same is true with retailers. Essentially there are two types of retail formats: store-based and nonstore-based formats. *Store-based retailers* operate from a fixed location that requires consumers to travel to the store to view and select merchandise and/or services. Essentially, the retailer requires that the consumer perform part of the transporting activity. *Nonstore-based retailers* attempt to reach the consumer at home, work, or any place other than a store where they might be susceptible to purchasing. Today, many retailers are trying to reach consumers on the Internet.

There are many examples of retailers operating successfully in more than one type of format by using different marketing strategies, each making use of a unique blend of product, price, promotion, and place. Saks Incorporated, the parent company of Saks Fifth Avenue stores, Saks Off 5th stores, and the http://www.saksincorporated. com Web site, also operates stores in 39 states under the names of Parisian, Proffitt's, McRae's, Younkers, Herberger's, Carson Pirie Scott, and Bergner's. Each operation is tailored to meet the needs of a local market.[9]

Store-Based Retailers

The six retailers using the store-based format today are department stores, specialty stores, supermarkets, supercenters, category killers, and convenience stores (see Figure 12.7).

Six Basic Types of Store-Based Retailers	Figure 12.7

- **Department stores:** Large-scale operations that contain a broad product mix consisting of many different product lines that each have above-average depth.
- **Specialty stores:** Relatively small-scale stores offering a great deal of depth in a narrow range of product lines.
- **Supermarkets:** Retailers that sell groceries and some general-merchandise products through large-scale physical facilities with self-service and self-selection displays that enable the retailer to shift the performance of some marketing functions to the consumer.
- **Supercenters:** Cavernous, one-stop combinations of supermarkets and discount department stores that range in size from 120,000 to 160,000 square feet, and carry between 80,000 to 100,000 products, ranging from televisions to peanut butter to fax machines.
- **Category killers:** Carry such a large amount of merchandise in a single category at such good prices that they make it impossible for customers to walk out without purchasing what they need, thus "killing" the competition.
- **Convenience stores:** Stock frequently purchased products such as gasoline, bread, tobacco, and milk that tend to be consumed within 30 minutes of purchase, as well as offering services such as ATMs and car washes.

Department Stores

Department stores were first introduced in the mid-1800s, about the time of the Civil War. Today Sears, May Company, JCPenney, Federated Stores, and Dillard's are some of the well-known traditional department stores operating in the United States. These stores generally have 120,000 to 300,000 square feet of selling space. The various related product lines carried in the store's product mix are merchandised in separate departments (including men's wear, women's wear, jewelry, toys, sporting goods, home furnishings, and furniture). Department stores offer many customer services, such as knowledgeable and helpful sales clerks, delivery and wrapping services, liberal return policies, and store credit cards.

Despite its past successes, the future of the traditional department store is clouded. Squeezed by discounters at the low end of the price spectrum and specialty stores at the high end of the selection spectrum, today's department stores are only managing to achieve a very low rate of sales growth. However, as consumers turn to alternative formats that are more convenient or offer a stronger value or lifestyle appeal, department stores are beginning to fight back by using technology to better manage their marketing channels in order to lower prices.

Discount department stores, commonly called *discounters,* are an outgrowth of the traditional department store. These stores first appeared in the mid-1940s, just after World War II, and featured low prices in a no-frills low-service setting. Like traditional department stores, discounters carry a variety of product lines and use departmental merchandising techniques. However, they do so at lower prices than traditional department stores. Their lower prices are the result of offering fewer customer services, having less upscale facilities, and using self-service to reduce operating expenses. Examples include Target, Kohl's, and Wal-Mart. These stores usually range in size from 40,000 to 100,000 square feet. Most communities with a population of more than 10,000 have either a traditional department store or a discount department store. Strong growth is forecasted for this format as the discounters open new stores, including supercenters, add new product categories, and use their scale efficiencies and purchasing power to lower prices.

Natural Forces

Many apparel retailers have seen their profits vanish when they failed to take early markdowns and, in mid-to-late July, they were still using their valuable endcaps to sell excess summerwear. This was occurring when high-markup and high-impulse "back to school" clothing was arriving at their docks.

The Grinch that Stole Christmas in 2002

Since 25–30% of a retailer's annual sales (excluding grocery operations) occur in November and December, it is easy to see why Christmas is the retailer's most important season. No wonder retailers spend a great deal of time forecasting and planning for this season. Such was the case in 2002, when retailers entered the season with the lowest expectations in more than a decade. However, traditional retailers were blindsided by an unforeseen action taken by a new breed of seller.

Back in June 2002, retailers were already making plans for a poor Christmas season. Most experts predicted that, since consumers were tightening their purse strings, retailers would be happy with a sales increase of only 3% more than the prior year. Several factors contributed to this dismal forecast.

- The traditional Thanksgiving-to-Christmas shopping period would be six days shorter, as Thanksgiving in 2002 was on November 28, compared to November 22 in 2001.
- The country was in the third year of an economic recession, September 11 was still in the minds of most consumers, and the unemployment level had reached a six-year high.
- The stock market was down by more than 50% since January 2000, resulting in a loss of $8 trillion in personal wealth.
- The nation was preparing for a possible war with Iraq.
- A dockworkers' strike was expected that would cause inventory problems for retailers.

Despite these problems, retailers hoped to save Christmas with a higher-than-average number of promotional activities built around hot-selling items. In fact, some experts joked that the post-Christmas sales actually began the Friday after Thanksgiving. That's when retailers first noticed their problem: They were out of all their hot items by early December. The grinch was eBay.

eBay is the leading online marketplace for the sale of goods and services by a diverse community of individuals and businesses, with 49.7 million registered users. It is the most popular shopping site on the Internet when measured by total user minutes, according to Media Metrix. Since its founding in September 1995, eBay has become the new arena for "microretailers" operating out of their homes to reach a global marketplace. Microretailers are small one- or two-person retail organizations.

Imagine, for a moment, competing against the world's best-known retailers from your living room. But that is what happened. When consumers started hunting for the popular toys, such as a FurReal Friend, a $35 robotic cat that purrs when you pet it, they could not find any in the stores. However, there were plenty on eBay for more than $100 each. It seems a combination of advance planning, intuition, and advice from eBay Inc. prompted these micromerchants to stock up on these hot items. In fact, in late October, eBay sent its micromerchants a list of 20 toys it expected to be big sellers and encouraged them to stock up.

Soon these "mom-and-pop" retailers went into action by picking up all the hot items whenever they arrived at neighborhood stores. In the past, eBay was considered a last chance for hot items like "Tickle Me Elmo." In 2002, though, eBay became the merchant of last resort because it encouraged its microretailers to scour stores and other potential sources before the masses began snapping everything up after Thanksgiving.

In the weeks before Christmas, consumers around the country were writing letters to their editors complaining about the unethical behavior of both eBay and its eBayers. These writers claimed that the behavior of eBay and it members kept their little darlings from getting the toys they wanted. What especially angered some writers was the fact that, since eBayers were operating with very low overhead and really were not taking a big risk on being stuck with excess inventory, why should they be allowed to take such high markups?

DISCUSSION QUESTIONS

1. Were the eBayers behaving unethically?
2. Many economists believe that economic freedom is a good thing. Would a ban on eBayers performing as they did be bad for our country's economic system?

Specialty Stores

Specialty stores are relatively small-scale stores offering a great deal of product depth within a narrow range of product lines. Specialty stores are common in women's wear, men's wear, jewelry, footwear, electronics, furniture, sporting goods, automotive supplies, painting supplies, flowers, liquor, pets, bridal wear, and fabrics. Many specialty stores range from 3,000 to 7,500 square feet, although some are much smaller, and others, such as furniture stores, which can occupy more than 100,000 square feet, are much larger. Some popular specialty stores are The Gap (leisure wear), Hickory Farms (specialty cheeses and snacks), AutoZone (automotive supplies), Walgreens (drugstores), and Foot Locker (jogging and athletic shoes).

Most successful specialty stores pursue a strong store-positioning strategy. Here, all the elements of the store's marketing mix are aimed at a well-defined target mar-

dELiA's is a specialty store that reaches its customers through 65 retail stores, a catalog, and delias.com. The marketing mix at dELiA's is carefully aimed at teenage girls interested in trendy clothing.

ket, which is segmented from the total market based on some specific demographic or lifestyle variable. Christopher & Banks, formerly known as Braun's, for example, is a specialty apparel retailer where fashion is not a strong draw. Instead, the chain offers moderately priced, private-label apparel for working women age 35 to 55 with families. dELiA's, on the other hand, caters to the special whims of teenage girls through its retail stores, catalogs, and Web site.

Given the continued aging of the U.S population, the record introductions of new remedies and drugs, and the record number of Americans with health insurance, drugstores are one of the types of specialty stores for which sales volume is expected to surge over the next decade.

Supermarkets

The *supermarket* concept of retailing developed in the 1930s, when the Great Depression forced many grocers to replace their small, inefficient, traditional, mom-and-pop corner stores in order to offer consumers lower prices. Selling groceries and some general-merchandise products through large-scale physical facilities with self-service and self-selection displays enabled the supermarket retailer to shift the performance of some distribution functions to consumers. Today, most grocery retailing is still done through supermarkets such as Safeway, Albertsons, and Kroger, although supercenters are rapidly gaining market share. Wal-Mart, however, with its new neighborhood stores, as well as its supercenters (discussed next), is now the nation's volume leader in grocery sales.

The supermarket concept involves five basic principles directed at improving retail productivity and reducing the cost of distribution:

1. Self-service and self-selection displays
2. Centralization of customer services at the checkout counter/desk
3. Large-scale, low-cost physical facilities
4. A strong price emphasis
5. A broad assortment of merchandise to facilitate multiple-item purchases

Recently, the supermarket retailing concept has been used in developing two new types of nonfood retailing, which are discussed later: the supercenter and the category

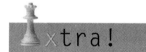

Scrambled merchandising
Is the handling of merchandise lines based solely on the profitability criterion without regard to the consistency of the product or merchandise mix.

killer. In addition to expanding the supermarket concept to include new types of stores, the traditional food supermarket's product mix is being expanded to include prepared, or ready-to-eat, foods. For example, many supermarkets now offer HMRs (home-meal-replacements) to compete with fast-food operators, as well as nonfood items such as clothing, small appliances, automotive supplies, nonprescription drugs, cosmetics, and fragrances. This phenomenon is referred to as **scrambled merchandising**. This results in unrelated lines of merchandise being carried by a single retailer. For example, convenience stores today sell gasoline, bread, milk, beer, cigarettes, phone cards, lottery tickets, magazines, and even fast food. Supermarkets sell HBA (health and beauty aid) products, videos, some apparel items, stamps, and prescription drugs.

Over the next decade, as more supercenters and wholesale clubs are opened and Americans eat out more often, thereby lowering their need for groceries, the growth in supermarket sales is not expected to match the overall level of inflation. The growth of wholesale clubs such as Sam's Club and Costco is particularly alarming for supermarkets, since the demographics of club shoppers are actually more similar to heavy users of supermarkets. And, the club channel is driving sales in categories like fresh meat and fresh produce that have traditionally been a real stronghold for supermarkets. This lower level of sales growth should foster industry consolidation as the remaining players seek to become more competitive.

Supercenters

One of the newest competitive retail types within the store-based format is the *supercenter*. These cavernous, one-stop, combination supermarkets and discount department stores, which range in size from 120,000 to 160,000 square feet, carry between 80,000 and 100,000 products, ranging from televisions to peanut butter to fax machines to tires and gasoline. In addition, these retailers often lease space to noncompetitors offering services, such as in-store banking, hair styling, fast food, and eye-care.[10] Cross-shopping is a major appeal, as the customer has the availability of general merchandise, services, prescriptions, and gas at one location. The availability of such one-stop shopping draws customers from a 30- to 50-mile radius in some rural areas and lowers the customer's total cost of purchasing in terms of time and stores visited, without sacrificing service and variety.

Wal-Mart, Kmart, and Target are banking their future on this new format. Yet, while they are adding a combined 500 new supercenters a year, some retail analysts question whether older consumers can get around in these stores, whether younger ones will take the time to shop in these mammoth stores, and whether folks will buy tires, apparel, and tomatoes on the same shopping trip. Nevertheless, since the country's major retailer, Wal-Mart, is using supercenters as its vehicle for growth over the next decade, it is difficult to predict failure. Some retailers are prepared for customer dissatisfaction with supercenters. For example, as mentioned earlier, Dollar General has revamped its 6,000 small-sized discount stores to handle more paper goods and other frequently purchased general merchandise. In addition, supermarkets, which have always operated with paper-thin net-profit margins, are seeking to match, if not beat, the supercenters' prices.

Category killers
Get their name from their marketing strategy of carrying such a large amount of merchandise in a single category at such good prices that they make it impossible for customers to walk out without purchasing what they need, thus "killing" the competition.

Category Killers

Essentially the ultimate in specialty stores, the **category killer** got its name from its marketing strategy: carry such a large amount of merchandise in a single category at such good prices that it makes it impossible for customers to walk out without purchasing what they need; thus "killing" the competition.

Toys "R" Us, which began operations in the 1950s as an out-growth of a baby furniture store, has the distinction of being the first category killer. Today, Toys "R" Us operates more than 700 toy stores in the United States and has a presence in more than 28 countries.[11]

Over the last two decades, the category-killer retail format exploded. Some other well-known category killers include: Best Buy, Home Depot, Lowe's, Blockbuster Video, Circuit City, Office Depot, Office Max, PetsMart, Bed Bath & Beyond, Auto-Zone, Barnes & Noble, and Sports Authority. Many category killers are also diverting business away from traditional wholesale supply houses. For example, Home Depot and Lowe's appeal to professional contractors and Office Depot and Office Max to business owners who traditionally purchased supplies from hardware wholesalers and office supply and equipment wholesalers.

Convenience Stores

Convenience stores (c-stores) are generally small (2,000 to 4,000 square feet) and offer products such as fast food, beverages, household staples, and gasoline. C-stores serve the neighborhood within 1.5 miles of the store. Because these stores offer greater time, place, and possession utility to the consumer, while operating with a lower inventory-turnover rate than do larger grocery stores, c-stores often charge higher prices on comparable items. 7-Eleven, the originator of the c-store concept, is still this country's largest c-store chain, although it is now owned by Japan's Ito-Yokado Corporation. Unit growth of this format is coming from the major oil companies, such as ChevronTexaco and Conoco, which have been rapidly converting conventional gasoline stations into modern convenience stores. In addition, sales of lottery tickets, beverages, candy, and snacks, as well as food services, should offset the loss of tobacco sales and the uncertainty of future gasoline prices.

Nonstore-Based Retailers

Several industry analysts contend that changes in nonstore-based operators will lead to the next revolution in retailing. The mechanics for such a revolution are already in place as a variety of established selling techniques permit consumers to purchase goods and services without having to leave home. With accelerated communications technology and changing consumer lifestyles, the growth potential for nonstore retailing is explosive. Five types of nonstore retailing will be discussed: street peddling, direct selling, mail-order, automatic-merchandising machine operators, and electronic shopping.

In addition, the move into multiformat retailing has accelerated over the past few years. The previously mentioned dELiA's now reaches its consumers through the dELiA's catalog, dELiAs.com Web site, and 65 dELiA's retail stores. These retailers have successfully expanded onto the Internet by leveraging their direct-marketing skills and established distribution network. Other Internet operators, such as the nation's number-one online stockbroker, Charles Schwab, are adding physical outlets to generate additional traffic for their sites. (Interestingly enough, while Schwab does 80% of its transactions electronically, it opens 70% of its new accounts face-to-face in branch offices.)[12] Many store-based retailers, such as Target, are not only continuing to build traditional stores but are developing and enhancing their Web sites. This latter group has found that their Internet sites not only generate online sales but also increase sales in their traditional store-based outlets. According to one study, consumers who visit a retailer's Web site before shopping in the store spend 33% more on an annual basis than regular in-store shoppers.[13]

Street Peddling. Retailing has changed drastically throughout the history of this country. The United States has evolved from a nation dependent on *street peddlers* selling their products in the streets, open markets, or via covered wagons, to small stores near the geographic center of the town, to neighborhood shopping strips, and today to massive supercenters and indoor shopping malls in the suburbs.

Street peddling is still common in many parts of the world. To this day, peddlers sell their merchandise from pushcarts or temporary stalls set up on a street. Even today, in the United States, street peddlers are commonly seen on street corners in

Sociocultural Forces

The increase in the number of street peddlers is an outgrowth of the increase in the number of pedestrians with disposable income.

major metropolitan areas. Here they sell inexpensive items such as T-shirts, watches, books, magazines, tobacco, candy, and hot dogs, or provide a service, as do street-side sketch artists and musicians.

Many cities view the presence of street peddlers as positive. It gives an area a distinctive flavor not unlike that of New Orleans' French Quarter. Other cities, due to pressure from store-based retailers who pay higher taxes and support many community activities, are considering a ban on this retail format.

Direct Selling. Direct selling establishments engage in the sale of a consumer product or service on a person-to-person basis away from a fixed retail location using party plans (The Pampered Chef Ltd.) or one-to-one selling in the home or workplace (Avon Products Inc.). In the United States, more than 12.2 million independent distributors, also called representatives, consultants, and small business owners, who are not employed by the organization they represent, generate direct sales that total about $26.69 billion annually. More than 90% of all direct sellers operate their businesses part-time. Currently, the United States is the leading market followed by Japan ($24.5 billion) and Korea ($4.62 billion) in worldwide sales from direct selling in 43 countries that total about $83 billion annnually. Major product categories include cosmetics and skin care items (Mary Kay Inc., Nu Skin Enterprises), decorative home products (Princess House Inc., CUTCO Corp.), and Nutritional Supplements (Herbalife International, Shaklee Corp.).

Some of today's direct selling companies are incorporating additional marketing channels, such as catalogs, kiosks, and the Internet to augment sales from traditional direct selling. The major attributes of direct selling remain the same: product quality and uniqueness, knowledge and demonstration of the product by the salesperson, excellent warranties and guarantees, and the person-to-person component.[14]

Mail-Order. *Mail-order houses,* which generate annual sales of $65 billion, are primarily engaged in the retail sale of products by catalog and mail-order. Included are book and music clubs, jewelry firms, novelty-merchandise firms, and specialty merchandisers, such as sporting goods (L.L. Bean), children's apparel retailers (Right Start), and kitchenware (Williams-Sonoma). Although mail-order retailers continue to offer their merchandise via print catalogs, which produce a profit of $2.20 per mailed catalog,[15] almost all have also begun to offer their merchandise online.

While mail-order houses have done a great job of segmenting the overall market for their particular offerings, increasing postal and paper costs may negatively affect the future of this retail format. To combat these cost increases, many catalog operations are relying on the use of new printing strategies that lower the overall cost of printing.

A modern form of mail-order retailing is the television shopping network. While they use a video/electronic presentation with a different medium, they operate the same as their mail-order counterparts.

Automatic-Merchandising Machine Operators. Automatic-merchandising machine operators are primarily engaged in the retail sale of products by means of automatic-merchandising units, or vending machines. Surprisingly, such machines have been with us since about 215 B.C., when Egyptians devised a coin-operated water dispenser for places of worship.[16] To be designated a vending machine, a machine must dispense a product in exchange for money, and operate unattended, except for refills and repairs. Therefore, sales made by coin-operated service machines, such as amusements, videos, and game machines, are not included.

Because laws in every state prohibit the sale of tobacco products to persons under the age of 18, retailers or owners of businesses that sell cigarettes or other tobacco products are required to post a conspicuous sign stating that tobacco sales to minors are illegal and that proof of age is required to purchase tobacco products. Such requirements are expected to limit the use of vending machines for cigarette sales, which will negatively affect total vending-machine sales in the future.

Electronic Shopping. Many of the early e-tailers may have forgotten an important marketing lesson from the past. Being first into a market does not guarantee success. Most of the early entrants into e-tailing had a problem with their marketing plan: They believed that market share was more important than profits. As a result, they not only gave away cameras in an attempt to sell film but also gave away the film, free developing, and postage. Their marketing plan forgot one of the simple rules of any business: Cash in must exceed cash out. Little wonder, then, that according to http://www.webmergers.com, a total of 895 Internet companies shut down or declared bankruptcy between January 2000 and September 30, 2002. Additionally, the study tracked more than 3,700 healthy or distressed Internet companies that have been acquired by or merged with other companies.[17]

Still, out of these failures will come businesses that will truly introduce a "new economy." As the Internet grows to allow real-time, fully immersive, three-dimensional video, Americans will spend more of their time in cyberspace. This in turn will create a whole new shopping experience. Future shoppers will opt for the convenience and heightened experience of virtual shopping. Browsing will be even easier and the choices more extensive. As a result, conversion rates—the percentage of shoppers who actually make a purchase—will increase to the rates enjoyed by brick-and-mortar retailers.

Consumers will still want social activity and connections outside the home; however, e-tailing will likely evolve beyond shopping to include real entertainment, such as attending a sporting event or concert where, incidentally, a lot of merchandise and food will be offered for sale. The Internet will allow consumers to shop with family and friends, even if they live half the world away. In fact, the most encouraging news about the Net's future may be that online shoppers are getting poorer and older. What is so good about that? Currently, most Net shoppers are young and affluent. This new projection means that e-tailers selling to the mass market will stand to gain.[18]

However, before conceding that e-tailing will replace the traditional store, it may be advisable to consider several key facts:

1. The Internet will not increase overall consumer demand. In terms of overall consumer spending, online sales will definitely affect store and catalog sales. This cannibalization of sales will vary across product categories. Online shopping, which in 2002 accounted for less than 2% of retail sales, will be big for airline tickets, PCs, hotel reservations, books, music, and video. However, online shopping will remain a minor player for all other categories, at least until technology dramatically improves.

2. Clicks-and-brick strategies that integrate a single message will be more powerful than a pure e-tailing strategy. This will be especially true once clicks-and-brick retailers, who operate both online and from traditional stores, learn the importance of reinforcing their Internet presence with in-store kiosks.

3. E-tailers must pay better attention to customer service. Most e-tailers tend to do a good job during busy seasons, such as Christmas. However, in an effort to reduce operating costs, they reduce their service standards at other times. Customers are demanding such basic services as e-mail confirmation of orders, availability of real-time inventory, and more product information, including the ability to view close-up product images online.

4. Internet shoppers would probably buy more online if they could return items more easily. Until e-tailers copy catalog retailers in offering free shipping and returns, the Internet will never reach its true potential.

Retail mix
Is a retailer's combination of merchandise, prices, advertising, location, customer services, selling, and store layout and design that is used to attract customers.

Managing the Retail Mix

Like all marketers, retailers must first identify their target market and then determine the specific **retail mix** that will appeal to this target market in order to perform the first two retailing tasks discussed earlier in this chapter: (1) attract consumers to come inside their store, and (2) turn these consumers into loyal customers by enticing them to make a purchase. A retail mix is a combination of merchandise, price, advertising and promotion, customer services and selling, and store layout and design.

Atmospherics

When developing their retail mix, retailers must begin by realizing that the store (or Web site) is a major part of their offering. After all, the retailer must create a positive image for the store/Web site. *Atmospherics* is the use of merchandise, level of service offered by employees, fixtures, floor layout, sound, and odor to influence customers' perceptions. Brick-and-mortar retailers, for example, need to be concerned with how customers perceive the in-store environment and whether they are comfortable in it. Customers are more likely to make larger and more frequent purchases if a store's total environment is comfortable and welcoming and encourages browsing.

Attracting Consumers

Many retailers think this is one of their most difficult tasks—getting people to visit their Web site or to come into their store. Research has pointed out that it costs the average retailer five times as much to get a consumer to enter a store for the first time than it does to keep one or even get an unhappy customer to return. In the chapter's opening vignette, we discussed how supermarkets are organized to move merchan-

xtra!

Atmospherics is the use of merchandise, floor layout, odor, and sound to influence customers' perceptions. To attract customers inside its store and make them feel comfortable, L.L. Bean uses bright, colorful displays that showcase their merchandise.

© Susan Van Etten

dise inside the store. But what got customers inside that store in the first place? The starting point is the store's image in the mind of the consumer. A store's image includes the merchandise carried in the store, along with the retailer's promotional activities, customer service, the salesforce, and the physical appearance of the store itself. For example, furniture retailers that want to project a high-status image will carry Heritage, Henredon, and other upscale furniture lines. Austrian crystal and Irish linen are not likely to be found in the same housewares department as plastic glasses and oilcloth table coverings. Customers select where to shop for particular items according to their overall perception of the available stores. Mothers might well go first to Target or Wal-Mart for children's playwear, but would probably skip over these stores in favor of Dillard's, Bloomingdale's, or a specialty store when shopping for their daughter's dress for a school dance.

Store fixtures must also be consistent with the overall image the retailer wishes to project. Suits crowded together on plastic coat hangers do not reflect the image of quality that similar suits project when hung on wooden hangers with ample space on the rack to facilitate customer browsing. If a retailer wants the store to project a quality image, the display units themselves must be adequately spaced and accessible. The aisles must be uncongested and well laid out, and related products should be placed close enough to promote ancillary purchases (e.g., a handbag to complement a newly purchased pair of shoes).

Effective store design must appeal to the human senses of sight, sound, smell, and touch. Obviously, as pointed out in the opening vignette, the majority of design activity in a retail store is focused on affecting sight, but research has shown that the other senses can also be very important. Since smell is believed to be the most closely linked of all the senses to memory and emotions, retailers hope that its use as an in-store marketing tool will put consumers in the "mood," such as Victoria's Secret, with its potpourri caches deployed throughout its stores.

Retailers have piped music, such as Muzak, into their stores for generations, believing that a musical backdrop will create a more relaxing environment and encourage customers to stay longer. However, the music must match the merchandise being offered. For example, a jeans retailer might play hip-hop over the baggies and classic rock over the Dockers. Also, while soothing classical music has been shown to encourage customers to shop longer and select more expensive merchandise, it may be inconsistent with the desired ambience of a trendy fashion store catering to college-age women.

However, other factors beyond the control of the retailer and the store's atmospherics can affect the traffic level. The factors that affect the retailer's ability to attract customers include the following:

- **Store compatibility.** Research has found that retailers experience a benefit from *store compatibility*. That is, when two compatible, or very similar, businesses (e.g., two shoe stores) locate near each other, they will show an increase in sales volume greater than what they would have achieved if they were located apart from each other.[19] Today we see this clustering with shoe stores in malls, auto dealerships, furniture stores, and restaurants. Clustering of stores allows customers to walk from store to store, comparing prices, goods, and service.
- **Natural forces.** Probably the major uncontrollable factor facing any retailer is the weather. Retailers want it warm in the spring so they can sell spring/summer clothing and cool in the early fall so they can sell those sweaters and jackets. Otherwise, consumers will tend to postpone these purchases. In fact, a retailer's Christmas season can be ruined by a blizzard the weekend before Christmas.
- **Economic Forces.** Any type of change in the economy, either slowdown or pickup, will affect the ability of retailers to get consumers into their store.

Competitive Forces

About the only situation where compatible retailers do not achieve a greater sales volume when located in close proximity to each other is with membership retailers, such as wholesale clubs and fitness centers. After all, consumers have already paid to use one of the retailers, so it is doubtful that they will pay to shop at the other.

Political and Legal Forces

The impact of political and legal forces has been made more evident by the events of September 11. Some shoppers will avoid shopping in a major mall or store for fear of security[20] and others may stay home because of what is now called the "CNN Effect," where shoppers stay home watching television for late-breaking news. This was true in the weeks and months immediately after September 11 and also for the 30 days of ballot counting in Florida in 2000.

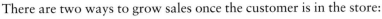

Turning Consumers into Loyal Customers

There are two ways to grow sales once the customer is in the store:

1. Increase the average number of units sold of typically purchased product lines.
2. Motivate the customer to purchase additional products not normally purchased in this store.

To achieve these dual objectives, retailers need the right merchandise, the right layout and display, and the right salesforce. In this vein, the success of Dollar General and Family Dollar is not just about people on budgets or the result of a soft economy. They thrive because consumers enter the stores for convenience and they realize that it's human nature to want to get something for (almost) nothing. Thus many of the purchases here tend to be incremental because of the way the store is laid out.

Another simple retailing strategy for creating a competitive advantage is the delivery of high-quality service. Good service must meet or exceed the customer's expectations. Most retailers never actually measure customer service. They just believe their employees when they claim that they give the customers good service. Yet, one research study found that one-third of customers who entered a store with the expressed intent of making a specific purchase walked out without making any purchase. The reason was that the shoppers either had no contact with sales personnel or, if they had contact, it was probably the wrong kind.[21] It is obvious that a small increase in converting these nonpurchasing consumers into customers will increase sales dramatically, even if the shopper is only in the store as a way to combat loneliness.

Operating in the Most Efficient Manner

A store's environment must maximize its space productivity, a goal summarized in a simple but powerful truism in retailing: The more merchandise customers are exposed to that is presented in an orderly manner, the more they tend to buy. The typical shopper in a department store goes into only two or three shopping areas per trip. Through careful planning of the store environment, the retailer can encourage customers to flow through the entire store, or at least more shopping areas, and see a wider variety of merchandise. The proper use of in-store advertising and displays will let customers know what is happening in other shopping areas and encourage visits to those areas. Conversely, however, the store does not want to push merchandise into every conceivable nook and cranny of the store so that customers cannot get to it.

Today's successful retailers are aware that most of a product's cost gets added after the item is produced and moves from the factory to the retailer's shelf and finally to the consumer. Thus, good strategies to reduce operating costs while providing the appropriate level of service present significant opportunities for retailers. Sam Walton found out early that when your costs are low, your prices can be low, and your profits will increase. Wal-Mart's success can be attributed to being the first discounter to make a major commitment to its integrated use of the computer. It changed the way retailers now do business. Today, Wal-Mart's computers enable it not only to scan sales but also to make certain that inbound shipments coming in one side of a distribution center are transferred to the correct dock on the other side of the center for shipment to more than 3,000 stores.

Another means of cutting costs is by having happy employees. As was pointed out in Chapter 10, employee satisfaction and customer satisfaction are directly related. Therefore, a critical job for retailers today is retaining current employees.[22] A recent study of the supermarket industry found, for example, that the median

Technological Forces
Wal-Mart's computers not only manage product movement within the distribution centers but also connect the stores, distribution centers, and vendors to Wal-Mart's headquarters in Arkansas via satellite.

Do Retailers Really Understand the Latino Consumer?

It is important that all marketers understand the purchase behavior of their targeted Latino consumer, their attitudes and beliefs, and the size of the opportunity, before they can think of successfully marketing to Latinos. Given the size of the opportunity and its importance to the future growth of many companies, it is crucial that food marketers begin to understand the Latino consumer now or potentially miss out on the largest opportunity of this century.

Consider, for example, the grocers catering to Latino consumers. One of the very successful operators is San Jose's Mi Pueblo Foods. While many outside observers would attribute Mi Pueblo's success to the layout and design of its stores—an intricate floor-tile pattern, stucco textured walls, faux windows, adobe roof tiles, faux balconies, large bins of beans, walls of spices, and hanging sides of meat—that is not the case. What really sets Mi Pueblo apart from other grocers is its understanding of the Latina female and her shopping habits.

Most grocery stores in the United States, recognizing the time poverty of the average household, feature prepared foods. Yet, as a study by ACNielsen and Cultural Access Group found out, this is not always the case. Less acculturated Latina women feel it is easier to cook from scratch, since that is what they have always done. Such dishes made with traditional ingredients are less stressful to prepare. However, for more acculturated women, who are more likely to be working and familiar with the benefits of prepared foods, the opposite is true. Prepared foods for these shoppers, who are more likely to shop mainstream stores such as Safeway, are fast, easy, and consistent with their new lifestyle.

Value orientation also plays a big role. For the less acculturated Latina, detailed food preparation is an expression of love for her family and goes to the heart of her identity as a Latino woman and mother. Cooking is also a vehicle for passing on traditions. A fully acculturated Latina understands that simplified food preparation allows her to focus on her career and other interests and is guilt free. Therefore, while a Latina woman who is less acculturated may quickly understand the benefits of prepared foods from a convenience standpoint, her values will be more difficult to change, and even when prepared foods are served, she will feel significant guilt. An interesting point that should not be lost in this discussion is that the second- or third-generation homemaker, while fully acculturated in American society, will still want to prepare traditional holiday foods from scratch for her family.

Source: Based on material supplied by Phil Lempert, editor of the FMI/ACNielsen/Lempert E-Newsletter; Mike Tolley, Mi Pueblo Foods; and Paul Adams.

---

retention rate of hourly supermarket employees was 97 days. That is, one-half of all new supermarket hires terminate their employment within 97 days of starting work.[23] The study further found that the cost (including both direct and opportunity costs) of replacing an hourly employee was $4,291 for a union store and $3,372 for a nonunion store.[24] In all, employee turnover costs the average supermarket almost $190,000 annually in direct and opportunity costs.[25] Turnover is thought to be an even more serious problem in specialty stores, since they typically hire part-timers in entry-level positions.

Other innovative ways of cutting expenses are to build stores with roll-up doors to let fresh air in and help cool the store, place windows just under the roofline to cut lighting costs, and use unthirsty plants.[26]

Another factor that hurts a store's productivity is shrinkage, or the loss of merchandise through theft, loss, and damage. It is called **shrinkage** because you usually do not know what happened to the missing items, only that the inventory level in the store has somehow shrunk. Even stores that move customers through the entire space and effectively use in-store marketing techniques to maximize sales can fall victim to high shrinkage. Remember, when a store sells an item for $1.29, it earns only a small percentage of that sale, perhaps ranging from 15 to 60 cents. When an item is stolen, lost, or damaged, however, the store loses the cost of that item (e.g., 69 cents in the case of the $1.29 item), and this loss is deducted from the store's overall sales. Shrinkage ranges from 1–4% of retail sales. While this may seem like a small number, consider that many retailers' after-tax profit is little more than 4%, so high shrinkage alone can make the difference between a profit and a loss.

Shrinkage
Refers to reduction of merchandise through theft, loss, and/or damage.

Xtra!

Category management
Is a process of managing and planning all SKUs in a product category as a distinct business.

SKU
Is a stock-keeping unit and refers to a distinct merchandise item in the retailer's merchandise assortment.

Category Management

One way to reduce costs is to use category management. Because of the increasing cost of carrying inventory, the shortening of retail life cycles, the more rapid turning of the wheel of retailing, and the rapid growth of hypercompetitive retailers (especially category killers, supercenters, and Internet-based competitors), retailers have turned their attention to category management as the best way to reduce unnecessary costs. **Category management** is a process of managing and planning all SKUs within a product category as a distinct business so that the store can optimally use shelf space to generate the highest profits. A **SKU**, or stock-keeping unit, refers to a distinct merchandise item in the retailer's merchandise assortment. When all SKUs in a category are managed as a business unit, every store has the proper assortment to match its customers' preferences. The end result is an increased ability to get consumers from the retailer's trading area into their store, convert these consumers into paying customers, while operating in the most efficient manner so as to reduce operating costs.

Because retailers handle thousands of SKUs, they have found category management to be an extremely effective marketing tool. For example, a grocery-store chain that stocks up to 35,000 SKUs may decide to have a category manager for laundry products. This category manager would first need to define the category, perhaps as detergent and soap products. Next, it would be important to determine where customers purchased detergent/soap products. Although in the past, consumers may have primarily purchased these items at grocery stores, the category manager would now find that detergent/soap products are also frequently purchased at discounters, supercenters, and warehouse clubs. The category manager would also be interested in the major brands and their share of the market. For example, within this category, Procter & Gamble alone manufactures seven products—Bold, Cheer, Dreft, Era, Gain, Ivory, and Tide. It would be helpful to know if these brands have different penetration levels in different marketing channels as well.

Each of the brands would have certain attributes that influence purchases, including price, added softening agents, whitening/brightening powers, stain-removal power, and whether the product is color-safe. With this knowledge and an understanding of the store's target market and its competition, the category manager would develop a coordinated retail mix for the detergent/soap category, including which brands to stock, price points and price lines to establish, in-store display and shelf-space allocation, and advertising expenditures and promotional activities, such as couponing.

But how does a category manager make these marketing decisions? Retailers track what is selling by scanning products at checkout. The information goes into databases, then into category-management software programs that analyze what shoppers are buying and what they're leaving on the shelves. The major goal of the category manager is to achieve a certain level of profit per square foot of space (allocated to the product category) and profit per dollar or linear foot of inventory investment (in the product category). These two measures of financial performance guide all marketing decisions. The category manager quickly realizes that he or she cannot infinitely increase the number of SKUs to better serve customers. This would require more inventory and space resources, which are extremely valuable and constrained. There are approximately 300 different detergent/soap SKUs; by stocking all these SKUs, the retailer would certainly increase the likelihood of serving its customers. However, that might not be very profitable. More likely, the category manager may determine that 40 to 50 SKUs will serve 80–90% of the retailer's customer base or target market. Therefore, determining the retailer's target market, which will be a particular socioeconomic class, will help to determine the most popular detergent/ soap SKUs that should be stocked and promoted.

Wholesaling in the U.S. Economy

4 **LEARNING OBJECTIVE**

As noted at the beginning of this chapter, **wholesaling** is a larger sector of the U.S. economy than retailing. Total wholesale sales by the nation's 460,000 wholesalers are almost $4.3 trillion,[27] compared to retailing's $3.3 trillion. Why are wholesale sales greater than retail sales? The answer lies in the fact that wholesalers sell not only to retailers but also to manufacturers and other wholesalers. In fact, wholesalers can and do operate differently in the various types of marketing channels discussed in the previous chapter.

Wholesaling
Involves the activities of persons or establishments that sell to retailers and/or other organizational buyers for industrial, institutional, and commercial use, but do not sell in significant amounts to final consumers.

Types of Wholesalers

Some wholesalers provide a wide range of services or handle broad lines of goods. Others specialize in selling only to other wholesalers or manufacturers, and still others never take title to or physical possession of the merchandise they are selling. As shown in Figure 12.8, wholesalers can be grouped into three broad categories: manufacturer's sales branches, merchant wholesalers, and agent/brokers.

Figure 12.9 shows the state of wholesaling today. Three facts and trends are apparent from this figure:

- Manufacturer's sales branches have the highest sales per establishment.
- Merchant wholesalers now account for about 50% of sales.
- Agents and brokers are the smallest category, when considering both total sales and establishments.

Types of Wholesalers		Figure 12.8
• **Manufacturer's sales branches**	Include both sales outlets (which carry inventory) and sales offices (which don't carry inventory) owned by the manufacturer.	
• **Merchant wholesalers**	Independent firms that purchase a product from the manufacturer and resell it to other manufacturers, wholesalers, or retailers, but not to the final consumer. Merchant wholesalers can be categorized as full-service or limited-service wholesalers: Full-service merchant wholesalers provide a wide range of services for retailers and business purchasers. Limited-service merchant wholesalers perform only a few services for manufacturers or their customers or perform all of them on a more restricted basis than do full-service wholesalers.	
• **Agents/brokers**	Never take title to the merchandise. Their key function is to help bring potential buyers and sellers together.	

| Figure 12.9 | Percentage of Sales and Establishments by Type of Wholesaler, 1929–1997 |

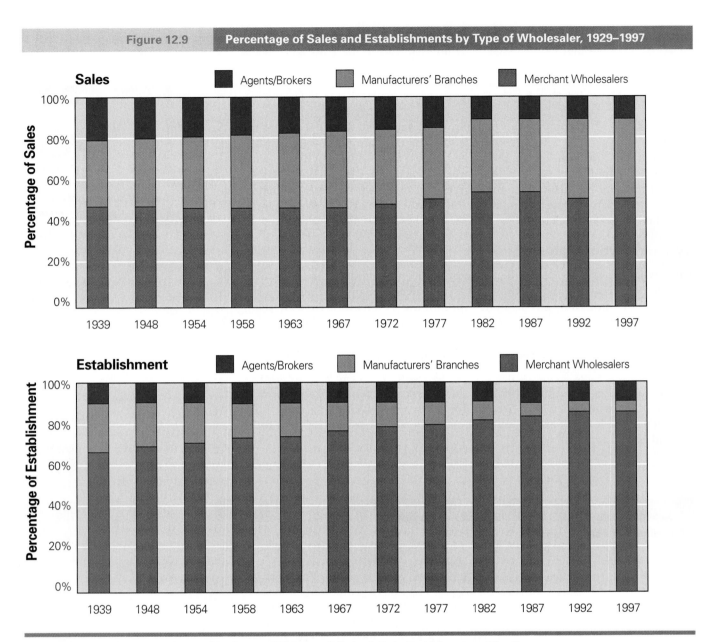

Source: Department of Commerce, Bureau of the Census, 1997 Census of Wholesale Trade, Establishments and Firm Size.

Manufacturers' sales branches

Are sales outlets owned by the manufacturer.

Manufacturers' Sales Branches

Manufacturers' sales branches actually include both *sales outlets* (which carry full inventory) and *sales offices* (which do not carry inventory) that are owned by the manufacturer. The reasons why a manufacturer might choose to distribute its goods directly through company-owned facilities include:

- Distribution of some perishable goods needs to be rigidly controlled to avoid spoilage.
- The goods have a high value per unit, causing other middlemen not to want to handle the line.
- The goods require complex installation or servicing.
- The goods need aggressive promotion.

When inventory is carried at these outlets, the manufacturer is essentially performing most, if not all, of the wholesaling function. Predictably, the operating expenses of these outlets increase as the value of the inventory carried in stock increases. Black & Decker is an example of a manufacturer that uses its own sales branches and sales force to strengthen customer relations with key accounts, such as Home Depot and Lowe's. In addition, these branch outlets provide service and display merchandise for other local dealers.

As Figure 12.9 points out, manufacturers' sales branches comprise less than 7% of wholesale establishments[28]—but these operations account for nearly one-third of all wholesale sales. A major reason for the high sales per branch outlet is that they are usually placed in the largest metropolitan markets and serve as a base of operation for the manufacturer's sales staff when calling on a large customer base.

Merchant Wholesalers

Some manufacturers have found that it is more profitable to use merchant wholesalers rather than their own outlets to sell directly to retailers or other business firms. **Merchant wholesalers**, which are independent firms, purchase a product from a manufacturer, take title to that product, and resell it to other manufacturers, wholesalers, or retailers, but not to the final consumer. These middlemen are used when it is not economical for the manufacturer's salespeople to call directly on its users or to send them separate shipments. Thus, the merchant wholesaler provides economies of scale to the manufacturer. For example, if each merchant wholesaler has 200 accounts, the manufacturer can reach 2,000 customers by selling to only 10 wholesalers, thereby reducing selling and distribution costs. Merchant wholesalers can be categorized as full-service or limited-service wholesalers.

A **full-service merchant wholesaler** provides a wide range of services for retailers and business purchasers, such as storing merchandise in a convenient location and allowing customers to make purchases on short notice, thus minimizing their inventory costs. The full-service wholesaler typically maintains a sales force to call on retailers, manufacturers, and other wholesalers; make deliveries; and extend credit to qualified buyers. The three most common full-service wholesalers are:

> **Merchant wholesalers**
> *Are independent firms that purchase a product from a manufacturer and resell it to other manufacturers, wholesalers, or retailers, but not to the final consumer.*

> **Full-service merchant wholesalers**
> *Provide a wide range of services for retailers and business purchasers.*

1. *General merchandise wholesalers,* which carry a complete line of nonperishable items such as hardware, drugs, and plumbing supplies. McLane Company, which supplies convenience stores with a wide variety of products in smaller quantities, is an example of this type of wholesaler.
2. *Single-line wholesalers,* which carry a particular line of goods. For example, Alpine Lace distributes and markets low-salt and low-fat cheeses through 45,000 retail outlets, including supermarkets and specialty food stores.
3. *Specialty wholesalers,* which carry a rather limited range of items. McKesson, for example, distributes and markets ethical and proprietary drugs and health- and beauty-care products to 17,000 retail outlets; in addition, it sells to hospitals and HMOs.

In the industrial-goods market, full-function merchant wholesalers are often called *industrial distributors.* Products handled by these distributors, which were also discussed in Chapter 9, include machinery, inexpensive accessory equipment, and supplies. Industrial distributors can handle either a broad line of products or a narrow one. Bearings, Inc., for example, handles a broad line of more than 100,000 different (SKUs) industrial bearings, primarily to original equipment manufacturers and to the repair and maintenance industry. W.W. Grainger, which handles a narrow line, is a nationwide industrial distributor of maintenance, repair, and operating supplies to commercial, industrial, contractor, and institutional customers. Grainger stocks over 500,000 SKUs through 340 branches in 50 states. As a rule, full-service wholesalers generally have a gross margin of 15%.

Limited-service merchant wholesalers perform only a few services for manufacturers or their customers, or they perform all of them on a more restricted basis than do full-service wholesalers. Limited-service wholesalers avoid some of the marketing functions by eliminating them entirely or passing them on to another marketing channel member or to the customer. Clearly, the fewer services performed by the wholesaler, the lower the markup it can charge on the merchandise it sells. Some of the more popular types of limited-service wholesalers are:

- *Drop-shippers (desk jobbers),* which pass on customer orders with instructions that the manufacturer ship directly to a location specified by the customer. They have no warehouse or inventory and do not have physical possession of the goods. They usually contact customers by phone, so a sales force may not be necessary. In addition, they may be much less active in generating promotion. These limited-service wholesalers are particularly useful in handling bulky goods and where merchandise typically moves in car-lot quantities; in fact, they are sometimes called "car-lot wholesalers."
- *Cash-and-carry wholesalers,* which do not provide customers with credit or delivery. The customer must pick up the merchandise from the wholesaler and pay for it with cash or a check. This type of wholesaler typically does not have a sales force. Customers are usually small retailers or small industrial accounts. An example of a cash-and-carry wholesaler is Smart & Final, Inc., which distributes food-service supplies through more than 150 outlets primarily located in the western United States. Smart & Final primarily supplies small restaurants, schools, and churches.
- *Truck jobbers (wagon jobbers),* which use their truck as a warehouse. Usually they are self-employed with little capital and they generally do not extend credit to customers. Truck jobbers may own their own goods, but usually get their merchandise on consignment from a large full-service wholesaler. They travel to customers and sell directly from the back of their truck. An example of a truck jobber that many students are familiar with is Snap-on, Inc. Snap-on distributes hand and power tools, diagnostic and shop equipment, and tool-storage products to automotive service centers and repair shops. Sales are through a dealer-van (truck) system that operates in more than 100 countries.
- *Rack jobbers,* which maintain racks stocked with merchandise at the retailer's location. Rack jobbers assume heavy risk, since the jobber holds title and the retailer holds goods sold from the rack. The retailer's only investment is in the space allotted to the rack. Most consumers are only aware of this type of limited-service wholesaler because they see rack jobbers filling the bread rack at grocery stores or the newspaper rack at convenience stores. Frito-Lay, as discussed in the opening vignette, distributes snacks to supermarkets, convenience stores, discounters, and supercenters.

Limited-service wholesalers generally have a gross margin of 4–6% of sales. However, it is important to remember that when a manufacturer chooses to use a limited-service wholesaler, he is not saving 10%. After all, the manufacturer must now assume responsibility for those services not performed by the wholesaler.

Agents/Brokers

The key difference between agents/brokers and merchant wholesalers is that **agents/brokers** never take title to the merchandise. Their key function is helping to bring potential buyers and sellers together. Like merchant wholesalers, they may or may not take possession of the merchandise they handle or provide all the services a full-service wholesaler performs. As was shown in Figure 12.9, agents and brokers today account for a little more than 10% of wholesale sales.[29]

Manufacturers' agents are independent middlemen who handle a manufacturer's marketing functions by selling part or all of a manufacturer's product line in an assigned geographic area. They are paid on commission, but have little or no control over prices and terms of sale and may work for a number of firms that produce related, noncompeting products. Agents can earn 2–20% on sales, depending on industry norms and how costly it is for them to perform the selling function. Manufacturers' agents are most likely to be used by manufacturers who want to enter a new geographic market area, those with a limited product line, those with insufficient resources to develop their own sales force, and those seeking to enter a new market with a product unrelated to their existing product line.

Brokers are independent middlemen who bring buyers and sellers together and provide market information to one or both parties. While most brokers work for sellers, some work for buyers. Brokers, who normally earn less than 5% of sales, simply negotiate a sale and are paid a fee only if the transaction is completed. Most brokers today operate in the food industry; however, they are also common in the industrial-equipment industry. Many students are familiar with mortgage brokers. Most home mortgages are initiated and then brokered into mortgage-backed securities. The mortgage broker receives some of the points or prepaid interest as a fee.

Selecting and Working with Wholesalers

A major decision in designing any channel is selecting the right wholesalers for the tasks to be performed and determining how to manage the wholesalers chosen.

Selecting Wholesalers

Manufacturers need screening devices to help assess the quality of potential wholesalers on at least five broad dimensions:

1. Management skills—Wholesalers should be screened on such points as their record and reputation, their planning and management systems, procedures used, cooperation and helpfulness, and receptiveness to constructive management suggestions.

2. Financial characteristics—The wholesaler's financial strength, integrity, history, and future prospects must also be considered. For example, wholesalers in a poor financial position may not be able to perform the necessary marketing functions and services. Therefore, it is important to assess financial characteristics, such as whether the wholesaler is making a profit, if it is sufficiently capitalized, if credit is adequate, and whether it can afford to keep adequate stocks on hand.

3. Physical facilities—The wholesaler's equipment and facilities should be assessed carefully. Considerable variation exists among wholesalers on this dimension. Here, it is necessary to know if the wholesaler has the needed facilities and equipment to handle a product, the age and condition of the facilities and equipment, the maintenance schedule, the wholesaler's reputation regarding service standards, and whether the office setup is adequate to handle the manufacturer's business.

4. Objectives and policies—To what extent are the wholesaler's objectives and policies compatible with the manufacturer's marketing channel? In evaluating this dimension, the wholesaler's managerial objectives and policies must be assessed with respect to growth, the stability and reliability of the organization, and the possibility of conflicts.

5. Marketing skills/strengths—Wholesalers need to have the marketing expertise and stamina to successfully market and distribute the manufacturer's product line. Therefore, the wholesaler's marketing know-how and the size, reputation, credibility, and attitude of its sales force must be assessed. Many wholesalers, such as those in the medical and industrial equipment area, have excellent long-term marketing relationships with their customers and can be very helpful to manufacturers in the introduction of new products.

By carefully assessing wholesalers on these five dimensions, the manufacturer should be able to maximize the chances of selecting the best wholesalers. Unfortunately, the best available wholesalers may not always be willing to handle the manufacturer's product line. Consequently, it is important for the manufacturer to know how to properly manage wholesalers in order to obtain their commitment to the manufacturer's products.

Managing Wholesalers

As pointed out earlier, manufacturers that operate through wholesalers typically do so because they find it more efficient and less expensive than doing the wholesaling activities themselves. However, manufacturers can only use wholesalers successfully if they get the wholesalers' cooperation in marketing their products. To accomplish this, manufacturers must obtain some degree of control over wholesalers.

If manufacturers want the cooperation and commitment of wholesalers, they must offer them financial, promotional, training, and general-management aids. Depending on the line of trade, some or all of these may be offered. The most important financial assistance that manufacturers can offer wholesalers is the planned gross margin, which must be large enough so that wholesalers can achieve an adequate profit after performing all the activities desired by manufacturers. Other important forms of financial assistance include inventory financing through liberal purchase terms, rebates, bonuses if quotas are achieved, seasonal dating to get wholesalers to stock up early in the season, and extra discounts for performing special services such as product recall or warranty services.

Frequently offered forms of promotional assistance include national or regional advertising that mentions the wholesaler's name; advertising allowances for local advertising; brochures, pamphlets, and other sales material to be distributed to potential customers; suggested advertising layouts or content for local advertising (i.e., prepared advertising mats); and salespeople employed by manufacturers to generate new accounts for the wholesaler.

If the wholesaler has neither the human nor financial resources to properly train salespeople, the manufacturer may offer a sales-training program. A good training program will help the wholesaler service the manufacturer's merchandise line by informing sales representatives about the strengths and weaknesses of the manufacturer's products and those of competing products, and by teaching them how to make effective sales presentations. Training of service personnel may also be advantageous, especially if the manufacturer's product line is technically complex and needs pre- or post-installation service.

Wholesalers are becoming more concerned about internal operating problems, including problems of credit and collection, inventory control, finance, planning, and personnel. Consequently, some manufacturers are designing management-development programs to help wholesalers solve their operating problems. By offering such programs, manufacturers are recognizing the fact that their marketing efforts can only be successful if the wholesaler survives and prospers.

Finally, all wholesale distributors should be given a sales goal based on the market potential and competitive intensity in the geographic territory the wholesaler serves. The manufacturer and wholesaler must discuss this goal and arrive at some agreement on its reasonableness. Once wholesale distributors are selected and offered the proper mix of assistance, they should be expected to meet their targeted goals. To assess their performance, an objective annual evaluation should be conducted.

Chapter Summary

Learning Objective 1: *Understand the role of retailing in the U.S. economy, differentiation strategies used by retailers, and the retail life cycle.* Retailing is a diverse business activity. There are several ways to categorize retailers on a variety of dimensions that explain the reasons why retailers behave as they do. These dimensions are number of outlets, margin versus turnover, and location. Since it is relatively easy to open a retail store, new retail institutions appear continuously. Scholars studying retailing have developed several theories to explain and describe the evolution of competition in retailing. Two of the most popular theories include the wheel of retailing and the retail life cycle.

Learning Objective 2: *Describe the major types of retail formats, including traditional stores and e-tailers.* When discussing the various types of retailers, it is first necessary to determine if the retailer is selling from a fixed physical location. There are six basic types of store-based retailers: department stores, specialty stores, supermarkets, supercenters, category killers, and convenience stores. There are five types of nonstore-based retailing: street peddling, direct selling, mail-order, automatic-merchandising machines, and electronic shopping. Many experts believe that nonstore retailing is where the next revolution in retailing will occur.

Learning Objective 3: *Recognize the components of the retailing mix and how it is designed to attract and retain customers.* Like all marketers, retailers identify their target market and make marketing decisions to satisfy the needs of that market. When doing this, retailers must realize that the store and the image it projects is a major part of their offering. A positive store image (the overall feeling or mood projected by a store through its aesthetic appeal to human senses) depends on its retail mix—that combination of merchandise, prices, advertising, location, customer services, selling, and store layout and design.

Due to intensified retail competition, retailers have been increasingly using category management. This is where all of the SKUs in a merchandise category are managed as a distinct business. Category managers are guided by the twin goals of increasing space and inventory productivity, because space and inventory resources are constrained in retailing.

Learning Objective 4: *Understand the role of wholesaling in the U.S. economy.* Wholesaling involves the activities of those persons or establishments that sell to retailers and/or other organizational buyers for industrial, institutional, and commercial use, but do not sell in significant amounts to final consumers. Wholesalers can be grouped into three broad categories: manufacturers' sales branches, merchant wholesalers, and agent/brokers.

For manufacturers to operate successfully through wholesalers, they must be able to select and work with the chosen wholesalers. To select the best wholesalers, manufacturers need a screening device that assesses the quality of potential wholesalers on at least five broad dimensions: management skills, financial characteristics, physical facilities, objectives and policies, and marketing skills/strengths.

Manufacturers that want their wholesalers' cooperation and commitment must offer them financial, promotional, training, and general-management aids.

Key Terms

For interactive study: visit http://bestpractices.swlearning.com.

Agents/brokers, 418
Anchor stores, 396
Balanced tenancy, 396
Category killers, 406
Category management, 414
Full-service merchant
    wholesalers, 417
Gross margin, 393
Gross margin percentage, 393

Inventory turnover, 393
Limited-service merchant
    wholesalers, 418
Manufacturers' agents, 418
Manufacturers' sales branches, 416
Merchant wholesalers, 417
Operating expenses, 393
Retailing, 390
Retail life cycle, 401

Retail mix, 410
Scrambled merchandising, 406
Shrinkage, 413
SKU, 414
Wheel of retailing theory, 400
Wholesalers, 390
Wholesaling, 415

Questions for Review and Discussion

1. Why are convenience stores able to charge higher prices for the same merchandise than supercenters do?

2. What are the three basic tasks of retailers? Provide an example of a retailer who does an excellent job at each of these tasks. (You may use a different retailer for each task.)

3. What are atmospherics? How do a store's atmospherics affect its image and its ultimate success or failure?

4. According to the wheel of retailing theory of competitive evolution in retailing, what new type(s) of retail operation might be seen in the future?

5. Why has category management become more important in retailing?

6. What major goals does the category manager focus on in developing a retail mix for a category? Why?

7. If wholesalers sell to retailers and retailers sell to final consumers, why are total wholesaler sales greater than total retail sales?

8. What are the key differences between a limited-service merchant wholesaler and a full-service merchant wholesaler?

In-Class Team Activities

1. Form teams and debate your position on the following statement: "Scrambled merchandising is really a very inefficient way of retailing. Retailers should specialize in the line(s) of merchandise they carry. Therefore, the use of scrambled merchandising should decrease over the remainder of this decade." Support your position.

2. Today many retailers such as Home Depot and Wal-Mart have turned over the responsibility for setting up merchandise displays to wholesalers. Does this mean that we may not need retailers in the future?

Internet Questions

1. Begin by ranking the national retail chains in either your hometown or campus town with regard to their service. (Remember, banks are retailers.) Then go to the Web site for the University of Michigan Business School at http://www.bus.umich.edu and search the site for the "American Customer Satisfaction Index" to see the recent data on customer satisfaction for the nation's leading retailers. Next, look for differences between your ratings and the national survey. Finally, explain any differences between the two. This site is updated quarterly. If you want to learn how to conduct a customer satisfaction survey, go to http://customersat.com.

2. Go to the home page for the U.S. Census Bureau (http://www.census.gov). Then go to the economic census link, then the retail/wholesale link, then the PDF (free version) link. Access this site and locate the summary retail statistics (sales and number of stores) for your state. Identify the line of retail trade in your state that had the most rapid sales growth over the most recent five years of available data and the one that had the slowest growth. Why do you believe the fastest-growing line of retail trade grew faster than the slowest line of retail trade? Try to develop several hypotheses or explanations.

3. Go to the home page for the U.S. Census Bureau (http://www.census.gov). Then go to the economic census link, then the retail/wholesale link, then the PDF (free version) link. Access this site and locate the summary statistics (sales and number of establishments) for your state. Identify the line of wholesale trade in your state that had the most rapid sales growth over the most recent five years of available data and the one that had the slowest growth. Why do you believe the fastest-growing line of wholesale trade grew faster than the slowest line of wholesale trade? Try to develop several hypotheses or explanations.

CHAPTER CASE

The Changing Face of Tobacco Retailers

Over the last half century, Americans have become accustomed to the idea of being able to buy cigarettes at a variety of retail outlets ranging from vending machines in bars, restaurants, and airports, to supermarkets, convenience stores, gas stations, and discount stores. However, federal legislation may soon change the way tobacco is sold in the United States.

Wal-Mart was one of the first major retailers to address the tobacco issue. In 1990, Sam Walton admitted in a letter to a consultant that he was ". . . still in a quandry (sic) on our direction for this very important issue." The next year the retailer announced a ban on smoking on all Wal-Mart property, including the stores, as well as the removal of any cigarette-vending machines. At the time, Walton was not aware of any vending machines, but as a precaution, he issued the "ban" order. Later, when Wal-Mart expanded into Canada by purchasing 127 Woolco stores, Walton met with the pharmacists from the newly acquired stores. They informed Walton that their job involved helping people get well, not causing health problems, which tobacco did. At their request, Wal-Mart dropped the sale of tobacco in its Canadian stores. A member of the chain's Executive Committee decided to continue with the sale of cigarettes after Mr. Walton's death.

At the same time, various state and local agencies began to enforce age restrictions on the sale of cigarettes and other products such as firearms, spray paint (which was used for painting gang slogans), and even glue. Wal-Mart introduced a program into its scanners that froze the cash register when the SKU for one of these products was recorded until the clerk ascertained the age of the purchaser. As a result of this increased enforcement of the laws regulating the sale of tobacco, some retailers, especially supermarkets and drugstores, began to drop tobacco. How would this affect the sale of these legal products, which accounted for more than $60 billion each year?

If such a change were to occur, what retailers would benefit? Some experts think that one of the retailers best prepared for cigarettes being dropped by mass sellers is John Roscoe's family-owned Cigarettes Cheaper chain. This is a 400-store operation already doing $50 million in sales each year.

Cigarettes Cheaper, which only sells cigarettes in 1,200-square-foot outlets primarily located in strip malls, and is second only to Wal-Mart in total cigarette sales, is a spin-off of Roscoe's Customer Company convenience-store chain. The name Customer Company was a reflection of Roscoe's appreciation for his consumers, and as a result he offered the lowest prices on everything in the store. His tobacco stores follow the same philosophy by charging 20% less on the average pack or carton of cigarettes.

The chain is able to charge such prices by taking advantage of every manufacturer discount available and realizing that its consumers are not apt to buy just a pack or even a carton, but more likely to purchase 10 to 12 cartons at a time. But low prices are not the only thing. Roscoe's store and similar operations have a broader range of brands and packaging than other retailers, a regular diet of promotions, and a welcoming attitude towards smokers that is not always the case elsewhere.

However, what is most impressive about Roscoe's operation are these facts:

- No members of the family smoke, nor do they encourage anyone to smoke.
- The stores put in a great deal of effort to control "underage" customers. All stores have a large sign stating "NO MINORS ALLOWED INSIDE" and a manager could lose his/her job for violating this rule.

Case Questions

1. Should retailers be permitted to sell cigarettes to anyone who is of legal age, even if the retailer is located near a highly traveled area for minors?
2. If the sale of cigarettes is banned from retailers located near high schools and college campuses, as some lawmakers are proposing, should the same thing be done with beer?
3. Some cities have just banned smoking in all restaurants. Is this fair to the individual property owners of the restaurants? Whose rights are most important: the owners or the consumers?

VIDEO CASE

Neiman Marcus' Premier Customer Service

You've probably never spent $3,000 for a suit, even if the label came from a designer and the quality was impeccable. But would you drive several hours to shop at a store that carried all the clothing brands and styles you loved? Maybe, if you were a die-hard shopper and you felt a strong bond with the store. What if the store offered you a trip to Paris for your loyalty? It might happen if you're a Neiman Marcus shopper.

Neiman Marcus. The name tumbles off the tongue, conjuring up visions of affluence, high fashion, and an anxiously awaited annual catalog featuring exotic—and expensive—holiday gifts for the recipient whose closets and carports are already filled with clothing and cars most of us would die for. The specialty retailer that traces its beginnings to Dallas opened in the early part of the 20th century and has gradually expanded nationally to 15 states and more than 30 locations from Boston to Southern California. Neiman Marcus is known around the world as a specialty retailer offering high-end fashion, jewelry, gifts, and home furnishings. Billy Payton, vice president of marketing and customer programs, identifies Neiman's customers as consumers—mostly women—whose household income is $150,000 and above, who are between the ages of 35 and 55, and who like the one-to-one relationship that Neiman's tries to build with them. He says that the Neiman's customer "appreciates fashion and appreciates quality in merchandise and gifts and apparel." Burton Tanksy, president of the Neiman Marcus Group, targets his customers this way: "Our customer wants designer clout. She wants something easily recognizable so that people will know she paid a lot for it." Payton further identifies two main categories of customer: long-term customers who have shopped with the store for years and occasional customers who visit the store for a specific need, such as a wedding gift.

How does Neiman Marcus develop relationships with customers who could shop anywhere they want? First, by recognizing the very fact that these customers can afford to shop anywhere, then by looking for ways to create greater utilities for them. "Neiman Marcus is all about developing relationships with customers, through our sales associates, through our marketing efforts, through editing the selection of quality merchandise and fashion. So it's all about a one-to-one relationship," explains Payton. One important way of doing this is attracting customers to the InCircle Program, a frequent-buyer program that was the first of its kind when it was launched in 1984. For every dollar a customer spends at Neiman Marcus, one point is added to the customer's InCircle account. Later, customers can redeem points for gifts and purchasing privileges—say, that trip to Paris. So a long drive to a Neiman's store becomes worthwhile to many customers. Neiman's has also upgraded the old-fashioned gift certificate, replacing it with a plastic card that looks like a credit card. The new card has a new name: the NM Gift Card.

To increase personal service even more, Neiman's sales associates develop exclusive relationships with particular customers. Pat Ames, a sales associate, notes that she often drops off a purchase at a customer's home or workplace or selects appropriate gifts for customers when they are short on time or ideas. Finally, there's Neiman's famous "The Book," a large, glossy fashion publication that is more idea book than catalog; customers are encouraged to sift through its pages, glean fashion and gift ideas, then visit the stores themselves for personal service. Customers treasure their copies as if they were first editions of literary classics.

Although Neiman's traditionally focused on developing long-term customer relationships, recently the company has broadened its marketing focus to include the occasional customer. Payton notes, "The new buzz term is *CRM*, continuous relationship management, meaning, are we serving the occasional customer—all of their needs? All of their shopping needs, or fashion needs, their gift needs, their accessory needs, their cosmetic needs? Are we maximizing the servicing and our selling opportunity to all of our customers?" The NM Gift Card is a result of this thinking, and Payton notes that every holiday—or occasion—counts at Neiman's. In fact, he refers to the company's new focus on occasions as a "year-round business." Another new area of focus is "the whole culture of successful young Gen-Xers craving high-fashion, high-quality merchandise who may not think of Neiman Marcus as a place for them," says Payton. The trick, he says, is to attract the younger shoppers without alienating the older ones.

Not willing to be left behind in the wake of Internet technology, Neiman Marcus has already launched its own online shopping site at http://www.neimanmarcus.com and has joined forces with other organizations on the Internet. Neiman's and several other retailers have signed up with a wedding registry site called http://www.dellajames.com, which allows wedding guests to buy gifts directly online from the group of retailers. As for the company's regular Web site, Billy Payton notes, "We definitely recognize and know that the Web will play a major part in our marketing in the future. . . . We're trying to reach a very sophisticated customer, who appreciates technology, who understands technology and responds to it." Will Neiman's be able to replicate its bricks-and-mortar presence and also become a leading upscale Internet retailer? If its sales associates can still offer the personal touch, if customers still believe they are getting the best of the best, and if occasional customers like the idea of buying a wedding gift with the click of a mouse, the company could do very well online. Still, it is probably safe to predict that not a single Neiman's customer will give up that precious copy of "The Book."

Case Questions

1. In what ways does Neiman Marcus create time, place, and ownership utilities for its customers?
2. Describe the typical Neiman Marcus customer. How well do you think Neiman Marcus meets the needs of this market?

3. In what ways might technology affect Neiman's marketing strategy?
4. Neiman's sales associates are known for providing excellent personal service for their customers. Describe how Neiman's Web site (http://www.neimanmarcus.com) attempts to integrate a "personal touch" for their customers.

Sources: Neiman Marcus company Web site, http://www.neimanmarcus.com, http://www.neimanmarcusgroup.com, accessed 15 February 2000.

Bruce Horovitz, "Neiman Marcus Spins Own Webcast," *USA Today,* 30 August 1999, http://www.usatoday.com.

"My Biggest Mistake: Stanley Marcus," *Inc.com,* 1 July 1999, http://www.inc.com.

Wendy Bounds, "Retailers Say 'I Do' to Wedding Web," *The Wall Street Journal,* 9 June 1999, B9.

In Chapter 13, **Terence Shimp**, University of South Carolina, reveals how marketing communications tools can enhance brand equity, create sales, and deliver acceptable returns on investment. Professor Shimp provides insights into how marketing communicators can use various communication methods to reach audiences with interesting and persuasive messages. Recognizing the importance of sales in today's organization, Chapter 14 highlights the role of the sales force in building customer relationships and solving customer problems. In this chapter, **Judy Siguaw**, Cornell University, describes personal

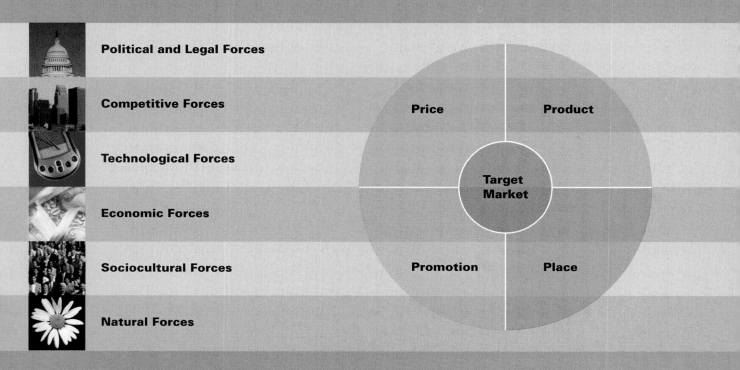

Political and Legal Forces

Competitive Forces

Technological Forces

Economic Forces

Sociocultural Forces

Natural Forces

Price

Product

Target Market

Promotion

Place

selling as a critical component of the promotional strategy, reviews the sales process, and studies the role of sales management. In Chapter 15, **Joel Urbany**, University of Notre Dame, presents contemporary pricing practices and then takes a glimpse into the factors that determine prices: cost, competitors, and customer price sensitivity or elasticity. Professor Urbany also explores the environmental context that makes pricing decisions complex, as well as Web-based developments in pricing.

Integrated Marketing Communications and Pricing Strategy

 Political and Legal Forces Many abuses of e-mail advertising exist, especially companies sending unsolicited messages and selling e-mail addresses to list brokers. U.S. Congressional committees are debating the merits of regulating e-mail advertising, although no major statutes have as yet been passed. Even the Direct Marketing Association, a powerful trade association that represents direct marketers, favors federal legislation that restricts spam.

 Competitive Forces Because competitive brands such as the Toyota Matrix and Pontiac Vibe will also heavily advertise their own brands, gaining consumer awareness of a new market entry is not an easy task in a cluttered media environment. This is why more than $15 million will be invested in first-year advertising for the Element.

 Technological Forces Salespeople at Hewlett-Packard use the Internet to customize presentations, obtain on-the-spot answers to customer questions, and follow up with customers. As a result, HP salespeople are more productive than their less "wired" counterparts.

 Economic Forces As firms experience stress due to multiple environmental pressures, they may respond by trying to force customers to purchase their products. This strategy, however, may harm the firms' relationships with their customers and result in a decrease in performance over the long term.

 Sociocultural Forces Companies like Merrill Lynch and American Express are proactive in bringing diversity to their workforces. Organizations such as these recognize that diversity makes economic sense.

 Natural Forces Canadian companies are somewhat more concerned about environmental issues than U.S. companies, suggesting that concern over the environment is a more important part of the "social contract" and culture in Canada.

Integrated Marketing Communications: Advertising, Promotions, and Other MarCom Tools

xtra!

Interactive Marketing Activity

Go to Xtra! to access this Interactive Marketing Activity at http://bestpracticesxtra.swlearning.com.

In 2003, Honda introduced the Element, a boxy-looking, inexpensive, crossover vehicle targeted to active Generation Y males. Honda has projected sales of 50,000 Elements in 2003. To accomplish this objective and build the Element's brand equity, Honda has invested $15–20 million in television and online advertising and sponsorships of snowboarding, surfing, and bicycling events. Competitive vehicles, such as the Toyota Matrix and the Pontiac Vibe, however, hope to prevent Honda from reaching its goals for the Element.

You Decide. After reading the opening vignette and paying special attention to the sections of this chapter marked with the chess piece, answer these questions:

1. Based only on the information contained in the opening vignette of this chapter, which "key aspect of integrated marketing communications" (IMC) did Honda most obviously use in its promotion of the Element?

2. Television advertisements used to introduce the Honda Element featured friends enjoying road trips to surfing and mountain-biking activities in an effort to portray the Element as a cool, hip, and even radical product. What is the primary purpose of these introductory ads?

3. Honda has invested $15–20 million in advertising the Element. How might Honda best assess the effectiveness of these introductory ads?

AP Topic Gallery

A Dorm Room on Wheels for Generation Y: The Honda Element

Honda's research-and-development (R&D) team began work back in 1998 on a new vehicle that in the early stages of development was given the code name "Model X." Marketing researchers at Honda had learned from their studies that many entry-level consumers were looking for a different, more functional type of vehicle than provided by traditional sport utility vehicles, minivans, or pickup trucks. With input and direction from the marketing research department, Honda's R&D team proceeded to develop what eventually became the Honda Element. This unique vehicle was introduced to the American market in early 2003. With a base price of nearly $17,000, the Element was targeted to so-called Generation Y young males who were single, active, college graduates. It was expected that the vehicle would also appeal to slightly older Generation X customers.

As you learned in the chapter opener for Chapter 1, the Element is a rather boxy-looking vehicle designed to appeal less to "good looks" and more to young drivers' need for a vehicle that has abundant interior space for hauling mountain bikes, surfboards, and other items suitable for active lifestyles and also providing enough room for two adults to sleep in it. The Element falls in the category of "crossover" vehicles that combine features of pickup trucks, SUVs, and minivans. The demand for crossovers grew from less than 2% of the market for light vehicles in 1999 to more than 7% by 2003. Designed mostly for active males, the Element represents a dorm room on wheels—providing plenty of storage space, wide-opening cargo doors, easy-to-clean interiors, and seats that fold flat to create "beds."

Honda projected sales of 50,000 Elements for 2003, the introductory year. Approximately $15–20 million was invested in TV and online advertising, and sponsorships of snowboarding, surfing, and bicycling events. Aggressive marketing communications efforts were essential to build the Element's brand equity and achieve the ambitious goal of selling 50,000 vehicles in the first year of marketing—especially considering the competition from other crossover vehicles such as the Toyota Matrix and Pontiac Vibe. Introductory television advertisements for the Element featured friends enjoying the thrill of road trips to participate in surfing and mountain-biking activities. Only time will tell whether this highly functional but somewhat odd-looking vehicle will achieve its ambitious sales goal and claim the imagination of America's active Gen Y generation.[1]

LEARNING OBJECTIVES

After you have completed this chapter, you should be able to:

1. *Appreciate the variety of marketing-communications tools and how they work together to accomplish communication objectives.*

2. *Understand the nature, importance, and features of integrated marketing communications.*

3. *Describe the concept of brand-equity enhancement and the role of marketing communications in facilitating this objective.*

4. *Comprehend the factors that determine how different marketing-communications elements are effectively combined.*

5. *Discuss the primary decision spheres involved in managing the marketing-communications process.*

6. *Evaluate the nature and function of the major marketing-communications tools: (a) advertising, (b) sales promotion, (c) public relations, and (d) sponsorship and event marketing.*

VOICE OF THE EXPERT
Terence A. Shimp, University of South Carolina

The field of marketing communications has changed rather dramatically during the past decade, largely as a function of spectacular disruptions in the social and economic landscapes of America, Asia, and Europe—developments such as stock market devaluations; thousands of dot-com companies going out of business after blowing billions of startup funds provided by overeager venture capitalists; terrorist attacks on the World Trade Center and the Pentagon; accounting scandals involving companies such as Enron, Tyco, WorldCom, Adelphia, and Arthur Andersen; and many individuals' growing apprehension and uncertainty about their personal safety and economic future. Among other effects on marketing-communication practices, advertising budgets have shrunk; indeed, the years 2001 and 2002 witnessed the biggest proportionate reductions in advertising expenditures since the Great Depression, more than 70 years ago.

Within this milieu, marketing managers realize now more than ever that advertising and other marketing-communications investments must be held financially accountable. Companies are continuously seeking more effective ways of communicating effectively and efficiently with their targeted audiences. The competition is more intense than ever, and the marketplace is filled with communications clutter. Marketing communicators are challenged to use communication methods that will break through this clutter, reach audiences with interesting and persuasive messages, and assure that marketing-communications investments yield an adequate return on investment. In meeting these challenges, companies are increasingly embracing a strategy of integrated marketing communications (IMC). It is my hope that, by reading this chapter, you will gain an increased understanding of the role and scope of marketing communications and heightened appreciation of marketing communications' importance in building brand equity, creating sales, and delivering acceptable returns on investment.

Consumers are rushed for time; their lives are pressured; they often do not have the inclination to leisurely walk up and down store aisles and peruse every stock-keeping unit available on the shelves or to visit every possible supplier of dental, automotive repair, eye care, or other services. A brand may be of high quality and fairly valued, but it will fail to achieve sales and profit objectives if potential customers are unaware of it or do not perceive it favorably. Effective advertising and other forms of marketing communications are absolutely crucial to creating brand awareness, establishing positive brand identities, moving products off store shelves, and encouraging more people to use a particular provider's services. The introduction of the Honda Element in the opening vignette illustrates the crucial role that advertising, events, and other marketing-communications tools play in achieving successful product launches and sustaining sales over time.

Marketing communications are also critical to the success of business-to-business (B2B) marketers in their efforts to achieve market share and profit objectives. Many B2B products share similarities from one supplier to the next; product quality generally is not that different among competitors, and prices often are nearly equal. The real distinctions among B2B competitors frequently amount to created differences achieved through effective advertising and, more importantly, superior service and personal selling efforts. Regardless of the nature of the product category or type of business, marketing communications are key to a company's overall marketing mission and represent a major determinant of its success.

It is not just major corporations involved in consumer-oriented marketing (B2C) or B2B marketing that use marketing communications as an important part of their business or organizational activities. For example, small businesses involved in retailing goods and services must communicate their offerings and attempt to maintain or build their businesses. Such firms advertise, hold special events, and occasionally offer promotional deals. Likewise, not-for-profit organizations (religious institutions, museums, orchestras, dance groups, philanthropic organizations, and many others) also rely on the tools of marketing communications to inform potential clients of their offerings and encourage behaviors such as museum attendance, donations to charities, and volunteer efforts.

In addition to formal and sustained marketing-communications efforts, business organizations, both large and small, and not-for-profit organizations must rely on favorable word-of-mouth communications from satisfied customers to accomplish their communication objectives. Indeed, word of mouth is perhaps the ideal form of communications because recommendations from friends and family members have considerable credibility. But because word-of-mouth communication is sporadic and undependable, business and nonbusiness organizations must undertake formal and systematic communications to get the job accomplished.

The objective of this chapter is to identify and hopefully forge greater appreciation for the more formal and systematic aspects of marketing communications, which hereafter are abbreviated as *MarCom*. The various tools that are part of managers' MarCom repertoire are discussed first. The two following sections discuss the nature of integrated MarCom and the challenge of enhancing brand equity. Next, the chapter describes the factors that influence the choice of MarCom tools most appropriate for a particular brand-marketing situation. The chapter concludes with a discussion of managing the MarCom process and the major MarCom tools: advertising, sales promotion, public relations, and sponsorship marketing.

LEARNING OBJECTIVE 1   ## The Tools of Marketing Communications

This section provides an overview of each of the MarCom elements. First, however, it will be useful to draw an analogy between getting the most out of the players on a basketball team and the challenge of mixing the MarCom tools to achieve maximum success.

In brief (and simplistically), a basketball team includes 10–12 players, five of whom play as a unit at any time. The players differ in the roles expected of them and the strengths they offer. One player, the point guard, has primary responsibility for dribbling, controlling the tempo of the offense, and setting up plays. Another guard, the shooting guard, has a greater scoring responsibility. Both guards play defense as well as offense. The center, who typically is the tallest player on the team, has major responsibility for inside scoring (i.e., close to the basket), rebounding, and defending against opponents' offensive efforts. Two other players, the forwards, typically score points from intermediate range and also have responsibility for rebounding and defending. The quality of a basketball team depends on all players working together and playing as a unit. Offense is important, but so is defense. Players who can score points quickly and in spurts are important, but so are those who are steady and dependable, rather than erratic. A basketball team would not be very good if it consisted only of five Shaquille O'Neals, or five Allan Iversons, five Kobe Bryants, five Yao Mings, five Lisa Leslies, or five of any single type of player. An outstanding team requires players representing contrasting dimensions—quickness, shooting skill, rebounding savvy, shot-blocking ability, and so on—who complement each other.

So it is with the MarCom mix and the various elements that comprise the mix. Personal selling, in a sense, is like a basketball team's point guard. It sets the tempo for all other MarCom elements. Advertising is like a flamboyant shooting guard—the Allen Iverson of marketing communications. Public relations is an adjunct to advertising, working together, assisting, and augmenting advertising to accomplish mutual goals. Public relations (PR) also is great when the need for defense is especially important—such as when a firm or one of its brands is surrounded with negative publicity. Sales promotion is like the player who scores a lot of points quickly; it can achieve sales results in a shorter period than can other MarCom elements.

There is no need to strain the analogy further. The point should be clear: The MarCom mix is like a team that consists of players who provide distinct abilities and perform different but mutually reinforcing roles. Now we will briefly describe each tool and reserve detailed discussion for later sections.

Personal Selling

B2B marketers rely especially heavily on personal selling. **Personal selling** is person-to-person communication in which a seller informs and educates prospective customers and attempts to influence their purchase choices. In the consumer market, products such as insurance, automobiles, and real estate are sold mainly through personal selling efforts. Historically, personal selling involved face-to-face interactions between salesperson and prospect, but phone sales and other forms of electronic communications are being used increasingly. Chapter 14 focuses exclusively on personal selling and sales management, so this chapter will emphasize the other MarCom elements.

Personal selling
Is person-to-person *communication in which a seller informs and educates prospective customers and attempts to influence their purchase choices.*

Advertising

The purpose of advertising is to inform the end consumer or the B2B customer about the advertiser's products and brand benefits and ultimately to influence brand choice. **Advertising**, *nonpersonal* communication paid for by an identified sponsor, involves either *mass communication* via newspapers, magazines, radio, television, or other media (e.g., billboards, bus stop signage) or *direct-to-consumer communication* via postal or electronic mail. Advertising is considered nonpersonal because the sponsoring firm is simultaneously communicating with multiple receivers, perhaps millions, rather than talking with a specific person or small group. Advertising—such as Honda's effort with the Element in the opening vignette—attempts to keep the brand's name and image in the customer's mind over a long period of time.

Advertising
Is nonpersonal *communication that is paid for by an identified sponsor, and involves either* mass communication *via newspapers, magazines, radio, television, and other media (e.g., billboards, bus stop signage) or* direct-to-consumer communication *via postal or electronic mail.*

Public Relations

Publicity
Like advertising, is nonpersonal communication to a mass audience, but unlike advertising, publicity is not directly paid for by the company that enjoys the publicity.

Publicity, which is the major PR tool, usually comes in the form of news items or editorial comments about a company's products. **Publicity**, like advertising, is *nonpersonal* communication to a mass audience, but unlike advertising, publicity is not directly paid for by the company that enjoys the publicity. The news items or editorial comments receive free print space or broadcast time because media representatives consider the information pertinent and newsworthy for their reading or listening audiences. It is the job of a firm's PR personnel to garner positive publicity for the company and its brands. These personnel also face the challenge of overcoming negative publicity when a company is faced with a product disaster or confronted with claims of unfavorable business practices.

Sales Promotion

Sales promotion
Consists of all marketing activities that attempt to stimulate quick buyer action, or, in other words, attempt to promote immediate sales of a product (thereby yielding the name sales promotion).

Sales promotion is intended to create an immediate response from the market, while advertising and publicity, by comparison, are more designed to favorably influence customer expectations and attitudes over the long term. **Sales promotion** consists of all marketing activities that attempt to stimulate quick buyer action, or, in other words, attempt to promote immediate sales of a product. *Trade-oriented sales promotions* include the use of various types of allowances and merchandise assistance that activate wholesaler and retailer response. *Consumer-oriented sales promotions* include coupons, premiums, free samples, contests/sweepstakes, rebates, and other devices.

Sponsorship Marketing

Sponsorship marketing
Is the practice of promoting the interests of a company and its brands by associating the company with a specific event *(e.g., a golf tournament) or a charitable* cause *(e.g., the Leukemia Society).*

In general, sponsorship marketing represents an opportunity for a company and its brands to directly target communications toward narrow, but highly desirable, audiences. **Sponsorship marketing** is the practice of promoting the interests of a company and its brands by associating the company with a specific high-profile *event* (e.g., a golf tournament or a symphony concert) or a charitable *cause* (e.g., the Leukemia Society). The use of sponsorship marketing is generally not expected to substitute for more traditional forms of marketing communications, such as advertising, but

The Revlon Run/Walk For Women is an example of sponsorship marketing and has grown to become one of the nation's largest 5K fundraising events. To date, the Run/Walks have raised more than 26 million dollars for cancer research, counseling, and outreach programs.

© Trapper Frank/CORBIS SYGMA

rather to complement these activities. Many marketing communicators use traditional mass-media advertising, but then supplement the advertising with a brand presence at events where samples are distributed.

The Philosophy and Practice of Integrated Marketing Communications

The person in charge of advertising and other MarCom elements in small companies may be the business owner him- or herself or someone with a title such as sales and marketing manager. In not-for-profit companies, the individual responsible for Mar-Com decisions may be the business manager.

In large corporations, a vice president of marketing generally has overall responsibility for all aspects of a firm's marketing programs. However, most day-to-day, or tactical, marketing decisions occur at the product- or brand-management levels. Product managers for B2B companies and brand managers for B2C companies have profit-and-loss responsibility for the particular product or brand they manage. However, the various MarCom decisions are not the sole responsibility of the product brand manager; instead, in most large organizations, department managers are responsible for planning and implementing decisions pertaining to individual Mar-Com elements. Sales management, for example, is responsible for the personal selling function (more on this in Chapter 14). Advertising managers have authority over the entire advertising function, much of which is performed in conjunction with independent advertising agencies. Public relations managers provide news media with positive messages about the company and its activities. As with advertising, public relations functions are often delegated to independent PR agencies. Likewise, sales promotion managers carry out various trade- and consumer-oriented promotions. Again, outside vendors that specialize in specific forms of promotions (e.g., premium consultants; sweepstakes, contests, and games administrators; coupon specialists) are often contracted with to perform these specialized services.

Regardless of the size of the organization or the number of managers or independent agencies involved in the MarCom process, one individual needs to have the programs' big picture at all times to ensure success. In the past, companies often treated the MarCom elements as virtually separate activities, but the current view is that integrating all elements is absolutely imperative for success. (Recalling the earlier basketball analogy, MarCom must be managed as a team rather than as a collection of individual players.) One of the significant marketing trends of recent years is a move toward fully integrating all business practices that communicate something about a company's brands to present or prospective customers. This development is known as integrated marketing communications (IMC). **Integrated marketing communications (IMC)** is a system of managing and integrating all marketing-communications elements—advertising, publicity, sales promotion, sponsorship marketing, and point-of-purchase communications—so that all elements adhere to the same message.

Some skeptics have suggested that IMC is little more than a short-lived management fashion,[2] but evidence to the contrary suggests that IMC is not fleeting but rather has become a permanent feature of the MarCom landscape around the world and in many different types of marketing organizations.[3] In the final analysis, the key to successfully implementing IMC is for brand managers, who represent the client side, to closely link their efforts with outside suppliers of MarCom services (such as ad agencies), and both parties must be committed to assuring that all communication tools are carefully and finely integrated.[4]

Integrated marketing communications (IMC)
Is a system of management and integration of marketing-communications elements—advertising, publicity, sales promotion, sponsorship marketing, and point-of-purchase communications—with the result that all elements adhere to the same message.

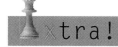

Key Aspects of Integrated Marketing Communications

The philosophy and practice of IMC can be described in terms of five key features that are listed in Figure 13.1 and discussed in this section. Before proceeding, it is

Figure 13.1	Five Key Features of IMC

1. Start with the customer or prospect
2. Use any form of relevant contact
3. Achieve synergy (speak with a single voice)
4. Build relationships
5. Affect behavior

important to note that these features are interdependent, with no particular sequence of importance attached to the ordering in Figure 13.1.

Start with the Customer or Prospect

An initial key feature of IMC is that the process should *start with the customer or prospect* and then work back to the brand communicator to determine the most appropriate messages and media for informing, persuading, and inducing customers and prospects to act favorably toward the communicator's brand. The IMC approach avoids an "inside-out" (from company to customer) approach in identifying how best to reach, or contact, customers. It instead starts with the customer ("outside-in") to determine those communication methods that will best serve customers' information needs and motivate them to purchase the marketer's brand. The next IMC feature is a natural extension of being customer focused.

Use Any Form of Relevant Contact

IMC uses all forms of communication and all sources of appropriate contacts as potential message-delivery channels. The term *contact* is used here to mean any message medium capable of reaching target customers and presenting the brand in a favorable light. The key feature of this IMC element is that it reflects a willingness on the part of the brand communicator to use any communication outlets (contacts) appropriate for reaching the target audience. Marketing communicators who practice this principle are not precommitted to any single medium or subset of media, such as depending exclusively on television advertising. Rather, the objective is to surround customers/prospects with the brand message at every possible opportunity and allow them to use whatever information about the brand they deem most useful.[5] An established advertising practitioner has referred to this as *360-degree branding*, an apt phrase indeed.[6]

IMC adherents use whichever media and methods of contact best enable the communicator to deliver the brand message to the targeted audience. Direct-mail advertising, promotions at sporting and entertainment events, advertisements on packages of other brands, in-store displays, and online ads are just some of the contact methods for reaching present and prospective customers. The IMC objective is to reach the target audience efficiently and effectively using whatever contact methods are appropriate. Television advertising, for example, may be the best medium for contacting the audience for some brands, while less traditional (and even unconventional) contact methods may best serve other brands' communication and financial needs.

Achieve Synergy

Inherent in the definition of IMC is the need for *synergy*. A brand's assorted communication elements (advertisements, point-of-purchase signage, sales promotions, event sponsorships, direct mailings, online advertisements, and so on) must all strive to present the same brand message and convey that message consistently across diverse message channels, or points of contact. Marketing communications for a brand must, in other words, *speak with a single voice*. Coordination of messages and media is absolutely critical to achieving a strong and unified brand image and moving customers to action. The failure to closely coordinate all communication elements can result in duplicated efforts or—worse yet—contradictory brand messages. A vice president of marketing at Nabisco fully recognized the value of speaking with a single voice when describing her intention to integrate all of the marketing-communications contacts for Nabisco's Oreo brand of cookies. This executive captured the essential quality of synergy when stating that under her leadership, "Whenever consumers see Oreo, they'll be seeing the same message."[7] A general manager at Mars Inc., the maker of candy products, expressed a similar sentiment when stating: "We used to look at advertising, PR, promotion plans, each piece as separate. Now every piece of communication from package to Internet has to reflect the same message."[8]

Build Relationships

A fourth characteristic of IMC is the belief that successful marketing communications require building a relationship between the brand and the customer. A relationship is an enduring link between a brand and its customers.[9] Successful relationships between customers and brands lead to repeat purchasing and perhaps even loyalty toward a brand.

There are myriad ways to build brand/customer relationships. One, perhaps overused, method is the use of frequent-flier and other so-called frequency, loyalty, or ambassador programs. All of these programs are dedicated to retaining existing customers and encouraging them to satisfy most of their product needs from the organization making the offer. Airlines, hotels, supermarkets, and many other businesses provide customers with bonus points for their continued patronage. Relationships between brand and customer also are nurtured by creating brand experiences that make positive and lasting impressions. This is done with the use of special events, sometimes called *experiential programs,* that attempt to create the sensation that a sponsoring brand is relevant to the consumer's life and lifestyle. Companies such as Saturn automobiles and Harley-Davidson motorcycles, for example, have held retreats where they invite brand owners to celebrate the brand, learn about new product offerings, and to generally enjoy the occasion in a festival-like atmosphere.

Harley-Davidson Motorcycles build relationships with customers by hosting special events for Harley owners to celebrate the brand, learn about new product offerings, and enjoy socializing with other Harley owners.

© Mark Hunt/Index Stock Imagery

Affect Behavior

A final IMC feature is the goal of affecting the behavior of the communications audience. This means that marketing communications must do more than just influence brand awareness or enhance consumer attitudes toward the brand. For example, it is not enough that marketers of the Honda Element merely make targeted consumers aware of this automobile and whet their appetites; rather, it is crucial that thousands of young men (and women) actually plop down cash or, more likely, finance the acquisition of new Element vehicles. A new restaurant must do more than make itself familiar to potential consumers and influence them to think this might be a good place to have dinner; instead, it must get people to actually dine at the restaurant, enjoy the experience, and hopefully return.

The objective, in other words, is to *move people to action*. We must be careful not to misconstrue this point. An integrated marketing-communications program ultimately must be judged in terms of whether it *influences behavior*, but it would be simplistic and unrealistic to expect an action to result from every communication effort. Prior to purchasing a new brand, consumers generally must be *made aware* of the brand and its benefits and influenced to have a *favorable attitude* toward it. Communication efforts directed at accomplishing these intermediate, or prebehavioral, goals are fully justified. Yet eventually—and preferably sooner rather than later—a successful marketing-communications program must get people to undertake a desired (from the communicator's viewpoint) action—buy a particular brand, make a contribution to a worthy cause, engage in a behavior advocated by public health officials (exercising, stopping smoking, etc.).

Key Changes in MarCom Practice Resulting from the IMC Thrust

The adoption of an IMC mind-set necessitates some fundamental changes in the way MarCom has traditionally been practiced. The following changes are particularly prominent:[10]

1. **Reduced Dependence on Mass-Media Advertising.** Many marketing communicators now realize that communication methods other than mass-media advertising often better serve the needs of their brands. Media advertising is not always the most effective or financially efficient medium for contacting customers and prospects. This is not to say that mass-media advertising is fading away; the point instead is to emphasize that MarCom professionals and brand managers are increasingly turning to alternative methods for contacting present or prospective customers and relying less on mass-media advertising.

2. **Increased Reliance on Highly Targeted Communication Methods.** Direct mail, special-interest magazines, cable TV, event sponsorships, and e-mail messaging (so-called permission, or opt-in, e-mailing) are just some of the contact methods that facilitate communications pinpointed to specific target groups rather than blanketed to the masses. The use of database marketing is a key aspect of targeted communications. **Database marketing** involves collecting and electronically storing (in a database) information about present, past, and prospective customers. Almost all sophisticated B2B and consumer-oriented companies maintain large, up-to-date databases of present and prospective customers.

3. **Expanded Efforts to Assess Communications' Return on Investment.** A final change is IMC's insistence on systematic efforts to determine whether marketing communications yield a reasonable return on investment (ROI). All managers—and marketing communicators are no exception—must be held financially responsible for their actions. Marketing communicators, perhaps especially advertisers, long held onto the assumption that advertising's influence on sales and profits cannot be adequately measured, but in a world where financial accountability is the watchword of business efficiency, marketing communicators have been forced to justify their efforts. A marketing consultant has clearly

Database marketing
Involves collecting and electronically storing (in a database) information about present, past, and prospective customers.

stated the ROI imperative for today's marketing communicators: "In the age of ROI, you must speak the language of the CEO [chief executive officer] and CFO [chief financial officer]: cost and benefits, investment and earnings."[11]

A MarCom Challenge: Enhancing Brand Equity

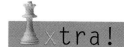

We live in a world of brands. It just so happens that some brands are better known and more respected than others. A brand (as introduced in Chapter 9) comes into existence when a product, retail outlet, or service receives its own name, term, sign, symbol, design, or any particular combination of these elements. Coca-Cola, Levis, Lexus, Sony, Adidas, Target, the New York Yankees, and *The Wall Street Journal* exemplify well-known and respected brand names. The Honda Element, which was introduced in the opening vignette, is a relatively unknown brand in comparison to the above-mentioned brands. Some brands, however, have greater equity than others. Looked at from the customers' perspectives, a brand possesses equity to the extent that customers are familiar with the brand and have stored in their memories favorable, strong, and unique brand associations.[12] That is, *brand equity* from the customer's perspective consists of two forms of knowledge: *brand awareness* and *brand image*. Figure 13.2 graphically portrays these two dimensions of brand knowledge; subsequent discussion will fill in the details.[13]

A Model of Brand Equity   Figure 13.2

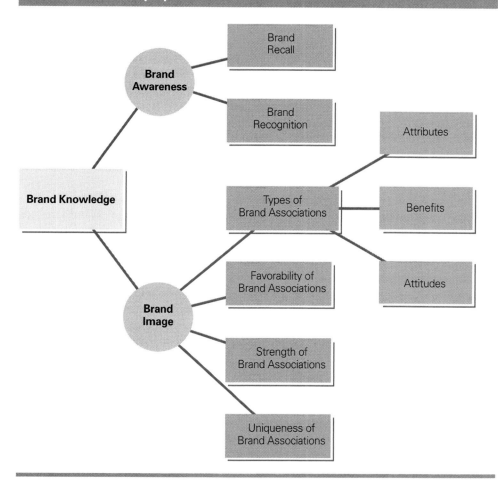

Source: Kevin Lane Keller, "Conceptualizing, Measuring, and Managing Customer-Based Brand Equity," *Journal of Marketing* 57 (January 1993): 7.

SHIFT_joy

Courtesy, Nissan North America, Inc.

Nissan increases brand awareness with an integrated marketing communications campaign that features the SHIFT_ tagline.

Competitive Forces

Because competitive brands such as the Toyota Matrix and Pontiac Vibe will also heavily advertise their own brands, gaining consumer awareness of a new market entry is not an easy task in a cluttered media environment. This is why more than $15 million will be invested in first-year advertising for the Element.

Brand Awareness

Brand awareness is based on whether a brand name comes to mind when customers think about a particular product category and the ease with which the name is evoked. It is the basic dimension of brand equity, in that a brand has no equity unless the customer is at least aware of it. Thus, achieving brand awareness is the initial challenge for new brands, and maintaining high levels of brand awareness is the task faced continuously by all established brands.

Marketing communications are instrumental in confronting both these challenges. Consider the challenge facing brand managers of Honda's crossover vehicle, the Element, when introducing it to college students and other members of the target market in 2003. The first task was to increase brand awareness. First-year advertising and event sponsorships costing $15–20 million were considered crucially important for this purpose.

Figure 13.2 shows two levels of awareness: brand recognition and brand recall. *Brand recognition* reflects a relatively superficial level of awareness, whereas *brand recall* reflects a deeper level. Customers may be able to identify a brand if it is presented to them on a list or if hints/cues are provided; however, fewer customers are able to retrieve a brand name from memory without any reminders or cues. It is this deeper level of awareness— recall—to which marketers aspire. Through effective and consistent MarCom efforts, some brands are so well known that virtually every living person of normal intelligence can recall the brand. For example, asked to name brands of athletic footwear, most people would mention Nike, Reebok, and Adidas. The MarCom imperative is thus to move brands from a customer's state of unawareness, to recognition, on to recall, and ultimately to top-of-mind awareness (TOMA). This pinnacle of brand-name awareness (i.e., TOMA status) exists when a brand is the first recalled when customers think of the available options in a particular product category.

Brand Image

The second dimension of customer-based brand knowledge is a brand's image. *Brand image* can be thought of in terms of the types of associations that come to the customer's mind when contemplating a particular brand. A *brand association* is simply the particular thoughts and feelings that a customer has about a brand, much in the same way that we have thoughts and feelings about other people. For example, what thoughts/feelings come immediately to mind when you think of your best friend? You undoubtedly associate your friend with certain personality, physical, and intellectual characteristics—strengths as well as weaknesses. Likewise, brands are linked in our memories with specific thought-and-feeling associations. As shown in Figure 13.2, these associations can be conceptualized in terms of (1) type, (2) favorability, (3) strength, and (4) uniqueness.

Efforts to enhance a brand's equity are initially accomplished through the careful choice of positive brand identity (that is, the selection of a good brand name or logo). But they must be reinforced by MarCom programs that forge favorable, strong, and unique associations in the customer's mind between a brand and its attributes/benefits. It is impossible to overstate the importance of efforts to enhance a brand's equity. Products that are high in quality and represent a good value potentially possess high brand equity. But effective and consistent MarCom efforts are needed to build on and maintain brand equity. A favorable brand image does not

The Wi-Fi Revolution

College students a half century ago listened to music on stereos which, at the time, were referred to as Hi-Fi players, which stood for high-fidelity performance. College students today, along with millions of other people around the world, can gain access to the Internet via Wi-Fi, which is short for wireless fidelity. Wi-Fi enables computers to connect to the Internet via low-power radio signals instead of cables. Thus, users can have Internet access at base stations, or so-called "hot zones," that are Wi-Fi equipped. As long as he has a Wi-Fi-enabled laptop computer (and most new laptops, and even desktops, now come Wi-Fi ready), the user can surf the Net at public access points throughout the United States and elsewhere around the world. In addition to Internet access, Wi-Fi technology allows computers within the same hot zone to communicate with each other. It is estimated that by 2006 there will be well over 100,000 public hot spots in the U.S.

What are the MarCom implications of Wi-Fi? Early developments in Wi-Fi usage portend future applications that are even more exciting than present uses. Perhaps the most outstanding application of Wi-Fi technology at this time is the availability of hot zones at Starbucks coffee shops. Wireless Internet connections are available in more than 2,000 Starbucks stores in the U.S. and Europe. Early experience indicates that customers who purchase Wi-Fi accounts at Starbucks spend more time in the stores and purchase more products. Real estate professionals are among the earliest heavy users of Starbucks Wi-Fi accounts. The coffee shops provide an excellent venue for realtors to meet clients and view Internet-accessed property listings in a leisurely environment. In addition to Starbucks, the sandwich chain Schlotzky's offers free Wi-Fi access in a limited number of stores.

Companies that advertise via the Internet will have greater access to millions of customers who, before wireless-enabled Internet access, could be reached only in their homes or offices and not when they were actually in the marketplace to make product and brand selections. Now customers can be contacted at the point of purchase, where advertising can have a greater impact in influencing brand choice. For example, an advertising message received at home late at night several days prior to going to the mall may be forgotten before the customer is ready to make product and brand choices. In contrast, imagine sitting on a comfortable bench at the mall surfing the Web wirelessly and being exposed to an ad announcing a sale at a store 100 yards away. This ad is likely to be substantially more effective than one received at a time and place separate from the buying decision. Wi-Fi has a huge future as an advertising medium for reaching business customers and everyday consumers.

Sources: "In the Zone," *Advertising Age,* 27 January 2003, S–1, S–4.

Kate Fitzgerald, "Wi-Fi Connects as a Marketing Tool," *Advertising Age,* 27 January 2003, S–2.

Judith Nemes, "Cellular Picks Its Hot Spots," *Advertising Age,* 27 January 2003, S–4.

Michael Krauss, "Starbucks Adds Value by Taking on Wireless," *Marketing News,* 3 February 2003, 9.

happen automatically. Sustained marketing communications are generally required. For example, it could be claimed that one of the world's greatest brands, Coca-Cola, is little more than colored sugar water. This brand nevertheless possesses immense brand equity—with a market share in excess of 40% of the U.S. soft-drink market[14]—because its managers are ever mindful of the need for continuous advertising executions that sustain the Coca-Cola story and build the image around the world. Consumers don't buy this "colored sugar water" merely for its taste; they instead purchase a lifestyle and an image when selecting Coca-Cola over other available brands. It is effective advertising, exciting sales promotions, creative sponsorships, and other forms of marketing communications that are responsible for Coca-Cola's positive image and massive market share.

Research has shown that when firms communicate unique and positive messages via advertising, personal selling, sales promotion, and other means, they are able to effectively differentiate their brands from competitive offerings and insulate themselves from future price competition.[15] Marketing communications play an essential role in creating positive brand equity and building strong brand loyalty. However, this is not always accomplished with traditional advertising or other conventional forms of marketing communications. For example, Starbucks, the virtual icon for upscale coffee, does very little advertising, yet this brand has a near cultlike following.

Let us return to the Honda Element for further discussion of brand image. If you were brand manager of the Element, how would you want consumers to think of your brand? What attributes and benefits would you like to lodge in consumers' memories? Stated alternatively, what image would you want for the brand? Introductory advertising portrayed this crossover vehicle as a cool, hip, and even radical

Sociocultural Forces

The Element stands a good chance of succeeding because it is a brand that is congenial with demographic and social/cultural developments. In particular, the age category to which the Element appeals numbers nearly 20 million. Also, young males in this category are increasingly on the go for social and recreational pursuits. The Element accommodates their active lifestyles.

product. The Element's boxiness is advantageous because it allows the driver or passengers to nearly stand up, perhaps while changing clothes after an active outing. The seats can be reconfigured to meet the owner's exact needs. And doors that open wide allow big objects to be hauled in the vehicle. Front seat covers protect against stains, and interior surfaces are coated with urethane for cleaning ease and water resistance. All of these product features provide benefits that are much sought after by members of the target audience, who desire a vehicle that is functional as well as cool. The Honda Element stands a very good chance of developing strong brand equity due to an image that is perceived as exciting, modern, rugged, and fitting in with active lifestyles—a dorm room on wheels.[16]

Determining an Appropriate Mix of IMC Tools

In determining an appropriate mix of MarCom elements for a specific brand in a particular product category, a product or brand manager must weigh a variety of factors related to the category, the brand, and the market. The manager typically has considerable discretion in determining which elements to use and how much relative emphasis each should receive. Should the entire budget go toward supporting the sales force, or should some be allocated to mass-media advertising? Are point-of-purchase materials needed at retail? Will coupons or bonus packs help move more product? There is no right formula for determining an optimum blend of elements. The manager must thoroughly analyze the product, the competition, the brand's strengths and weaknesses, and the target market to determine the brand's MarCom needs and opportunities. The decision is guided by systematically considering the following questions:

1. What is the intended market?
2. What objectives must the MarCom initiative achieve?
3. What is the product life-cycle stage?
4. What are competitors doing?
5. What is the available budget for marketing communications?

What Is the Intended Market?

The blend of MarCom activities will differ considerably depending on the character of the intended market. An earlier chapter established that, in the B2B market, the number of organizational buyers are fewer, decisions are often made in groups, and buyers are more geographically concentrated. The marketing budget would be more effectively used in personal selling to reach this target market. However, to reach buyers in the consumer market—where individual buyers often number in the millions, where decisions are made by each consumer individually or in small groups, and where consumers are widely dispersed—the marketing budget is more effectively spent on advertising, sales promotion, and other communication approaches that can contact the masses. Thus, a clear understanding of the product's target market is vital to determine how best to allocate the MarCom budget.

Consider, for example, an industrial machine marketed to a small segment of B2B customers. Although the industrial-machine marketer might use some advertising and sales promotions, personal selling would provide the primary means by which the marketer would reach prospective customers. In this case, the marketer's budget may be divided as follows: 70% to personal selling; 20% to trade-oriented media advertising; and the remaining 10% to direct-mail advertisements, a Web site, and telemarketing efforts. By comparison, consider the allocation of the MarCom budget for a consumer convenience good that is sold in supermarkets. In this case, the marketer's budget might be allocated this way: 10% to personal selling to gain product distribution in retail outlets; 20% to trade-oriented sales promotions to achieve favorable shelf space; 25% to consumer-oriented sales promotions to encourage product trial and repeat purchasing; 40% to mass-media advertising to build brand awareness and create a favorable image; and 5% to point-of-purchase materials to encourage impulse buying. In these scenarios, no one element within the mix will be omitted completely from the B2B or B2C budgets. The focus on each element will change, though, depending on the nature of the intended market.

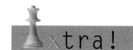

What Objectives Must the MarCom Initiative Achieve?

Figure 13.3 presents a *hierarchy-of-effects* framework that provides a useful way of thinking about the objectives that MarCom can accomplish. The hierarchy framework captures the idea that marketing communications are designed to advance B2B customers, B2C consumers, and not-for-profit clientele from an initial stage of brand awareness, to learning about the brand (i.e., brand-related beliefs and knowledge), to forming positive attitudes toward the brand, to intending to purchase it, and ultimately to making purchase decisions that favors the marketing communicator's brand versus competitive offerings.

The different stages in the hierarchy are best understood by examining an actual MarCom situation. Have you ever heard of a company called American Family Life Assurance Company? I'll bet you haven't. Have you ever heard of a company called AFLAC? You probably have. (AFLAC is, of course, an acronym for American Family Life Assurance Company.) Do you recall seeing TV commercials featuring a white duck that seems to go unnoticed by the participants *in* the commercial but not to viewers of the commercial who see and hear the talking duck exclaim repeatedly "AFLAAAAAC!" Let's now assess what the advertiser is attempting to accomplish.

First, most consumers are not that interested in thinking about insurance or learning about different companies that compete in this industry. AFLAC, although

The Hierarchy of Effects   Figure 13.3

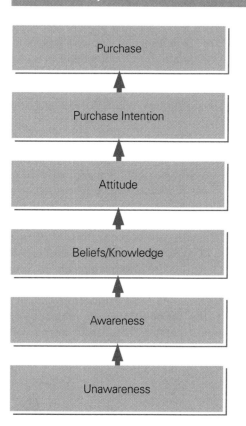

a huge company in the so-called supplemental insurance business—the business that sells insurance policies to people to augment their inadequate health, life, and disability coverage from employer-funded insurance programs—generates annual revenues of $10 billion or more, yet most consumers were unaware of AFLAC prior to its "duck" advertising campaign.[17] The campaign was designed to familiarize consumers initially with the AFLAC name (*create brand awareness*). Interestingly, the ad agency responsible for the campaign came up with the idea of using a duck after one of its creative people observed that AFLAC, when spoken, sounds like a squawking duck. Second, the campaign intended to make consumers knowledgeable about situations where supplemental insurance might be necessary (*build brand knowledge*). For example, in one advertisement, a couple is shown riding in the front of a roller coaster. The duck in the car behind the couple reassures them about their supplemental insurance coverage in the event the coaster has a disaster. Third, the reassuring advertising should have the effect of influencing consumers to like AFLAC's advertising and thus the company itself (*positive attitude formation*). Fourth, having now learned about supplemental insurance and recognizing that their own employer-based insurance coverage is inadequate, many consumers could be expected to contemplate the possibility of acquiring supplemental insurance, perhaps from AFLAC (*purchase intention*). Finally, some consumers will act upon the intention by meeting with an AFLAC sales representative and purchasing a supplemental insurance policy (*purchase*). AFLAC's duck campaign apparently accomplished its goal of moving consumers up the hierarchy of effects, since sales increased by a whopping 27% within 18 months of the start of the advertising campaign.[18]

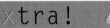

What Is the Product Life-Cycle Stage?

Is the brand well established and in the maturity stage of the product life cycle, or is it a new brand in the introduction stage? In the introduction stage, advertising is especially critical to create awareness and to inform consumers about the brand and its benefits (i.e., influence beliefs/knowledge). Trade-oriented sales promotions are essential for gaining wholesaler and retailer support, and consumer sales promotions (such as samples, coupons, and cents-off deals) are also important for achieving consumer trial, especially when marketing packaged goods. Later on, as the product reaches the maturity stage, advertising and sales promotion remain crucial, but both undergo qualitative changes. Advertising is now needed to maintain a positive brand image and differentiate the brand from competitive offerings, while sales promotion is used to encourage repeat purchase behavior.

What Are Competitors Doing?

Competitive action generally dictates what can or must be done. A useful yardstick, or metric, for measuring competitive action with respect to advertising activity within a particular product category is referred to as *share of voice*, or SOV for short. Consider the situation in Figure 13.4 that lays out the advertising expenditures, SOVs, and shares of market for the top 10 fast-food burger brands. Note first that each brand's SOV is simply calculated as ad expenditures as a percentage of total advertising expenditures for all 10 burger brands. The important point to note is the strong correlation between shares of voice and shares of market. Hence, brand marketers need to closely follow competitors' advertising (and promotion) activity so as to not fall into a competitive disadvantage. If a major competitor substantially increases its ad budget during a particular business quarter, then "our" brand will have to retaliate the next quarter, or else it stands to lose market share that may be very difficult to regain.

What Is the Available Budget?

This determinant of how MarCom tools should be mixed is closely tied to considerations of what competitors are doing. The available MarCom budget will determine

Shares of Voice and Market for Top 10 Burger Brands				Figure 13.4
Brand	**Ad Expenditures (in millions)**	**Share of Voice**	**Share of Market**	
McDonald's	$664.8	44.0	43.1	
Burger King	385.3	25.5	21.1	
Wendy's	241.8	16.0	12.7	
Hardee's	36.3	2.4	5.3	
Jack in the Box	70.6	4.7	4.4	
Sonic Drive-Ins	41.9	2.8	4.0	
Carl's Jr.	41.6	2.7	2.1	
Whataburger	10.4	0.7	1.4	
Steak 'n Shake	8.3	0.5	1.1	
White Castle	10.8	0.7	1.1	
TOTAL TOP 10	$1,512.1	100.0%	96.3%	

Source: Adapted from "Leading National Advertisers," *Advertising Age,* 24 September 2001, S8.

what elements can and cannot be emphasized in the communications program. In the B2B market, a marketer may emphasize personal selling and forgo advertising if the total MarCom budget is limited due to poor performance the previous year or an unattractive economic forecast for the coming year. The sales force is a relatively fixed expense, whereas advertising can be increased or decreased depending on the situation and financial circumstances. (During the economic slowdown of 2000–2003, many marketers substantially reduced their advertising budgets.) In the consumer market, on the other hand, the competition forces nationally distributed brands to devote some funds to advertising and sales promotion. The actual amount varies depending on the product category and economic situation, but most brands invest anywhere from 1–15% of sales revenue on advertising and an equal or greater amount to trade- and consumer-oriented sales promotions, collectively.

Managing the MarCom Process   5 **LEARNING OBJECTIVE**

As the previous sections illustrate, many factors must be considered to create an effective mixture of MarCom elements. Marketing communications—like any other business process—must be managed. Managing marketing communications for a brand involves six primary areas of decision influence. The Honda Element introduced in the opening vignette provides a suitable medium for illustrating each of these decision spheres.

1. Selecting target markets
2. Establishing objectives
3. Setting budgets
4. Formulating positioning strategies
5. Establishing and implementing message and media strategies
6. Evaluating program effectiveness.

Selecting Target Markets

Selecting target markets is the critical first step toward effective and efficient marketing communications. Targeting allows marketing communicators to pinpoint the product's potential audience and to precisely deliver messages to this group. Targeting attempts to avoid wasting valuable promotional dollars on those consumers outside the target market. As discussed in Chapter 8, companies identify potential target markets in terms of a combination of characteristics—demographics, lifestyles, product-usage patterns, geographical location—that will cause these consumers to act in a similar fashion. For example, the target market for Honda Element consists primarily of young males who are single, enjoy active lifestyles, and participate in outdoor activities such as surfing, mountain biking, and skiing. The target market for AFLAC likely consists primarily of younger families in the 25–39 age range who are of average socioeconomic status, are somewhat risk averse, and believe in the importance of insurance.

Establishing Objectives

As discussed earlier in the chapter, it is important for marketing communicators to establish clear and achievable objectives as a prelude to designing messages and executing communication programs. MarCom objectives must fit within the company's overall corporate and marketing objectives. The objectives must also be realistic and stated in quantitative terms, with the amount of projected change and the time duration specified. For example, the objective "to increase brand awareness for the Honda Element" is too general to be of much value. A much better objective would be "to increase within the next six months consumers' awareness of the Element from the present (hypothetical) level of 40% to 50%." This objective is specific, measurable, realistic, and achievable given sufficient advertising and other MarCom expenditures. As the prior statement suggests, the objectives to be achieved by Mar-Com efforts are inextricably related to the budget available for such efforts.

Setting the Budget

An organization's financial resources are budgeted to specific MarCom elements to accomplish the sales and profit objectives established for its various brands. The discussion of the Honda Element in the opening vignette indicated, for example, that the first-year advertising budget for this brand fell in the range of $15–20 million. The resources allocated to specific MarCom elements is typically the result, in most sophisticated corporations, of an involved process. Companies use different budgeting processes in allocating funds to brand managers. At one extreme is *top-down budgeting,* in which senior management decides how much each subunit receives. At the other extreme is *bottom-up budgeting,* in which managers of subunits (such as brand managers) determine how much is needed to achieve their objectives; these amounts are then combined to establish the total marketing budget.

Most budgeting practices involve a combination of top-down and bottom-up budgeting. For example, in the *bottom-up/top-down process,* brand managers submit budget requests to a chief marketing officer (say, a vice president of marketing), who coordinates the various requests and then submits an overall budget to top management for approval. The *top-down/bottom-up* process reverses the flow of influence by having top managers first establish the total size of the budget and then divide it among the various brand managers. The *bottom-up/top-down* process is by far the most frequently used, especially in more sophisticated firms where marketing-department influence is high compared to finance-department influence.[19]

Formulating a Positioning Strategy

Brand positioning is an essential activity in developing successful MarCom programs. It is only by having a clear positioning statement that marketers know to whom a brand should be targeted, what should be said about the brand, and what media and message vehicles should be selected for contacting target customers.

Positioning is both a useful conceptual notion and an invaluable strategic tool. Conceptually, the term *positioning* suggests two interrelated ideas. First, the marketing communicator wishes to create a specific meaning for the brand and to have that meaning clearly lodged in the customer's memory (think of this as "positioned in").

The second aspect of positioning is that the brand's meaning in customers' memories stands in comparison to what they know and think about competitive brands in the product category (think of this as "positioned against").

Strategically and tactically, positioning is a short statement—even a word—that represents the message you want to "imprint in the minds of customers and prospects."[20] This statement tells how your brand differs from and is superior to competitive brands. It gives a reason why customers should buy your brand rather than a competitor's and promises a solution to the customer's needs or wants. A good positioning statement should (1) reflect a brand's competitive advantage and (2) motivate customers to action.[21] The **positioning statement** is the key idea that encapsulates what a brand is intended to stand for in its target market's mind and then consistently delivers the same idea across all media channels. Ultimately, a positioning statement for a brand represents how you want customers and prospects to think and feel about your brand. These thoughts and feelings should stand out in comparison to competitive offerings and motivate the customer/prospect to want to try your brand. The Honda Element, for example, is positioned as a dorm room on wheels, that is, as a vehicle that is ideal for hauling possessions and recreational equipment, and even serving as rough sleeping quarters when the occasion arises.

Positioning statement
Is the key idea that encapsulates what a brand is intended to stand for in its target market's mind and then consistently delivers the same idea across all media channels.

Formulating and Implementing Message and Media Strategies

Decisions must be made regarding the message to be communicated and the media within which the message will be carried. The message is a critical component of MarCom effectiveness. Marketers must decide how best to present their ideas to achieve the established objectives and implement the positioning strategy that has been formulated. In creating a message, a marketer may choose from a variety of message alternatives, including what image to create and what types of appeals to use such as humor, nostalgia, and so on. Introductory television advertisements for the Element featured friends enjoying the thrill of road trips to participate in surfing and mountain-biking activities.

Marketing communicators need also consider various media strategies. A **media strategy** consists of four sets of interrelated activities: (1) selecting the target audience, (2) specifying media objectives, (3) selecting media categories and vehicles, and (4) buying media. Media typically connote modes of advertising such as television, radio, or magazines. But the term *media* can be applied to every MarCom element. Point-of-purchase materials, for example, can be a simple cardboard shelf talker, a take-one pad, or a sophisticated display. A sales promotion can range from a simple coupon distributed via freestanding inserts to a more involved sweepstakes offer. Each of these alternatives is a different medium that has a unique rate of effectiveness, as well as cost. Brand managers must determine which message and media will be most effective—from both a communications and a cost standpoint—in delivering the desired message.

Media strategy
Consists of four sets of interrelated activities: (1) selecting the target audience, (2) specifying media objectives, (3) selecting media categories and vehicles, and (4) buying media.

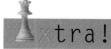

Evaluating Program Effectiveness

Once a MarCom program is in place and being implemented, the program must be evaluated for its effectiveness. Only through evaluation can you learn what works, what does not work, and why. This information will be critical in creating future programs and taking corrective action when necessary.

A program is evaluated by measuring the results of the program against the objectives established in the planning stage. For some elements, it is relatively simple to assess effectiveness, because the results generated are easily attributable to just that element. Consider a direct-mail campaign, where the measure of effectiveness is the actual response rate, or the number of orders received as a percentage of the

What Role Does Sex Play in Advertising?

Sexual material in advertising is used for several reasons. First, such content serves to both lure and retain consumers' attention to the advertising message. A second potential role is to enhance recall of message points, although it has been found that sexual content in advertising enhances recall only if it is appropriate to the product category and the creative advertising execution. A third role performed by sexual content is to evoke emotional responses, such as romance-relevant feelings. These reactions can increase an ad's persuasive impact, with the opposite occurring if the ad elicits negative feelings, such as disgust, embarrassment, or uneasiness.

A TV advertisement for Miller Lite beer (dubbed "Catfight") perhaps typifies the various roles performed by sexual content in advertising. The ad, which was created by the Ogilvy & Mather advertising agency, aired on many occasions during NFL football games in the 2002–03 season. You may recall seeing the ad, which portrayed two attractive and bosomy women literally ripping each other's clothes off in a swimming pool and later in wet cement, as they supposedly fought over whether Miller Lite beer is the beer of choice because it is "better tasting" than other light beers or because it is "less filling." This ad doubtlessly caught the attention of millions of men (and women) who view NFL football, and perhaps aroused emotions and aided brand-name recall. Although the ad likely achieved positive objectives for the makers of Miller Lite, it raised distinct ethical issues about advertising propriety. Notably, the ad achieved such a degree of success that the makers of Miller Lite subsequently launched sequel advertisements featuring other bosomy models.

The fact remains that many people—men as well as women—are offended by advertisements that portray women (and men) as brainless sex objects. Sex in advertising can be demeaning to females (and males) and, for this reason, should be used cautiously. Indeed, the use of sex in advertising is a matter of concern to people and regulatory bodies throughout the world. Three categories of indecency include advertisements that are sexist, sexy, or that sexually objectify their models. *Sexist ads* are those that demean one sex in comparison with the other, particularly through sex-role stereotyping; *sexy ads* use sexual imagery or suggestiveness; and *sexual objectification* occurs when ads use women (or men) as decorative or attention-getting objects with little or no relevance to the product category. It would seem that the Miller Lite "Catfight" commercial is guilty of sexual objectification along with being sexist.

DISCUSSION QUESTIONS

1. Discuss the pros and cons of using sex in advertising.
2. Would you prefer that advertisers use more "average-looking" actors in their ads to promote their products? Why or why not?

Source: Hillary Chura, "Miller Set to Roll Catfight Sequels," *Advertising Age*, 17 February 2003, 1, 35.

---

number of mailings (e.g., a 2% response rate). Effectiveness is evaluated by comparing the actual response rate with the objective established in the form of a projected response rate. For a premium offer, the total number of consumers sending in proofs-of-purchase can be compared against the number of submissions contained in the original objective. In either event, corrective action is called for if the actual response rate falls significantly below that which was projected.

Other promotional elements, such as advertising, are more difficult to evaluate, since objective outcomes—such as the amount of sales generated in a period—are not directly or exclusively attributable to the ads per se. In other words, sales are the result of all marketing-mix variables, not just advertising. Moreover, current sales are due to past marketing efforts, and are not solely attributable to current advertising; that is, the advertising and sales relationship is typically lagged, with advertising in the current period influencing sales at later times, as well as in the current period. Due to these complications, advertisers typically assess advertising effectiveness in terms of so-called *communication outcomes* such as changes in customers' awareness of the advertised brand, knowledge of copy points, or attitudes toward the brand. All of these factors, if known before an advertising campaign begins, can be measured again at the end of the campaign and compared with objectives to determine effectiveness. For example, when Honda introduced the Element in 2003, the initial level of brand awareness was virtually zero. One of several communication objectives may have been to increase the first year's brand awareness in the target market to a level of 40%, for example.

Nature and Function of Major MarCom Tools

The last section of this chapter provides an in-depth overview of each of the Mar-Com tools. Numerous advertising issues are addressed including setting advertising objectives, budgeting, brand positioning, ad creation, media selection, online advertising, point-of-purchase advertising, and evaluating advertising effectiveness. The shift from advertising to sales promotion is presented in the sales promotion section as are the roles and objectives of sales promotion, and the various types of trade and consumer promotions. Public relations are discussed in terms of proactive and reactive marketing public relations. Finally, sponsorship and event marketing activities are introduced as one of the fastest-growing aspects of marketing communications.

Advertising

There are three basic ways by which companies can add value to their offerings: *innovating, improving quality,* or *altering consumer perceptions*. These three value-added components are completely interdependent. Advertising adds value to brands by influencing customers' perceptions. Effective advertising causes brands to be viewed as more elegant, more stylish, more prestigious, and/or perhaps superior to competitive offerings, and, in general, of higher perceived quality and/or value. When advertising is done effectively, brands are perceived as more desirable, which in turn can lead to increased market share and greater profitability. It is little wonder that Procter & Gamble, perhaps the leading consumer-goods firm in the world, fully appreciates advertising's value-adding role. Indeed, a P&G vice president of worldwide advertising has characterized *effective* advertising as "a deposit in the brand equity bank."[22] Please note that not *all* advertising represents a deposit in the BE bank, only strong, effective advertising—the creation of which is the goal of brand managers and their advertising agencies. When done well, advertising can be incredibly effective and represent a good return on stockholders' investments; when done poorly, advertising is virtually a wasted expenditure.

Advertising can also be considered an economic investment that is regarded favorably by numerous large and small businesses and not-for-profit organizations throughout the United States and around the world. In recognition of advertising's invaluable role, companies in the U.S. invested approximately $230 billion on advertising in one recent year.[23] This amounts to more than $800 in advertising for each of the nearly 280 million men, women, and children in the United States at the onset of the new millennium. Advertising spending is also substantial in other major industrialized countries, but not nearly to the same magnitude as in the U.S. The biggest advertising spenders after the United States are Japan, Germany, the United Kingdom, France, and Canada.

Some companies invest more than $1 billion a year on worldwide advertising spending. In one recent year, for example, the top five worldwide advertising spenders were:

- Procter & Gamble, $3.82 billion worldwide ($1.7 billion in the U.S.)
- General Motors, $3.03 billion ($2.21 billion in the U.S.)
- Unilever, $3.01 billion ($571 million in U.S.)
- Ford, $2.31 billion ($1.27 billion in U.S.)
- Toyota, $2.21 billion ($770 million in U.S.)[24]

Even the U.S. government invests more than $1 billion in advertising directed at such initiatives as controlling drug use and smoking, recruiting young people into the military, increasing use of the U.S. Postal Service, and increasing the number of people taking government-funded Amtrak trains.[25] In 2003, the U.S. Department of Homeland Security introduced a $40–50 million TV and print advertising campaign to prepare Americans for the possibility of terrorist attacks. The campaign was aided by a public service group known as the Ad Council, which procured free ad placements on TV and in the print media.[26]

The U.S. spends over $1 billion in advertising and includes ads promoting the U.S. Postal Service.

The actual advertising process for a particular brand can be thought of as the development and implementation of an advertising strategy. *Advertising strategy* entails five major activities: objective setting, budgeting, positioning, planning message strategy, developing media strategy, and assessing advertising effectiveness. The first three activities—objective setting, budgeting, and positioning—were described earlier in context of the overall MarCom process and are discussed only briefly in the present advertising situation. Suffice it to say that the objective-setting, budgeting, and positioning processes are fundamentally the same regardless of which MarCom element is involved.

Setting Advertising Objectives

Advertising objectives provide the foundation for all remaining advertising decisions. There are three major reasons for setting advertising objectives:[27]

1. The process of setting objectives literally forces top marketing and advertising managers to agree on the course that advertising should take for the upcoming planning period, as well as the tasks that advertising is expected to accomplish for a brand.
2. Objective setting guides the budgeting, message-creation, and media-selection aspects of advertising strategy.
3. Advertising objectives provide standards against which results can be measured.

Advertisements are created to accomplish goals such as (1) making the target market aware of a new brand, (2) facilitating customer understanding of a brand's attributes, (3) creating expectations about a brand's benefits, (4) enhancing attitudes toward the brand, (5) influencing purchase decisions, and (6) encouraging product trial and repeat purchasing.

Budgeting for Advertising

The budgeting decision for advertising is, in many respects, the most important decision advertisers make. If too little money is spent on advertising, sales volume will not be as high as it could be, and profits will be lost. If too much money is spent, expenses will be higher than they need to be, and profits will be reduced.

Budgeting is also one of the most difficult advertising decisions. This difficulty arises because it is hard to determine precisely how effective advertising has been in the past or might be in the future. The sales response to advertising is influenced by a multitude of factors (quality of advertising execution, intensity of competitive advertising efforts, customer taste, and other considerations), thereby making it difficult, if not impossible, to know with any certainty what volume of sales a particular advertising effort will generate.

Companies ordinarily set budgets by using their best judgment, applying their experience with analogous past situations, and using simple rules-of-thumb, or *heuristics*. Although criticized because they do not provide a basis for advertising budget setting that is directly related to the profitability of the advertised brand, heuristics continue to be widely used. The two most pervasive heuristics, in use by both B2B and B2C advertisers, are the percentage-of-sales and objective-and-task methods.[28] The *percentage-of-sales method* involves allocating a fixed percentage of past or anticipated sales revenue to advertising. For example, a company may allocate 5% of the next fiscal period's anticipated sales to advertising. If sales are estimated to be $100 million for the upcoming year, the advertising budget will be $5 million. The *objective-and-task method* involves the following three-step procedure:

(1) specifying the objectives that a particular ad or entire ad campaign is intended to achieve, (2) identifying the specific tasks that must be accomplished in order to reach these objectives, and (3) estimating the anticipated cost of achieving the specified tasks. The outcome of this systematic, three-step process is an advertising budget that should be sufficient to achieve critical objectives.

Establishing the Brand Positioning

Managers work with their advertising agencies to formulate specific meanings for their brands. This meaning, or positioning, establishes how the company wants the brand to be thought of by members of the target market and how the company wants the brand to be perceived compared to competitive brands in the product category. To illustrate positioning strategies: Volvo is basically synonymous with safety, Absolut vodka has built a reputation for being cosmopolitan and hip, Godiva chocolate represents pleasurable indulgence in the minds of many consumers, and Nike is *the* brand for serious athletes.

Creating Advertising Messages

Advertisers use a vast array of techniques to present their brands in the most favorable light and persuade customers to contemplate purchasing these brands. Frequently used techniques include:

Houston Rockets center, Yao Ming, provides celebrity endorsements for a variety of products including the Apple iMac, Visa Check Card, and Gatorade.

1. Informational ads (such as automobile ads in the classified pages of a newspaper).
2. Emotional ads appealing to consumers' nostalgic sentiments, love for family, sense of humor, excitement, and so forth.
3. Sex appeal (e.g., TV commercials for Victoria Secret's lingerie items displaying barely clad women in provocative poses that previous generations would have considered virtually pornographic).
4. Celebrity endorsements (e.g., advertisements featuring athletes such as Tiger Woods and Yao Ming).

The techniques to persuasively advertise brands are limited only by advertisers' creativity and ingenuity. It is beyond the scope of this text to go into detail concerning these and other advertising techniques. Rather, we pose a more straightforward question: What makes an advertisement good or effective? Although it is impractical to provide a singular, all-purpose definition of what constitutes effective advertising, it is meaningful to talk about general characteristics.[29] At a minimum, good or effective advertising satisfies the following considerations:

1. *It extends from sound marketing strategy.* Advertising can be effective only if it is compatible with other elements of an integrated and well-orchestrated MarCom strategy.
2. *It takes the customer's view.* Customers buy product benefits, not attributes. Therefore, advertising must be presented in a way that relates to the customer's needs, wants, and values, and not strictly in terms of product characteristics.
3. *It is persuasive.* Persuasion usually occurs when there is a benefit for the customer, and not just for the marketer. Advertisements that present customers with meaningful benefits enhance brand attitudes, increase purchase intentions, and drive purchase behavior. Such ads are, in short, persuasive.
4. *It finds a unique way to break through competitive clutter.* Advertisers continuously vie with competitors for the customer's attention. This is no small task,

These ads demonstrate creative advertising. The milk-mustached campaign that associates drinking milk with a wide variety of interesting celebrities appeals to a variety of target markets. Absolut vodka's continuing magazine campaign focuses on this brand's "hip" image by portraying the brand's unique bottle shape in trendy situations.

Absolut Country of Sweden Vodka & Logo, Absolut, Absolut Bottle design and Absolut calligraphy are trademarks owned by V&S Vin & Sprit AB. © 2003 V&S Sprit AB.

considering the massive number of print advertisements, broadcast commercials, and other sources of information that are routinely available. Consumers, purchasing agents, and other buyers have more important things to do in their lives than processing advertisements. Accordingly, effective advertisements must provide informational and/or entertainment value to overcome the cluttered mass of ads and other media content that literally surround us.

5. *It never promises more than it can deliver.* This point speaks for itself, both in terms of ethics and in terms of smart business sense. Customers learn quickly when they have been deceived, and resent it. In some situations, an advertiser can succeed *in the short term* by presenting misleading promises in advertising that a brand cannot deliver. Customers who have been led to buy a particular product that doesn't live up to its advertising claims inevitably become dissatisfied and are unlikely to repurchase the same brand in the future. So, although the misleading/deceptive advertising has encouraged a single purchase, it is unable to forge a long-term relationship with the customer. And, as previously discussed when describing features of IMC, long-term relationships are the stuff of successful marketing and MarCom programs.

6. *It prevents the creative idea from overwhelming the strategy.* The purpose of advertising is to persuade and influence; the purpose is not to be cute for cute's sake or humorous for humor's sake. The ineffective use of humor, for example, results in people remembering the humor, but forgetting the selling message.

Effective advertising is usually *creative*. That is, it differentiates itself from the mass of mediocre advertisements; it is somehow different and out-of-the-ordinary. Advertising that is the same as most other advertising is unable to break through the competitive clutter and fails to grab the customer's attention. It is easier to give examples of creative advertising than to define exactly what it is.

Selecting Advertising Media

Outstanding message execution is of no avail unless the messages are delivered to the right customers at the right time, and with sufficient frequency. In other words, advertising messages stand a chance of being effective only if the media strategy itself is effective. Good messages and good media go hand in hand; they are inseparable—a true marriage. Improper media selection can doom an otherwise promising advertising campaign.

Creative advertisements are more effective when placed in media whose characteristics enhance the value of the advertising message and reach the advertiser's targeted customers at the right time. A variety of decisions must be made when choosing media. In addition to determining which media to use (television, radio, magazines, online, etc.), the media planner must also pick *vehicles*, or ad carriers, within each medium (e.g., specific magazines, such as *Cosmopolitan* and *Business Week*; TV programs, such as *ER* and *20/20*; and newspapers, such as *USA Today*), and decide how to allocate the available budget among the various media and vehicle alternatives. Additional decisions involve determining when to advertise, choosing specific geographical locations, and deciding how to distribute the budget over time and across geographic locations.

Successful media strategy requires, first, that the target audience be clearly pinpointed. Failure to precisely define the audience results in wasted exposures; that is, some nonpurchase candidates are exposed to advertisements, while some prime candidates are missed. Target audiences are usually selected based on *demographic* considerations (e.g., the Honda Element's advertising is directed primarily to young men in the Gen X age category); *psychographic* characteristics (e.g., Honda Element ads are directed to guys who enjoy active, outdoor lifestyles); *geographic* factors (e.g., the ads are directed more at young men living in areas known for their active, outdoor lifestyles—e.g., California, Colorado, Florida); and *buyographic* (a word implying past buying behavior) considerations, such as identifying young men who already own a pickup truck or an SUV.

A second aspect of media strategy is establishing specific objectives. Four objectives are fundamental to media planning: reach, frequency, timing, and cost. Media planners seek answers to the following types of questions:

1. What portion of the target audience do we want to see (or read, or hear) the advertising message? (a *reach* issue)
2. How often within a particular period of time (say, four weeks) should the average target audience member be exposed to the advertisement? (a *frequency* issue)
3. When are the best occasions (times of year, days of week, times of day) to reach the target audience? (a *timing* issue)
4. What is the least expensive way to accomplish the other objectives? (a *cost* issue)

Advertisers work with statistics such as ratings, gross rating points, and cost per thousand to compare different vehicles within the same medium and to make intelligent selections. For example, AFLAC (of white duck fame) advertises its insurance on evening news programs such as *NBC Nightly News* with anchor Tom Brokaw. Assume that this particular program reaches an average of 10 million households each night. Since there are approximately 107 million households in the U.S., this means that an AFLAC ad carried on *NBC Nightly News* would produce an average *rating* of 9.3 percentage points ($10 \div 107$). If during a four-week period a total of 20 AFLAC commercials were aired on *NBC Nightly News*, this program would accumulate a total of 186 *gross rating points*, or *GRPs*; i.e., 20 ads at an average rating of 9.3. **Gross rating points (GRPs)** are the accumulation of rating points including all vehicles in a media purchase over the span of a particular campaign. GRPs simply represent the mathematical product of individual ratings times the number of times that an advertisement is aired on a TV program (or placed in a magazine or other medium). In equation form, GRPs = R × F, where R equals reach and F equals frequency of ad placement.

Cost per thousand (CPM) (where the *M* is the Roman numeral for 1,000) is a useful statistic for comparing the cost efficiency of vehicles in the same medium. **Cost per thousand (CPM)** is calculated by dividing the cost of an ad placed in a particular ad vehicle (e.g., certain magazine) by the number of people (expressed in thousands)

Gross rating points (GRPs)
Are the accumulation of rating points, including all vehicles in a media purchase, over the span of a particular campaign.

Cost per thousand (CPM)
Is calculated by dividing the cost of an ad placed in a particular ad vehicle (e.g., certain magazine) by the number of people (expressed in thousands) who are exposed to that vehicle.

who are exposed to that vehicle. For example, in a recent year, a single four-color full-page advertisement placed in *Sports Illustrated* cost the advertiser about $203,000 and reached approximately 20,383,000 male readers of this magazine. Therefore, the CPM = cost of ad placement ($203,000) ÷ size of audience expressed in thousands (20,383) = $9.96.[30]

The advertiser would compare this value with the CPM to advertise in alternative vehicles. For example, in this same year, a full-page four-color ad placed in *Golf Digest* magazine cost $126,930 and reached 5,413,000 readers. *Golf Digest*'s CPM is $23.45 (i.e., $126,930 ÷ 5,413). *Sports Illustrated* is a less expensive vehicle on a per-thousand basis than *Golf Digest* and is the obvious better buy when considering cost alone. However, the decision on which magazine to select is based on considerations other than cost. Also crucial are factors such as how closely a vehicle's readers/viewers match the brand's target audience and the fit between the image of the vehicle and the brand's desired image.

Advertisers have a variety of media from which to choose. These include the major mass media (television, radio, magazines, and newspapers), out-of-home media (billboards, transit advertising, etc.), advertising via various "alternative" media (product placements in movies and TV programs, advertising via CD-ROMS, logo advertising on automobiles, etc.), online advertising, and point-of-purchase advertising. There are as many advertising media as there are unique spaces for locating advertisements. For example, boxers sometimes appear in the ring with the names of casinos or other brands temporarily tattooed on their backs. A London ad agency has recruited university students to get their foreheads temporarily tattooed with brand logos (temporary tattoos last about a week). Students get paid approximately $7 an hour to walk around in locales where potential customers of their tattooed brands are likely to be situated.[31]

Each advertising medium possesses various strengths and weaknesses. Figure 13.5 provides a detailed listing of the strengths and weaknesses for each of the major mass media.[32] Because students are more familiar with advertising in traditional mass media (who could escape it?), we will focus instead on two forms of advertising that are relatively new in one case (i.e., online advertising) and relatively unknown in the other (i.e., point-of-purchase advertising).

Online Advertising. Conventional advertising media have served advertisers' needs for many years, but recently advertisers and their agencies have increased their efforts to identify new advertising media that are less costly, less cluttered, and potentially more effective than established media. The Internet provides one such medium. Various commentators have claimed that the Internet as a communications medium is more versatile than other media and superior at targeting customers.[33]

Although it dates back only to 1994, commercial use of the Internet has the potential to become an invaluable advertising medium. More than 60% of the U.S. population, or nearly 170 million people, have Internet access at home or at work. Other countries with high Internet usage include Germany (28 million), the United Kingdom (24 million), Italy (18 million), Taiwan (12 million), and Australia (10 million).[34] In comparing the Internet to other ad media, here is what the CEO of the Internet Advertising Bureau (IAB), the trade association for Internet advertising, had to say:

The Internet is a medium that consumers spend more time with than either newspapers or magazines and is the only medium where consumers are one click from a purchase. It has all the capabilities of direct mail at a fraction of the cost, and reaches the most educated and affluent Americans where they live and work.[35]

Individualization and interactivity (the Internet's two Is) are key features of the Internet and of advertising in that medium.[36] *Individualization* refers to the fact that the Internet user has control over the flow of information. This feature enables advertisers, in turn, to target relevant advertisements and promotions to specific cus-

Comparative Strengths and Weaknesses of Major Advertising Media		Figure 13.5

Medium	Strengths	Weaknesses
Television	• Dramatic presentation and demonstration ability • High reach potential • Attain rapid awareness • Relatively efficient • Intrusive and impactive • Ability to integrate messages with other media such as radio	• Relatively downscale audience profile • Network audience erosion • Growing commercial clutter • High out-of-pocket cost • High production costs • Long lead time to purchase network time • Volatile cost structure
Radio	• Target selectivity • High frequency • Efficient • Able to transfer image from TV • Portable, personal medium • Low production cost • Use of local personalities • Ability to integrate messages with other media such as TV	• Commercial clutter • Some station formats relatively uninvolving for listeners • Relatively small audiences • High out-of-pocket cost to attain significant reach • Audience fractionalization
Magazines	• Efficient reach for selective audiences • Ability to match advertising with compatible editorial content • High-quality graphics • Reach light TV viewers • Opportunity to repeat ad exposure • Flexibility in target-market coverage • Can deliver complex copy • Readership is not seasonal	• Not intrusive; reader controls ad exposure • Slow audience accumulation • Significant slippage from reader audience to ad-exposure audience • Clutter can be high • Long lead times to purchase magazine space • Somewhat limited geographic options • Uneven market-by-market circulation patterns
Newspapers	• Rapid audience accumulation • Timeliness • High single-day reach attainable • Short lead times to purchase newspaper space • Excellent geographic flexibility • Can convey detailed concepts • Strong retail trade support • Good for merchandising and promotion • Low production cost • Excellent local market penetration	• Limited target selectivity • High out-of-pocket costs for national buys • Significant differential between national and local rates • Not intrusive • Cluttered ad environment • Generally mediocre reproduction quality
Online Advertising	• Broad reach • Relatively low cost • Timeliness • Ability to reach both targeted and mass audiences • Around-the-globe coverage	• Cluttered media environment • Sometimes excessive intrusion • Limited demonstration ability • Difficulty measuring effectiveness

Source: Adapted from *Marketer's Guide to Media*, Fall/Winter 1994–1995, 17, 2 (New York: ADWEEK): Copyright © 1994 VNU Business Media Inc.

tomers. *Interactivity*, which is intertwined with individualization, allows users to select the information they perceive as relevant and advertisers to build relationships with customers via two-way communication.

Contrary to the early hype, when many businesspeople thought the Internet would be an advertising panacea, it can be argued that this medium's interactivity feature may represent a disadvantage rather than an advantage. That is, the Internet user is in a "leaning forward" mind-set compared with, say, the TV viewer who is "leaning back." In other words, whereas the TV viewer is casually watching TV programs and advertisements in a relaxed mood (leaning back, so to speak), the Internet user is goal driven and on a mission to obtain information (leaning forward). In this mind-set, banner ads and pop-ups simply represent an interruption, an obstacle to the user's primary mission for connecting to the Internet.[37] Advertisements seen while in a leaning-forward mission mind-set are actively avoided and may accomplish little more than achieving brand identification.

It has been estimated that the average Internet user will be exposed to more than 900 banner ads daily by 2005.[38] The vast majority of these ads never receive our attention, and click-through rates average less than 0.5%. In other words, online users attend to and solicit information from only a small percentage of all the banner ads to which they are exposed. Internet advertisers, like advertisers in all other media, have to fight through the clutter to find ways to attract the online user's attention. Bigger ads, ads popping up, and ads that offer sound and gyrating visuals are just some of the ways that have been devised to attract and hold the Internet user's attention.

The major growth area in online advertising is not mass-oriented advertising via banner ads, pop-ups, and various forms of moving ads, but rather advertising via e-mail. *E-mail advertising* involves using the Internet to send commercial messages via e-mail messages. As with any other advertising medium, there is no such thing as a single type of e-mail message; rather, e-mail messages appear in many forms, ranging from pure-text documents to more sophisticated versions that use all the audio-video powers of the Internet. E-mail is the most heavily used form of Internet advertising and far exceeds the amount invested in alternative advertising forms such as banners and pop-ups.

It has been estimated that more than 20% of the e-mail that people receive is marketing related.[39] Expenditures on e-mail advertising are expected to exceed $9 billion by 2006.[40] Roughly half of the marketing-related e-mail is opt-in, or permission-granted, e-mail, while the remainder is unsolicited, or so-called spam. **Opt-in e-mailing** is the practice of marketers asking for and receiving customers' permission to send them messages on particular topics. The customer has agreed, or opted-in, to receive messages on topics of interest rather than receiving messages that are unsolicited. E-mail advertising is stringently regulated in Europe. European Union countries require companies to inform customers about data being collected and retained, explain to customers how the data will be used in the future, and provide customers with the opportunity to opt-in or out of the process.

Imagine, for example, that a consumer interested in purchasing a CD player that holds 400 CDs conducts a Google.com search by inputting "CDs + 400." Google quickly displays a number of sites, and she proceeds to click through one particularly promising Web site. While logged into this site, which is quite informative, she receives a query that asks whether she would be interested in receiving more information about CD players. She replies "yes" and provides her e-mail address, as well as other information. The Web site electronically records her "permission granted" and, unknown to this unsuspecting shopper, sells her name and address to a broker that specializes in compiling lists. This list broker, in turn, sells her name and e-mail address to companies that market CD players and other home electronic equipment and supplies. Our hypothetical Internet user's name and e-mail address eventually appears on a variety of lists, and she will receive regular e-mail messages for audio equipment and supplies—many of which are of no interest whatsoever to her.

In theory, opt-in e-mailing serves both the marketer's and the customer's interests. However, the frequency and quantity of e-mail messages can become intrusive as more and more companies have access to your name and areas of interest. Customers feel especially violated when e-mail messages deal with topics that are tangential to their primary interests. For example, when granting the original Web site permission to send audio-related messages, our unsuspecting consumer may have

Opt-in e-mailing

Is the practice of marketers asking for and receiving customers' permission to send them messages on particular topics. The customer has agreed, or opted-in, to receive messages on topics of interest rather than receiving messages that are unsolicited.

Political and Legal Forces

Many abuses of e-mail advertising exist, especially companies sending unsolicited messages and selling e-mail addresses to list brokers. U.S. Congressional committees are debating the merits of regulating e-mail advertising, although no major statutes have as yet been passed. Even the Direct Marketing Association, a powerful trade association that represents direct marketers, favors federal legislation that restricts spam.[41]

been interested only in information about CD players, but may then be subsequently bombarded with messages involving more aspects of audio products than she ever could have imagined. She did not realize what she had opted for—some of the information she received was relevant, but most was not.

Although this example may appear to cast a negative light on opt-in e-mail, the fact remains that advertisers that send messages to individuals whose interests are known, if only somewhat broadly, increase their odds of providing customers with relevant information. Moreover, sophisticated marketers are using a more detailed opt-in procedure so they can better serve both their own needs for accurate targeting and customers' needs for relevant information.

Compare this with the practice of sending unsolicited e-mail messages, the practice pejoratively referred to as *spam*. Such messages offer little prospect that recipients will do much more than click on and then rapidly click off. It could be argued that spam at least has a chance of influencing brand awareness, perhaps much like what may happen when the customer is perusing a magazine and unintentionally comes across an ad for a product in which he has little interest. However, while customers expect to see ads in magazines and realize that this is part of the "cost of entry," customers do not, at least at the present time, expect to receive unsolicited e-mail messages. Thus, any brand awareness gain a marketer might obtain from e-mailing unsolicited messages is likely to be offset by the negative reaction customers have to this form of advertising.

Point-of-Purchase Advertising. Marketers use a variety of items at the point-of-purchase to draw attention to their brands and activate customer purchases. These include signs, mobiles, plaques, banners, shelf "talkers," mechanical mannequins, lights, mirrors, plastic product reproductions, checkout units, full-line merchandisers, wall posters, motion displays, and other materials. Retailers and brand managers recognize the value of point-of-purchase (P-O-P) advertising; indeed, Point of Purchase Advertising International (POPAI), the trade association for this form of advertising, estimates that in one recent year marketers in the U.S. spent $17 billion on P-O-P advertising.[42] This level of expenditure can be justified by the fact that point-of-purchase materials provide a useful service for all participants in the marketing process—manufacturers, retailers, and consumers. Effective P-O-P advertising serves to attract the consumer's attention, increase his or her interest in shopping, and extend the amount of time spent in the store—all of which mean increased sales. P-O-P advertising also keeps brand names before the consumer and reactivates and reinforces brand information the consumer has previously received through mass-media advertising. P-O-P calls attention to special offers such as sales promotions and stimulates impulse purchasing. P-O-P serves to reinforce the job already performed by advertising before the consumer enters a store. Indeed, P-O-P advertising represents the capstone for an integrated MarCom program.

Because many product- and brand-choice decisions are made while the consumer is in the store, rather than before he arrives, point-of-purchase materials play a role, perhaps the major role, in influencing unplanned purchasing. POPAI performed a major study based on a national sample of supermarkets and mass-merchandise outlets (e.g., Wal-Mart) and determined that 70–74% of purchase decisions for items carried in these types of retail outlets are made by shoppers while in the store.[43]

Assessing Advertising Effectiveness

Assessing advertising effectiveness is a final critical aspect of advertising strategy to determine if advertising objectives have been accomplished. This often requires that baseline measures be taken before an advertising campaign begins (to determine, for example, what percentage of the target audience is aware of the brand name), and then afterwards to determine whether the objective was achieved. Advertisers do, or at least should, go to great lengths to measure the effectiveness of their advertise-

Teenagers Purchasing Online Without a Credit Card

There are more than 25 million 13- to 19-year-olds in the United States. Needless to say, they have tremendous earning power and considerable influence on both personal and household purchases. Teenagers are a large subset of the age group often referred to as the *Millennial Generation* or *Generation Y* (in contrast to the generation that preceded it, *Generation X*). Technically speaking, Gen Y consists of individuals born between 1979 and 1994. Thus, as of 2003, Gen Yers include all people between the ages of 9 and 24, approximately 60 million Americans. The present discussion focuses just on the Gen Y subset of teenagers.

A study by Teenage Research Unlimited, which follows teen trends and attitudes, estimated that American teenagers spent $155 billion in one recent year. Teenagers have far more purchasing influence and power than ever before, which accounts for the growth of MarCom programs aimed at this group.

An accepted product can become a huge success when the teenage bandwagon selects a brand as a personal mark of the in-crowd. However, today's accepted product or brand can easily become tomorrow's passé item. It is said that teenagers don't like to be "marketed to." As with all consumers, it is important that marketing communicators provide useful information, but teens like to acquire the information themselves—such as on the Internet or from friends—rather than having it imposed on them. MarCom personnel thus walk a precarious plank in communicating useful information to teens while avoiding being overbearing. The Internet is an obvious communication medium for reaching teens, but an interesting issue arises: How do teenagers make online purchases if they don't have their own credit cards?

Rocketcash.com was launched to solve this problem. Here is how it works: Parents or other relatives deposit money into an account held in the teenager's name. The teenage user contacts the Rocketcash.com site, which is linked to dozens of Web merchants such as adidas.com, bestbuy.com, dell.com, jcrew.com, oldnavy.com, and other popular online merchants. Kids thus have the freedom to shop online and gain a sense of fiscal responsibility, and parents don't have to worry about their children running up excessive credit-card bills. Seventeen is the average age of Rocketcash's customers. Rocketcash's revenue source is commissions from its merchant partners that range from 5% to 15% of the purchase amount.

Sources: Dan Lippe, "It's All in Creative Delivery," *Advertising Age,* 25 June 2001, S-8.
  Adam Bryant, "Where's My E-llowance?" Grok (http://www.thestandard.com/grok), February–March 2001, 58–59; http://www.thestandard.com; http://www.rocketcash.com, (accessed February 2001).

ments. There is literally an entire industry of companies that are in business to measure advertising effectiveness. For example, two competitive companies, Simmons Market Research Bureau (SMRB) and Mediamark Research, Inc. (MRI), specialize in measuring magazine readership. Nielsen Media Research measures television audience size and provides advertisers with audience-size statistics such as program *ratings* (as discussed above). Then there are services that assess consumer recognition and recall of magazine ads (Starch Readership Service) and of television commercials (Burke Day-After Recall), and measures of the persuasive impact of TV commercials (such as performed by Ipsos-ASI and RSC).[44]

All of the above services are designed to measure advertising effectiveness of B2C companies. Unfortunately, companies involved in B2B advertising do not have the same quality of research services available. However, it is worth noting that many B2B companies pay for outside vendors to perform *clipping services*. That is, these vendors literally track all advertisements in trade publications that are directed at potential buyers in a particular line of business. Thus, a B2B marketer may pay to have an outside vendor track its competitors' advertising efforts in select trade magazines in order to know how extensively competitors are advertising, as well as what they are saying about their products.

Finally, small businesses such as retailers of goods and services typically do not have the luxury of conducting sophisticated advertising research or paying for the services of outside suppliers that specialize in such research. However, it is critical to note that every business, as well as not-for-profit organization, can conduct its own advertising research, even if informally. For example, consider the situation of a new retail furniture store that has not yet advertised during its first six months of operation. The retailer now decides to advertise in the local newspaper in hopes of getting more shoppers to the store. Rather than assuming that the advertising will be effective, this furniture retailer should conduct an "empirical test." In particular, it should record the number of prospective customers who visit the store *after* the advertisement is placed in the newspaper and compare that number to the number of shoppers who visited the store *before* the ad was placed. In other words, this retailer should take a baseline measurement of average store traffic for, say, two weeks before placing the newspaper ad and then compare that baseline level with the average store traffic for two weeks after the ad has run in the newspaper. Needless to say, actual sales receipts also can be compared for these "before" and "after" periods. Regardless of exactly how the retailer decides to do it, efforts to measure advertising effectiveness can and should be made by *any* business or not-for-profit organization, regardless of size. Failure to measure ad effectiveness is tantamount to merely wishing that advertising will be successful or assuming, after the fact, that it has been effective. Sophisticated managers, regardless of the size of their organizations, should do everything possible to measure advertising effectiveness. And students such as you who are receiving formal training in business education are especially obligated to measure advertising effectiveness.

Sales Promotion

Sales promotions involve incentives offered by a manufacturer to induce the trade (wholesalers and retailers) and/or consumers to buy a brand and/or to encourage the sales force to aggressively sell it. Retailers also use promotions to encourage greater purchasing by their customers. The incentive is in addition to the basic benefits provided by the brand and temporarily changes its perceived price or value. By definition, sales promotions involve *incentives* that are additions to, not substitutes for, the basic benefits a purchaser typically acquires when buying a particular brand. The target of the incentive is the trade, final consumers, the sales force, or all three. The incentive changes a brand's perceived price/value, but only temporarily. In other words, a sales-promotion incentive for a particular brand applies to a single purchase or perhaps several purchases during a particular period, but not to every purchase a customer makes over an extended period.

A Shift from Advertising to Sales Promotion

Historically, the promotional emphasis in many consumer-goods firms was on creating promotional pull. That is, manufacturers advertised heavily, especially on network television, and literally forced retailers to handle their products by virtue of the fact that consumers demanded heavily advertised brands. This advertising served, in other words, to pull the manufacturer's product through the channel of distribution. However, over the past two decades, *pull-oriented* marketing has become less effective as a result of fragmented media. Along with this reduced effectiveness has come an increase in the use of *push-oriented* sales-promotion practices by which manufacturers have targeted increased efforts, including promotional incentives, directly to the trade (wholesalers and retailers) rather than to the ultimate consumer. This does not mean that manufacturers no longer advertise to final consumers; rather, the point is that proportionately less of the total MarCom budget is being directed to final consumers and proportionately more is being directed to the trade.

The result of these developments is that advertising expenditures in mass media (television, radio, magazines, newspaper, and outdoor advertising) have declined in most firms as a percentage of their total MarCom expenditures. On the other hand, expenditures on sales promotions, direct marketing, and sponsorships have steadily increased. In fact, annual studies have shown that media advertising expenditures as a proportion of companies' total MarCom spending have declined steadily for more than a decade. While media advertising used to average more than 40% of companies' MarCom budgets, its portion of the total budget has fallen to about 25%. By comparison, trade promotions now constitute, on average, at least 50% of companies' total MarCom budgets.[45]

Increased investment in sales promotions, especially trade-oriented promotions, has gone hand-in-hand with the trend toward greater push-oriented marketing. The factors listed below account for the shift in allocating promotion budgets away from advertising toward sales promotion and other forms of marketing communications. These are summarized in Figure 13.6.

1. *Balance-of-Power Transfer.* Until recently, national manufacturers of consumer goods used to be more powerful than the supermarkets, drugstores, and mass merchandisers that carried the manufacturers' brands. However, the balance of power began shifting when network television dipped in effectiveness as an advertising medium and, especially, with the advent of optical scanning equipment, which allowed retailers to attain as much market power via market information as previously had been possessed only by manufacturers. The consequence for manufacturers is that for every promotional dollar used to support retailers' advertising or merchandising programs, one less dollar is available for the manufacturer's own advertising.

2. *Increased Brand Parity and Price Sensitivity.* In earlier years when truly new products were being offered to the marketplace, manufacturers could effectively advertise their products' unique advantages over competitive offerings. As product categories have matured, however, most new offerings represent only slight changes from existing products, resulting in more similarities than differences between competitive brands. With fewer distinct product differences, consumers rely more on price and price incentives (coupons, cents-off deals, refunds, automobile and computer rebates, etc.) as a way of differentiating alternative parity brands. Because real, concrete advantages are often difficult to obtain, firms have turned increasingly to sales promotion as a means of achieving at least temporary advantages over competitors.

3. *Reduced Brand Loyalty.* Consumers have become less loyal to brands than they once were. This is partly due to the fact that brands have grown increasingly similar, thereby making it easier for consumers to switch among brands. Also, marketers have effectively trained consumers to expect that at least one brand in a product category will always be on deal with a coupon, cents-off offer, or refund; thus, many consumers rarely purchase brands other than those that offer a deal. The upshot of all of this dealing activity is that marketers' extensive use of sales promotions has reduced brand loyalty and increased switching behavior, thereby requiring even more dealing activity to feed consumers' insatiable desire for deals.

4. *Splintering of the Mass Market and Reduced Media Effectiveness.* Advertising efficiency is directly related to the degree of homogeneity in consumers' consumption needs and media habits. The more homogeneous these needs and habits are, the less costly it is for mass advertising to reach target audiences. However, as consumer lifestyles have become more diverse and advertising media have narrowed in their appeal, mass-media advertising is no longer as efficient as it once was. On top of this, advertising effectiveness has declined with simultaneous increases in ad clutter and escalating media costs. These combined forces have influenced many brand managers to devote proportionately larger budgets to sales promotions.

Figure 13.6	Factors Giving Rise to the Growth of Sales Promotions

1. Balance-of-power transfer
2. Increased brand parity and price sensitivity
3. Reduced brand loyalty
4. Splintering of the mass market and reduced media effectiveness
5. Short-term orientation and corporate reward structures
6. Trade and customer responsiveness

5. *Short-Term Orientation and Corporate Reward Structures.* The brand-management system and sales promotion are perfect partners. The reward structure in firms organized along brand-manager lines emphasizes short-term sales response rather than slow, long-term growth, and sales promotion is incomparable when it comes to generating quick sales response. In fact, the majority of sales for many brands of packaged goods are associated with some kind of promotional deal.

6. *Trade and Consumer Responsiveness.* A final force that explains the shift toward sales promotion at the expense of advertising is that retailers and wholesalers (the trade) and consumers respond favorably to money-saving opportunities.

Sales Promotion: Roles and Objectives

Sales promotion is well suited for accomplishing the following 10 tasks, which are summarized in Figure 13.7.

1. *Facilitating the Introduction of New Products to the Trade.* Sales promotions to wholesalers and retailers are often necessary to encourage the trade to handle new products. In fact, many retailers refuse to carry new products unless they receive extra compensation in the form of trade allowances, display allowances, and other forms of allowances.

2. *Obtaining Trial Purchases from Consumers.* Marketers depend on free samples, coupons, and other sales promotions to encourage trial purchases of new products. Many consumers would never try new products without these promotional inducements.

3. *Stimulating Sales-Force Enthusiasm for New, Improved, or Mature Brands.* Exciting sales promotions give salespeople extra ammunition when interacting with buyers; they revive enthusiasm and make the salesperson's job easier and more enjoyable.

4. *Invigorating Sales of a Mature Brand.* Sales promotion can stimulate sales of a mature brand that requires a shot in the arm.

5. *Increasing On- and Off-Shelf Merchandising Space.* Trade-oriented sales promotions enable a manufacturer to obtain extra shelf space for a temporary period. This space may be in the form of extra facing (i.e., rows of shelf space) or off-shelf space in, for example, an end-aisle display.

6. *Neutralizing Competitive Advertising and Sales Promotion.* Sales promotions can be used to offset competitors' advertising and sales-promotion efforts. For example, one company's 50-cents-off coupon loses much of its appeal when a competitor simultaneously comes out with a $1 coupon.

7. *Holding Current Users by Encouraging Repeat Purchases.* Brand switching is a fact of life faced by all brand managers. The strategic use of certain forms of sales promotion can encourage at least short-run repetitive purchasing. Premium programs, refunds, and various other devices are used to encourage repeat purchasing.

Sales Promotion's Capabilities	Figure 13.7

1. Facilitate introduction of new products to the trade
2. Induce trial purchases by customers
3. Stimulate sales-force enthusiasm
4. Invigorate sales of mature brand
5. Increase merchandise space
6. Neutralize competitive advertising and sales promotions
7. Hold current customers by encouraging repeat purchasing
8. Increase product usage by loading customers
9. Preempt competition by loading customers
10. Reinforce advertising

8. *Increasing Brand Usage by Loading Consumers.* Consumers tend to use more of certain products (e.g., snack foods and soft drinks) when they have more of them available in their homes. Thus, sales-promotion efforts that encourage consumers to stock up with greater quantities than they normally would buy on a particular purchase occasion generate temporary increases in brand usage. This practice is referred to as *loading* consumers. Bonus packs and two-for-the-price-of-one deals are particularly effective loading devices.
9. *Preempting Competition by Loading Consumers.* When consumers are loaded with one company's brand, they are temporarily out of the marketplace for competitive brands. Thus, one brand's sales promotion serves to preempt sales of competitive brands.
10. *Reinforcing Advertising.* A final can-do capability of sales promotion is to reinforce advertising. An advertising campaign can be strengthened greatly by a well-coordinated sales-promotion effort.

Sales promotions are clearly capable of performing important tasks. There are, however, distinct limitations that are beyond the capability of sales promotions. In particular, sales promotions cannot (1) compensate for a poorly trained sales force, (2) give the trade or consumers any compelling long-term reason to continue purchasing a brand, or (3) permanently stop an established brand's declining sales trend, or change the basic nonacceptance of an undesired brand.

Trade Promotions: Role and Objectives
As earlier noted, manufacturers use some combination of push and pull strategies to accomplish both retail distribution and consumer purchases. **Trade promotions**, typically in the form of off-invoice allowances, are directed at wholesalers, retailers, and other marketing intermediaries. This form of promotion represents the first step in any promotional effort. Consumer promotions are likely to fail unless trade-promotion efforts have succeeded in getting wholesalers to distribute the product and retailers to stock adequate quantities. The special incentives offered by manufacturers to their distribution-channel members are intended to be passed along to consumers in the form of price discounts offered by retailers, which in turn are often stimulated by advertising support and special displays. As we will see, this does not always occur.

A manufacturer's objectives for using trade-oriented sales promotions may be to: (1) introduce new or revised products, (2) increase distribution of new packages or sizes, (3) build retail inventories, (4) maintain or increase the manufacturer's share of shelf space, (5) obtain displays outside normal shelf locations, (6) reduce excess inventories and increase turnover, (7) achieve feature space in retailers' advertisements, (8) counter competitive activity, and/or, ultimately, (9) sell as much as possible to final consumers.[46]

Trade Allowances. Manufacturers use a variety of trade-oriented promotional inducements, most of which are some form of trade allowance. **Trade allowances**, or trade deals, come in a variety of forms and are offered to retailers simply for purchasing the manufacturer's brand or for performing activities in support of the manufacturer's brand. These allowances/deals are needed to encourage retailers to stock the manufacturer's brand, discount the brand's price to consumers, feature it in advertising, and/or provide special display or other point-of-purchase support. The most frequently used allowance is an off-invoice allowance. **Off-invoice allowances** are deals offered periodically to the trade that allow wholesalers and retailers to simply deduct a fixed amount, say 15%, from the full price at the time the order is placed. By using off-invoice allowances, manufacturers hope to increase retailers' purchases of the manufacturers' brands and increase consumers' purchases of the manufacturers' brands from retailers. This latter objective is based on the expectation that retailers will in fact pass along to consumers the discounts they receive from manufacturers, which unfortunately does not always happen.

Trade promotions
Typically in the form of off-invoice allowances, are directed at wholesalers, retailers, and other marketing intermediaries. This form of promotion represents the first step in any promotional effort.

Trade allowances
Or trade deals, come in a variety of forms and are offered to retailers simply for purchasing the manufacturer's brand or for performing activities in support of the manufacturer's brand.

Off-invoice allowances
Are deals offered periodically to the trade that allow wholesalers and retailers to simply deduct a fixed amount (e.g., 15%), from the full price at the time the order is placed.

Off-invoice trade allowances create significant problems for the manufacturers that use them. One particular problem is that off-invoice allowances often induce the trade to stockpile products in order to take advantage of the temporary price reduction. This merely shifts business from the future to the present. Two prevalent practices are *forward buying* and *diverting,* both of which represent wholesalers' and retailers' efforts to earn money from *buying* on deal rather than from selling merchandise at a profit.

Manufacturers' off-invoice allowances typically are available every four weeks of each business quarter (which translates to about 30% of the year), and a number of manufacturers sell upward of 80–90% of their volume at less than full price. **Forward buying** or **bridge buying**, is when retailers purchase enough product during a manufacturer's off-invoice allowance period to carry the retailers over until the manufacturer's next regularly scheduled deal. When a manufacturer marks down a product's price by, say, 10%, wholesalers and retailers commonly stock up (i.e., *forward buy*) with a 10- to 12-week supply. Wholesalers and retailers are rational businesspeople: They take advantage of deals!

A related buying practice, **diverting**, occurs when a manufacturer restricts an off-invoice allowance to a limited geographical area, resulting in some wholesalers and retailers buying abnormally large quantities at the deal price and then transshipping the excess quantities to other geographical areas. The transshipping retailer earns a small profit on each item when engaging in this practice. Interestingly, the practice of diverting in a marketing context is equivalent to what is known as *arbitrage* in finance circles, where financiers simultaneously buy and sell securities or foreign exchange in different markets to profit from unequal prices.

Trade Shows. A specialized form of trade promotion is the trade show. A **trade show** is a temporary forum (typically lasting several days) for sellers of a product category (such as small appliances, toys, clothing, furniture, industrial tools, food products, or sporting goods) to exhibit and demonstrate their wares to present and prospective buyers. Trade shows provide an extremely effective mechanism for assisting customers in learning about and trying new products. Thousands of trade shows are conducted annually in North America, and these shows attract millions of attendees to the booths of the more than one million companies that exhibit their products at these shows. Trade show activity is even greater in Europe, representing approximately one-fourth of the total marketing communications budgets for European business-to-business firms (compared to one-fifth among North American companies).[47] Business-to-business firms are especially likely to allocate a relatively large percentage of their MarCom budgets to trade shows.

Trade show attendees include most of an industry's important manufacturers and major customers. This enables the trade show exhibitor to accomplish both selling and nonselling functions. Specific functions include (1) servicing present customers, (2) identifying prospects, (3) introducing new or modified products, (4) gathering information about competitors' new products, (5) taking product orders, and (6) enhancing the company's image.[48]

Trade shows are an excellent forum for introducing new products. Products can be demonstrated and customer inquiries can be addressed at a time when customers are actively soliciting information. This allows companies to gather useful feedback. Positive information can be used in subsequent sales presentations and advertising efforts, while negative information can guide product improvements or changes in the marketing program. Trade shows also provide an ideal occasion to recruit dealers, distributors, and sales personnel.

A recent innovation is the conduct of trade shows online (*digital trade shows*). The traditional trade show is typically conducted at a convention center in a major city. Representatives for the numerous exhibitors, along with hundreds, if not thousands, of potential customers, travel to the trade show site to participate in a two-day or longer event. Needless to say, millions of dollars are invested to rent space, set

Forward buying or bridge buying
Is when retailers purchase enough product during a manufacturer's off-invoice allowance period to carry the retailers over until the manufacturer's next regularly scheduled deal.

Diverting
Occurs when a manufacturer restricts an off-invoice allowance to a limited geographical area, resulting in some wholesalers and retailers buying abnormally large quantities at the deal price and then transshipping the excess quantities to other geographical areas.

Trade show
Is a temporary forum (typically lasting several days) for sellers of a product category (such as small appliances, toys, clothing, furniture, industrial tools, food products, or sporting goods) to exhibit and demonstrate their wares to current and prospective buyers.

up exhibits, and pay for travel, lodging, dining, and so on. The online trade show eliminates most of these expenses, but also lacks the opportunity for potential customers to physically inspect products and interact with trade-show exhibitors on a personal, one-to-one basis. While online trade shows will not eliminate their traditional counterparts, they do represent a promotional growth area.

Consumer Promotions: Roles and Objectives

A variety of sales-promotion methods are used to encourage consumers to purchase one brand over another, purchase a particular brand more often, and purchase in larger quantities. **Consumer promotions**, which are directed at end users rather than the trade, include such activities as sampling, couponing, refunding, rebating, and offering premiums, sweepstakes, and contests.

Consumers would not be responsive to sales promotions unless there were something in it for them—and, in fact, there is. All sales-promotion techniques provide consumers with incentives or inducements that encourage certain forms of behavior desired by brand marketers and/or retailers. Rewards are typically in the form of cash savings or free gifts. Sometimes rewards are immediate, while other times they are delayed. An *immediate reward* is one that delivers the savings or gift as soon as the consumer performs a marketer-specified behavior. For example, you receive cash savings at the time you redeem a coupon and you receive pleasure immediately when you try a food sample while shopping in a grocery store. *Delayed rewards* are those that follow the behavior by a period of days, weeks, or even longer. For example, you may have to wait a month or more before a free-in-the-mail premium object can be enjoyed. Generally speaking, consumers are more responsive to immediate rewards rather than delayed ones. Of course, this is in line with the natural human tendency to seek immediate rather than delayed gratification.

Manufacturers use sales promotions to accomplish three general categories of objectives: generating trial purchases, encouraging repeat purchases, and reinforcing brand image. **Generating trial purchases** refers to inducing nonusers to try a brand for the first time, or encouraging retrial by consumers who have not purchased the brand for an extended period. **Encouraging repeat purchases** includes manufacturers' efforts to hold on to their current users by rewarding them for continuing to purchase the promoted brand, or to load them up with the product so they have no need to switch to another brand. **Reinforcing brand image** involves carefully selecting the right premium object, or appropriate sweepstakes prize, to support a brand's desired image. Figure 13.8 classifies sales-promotion techniques by the specific objective each is primarily responsible for accomplishing, and by the type of reward, either immediate or delayed, that is provided to consumers.[49] It is important to recognize that most forms of sales promotions perform more than a single objective. For example, refunds and rebates are classified as providing a delayed reward to encourage repeat purchasing; however, on some occasions, rebates/refunds may also stimulate trial purchasing. Note also that two techniques, coupons and premiums, have multiple entries in Figure 13.8. This is because these techniques achieve different objectives depending on the specific form of delivery vehicle. The choice of which sales-promotion tool to use depends on the specific objectives that must be accomplished for a brand at a particular point in time, and an evaluation of the relative expense of using different tools. Let us now briefly discuss some of the major sales-promotion methods that fall under each of the six cells in Figure 13.8.

Cell 1: Generating trial purchases by providing consumers an immediate reward. Free samples, instant coupons (i.e., coupons that peel off product packages), and shelf-delivered coupons (from those red "machines" on store shelves) are the three forms of promotions that provide consumers with immediate rewards and serve marketers by generating trial purchases. Space does not permit a discussion of all these promotions, but the importance of sampling requires some elaboration.

Consumer promotions
Are directed at end users rather than at the trade. These promotions include sampling; couponing; refunding; rebating; and offering premiums, sweepstakes, and contests.

Generating trial purchases
Refers to inducing nonusers to try a brand for the first time, or encouraging retrial by consumers who have not purchased the brand for an extended period.

Encouraging repeat purchases
Includes manufacturers' efforts to hold on to their current users by rewarding them for continuing to purchase the promoted brand, or to load them up with the product so they have no need to switch to another brand.

Reinforcing brand image
Involves carefully selecting the right premium object, or appropriate sweepstakes prize, to support a brand's desired image.

Major Consumer-Oriented Promotions			Figure 13.8
	Brand Manager's Objective		
Consumer Reward	**Generating Trial Purchases**	**Encouraging Repeat Purchases**	**Reinforcing Brand Image**
Immediate	**Cell 1** • Samples • Instant coupons • Shelf-delivered coupons	**Cell 3** • Price-offs • Bonus packs • In-, on-, and near-pack premiums • Games	**Cell 5**
Delayed	**Cell 2** • Scanner-delivered coupons • Media- and mail-delivered coupons • Online coupons • Mail-in premiums • Free-with-purchase premiums	**Cell 4** • In- and on-pack coupons • Rebates/refunds • Phone cards • Continuity programs	**Cell 6** • Self-liquidating premiums • Sweepstakes and contests

Source: Terence A. Shimp, *Advertising, Promotion, and Supplemental Aspects of Integrated Marketing Communications*, 6th ed. (Cincinnati: South-Western, 2003), 524. © 2003. Reprinted with permission of South-Western, a division of Thomson Learning: www.thomsonrights.com. Fax 800-730-2215.

Most practitioners agree that sampling is the premier sales-promotion device for generating trial usage. In fact, sampling is virtually a necessity when introducing truly new products. Sampling is effective because it provides consumers with an opportunity to personally experience a new brand; it allows an active, hands-on interaction with the sampled brand rather than a passive encounter, as is the case with promotional techniques such as coupons.

By definition, *sampling* includes any method used to give consumers an actual- or trial-sized product. Most manufacturers of consumer packaged goods use sampling as part of their sales-promotion mixes. In fact, brand managers in the United States spend more than $1.2 billion annually on product sampling.[50]

Marketers use a variety of distribution methods for delivering samples. These include direct mail; newspapers and magazines; door-to-door sampling by distribution crews; on- and in-package sampling; sampling at high-traffic locations and events (e.g., at shopping centers, movie theaters, airports, and athletic or entertainment events); in-store sampling; and sampling via the Internet. Increasingly, brand managers are distributing samples online. They typically use the services of companies that specialize in online sample delivery, such as Amazing Freebies!, FreeShop.com, Sampleville, StartSampling, and TheFreeSite.com. Interested consumers are directed to online sampling sites and register to receive free samples of brands that interest them. Samples are then mailed in a timely fashion. Because mailing represents a major cost element, online sampling costs are estimated to be three times greater than sampling in stores or at special events.[51] The justification for this added expense is that people who go online to request a particular sample are really interested in that brand—and eventually may purchase it—in comparison to people who receive a sample through the mail or at an event.

Cell 2: Generating trial purchases but delaying the consumer's reward. In contrast to the promotional methods listed in cell 1 (Figure 13.8), the tools in cell 2 also generate trial purchases from consumers, but delay the reward. Marketers use scanner-delivered coupons, coupons delivered via the mail and mass media (newspapers and magazines), online coupons, mail-in premiums, and free-with-purchase premiums to encourage trial purchases. Consumers are not as responsive to these promotions as those mentioned in cell 1, but these methods still perform important functions for brand marketers. While space limitations do not permit detailed discussion of each of these techniques, several are briefly described for illustrative purposes.

The method of coupon distribution preferred by brand managers is the *freestanding insert (FSI)*. FSIs, which appear in Sunday newspapers, account for 82% of all coupons distributed in the United States. The other media for coupon distribution are handouts at stores or other locations (about 8%), magazine and newspaper distribution (approximately 4%), inside or on product packages (3%), direct mail (2%), and in the store or via the Internet (1%).[52] Because freestanding inserts capture the consumer's attention more readily than non-freestanding inserts (e.g., regular newspaper advertising), they are superior in overcoming competitive clutter.

Scanner-delivered coupons are dispensed at the point of purchase by determining (via optical scanner) what brands a consumer has purchased on the present shopping trip and then issuing a coupon that can be redeemed on a subsequent trip. For example, the Catalina Marketing Corporation has developed a scanner-delivered couponing method that dispenses coupons for a participating manufacturer's brand when optical scanners at grocery store checkouts record that shoppers have purchased a *competitor's brand*. For example, purchasers of Hunt's ketchup would receive a coupon for Heinz ketchup. By targeting competitors' customers, Catalina's program ensures that the couponer (Heinz in this case) will reach people who buy in the product category and influence them on a subsequent purchase occasion to switch from buying a competitor's brand to their brand.

Turning from couponing to premiums, many companies provide articles of merchandise or services (e.g., travel) to encourage consumers to purchase a particular brand. *Mail-in offers* give consumers a free item from the sponsoring manufacturer in return for submitting a required number of proofs of purchase. Although children and their parents are the targets of numerous mail-in premium offers, this promotional tool is not limited to children. Perhaps as few as 2–4% of consumers who are exposed to free mail-in offers actually take advantage of these opportunities. However, mail-in premiums can be effective if the premium item is appealing to the target market.

Whereas mail-in premiums typically are offered by packaged-goods brands, *free-with-purchase premiums* are more often provided by durable-goods brands. Examples of this type of free-with-purchase premium include an offer from Michelin to receive a $100 retail-value emergency roadside kit with the purchase of four Michelin tires. Compaq offered a free Rio 600 MP3 digital audio player with the purchase of select computer models. Attractive premiums such as these might provide indecisive consumers with added reason to purchase the premium-offering brand rather than a competitive option.

Cell 3: Encouraging repeat purchases by providing consumers an immediate reward. Marketers often use sales promotions to reward a brand's present consumers rather than to attract new, or trial, customers. Using promotions to encourage repeat purchasing is harmonious with the IMC concept discussed earlier in the chapter that successful marketing communications require building a *relationship* between the brand and the consumer. What promotion methods encourage repeat purchasing by providing consumers with an immediate reward? As shown in Figure 13.8, these include price-offs; bonus packs; in-, on-, and near-pack premiums; and games. *Price-offs* are periodic deals clearly labeled as such on the package that reduce a brand's price, typically in the range of 10–25%. Consumers who have previously purchased the brand offering the deal are the ones most likely to buy the brand again when it is on deal and thus be rewarded with an attractive price reduction. *Bonus packs* also reward a brand's present users by providing them with extra quantities of the brand at the regular price. For example, Listerine mouthwash provided consumers with a free 250-milliliter bottle along with the purchase of a 1.7-liter bottle. *In-, on-, and near-pack premiums* provide brand purchasers with the gift of a premium item (either in-, on-, or near the brand that offers the gift) when they purchase the brand. Again, current brand users are the consumers most likely to avail themselves of such offers and thus be rewarded for their continuing purchase of the brand. Finally, consumers receive an immediate reward (or learn that they have not won a prize) when participating in *games*.

Cell 4: Encouraging repeat purchases but delaying the reward. In- and on-pack coupons, rebate and refund offers, phone cards, and continuity programs (Figure 13.8) are the sales promotion methods that provide consumers with a reward for continuing to purchase a brand, but expect the consumer to wait to receive the reward. For example, when a consumer purchases a brand that has a coupon either in or on the brand package, she is rewarded with a discount (the coupon's face value) if she redeems it on a subsequent purchase occasion; however, that price savings is delayed in the sense that it is realizable only at a later date. Likewise, refund and rebate offers provide attractive savings; however, it may take months after a consumer has submitted a proof of purchase for a particular brand before a refund check is mailed. Since these techniques delay the reward, they appeal more to present brand users rather than attracting new users.

Cells 5 and 6: Reinforcing brand image. A final reason for offering sales promotions is to reinforce (or even bolster) a brand's image. No sales-promotion tools are able to accomplish this objective while providing consumers with an immediate reward, which explains why cell 5 is empty in Figure 13.8. However, several promotional tools are able to reinforce a brand's image while delaying the reward to consumers. With *self-liquidating premiums,* the consumer mails in a stipulated number of proofs of purchase along with sufficient money to cover the manufacturer's costs for purchasing, handling, and mailing the premium item. In other words, the actual cost of the premium is paid for by consumers; from the manufacturer's perspective, the item is cost-free, or, in other words, self-liquidating. Attractive self-liquidating offers can enhance a brand's image—by associating the brand with a positively valued premium item—and also encourage repeat purchasing by requiring multiple proofs of purchase to be eligible for the premium offer. For example, for 12 Gerber baby food proofs of purchase and $8.95, consumers received a cup engraved with their child's name and birth date. This item at retail would have sold for around $25. Many parents likely purchased Gerber exclusively until they acquired the requisite proofs of purchase.

Sweepstakes and contests are two additional sales promotions that may serve to reinforce a brand's image. In a *sweepstakes*, winners are determined purely on the basis of chance from names submitted for an opportunity to win a prize—e.g., a trip for two to the Super Bowl—sponsored by the participating brand. Because, as will be seen, sweepstakes require less consumer effort and generate greater participation, brand managers much prefer this form of promotion over contests. In a *contest*, the participant must act according to the rules of the contest and may or may not be required to submit proofs of purchase. For example, Hershey's Syrup brand managers created a contest that appealed to soccer moms and their children. The rules required submitting an action photo of a 6- to 17-year-old child/teen playing soccer, along with an original store receipt for the purchase of a 24-ounce bottle of Hershey's Syrup. This promotion associated Hershey's Syrup with a sport cherished by millions of families and also encouraged brand purchasing by customers interested in participating in the contest and thus becoming eligible to win any of the numerous prizes. A contest such as this fits with the brand's wholesome image and matches the interests of many consumers in its target market.

Public Relations

Public relations, or *PR* for short, is the MarCom tool uniquely suited to fostering *goodwill* between a company and its various publics. When effectively integrated with advertising, personal selling, and sales promotion, public relations is capable of accomplishing objectives other than goodwill. It can also increase brand awareness, build favorable attitudes toward a company and its products, and encourage purchase behavior. PR is similar to advertising because both are forms of mass communication; the difference is that the publicity generated by PR receives free news space or broadcast time in comparison to advertising's paid-for space and time. The PR department serves as the prime source of an organization's contact with the news media.

PR efforts are aimed primarily at customers, employees, suppliers, stockholders, governments, the general public, labor groups, and citizen action groups. Our concern, however, is only with the more narrow PR aspect that involves an organization's interactions with customers. This marketing-oriented aspect of public relations is called *marketing PR*, or *MPR* for short. Marketing PR can be further delineated as involving either proactive or reactive public relations.

Proactive MPR

Proactive MPR is a MarCom tool in addition to advertising and sales promotion that can give a brand additional exposure, newsworthiness, and credibility. **Proactive marketing public relations (proactive MPR)** is offensive, rather than defensive, and opportunity-seeking rather than problem-solving. The major role of proactive MPR is in the areas of product introductions or product revisions. This last factor, *credibility*, largely accounts for the effectiveness of proactive MPR. Whereas sales and advertising claims are sometimes suspect—because we question salespeople's and advertisers' motives, knowing they have a personal stake in persuading us—product announcements by a newspaper editor or television broadcaster are significantly more believable. Customers are less likely to question the motivation underlying an editorial-type endorsement.

Publicity is the major tool of proactive MPR. Like advertising and personal selling, the fundamental purposes of marketing-oriented publicity are to engender brand awareness, enhance attitudes toward a company and its brands, and possibly influence purchase behavior. Companies obtain publicity by using various forms of news releases, press conferences, and other types of information dissemination. News releases concerning new products, modifications to old products, and other newsworthy topics are disseminated to editors of newspapers and magazines, station managers of television and radio, and en masse to Web sites. Press conferences announce major news events of interest to the public. Photographs, tapes, and films are used to illustrate product improvements, new products, advanced production techniques, and so forth. Of course, all forms of publicity are subject to the control and whims of the media. However, by preparing PR materials that fit the media's needs, a company increases its chances of obtaining beneficial publicity.

Reactive MPR

Reactive MPR is undertaken as a result of external pressures and challenges brought by competitive actions, changes in consumer attitudes, changes in government policy, or other external influences. **Reactive MPR** is a form of defensive PR that deals with dramatic developments such as product defects or flaws that have negative consequences for the organization. Reactive MPR attempts to repair a company's reputation, prevent market erosion, and regain lost sales.

A number of negative-publicity cases have received widespread media attention in recent years. For example, Food Lion, a regional supermarket chain, suffered grave losses and was forced to close some stores after news reports charged that Food Lion stores were unsanitary and that they sold out-of-date meat, fish, and poultry products. Cans of Pepsi-Cola were rumored to be contaminated with hypodermic needles, but skillfully designed MPR quickly dispelled this hoax. An accident in a Coca-Cola bottling plant in Belgium introduced some tainted carbon dioxide into bottles, and European consumers reported becoming ill after drinking the bever-

Proactive marketing public relations (proactive MPR)

Is offensive rather than defensive, and opportunity-seeking rather than problem-solving. The major role of proactive MPR is in the areas of product introductions or product revisions.

Reactive MPR

Is a form of defensive PR that deals with developments such as product defects or flaws that have negative consequences for the organization. Reactive MPR attempts to repair a company's reputation, prevent market erosion, and regain lost sales.

age. Coca-Cola's initial response was to deny that its product was at fault, which prompted a public outcry in reaction to this corporate denial and created feelings among consumers that Coca-Cola officials did not care about their health and safety. Media throughout Europe wrote articles asserting that Coca-Cola products had poisoned consumers. Senior officers at Coca-Cola eventually got the message, and its PR people were put to work to offset the considerable damage to Coke's brand equity and profitability. This incident resulted in millions of dollars of lost revenue, much more than likely would have been lost had the company responded more quickly and apologetically.[53]

Intel, the huge computer-chip manufacturer, was embarrassed by reports that its new Pentium chip failed to correctly perform some mathematical calculations. Although corrective technical alterations were made, Intel was slow in reacting to this negative publicity and suffered a temporary loss of credibility. Both Ford Motor Company and particularly Bridgestone/Firestone suffered considerable financial losses after numerous rollover accidents involving Ford Explorers equipped with Firestone tires. Bridgestone/Firestone issued a massive recall of its 15-inch tires in the wake of news reports that these tires, when fitted on Ford Explorer SUVs, were responsible, at least in part, for hundreds of vehicle rollovers and deaths.[54]

Sponsorship Marketing

One of the fastest-growing aspects of marketing and marketing communications is the practice of corporate sponsorships. **Corporate sponsorships** involve investments in *events* or *causes* for the purpose of achieving various corporate objectives, such as increasing sales volume, enhancing a company's reputation or a brand's image, and increasing brand awareness. Sponsorships range from supporting athletic events (golf and tennis tournaments, college football bowl games, etc.), to underwriting rock concerts, to throwing corporate weight behind worthy causes such as efforts to generate funds for cancer research.

At least four factors account for the growth in sponsorships. First, by attaching their names to special events and causes, companies are able to *avoid the clutter* inherent in advertising media. Second, sponsorships help companies *respond to consumers' changing media habits*. For example, with the decline in network television viewing, sponsorships offer a potentially effective and cost-efficient way to reach consumers. Third, sponsorships help companies *gain the approval of various constituencies*, including stockholders, employees, and society at large. Finally, the sponsorship of special events and causes enables marketers to *target their communication and promotional efforts* to specific geographic regions and/or to specific lifestyle groups. For example, the Honda Element's brand marketers have sponsored events such as the Alternative Games, which reach the young male target audience to which this brand appeals.

Event Marketing

Thousands of companies invest in some form of event sponsorship. Event-related marketing is separate from advertising, sales promotion, point-of-purchase merchandising, or public relations, but it generally incorporates elements from all of these promotional tools. **Event-related marketing** is a form of brand promotion that ties a brand to a meaningful cultural, social, athletic, or other type of high-interest public activity. It is growing rapidly because these sponsorships provide companies with alternatives to the cluttered mass media, an ability to segment on a local or regional basis, and opportunities for reaching narrow lifestyle groups whose consumption behavior can be linked with local, regional, or national/international events. Events are effective because they reach people when they are in a relaxed atmosphere and receptive to marketing messages.

As with every other MarCom decision, the starting point for effective event sponsorship is to clearly specify the objectives that an event is designed to accomplish.

Technological Forces

With the near-viral proliferation of information made possible by the Internet, it is difficult for companies to control the spread of negative information. According to some observers, the Internet magnifies customer concerns, thus making it especially difficult to manage bad publicity in the Internet age.

Corporate sponsorships
Involve investments in events *or* causes *to achieve various corporate objectives, such as increasing sales volume, enhancing a company's reputation or a brand's image, and increasing brand awareness.*

Event-related marketing
Is a form of brand promotion that ties a brand to a meaningful cultural, social, athletic, or other type of high-interest public activity.

Event marketing has no value unless it accomplishes these objectives. For example, to create a fun and exciting image for Cool Mint Listerine mouthwash, Warner-Lambert literally pitched tents at ski resorts. Product samples and Cool Mint headbands were distributed from the tents. The event was further tied in to retail displays that offered lift-ticket discounts to consumers who appeared at ski resorts with a Cool Mint proof-of-purchase.

Cause-Related Marketing

Cause-related marketing (CRM)

Is a form of corporate philanthropy that links a company's contributions (usually monetary) to a predesignated worthy cause with purchasing behavior of consumers.

Cause-related marketing is a relatively narrow aspect of overall sponsorship. **Cause-related marketing (CRM)** is a form of corporate philanthropy that links a company's contributions (usually monetary) to a predesignated worthy cause with customer purchasing behavior. It involves an amalgam of public relations, sales promotion, and corporate philanthropy; however, the distinctive feature of cause-related marketing is that a company's contribution to a designated cause is linked to customers engaging in *revenue-producing exchanges* with the firm.[55] The contribution is contingent on the consumer performing a behavior (such as buying a product or redeeming a coupon) that benefits the firm.

The following examples illustrate how cause-related marketing operates. For each Heinz baby-food label mailed in by consumers, H. J. Heinz Company contributed six cents to a hospital near the consumer's home. Nabisco Brands donated one dollar to the Juvenile Diabetes Foundation for each one-dollar donation certificate redeemed with a Ritz brand proof of purchase. Hershey donated 25 cents to local children's hospitals for each redeemed Hershey coupon. Dutch Boy paint contributed 25 cents to Healthy Families America for each gallon of paint it sold during a designated period. Stride Rite made a donation to Save the Children in the amount of 3–4% of the retail price for each pair of specially designed footwear sold.

Chapter Summary

Learning Objective 1: *Appreciate the variety of marketing communications tools and how they work together to accomplish communication objectives.* The five basic tools of marketing communications (MarCom for short) include personal selling, advertising, sales promotions, public relations, and sponsorship marketing. The use of these tools in MarCom efforts is analogous to organizing a basketball team with different players of varying sizes, capabilities, and limitations effectively combined to achieve success.

Learning Objective 2: *Understand the nature, importance, and features of integrated marketing communications.* The philosophy and practice of integrated marketing communications (IMC) involve five guiding principles: (1) begin all MarCom efforts by first understanding how and where the customer or prospect will come into contact with the brand's communication messages; (2) use any and all relevant ways to contact customers and prospects; (3) work toward delivering a coordinated, unified message regardless of which MarCom tools are used; (4) attempt to build long-term relationships with customers so that it is unnecessary to always recruit new customers; and (5) make the ultimate goal of MarCom efforts affecting customer behavior rather than merely influencing the antecedents of that behavior. The practical thrust toward IMC has resulted in less dependence than in past years on mass-media advertising, increased use of highly targeted MarCom methods, and heightened efforts to assess MarCom's ROI (return on investment).

Learning Objective 3: *Describe the concept of brand-equity enhancement and the role of marketing communications in facilitating this objective.* From the customer's perspective, a brand possesses equity to the extent that the customer is familiar with the brand and has favorable, strong, and unique brand associations stored in his or her memory. That is, brand equity from the customer's perspective consists of two forms of knowledge: brand awareness and brand image. MarCom efforts serve to enhance a brand's equity both by making customers aware of brands and by forging in their collective memories thoughts, feelings, and beliefs (collectively, associations) that are both positive and somewhat strongly held.

Learning Objective 4: *Comprehend the factors that determine how different marketing communications elements are effectively combined.* Five factors play major roles in determining the circumstances that call for using different MarCom tools: (1) the nature of the intended market toward which communication efforts are directed, (2) the objectives to be accomplished, (3) the product life stage a brand is in, (4) competitive MarCom efforts, and (5) the amount of money available for accomplishing the MarCom objectives.

Learning Objective 5: *Discuss the primary decision spheres involved in managing the marketing communications process.* Managing the MarCom process involves selecting target markets, establishing marketing communications objectives, setting overall budgets for the MarCom program, establishing and implementing message and media strategies, and evaluating MarCom programs to ascertain whether they have been effective in accomplishing program goals.

Learning Objective 6: *Evaluate the nature and function of the major MarCom tools: (a) advertising, (b) sales promotion, (c) public relations, and (d) sponsorship and event marketing.* Advertising includes mass-media advertising, online advertising (including opt-in e-mail advertising), and point-of-purchase advertising. The use of sales promotions has increased, since sales promotions can accomplish many marketing objectives. Trade-oriented promotions include trade shows, as well as other methods. Customer-oriented sales promotions include an array of different techniques. Marketing-oriented public relations include proactive efforts conducted primarily through publicity campaigns and reactive efforts to ward off negative publicity and to respond to product failures and defects. Sponsorship marketing includes event marketing and cause-related marketing initiatives.

In sum, in today's highly competitive and dynamic marketing world, effective communications are critical to a company's success. Marketing managers have considerable discretion in determining which MarCom elements to use and how much each should be emphasized. Various factors such as the target market, product lifecycle stage, objectives, competitive activity, and available budget all affect the appropriate mix of MarCom elements. While many marketing communication decisions were once treated disparately and managed by independent departments that failed to carefully coordinate their activities, recently integrated marketing communications, or IMC, have taken hold. When used appropriately and effectively, the various MarCom tools can enhance a brand's equity and move customers and prospects to action.

Key Terms

For interactive study: visit http://bestpractices.swlearning.com.

Advertising, 431
Cause-related marketing (CRM), 468
Consumer promotions, 462
Corporate sponsorships, 467
Cost per thousand (CPM), 451
Database marketing, 436
Diverting, 461
Encouraging repeat purchases, 462
Event-related marketing, 467
Forward buying or bridge buying, 461

Generating trial purchases, 462
Gross rating points (GRPs), 451
Integrated marketing communications (IMC), 433
Media strategy, 445
Off-invoice allowances, 460
Opt-in e-mailing, 454
Personal selling, 431
Positioning statement, 445
Proactive marketing public relations (proactive MPR), 466

Publicity, 432
Reactive MPR, 466
Reinforcing brand image, 462
Sales promotion, 432
Sponsorship marketing, 432
Trade allowances, 460
Trade promotions, 460
Trade show, 461

Questions for Review and Discussion

1. One key feature of the integrated marketing communications (IMC) philosophy is that the IMC process should start with the customer. Compare this perspective with "the marketing concept" you studied in Chapter 1.

2. Assume you are the head of marketing communications for a sorority, fraternity, or other campus organization. Your responsibility is to recruit 25% more members than you presently have. Explain how "starting with the customer" would apply to your choice of ways to recruit new members.

3. List your mental associations for each of the following "brands" and prepare to share them in class: (1) Norah Jones (a multiple Grammy winner in 2003), (2) Levi jeans, (3) Michael Jackson, (4) Silk soy milk, (5) Harvard University, and (6) *The Wall Street Journal*.

4. Compare and contrast the brand-equity model (Figure 13.2) with the hierarchy-of-effects framework (Figure 13.3). What are the specific similarities and differences between these models?

5. Locate two magazine advertisements that you consider to be good illustrations of creative advertising. Explain precisely why you regard each to be especially creative.
   a. Assume that a one-page, four-color advertisement in *Ebony* magazine cost $75,000 in 2003. A syndicated service that measures magazine readership estimated that *Ebony*'s total readership that year was approximately 12 million adults. What was *Ebony*'s CPM in 2003?
   b. Advertisements for a particular brand are run on each of four television programs on a Thursday evening. Designating these programs as P1, P2, P3, and P4, assume that the ratings for each program are: P1=13.5, P2=15.3, P3=17.4, and P4=19.8. How many gross rating points (GRPs) would this advertiser accumulate on this one evening of advertising?

6. The term *promotional inducement* has been suggested as an alternative to *sales promotion*. Explain why the former term is more descriptive than the latter, but why promotion practitioners may favor the latter.

7. Several examples of negative publicity were listed in the reactive MPR section of the chapter. Are you familiar with any other examples of companies that have suffered such negative press? Discuss the effectiveness of the companies' "reactive MPR." Provide your views on how well Firestone and Ford Motors handled the Ford Explorer rollover problem.

8. Go to a local supermarket and pay careful attention to the point-of-purchase materials in use. Provide examples of three P-O-P practices in this store that you consider particularly effective. Offer an explanation as to why these practices are effective.

9. Hundreds of millions of coupons are distributed annually in the U.S. Why do you think that brand managers use coupons so frequently? Since coupons represent a form of price reduction, wouldn't it make more sense for brand managers to directly reduce prices rather than requiring consumers to redeem coupons? Do you think consumers are most likely to redeem coupons for brands they regularly purchase or for brands they purchase infrequently?

10. If you were the brand manager of the Honda Element, what cause might you sponsor to appeal to this brand's target market? Name (and justify) an event that might be sponsored by the Element.

In-Class Team Activities

1. As a group, assume you represent the marketing communications staff for a new company that manufactures and markets graduation rings for high school and college students and competes against established brands such as Balfour and Jostens. You are in the process of developing a MarCom strategy aimed specifically at high school students to build your brand's equity and thus encourage purchases of "your" brand over the well-known established brands.

   a. With an advertising budget of $5 million, identify the specific media you would advertise in and the specific vehicles in these media that you would select. Also, discuss when you would advertise.
   b. What forms of sales promotions would you use to encourage consumers to select your brand over better-known competitors? Be specific.
   c. How might you generate "buzz" about your brand in order to create positive word-of-mouth influence among high school students?

2. The advertising industry is often accused of various ethical violations. Typical criticisms include claims that advertising is (1) untruthful and deceptive, (2) manip-

ulative, (3) offensive and in bad taste, (4) a perpetrator of stereotypes, (5) a cause of consumers' buying things they really do not need, and (6) a contributor to people's fears and insecurities. Randomly divide the class into two subgroups and then participate in a debate about these alleged ethical violations. One group should criticize advertising, while the other should defend advertising on such grounds as "yes, some advertisers do indeed commit ethical breaches, but the same can be said of other institutions in an open society."

Internet Questions

1. As with all forms of advertising, Internet advertisements must go to considerable lengths to draw attention away from consumers' primary goals for using the Internet—namely, entertainment and informational pursuits. Spend some time online and identify and describe at least three specific techniques that online advertisers use to grab attention. What are the pros and cons of each technique?

2. You may have noticed that Web sites seem to know more and more about you each time you visit. They accomplish this with the use of so-called "cookies." A cookie is a small piece of information that's sent to your browser along with an HTML page when you access a particular site. When a cookie arrives, your browser saves this information to your hard drive; when you return to that site, some of the stored information is sent back to the Web server, along with your new request. The Web site **http://www.cookiecentral.com** is dedicated to explaining what cookies are and what they can do. Visit this site and discuss how cookies are used to compile lists of contacts for direct-marketing purposes. Also, provide your views on the ethical issues surrounding the use of cookies. Is this an invasion of your privacy?

CHAPTER CASE

Getting American Consumers to Accept and Use Recyling Kiosks

Tomra Systems is a Norwegian company that specializes in recycling. After conducting an intensive analysis of American recycling practices, Tomra launched a chain of recycling kiosks in a test market in southern California. Tomra has ambitious plans to expand its *rePlanet* kiosks across the United States. The rePlanet kiosks have several features that should appeal to Americans: They are clean, conveniently located in supermarket parking lots, and brightly lit to provide the user with a sense of safety. Plus, the recycler gets paid for depositing used recyclable cans and bottles. Attendants are available during daytime hours and are trained to be friendly, accommodating, and efficient. But even when daytime attendants are not available, a "reverse" vending machine accepts containers and then issues a machine-printed receipt the recycler can later redeem for cash at a participating grocery store.

Tomra's marketing representatives offer several reasons why consumer recycling efforts are important in the U.S.:

- Americans use 2.5 million plastic bottles every hour, which translates into 60 million plastic bottles per day and nearly 22 billion per year!

- Because plastic degrades very slowly, plastic rings from Colonial times would still be with us if the Pilgrims had had six-packs and discarded the plastic rings.

- Fifteen hundred aluminum cans are recycled every second in the U.S., which translates into about 130 million cans per day, or more than 47 billion per year!

- It takes 500 years for aluminum to biodegrade.

- The energy saved from recycling one aluminum can would power a TV set for three hours or light a 100-watt bulb for 20 hours.

- Recycling aluminum requires 90–95% less energy than mining and processing bauxite ore, which is the source of aluminum.

Tomra has its sights on a potentially huge recycling market in the United States. Fewer than half of all Americans have access to curbside recycling services. The consequence of this is that plastic bottles and aluminum cans end up in landfills, creating a huge environmental problem both in terms of landfill space and the energy required to produce replacement containers. Tomra would like to convert millions of people who now deposit cans and bottles in their curbside trash into enthusiastic recyclers. This can be accomplished, according to Tomra's business plan, by rewarding consumers with modest cash payments for each recycled container and by providing convenient, efficient, and safe recycling services.

What will it take for Tomra to succeed? The basic business model requires annual revenues from each kiosk of approximately $100,000. The rePlanet kiosks cost the company about $40,000 to $50,000 each to install and another $25,000 annually for payroll and pickup expenses. Tomra needs to process an average of 200,000 to 230,000 containers per month at each kiosk to be economically viable. This volume is essential for achieving reasonable profit goals. In addition to its California kiosks, Tomra has also tested the viability of the concept in metropolitan areas such as Atlanta, Orlando, and Tampa. There are rePlanet facilities outside the U.S. in Japan and Brazil, as well as Norway.

An executive of Tomra's North American operation claims that the company hopes to market recycling as an "experience" rather than an unpleasant chore. "We want to be the Starbucks of the recycling business." Though perhaps a bit idealistic, this nonetheless represents a worthwhile goal both in terms of environmental benefits and profit opportunities for the company. The challenge, however, involves convincing the American masses to change their recycling attitudes and behavior. Will Tomra's attractive and convenient kiosks provide people with sufficient reason to slightly complicate their lives in return for environmental enrichment and a relatively small economic incentive? Will the rePlanet kiosks indeed become the Starbucks of recycling? What role must MarCom efforts play to make this happen?

Case Questions

1. Figure 13.1 and the surrounding text identified five key features of an integrated marketing communications program. Assume that rePlanet kiosks have just recently opened in your home state or province. Also assume that you are in charge of marketing communications for Tomra's marketing efforts in your home state/province. Use the five key IMC features to propose an integrated marketing-communications program that would help produce rapid success for Tomra's rePlanet kiosks.

2. A good brand name generally must satisfy several criteria, including (1) distinguishing the brand from competitive offerings, (2) describing the brand and its attributes/benefits, (3) providing compatibility with the brand's desired image, and (4) achieving memorability and being easy to pronounce. With these considerations in mind, evaluate the rePlanet name for Tomra's recycling kiosks.

3. Develop a precise positioning statement that could be used to design advertisements and other forms of marketing communications for rePlanet kiosks.

4. Recommend a specific sales promotion you would use to generate trial usage of the rePlanet kiosks. Similarly, recommend a promotion that would encourage repeat usage of your kiosks.

5. Identify an event Tomra could sponsor as a way to enhance the brand equity of the rePlanet kiosks. Justify the choice of this particular event.

Sources: Adapted from Jim Carlton, "Norway's Tomra Redefines Recycling with Bright, Clean, Accessible Kiosks," *The Wall Street Journal Interactive Edition,* 6 March 2001, http://www.interactive.wsj.com.

Supplemented with information from Tomra's Web site (http://www.tomra.no), and from Sarah Nichols, "Recyling: ReThinking Recyling," *Waste Age,* 1 August 2001 (available online at http://www.wasteage.com).

VIDEO CASE

Polaroid I-Zone's Zoom to the Top

"Where will you stick it?" If you hear those words from a young teen brandishing a brightly colored camera, relax. You aren't being attacked or insulted. To the contrary, your friend probably just wants to take your picture. "Where will you stick it?" is Polaroid's slogan for its I-Zone pocket camera, the firm's first new consumer-product introduction in more than 20 years. It's also a new target market for Polaroid product: teens. Polaroid, famous for its instantly developing film, has come up with a new filmstrip with a sticky back that turns tiny photos into instant stickers. Kids can snap a photo, pull out the strip, wait a few seconds for the picture to develop, then peel it off the strip and stick it anywhere—on a notebook,

a jacket or hat, a key chain, a purse, or a bicycle. Within months of its launch, the I-Zone became the No. 1-selling camera in the United States.

How did the I-Zone zoom to the top of the charts so quickly? Polaroid made a commitment to integrated marketing communications (IMC) in researching the market, getting the product to the right consumers, and promoting it. First, they did the research, and discovered that teens now have more spending power than any other generation of teens before them. "Polaroid decided to enter the kids market because the kids market right now is the biggest it's ever been in history," says Mary Courville. Second, they divided the market further, into preteens—

tweens—and older teenagers. Girls seem to be most interested in taking pictures, so the Polaroid team focused there. Third, they thought "outside the box" about different uses for a camera. For instance, the younger girls actually view the camera as a fashion accessory—so a sleek design in fashion-bright colors was important. By thinking creatively, the team came up with whole new ways to use a camera. "It's not about taking pictures to put in a photo album," explains Courville. This is "a cool camera that allows kids to be creative and have fun. It's about play and doing what you want to do." The I-Zone's sticky film lets young photographers become artists. They can take their camera anywhere and stick their pictures anywhere.

Courville stresses that Polaroid couldn't have come up with either the product or the promotion that followed without integrated communications among the marketing, public relations, advertising, and promotion staff. "We're a very tight group," she says. "We're always together." They conducted focus groups and field tests together. They met with the advertising agency together. "We are just always talking to each other," she says. "Always, always, always." Not only does this increase the efficiency with which the product is launched, it keeps the message to the consumer consistent. The consumer sees the same message through television commercials, magazine or Internet ads, and various promotions.

What exactly is the message? For Polaroid in general, says Courville, it's about instant gratification. "Only Polaroid can give you that photograph instantly. Only Polaroid can enliven your time, your party, right then. Polaroid is the only one that allows you to capture the moment instantly." I-Zone takes it a step farther by giving kids instant pictures that they can use to transform and personalize something else—a backpack, a belt buckle, a baseball cap.

In addition to advertising in traditional media and the Internet, Polaroid decided to hook up with the popular teen group the Backstreet Boys, becoming a sponsor of their Into the Millennium tour. "Sponsorship allowed us

wonderful promotional opportunities," comments Courville. Because the group's biggest fans are girls age 14 to 17, the match was perfect. The Backstreet Boys actually used the I-Zone cameras during their concerts, and girls were invited onstage to have their pictures taken with band members, with I-Zone cameras, of course. Polaroid distributed cameras to fans at concerts so they could take pictures of each other and the band. Results were so positive that Polaroid decided to sponsor another pop singer, Britney Spears, the following year. "This sponsorship is the perfect combination of music, fun, and friendship—all key aspects of our target consumers' lifestyle. Polaroid is committed to giving teens and tweens exactly what they want." Even the stars themselves seem hooked on I-Zone. "I'm psyched to be working with Polaroid," says Spears. "The I-Zone is the coolest way for me and my fans to have fun taking pictures. We can stick them everywhere." That's just what Polaroid has in mind.

Case Questions

1. Describe Polaroid's IMC approach to marketing the I-Zone.
2. What steps might Polaroid's IMC group take to market I-Zone overseas? Would it be successful? Why or why not?
3. Did Polaroid's sponsorship of the Backstreet Boys succeed according to standard sponsorship objectives? Why or why not?
4. Visit the Polaroid Web site (http://www.polaroid.com) to find out more about I-Zone. Imagine that you are part of the IMC group and write a slogan for the site with suggestions for more ways to use the I-Zone and more places to stick the photos. Where else besides the Web would you advertise or conduct a promotion?

Sources: Polaroid Web site, http://www.polaroid.com, accessed 10 March 2000.
"Polaroid and Britney Spears Will Drive You Crazy," *PR Newswire,* 3 March 2000.
Cara Beardi. "Targeting Teens Pays Off for Polaroid." *Advertising Age,* 6 March 2000, 16.
"Polaroid's New I-Zone Pocket Camera #1 Selling Camera in the United States," *PR Newswire,* 2 December 1999.

Personal Selling and Sales Management

The Xbox game console, although innovative, has not been a profitable venture for Microsoft to date. Not only has the game market produced product and logistical challenges that Microsoft had not previously faced with its business software, but the game market has also required Microsoft to develop relationships with retailers it previously had not needed. The initial development of these relationships went poorly, resulting in many complaints about poor service and a greater need for face-to-face interaction. Microsoft has now reorganized its sales force with the goal of better understanding and serving its markets. However, to surpass Sony, its top competitor in the electronic game market, the Microsoft sales force must provide superb performance.

You Decide. After reading the opening vignette and paying special attention to the sections of this chapter marked with the chess piece, answer these questions:

1. Which element of sales management, other than reorganization, might Microsoft use to best ensure that the Xbox sales force reaches its objectives?

2. What is the primary territory realignment issue facing Xbox sales managers?

3. In the face of competition from Sony, as well as other competitors such as Nintendo, Electronic Arts, Activision, and THQ Interactive, what is the primary competitive advantage of the sales-force reorganization?

© AFP/CORBIS

You've Been X-ed!
Xbox is a game console designed to bring the most powerful game experiences to Gen Y buyers. Xbox is one of many innovative products developed by Microsoft, the global leader in software, services, and Internet technologies. In 2002, Xbox Live Starter Kits were introduced to create the first high-speed online console gaming service. Using high-speed Internet connections, Xbox Live allowed players to compete against other gamers all over the United States and Canada. In 2003, Xbox players in France, Germany, United Kingdom, Belgium, Italy, Netherlands, Spain, Sweden, New Zealand, and Japan were able to enter the online playing arena. Although extremely popular, Xbox has not been a profitable venture for Microsoft because of its high initial development costs and some major differences between game and PC software that have required modifications and adjustments. Altering the direction of the Xbox's financial performance will hinge largely on the productivity of the sales force.

Microsoft employs approximately 6,500 sales people in the United States alone. Recently, in response to customer complaints about poor service, and in recognition of the fact that customers need the face-to-face interaction that can only be provided through personal selling, Microsoft organized itself into seven product groups. Microsoft then reorganized its sales force into 12 vertical industries: professional services, media and entertainment, oil and gas, high-tech manufacturing, automotive manufacture, retail, health care, education, federal government, local and state governments, telecommunications, and financial services. Xbox falls under the media and entertainment product group.

Kevin Johnson, senior vice president of Microsoft's Americas division, noted that the purpose of the reorganization was to "help the company better understand and serve its markets." By dividing the sales force into 12 teams, each of which specializes in a particular industry, it is hoped that the sales force will become more knowledgeable about their assigned industries and therefore provide the best Microsoft solutions for each customer. Furthermore, the reorganization has increased the sales team's interaction with customers, which in turn should enhance customer relationships and increase customer-satisfaction levels.

The sales force responsible for selling Xbox currently consists of 12 people who are split into three regions—East, Central, and West—across the U.S. Each region has its own director and set of account executives. The sales efforts of the account executives are focused on 18 key customers that account for 90% of the electronic game sales in the U.S. The seven largest accounts include Wal-Mart, Best Buy, Circuit City, Game Stop, Target, Electronics Boutique, and Toys "R" Us. The remaining 10% of electronic gaming sales are made through four key distributors that in turn sell to independent stores. Account executives are customer-centrically located, meaning they are based in the same area as the headquarters for the key account served. The Xbox sales force is charged with building relationships with the category buying teams of the assigned key accounts. They also introduce and obtain orders for new games just prior to launch. In conjunction with the Xbox channel marketing team, the account executive is also responsible for retail marketing, that is, ensuring that Xbox games and consoles are appropriately placed on the shelves and that interactive kiosks are in place. The interactive kiosks are critical, because 80% of Xbox's target market—young males between 16 and 26 years of age—try the product before buying.

Much of Xbox's success and long-term viability is being shouldered by the Microsoft sales force. Ed Bland, senior director of U.S. sales and channel marketing for Microsoft's Xbox, has identified five goals for the team: "Focus on games, learn about the game market, embrace the learning, build, and develop efficiencies." Bland believes that achieving these broad objectives will lead to greater performance and profitability for Xbox.

LEARNING OBJECTIVES

After you have completed this chapter, you should be able to:

1. *Identify and understand the factors that make personal selling such a critical component of promotion.*

2. *Describe the selling contexts and types of salespeople.*

3. *Understand and explain the sales process.*

4. *Comprehend the diverse tasks and functions of the sales manager.*

VOICE OF THE EXPERT
Judy Siguaw, Cornell University

If your first reaction to hearing the word "salesperson" is a negative one, you are not alone. The old stereotype of the fast-talking, scamming salesperson is a difficult one to erase. My goal in writing this chapter is to illustrate to you that (1) selling is a critical company function that is directly responsible for top-line revenues; (2) the sales forces of the best companies practice professional, consultative selling; and (3) companies invest huge sums into their sales forces through compensation, technology, and other perquisites. The importance of sales within an organization is formally recognized by the rapidly growing number of undergraduate and graduate courses in sales, often driven by pressure from corporations in desperate need of skilled salespeople, and by the increase in theory and research in the area of sales. Furthermore, the sales profession is now focused on building long-term customer relationships and solving customer problems, since time has demonstrated that a sales force with a strong customer orientation produces far more top-line revenues. Thus, sales has developed into a highly lucrative and rewarding career path.

After reading this chapter, I hope you will come away with a more positive view of salespeople in general and that you will use the knowledge you have acquired to begin critically analyzing your own sales encounters. Also, I sincerely hope that this chapter may spark enough interest that you will seek to gain sales skills and sales knowledge by enrolling in a college-level sales course. I can promise you that you will not regret it and that you will use the acquired sales skills throughout your lifetime.

Only time will tell whether the Xbox sales force will meet its objectives and catapult Microsoft's Xbox to number-one game console in the world—a position currently held by Sony's PlayStation. If you think you would be interested in helping Microsoft build the Xbox brand, go to http://www.microsoft.com/careers.[1]

The act of selling is pervasive in society. If you have ever interviewed for a job, you were "selling" yourself by trying to persuade the interviewer that you would be the best person for the job. If you have ever tried to persuade a friend to do some activity that you wanted to do, you were "selling" your idea. When you were younger, you were "selling" every time you tried to persuade Mom or Dad to buy you something you wanted, and you were probably quite persistent in order to obtain what you desired. As an adult, you will find that you must "sell" regardless of what your job title is—whether it is selling your ideas to your boss, convincing your supervisor that you deserve a raise or promotion, persuading customers to purchase your products, or persuading investors to invest in your firm. Not just salespeople sell—so do accountants, engineers, financial analysts, insurance agents, stockbrokers, computer programmers, scientists, and nearly all other professionals.

In the everyday selling situations mentioned previously, you have probably been successful in achieving your goals sometimes, but at other times you have not been as successful. How can you improve your success rate? By learning to excel in sales through the acquisition of good selling skills. This chapter provides you with a good start in that direction. First, we define personal selling and explain its importance in the promotion mix. Next, we discuss the evolution of personal selling and the pros and cons of the selling profession. We then present the various types of personal selling, selling environments, and the sales process. An explanation of the growing professionalism of selling through certification follows. We then discuss the sales-management function, including the characteristics and duties of a good sales manager. We conclude by discussing sales-force technology, team selling, and legal and ethical issues.

LEARNING OBJECTIVE   1

Personal selling
Is direct person-to-person communication designed to explain how an individual's or firm's goods, services, or ideas fit the needs of one or more prospective customers.

Consultative selling
Is the process of helping customers reach their strategic goals by using the products and expertise of the sales organization.

Sales and Marketing in the 21st Century

Personal selling is direct person-to-person communication designed to explain how an individual's or firm's goods, services, or ideas fit the needs of one or more prospective customers. Consequently, personal selling is one of the most important elements of the promotional mix and a critical activity of marketing management; it is also the most expensive form of promotion that a firm can undertake. Recent figures indicate that the average sales call—factoring in compensation, benefits, and travel and entertainment expenses—costs the organization $169.64.[2] For firms emphasizing **consultative selling**, the process of helping customers reach their strategic goals by using the products and expertise of the sales organization, the average price of a sales call is even higher, $211.56.[3] Furthermore, across all industries, only one sales call in three is successful. Why then would a firm choose to use personal selling and incur the associated costs?

The Strategic Importance of Personal Selling

There are three primary reasons why personal selling is such an important component of a promotional strategy. First, since personal selling involves direct communication between a sales representative and a prospective customer, it is the only form of promotion that allows a firm to respond immediately to the needs of the prospect. That is, as the salesperson makes his or her presentation, the salesperson can continuously adapt the presentation to the needs of the prospect. The ability to constantly adapt to the prospective customer results in a greater number of sales. Second, personal selling allows for immediate customer feedback, so a firm has timely information regarding customer satisfaction with its offerings. Other forms of promotion, such as advertising, are company-sponsored communications aimed toward the target market, but *immediate,* person-to-person feedback from customers is not usually possible. Finally, personal selling results in an actual sale—the salesperson can leave a customer's office with an order in hand. Thus, personal selling is one of the few forms of promotion to which the sale of a specific product can be *directly* traced. Consequently, successful companies truly value their sales forces.

Due to the costs associated with personal selling, this form of promotion is not used as often for consumer markets where there are many, geographically dispersed buyers whose individual purchases will not support the average cost of a sales call. Personal selling, however, is often a must in the business-to-business market, and may be used in consumer markets where buyers tend to be fewer in number, more geographically concentrated, and more inclined to purchase in larger quantities and dollar amounts. Additionally, personal selling is usually a necessity for *complex products, high-involvement buying situations,* and *transactions involving trade-ins.*

The Evolution of Personal Selling and the Changing Face of Sales

At one time, sales companies believed customers had to be forced into making a purchase. Salespeople using the **hard sell** tried every means to get the prospect to buy, regardless of whether it was in the prospect's best interest. This type of selling attitude resulted in singular transactional exchanges. That is, when customers purchased from these "hard-sell" representatives, and learned that the products truly did not meet their needs, they recognized that the salespeople were not working to satisfy them. Consequently, these customers would not purchase from these salespeople again, so the salespeople gained only a one-time transaction. Additionally, the hard sell sometimes bordered on the unethical or even illegal. Even today, when certain macroenvironmental factors combine forces, such as a hypercompetitive environment operating in conjunction with an economic downturn, firms may feel compelled to return to the hard sell.[4]

Many businesses, however, are experimenting with approaches other than the hard sell; thus, personal selling has begun to focus on the important concept of **relationship selling**. That is, the salesperson focuses on developing a trusting partnership by providing long-term customer satisfaction through listening, gathering information, educating, and adding value for the customer. When the salesperson clearly identifies customer needs and seeks to provide the best product to meet those needs, the salesperson is able to develop a long-term relationship with the customer. Not only does the customer benefit from this relationship, but the salesperson also benefits by way of the future sales yielded from this relationship over time. In today's business environment, the goal is to develop long-term relationships with customers. However, to help firms identify the best customers on which to focus their sales efforts, companies are adopting *customer-relationship-management*

Figure 14.1	Sales-Force Diversity in the United States

Gender Composition

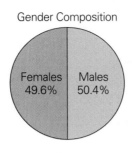

Racial/Ethnic Composition

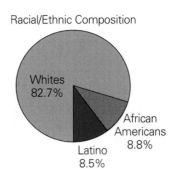

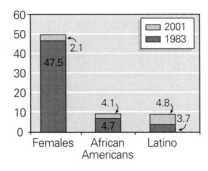

Sources: U.S. Bureau of Labor Statistics, *Employment and Earnings,* January 2001. http://www.bls.gov, accessed 1 July 2003.

(CRM) strategies and applications that rely on systematized processes to profile key segments so that marketing and retention strategies can be customized for these prospective buyers.

Similar to the way in which sales have evolved from a hard-sell to a relationship selling approach, the face of the sales force has also changed. In 1983, men represented the majority of the U.S. sales force, but women have made strong inroads (see Figure 14.1). Largely due to sociocultural environmental factors, females now comprise approximately half of all those employed in sales occupations.[5] Furthermore, African Americans now represent 8.8% of the total U.S. sales force, up 4.1% from 1983, while Latinos constitute 8.5%, up 4.8% since 1983.[6] In addition, 40.3% of sales manager positions are now held by women, an increase of approximately 12% over the past two decades.[7]

The Sales Professions: Rewards and Drawbacks

Several studies suggest that college students are not interested in pursuing careers in the sales profession.[8] Unfortunately, the all-too-frequent portrayal of salespeople as fast-talking, glad-handing, slick characters with highly questionable ethics has tainted the sales profession to the point where many people think of selling as an undesirable profession. They fail to realize how highly dependent large and small companies are on the revenues that salespeople generate. If you do not think this is true, try staying in business without selling something! Further, salespeople provide expertise in the field to customers seeking product information. Salespeople also spot

Sociocultural Forces

Companies like Merrill Lynch and American Express are proactive in bringing diversity to their workforces. Organizations such as these recognize that diversity makes economic sense.

and report potential competitive and market trends so their companies can respond appropriately. Consequently, salespeople are truly vital to the business world.

The future for sales professionals looks great! Employment in sales occupations continues to grow. Today, approximately 13 million people hold sales-related jobs.[9] By the year 2010, the U.S. Department of Labor expects the number of people employed in sales positions to increase to 17 million.[10] Thus, in the next decade, the profession of selling probably offers more employment opportunities than almost any other career choice, although, as with all other professions, employment in the sales arena will be heavily influenced by macroenvironmental forces, especially economic factors.

Sales positions also offer many advantages, which are summarized in Figure 14.2. There is great flexibility in sales activities, so no two workdays are alike.[11] Intrinsic rewards are gained by meeting the needs of customers and feeling you have helped someone else. There are also extrinsic rewards. First, potential compensation is quite high.[12] In 2001, even in the midst of an economic recession, sales representatives averaged $80,023, including $25,571 in bonuses and commissions.[13] Frequently, the compensation includes a company car, laptop computer, and cell phone to make the total compensation package even more valuable. For top-performing sales representatives, salaries average $139,459 per year.[14] Further, sales positions frequently offer travel opportunities, increasing responsibility, and limited supervision. Finally, a sales position is also a great career track because of its high visibility. Good salespeople stand out in an organization because they are directly responsible for the revenues of the company.

Sales, like all professions, also presents a few drawbacks. The hours can be long, and it is not unusual for salespeople to experience **role conflict**, which is anxiety caused by conflicting job demands (e.g., the firm's demands that the salesperson obtain a high price for the firm's product and the customer's demands for a low price). **Role ambiguity**, which is anxiety caused by inadequate information about job responsibilities and performance-related goals, may influence the salesperson's activities and create uncertainty about what is expected of her. One source of role ambiguity can stem from a salesperson trying to cooperate and work successfully with many organizational departments—billing, shipping, production, marketing, and public relations. Finally, salespeople may experience **job anxiety**, which is tension caused by the pressure of the job. Pressure may stem from the challenge of performing multiple tasks: meeting sales objectives, servicing old accounts and producing new accounts, developing and conducting effective sales presentations, developing product and competitor knowledge, submitting timely reports to the company, and controlling sales expenses.[15]

Desirable Salesperson Traits

Good salespeople must be self-motivated, organized, enthusiastic, adaptive, competitive, goal-oriented, empathetic, learning-oriented, and most importantly, customer-oriented, as shown in Figure 14.3. This last trait has been found to be the most significant differentiating factor between successful and mediocre salespeople.

Economic Forces

Sales occupations have been projected to be a growth area for many years to come. However, while growth projections still look good, the U.S. Department of Labor has determined that the number of people employed in sales has declined by almost 19% from just two years ago because of current worldwide economic difficulties.

Role conflict
Is the anxiety caused by conflicting job demands (e.g., the firm demands that the salesperson obtain a high price for the firm's product, while the customer demands a low price).

Role ambiguity
Is anxiety caused by inadequate information about job responsibilities and performance-related goals (e.g., many organizational departments—billing, shipping, production, marketing, and public relations—may influence the salesperson's activities and create uncertainty about what is expected of the salesperson).

Job anxiety
Is tension caused by the pressures of the job (e.g., the salesperson must perform, often simultaneously, many tasks: meeting sales objectives, servicing old accounts and producing new accounts, developing and conducting effective sales presentations, developing product and competitor knowledge, submitting timely reports to the company, and controlling sales expenses).

Benefits of Sales Occupations		**Figure 14.2**
• Flexibility in day-to-day activities	• Limited supervision	
• Intrinsic reward from helping customers	• Increasing responsibilities	
• Good compensation	• High-visibility career track	
• Travel opportunities	• Promotion potential	

As an alternative to a time machine, this ad promotes IBM Consulting Services to help companies understand and respond to customer needs.

Once upon a time,

there was a company in desperate danger of getting left behind. Their customers were demanding much more personal service. More customization. More value. Instantly. *On demand.* So they bought a Time Machine. That's right, a Time Machine. Flick a switch, and they could immediately go forward in time – and understand what their customers were going to need before they actually needed it. Touch a button, they could *go back* and integrate systems and processes that were creating customer snafus. Instead of being left behind, they could catch up. *They were jazzed.* There was only one problem: the Time Machine was a dud. A flop. Kaput. It didn't work.

AND THAT'S WHEN THEY CALLED IBM.

IBM can prepare you for the future of e-business *on demand* right now. With deep expertise in 18 industries and resources in 160 countries, the people of IBM Business Consulting Services can help you see where this world is headed. IBM is also pioneering new technologies that are easy to integrate and self-healing. By putting it all together, IBM is helping companies of all sizes and shapes plan for success in the *on demand* world. Learn more at **ibm.com**/ondemand

IBM.
@ business on demand

Learning-oriented
Is the trait of being open to and excited about acquiring new knowledge and skills.

Customer-oriented
Means the salesperson seeks to elicit customer needs/problems and then takes the necessary steps to meet those needs or solve the problem in a manner that is in the best interest of the customer.

Learning-oriented salespeople are open to and excited about acquiring new knowledge or skills, while **customer-oriented** salespeople seek to elicit customer needs/problems and then take the necessary steps to meet those needs or solve the problems in a manner that is in the best interest of the customer.

Figure 14.3	Desirable Salesperson Traits

Selling Contexts and Types of Salespeople

Personal selling occurs in different contexts, and each context determines which types of selling are used. The three contexts in which personal selling may occur are telemarketing, over-the-counter selling, and field selling (see Figure 14.4).

Telemarketing

Telemarketing uses the phone for prospecting, selling, and/or following up with customers. Two types of salespeople are generally found in this environment. *Outbound telemarketers* are salespeople who use the phone to call customers and close deals. *Inbound telemarketers,* on the other hand, are those salespeople who answer phone calls from customers and help them place orders. Firms that employ inbound telemarketers often have toll-free phone numbers as a convenience for their customers. Of the three selling contexts, telemarketing, in general, tends to rely less on developing relationships with customers.

Over-the-Counter Selling

Over-the-counter selling is usually conducted in retail outlets. As a consumer, you choose to enter a store, where you may be greeted by a retail salesperson. The salesperson may be an **order taker**, who only processes the purchase the customer has already selected, or an **order getter**, who seeks to actively provide information to prospects, persuade prospective customers, and close sales. If the store you have selected is heavily oriented toward self-service, your only interaction with a salesperson may be when you have to track one down to obtain an answer to a specific question you have regarding the merchandise. In this type of store, the over-the-counter salesperson will usually act only as an order taker, ringing up and appropriately packaging what you wish to purchase without imparting any product-specific knowledge. On the other hand, if the store is oriented toward personal service, the salesperson is likely to try to identify what it is you are seeking and to help you with merchandise selection. In these situations, the salesperson is acting as an order getter. The salesperson may even practice **suggestion selling** by pointing out available complementary items in line with the selected item, in order to encourage an additional purchase. For example, if you go into a store with the intention of purchasing a business suit, the salesperson may make suggestions regarding styles and colors. After your selection is made, the salesperson may suggest a tie or blouse that will match the suit.

Field Selling

Field selling involves calling on prospective customers in either their businesses or their homes. As in over-the-counter selling, salespeople involved in field selling may

Selling Environments and Types of Salespeople		Figure 14.4
Selling Environment	**Types of Salespeople**	
Telemarketing	Outbound Telemarketers Inbound Telemarketers	
Over-the-Counter	Order Takers Order Getters	
Field Selling	Professional Salespeople National Account Managers Missionary Salespeople Support Salespeople	

Listening in on the Web

Listening to the customer is a basic tenet for sales success. Procter & Gamble (P&G) has improved upon this principle by finding a way to hear its customers beyond those residing in one or two test market areas. In essence, P&G has used the Internet to create a global test market. When P&G first introduced Whitestrips, an oral-care product made of thin plastic material coated with hydrogen peroxide, it started selling the product through dentist offices and two typical test-market cities: Grand Junction, Colorado, and Pittsfield, Massachusetts. Shortly thereafter, it also launched the http://www.whitestrips.com Web site. The Web site allowed customers around the world to purchase the product at the same price it was offered at retail. Within nine months, the Web site had yielded more than a million purchases. Further, the site allowed the Whitestrips brand team to collect demographic data on prospective buyers and to listen to their responses to the product. This feedback ensured a successful national retail introduction. Additionally, the Web site allowed P&G to reach a much broader demographic group than the classic test markets, so P&G was able to hear from more customers of color, from nontraditional families, and from major urban areas—all previously underrepresented groups. Finally, P&G used the Internet to identify its best promotional outlets. The Whitestrips brand manager placed ads in various magazines, including *People,* an outlet not usually used by P&G. Each ad carried a code that linked it to a specific magazine and the ad offered a product discount if the buyer would enter the code on the Whitestrip Web site. By tracking the codes, the brand manager was able to learn that many of the site hits were generated by *People* readers. This finding resulted in a major change in the way P&G purchases promotional media.

Source: Fara Warner, "Don't Shout, Listen," *Fast Company* 49 (August 2001), 130–138.

act as order takers, such as in the food industry, or as order getters, such as in the encyclopedia business. Many salespeople in the field-selling environment, however, are categorized as professional salespeople, national account managers, missionary salespeople, or support salespeople.

Professional Salespeople

Professional salespeople may be found in all industries, but especially in industries where products are adapted to individual customer needs, such as high-tech computers. The companies for which they work may assign professional salespeople a variety of job titles, including account executive, sales consultant, or sales representative.

National Account Managers

National account managers are highly skilled salespeople who call on key customers' headquarters, develop strategic plans for the accounts, make formal presentations to top-level executives, and assist with all the product decisions at that level. Consequently, important customers associate one key person—the national account manager—with the vendor company, and the vendor company does not need to have its other salespeople call on all the local branches of a large, diverse customer. For example, the Procter & Gamble national account manager for Wal-Mart conducts sales presentations at the company's Arkansas headquarters, and any decisions made pertaining to Procter & Gamble products at headquarters will then be passed down to all of Wal-Mart's retail outlets. This way, Procter & Gamble does not need to have individual salespeople calling on every Wal-Mart store to try to influence decision makers at that level.

National account managers are expected to know their customers' businesses intimately; consequently, national account managers call on very few accounts. Indeed, it is not unusual for a national account manager to be responsible for just one customer, if the customer is a very large one. Customers that are assigned national account managers have enormous sales potential and more complex buying behaviors, due to their multiple locations and various operating units. The national account manager's job is to provide these special accounts with significant attention and service to ensure that a partnership develops between the two organizations.

Missionary Salespeople

Missionary salespeople differ from other sales professionals in that they do not seek to obtain a direct order from their customers. Although they are charged with providing product information to customers, their primary goal is to persuade customers to place orders with distributors or wholesalers. For example, the goal of Kraft Foods salespeople is to convince the managers of grocery stores to place orders with food wholesalers for Kraft products. Pharmaceutical representatives are also missionary salespeople. Their job is to provide detailed information to physicians, so that the physicians will prescribe their drug to their patients. These patients, in turn, will purchase the prescription from one of the pharmaceutical firm's resellers, such as a drug store.

Support Salespeople

Support salespeople do not actually perform all the steps in the sales process; instead, their job is to support the sales force in a number of ways. Technical support salespeople serve as technical advisors to the sales force and prospective customers on complex products such as data networking systems. They are often teamed with a sales representative to assist with the technical aspects of sales presentations. Other support salespeople, sometimes known as merchandisers, set up product displays in the customer's business after the sales representative has obtained the customer's permission to do so. Still other types of support salespeople complete and follow up on order processing, and do other related administrative tasks in order to free the salesperson to spend more time with customers.

Sales Certification

As selling evolves into the development of strategic partnerships with customers, salespeople are heralding a new level of professionalism through sales certification. Several organizations now offer certification programs that are designed to increase the professionalism and expertise of salespeople. Applicants for sales certification must meet a specified point criterion based on a combination of education, sales experience, and industry service; pass a challenging written exam; write a 2,500-word original research paper; provide professional references; and agree to adhere to a code of ethics.[16] They are also encouraged to participate in continuing education programs to maintain certification. Three organizations that offer salesperson certification programs are Hospitality Sales and Marketing Association International (HSMAI), the National Association of Sales Professionals (NASP), and Sales and Marketing Executives International (SMEI).[17] These certification programs are designed to increase the credibility and professionalism of the salesperson, and earn the public's respect for the sales profession.

The Sales Process

3 **LEARNING OBJECTIVE**

There are eight basic steps in the sales process: prospecting, the preapproach, the approach, need identification, presentation, handling objections, gaining commitment, and follow-up (see Figure 14.5). In the *traditional selling method,* little time is spent on the early stages of the process—especially the approach and need identification. Consequently, the prospective buyer is not usually convinced that he or she really needs the product, so gaining commitment from the buyer is difficult, tedious, and time-consuming. In the *professional selling method,* a great deal of time is spent on the early stages—prospecting, preapproach, approach, and need identification—so that commitment is gained as a very natural, or logical, next step. Essentially, customers are convinced that the product will solve their problem, or meet their need, because early in the sales process care has been taken to establish that need and link it to the benefits of the product. In the following sections, each of the eight steps of the sales process is discussed.

| Figure 14.5 | The Sales Process |

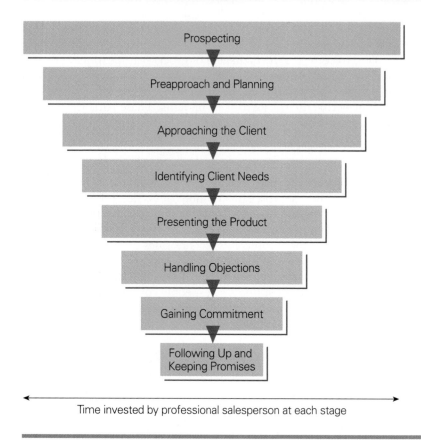

Time invested by professional salesperson at each stage

Prospecting

Qualified sales leads

Are potential customers who have a need for the salesperson's product, the financial means to purchase the product, and the authority to make the buying decision.

Prospecting involves finding **qualified sales leads**, which are potential customers who have a need for the salesperson's product, the financial means to purchase the product, and the authority to make the buying decision. The importance of prospecting cannot be overstated. The greatest cause of failure in a sales career and the most common source of inconsistent earnings have been linked to a failure to consistently and continuously prospect for new customers.[18]

There are many ways to find sales leads: making cold calls, working trade shows, networking through industry associations or social organizations, offering educational seminars, reading trade journals and newspaper business pages, and buying leads from online providers. One of the better means of finding leads, though, is through **referrals**, which are obtained by the salesperson asking current customers if they know of someone else, or another company, who might need the salesperson's product. The most successful salespeople build their sales practices largely through referrals, and referrals are the most efficient means of producing new sales.[19] Indeed, in financial services, one sale is gained for every 3.3 referrals, compared to every 10 seminar attendees, every 50 cold calls, or every 60 letters.[20]

Referrals

Are obtained by the salesperson asking current customers if they know of someone else, or another company, who might need the salesperson's product.

Prior to asking for referrals, a salesperson should ensure that the current customer is satisfied. But once a strong relationship has been established, the salesperson should not hesitate to ask for a referral. Referred leads usually mean faster closings, shorter sales cycles, and larger initial transactions. Unfortunately, few salespeople ask for referrals, although customers generally indicate they would gladly provide them.

Technology makes obtaining customized, qualified leads easily available so a salesperson can be more efficient and productive. D&B's Zapdata.com, for example, offers a business-to-business database for salespeople looking for leads.

Although most salespeople dislike making **cold calls**—contacting prospective customers without a prior appointment—nearly all salespeople must perform some cold-calling during their careers. Cold-calling is occasionally conducted by phoning prospects. When using the phone for cold calls, most salespeople attempt only to secure a definite appointment with the prospect, although other salespeople will attempt to complete the sale over the phone. Cold-calling may also involve stopping by the customer's business or home without a prearranged appointment. While this face-to-face interaction can be quite effective, some companies have strict rules about salespeople seeing their employees for solicitation purposes. Salespeople should familiarize themselves with company policies before dropping in to visit.

Many salespeople have a fear of cold-calling because they fear rejection. On average, a salesperson has to make three to five sales calls for every one sale; however, for some industries, the ratio may be 1 in 10 or 1 in 25 calls. In a difficult economic environment, identifying and calling on even more prospects are essential for maintaining the company's sales volume.[21] Consequently, salespeople should not become discouraged. They can remain motivated by remembering that sales is a numbers game—sales representatives will likely hear many "nos" before they hear a "yes."

Once prospects have been identified, these potential buyers should be incorporated into a customer-relationship-management database that will help salespeople have the right information, including the most effective contact method, at the right time.[22]

Cold calls
Mean contacting prospective customers without a prior appointment.

Economic Forces
Although prospecting is often the least favorite task of salespeople, it becomes an even more critical skill during an economic recession. Because current customers often reduce their level of buying during trying times, an organization's very survival may rely on the sales force's ability to identify and qualify prospects that are capable of offsetting declining revenues.

Preapproach and Planning

The preapproach is the collection of information about the potential customer and the customer's company prior to the initial visit. In very much the same way that job candidates should research any firm that they are going to interview with, salespeople should also research any prospective client and the client's company.[23] A salesperson should seek answers to the following questions:

- Who will make the purchase decision?
- What are that person's interests?
- What is that person's job title?

- What does the company do?
- Who are the company's primary competitors?
- Which of the vendor's direct competitors are currently doing business with the prospective customer?
- What rules does the prospective customer have regarding salespeople?

In other words, the sales representative should obtain as much information as possible about prospects and their respective companies. One quick source for this information may be the local library or the Internet. Many firms have Web sites that provide useful company information. Figure 14.6 illustrates how the Internet might be used throughout the sales process.

Researching the prospect and the prospect's company will demonstrate that the salesperson is serious about earning the prospect's business, and helps ensure that the prospect is a qualified buyer. This information also assists the salesperson in planning the initial presentation to the prospective customer. Failure to do precall planning has a direct and negative effect on long-term sales success.[24]

Approaching the Client

The approach is the development of rapport with the customer. Using the information he has already gathered, the salesperson begins developing a relationship with the customer. The salesperson wants to illustrate that he is working to understand and help meet the prospective customer's needs. In this stage, it is important for the salesperson to adapt to the potential customer's social style.

Social Styles

There are four basic social-style categories,[25] which are depicted in Figure 14.7.

1. The *driver* is action- and goal-oriented, and makes quick decisions. To adapt to this social style, the salesperson should provide the bottom-line information first, and then work backward to fill in essential details. The driver will want only the basic facts and will not want to socialize a great deal.
2. The *analytical* is fact- and detail-oriented. This individual will require time to make decisions, while carefully weighing all the facts. To adapt to this social style, the salesperson should inundate the analytical prospect with facts and figures that can be supported with documentation. Like the driver, the analytical is not very interested in developing a personal relationship with the salesperson.
3. The *expressive* loves to socialize and will frequently base the purchase decision on her relationship with the salesperson. To adapt to this social style, the salesperson should be prepared to establish a personal relationship with the expres-

Figure 14.6	Steps in the Personal Selling Process Adapted to the Web	
	Personal Selling	**Web Selling**
Prospecting	Names from databases, referrals, past customers, other sources	Search engines, listserv(es), e-mail, links
Preapproach	Information gathering on needs, wants, preferences	Data collection online, site searches, screening links
Approach	Method of contact, atmospherics, initial impressions, cold call	URL, opening Web screen, navigation
Presentation	Discussing the options, listening, and replying to objections	Graphics, screen design, links to other products
Closing the Sale	Asking for the sale Filling out the order	Taking the order online, self-service
Follow-Up	Determining customer satisfaction	E-mail, other follow-up

Social Styles Figure 14.7

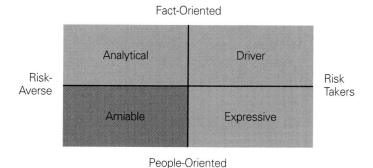

Source: Adapted from David Merrill and Roger Reid, *Personal Styles and Effective Performance* (Radnor, PA: Chilton, 1981).

sive prospect by telling anecdotal stories, socializing outside the office, and relating personal information.

4. The *amiable* tends to be a visionary with big ideas for the future, but is not a detail-oriented individual. The amiable prospect is hesitant to make quick decisions and will seek consensus from others before reaching a purchase decision. The amiable also seeks to have a personal relationship with the salesperson, as this relationship helps reduce some of the anxiety he feels about making a decision. To adapt to this social style, the salesperson should establish a personal relationship and provide assurances that will reduce the amiable's feeling of risk. Further, the sales representative should present the product based on what it will do for the customer in the "big picture," and avoid getting into discussions of minute details.

Other factors must be considered in the approach stage. This is the salesperson's chance to make a good first impression. Consequently, the salesperson should dress neatly and professionally. Prospects should be greeted with a firm handshake and direct eye contact. Throughout the sales interview, the salesperson should maintain an open body posture to indicate interest and openness to the customer; that is, the salesperson should keep feet flat on the floor; body leaning slightly forward, if seated; direct eye contact; arms open (uncrossed); and hands open, palms slightly upward. The salesperson should also let the customer know that she is actively listening by rephrasing or summarizing important points the customer has made.

Identifying Client Needs Through Probing Questions

Success at the need-identification stage of the sales process requires asking probing questions of prospective customers to determine their needs. Determining and addressing customer needs throughout the sales process is crucial to a successful sales call. Customer needs may be *organizational* and/or *personal*. Organizational needs may involve finance, image, or performance issues, whereas personal needs may involve ego or self-image.

To obtain information about the prospect's needs, the salesperson should ask open-ended questions. Such questions are designed to elicit a true expression of the prospect's opinions and feelings, regardless of whether these opinions are favorable or unfavorable in the salesperson's view. The salesperson should use open-ended, or probing, questions frequently throughout the sales presentation to ensure that the prospective buyer's needs and potential concerns are addressed. The key here is to learn what prospective customers want, not just to try to sell whatever the salesperson has to offer.[26] Figure 14.8 illustrates the difference between open and closed questions.

Figure 14.8	Open- versus Closed-Question Formats

Open-Ended		**Close-Ended**	
Salesperson:	What are you looking for in a new car?	Salesperson:	Do you want to look at our full-size four-wheel-drive vehicles?
Buyer:	I want an economic car that is easy to park, but handles well on icy roads. I don't want a big four-wheel drive vehicle, though. I also want to keep my monthly payments down.	Buyer:	No, I'm not interested in that.
Salesperson:	Excellent! I think you will find our new Subaru model is exactly what you're looking for. Let me show it to you.		

Presenting the Product

After needs have been identified, the salesperson should gain the prospect's permission to begin the presentation. The presentation should be adapted to address the specific customer needs identified in the previous stage.

Features versus Benefits

Customers buy products not because of the features they offer, but because of the customer needs these features satisfy. Therefore, the focus of the sales presentation should be the salesperson's explanation of how a product's features provide "benefits" that specifically address the prospect's previously identified needs or problems. These benefits should answer the buyer's often unvocalized question, "What's in it for me?" For example, rather than simply telling buyers that a shampoo contains special conditioners (feature), the marketer must tell the buyers that their hair will be softer and shinier (benefit) because of these special conditioners.

Types of Presentations

Presentations may be flexible or memorized (see Figure 14.9). *Flexible presentations* allow the salesperson to identify the customer's needs and customize the presentation specifically for the individual customer. This type of presentation is sometimes

Focusing on customer benefits and providing evidence of these benefits is key to a strong sales presentation.

© Michael Newman/PhotoEdit, Inc.

Presentation Styles	Figure 14.9

Flexible Presentations

- Identify customer needs
- Customize presentation

Memorized Presentations

- Do not address specific needs of customer
- Scripts feature key benefits and selling points

called a *need-satisfaction presentation,* and is the preferred method for professional salespeople. *Memorized presentations* require that the salesperson commit a scripted presentation to memory. This type of presentation, sometimes called a *canned presentation,* does not address the specific needs of each customer; however, the script is built around the best key benefits and selling points of the company and the product. Salespeople who sell to consumers in their homes may use this method of presentation. For example, book companies that sell door-to-door often have their sales representatives use memorized presentations with successful results. This approach should be used with caution since it may create a perception of unoriginality, thereby making customers feel as if they are not special or important.

To improve the effectiveness of their presentations, many salespeople now incorporate the latest technology via laptop computers. Thus, sales representatives may use computer graphics and/or Web sites in their sales presentations to generate increased attention and interest from prospective customers.

Handling Objections

Prospective buyers frequently raise objections about buying a particular product. However, these objections do not necessarily mean that the prospect is uninterested in the product. Instead, objections may indicate that the salesperson has failed to provide adequate information to the buyer, or has not demonstrated how the product meets the prospect's needs. Consequently, the prospective customer is afraid that he may make a mistake by purchasing the product. When faced with objections, the salesperson should approach the objection as a sign of interest on the part of the prospect, and provide information that will ensure the prospect's confidence in making the purchase.[27] As he gains experience, the salesperson will recognize that certain objections occur on a regular basis. After discerning what these common objections are, the salesperson should work to provide information early in the presentation that will counter these objections. For example, if the salesperson routinely hears prospective buyers say, "The price is too high," the salesperson should strive to emphasize the higher quality or special attributes offered by the product. Consequently, the prospect will recognize that added features and increased quality compensate for the higher price; thus, good value is still offered.

Providing Supporting Evidence
During the presentation, the salesperson should be prepared to document any statements of fact that are made. This documentation can come from a variety of sources, including letters of testimony from satisfied customers, independent reports, newspaper or magazine articles, company brochures or other literature, and product demonstrations. For example, a hotel sales manager might explain to a potential client that numerous companies have used the hotel's facilities to hold their annual meetings and have been quite satisfied. The salesperson should then produce letters of testimony from various companies that support the claim of satisfied corporate clientele.

Hooked on Credit

Credit cards for teens—Apply today—30-second approval!

Plus, $0 liability on unauthorized charges and 8.9% introductory APR on all purchases!

You will always receive the lowest prices when you shop online GUARANTEED!

The credit card for teens carries more benefits than most standard credit cards.

There is no application fee!

Look familiar? Statistics indicate that 70% of college undergraduates carry credit cards in their own names, and almost a quarter of these students obtained their first credit card while still in high school. When did teens begin carrying cards? When credit-card companies decided they wanted to tap into the $155 billion a year spent by Americans under the age of 18. Credit-card companies are so desperate to win a piece of teen spending that they give away t-shirts, place full-page ads in campus newspapers, and offer preapproved applications. Across the country on college campuses, credit-card companies make mutually lucrative deals with university administrators so that the companies can hawk their credit cards to a constant parade of college students in high-traffic campus areas; similarly, these same companies are ruthlessly pursuing high school students 16 or older, and, in some cases, seek teens as young as 13. Frequently, obtaining a credit card in the student's name requires no more than the student's signature on an application. However, credit cards targeted toward students tend to have high interest rates and other unfavorable terms because students have limited credit histories and high default rates.

Further, major credit card companies are actively pursuing teens despite numerous stories of out-of-control credit-card spending by teens that resulted in massive debt and sometimes suicide. One high school student reported finding herself $60,000 in debt by the time she was 18. A college student amassed $40,000 in credit-card debt during his college years; the stress he felt trying to pay off his debt led him to create the Web site called **http://www.cardratings. org**. Similarly, yet another college student found himself so much in debt to credit-card companies that he was not even able to work enough hours to meet the minimum payments:

He had to leave school for a year to pay down his credit-card debt.

While no one is twisting the arms of teens to get them to use credit cards, many teens report that it felt like someone had just given them a lot of money and they had plenty of time to pay it back. Indeed, a recent survey by the National Consumers League indicated that more than 50% of surveyed teens did not recognize that they had a legal obligation to repay credit-card debt. Furthermore, most teens do not realize that if they purchase a $2,000 item and then choose to pay the minimum balance each month, it will take more than 30 years to pay off the debt, during which time they will have paid $5,000 in interest alone. To protect U.S. teens, some members of Congress are considering legislation that would restrict the sales practices of credit-card companies.

DISCUSSION QUESTIONS
1. Should credit-card companies be allowed to specifically target teens in their sales strategies?
2. What are the ethical issues underlying selling easy credit to teens?

Sources: Robin Marantz Henig, "Teen Credit Cards Actually Teach Responsibility," *USA Today* (31 July 2001), A15.

Bob Tgedeschi, "Charge It!," *The New York Times,* Teacher's Ed. (25 March 2002), 12–13.

Jeffrey Green and Lavonne Kuykendall, "Teens: Paying Their Own Way," *Credit Card Management* 13 (September 2000), 56–61.

Kristin Nemsick, "Credit Cards Ruined My Life," *Teen* 43 (May 1999), 84–86.

Anonymous, "Credit Card Debts Mortgaging U.S. Middle Class' Future," *USA Today* (15 June 1999), 23.

Anonymous, "Teens: I Really Have to Pay This Back," *Medical Economics* (21 June 2002), 10.

Christine Dugas, "Teens Need Some Training Wheels," *USA Today* (18 August 2000), http://www.usatoday.com/money/wealth/consumer/mcw074.htm (accessed 16 December 2002).

Anonymous, "Don't Let 'Spring Break' Expenditures 'Break' You!" March 2000, http://www.cardratings.com/mar00new.html (accessed 16 December 2002).

Anonymous, "The High Cost of Using Credit Cards," 2002, http://financialplan.about.com/library/weekly/aa071000a.htm (accessed 16 December 2002).

Amy Simmons, "LaFalce: Legislation Aimed at Credit Card Abuses Is Long Overdue: Calls on Regulators to Investigate Use of Credit Cards in Internet Gambling," 1 November 2001, http://www.house.gov/banking_democrats/pr_011101.htm (accessed 16 December 2002).

Gaining Commitment

Commitment is gained when the prospect agrees to take the action sought by the salesperson. Usually, this means the buyer purchases the product, or at least signs a purchase agreement. However, prospects will not usually come right out and say they want to buy what the salesperson is offering; the salesperson must ask for commitment. In other words, *the salesperson must ask for the order*, just as the interviewee should ask for the job.[28] Failure to ask for an order is frequently the cause of a salesperson's unsuccessful presentation. Indeed, 55% of sales managers report that their salespeople have difficulty closing sales.[29] Yet, the sales profession recognizes

Closing the sale is a critical step in the sales process, frequently overlooked. Closing the sale on a new car means asking the customer to make the purchase or to sign a purchase agreement.

the importance of this stage of the sales process, as evidenced by the numerous book chapters devoted to gaining commitment.[30]

Following Up and Keeping Promises

The last step in the sales process, follow-up, requires that the salesperson complete any agreed-upon actions. Unfortunately, while salespeople may work very hard to get a customer, they frequently fail to follow through on their promises, so they cannot keep these customers. Sales experts suggest that it is more cost-effective to keep customers that the sales force knows well; consequently, it is imperative that salespeople keep any promises they make to customers.[31]

Additionally, salespeople should stay in touch after a sale by writing thank-you notes, clipping and mailing newspaper articles of interest to the prospect, or occasionally calling on customers just to ensure that they are still happy with their purchase decisions. The technological environment also enhances the follow-up phase of selling by providing a cost-effective tool for sending e-mail newsletters to opt-in customers, placing solutions to common problems or answers to frequently asked questions on the selling company's Web site, and e-mailing notices of specials or promotions to customers whose past behaviors indicate they would have an interest in a particular product.[32]

Technological Forces

MicroStrategy is leveraging technology to strengthen relationships with customers, suppliers, and partners by converting and distributing all sorts of information through wireless devices so it can be accessed at any time and anywhere.

Building and Managing the Sales Force

4   **LEARNING OBJECTIVE**

Selling is the revenue stream of the corporation. Managing this vital function requires strong skills so that the sales force will continue to generate the money to fund the rest of the organization. Sales management is the process of planning, directing, controlling, and implementing the personal-selling function of the organization.

Sales managers must be good leaders who can recruit, train, motivate, and evaluate their sales representatives; manage territories; and develop sales plans and sales forecasts while accomplishing the goals of the organization (see Figure 14.10).[33] They also need to be able to identify business opportunities and create and implement optimum sales strategies.

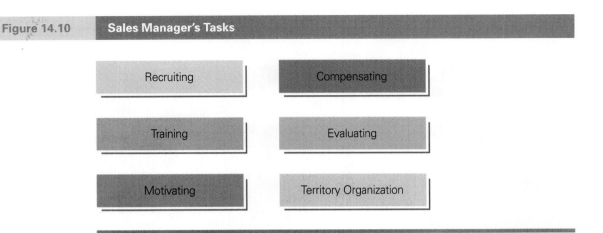

Figure 14.10   Sales Manager's Tasks

Recruiting

Sales managers must recruit the appropriate individuals for any open sales positions. A sales force composed of the right people makes a big difference in how large a company can grow. The individuals the sales manager hires should possess the attributes previously discussed: empathy, competitiveness, goal orientation, customer orientation, enthusiasm, learning orientation, organization, and self-motivation. In addition, the sales manager should recruit individuals whose values and goals match those of the firm. This congruency will facilitate greater job satisfaction among new recruits.

To hire the best salespeople, the sales manager should not rely solely on résumés, but should pay close attention to how candidates conduct themselves throughout the interview process. For example, if the first contact is by phone, the candidate should ask for an appointment. Candidates who do not ask are unlikely to ask for orders from prospective customers. Candidates should also demonstrate persistence by staying in touch with the sales manager, not just waiting for the sales manager to call back. Additionally, candidates should be good listeners. Candidates who talk more than 50% of the time may not be effective at listening to prospects and customers. Finally, candidates should ask for the job. Candidates who do not ask for the job will probably be too timid to ask for commitment from prospective customers.

Many sales organizations have resorted to objective tests to assist them in selecting the best sales candidates. Some companies, such as The Breakers, and Ramada Franchise Systems, have determined that certain personality types perform better in their industries; therefore, after passing initial screening interviews, candidates are subjected to personality tests. Only those candidates who fit a certain personality profile move on to the next level in the selection process. Other companies, such as Procter & Gamble, General Mills, and PricewaterhouseCoopers, test for certain sales skills such as critical thinking, adaptability, or intellect. Candidates who do not obtain an adequate score are dropped from the pool of eligible candidates. Still other organizations, such as McKinsey & Company, subject their job candidates to role-playing early in the selection process. Those candidates who perform well in the role-play progress to the next step. These somewhat more objective methods for selecting sales recruits are designed to reduce some of the difficulty that firms have in finding the best candidates for their sales forces.

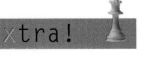

Sales-Force Training

Training is essential to the success of the sales force. Consequently, all sales representatives, regardless of how long they have been selling, should periodically receive training to stay up-to-date and to keep their skills honed. Sales-force training includes learning the corporate culture, building product knowledge and sales skills, and using technology to fulfill job responsibilities.

Technology is a key tool for increasing sales performance, but the selected technology must fit the needs of the sales force.

Corporate Culture

After hiring the best candidates, sales managers must orient recruits to the company culture. Additionally, sales managers must train new sales representatives on product and customer knowledge and selling skills. Although sales training is expensive—in 2002, U.S. companies spent $14.2 billion on training[34]—the payoff is worth it.[35] Indeed, experts note that employees achieve a 30% increase in productivity following effective training.[36]

Product Knowledge and Sales Skills

The focus of initial sales training should be on product knowledge and sales skills. Good product knowledge is essential for making presentations and handling objections while the acquisition of good sales skills is necessary to move effectively through the sales process. Sales representatives should be taught to identify the social styles of customers and alter their presentations for each customer type. In other words, sales representatives should know and practice *adaptive selling*. In addition, the sales force should learn to develop attention-getting openings and good listening skills, focus on customer needs, handle objections, and be able to close the sale. More advanced salespeople should be trained in strategic account management and the development of long-term customer relationships. They should understand the importance of identifying the organizational structure, key decision makers, and decision influencers in their customers' organizations. They must learn more about their customers' businesses and how they can help customers be more profitable. Finally, all salespeople should receive training to understand the competitive and technological environments in which they operate. This knowledge should provide salespeople with strategies and tactics for managing these environmental forces so there is no negative impact on the sales force's ability to effectively serve customers.

Sales-Force Technology

As the widespread and increasing use of technology among sales forces indicates, the technological environment has had a major impact on the daily lives of salespeople. Many companies are mandating that their sales forces operate from "virtual offices" equipped with laptop computers, cell phones, and portable printer-copier-fax machines, rather than driving to corporate headquarters each day.[37] These virtual

Technological Forces

Salespeople at Hewlett-Packard use the Internet to customize presentations, obtain on-the-spot answers to customer questions, and follow up with customers. As a result, HP salespeople are more productive than their less "wired" counterparts.

Technological Forces

Well-known companies such as American Express, Aetna, Scudder Kemper Investments, and Dain Rauscher Corp. have struggled to integrate technology into their organizations. These companies learned that they had to obtain input from their sales forces *before* the technology integration could take shape.

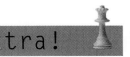

offices allow a sales force to spend more time in the field with customers. Salespeople use laptop computers to communicate electronically with their corporate office several times a day. Indeed, sales data are now routinely processed electronically for faster customer service.

Computers are also used to prepare and deliver sales presentations to customers and receive continuous updates on products and pricing, and may be a vehicle for sales training.[38] Cell phones are standard equipment for most sales forces, and those phones with advanced features, such as Internet capabilities, are becoming increasingly popular, as are electronic organizers.[39] The Internet is also being used to reduce operating expenses and provide salespeople with more selling time. Major accounts still receive high levels of personalized service, while small accounts or individuals who previously consumed valuable sales time, but did not purchase in sufficient quantities to warrant personalized sales service, can now be tactfully directed to the Web. Further, the Internet assists a sales force in efficiently communicating with its customers by making contracts, designs, and blueprints available to customers on the Web.[40] In turn, the sales force saves hours of driving time. This saved time can be used to pursue new business and to develop stronger relationships with current customers.

Sales representatives must be knowledgeable regarding spreadsheet software and other sophisticated software applications specific to their industry. Also, sales managers ensure that their representatives have a competitive edge by using a CRM database that maintains customer information and tracks customer purchase behaviors.[41] As explained in previous chapters, CRM systems allow a sales force to match customers with a customized marketing plan, identify customers at risk of defecting to competitors, track changing customer preferences, improve customer relationships, and determine customers' profitability to the firm.[42] Rapidly advancing technology is allowing sales forces to access real-time customer data through wireless platform applications. As a result, sales can be closed faster and more often because sales representatives have all the information they need right at their fingertips.[43]

Finally, some sales managers are also suggesting that their sales forces use a software program that allows sales representatives to enter a geographical location and immediately receive a listing and location of all current and potential accounts in the area. Such a program allows sales representatives to use their time more efficiently.

Frequently, sales training requires travel to a distant location and overnight stays in a hotel. For companies with large sales forces, the cost of such training can run into millions of dollars, which precludes frequent training. In today's high-tech world, though, many companies are turning to online or Web-based learning to train their sales forces.[44] The salespeople involved are able to use their own computers to link into a training session from their homes or hotel rooms if they are on the road visiting clients. Some companies combine these Web-based sessions with standard classroom training,[45] while others allow their sales forces to tap into the Internet whenever the need arises to become informed about new offerings or to refresh themselves on a particular product.[46] Consequently, firms are now able to offer their salespeople more frequent training, without requiring that the representatives leave their sales territories and customers.

Unfortunately, despite some of its obvious benefits, automating the sales force through the use of technology has met some resistance. Recent studies indicate that approximately three out of five attempts at introducing new technology into the operations of sales forces have failed.[47] This high failure rate can be partially attributed to a lack of fit between the technological tools and the sales process.[48] Consequently, salespeople are often initially enthusiastic about new technology, but develop negative attitudes after using the new technological tool for six months.[49]

Motivating the Sales Force

Sales representatives are individuals, and what motivates one may not motivate another.[50] Sales managers have to use a variety of methods to keep all of these diverse individuals motivated to put forth maximum effort. After all, the sales profession can

Avon calling! Avon ringer på! Avon toca la puerta! Avon frappe a la purte!

Avon is the worldwide leader in direct sales of beauty products, with more than 65% of Avon's sales coming from outside the United States. Currently, Avon's direct sales force is active in more than 140 countries and the company looks to continue strong financial performance by continuing to expand into emerging markets. Indeed, in 2002, central and eastern Europe were the fastest growing sales regions for Avon, and Avon is one of the strongest cosmetic brands in Brazil.

Financial analysts note that international shoppers tend to be extremely loyal to the Avon brand, whose primary target market has been women in the lower- to middle-class markets, and Avon maintains this loyalty through new marketing campaigns. However, Avon is now seeking a new target market: young women between the ages of 16 and 24. Avon's strategy involves using teenage girls to sell a new line of teen-oriented products to other teens through direct selling channels, catalogs, and the Internet. The company has had some previous success in attracting young sales agents and customers. For example, in China, 75% of Avon customers are in the 15-to-34 age category. Nevertheless, Avon will find that attracting and holding Gen Y customers is a challenge, as this market segment is always looking to identify and follow the latest fad. To be successful, Avon will have to be highly flexible in its product offerings, as well as its marketing promotions. Yet, capturing this market segment will be highly profitable—teens account for 20% of the cosmetic sales volume in countries such as the United States, France, United Kingdom, and Germany. For the United States market alone, teen cosmetic purchases amount to $5.6 billion dollars a year. That's real teen power!

Sources: Allison Krampf, "Makeover Magic: Look for More Growth from the Retouched Avon," *Barron's* (4 November 2002), 26.
Anonymous, "Avon to Target Teens," *Direct Marketing* 64 (November 2001), 22.
Sonoo Singh, "Avon Plans Global Teen Assault," *Marketing Week* (16 August 2001), 5.
Fernando Agos, "Brazil: Making Progress," http://www.globalcosmetic.com (March 2000), 70–75 (accessed 16 December 2002).
Sally Beatty, "Avon Is Set to Call on Teens—Cosmetics Maker Creates Line It Hopes 16-to-24-Year-Olds Will Not Only Buy But Sell," *The Wall Street Journal* (17 October 2002), B1.
Regina Molaro, "Teen Beat," *Global Cosmetic Industry* (July 2001), 20–22.

be a high-pressure job that involves frequent rejection. For some salespeople, working to beat the set quota and winning sales contests is a great motivator. Winning builds confidence and reinforces the notion that the individual is a great sales representative. Other salespeople are motivated by extra training sessions that challenge them and groom them for upper-management positions. Sales managers may also find that some top-performing individuals are motivated by acting as mentors to newer sales representatives, or by being sought for their advice and wisdom. Some salespeople are most motivated when their strong customer-service efforts are recognized throughout the company by plaques and awards.[51] Finally, salespeople may be driven to perform at a high level when they are having fun at work. Several companies—including Southwest Airlines, LEGO Systems, and Auto Glass Plus—ensure that their sales staff's morale is routinely boosted by theme days, games, and humor.[52] In summary, sales managers must identify what best motivates each of their sales representatives and then strive to motivate and reward them accordingly. The use of sales quotas and sales coaching are two proven techniques for improving sales performance.

Sales-Force Quotas

Sales-force quotas are used throughout the sales industry to further motivate salespeople and encourage them to focus on company priorities. Basically, the sales manager provides each sales representative with a reward when the sales representative, or in some cases the sales team, reaches a challenging performance objective called a *quota*.[53] The quota usually represents an aspect of sales volume that the sales representative is expected to achieve.[54] The quota should be high enough to encourage the sales force to put forth greater effort, yet low enough to appear attainable. Otherwise, the quotas that the sales manager sets may serve to discourage rather than motivate the sales force. Similarly, the reward offered for meeting or exceeding the quota should be of sufficient value to provide motivation. If it is too low, the sales force may deem that it is not worth their extra effort to achieve. The competitive environment may affect the salesperson's evaluation of the equity of the quota, as the

Competitive Forces

To retain the best salespeople, a firm's overall compensation and benefits must meet or exceed those of competitive firms. NCR, Verizon, Carnival Cruise Lines, E&J Gallo Winery, Motorola, Unison Industries, MSA, Marriott International, Misys Healthcare Systems, and Follet Library Resources have been recognized for their top sales forces.

Sales managers must customize incentives to keep each salesperson motivated. Prizes, such as Home Depot gift cards, are frequently used to integrate creativity and fun into the salesperson's job.

Sales-call anxiety
Is a fear of negative evaluation and rejection by customers.

sales force is likely to make comparisons with counterparts in other firms.[55] If quotas are deemed too high by comparison, salespeople may leave the firm. Successful sales managers also suggest providing extra, individualized incentives for those salespeople who exceed their sales quotas.[56]

Sales Coaching

Coaching involves facilitating the development of sales skills through mentoring, modeling behavior, and one-on-one interaction.[57] The goal of the sales coach is to develop a relationship of mutual trust and respect with the sales force, which in turn encourages the sales force to listen to and follow directives from the sales manager. Good sales-manager-salesperson interaction has also been found to reduce the role conflict and ambiguity often associated with the sales profession. Finally, the sales manager serves as a model to the sales force so they know what behavior and actions to emulate. Sales-manager coaching has been found to motivate salespeople to improve their performance.[58]

As part of the coaching function, sales managers should help sales representatives overcome **sales-call anxiety (SCA)**.[59] Most often, sales-call anxiety surfaces during the prospecting or closing phases of the sales process, and can be quite debilitating for the salesperson. Sales managers should familiarize themselves with the various strategies that exist for overcoming SCA and work with sales representatives who may be avoiding either initiating customer contact or gaining customer commitment.

Compensating the Sales Force

Sales managers are responsible for determining how the sales force will be compensated for their efforts. Sound execution of this management task is crucial, since compensation is a key factor in ensuring sales-force motivation, satisfaction, and retention.

Continuum: Straight Salary to Straight Commission

The level of compensation may be established anywhere on a continuum from straight salary on one end to straight commission on the other (see Figure 14.11). That is, the sales manager may choose to pay the sales force a *straight salary*, in which pay is based on units of time (year, month, week, or hour). This form of compensation provides the sales force with greater security, but may reduce their desire to put forth extra efforts because they will not receive a direct reward for this effort. Or, the sales manager may choose to compensate the sales force on the basis of *straight commission*, in which pay is based on units of results. In this case, the sales representatives' pay is based solely on how much they sell. For many companies, this

Figure 14.11	The Salary Continuum

Straight Salary ◆━━━━━━━━━━━━━━━◆ **Straight Commission**

Low Risk/ Low Reward   High Risk/ High Reward

has been the traditional means of rewarding the sales force. Straight commission, however, can create a great deal of insecurity in sales representatives since some factors that they have no control over, like an economic recession, may cause a downturn in their sales, and thus a reduction in their salary. The third and most popular method of sales-force compensation is through a combination of the previous two: *salary plus commission*. Accordingly, the sales manager pays the sales force a sufficient base salary to provide for a basic standard of living, but also pays a commission on sales that is high enough to serve as an incentive for extra sales efforts. This base salary plus high commission can allow a motivated salesperson to earn a six-figure income. (see Figure 14.12).[60]

In today's environment, where the focus is on long-term relationships and where e-commerce is altering the sales landscape, many companies are finding it necessary to change their method of compensating the sales force. Compensation plans that incorporate high commissions on sales units encourage the sales force to make quick sales without regard to actual customer needs; they do not encourage the sales force to take the time to establish relationships with their customers. Furthermore, customers are determining the sales channel (i.e., Internet, telemarketing, face-to-face) most appropriate for their particular needs. Consequently, some companies have set up different types of compensation plans in which a portion of commission money may be tied to the following:

- Customer satisfaction
- Customer retention rates
- Share of customer's business
- Training of new salespeople
- Other nonrevenue objectives

Only a small portion is linked directly to sales dollars.[61] At the same time, other incentives encourage the sales force to integrate their efforts with e-commerce and support rapid, continuous corporate change.[62] Such a compensation plan facilitates long-term relationships between the salesperson and the customer, and in the long run will better benefit the company.

Evaluating Sales Performance Using Qualitative and Quantitative Factors

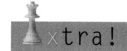

Another task of the sales manager is to evaluate sales-force performance. Evaluation of the sales force should not be performed only once a year. In conjunction with sales-coaching guidelines, sales managers should provide continual guidance and feedback.

Comparison of Compensation Plans	Figure 14.12

Straight Salary
- Provides security
- Reduces motivation

Straight Commission
- Increases motivation
- Creates insecurity

Salary Plus Commission
- Provides job security
- Provides motivation

The sales manager may choose to evaluate the sales force on a combination of *quantitative* or *qualitative* factors. However, past studies have found that sales managers weight subjective, qualitative factors more heavily than quantitative variables when assessing salesperson performance. The most popular *qualitative factors* used include:

- Communication skills
- Product knowledge
- Attitude
- Selling skills
- Initiative/assertiveness
- Appearance/manner
- Knowledge of the competition

The most commonly used *quantitative factors* include:

- Sales volume in dollars
- Sales volume compared to previous year's sales
- Number of new accounts
- Net dollar profits
- Sales volume by dollar quota

A promising metric that assesses a salesperson's ability to focus on both customer satisfaction and revenue maximization appears to be *RevPASH* (revenue per available salesperson hour).[63] RevPASH evaluation encourages salespeople to focus their sales efforts on customer segments that will generate the highest income while accounting for customer expectations regarding sales-force time.

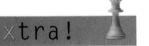

Organizing and Managing Sales Territories

Sales managers must devote time to ensuring that sales territories are well organized and aligned so that they maximize profitability for the company. The following discusses territory organization, territory allocation, territory potential, and a review of territory allocation.

Geographical and Product-Line Organization

Sales managers have a number of options when it comes to organizing the sales territories of their salespeople. Sales territories organized by product line or by geographical area are the more traditional means of organizing sales forces. Under *geographical* and *product-line* territory organization, salespeople are often required to sell to *all* customers within a geographic area, although their product line may be somewhat limited. In either case, though, they call on customers in dozens of different industries.

Today, however, more and more sales managers are organizing sales territories around *customers*. In this case, the salesperson is asked to call on customers in one or two specific industries, regardless of where the customer is located geographically. This allows the salesperson to become an expert in the particular industry to which he or she is assigned. Consequently, the salesperson can develop a better understanding of the customer's problems, which facilitates the development of a close, long-term relationship between the sales representative and the customer.

Territory Allocation

After deciding which method to organize the territories, the sales manager must then divide up the territories among the company's salespeople. There are two criteria that should guide territory allocation: (1) all salespeople should feel that their territory offers as much potential as their colleagues' territory, and (2) all should feel the territory division does not require that they work harder than any other salespeople. To achieve these goals, the sales manager must determine the *revenue potential* of each account (regardless of whether the account is a current or a potential customer), and how much of the sales representative's time is required to service each account. Then, individual sales territories can be allocated to sales representatives in an equitable manner.

Territory Potential

The sales manager should also help the sales force maximize their territories' potential. The sales manager can accomplish this by encouraging sales representatives to devote their time and efforts to profitable accounts, and not waste their efforts on accounts that are not potentially profitable to the company.[64] Sales managers need to ensure that sales representatives get the maximum potential from all their accounts, and not just meet their quotas because of the large purchases of one key buyer. Finally, sales managers need to use market research to ensure that no potential accounts are overlooked in any given territory.

Review of Territory Allocations

Once territories are established, the sales manager should review them on a quarterly basis. This will not only assist the sales manager with the sales budget, but may also indicate where realignment of territories needs to occur. Appropriate alignment is critical, as studies indicate that companies may lose 2–7% of sales as a result of poor territory alignment.[65] Key areas to check are those territories where the salesperson consistently exceeds, or fails to make, quota. When a salesperson regularly exceeds the set quota, the sales manager should ensure that this is not due to the territory potential being so large that the sales representative has to make virtually no effort to reach quota. If this is the case, the quota should be raised, or if the territory potential warrants it, a new representative should be added to the area. In the case of the salesperson who never makes quota, the sales manager must determine if this is a function of a person's lack of sales ability or a territory with truly poor potential. In the former situation, the salesperson should receive additional training; in the latter situation, the representative's territory should be expanded to include new accounts.[66]

Territories should not be changed on a whim, however. Customers identify "their" salesperson as the selling company. In other words, to the customer, the salesperson *is* the selling company. Consequently, when territories are changed and a new salesperson is put in place, the selling company loses the continuity of the relationship with the customer. This event can have serious repercussions and business may be lost if the new salesperson is unable to rapidly develop a good relationship with the customer. Sales managers should make every effort to ensure that changes in sales personnel, whether due to realignments or other factors, result in smooth transitions for the affected customers. Further, territory realignment can influence salesperson motivation; therefore, sales managers need to justify any territory change on the basis of fairness.[67]

Pros and Cons of Team Selling

As products and competitive environments have become increasingly complicated, the somewhat controversial use of selling teams has become more commonplace, especially in business-to-business contexts. Selling teams usually consist of a salesperson, who is responsible for managing the sales cycle, and a technical expert, who provides subject-matter credibility for the customer. However, selling teams may take other forms as well. For example, a sales team may consist of all company representatives who will have any effect on a customer, or the sales team may comprise sales representatives who are responsible for the same territory, but different products.

Why use selling teams? Salespeople often do not have the extensive technical knowledge necessary to understand customer requirements for highly complex products; engineers and technicians usually lack the skills necessary to guide the customer through the sales process. In combination, however, salespeople and technical experts can form a powerful team that serves to better address customer needs and ensures that the sales team can speak the technical language of some of the key players in the buying-decision process. Consequently, selling teams are most likely to be used when the customer is purchasing a complex product for the first time, when the customer warrants special treatment, or when several people are involved in the purchasing decision.

The implementation of team selling within an organization, however, is not easy. Sales representatives may want total control over the sales process and feel uncomfortable with involving a technical expert. Similarly, technicians and engineers may resent being forced to participate in the more "earthy" business of sales. Consequently, sales teams are not always as productive as they could be. For companies that have formulated winning strategies for their sales teams, however, the payoffs can be huge.[68]

Chapter Summary

Learning Objective 1: *Identify and understand the factors that make personal selling such a critical component of promotion.* Personal selling involves direct communication between the sales representative and the customer. It is one of the most important elements of the promotion mix and a critical element of marketing, but it is also the most expensive form of promotion a firm can undertake. Personal selling offers several advantages: Salespersons can adapt their presentations to suit the needs of individual customers, immediate feedback from the customer can be responded to during sales presentations, and the effectiveness of personal selling can be more easily measured. It also provides exciting and challenging career opportunities, with a focus on relationship selling and the development of partnerships based on the long-term satisfaction of customers' needs.

Learning Objective 2: *Describe the selling contexts and types of salespeople.* Personal selling occurs in different contexts, and each context determines which types of salespeople are used. The three contexts in which personal selling may occur are telemarketing, over-the-counter selling, and field selling. Types of salespeople include inbound or outbound telemarketers, order getters, order takers, professional salespeople, national account managers, missionary salespeople, and support salespeople.

Learning Objective 3: *Understand and explain the sales process.* The sales process is composed of eight basic steps: prospecting, preapproach and planning, approaching the client, identifying client needs, presenting the product, handling objections, gaining commitment, and following up on and keeping promises. In the traditional selling method, little time is spent on the early stages of the process. In the professional selling method, a great deal of time is spent on the early stages so that commitment is gained as a very natural, or logical, next step.

Learning Objective 4: *Comprehend the diverse tasks and functions of the sales manager.* Sales management requires the skills of planning, directing, controlling, and implementing the personal-selling function. Sales managers are responsible for many tasks, including recruiting, training, motivating, compensating, and evaluating the sales force, as well as organizing and allocating territories, and updating the sales force's technological capabilities.

Key Terms

For interactive study: visit http://bestpractices.swlearning.com.

Cold calls, 485
Consultative selling, 476
Customer-oriented, 480
Field selling, 481
Hard selling, 477
Job anxiety, 479

Learning-oriented, 480
Order getter, 481
Order taker, 481
Personal selling, 476
Qualified sales leads, 484
Referrals, 484

Relationship selling, 477
Role ambiguity, 479
Role conflict, 479
Sales-call anxiety, 496
Suggestion selling, 481

Questions for Review and Discussion

1. In your day-to-day routine, identify situations in which you have had to persuade someone to accept your ideas or suggestions. What did you do? Were you successful or unsuccessful? Can you identify other ways that might have worked better?

2. As regional sales manager for a large consumer goods company, you are interested in attracting college graduates to your sales force. Develop a marketing plan to do so. Determine why students are often not interested in sales as a profession and then develop the benefits of the sales position that will overcome these objections. What steps should be taken by your company to encourage more students to seek jobs in sales?

3. Think about the best salesperson you have ever met. What did you like about this individual? What traits did he or she possess? What made this salesperson better than others you have met? Describe the worst salesperson you have ever met. What did this individual do that you disliked? What made him or her the worst?

4. There are many methods of prospecting, that is, finding qualified individuals who may become customers. A few methods are listed in this chapter; however, do a little brainstorming and see how many more methods you can identify.

5. Pretend you want to convince a friend to join a school organization with which you are affiliated. What might you say? Using the steps in the sales process, outline your presentation to your friend. Next, role-play with a classmate to see if you can present a valid argument based on the classmate's needs.

6. Assume that the president of your firm, a life insurance company, still believes in pushing his agents to use the hard sell. As the sales manager, how could you convince him that relationship selling is a better way of doing business? Compare the two methods of selling and write convincing arguments to support the use of relationship selling.

7. As vice president of sales and marketing for a large hotel chain, you are reviewing the current compensation plan for the national sales force. Sales representatives are presently hired at a low base pay of $21,000. After three months of training, these representatives are eligible for 20% commissions on their sales, but their base pay disappears. Quotas are also set for each representative; those who fail to achieve at least 80% of their quota objective for three of four quarters are terminated. What do you think of this plan? Should you support it or should you develop a new one? If you choose to create a new compensation plan, what arguments will you make to the president of your hotel chain to persuade her to accept it?

8. As a good salesperson, you should prepare responses to objections that you expect will be forthcoming from potential customers. Two of the most common objections heard in sales are "Your price is too high" and "I need to think about it." Assuming you sell cell phones, prepare a brief list of responses for each objection that will assist you in moving the customer toward commitment.

9. Automation and the Internet are rapidly changing the way selling is conducted. As this trend continues, do you think salespeople will be phased out of business? Why or why not?

10. A female sales representative, Carol, has been working for you less than six months. During this time, as part of an overall training program, you have placed her in the field for month-long stints with several experienced sales representatives. Last night, Carol called your home and requested an immediate meeting with you. You agreed to meet with her first thing in the morning. At the meeting, she informs you that one of the sales representatives you had assigned her to work with made sexually explicit suggestions to her. You are surprised, as this particular representative, Jim, has always been one of your top salespeople, and has a reputation for being a solid family man. He is also at least 20 years older than Carol. What should you do now?

In-Class Team Activities

1. With a group of classmates, brainstorm the benefits of your particular college or university. Were these benefits explicitly used to "sell" you when you were a prospective student? How could your college or university do a better job of selling to prospects?

2. Discuss sales jobs you and your classmates have previously held. These may be jobs where you sold goods to raise money for an organization (church, band, etc.), or an actual sales position. What did you like about these jobs? What did you dislike? What could have made the job more enjoyable? What did you learn about selling from the experience?

Internet Questions

1. Visit http://www.sellingpower.com. This Web site supports the popular sales magazine *Selling Power* and is chock-full of helpful advice for experienced and novice salespeople. Take time to play a sales game as part of a contest to win a trip. Also, check out these other top sales sites:

   - Just Sell at http://www.justsell.com
   - Guerilla Marketing Online at http://www.gmarketing.com
   - Sales Dog at http://www.salesdog.com

2. Visit http://www.monster.com, http://www.hotjobs.yahoo.com, or http://www.jobs.com, which contain hundreds of thousands of job listings for the United States and several other countries. Select entry-level sales jobs that may be of interest to you. What type of salesperson is needed for each job? What qualifications are being sought? What do you need to do to prepare yourself for these positions?

3. Visit http://www.zapdata.com and click on "Prospect Lists" to understand how to customize lists of prospective customers. How might this Web site benefit a salesperson?

4. Just for fun, go to http://www.pg.com and click on "Try & Buy Store," which lets you view and purchase new products before they are available in retail stores. Then try http://www.tide.com and click on "Stain Detective," which explains how to get rid of almost any fabric stain. Finally, check out http://www.reflect.com, the number-one cosmetics Web site, which allows buyers to customize makeup and skin-care products. How do these Web sites assist Procter & Gamble with its sales?

CHAPTER CASE

Padding Expense Accounts

Stephanie Heller, senior vice president of sales for Logix-Tech, spun her office chair around to stare out the window. The accounting department had phoned a short time ago to tell her that one of her top salespeople, Michelle May, has been inflating her expense report by at least 20% over the last quarter. Further, the accounting department has also intimated that, during the same time frame, Michelle may have been playing games with customer orders in order to increase the size of her commissions. The CEO of LogixTech has sent Heller an e-mail telling her that the problem is to be corrected immediately or her own job will be on the line. However, Heller has been given the freedom to decide how to handle the situation. Now Heller must come up with the appropriate strategy quickly.

Heller's first impulse is to fire Michelle to show the other sales team members that such behavior will not be tolerated, no matter what the circumstances may be. On the other hand, Michelle has not only been one of LogixTech's best long-term performers, she has also been a great organizational citizen. She is always willing to help train new representatives; she is friendly to all the support staff; and she is a good contributor to discussions at sales meetings. She has also won an award from Raython, one of LogixTech's largest customers, for providing the best vendor service.

In addition to these issues, Heller is under pressure to meet LogixTech's sales goals. The company failed to meet last year's goals by 8%; consequently, LogixTech's stock value has fallen. Heller has implemented some new sales tactics and, with her well-seasoned sales team, was on target to meet this year's sales objectives. Heller knows that a new salesperson would be unable to step in and immediately make the kind of sales that Michelle learned to produce over the years. Consequently, LogixTech would likely fail to meet its sales goals two years in a row. This repeated failure could jeopardize Heller's job and her anticipated bonus. In addition, LogixTech would risk losing the Raython business, since that customer places high value on its relationship with Michelle. Damaging the relationship with Raython could result in long-term financial difficulties for the company.

Heller has heard through office chatter that Michelle has been going through a very nasty divorce and has been involved in an acrimonious custody fight for her young son. Rumor has it that Michelle has been forced to hire a very expensive attorney to battle her soon-to-be ex-husband. Heller, in fact, had been silently applauding the way Michelle had managed to keep this personal business out of the office and had not let her sales performance slip.

This is the first time Michelle has ever been in any trouble with the company, and Heller really likes Michelle. If Heller does not come up with a suitable solution, however, she could find herself out of a job.

Case Questions

1. On a scale of 1 to 5, with 1 = completely unethical and 5 = completely ethical, how ethical do you believe Michelle's behavior is? Why?
2. What decision should Heller make regarding Michelle?
3. In the future, what measures should Heller put in place to prevent this type of problem from occurring again?

4. If Heller chooses to fire Michelle, what strategies might she use to improve the chances that LogixTech can meet its sales goals this year?

5. How might Heller lessen the damage to the company's relationships with Michelle's former accounts if she decides to replace Michelle with a new salesperson?

VIDEO CASE

Concept2 Coaches Customers Toward Better Health

Concept2 is the story of two brothers who turned their passion for a sport into a passion for a business, involving their wives, children, friends, and relatives. In 1976, Pete and Dick Dreissigacker, avid rowers, were training to make the final cut for the U.S. Olympic Team in rowing. During training, they started tinkering with a design for a new oar—Pete is a design engineer; Dick is a mechanical engineer. They didn't make the Olympic team, but they came up with an oar design that has since swept through the sport around the world. Made from synthetic materials instead of wood, the oars are stronger, lighter, and cheaper than their traditional counterparts, and rowers worldwide love them. Within a few years, the brothers, who had settled in Vermont, were kicking around ideas for an indoor rowing machine that would allow them to continue their beloved pastime during the winter, when Vermont's rivers and lakes were frozen. So they turned Pete's old bicycle upside down, nailed it to the floor, added a handle and seat that would slide, and presto—they had the first indoor rowing machine.

Twenty years later, the Concept2 Indoor Rower is still sold directly from the Dreissigacker's factory in Morris-ville, Vermont. Customers can place orders via phone or the Web site, and although miles may separate Concept2 from its customers, the company has worked hard to develop relationship selling so that everyone who buys a Concept2 rower will feel like part of the Concept2 "family." Customer service is a top priority. "We aren't trying to sell a lot of machines," explains Judy Geer, wife of cofounder Dick Dreissigacker. "We're trying to have a lot of satisfied customers." Although the Web site has a section containing answers to most-asked questions, customers can contact someone at Concept2 for in-person answers anytime. Shawn Larose is a service technician who handles problems or warranty questions for customers who call: "When people call with what they think is a very serious problem and it turns out to be a 30-second answer, that's very rewarding."

Concept2 also has an on-staff "coach," Larry Gluck-man, to help customers learn how to use the rower and improve their individual workouts. Concept2 publishes a semi-annual newsletter called *Ergo Update,* with product and company news, rowing stories from customers, and letters the company receives. "We get letters [that describe how] we've changed someone's life, we've really improved their health, and that definitely makes it," notes Judy Geer. To make the sport of indoor rowing a bit more interesting—and to keep customers connected with each other and the company—Concept2 started a world rank-ing system, in which rowers from anywhere in the world can send in their best times achieved rowing a virtual distance on their rower. *Ergo Update* publishes the rankings once a year. Finally, anyone can take a tour of the Concept2 factory. They just need to call or show up. All of these approaches help build continuous relationships with customers by keeping them connected to Concept2 in personal ways, no matter where they live.

Concept2 makes ordering a rower easy, but the company had to find ways to provide demonstrations for potential buyers to sell their product. After all, at roughly $800 plus shipping, an indoor rower is not a small purchase for most individuals, no matter how passionate they are about the sport. Once the questions are answered, people still want to see how the equipment works before making a purchase. So Concept2 has a 22-minute promotional video that shows how the machine functions—how it's built, how to assemble it, and how to use it. Anyone who watches the short film—narrated by Dick and Judy's 8-year-old daughter, Hannah—will pull out a credit card in a single stroke.

Case Questions

1. Concept2 focuses on relationship selling. As the company grows, in what ways might it use consultative selling and telemarketing? If you think either of these approaches would be a poor choice for the company, explain why.

2. Why is demonstration an important part of the Concept2 sales process? Do you think that Concept2 handles this well? Why or why not? Go to the Concept2 Web site at **http://www.rowing.concept2.com**.

3. How does Concept2 use its Web site to enhance the customer's indoor-rowing experience? What benefits does the company derive from improving the customer experience?

4. Browse through the Concept2 Web site for ways the company uses the site to develop its relationship with customers. Discuss your findings in class.

Sources: Concept2 Web site, http://www.rowing.concept2.com, accessed 23 March 2000.
    Concept2 video and promotional materials, 1999.
    Sean Thomas Langan, "The Big Blade," *Vermont Inc.,* February 2000, 22–23, 59.
    David Churbuck, "Virtual Racing," *Forbes.com,* 6 May 1996, http://www.forbes.com.

15

Pricing Strategies and Determination

A number of airlines are now struggling to remain solvent in light of a dual pricing structure. On the one hand, airlines have historically demanded, and obtained, significantly higher rates for travelers, especially business travelers, who book flights at the last minute. On the other hand, airlines have used low fares to entice leisure travelers, who are more likely to plan ahead and book travel far in advance. Recent changes in the environment, such as increased price sensitivity in an uncertain economy, competition from low-cost airlines, and increasing costs, are now challenging this traditional pricing structure for long-time major airlines.

You Decide. After reading the opening vignette and paying special attention to the sections of this chapter marked with the chess piece, answer these questions:

1. What is the greatest challenge facing traditional airlines in developing an innovative pricing structure to better compete with newer low-cost airlines?

2. Which strategic concern is likely to have the greatest impact on determining any short-range changes to the pricing structure for long-time airline companies?

3. Which pricing-adjustment tactic offers the best potential for future price flexing in the airline industry?

David Young-Wolff/PhotoEdit, Inc.

Blue Sky Pricing

We're going to test the theory that the convoluted nature of airline pricing is a major deterrent to flying . . . many business travelers are no longer flying and those who are flying often modify their itineraries in order to qualify for the lowest possible fare.

Gregg Saretsky,
Executive Vice President of
Marketing and Planning
Alaska Airlines

Gregg Saretsky's comments relate to an important strategy that some airlines are experimenting with today. These airlines are identifying ways to lower airfares for business travelers who purchase tickets with far less advance notice than leisure travelers.

Business travelers flying to the same destinations as vacationers and other leisure travelers frequently pay vastly more expensive airfares. Why? The first and foremost reason is "time." Dating back to super-saver fares in the 1980s, an airline flight is likely to have a variety of different fares. How many days in advance you make your reservation has a big effect on the fare you pay. Fares booked closer to the flight are more expensive than fares booked earlier.

If airlines priced all of their seats at a low price, they would sell the vast majority of their tickets several weeks in advance. Yet, such a pricing strategy would fail to meet the needs of the traveler who requires greater flexibility in scheduling travel. If all flights were booked several weeks in advance, there would be no way to accommodate a business-person who decides today to travel tomorrow to quickly rectify a customer's problem or build a new relationship.

Travelers who truly need those last-minute seats tend to be less sensitive to paying higher prices. In addition, throughout the boom period of the 1990s, travel budgets were generous and businesspeople felt compelled to spend them freely. The pace of business became more frenzied as competition heated up, new product development cycles shrank dramatically, and businesses began to spend more time listening to customers. All of these factors placed an emphasis on air travel, the flexibility to fly at a moment's notice, and a growing insensitivity to higher airfares, particularly those paid on short notice.

At the same time, consumers gained access to a wide variety of new online services that would assist them in getting good airfares (e.g., priceline.com, travelocity.com, expedia.com). With this new access to prices, leisure travelers became more sensitive to the price of an airline ticket.

Challenges in 2003

Pressure to reduce the gap between business and leisure airfares has emerged today primarily because business travelers have begun to balk at high fares. Airlines are feeling an intense pressure to lower their fares because of recessionary conditions that have shrunk travel budgets, the rise of discount airlines like Southwest and Frontier, and the proliferation and increasing credibility of Web-based "do-it-yourself" travel services.

Buyer Behavior, Price Sensitivity. As the economy moved into recession, the pie for overall corporate travel spending shrank. This led business customers to seek new sources for travel—planning trips in advance to take advantage of leisure fares, or surfing the Internet for travel deals. In addition, companies simply changed travel policies, encouraging travel by car where possible. According to a recent survey, 77% of travel and purchasing managers are directing greater use of rental cars and trains for shorter trips. In fact, 16% of the companies surveyed were requiring employees to drive on shorter-haul trips.

Competition. Tougher economic times have turned business travelers' attention to airlines that have creatively built their businesses around a cost-leadership model. Southwest Airlines consistently underprices other firms and is driven to continual process and cost improvement. *CFO* magazine reports that the

LEARNING OBJECTIVES

After you have completed this chapter, you should be able to:

1. *Define price, explain why cost-based pricing methods are used so widely, and understand the drawbacks of these methods.*

2. *Incorporate demand considerations into pricing and determine a short-term profit-maximizing price.*

3. *Identify and explain strategic drivers of prices.*

4. *Explain and evaluate reasons why base prices change over time in both business and consumer markets.*

5. *Explain basic legal and ethical constraints on pricing behavior.*

VOICE OF THE EXPERT

Joel E. Urbany, University of Notre Dame

My job at this moment is to get you pumped up about the study of pricing. That's a tough job because, well . . . there's some **math**! Yes, the first part of the chapter is about costs, demand, breakeven, and profit maximization and looks a bit on the boring side (hey, you didn't hear that from me!!). **Do not** skip it, however! There are many fundamentals and definitions in the chapter that you **really** need to pay attention to. Trying to understand more contemporary pricing practices without a firm grasp on the fundamentals is as perilous as trying to play a Dave Matthews song without first learning scales.

There is a lot in the chapter about current pricing practice, designed to give you a feel for the dynamics and complexity in the pricing issues that firms face today. The marketplace is an exciting and rapidly changing place, and pricing is playing an increasingly important role in business. Charles Fishman described this very well in a recent *Fast Company* article: "Business is at the start of a new era of pricing. This era is being shaped by a new set of insights into business strategy and human behavior, and these insights are turbocharged with software, mathematics, and rapid experimentation. . . . Changes in pricing will alter every part of the economy . . . companies will flourish or be crushed based in part on their ability to grasp and master the new science of pricing." ("Which Price is Right," *Fast Company* 68, March 2003, 92.)

The new "science," though, is in the end about understanding and extracting value in an exchange. Many pricing moves that companies make today consider only short-term value—like having temporary price promotions (very popular, but often dangerous). It takes courage to back away from that. And it takes some sophistication to get your hands around the new Web-based developments in pricing.

cost basis varies tremendously across airlines. Frontier Airlines' break-even point—the proportion of seats that have to be sold to cover all costs—is 55% of available seats. In contrast, United Airlines has to fill 91% of available seats to cover all costs.

Costs. The airline industry is extremely cost-intensive, with a large proportion of fixed costs tied up in fleet, labor, and jet fuel. There is an oversupply of airplanes, labor costs have increased, and, prior to the war with Iraq, jet-fuel prices went from $.70 to $1.25 per gallon. Labor costs have been particularly problematic for the larger airlines. Ironically, just as the industry moved out of the heady 1990s and into more challenging economic times, United's pilots negotiated significant pay increases that raised their salaries by as much as 28.5%. At the same time, American Airlines signed flight attendants and ground workers to "industry-leading deals." Labor costs at American are 40% of total expenses, while they account for a significantly lower 25% and 30% respectively, at Frontier and Southwest.

The Pricing Paradox. The airline industry is currently in dire straits in part because of these issues: price sensitivity, increased competition, and rising costs. In addition, air travel declined 20–25% between 2000 and 2003. Some analysts believe that much of this decline is permanent. Second, price changes are constrained by increasing price sensitivity on the low end (due in part to better informed buyers with more choices) and heavy cost structures on the high end. In short, the airlines have a hard time lowering the higher, time-sensitive prices and even more difficulty raising the lower price points aimed at the leisure market. Still, efforts are being made—as reflected in the quote from Greg Saretsky—to lower those prices on the high end that are aimed at more time-sensitive customers.

However, many believe that the airlines are stuck with the current pricing structure and overall unprofitable results. Short of complete restructuring of the major cost categories, the airlines operating without low-cost models are in for a turbulent ride ahead.[1]

Of the traditional marketing-mix variables, the development of effective pricing strategies remains perhaps the most elusive. Consider the following sample of opinions about pricing practices over the last 50 years:

. . . pricing policy is the last stronghold of medievalism in modern management . . . [Pricing] is still largely intuitive and even mystical in the sense that the intuition is often the province of the big boss."[2]

. . . for marketers of industrial goods and construction companies, pricing is the single judgment that translates potential business into reality. Yet pricing is the least rational of all decisions made in this specialized field."[3]

. . . pricing is approached in Britain like Russian roulette to be indulged in mainly by those contemplating suicide."[4]

Perhaps it is reasonable that marketers have only recently begun to focus seriously on effective pricing. Only after managers have mastered the techniques of creating value do the techniques of capturing value become important."[5]

Pricing decisions are complex, driven by many different factors. In the opening vignette and throughout the chapter, we will see that firms are influenced by political/legal concerns (legal requirements, unions); competitive concerns (price wars); socio-cultural factors (environmental and social concerns and their impact on cost); technology (smart pricing); economic concerns (impact of recession on airlines); and natural concerns (environmental concerns, demand and willingness to pay for environmentally friendly cars).

This environmental context makes pricing decisions complex and even volatile. Yet, despite that complexity, prices are still driven by the fundamentals: cost, competitors, and customer price-sensitivity or elasticity—all of which play a prominent role in the evolution of prices in the airline industry, as just discussed. This chapter provides insight into how these fundamentals should be taken into account in both setting initial prices and in designing price-adjustment strategies.

The first portion of the chapter examines the basics behind setting base prices, the usual approaches that firms take, and how those approaches can be improved. The rest of the chapter focuses on the factors that determine why base prices change over time. We begin, though, with a definition of price.

Defining Price and Determining Base Prices

So what is *price*? It is not just the number on the price tag in the store (although that is clearly what most customers think of). In general terms, any exchange involves a price, and it is not always monetary. As such, price can be or can incorporate rent, tuition, wages, fees, fares, lease payments, interest rates, or time donated. In short, price is an exchange rate—it defines the sacrifice that one party makes to another to receive something in exchange.[6] Our specific focus will be on **price** *as a monetary value charged by an organization for the sale of its products.* In this chapter, we will distinguish between two general categories of pricing decisions: (1) setting a base price for a product and (2) making adjustments to that product's price over time (see Figure 15.1).

Classic economics holds some important insights about how prices should be determined. Figure 15.2 illustrates simple tools that help explain the interaction between buyer and seller behavior. Consider a new college student named Andrew who is thinking about the purchase of one or more pairs of jeans for the coming school year. Figure 15.2 shows varying prices on the vertical axis and quantities on the horizontal axis. The curve labeled D illustrates the number of pairs of jeans Andrew is willing to pay at a given price. So, at a price of $50, he would be willing to buy three pairs. If the jeans cost $75, he is only willing to buy two pairs. (This willingness to buy is determined by many factors, including Andrew's income and tastes,

1 **LEARNING OBJECTIVE**

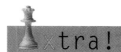

Price
Is some unit of value given up by one party in return for something from another party.

Basic Pricing Decisions and Primary Driver: Cost　　　　　　　　　　　　　　**Figure 15.1**

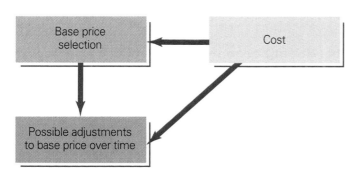

Figure 15.2	Demand and Supply Curve: Jeans

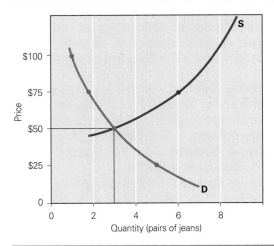

Source: Professor Kim Sosin, College of Business Administration, University of Nebraska at Omaha, Omaha, NE 68182. Reprinted with permission.

and the cost of other types of clothing.) However, market prices are determined by both the buyer's choice behavior and the seller's willingness to supply the product. The curve labeled S in Figure 15.2 captures this. It's called a supply curve and it indicates how many pairs of jeans a seller (say, Levi's) would be willing to supply at a given price. Over time, the market price would be determined by the intersection of supply and demand. In this case, demand and supply are matched up at $50.[7]

Cost-Plus Pricing: The Natural (But Sometimes Wrong) Way to Set Base Prices

We will return to demand and many other factors that influence pricing decisions later in the chapter. At the moment, though, we'll focus on cost, which in the minds of businesspeople is probably the most fundamental determinant of price:

. . . the easiest way to think about a price is first to think like an accountant: price equals costs plus overhead plus a fair profit. Cost-plus pricing, furthermore, is a useful ritual, with great public-relations advantages . . . (a smart, prudent businessman) . . . admits only to wanting a "fair" return.[8]

It is no surprise that costs come into play quite significantly in setting *base prices*. Managers are generally (although not always) aware of their costs of doing business. As a result, the practice of setting prices based on costs has become firmly established in the American marketplace. Both early and fairly recent studies of managerial pricing have found cost to be a dominant consideration in pricing decisions.[9] Below, we illustrate cost-plus pricing and evaluate its advantages and drawbacks. We then use the following example as a springboard to discuss other pricing methods and factors that influence pricing.

An Example of Cost-Plus Pricing: Symphony Tickets

Let's say you're a manager for a symphony orchestra.[10] The symphony season is just starting in this town, and you've been hired as marketing director. One of your early assignments is to figure out a ticket price for a new concert series in the coming months. You have information about demand in the past (for several programs in the past, the symphony sold about 950 of its 1,100 seats). In addition, the following costs have been identified:

Fixed overhead	$1,500
Rehearsal costs	$4,500

Performance costs	$2,000
Variable costs (programs, tickets)	$1 per patron

Note that some of these costs are fixed and some are variable. *Fixed costs* are costs that have no relationship to volume. They are, by definition, fixed. They do not change if more customers come to the show. The first three cost categories in our example (fixed overhead, rehearsal costs, and performance costs), totaling $8,000, are all fixed. *Variable costs,* on the other hand, are costs that are incurred for each customer. In this case, they are fairly small—only $1 per customer for tickets and programs.

To determine a price per patron using a cost-plus rule, you need to evenly spread all costs over each patron. Again, past history suggests average attendance of 950 people. *Average total cost* can be calculated simply by adding an "average" fixed-cost figure to variable cost.

$$\text{Average total cost} = \text{Variable cost} + \frac{\text{Fixed Cost}}{\text{Unit Sales}}$$

In the current case, the average total cost would be:

$$\$1 + \frac{(\$1,500 + \$4,500 + \$2,000)}{950} = \$9.42$$

So, for every "unit" you sell (in this case, each of the 950 seats), the orchestra incurs a cost of $9.42, accounting for both fixed and variable costs.

Cost-Based Pricing Approaches

There are two common approaches to setting prices based on cost. One is to use a standard rule-of-thumb markup. The second is to build up the price by adding together both cost per unit and desired profit.

Standard Mark-Up. Let's say that the orchestra has always used this rule-of-thumb in the past: Mark up costs by 20%. This is effectively saying that, "for every unit we sell, we want 20 percent of the selling price to represent profit over and above costs." The price can be easily calculated as follows:

$$\frac{\text{Unit cost}}{\text{Selling price}} = \frac{\text{Unit cost}}{(1 - \text{Markup \%})} = \frac{\$9.42}{(1-20\%)} = 11.775$$

So, you might charge a price of $11.75 (rounded off to the nearest quarter). Keep in mind that all this means is that the profit you get from each ticket ($11.75–$9.42 = $2.33) is 20% of the selling price ($2.33/$11.75). In fact, the 20% in this case refers to *markup on retail price* (it's simply the "markup" as a percentage of the retail price calculated by: [(Retail price-cost)/retail]). For the sake of clarity, it is important to distinguish this from *markup on cost*. You may have heard that the common rule for some retailers is that they determine the retail price by "doubling costs" (i.e., multiply them by two). This reflects a simple 100% markup *on cost*. In the orchestra example, such a 100% markup rule would produce a ticket price of $18.84. Using the example we've already calculated—a retail ticket price of $11.75—we calculate the markup on cost to be 24.7% calculated by: [(Retail price–cost)/cost](i.e., $2.33/$9.42 = 24.7%).

Target Return Pricing. Another similar approach would be for the orchestra to add a target profit to the unit-cost figure (to cover both cost and profit):

$$\text{Selling price} = \text{Unit cost} + \text{Desired profit per unit}$$

The desired-profit figure could come from a couple of places. First, there may be a rule-of-thumb that "we'd like to earn $2 a head coming in" (which would make the price $9.42 + $2.00 = $11.42). Alternatively, the desired profit per unit may be determined based on the company's desired return on investment.[11]

Let's say you apply the standard markup (as many retailers do, for example), and you set your price at $11.75. Have you done a good job? Well, yes and no.

- You have been smart in accounting for your costs, both fixed and variable.
- The pricing method is fair—it is steeped in tradition and is a widely accepted business practice.

For these reasons, no one could argue with your approach. However, there are some drawbacks:

- The fundamental flaw of this approach to pricing is that *it ignores demand*. This approach assumes that a certain demand level is a given, independent of price. This is at odds with one of the most fundamental relationships in all of business: Quantity sold is a function of price. Generally speaking, as price goes up, demand goes down (and vice versa). Yet, you're assuming that 950 seats will be sold no matter what the price! Note what happens if different demand levels are assumed. The average unit cost would be much higher if we assumed sales of only 850 tickets (in fact, in this case, average unit cost would be $1 + [$8,000/850] = $10.41, rather than $9.42). This means that the $11.75 price would not be high enough to produce the 20% profit markup you desired. Alternatively, if ticket sales were 1,050, your unit cost would actually end up being lower ($1 + [$8,000/1,050] = $8.62), and your price could be lower than $11.75 and still produce the desired markup return on sales. In the marketplace, because price influences customer perception of value, demand is a function of price. In other words, price determines demand, not the other way around.
- In addition, a cost-plus pricing rule *fails to account for competition*. Competitors' prices have a significant impact on sales and profit outcomes as well, since consumers make choices from competitive sets of alternatives rather than a single one. For example, if a new symphony was started in a nearby city, it might well compete for the dollars that patrons might normally spend on your symphony. As such, this might have implications for how high you set your price compared to competing alternatives. In fact, failing to consider these issues can have devastating consequences. Wang Laboratory developed and introduced the world's first word-processing software in 1976. The product was a great success and Wang came to dominate the market. The company's pricing, though, was cost-driven. Competition eventually increased and growth slowed, yet the company did not bring down prices to maintain the value position of their software. The reason? Their pricing was basically cost-driven. Wang managers constantly recalculated unit costs and prices to capture increasing overhead cost allocations. Prices remained high and customers made their way to less expensive alternatives.[12]

Competitive Forces

Competitors' prices have a significant impact on sales and profit outcomes, since consumers make choices from competitive sets of alternatives, rather than a single one.

As you can see, cost-plus pricing takes into account neither price sensitivity nor competition, both of which are essential considerations in setting prices effectively. Further, as noted earlier, cost-plus pricing generally involves allocating fixed costs on a per-unit basis—that is, treating them as variable costs—even though fixed costs do not change with the number of units sold.

The next sections provide some detail on the factors that can and should be considered in pricing. They review additional techniques and considerations for setting an initial base price for a product. Next, we discuss the most fundamental of all pricing concepts.

LEARNING OBJECTIVE 2

Demand Considerations:
The Relationship Between Price and Sales

Your price of $11.75 is designed to cover average total costs for the projected 950 seats sold and produce a 20% profit markup on costs. Yet, as discussed above, in setting the price this way you have failed to consider one of the fundamental principles of economics: that price causes demand (not the other way around!). If your price is lower, demand usually is higher, and vice versa. Economists have made this concrete for us by articulating a simple concept called **elasticity of demand**, which helps us better understand the *relationship* between changes in price and quantity sold.

Elasticity of demand may be difficult to estimate. However, even the first few steps of thinking in terms of market response are very important and always helpful, even without precise knowledge of it. In fact, let's start with the assumption that you know very little about how much demand you'll get at different prices. Even under these circumstances, there is one brief analysis you can and should do before anything else, since it will help you frame good questions about potential demand. This is break-even analysis.

Break-Even Analysis

Break-even analysis (BEA) is a standard analysis technique that should be performed for nearly every business decision, particularly those for new products. BEA doesn't tell you what your demand will be at a given price point, but it does tell the very important tale of what sales level you *need* for a particular price to be profitable. The key question in this analysis is, "At a price of $11.75, how many units (seats) do we need to sell to break even?"

The calculation for the break-even point is straightforward:

$$\text{Break-even sales} = \frac{\text{Fixed Costs}}{\text{Selling Price} - \text{Variable Costs}}$$

In the BEA, you treat fixed and variable costs separately (as we generally should). The numerator of the equation includes all fixed costs, which you have to pay regardless of how many seats you fill. The denominator contains your *contribution margin*. For each seat, you make $11.75–$1.00 = $10.75, which captures the contribution of each ticket sold to covering fixed costs and producing a profit. At the $11.75 price, your break-even sales are:

Break-even sales = $8,000 ÷ ($11.75–$1.00) = 744.2 tickets

If you sell 745 tickets at a price of $11.75, you will just break even—that is, your total costs will equal your total revenues. Note that you can vary price and see how BE sales change. In Figure 15.3, the break-even sales figures at various prices appear in column E. If you go with the highest price under consideration ($15), you need to sell a minimum of 571 seats—just to have zero profit at the end. At $8 per ticket, you would have to sell more seats than the auditorium's capacity (which is 1,100) just to break even. You may have anticipated the next step. Since you clearly do not want to just break even, how can you account for profit in this analysis? Let's say the symphony board views this series as the group's big money maker and would like to bring in a profit of $2,000 per show. How many tickets do you have to sell at each price to cover fixed costs and produce a $2,000 profit? To determine this, you simply add the $2,000 profit figure to the fixed costs and again divide by the contribution margin. So, at a price of $10, you would need to have "standing room only" (sales of 1,111 seats) to cover fixed cost and meet the profit goal, while at a price of $11, you would need to sell 1,000 seats.

Some very important information emerges from the figures in column G of Figure 15.3. Again, since the auditorium has only 1,100 seats, a price of $10 or less is not feasible. The price of $11.75 determined earlier could cover fixed costs and produce the desired total profit if 930 tickets can be sold ($10,000/[$11.75 – $1.00]). At a $15 price, you would need to sell 714 tickets to meet the profit objective.

At this point, you simply know what sales will be required at each price to cover costs and meet the profit objective. But the analysis also forces you to face an extremely important question: For a given price, *can you sell the requisite number of tickets?* (Can you sell at least 930 tickets at a price of $11.75?) In other words, what

Elasticity of demand
Is the relationship between changes in price and quantity sold.

Break-even analysis (BEA)
Is an analysis technique that literally means "to have zero profit." It is that point at which total cost and total revenue are equal.

Figure 15.3				Break-Even Analysis for the Symphony		
A	B	C	D	E	F	G
Price	Variable Cost	Contribution Margin	Fixed Costs	Units Needed to Break Even	Fixed Costs Plus $2,000 Profit Goal	Units Needed to Cover FC and Profit Goal
$8	$1	7	$8,000	1,143	$10,000	1,429
$9	$1	8	$8,000	1,000	$10,000	1,250
$10	$1	9	$8,000	889	$10,000	1,111
$11	$1	10	$8,000	800	$10,000	1,000
$12	$1	11	$8,000	727	$10,000	909
$13	$1	12	$8,000	667	$10,000	833
$14	$1	13	$8,000	615	$10,000	769
$15	$1	14	$8,000	571	$10,000	714

will demand be at each price point? To consider this question in more detail, let's take a short side road here and introduce the concepts of the demand schedule and elasticity of demand.

The Demand Schedule

Demand schedules

Provide a systematic look at the relationship between price and quantity sold.

Generally, as price goes up, fewer people will buy a product. As prices go down, the opposite usually happens. Figures 15.4, 15.5, and 15.6 present hypothetical demand schedules for wheat, automobiles (back in the Model T era), and movies.[13] **Demand schedules** provide a systematic look at the relationship between price and quantity sold. The first three columns of each of these tables show what quantity (B) is projected to be sold at each price (A), and then the resulting total revenue (C = A*B). Figures 15.4, 15.5, and 15.6 also show the three demand schedules graphically. Consider the demand schedule for wheat, shown in Figure 15.4. If wheat is priced at $5 a bushel, nine million bushels a month will be demanded by customers. If the price drops to $4, demand jumps up, but only to 10 million bushels and total revenue actually drops. Total revenue drops for every lower price point in this table.

In contrast, Figure 15.5 illustrates Henry Ford's belief that consumers would be very responsive to the lowering of automobile prices. Dropping the price from $2,500 to $2,000 increases sales by a factor of six (10,000 cars demanded jumps to 60,000). For nearly every price-point reduction, the total revenue in column C increases.

Finally, Figure 15.6 indicates that the demand for movies changes at the exact same rate as does price. When this happens, total revenue is the same regardless of the price charged.

Elasticity of Demand

Economists quantify the relationship between price and quantity sold using a concept called *elasticity*. The *elasticity coefficient* is simply the absolute value of the percentage change in quantity divided by the percentage change in price.

$$\text{Elasticity coefficient } E = \frac{\text{Percentage change in Q}}{\text{Percentage change in P}}$$

Inelastic demand is reflected by an elasticity coefficient of less than 1. Take a look again at Figure 15.4. Columns D, E, and F calculate these percentage changes (using the higher price point as the basis for the calculations[14]), as well as the elasticity. The demand for wheat is inelastic; that is, the absolute values of the elasticity coefficients are less than 1.0. If the price of wheat were to drop, total revenue would drop. Note that the other side of this is that if the price increases from a market price of $1, for example, total revenue *increases*. If you're looking only at total revenue, then *higher prices are favored when demand is inelastic*.

Demand Schedule and Demand Curve for Wheat				**Figure 15.4**	
A	B	C	D	E	F
Price per Bushel	Quantity Demanded (million bushels per month)	Total Revenue (mil. $) (A*B)	Percentage Change in Price	Percentage Change in Quantity	Elasticity (E)
$1	20	$20	−50.0%	25.0%	−0.5
$2	15	$30	−33.3%	20.0%	−0.6
$3	12	$36	−25.0%	16.7%	−0.7
$4	10	$40	−20.0%	10.0%	−0.5
$5	9	$45	0.0	0.0	0.0

Note: In calculating the percentage changes, we use the biggger number of the pair as the "base." Alternatively, the base could be the average of the two Ps or the two Qs being compared. This produces similar results.

Source: Paul A. Samuelson, *Economics: An Introductory Analysis,* 4th Ed. (New York: McGraw-Hill, 1958), 370–374. Reprinted with permission of McGraw-Hill Companies.

Demand Schedule and Demand Curve for Model T Automobiles				**Figure 15.5**	
A	B	C	D	E	F
Price per Auto	Quantity Demanded (thousands per year)	Total Revenue (A*B)	Percentage Change in Price	Percentage Change in Quantity	Elasticity (E)
$500	300	$150,000	−50.0%	33.3%	−0.7
$1,000	200	$200,000	−33.3%	40.0%	−1.2
$1,500	120	$180,000	−25.0%	50.0%	−2.0
$2,000	60	$120,000	−20.0%	83.3%	−4.2
$2,500	10	$25,000	0.0	0.0	0.0

Notes: Add (00) to the y axis for total and total contribution. R = Total revenue. P = Total Contribution (profit before fixed costs).

Source: Paul A. Samuelson, *Economics: An Introductory Analysis,* 4th Ed. (New York: McGraw-Hill, 1958), 370–374. Reprinted with permission of McGraw-Hill Companies.

| Figure 15.6 | Demand Schedule and Demand Curve for Movies | | | | |
A	B	C	D	E	F
Price per Ticket	**Quantity Demanded per day**	**Total Revenue per day (A*B)**	**Percentage Change in Price**	**Percentage Change in Quantity**	**Elasticity (E)**
$1	1,200	$1,200	−50.0%	50.0%	−1.0
$2	600	$1,200	−33.3%	33.3%	−1.0
$3	400	$1,200	−25.0%	25.0%	−1.0
$4	300	$1,200	−20.0%	20.0%	−1.0
$5	240	$1,200	0.0	0.0	0.0

Source: Paul A. Samuelson, *Economics: An Introductory Analysis,* 4th Ed. (New York: McGraw-Hill, 1958), 370–374. Reprinted with permission of McGraw-Hill Companies.

Elastic demand is reflected by an elasticity coefficient of greater than 1. Demand is elastic in the automobile example for price changes, except the change from $1,000 to $500 (Figure 15.5). Generally speaking, *when demand is elastic, lower prices are favored* (again, when considering total revenue). An excellent illustration of highly elastic demand is seen in the number of new customers entering the computer market with the advent of personal computers that cost less than $1,000. By year-end 1997, sub-$1,000 PCs accounted for 30% of all U.S. computer sales, and one-third of those sales were to consumers who had never purchased a PC before.[15]

Unitary elasticity means that the coefficient is exactly equal to 1. Figure 15.6 shows that movies have unitary elasticity. In these cases, quantity demanded changes at the same rate as price does.

Profit Maximization

Given the information contained in a demand curve, a firm can determine the *profit-maximizing price* by simply calculating the profit at each price point and determining which price produces the highest profit. To illustrate, see Figure 15.7, which extends the Model T example from Figure 15.5 by factoring in a variable cost per car of $350. With this additional information, the price that produces the maximum profit can be easily determined by identifying which price produces the largest *total contribution* (which equals [column C] Total Revenue minus [column D] Total Variable Cost). Given this demand schedule, the company would maximize profit for the car by pricing it at $1,500, which produces a total contribution of $138,000.[16] You can verify this by looking at *marginal revenue* and *marginal cost* (columns F and G in Figure 15.7). **Marginal revenues** are the changes in a firm's total revenue per unit change in its sales level. **Marginal costs** are the changes in a firm's total costs per unit in its output level. These reflect the *changes* in total revenue and total cost from price to price. Lowering the price from $2,500 to $2,000 is good: Revenue jumps $95,000, while costs only jump $17,500 (marginal revenue exceeds marginal cost).

Marginal revenues

Are the change in a firm's total revenue per unit change in its sales level.

Marginal costs

Are the change in a firm's total costs per unit change in its output level.

Calculating Maximum Profits for the Model T					Figure 15.7	
A	B	C	D	E	F	G
Price per Auto	Quantity Demanded (thousands per year)	Total Revenue (A*B)	Total Variable Cost (B*$350)	Total Contribution	Marginal Revenue	Marginal Cost
$500	300	$150,000	$105,000	$45,000	($50,000)	$35,000
$1,000	200	$200,000	$70,000	$130,000	$20,000	$28,000
$1,500	120	$180,000	$42,000	$138,000	$60,000	$21,000
$2,000	60	$120,000	$21,000	$99,000	$95,000	$17,500
$2,500	10	$25,000	$3,500	$21,500	0	0

Variable cost: $350

The same goes for dropping the price from $2,000 to $1,500 (MR = $60,000, MC = $21,000). But, when you drop to a price of $1,000, the marginal revenue generated is just $20,000, and is exceeded by marginal cost ($28,000), indicating that this would not be a profitable move. Figure 15.5 provides a graphic representation of total revenue (R) and total contribution (P), illustrating that while a price of $2,000 produces maximum revenue, $1,500 produces the most profit.

If calculating maximum profit is this easy, why don't more companies set prices this way? In reality, other pricing goals—like meeting competition or achieving market-share goals (discussed below)—tend to be used more frequently than profit maximization. This is partly because demand curves are difficult to estimate. While managers are likely to apply their own intuitive sense of market price response in their pricing, they rarely have the nice, neat information about demand provided in Figure 15.5. So many variables affect sales in a given market that isolating the effect of price is quite difficult. However, it can be done in several ways:

1. **Analytic Modeling.** The most sophisticated approach is to develop a statistical model that predicts sales based on historical observations of sales and such variables as the firm's price, advertising, sales-force levels, competitive tactics, and other variables that may influence demand (e.g., variables capturing economic conditions). This approach allows you to isolate the effect of price on demand.
2. **Experiments.** Firms can run experiments where they change prices in certain markets but not in others, allowing them to see more precisely how such price changes influence sales.
3. **Customer Surveys.** Another approach to identifying a demand curve is to survey customers or present them with purchase scenarios in which they evaluate the product and indicate their intention to purchase at various prices. You have to be careful about interpreting these results, though, as customers may overstate intentions. However, such an approach can be helpful in estimating price response.[17]
4. **Managerial Judgment.** Often, managers have good insight into sales response in a market. Although there may be some error in assessment, obtaining consensus estimates of demand from several managers who are familiar with a market can provide a useful picture of the demand curve.

At long last, let's return to your symphony pricing problem. Assume that you ask a convenience sample of target symphony customers to evaluate the likelihood that they would go to the symphony at different prices. You present the symphony as an alternative against other activities (e.g., baseball games, going out to eat, going to the art museum, going to a movie). Projecting your results to the larger population, you are able to estimate demand at each price point (see Figure 15.8, columns A and B).

Note that the prices under $11 have been dropped from consideration, since the break-even analysis showed them to be infeasible. You ask a few local experts in the

Figure 15.8		Elasticity and Total Revenue: Symphony Problem			
A	**B**	**C**	**D**	**E**	**F**
Price	**Estimated Demand**	**Percentage Change in Price***	**Percentage Change in Quantity**	**Elasticity**	**Total Revenue (A*B)**
$11	1,129	−8.3%	2.6%	−0.31	$12,419
$12	1,100	−7.7%	3.2%	−0.41	$13,200
$13	1,065	−7.1%	5.0%	−0.70	$13,845
$14	1,012	−6.7%	3.9%	−0.58	$14,168
$15	973	0.0	0.0	0.00	$14,595

*Uses the higher-price numbers as base for calculating percentage changes.

industry to look your estimates over, and everyone agrees that they are reasonable. The elasticities calculated between price points (columns C-E in Figure 15.8) clearly indicate that demand is inelastic (i.e., since the absolute values of all of the elasticity coefficients are less than 1). As in the wheat example earlier, this suggests that customers are not highly responsive to price. Demand does not drop off significantly when price is raised, nor does it increase substantially when price is cut. Note that total revenue drops only as you go from higher to lower prices.

However, you are not seeking to maximize total revenue. Instead, you are seeking to maximize profit. As you know, variable cost is $1.00 and fixed costs are $8,000. What price produces the maximum profit? (Don't read ahead or look at Figure 15.9 until you figure this out.)

The answer, perhaps not surprisingly, is the highest price ($15), which produces a total contribution of $13,622 compared to the next highest, $13,156, when the price is $14 (see column E of Figure 15.9). The figure also provides fixed costs in column F and a total profit calculation in column G to confirm that the same price point ($15) is selected as profit-maximizing whether fixed costs are included or not. Incorporating fixed costs here is equivalent to subtracting a constant, which illustrates why fixed costs are not relevant to determining the profit-maximizing price in this example.

So, the profit-maximizing approach would have you setting the price at $15,[18] selling approximately 975 tickets, and earning substantially more than the $2,000 profit goal.

How do you like the $15 price? A little further consideration illustrates why pricing is a little bit science and a little bit art. There actually are other considerations to be taken into account that suggest that the short-term profit-maximizing price would not be the "right" price. In this case, the issue is auditorium capacity. The symphony board may be willing to give up some profit (as long as you've reached the $2,000 goal) in

Figure 15.9		Total Contribution and Total Profit: Symphony Problem				
A	**B**	**C**	**D**	**E**	**F**	**G**
Price	**Estimated Demand**	**Total Revenue (A*B)**	**Total Variable Cost (B*$1)**	**Total Contribution**	**Fixed Costs**	**Total Profit**
$11	1,129	$12,419	$1,129	$11,290	$8,000	$3,290
$12	1,100	$13,200	$1,100	$12,100	$8,000	$4,100
$13	1,065	$13,845	$1,065	$12,780	$8,000	$4,780
$14	1,012	$14,168	$1,012	$13,156	$8,000	$5,156
$15	973	$14,595	$973	$13,622	$8,000	$5,622

Variable cost: $1

Determinants of Price   **Figure 15.10**

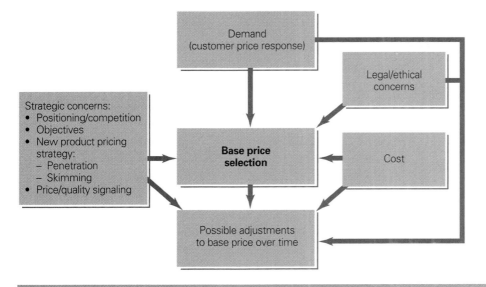

Source: Adapted from Peter R. Dickson, *Marketing Management,* 2nd Ed. (Mason, Ohio: South-Western, 1996): 629.
© 1997. Reprinted with permission of South-Western, a division of Thomson Learning: www.thomsonrights.com.
Fax 800-730-2215.

order to fill up the auditorium. Filling up the auditorium would be a public relations victory, allowing you to promote the fact that the performances are "sold out" and improving the symphony's outcomes in the longer term. Thus, other strategic considerations or objectives come into play. Figure 15.10 displays a larger set of factors that may influence the selection of a base price. We examine these factors next.

Strategic Drivers of Price

3 LEARNING OBJECTIVE

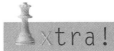

Important strategic factors that will play a role in setting a base price are positioning strategy, objectives, specific new product-pricing strategies, and price-quality inferences.

Positioning Strategy/Competition

Envision two different home-furnishing stores in Atchison, Kansas (population 11,000). One store has reasonably inexpensive household goods (e.g., dishes, glasses, towels, bedding, and decorating items) and small pieces of furniture, many from national manufacturers. The store is neat and clean. It has something of a "warehouse" feel to it, with wire shelving, wide aisles, and bright lighting. Employees make a little above minimum wage, and management makes every effort to keep costs low to maintain low prices for consumers. In contrast, another local store called Neil Hill's is set in a turn-of-the-century bank building in the downtown area and is run by an entrepreneur named Mary Carol Garrity. Inside, the store looks like a home, with high walls and many different rooms with carpeted floors. It doesn't have shelves. Instead, it has merchandise hanging from walls and ceilings, ranging from $2 candle holders to $7,000 French antiques. It sells the same kinds of products as the first store (home furnishings), but the merchandise is all very unique. Products come from large city markets and are hand-selected by the owner, who has the unusual knack of being able to identify and buy merchandise that will become popular before it becomes trendy. She changes the merchandise frequently, and regularly redecorates the store, often repainting the walls and changing the look of every room. The owner greets many of her customers by name, and works closely with

Stores such as Target and Nord-strom represent opposite ends of a competitive strategy positioning continuum. Target features every-day low prices. Nordstrom caters to customers who are far less sensitive to price because of its unique merchandise.

them (many times after hours) on decorating ideas. Incredibly, 95% of this store's sales are made to people who live more than 50 miles away, primarily in Kansas City. Mary Carol recently won a tourism award from the Atchison Chamber of Commerce for the thousands of people her store draws to the town each year.[19]

The two stores represent opposite ends of a *competitive strategy positioning continuum* anchored by "low-cost leadership" on one end and "differentiation" on the other.[20] The first store might be any local, regional, or national competitor that competes by maintaining very low purchasing and operation costs. Neil Hill's, however, seeks to create an absolutely unique (if not unusual) shopping experience for customers. As a result, the two stores have very different pricing policies. The first store would likely attempt to maintain everyday low prices and have frequent sales. Neil Hill's, on the other hand, would have much higher prices, in part because the cost of its unique merchandise is higher, but also because customers are *far less sensitive* to price than they would be at the more mundane price-oriented store.[21] One can find this strategic distinction between brands in almost any product category (e.g., Timex versus Rolex, Honda versus Harley Davidson, private-label cookies versus Pepperidge Farms). With uniqueness comes a price premium, as explained in Chapter 8.

Returning to the symphony example, it is not likely, given the nature of the product category and the audience, that a cost-leadership strategy would generally be effective. Differentiation, though, might involve positioning the symphony experience as distinct and prestigious; making it fun and unique—perhaps offering dinner and wine with performances, an opportunity to meet with members of the orchestra or special guest stars, or rotating concert locations among very unique, attractive locations. Such efforts would merit higher prices in part because costs would be higher, but also because of the higher perceived value being returned to patrons.

A concrete illustration of how these different strategies capture value is provided in Figure 15.11, which contrasts estimated income statements for Suave and Vidal Sassoon. Suave's high volume compensates for its very low price and margin. Vidal Sassoon, in contrast, offers a more distinctive and higher-quality shampoo (along with a more intensive advertising campaign to support it), and as such charges retailers a price per ounce more than *four times* that of Suave's. Interestingly, Sassoon has only one-tenth the sales volume that Suave does, yet Vidal Sassoon is estimated to be

Contrasting Prices, Volumes, and Margins: Suave (Low Cost Leader) vs. Vidal Sassoon (Differentiator), 1984			Figure 15.11
Price, Cost, Volume	**Suave**	**Vidal Sassoon**	
Unit Price (to retailers, per ounce)	.063	.266	
Unit Cost	.036	0.72 (est.)	
Volume (million ounces)	1,161	133	
Income Statement (all $ figures in millions)			
Total Revenue	$73.1	$35.4	
Total Variable Cost	$41.8	$9.6	
Total Contribution to Fixed Costs	$31.3	$25.8	
Advertising	$6.0	$13.5	
Promotion	$17.9	$5.8 (est.)	
Operating Profit	$7.4	$6.5	
Return on Sales	10.1%	18.4%	

more profitable (as measured by return on sales) because of its substantially higher prices and margin. Each brand is profitable, but they travel different routes to profitability: one through volume and one through margin. Clearly, a competitive positioning strategy is an important determinant of base-price level.

Pricing to Meet Objectives

You saw in the symphony example that $15 was the profit-maximizing price. Yet, management may have another goal in mind: fill up the auditorium (i.e., maximize sales). *Goal-setting* (or *objective-setting*) is an important part of a firm's strategic planning process. Plans are developed at both the corporate and business levels, and the objectives for a particular brand or business (like Suave) are in part a function of the corporation's objectives (Helene Curtis). In a classic Brookings Institution study on pricing in large corporations, four predominant pricing objectives were identified:

- Achieve a target **return on investment (ROI)**. (Return on investment is explained below and in detail in the appendix.)
- Stabilize price and margin.
- Reach a market-share target.
- Meet or prevent competition.

Each of these will be addressed individually, as will two other commonly discussed objectives (profit maximization and survival).

Pricing to Achieve a Target ROI

This was found to be the most common approach to pricing in the Brookings' study. Assuming a standard volume, firms add a particular margin to standard cost that is expected to produce a target profit return on investment. Across 20 firms, the target return figure averaged 14%, with a range of 8–20%.

Pricing to Stabilize Price and Margin

Generally, this approach reflects the goal of avoiding the price fluctuations characteristic of a commodity market. Managers in the Brookings' study reflected a desire to "refrain from upping the price as high as the traffic will bear in prosperity." This motive raises questions about the fairness of frequent price changes (particularly increases), a point which has been raised more recently in an economic theory labeled dual entitlement.[22] The **theory of dual entitlement**, in fact, argues similarly that concerns about fairness may constrain price increases. This is supported by the

Return on investment (ROI)
Is the percentage of the dollar profit generated by each dollar invested in the business.

Theory of dual entitlement
Holds that consumers believe there are terms in a transaction to which both consumers and sellers are "entitled" over time. Cost-driven price increases are believed to be fair because they allow the seller to maintain her/his profit entitlement. Demand-driven price increases are not believed to be fair, however, since they allow a seller to increase per-unit profit, while the buyer receives nothing in return.

Two major pricing challenges have recently begun to be addressed via new Web-based pricing technologies. First, it is extremely difficult to obtain information about the sales and costs of all types of units sold by a company across different regions and retailers. Systems exist that capture this information in bits and pieces, but they generally tend to be disconnected. Second, the math used to identify "optimal" prices can get very complex, particularly when you're considering the effects of decisions on a product's own sales, sales of other products, competitive behavior, seasonal effects, and differences across various regions of the country.

Consider even a simple-sounding pricing decision:

It's early to mid-summer, but we at Casual Male retail group are looking ahead at an age-old planning question: At what point do we begin to reduce prices to move our bathing suits and make way for fall merchandise?

There are rules of thumb in the company for these sorts of decisions (e.g., our pricing people might simply have a rule about "taking off 50% of the slowest-moving items in the first week of August"). However, no one has ever taken a systematic look at this decision, asking questions like "Specifically when will demand for bathing suits begin to fade?" and "At what point does the incremental cost of holding inventory exceed the incremental margin being obtained from having bathing suits on the shelves?"

These basic questions are very difficult to answer without the right information. About 50 companies have adopted different versions of new "smart-pricing" systems that provide a Web-based method for organizing an enormous amount of sales, price, sales-promotion, and inventory data, and for applying mathematical models to answer questions like those above. Developed and marketed by vendors such as SAP, DemandTec Inc., and ProfitLogic Inc., these systems are expensive, typically beginning at upward of $3 million, and require a tremendous change in the way sales and pricing information is collected and used in a company.

Yet, some big players are adopting such systems and producing good results:

- JCPenney has reportedly experienced gains of $15–$20 million in the sales of marked-down items since 2001, when their system was installed.
- Dillard's has experienced a 5–6% increase in gross margins in 17 departments in the same time frame, according to analysts.
- Hewlett-Packard was able to adjust the timing of its software price reductions and increased sales 1–1.5% in 2002.
- DHL used a model to test the sensitivity of customers to price changes and was able to convert 25% of its cold calls to sales (vs. 17% prior to the new system being in place). Revenue increased 13.2%, while gross margins jumped 5.4%.

And how about our friends at Casual Male retail group? To quote *Business Week:*

. . . as senior vice-president for planning, Steve Schwartz looked to Web-based pricing tools to eliminate (the guesswork). After loading gobs of sales data into the system a year ago, he spotted enormous regional variation. Northeasterners slowed down on bathing suits in July, but Midwesterners kept buying until August. And Sunbelt shoppers never stopped. While the previous sales system allowed only one chainwide price, Schwartz now had tools—and analysis—to slice and dice prices on all sorts of clothes. "We're doing much better than last year," he says. Gross margins for the chain rose 25% in the nine months ended November 2002, thanks in part to the new pricing system.

While firms are being guarded about their involvement in and results from experimentation with such systems, results look very, very promising.

Source: Faith Keenan "The Price Is Really Right," *BW Online*, http://www.businessweek.com, accessed 31 March 2003.

observation that at times prices are lower than they would be if price-setters were strictly following economic theory. Fairness may be an issue even when companies do not openly increase prices. In response to electricity rationing in May 2001, some Brazilian companies reduced the amount of product in their packaging without changing price (for example, the Danone company reduced cookie packages by near one ounce and relaunched them under a new brand name). Consumer protection groups have been quite vocal in their opposition to such practices, which in turn has led to government investigations.[23]

Pricing to Reach a Market-Share Target

Particularly when there is no patent protection on a product, firms may pursue a market-share target. In most cases, firms will seek a significant share on entering the market. For example, 3M's Scotch Brite Never Rust soap pad was priced aggressively enough to gain a 15.4% market share upon introduction, taking significant share from SOS and Brillo.

Pricing to Meet or Prevent Competition

The logic behind meeting competitors' prices is straightforward. Meeting price cuts will eliminate a competitive disadvantage, while meeting price increases (although less likely) can fatten margins. This reflects a classic tit-for-tat strategy that has been found to be effective in promoting higher profits for all players.[24] An additional benefit is that a consistent pattern of matching competitors' price moves sends rivals the signal that "undercutting price is not a good idea because we will simply match you." In the 1980s, following a horrific price war in a regional soft drink market, Brian Dyson of Coca-Cola Enterprises (a major Coke bottler in Atlanta) made it clear in an interview in *Beverage World* that CCE would not tolerate further aggressive pricing from rivals, noting that ". . . if somebody attempts to lowball the price on us, we will meet that. We insist on a level playing field."

Pricing for Profit Maximization

As noted, the pursuit of this objective requires substantial cost and demand information. It is rarely articulated as a goal by executives being interviewed about their pricing.

Pricing for Survival

A company experiencing trouble may seek to produce an acceptable cash flow to cover marginal costs and simply survive. This may result when competition is especially intense, when consumer needs are changing, and/or when substantial excess capacity exists. Chipmaker Advanced Micro Devices reported a loss of $64.6 million in the second quarter of 1998 in the face of price-cutting by rival Intel, a slowdown in demand for personal computers, and downturns in its other semiconductor businesses. In order to hang on in the face of competing with Intel's value, the company dropped average microprocessor prices from $105 to $86 in the second quarter, significantly cutting into margins.[25]

In order to meet the pricing objective of reaching a target market share, Dodge has implemented a value pricing strategy.

New Product Pricing

Two classic pricing strategies are commonly discussed for new products: skimming and penetration.

Price Skimming

Market (price) skimming is a strategy of pricing the new product at a relatively high level and then gradually reducing it over time. To be successful, this strategy requires that a large segment of the customer market be willing to pay the high price for the unique value the product provides and that competitors cannot quickly enter with similar products at lower prices. For example, VCRs were initially priced as high as $800–$900, but have gradually come down to around $200. Other products that followed similar price patterns are compact disc players, cell phones, and multimedia computers. Intel is also well known for this strategy, pricing its microprocessors for up to $1,000 per chip, but then dropping that price as new superior chips are developed. Price skimming is a strategy that is likely to be followed by a firm pursuing a clear differentiation strategy. In addition, a skimming strategy tends to be pursued in the introduction phase of the product life cycle (see Chapter 9).

Market (price) skimming
Is a strategy of pricing the new product at a relatively high level and then gradually reducing it over time.

Chapter 11 is a discount bookstore that thrives against Borders and Barnes & Noble because of its low prices. Using a penetration strategy, Chapter 11 targets customers who are price sensitive.

Chapter 11 Bookstore

Penetration strategy

Requires that the firm enter the market at a relatively low price in an attempt to obtain market share and expand demand for its product.

Price Penetration

A **penetration strategy** requires that a firm enter the market at a relatively low price in an attempt to obtain market share and expand demand for its product. By pursuing a penetration strategy in the face of a retail book marketplace dominated by Borders and Barnes & Noble (together having 13 super stores in Atlanta alone), a small bookseller called *Chapter 11* thrives with price-cutting.[26] The store's slogan is "Prices So Low, You'd Think We Were Going Bankrupt" and it prices aggressively, discounting best sellers 30% and all books at least 11%. Its new stores are small, in low-cost locations, and designed for quick shopping, all tactics quite different from the larger competitors. Such a "penetration" strategy is the opposite of a skimming strategy. Firms following such a strategy sometimes even enter a market at a loss, hoping to make up initial losses with longer-term repeat purchases. This strategy makes sense when competitive imitation will occur quickly, costs are likely to drop a good deal with increases in volume, and target consumers are relatively price sensitive. Southwest Airlines was able to obtain 75% of Florida's intrastate air traffic, while simultaneously increasing the size of the market, through its low pricing.[27] Penetration pricing is the standard strategy followed by low-cost leaders.

One of the downsides of penetration pricing is that customers may infer low quality from low price. This is most likely to happen under the following circumstances:

1. **When customers are uncertain about brand quality prior to purchase.** The quality of some products is difficult to judge because of their complexity (e.g., computers and cameras), while other products are difficult to assess simply because you cannot "try them out" prior to buying them (e.g., many consumer package goods like food products). A fascinating example is reported by Kent Monroe of a company named Tripledge Wiper Corporation, taken over by an entrepreneur named Jennifer Runyeon in 1988. The core product was a multiedged windshield wiper that worked better and lasted longer than conventional wipers. The firm was renamed Life-time Products, and an aggressive marketing communications and distribution program was put into place. More significantly, however, is the fact that the price was doubled (from $9.95 to $19.95)! Remarkably, sales increased tenfold to $20 million. The substance behind this change, however, was that Life-time had a superior product and a warranty behind it. These advantages were what produced customer perceptions of value that the company

had not been previously capturing with its pricing.[28] In contrast, Omega damaged a brand name more prestigious than Rolex in the 1970s, by pursuing a penetration-pricing strategy with a series of lower-priced products.[29] The latter case is a particularly frightening scenario in that the negative perceptions created by the low price overpowered a great brand name.

2. **When the risk to customers of a bad decision is high.** When the risk of a bad choice is high, customers will often rely on price to suggest quality. Risk may vary across product categories (e.g., in general, the perceived risk associated with service purchases is higher than that for goods), perceived variance among products within the category (e.g., risk is low if all refrigerators are perceived to provide roughly the same performance), and consumption situations (e.g., higher risk when a disposable camera is used to take pictures at a wedding or on the first day of first grade).

Although there continues to be a debate about how frequently (and when) customers use price as a signal of quality, it is fairly safe to assume that customer uncertainty about quality for a new brand is often very high, so that price-quality inference is a concern. It is also clear that firms pursuing differentiation strategies should maintain relatively high prices, for an additional reason beyond those discussed earlier: to credibly communicate their high quality to customers who may have uncertain quality assessments.

Explaining Adjustments to Base Price Over Time

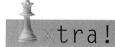

Most of the pricing decisions made for a product in its lifetime are *price-change decisions*. Base price may change as a natural function of different objectives over the product life cycle in response to specific *competitive price moves* or as a function of special pricing tactics that may create a "schedule" of prices or even unique prices for different customers. In addition, prices may change for short periods of time as a result of the ever-popular practice of price promotion. Figure 15.12 summarizes each of these factors. We examine them in turn.

Variation in Objectives over the Product Life Cycle

As discussed in Chapter 9, the firm's objectives in pricing and other elements of the marketing mix will vary over the product life cycle. DuPont's classic strategy is described as follows:

DuPont's strategy for the best part of 50 years was to develop "proprietary" products and to charge all it could get for them as long as the getting was good. So were the giants in data processing, pharmaceuticals, machine tools, and other high technologies. But these proprietary profits inevitably fire up competition, which invades the market with innovations of its own.[30]

In the introductory phase, paying attention to costs is important, and the firm may choose to pursue a skimming or penetration strategy (see earlier sections). In the growth phase, the firm is faced with the opposing forces of growing demand while increasing competition. This necessitates aggressive pricing if the firm cannot maintain a unique product advantage. Maturity is likely to bring either stable, competitive prices or price wars if some rival attempts to get aggressive (again, this assumes no unique advantage of any rival). The firm should do its best to maintain stable prices and not rock the boat in maturity. Alternatively, some firms will attempt innovations to break out of the commodity trap. In decline, the firm should try to keep prices up if the decision has been made to harvest the brand. The DuPont example above illustrates that there is likely to be a declining trend in prices over time as an industry matures. Predicting when and how much to cut prices is an important task.

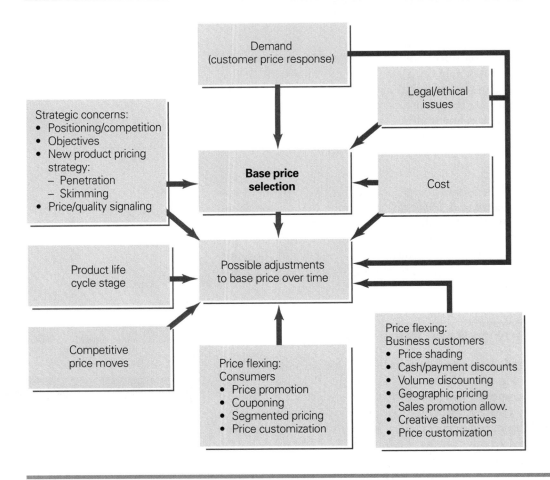

Figure 15.12   Determinants of Price Adjustments Over Time

Source: Adapted from Peter R. Dickson, *Marketing Management* (Fort Worth, TX: Dryden Press, 1996).

Competitive Price Moves

Very often, one firm's price change prompts a reaction from another. This is particularly true today as markets move quickly into maturity and face commodity status. Even brands as strong as Rubbermaid are affected by such competitive forces. Once a Wall Street darling and able to charge a price premium for its innovative new products, Rubbermaid (now Newell-Rubbermaid) has maintained lower prices in the face of growing competition and increasing retailer pressure to discount.[31] In homage to Wal-Mart (which accounts for 15% of Newell-Rubbermaid sales), CEO Joe Galli recently noted that "the days of the price increase are over."[32] Similarly, Nucor Corporation was faced with record steel imports coming from Russia and Japan (among others), leading in some cases to deep price cuts.[33] When competitors enter the market and improve products as an industry moves into the growth phase of its life cycle, the incumbent almost always has to respond with price and/or innovation. This is dramatically illustrated in the case of Johnson & Johnson, which, after seven years of R&D, completed a workable stent. A *stent* is a unique device that cardiologists use to keep arteries propped open following an angioplasty procedure. Incredibly, in just 37 months following introduction, J&J had 1996 sales of $1 billion and a 91% share of this market that it had created. Yet, J&J's pricing remained quite high, and it was initially reluctant to give hospitals—even those accounting for a substantial volume of stents—breaks on price. As competitors (Guidant and Arterial Vascu-

Technological Forces

Johnson & Johnson has persevered in the stock market, innovating with a drug-covered stent that has just recently been approved by the FDA (the drugs help to eliminate future blockage). This product is unmatched by competitors, gets a price of $3,195 (three times today's price for bare-metal stents), and is projected to have 60% of the U.S. market by the end of 2003.[34]

Societal Impact of Pricing Decisions

In 1996, Merck introduced Crixivan, a drug that combats the HIV virus and related infections in people with AIDS. This drug costs approximately $12 per day. Guy MacDonald, head of Merck's anti-infectives franchise (responsible for the HIV/AIDS products), knew that 90% of the people that need Crixivan could not afford it.

Among the most vivid ethical concerns in pricing occurs in product categories that represent vital life services or in cases where the price requires a significant portion of household expenditures. In both of these cases, pricing decisions may have a significant societal impact. The application of standard economics (i.e., pricing at a level the market will bear, profit maximization) seems to be out of place. But is it?

Pharmaceutical Pricing

Pharmaceutical companies have an inherently challenging ethical dilemma with almost every new drug developed for populations that desperately need them: How does the firm price a new drug in a manner that produces an acceptable profit, but does not make the cost too high for the people who really need it? Critics are quick to cry foul when prescription prices appear too high, particularly for drugs targeted to populations with very few choices. In an interesting analysis of pricing prescription drugs, Terri Bernacchi makes the business case very clear:

. . . what (critics) refuse to acknowledge is that the pharma industry fosters innovation that cannot be subjected to external price regulation without a loss or at least a diminution of vital research and development. In the past 100 years, the frequently maligned pharma profit motive . . . has yielded life- and society-changing dividends.

Logically, Bernacchi notes, any business must price at a level that exceeds costs. There are a myriad of costs that pharmaceutical firms need to cover, including innovation (R&D), government approval and regulation, marketing, production, access to retail markets, and potential problems (e.g., costs related to potential patent issues, liability issues, etc.). Some of these costs (particularly R&D) are incurred over a period of years, raising price levels higher than would appear necessary just based on existing variable costs.

Yet, Bernacchi also accepts that there are very real perceptual barriers to treating pharmaceutical pricing strictly as an exercise in equating marginal revenue and marginal cost. She notes that high prices can dilute doctors,' patients,' and managed care plans' acceptance, as well as sully the firm's reputation. Prices that are too high "create unwelcome criticism and makes stockholders unhappy, not to mention that it puts their drugs out of reach for many patients."

So, firms' pricing decisions must take into account these less quantifiable considerations, particularly for a problem as important as AIDS/HIV. Consideration of larger societal impact is clear in these examples:

1. What has Merck done with Crixivan? The company is currently providing Crixivan and Stocrin at prices where the company makes no profit. Beyond pricing, the company has contributed funding for the establishment of regional AIDS treatment centers, and has joined the government of Botswana to create a comprehensive HIV/AIDS program, teaming up with the Gates Foundation, which along with the Merck Foundation is donating $50 million.
2. Other companies have followed suit. Roche also has other less expensive AIDS drugs that it is selling in poorer countries at cost (Viracept). Viracept will now cost about $900 a year for each patient, compared to $3,300 before prices were cut recently. In developed nations, such as Switzerland, the price will remain at $6,000 a year.
3. In early 2003, the California Public Employees Retirement System (CalPERS) sent a letter to Glaxo CEO Jean-Paul Garnier, urging the company to examine its pricing in developing countries. Glaxo subsequently cut prices by up to 47%.

Do the economics disappear in such cases? The answer is no. For example, Glaxo was responsive to the urging of CalPERS because that organization is a significant Glaxo stockholder that was greatly concerned about Glaxo's reputation and future growth prospects!

Finally, Roche's pricing of Viracept is very interesting in light of a new dilemma with a recently developed AIDS drug that has proven effective for some patients who have not responded to more standard treatments. The company said in February 2003 that it will price its AIDS drug Fuzeon in Europe at $20,424 for a year's supply, doubling the price of the most expensive treatment in the market.

DISCUSSION QUESTIONS

1. Is Roche wrong in requiring such a high price for Fuzeon? Why or why not? In formulating your response, consider that the development of the drug (a synthetic peptide) required a $600-million investment and its 106-step production process is more complex and costly than other drugs in this category.
2. Should executives who are fully aware of the societal consequences of their decision making ignore the economic fundamentals involved in pricing? Why or why not?

Sources: Vanessa Fuhrmans and Rachel Zimmerman, "Roche to Sell Drug for AIDS at Cost in Poorer Nations," *The Wall Street Journal*, 13 February 2003, D3.

Vanessa Fuhrmans, "Steep Price of Roche AIDS Drug May Put It Outside of Patient's Reach," *The Wall Street Journal*, 24 February 2003, A1.

Terri Bernacchi, "The Challenge of Prescription Drug Pricing," *Pharmaceutical Executive*, 21 (3) (1 March 2001), 56–68.

Merck Corporate News Release, "Merck's Commitment to Research Remains Key to Success, Chairman Tells Stockholders," Merck News Item, 22 April 2003, http://www.merck.com, accessed 16 July 2003.

Gilbert Chan, "GlaxoSmithKline Slashes AIDS Drug Costs," *Sacramento Bee*, 29 April 2003, D3.

lar Engineering) entered the market with equivalent or superior products, J&J did not respond quickly enough with product innovation or pricing, and its market share went into a free fall.[35]

Of all the marketing-mix decisions, price is the one most likely to motivate a response from competitors.[36] Companies tend to keep a sharp eye on competitors' prices, especially in mature markets where overall demand is price inelastic. More recently, it has been found that management's decision to follow a competitor's price change is affected by the decision-maker's perception of product-price elasticity, as well as the behavior of other competitors.[37]

Price Flexing: Different Prices for Different Buyers

A naive look at pricing would lead to the assumption that once price is set, it then remains constant and is the same for all buyers. We have seen above that prices are not static—they may change in response to changes in the firm's objectives over the product life cycle and in response to competitive price moves. Yet, even more variation in prices is introduced by both established promotion and discount practices, and innovative pricing practices related primarily to new information technology.

Price Flexing to Business Customers

Political and Legal Forces
The Robinson-Patman Act places constraints on manufacturers' ability to charge business customers different prices.

Although the Robinson-Patman Act places constraints on manufacturers' ability to charge business customers different prices, a tremendous amount of price flexing takes place in the form of a wide variety of discounts and allowances. For example, *Computerworld* has reported that instead of using fixed pricing, "IBM will negotiate software charges on a case-by-case basis in emerging application areas such as electronic commerce and enterprise resource planning."[38] To IBM, this policy may have some appeal because potential customers view it as an opportunity to save money and as an incentive to try new applications. The cost to IBM, though, is the hassle of negotiating every deal and then managing nonstandard bid licenses. There are many other ways that a supplier can sell to different buyers for different prices.

Price Shading. Price shading occurs when, during negotiation, a salesperson reduces the base price of a product. This may occur for a variety of reasons, but is most likely due to the attractiveness of obtaining the business of the particular customer under discussion (e.g., a large customer or one who promises a potentially profitable long-term relationship). It may be common for some haggling to take place and may, in fact, be a badge of honor among purchasing agents to achieve some discount off-list price. For companies attempting to pursue a strategy of differentiation, though, price shading is not desirable. Booklet Binding, Inc. is a company that, through sales training, reinvented its sales culture to get the sales force (and customers!) focused more on value-added goods and services and less on price shading.[39]

Cash or Payment Discounts. These are discounts the buyer receives for either paying in cash or paying promptly. A standard payment term is "two-10, net 30," meaning that the buyer gets a 2% discount for paying in less than 30 days (otherwise, they pay the total net cost). This practice effectively price discriminates between slow- and fast-paying customers.

Volume Discounting. Customers who buy in larger volumes are often given more favorable terms. In fact, this is one of the key justifications for price discrimination in the eyes of the Robinson-Patman Act: Total handling, shipping, and clerical expenses are lower (per unit) for larger volumes sold. Providing such discounts also encourages customers to purchase in large volumes, which has the added benefit of reducing the customer's probability of doing business with competitive firms.

Geographic Pricing. It is common for business customers in different regions to receive different prices, since transportation costs may be accounted for in pricing.

Sellers deal with freight charges in different ways. **Free on-board (FOB) pricing** requires the customer to pay for all costs of transportation. This simplifies things for the seller, but also creates a disadvantage in that its products become increasingly expensive for buyers who are geographically further away. An alternative to FOB pricing is **uniform delivered pricing**, where the seller averages the costs of transportation across all customers. A good example of this is postage-stamp pricing—it costs 37 cents to send a letter anywhere in the United States.

Sales-Promotion Allowances. These are discounts that business customers (like retailers) receive for putting the manufacturer's product on sale to consumers for a particular period of time. As discussed in Chapter 13, such allowances have become a staple in business today, particularly in consumer packaged goods.

Creative Alternatives to Discounting.[40] Consider the following scenario:

Peregrine Inc., a Southfield, Michigan, auto-parts maker, is about to close a big contract with a paint supplier. In the old days, it would be pushing for an up-front price discount. But today, the company is getting very different concessions: a multiyear contract with guaranteed on-time deliveries, low reject rates, and no down-the-road price hikes.

Suppliers are getting very creative today with their price-flexing, so that the list price appears to stay fairly constant, but other tactics provide the flex. A few examples:

1. Some manufacturers provide generous financing for buyers. For example, Lucent Technologies, Inc. will sell equipment to startups in return for some negotiated share of the startup's (sometimes shaky) revenue.
2. Some customers are requiring suppliers to give them long-term contracts that guarantee no price increases for the life of the deal.
3. Suppliers may provide services (e.g., repairs) at no cost.
4. An increasing number of customers are demanding promises of quality improvement at the same or lower price over the course of a contract.

Similarly, economist Alan Blinder found in a series of interviews with executives in the 1980s that the most plausible explanation of why list prices often don't change very much is that, instead of changing prices, sellers adjust delivery lags or service.[41]

Price Customization. While price shading, discounting, and the creative approaches to price flexing discussed above clearly reflect some degree of "customizing" price for customers, new technology may make it possible for prices to be literally customized on a transaction-by-transaction basis, depending on the conditions of supply and demand at the moment. In the free market, prices are determined by the interplay of supply and demand. Prices will be higher when demand exceeds supply and they will drop as more suppliers (or more supply) enter the market. Traditionally, supply-and-demand adjustments have taken days, weeks, or months to occur as information about current supply and demand slowly found its way to buyers and sellers. However, new technology has made sharing supply-and-demand information nearly instantaneous, as "the Internet, corporate networks, and wireless setups are linking people, machines, and companies around the globe—and connecting sellers and buyers as never before."[42] Consider the following examples:

- In some cases, this new, more customized pricing comes in the form of *online auctions*. CRN reports that "Once known as the epicenter of the Beanie Baby and baseball card online trading world, eBay has emerged as a force to be reckoned with in B2B IT sales." eBay's ratings capability, along with its ability to provide access to hard-to-find equipment, along with "storefronts" for IBM, Compaq, and Sun Microsystems make it a very attractive supply option.

Free on-board (FOB) pricing
Leaves the cost and responsibility of transportation to the customer.

Uniform delivered pricing
Means that the seller charges all customers the same transportation cost regardless of their location.

Technological Forces
Sherlock Systems does 150 transactions and spends $25,000 a month on computer products and parts on eBay.[43] With its recent acquisition of PayPal (a system that facilitates payments over the Internet), eBay's revenue grew more than 90% in the first quarter of 2003.[44]

Pricing Hybrid Vehicles

The auto industry sold almost 17 million cars in the U.S. in 2002. A tiny fraction of those sales (36,000 in total) were in a new category of car called the "hybrid" technology. Foremost among the hybrids is the Toyota Prius, on the market for five years and selling about 20,000 units in 2002.

Hybrid technology combines a gas engine with an advanced electric motor to simultaneously power the car and recharge the vehicle's batteries. Each system is monitored to maximize fuel efficiency and the benefits are numerous: The car has the look of a subcompact, gets 48 miles to the gallon, produces very low emissions, (up to 90% cleaner for smog-forming emissions than an ultra-low-emission vehicle), and never needs to be plugged in for recharging. Due to IRS incentives, buyers get a tax deduction of $2,000 when they purchase the car.

How would you price a car with all of these unique features? One option is to set a very high price and skim the market, achieving profitability by selling a small number of high-margin cars. A second option is to pursue significant market penetration by pricing low and attempting to generate large volume, hoping that the car will "catch on," achieving profitability through high volumes but at lower margins. While determining the price of the Prius, you'll want to take note of the gas-powered cars that might be perceived as competitors. The Nissan Sentra is priced at about $14,000, and the Honda Civic and Toyota Corolla LE are both priced at approximately $15,000.

Would you believe that Honda and Toyota have adopted a price-skimming strategy that actually loses money on every car sold? Yes, it's true—the new technology in this emerging market is actually producing a new hybrid pricing strategy! Both the Toyota Prius and the recently introduced Honda Civic hybrid are being sold for about $20,000. This retail price is $4,000 to $5,000 higher than comparable gas-powered models, yet—according to estimates—it is $3,000 to $4,000 below the cost of producing cars with hybrid technology. The unit costs of producing the hybrid tend to be higher because the engine is more complex than standard gas-powered cars.

At this point, the pricing is clearly aimed at penetrating the market in hopes that experience and economies in production will drive down costs of producing the cars. The companies are counting on conservative estimates that, by 2007, 500,000 hybrid automobiles will be sold in the U.S.

Sources: Laurie Willis, "Interest Is Growing in High-Mileage Hybrid Vehicles," *The Baltimore Sun,* 27 March 2003.
Royal Ford, "Toyota, Honda Take Lead in Bringing Hybrids Mainstream," *The Boston Globe,* 30 November 2002.
Robert Bostelaar, "Great Escape to Hybrid Power," *The Ottawa Citizen,* 17 January 2003, C2.
Kathleen Kerwin, "How Detroit Can Gun the Engines," *Business Week,* 17 February 2003, 80.

- Enermetrix is a company that creates an online market for buying and selling energy. The Web site provides an auction forum for sellers of energy to link up with (primarily large) buyers that can lock very good rates into contracts. Buyers have the ability to post secure buy orders for real-time, competitive bidding, as well as the ability to digitally sign electronic contracts with counter parties.[45] The company's service went live in January 1998 and in the ensuing year-and-a-half produced contracts worth more than $70 million.[46] In 2001, the value of Enermetrix's retail business was $650 million.[47]

- Arbitrage Networks has developed a technology—currently available in carrier-to-carrier exchanges—that will allow every long-distance call to be instantaneously placed on the carrier that has the lowest price. This is accomplished by having carriers supply moment-to-moment information about their network availability and price, and then accessing computers and switching networks powerful enough to match incoming calls with lowest-cost carriers at any given time.[48] As of the first quarter of 2003, the company's trading incorporates 250 telecommunications partners and now exceeds seven billion minutes per year.[49]

In short, new technology presents the capability of bringing supply and demand together in real time, producing highly efficient markets and potentially placing significant downward pressure on price. Such customization has become increasingly available in consumer markets as well.

Price Flexing to Consumers

While there are some circumstances in which consumers negotiate pricing (e.g., new or used automobiles), you may think that retailers use a "one-price" approach almost exclusively. With a few exceptions—particularly smaller local shops, antique stores, and used-goods dealers—sellers do appear to charge fixed prices for products. Even the automobile industry is seeing a trend toward *single-pricing*, both with

Sociocultural Forces

Manufacturers are increasingly adopting a single-price policy to lure customers who do not like the traditional adversarial sales process.

Saturn's innovative sales approach and with the online car vendors (e.g., Auto-By-Tel, AutoVantage, or Microsoft's CarPoint) that each sell products at no-haggle prices.[50] This has not come without its challenges—Toyota had trouble seeking to control dealer pricing in Canada—but this pricing approach is valued by customers who do not like the adversarial sales process.[51]

Interestingly, though, there is more price-flexing taking place in consumer markets than meets the eye. It takes the form of price promotion, couponing, segmented pricing, and, as we saw earlier with the business market, an increasing trend toward customization.

Price Promotion. **Price promotion** is a ubiquitous and effective practice in many situations, particularly early in a product's life, where the objective is to encourage trial and to allow the seller to maintain a higher list price. The dangers of price promotion in more mature markets can be illustrated with a simple example.

Let's say that you and your competitor sell widgets to the consumer market, and you each have a reasonable market share and comfortable profit of $20 million per period. Your competitor, though, decides to try a 10% temporary price reduction and boosts his profit to $27 million for the period. This is fine for your rival, but you lost market share and your profit dropped to $13 million for that same period, since the competitor stole some of your market share. So, what do you do? You retaliate with a price promotion of your own! You and your competitor go back and forth like this a few times, and you find that you're both promoting at 10% off most of the time and that you're now each making $18 million each period, instead of the $20 million that you were making before the price promotions were initiated!

This is a version of the famous *prisoner's dilemma* from game theory, which poses the paradox of a joint decision-making situation in which the players do best by cooperating (not promoting), but each player has an individual incentive to "defect" (in our case, to do a price promotion). If both players defect, both are worse off. Once promotions get started, it may become clear to the firms that their profitability is lower, but they have a hard time raising prices back up again. Why is this so?

The reason is that consumers respond well to promotions, which encourages manufacturers to do more of them. As consumers grow accustomed to such price specials, any firm who does not price-promote is likely to lose sales. So, promotions tend to increase over time, leading consumers to be more sensitive to price.[52] As this happens, retailers adapt to promotions by *forward-buying* or *diverting product*. All in all, everyone's attention goes to price when price is highlighted through increasing promotion. As a response to this vicious cycle of competitive promotions—and its related inefficiency—Procter & Gamble instituted **everyday low pricing (EDLP)** in the early 1990s (also known as *value pricing*). This pricing initiative was led by Edwin Artzt, a Procter & Gamble leader.

Couponing. *Couponing* provides another means of price discrimination in that it gives some consumers—those who wish to take the time and effort to clip coupons—the capability of paying lower prices. Most coupons come from *freestanding inserts (FSI)* in the weekend newspaper, but increasingly coupons are available at the point-of-purchase and printed on grocery-register tapes. Into the early 1990s, manufacturers were following a trend of continuously increasing the number of coupons distributed per year. A significant change has occurred more recently in that

Couponing gives consumers the option of paying lower prices. Marketers use coupons to speed up the entry of a new product, like the new flavors of French's Mustard, to market.

Price promotions
Are short-term price reductions designed to create an incentive for consumers to buy now rather than later and/or stock up on the product.

Everyday Low Pricing (EDLP)
Refers to the pricing strategy in which a firm charges the same low price every day.

Coupon distribution has declined as large firms such as Procter & Gamble cut back on incentives.

© Susan Van Etten

Technological Forces

Redemption rates for paper coupons have become more anemic (1.1%), while redemption of online coupons is higher, although still surprisingly low (3.1%).[55]

consumer packaged-goods firms, led again by Procter & Gamble, are looking into cutting back many incentives, including coupons.[53] *Advertising Age* reports that coupon distribution declined 10% to 276 billion coupons in 1997, attributing the change to a shifting of funds into frequent-shopper cards and electronic discounts. Note that coupon redemption fell 18% to 4.8 billion in 1997, reflecting an overall paltry 1.7% redemption rate.[54] In 2002, however, the industry has blossomed overall with 335 billion paper coupons distributed and 242 million coupons downloaded from the Web (the latter reflects an increase of 111%).

Pricing for Different Segments. Marketers very often have different marketing programs for different consumer segments.

- **Geographic Segments.** Price sensitivity sometimes varies across geographic regions. For example, some grocery retailers have different price zones, with prices likely to vary across those zones. Competition and consumer profiles may differ among geographic areas. To generate interest among potential patrons in outlying areas, the symphony (discussed earlier) might plan smaller, fun ensemble concerts at performance halls or public places in other locales priced at or below variable cost.
- **Usage Segments.** It is common for marketers to recognize high-volume users and reward them with different prices. For example, regular customers at a particular grocery store who carry the store's frequent-shopper card receive discounts at checkout that other shoppers do not receive. Where capacity is an issue for the manufacturer or service provider, the heaviest users may actually pay more. IBM has applied this strategy for its Internet service, where accounts exceeding a threshold level of usage are charged an hourly fee in addition to the base monthly rate. In contrast, symphonies and theatres often have packages whereby patrons who commit to coming to a certain number of events receive a reduced price.
- **Demographic Segments.** A symphony may provide special prices for students or children to encourage attendance, or may give discounts to senior citizens. This is a common strategy used by museums, athletic events, and amusement parks.
- **Time Segments.** There are many examples of how "time" provides a relevant basis for segmenting markets for pricing. Resort hotels have on- and off-season rates, reflecting differences in demand for those seasons. Similarly, plumbers have regular and overtime, or weekend rates, capturing the same concept. A bakery might lower prices at the end of the day to move leftover merchandise. A symphony might have a Saturday morning or afternoon concert to reach new markets, accompanied by lower pricing. *Forbes* magazine reports that the cities of Singapore, San Diego, and Toronto all engage in "congestion pricing" on their toll roads. This is where higher toll rates are charged during rush hour to reallocate traffic to less busy times.[56]

Customization. As discussed above for business markets, new technology may have a significant effect on the prices consumers pay for products and may lead to significant variation in the prices that consumers pay for the same item. Consumers can participate in the Internet auctions described earlier. Further, Arbinet's services (linking callers to the lowest-cost long-distance provider) may be available for consumers in two years. In fact, some envision a "smart" phone that automatically seeks the lowest-cost carrier each time a long-distance call is placed. Beyond this, the Internet is affecting consumers' ability to search for and access low prices. For example, airlines today often send out e-mail alerts of last-minute fare specials to fill up unfilled seats. Only consumers on the airline's e-mail list receive notice of these fares. Yet, Priceline.com allows consumers to specify their travel plans and then name their price for the flight(s). Priceline acts as a go-between for participating airlines and consumers, forwarding bids to the airlines and relaying acceptances or refusals to consumers. The Priceline Web site received more than one million visits in the week after it was launched, and within two months had sold 100,000 tickets.[57] While the company experienced challenges in 2000, Priceline reported record sales of $364.8 million in the second quarter of 2001.[58] However, with air travel down and Priceline's ticket sales down 44%, the company reported sales of $195.3 million, a net loss of $8.0 million, or four cents per share, in the quarter ended March 31, 2003.[59] *The Economist* has argued that companies will continue to use new technology to manage customer relationships and track customer loyalty (as well as shape offers for loyal customers) and to use lower prices where appropriate as a tool to maintain loyalty. They note that "in future, 'good' customers will routinely expect to pay less for a service (or get more for their money) than the rest of us."[60]

Legal and Ethical Issues in Pricing

5 LEARNING OBJECTIVE

The laws of the land represent an additional set of considerations that influence the setting of base price. Prudent marketers must be attentive to legal and ethical concerns in pricing. As proof, consider a case involving John Taylor,[61] who in 1983 was an honest, hard-working division manager at Allegheny Pepsi, a large bottling company that controlled numerous Pepsi franchises. In late spring of that year, Taylor traveled to Norfolk, Virginia, at the request of his boss, George Goodwin, to meet with Bob Miller, the regional division manager for their competitor, Mid-Atlantic Coke. Taylor listened at the meeting as George Goodwin described the significant price-cutting that had been taking place in the market and how it was hurting both firms' profit. Goodwin suggested ". . . let's forget all the problems we've had up to this point . . . let's just agree not to have it continue on." He then pulled out a notepad and wrote down prices for each different size of soda bottle, and these prices were agreed upon by both competitors.

Such **price-fixing** was fairly common in the soft-drink industry at this time. Yet, price-fixing is illegal because it restricts competition and leads to higher prices for customers. John Taylor did not design the price-fixing scheme, but he did help to implement it. On occasion, he would make sure his sales reps did not give customers any deals that would break the implicit agreement with Coke. When one disgruntled customer learned about the agreement, he contacted the police and the FBI. In the legal proceedings that followed, Taylor declined offers of immunity. Ironically, his boss, George Goodwin—architect of the price-fixing plan—took an immunity offer and became a star witness in the federal government's case *against* John Taylor. In spite of recognizing Mr. Taylor's good character and the awkward situation in which the price-fixer received immunity, the judge was compelled to sentence Taylor to three years in prison and a $15,000 fine. Several others also went to jail over this incident.[62]

This case illustrates the dramatic personal and professional consequences that can result from illegal pricing behavior. Ironically, Mr. Taylor did not benefit financially from the price-fixing arrangement, as he was just doing his job. A similar situation involved two of the most famous auction houses in the world. In this case, executives from Christie's and Sotheby's were alleged to have discussed and agreed to increasing buyer's fees before they announced these pricing-policy changes for their respective companies. By setting identical commission rates, they would effectively limit competition, as well as increase the amount that buyers paid when they

Price-fixing
Is a conspiracy to fix competitive prices.

Political and Legal Forces
Certain illicit practices can become commonplace in an industry and seem legitimate because "this is the way we've always done it." That's a slippery slope to walk, however. An understanding of the law is vital to making pricing decisions.

bought fine art and antiques from each auction house. The completion of a U.S. Department of Justice investigation resulted in a guilty plea for Diana Brooks, Sotheby's chief executive officer.[63] Several types of pricing behavior are illegal in the United States.[64]

Price Fixing

Price fixing is a violation of the **Sherman Antitrust Act,** which prohibits any contract, combination, or conspiracy that restrains trade. It is one of the key reasons for the existence of **cartels,** organizations of firms in an industry where the central organization makes certain management decisions and carries out functions that would normally be performed with the individual firms. Archer Daniels Midland (ADM) pleaded guilty in 1996 to criminal charges of price fixing in the distribution of lysine (an amino acid that speeds livestock growth). ADM paid $100 million in penalties. In their individual trials, ADM executives were found guilty in September 1998 and one executive was sentenced to a three-year sentence in a federal prison camp.[65]

Price Discrimination

Price discrimination occurs when a seller offers a lower price to some buyers than it does to other buyers. It is *not* illegal when the buyers are consumers (who do not compete with each other). But, if a manufacturer offers different retailers different prices without economic justification, this behavior violates the Robinson-Patman Act (1936), which amended the earlier Clayton Act (1914). Price discrimination is legal when:

1. **It is cost-justified.** For example, there may be cost differences in selling to two different customers. Wal-Mart, for example, obtains more favorable prices than smaller retailers because of its sheer size and the economies that manufacturers obtain in selling in such high volumes. Alternatively, if the manufacturer's costs go up, one customer may be charged a higher price than another customer who bought before the price increase.
2. **The seller is attempting to match a competitor's lower prices.** The Robinson-Patman Act has a "good-faith clause" that allows a seller to charge a lower price to Store X than to Store Y if a competitor is already charging Store X a lower price.
3. **There is no apparent harm to competition.**

Resale Price Maintenance

If I'm a manufacturer and you're a retailer selling my product, we are in violation of the law if we get together and *agree upon* some minimum price to be charged to consumers at retail. I can, however, suggest retail-price levels to you. Further, I can stop dealing with you if you do not follow my recommendation.[66] The primary concern about *resale price maintenance* is that retail price competition should not be eliminated by manufacturers and retailers should not agree on specific minimum prices.

Predatory Pricing

Predatory pricing is a practice where one firm attempts to drive out rivals by pricing at such a low level that the rival cannot make any money. Some have accused the airlines of predatory pricing. Spirit Airlines abandoned its Detroit-Philadelphia service when Northwest Airlines cut its one-way fares to $49 on all seats and added 30% more seats. Following Spirit's departure from the route in September 1996, Northwest's one-way fare climbed to more than $230 and the number of seats available dropped.[67] This is the classic pattern of predatory pricing, in which an incumbent firm apparently attempts to drive out newer, smaller rivals with aggressive pricing. The practice of aggressive pricing and capacity expansion has come under intense scrutiny recently in the airline industry[68]—although no convictions have been made.

It is quite difficult to prove predatory behavior, as federal law requires demonstrating that the alleged predator priced below an appropriate measure of its average cost and that it had a reasonable expectation that it would recoup its losses.[69] Northwest has argued that it is competing "fairly but aggressively" and that smaller airlines often survive in spite of these aggressive tactics. Predatory pricing continues to be "rarely tried and even more rarely successful."[70]

Markup laws are state laws that require a certain markup above cost in particular industries to protect consumers and small businesses from predatory pricing. For example, Wal-Mart ran into significant regulatory trouble in several states in spring and summer 2001 when it opened up parking-lot gas pumps to lure consumers to the store. Thirty-seven states have laws that either prohibit selling gas below cost or general fair-marketing laws that apply more broadly. These laws are specifically designed to protect consumers and small businesses from predatory pricing. In many states, the laws prevented Wal-Mart from exploiting its natural cost advantage with aggressive pricing at levels that would be below the costs of other gasoline retailers. Wal-Mart has tried but been unsuccessful in lobbying states to repeal these laws.[71]

Political and Legal Forces
Political/legal forces significantly affect pricing strategy. Laws that outlaw price fixing, price discrimination, and predatory pricing protect competition, as well as consumers.

Markup laws
Are state laws that require a certain markup above cost in particular industries to protect consumers and small businesses from predatory pricing.

Exaggerated Comparative-Price Advertising

A very common price-advertising tactic is to compare an advertised sale price to a former price; for example: Was $49.99, Now $29.99. Adding a comparison price has been found to significantly improve consumers' perception of savings and value in an advertised offer.[72] If such a comparative price is bona fide and "was offered to the public on a regular basis for a reasonably substantial period of time," it is perfectly legal.[73] Yet, many retailers appear to stretch this guideline, using comparison prices of questionable validity. While such charges have been considered by many state attorneys general, few cases have gone to trial. An exception was a case against May D&F that resulted in a judgment against the retailer. May D&F had institutionalized a policy in which a profitable "intermediate markup" price was set for a product (e.g., $79.99 for a Krups coffee maker), but a much higher "promotional markup" price was also set ($119.99) that would be charged for as few as 10 days at the beginning of the six-month selling season. After the initial 10 days, the store would promote the item as "originally $119.99, now $79.99" for much of the remaining season. May D&F was found to be in violation of FTC standards for comparative price advertising.

Ethical Concerns

Customers and public policy groups raise many questions about pricing practices, primarily about what often appear to be exorbitant prices. The cereal industry has been the target of such criticism, as has the pharmaceuticals industry and the banking industry (for excessive ATM fees). Consider these additional pricing scenarios:

- A hardware store raises its price for snow shovels on the morning after a big snow storm.
- A supermarket chain charges higher prices in its inner-city stores than in its stores in the suburbs.
- A microchip manufacturer charges initially high prices for its new-generation chip and then sharply reduces prices after the less price-sensitive buyers have purchased it.
- A retailer prices dresses at 400% above cost.
- A consultant prices her services at $5,000 per day.
- A bank charges a $1.50 fee for ATM usage to customers who do not have an account with the bank.

Are these all ethical pricing practices? Are they all unethical? People from different backgrounds are likely to apply very different frameworks and standards in making their judgments. Further, we may judge them differently depending upon

Higher prices—even when justified on the basis of supply and demand—may be viewed as unfair by customers. Some gas stations hiked their prices up to $6 per gallon following the terrorist attacks of September 11, causing resentment for customers and new price-gouging laws.

© Susan Van Etten

whether we are buyers or sellers! All of the above behaviors can be justified from a business perspective in one of two ways: (1) demand exceeds supply, so equating the two (specifically, rationing demand) requires high prices, and/or (2) the value or return that the buyer receives from each transaction merits these higher prices. These are powerful arguments, yet it should be noted that customers do not always buy into them. Higher prices—even those justified on the basis of supply and demand—may be viewed as unfair by customers and may create resentment, which will affect long-term business. For example, a majority of consumers surveyed felt that the hardware-store owner in the first example behaved unfairly.[74] Two-thirds of the consumers surveyed about recent ATM fees said they changed their usage in response to the fees, with 11% saying they stopped using ATMs altogether.[75]

The law defines minimally acceptable behavior. In some states, there are *gouging laws* that attempt to prevent substantial price increases in response to special circumstances.[76] In the wake of the September 11 terrorist attacks, panic buying by consumers fearful of gas shortages led to prices as high as almost $6 a gallon in some locations. States of emergency were declared in Texas, Mississippi, and Florida to trigger emergency price-gouging laws and Michigan's attorney general accused several gas stations of charging prices "grossly in excess" of normal.[77]

Business common sense defines another standard: You do not want to alienate customers and lose them. There are also personal standards of ethics that each of us needs to think about and develop:

Firms can facilitate ethical marketing behavior from their employees by suggesting that employees apply each of the following tests when faced with an ethical predicament: (1) act in a way that you would want others to act toward you (the Golden Rule), (2) take only actions which would be viewed as proper by an objective panel of your professional colleagues (the professional ethic), and (3) always ask, would I feel comfortable explaining this action on TV to the general public? (the TV test).[78]

Chapter Summary

Learning Objective 1: *Define price, explain why cost-based pricing methods are used so widely, and understand the drawbacks of these methods.* Price is a monetary value charged by an organization for the sales of its products. Because managers are generally aware of their costs of doing business, cost has become a common factor in price setting. There are two common approaches to cost-based price-setting. One is the standard markup and the second is achieved by adding together both cost per unit and desired profit. However, cost-plus pricing does not address price sensitivity or competition, both of which are essential considerations in setting prices effectively. Also, cost-plus pricing generally involves allocating fixed costs on a per-unit basis and treating them as variable costs, even though fixed costs do not change with the number of units sold.

Learning Objective 2: *Incorporate demand considerations into pricing and determine a short-term profit maximizing price.* Pricing decisions must take into account the relationship between price and demand. The transition from a cost-based approach to a more market-driven approach begins with a break-even analysis, which asks the question "can we sell the number of units needed at this price to make the desired profit?" From here, estimates of a demand schedule provide important input into pricing decisions.

Learning Objective 3: *Identify and explain strategic drivers of prices.* Prices may be determined based on a competitive-positioning strategy that involves the uniqueness of the product. Customers are far less sensitive to price when they are seeking unique goods and services. Pricing may be determined based on management's goals and objectives. These objectives may include achieving a target ROI, stabilizing price and margin, reaching a market-share target, and meeting or preventing competition. Two strategies for new-product pricing include price skimming and price penetration.

Learning Objective 4: *Explain and evaluate reasons why base prices change over time in both business and consumer markets.* There are many reasons why firms change base prices over time. Prices change because objectives change over the product life cycle and because competitors change prices. Price flexing occurs with promotion and discount practices or innovative pricing practices due to new information technology. Although the Robinson-Patman Act constrains manufacturers' ability to charge business customers different prices, price flexing takes place in the form of a wide variety of discounts and allowances. Price flexing in the consumer market takes the form of price promotion, couponing, pricing for different markets, and customization through Internet auctions.

Learning Objective 5: *Explain basic legal and ethical constraints on pricing behavior.* Every manager should be aware of pricing behavior that is considered illegal in the United States. This includes price fixing, price discrimination, retail price maintenance, and predatory pricing. In addition to understanding these legal constraints to pricing, every manager should be sensitive to the ethical dilemmas related to pricing.

Key Terms

For interactive study: visit http://bestpractices.swlearning.com.

Break-even analysis (BEA), 511
Cartel, 532
Demand schedules, 512
Elasticity of demand, 511
Everyday low Pricing (EDLP), 529
Free on-board (FOB) pricing, 527
Marginal costs, 514

Marginal revenues, 514
Market (price) skimming, 521
Markup laws, 533
Penetration strategy, 522
Predatory pricing, 532
Price, 507
Price discrimination, 532

Price-fixing, 531
Price promotions, 529
Return on investment (ROI), 519
Sherman Antitrust Act, 532
Theory of dual entitlement, 519
Uniform delivered pricing, 527

Questions for Review and Discussion

1. A manufacturer of golf equipment has developed a new golf club called the Big Bomber. The Bomber produces 15% longer drives based on new shaft technology. The company has $80 million invested in operating capital. The fixed cost of promoting the driver is $4.5 million. The unit cost of producing the driver is $100.
   a. If the selling price to retailers is $250, how many drivers have to be sold to break even on these fixed expenses? How does that number change if the selling price is $300? $350?
   b. If the company were to price the golf club by applying a 75% markup on cost, what would the selling price to retailers be?
   c. Assume that the company is seeking to produce a first-year profit of 30% for this club. It projects that it will sell 300,000 drivers. What should be the selling price to retailers?

d. The company has some rough estimates of demand at different price levels, based on a survey it conducted. It projects that pricing at $250 to retailers will produce first-year sales of 350,000, at $300, 295,000 will be sold, and at $350, 248,000 will be sold. Assuming that these estimates are accurate, what should the price be?

2. If cost-plus pricing is used by oligopolistic rivals consistently over time with adjustments made in markup levels as sales figures are studied, could it lead to profit-maximizing prices?

3. Answer the following questions, explaining the relationships among changes in price, demand (units sold), and profit. Explain whether demand appears to be elastic or inelastic in each case.

   a. Hewlett-Packard dropped prices on personal computers during 1997 by offering customers discounts of up to 50%. Unit sales shot up 70% during this period. Yet the personal computer division *lost $50 million*. What would explain this odd combination of performance outcomes? (Note: There were no especially large accounting write-offs for the PC business during this period.)

   b. Heublein, Inc. raised prices 8% on its Popov brand of vodka to an average of $4.10 for a fifth of vodka. Popov lost 1% of its market share. What would determine whether or not Popov actually lost money?

   c. Scott Mt. Joy is cofounder of Nieto Computer Services, a three-year old Houston computer and network-services company. In 1995, the company charged $35 to $50 an hour for its contract work. By 1998, those rates were $75 to $150. "We raised hourly rates (two years in a row) and lost one or two clients out of 130," says Mr. Mt. Joy. What would explain this inelastic demand?

4. Given the data below, at what price does this manufacturer of barbecue grills maximize profit?

A Estimated Price	B Sales Quantity	C Variable Cost
$125	100,000	$70
$130	95,000	$70
$135	85,000	$70
$140	75,000	$70

5. Diamonds are a luxury. Water is an essential requirement for human life. Why are diamonds so much more expensive than water?

6. Consider your answer to question 5, then answer the following two questions:

   a. *Business Week,* 2 March 1998: "Step into a Kmart or Wal-Mart store these days and you can pick up a diamond bracelet for $29.99—about the same price as a toaster . . . prices of smaller diamonds are plunging."* Why do you think this is happening?

   b. In contrast, water is more expensive (bottled water). What makes consumers willing to pay $1.09 for a 16-ounce bottle of water?

*Heidi Dawley and William Echikson, "Cracks in the Diamond Trade: A Flood of Low-Quality Gems Has Shaken DeBeers' Iron Grip," *Business Week,* n.3567, March 2, 1998, 106.

In-Class Team Activities

1. The prices shown are for a unique product. Assume that it is sold in grocery stores, but has no in-store competition. No nearby stores carry it either. Customers buy just enough of the product, but do not stock up. They consume all of the product. Discuss in small teams the implications of each of these assumptions for pricing decisions. Then, as a team (and applying these assumptions), determine the best prices for this product in the coming 13 weeks.

   At the right is (a) the cost schedule for the next 13 weeks—that is, the price that you will pay to the manufacturer to get the product. Next is a table (b) listing prices and demand (units sold) for the previous 26 weeks. What prices would your team recommend for the coming 13 weeks, and why?

   a. Cost schedule for the upcoming 13 weeks

Week	Your Cost from the Supplier	What Price Should You Charge?
1	$1.00	
2	$1.00	
3	$0.75	
4	$1.00	
5	$1.00	
6	$1.00	
7	$0.75	
8	$1.00	
9	$0.50	
10	$0.50	
11	$1.00	
12	$1.00	
13	$1.00	

b. Prices and demand for the previous 26 weeks

Week	Retail Price	Your Sales
1	$1.49	448
2	$1.49	392
3	$1.19	688
4	$1.04	752
5	$1.49	408
6	$1.19	672
7	$1.49	416
8	$1.49	408
9	$1.34	544
10	$1.49	432
11	$1.49	440
12	$1.49	416
13	$1.34	528
14	$1.49	432
15	$1.19	680
16	$1.34	560
17	$1.49	392
18	$1.49	416
19	$1.19	664
20	$1.49	384
21	$1.04	800
22	$1.49	424
23	$1.49	440
24	$1.04	768
25	$1.49	424
26	$1.49	408

2. Play the following promotion game. Get four or six people together and make up two teams. The teams will compete in a "promotion game." You sell a nondescript product for $200, with a variable cost of $100. Your fixed costs are $400 million. The two teams will compete for several periods. There's only one decision you make in this game. What price-promotion (temporary price-reduction) level would you pick each period? You can choose the following levels: 0%, 5%, 10%, 15%, or 20%. Your team should decide your promotion level by quietly consulting with each other (without the other team hearing), writing down your decision, and placing it in a hat or in the middle of the table (concealed). When each team has finished, the decisions are revealed, and you each determine your profit for that period using the table below. Continue play until your instructor tells you to stop. The team that wins is the one that has the most profit.

Payoff Matrix for Both Teams

Numbers in the Table are in Millions of dollars

Your Promotion Level	Competitor's Promotion Level				
	0%	5%	10%	15%	20%
0%	20	12	3	−6	−15
5%	27	18	10	1	−8
10%	29	21	12	3	−6
15%	26	18	9	0	−9
20%	15	7	−2	−10	−19

Source: Adapted from John Hauser, *Enterprise: An Integrating Management Exercise* (Redwood City, CA: Scientific Press, 1989).

Discussion Questions

a. What are your thoughts as you make the promotion decisions? What are all the factors that you and your teammates discussed?
b. What do you believe your opponents were thinking during each period of the game?
c. How would the game have gone differently if you had a different objective (e.g., if you were given the goal of averaging profits of $14 million each period instead)?
d. Describe how this exercise captures the prisoner's dilemma.

Internet Questions

1. Identify two services that sell automobiles via the Internet. How do they communicate price information? Why? What impact do you think these services will have on the cost of purchasing automobiles in the future?

2. Go to http://www.netgrocer.com. Sign up for the service (you don't need to give them a credit-card number) and then go shopping for breakfast. How much would it cost if you ordered a box of Wheaties, a box of Nutrigrain bars, and Orange Tang in the 31.70-ounce container? Compare this to your local grocery store and explain the differences in pricing.

3. Go shopping for a video of the following movies: *It's a Wonderful Life, Gone with the Wind, Good Will Hunting,* and the Beatles' *Yellow Submarine.* (Hint: http://www.yahoo.com, http://www.excite.com, http://www.junglee.com) What are your best prices for each of these items? What are the implications of this search capability for the pricing of goods and services in the future?

CHAPTER CASE

Dell Computers: Starting a Price War

Dell Computer Corporation is world-renowned for its business model and is creating a pricing firestorm in the personal computer industry. This case asks you to evaluate this decision and then provides you with a hindsight view. So, we ask you to look back to 2001. First, some background on the company.

Dell's business model is a "direct-sales" model in which it designs, manufactures, and customizes goods and services to customer requirements, and offers an extensive selection of software and peripherals. Business customers or consumers order their computers directly from the company via catalogs, phone, or the Web. The company is an assembler. It keeps a small inventory of component parts but relies on close relationships with suppliers that provide real-time order-supply capability. Its expertise is in developing systems and technology that allow it to take a customer's order and assemble and ship a made-to-spec product within a few days.

What are the key elements of Dell's business model and what do they have to do with pricing? There are three key themes: cost, flexibility, and competitive position.

Cost

Dell's business model affords it the lowest-cost position in the market. One story holds that Michael Dell gave a hard time to a supplier who brought cinnamon rolls to a meeting with Dell employees, telling the supplier that he ought to save the money to keep his own prices down. The direct-sales model eliminates the costs of dealing with retailers and is based on a quick turnover of inventory. At one point of comparison, Dell's inventory was turning over 79.7 times per year, compared to 23.9 for Compaq, 30.5 for Gateway, and 8.6 for Hewlett-Packard. The Wall Street Journal reports that Dell's overhead costs were just 11.5% of every sales dollar in 2001, versus an average of 19.8% for these other competitors. Dell has no retailers to deal with and has developed a forecasting system and information-sharing routines (with suppliers) that allow a careful focus on current and future costs. The company constantly focuses everyone's attention on "how can we drive down costs to allow lower prices?" Dell could immediately capitalize on the cost savings and pass on the savings to their customers.

High inventory turnover has had a significant impact on Dell's cash management. Since 1999, Dell has improved its accounts receivable from 36 to 32 days, while simultaneously extending its account payable aging from 54 to 58 days. Meanwhile, inventory-supply days were reduced from six to five. As a result, Dell enjoys a "negative cash conversion cycle." In other words, Dell gets paid for products it ships before having to pay for its component costs. In 2001, Dell's cash-conversion cycle improved to a negative 21 days from a negative 18 days in fiscal year 2000, and that number has improved significantly since then.

Flexibility

The real-time cost-information systems that the company has developed, along with its close supplier relationships, has produced great flexibility in Dell's ability to adjust prices in response to changes in costs and customer demand. The company is pushing hard to adapt quickly to changes in costs, passing them along in the form of lower prices to customers. In fact, prices are so flexible that you can often find the same product at different prices on Dell's own Web site! One story holds that a Dell phone sales rep in the past year actually quoted a PC price $50 lower than the price that had been advertised in The New York Times that morning.

Competitive Position

Dell is the industry's cost leader. The innovative dimensions of its business model are the source of its strong competitive position. The cost-leader position creates a very clear advantage—you can withstand a price war longer than your competitors because you have a lower cost floor.

Dell also applies this basic business model to other product lines. Other related product lines include servers and storage products, the prices of which are also being driven down over time.

Price Aggression

Dell's strategy is collapsing profit margins throughout the PC market, a dire development for rivals who can't keep up. Dell is pricing its machines not so much like lucrative high-tech products, but more like airline tickets and other low-margin commodities. (The Wall Street Journal, 8 June 2001)

In late 2000, Dell began reducing prices by as much as 20%, aiming to take sales away from competitors. By summer 2001, Dell's average PC price had fallen to $1,850 from the average price of $2,256 a year before. Dell's gross margin on PCs dropped to 17.5% of sales in 2001, from 21.4% the year before.

As a result, in what had been a soft market, shipments for the industry grew by 852,000 units to 31.6 million in the first quarter of 2001. Dell's shipments grew by 957,000 units. During that year, Dell was poised to earn more than $1.7 billion, accounting for almost every dollar of profit among makers of Windows–based PCs.

Dell has continued to maintain price pressure on the industry.

During 2001 and especially after the events of September 11, the world economy suffered a severe downturn. Global PC unit sales declined to 125 million in 2001 from what had been 130 million the year before. Amazingly, during that year, Dell's global market share grew from 10% in fiscal year 2000 to 13% in 2001. In addition, Dell's U.S. total market share grew from 6.8% in 1996 to 24.5% in 2001.

In spite of these positive effects on market share, Dell's price-cutting strategy flies in the face of the conventional wisdom of how a firm should compete in a mature market. That wisdom holds that price-cutting simply lowers margins for all players in the industry, leaving everyone less profitable. In fact, Dell has been called "irrational" by some analysts and competitors. Roger Kay, director of PC hardware at International Data Corp., a research firm, summed up that point of view in *Chief Executive* magazine:

A lot of people are scratching their heads, saying they don't know why Dell is doing what they're doing. Start-ing a price war hurts everyone else, but it doesn't help them much. They can't hope to come out a monopoly.

Case Questions

1. Do you agree or disagree with Dell's aggressive pricing strategy? What are the arguments for and against this strategy? (Issues to think about include competitive strategy position, consistency with Dell's business model, industry/competitive environment, customer expectations, and profitability.)

2. When overall growth in the combined PC market had slowed substantially, how did Dell's sales go up in the first quarter of 2001 by more than total industry sales?

Sources: "Disclosure's SEC Data Bases," *Pirahana Web* (Thomson Financial).

Gary McWilliams, "Dell Fine-Tunes Its PC Pricing to Gain an Edge in Slow Market," *The Wall Street Journal* (8 June 2001), A1.

"As More Buyers Suffer from Upgrade Fatigue, PC Sales are Falling," *The Wall Street Journal* (24 August 2001), A1.

Chris Kraeuter, "Dell Dips with Market Despite Results," http://www.cbs.marketwatch.com (15 February 2002).

J. William Gurley, "Why Dell's Wart Isn't Dumb," *Fortune* (7 July 2001), 134.

Bob Brewin, "Top PC Makers Preparing for Price War, *Computerworld* (14 May 2001), 25.

http://www.moneycentral.msn.com.

VIDEO CASE

Learjet Takes Off with Shared Ownership

Bombardier Aerospace would be happy to sell you a sleek little Learjet so you can hop from customer to customer over a wide geographic area with ease and style. If you don't have $10 million, but can come up with $1 million, Bombardier can still accommodate you. Here's how.

In 1994, Bombardier built about 60 jets; five years later, it turned out 183. And while there is now more demand for these aircraft, industry executives also claim they are building better planes, so that increased quality is also increasing demand. But Bombardier and other manufacturers have figured out a way to increase demand even further by spreading the price of a single plane among several owners. Called fractional ownership, the pricing program works like this: A business customer buys a share of a Learjet; a share of the Model 60 would be about $1.4 million, with $300,000 a year in operating costs. The share comes with a guaranteed 100 hours of annual flying time. Bombardier maintains a fleet of 83 Learjets ready at all times so that each customer has access to a plane within 10 hours of a request. Since the $10-million price tag for a jet and roughly $1 million annually in running costs is more than many small businesses can afford—not to mention the fact that they are paying for the plane's down time—fractional owner-ship is becoming increasingly popular. When the fractional ownership business began in 1993, the aircraft industry sold three planes for this purpose. In 1999, more than 90 planes were sold into fractional-ownership programs. "There is no sign of it leveling off in the next few years," predicts John Lawson, sales president of Bombardier.

Bombardier is also looking at other ways to manage the pricing function of its Learjets by managing supply-chain costs. Recently, the company signed a contract with Optum, Inc. for Optum's supply-chain software to improve logistics at Learjet's manufacturing facility in Wichita, Kansas. Optum's warehouse management software (WMS) will help Learjet manage its aircraft-inventory levels as well as improve its receiving and shipping processes. The distribution software is intended to help Learjet track shipping in real time as well as detail individual aircraft parts as they move from the warehouse stock room to the assembly floor. Better logistics efficiency should help the company reduce the time it takes to assemble or repair an aircraft, reduce the cost of mistakes, and increase customer satisfaction. "Bombardier is looking to leverage supply-chain automation and real-time inventory visibility to improve our manufacturing and service operations, and work more quickly and profitably," explains Alan Young, director of work and material planning for Bombardier Aerospace in Wichita. If the company can build more planes, more quickly—and reduce turnaround time on repairs—then it has the freedom to either invest the savings elsewhere in the business or reduce the price of the Learjet.

If you purchase a Learjet, what benefits do your millions buy you? First, Learjet offers what it calls a "strong warranty," which includes five years on major parts like airframe and structure and two years on smaller parts like windshields and paint. Second, the company offers several maintenance programs and says that operating costs are predictable because of the reliability of the plane's parts. Finally, there is a guaranteed trade-in-value program. Of course, availability of some of these programs vary between outright ownership and fractional ownership, but Bombardier remains committed to customer support for all of its Learjets. "Our mission is to provide the finest support in the industry by understanding and fulfilling customer needs," notes the company Web site. That's a lofty goal, at any price.

Case Questions

1. If Bombardier could reduce its manufacturing and distribution costs and thus reduce the price of a Learjet, do you think that more or fewer of the planes would sell? Why?

2. Can you think of another high-priced product that would benefit from a fractional ownership program (excluding time-share condominiums)? Describe your idea.

3. Visit the Learjet Web site at http://www.learjet.com and browse through the sections on Business Aircraft for some of the Learjet models, including the Ownership link, which provides information on operating cost, maintenance programs, and warranties. Does Bombardier appear to be practicing product-line pricing with its Learjets? Why or why not?

Sources: Bombardier Web site, http://www.learjet.com, accessed 16 March 2000; "Learjet Flies High With Optum Supply Chain Software," *PR Newswire,* 6 March 2000.
    "Heady Days for Bizjet Makers," *Reuters Company News,* Reuters Limited, 27 February 2000.
    "Bombardier Aerospace Enjoys Record Growth in Asia-Pacific and Continues to Invest in Strategic Partnerships," *PR Newswire,* 22 February 2000.
    "Bombardier Provides an Update on Its Deliveries and Backlogs," *Business-Wire,* 16 February 2000.

Marketing Arithmetic

LEARNING OBJECTIVES

After you have completed this appendix, you should be able to:

1. *Understand and interpret the components of an income statement.*

2. *Determine the productivity of investments by using the return-on-investment percentage.*

3. *Develop a strategic profit model that analyzes marketing performance by looking at the relationships among net profit, asset turnover, and financial leverage.*

4. *Calculate the break-even point and determine the sales units, sales dollars (price), profit units, and market share needed to break even and/or meet specific objectives.*

5. *Determine cost per thousand (CPM) of an advertising medium, and choose the medium that produces the greatest exposure of a company's message for the lowest cost.*

6. *Calculate the lifetime value of a customer.*

7. *Ascertain the amount that should be profitably spent to acquire new customers.*

Marketing strategy is influenced and constrained by available resources. A firm's resources include finances, technological and production capabilities, managerial talent, and so on. Resource constraints prevent marketing managers from pursuing every available opportunity. For example, the return on investment from previous plant expansion may limit investments in future expansion; financial restrictions can prevent a firm from running a prime-time television campaign for a new product introduction, but it may be able to afford a national radio campaign instead; and/or additional investments in enhancing customer satisfaction may be warranted, since past investments have paid off handsomely.

The bottom line is that successful businesses quantify their actions through the use of financial analyses. This appendix provides examples of just a few of the helpful financial analyses that are available to help marketing managers make informed decisions. If a firm is fully aware of its financial position, marketing strategies can be developed and opportunities pursued that *are* within the company's limits and therefore have the company's best interest at heart.

Income Statement

1 LEARNING OBJECTIVE

The **income statement** is a financial tool used to determine how much income is available for marketing and other operations.

Applications in Marketing

The income statement is used in marketing to:

1. Summarize the revenue generated by the marketer and the amount he spent to generate the revenue.
2. Show the marketer how well he is doing in terms of profit and customer satisfaction.
3. Identify which marketing activities are generating the most revenue and profit.
4. Guide the marketer in evaluating the success of the enterprise.

Example

On December 30, 2003, Greenstown Sheet Metal Inc.'s owner, Mrs. Thomas, was considering whether to expand her business to the northwestern part of the state. The company deals in preengineered metal buildings, construction services, metal roofing, and wall panels. Northwest North Carolina had witnessed a rapid increase in both residents and businesses in the past four years. A successful retail expansion required at least $150,000. Mrs. Thomas needed to know how much money to borrow from the bank to add to the company's annual profit to complete the expansion. The financial record for 2003 showed the following:

1. Gross sales = $393,671
2. Returns and allowances = $16,300
3. Cost of goods sold = $213,255
4. Operating expenses = $118,088
5. Profit from the lease of a parking lot = $740
6. Earned bank interest = $3,377
7. Corporate income tax = 35%

Mrs. Thomas used the company's financial statement to set up the following income statement.

Greenstown Sheet Metal
Income Statement

		Percentage
Gross Sales	$393,671	
Return and allowance	−$16,300	
Net Sales	$377,371	100.0%
Cost of goods sold	−$213,255	56.5%
Gross Margin	$164,116	43.5%
Operating expenses	−$118,088	31.3%
Operating Profit	$46,028	12.2%
(Plus) other income	$4,177	1.1%
Profit Before Taxes	$50,205	13.3%
Income Tax Expense (35% of profit before taxes)	−$17,572	
Net Income	$32,633	8.6%

Interpretation of the Results

1. Greenstown Sheet Metal had a cost of goods sold of 56% of sales.
2. The company had operating expenses of 31.3% of sales.
3. The net profit before tax is $50,205, or 13.3% of sales.
4. The net income is $32,633, or 8.6% of sales.
5. Mrs. Thomas had to seek a loan for $117,367 ($150,000-$32,633).

Calculation Steps

1. Determine the gross sales for the year.
2. Subtract the returns and allowances from gross sales to find the net sales.
3. Subtract the cost of goods sold from the net sales to find the gross margin.
4. Subtract the operating expenses from the gross margin to find the operating profit.
5. Add other incomes to the operating income to find the profit before taxes.
6. Multiply the profit before taxes by the income tax percentage to find the income tax expense.
7. Subtract the income tax expense from the profit before taxes to find the net income or the "bottom line."
8. Find out the percentage make-up of each item in net sales by dividing the item by net sales and multiplying by 100.
9. Determine the amount of the loan by subtracting the net income from the required loan amount.

Return on Investment

The **return on investment (ROI)** is the percentage of the dollar profit generated by each dollar invested in the business.

Applications in Marketing

Return on investment is used to:

1. Measure the productivity of new market areas and new accounts or market investment by looking at sales output and the cost of sales.
2. Measure how efficient salespeople are.

Example

American Plumbing Supplies Inc. makes porcelain toilet bowls, seats, and toilet paper holders. The company is located in Freetown, NC. It sells to wholesalers that resell to retailers. In 2002, American Plumbing Supplies invested $9.4 million to build two additional production plants in Michigan and California. In 2003, sales from the two plants totaled $3,151,211, with total expenses of $952,451. As usual, the company wanted to know the return on investment for the year in order to decide whether to continue the expansion. It did the following.

American Plumbing Supplies Inc.

Return on Investment (%)

$$\text{Return on Investment (\%)} = \frac{\text{Profit before taxes} \times 100}{\text{Investment}}$$

$$= \frac{\$2,198,760}{\$9,400,000} \times 100 = 23.39\%$$

Interpretation of the Results

1. American Plumbing Supplies Inc. had a 23.39% return on investment in 2003.
2. America Plumbing Supplies made approximately 23 cents for every $1 sales it invested in 2002.

Calculation Steps

1. Find the profit before taxes by subtracting total expenses from total sales.
2. Divide the profit before taxes by the total investment and multiply by 100.

Strategic Profit Model

The **strategic profit model** is a technique that shows the mathematical relationship among net profit, asset turnover, and financial leverage.

Applications in Marketing

The strategic profit model provides a marketer with a performance measure termed return on net worth that is used to plan and control assets.

Example

Lagos Refrigeration Services Inc. sells, installs, and services commercial and industrial ice machines, coolers, and freezers. Located in Los Angeles, CA, the company serves more than 60% of the city's institutional and commercial refrigerator users, such as restaurants, convenience stores, offices, schools, and churches.

The economy of scale that results from its large customer base gives Lagos Refrigeration Services the advantage of low prices and high sales. Net sales in 2003 were $11.4 million, and net profit was $6.1 million. The company invested a part of this profit to acquire assets, as it has done since it began in 1968. It now owns about $82 million in assets, with a total liability of $28 million. Lagos Refrigeration Services needed to know how much to manipulate the market to achieve desired success levels. For example, how much increase in the return on net worth would result from a given amount of increase or decrease in the net profit margin, or asset turnover, or financial leverage? It calculated this by using the strategic profit model as shown below.

Lagos Refrigeration Services

Strategic Profit Model

$$\text{Return on net worth (RONW)} = \text{Net Profit Margin} \times \text{Asset Turnover} \times \text{Financial Leverage}$$

$$\text{RONW} = \frac{\text{Net Profit}}{\text{Net Sales}} \times \frac{\text{Net Sales}}{\text{Total Assets}} \times \frac{\text{Total Assets}}{\text{Net Worth}}$$

$$\text{RONW} = \frac{\$6,100,000}{\$11,400,000} \times \frac{\$11,400,000}{\$82,000,000} \times \frac{\$82,000,000}{\$54,000,000}$$

$$\text{RONW} = .5351 \times .1390 \times 1.519$$
$$\text{RONW} = .1130 \text{ or } 11.30\%$$

To increase the RONW to 18.30% by using the net profit margin

Furthermore, Lagos Refrigeration Services wanted to increase the return on net worth by 7%, to 18.30%. It needed to know how much to increase the net profit margin in order to achieve an 18.30% return on net worth. It calculated it as follows.

$$\textbf{RONW} = \frac{\$9,878,950}{\$11,400,000} \times \frac{\$11,400,000}{\$82,000,000} \times \frac{\$82,000,000}{\$54,000,000}$$

$$= .8666 \times .1390 \times 1.519$$

$$= .1830 \text{ or } 18.30\%$$

Thomas Electronics Purchase History for 2003

Customer Lifetime Value

# of repeat purchases	×	% of your customers (in decimals)	=	Weighted average customer
0		.19		0.00
1		.23		.23
2		.20		.40
3		.14		.42
4		.05		.20
5		.12		.60
6		.07		.42
		1.00		2.27

Lifetime Value of Customer = (Average number of repeats × Average sales × Average variable-contribution margin) + Variable-contribution margin on initial sale.

$$= (2.27 \times \$120 \times .60) + \$66 = \$229.44$$

Interpretation of the Results

The lifetime value of each customer in 2003 was \$229.44. This was far above the \$56.40 it costs to attract one new customer.

Calculation Steps

1. Based on historical purchase data, group customers according to the number of times they make repeat purchases and calculate the percentage of repurchase by customers in each group.
2. Add the percentage of repurchase in decimals by all segments to make sure it totals 1.0.
3. Calculate the weighted average of each segment by multiplying the number of repeat purchases by the percentage of repurchase customers in decimals. Add all the segments' weighted averages.
4. Multiply the average number of repeat purchases by the average sales and the average variable-contribution margin. Add this to the variable-contribution margin on initial sales to get the lifetime value of the customer.

Profit Impact of Customer Satisfaction

7 LEARNING OBJECTIVE

The **profit impact of customer satisfaction** is the relationship between the increase or decrease in the type and amount of customer service and the change in profit.

Applications in Marketing

Calculating the profit impact on customer satisfaction helps to:

1. Determine when the right decision is made in future customer-service efforts.
2. Know how much to spend on customer service.

Example

Unique Web Works Inc. started in May 2000. The company designs and develops Web sites, and offers online marketing support to businesses. In December 2000, Unique Web Works surveyed its customers to measure the level of their satisfaction with the company's offerings and services. The research showed that 65% of the

100,000 existing customers were first-time buyers. Forty-five percent of the first-time buyers were satisfied. Based on customer tracking, Unique Web Works sensed that 33% of the satisfied customers would return on an average of three times in a year. The variable-contribution margin (sales minus variable cost divided by units sold) per customer was $500. Unique Web Works believed that spending $1.4 million to improve equipment and technical service would result in an increase in the number of total customers by 10% and increase satisfied first-time customers to 55% in 2003. The company wanted to know how much impact this increase in first-time and first-time satisfied customers would have on future profit. It did the following.

Unique Web Works Inc.

Profit Impact on Customer Satisfaction

	2000 Actual	2001 Target
1. Total buyers	100,000	110,000
2. Multiplied by % of 1st time buyers	x 65%	x 65%
3. Total # of new buyers	65,000	71,500
4. Multiplied by % of satisfied buyers	x 45%	x 55%
5. Total satisfied new buyers (accounts)	29,250	39,325
6. Multiplied by probability of repeat purchase	x 33%	x 33%
7. Expected number of repeaters	9,652.5	12,977
8. Multiplied by average number of repeat visits	x 3	x 3
9. Total number of visits	28,957.5	38,931
10. Multiplied by unit contribution margin ($500)	$14,478,750	$19,465,500
11. Expected increased contribution from improved customer satisfaction ($19,465,500 –$14,478,750)		$4,986,750
12. Expenses to improve equipment & services		1,400,000
13. Net gain in contribution (11–12)		$3,586,750

Interpretation of the Results

Unique Web Works would generate $3,586,750 in future contribution to profit if it improved the number of total customers by 10% and increased satisfied first-time customers to 55% in 2003.

Calculation Steps

1. Determine the total number of buyers from the sales records.
2. Multiply #1 by the percentage of first-time buyers to find the total number of new buyers.
3. Multiply #3 by the percentage of satisfied buyers to find the total number of satisfied new buyers (accounts).
4. Multiply #5 by the probability of repeat purchases to find the expected number of repeat customers.
5. Multiply #7 by the average number of repeat visits and the variable-contribution margin to find the increase in the contribution from repeat purchases by first-time customers.
6. Subtract the actual increase in the contribution from repeat purchases by first-time customers from the resulting future increase to find the expected increased contribution from improved customer satisfaction.
7. To find the net gain in contributions, subtract the expenses to improve equipment and service from the expected increased contribution from improved customer satisfaction.

Marketing Arithmetic Exercises

Income Statement

Develop an income statement for Jim's Food Store based on the following:

1. Gross sales $4,000,000
2. Cost of goods sold $2,010,000
3. Other income $123,000
4. Returns and allowance $14,000
5. Income tax 35%
6. Operating expenses $35,000

Return on Investment

Cooper Tire Company manufacturers and sells tires to wholesalers that resell the tires to retailers. In 2002, Cooper Tire invested $50 million to build a new manufacturing plant. In 2003, sales from the new plant totaled $15,750,000 and total expenses amounted to $1,952,000. Calculate the return on investment for 2003.

Strategic Profit Model

In 2003, Jimboy Computers, a computer retailer, wanted to know how it had performed after completing the first year of a strategic marketing plan. Net sales were $1.8 million and net profit was $895,100. Total assets were $3.9 million and total liability was $1.2 million.

- What is the net profit?
- Calculate the profit margin.
- Calculate the asset turnover.
- Calculate the financial leverage.
- Calculate the return on net worth.

Break-Even Point

In the city of Johnstown, 120,000 cars were repaired in 2003. Mr. Baker started a car repair shop during the year and by the end of the year had a total fixed cost of $75,000, a variable cost of $100 per car, and an average repair price of $750. Mr. Baker wanted to make a profit of $10,000.

- How many cars will Mr. Baker need to repair to cover his costs or break even?
- What amount of money does he need to make to break even?
- How many cars would Mr. Baker need to repair to make a $10,000 profit?
- What market share is needed to break even and make $10,000 in profit?

Cost per Thousand (CPM)

- What is the cost per thousand (CPM)?
- Calculate CPM for a radio advertisement that costs $1,230 to reach 568,700 people.
- Calculate CPM for a television advertisement that costs $5,500 to reach 3,000,000 people.

Lifetime Value of a Customer

Destin Seafood Inc. had 300 customers during 2003. The average customer made 3.33 repeat purchases (0=.29; 1=.38; 2=.20; 3=.32; 4=.12; 5=.09; 6=.11), with an average buy of $250. The average-contribution margin was .39. The variable-contribution margin on the initial sales was $71. The company spent $40,000 in promotion for a total acquisition cost of $133 ($40,000/300). What was the lifetime value for each customer?

Profit Impact on Customer Satisfaction

A firm needed to increase its market share by improving customer satisfaction. It had 6,000 customers. Forty percent of the customers were first-time buyers. Sixty percent of the first-time buyers were satisfied. Eighty percent of the satisfied first-time buyers repurchased by visiting the store four times a year. The variable-contribution margin (sales minus variable costs/units sold) per customer is $350. Suppose that the firm planned to spend $10,000 to improve its total customer base by 5% and satisfied first-time buyers to 65%. What would be the net contribution of the first-time buyers to profit?

Answers to Questions and Problems

Income Statement

		Percentage
Gross Sales	$4,000,000	
Return and allowance	−$14,000.00	
Net Sales	$3,986,000	100%
Cost of goods sold	−$2, 010,000	50.4%
Gross Margin	$1,976,000	49.5%
Operating expenses	−$35,000.00	.88%
Operating Profit	$1, 941,000	48.7%
(Plus) other income	$123,000	3.1%
Profit Before Taxes	$2,064,000	51.8%
Income Tax Expense		
(35% of profit before taxes)	−$722,400	
Net Income	$1,341,600	33.7%

Return on Investment

$$\frac{\text{Net profit before taxes}}{\text{Investment}} \times 100 = \frac{15,750,000\text{–}1,952,000}{50,000,000} \times 100 = 27.5\%$$

Strategic Profit Model

Net profit	Profit margin	Asset turnover	Financial leverage
	$895,100	$1,800,000	$3,900,000
=$895,100	$1,800,000	$3,900,000	$2,700,000
	= .4972	= .4615	= 1.444

Return on net worth
$.4972 \times .4615 \times 1.444 = 33.13\%$

Break-Even Point

BEP (unit sales)	BEP (sales dollars)	BEP (profit)	BEP (market share)
$\dfrac{\$75,000}{750\text{–}100}$	115 cars × $750	$\dfrac{\$75,000 + \$10,000}{750\text{–}100}$	$\dfrac{131 \text{ cars}}{120,000 \text{ cars}} \times 100$
= 115 cars	= $86,250	= 131 cars	= .11%

Cost Per Thousand

$$\text{CPM radio} = \frac{1,230 \times 1,000}{568,700} = \$2.16 \text{ per thousand}$$

$$\text{CPM TV} = \frac{5,500 \times 1,000}{3,000,000} = \$1.83 \text{ per thousand}$$

Lifetime Value of a Customer

$$(3.33 \times \$250 \times .39) + \$71 = \$395.68$$

Profit Impact on Customer Satisfaction

		Actual	Target
1.	Total buyers	6,000	6,300
2.	Multiplied by % of 1st time buyers	× 40%	× 40%
3.	Total # of new buyers	2,400	2,520
4.	Multiplied by % of satisfied buyers	× 60%	× 65%
5.	Total satisfied new buyers (accounts)	1,440	1,638
6.	Multiplied by probability of repeat purchase	× 80%	× 80%
7.	Expected number of repeaters	1,152	1,310.40
8.	Multiplied by average number of repeat visits	× 4	× 4
9.	Total number of visits	4,608	5,241.60
10.	Multiplied by unit contribution margin ($350)	$1,612,800	$1,834,560
11.	Expected increased contribution from improved customer satisfaction ($1,834,560–$1,612,800)		$221,760
12.	Expenses to improve equipment and services		$10,000
13.	Net gain in contribution (11–12)		$211,760

Glossary

A

Advertising is *nonpersonal* communication that is paid for by an identified sponsor, and involves either *mass communication* via newspapers, magazines, radio, television, and other media (e.g., billboards, bus stop signage) or *direct-to-consumer communication* via postal or electronic mail.

Agent is a marketing intermediary that does not take title to products, but instead develops marketing strategy and establishes contacts abroad.

Agents/brokers are independent middlemen who bring buyers and sellers together, provide market information to one or both parties, but never take title to the merchandise. While most agents/brokers work for the seller, some work for buyers.

Alternative-evaluation is the stage in the consumer buying-decision process when consumers select one of several alternatives (brands, dealers, and so on) available to them.

Anchor stores are dominant, large-scale stores that are expected to draw customers to a shopping center.

Antidumping laws are designed to help domestic industries injured by unfair competition from abroad due to imports being sold at less than fair value.

Attitudes are learned predispositions to respond to an object or class of objects in a consistently favorable or unfavorable way.

B

Balanced tenancy occurs where the stores in a shopping center complement each other in merchandise offerings.

Behavior or usage segmentation is the segmentation of markets based on usage patterns, such as heavy users, medium users, and light users, or loyalty toward a product, or the way in which a customer uses a product.

Benefits-sought segmentation is the segmentation of markets based on consumer preference for a specific product attribute or characteristic.

Brand equity is the marketplace value of a brand based on reputation and goodwill.

Brands are the name, representative symbol or design, or any other feature that identifies one firm's product as distinct from another firm's. Trademark is the legal term for a brand. Brands may be associated with one product, a family of products, or with all of the products sold by a firm.

Break-even analysis (BEA) is an analysis technique that literally means "to have zero profit." It is that point at which total cost and total revenue are equal.

Build strategy refers to the resource allocation strategy for which the goal is to improve the SBU's current position in the marketplace.

Business market consists of all organizations that buy goods and services for incorporation into other goods for consumption, use, or resale.

Business-to-business customers are defined as customers who resell the product, customers who use products as component parts for the production of finished products, and customers who are final users of products in their daily business operations.

Buyers are the consumers who actually purchase the product.

Buying center consists of those individuals who participate in the purchasing decision and who share the goals and risks arising from the decision.

C

Cartel is an organization of firms in an industry where the central organization makes certain management decisions and carries out certain functions (often regarding pricing, outputs, sales, advertising, and distribution) that would otherwise be performed by the individual firms.

Cash cows are SBUs that enjoy high market share but undergo low levels of market growth.

Categorical imperative asks whether the proposed action would be ethical and right if everyone did it.

Category killers get their name from their marketing strategy of carrying such a large amount of merchandise in a single category at such good prices that they make it impossible for customers to walk out without purchasing what they need, thus "killing" the competition.

Category management is a process of managing and planning all SKUs in a product category as a distinct business.

Causal research also known as cause-and-effect studies, is used when the research question specifically hypothesizes that X "causes" Y.

Cause-related marketing (CRM) is a form of corporate philanthropy that links a company's contributions (usually monetary) to a predesignated worthy cause with purchasing behavior of consumers. Cause-related marketing is an activity that governments, public service organizations, companies, and individuals undertake to encourage target customer participation in socially redeeming programs.

Change agent is a person or institution that facilitates change in a firm or in a host country.

Channel intensity refers to the number of intermediaries at each level of the marketing channel.

Channel length is the number of levels in a marketing channel.

Channel strategy is the broad set of principles by which a firm seeks to achieve its distribution objectives to satisfy its customers.

Channel structure consists of all of the businesses and institutions (including producers or manufacturers and final customers) who are involved in performing the functions of buying, selling, or transferring title.

Cluster samples are probability samples where researchers randomly choose geographic clusters and then randomly select samples within the clusters.

Code law is based on a comprehensive set of written statutes.

Coding is categorizing customers based on how profitable their past business has been.

Cold calls mean contacting prospective customers without a prior appointment.

Commercial enterprises are the sector of the business market represented by manufacturers, construction companies, service firms, transportation companies, professional groups, and resellers that purchase goods and services.

Common law is based on tradition and depends less on written statutes and codes than on precedent and custom.

Competitively advantaged product is a product that solves a set of customer problems better than any competitor's product. This product is made possible due to this firm's unique technical, manufacturing, managerial, or marketing capabilities, which are not easily copied by others.

Complementary marketing is a contractual arrangement where participating parties carry out different but complementary activities.

Concentrated strategy is the target-marketing strategy where only one marketing mix is developed and directed toward one market segment.

Concentration strategy is the market-development strategy that involves focusing expansion on a smaller number of markets.

Concept is a written description or visual depiction of a new product idea. A concept includes the product's primary features and benefits.

Conflict in marketing channels occurs when one channel member believes that another channel member is impeding the attainment of its goals.

Conquest marketing is a strategy for constantly seeking new customers by offering discounts and markdowns and developing promotions that encourage new business.

Consultative selling is the process of helping customers reach their strategic goals by using the products and expertise of the sales organization.

Consumer behavior is the process by which individuals or groups select, use, or dispose of goods, services, ideas, or experiences to satisfy needs and wants.

Consumer buying-decision process typically involves whether to purchase, what to purchase, when to purchase, from whom to purchase, and how to pay for a purchase.

Consumer promotions are directed at end users rather than at the trade. These promotions include sampling; couponing; refunding; rebating; and offering premiums, sweepstakes, and contests.

Contract manufacturing is using another firm to manufacture goods so that the marketer may concentrate on research and development, as well as the marketing, aspects of the operation.

Convenience sample is a sample of consumers who are not randomly sampled from a population (e.g., users of the product) but who are readily available.

Coordinated marketing effort represents the business mindset that adopting and implementing a market orientation should not be the sole responsibility of the marketing department.

Core benefit proposition (CBP) is the primary benefit or purpose for which a customer buys a product. The CBP may reside in the physical good or service performance, or it may come from augmented dimensions of the product.

Corporate sponsorships involve investments in *events* or *causes* to achieve various corporate objectives, such as increasing sales volume, enhancing a company's reputation or a brand's image, and increasing brand awareness.

Cost per thousand (CPM) is calculated by dividing the cost of an ad placed in a particular ad vehicle (e.g., certain magazine) by the number of people (expressed in thousands) who are exposed to that vehicle.

Customer focus pertains to obtaining information about customer needs and wants and then providing products that address these needs and wants.

Customer prototypes are the detailed pictures and descriptions of individuals or firms in the target market for a product. Creating these descriptions helps firms envision how products and the marketing mix might best be combined to maximize profits.

Customer relationship management (CRM) is the process of identifying, attracting, differentiating, and retaining customers.

Customer retention refers to focusing a firm's marketing efforts toward the existing customer base.

Customer satisfaction is a short-term, transaction-specific measure of whether customer perceptions meet or exceed customer expectations.

Customer-oriented means the salesperson seeks to elicit customer needs/problems and then takes the necessary steps to meet those needs or solve the problem in a manner that is in the best interest of the customer.

Customer-relationship management is the process of identifying, attracting, differentiating, and retaining customers.

D

Data mining is a technique of exploring data for patterns.

Database marketing involves collecting and electronically storing (in a database) information about present, past, and prospective customers.

Decision-support system (DSS) is a set of computer software programs built into a user-friendly interface package, such as Windows, that helps a manager make marketing-mix decisions.

Degree of individualism is the extent to which individual interests prevail over group interests.

Demand schedules provide a systematic look at the relationship between price and quantity sold.

Demand-side market failure is the cumulative effect of the marketing practices of many thousands of advertising campaigns, which has a residual negative impact on the values of buyers and the demand for various products (e.g., voting).

Demographic segmentation is the division of groups of consumers into segments based on demographic characteristics such as age, income, gender, ethnic background, and occupation.

Derived demand is the direct link between the demand for an industrial product and the demand for consumer products.

Descriptive research also known as survey research, is characterized by a more formal research process of exploration and is typically used for product-usage and customer-satisfaction research.

Differentiated strategy is the target-marketing strategy where a firm develops different marketing-mix plans specially tailored for each market segment.

Discrepancies between production and consumption are differences in quantity, assortment, time, and place that must be overcome to make goods available to final customers.

Displacement is the act of moving employment opportunities from the country of origin to host countries.

Distributor is a marketing intermediary that purchases products from the domestic firm and assumes the trading risk.

Diversification strategy is the market-development strategy that involves expansion to a relatively large number of markets.

Diverting occurs when a manufacturer restricts an off-invoice allowance to a limited geographical area, resulting in some wholesalers and retailers buying abnormally large quantities at the deal price and then transshipping the excess quantities to other geographical areas.

Divest strategy refers to the resource allocation strategy where investment in an SBU is discontinued.

Dogs are SBUs characterized by low market shares and low market-growth rates.

E

E-procurement systems enable individual employees to buy online while the company retains control of the entire purchasing process.

Economies of scale and economies of scope are obtained by spreading the costs of distribution over a large quantity of products (scale) or over a wide variety of products (scope).

80/20 principle states that about 20% of a firm's customers are responsible for generating 80% of the firm's revenue.

Elasticity of demand is the relationship between changes in price and quantity sold.

Emotions are strong, relatively uncontrolled feelings that affect our behavior.

Encouraging repeat purchases includes manufacturers' efforts to hold on to their current users by rewarding them for continuing to purchase the promoted brand, or to load them up with the product so they have no need to switch to another brand.

Environmental forces exist outside the walls of the firm, are uncontrollable, and include sociocultural, economic, natural, technological, political, legal, and competitive forces.

Environmental scanning identifies important trends in the environment and considers the potential impact of these changes on the firm's existing marketing strategy.

Ethical vigilance means paying constant attention to whether one's actions are "right" or "wrong," and if ethically "wrong," asking why one is behaving in that manner.

Ethics ombudsman is someone senior in an organization whom managers can go to and know they will receive a sympathetic hearing: someone who can help them with an ethical quandary, take up the concern, and protect the manager (whistle-blower) from any negative repercussions.

European Article Numbering (EAN) is the European version of the Universal Product Code on a product package that provides information read by optical scanners.

Evaluative criteria are specifications that organizational buyers use to compare alternative goods and services.

Event-related marketing is a form of brand promotion that ties a brand to a meaningful cultural, social, athletic, or other type of high-interest public activity.

Everyday Low Pricing (EDLP) refers to the pricing strategy in which a firm charges the same low price every day.

Exchange process takes place when two or more parties give something of value to each other to satisfy perceived needs or wants.

Exclusive distribution occurs when only one intermediary is used at a particular level in the marketing channel.

Exploratory research is appropriate when the research question needs to be further defined and/or if researchers want additional information before they venture into more formal and extensive data-collection procedures.

Export management companies (EMCs) specialize in performing international services as commissioned representatives or as distributors.

Expropriation is a government takeover of a company's operations, frequently at a level lower than the value of the assets.

F

Family life cycle (FLC) is a segmentation variable that incorporates income and lifestyle to explain differences in spending patterns based on family role and transitions among roles.

Features are the way that benefits are delivered to customers. Features provide the solution to customer problems.

Field selling involves calling on prospective customers in either their business or home.

Flows in marketing channels are the movement of products, negotiation, ownership, information, and promotion through each participant in the marketing channel.

Focus group is a carefully recruited group of six to 12 people who participate in a freewheeling, one- to two-hour discussion that focuses on a particular subject, such as product usage, shopping habits, or warranty experiences.

Foreign direct investment is an international entry strategy achieved through the acquisition of foreign firms.

Form utility pertains to the transformation of raw materials and/or labor into a finished product that the consumer desires.

Forward buying or **bridge buying** is when retailers purchase enough product during a manufacturer's off-invoice allowance period to carry the retailers over until the manufacturer's next regularly scheduled deal.

Franchising is a form of licensing that grants a wholesaler or a retailer exclusive rights to sell a product in a specified area.

Free on-board (FOB) pricing leaves the cost and responsibility of transportation to the customer.

Full-service merchant wholesalers provide a wide range of services for retailers and business purchasers.

G

Generating trial purchases refers to inducing nonusers to try a brand for the first time, or encouraging retrial by consumers who have not purchased the brand for an extended period.

Geodemographics is the combination of demographic and geographic segmentation.

Geographic segmentation is the division of groups of consumers into segments based on where those consumers live.

Globalization approach is the approach to international marketing in which differences are incorporated into a regional or global strategy that will allow for differences in implementation.

Goods are objects, devices, or things.

Governmental units comprise the sector of the business market represented by federal, state, and local governmental units that purchase goods and services.

Gray marketing is the marketing of authentic, legally trademarked goods through unauthorized channels.

Gross margin equals net sales minus the cost of goods sold.

Gross margin percentage shows how much gross margin a retailer makes as a percentage of sales.

Gross rating points (GRPs) are the accumulation of rating points, including all vehicles in a media purchase, over the span of a particular campaign.

H

Hands-on consumer research is conducted by managers directly observing the way current customers use specific products and brands. The opposite is arm's-length research, which is undertaken by external suppliers.

Hard selling involves trying every means to get the prospective customer to buy, regardless of whether it is in the prospect's best interest.

Harvest strategy refers to the resource allocation strategy in which an SBU is primarily used to generate resources to fund other SBUs.

Heterogeneity is a distinguishing characteristic of services that reflects the variation in consistency from one service transaction to the next.

Heterogeneous demand occurs when a group of consumers have differing needs from a specific product.

Household consumers are defined as the consuming public.

Household decision making occurs when significant decisions are made by individuals jointly with other members of their household and purchases are made for joint use by the members of the household.

I

Inefficient targeting results when advertising and distribution reach too broad an audience, most of whom are not interested in the product.

Information search is the stage in the consumer buying-decision process when consumers collect information on a select subset of brands.

Inseparability is a distinguishing characteristic of services that reflects the interconnection among the service provider, the customer receiving the service, and other customers sharing the service experience.

Institutional customers comprise the sector of the business market represented by health-care organizations, colleges and universities, libraries, foundations, art galleries, and clinics that purchase goods and services.

Intangibility is a distinguishing characteristic of services that makes them unable to be touched or sensed in the same manner as physical goods.

Integrated marketing communication (IMC) is a system of management and integration of marketing communication elements—advertising, personal selling, publicity, sales promotion, sponsorship marketing, and point-of-purchase communications—with the result that all elements adhere to the same message.

Intensive distribution occurs when all possible intermediaries at a particular level of the channel are used.

International intermediaries are marketing institutions that facilitate the movement of goods and services between the originator and the customer.

International marketing is the process of planning and conducting transactions across national borders to create exchanges that satisfy the objectives of individuals and organizations.

International Organization for Standardization (ISO) is a nongovernmental organization that promotes the development of standardization to facilitate the international exchange of goods and services.

Interorganizational context refers to channel management that extends beyond a firm's own organization into independent businesses.

Inventory turnover refers to the number of times per year, on average, that a firm sells its inventory.

Involvement is a product's degree of personal relevance to a consumer.

J

Job anxiety is tension caused by the pressures of the job (e.g., the salesperson must perform, often simultaneously, many tasks: meeting sales objectives, servicing old accounts and producing new accounts, developing and conducting effective sales presentations, developing product and competitor knowledge, submitting timely reports to the company, and controlling sales expenses).

Joint ventures result from the participation of two or more companies in an enterprise in which each party contributes assets, owns the new entity to some degree, and shares risk.

Judgment sampling refers to a nonprobability sampling technique where the respondent's selection is based on the arbitrary judgment of the researcher.

K

Key buying influentials are those individuals in the buying organization who have the power to influence the buying decision.

L

Leaky bucket theory is traditionally associated with conquest marketing, where new customers replace disloyal customers at the same rate; hence, the firm never grows.

Learning is a change in the content of long-term memory.

Learning-oriented is the trait of being open to and excited about acquiring new knowledge and skills.

Level of equality is the extent to which less powerful members accept that power is distributed unequally.

Licensing agreement is an arrangement in which one firm permits another to use its intellectual property in exchange for compensation, typically a royalty.

Limited-service merchant wholesalers perform only a few services for manufacturers or other customers, or they perform all of them on a more restricted basis than do full-service wholesalers.

Line extensions are new products that are developed as variations of existing products.

Logistical service standards are the kinds of quantifiable distribution services performed by a logistical system to meet customer needs.

Logistics (or physical distribution) is planning, implementing, and controlling the physical flows of materials and final products from points of origin to points of use to meet customers' needs at a profit.

Long-term success focuses on building and maintaining customer relationships that can last a lifetime.

M

Maintain strategy refers to the resource allocation strategy for which the goal is to hold the SBU's current position steady in the marketplace.

Manufacturers' agents are independent middlemen who handle a manufacturer's marketing functions by selling part or all of a manufacturer's product line in an assigned geographic area.

Manufacturers' sales branches are sales outlets owned by the manufacturer.

Marginal costs are the change in a firm's total costs per unit change in its output level.

Marginal revenues are the change in a firm's total revenue per unit change in its sales level.

Market (price) skimming is a strategy of pricing the new product at a relatively high level and then gradually reducing it over time.

Market is any individual, group of individuals, or organization willing and able to purchase a firm's product.

Market development represents the firm's attempt to sell more of its existing products to new markets.

Market penetration represents the firm's attempt to sell more of its existing products to existing markets.

Market research is the process of gathering information pertaining to customers, competitors, channels, and public policy for the purpose of specific decision making.

Market segment is a group of consumers that are alike based on some characteristic(s).

Market segmentation is the process of dividing markets into distinctive groups based on homogeneous (similar) sets of needs.

Market-research process as presented in Figure 5.1, offers a systematic approach to designing, collecting, interpreting, and reporting information that helps marketers explore opportunities and make specific marketing decisions.

Marketing is the process of planning and executing the conception, pricing, promotion, and distribution of ideas, goods, and services to create exchanges that satisfy individual and organizational goals.

Marketing channel is the network of organizations that create time, place, and ownership utilities for household consumers and business customers.

Marketing channel management refers to analyzing, planning, organizing, and controlling a firm's marketing channels.

Marketing channel power is the capacity of one channel member to influence the behavior of another channel member.

Marketing concept promotes the business philosophy of "making what we can sell" and is built upon the three pillars of customer focus, coordinated marketing, and long-term success.

Marketing information systems (MIS) provide organized and continuous data collection and analysis to facilitate ongoing marketing intelligence.

Marketing mix comprises four key areas of decision making—product, place (distribution), promotion, and price—also known as the four Ps.

Marketing network includes the company and its stakeholders, who form mutually profitable business relationships.

Marketing planning has a shorter planning horizon (typically one year) and is performed at the marketing level or product or product-line level of the organization.

Marketing strategy involves: (1) identifying target markets (2) tailoring marketing mixes that meet the needs and wants of each specific target market and (3) developing marketing mixes that reinforce the product's positioning strategy in the marketplace.

Markup laws are state laws that require a certain markup above cost in particular industries to protect consumers and small businesses from predatory pricing.

Material achievement is the extent to which the dominant values in society are success, money, and things.

Media strategy consists of four sets of interrelated activities: (1) selecting the target audience, (2) specifying media objectives, (3) selecting media categories and vehicles, and (4) buying media.

Merchant wholesalers are independent firms that purchase a product from a manufacturer and resell it to other manufacturers, wholesalers, or retailers, but not to the final consumer.

Micromarketing is the process of targeting small, narrowly defined market segments, such as zip codes or even neighborhoods.

Micromarkets are very small market segments, such as zip code areas or even neighborhoods.

Mission statement is a guideline for the organization's decision making for both the short and long run and provides direction to the strategic planning and marketing planning processes.

Modified rebuy is a purchase where the buyers have experience in satisfying the need but feel the situation warrants reevaluation of a limited set of alternatives before making a decision.

Moods are emotions that are less intense and transitory.

Motivating channel members is the action taken by a manufacturer or franchiser to get channel members to implement its channel strategies.

Motivation is the state of drive or arousal that moves us toward a goal-object.

Motivational research is directed at discovering the conscious or subconscious reasons for a person's behavior.

Multidomestic approach is the approach to international marketing whereby local conditions are adapted to in each and every target market.

Multinational corporations are companies that have production operations in at least one country in addition to their domestic base.

N

Needs are unsatisfactory conditions that prompt consumers to an action that will make the conditions better.

New-task buying situation is a purchase situation that results in an extensive search for information and a lengthy decision process.

Niche is a relatively small market segment.

Niche marketing is the process of targeting a small market segment with a specific, specialized marketing mix.

Niche strategy refers to the resource allocation strategy where the scope of the SBU is more narrowly focused on smaller, more well-defined target markets.

Nonresponse error or *participation bias* occurs when a particular customer group is under- or overrepresented in a sample.

O

Off-invoice allowances are deals offered periodically to the trade that allow wholesalers and retailers to simply deduct a fixed amount (e.g., 15%), from the full price at the time the order is placed.

Omnibus surveys refers to the sampling method whereby several firms studying different product markets participate in the same survey.

Operating expenses are the costs a retailer incurs in running a business, other than the cost of merchandise.

Opt-in e-mailing is the practice of marketers asking for and receiving customers' permission to send them messages on particular topics. The customer has agreed, or opted-in, to receive messages on topics of interest rather than receiving messages that are unsolicited.

Order getter is a salesperson who seeks to actively provide information to prospects, persuade prospective customers, and close sales.

Order taker is a salesperson who just processes the purchase the customer has already selected.

Outsourcing is using another firm for the manufacture of needed components or finished goods or delivery of a service.

Ownership utility involves transferring the title for a product from producer to consumer.

P

Partial employees are customers who coproduce their service via a cooperative effort with service providers.

Payers are the consumers who actually pay for the product.

Penetration strategy requires that the firm enter the market at a relatively low price in an attempt to obtain market share and expand demand for its product.

Perception is the process by which an individual senses, organizes, and interprets information received from the environment.

Perceptual map is a commonly used multidimensional scaling method of graphically depicting a product's performance on selected attributes, or the "position" of a product against its competitors on selected product traits.

Perishability is a distinguishing characteristic of services in that they cannot be saved, their unused capacity cannot be reserved, and they cannot be inventoried.

Personal selling is *person-to-person* communication in which a seller informs and educates prospective customers and attempts to influence their purchase choices. Personal selling is direct person-to-person communication designed to explain how an individual's or firm's goods, services, or ideas fit the needs of one or more prospective customers.

Place utility makes the product available where the consumer wants or needs it.

Planned obsolescence is the design of a product with features that the company knows will soon be superseded, thus making the model obsolete.

Polygamous loyalty reflects the notion that customer loyalty tends to be divided among a number of providing firms.

Positioning is the image customers have about a product in relation to the product's competitors.

Positioning statement is the key idea that encapsulates what a brand is intended to stand for in its target market's mind and then consistently delivers the same idea across all media channels.

Postpurchase behavior is the last stage in the consumer buying-decision process, when the consumer experiences an intense need to confirm the wisdom of that decision.

Predatory pricing is a practice where one firm attempts to drive out rivals (usually smaller ones) by pricing at such a low level that the rival cannot make money.

Price is some unit of value given up by one party in return for something from another party.

Price discrimination occurs when a seller offers a lower price to some buyers than it does to other buyers.

Price promotions are short-term price reductions designed to create an incentive for consumers to buy now rather than later and/or stock up on the product.

Price-fixing is a conspiracy to fix competitive prices.

Primary data pertain to the generation of new data collected to address specific market-research problems.

Principle of utility is when "ethical behavior" is the behavior that produces the most good for the most people in a specific situation.

Proactive marketing public relations (proactive MPR) is offensive rather than defensive, and opportunity-seeking rather than problem-solving. The major role of proactive MPR is in the areas of product introductions or product revisions.

Problem children are SBUs that enjoy rapid growth but are characterized by low market shares and poor profit margins.

Problem recognition is a consumer's realization that he or she needs to buy something to get back to a normal state of comfort.

Product concept also known as the better-mouse-trap fallacy, is the belief that customers will favor the best-quality products on the market.

Product development represents the firm's attempt to sell new products to existing markets.

Product diversification represents the firm's attempt to sell new products to new markets.

Product life cycle is the cycle of stages that a product goes through from birth to death: introduction, growth, maturity, and decline.

Product line is the set of products a firm targets to one general market. These products are likely to share some common features and technology characteristics or be complementary products. They also are likely to share several elements of the marketing mix, such as distribution channels.

Product mix is the full set of a firm's products across all markets served.

Product-development process consists of a clearly defined set of tasks and steps that describes the normal means by which product development proceeds. The process outlines the order and sequence of the tasks and indicates who is responsible for each.

Production concept is based on the belief that products that are widely available and affordable will sell themselves.

Products are the set of features, functions, and benefits that customers purchase. Products can be goods, services, people, places, and ideas.

Profile is a detailed picture of a market segment based on multiple segmentation descriptors.

Profit repatriation limitations are restrictions set up by host governments in terms of a company's ability to pay dividends from its operations back to its home base.

Project strategy sometimes called a protocol, is a statement of the attributes the project is expected to have, the market to which it is targeted, and the purpose behind commercializing the product.

Prototype is a product concept in physical form. A prototype may be a full working model that has been produced by hand or a nonworking physical representation of the final product. It is used to gather customer reaction to the physical form (aesthetics and ergonomics) or to initial operating

capability. It is also used in internal performance tests to ensure that performance goals have been met.

Psychographic segmentation is the segmentation of markets by social class, lifestyles, and psychological characteristics, such as attitudes, interests, opinions, and values.

Psychographics are characteristics of individuals that describe them in terms of their psychological and behavioral makeup.

Publicity like advertising, is *nonpersonal* communication to a mass audience, but unlike advertising, publicity is not directly paid for by the company that enjoys the publicity.

Purchase is the stage in the consumer buying-decision process when transaction terms are arranged, ownership title is transferred, the product is paid for, and the consumer takes possession of the product from the seller.

Q

Qualified sales leads are potential customers who have a need for the salesperson's product, the financial means to purchase the product, and the authority to make the buying decision.

Quota samples are nonprobability samples where researchers conveniently match characteristics in the population with quotas to ensure that respondents are not under- or over-represented.

R

Reactive MPR is a form of defensive PR that deals with developments such as product defects or flaws that have negative consequences for the organization. Reactive MPR attempts to repair a company's reputation, prevent market erosion, and regain lost sales.

Reference groups are the formal and informal groups that affect a consumer's purchase decision.

Referrals are obtained by the salesperson asking current customers if they know of someone else, or another company, who might need the salesperson's product.

Reinforcing brand image involves carefully selecting of the right premium object, or appropriate sweepstakes prize, to support a brand's desired image.

Relationship marketing concept seeks to create and sustain mutually satisfying long-term relationships not only with customers but also with other key players, such as employees, suppliers, distributors, retailers, the surrounding community, and society as a whole.

Relationship selling requires the development of a trusting partnership in which the salesperson seeks to provide long-term customer satisfaction by listening, gathering information, educating, and adding value for the customer.

Reliability is a measure of the stability or consistency of customer responses. In other words, a research technique is reliable if it produces almost identical results when the same question is asked again of the same respondents, or when several similar customer questions produce similar customer responses.

Repositioning is the process of creating a new image about an existing product in consumers' minds.

Retail life cycle is a description of competitive development in retailing that assumes that retail institutions pass through an identifiable cycle that includes four distinct stages: (1) introduction, (2) growth, (3) maturity, and (4) decline.

Retail mix is a retailer's combination of merchandise, prices, advertising, location, customer services, selling, and store layout and design that is used to attract customers.

Retailing consists of the final activity and steps needed to place merchandise made elsewhere into the hands of the consumer or to provide services to the consumer.

Return on investment (ROI) is the percentage of the dollar profit generated by each dollar invested in the business.

Reverse auction involves one buyer who invites bids from several prequalified suppliers.

Role ambiguity is anxiety caused by inadequate information about job responsibilities and performance-related goals (e.g., many organizational departments—billing, shipping, production, marketing, and public relations—may influence the salesperson's activities and create uncertainty about what is expected of the salesperson).

Role conflict is the anxiety caused by conflicting job demands (e.g., the firm demands that the salesperson obtain a high price for the firm's product, while the customer demands a low price).

Routing is the process of directing incoming calls to customer-service representatives in a way that ensures that more profitable customers are more likely to receive faster and better customer service.

Royalty is the compensation paid by one firm to another under licensing and franchising agreements.

S

Sales promotion consists of all marketing activities that attempt to stimulate quick buyer action, or, in other words, attempt to promote immediate sales of a product (thereby yielding the name *sales promotion*).

Sales-call anxiety is a fear of negative evaluation and rejection by customers.

Scrambled merchandising is the handling of merchandise lines based solely on the profitability criterion without regard to the consistency of the product or merchandise mix.

Secondary data refers to data that already exist.

Selection criteria are the factors that a firm uses to choose which intermediaries will become members of its marketing channel.

Selective distribution means that a carefully chosen group of intermediaries is used at a particular level in the marketing channel.

Self-concept refers to a person's self-image.

Selling concept promotes the business philosophy of "selling what we make."

Service gap is the gap between customers' expectations of service and their perception of the service actually delivered, which is a function of the knowledge gap, the standards gap, the delivery gap, and the communications gap.

Service quality is an attitude formed by a long-term, overall evaluation of performance.

Service recovery is a firm's reaction to a complaint that results in customer satisfaction and goodwill.

Services are deeds, efforts, or performances.

Servicescape refers to the use of physical evidence to design service environments.

Sharing involves making key customer information accessible to all parts of the organization, and in some cases selling that information to other firms.

Sherman Antitrust Act prohibits any contract, combination, or conspiracy that restrains trade. It was passed by Congress in 1890 in an effort to prevent companies from controlling (monopolizing) an industry.

Shrinkage refers to reduction of merchandise through theft, loss, and/or damage.

Simple random sample is a probability sample where respondents are chosen from a complete list of the population.

Situation segmentation is segmentation of markets based on purchase situation or occasion.

Situational ethics is that societal condition where "right" and "wrong" are determined by the specific situation, rather than by universal moral principles.

SKU is a stock-keeping unit and refers to a distinct merchandise item in the retailer's merchandise assortment.

SMART refers to well-developed organizational objectives that are specific, measurable, achievable, relevant, and time-bound.

Social contract is a philosophical belief that part of the price you pay or what you owe for being able to conduct business in a society and profit from such business is to care about the society and contribute to its betterment.

Social responsibility is the collection of marketing philosophies, policies, procedures, and actions intended primarily to enhance society's welfare.

Societal marketing concept is defined as satisfying customer needs and wants in a manner that is in the best interest of consumers and society-at-large.

Specialization or division of labor occurs when each participant in the marketing channel focuses on performing those activities at which it is most efficient.

Sponsorship marketing is the practice of promoting the interests of a company and its brands by associating the company with a specific *event* (e.g., a golf tournament) or a charitable *cause* (e.g., the Leukemia Society).

Stage-gate™ process is a common new product-development process that divides the repeatable portion of product development into a time-sequenced series of stages, each of which is separated by a management-decision gate.

Standardized approach is the approach to international marketing in which products are marketed with little or no modification.

Stars are SBUs characterized by high market-growth rates and high market shares.

Straight rebuy is routine reordering from the same supplier of a product that has been purchased in the past.

Strategic alliances are informal or formal arrangements between two or more companies with a common business objective.

Strategic business units (SBUs) facilitate planning and have a clear market focus, an identifiable set of competitors, independent management teams, and SBU-specific operational goals.

Strategic planning or the organization's overall game plan, has a longer planning horizon (typically three to five years) than marketing planning and is performed at the corporate and business levels of the organization.

Stratified sample is a probability sample where researchers divide the complete population into groups and then use simple random-sampling techniques on the subgroups.

Suggestion selling occurs when the salesperson points out available complementary items in line with the selected item(s), in order to encourage an additional purchase.

Sugging refers to the illegal practice of selling under the guise of research.

Supply-chain management also known as logistics and physical distribution, refers to the planning, implementation, and control of the physical flows of materials and finished products from points of production to points of use. Supply-chain management is a technique for linking a manufacturer's operations with those of all its strategic suppliers, key intermediaries, and customers to enhance efficiency and effectiveness. Supply-chain management is managing logistical systems to achieve close cooperation and comprehensive interorganizational management, so as to integrate the logistical operations of different firms in the marketing channel.

Supply-side market failure results when the individual activities of a supplier inadvertently lead to destructive effects on the overall supply.

Sustainable competitive advantage is a competitive edge that cannot be easily or quickly copied by competitors in the short run.

Systems concept of logistics entails viewing all components of a logistical system together and understanding the relationships among them.

T

Tacit knowledge is knowledge implied by or inferred from actions or statements.

Tactical planning involves specifying details that pertain to the organization's activities for a certain period of time.

Target market is the specific group of customers toward which a firm directs its marketing efforts.

Target marketing is the process of matching a specialized marketing mix to the needs of a specific market segment.

Targeting involves offering the firm's most profitable customers special deals and incentives.

Theory of dual entitlement holds that consumers believe there are terms in a transaction to which both consumers and sellers are "entitled" over time. Cost-driven price increases are believed to be fair because they allow the seller to maintain her/his profit entitlement. Demand-driven price increases are not believed to be fair, however, since they allow a seller to increase per-unit profit, while the buyer receives nothing in return.

Time utility makes the product available when the customer wants or needs it.

Time, place, and possession utilities are conditions that enable consumers and business users to have products available for use when and where they want them and to actually take possession of them.

Total cost of ownership considers not only the purchase price but also an array of other factors, such as the quality and other attributes of a product over its complete life cycle.

Total-cost approach is calculating the cost of a logistical system by addressing all of the costs of logistics together rather than individual costs taken separately, so as to minimize the total cost of logistics.

Trade allowances or trade deals, come in a variety of forms and are offered to retailers simply for purchasing the manufacturer's brand or for performing activities in support of the manufacturer's brand.

Trade promotions typically in the form of off-invoice allowances, are directed at wholesalers, retailers, and other marketing intermediaries. This form of promotion represents the first step in any promotional effort.

Trade show is a temporary forum (typically lasting several days) for sellers of a product category (such as small appliances, toys, clothing, furniture, industrial tools, food products, or sporting goods) to exhibit and demonstrate their wares to current and prospective buyers.

Trading company is a marketing intermediary that undertakes exporting, importing, countertrading, investing, and manufacturing.

Tragedy of the commons is the name given to the process in which individuals, pursuing their own self-interest, overuse a common good to such an extent that the common good is destroyed.

Transaction efficiency refers to designing marketing channels to minimize the number of contacts between producers and consumers.

U

Uncertainty avoidance is the extent to which people feel threatened by ambiguous situations and have created beliefs and institutions to try to avoid these feelings.

Undifferentiated targeting strategy is the targeting strategy where one marketing-mix strategy is used for all members of the total market.

Uniform delivered pricing means that the seller charges all customers the same transportation cost regardless of their location.

Universal Product Code (UPC) is a bar code on a product's package that provides information read by optical scanners.

Users are the consumers who actually use the product.

V

Validity refers to the relevance of the measure.

VALS™ is a psychographic profiling scheme developed by SRI Consulting Business Intelligence.

Value represent the trade-off between the perceived benefits of the product to be purchased and the perceived sacrifice in terms of the costs to be paid.

Value analysis is a method of weighing the comparative value of materials, components, and manufacturing processes from the standpoint of their purpose, relative merit, and cost in order to uncover ways of improving products, lowering costs, or both.

Value chain is formed by combining the supply chain with the marketing channel and represents what most practitioners are talking about when they discuss supply chain management.

Value proposition is the bundle of benefits the product provides to fulfill customer needs and wants.

Value proposition is a program of goods, services, ideas, and solutions that a business marketer offers to advance the performance goals of the customer organization.

Voice of the customer (VOC) is a one-on-one interviewing process used to elicit an in-depth set of customer needs. Voice of the customer (VOC) is the expression of the preferences, opinions, and motivations of the customer that need to be listened to by managers.

W

Wants are desires to obtain more satisfaction than is absolutely necessary to improve an unsatisfactory condition.

Wheel of retailing theory is a pattern of competitive development in retailing that states that new types of retailers enter the market as low-status, low-margin, low-price operators. However, as they meet with success, these new retailers gradually acquire more sophisticated and elaborate facilities, thereby becoming less efficient and vulnerable to new types of low-margin retail competitors that progress through the same pattern.

Wholesalers are persons or establishments that sell to retailers and/or other organizational buyers for industrial, institutional, and commercial use, but do not sell in significant amounts to ultimate consumers.

Wholesaling involves the activities of persons or establishments that sell to retailers and/or other organizational buyers for industrial, institutional, and commercial use, but do not sell in significant amounts to final consumers.

World Trade Organization (WTO) is the institution that administers international trade and investment accords. It supplanted the General Agreement on Tariffs and Trade (GATT) in 1995.

Endnotes

Chapter 1

[1] Developed from James R. Healey, "Versatile, oh-so-cool Element Rocks," http://www.usatoday.com/money/autos/reviews/healey/2002-11-21-element_x.htm, accessed 16 January 2003; Daniel Pund, "Honda Element," http://www.caranddriver.com/xp/Caranddriver/previews/2002/november/0211_preview_element.xml?keywords=Element, accessed 16 January 2003; Lindsey Chappel, "Hey Dude, Honda Wants to Get You," http://www.autonews.com/news.cms?newsId=4166, accessed 16 January 2003.

[2] http://www.google.com, accessed 1 April 2003.

[3] Nicholas Stein, "America's Most Admired Companies," *Fortune*, 3 March 2003, 81.

[4] Developed from Ajay K. Kohli and Bernard J. Jaworski, "Market Orientation: The Construct, Research Propositions, and Managerial Implications" *Journal of Marketing* 54 (2) April 1990: 1–18; Ronald A. Fullerton, "How Modern is Modern Marketing? Marketing's Evolution and the Myth of the 'Production Era'," *Journal of Marketing* 52 (1) January 1988: 108–125; George S. Day, "The Capabilities of Market-Driven Organizations," *Journal of Marketing* 58 (4) October 1994: 37–52; John C. Narver and Stanley F. Slater, "The Effect of Market Orientation on Business Profitability," *Journal of Marketing* 54 (4) October 1990: 20–36.

[5] Jakki Mohr, *Marketing of High-Technology Products and Innovations* (Upper Saddle River, NJ: Prentice-Hall, 2001), 97–103.

[6] http://www.crmcommunity.com/library/fundamentals.cfm, accessed 31 March 2003.

[7] Peter D. Bennet, ed., *Dictionary of Marketing Terms* (Chicago: American Marketing Association, 1988), 54.

[8] Lorrie Grant, "Wal-Mart Moves Up," *USA Today*, http://www.usatoday.com/money/industries/retail/2002-09-24-walmart_x.htm, accessed 27 January 2003.

[9] http://www.shomotion.com/index_html.htm, accessed 27 January 2003.

[10] http://www.fsis.usda.gov/oa/pubs/ingrade.htm, accessed 27 January 2003.

[11] http://www.nielsenmedia.com/main_frame.html, accessed 27 January 2003.

[12] John C. Narver and Stanley F. Slater, "The Effect of Market Orientation on Business Profitability," *Journal of Marketing* 54 (4) October 1990: 20–36.

[13] K. Douglas Hoffman et al., *Marketing: Best Practices* (Mason, OH: South-Western, 2003), 64.

[14] William M. Pride and O. C. Ferrell, *Marketing: Concepts and Strategies* (Boston, MA: Houghton Mifflin, 2003), 16.

[15] U.S. Bureau of the Census, *Statistical Abstract of the United States: 2000*, Table nos. 1271 and 1274.

[16] K. Douglas Hoffman, L. W. Turley, and Scott W. Kelley, "Pricing Retail Services," *Journal of Business Research* 55 (2002): 1015–1023.

[17] The framework for developing the discussion around researching the market, identifying current and potential competitors, and anticipating competitive actions was taken from John H. Lindgren Jr., and Terence A. Shimp, *Marketing: An Interactive Learning System* (Fort Worth, TX: Dryden Press, 1996), 41–46.

[18] Developed from Bob Nardelli, "A Do-It-Yourself Disaster," *Economist* (11 January 2003), 54–55; Aixa M. Pascual, "Lowe's is Sprucing Up its House," *Business Week* (3 June 2002), 56–57.

[19] World POPClock, U.S. Census Bureau, http://landview.census.gov/main/www/popclock.html, accessed 27 January 2003.

[20] Taken from The World Village Project Web site, http://www.WorldVillage.org, accessed, 27 January 2003.

[21] Developed from Daniel Joelson, "U.S. Financial Firms Cater to Latinos," *Bank Technology News* 14 (3) (March 2001); Bonnie McGreer, Banks Focus on Minority Merchants," *American Banker* 166 (87) (7 May 2001); Rodney Moore, "1-To-1 An Ethnic Star," *Advertising Age* 72 (44) (29 October 2001); Geng Cui, "Marketing to Ethnic Minority Consumers: A Historical Journey (1932–1997)," *Journal of Macromarketing* 21 (1) (June 2001); John Kerrigan, "Playing to Hispanics Garners Rewards," *Marketing News* (22 July 2002): 20.

[22] Lisa Benenson, "The State of the Union," *Ladies Home Journal* March 2003, 108–114; Brent Schlender, "Peter Drucker Takes the Long View," *Fortune* 138 (6) (28 September 1998), 162–173.

[23] Developed from James W. Gentry, Suraj Commuri, and Sunkyu Jun, "Review of Literature on Gender in the Family," *Academy of Marketing Science Review* [Online] (1) (2003), available http://www.amsreview.org/articles/gentry01-2003.pdf; Ellen Neuborne and Kathleen Kerwin, "Generation Y," *Business Week* (15 February 1999), 80–88; John H. Lindgren Jr., and Terence A. Shimp, *Marketing: An Interactive Learning System* (Fort Worth, TX: The Dryden Press, 1996), 58; "Microsoft Accessibility: Technology for Everyone," http://www.microsoft.com/enable/business/value-u.htm, accessed 27 January 2003.

[24] U.S. Bureau of the Census, "Statistical Abstract of the United States: 2000," http://factfinder.census.gov/bf/_lang=en_vt_name=DEC_2000_SF3_U_DP3_geo_id=01000US.html, accessed 22 January 2003; *The World Factbook 2002*, http://www.cia.gov/cia/publications/factbook/geos/us.html, accessed 12 January 2003; and John H. Lindgren Jr., and Terence A. Shimp, *Marketing: An Interactive Learning System* (Fort Worth, TX: Dryden Press, 1996), 41–46.

[25] Developed from the Web site for J. Ottman Consulting Inc., http://www.greenmarketing.com/Green_Marketing_Book/Green_Marketing_Book.html, accessed 31 March 2003.

[26] Developed from Judy Strauss, Adel El-Ansary, and Raymond Frost, *E-Marketing*, 3rd ed. (Upper Saddle River, NJ: Prentice-Hall, 2003), 1–19.

[27] Developed from Paul N. Bloom and Gregory T. Gundlach, eds., *Handbook of Marketing and Society*, (Thousand Oaks, CA: Sage Publications, 2001), 34–47; and John H. Lindgren Jr., and Terence A. Shimp, *Marketing: An Interactive Learning System* (Fort Worth, TX: Dryden Press, 1996), 41–46.

Chapter 2

[1] http://www.Viacom.com/thefacts.tin (6 February 2003); John Horn, "Sayonara, SpongeBob," *Newsweek* 139 (21) (27 May 2002), 81; Daisy Whitney, "Spotlight on: SpongeBob SquarePants," *Electronic Media*, 21 (43) (28 October 2002), 16; Anne D'Innocenzio, "Nickelodeon Finds Success with Cast of Quirky Characters," *The Rocky Mountain Collegian* (6 February 2003), 4B; Sally Beatty, "Something about 'SpongeBob' Whispers 'Gay' to Many Men," *The Wall Street Journal Online* (8 October 2002), http://online.wsj.com/article/o,,SB1034028869241478240.dgm,oo.html.

[2] The framework and specific sections of this chapter were adapted or modified from John H. Lindgren, Jr., and Terence A. Shimp, *Marketing: An Interactive Learning System* (Fort Worth, TX: Dryden Press, 1996) and previous editions of *Marketing Principles and Best Practices* (Mason, OH: South-Western, 2003).

[3] For more information, see P. Rajan Varadarajan and Terry Clark, "Delineating the Scope of Corporate, Business, and Marketing Strategy," *Journal of Business Research* 31 (1994): 93–105; and Donald R. Lehmann and Russel S. Winer, *Analysis for Marketing Planning*, 5th ed. (Boston: McGraw-Hill Irwin, 2002).

[4] For more information about Starbucks' mission statement and company history, go to http://www.starbucks.com/aboutus/overview.asp, accessed 14 February 2003.

[5] For more information about Doritos® Brand Tortilla Chips, go to http://www.doritos.com/products/index.cfm, accessed 14 February 2003.

[6] For a more detailed discussion of how to write smart objectives, see Gary Platt, "Smart Objectives," *Training & Conference Center: 01926 336621*, http://www.wgrange.com/news/smart.html, accessed 14 February 2003.

[7] This discussion is adapted from George S. Day, "Diagnosing the Product Portfolio," *Journal of Marketing* 41 (April 1977): 29–38.

[8] J. Scott Armstrong and Roderick J. Brodie, "Effects of Portfolio Planning Methods on Decision Making: Experimental Results," *International Journal of Research in Marketing* (1994): 73–84.

[9] For more information about the Starbucks Loyalty Card program, go to http://www.starbucks.com/card/default.asp, accessed 14 February 2003.

[10] Sources: Catherine Arnold, "Technology Reels 'em In," *Marketing News* (14 October 2002), http://www2.exxonmobil.com/corporate/Newsroom/NewsReleases/Corp_NR_PressKitSpeedpass.asp, accessed 4 December 2002.

[11] For more information about Yum! Brands Inc., go to http://www.yum.com/help.htm, accessed 14 February 2003.

[12] For further reading on marketing planning, see Donald R. Lehmann and Russel S. Winer, *Analysis for Marketing Planning*, 5th ed. (Boston: McGraw-Hill Irwin, 2002).

[13] For more information about Pringles Brand Potato Chips, see http://www.pringles.com/meet.shtml, accessed 14 February 2003.

[14] For more information about Rold Gold® Pretzels, see http://www.frito-lay.com/consumer.html, accessed 14 February 2003.

[15] *All-commodity volume (ACV)* is a term used by marketing and advertising practitioners to refer to total sales of a product. For example, an 85 ACV level for Rold Gold® simply means that brand has obtained 85% distribution in retail outlets.

Chapter 3

[1] Jeffrey M. Laderman, "Wall Street's Spin Game" *Business Week*, 5 October 1998, 148–156; David Rynecki, "The Price of Being Right," *Fortune*, 5 February 2001, 126–141.

[2] "Lots About It," *The Economist*, 14 December 2002, 62–64.

[3] Booz-Allen & Hamilton, *New Product Management for the 1980s* (New York: Booz-Allen & Hamilton, 1982).

[4] Stephen Manes, "Windows: The Fix Is Not In, " *Forbes*, 13 May 2002, 160.

[5] Steven H. Star, "Marketing and Its Discontents," *Harvard Business Review* (November–December 1989): 148–154.

[6] See "Turning Off the Tap," *The Economist*, 14 November 1998, 29.

[7] From the results of a survey of 511 Wisconsin adults surveyed two weeks before the 1998 elections, reported in the *Wisconsin State Journal*, 31 October 1998, 1.

[8] Michael McCarthy, "Miller Lite's Catfight Ad Angers Some Viewers," *USA Today*, 15 January 2003, B1.

[9] Jim Guest, "Consumers Need to Know More About Faulty Products," *Consumer Reports* 66 (July 2001), 6.

[10] FDCH Regulatory Intelligence Database, *Lane Company Agrees to Pay $900,000 Civil Penalty for Delay in Reporting Child Entrapment Fatalities in Cedar Chests*, 6 July 2001.

[11] FDCH Regulatory Intelligence Database, *Indiana Company to Pay $150,000 Fine for Failure to Report Ride-On Toy Defects*, 7 June 2002.

[12] "Good Grief," *The Economist*, 8 April 1995, 57.

[13] Some of the questions are based on the thinking of Gene R. Laczniak, "Framework for Analyzing Marketing Ethics," *Journal of Macromarketing* (Spring 1983): 7–18; and William David Ross, *The Right and the Good* (Oxford: Clarendon Press, 1930).

[14] Sir Adrian Cadbury, "Ethical Managers Make Their Own Rules," *Harvard Business Review* 87 (5) (September/October 1987): 69–75.

[15] Miles Moore, "Industry to Face Treat Act Ramifications Over Long Haul: *Rubber and Plastic News*, 10 December 2001, 18.

[16] Kate Fitzgerald, "Antitrust Case Threatens the Image of Toys "R" Us," *Advertising Age*, 27 May 1996, 6.

[17] Peter R. Dickson and Philippa K. Wells, "The Dubious Origins of the Sherman Antitrust Act: The Mouse That Roared," *Journal of Public Policy and Marketing: Special Issue on Competition* (Spring 2001): 1–12.

18 Stephen Cook, "Who Cares Wins," *Management Today,* January 2003, 40–48.

19 Claudia Gaines, "Next Step in Cause Marketing: Businesses Start Own Nonprofits," *Marketing News,* 12 October 1998, 4.

20 John A. Bryne, "The New Face of Philanthropy," *Business Week,* 2 December 2002, 82–86.

21 See Michael L. Rothschild, "Promises, Carrots, and Sticks: A Conceptual Framework for the Management of Public Health and Social Issue Behaviors," *Journal of Marketing* 63 (4) (1999): 24–37, for an excellent review of contemporary social marketing issues and practices.

22 See Richard Behar, "SCF's Little Secret," *Forbes,* 21 April 1986, 106–107.

23 Richard W. Pollay et al., "The Last Straw? Cigarette Advertising and Realized Market Shares among Youths and Adults, 1979–1993," *Journal of Marketing* 60 (April 1996): 1–16.

24 See Christine Gorman, "A Web of Deceit," *Time,* 9 February 1999, 76.

Chapter 4

1 "Think Local," A Survey of Television, *The Economist,* 13 April 2002, 12–14; "Culture in Peril? Mais Oui," *Fortune,* 13 May 2002, 51; "The American Connection," *The Washington Post,* 25 May 2002, E1–E2; "Rebels Without a Cause," *The Economist,* 27 April 2002, 65; "At Vivendi Universal, A French Evolution," *The Washington Post,* 24 April 2002, E1, E3.

2 Robert W. Armstrong and Jill Sweeney, "Industrial Type, Culture, Mode of Entry, and Perceptions of International Marketing Ethics Problems: A Cross-Culture Comparison," *Journal of Business Ethics* 13 (1944): 775–785.

3 J. David Richardson and Karin Rindal, *Why Exports Matter: More!* (Washington, DC: Institute for International Economics and The Manufacturing Institute February 1996).

4 U.S. Department of Commerce and Small Business Administration, Exporter Data Base, (Washington DC, April 2002).

5 http://www.ctw.org; and "Puppet Politics," *Time,* 30 September 2002, 68.

6 Jagdish N. Sheth and S. Prakash Sethi, "A Theory of Cross-Cultural Buying Behavior," in *Consumer and Industrial Buying Behavior,* eds. Arch G. Woodside, Jagdish N. Sheth, and Peter D. Bennett (New York: Elsevier North-Holland, 1977), 369–386; and Michael R. Czinkota, and Ilkka A. Ronkainen, "Global Marketing 2000: A Marketing Survival Guide," *Marketing Management* 1 (Winter 1992): 36–45.

7 Geert Hofstede, *Culture's Consequences: International Differences in Work-Related Values* (Beverly Hills, CA: Sage Publications, 1984). For ease of understanding, Hofstede's term for "power distance" was changed to "level of equality," and "masculinity" to "material achievement."

8 Sudhir H. Kale, "Grouping Euroconsumers: A Culture-Based Clustering Approach," *Journal of International Marketing* 3 (3), 1995: 35–48.

9 W. Chan Kim and R. A. Mauborgne, "Cross-Cultural Strategies," *Journal of Business Strategy* 7 (Spring 1987): 28–37.

10 "On-Line Learning," Special Advertising Section, *Fortune,* 1 July 2002, S1–S19; and Peter T. Burgi and Brant R. Dykehouse, "On-line Cultural Training: The Next Phase," *International Insight* (Winter 2000), 7–10.

11 www.levistrauss.com/brands/dockers.htm

12 Dana James, "B2–4B Spells Profits," *Marketing News,* 5 November 2001, 1, 11–12.

13 Office of the U.S. Trade Representative, *2001 National Trade Estimate Report on Foreign Trade Barriers* (Washington, DC: GPO, 2001), 94–95.

14 Igal Ayal and Jehiel Zif, "Marketing Expansion Strategies in Multinational Marketing," *Journal of Marketing* 43 (Spring 1979): 84–94.

15 Warren J. Bilkey and George Tesar, "The Export Behavior of Smaller Sized Wisconsin Manufacturing Firms," *Journal of International Business Studies* 8 (Spring–Summer 1977): 93–98.

16 Finn Weidersheim-Paul, H. C. Olson, and L. S. Welch, "Pre-Exports Activity: The First Step in Internationalization." *Journal of International Business Studies* 9 (Spring–Summer 1978): 47–58.

17 Wallace Doolin, "Taking Your Business on the Road," *The Wall Street Journal,* 25 July 1994, A14.

18 United Nations, *Multinational Corporations in World Development* (New York: United Nations, 1973), 23.

19 W. G Friedman and G. Kalmanoff, *Joint International Business Ventures* (New York: Columbia University Press, 1961).

20 Oded Shenkar and Shmuel Ellis, "Death of the 'Organization Man': Temporal Relations in Strategic Alliances," *The International Executive* 37 (6) (November/December 1995), 537–553.

21 John Hageddoorn, "A Note on International Market Leaders and Networks of Strategic Technology Partnering," *Strategic Management Journal* 16 (1995): 241–250.

22 Richard Gibson, "Cereal Venture Is Planning Honey of a Battle in Europe," *The Wall Street Journal,* 14 November 1990, B1, B8.

23 Dori Jones Yang, Michael Oneal, Charles Hoots, and Robert Neff, "Can Nike Just Do It?" *Business Week,* 18 April 1994, 86–90.

24 Carl A. Sohlberg, "The Perennial Issue of Adaptation or Standardization of International Marketing Communication: Organizational Contingencies and Performance," *Journal of International Marketing* 10 (3), (2002): 1–21.

25 Stephen C. Messner, "Adapting Products to Western Europe," *Export Today* 10 (March/April 1994), 16–18. See also *http://www.murray.com.*

26 Drew Martin and Paul Herbig, "Marketing Implications of Japan's Social-Cultural Underpinnings," *Journal of Brand Management* 9 (January 2002): 171–179.

27 Davis Goodman, "Thinking Export? Think ISO 9000," *World Trade* (August 1998), 48–49.

28 Doug Bartholomew, "Beyond the Grave, *Industry Week,* March 2002, 34–40.

29 "The Puff, the Magic, the Dragon," *The Washington Post,* 2 September 1994, B1, B3.

30 "Teach Me Shopping," *The Economist,* 18 December 1993, 64–65.

31 Rahul Jacob, "The Big Rise," *Fortune,* 30 May 1994, 74–90.

32 "Divide and Conquer." *Export Today* 5 (February 1989): 10.

33 Ilkka A. Ronkainen and Ivan Menezes, "Implementing Global Marketing Strategy," *International Marketing Review* 13 (3) (1996), 56–63.

34 Ingo Theuerkauf, David Ernst, and Amir Mahini, "Think Local, Organize . . . ?" *International Marketing Review* 13 (3) (1996), 7–12.

Chapter 5

1 John Motavalli, *Bamboozled at the Revolution: How Big Media Lost Billions in the Battle for the Internet* (New York: Viking, 2002), 301.

2 Arie P. DeGeus, "Planning as Learning," *Harvard Business Review* (March/April 1988): 70–74.

[3] Turley, L. W. and Ronald E. Milliman (2000), "Atmospheric Effects on Shopping Behavior: A Review of the Experimental Evidence," *Journal of Business Research,* 49 (2), 193–211.

[4] This list is based in part on advice from "The Art of Obtaining Information," Washington Researchers, Washington, DC.

[5] Edward F. McQuarrie and Shelby H. McIntyre, *The Customer Visit: An Emerging Practice in Business-to-Business Marketing* (Cambridge, MA: Marketing Science Institute, 1992), 92–114.

[6] Johny K. Johannson and Ikujiro Nonaka, "Market Research the Japanese Way," *Harvard Business Review* (May/June 1987): 16–22; Lance Ealey and Leif Soderberg, "How Honda Cures Design Amnesia," *The McKinsey Quarterly* (Spring 1990): 3–14; and Kenichi Ohmae, *The Borderless World* (New York: Harper Business, 1990).

[7] B. Dumaine, "Creating a New Company Culture," *Fortune,* 15 January 1990, 127–131.

[8] B. Dumaine, "Corporate Spies Snoop to Conquer," *Fortune,* 7 November 1988, 68–76.

[9] Robert A. Westbrook, "A Rating Scale for Measuring Product/Service Satisfaction," *Journal of Marketing* 44 (Fall 1980): 68–72; and Richard L. Oliver and John E. Swan, "Consumer Perceptions of Interpersonal Equity and Satisfaction in Transactions: A Field Survey Approach," *Journal of Marketing* 53 (April 1989): 21–35.

[10] The calculation is based on the statistic $p \pm 3 \yen s.d._p = 50\% \pm (3 \yen (0.5 \yen 0.5/400)^{1/2}) \yen 100\%$.

[11] The calculation is $50\% \pm (3 \yen (0.5 \yen 0.5/10,000)^{1/2}) \yen 100\%$.

[12] See Angelina Herrin, "Food Survey Called Flawed," *Wisconsin State Journal* (11 September 1991), 3A; and Gilbert A. Churchill, Jr., *Marketing Research* (Fort Worth, TX: Dryden Press, 1995), 654.

[13] See Gilbert A. Churchill, Jr., and J. Paul Peter, "Research Design Effects on the Reliability of Rating Scales: A Meta-Analysis," *Journal of Marketing Research* 21 (November 1984), 360–375.

[14] David Greising, "Quality: How to Make It Pay," *Business Week,* 8 August 1995, 54–59.

[15] The bad news is that it took the hotel 15 years to discover the ironing problem. See Leonard L. Berry, "Improving America's Service," *Marketing Management* 1 (3) (1992): 29–37.

[16] Much of the material in this section is drawn from the following book which is an excellent review of the new high-tech use of scanner data: David J. Curry, *The New Marketing Research Systems* (New York: John Wiley & Sons, 1993).

[17] Leonard M. Lodish et al., "How Advertising Works: A Meta-Analysis of 389 Real World Split Cable TV Advertising Experiments," *Journal of Marketing Research* (May 1995), 125–139

[18] Thomas W. Miller and Peter R. Dickson, "On-line Market Research," *International Journal of Electronic Commerce* 5 (3) (Spring 2001), 139–167.

[19] M. Blackwood, "Taking Action on Satisfaction Measurement" (paper presented at the 1999 Explor Forum, Madison, WI, October 1999).

[20] See Peter R. Dickson, Paul W. Farris, and Willem J. M. I. Verbeke, "Dynamic Strategic Thinking," *Journal of the Academy of Marketing Science* 29 (3) (2001): 216–237.

[21] James M. Utterback, *Mastering the Dynamics of Innovation* (Cambridge, MA: Harvard Business School Press, 1994).

[22] Gloria P. Thomas and Gary F. Soldow, "A Rules-Based Approach to Competitive Interaction," *Journal of Marketing* 52 (April 1988): 63–74.

[23] Michael E. Porter, *Competitive Strategy* (New York: The Free Press, 1980).

[24] Thomas W. Dunfee, Louis Stern, and Frederick D. Sturdivant, "Bounding Markets in Merger Cases: Identifying Relevant Competitors," *Northwestern University Law Review* 78 (November 1983): 733–773.

[25] Subrata N. Chakravarty and Carolyn Torcellini, "Citizen Kane Meets Adam Smith," *Forbes,* 20 February 1989, 82–85.

[26] Michael E. Porter, *Competitive Advantage* (New York: The Free Press, 1985).

[27] Howard Sutton, *Competitive Intelligence* (New York: The Conference Board, 1988), 31, 37.

[28] Richard Harwell, *Washington* (New York: Collier Books, 1992), 511–512.

Chapter 6

[1] Adapted from Michael J. Silverstein and Neil Fiske, "Luxury for the Masses," *Harvard Business Review,* 81, no. 4 (2003): 48–57.

[2] Eugene Sivadas, Rajdeep Grewal, and James Kellaris, "The Internet as a Micro Marketing Tool: Targeting Consumers through Preferences Revealed in Music Newsgroup Usage," *Journal of Business Research* 41 (3) (March 1998): 179–186.

[3] Hillel J. Einhorn, "Use of Nonlinear, Noncompensatory Models in Decision Making," *Psychological Bulletin* 73 (1970): 221–230.

[4] Richard P. Bagozzi, Mahaesh Gopinath, and Prashant U. Nyer, "The Role of Emotions in Marketing," *Journal of the Academy of Marketing Science* 27 (Spring 1999): 184–206.

[5] Gordon W. Allport, "Attitudes," in *A Handbook of Social Psychology,* ed. C. A. Muchinson (Worcester, MA: Clark University Press, 1935), 798–844.

[6] Lynn R. Kahle, Sharon E. Beatty, and Pamela Homer, "Alternative Measurement Approaches to Consumer Values: The List of Values (LOV) and Values and Lifestyle (VALS)," *Journal of Consumer Research* 13 (December 1986): 405–409.

[7] VALS description on the Internet, SRI Consulting Business Intelligence Web site, http://www.sric-bi.com/vals, accessed 31 March 2003.

[8] Based on U.S. Census estimates, obtained from the U.S. Census Bureau Web site, http://www.census.gov/main/www/cen2000.html, accessed 24 April 2002.

[9] Jagdish N. Sheth, "A Theory of Family Buying Decisions," in *Models of Buyer Behavior: Conceptual, Quantitative, and Empirical* (New York: Harper & Row, 1974), 17–33.

[10] Joel Garreau and John Garreau, *Nine Nations of North America* (Boston: Avon Books, 1981).

[11] Rajeev Batra and Douglas M. Stayman, "The Role of Mood in Advertising Effectiveness," *Journal of Consumer Research* 17 (2) (September 1990): 203–214.

Chapter 7

[1] William M. Bulkeley, "These Days, Big Blue is About Big Services Not Just Big Boxes," *The Wall Street Journal,* 11 June 2001, A1, A10.

[2] "Land's End Embarks on Voyage to Deliver More Customer Value with DB2," http://www.ibm.com/services, accessed 22 January 2003.

[3] "Michigan State Government Implements ePortal to Make Services Available to Constituents," http://www.ibm.com/services, accessed 22 January 2003.

[4] "Washington Mutual Evolves to National Presence with Help from IBM Global Services," http://www.ibm.com/services, accessed 22 January 2003.

[5] Larry Schiff, "How Customer Satisfaction Improvement Works to Fuel Business Recovery at IBM," *Journal of Organizational Excellence* 20 (Spring 2001): 8.

[6] Anne Millen Porter, "The Top 250: Tough Measures for Tough Times," *Purchasing*, 7 November 2002, 31–35.

[7] U.S. Department of Commerce, Bureau of the Census, *Statistical Abstract of the United States, Annual Survey of Manufacturers: 2001* (Washington, DC: 2001).

[8] U.S. Department of Commerce, Bureau of the Census, "2000 County Business Patterns," http://www.census.gov, accessed 1 February 2003.

[9] Ibid.

[10] Thomas H. Davenport, Jeanne G. Harris, and Ajay K. Kohli, "How Do They Know Their Customers So Well?" *MIT Sloan Management Review* 42 (Winter): 65.

[11] Anne Millen Porter, "Big Spenders: The Top 250," *Purchasing*, 6 November 1997, 40–52.

[12] Porter, "The Top 250," 31.

[13] Nicole Harris, "'Private Exchanges May Allow B-to-B Commerce to Thrive After All," *The Wall Street Journal*, 16 March 2001, B4.

[14] "What's Happening in High-Tech Markets," *Purchasing*, 17 May 2001, 5.

[15] "Case Study: Cooper Industries," 9 January 2001, http://www.freemarkets.com.

[16] U.S. Department of Commerce, Bureau of the Census, *Statistical Abstract of the United States: 2001* (Washington, DC: 2001), 260.

[17] Stephanie N. Mehta, "Small Firms Are Getting More Government Contracts," *The Wall Street Journal*, 27 April 1995, B2.

[18] Richard Walker and Kevin McCaney, "Reverse Auctions Win a Bid of Acceptance," *Buyers.Gov*, December 2001, accessed January 2002.

[19] Laura M. Holson, "Pushing Limits, Finding None," *The New York Times*, 1 November 2001, C1, C6.

[20] U.S. Department of Commerce, Bureau of the Census, *Statistical Abstract of the United States: 2001*, (Washington, DC: 2001), 91, 133.

[21] Joseph Kahn, "Made in China, Bought in China," *The New York Times*, 5 January 2003, 3–1, 3–10.

[22] Subhash C. Jain, "Standardization of International Marketing Strategy: Some Research Hypotheses," *Journal of Marketing* 53 (January 1989): 70–79.

[23] "History of SIC/NAICS," http://www.naics.com, accessed 1 February 2003.

[24] Larry Yu, "Successful Customer-Relationship Management," *MIT Sloan Management Review* 43 (Summer 2001): 18.

[25] Darrel K. Rigby, Frederick F. Reichheld, and Phil Schefter, "Avoid the Four Perils of CRM," *Harvard Business Review* 80 (January/February 2002): 102.

[26] Frederick F. Reichheld, "Lead for Loyalty," *Harvard Business Review* 79 (July/August 2001): 76–84.

[27] Kevin R. Fitzgerald, "For Superb Supplier Development: Honda Wins!" *Purchasing*, 21 September 1995, 32–40.

[28] Rick Mullin, "Managing the Outsourced Enterprise," *Journal of Business Strategy* (July/August 1996): 32.

[29] Tim Minahan, "JIT: A Process with Many Faces," *Purchasing*, 4 September 1997, 42–48.

[30] Patrick J. Robinson, Charles W. Faris, and Yoram Wind, *Industrial Buying and Creative Marketing* (Boston: Allyn & Bacon, 1967).

[31] Robinson, Faris, and Wind, *Industrial Buying and Creative Marketing*; see also Erin Anderson, Wujin Chu, and Barton Weitz, "Industrial Purchasing: An Empirical Exploration of the Buyclass Framework," *Journal of Marketing* 51 (July 1987): 71–86; and Morry Ghingold, "Testing the 'Buygrid' Buying Process Model," *Journal of Purchasing and Materials Management* 22 (Winter 1986): 30–36.

[32] The discussion of buying-decision approaches in this section is drawn from Michele D. Bunn, "Taxonomy of Buying Decision Approaches," *Journal of Marketing* 57 (January 1993): 38–56.

[33] The levels of decision making discussed in this section are drawn from John A. Howard and Jagdish N. Sheth, *The Theory of Buyer Behavior* (New York: John Wiley and Sons, 1969).

[34] Christopher P. Puto, Wesley E. Patton III, and Ronald H. King, "Risk Handling Strategies in Industrial Vendor Selection Decisions," *Journal of Marketing* 49 (Winter 1985): 89–98.

[35] Somerby Dowst, "CEO Report: Wanted: Suppliers Adept at Turning Corners," *Purchasing*, 29 January 1987, 71–72.

[36] Timothy M. Laseter, *Balanced Sourcing: Cooperation and Competition in Supplier Relationships* (San Francisco: Jossey-Bass, 1998), 224.

[37] Gary S. Vasilash, "The '03 Accord: Why Smart Designers Make All the Difference," *Automotive Design & Production* 114 (September 2002): 50–53.

[38] Matthew G. Anderson and Paul K. Katz, "Strategic Sourcing," *International Journal of Logistics Management* 9 (1) (1998): 1–13.

[39] Tom Stundza, "How Chrysler Will Cut Costs," *Purchasing*, 8 February 2001, 30–32.

[40] Allen M. Weiss and Jan B. Heide, "The Nature of Organizational Search in High Technology Markets," *Journal of Marketing Research* 30 (May 1993): 220–233; see also Jan B. Heide and Allen M. Weiss, "Vendor Consideration and Switching Behavior for Buyers in High-Technology Markets," *Journal of Marketing* 59 (July 1995): 30–43.

[41] Weiss and Heide, "The Nature of Organizational Search," 221.

[42] Michael Fredette, "An Interview with Judith Hollis," *The Journal of Supply Chain Management* 37 (Summer 2001): 3.

[43] For a comprehensive review of buying center research, see Wesley J. Johnston and Jeffrey E. Lewin, "Organizational Buying Behavior: Toward an Integrative Framework," *Journal of Business Research* 35 (January 1996): 1–15; and J. David Lichtenthal, "Group Decision Making in Organizational Buying: A Role Structure Approach," in *Advances in Business Marketing*, vol. 3, ed. Arch G. Woodside (Greenwich, CT: JAI Press, 1988), 119–157.

[44] For example, see Robert D. McWilliams, Earl Naumann, and Stan Scott, "Determining Buying Center Size," *Industrial Marketing Management* 21 (February 1992): 43–49.

[45] Arch G. Woodside, "Conclusions on Mapping How Industry Buys," in *Advances in Business Marketing and Purchasing*, vol. 5, ed. Arch G. Woodside (Greenwich, CT: JAI Press, 1992), 283–300; see also Gary L. Lilien and M. Anthony Wong, "Exploratory Investigation of the Structure of the Buying Center in the Metalworking Industry," *Journal of Marketing Research* 21 (February 1984): 1–11.

[46] Anderson, Chu, and Weitz, "Industrial Purchasing," 82.

[47] Ibid.

[48] Frederick E. Webster Jr. and Yoram Wind, *Organizational Buying Behavior* (Englewood Cliffs, NJ: Prentice-Hall, 1972), 77. For a review of buying role research, see J. David Lichtenthal, "Group Decision Making in Organizational Buying," 119–157.

[49] B. G. Yovovich, *New Marketing Imperatives: Innovative Strategies for Today's Marketing Challenges* (Englewood Cliffs, NJ: Prentice-Hall, 1995), 4–5.

[50] Philip L. Dawes and Paul G. Patterson, "The Use of Technical Consultancy Services by Firms Making High-Technology Purchasing Decisions," in *Twenty-First Annual Conference of the European Marketing Academy,* ed. Klaus G. Grunert and Dorthe Fuglede (Aarhus, Denmark: Aarhus School of Business), 261–275.

[51] John R. Ronchetto, Michael D. Hutt, and Peter H. Reingen, "Embedded Influence Patterns in Organizational Buying Systems," *Journal of Marketing* 53 (October 1989): 51–62; see also Ajay Kohli, "Determinants of Influence in Organizational Buying: A Contingency Approach," *Journal of Marketing* 53 (July 1989): 50–65; and Daniel H. McQuiston and Peter R. Dickson, "The Effect of Perceived Personal Consequences on Participation and Influence in Organizational Buying," *Journal of Business Research* 23 (September 1991): 159–177.

[52] McQuiston and Dickson, "The Effect of Perceived Personal Consequences on Participation and Influence in Organizational Buying," 159–177.

[53] Jagdish N. Sheth, "A Model of Industrial Buyer Behavior," *Journal of Marketing* 37 (October 1973): 51; see also Sheth, "Organizational Buying Behavior: Past Performance and Future Expectations," *Journal of Business and Industrial Marketing* 11 (3/4) (1996): 7–24.

[54] Sheth, "A Model of Industrial Buyer Behavior," 52–54.

Chapter 8

[1] Brad Dorfman, "Colgate to Take on P&G with Teeth Whitening System," *News.Com,* 21 August 2002, http://www.cnet.com/investor/news/newsitem/0-9900-1028-20324683-0.html, accessed 15 January 2003; Jason Fagone, "The Great White Hope," *Cincinnati,* September 2002, 60–65; Aparna Narayanan, "Whiter, Brighter Smiles Add Up to Blacker Ink," *Knight Ridder Tribune Business News,* 2 January 2003; Ameet Sachdev, "Teeth Whiteners Clean Up in Oral-Care Business," *Chicago Tribune,* 23 April 2002.

[2] Peter R. Dickson and James I. Ginter, "Market Segmentation, Product Differentiation, and Marketing Strategy," *Journal of Marketing* (April 1987): 1–10.

[3] Rebecca Gardyn, "Swap Meet," *American Demographics,* July 2001, 50–55.

[4] Ameet Sachdev, "Marketers Harvest Census Numbers to Target Consumers' Demand," *Chicago Tribune,* 26 April 2001.

[5] Rebecca Gardyn, "Swap Meet," *American Demographics,* July 2001, 50–55.

[6] Adapted from Jock Bicker, "Cohorts II: A New Approach to Market Segmentation," *Journal of Consumer Marketing* (Fall–Winter 1997): 362–380.

[7] Christine Y. Chen, "Darius Bikoff vs. Coke and Pepsi," http://www.fortune.com, 21 January 2003, accessed 24 January 2003.

[8] Kevin Sheridan, "Segs and the Single Card," *Bank Marketing,* August 1997, 5.

[9] Ned Anschuetz, "Building Brand Popularity: The Myth of Segmenting to Brand Success," *Journal of Advertising Research* (January/February 1997): 63–67.

[10] Sally Dibb and Lyndon Simkin, "A Program of Implementing Market Segmentation," *Journal of Business & Industrial Marketing* (Winter 1997): 51–66.

[11] Yoram Wind, "Issues and Advances in Segmentation Research," *Journal of Marketing Research* (August 1978): 317–337.

[12] Erwin Daneels, "Market Segmentation: Normative Model Versus Reality," *European Journal of Marketing* (June 1996): 36–42.

[13] John Fetto, "Guys Who Shop," *American Demographics,* November 2002, 16.

[14] Paul E. Green and Abba M. Krieger, "Segmenting Markets with Conjoint Analysis," *Journal of Marketing* (October 1991): 20–31; Dickson and Ginter, "Market Segmentation, Product Differentiation, and Marketing Strategy," 1–10.

[15] Adapted from Green and Krieger, "Segmenting Markets with Conjoint Analysis," 20–31.

[16] Daniel Rogers and Mark Kleinman, "Pepsi Music Stars Take Fight to Coke," *Marketing,* 14 November 2002.

[17] Vincent-Wayne Mitchell and Sarah Haggett, "Sun-Sign Astrology in Market Segmentation and Empirical Investigation," *Journal of Consumer Marketing* (Spring 1997): 113–132.

[18] See Morris B. Holbrook and Robert M. Schindler, "Market Segmentation Based on Age and Attitude Toward the Past: Concepts, Methods, and Findings Concerning Nostalgic Influences on Customer Tastes," *Journal of Business Research* (September 1996): 27–40.

[19] Charles M. Schaninger and William D. Danko, "A Conceptual and Empirical Comparison of Alternative Household Life Cycle Models," *Journal of Consumer Research* (March 1993): 580–594.

[20] Lynn R. Kahle, "The Nine Nations of North America and the Value Basis of Geographic Segmentation," *Journal of Marketing* (April 1986): 37–47.

[21] Glenn Rosen, "4Runner is Born to be Wild," *The Dallas Morning News,* 19 January 2003, 23D.

[22] Russell I. Haley, "Benefit Segmentation: A Decision-Oriented Research Tool," *Journal of Marketing* (Summer 1995): 59–62.

[23] Russell W. Belk, "Situational Variables and Consumer Behavior," *Journal of Consumer Research* (December 1975): 157–164.

[24] Ann M. Raider, "Pointing to Customer Needs and Retailers' Profits," *Progressive Grocer,* June 1999, 17.

[25] Frederick F. Reichheld and W. Earl Sasser, Jr., "Zero Defections: Quality Comes to Services," *Harvard Business Review,* September 2002, 105–111.

[26] Werner Reinartz and V. Kumar, "The Mismanagement of Customer Loyalty," *Harvard Business Review,* July 2002, 86–94.

[27] Susan Pigg, "Diapers, Drinking and Data," *Toronto Star,* 16 August 2002.

[28] Susan Pigg, "Diapers, Drinking and Data," *Toronto Star,* 16 August 2002.

[29] "Real Men Don't Litter," *Time,* 19 January 1987, 25.

[30] The Louisiana Board of Regents Statewide Student Profile System Enrollment Data, http://www.regents.state.la.us/Reports/sspshome.htm, accessed 19 January 2003.

[31] Bruce Horovitz, "McDonald's Looks Beyond Burgers," *USA Today,* 23 May 2002.

[32] Louise Kramer, "Mountain Dew Stays True to Its Brand Positioning," *Advertising Age,* 18 May 1998, 26; Joan Raymond, "Going to Extremes," *American Demographics,* June 2002, 28–30.

[33] Benson P. Shapiro and Thomas V. Bonoma, "How to Segment Industrial Markets," *Harvard Business Review* (May/June 1984): 104–110.

[34] Section adapted from Shapiro and Bonoma, "How to Segment Industrial Markets," 104–110.

[35] Thomas S. Robertson and Howard Barich, "A Successful Approach to Segmenting Industrial Markets," *Planning Review* November/December 1992, 4–12.

36 For more detail, see Arun Sharma and Douglas M. Lambert, "Segmentation of Markets Based on Customer Service," *International Journal of Physical Distribution and Logistics Management* (May 1994): 50–58.

37 Peter G. P. Walters, "Global Market Segmentation: Methodologies and Challenges," *Journal of Marketing Management* (January/April 1997): 165–177

38 Hallie Mummert and Lisa Yorgey, "Selling Around the World," *Target Marketing* January 1995, 28–32.

39 Deborah L. Vence, "Mexican Bill Could Affect U.S. DMers," *Marketing News,* 14 October 2002, 5.

Chapter 9

1 Markos Kounalakis, *Defying Gravity: The Making of Newton* (Hillsboro, OR: Beyond Words Publishing, 1993).

2 *Product* refers to both physical goods such as cars and shampoos and to services such as banking, dining, and consulting, as well as to ideas and people. For example, graduates are a college "product." Developing new services frequently requires developing both a physical good and the intangible benefits. For example, a new hotel requires the physical building, including the room layout, the software and hardware infrastructure to handle reservations and billing, and ancillary physical spaces such as outdoor recreation and parking facilities. Chapter 10 presents additional information about the marketing impacts of the special aspects of services.

3 This section is adapted from John H. Lindgren, Jr. and Terry Shimp, *Marketing: An Interactive Learning System* (Fort Worth: The Dryden Press, 1996), 227–235.

4 The section "Managing the Product Portfolio," also in this chapter, presents more on this topic.

5 Abbie Griffin, "PDMA Research on New Product Development Practices: Updating Trends and Benchmarking Best Practices," *Journal of Product Innovation Management* 14 (6) (1997): 429–458.

6 The section "Managing Products Through Their Life Cycle," also in this chapter, presents more on this topic.

7 Abbie Griffin and Albert L. Page, "The PDMA Success Measurement Project: Recommended Measures for Product Development Success and Failure," *Journal of Product Innovation Management* 13 (November 1996): 478–496.

8 Cupplerobe—For Two People to Share, http://www.hotproductnews.com/npn_detail.tpl?command=search&skudata=10521&db=Products.db&News_Categories=Products&, accessed 29 April 2003.

9 Abbie Griffin, "PDMA Research on New Product Development Practices," 429–458.

10 Ibid.

11 "Tankless" Water Heater, http://www.hotproductnews.com/npn_detail.tpl?command=search&skudata=10614&db=Products.db&News_Categories=Products&, accessed 29 April 2003.

12 Dog Travel Guide, http://www.hotproductnews.com/npn_detail.tpl?command=search&skudata=10650&db=Products.db&News_Categories=Products&, accessed 29 April 2003.

13 Abbie Griffin and John R. Hauser, "The Voice of the Customer," *Marketing Science* 12 (1) (1993): 1–27; Gerald Zaltman and Robin A. Higgie, "Seeing the Voice of the Customer: The Zaltman Elicitation Technique," Working Paper 93–114, Cambridge, MA: Marketing Science Institute, 1993.

14 Body Mint All-Body Deodorizer, http://www.hotproductnews.com/npn_detail.tpl?command=search&skudata=10655&db=Products.db&News_Categories=Products&, accessed 29 April 2003.

15 Griffin, "PDMA Research on New Product Development Practices," 429–458.

16 Ibid.

17 A fuller explanation of each of these may be found in Chapters 6 and 8 of Robert G. Cooper, *Winning at New Products,* 2nd ed. (Reading, MA: Addison Wesley, 1993), 121–162 and 205–226.

18 Griffin, "PDMA Research on New Product Development Practices," 429–458.

19 Kim B. Clark and Steven C. Wheelwright, *Managing New Product and Process Development* (New York: Free Press, 1993), 519–594.

20 Stephen Markham and Abbie Griffin, "The Breakfast of Champions: Associations between Champions and Product Development Environments, Practices and Performance," *Journal of Product Innovation Management* 14 (6) (1998): 436–454.

21 Michael E. McGrath, Michael T. Anthony, and Amram R. Shapiro, *Product Development: Success through Product and Cycle-Time Excellence* (Boston: Butterworth-Heinemann, 1992).

22 Parts of this section are adapted from Peter R. Dickson, *Marketing Management* (Fort Worth, Dryden Press, 1994), 310–322.

23 See Chapter 8 of this book for additional information on product positioning.

24 Extreme Sports Games on Mobile Phones, http://www.hotproductnews.com/npn_detail.tpl?command=search&skudata=10646&db=Products.db&News_Categories=Products&, accessed 29 April 2003.

Chapter 10

1 Catherine Arnold, "Technology Reels 'em In," *Marketing News* (14 October 2002); 13. http://www2.exxonmobil.com/corporate/newsroom/newsreleases/corp_nr_presskitspeedpass.asp, accessed 4 December 2002; https://www.starbucks.com/card/default.asp accessed 4 December 2002; http://www.timex.com/speedpass, accessed 4 December 2002.

2 K. Douglas Hoffman and John E. G. Bateson, *Essentials of Services Marketing: Concepts, Strategies, and Cases,* 2nd ed. (Mason, OH: South-Western, 2002), 3.

3 "The Final Frontier," *The Economist,* 20 February 1993, 63.

4 Leonard L. Berry, "Services Marketing Is Different," *Business Magazine,* May-June 1980, 24–29.

5 G. Lyn Shostack, "Breaking Free from Product Marketing," *Journal of Marketing* 41 (April 1977): 73–80.

6 This section adopted from Hoffman and Bateson, *Essentials of Services Marketing,* 2nd ed., 26–51; and Valerie A. Zeithaml, A. Parasuraman, and Leonard L. Berry, "Problems and Strategies in Services Marketing," *Journal of Marketing* 49 (Spring 1985): 33–46.

7 Asra Q. Nomani, "In the Skies Today, A Weird New Worry: Sexual Misconduct," *The Wall Street Journal,* 10 June 1998, A1; Frances Fiorino, "Passengers Who Carry Surly Bonds of Earth Aloft," *Aviation Week and Space Technology* 149 (5), 28 December 1998, 123.

8 Julie Scelfo, "Remain Seated," *Newsweek,* 139 (22) 3 June 2002, 10, 1/4p.

9 This section adopted from Hoffman and Bateson, *Essentials of Services Marketing,* 2nd ed., 4–16; and E. Langeard, J. Bateson, C. Lovelock, and P. Eigler, *Marketing of Services: New Insights from Consumers and Managers,* Report No. 81–104 (Cambridge, MA: Marketing Science Institute, 1981).

10 Mary Jo Bitner, "Servicescapes: The Impact of Physical Surroundings on Customers and Employees," *Journal of Marketing* 56 (April 1992): 57–71.

[11] Michael R. Solomon, "Packaging the Service Provider," in *Managing Services Marketing, Operations, and Human Resources,* ed. Christopher H. Lovelock (Englewood Cliffs, NJ: Prentice-Hall, 1988), 318–324.

[12] Alan J. Dubinsky, Roy D. Howell, Thomas N. Ingram, and Danny N. Bellenger, "Salesforce Socialization," *Journal of Marketing* 50 (4) (1986): 192–207.

[13] Solomon, "Packaging the Service Provider," 318–324.

[14] K. Douglas Hoffman et al., *Marketing Principles and Best Practices,* 3rd ed. (Mason, OH: South-Western, 2003).

[15] "Plane Seats Get Bigger, Cost More: Airlines Betting Fliers Will Pay Extra for Added Legroom," *Denver Rocky Mountain News,* 28 February 2000, 2A, 31A.

[16] Keith Naughton, "Try Lounging in Leather," *Newsweek,* 137 (17) 23 April 2001, 40, 1/2p.

[17] Solomon, "Packaging the Service Provider," 318–324.

[18] For more information, see Hoffman and Bateson, *Essentials of Services Marketing,* 2nd ed., 247–269.

[19] Ron Zemke and Kristen Anderson, "Customers from Hell," *Training* (February 1990): 25–29.

[20] John E. G. Bateson and K. Douglas Hoffman, *Managing Services Marketing,* 4th ed. (Fort Worth, TX: Harcourt College Publishers, 1999).

[21] For more information, see Charles L. Martin, "Consumer-to-Consumer Relationships: Satisfaction with Other Consumers' Public Behavior," *Journal of Consumer Affairs* 30 (1) (1996): 146–148; and Stephen J. Grove and Raymond P. Fisk, "The Impact of Other Customers on Service Experiences: A Critical Incident Examination of Getting Along," *Journal of Retailing* 73 (1) (1997): 63–85.

[22] Bateson and Hoffman, *Managing Services Marketing,* 4th ed.

[23] Jim Kelly, "From Lip Service to Real Service: Reversing America's Downward Service Spiral," *Vital Speeches of the Day* 64 (10) (1998), 301–304.

[24] Joseph B. Pine II and James H. Gilmore, *The Experience Economy* (Boston, MA: Harvard Business School Press, 1998).

[25] Andy Cohen, "Marketing Hits and Misses," *Sales & Marketing Management,* 154 (2), February 2002, 14.

[26] http://www.theacsi.org/overview.htm, accessed 5 December 2002.

[27] David Stires, "Fast Food, Slow Service," *Fortune,* 146 (6) 30 September 2002, 38, 1/3.

[28] Karl Albrecht and Ron Zemke, *Service America! Doing Business in the New Economy* (Homewood, IL: Business One Irwin, 1985), 6.

[29] Jim Pavia, "Just Thinking," *National Jeweler,* 96 (18) 16 September 2002, 18.

[30] Bob Romano and Barbara Sanfilippo, "A Total Approach: Measure Sales and Service," *Texas Banking* 85 (8), 1996, 16–17.

[31] Leonard L. Berry, A. Parasuraman, and Valerie A. Zeithaml, "Improving Service Quality in America: Lessons Learned," *Academy of Management Executive* 8 (2), 1994, 36.

[32] Robert Levering and Milton Moskowitz, "The 100 Best Companies to Work For in America," *Fortune* 137, 12 January 1998, 84.

[33] This section developed from Diane Brady, "Why Service Stinks," *Business Week,* 23 October 2000, 118–128.

[34] Ibid., 124.

[35] Ibid.

[36] J. Joseph Cronin, Jr., and Steven A. Taylor, "Measuring Service Quality: A Reexamination and Extension," *Journal of Marketing* 56 (July 1992): 55.

[37] Thomas A. Stewart, "After All You've Done for Your Customers, Why Are They Still NOT HAPPY?" *Fortune,* 11 December 1995, 178–182.

[38] A. Parasuraman, Valerie A. Zeithaml, and Leonard L. Berry, "A Conceptual Model of Service Quality and Its Implications for Future Research," *Journal of Marketing* 49 (Fall 1985), 41–50.

[39] C. Brune, "E-business Misses the Mark on Customer Service," *Internal Auditor* 57 (3), June 2000, 13–15; "Rainer: Top Companies Lax in Replying to Email," http://www.nua.ie/surveys, accessed 3 August 2000.

[40] Frederick F. Reichheld and W. Earl Sasser, Jr., "Zero Defections: Quality Comes to Services," *Harvard Business Review,* September–October 1990, 105–111.

[41] Grahame R. Dowling and Mark Uncles, "Do Customer Loyalty Programs Really Work?" *Sloan Management Review* 38 (4), September 1997, 71–82.

[42] Beth Armknecht Miller, "Social Initiatives can Boost Loyalty," *Marketing News,* 14 October 2002, 14–15.

[43] Christopher W. L. Hart, Leonard A. Schlesinger, and Don Maher, "Guarantees Come to Professional Service Firms," *Sloan Management Review,* Spring 1992, 19–29.

[44] Adapted from K. Douglas Hoffman and Scott W. Kelley, "Perceived Justice Needs and Recovery Evaluation: A Contingency Approach," *European Journal of Marketing* 34 (3/4) (2000): 418–432; and Christopher W. L. Hart, James L. Heskett, and W. Earl Sasser, "The Profitable Art of Service Recovery," *Harvard Business Review,* July–August 1990, 148–156.

[45] http://www.sfgate.com/cgi-bin/article.cgi?file=/news/archive/2002/12/05/financial 1112ESTo092.DTL, accessed 7 December 2002.

Chapter 11

[1] Cathleen Egan, "Altoids Mint Success Opens Door for Candy Market Niche Players," *The Wall Street Journal,* 20 August 2001, B8.

[2] Bert Rosenbloom, *Market Channels: A Management View,* 7th ed. (Mason, OH: Thomson/South-Western, 2003), 80–81.

[3] Robert D. Hof and Heather Green, "How Amazon Cleared That Hurdle," *Business Week,* 4 February 2002, 53.

[4] Sean Donahue, "B-To-B Better Be Patient," *Business 2.0,* 26 December 2000, 44.

[5] Rosenbloom, *Market Channels: A Management View,* 4.

[6] For a related discussion, see Jeff Bailey, "Web Sites Force Middlemen to Redefine Markets," *The Wall Street Journal,* 11 June 2002, B4.

[7] Jeanette Brown, Heather Green, and Wendy Zellner, "Shoppers Are Beating a Path to the Web," *Business Week,* 24 December 2001, 41.

[8] Gary L. Frazier, "Organizing and Managing Channels of Distribution," *Journal of the Academy of Marketing Science* (Spring 1999): 226–240.

[9] Bert Rosenbloom and Trina Larsen, "A Functional Approach to International Channel Structure and the Role of Independent Wholesalers," *Journal of Marketing Channels* (Summer 1993): 65–82.

[10] Wroe Alderson, *Marketing Behavior and Executive Action* (Homewood, IL: Richard D. Irwin, 1957).

[11] See, for example, Aviv Shoham, Gregory M. Rose, and Frederic Kroff, "International Channels of Distribution and the Role of Centralization," *Journal of Global Marketing* 13 (1) (1999): 87–103.

[12] Rosenbloom *Market Channels: A Management View,* 5–7.

13 Keysuk Kim, "On the Effects of Customer Conditions on Distributor Commitment and Supplier Commitment in Industrial Channels of Distribution," *Journal of Business Research* 51 (2001): 87–99.

14 Rekha Balu, "Big Brewers Find Price War Seems to Have No End," *The Wall Street Journal*, 2 July 1998, B6.

15 John O'Dell, "Land Rover's Mini-SUV Relies on Internet Marketing," *Philadelphia Inquirer*, 9 September 2001, F27.

16 Louis W. Stern and Jay W. Brown, "Distribution Channels: A Social Systems Approach," in *Distribution Channels: Behavioral Dimensions*, ed. Louis W. Stern (New York: Houghton Mifflin, 1969), 6–19.

17 Richard Gibson, "Franchisee's Suit Blames McDonald's for Failure," *The Wall Street Journal*, 18 June 2002, B4.

18 John R. Wilke, "Microsoft Antitrust Case Heads Back to Trial Court," *The Wall Street Journal*, 3 August 2001, A3.

19 John R. Wilke, Rebecca Buskman, and Gary McWilliams, "Microsoft Lets PC Firms Remove Browser," *The Wall Street Journal*, 12 July 2001, A3, A8.

20 Arlene Weintraub, "Why Rivals Are Thanking HP and Compaq," *Business Week*, 22 April 2002, 90.

21 Bert Rosenbloom, "Channel Management," in *Encyclopedia of Marketing*, ed. Michael J. Baker (London: Thomson Business Press, 1999), 407–419.

22 Michael E. Porter, "Strategy and the Internet," *Harvard Business Review* (March 2001): 63–68.

23 Nikhil Deogun, "PepsiCo Chief's Stand on Exclusive Pacts Adds to Cola War's Charged Atmosphere," *The Wall Street Journal*, 15 May 1998, A4.

24 Denise D. Schoenbackler and Geoffrey L. Gordon, "Multi-Channel Shopping: Understanding What Drives Channel Choice," *Journal of Consumer Marketing* 19 (1) (2002): 42–53.

25 "Integrating Multiple Channels," *Chain Store Age*, August 2001, 24A–25A.

26 Andrew Park, Faith Keenan, and Cliff Edward, "Whose Lunch Will Dell Eat Next?" *Business Week*, 12 August 2002, 66–67.

27 Debbie Howell, "Fleming Takes Distribution Service to Next Level," *DSN Retailing Today*, 2 November 2001, 3.

28 Ann Zimmerman, "Taking Aim at Costco, Sam's Club, Marshalls, Diamonds and Pearls," *The Wall Street Journal*, 9 August 2001, A1, A4.

29 Pui-Wing Tam and Gary McWilliams, "Apple Is Mulling Own Store Chain to Expand Sales," *The Wall Street Journal*, 29 September 2000, B1, B2.

30 Peter Burrows, "How to Milk An Apple," *Business Week*, 3 February 2003, 44.

31 See, for example, Kenneth H. Wathne, Harold Biong, and Jan B. Heide, "Choice of Supplier in Embedded Markets: Relationship and Marketing Program Effects," *Journal of Marketing* (April 2001): 54–66.

32 Richard Gibson, "McDonald's Finds Angry Customers on Its Menu," *The Wall Street Journal*, 16 July 2001, A14.

33 Henry Adobor and Ronald S. McMullen, "Strategic Partnering in E-Commerce: Guidelines for Managing Alliances," *Business Horizons*, March-April 2002, 67–76.

34 Bert C. McCammon, Jr., "Perspectives for Distribution Programming," in *Vertical Marketing Systems*, ed. Louis P. Bucklin (Glenview, IL: Scott, Foresman, 1970), 43.

35 McCammon, 43–44.

36 Gary L. Frazier, "Organizing and Managing Channel of Distribution," *Journal of the Academy of Marketing Science* 27 (3) (1999): 226–240.

37 Rosenbloom, *Market Channels*, 309.

38 J. Miguel Villas-Boas, "Product Line Design for a Distribution Channel," *Marketing Science* 17 (2) (1998): 156–169.

39 Tom Lowry, "Island Def Jam Brings On Da Noise," *Business Week*, 28 October 2002, 74–76.

40 Frederick F. Reichheld and Phil Schefter, "E-Loyalty: Your Secret Weapon on the Web," *Harvard Business Review* (July–August 2000): 105–113.

41 Philip Kotler, *Marketing Management, Analysis, Planning, Implementation, and Control*, 11th ed. (Upper Saddle River, NJ: Prentice-Hall, 2003), 551.

42 "Supply Chain: Focus on the Future," *Business Week*, 7 October 2002, 75–82.

43 See, for example, Rick Brooks, "Air Shipping Hurt by Penny-Pinchers, Better Ground Services," *The Wall Street Journal*, 15 July 2002, B1, BC.

44 Carol Casper, "Flow-Through: Mirage or Reality?" *Food Logistics*, October/November 1997, 44–58.

45 Rhonda L. Rundle, "Hospital Cost Cutters Push Use of Scanners to Track Inventories," *The Wall Street Journal*, 10 June 1997, A1, A8.

46 Pete Engardio, "Why the Supply Chain Broke Down," *Business Week*, 19 March 2001, 41.

47 Ray A. Smith and Sheila Muto, "Dot-Coms' New Dilemma: Vacant Warehouses, *The Wall Street Journal*, 22 August 2001, B10.

48 Bert Rosenbloom, "The Ten Deadly Myths of E-Commerce," *Business Horizons*, March/April 2002, 61–66.

49 Rakesh Niraj, Mehendra Gupta, and Chakravarthi Narasimhan, "Customer Profitability in a Supply Chain," *Journal of Marketing* (July 2001): 1–16.

50 Carol C. Bienstock, John T. Mentzer, and Monroe Murphy Bird, "Measuring Physical Distribution Service Quality," *Journal of the Academy of Marketing Science* (Winter 1997): 31–44.

Chapter 12

1 U.S. Bureau of Census, *Statistical Abstract of the United States: 2001*, Table Nos. 2, 1020, and 1024.

2 Ibid.

3 "Spamouflage and Cajun Crawtators," *Forbes*, 29 October 2001, 85–88.

4 "Wal-Mart in the Inner City," http://www.morningnewsbeat.com, accessed 4 December 2002.

5 "In a Giant's Shadow," *Shopping Center Today*, October 2002, 37.

6 "Philadelphia Marketplace Opens June 4th at Philadelphia International Airport," http://www.phl.org/news/980604.html, 15 December 2002.

7 "Retailing 101," *Progressive Grocer*, January 2000, 50–56.

8 Malcolm P. McNair, "Significant Trends and Developments in the Postwar Period," in A.B. Smith, ed., *Competitive Distribution in a Free High-Level Economy and Its Implications for the University* (Pittsburgh, PA: University of Pittsburgh Press, 1958).

9 http://www.saksincorporated.com.our-stores.html, accessed 11 December 2002.

10 "Retailers As Landlords," *Chain Store Age*, May 2002, 55–58.

11 Rebecca Caniso, "Toy Story III: The Toys "R" Us Story" (speech given at the Fifth Conference on Corporate Communications, University of Notre Dame, (Notre Dame, IN, September 2001).

12 Based on sections of David S. Pottruck and Terry Pearce, *Clicks and Mortar: Passion Driven Growth in an Internet Driven World* (San Francisco: Jossey-Bass, 2000), and the authors' experiences with Schwab.

13 "E-tailers Channel Sales Effort," *The Globe and Mail,* 17 November 2000, 2.

14 The information in this section was provided by Ms. Robin Diamond at the Direct Selling Association, Washington DC.

15 Information supplied by John Schulte, chairman of the National Mail Order Association, 30 June 2001.

16 Fact Sheet from the National Automated Merchandising Association, Chicago.

17 http://www.webmergers.com, accessed 17 December 2002.

18 "Online Shoppers Getting Poorer: Hooray!" *Shopping Centers Today,* May 2002, 17.

19 Richard L. Nelson, *The Selection of Retail Locations* (New York: F.W. Dodge, 1958), 66.

20 "Can Shoppers Be Kept Safe?" *The Wall Street Journal,* 5 December 2002, B1.

21 Based on information supplied by the National Retail Federation (NRF) and Marvin Rothenberg.

22 "Labor of Love," *Progressive Grocer,* May 2000, 59–68.

23 Blake Frank, *New Ideas for Retaining Store-Level Employees* (a study for The Coca-Cola Retailing Research Council, University of Dallas, 2000), 10.

24 Ibid., 6.

25 Ibid., 5.

26 "The Frugal Mall," *Shopping Center Today,* December 2002, 27–30.

27 U.S. Bureau of Census, *Statistical Abstract of the United States: 2001,* Table No. 722.

28 Ibid., Table No. 1048.

29 Ibid.

Chapter 13

1 Sources: Karl Greenberg, "Déjà Vu," *Brandweek,* 16 December 2002, 1, 6; John Porretto, (The Associated Press), "Crossover Vehicles Snare Drivers" http://www.thestate.com 27 February 2003; Sue Mead, "2003 Honda Element SUV Feature," *Truckworld Online,* http://www.truckworld. com; Michael Frank, "2003 Honda Element EX," *Forbes Online* http:// www.forbes.com; Kim Wolfkill, "2003 Honda Element," *Road & Track Online* http://www.roadandtrack.com (accessed December 2002).

2 Joep P. Cornelissen and Andrew R. Lock, "Theoretical Concept or Management Fashion? Examining the Significance of IMC," *Journal of Advertising Research* 40 (September/October 2000): 7–15. For counter positions, see Don E. Schultz and Philip J. Kitchen, "A Response to 'Theoretical Concept or Management Fashion'," *Journal of Advertising Research* 40 (September/October 2000): 17–21; Stephen J. Gould, "The State of IMC Research and Applications," *Journal of Advertising Research* 40 (September/October 2000): 22–23.

3 Don E. Schultz and Philip J. Kitchen, "Integrated Marketing Communications in U.S. Advertising Agencies: An Exploratory Study," *Journal of Advertising Research* 37 (September/October 1997): 7–18; Philip J. Kitchen and Don E. Schultz, "A Multi-Country Comparison of the Drive for IMC," *Journal of Advertising Research* 39 (January/February 1999): 21–38.

4 Stephen J. Gould, Andreas F. Grein, and Dawn B. Lernan, "The Role of Agency-Client Integration in Integrated Marketing Communications: A Complementary Agency Theory-Interorganizational Perspective," *Journal of Current Issues and Research in Advertising* 21 (Spring 1999): 1–12.

5 David Sable, "We're Surrounded," *Agency* (Spring 2000), 50–51.

6 The practitioner is Shelly Lazarus, whose career at advertising agency Ogilvy & Mather has extended over a quarter century. Lazarus was quoted by Laurie Freeman, "Internet Fundamentally Changes Definition," *Marketing News,* 6 December 1999, 15.

7 Judann Pollack, "Nabisco's Marketing VP Expects 'Great Things,'" *Advertising Age,* 2 December 1996, 40.

8 Stephanie Thompson, "Busy Lifestyles Force Change," *Advertising Age,* 9 October 2000, s8.

9 For an insightful discussion of different forms of consumer-brand relationships, see Susan Fournier, "Consumers and Their Brands: Developing Relationship Theory in Consumer Research," *Journal of Consumer Research* 24 (March 1998): 343–373.

10 Glen J. Nowak and Joseph Phelps, "Conceptualizing the Integrated Marketing Communications' Phenomenon: An Examination of Its Impact on Advertising Practices and Its Implications for Advertising Research," *Journal of Current Issues and Research in Advertising,* 16 (Spring 1994): 49–66.

11 William Band, "Marketing Accountability: New Rules for ROI," *Brandweek,* 10 February 2003, 19.

12 The following discussion borrows liberally from Kevin Lane Keller, *Strategic Brand Management* (Upper Saddle River, NJ: Prentice Hall, 1998, chapter 2), and Kevin Lane Keller, "Conceptualizing, Measuring, and Managing Customer-Based Brand Equity," *Journal of Marketing* 57 (January 1993): 1–22.

13 This figure is from "Conceptualizing, Measuring, and Managing Customer-Based Brand Equity," 7.

14 Betsy McKay, "Coke's U.S. Lead Widens as Share of Market Grows," *The Wall Street Journal Online* http://www.interactive.wsj.com 25 February 2003 (accessed February 2003).

15 William Boulding, Eunkyu Lee, and Richard Staelin, "Mastering the Mix: Do Advertising, Promotion, and Sales Force Activities Lead to Differentiation?" *Journal of Marketing Research* 31 (May 1994): 159–172.

16 Karl Greenberg, "Déjà Vu," *Brandweek,* 16 December 2002, 1, 6.

17 Lisa Bertagnoli, "Duck Campaign Is Firm's Extra Insurance," *Marketing News,* 27 August 2001, 5–6.

18 Ibid., 6.

19 Nigel F. Piercy, "The Marketing Budgeting Process: Marketing Management Implications," *Journal of Marketing,* 51 (October 1987): 45–59.

20 Kevin J. Clancy and Peter C. Krieg, *Counter-Intuitive Marketing: Achieve Great Results Using Uncommon Sense* (New York: The Free Press, 2000), 110.

21 Ibid., 111.

22 John Sinisi, "Love: EDLP Equals Ad Investment," *Brandweek,* 16 November 1992.

23 Suzanne Vranica, "Industry Forecaster Cuts Projections for U.S. Ad-Spending Growth to 2.5%," *The Wall Street Journal Online* http://www. interactive.wsj.com 15 June 2001 (accessed June 2001). Also, Laurel Wentz and Mercedes M. Cardona, "Ad Fall May Be Worst Since Depression," *Advertising Age,* 3 September 2001, 24.

24 "Top 100 Global Marketers," *Advertising Age,* 11 November 2002, 30.

25 "100 Leaders by U.S. Advertising Spending," *Advertising Age,* 24 September 2001, s2.

26 Vanessa O'Connell and Nicholas Kulish, "Duct Tape Part Deux: Government Rolls Out Ads," *The Wall Street Journal Online* http://www. interactive.wsj.com 19 February 2003 (accessed February 2003).

27 For further discussion, see Terence A. Shimp, *Advertising, Promotion, and Supplemental Aspects of Integrated Marketing Communications,* 6th ed. (Cincinnati: South-Western, 2003), Chapter 8.

28 Gary L. Lilien, Alvin J. Silk, Jean-Marie Choffray, and Murlidhar Rao, "Industrial Advertising Effects and Budgeting Practices," *Journal of Marketing* 40 (January 1976): 21; Kent M. Lancaster and Judith A. Stern, "Computer-Based Advertising Budgeting Practices of Leading U.S. Consumer Advertisers," *Journal of Advertising* 12 (4) (1983): 6.

29 For further discussion, see Shimp, *Advertising, Promotion and Supplemental Aspects of Integrated Marketing Communications,* Chapter 9.

30 These statistics are from *Marketers Guide to Media,* Vol. 25 (New York: VNU Business Publications USA, 2002). Please note that the ad cost of $203,000 is based on a one-time placement in *Sports Illustrated.* The rate would be lower for an advertiser that advertised in *Sports Illustrated* on multiple occasions during a calendar year. Also note that the male readership figure of 20,383,000 is based on the average of estimates provided by two sources that estimate magazine readership audiences: Simmons Market Research Bureau and Mediamark Research.

31 Erin White, "Foreheads for Hire: Ad Agency Uses Face Tattoos to Push Brands, *The Wall Street Journal Online* http://www.interactive.wsj.com 10 February 2003 (accessed February 2003).

32 For more details, see Shimp, *Advertising, Promotion, and Supplemental Aspects of Integrated Marketing Communications,* Chapter 12.

33 For example, Rafi A. Mohammed, Robert J. Fisher, Bernard J. Jaworski, and Aileen M. Cahill, *Internet Marketing: Building Advantage in a Networked Economy* (New York: McGraw-Hill, 2002), 370.

34 http://www.nielsen-netratings.com (accessed February 2003).

35 Robin Webster, "IAB Aim Is to Lower Interactive Ad Hurdles," *Advertising Age,* 19 March 2001, 28.

36 Mohammed et al., *Internet Marketing: Building Advantage in a Networked Economy,* 371.

37 Terry Lefton, "The Great Flameout," *The Industry Standard,* 19 March 2001, 75–78.

38 Dana Blankenhorn, "Bigger, Richer Ads Go Online," *Advertising Age,* 18 June 2001, T10.

39 Jodi Mardesigh, "Too Much of a Good Thing," *The Industry Standard,* 19 March 2001, 84–85.

40 This estimate is from Jupiter Media Metrix as cited in Suzanne Vranica, "Marketers Face Problem as Consumers Gripe About Receiving E-Mail Pitches," *The Wall Street Journal Online,* http://www.interactive.wsj.com 2 November 2001 (accessed February 2003).

41 Mylene Mangalindan, "Direct Marketers Join Fight Against Surging Tide of Spam," *The Wall Street Journal Online* http://www.interactive.wsj.com 25 February 2003 (accessed February 2003).

42 Cara Beardi, "POP Ups Sales Results," *Advertising Age,* 23 July 2001, 27.

43 *Measuring the In-Store Decision Making of Supermarket and Mass Merchandise Store Shoppers* (Englewood, NJ: Point-of-Purchase Advertising Institute, 1995). Please note that POPAI recently changed its name from the Point-of-Purchase Advertising Institute to Point-of-Purchase Advertising International.

44 For more details, see Shimp, *Advertising, Promotion, and Supplemental Aspects of Integrated Marketing Communications,* Chapter 11.

45 Jack Neff, "Coupons Get Clipped," *Advertising Age,* 5 November 2001, 1. Another source that used to track advertising, trade, and consumer promotions, but which no longer is published is *Cox Direct 20th Annual Survey of Promotional Practices* (Largo, FL: Cox Direct, 1998).

46 Chakravarthi Narasimhan, "Managerial Perspectives on Trade and Consumer Promotions," *Marketing Letters,* 1 (3) (1989), 239–251.

47 Srinath Gopalakrishna, Gary L. Lilien, Jerome D. Williams, and Ian K. Sequeira, "Do Trade Shows Pay Off?" *Journal of Marketing* 59 (July 1995): 75. For discussion of trade shows in the U.K., see Jim Blythe, "Does Size Matter?—Objectives and Measures at UK Trade Exhibitions," *Journal of Marketing Communications* 3 (March 1997): 51–59. For a comparison of trade shows in the U.K. and U.S., see Marnik G. Dekimpe, Pierre Francois, Srinath Gopalakrishna, Gary L. Lilien, and Christophe Van den Bulte, "Generalizing About Trade Show Effectiveness: A Cross-National Comparison," *Journal of Marketing* 61 (October 1997): 65–73.

48 Roger A. Kerin and William L. Cron, "Assessing Trade Show Functions and Performance," *Journal of Marketing* 51 (July 1987): 88.

49 For further discussion, see Shimp, *Advertising, Promotion, and Supplemental Aspects of Integrated Marketing Communications,* Chapter 18.

50 "Give and Take," *Promo's 8th Annual Sourcebook 2001,* 41.

51 Dan Hanover, "We Deliver," *Promo,* March 2001, 43–45.

52 Based on Nielsen Clearing House estimates as published in *Promo's 9th Annual Sourcebook 2002,* 23.

53 Amie Smith, "Coke's European Resurgence," *Promo,* December 1999, 91.

54 Jean Halliday, "Firestone's Dilemma: Can This Brand Be Saved?" *Advertising Age,* 4 September 2000, 1, 54; William H. Holstein, "Guarding the Brand Is Job 1," *U.S. News & World Report,* 11 September 2000; Karen Lundegaard, "The Web @ Work? Ford Motor Company," *The Wall Street Journal Online,* 16 October 2000, http://interactive.wsj.com.

55 P. Rajan Varadarajan and Anil Menon, "Cause-Related Marketing: A Coalignment of Marketing Strategy and Corporate Philanthropy," *Journal of Marketing,* 52 (July 1988): 58–74.

Chapter 14

1 Sources: Todd R. Weiss, "Microsoft to Boost Sales Force, Focus on Closer Ties to Customers," http://www.computerworld.com/softwaretopic, accessed 27 June 2002; "Xbox Live Starter Kits Virtually Sell Out in First Week of Sales, http://www.microsoft.com/presspass/press/2000/Nov02/11–22XboxLiveStarterPR.asp, accessed 2 November 2002; Mike Ricciuti, "Microsoft Plans Sales Force Expansion," http://www.asia.cnet.com/newstech/applications, accessed 25 June 2002; phone interview with Ed Bland, senior director of U.S. sales and channel marketing for Microsoft Xbox, 20 December 2002.

2 Michelle Marchetti, "What a Sales Call Costs," *Sales & Marketing Management* (September 2000): 80.

3 Ibid., 80.

4 Michael Weinreb, "A Fine Line," *Sales & Marketing Management* (October 2002), 49–54.

5 Bureau of Labor Statistics, *Employment and Earnings* (January 2001). http://www.bls.gov (accessed 30 June 2003).

6 U.S. Census Bureau, *Statistical Abstract of the United States,* Labor Force Employment and Earnings; Bureau of Labor Statistics, *Employment and Earnings* (January 2001). http://www.bls.gov (accessed 30 June 2003).

7 Bureau of Labor Statistics, *Employment and Earnings.* http://www.bls.gov (accessed 1 July 2003).

8 Susan DelVecchio and Earl D. Honeycutt, Jr., "Explaining the Appeal of Sales Careers: A Comparison of Black and White College Students" *Journal of Marketing Education* 24 (April 2002): 56–63; Susan DelVecchio and Earl D. Honeycutt, Jr., "An Investigation of African-American Perceptions of Sales Careers," *The Journal of Personal Selling & Sales*

Management 20 (Winter 2000): 43–52; Susan DelVecchio, Earl D. Honeycutt Jr., and Erika Rasmusson, "Does Your Sales Force Need a New Look?" *Sales & Marketing Management* (May 2000), 13.

9 Bureau of Labor Statistics, "Occupational Employment Statistics," http://stats.bls.gov/oes/home.htm (accessed 3 December 2002).

10 Bureau of Labor Statistics, "Employment by Major Occupational Group, 2000 and Projected 2010," http://stats.bls.gov/news.release/ecopro.t02.htm (accessed 3 December 2002).

11 Nancy Smith, "Waking Up to Your Dreams," *Black Collegian* 31 (October 2000), 61–63.

12 Louise M. Kursmark and Edward R. Newill, *Sales Careers: The Ultimate Guide to Getting a High-Paying Sales Job* (Indianapolis: Jist Works, 2003).

13 Christine Galea, "2002 Salary Survey" *Sales & Marketing Management* (May 2002), 32–36.

14 Ibid.

15 Many articles and books have been published about the effects of role conflict, role ambiguity, and job anxiety. See, for example, Ken Grant, David W. Cravens, George S. Low, and William C. Moncrief, "The Role of Satisfaction with Territory Design on the Motivation, Attitudes, and Work Outcomes of Salespeople," *Journal of the Academy of Marketing Science* 29 (Spring 2001): 165–178; George S. Low, David W. Cravens, Ken Grant, and William C. Moncrief, "Antecedents and Consequences of Salesperson Burnout," *European Journal of Marketing,* 35 (5/6) 2001: 587–611; Julie T. Johnson, Rodger W. Griffeth, and Mitch Griffin, "Factors Discriminating Functional and Dysfunctional Salesforce Turnover," *The Journal of Business & Industrial Marketing,* 15 (6) 2000: 399–415.

16 HSMAI Web site, http://www.hsmai.org/resources/certification.cfm (accessed 2 December 2000).

17 These organizations can be contacted as follows: Hospitality Sales & Marketing Association International, 8201 Greensboro Dr., #300, McLean, VA 22102, (703) 610–9024, http://www.hsmai.org; National Association of Sales Professionals, 8300 North Hayden Rd., Scottsdale, AZ 85288–2458, (602) 951-4311 http://www.nasp.com; and Sales & Marketing Executives International, 5500 Interstate North Parkway #545, Atlanta, GA 30328, http://www.smei.org.

18 Bill Brooks, "20 Ways to Derail a Successful Sales Career," *The American Salesman* (September 2002), 3–6.

19 Patrick Leone, "The Right Way to Get Referrals," *Advisor Today* (October 2002), 84.

20 Ibid.

21 Michael Weinreb, "Don't Waste Your Time," *Sales & Marketing Management* (November 2002), 70.

22 Wendy O'Connell, "The E-vangelist: Prospective Customer Relationship Management," *Sales and Marketing Management* (March 2001), 29.

23 Weinreb, "Don't Waste Your Time," 70.

24 Brooks, "20 Ways to Derail a Successful Sales Career, 3–6.

25 David Merrill and Roger Reid, *Personal Styles and Effective Performance* (Radnor, PA: Chilton, 1981).

26 See Christine Canabou, "Fast Talk: Tough Sell," *Fast Company* 64 (November 2002), 59–62; Fara Warner, "Don't Shout, Listen" *Fast Company* 49 (August 2001), 130–138.

27 Barry Higgins, "Answering a Prospect's Objections," *National Underwriter* 106 (10 June 2002): 33.

28 Anonymous, "Shift to Consultative Selling Now Seen as Biggest Challenge," *The American Salesman* (November 2002), 13–14.

29 Higgins, "Answering a Prospect's Objections," 33.

30 See, for example, James W. Pickens, *The Art of Closing Any Deal: How to Be a Master Closer in Everything You Do* (New York: Warner Books, 2002); Tim Breithaupt, *Ten Steps to Sales Success* (New York: AMACOM, 2003); William 'Skip' Miller, *Proactive Selling: Control the Process—Win the Sale* (New York: AMACOM, 2002).

31 Laura Mazur, "So What Are You Doing about This Customer Thing?" *Marketing* (3 October 2002), 16.

32 David Garfinkel, "Making the Most of IT: How To Squeeze More Profits from the Web," *Sales & Marketing Management* 154 (March 2002), 19–20.

33 Dawn R. Deeter-Schmelz, Karen Norman Kennedy, and Daniel J. Goebel, "Understanding Sales Manager Effectiveness: Linking Attributes to Sales Force Values," *Industrial Marketing Management* 31 (October 2002), 617–626; Rolph Anderson, Rajiv Mehta, and James Strong, "An Empirical Investigation of Sales Management Training Programs for Sales Managers," *Journal of Personal Selling & Sales Management* 17 (Summer 1997): 53–66.

34 Phillip H. Wilson, David Strutton, and M. Theodore Farris II, "Investigating the Perceptual Aspect of Sales Training," *Journal of Personal Selling & Sales Management* (Spring 2002): 77–86.

35 Ashraf M. Attia, Earl D. Honeycutt, Jr., and Magdy Mohamed Attia, "The Difficulties of Evaluating Sales Training," *Industrial Marketing Management* 31 (April 2002), 253–259.

36 Malcolm Campbell, "Training on Track," *Selling Power* (March 2000), 84–86.

37 Olivia Thetgyi, "Radical Makeovers," *Sales & Marketing Management* (April 2000), 78–88.

38 Christine Galea, "2002 Sales Training Survey," *Sales & Marketing Management* 154 (July 2002), 34–37; Mark McMaster, "Homework for Salespeople," *Sales & Marketing Management* 154 (October 2002), 58.

39 Scott M. Widmier, Donald W. Jackson, Jr., and Deborah Brown McCabe, "Infusing Technology into Personal Selling," *Journal of Personal Selling & Sales Management* 22 (Summer 2002), 189–198.

40 Alastair Ray, "How to Encourage Internet Shopping," *Marketing* 3 (May 2001), 41–42.

41 Eric Norlin "In CRM, Size Matters and Smaller is Better," Inc.com (25 May 2001) at http://www.inc.com/customer_service/advice/22444.html, (accessed 11 December 2002); Craig Woirhaye, "How to Add Value to Customer Relationships," (29 June 2001), http://www.inc.com/customer_service/advice/23137.html, (accessed 11 December 2002).

42 James H. Drew, D. R. Mani, Andrew L. Betz, and Piew Datta, "Targeting Customers with Statistical and Data-Mining Techniques," *Journal of Service Research* (February 2001): 205–219; Owen P. Hall, Jr., "Mining the Store," *Journal of Business Strategy* (March/April 2001): 24–27.

43 Phat X. Chiem, "Wireless CRM Starting to Support Sales Forces," *B to B,* 19 February 2001, 29.

44 Mark McMaster, "Online Learning from Scratch," *Sales & Marketing Management* 154 (November 2002), 60.

45 Mark McMaster, "Homework for Salespeople," *Sales & Marketing Management* 154 (October 2002), 58.

46 Julie Hill, "E-Briefings Change Training for a Firm in Transition," *Presentations* (February 2001), 20.

47 Widimier et al., "Infusing Technology Into Personal Selling, 189–198.

48 Cheri Speier and Viswanath Venkatesh, "The Hidden Minefields in the Adoption of Sales Force Automation Technologies," *Journal of Marketing* 66 (July 2002), 98–111.

49 Ibid.

50 Vincent Alonzo, "Role Call," *Sales and Marketing Management* 153 (June 2001), 34–35; Erin Strout, "By the Book: Managing to Motivate," *Sales and Marketing Management* 154 (November 2002), 73.

51 Alonzo, "Role Call," 34–35.

52 Julie Sturgeon, "Fun Sells," *Selling Power* (20 March 2000), 56–65; Julia Chang, "Relieving Anxiety in Anxious Times," *Sales & Marketing Management* 154 (November 2002), 16.

53 René Y. Darmon, "Optimal Salesforce Quota Plans Under Salesperson Job Equity Constraints," *Canadian Journal of Administrative Sciences* 18 (2001), 87–100; David J. Good and Charles H. Schwepker, "Sales Quotas: Critical Interpretations and Implications," *Review of Business* (Spring 2001), 32–36.

54 Good and Schwepker, "Sales Quotas: Critical Interpretations and Implications," 32–36.

55 Darmon, "Optimal Salesforce Quota Plans Under Salesperson Job Equity Constraints," 87–100.

56 Betsy Cummings, "Quota Busters: Getting Reps to Exceed—Not Just Meet—Their Goals," *Sales & Marketing Management* (July 2001), 67.

57 Deeter-Schmelz et al., "Understanding Sales Manager Effectiveness: Linking Attributes to Sales Force Values," 617–626.

58 Ibid.

59 Willem Verbeke and Richard P. Bagozzi, "Sales Call Anxiety: Exploring What It Means When Fear Rules a Sales Encounter," *Journal of Marketing* (July 2000): 88–101; William F. Kendy, "Overcoming Cold-Calling Fear," *Selling Power* 22 (November/December 2002), 52.

60 Donald L. Caruth and Gail D. Handlogten-Caruth, "Compensating Sales Personnel," *The American Salesman* 47 (April 2002), 6–15.

61 David J. Cocks and Dennis Gould, "Sales Compensation: A New Technology-Enabled Strategy," *Compensation & Benefits Review* (January/February 2001), 27–31.

62 Bill Weeks, "Setting Sales Force Compensation in the Internet Age," *Compensation & Benefits Review* (March/April 2000), 25–34.

63 Judy A. Siguaw, Sheryl E. Kimes, and Jule B. Gassenheimer, "Sales Force Productivity: The Application of Revenue Management Strategies to Sales Management," *Industrial Marketing Management* (2003), forthcoming.

64 Andris A. Zoltners and Sally E. Lorimer, "Sales Territory Alignment: An Overlooked Productivity Tool," *Journal of Personal Selling & Sales Management* 20 (Summer 2000), 139–150.

65 Ibid.

66 Zoltners and Lorimer, "Sales Territory Alignment: An Overlooked Productivity Tool," 139–150; Kirk Smith, Eli Jones, and Edward Blair, "Managing Salesperson Motivation in a Territory Realignment," *Journal of Personal Selling & Sales Management* 20 (Fall 2000), 215–226.

67 Smith, et al., "Managing Salesperson Motivation in a Territory Realignment," 215–226.

68 Dave Downey, Mike Jackson, and Marilyn Holschuh, "Strategic Selling: Team Selling=Greater Success with Key Accounts," *Agri Marketing* (September 2000), 18–19.

Chapter 15

1 Sources: Charles Fishman, "Which Price is Right?," *Fast Company* 68 (March 2003), 92. "Wide Gap in Business, Leisure Fares Drawing Fire," *Airline Financial News*, (3 June 2002), http://www.aviation.com, accessed 16 July 2003; Lori Calabro, "Making Fares Fairer: Why Airline Pricing Can't be Fundamentally Changed Without an Overhaul of Industry Cost Structures, *CFO*, 18 (9) (1 September 2002), 105; Eric Torbenson, "Recession, Cheaper Tickets Online Fuel American Airlines' Slide," *Dallas Morning News*, http://www.dallasnews.com, accessed 31 March 2003.

2 J. Dean, "Research Approach to Pricing," in *Planning the Price Structure*, Marketing Series No. 67, Management Association, (New York: American Management Association, 1947), 4.

3 A. W. Walker, "How to Price Industrial Products," *Harvard Business Review* 45 (1967): 8–45.

4 "Finding the Right Price Is No Easy Game to Play," *Chief Executive*, September 1981, 16–18.

5 Thomas T. Nagle and Reed K. Holden, *The Strategy and Tactics of Pricing*, 2nd ed. (Englewood Cliffs, NJ: Prentice-Hall, 1995), 15.

6 John H. Lindgren, Jr. and Terence A. Shimp, *Marketing: An Interactive Learning System* (Fort Worth, TX: Dryden Press, 1996), 378.

7 Example used with permission from Professor Kim Sosin, UNO Center for Economic Education, College of Business Administration, University of Nebraska at Omaha, NE 68182.

8 Gilbert Burck, "The Myths and Realities of Corporate Pricing," *Fortune*, April 1972, 85+. See also, Richard Thaler, "Mental Accounting and Consumer Choice," *Marketing Science* (Summer 1985), 199–214.

9 R. Hall and C. Hitch, "Price Theory and Business Behavior," *Oxford Economic Papers*, 1939; and Thomas V. Bonoma, Victoria L. Crittenden, and Robert J. Dolan, "Can We Have Rigor and Relevance in Pricing Research?" in *Issues in Pricing: Theory and Research*, ed. T. DeVinney (Lexington, MA: Lexington Books, 1988), 337.

10 This example is adapted from Thomas T. Nagle and Reed K. Holden, *The Strategy and Tactics of Pricing*, 2nd ed. (Englewood Cliffs, NJ: Prentice-Hall, 1995), 19–22.

11 For target ROI pricing, the desired profit per unit is calculated as follows:

$$\text{Desired profit per unit} = \frac{(\text{Target Return} + \text{Investment})}{\text{Projected Unit Sales}}$$

12 Nagle and Holden, *The Strategy and Tactics of Pricing*, 3.

13 Tables 14.2, 14.3, and 14.4 are taken from Paul A. Samuelson, *Economics: An Introductory Analysis*, 4th ed. (New York: McGraw-Hill, 1958), 370–374.

14 For example, the percentage of the price change from $5 to $4 in Table 14.2 is ($5–$4)/$5 = 20%. The percentage change in quantity sold is (10–9)/10 = 10%.

15 "Cheap PCs," *Business Week*, 23 March 1998, 28.

16 Note that there are no fixed costs included in Table 14.3, which may seem a bit odd. It is important to recognize that fixed costs do not help in determining the profit-maximizing price for one simple reason: They are the same no matter what price you charge. As such, the only fixed costs that would be relevant would be those that change as a function of pricing. For example, going with a very low price for a product may require extra investment in production capacity to make sure enough product is available. The fixed costs associated with additional production would then be relevant and should be accounted for.

17 Simulated purchase tasks have been found to provide reasonably accurate assessments of consumer response to price. See John R. Nevin, "Laboratory Experiments for Estimating Consumer Demand: A Validation Study," *Journal of Marketing Research* (August 1974): 261–268; and Raymond R. Burke, Bari A. Harlam, Barbara E. Kahn, and Leonard M. Lodish, "Comparing Dynamic Consumer Choice in Real and Computer-Simulated Environments," *Journal of Consumer Research* (June 1992): 71–82.

[18] One could argue that the symphony should consider an even higher price, since profits show a continual upward trend as the price gets higher.

[19] AtchisonNet, http://www.atchisonkansas.net/News/Awards.asp, accessed 15 February 2003.

[20] Michael Porter, *Competitive Strategy* (New York: Free Press, 1980), 39.

[21] We should note that, although Neil Hill's prices are likely to be equal to or lower than a similar store in Kansas City because of the lower costs of doing business in Atchison, driving from Kansas City is part of the price of shopping at Neil Hill's. The combination of an absolutely unique shopping experience and fair prices (relative to Kansas City alternatives) is likely a strong draw. See Kevin Helliker, "Word of Mouth Makes Kansas Store a Star," *The Wall Street Journal,* 7 November 1997, B1.

[22] See Daniel Kahneman, Jack L. Knetsch, and Richard H. Thaler, "Fairness as a Constraint on Profit Seeking: Entitlements in the Market," *American Economic Review* 70 (September 1986): 728–741.

[23] Miriam Jordan, "Brazilian Producers Economize, and Some Consumers Cry Foul," *The Wall Street Journal,* 27 August 2001, A8.

[24] Robert Axelrod, *The Evolution of Cooperation* (New York: Basic Books, 1984), 35.

[25] Dean Takahashi, "AMD Posts Loss Amid Price War, Sluggish Demand," *The Wall Street Journal,* 9 July 1998, B3.

[26] Jeffrey Tannebaum, "Small Bookseller Beats the Giants at their Own Game," *The Wall Street Journal,* 4 November 1997, B1.

[27] Scott McCartney, "Southwest Airlines Lands Plenty of Florida Passengers," *The Wall Street Journal,* 11 November 1997, B4.

[28] Kent B. Monroe, *Pricing: Making Profitable Decisions,* 3rd ed. (New York: McGraw-Hill, 2003), 163.

[29] Reed K. Holden and Thomas T. Nagle, "Kamikaze Pricing," *Marketing Management* 7(2) (1998): 30–40.

[30] Gilbert Burck, "The Myths and Realities of Corporate Pricing," *Fortune,* April 1972, 87.

[31] Timothy Aeppel, "Rubbermaid Is on a Tear, Sweeping Away the Cobwebs," *The Wall Street Journal,* 8 September 1998, B4.

[32] Jerry Useem, Julie Schlosser, and Helen Kim, "One Nation Under Wal-Mart; How Retailing's Superpower—and Our Biggest Most Admired Company—Is Changing the Rules for Corporate America," *Fortune* 147 (4), 3 March 2003, 64.

[33] Chris Adams, "Nucor Cuts Steel Prices Amid Rush of Imports," *The Wall Street Journal,* 11 September 1998, A2.

[34] Daniel Rosenberg, "Traditional Stents Still Have Market In US, Doctors Say," *The Wall Street Journal,* 29 April 2003.

[35] Ron Winslow, "How a Breakthrough Quickly Broke Down for Johnson & Johnson," *The Wall Street Journal,* 18 September 1998, A1.

[36] Venkataraman, Chen, and MacMillan, in a study of the airline industry, find that price moves produce a competitive reaction with 75% probability. The probability that a competitor would match a nonprice move was 17%. S. Venkataraman, Ming-Jer Chen, and Ian C. MacMillan, "Anticipating Reactions: Factors that Shape Competitor Responses," in *Wharton on Dynamic Competitive Strategy,* George S. Day and David J. Reibstein, eds. (New York: John Wiley, 1997), 198–219.

[37] Peter R. Dickson and Joel E. Urbany, "Retailer Reactions to a Competitor's Price Change," *Journal of Retailing* 70 (Spring 1994): 1–22; Joel E. Urbany and Peter R. Dickson, "Competitive Price-Cutting Momentum and Pricing Reactions," *Marketing Letters* 2(4) (1991): 393–402.

[38] Jaikumar Vijayan, "IBM Proposes Flexible Software Pricing," *Computerworld,* 6 April 1998, 57.

[39] Joshua Hyatt, "Hot Commodity," *Inc.,* February 1996, 50–60.

[40] This short section is based on Howard Gleckman and Gary McWilliams, "Ask and It Shall Be Discounted," *Business Week,* 6 October 1997, 116–120.

[41] Alan S. Blinder, "Why Are Prices Sticky? Preliminary Results from an Interview Study," *American Economic Association Papers and Proceedings,* May 1991, 89–96.

[42] Amy Cortese and Marcia Stepanek, "E-commerce: Good-Bye to Fixed Pricing?" *Business Week,* 4 May 1998, 71.

[43] Amy Rogers, "e-Bay: The New Kid in Town," *CRN,* 12 November 2001, 16–20.

[44] Nick Wingfield, "eBay Profit, Revenue Soar Despite Tough Environment," *The Wall Street Journal,* 23 April 2003.

[45] Prime Media, Inc., "Enermetrix Announces New Methods for Companies to Access World's Leading Retail Exchange," 29 July 2002; "Energy & Utilities," *Forbes,* 17 July 2000, 136–138; Clinton Wilder, "The Power of the Net," *Informationweek,* 23 August 1999, 63–64.

[46] "Energy & Utilities," *Forbes,* 17 July 2000, 136–138.

[47] Wilder, "The Power of the Net," 63–64.

[48] Cortes and Stepanek, "E-commerce: Good-Bye to Fixed Pricing?", 71.

[49] "At PTC2003, Teleglobe, Arbinet-thexchange Detail The Future," *Fiber Optics News,* 23 (4), 27 January 2003; http://www.arbinet.com.

[50] Jim O'Brien, "Hot Off the Wire," *Computer Shopper,* August, 1998, 474; and Mary Connelly, "Philosophy of Car Pricing Is Clear: Cut Out Games," *Advertising Age,* 28 March 1994, S28–34.

[51] Ellen Roseman, "No-Haggle Policy Can Be a Hard Sell, Toyota Discovers," *Toronto Star,* 12 April 2003, d4.

[52] Carl F. Mela, Sunil Gupta, and Donald R. Lehmann, "The Long-Term Impact of Promotion and Advertising on Consumer Brand Choice," *Journal of Marketing Research* (May 1997): 248–61.

[53] Kenneth Hein and Vincent Alonzo, "P&G Scales Back Promotions," *Incentive,* April 1997, 15.

[54] "Distribution of Coupons Falls 10% to 276 Billion," *Advertising Age,* 23 March 1998, 32.

[55] "Online Coupon Category Is Growing," *The Food Institute Report,* 24 March 2003, 2.

[56] Peter Huber, "The Four-Hour Energy Crisis," *Forbes,* 17 September 2001, 88.

[57] David Leonhardt, "Make a Bid, but Don't Pack Your Bags," *Business Week,* 1 June 1998, 164.

[58] Kent German, "Priceline on the Rise," *Upside,* December 2001/January 2002, 16; and Monica Roman, "Priceline Shocker: Black Inc.," *Business Week,* 13 August 2001, 40.

[59] "Priceline Posts Loss as Revenues Fall, Hotel Sales Grow," *Factiva Advertising & Media Digest,* 2 May 2003; "With Air Travel Soft, Priceline Widens Its Loss," *The New York Times,* 11 February 2003, 5.

[60] F. T. McCarthy, "Managing Customers: All Customers Are Important, But Some Are More Important than Others," *The Economist,* 13 August 2001.

[61] These individuals' names have been changed.

[62] Andrew Galvin, "The Price of Fixing Prices," *Journal of Pricing Management* (Summer 1990): 46–51.

63 Kathryn Kranhold, "Taubman Lawyers Seek Evidence He Didn't Know of Pricing Talks," *The Wall Street Journal,* 20 August 2001, B2.

64 See the Federal Trade Commission's publication, "Promoting Competition, Protecting Consumers: A Plain English Guide to Antitrust Laws," at the FTC's Web site: http://www.ftc.gov/bc/compguide/index.htm, accessed 24 July 2003.

65 Scott Kilman, "Federal Jury Convicts Ex-Executives in Archer-Daniels-Midland Lawsuit," *The Wall Street Journal* 18 September 1998, A3; Scott Kilman, "ADM Says Ex-Chief Dwayne Andreas will Leave Board," *The Wall Street Journal,* 13 August 2001, A6.

66 See, for example, *Ben Elfman & Son, Inc. et al. v. Criterion Mills, Inc., et al.,* CCH 69, 611 (DC MA, October 1991); BNA ATRR No. 1538 24 October 1991, 507, summarized in the *Journal of Marketing* (July 1992): 100.

67 Wendy Zellner, "How Northwest Gives Competition a Bad Name," *Business Week,* 16 March 1998, 34.

68 In fact, the U.S. Department of Transportation has instituted a policy that defines "unfair exclusionary tactics" and penalizes any airline engaging in such tactics. See "Department of Transportation to Major Airlines: Forewarned Is Fair Warned," *Airline Financial News,* 13 April 1998.

69 Joseph P. Guiltinan and Gregory T. Gundlach, "Aggressive and Predatory Pricing: A Framework for Analysis," *Journal of Marketing* (July 1996): 88.

70 Wendy Zellner, "How Northwest Gives Competition a Bad Name," 34; and "Majors Fault DOT for Ignoring Law, History, Real-World Economics," *Aviation Daily,* 30 July 1998, 180.

71 Russell Gold, and Ann Zimmerman, "Pumped Out: Wal-Mart's Defeat in Low-Cost Gas Game," *The Wall Street Journal,* 13 August 2001, A14.

72 Joel E. Urbany, William O. Bearden, and Dan C. Weilbaker, "The Effect of Plausible and Exaggerated Reference Prices on Consumer Perceptions and Price Search," *Journal of Consumer Research* (June 1988): 95–110; and Kent B. Monroe, *Pricing: Making Profitable Decisions,* 2nd ed. (New York: McGraw-Hill, 1990), 82.

73 These are the Federal Trade Commission Guides, as cited in *The State of Colorado* vs. *The May Department Stores Company,* Case No. 89 CV 9274, District Court, City and County of Denver, Colorado, 1990.

74 See Daniel Kahneman, Jack L. Knetsch, and Richard H. Thaler, "Fairness as a Constraint on Profit Seeking: Entitlements in the Market," *American Economic Review* 70 (September 1986): 728–741.

75 Christine Dugas, "Consumers Walking Away from ATM Charges," *USA Today,* 16 August 1996, 1B.

76 For example, the Georgia Legislature passed a price-gouging law in 1994 to prevent hotels and wholesalers from taking advantage of visitors to the Olympics in Atlanta in 1996. It is unclear how successful the law was, as many hotels still doubled or tripled their room rates. See Donna Rosato, "Some Room Rates have Done a Triple Jump," *USA Today,* 15 July 1996, 1B.

77 Alexei Barrionuevo, Gary McWilliams, and Russell Gold, "Gasoline Gouging Draws Ire of Officials," *The Wall Street Journal,* 13 September 2001, A2; and "Michigan Joins Attack on Gasoline Sellers Who Gouge Prices," *The Wall Street Journal,* 14 September 2001, A2.

78 John H. Lindgren, Jr. and Terence A. Shimp, *Marketing: An Interactive Learning System* (Fort Worth, TX: Dryden Press, 1996), 403.

J. Backman, *Price Practices and Price Policies* (New York: Ronald Press, 1953).

"Finding the Right Price Is No Easy Game to Play," *Chief Executive* (September 1981), 16–18.

J. Dean, "Research Approach to Pricing," in *Planning the Price Structure,* Marketing Series No. 67. (New York: American Management Association, 1947).

A. Marhall, *More Profitable Pricing* (London: McGraw-Hill, 1979).

Thomas T. Nagle and Reed K. Holden, *The Strategy and Tactics of Pricing* (Englewood Cliffs, NJ: Prentice-Hall, 1995).

A. W. Walker, "How to Price Industrial Products," *Harvard Business Review* 45 (1967): 38–45.

Company Index